1999 COMPLETE GUIDE TO CRUISING AND CRUISE SHIPS

by
DOUGLAS WARD
President
The Maritime Evaluations Group (MEG)

Berlitz Publishing Company, Inc.
Princeton Mexico City Dublin Eschborn Singapore

Berlitz 1999 Complete Guide to Cruising and Cruise Ships

Berlitz Publishing Company, Inc.
400 Alexander Park, Princeton, NJ 08540 USA
9–13 Grosvenor Street, London W1X 9FB UK

Cover design: Suzanne Noli
Cover photo: © courtesy Norwegian Cruise Line
Interior design: Media Content Marketing, Inc.

ISBN 2-8315-6229-5

Publisher's Note

The Maritime Evaluations Group (MEG) has evaluated cruise ships since 1980, issuing annual reports on the world's best cruise fleet. All professional opinions and ratings are strictly those of the author and not of the publisher, Berlitz, which makes this survey available in bookstores.

Printed in Canada.

Contents

STOP PRESS

The very nature of a book such as this, which contains so much factual information, is subject to constant change, just as many parts of the cruise industry itself constantly change. The book is up-to-date and as accurate as possible, until August 1998, when it was completed, although last-minute changes received are noted below.

- Wind Star (Windstar Cruises) has canceled her schedule of ten-day Southeast Asia cruises. Instead, she will sail in the Caribbean during the winter of 1999.

- Expect a change of name for Royal Viking Sun (Cunard) in the latter half of 1999. The highly rated ship is expected to change her name to one of the famous Cunarders of the past.

- The new sailing vessel (the world's largest), Royal Clipper (Star Clippers), will be based on Barbados during the winter and Cannes during the summer.

- Thomas Cook and Union Castle Line, which has been dormant for twenty-one years, plan to operate cruises by the year 2000.

- Bali Sea Dancer has been sold and is now operating in the Galapagos Islands.

- *SuperStar Sagittarius* was sold by Star Cruises to Hyundai Merchant Marine and delivered September 20, 1998. *SuperStar Capricorn* (Star Cruises) has also been chartered by Hyundai for four years from September 5, 1998.

All evaluations of cruise ships in this book were made without bias, partiality, or prejudice. In almost all instances, the ships have been visited recently by the author to update earlier ratings or to assess current status. Most of the information contained in the profiles in Part Two was supplied and checked by the cruise lines and shipowners. Any errors or updated information (including upgrading work, structural changes, and improvements to ships) should be sent to the author at the address below.

The author regrets that he is unable to answer any letters that do not include full return postage. Further note that absolutely no correspondence will be entered into regarding the ship ratings and evaluations.

Mr. Douglas Ward
The Maritime Evaluations Group
Canada House
1 Carrick Way
New Milton
Hampshire BH25 6UD
ENGLAND

During the early part of his seagoing career, starting in 1965, Douglas Ward worked aboard fifteen well-known liners (most of which are no longer in service) as follows:

Andes, 25,689 grt; scrapped in 1971
Black Watch, 11,209 grt; withdrawn
Blenheim, 10,240 grt; presently *Discovery I*
Calypso, 20,204 grt; presently *OceanBreeze*
Cunard Countess, 17,593 grt; presently *Olympic Countess*
Cunard Princess, 17,495 grt; presently *Rhapsody*
Franconia, 22,637 grt; presently *Fedor Shalyapin* (scrapped in 1997)
Kenya Castle, 19,904 grt; presently *Amerikanis* (presently laid up)
Ocean Monarch, 22,552 grt; withdrawn in 1966, scrapped at Kaohsiung in 1975
Oronsay, 27,632 grt; withdrawn in 1973, scrapped at Kaohsiung in 1974
Queen Elizabeth, 83,673 grt; withdrawn in 1968, caught fire in Hong Kong under suspicious circumstances February 9, 1972
Queen Elizabeth 2, 70,327 grt; still in service
Queen Mary, 81,237 grt; withdrawn in 1967, moored alongside at Long Beach, California; still in use as a floating hotel and attraction
Reina del Mar, 21,501 grt; withdrawn in 1975, scrapped at Kaohsiung in 1975
Southern Cross, 20,204 grt; presently *OceanBreeze*

INTRODUCTION

Why be land-bound when you can be cruise-bound? Ever since my first transatlantic crossing, in July 1965, aboard Cunard's 83,673-grt (gross register tonnes) ocean liner RMS *Queen Elizabeth*, then the largest passenger ship ever constructed, I have been captivated by passenger ships and the sea. More than 4,200 days at sea, involving over 800 cruises, 145 transatlantic crossings, and countless Panama Canal transits, shipyard visits, ship christenings, maiden voyages, and ships later, I am even more fascinated by and absorbed in every aspect of cruising and passenger-ship travel.

Cruising is truly the vacation of the 1990s. There is simply no better way to get away from it all than on a cruise. Speak to anyone who has taken a cruise before—they'll be very enthusiastic in their praise. So will you—that is, ***if* you choose the *right* ship, for the *right* reasons.** That brings me to the purpose of this book: it is intended to be a primary and comprehensive source of information about cruising and the ships and companies that offer to take you away from the pressures, stresses, and confines of daily life ashore.

When you first look into taking a cruise, you will be confronted by an enormous and bewildering choice. Don't panic. Simply read through this book carefully. At the end you will be nearer to making the right choice and will leave for your cruise as well informed as most specialists in the industry! In fact, any professional cruise sales agent will also find this book a valuable reference source about ships and cruising.

The book is divided into two distinct sections. Part One is composed of 22 chapters; it introduces you to the world of cruising, helps you define what you are looking for in a cruise vacation and what kind of accommodation to choose, and provides valuable advice on what to know before you go.

There is a complete picture of life aboard ship and how to get the best from it; the well-known cuisine; the evolution of cruising; nautical terminology; amusing anecdotes; who's who on board; and advice about going ashore. If you are looking for the cruise with a difference—along a river or an adventurous expedition—there is a discussion of these aspects, too, culminating with that ultimate travel experience: the world cruise and other grand voyages.

Part Two contains profiles of 225 oceangoing cruise ships (including expedition cruise vessels, "soft" expedition cruise vessels, and sail-cruise vessels). From large to small, from unabashed luxury to ships for the budget-minded, old and new, they are all here.

The ratings and evaluations are a painstaking documentation of my personal work, much of it undertaken incognito. To keep this book up-to-date and as accurate as possible, I travel constantly throughout the world and inspect over seventy ships each year, including the "behind the scenes" areas that passengers do not normally see but that are an important part of the overall evaluation. This translates to being "on the road" for more than ten months each year. The ratings are best used selectively, according to your personal tastes and preferences. If cuisine is important to you, or your concern is for entertainment, then these aspects of the ratings will obviously be more significant for you than the overall score or number of stars achieved. The attraction of cruising is in the variety of opportunities available. This book is intended to help you make an informed choice, given the enormous differences between ships, service standards, and cruise lines today.

This book is a tribute to everyone who has made my seafaring experiences possible, and a thank-you to all the cruise lines for their cooperation.

Douglas Ward

August 1998

WHY TAKE A CRUISE?

WHY IS A CRUISE VACATION SO POPULAR?

Well, more than 7.6 million people can't be wrong (that's how many people took a cruise last year)! Cruising is a popular vacation today, because it takes one away from the pressures and strains of contemporary life by offering an escape from reality. Cruise ships are really self-contained floating resorts, without the crime, which can take you to several destinations in the space of just a few days. The sea has always been a source of adventure, excitement, romance, and wonder. It is beneficial and therapeutic, and, because you pay in advance, you know what you will spend on your vacation without any hidden surprises. There is no traffic (unless you go ashore in ports of call), no pollution, no telephone. And the hassles of ordinary travel are almost completely eliminated in one pleasant little package. It's no wonder that 85 percent of passengers want to go again. And again. And again.

ISN'T CRUISING EXPENSIVE?

Cruising can be an all-inclusive vacation, or an almost all-inclusive vacation. If you compare what it would cost on land to have all your meals and entertainment provided, as well as your transportation costs, fitness and sports facilities, and social activities, educational talks, parties, and other functions, you will soon realize the incredible value of a cruise vacation. Remember, a ship is a destination in itself that moves to other destinations. No land-based resort could ever do that! Ask anyone who has been on a cruise recently and you will see. Finally, give yourself a vacation budget and go to your professional travel agent with it. The rest, as they say, will be taken care of. If you want to take a cruise now but want to pay later, Carnival Cruise Lines, Celebrity Cruises, Princess Cruises, and Royal Caribbean International have programs for you, and I am sure other lines will follow (U.S. residents only). Payments can be made over 24, 36, or 48 months. It's as easy as that!

JUST WHO TAKES A CRUISE?

Singles, couples, families with children of all ages (including single parents and grandparents), honeymooners, second or third honeymooners, groups of friends, and college buddies are all passengers. In fact, today's passengers are probably your next-door neighbors.

WHERE CAN I GO ON A CRUISE?

Pick any of the 500-plus destinations in the world, and you will find a ship and cruise to take you there. A cruise can also take you to places inaccessible by almost any other means, such as Antarctica, the North Cape, the South Sea islands, and so on.

BUT ISN'T CRUISING FOR WRINKLY OLD PEOPLE?

Nothing could be further from the truth. Indeed, the average age of passengers is younger each year. Although those of silver years have found cruising to be a very safe way to travel the world, the average age of first-time passengers is now well under forty. But do remember that even wrinkly old people can have a lot of fun, too, and many of them have more get-up-and-go than many people under the age of forty!

I see seven-day cruises advertised for $400 per person. Is this too good to be true?

As a rule, yes! When you consider that a decent hotel room in New York costs at least $200 per night without meals (taxes additional), it stands to reason that something is not quite as it seems. Before jumping into anything, read the fine print. Look at all the additional costs (tipping to cabin and dining room stewards and others, 15 percent drink gratuity, shore excursions, getting to and from the ship, and so on). That $400 per person could well be for a four-berth cabin adjacent to the ship's laundry or above the disco, but in any event, not in a desirable location (just as a $50 hotel room in New York would be).

How many different cruises can I choose from?

The cruise industry operates more than 20,000 cruises each year throughout the year. One of them should fit your needs.

Won't I get bored?

Usually it's men who ask this. But get them aboard, and it is almost guaranteed that there won't be enough time in the day to do all the things they want to do (as long as you choose the right ship, for the right reasons). So, whether you want to lie back and be pampered, or go nonstop, you can do it on a cruise vacation, and you will only have to pack and unpack once.

Why does it cost more to cruise in Europe and the Far East than in the Caribbean?

The answer is twofold:

- 1. Almost all aspects of operations, including fuel costs, air transportation, and supplying food to the ships, are higher.
- 2. Cruise companies want to make more money (called yield) than in the cut-price Caribbean, where sun, sea, and sand are the principal delights, whereas sightseeing, architecture, culture, and other things are part of a more enriching cruise experience.

Can I learn about computers while on a cruise?

Absolutely. Crystal Cruises and Cunard are just two examples of cruise companies that provide computers and lectures. Indeed, Cunard's Computer Learning Center aboard *QE2* is always full. And unlike learning centers on land, this one serves caviar and smoked salmon to its participants.

Is cruising for singles?

Yes, indeed. A cruise vacation is ideal for people traveling alone (over 25 percent of all passengers are single, or solo, travelers), because it is easy to meet other people in a noncompetitive environment. Many ships also have special cabins for singles as well as special add-on rates for single occupancy of double cabins. Some cruise lines will even find a cabinmate for you to share with, if you so desire.

Are cruises for honeymooners?

Couldn't be better. In fact, cruising is the ideal setting for romance, shipboard weddings (these can be arranged in some ports, depending on local regulations), receptions, and honeymoons. Most decisions are already made for you, so all you have to do is show up.

Most ships have accommodation in double-, queen-, or king-sized beds, too. And for those on a second honeymoon, many ships now perform a "renewal of vows" ceremony (some ships charge for this, some do not).

Are cruises for children, too?

Absolutely! In fact, a cruise provides families with more quality time than any other type of vacation. Events on board are tailored to various age groups (even Disney has special cruise ships). In addition, a cruise is very educational, allows children to interact in a safe, crime-free environment, and takes them to destinations in comfortable and familiar surroundings. Take children cruising to Alaska, for example, and they will get to go kayaking, participate in Native American craft-making sessions, take train and tram rides, share in wildlife learning excursions, or go to the Alaska Raptor Rehabilitation Center. In fact, kids have such a good time ashore and aboard ship, you will have difficulty getting them off the ship at the end of the cruise, if you choose the right ship. And you as parents (or as a single parent) will be able to get time to enjoy life, too. Again, choosing the right ship is most important.

Can I find a quiet, serene cruise, away from children and noise?

Yes, indeed. If you don't like crowds, noise, or long lines, there are some beautiful small ships ready to cater to your every whim. Perhaps a sail-cruise vessel or a river or barge cruise could provide the right antidote. There are so many choices.

Is there a cruise with no ports of call?

Yes, but it is not a cruise, it is a transatlantic crossing from New York (United States) to Southampton (England) aboard Cunard's *Queen Elizabeth 2*. I have, however, been telling cruise lines for years that a ship doing occasional three-, four-, or seven-day cruises to nowhere would be most welcome for many repeat passengers, but no cruise line has yet to take the initiative. So many passengers are "allergic" to places such as Nassau (Bahamas) or other tourist rip-off destinations that they really want nothing more than to be aboard a ship at sea, with all the creature comforts of home.

Are there different classes aboard ship?

Not any more. Gone are the class distinctions and the pretensions of formality of the past. Differences, however, can be found in the type of accommodation chosen, in the price you pay for a larger cabin (or suite), and in the location of your cabin (or suite).

Isn't it difficult to find one's way around large ships?

Yes, it can take at least a few hours, or a day or so. In general, however, remember that decks are horizontal and stairs are vertical. The rest comes naturally or with practice.

Can I go shopping in ports of call

Yes, you can. In fact, many passengers engage in "retail therapy" when visiting ports of call such as Hong Kong, Singapore, St. Maarten, and St. Thomas, among so many others. Just remember that you will have to carry all those purchases home at the end of your cruise, as the luggage companies know well enough.

Aren't all ships and cruises quite similar?

Indeed, no—far from it! Look through this book and you will see that ships range from under 200 feet (60.9 m) to over 1,000 feet (304.8 m) in length. They carry from under 100 to more than 3,000 passengers; facilities, food, and service will vary, quite naturally, according to the size of the ship. The ambience ranges from ultra-casual to very formal (starchy and reserved). The entertainment, likewise, ranges from amateur dramatics to full-fledged high-tech production shows, from the corner cabaret to a world-famous headliner, and everything in between.

As a repeat passenger who likes large ships, I find it difficult to get away from constant noise. What do you suggest?

Believe me, I understand your problem. If I weren't doing what I'm doing, I would sue certain cruise lines for hearing loss caused by loud music (and announcements) aboard their ships! Seriously, though, simply contact the hotel manager and let him or her know that the volume level is unacceptable and to please do something about it. If enough people do this, things will have to change for the better.

As a repeat passenger, I've noticed standards dropping. Why?

Well, prices are the same as ten years ago, but operation and crew costs have risen considerably. So somewhere along the line, something has to give. It is usually the little details that cruise lines think passengers will not notice, like standards!

Can I get pizzas delivered?

As a matter of fact, you can, delivered in a box right to your cabin, aboard Celebrity Cruises' ships *Century*, *Galaxy*, and *Mercury*. Actually, many ships have pizza parlors, but last year Celebrity Cruises became the first to deliver pizzas, in boxes and insulated pouches, to cabins, until 1 a.m.

What if I don't like it?

I'm almost certain that you will enjoy your cruise vacation. Actually, the world's biggest cruise company (Carnival Cruise Lines) has a Vacation Guarantee that states that if you do not like the cruise, the ship, or other aspect of the vacation, you can disembark in the first port of call, and the line will return all your money. Now that's an excellent guarantee that less than one-tenth of 1 percent of its passengers take up. I expect other lines to follow suit.

WHERE TO?

With approximately 500 destinations available to cruise ships, there is almost certainly a ship to take you wherever you want to go. Because itineraries vary widely, depending on each ship and cruise, it is wise to make as many comparisons as you can by reading the cruise brochures for descriptions of the ports of call. If, for example, you would like a Caribbean or a Mediterranean cruise, it is possible to choose from over 100 itineraries.

Several ships may offer the same or similar itineraries simply because these have been successfully tried and tested. Narrow the choice further by noting the time spent at each port and whether the ship actually docks in port or lies at anchor. Then compare the size of each vessel and its facilities.

Caribbean Cruises

There are 7,000 islands in the Caribbean Sea, although many of them are too small or uninhabited. Caribbean cruises are usually destination-intensive cruises in a normally sunny climate that cram between four and eight ports into one week, depending on whether you sail from a Florida port or from a port in the Caribbean, such as Barbados or San Juan. This means you could be visiting at least one port a day, with little time at sea for relaxation.

This kind of intensive "island hopping" leaves little time to explore a destination before you have to be back on board. Although you see a lot of places in a week, by the end of the cruise you may need another week to unwind. Ultimately, this is not the best way to cruise, unless you really wish to cover a lot of ground in a short space of time.

An eastern Caribbean cruise would typically include ports such as Barbados, Dominica, Martinique, Puerto Rico, St. Croix, St. Kitts, St. Maarten, and St. Thomas.

A western Caribbean cruise would typically include ports such as Calica, Cozumel, Grand Cayman, and Playa del Carmen.

Courtesy Douglas Ward

"Bahamaramamama" is a special shore tender used to take passengers ashore to a "private island" for a day on the beach.

A southern Caribbean cruise would typically include ports such as Antigua, Aruba, Barbados, La Guaira, and Grenada.

Although not stated in any cruise line brochure, you should be aware that the months from June to November in the Caribbean region are hurricane season.

Private Islands

Several cruise lines featuring Bahamas/Caribbean itineraries have their own "private island" (often called an "out-island")—a small island in the Bahamas close to Nassau (or the Turks and Caicos Islands) that is outfitted with all the ingredients to make an all-day beach party a memorable occasion. These are extremely popular with passengers, with watersports, scuba, snorkeling, crystal-clear waters, warm sands, and even a hammock or two (many of these are extra-cost items). There are no reservations to be made, no tickets to purchase, and no hassles with taxis.

Norwegian Cruise Line was the first to use a private island in 1977. But Disney Cruise Line, whose first ship debuted in March 1998, has fulfilled its promise to have the most extensive facilities of all on its private island (which is wholly owned, not leased, unlike most).

Some private islands change names, depending on what day of the week it is, and what ship is in. You should note that the beaches, though idyllic for 200 passengers, can prove extremely noisy and crowded when filled with 2,000 or more passengers from one of the large ships, anchored for a "Beach Barbecue Day." Cruise lines have their own inventive names for these islands, such as Blue Lagoon Island (Dolphin Cruise Line), Castaway Cay (Disney Cruise Line), Little Stirrup Cay (Norwegian Cruise Line), Half Moon Cay (Holland America Line), Princess Cays (Princess Cruises), and Serena Cay (Costa Cruises).

The good thing is that the private island will not be cluttered with hawkers and hustlers, as are so many beaches in the Caribbean today. And, because they are private, there is security—and no fear of passengers being mugged, as has happened in some Caribbean islands.

These private island beach days are not all-inclusive, and cruise lines (or their shore-based operating concession partners) now charge high rates for everything, including snorkel gear (and mandatory swim vest), all pleasure craft, and such things as "banana" boat fun rides. It has become yet another way for the cruise lines to make money. However, this is because it costs a lot of money to develop a private island, as in the case of Disney Cruise Line, which spent $25 million developing and outfitting Castaway Cay (formerly known as Gorda Cay), or Holland America Line, which spent $16 million developing Half Moon Cay.

Europe/Mediterranean Cruises

If you are planning to go to Europe (including the Baltic, Black Sea, Mediterranean and Norwegian fjord areas), traveling there by cruise ship makes economic sense.

Europe/Mediterranean cruises are popular because:

- So many of Europe's greatest cities—among them Amsterdam, Barcelona, Copenhagen, Genoa, Helsinki, Lisbon, London, Monte Carlo, Nice, Oslo, St. Petersburg, Stockholm, and Venice—are on the water, and it is much less expensive to take a cruise than to fly and stay in decent hotels (and have to pay for food and transport).
- You will not have to try to speak or understand different languages when you are aboard ship as you would ashore (if you choose the right ship).
- Aboard ship you use a single currency.
- A wide variety of shore excursions are available.
- Lecture programs provide you with insights before stepping ashore.

- Ships with under 1,000 passengers are arguably better than larger ships, as they will be able to obtain berthing space (larger ships may have to anchor in more of the smaller ports, which means it will take you more time to get to and from shore—a frustrating inconvenience at times). Be aware that many of the Greek islands do not have docking facilities and are only accessible by shore tender. When looking at itineraries, one company may give you more time ashore than another company, so it pays to compare the cruise brochures. Aboard ships that cater to passengers of different nationalities, daily programs and announcements will be in as many as six different languages.

Alaska Cruises

For a real cold rush, try an Alaska cruise. Alaska cruises are popular because:

- They offer the best way to see Alaska's magnificent shoreline and glaciers.
- It is a vast, relatively unexplored region.
- There is a wide range of shore excursions to choose from, including many floatplane and helicopter tours.
- There is an extensive array of excursions to add on to your cruise. These can include "dome car" rail journeys to Denali National Park to see North America's highest peak, Mt. McKinley.
- Pre- and post-cruise journeys to Banff and Jasper National Parks can be made from Vancouver.

There are two popular cruise routes:

- **Inside Passage Route:** usually includes visits to tidewater glaciers, such as those found in Glacier Bay's Hubbard Glacier or Tracy Arm (just two of the fifteen active glaciers along the 62-mile-long Glacier Bay coastline). Typical ports of call might include Juneau, Ketchikan, Skagway, and Haines.
- **Glacier Route:** which usually includes the Gulf of Alaska during a seven-day one-way cruise between Vancouver and Anchorage. Typical ports of call might include Seward, Sitka, and Valdez.

Two major cruise lines, Holland America Line and Princess Cruises, have such comprehensive shoreside facilities (hotels, tour buses, and even trains) that they are committed to Alaska for many years. Holland America Line-Westours and Princess Tours (a division of Princess Cruises), have between them invested over $250 million in Alaska; Holland America Line-Westours is the state's largest private employer. Other lines must therefore depend on what's left of the various forms of local transportation for their shoreside tours. Holland America Line took 148,300 passengers to Alaska in 1997, while Princess Cruises took 171,000.

Some ships must anchor rather than dock in several ports of call, because of the limited amount of docking space. Some lines also may pay more in fees so that their ships can dock alongside, making it easier for passengers to go ashore; this is useful when the weather is poor. Most cruise brochures unfortunately do not indicate which ports are known to be anchor (tender) ports (European, particularly German, brochures are much better at providing this information).

Sadly, there is now so much congestion in the tiny Alaskan ports (more than 400,000 passengers visited Alaska in 1997), where there can be several large ships in port on any one day, that avoiding crowded streets becomes an unpleasant part of the cruise experience. Even nature is retreating; with more humans around, wildlife is becoming harder to spot. And some of the same shops can now be found in Alaska as well as the Caribbean.

For those of a more adventurous nature, consider one of the more unusual Alaska cruises to the far north, around the Pribiloff Islands (superb for bird spotting) and into the Bering Sea.

Transcanal Cruises

Transcanal cruises will take you through the Panama Canal, which was constructed by the United States after the failure of a French effort started by Ferdinand de Lesseps. The French labored for twenty years, beginning in 1880, but disease and financial problems defeated them. The United States took over the canal-building effort in 1904 and the waterway opened just ten years later on August 15, 1914. The Panama Canal runs from northwest to southeast, and the best way to experience this engineering wonder is from the deck of a cruise ship.

Cruising from the Caribbean to the Pacific, your ship will be lifted 85 feet (26m) in a continuous flight of three steps at Gatun Locks to Gatun Lake, through which it will travel to Gaillard Cut where the Canal slices through the Continental Divide. It will be lowered 31 feet (9.4 meters) in one step at Pedro Miguel Locks to Miraflores Lake and then the remaining two steps to sea level at Miraflores Locks before passing into the Pacific Ocean. Ships move through the locks under their own power guided by towing locomotives; the 50-mile (80-km) trip across the Isthmus of Panama takes about nine hours.

Panama Canal cruises typically depart from Ft. Lauderdale or San Juan, calling at one or two Caribbean islands before entering the canal and ending in Acapulco, Los Angeles, or San Francisco.

Australia and Orient Cruises

If you like the idea of Australasia, Southeast Asia, and the Orient and you live in Europe or North America, be aware that the flying time to get to your port of embarkation and ship will be long. It is advisable to arrive at least two days before the cruise, as the time changes and jet lag can be quite severe. The area has so much to offer that it is worth taking a minimum fourteen-day cruise to make the most of it.

Choose an itinerary that appeals to you, and then read about the proposed destinations and their attractions. Your cruise or travel agent will be able to provide some of the essential background on destinations and help you select an itinerary. Australia, New Zealand, the islands of the South Pacific, Hong Kong, China, Japan, Indonesia, Malaysia, and Thailand offer superb cruise destinations.

WHERE TO?

With over 500 destinations to choose from, today's cruise ships do indeed roam all over the world. For the sake of simplicity, some of the major cruise areas are grouped together on the following pages, together with the names of the companies and, in most cases, the ships that will take you there.

Note that large cruise lines that operate several ships tend to switch ships to operate certain itineraries from year to year, and so the names of the ships are not provided. When it was compiled, the chart was as accurate as it was possible to make it, given the fact that many companies had not released their 1999 itineraries.

Finally, some ships just seem to roam the world constantly, on long cruises, with no fixed base ports.

When Is the Best Cruise Season?

MONTH	Alaska	Amazon	Antarctica	Arctic/Greenland	Around Great Britain	Around South America	Australia/New Zealand	Bahamas	Bermuda	Black Sea	Caribbean
January		★	★			★	★	★			★
February		★	★			★	★	★			★
March		★				★	★	★			★
April								★		★	★
May					★			★	★	★	★
June	★				★			✧	★	★	✧
July	★			★	★			✧	★	★	✧
August	★				★			✧	★	★	✧
September	★				★			✧	★	★	✧
October						★	★	✧	★		✧
November			★			★	★	✧			✧
December		★	★			★	★	★			★

Key:

★ = this is the best cruise season

✧ = this is hurricane season, which can mean unpredictable weather patterns in this region

✪ = this is cyclone season, which can mean unpredictable weather patterns in this region

Did You Know...?

...that Alaska has two time zones? Most of Alaska is 1 hour behind Pacific Standard Time, whereas the Aleutian Islands are 2 hours behind Pacific Standard Time.

...that the Pacific Ocean has a tide of 22 feet (6.7 meters) and the Atlantic Ocean has a tide of only 8 inches (20.3 centimeters)?

...that the Wallace Line is not a new cruise company but the scientific demarcation separating Asia and Oceania?

...that the average time for a ship to pass through the Panama Canal is 8 hours? The fastest transit time was set by the *uss Manley* at 4 hours and 38 minutes.

Egypt/Israel	Galapagos Islands	Mediterranean	Mexican Riviera/U.S. West Coast	New England/Canada	North Cape/Norwegian Fjords/Iceland	Northwest Passage	Red Sea/East Africa/Indian Ocean	Southeast Asia	South Pacific	U.S. East Coast	World Cruises
★			★				★	★			★
★			★				★	★			★
★			★				★	★			★
★		★							★		★
		★							★	★	
		★			★				★	★	
		★			★	★			✪	★	
		★		★	★	★			✪	★	
		★		★					★	★	
★		★		★			★	★		★	
★			★				★	★			
★			★				★	★			★

Where To?

Key(*)=Year-Round

See NOTES on page 18

	Bahamas ➢	Bermuda ⇨ (summer)	New England/Canada ⬘	Caribbean ✔	Alaska ✦	Mexican Riviera✕ (Year-round: 3, 4, and 7 days)	Hawaii ✖
Abercrombie & Kent					X		
Airtours Sun Cruises				X			
Alaska Sightseeing/Cruise West					X		
American Canadian Caribbean Line			X	X			
American Hawaii Cruises							X*
Arcalia Shipping				X			
Arkona Reisen				X			
Canaveral Cruise Line	X*						
Carnival Cruise Lines	X*			X*	X	X*	X
Celebrity Cruises	X*	X		X*	X		
Classical Cruises			X	X			
Clipper Cruise Line			X	X	X		
Club Med Cruises				X			
Commodore Cruise Line				X*			
Compagnie des Isles du Ponant				X			
Costa Cruises				X			
Crystal Cruises			X	X	X		X
Cunard			X	X*	X		X
Curnow Shipping							
Deilmann Reederei				X			
Deilmann Seerederei							
Delphin Seereisen			X	X			
Deutsche Seerederei							
Deutsche Seetouristik			X	X			
Disney Cruise Line	X*						
Dolphin Hellas Cruises							
Far East Shipping							
Festival Cruises							
Fred Olsen Cruise Lines			X	X*			
Fritidskryss							
Grimaldi Cruises							
Hanseatic Tours							
Hapag-Lloyd Cruises							
Hapag-Lloyd Seetouristik			X		X		
Holland America Line	X*		X	X*	X		X

Mediterranean (including Black Sea/Greek Isles)	North Cape/Baltic Sea	Atlantic Isles (Canary Isles/Madeira)	Arabian Gulf (Red Sea)	Indian Ocean	Southeast Asia	Australia/New Zealand/South Pacific	Amazon	Galapagos	Antarctica ✘	Around Britain	Around Africa	South America (East Coast)	Around South America	Around-the-World Cruises (1999)	Roaming Ships ✚	Northwest Passage
									X						X	
X		X														
X	X											X				
X			X													
X																
							X									
									X	X						
X		X			X											
X																
X	X	X										X				
X	X	X		X	X	X	X					X	X	X	X	
X	X	X		X	X	X	X			X		X	X	X	X	
										X						
	X	X	X							X						
X																
X							X					X	X	X	X	
X	X															
															X	
X																
					X*	X										
X	X	X														
X	X	X									X					
	X															
X		X														
																X
X											X					
	X			X	X	X	X		X	X		X	X	X	X	X
X	X	X				X						X	X	X		

Where To?

Key(*)=Year-Round

See NOTES on page 18

	Bahamas	Bermuda (summer)	New England/Canada	Caribbean	Alaska	Mexican Riviera (Year-round: 3, 4, and 7 days)	Hawaii
Ivaran Lines							
Leisure Cruises							
Louis Cruise Lines							
Majestic International Cruises							
Mano Cruises							
Marine Expeditions					X		
Mediterranean Queen Lines							
Mediterranean Shipping Cruises				X			
Metropolitan Touring							
Mitsui OSK Passenger Line							
Neckermann Seereisen			X	X			
New Century Tours							
Nina Cruise Line				X			
Noble Caledonia							
Norwegian Capricorn Line							
Norwegian Cruise Line	X*	X		X*	X		X
NYK Cruise Line							
Orient Lines							
P&O Cruises			X	X			
P&O Holidays							
P&O Spice Island Cruises							
Paquet Cruises				X			
Peace Boat							
Peter Deilmann Reederei							
Phoenix Seereisen			X	X	X		
Plantours							
Premier Cruises	X*		X	X*			
Primexpress Cruises							
Princess Cruises	X*		X	X*	X		X
Quark Expeditions							
Radisson Seven Seas Cruises			X	X			
Raymond & Whitcomb							
Regal Cruises			X	X			
Renaissance Cruises				X			
Royal Caribbean International	X*	X		X*	X	X*	X

Mediterranean (including Black Sea/Greek Isles)	North Cape/Baltic Sea	Atlantic Isles (Canary Isles/Madeira)	Arabian Gulf (Red Sea)	Indian Ocean	Southeast Asia	Australia/New Zealand/South Pacific	Amazon	Galapagos	Antarctica ✖	Around Britain	Around Africa	South America (East Coast)	Around South America	Around-the-World Cruises (1999)	Roaming Ships ✚	Northwest Passage
												X				
X	X									X				X	X	
X*																
X																
X																
							X		X	X		X		X		X
X																
	X															
								X								
					X*											
X	X			X								X	X	X	X	
					X*											
X																
	X		X	X	X				X	X						
						X*										
				X	X*	X								X		
X				X	X	X			X			X			X	
X	X	X	X	X		X								X		
						X										
					X*											
X	X													X		
														X		
							X					X				
X	X	X	X								X	X	X	X	X	
											X				X	
												X				
X	X			X												
X	X			X	X	X	X			X		X	X	X	X	
									X			X				X
X	X	X		X	X	X*				X						
										X						
													X			
X	X	X	X	X	X											
X	X				X*					X						

Where To?

Key(*)=Year-Round.

See NOTES on page 18

	Bahamas	Bermuda (summer)	New England/Canada	Caribbean	Alaska	Mexican Riviera (Year-round: 3, 4, and 7 days)	Hawaii
Royal Hispania Cruises							
Royal Olympic Cruises				X			
Royal Seas Cruise Line				X*			
Saga Shipping				X			
Sea Cloud Cruises				X			
Seabourn Cruise Line			X	X	X		X
Seawind Cruise Line				X*			
Seetours			X	X			
Siam Cruise Line							
Silversea Cruises			X	X			
Society Expeditions					X		
Soviet Danube Shipping							
Special Expeditions					X		
Star Clippers				X			
Star Cruises							
Star Line Cruises							
Sun Cruises							
SunFest Cruises							
Swan Hellenic Cruises							
Tall Ship Adventures				X*			
Thomson Cruises							
Transocean Cruise Lines							
Transocean Tours			X	X	X		
Venus Cruise Line							
Windjammer Barefoot Cruises				X*			
Windstar Cruises				X			
World Cruise Company							
World Explorer Cruises					X		

Mediterranean (including Black Sea/Greek Isles)	North Cape/Baltic Sea	Atlantic Isles (Canary Isles/Madeira)	Arabian Gulf (Red Sea)	Indian Ocean	Southeast Asia	Australia/New Zealand/South Pacific	Amazon	Galapagos	Antarctica ✖	Around Britain	Around Africa	South America (East Coast)	Around South America	Around-the-World Cruises (1999)	Roaming Ships ✚	Northwest Passage
X		X														
X*			X				X					X				
X	X	X												X	X	
X	X			X	X	X	X			X		X	X		X	
X	X	X			X*		X					X	X	X	X	
					X*											
X	X	X		X	X	X	X			X		X	X		X	
									X						X	
X																
							X	X*								
		X														
					X*	X										
X				X												
					X*											
X																
X	X		X	X	X					X						
X		X	X	X												
														X		
X	X	X		X	X		X			X		X	X		X	
					X											
X					X	X*										
														X		

NOTES FOR WHERE TO? CHART

➢ Bahamas: Only those ships that feature year-round cruises to the Bahamas are included.

➾ Bermuda: Only the three cruise lines (featuring five ships) that have long-term Bermuda government contracts for weekly summer season cruises to Bermuda are included, although several other companies operate cruises that include Bermuda infrequently during the summer season.

➭ New England/Canada: These cruises are normally seven-day northbound voyages between New York and Montreal or southbound voyages from Montreal to New York. These can be combined to make a fourteen-day round-trip voyage.

✔ Caribbean: Note that there are several more companies than those included here whose ships visit the Caribbean infrequently, but their schedules are seldom known far enough in advance to be included.

✦ Alaska: These cruises are operated generally between May and September.

✕ Mexican Riviera: Ships based on the U.S. west coast.

✖ Hawaii: A number of cruise lines have ships that call at Hawaii, but none on a regular basis, due to the archaic Jones Act (U.S. cabotage laws), which states that only U.S. flag ships (there is only one major oceangoing U.S. flag ship at present) can embark and disembark passengers in a U.S. port without first going to a foreign port. Note that a U.S. flag ship is a ship that is registered in the United States. It has nothing to do with being a flag ship.

✘ Antarctica: The Antarctic is no place for normal cruise ships. To operate in this region, where ice can easily crush a ship within an hour should the weather deteriorate (as it often does), a ship must have an "ice-strengthened" or "ice-hardened" hull capable of breaking through pack ice in the formative stage. Rubber-inflatable Zodiac landing craft are used for venturing ashore (there is no such thing as a dock on the Antarctic continent). All the companies listed here provide the right facilities, but some are better than others. The austral summer is the only time ships can get close to the Antarctic Peninsula (where many nations have their research stations), as the ice is so dense during the winter months that the continent (which, at its smallest, is the size of North America) swells to twice its summer size.

✙ Roaming Ships: You are just as likely to see the ships of the following companies in Nosy-Be (Madagascar) as in the Amazon, Greenland, Barcelona, Oslo, Singapore, the Maldives, or Seychelles. In fact, all they do all year long is roam the oceans of the world, mostly on nonrepeating itineraries of varying cruise lengths.

Part One:

THE WORLD OF CRUISING

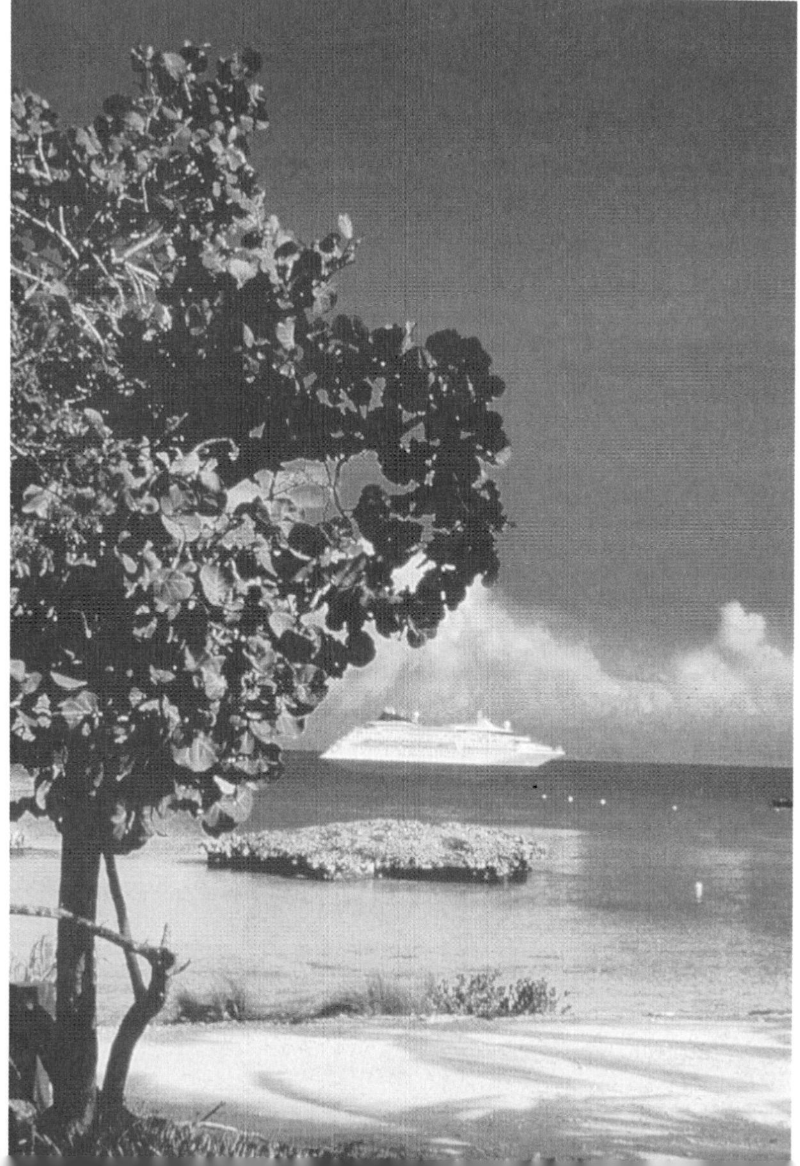

© Courtesy Norwegian Cruise Line

YOUR FIRST CRUISE: WHAT TO EXPECT

Well before the cruise, make sure you have your passport and any visas required (in some countries, you might go ashore under a group visa, although in such cases you would have to go with the group on organized excursions). Remember to pack any medication you may need, and advise family members and friends where you are going.

With anticipation and excitement running high, if you've never been on a cruise before, allow me to take you through a typical initial embarkation process.

You already have been sent your cruise tickets and documents by the cruise line or your travel agent. A typical document package might include:

- Flight ticket
- Cruise ticket
- Luggage tags
- Embarkation card (fill it out before you get to the embarkation point)
- Discount coupons for the onboard shops
- Bon Voyage gift selection form
- Shore excursion brochure
- On-board credit account form
- Guide to onboard services
- Ship's telephone and fax contact numbers
- Coupon for tuxedo rental

Let's now assume that you've arrived at the airport closest to your ship's embarkation point and retrieved your luggage. It is probable that there will be a representative from the cruise line waiting, holding up a sign that says "Condor Cruise Lines" or something similar. You will be asked to place your luggage in a cluster together with those of other passengers on the same flight as you, or perhaps with passengers on other flights of the same airline arriving at roughly the same time as yours.

Alternatively, you could have perhaps driven to the port of embarkation (or taken a train or specially chartered bus), in which case you would hand over your luggage to a representative of the cruise line or to a baggage handler (who would probably expect a tip, even for moving it a few feet).

In any case (no pun intended), the next time you see your luggage should be aboard ship, where it will be delivered to your cabin. Now, let's proceed to the check-in point.

Head to the registration (check-in) area in the terminal building. For large ships, numerous desks will be set up (with the alphabet split into several parts), probably with long lines of people at each of them. Go to the desk that displays the letter of your surname, wait in line (having filled out all embarkation, registration, and immigration documents), and then check in. If your accommodation is designated as a "suite," there should be a separate check-in facility (sometimes called gold card service).

If you are cruising from a U.S. port and you are a non-U.S. citizen or "Resident Alien," you will go to a separate desk to check in. You will be asked for your passport, which you leave with the check-in personnel (remember to ask for a receipt for it—it is, after all, a valuable document). If you are cruising from any other port in the world that is not a U.S. port, be advised that each country has its own check-in requirements, setups, and procedures (passport control and inspection, for example). In any event, once you've checked in, you will be only a few steps away from your ship and cruise.

Documents in hand, you will probably go through a security screening device, for both your person and carry-on (hand) luggage (just like airports). Next, you'll walk a few paces toward the gangway. This may be a covered, airport-type gangway, or an open gangway (hopefully with a net underneath it in case you drop something over the side). The gangway could be flat, or you may have to walk up a steep incline, depending on the

Courtesy Douglas Ward

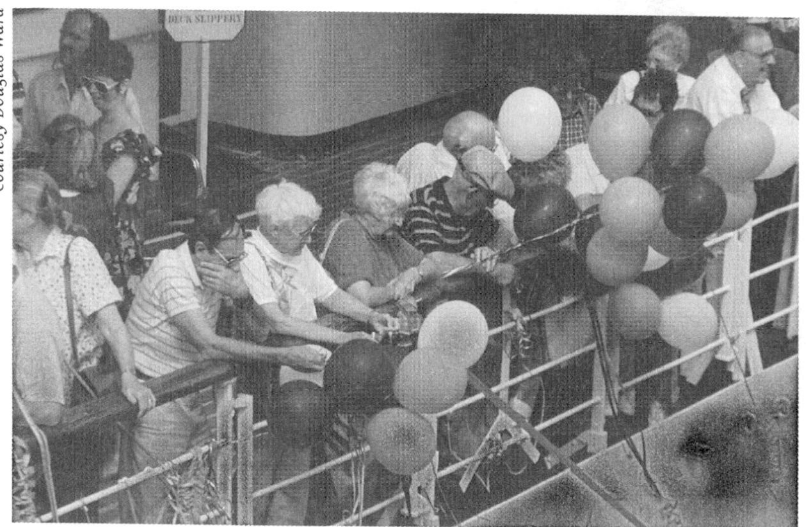

Bon Voyage!

location of the gangway, the tide, and so on. When you get to the gangway, you will probably be greeted by the ship's photographers, a snap-happy team ready to take your photograph, bedraggled as you may appear after possibly having flown or otherwise traveled for hours. If you do not want your photograph taken, say "no" firmly, and proceed.

Once on the gangway, you will feel a heightened sense of anticipation. At the ship side of the gangway, you will find a decorated (hopefully) entrance, and the comfortable feel of cool air-conditioning if the weather is hot. You should also be greeted by well-dressed young men and women of the cruise staff and an officer or security personnel, who will ask for your boarding pass and your cabin number. Show them your cabin number, and a steward should magically appear to take your carry-on luggage (or perhaps a winter coat) from you and take you directly to your cabin. At last you've arrived.

The door to your cabin should be unlocked and open. If it is locked, ask the steward to obtain the key to open the door. On the newest ships, you will probably be handed an electronically coded key card, which you insert into the door lock. Once inside the cabin, put down your personal effects and take a good look. Is it clean? Is it tidy? Are the beds properly made? Check under them to make sure the floor is clean (on one cruise I found a pair of red ladies' shoes, but, alas, no one to go with them!). Make sure there is ice in the ice container. Check the bathroom, bath (if there is one), and shower. Make sure there are towels and soap. If all is clean and shipshape, fine.

If there are problems, bring them to the attention of your cabin steward immediately. Or call the purser's office (or reception desk) and explain the problem, then quietly but quite firmly request that someone in a supervisory position see you to resolve it. The housekeeping on cruise ships is generally very good, but sometimes when "turnaround" time is tight, when passengers disembark in the morning and new passengers embark in the afternoon, little things get overlooked. They shouldn't, but they do (just as in any hotel ashore).

One thing you also should do immediately is to memorize the telephone number for the ship's hospital, doctor, or medical emergencies, just so you know how to call for help should any medical emergency arise.

Your luggage probably will not have arrived yet (if it is a ship carrying more than 500 passengers) so don't sit in the cabin waiting for it. Once you've oriented yourself with the cabin and its features, put your carry-on luggage away somewhere, and, deck plan in hand, take a walk.

Familiarize yourself with the layout of the ship. Learn which way is forward, which way is aft, and how to reach your cabin from the main stairways. This is also a good time to learn how to get from your cabin to the outside decks in case of an emergency. It is more than likely that a Passenger Lifeboat Drill will be held before the ship sails. This is good, in that the drill will not disturb your cruise (or your sleep) should it be held next morning. In any case, the drill must take place within 24 hours after the ship sails from the port of embarkation.

After the drill (you'll find your lifejacket in the cabin, and directions to your assembly station will be posted on the back of the cabin door), you can take off the lifejacket and relax. By now your luggage probably will have arrived.

Unpack, and then go out on deck just before the ship sails. It's always a magical moment, and a good time to meet some new faces. Now, enjoy yourself. You're on a wonderful cruise vacation. No cares. No hassle. No hype. Just you (and maybe a loved one) and that bracing sea air. You'll soon be ready for that first night's dinner. It is simply amazing how the sea air gives you an appetite, although there's no truth to the rumor that the sea air seems to shrink your clothes by the end of the cruise.

WHAT'S NEW IN CRUISING

INTRODUCTION

The cruise industry is truly alive, vibrant, and continuing to grow at a healthy pace (more than 10 percent a year in Europe and Asia, though a little less in North America). For 1999 and beyond, the introduction of new ships continues at a dizzying rate. Some twenty-seven new ones are due to be delivered in the two years between January 1999 and December 2000 alone, at a cost of almost $8 billion, fueled by the increase in demand for the high-value cruise vacation product.

New ships incorporate the very latest in sophisticated high-tech electronic equipment and safety equipment, and the best in advanced ship design and construction, offering passengers an unprecedented number of options, choice of facilities, and dining and entertainment experiences.

New in 1998 were the first two ships for Disney Cruise Line—two 85,000-tonne vessels that provide an encapsulated floating entertainment package for families with children, sailing three- and four-day Bahamas cruises from Port Canaveral (not far from Walt Disney World in Orlando, Florida).

New for 1999 is what will be the world's largest cruise vessel, a 142,000-tonne floating resort/hotel playground for Royal Caribbean International, to be based in Miami and aimed at the standard cruise marketplace for the Caribbean, with orders for two more to follow. Is bigger better? Well, that's up to the individual, but it is rather like being in a big shopping mall environment as opposed to a small boutique environment.

PROPULSION

Most new ships are driven by either diesel-electric or diesel-mechanical propulsion systems that propel them at speeds of about 25 knots (few ships can go faster, or need to, except for Cunard's *QE2*, which has a service speed of just under 30 knots). This, in turn, better equips these ships for the more attractive long-distance itineraries and gives them the capacity of having reserve speed when crossing vast stretches of water, such as those of the Atlantic, Indian, and Pacific oceans, or simply adding more ports and a longer stay in port in areas like the Aegean/Mediterranean.

Several new ships are capable of 25 knots or more: *Enchantment of the Seas*, *Grandeur of the Seas*, *Legend of the Seas*, *Oriana*, *Rotterdam*, *Splendour of the Seas*, and *Vision of the Seas*. Their shape is also sleeker from an aerodynamic viewpoint. Diesel-electric power systems have increasingly become the power philosophy of choice, because of their varied service profile and the tough requirements placed on power used by the various departments of the latest breed of floating hotel. However, it will not be long before gas turbine powerplants are introduced to cruise ships; indeed, the first will be with us before the millennium.

One new technology now incorporated into propulsion design is called the Azipod system. Briefly, Azipod units replace internal electric propulsion motors, shaft lines, rudders, and their machinery, as well as stern thrusters, and are compact, self-contained units that weigh about 170 tonnes each. Azipod units pull rather than push a ship through the water, and save space. When going ahead, the Azipod units face with the propeller forward (ships can go astern either by rotating the Azipod units 180 degrees or by reversing the thrust). A vessel's turning circle diameter is reduced considerably, as is stern vibration. The first cruise ships to employ the technology are Carnival Cruise Lines' 70,367-tonne *Elation* and *Paradise* (Royal Caribbean International's 142,000-tonne *Voyager of the Seas* will have three of them), although it should become standard aboard many other new ships in future.

Exteriors

The cascading, curved, and indented afterdecks of ships such as P&O Cruises' *Oriana* are practical as well as stunning, overlooking an aft pool area (more dramatic, but no less practical, than the terraces aboard *Norwegian Dream* and *Norwegian Wind*). Other cruise ships take the "block" approach and fill in their stern areas with cabins that have an aft-facing view (*Carnival Destiny, Century, Galaxy,* and *Mercury*), or multilevel dining rooms with a huge expanse of glass windows, or other public rooms and facilities. Indeed, more glass areas are being created to provide a perceived link between passenger and sea. *Dawn Princess, Enchantment of the Seas, Grandeur of the Seas, Legend of the Seas, Ocean Princess, Splendour of the Seas,* and *Sun Princess*, for example, all have great expanses of glass.

Play golf? Try the 6,000-sq. ft. (557.5 m²), 18-hole miniature golf course aboard *Legend of the Seas* and *Splendour of the Seas*. The courses are equipped with the foliage, grass, sand traps, bridges, water hazards, and other "trappings" of a traditional miniature golf course, although there is no room for caddies! Holes range from 155 to 230 sq. ft. (14.3-21.4 m²). The courses were designed by the same firm that designed the course for the world's largest shopping center, the Mall of America in Bloomington, Minnesota.

Several ships have electronic golf simulators (*Century, Dawn Princess, Galaxy, Mercury, Royal Viking Sun, and Sun Princess*), at which you can play some of the world's best golf courses (for a fee). *Dawn Princess* and *Sun Princess* feature a basketball court in the base of the huge funnel structure, and aboard *Disney Magic* and *Disney Wonder*, one entire funnel structure (there are two funnels, one of which is a dummy) houses a large sports facility and sports bar. Meanwhile, the uppermost, forwardmost outside deck aboard *CostaVictoria* features a huge, gentle "rain shower" unit to keep sunbathers cool, and, thankfully, no music.

It's back to the future with the Stargazing Deck aboard Royal Caribbean International's *Legend of the Seas* and *Splendour of the Seas*. Both feature a "planiwheel" (starwheel) created specifically for the line. It is located on a forward-facing outdoor deck; passengers can look at the night sky, with charts of the stars and planets in two sections, one for the Northern Hemisphere and one for the Southern Hemisphere. *Century* and *Galaxy* (but not *Mercury*) feature telescopes mounted in their spacious forward observation lounges, which also double as noisy discotheques by night.

Still, the most instantly recognizable exterior is that of the German ship *Aida* (from Verdi's opera of the same name), where huge, bold, red lips and brown eyes adorn her prow. When she leaves port on the first day of a cruise, the laser light show on deck is quite stunning.

Interiors

Contemporary is out. Retro is in! More than ever before, interior designers are changing tack to create luxurious, welcoming interiors reminiscent of London's grand hotels, particularly in the small and medium-sized ships, where the sense of intimacy can genuinely be established.

Large ship interiors include such things as ten-deck-high atriums (*Legend of the Seas* and *Splendour of the Seas*), large theaters with revolving stages, hydraulic orchestra pits, and huge scenery stowage spaces (*Carnival Destiny, Century, Dawn Princess, Galaxy, Grand Princess, Oriana,* and *Sun Princess*), and interactive television in cabins. *Oriana*'s show lounge even has individually air-conditioned seats (the air exits from each seatback), while grand atriums in ships such as *Legend of the Seas* and *Splendour of the Seas* connect with a midship Viking Crown Lounge (day lounge/bar and nightclub) high up, at the base of the funnel.

Several ships now feature two atrium lobbies instead of just one (*Carnival Destiny, Carnival Triumph, Galaxy,* and *Mercury*), while *CostaVictoria* has a forward observation lounge complete with a waterfall that spans three decks. In *Century* and *Galaxy*, the main atrium contains a gentle waterfall with a background of nine large video screens. *Oriana*'s

Courtesy Norwegian Cruise Line

Romantic moments aboard Norway *(Norwegian Cruise Line).*

atrium contains what is, at present, the only two-level shop at sea, appropriately called Knightsbridge; both levels are linked by a spiral stairway.

As in all new ships, the interior decor continues to evolve, with designers seeking out new themes and trying out new stylistic innovations to differentiate "their" ships. Some of the most stunning, bold, and graphic interiors continue to be found in the ships built for Carnival Cruise Lines. *Imagination*, for example, has ancient mythological figures such as sphinxes, Medusas, cherubs, and winged Mercury figures to reflect the refinement of civilizations past. Somehow, lilac neon, fiberoptics, mosaics, and multicolored carpeting go together here, although they never would in any setting other than a glitzy Las Vegas hotel. It is all a feast for the eyes and mind (entertainment architecture, as the interior designer calls it), but for many (especially for European passengers) it could be sensory overkill (but a good advertisement for the fiberoptics and lighting industries).

One of the most innovative cruise ships of late is the German cruise ship *Aida*, where zany theatrics become spontaneous explosions in her two large self-service "island" buffet restaurants, or elsewhere around the ship, not to mention superb laser light shows on deck and in the show lounge. The element of surprise is done so well by the Germans, whose youth have a great sense of humor. Alternatively, the interiors in the new German cruise ship *Deutschland* (which debuted in May 1998) are completely decorated in true 1920s ocean-liner style (which should prove very popular with those who remember oceangoing voyages as they used to be).

The latest ships have also become instant floating museums (some are better than others, however), with collections of artwork costing several million dollars for each vessel; for example: $4 million *(Enchantment of the Seas)*; $3.8 million *(Century)*, $3 million *(Galaxy)*, $2.5 million *(Sun Princess)*, $2 million *(Veendam)*, $1 million *(Aida, Inspiration)*. However, it is not the money spent that's important; it is the fact that artwork now forms a more important part of the physical interior decor than ever before, and particularly so with large ships, with ever larger wall spaces to cover.

Mercury's art collection, for example, consists of over 400 works of art by some of today's most celebrated artists. Some ships (*Century, Dawn Princess, Galaxy, Mercury, and Sun Princess*, for example) have artwork along the passenger accommodation hallways, whereas other ships (*CostaVictoria*, for example) leave their hallways completely bare. Artwork can add to (or possibly detract from) the subliminal value of the total cruise experience. Shipboard art must fit the available spaces, it must be properly lighted, and safety must be taken into consideration (most artwork is highly flammable).

Computer-Driven Cruising

Computer users should note that many cruise lines can be reached on the Internet. Some of the major cruise lines have over 100 pages for browsing, including good information about ports of call (more information than is given in the company's brochures).

Computers now link almost all departments and functions aboard today's new ships, and the latest in-cabin interactive systems let you order wine and shore excursions, play casino games, go shopping, and order pay-per-view movies, all from the comfort of your cabin. The only thing computers cannot do yet is pour you a drink (although you can order one) accompanied by a light snack. However, order a croissant with your Continental breakfast and the "point and select" system probably will not bother to ask whether you'd like it warm or cold. Oh, well, that's technology for you; as long as you are a "standard" photofit passenger, it'll work for you. Otherwise, call room service (sort of defeats the object, doesn't it?). SeaVision, an U.S.-based company that is really a network provider, produces the leading interactive systems for cruise ships.

Floating Spas

Health and fitness spas are among the hottest passenger facilities in the latest cruise ships, with more space than ever devoted to them. In recent years, the basic sauna and massage facility has given way to specially designed marine spas providing the latest in high-tech muscle exercising, aerobic and weight-training machines, and relaxation treatments in a completely "themed" environment. Close by will be the ship's swimming pools and whirlpools.

The latest shipboard spas contain a combination of all or several of the following: reception desk, changing area, aerobics exercise room, gymnasium, and sauna, steam, massage, and other treatment rooms. Facilities include all or some of these: hydrotherapy and thalassotherapy baths, jet blitz, rasul (graduated steam and all-over body mud cleansing), and other treatment rooms. In some ships, the beauty salon is adjacent to the spa complex, or contained within it. The latest spas, with their personal treatments and affiliated beauty salon, have become significant revenue-producing areas for both cruise line and concession.

The most common (and popular) location for spas in the latest ships is on an upper-deck area with large floor-to-ceiling windows that provide ocean views, particularly for exercise areas. Treatment rooms must be flexible so that they can be adapted to incorporate the latest trends (and gimmicks). Traditional Japanese design elements, including a rock garden and shoji screens, provide a serene environment for passengers in the 9,340 sq. ft. (867.6 m^2) AquaSpa aboard Celebrity Cruises' *Century*, *Galaxy*, and *Mercury*. You will find a thirty-person coed sauna, with a huge glass wall overlooking the port side of the German ship *Aida*.

In the Swim

In *Dawn Princess* and *Sun Princess*, an aft swimming pool is "layered" over two decks, partly open, partly covered by glass. Several new ships now feature a magrodome—a glass-enclosed structure that is used to cover swimming pools in case of inclement weather (found on *Carnival Destiny*, *Galaxy*, *Legend of the Seas*, *Mercury*, and *Splendour of the Seas*). These are not new facilities (*Europa* has one and *QE2* had one until it was removed in a 1994 refit), but they do make it possible for passengers to enjoy all-weather swimming. Unlike the sliding multifold magrodomes that are installed aboard various other ships, the glass structures used aboard *Legend of the Seas* and *Splendour of the Seas* are one-piece affairs.

Other New Things

What else? Carnival Cruise Lines was the first, in the spring of 1995, to introduce cash-dispensing ATMs (automated teller machines) aboard some of its largest ships. Celebrity Cruises also has them aboard its ships. I expect other lines to follow.

Other unusual items include marine-quality binoculars for passengers in the top suites aboard *Oriana* and in all passenger "club" category suites in *Asuka*. Umbrellas are provided in all cabins aboard *Silver Cloud, Silver Wind,* and *Song of Flower*. Electric shoe-cleaning machines can be found in all men's public toilets aboard *Delphin*. The day's weather report is provided in each cabin every morning on the small luxury cruise ships such as *Sea Goddess I, Sea Goddess II,* and *Song of Flower*. The Japanese cruise ships *Asuka, Fuji Maru,* and *Nippon Maru* all have pull-out (spring-loaded) flashlights for emergency use (something that should be adopted aboard all cruise ships).

Holland America Line has reintroduced the cigar humidor service (it had been discontinued for a couple of years) for which it had been known for many years, in its "Cigars Under the Stars" program. Cigar smokers now have special clubs aboard Celebrity Cruises' *Century, Galaxy, Horizon, Mercury,* and *Zenith,* with all the attendant ceremonies performed by specialists. As for totally nonsmoking ships, Renaissance Cruises has two 702-passenger ships that are totally nonsmoking throughout (cabins, all public rooms and areas, and open decks)—a cruise industry first. Meanwhile, nonsmokers will be pleased that most ships, particularly those cruising in the Caribbean and Alaska areas, now feature totally nonsmoking dining rooms.

Hot destinations? Apart from the popular Caribbean and Alaska cruising areas, there is Europe, with the Baltic and Russia, the Black Sea, and the eastern Mediterranean. But perhaps the hottest "new" area to be discovered, particularly for European passengers, is the Arabian Gulf. And then there is the mystical area of Southeast Asia, including China, Japan, Thailand, Malaysia, Singapore, and Vietnam. Who said cruising was boring?

Royal Caribbean International has established "Crown and Anchor Clubs" in St. Thomas and San Juan. This is to a Royal Caribbean International passenger what private lounges are to frequent flying businesspeople. There is no charge for the use of the "club," where passengers can enjoy complimentary tea and coffee, rest in comfortable seating areas, check their shopping purchases, purchase spirits, and discuss shopping and tourism questions with the Royal Caribbean International staff in attendance. A fine, practical idea.

Another shoreside idea is a definite back-to-the-future project. It is the terminal constructed at Port Canaveral, Florida, for the two Disney Cruise Line ships. The terminal is an updated recreation of the Ocean Terminal in Southampton, England, built in the post-war years for Cunard passengers for *Queen Elizabeth* and *Queen Mary*.

Living Spaces

Although most "standard" cabins are dimensionally challenged when compared to many land-based hotels, some are getting a little larger, thank goodness, in many new ships. For example, at 170 sq. ft. (15.7 m²) the cabins in *Legend of the Seas* and *Splendour of the Seas* are larger than those in any other ships in the Royal Caribbean International fleet to date. Those two ships also have huge suites measuring some 1,148 sq.ft. (106.6m²), almost as large as the largest living quarters aboard any current cruise ship. Those in Celebrity Cruises' *Century, Galaxy,* and *Mercury* have two penthouse suites of 1,173 sq. ft. (109.0 m²) that can be expanded to an apartment-sized 1,515 sq. ft. (140.7 m²) by using the adjacent minisuite and its lockable, interconnecting door. These penthouses also have built-in teleconferencing capabilities. In many ships, more cabins have private balconies than ever before. In *Dawn Princess* and *Sun Princess*, for example, there are 750 outside cabins with private balconies. Cruise ships now on order will have more.

Cabin bathrooms in *Aida* and *Arkona* (for German-speaking passengers) feature wall-mounted soap/shampoo dispensers so there is no wastage of environmentally unsound plastic bottles; real, normal, hand-held hairdryers are located in a drawer in the vanity desk where they should be, and not in the bathroom, as in most ships.

Dining and Service

What's hot (no pun intended!)? Several ships now feature twenty-four-hour casual dining, so you can eat what you want, when you want. Although the concept is good, the delivery often is not (in some ships, it is serve yourself—more like a freeway café experience).

Several cruise ships already have two-deck-high dining rooms *(Century, Dawn Princess, Galaxy, Legend of the Seas, Maasdam, Mercury, Nordic Empress, Rotterdam VI, Ryndam, Splendour of the Seas, Statendam, Sun Princess,* and *Veendam)*, and more will follow this expansion of the grand dining hall experience, complete with huge staircases that connect the two levels of these majestic dining rooms.

More ships now provide alternative dining spots. At present, *Asuka, Crystal Harmony, Crystal Symphony, Deutschland, Grand Princess, Norwegian Sea, R1, R2, Rotterdam, Silver Cloud, Silver Wind, Song of Flower, Star Aquarius, Star Pisces, SuperStar Leo, SuperStar Virgo, Vistafjord,* and *Wind Surf* already have them, and several cruise lines (Carnival Cruise Lines and Norwegian Cruise Lines, for example) have taken up the "bistro" concept, relieving pressure on the dining room and providing a (very) casual alternative. Most new ships will include more informal dining choices. *Dawn Princess* and *Sun Princess* both have five dining spots (*Star Aquarius* and *Star Pisces*, placed into service in 1993, have seven!). *SuperStar Leo* and *SuperStar Virgo* (Star Cruises) have Chinese and Japanese restaurants, as well as a main dining room, informal lido café, and other dining options. Some ships also have special theme bars/lounges, where delicacies such as caviar and champagne, cheese, and dessert and pastry items are served.

All Carnival Cruise Lines ships now sport 24-hour pizzerias, as well as beer round-the-clock! The latest Princess ships *(Dawn Princess, Grand Princess,* and *Sun Princess)* also have pizzerias, as have *Disney Magic* and *Disney Wonder.* Aboard Celebrity Cruises' *Century, Galaxy,* and *Mercury*, you can have your freshly baked pizza (in a box, of course) delivered to your cabin in an insulated pouch.

Note that in ships operating standard seven-day cruises, menu cycles are repeated each week, so if you are considering, for example, two back-to-back seven-day eastern and western Caribbean or Mediterranean cruises, you should be aware that the same menu generally will be repeated for the second week (and, more than likely, so will the whole entertainment program, the cruise director's spiel, jokes, and activities).

Generally, cruise ship food and service suffered somewhat in the past several years after deep discounting took a firm foothold in the North American marketplace. The standards of food quality, presentation, delivery, and service have fallen little by little, as ships have become larger and larger. Also, because of the acute shortage of waiters who speak good English (the majority of passengers being North American), many cruise lines have had to train personnel from the Caribbean basin and Central American countries whose command of English is often less than desirable. Although most of the major lines have now realized their mistakes and have made some advances in upgrading the food and service aspect of the cruise experience (actually playing "catch-up"), the large ships (those carrying over 1,000 passengers) cannot seem to deliver consistently what is portrayed in the cruise brochures.

What's not so hot

Sadly, much of the cruise industry now seems to insist on creating large floating resort hotels that travel at night and are usually in port during the day. There is, thus, little connection with the sea and nature. This floating hotel concept has spoiled the nature of the latest cruise ship designs—almost everything is designed to keep passengers inside the ship (hopefully to spend money, thus increasing on-board revenue and shareholders' dividends).

Keeping passengers inside the ship has created another problem—that of aggressive, so-called "cruise directors" who insist on interposing themselves into every part of your cruise, both day and night. Public address systems are consistently overused by these aggressive, bouncy youngsters and are often far too loud, which hardly makes for a restful cruise experience. Some of them have learned well from past masters, but most of today's cruise directors, who may make excellent cheerleaders, are unable to communicate with anyone over the age of twenty-five!

Another problem with the homogeneous new ships is the cabins. As identically-sized standard cabins are all the same shape and layout (good for incentive planners but not for individual passengers), they also tend to be the same basic color: eggshell white, off-white, or computer-colored light beige! Although such colors are welcome after days in the sun, they are tedious on voyages over long stretches of water. Only the bold bedspreads or the occasional color prints that adorn a spare wall bring relief. Plain ceilings are also boring. Close to useless are the wall-mounted hairdryers in the bathrooms (which seldom have enough directed pressure). They should, instead, be located in the vanity desk or dressing area.

Ships of identical size and layout also seem to assume that all passengers share the same basic likes and dislikes. Few cruise lines remain flexible enough to accommodate these different tastes, however.

Ships (particularly those in the standard cruise market) now charge for all sorts of things they never used to, such as bottled mineral water (few cruise lines make this clear in their brochures), cups of cappuccino and espresso coffee (even in the dining room), use of the electronic golf simulator, postcards, and pay-per-view movies. Prices seem to keep rising for such things as photos and medical services (free only aboard Russian- or Ukrainian-owned ships).

Anyone sailing aboard ships catering to Americans should note that the cool air-conditioning tends to be very powerful. Take a couple of sweaters or some thermal underwear!

Calling passengers "guests" is also confusing, and nautically incorrect. A guest in one's house is someone that doesn't pay. Passengers aboard ship pay to be there. On land, hotels have paying guests, but "guest" should be changed to "client" as in "clientele." Ships, however, are different (and they should always remain so). They provide a nautical experience and move through the water; passengers have cabins and suites, and decks, not floors. That's how it should remain, but some cruise lines think they are in the hotel business as hoteliers and accountants run them, not as shipping people do.

One thing that has almost gone by the wayside are the streamers and the free champagne provided at bon voyage parties on deck on sailing day (with the exception of world cruises and aboard some Japanese ships). Now it is a case of waiters hustling you to buy a "bon voyage" cocktail, or some "Bahamaramamaslammer" in a polystyrene sports cup. Shame!

One thing that should go by the wayside is the mildly theatrical, intrusive "Baked Alaska Parade." Popular with first-time passengers, it is old hat for many. It's time the cruise lines were more creative. The industry should also find a better way to sing "Happy Birthday" than the present waiter-induced chant that always seems to sound like a funeral dirge!

Finally, in the seven-day cruise market (particularly from U.S. ports) the disembarkation process still leaves much to be desired; it is more like a stampede after the word "go" is given. Passengers aboard large ships often complain that at the end of the cruise they are unceremoniously dumped ashore with no help after the trying procedure of locating their luggage and customs inspection, as well as an absence of representation once they get to their respective airport for check-in. Of particular concern is that the same procedure applies to all passengers, whether they are in the finest penthouse suites or in the smallest inside cabins. Last impressions of these seven-day cruises, therefore, are poor. Comment forms should also be sent to passengers two weeks after their cruise has ended to get a better feedback about this matter rather than asking passengers to complete their forms and hand them in just before disembarkation. Worst offenders: Ft. Lauderdale, Miami, and San Juan, with Los Angeles and San Francisco marginally better.

CRUISING: A BACKGROUNDER

In 1835, a curious advertisement appeared in the first issue of the Shetland Journal. Under the heading "To Tourists," it proposed an imaginary cruise from Stromness in Scotland round Iceland and the Faeroe Islands, and went on to suggest the pleasures of cruising under the Spanish sun in winter. So it is said that the journal's founder, Arthur Anderson, invented the concept of cruising. Just two years later, Anderson, along with his partner, Brodie Wilcox, founded the great Peninsular Steam Navigation Company (later to become P&O).

Sailing for leisure soon caught on. Even writers such as William Makepeace Thackeray and Charles Dickens boarded ships for the excitement of the voyage, and not just to reach a destination. The Victorians had discovered tourism, and they promoted the idea widely. Indeed, Thackeray's account of his legendary voyage in 1844, from Cornhill to Grand Cairo by means of the P&O ships of the day, makes fascinating reading, as does the account by Dickens of his transatlantic crossing aboard a Cunard ship in 1842. P&O's *Tagus*, which journeyed from London to the Black Sea in 1843, was the subject of Mark Twain's *The Innocents Abroad*, which was published in 1869.

In the 1920s, cruising became the thing to do for the world's well-to-do. Being pampered in such grand style was "in" and is still the underlying concept of cruising. The ship took you and your belongings anywhere and fed you, accommodated you, relaxed you, and entertained you. At the same time, it even catered for your servants who, of course, accompanied you.

Cruising for Americans was helped greatly by Prohibition in the 1930s. After all, just a few miles out at sea, you were free to consume as much liquor as you wanted. And cheap three- and four-day weekend "booze cruises" out of New York were preferable to "bathtub gin." Then came short cruises, with destinations as well as booze. In time, the short cruise was to become one of the principal sources of profit for the steamship companies of the day.

In the 1930s a battle raged between the giant cruising companies of the world, as Britain, France, Germany, and the United States built liners of unprecedented luxury, elegance, glamor, and comfort. Each country was competing to produce the biggest and best afloat. For a time, quality was somehow related to smokestacks: the more a ship had, the better. Although

Courtesy Douglas Ward

Cruise ships have interesting designs, even at the stern.

speed had always been a factor, particularly on the transatlantic run, it now became a matter of national ambition.

The first ship designed specifically for cruising from the United States after World War II was *Ocean Monarch* (Furness Withy & Company Ltd.), which was awarded a gold medal by the U.S. Academy of Designing for "outstanding beauty and unusual design features of a cruise ship." Her maiden voyage was from New York to Bermuda on May 3, 1951. I worked aboard her for a short time.

One of the most renowned cruise liners of all time was Cunard's *Caronia* (34,183 grt), which was conceived in 1948. She was designed and built to offer a transatlantic service in the peak summer months only and then spend the rest of the year doing long, expensive cruises. One of her outstanding features was a single giant mast and one smokestack, the largest of her time. Her hull was painted four shades of green, supposedly for the purposes of heat resistance and easy identification. Known for making extensive world cruises, she was one of the first ships to provide a private adjoining bathroom for every cabin—a true luxury. Lovingly known as the "Green Goddess," she was sometimes called the "millionaires' ship."

In June 1958 the first commercial jet aircraft flew across the Atlantic and completely altered the economics of transatlantic travel. It was the last year in which more passengers crossed the North Atlantic by sea than by air. In the early 1960s, passenger-shipping directories listed more than 100 oceangoing passenger ship lines with more than thirty ships featuring transatlantic crossings for the better part of each year. Until the mid-1960s, it was cheaper to cross the Atlantic by ship than by plane, but the appearance of the jet aircraft changed that rapidly, particularly with the introduction of jumbo jets in the early 1970s. In 1962 more than 1 million people crossed the North Atlantic by ship. In 1970 that number was down to 250,000.

The success of the jumbo jets created a fleet of unprofitable and out-of-work passenger liners that appeared doomed for the scrap heap. Even the famous big "Queens," noted for their regular weekly transatlantic service, found themselves at risk. Cunard's *Queen Mary* was withdrawn in September 1967. Her sister ship *Queen Elizabeth,* at 83,673-grt the largest passenger liner ever built (until 1996), made her final crossing in October 1968. I was aboard for the final voyage of this great ship.

The transatlantic shipping companies searched desperately for new ways to employ their aging vessels, but few survived the ever-successful growth of the jet aircraft. Ships were sold for a fraction of their value, and many lines simply went out of business. Those that survived attempted to mix transatlantic crossings with voyages south to the sun. The Caribbean became appealing, cruising became an alternative, and an entire new industry was born, with new lines being formed exclusively for cruising.

Then came smaller, highly specialized ships, capable of getting into the tiny ports of developing Caribbean islands (there were no commercial airlines taking vacationers to the Caribbean then, and few hotels). They were built to carry a sufficient number of passengers in a single class arrangement to make money.

Instead of cruising long distances south from northerly ports such as New York, the new lines established their headquarters in Florida. Having their ships based in Florida not only avoided the cold weather and rough seas of the northern ports, it also to enabled the lines to save on fuel costs with the shorter runs to the Caribbean. Cruising was reborn. California became the base for cruises to the Mexican Riviera, and Vancouver on Canada's West Coast became the focus for summer cruises to Alaska.

Flying passengers to embarkation ports was the next logical step, and there soon emerged a working relationship between the cruise lines and the airlines. The air/sea package came into being with the cruise lines using jumbo jets for their own purposes. The concept of fly-cruising was introduced in 1960 by Chandris Cruises in the Mediterranean cruise area; these days passengers are flown to almost anywhere in the world to join up with their cruises.

Courtesy Douglas Ward

The beautiful cascading aft decks of Crystal Harmony *(Crystal Cruises) are a delight to behold.*

Next came "sail 'n stay" packages—joint cruise and hotel vacations that were all-included in the cruise fare. Cruising had become an integrated part of tourism, with ships and hotels offering comfort and relaxation and the airlines providing quick access. Some of the old liners came out of mothballs and were purchased by emerging cruise lines. These ships were refurbished for warm-weather cruising operations, often with their interiors almost entirely redesigned and refitted.

During the late 1970s, the modern cruise industry grew at a rapid rate. It is still expanding today and is, in fact, the fastest-growing segment of the travel industry. Several brand-new cruise ships enter service each year, and the growth in new ships being built will continue strongly into the millennium.

Cruising Today

Today's cruise concept hasn't changed a great deal from that of earlier days, although it has been improved, refined, expanded, and packaged. Cruises now place more emphasis on destinations, onboard features, and choices. Modern ships are larger, on the whole, than their counterparts of yesteryear, yet cabin size has decreased to provide more space for entertainment and other public facilities.

Today's ships boast air-conditioning to keep heat and humidity out; stabilizers to keep the ship on an even keel; a high level of maintenance, safety, and hygiene; and more emphasis on health and fitness facilities.

Cruise ship design has moved from the traditional, classic, rounded profiles of the past to extremely boxy shapes with squared-off sterns and towering superstructures. Although ship lovers lament the changes in design, many were brought about by the need to fit as much as possible in the space provided (you can squeeze more in a square box than you can in a round one, although it may be less aesthetically appealing). Form follows function, and ships have changed in function from ocean transportation to floating vacation resorts.

Whatever you enjoy doing, you will find it on a cruise. Although ships have long been devoted to eating and relaxation in comfort (promulgating the maxim "Traveling slowly unwinds you faster"), cruise lines now offer so much more in the way of activities, as well as learning and life-enriching experiences, than were available years ago. Also, there are now so many more places you can visit on a cruise: from Antarctica to Acapulco, Bermuda to Bergen, Dakar to Dominica, Shanghai to St. Thomas, or if you wish, even nowhere at all. All told, the world's cruise fleet visits more than 500 ports (including 115 in the Aegean/Mediterranean area and 145 in Northern Europe alone).

Although small when compared with the figures for tourism in general, the cruise industry is a $13-billion business worldwide (over $7 billion in the United States alone) and growing. Clearly, cruising is in the mainstream of the vacation industry.

With well over six million gross registered tonnes of ships, the global cruise industry provides employment to an ever-growing number of personnel, both directly (there are over 60,000 shipboard officers, staff, and crew, as well as about 15,000 employees in cruise company head offices) and indirectly (as in the case of the suppliers of foodstuffs and mechanical and electrical parts, port agents, transport companies, and a wide variety of other peripheral workers).

The spin-off effect on tourism in those areas that are adjacent, or close to, the world's principal ports for the embarkation and disembarkation of passengers is tremendous, with direct and indirect benefits to both mainland and island destinations, airlines, railways, bus firms, other transportation systems, hotels, car rental companies, and so on.

In 1998, over 7.7 million people worldwide took an oceangoing cruise that was packaged and sold by cruise lines through tour operators and travel agents or cruise consultants. The most recent (1998) breakdown of passengers by nationality choosing to take an oceangoing cruise vacation is provided below (taken from figures supplied by the Maritime Evaluations Group):

United States	5,050,000
U.K.*	650,000
Asia (not including Japan)	500,000
Germany	283,000
Canada	250,000
Italy	250,000
Japan	225,000
France	150,000
Rest of Europe	100,000
Australasia	200,000
Cyprus**	75,000
TOTAL	**7,736,000**

* This figure includes 130,000 British passengers who took a two- to seven-day cruise from Cyprus in conjunction with a resort/hotel stay.

** Local Cyprus market

River Cruise Passengers:

Britain: 144,000; Germany: 107,500; France: 60,000; Japan: 30,000

In terms of popularity, the Caribbean (including the Bahamas and Bermuda) is still at the forefront of warm-weather cruising, followed closely by Europe (the Aegean, Mediterranean, and Baltic, all of which offer not only sunshine but also historical, cultural, and archaeological interest), then Alaska, then Southeast Asia.

No longer the domain of affluent retired people, the industry today is vibrant and alive with passengers of every age and socioeconomic background. Also, cruising is no longer the shipping business—it is the hospitality industry.

Constructing a Modern Cruise Ship

More than any other type of vessel, a cruise ship has to fulfill fantasies and satisfy exotic imaginations. It is the job of the shipyard to take those fantasies and turn them into a steel ship without unduly straining the laws of naval architecture and safety regulations, not to mention budgets.

Although there is no such thing as the perfect cruise ship, turning owners' dreams and concepts into ships that embody those ideals is the job of specialized marine architects and shipyards, as well as consultants, interior designers, and a mass of specialist suppliers. Computers have simplified this complex process, which seems to be mostly successful, though shipboard management and operations personnel very often become frustrated with shoreside designers who tend to be more idealistic than they are practical.

At one time, ships were constructed in huge building docks by being put together from the keel (backbone) up. Today's ships are built in huge sections, then joined together in an assembly area (as many as fifty sections for one of the current megaships). The sections may not even be constructed in the shipyard, but they will be assembled there.

Cost is the predominant factor in all ship design and size today. The larger the ship, the more cabins that can be incorporated; hence, the greater the potential in earnings, both in bookings and on-board revenue. It works thus: a 2 percent increase in cabin capacity in a 1,400-passenger ship could mean an increase of $1 – $1.5 million in annual income.

Ships today represent a compromise between ideals and restrictions of space and finance; the solution, according to some experts, is to design ships for specific conditions of service. That means making a ship fit a specific operating niche and cruise area, rather than for general use.

Traditionally, passenger spaces have been slotted in wherever there was space within a given hull. Today, however, computers provide the possibility of highly targeted ship design. Computer-aided design (CAD) is now standard and enables a new ship to be built within a two-year period instead of within the four or five years it took in the 1950s.

The maximum noise and vibration levels allowable in the accommodation spaces and recreational areas are stipulated in any owner's contract with the shipyard. Global vibration tests are carried out once a ship is built and launched, using what is termed a finite method element of evaluation, which embraces analyses of prime sources of noise and excitation: the ship's propellers and main engines.

In the outfitting of a large cruise ship today, prefabricated cabin modules, including in situ bathrooms complete with toilets and all plumbing, are used. When the steel structure of the relevant deck is ready, with main lines and insulation already installed, a specific cabin module is then affixed to the deck, and power lines and sanitary plumbing are swiftly connected. All the waste and power connections, together with hot/cold water mixing valves, are arranged in the service area of the bathroom and can be reached from the passageway outside the cabin module for maintenance.

Although accommodation modules in ships can be successfully systemized, the public spaces cannot. Areas such as food preparation galleys and pantries can, however, be supplied on a turnkey basis by outside contractors. They install these highly specialized areas during the fitting-out period. Electrical wiring is another area normally subcontracted today. In the building of the liner *France* (now *Norway*), for example, some 18,000 miles of electrical cabling had to be installed. Numerous contractors and subcontractors are involved during the fitting-out period of one of today's cruise vessels, a massive effort of coordination and timing. If just one or two contractors or subcontractors fall behind schedule, it can put the entire shipbuilding process behind, causing as many problems as a fire or strike would.

Courtesy Douglas Ward

Sun yourself and take a refreshing dip in the pool as you cruise.

Cruising Tomorrow

Less than 10 percent of any national population has discovered cruising, but more ships are being constructed every year because of the growing increase in popularity. This has led to an overcapacity of (or rather, less demand for) berths in some cruising areas during certain "soft" periods each year, which has kept prices modest and extremely competitive in favor of passengers (in 1999 several cruise lines offer two-for-one discounts and other incentives). Since 85 percent of people who take cruises are eager to go again, any overcapacity should decline as the margin increases, although not without some creative marketing.

The average age of all passengers is decreasing, with almost 40 percent of new passengers under the age of thirty-five. Clearly, this has meant a revamping of onboard facilities and activities aboard many ships, the provision of more and better health and fitness facilities and programs, and a higher, more international standard of entertainment.

In smaller ships equipped to cater to young, active passengers pursuing their hobbies or special interests (such as watersports), there is a definite trend toward "specialty" cruising. Cruise areas are developing for the islands of the South Pacific, the Far East, South America, and around East and West Africa.

As for ship design, current thinking in the industry follows two distinct paths, both based on the "economy of scale" and on market forces. The economy of scale helps the operator to keep down the cost per passenger. This is the reason for the move toward either large ships that can carry 2,000 passengers or more or smaller, more luxurious vessels that do not accommodate more than 250 passengers.

This presumes that some passengers will think, "bigger is better," whereas others will think "small and exclusive." Somehow, it is difficult to make a profit out of small or medium-sized ships in an economically variable environment such as in the U.S. (Caribbean) market (although they are ideal for the small ports of the Aegean and Mediterranean areas). Ships that have been delivered during the past few years are either large-capacity megaships or small-capacity yachtlike vessels, with only a sprinkling of medium-sized ships.

True, large ships can offer more facilities than small ships, but many ports simply cannot accommodate them. Although a metropolis at sea might be good for large conventions and meetings, it poses a challenge for the individual cruise passenger who simply wants to have a quiet, restful vacation. However, with three companies (Carnival Cruise Lines, Princess Cruises, and Royal Caribbean International) now building ships that measure over 100,000 grt each, the "bigger is better" principle is being pursued for all it is worth, even though these ships might be limited to the Caribbean as they are too wide to transit the Panama Canal.

Two fascinating new ship projects remain in the formative but well-developed stage (still awaiting firm contracts at press time, as are other more fanciful projects). One is the American Flagship Project, which would be a floating city accommodating 6,200 passengers in 2,800 cabins; thirteen international restaurants; 30,000 sq. ft. (2,787 m²) of specialty shops and boutiques; 100,00 sq. ft. (9,290 m²) of dedicated meeting space; a 2,000-seat theater; dozens of bars, cafés, and bistros; and an exhibition complex. The ship, named *America World City*, would be marketed and managed by Westin Hotels principally to the meeting and convention market, fly the U.S. flag, and cruise from the U.S. East Coast.

The second (more likely) project is for a ship of 95,000-tonnes, with just 250 huge apartments for purchase (a yearly maintenance fee is payable, just as it would be in an apartment complex ashore). The ship, named *The World of ResidenSea* (for which a letter of intent was signed on November 24, 1997), will have seven à la carte restaurants and will cruise the world for her exclusive owners, who will join and leave whenever they wish. Not that this would create a community; there would undoubtedly be cliques and the subject of exclusivity, which means there could be little ambience in the ship's public rooms or restaurants.

The "small is exclusive" concept, on the other hand, has now gained a strong foothold, particularly in the luxury category. New specialist lines offer very high-quality ships of low capacity. A small-draft vessel can enter ports larger ships cannot even approach, and it can provide a highly personalized range of quality services. However, small ships aren't as stable in bad weather, which is why they tend to follow itineraries close to shore.

Some lines have expanded by "stretching" their ships. This is accomplished by taking a ship into dry dock, literally cutting it in half, and inserting a newly constructed midsection. This instantly increases the vessel's capacity, enabling it to add more accommodation space and enlarge public room facilities, with the advantage of maintaining the same draft.

One interesting example of such a ship "stretch" can clearly be seen in Holland America Line's *Westerdam* (ex-*Homeric*), where the midsection that was built and inserted has larger windows than the fore and aft sections that formed the original ship. *Westerdam* was, in fact, the first ship ever to be stretched in dry dock (in the world's largest covered building dock at Papenburg, Germany).

Other examples of ships that have been stretched (all of them done in "wet" dock with the ship in the water and a new mid-

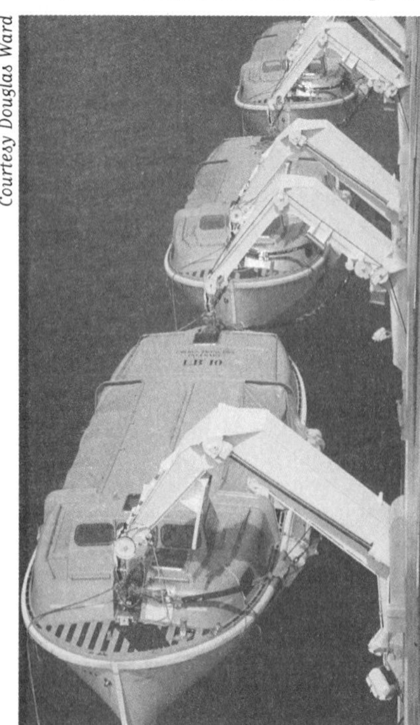

Courtesy Douglas Ward

The latest lifeboats, shown here lowered for action in a lifeboat drill.

section floated into place and then welded together) are *Black Watch* (ex-*Royal Viking Star*), *Carousel* (ex-*Nordic Prince*), *Norwegian Dream* (ex-*Dreamward*), *Norwegian Star* (ex-*Royal Viking Sea*), *Norwegian Wind* (ex-*Windward*), *SuperStar Capricorn* (ex-*Royal Viking Sky*), and *Sundream* (ex-*Song of Norway*).

Besides the traditional monohull construction of all but one cruise vessel up to now, a switch to multihull and "swath" (small water area twin hull) is most unlikely. Although multihull vessels can provide a sound, wide base on which a platform can be constructed, with both accommodation and public areas lying well above the water line (one such example is the twin semisubmersible-hulled *Radisson Diamond*), there has been no further attempt to extend this idea, the design being limited to low-speed vessels.

Whatever direction the design of cruise vessels takes in the future, ships and the companies that operate them have become increasingly environmentally friendly, and passengers need to be taught to behave accordingly. With growing concern about the environment, particularly in eco-sensitive areas such as Alaska and the South Pacific, better safeguards against environmental pollution and damage will have to be built into the vessels themselves.

The cruise industry is fast approaching "zero discharge," whereby nothing is discharged into the world's oceans at all, at any time. This is, naturally, an easier objective to attain for the latest batch of ships (particularly small vessels). Older ships will have a more difficult time of achieving zero discharge owing to now outdated equipment. The future, however, is in total environmental protection through zero discharge.

SAFETY FIRST

In an increasingly regulated world, the importance of safety cannot be overplayed. The training of crew members in relation to safety and security has become extremely important, so much so that new international regulations are due to come into force that will require all crew members to undergo basic safety training before they are allowed to join and work aboard any cruise ship. No longer will crew members be recruited with the intention of providing on-the-job training. Although a separate section for the rating of ships and their safety training has not yet been integrated into the evaluations and ratings in Part Two, safety is taken into consideration as part of the overall ratings.

Safeguards for passengers include lifeboats and life rafts. Since the introduction of the 1983 amendments to Chapter III of the Safety of Life at Sea (SOLAS) Convention 1974 (which actually came into effect in 1980), much attention has been given to safety. The SOLAS conventions are subscribed to by all 135 members of the United Nations, under the auspices of the International Maritime Organization (IMO).

All cruise ships built since July 1, 1986 must have either totally enclosed or partially enclosed lifeboats (only ships built before this date are allowed to have open lifeboats). These have diesel engines that will still operate when the lifeboat is inverted.

The 1990 SOLAS standards on stability and fire protection (mandating the enclosing of all stairways and the installation of sprinkler and smoke detection systems and "low-location" lighting) for all new ship construction took effect on October 1, 1997. Existing ships have another five years to comply (the retrofitting of sprinkler systems in particular is an expensive measure that may not be considered viable by owners of older ships).

October 1, 1997, was the deadline whereby all cruise ships must:

- Use smoke detectors and smoke alarms in all passenger cabins, corridors, stairway enclosures, and other public spaces.
- Have and use low-level lighting showing routes of escape (such as in corridors and stairways).
- Make all fire doors throughout the ship controllable from the ship's navigation bridge, and their status displayed thereon.

- Make all fire doors that are held open by hinges capable of release from a remote location (however, fire doors that slide are not required to have that capability until 2000).
- Use a general emergency alarm that is audible in all cabins.

In 2010, the use of combustible materials in cruise ship construction (allowed under the previous SOLAS 60 regulations) will be forbidden.

In any event, a Passenger Lifeboat Drill must be conducted on board within 24 hours of leaving port. You will hear an announcement from the bridge, which goes something like this:

"Ladies and Gentlemen, may I have your attention, please. This is the captain speaking to you from the bridge. In fifteen minutes' time, the ship's alarm bells will signal emergency lifeboat drill for all passengers. This is a mandatory drill, conducted in accordance with the requirements of the Safety of Life at Sea Convention. There are no exceptions.

"The emergency signal is a succession of seven or more short blasts followed by one long blast of the ship's whistle, supplemented by the ringing of the electric gongs throughout the ship. On hearing this signal, you should make your way quickly but quietly to your cabin, put on warm clothing and your lifejacket, then follow the signs to your emergency boat station, where you will be kept fully informed over the loudspeakers through which I am speaking to you now."

CHOOSING YOUR SHIP AND CRUISE

So you've decided your next vacation will be a cruise. Good choice! But the decisions do not stop there. Bombarded with glossy cruise literature tempting you with every imaginable lure and the overly abundant use of the phrases "five-star luxury," "gourmet dining," and "fabulous destinations," you may find it difficult to choose the right cruise for you. Whether you are traveling alone or with your loved one or family, there are different ships to suit different needs. Despite constant cruise company claims that theirs has been named the "Best Cruise Line" or "Best Cruise Ship," THERE REALLY IS NO SUCH THING, only what's best, and right, for you.

Most shipowners want to be "luxury" cruise operators, and most passengers want to sail aboard one of the top-rated "luxury" ships. But very few operators can really deliver a five-star product.

What a Cruise Is

A cruise is a vacation. It is an antidote to (and escape from) the stresses and strains of life ashore. It offers you a chance to relax and unwind in comfortable surroundings, with attentive service, good food, and a ship that changes the scenery for you. It is virtually a hassle-free and, importantly, a crime-free vacation. You never have to make blind choices. Everything's close at hand, and there are always polite people to help you.

What a Cruise Is Not

Some cruises simply aren't relaxing, despite cruise brochures proclaiming that "you can do as much or as little as you want to." Watch out for the high-density ships—ships that carry 3,000 or more passengers. They tend to cram lots of passengers into small cabins and provide nonstop activities that do little but insult the intelligence and taste buds and assault the wallet.

How do you begin to select the right cruise for the right price? Price is, of course, the key factor for most people. The cost of a cruise provides a useful guideline to the ambience, type of passengers, and degree of luxury, food, and service that you will likely find on board.

The amount you are prepared to spend will determine the size, location, and style of the shipboard accommodation to which you will be assigned. Be wary of cruise lines that offer huge discounts—it either means that the product was unrealistically priced at source or that there will be a reduction in quality somewhere. Remember, discount the price and you end up with discounted quality. Aside from cost, ships are as individual as fingerprints, and each one can change its "personality" from cruise to cruise, depending on the character of passengers aboard.

Fellow passengers encompass all types of personality and lifestyle, from affluent, reserved, and mature to active, athletic, fun-loving, and youthful, or family-oriented, or conservation-minded, or adventurous, or wild fun seekers. They may be well traveled, or honeymooners on their first cruise, or veteran passengers who cruise several times a year.

How Long?

In many ships, the standard of luxury, comfort, and service is generally in direct proportion to the length of the cruise. To operate long, low-density voyages, cruise lines must charge high rates to cover the extensive preparations, high food and transportation costs, port operations, fuel, and other expenditures. The length of cruise you choose will depend on the time and money at your disposal and the degree of comfort you are seeking.

The popular standard length of cruise is seven days, although cruises vary from two-day party cruises to a slow exotic voyage around the world lasting up to 180 days. If you are new to cruising and want to "get your feet wet," you might try a short cruise of three or four days first.

This will give you a good idea of what is involved, the kind of facilities and the lifestyle on board. Note that a three- or four-day cruise from an American port such as Miami, Fort Lauderdale, Los Angeles, or San Juan, or from the Greek port of Piraeus, could end up as a bit of an endurance test. It is fine if you like nonstop activities, noise, and razzle-dazzle stimulation, but it is hardly what you need if all you want to do is to relax.

Which Ship?

Because cruise ships (particularly large ones) are self-sufficient resorts, there really is a cruise line, cruise, and ship to suit virtually all tastes, so it is important to take into account your own personality and vacation requirements when selecting a ship.

Ships are measured (not weighed) in gross register tonnes (grt) and come in three principal size categories, as follows:

- **Small Ships:** for up to 500 passengers (generally 2,000–20,000 tonnes)
- **Medium Ships:** for 500–1,000 passengers (generally 20,000–50,000 tonnes)
- **Large Ships:** for over 1,000 passengers (generally 50,000–150,000 tonnes)

Perhaps there should also be a new category soon: Giga-Ships—for those carrying over 10,000 passengers, coming soon in the next century!

Whatever the physical dimensions, all cruise ships provide the same basic ingredients: accommodation, activities, entertainment, plenty of food, good service, and ports of call, although some of them do it much better than others (and charge more, accordingly).

There are a few "all-inclusive" ships where there really are no bar bills to pay, nothing to sign for, no gratuities to give, and no standing in line to sign up for shore excursions, but these tend to be the smaller "luxury" cruise ships that cost upward of $800 per person, per day (although some suites aboard larger "standard" market cruise ships can easily cost that). Once you are on board, you may never have to say, "How much?" Most of the larger cruise ships, however, will entice you to spend money on board, which is one way that cruise lines manage to support their low fares.

If you like or need a lot of space around you, it is of little use booking a cruise on a small, intimate ship where you knock elbows almost every time you move. If you like intimacy, close contact with people, and a homey ambience, you may feel lost and lonely aboard a large ship.

To get an idea of the amount of space you will have around you aboard ship, look closely at the Passenger Space Ratio given in the evaluation of each ship in Part Two of this book. A Passenger Space Ratio of 50 and above is the ultimate in terms of space per passenger; 30-50 can be considered very spacious; between 20 and 30 is moderately so; between 10 and 20 would be very high density; and below 10 is extremely cramped, as in "sardine-style."

Small Ships (up to 500 Passengers)

Choose a ship in this size category if you seek a more intimate cruise experience and want to cruise with a small number of passengers who share similar concerns.

Some of the most exclusive cruise ships in the world belong in this group. But so do most of the coastal vessels (with very basic, unpretentious amenities), the sail-cruise ships, and all of the expedition-style cruise vessels, which take passengers to see nature and wildlife in their natural settings. There is also one container-passenger vessel among this group.

Choose this group of ships if you do not really need much entertainment, large ship facilities, gambling casinos, or several restaurants or if you do not like to wait in lines. If you want to swim in the late evening, or have champagne in the Jacuzzi at midnight, it is far more possible aboard small ships than it is aboard medium or large ships, where more rigid programs provide the kind of inflexible thinking that many passengers detest.

Small Ships: Advantages

- More like small inns than mega-resorts.
- Easy to find your way around, and signage is usually clear and concise.
- At their best in warm weather areas.
- Capable of truly catering to the highest degree of culinary excellence, with fresh foods cooked individually to order.
- Most provide an "open seating" in the dining room; this means that you can sit with whomever you wish, whenever you wish, for all meals.
- Provide a totally unstructured lifestyle, offering a level of service not found aboard most of the larger ships, and no or almost no announcements.
- Provide an "open bridge" policy, allowing passengers to go to the navigational bridge at almost any time (except during difficult maneuvers and in cases of difficult weather conditions).
- Some small ships have a hydraulic marina watersports platform located in the stern and also carry equipment such as jet skis, windsurfers, a waterski powerboat, and scuba and snorkeling gear.
- When the ship is at anchor, going ashore is easy and speedy, with a continuous tender service.

Small Ships: Disadvantages

- Do not have the bulk, length, or beam to sail well in open seas in inclement weather conditions.
- Do not have the range of public rooms or open spaces that large ships can provide. Options for entertainment, therefore, are limited.

Medium Ships (500 to 1,000 Passengers)

Choose from this group of ships if you want to be among up to 1,000 passengers. Medium-size ships are particularly well suited to the smaller ports of the Aegean and Mediterranean and are more maneuverable than the large ships. Some of these ships operate around-the-world cruises and other long-distance cruising itineraries to more exotic destinations that are not really feasible aboard many of the ships in the "small ships" category.

The passenger-space ratio of ships in this group varies between 16.0 and 60.0. Thus, there is a tremendous difference in the amount of space available. Cabins vary from large "penthouse suites" with butler service to tiny inside cabins.

These ships will generally be more stable at sea than those in the "small ships" category, due to their increased size and draft. In addition, they provide more facilities, more entertainment, more dining options, and better food and service. There will be some passenger entertainment, and a more highly structured activities schedule than aboard smaller ships, but less so than aboard large ships.

Some ships in this category feature alternative dining spots, which make a change from the main restaurant and provide more choice.

Medium Ships: Advantages

- They are neither too large nor too small, but often strike a happy balance in terms of size and facilities.
- It is an easy matter to find one's way around.
- They generally sail well in areas of inclement weather, being neither high-sided like the large ships nor of too shallow draft like some of the small ships.

- Lines seldom form (except for ships that are approaching 1,000 passengers), but if they do, they are likely to be short.
- They appear more like traditional ships than most of the larger vessels, which tend to be more "boxy" in shape and profile.

Medium Ships: Disadvantages

- They do not offer as wide a range of public rooms and facilities as do large ships.
- Few have large show lounges for large-scale production shows; hence entertainment tends to be more of the cabaret variety.

Large Ships (over 1,000 Passengers)

Choose from among this group of ships if you enjoy being with lots of other people, in a large-scale city environment, out to have a good time. If you are really sociable and like to experience plenty of entertainment and dining options, these ships will certainly provide a well-packaged standard or premium cruise vacation experience, most probably in a seven-day cruise format.

Choose from among this group of ships if you want to have extensive and complete facilities and programs for families with children of all ages. However, if you meet someone on the first day and want to meet them again, make sure you appoint a place and time, otherwise you may not see them again all week (apart from the size of the ship, they may be on a different meal seating). The ships in this section will have a highly structured array of activities and passenger participation events each day, together with large entertainment venues, and the most lavish production shows at sea today.

The latest ships continue to evolve but feature basically the same public room space, facilities, and features. However, it is in the standard of service, entertainment, lecture programs, level of communication, and excellence in dining services that really can move these ships into high rating categories.

It is possible for these large ships to present a five-star product, but they must be exceptional to do so. Passengers who choose accommodation in the higher-priced suites will experience better service levels than those booking standard cabins. Thus, price is the deciding factor in whether you are, in effect, treated as a first-class or second-class passenger. Class distinction used to be clearly defined; today it is subtle, but it does exist, based on what you pay. Suite-class passengers often receive a gold card for special embarkation and priority disembarkation privileges.

Because these large ships are run on a highly programmed basis, it is difficult, for example, to be able to go swimming in the pools in the late evening or after dinner (they usually start cleaning the decks and putting nets over the pools at about 6 p.m.—far too early). Trying to get champagne delivered to outdoor Jacuzzis late at night is virtually impossible. Such things add to the frustration of passengers. The largest ships have lost the flexibility for which cruise ships were once known and have become victims of legislation, insurance company regulations, and potential lawsuits. Perhaps they will listen to their passengers again soon. We can only hope.

Large Ships: Advantages

- Have the widest range of public rooms and facilities, often an outdoorwrap-around promenade deck, and more space (but more passengers).
- Generally better flexibility in dining options.
- The latest ships have state-of-the-art electronic interactive entertainment facilities and options (good for those into computers and high-tech gadgetry).
- Generally sail well in open seas in inclement weather conditions.
- There are more facilities and activities for people of all ages, particularly for families with children.

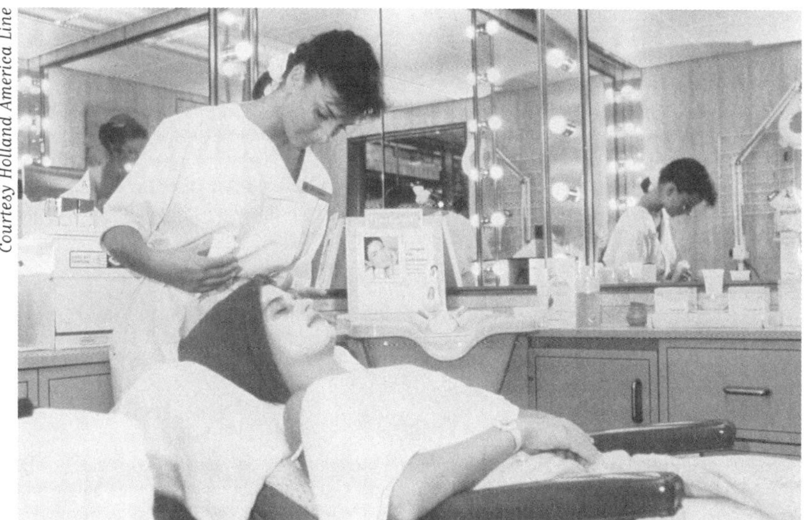

Courtesy Holland America Line

Pamper yourself in the beauty salons found aboard many cruise ships.

Large Ships: Disadvantages

- Trying to find your way around the ship can prove frustrating (at least for the first twenty-four hours).
- Plenty of lines to wait in: for embarkation, the purser's office, elevators, informal buffet meals, shore tenders, shore excursions, and disembarkation.
- Resemble floating hotels, with many items at extra cost.
- Signage is often confusing; there is a lack of elevators at peak times.
- The larger the ship, the more impersonal the service (unless you have "butler" service in a penthouse suite).
- There are simply too many announcements (worse, they could be in several languages).
- Difficult to meet people on different meal seatings (there will almost always be two).
- Dining room staff will be so programmed to provide speedy service, it is almost impossible to sit and dine in a leisurely fashion.
- Food may well be quite bland (cooking for 2,000 is not quite the same as cooking for a little dinner party of twenty).
- Telephoning room service can be frustrating (particularly in those ships with automatic telephone answering systems that state "your call will be answered by room service personnel in the order it was received").
- Room service breakfast is not generally available on the day of disembarkation.
- Almost all large ships close their swimming pools at 6 p.m.; some even take away the deck chairs.
- The in-cabin music aboard the latest batch of ships is supplied through the television set, and it is impossible to turn off the picture (so much for quiet, romantic late-night music and darkened cabins).
- When the ship is at anchor, you will probably need to stand in line, or wait in a lounge, with a "tender ticket"—then wait in the lounge until your ticket number is called—to go ashore by ship-to-shore craft. This can take an hour or more in some ships! Getting back on board could take some time, too.
- Some large ships have only two principal staircases. In the event of an emergency, the evacuation of more than 2,000 passengers could prove most difficult.

The Big Seven Cruise Lines

Cruise lines with large ships (those catering to more than 1,000 passengers) all offer one thing: a well-packaged cruise vacation (generally of seven days) that includes somewhat attractive itineraries, plenty of food, a decent standard of service, and a good standard of entertainment and production shows (mostly by the use of technical effects and great lighting). These ships also provide huge casinos and shopping malls, spa and fitness facilities, and other American mall-like features. Most ask you to pay port taxes, insurance, and gratuities to staff over and above the actual cruise fare, as well as for many additional items. Cruise-only fares are increasingly quoted in cruise brochures, rather than the cruise+air prices quoted for the past several years.

Where they differ, however, is in the facilities, space, food, and service they offer, together with subtle differences in the delivery of the cruise product. Although it is impossible to detail all the differences between these and other cruise lines, here are some of the principal ones between the "Big Seven" North America-based cruise lines. Please note that changes, the upgrading and downgrading of products and services, may have occurred since the completion of this book.

Carnival Cruise Lines

Carried 1.5 million passengers in 1997. This, the largest and most successful, cruise line in the world, specializes in cruises for the young at heart, with constant upbeat music and passenger participation games typically found in an adult summer camp atmosphere. Some could be taken to be potentially degrading, but they are well liked by passengers who associate such activities with "fun," the line's theme. All the ships have incredibly imaginative, multicolored, and very upbeat themed decor.

Carnival does not try to sell itself as an "upmarket" cruise line and consistently delivers exactly what it says it will in its brochures (nothing more, nothing less), for which there is a huge, growing first-time cruise audience. Carnival Cruise Lines provides a well-packaged cruise vacation, with smart new ships that have the latest high-tech entertainment facilities and features.

However, no longer do stewards show you to your cabin upon embarkation. Shore excursions are booked via the in-cabin television system ("Fun Vision"); there is no longer a shore excursion desk (and thus no one to answer questions).

With almost identical ships, the company does a fine job in providing activities to make you either thirsty or gamble. If you do not mind drinks in plastic glasses, and basic hamburger/hot dog and pizza-style fast foods in abundance, this line will provide them for you almost 24 hours a day. The company provides excellent "dazzle and sizzle" production shows and a lot of night-time entertainment options for party people, as well as excellent children's programming.

The cabins throughout the fleet are of a good standard size. Carnival will help you have fun all the way, but do not expect the finesse or small details you might find on other lines. One of the big sources of complaints from passengers is the way they are treated when embarking and disembarking (shoreside staff) and by the large number of security staff aboard ship; Carnival is not the only line to suffer from these complaints, however.

The company has grown dramatically over the last few years and has improved its product delivery substantially. In 1996, the company introduced its "Vacation Guarantee" program—the first of its kind in the industry—with great success. It is especially good for first-time passengers who do not know whether or not they will like cruising (perhaps the rest of the industry should follow suit if they believe in their product). Very, very few passengers consider leaving the cruise.

Celebrity Cruises

Carried 354,512 passengers in 1997. Celebrity Cruises has established an outstanding reputation for its cuisine, particularly in the dining rooms, with their formal service. All meals are made from scratch, and no prepackaged, boxed, or pre-prepared items are used at all—an admirable achievement, and different from all others in the Big Seven group. The sauces accompanying the main dishes, in particular, are excellent. Thus, there is a good degree of taste that is often lacking aboard the larger, standard market ships of today. The waiters (many of them from eastern European countries) are well trained, and it is easy to communicate with them. There are several tables for two in the dining room, although dining room chairs do not have armrests and would be more comfortable with them.

Another reason this line provides a high-quality cruise experience is the fact that each ship simply has many more staff members than other ships of comparable size and passenger number carry. This is particularly noticeable in the housekeeping and food and beverage departments, thus providing passengers with a superior product. The artwork in the latest ships in the fleet is also quite stunning and comprises what is probably the most stunning collection of contemporary art in the cruise industry today.

Two ships in its present five-ship fleet (*Horizon* and *Zenith*) have teak outdoors complete with wraparound promenade decks, while *Century*, *Galaxy*, and *Mercury* do not. The ships are always spotlessly clean, and passengers notice staff constantly vacuuming and polishing almost every hour of the day and night. There are more cleaners and service personnel aboard Celebrity Cruises' ships (per passenger) than in any of the other Big Seven cruise lines. In fact, there are more staff members per passenger than aboard any of the others in the Big Seven group.

Whether the high standards established can be continued under new owners Royal Caribbean International remains to be seen. At present, however, the standard of food and its delivery remains the best of any of the Big Seven.

Costa Cruises

Carried 361,000 passengers in 1997. This company specializes in cruises for Europeans (or passengers with European tastes), particularly Italians. The ships have a definite European feel to them, in their decor and manner of product delivery, which is very laid-back.

The food is very much standard banquet fare, quite disappointing and nonmemorable, as is the service, which displays little or no finesse (it is hard to find an Italian waiter anywhere—something the company was once known for). The company does, however, present good Italian pasta dishes, which are always popular, and, on formal nights, dining by candlelight. But there are no wine waiters! The buffets are particularly disappointing and arguably the worst of all the Big Seven.

The cabins tend to be on the mean side in size, but the decor is fresh and upbeat, and the bathrooms are very practical units (in some ships they have sliding doors, an excellent, practical, space-saving alternative to those that open inward, taking space from the bathroom).

What is good is the variety of public rooms, lounges, and bars, many of which provide fairly intimate spaces. With international passengers, those who speak English should remember that communication with many staff members could prove frustrating. Costa Cruises is the only company to have a chapel aboard each of its ships, with Roman Catholic Mass featured daily. Carnival Corporation, parent company of Carnival Cruise Lines, purchased the company in 1997.

Holland America Line

Carried 440,000 passengers in 1997. This line features teak outdoor promenade decks fleetwide, whereas most other cruise lines feature astroturf or some other form of indoor-outdoor carpeting. The ships are very clean.

The food is quite reasonable, though certainly not memorable, but the food quality, presentation, and service have become very standardized in recent years, and ingredients are mostly from prepackaged goods, although the menu variety has improved. The dining room service is provided much too fast by friendly, almost always smiling Indonesian waiters whose communication skills leave much to be desired. The company offers free ice cream during certain hours of the day aboard all ships and features Starbucks coffee, an American favorite, in certain areas (not all ships). Additionally, hot hors d'oeuvres are served in its bars, something other major lines seem to have discontinued.

When it comes to buffets, there are more canned fruits (liked by older passengers because they are soft) used by this line than by Celebrity Cruises or Princess Cruises, although it is about the same amount as you would find provided by Carnival Cruise Lines or Costa Cruises.

The company's claim to "five star" ships in its brochures is misleading. The ships are extremely pleasant and have an elegant feel to them, with some particularly high quality artwork from the Dutch East and West Indies. In addition, what is excellent is the fact that social dancing is always on the menu; older passengers, in particular, enjoy this availability. However, communication with many of the smiling staff can prove utterly frustrating.

The suites and cabins are of good proportions and come nicely equipped. They are extremely comfortable, and Holland America Line also provides a good array of personal toiletry amenities. An additional bonus item is the canvas tote bag provided to all passengers—a nice extra—useful for shopping or for going to the beach.

Carnival Corporation, the parent company of Carnival Cruise Lines, wholly owns Holland America Line.

Norwegian Cruise Line

Carried 507,304 passengers in 1997. This line provides a good product for a youthful, active, sports-minded audience. Most of the staff is from the Caribbean basin, and in general they do not have the finesse of those ships that have a greater percentage of European staff. The cabins are generally quite attractive and functional, although closet and drawer space is somewhat limited in the newest ships.

Although the dining room cuisine is generally not memorable, lighter fare is available in a "bistro" setting aboard all ships in the fleet for those who want to "eat and run" and do not want to bother with the more formal dining room setting. Sports fans in particular will see much evidence of sports bars and memorabilia aboard these ships. This is good for those young-at-heart sports fans and devotees, who are well catered to in this regard.

As for entertainment, the production shows are of the colorful, well-choreographed, if slightly belittling, high-energy type.

Princess Cruises

Carried 455,000 passengers in 1997. Despite billing itself as "The Love Boat," Princess Cruises does not have any tables for two in its dining rooms (exceptions: *Dawn Princess*, *Grand Princess*, *Sea Princess*, and *Sun Princess*).

Although Princess Cruises was once known for its good food, today it is very much run-of-the-mill fare and not memorable, with the exception of its pasta dishes, which are prepared daily by some talented headwaiters and are very good.

The cabins are of generous proportions (exceptions: *Dawn Princess*, *Sea Princess*, and *Sun Princess*) and well designed. They are all well equipped and very comfortable, with warm decor and practical, well-designed bathrooms. All ships have Filipino cabin stewardesses and plenty of European staff in front-line service areas, as well as their famous British bartenders.

The company's Shore Excursion Program is arguably the best-run of any of the Big Seven companies. Entertainment tends to be very traditional, with a mix of elegant production shows and the usual cabaret acts, but volume levels are thankfully quite moderate. The company now charges extra for airport transfers—shame.

The U.K.-based P&O Group, which also owns P&O Cruises, wholly own Princess Cruises.

Royal Caribbean International

Carried almost 1.3 million passengers in 1997. The standard cabins are small (the latest six ships, *Enchantment of the Seas, Grandeur of the Seas, Legend of the Seas, Rhapsody of the Seas, Splendour of the Seas*, and *Vision of the Seas* have slightly larger cabins). The company places more emphasis than most on passenger participation activities, such as a Passenger Talent Show, Masquerade Parade, Country & Western Jamboree, and so on. It is all very predictable, and the same programming is featured aboard all its ships because it is tried, tested, and proven, if perhaps a little "old hat" by now.

Although Royal Caribbean International's food is of a marginally better standard than that aboard Carnival Cruise Line ships, Carnival ships have larger cabins, as do the ships of Celebrity Cruises, Holland America Line, and Princess Cruises. French, Italian, Oriental, Caribbean, and American are the themes for the menus for different nights. Wine lovers should note that there are no vintages on the wine lists (because they are all so young).

At least the ships have lovely, well-rounded sterns and interesting design profiles that make them instantly recognizable. All the company's ships feature their trademark Viking Crown Lounge, set around the funnel stack—either in front of it or partway up it. The company also provides large, brightly lit casinos and shopping galleries that passengers have to walk through in order to get almost anywhere else—all cleverly designed to extract maximum revenue from you (in a nice way, of course).

Royal Caribbean International also owns Celebrity Cruises, although the two brands are kept reasonably separate as far as the onboard product is concerned.

New vs. Old Ships

Some executives in the cruise industry whose fleets comprise new tonnage are often quoted as saying that all pre-1970 tonnage should be scrapped. Yet, there are many passengers who like older ships. Although it is inevitable that some older tonnage cannot match the latest in high-tech ships, it should also be noted that ships today are simply not constructed to the same high standards, or with the same loving care, as in the past.

New Ships: Advantages

- Incorporate the latest in high-tech electronic equipment and the best in advanced ship design and construction
- Meet the latest safety and operating standards as laid down by the international maritime conventions
- Offer passengers more public room space, with public rooms and lounges built out to the sides of the hull, as open and closed promenade decks are no longer regarded as an essential requirement
- Have public room spaces that are easier to convert if necessary
- Offer more standardized cabin layouts and fewer categories
- Are more fuel-efficient
- Manage to incorporate the latest advances in technology, as well as the latest in passenger and crew facilities and amenities
- Do have a shallower draft, which makes it easier for them to enter and leave ports
- Have bow and stern thrusters, so they seldom require tug assistance in many ports, in this way cutting operating costs
- Have plumbing and air-conditioning systems that are new—and that work
- Have diesel engines mounted on rubber to minimize vibration
- Are usually fitted with the latest submersible lifeboats

The Big Seven Cruise Lines

A look at this chart shows just what cruise lines do (or do not) provide in your cabin and bathroom

Cruise Line	*Carnival Cruise Lines*		*Celebrity Cruises*		*Costa Cruises*
Cabin	Standard Cabins	Suites	Standard Cabins	Suites	Cabins
Bed Linen: Duvets (not sheets/blankets)	No	No	No	Yes	No
Bed Linen: 100% Cotton	No	No	No	No	Yes
Bed Linen: 50% Cotton/50% Polyester	Yes	Yes	Yes	Yes	No
Towels: 100% Cotton	No	No	Yes	Yes	Yes
Towels: 86% Cotton/14% Polyester	Yes	Yes	No	No	No
Non-Allergenic Pillows	No	No	No	No	Yes (2)
Fresh Fruit Bowl	No	No	No	Yes	Yes (2)
Fresh Flowers	No	No	No	Yes	Yes (2)
Telephone	Yes	Yes	Yes	Yes	Yes
Personal Safe	Yes	Yes	Yes	Yes	Yes
Personalized Stationery	No	No	No	Yes	No
Television	Yes	Yes	Yes	Yes	Yes
VCR Player	No	Yes	No	Yes	No
CD Player	No	No	No	Yes (7)	No
Shoe Shine	No	No	No	Yes	Yes
Continental Breakfast	Yes	Yes	Yes	Yes	Yes
Full In-Cabin Breakfast/Lunch/Dinner Service	No	No	No	Yes	No
Complimentary Espresso/Cappuccino Coffees	Yes	Yes	No	Yes	No
Free Local Newspaper in Port (when available)	No	No	No	Yes	No
Complimentary Pressing Service (First 24 Hours)	No	No	No	Yes	No
Cabin Bathroom					
Real Glasses in Bathroom	Yes	Yes	Yes	Yes	Yes
Plastic Glasses in Bathroom	No	No	No	No	No
Soap/Shampoo Dispenser Unit	No	No	No	No	Yes (3)
Soap	Yes	Yes	Yes	Yes	Yes
Shampoo	No	No	No	No	Yes
Conditioner	No	No	No	No	Yes
Combined Shampoo/Conditioner	No	Yes	Yes	Yes	No
Foaming Bath Oil	No	No	No	Yes	No
Hand Lotion	No	Yes	Yes	Yes	Yes
Mouthwash	No	No	No	Yes	No
Shower Cap	No	No	No	Yes	Yes
Loofah Sponge	No	No	No	Yes	No
Hairdryer	Yes (8)	Yes (8)	Yes	Yes	Yes
Weight Scale	No	No	No	Yes	No
Bathrobes	Yes (9)	Yes	No	Yes	No
Shaving/Make-Up Mirror	No	No	No	Yes	No

Key

(1) = Selected suites only

(2) = On request only

(3) = In the shower unit only: *CostaVictoria*

(4) = On back-to-back cruises only (turnaround day)

(5) = Deluxe cabins only

Costa Cruises	*Holland America Line*		*Norwegian Cruise Line*		*Princess Cruises*		*Royal Caribbean International*	
Suites	Standard Cabins	Suites	Standard Cabins	Suites	Standard Cabins	Suites	Standard Cabins	Suites
No	No	No	No	No	No	No	No	No
Yes	No	No	On request	On request	No	No	No	No
No	Yes	Yes	Yes	Yes	Yes	Yes	Yes	Yes
Yes	No	No	Yes	Yes	Yes	Yes	Yes	Yes
No	Yes	Yes	No	No	No	No	No	No
Yes (2)	No	No	No	No	Yes	Yes	Yes	Yes
Yes (2)	Yes	Yes	Yes (2)	Yes	Yes	Yes	No	No
Yes (2)	Yes	Yes	No	Yes	No	Yes	No	No
Yes	Yes	Yes	Yes	Yes	Yes	Yes	Yes	Yes
Yes	No	Yes	No	Yes	Yes	Yes	Yes	Yes
No	No	Yes	No	No	No	No	No	No
Yes	Yes	Yes	Yes	Yes	Yes	Yes	Yes	Yes
No	No	Yes	No	Yes (1)	No	No	No	Yes (6)
No	No	No	No	Yes (1)	No	No	No	Yes (6)
Yes	No	No	No	No	No	Yes	No	No
Yes	Yes	Yes	Yes	Yes	Yes	Yes	Yes	Yes
Yes	Yes	Yes	Yes	Yes	Yes	Yes	Yes	Yes
No	No	No	No	No	No	No	No	No
No	No	No	No	No	Yes (4)	Yes (4)	No	No
Yes	No	Yes	No	No	No	No	No	No
Yes	Yes	Yes	Yes	Yes	Yes	Yes	Yes	Yes
No	No	No	No	No	No	No	No	No
Yes (3)	No	No	No	No	No	No	No	No
Yes	Yes	Yes	Yes	Yes	Yes	Yes	Yes	Yes
Yes	No	No	No	No	Yes	Yes	Yes	Yes
Yes	No	No	No	No	Yes	Yes	No	Yes (5)
No	Yes	No	Yes	Yes	No	No	No	No
No	No	Yes	No	Yes (1)	No	No	No	No
Yes	Yes	Yes	Yes	Yes	Yes	Yes	No	Yes (5)
No	No	No	No	No	No	No	No	No
Yes	Yes	Yes	Yes	Yes	Yes (2)	Yes (2)	Yes	Yes
No	No	No	No	No	No	No	No	No
Yes	No	Yes	Yes	Yes	Yes	Yes	No	No
No	No	No	No	Yes (1)	No	No	No	No
Yes	No	Yes	No	Yes	Yes	Yes	No	Yes
No	No	No	No	No	No	No	No	No

(6) = Royal Suite only

(7) = Penthouse Suite only

(8) = *Carnival Destiny* only

(9) = Balcony cabins *Carnival Destiny* only

New Ships: Disadvantages

- Do not "take the weather" as well as older ships (the experience of sailing across the North Atlantic in November on one of the new mega-ships can be unforgettable)
- Because of their shallow draft, these ships roll—even when there is the slightest puff of wind
- Tend to have smaller standard cabins, which can mean narrow, and often short beds
- Have thin hulls and, therefore, do not withstand bangs and dents as well as older, more heavily plated vessels
- Have decor made mostly from synthetic materials (due to stringent fire regulations) and, therefore, could cause problems for those who are sensitive to such materials
- Are powered by diesel engines, which inevitably cause some vibration although on the latest vessels, the engines are mounted on pliable, floating rubber cushions and are, therefore, virtually vibration-free
- Have completely sealed cabin windows instead of portholes that can be opened

Older Ships (pre-1970): Advantages

- Have very strong, plated hulls (often riveted) that can withstand tremendously hard wear and tear; they can "take the weather" well
- Have large cabins with long, wide beds/berths, due to the fact that passengers of yesteryear needed more space, given that voyages were much longer
- Have a wide range of cabin sizes, shapes, and grades that are more suited to those families traveling with children
- Are powered by steam turbines, which are virtually free of vibration or noise and are considerably quieter and smoother in operation than modern vessels
- Have portholes that, in many instances, actually open
- Interiors are built from more traditional materials such as wood and brass, with less use of synthetic fibers (less likely to affect anyone allergic to synthetics)
- Have deep drafts, which help them to achieve a smooth ride in the open seas

Older Ships (pre-1970): Disadvantages

- Are not so fuel efficient and, therefore, are more expensive to operate than the new ships
- Need a larger crew because of the more awkward, labor-intensive layouts of the ships
- Have a deep draft (necessary for a smooth ride) but need tugs to negotiate ports and tight berths
- Have increasing difficulty in complying with the current international fire, safety, and environmental regulations
- Are usually fitted with older-type open lifeboats
- Ten years or older are more likely to have plumbing and air-conditioning problems in cabins and public areas

The International Maritime Organization (IMO), which is a United Nations agency, was formed in the late 1940s to vote in legislation among its 130-plus member nations regulating the safety of life at sea. The IMO Safety Committee has voted to bring older ships up-to-date by making various safety features, such as smoke detectors, mandatory in all cruise vessels. From 1994, and covering an eleven-year period, all vessels are required to fit sprinkler systems (an expensive but essential retrofit for many older ships) and to provide automatic navigation bridge control of fire doors.

The Crew

A ship's country of registration or parent company location can be a clue to the atmosphere on board, although there are many ships that are registered, for financial reasons, under a flag of convenience, such as Liberia or Panama. The nationality of the officers or management often sets the style and ambience of a ship and the cruise.

You can estimate the standard of service by looking at the crew-to-passenger ratio. You will find better service on those ships that have a ratio of one crew member to every two passengers, or higher.

Except for those ships with a single-nationality crew (as in the case of some German-, Greek-, Italian-, or Japanese-owned cruise lines, for example), the crew mixture can give the impression of the ship being like a miniature United Nations. On a ship carrying a multinational crew, you can expect the language proportions to be something like the following: 38 percent European, 36 percent North/South American, and 26 percent Asian.

In general, if the crew is a happy one, the ship will be happy, too, and passengers will certainly be able to sense it. The best way for any cruise ship to have a happy crew is for the cruise line to provide good accommodation, food, and relaxation facilities for them. The best ships in the world, from the point of view of crew living and working conditions, also tend to be the most expensive ones (the adage "you get what you pay for" tends to be true).

Theme Cruises

Many people are no longer satisfied with the standard kind of entertainment, such as production shows and cabaret acts. Now passengers seek amusements that better match their own tastes. Each year, there is an ever-richer variety of theme cruises available, with many cultural, ecological, and educational subjects.

If you still think that all cruises are the same, the following list will give you an idea of what is available in the way of special theme cruises:

Adventure
Antiques
Archaeological
Art Lovers
Astronomy
Backgammon
Ballroom and Latin Dancing
Big Band
Blues Festival
Bridge
Chess Tournament
Chocoholics
Classical Music
Computer Science
Cosmetology
Country and Western
Diet and Nutrition
Educational
Exploration
Fashion
Film Festival
Food and Wine
Gardening
Gay/Lesbian
Holistic Health
Jazz Festival
Maiden Voyage
Movie Buffs
Murder Mystery
Naturalist/Nude
Octoberfest
Ornithology (Bird Watching)
Photography
Sequence Dancing
Singles
Steamboat Race
Superbowl
Theatrical
Wine Tasting

Perhaps the most sought-after theme cruise will be the Millennium Cruise. All cruise lines will feature one, but not all will be spectacular. Golfers should note that there is a millennium cruise aboard Cunard's *QE2* to the Open Golf Championship, to be played on the Old Course at Scotland's St. Andrews.

Always check with your travel agent to see whether your proposed ship and sailing dates include a theme, particularly if you do not want to be with lots of theme cruise vacationers.

Signs You've Chosen The Wrong Ship

- When, after you've embarked, a waiter hands you a drink in a tall plastic glass from a whole tray of drinks of identical color and froth, then gives you a bill to sign and does not even have the courtesy to say "Welcome Aboard."
- When the so-called "luxury" cabin you booked has walls so thin you can hear your neighbors combing their hair.
- When what the brochure describes as a "full bathtub" actually means a large sink located at floor level.
- When you wanted a quiet, restful cruise, but your travel agent has booked you aboard a ship with 300 baseball fans and provided them all with signed baseball bats and ghetto blasters for their use (solution: read this book thoroughly first!).
- When you packed your tuxedo, but the ship's passengers take "formal" attire to mean clean cut-off jeans and a less-stained T-shirt. Check the brochure carefully.
- When the "medical facility" is in fact located in the purser's office and consists of a box of bandages with directions for their use in a foreign language.
- When the gymnasium equipment is kept in the maître d's office.
- When you have a cabin with an "obstructed view" (this will usually mean there is a lifeboat hanging outside it!), and it is next to or below the disco. Or the laundry. Or the garbage disposal facility.
- When the "Fresh Selected Greens" on the menu means a sprig of parsley on the entree plate at every lunch and dinner seating (boring even on a three-day cruise).
- When the cruise director tries to sell passengers a watch, or a piece of art, over the ship's public address system.
- When first-row seats at a rock concert would be quieter than a chaise longue at the poolside at midday.
- When you get to hear Achy Breaky Heart, Mary Ann, the Macarena, or Yellow Bird ten times during the first day of your cruise.
- When you have to buy shin pads to prevent injury just in case 600 children try to run you over in the passageways.
- When the cruise brochure shows your cabin with flowers and champagne, but you do not get either. If you want them, you get a bill, and in any case the flowers are never watered anyway.
- When the bottled water on your dining room table comes with a bill ever so quickly if you dare open the bottle.
- When "Fresh Catch of the Day" on the menu means that the fish is so old that it would be best used as a door wedge.
- When the brochure says "butler service," but you have to clean your own shoes, get your own ice, and still tip him twice the amount you would for a cabin steward.
- When the Beer Drinking Contest, Hog Calling Contest, Knobby Knees Contest, and Pajama Bingo are listed as "enrichment lectures."
- When the "fresh squeezed orange juice" you just ordered means fresh squeezed, but last week, or the week before that, on land, and then poured into industrial-size containers before transfer to your styrofoam cup on deck.
- When the brochure says tipping is not required, but your waiter and cabin steward tell you otherwise and threaten to break your kneecaps if you do not hand them something that approaches what to you is a large sum of money.
- When the cruise director thoughtfully telephones you at 2:30 a.m. to tell you that the bingo jackpot is up to $1,000!

- When, on the final day, the words "early breakfast" mean 5 a.m., and "vacate your cabin by 7:30 a.m." means you must spend about three hours sitting in the show lounge waiting for disembarkation, with 500 available seats, your carry-on luggage, and 2,000 other passengers, probably playing bingo.
- When the Lifeboat Drill consists of some crew member handing you a lifejacket and asks you to teach him how to wear it, and then asks you what the whistle is for.
- When you are out on deck, you look up and notice a big hole in the bottom of one or more of the ship's lifeboats.
- When the cabin steward tries to sell you a time-share in his uncle's coal mine in wherever he is from, at a greatly reduced price, or says you must go without soap and towels for a week.
- When the proclaimed "five-course gourmet meal" in the dining room turns out to be five courses of salty chicken noodle soup, and a potato.
- When the "Deck Buffet" literally means that there are no tables and chairs, only the deck, to eat off.
- When the brochure shows photos of smiling young couples, but you and your spouse/partner are the only ones under 80.
- When the library is located in the engine room.
- When the captain tells you he is really a concert pianist and his Trinity College diploma is for the piano, not navigation.

ACCOMMODATION

You should feel at home when at sea, so it is important to choose the right accommodation for your needs. Every ship has its strengths and weaknesses, and every cabin has its good and not so good points. So choose wisely, for if you find your cabin (incorrectly called a "stateroom" by some companies) is too small when you get to the ship, it may be impossible to change it or upgrade to a higher price category, as the ship could well be completely sold out.

Although you may request a specific cabin when you book, most lines now designate cabins only when deposits have been received and confirmed. They will, however, guarantee the grade and rate requested. If this is not done automatically, or if you come across a disclaimer such as one spotted recently—"All cabin assignments are confirmed upon embarkation of the vessel"—then I would advise that you get a guarantee in writing that your cabin will not be changed upon embarkation.

There are three main types of accommodation to choose from, with many variations on each theme: penthouse suites (the largest accommodation, with or without private balcony), suites and junior suites (with or without private balcony), outside cabins with a large picture window or one or more portholes (with or without private balcony), and inside cabins (so called because there is no window or porthole). Here are some tips that you should take into consideration when making your choice.

About private balconies

Cruise lines have devised a new gimmick—and a welcome one—private balconies. A private balcony (often called a "veranda") is just that: a balcony where you can sit, enjoy the view, dine, or even have a massage.

There's something quite wonderful about sitting on one's private balcony eating caviar and sipping champagne, or having breakfast à la deck in some exotic place. It is the height of exclusivity. It is also pleasant to get fresh air and to escape cold air-conditioned cabins. The value of a private balcony, for which you pay a premium price, comes into its own in warm-weather areas, but choosing a cabin with a balcony for cruises to cold-weather areas (such as Alaska) is all but pointless.

Some private balconies are not so private, however. Balconies that are not separated by full floor-to-ceiling partitions (as in the case of *Carnival Destiny, Carnival Triumph, Maasdam, Norway, Oriana, Ryndam, Statendam*, and *Veendam*, for example) don't quite cut it. You could get noise from your neighbor. You could also get mountains of smoke from a smoking neighbor in the cabin in front of your own. There is no guarantee. But when all things are in your favor, a balcony is a wonderful extra. Some ships have balconies that have full floor-to-ceiling privacy partitions and an outside light as well (*Century, Galaxy, Mercury*, and *Radisson Diamond*, for example), a real bonus (some partitions in *Century, Galaxy, and Mercury* are full, some are partial, depending on deck and location).

If you choose a ship with expensive suites that have forward-facing private balconies at the front of the ship (such as in *Seabourn Legend, Seabourn Pride, Seabourn Spirit, Silver Cloud*, and *Silver Wind*, for example), note that although the forward view may be good, when the ship is moving forward the wind speed can make these balconies all but unusable. In addition, be aware that when the ship drops anchor in ports of call, the noise can be very, very loud (better than any early morning alarm!).

Those ships with private balcony cabins (or suites) positioned along the port and starboard sides (such as *Asuka, Carnival Destiny, Century, Crystal Harmony, Crystal Symphony, Dawn Princess, Galaxy, Grand Princess, Mercury, Royal Princess, Royal Viking Sun, Silver Cloud, Silver Wind*, and *Sun Princess*, for example) may be better. If you really want sunshine, however, remember that this will depend on the direction the ship is traveling (and the time of day). The profiles in Part Two of this book give you the num-

Did You Know...?

...that the first "en suite" rooms (with private bathroom in cabin) were on board Cunard Line's *Campania* of 1893?

...that the first liner to offer private terraces with their first-class suites was *Normandie* in 1935?

...that the first single-berth cabins built as such were aboard Cunard Line's *Campania* of 1893?

...that the first ships to feature private balconies were a trio of ships built for the Compagnie des Messageries Maritimes, France? They were the 13,520-tonne *Cambodge, Laos,* and *Vietnam,* built in 1953.

...that the first ship to be fitted with interior plumbing was the 6,283-tonne *Normandie,* of 1883?

...that the first ship to be fitted with an internal electric lighting system was aboard the Inman liner *City of Berlin* in 1879?

...that cruising today is not the same as it was in the nineteenth century? On the first cruise ships there was little entertainment, and passengers had to clean their own cabins! Orders enforced on all ships sailing from Great Britain in 1849, for example, instructed all passengers to be in their beds by 10 p.m.!

ber of cabins with private balconies aboard each ship. You should look at the ship's deck plan carefully with your travel agent to find where your chosen cabin is located.

All private balconies have railings to lean on, but the balconies in some ships have solid steel plates between railing and deck, so you cannot look out to sea when you are seated (*CostaClassica, CostaRomantica, Dawn Princess,* and *Sun Princess,* for example). Better are those ships with balconies that have clear glass (*Century, Galaxy, Mercury,* and *Nordic Empress,* for example) or horizontal bars.

One thing is almost certain: if you have a private balcony once, you will want one again and again. You will probably never go back to a standard outside (or inside) cabin. Balconies are like cruises—totally addictive.

How much to pay

The amount you pay for accommodation aboard most cruise ships is directly related to the size of the cabin, the location within the ship, and the facilities provided. There are various other factors that are also taken into consideration when cruise lines grade their accommodation.

There are no set standards within the cruise industry; each line implements its own system according to ship size, age, construction, and the profit potential. It is unfortunate that many cruise lines still neglect to give cabin sizes in their brochures, but you will find the size range in The Ratings and Evaluations section in Part Two of this book.

Before you select your accommodation, decide how much you can afford to spend, including airfare (if applicable) and onboard expenses (remember to include the estimated cost of shore excursions, port charges, and tips), because this will determine the cabin categories available to you. It is advisable to choose the most expensive cabin you can afford, especially if it is your first cruise, as you will spend some time there. If it is too small (and most cabins are small), you just might suffer from "cabin fever," and so the cruise might fall short of your expectations. Alternatively, it is better to book a low-grade cabin on a good ship than a high-grade cabin on a poor ship. If you are in a party of three or more and do not mind sharing a cabin, you will achieve a substantial saving s per person, so you may be able to go to a higher-grade cabin without paying any extra money. In general, you will get precisely the kind of cabin you pay for.

Size of cabins

Ships' cabins should be looked upon as hotel rooms in miniature, providing more or less the same facilities. There is one difference—that of space. Ships necessarily have space limitations and, therefore, tend to utilize every inch efficiently. Viewed by many owners and designers as little more than a convenient place for passengers to sleep, shower, and change for dinner, a cabin's space is often compromised in favor of large public rooms and open areas. In some of the smaller inside and outside cabins, changing clothes is a challenge, and to take a shower, you'd need to be an acrobat!

There really is no such thing as an average cabin; cabin size will depend on the space that is allocated to accommodation within a ship of whatever tonnage measurement and principal dimensions. New ships are fitted with more standardized cabin sizes, because they are made in modular form. They also have integrated bathrooms, often made from non-combustible phenolic-glass-reinforced plastics and fitted into the ship during construction.

Generally, the larger the ship, the more generous it will be with regard to cabin space. Cabins can vary from the compact 121 sq. ft. (11.24 m^2) standard cabins in Royal Caribbean International ships to a magnificent 1,515 sq. ft. (140.7m^2) penthouse suite in Celebrity Cruises' *Century*, *Galaxy*, and *Mercury*. Remember that cruise ships are operated both for the pleasure of passengers and for the profit of the cruise companies. This is the reason why cabins in many new or modern ships are on the small side. The more cabins that a ship can provide, the more fare-paying passengers can be carried, and the greater the potential for on-board revenue.

Ships of yesteryear were able to offer passengers more spacious cabins simply because there were more days at sea, fewer ports of call, and fewer entertainment rooms. This encouraged many to spend a great deal of time in their cabins, very often entertaining other passengers. Although most modern ships have smaller cabins, they are certainly adequate for standard-length cruises, and they allow maximum space in public rooms for entertainment and social events.

Some cruise brochures are more detailed and specific than others when it comes to deck plans and cabin layouts. Deck plans do not normally show the dimensions, but they are drawn to scale, unless otherwise noted.

You can get a good idea of the space in a cabin by examining the cabin plan of the cruise category you are interested in. By looking at the beds (each twin bed is between 2 feet and 3 feet wide and 6 feet long), you can quite easily figure out how much empty or utilized space (bathroom, closets, and so on) there is. If the cabins appear to be the same size on the deck plan, it is because they are the same size, with the exception of suite rooms, which will be substantially larger. This is particularly true in some newer ships, where cabins are standardized.

Ask the cruise line, via your travel agent, for the dimensions of the cabin you have selected if it is not indicated on the deck plan. This will give you some idea of its size. Pace out a room at home as a means of comparison.

Location of your cabin

An "outside" cabin is preferable by far, especially if this is the first time you are to go cruising. An "inside" cabin has no portholes or windows, making it more difficult to orient yourself or to gauge the weather or time.

Cabins that are located in the center of a ship are more stable, and they also tend to be noise- and vibration-free. Ships powered by diesel engines (this applies to most new vessels) create and transmit some vibration, especially at the stern. For those who are technically minded, passenger cabins typically result in a noise level of 50-55 dba (this affects the standard cabins) and 40-50 dba (this affects the suites and upper-grade cabins).

Take into account your personal habits when choosing the location of your cabin. For example, if you like to go to bed early, do not pick a cabin close to the disco. And if you have trouble walking, select a cabin close to the elevator (and not on a lower deck, where there are none).

Generally, the higher the deck, the higher the cabin price and the better the service—an inheritance from the transoceanic times, when upper-deck cabins and suites were sunnier and warmer.

Cabins at the bow (front) of a ship are slightly crescent-shaped, given that the outer wall follows the curvature of the ship's hull. But they are usually roomier and cheaper. However, these forward cabins can be exposed to early morning noises, such as the anchor being dropped at ports where the ship cannot dock.

Connecting cabins are fine for families or close friends, but remember that the wall between them is usually thin, and each of the neighboring parties can plainly hear anything that's being said next door.

If you book a deluxe upper-deck cabin, check the deck plan carefully; the cabin could have a view of the lifeboats. Many cruise lines now indicate these "obstructed-view" cabins in the brochure. Make sure to read the fine print. Similarly, cabins on promenade decks may have windows that can easily be looked into by passing strollers on deck.

If you select a cabin that is on one of the lower decks, be advised that engine noise and heat become more noticeable, especially at the aft end of the vessel and around the engine casing. Be aware that in many older ships, elevators will probably not operate to the lowermost decks.

Facilities

Cabins will provide some, or all, of the following features:

- Private bathroom (generally small and compact) fitted with shower, sink, and toilet. Higher-priced cabins and suites often have full-size bathtubs—some may even have a whirlpool bath and/or bidet, a hairdryer, and considerably more space.
- Electrical outlets for personal appliances, usually U.S. standard, sometimes both 110 and 220 volts.
- Multichannel radio; in some ships, television (on regular or closed circuit) and video equipment.
- Two beds or a lower and upper berth (plus, possibly, another one or two upper berths) or a double-, queen-, or king-size bed (usually in suites or deluxe accommodation). In some ships, twin beds can be pushed together to form a double.
- Telephone, for intercabin or ship-to-shore communication.
- Depending on cabin size, a chair, or chair and table, or sofa and table, or even a separate lounge/sitting area (higher-priced accommodation only).
- Refrigerator and bar (higher-priced accommodation only).
- Vanity/desk unit with chair or stool.
- Personal safe.
- Closet space, some drawer space, plus storage room under beds for suitcases.
- Bedside nightstand/table unit.
- Towels, soap, shampoo, and conditioner. (Many of the ships, and particularly the more "upscale" ones, will provide a greater selection of items.)

Many first-time passengers are surprised to find their cabins furnished with twin beds. Double beds are a comparative rarity on the cruise ships except in the higher-priced suites. In some of the ships with small cabins (*Carousel*, *Olympic Countess*, *Rhapsody*, and *SuperStar Sagittarius*, for example), the twin beds convert to sofas for daytime use and at night are converted back by the steward.

The two beds are placed in one of two configurations: parallel (with little space in between) or, preferably, in an "L" shape, giving more floor space and the illusion that the cabin is larger.

Aboard some ships (especially the older ones) you will find upper and lower berths. A "berth" is a nautical term for a bed held in a wooden or metal frame. A "Pullman berth" tucks away out of sight during the day, usually into the bulkhead or ceiling. You climb a short ladder at night to get into an upper berth.

The Suite Life

Suites are the most luxurious and spacious of all shipboard accommodation. The definition of a suite is that it is a "suite of rooms" and should comprise a lounge or sitting room separated from a bedroom by a solid door (not just a curtain); a bedroom with a double-, queen-, or king-size bed, or large, movable twin beds; and one or more bathrooms. Be advised, however, that many cruise lines inaccurately describe some accommodation as suites when in fact they are simply nothing more than larger cabins with a curtain to divide the sitting area from the sleeping area. In ships, the best suites (usually the "owner's suite" or "penthouse suite") are located high and in the quietest part of the ship.

Some ships have whole decks or sections of decks devoted to suites. Shipowners and cruise line marketing companies know that some passengers will pay handsomely to stay in the best and quietest accommodation but will also expect the best service (usually provided by a butler), and preferential treatment throughout the ship.

Some of the most desirable suites on the smaller ships are those in the front of the ship, which have a private, forward-facing balcony. Not all are quiet, however, and some are downright noisy. The Royal Suites (701/702) in *Silver Cloud* and *Silver Wind*, for example, are subject to intense noise from the ship's winches, housed on an open deck directly in front of the suites. This means that you will be awakened in the early morning on every day that the ship docks. These suites are also subject to noise from the anchor going down or coming up, at anchor ports.

Is it the same in all of the smaller ships? Well, no, it is not, simply because ships such as *Sea Goddess I*, *Sea Goddess II*, *Seabourn Legend*, *Seabourn Pride*, and *Seabourn Spirit*, for example, have covered mooring decks; those in *Silver Cloud* and *Silver Wind* do not.

Most forward-facing suites have windows that can be covered not only by curtains but also additionally by electric or pull-down blinds for an almost complete blackout at night. Suite bathrooms are quite large (for a ship) and have a large bathtub (often with a whirlpool tub) and a shower, hairdryer, toilet, deluxe sink (or two), and (in some ships) a bidet. Some ships boast gold bathroom fittings in their best suites! Although this is the exception and not the rule, the bathrooms attached to the suites are usually excellent.

Suites should also be equipped with a stereo system, television, VCR player, CD player, refrigerator, and a partially or fully stocked bar, and occupants can command the very best of service round-the-clock (they should have butler service).

In ships such as *Norwegian Crown* and *QE2*, each suite is decorated in a different style, with authentic or reproduction period furniture, beautiful drapes, and fine furnishings. In *Century*, *Crystal Harmony*, *Crystal Symphony*, *Galaxy*, *Mercury*, *QE2*, and *Royal Viking Sun*, a personal butler will attend you (in some ships, however, butlers are nothing more than waiters in a different uniform).

Suites are best for a long voyage, when a ship crosses vast stretches of ocean for five or more days at a time. They are particularly suitable for impressing a loved one and for entertaining in. Be aware that in large ships (those carrying more than 1,000 passengers), there may well be a whole deck or two devoted to penthouses and suites, but you will have to share the rest of the ship with those in lower-priced accommodation. That means there is no preferential seating in the showroom, the dining rooms, on sunbathing decks, or anywhere else. You may, however, get separate check-in facilities and preferential treatment upon disembarkation, but your luggage will be lumped together with that of everyone else (not so "suite"!). No cruise line has yet recognized, nor properly catered to, the growing need for exclusivity for its suite occupants.

Most of the suites have their own balcony or veranda, although it is wise to check the deck plan in case the veranda faces the lifeboats or other obstructive apparatus. Suites are usually sheltered from the noise of the ship and the wind and should provide considerable privacy. Some of the best suites are the exclusive and very private owner's suites such as in *Seabourn Legend, Seabourn Pride, Seabourn Spirit,* and *Vistafjord.*

Reading a deck plan

Learning to read a deck plan is a relatively easy matter. The plan is always laid out so that the bow (front part of the ship) faces to your right or to the top of a page.

Traditionally, ships designated the central deck (which is equivalent to the main lobby of a hotel) as the Main Deck. This is where you will find the purser's office and the other principal business offices. Some of the modern ships, however, do not use the term "Main Deck," preferring a more exclusive- or attractive-sounding name. All ships also have a Boat Deck, so named because this is where the ship's lifeboats are stowed.

In the past, many ships also had a Promenade Deck, an enclosed walkway along the length of the deck on one or both sides of the ship. This was popular with passengers crossing the Atlantic, for when the weather was cold or foggy, they could still take their stroll. It is located between the Main Deck and the Boat Deck, except in some modern ships where Boat and Promenade is interchangeable. When the new generation of specialized cruise ships came into being in the 1970s, the Promenade Deck disappeared in favor of public entertainment lounges across the full beam of the ship, and the name of the deck was changed. Some of the ships that have been built recently have returned to the idea of a Promenade Deck.

The uppermost decks usually tend to be open and feature sunning space, multisports areas, and running or jogging tracks that may or may not encircle the ship.

The Restaurant Deck has undergone a metamorphosis, too. It used to be buried on one of the ship's lower decks so as to avoid the rolling motion of nonstabilized ocean liners. Even on the most luxurious liners, there were often no portholes, because the deck was placed below the waterline. As cruising replaced transportation as the prime source of revenue, newer ships were designed with restaurants set high above the waterline. Big picture windows provide diners with a panoramic view of the port or the surrounding sea. The Restaurant Deck can be either above or below Main Deck.

Traditionally, popular-priced cabins have been below Main Deck, with high-priced suites occupying space on one or two of the uppermost decks. Suites are always located where the view and privacy are best and the noise is least. In the latest ship designs, however, almost all accommodation areas are located above Main Deck to cut down on disturbing engine noise and vibration.

Older ships designated their accommodation decks A, B, C, D, and so on; most of the modern ships have given these decks more appealing names, such as Acapulco, Bimini, Coral, and Dolphin.

TYPICAL CABIN LAYOUT

The following rates are typical of those you can expect to pay for (a) a seven-day and (b) a ten-day Caribbean cruise aboard a modern cruise ship. The rates are per person, and include free roundtrip airfare or low-cost air add-ons from principal North American gateways.

Luxury outside suite with private verandah, separate lounge area, vanity area, extralarge double or queen-sized bed, bathroom with tub, shower, and extensive closet and storage space.

(a) $2,250 (b) $4,000

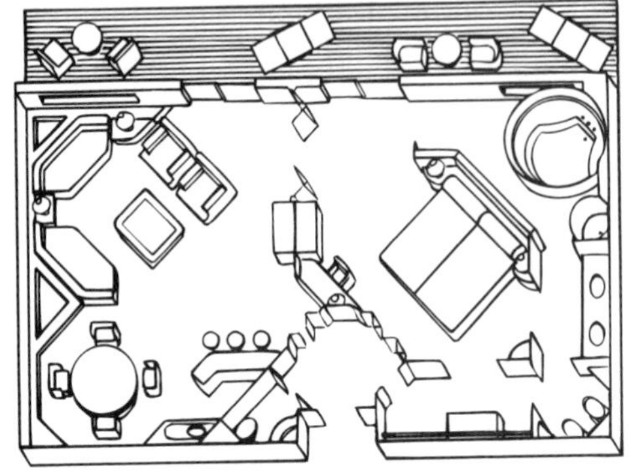

Deluxe outside cabin with lounge area, double or twins beds, bathroom with tub, shower, and ample closet and storage space.

(a) $2,250 (b) $2,850

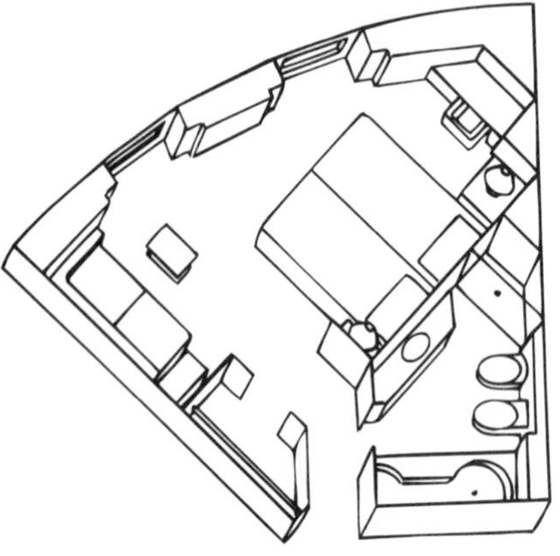

Note that in some ships, third- and fourth-person berths are available for families or friends wishing to share. The upper Pullman berths, not shown on these cabin layouts, are recessed into the wall above the lower beds.

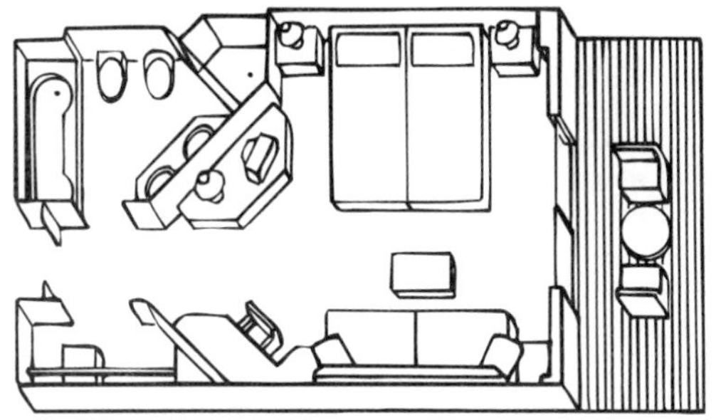

Large outside double with bed and convertible daytime sofabed, bathroom with shower, and good closet space.

(a) $1,750 (b) $2,450

Standard outside double with twin beds (plus a possible upper third/fourth berth), small sitting area, bathroom with shower, and reasonable closet space.

(a) $1,450 (b) $1,975

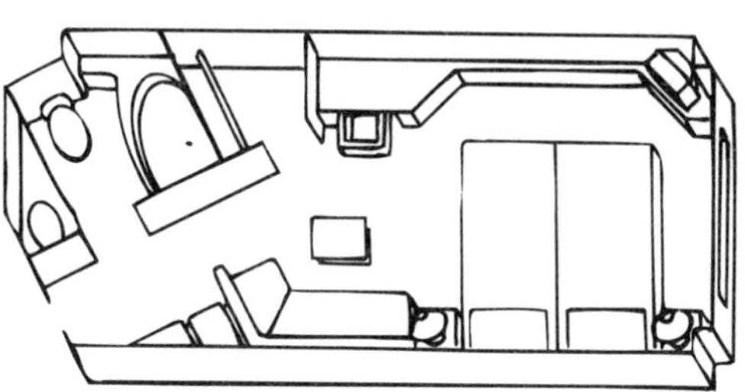

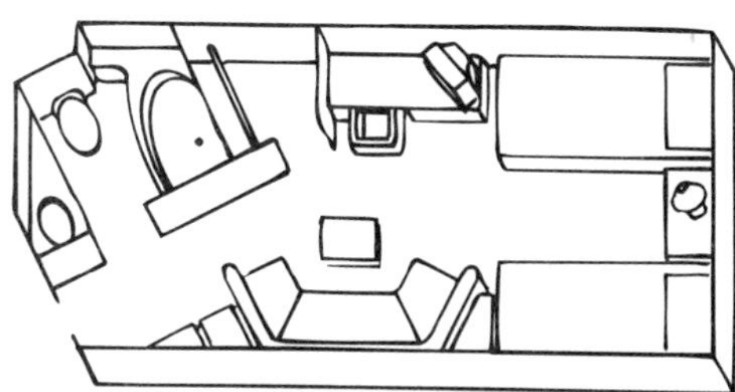

Inside double with two lower beds that may convert into daytime sofabeds (plus a possible upper 3rd/4th berth), bathroom with shower, and fair closet space.

(a) $1,250 (b) 1,750

BOOKING YOUR CRUISE

Travel agents

Many people think that travel agents charge for their services; they do not (perhaps they will soon), but they do earn commission from cruise lines for booking their clients on a cruise.

Can you do your own booking direct with the cruise line? Yes and no. Yes, you can book your cruise direct with a small number of cruise lines (mostly in Europe, Asia, and Japan), and no, because most cruise lines do not generally accept personal checks, thus in effect requiring you to book through a travel agent. In the United States, for example, 95 percent of cruise bookings are made by travel agents.

A good travel agent will probably ask you to complete a profile questionnaire. When this is done, the agent will go through it with you, and perhaps ask you some additional questions before making suggestions about the ships and cruises that seem to match your requirements.

Your travel agent will handle all matters relevant to your booking, and off you go. You may even find a nice flower arrangement in your cabin when you arrive or a bottle of wine or champagne for dinner one night, courtesy of the agency.

Consider a travel agent as your business advisor, and not merely as a ticket agent. As a business advisor, a travel agent should have the latest information on changes of itinerary, cruise fares, fuel surcharges, discounts, and any other related items, and should also be able to arrange insurance (most important) in case you have to cancel prior to sailing. Some cruise lines now have a totally automated computerized booking system. Some travel agents are linked into the computer systems of the major airlines, allowing them access to almost all shipboard information, including such details as the cabin dimensions and whether there is a porthole or window.

Ten questions to ask your travel agent

- Is air transportation included in the cabin rate quoted? If not, what will be the extra cost?
- What other extra costs will be involved? (These can include port charges, insurance, gratuities, shore excursions, laundry, and drinks)
- What is the cruise line's cancellation policy?
- If I want to make changes to my air arrangements, routing, dates, and so on, will the insurance policy cover everything in case of missed or canceled flights?
- Does your agency deal with only one, or several different insurance companies?
- Does the cruise line offer advance booking discounts or other incentives?
- Do you have preferred suppliers, or do you book any cruise on any cruise ship?
- Have you sailed aboard the ship I want to book or that you are recommending?
- Is your agency bonded and insured? If so, by whom?
- If you book the shore excursions offered and recommended by the cruise line, what insurance coverage is provided?

Cruise consultants

Remember, there is no "Best Cruise Line in the World" or "Best Cruise Ship"—only the ship and cruise that's right for you. It is the job of your cruise agent or travel agent to find exactly the right ship for your needs and lifestyle. They are all out there, but there is a more bewildering choice than ever before.

A number of cruise-only agencies, often called "cruise consultants," have sprung up in the last few years. Most cruise-only agencies are reputable, but some sell only a limited number of cruises. These are "preferred suppliers," because they may be receiving special "overrides" on top of their normal commission (but they probably know their limited num-

Courtesy Douglas Ward

Your cruise tickets and documents come nicely packaged.

ber of ships well). If you have chosen a ship and cruise, be firm and book exactly what you want, or change agencies. In the U.K. look for a member of the Guild of Professional Cruise Agents. The Passenger Shipping Association of Retail Agents (PSARA) provides in-depth agent training in the U.K. as well as a full "bonding" scheme to protect passengers from failed agencies or cruise lines. In the United States, look for a member of the National Association of Cruise Oriented Agencies (NACOA). Note that in the U.S. most agencies are not "bonded" in case of failure.

Many traditional travel agencies now have a special cruise section, with a knowledgeable consultant in charge. A good agent will help you solve the problem of cabin choice, but be firm in the amount you want to pay, or you may end up with a larger and more costly cabin than you had intended.

In the United States, Cruise Lines International Association (CLIA), a marketing organization with about three dozen member lines, does an admirable job providing training seminars for cruise and travel agent members (about 25,000) in North America.

Cruise brokers

Cruise brokers (often called cruise consolidators or cruise discounters) are useful for last-minute bookings. They often have unsold cabins at substantially discounted rates. Most brokers have low overheads, using only a phone and automated message services. British passengers can look at Teletext, on television channels 3 and 4, for travel companies offering discounts. Note: this is not an endorsement of these companies. The old saying "verbal agreements are only as good as the paper they are written on" applies here. Do not send any money to the cruise agency until you've first received a written invoice detailing all the key items.

If you are looking for full service and help in choosing a cruise, then a cruise broker is not for you; if you can book at the last minute, a cruise broker may save you a substantial amount of money. What you gain in price advantage you may lose in choice—of dinner seatings, cabin category and location, and other arrangements. You may also have to pay your airfare to join the cruise.

If you do book through a large consolidator or packager, you should know exactly who is responsible for getting you where you are supposed to be at the right time. Read the fine print.

The cruise line/operator/packager may seem initially responsible, but there is no set standard within the industry at present. The best advice is to read the fine print when booking. If you have complicated travel arrangements, make sure the cruise line provides you with a list of contacts for every stage of your journey. Standards and legal requirements also vary from country to country.

Reservations

Rule number one: plan ahead and book early. After choosing a ship, cruise, date, and cabin, the agency will ask for a deposit, roughly 10 percent for long cruises and 20 percent for short cruises (most cruise lines ask for a set amount, such as $250).

When you make your initial reservation, you should also make any special dining request known, such as your seating preference, whether you want the smoking or non-smoking sections, or any special dietary requirements. Prices quoted in cruise brochures are based on current taxes at the time the brochures are printed. All cruise lines reserve the right to change these prices in the event of tax increases, fluctuating rates of exchange, fuel surcharges, or other costs beyond their control.

Confirmation of your reservation and cruise fare will be sent to you by your travel agent. The balance is normally requested forty-five to sixty days prior to departure, depending on individual line policy. For a late reservation, you have to make payment in full as soon as space is confirmed. Shortly after the line has received full payment, your cruise ticket will be issued, along with baggage tags and other items.

When it arrives, check your ticket. In these days of automation, it is prudent to make sure that the ship, date, and cruise details you paid for are correctly noted. Also verify any connecting flight times.

Extra costs

Despite brochures boldly proclaiming that "everything's included," in most cases you will find this is not strictly true. In fact, on most standard Caribbean cruises "all-exclusive" would be a more appropriate term.

Your fare covers ship transportation, landing and embarkation charges, cabin accommodation, all meals, entertainment, and service on board. With few exceptions, it does not include alcoholic beverages, laundry, dry cleaning or valet services, shore excursions, meals ashore, gratuities, port charges, cancellation insurance (this covers you only if the cruise itself is canceled by the cruise line or the tour operator), optional onboard activities (such as skeet shooting, bingo, or horseracing and casino gambling), or special features or conveniences not mentioned in the cruise line's brochure.

Aboard most cruise ships, expect to spend about $25 per day per person on extras, plus another $10-$12 per day per person in gratuities. This can add up to as much as $500 per couple on a seven-day cruise. Genuine exceptions can be found in some of the small ships (those carrying fewer than 500 passengers), where just about everything is included.

Here are some examples of typical extra costs:

Bottled Water . . . . $2.50-$7 (per bottle)
Cappuccino/Espresso . . . . $1.50-$2.50
Cartoon Character bedtime "Tuck-In" Service $20
Wash one shirt . . . . $1.50-$3
Dry-Clean Dress . . . . $3-$7.50
Dry-Clean Jacket . . . . $4-$8
Golf Simulator . . . . $15 (30 minutes)
Hair Wash/Set . . . . $17-$28
Haircut (men) $20
Ice Cream . . . . $1-$3.75
In-cabin Movies $6.95

Laundry Soap . . . .$0.50-$1.50
Massage . . . .$1-plus per minute (plus tip)
Satellite Phone/Fax . . . .$6.95-$15.50 per minute
Sodas (Soft Drinks) . . . .$1-$2
Souvenir Photo . . . .$6-$8
Trapshooting (three or five shots) $5, $8
Wine/Cheese Tasting $5
Wine with Dinner . . . .$7-$500

To calculate the total cost of the cruise you've chosen, not including any extra-cost services you might decide you want once on board, read the brochure and, with the help of your travel agent, write down a list of the costs involved. Here are the approximate prices per person for a typical seven-day cruise on a well-rated medium or large cruise ship. This estimate is based on an outside two-bedded cabin:

Cruise fare $1500
Port charges . . . .$100 (if not included)
Gratuities $50
Total per person $1650

Divide this by seven and you get a rough cost of $235 per person per day. For this price, you wouldn't even get a decent hotel room in London, New York, Tokyo, or Venice!

Discounts and incentives

Looking at the fares listed in current cruise line brochures is just the starting point. Because of overcapacity in certain cruise markets, at specified times of the year (such as the beginning and at the end of the summer) cruise discounts and special incentives are widespread. It is wise to enlist the eyes and ears of a good travel agent and check out current discounts.

One way of saving money is to book well ahead, so that you can profit from one of many variations on the "super savers" theme. Many cruise lines now offer larger discounts for those who book the farthest ahead, with discounts decreasing as the date of the cruise comes closer. Another method is to reserve a cabin grade, but not a specific cabin—booked as "TBA" (to be assigned). Some lines will accept this arrangement and they may even upgrade (or possibly have to downgrade) you on embarkation day if all the cabins in your grade have been sold. It is useful to know that the first cabins to be sold out are usually those at minimum and maximum rates.

Another way of economizing is to wait for a "standby" cabin on sailing day or shortly earlier. Some lines offer standby fares thirty days before sailing (sixty days for transatlantic crossings). They may confirm a cabin (some lines even assign the ship) on the day of embarkation. Those who can go suitcase-in-hand to the dockside might be lucky enough to get on at minimum rate (or less) and be assigned a last-minute cancellation of a high-grade cabin.

For cruises to areas where there is year-round sunshine, there is an "on" and an "off" season. Naturally, the best cruise buys are in the off-season, while the on-season commands the highest prices. Some lines offer a "shoulder" season, which is somewhere between the on- and off-seasons. Peak season is during the Christmas and New Year vacation. Check with your travel agent to get the best rate for the time you wish to go.

Many of the cruise lines offer highly reduced rates for third and fourth persons sharing a cabin with two full-fare adults. Individual policy varies, so ask your travel agent for current rates. On some sailings, you might even go free.

Many cruise lines also have their own versions of "frequent passenger" clubs. You can join most without a fee (some, like Celebrity Cruises' Captain's Club, charge $35), and you will be notified first of any special offers that are being made. Discounts can frequently be as high as $1500 per cabin, so it is worth belonging to a club, especially if you like cruising with a particular line.

Most cruise fares are listed as "per person double occupancy" or "ppd." If you are single and wish to occupy a double cabin on your own, you may have to pay a single supplement (see Cruising for Romantics).

However, many lines will let you share a cabin at the standard ppd rate. The line will find you a cabin partner of the same sex, and you can both save money by sharing. The line cannot guarantee that you will like your partner, but they will invariably specify which cabin categories are available for sharing.

For those wishing to take their children on a cruise, there are some excellent bargains available for families (see Cruising for Families).

Cancellations and refunds

It is highly recommended that you take out full cancellation insurance (if it is not included), as cruises (and air transportation to and from them) must be paid in full before your tickets are issued. Without such insurance, if you cancel at the last minute, even for medical reasons, it generally means that you will lose the entire amount. Insurance coverage can be obtained from your travel agent for a nominal charge.

Cruise lines usually accept cancellations more than thirty days before sailing, but all charge full fare if you do not turn up on sailing day, whatever the reason. Other cancellation fees range from 10 to 100 percent, depending on the cruise and length of trip. Curiously, many lines do not return port taxes, which are not part of the cruise fare.

If you cancel with sufficient notice due to serious medical problems, a doctor's letter should be obtained. This is usually regarded sympathetically by cruise lines.

Medical insurance

Whether you intend to travel overseas or cruise down a local river, and your present medical insurance does not cover you, you should look into extra coverage for your cruise. A "passenger protection program" is a service usually prepackaged by the cruise line, and the charge for it will appear on your final invoice unless you decline. This is worth every penny, and it typically covers such things as evacuation by air ambulance, high-limit baggage, baggage transfers, personal liability, and missed departure.

Port taxes/handling charges

These are assessed by individual port authorities and are generally shown with the cruise rates for each itinerary. Port charges will be part of the final payment for your cruise, although they can be changed at any time up to the day of embarkation. The most expensive port charge at time of press was Bermuda, at $60 per passenger (in 1996, over half a million passengers visited the tiny island). The typical handling charges for a cruise ending in America, for example, include an U.S. Customs User/Federal Inspection Fee for each passenger.

Air/sea packages

When your cruise fare includes a one-way or round-trip air ticket, airline arrangements usually cannot be changed without paying considerably more toward the fare. This is because cruise lines often book space on aircraft on a special group basis to obtain the lowest rates. Changing your air ticket or flight within thirty days of your cruise will mean a surcharge to the cruise line of about $25 per person.

If you do change, remember that in the event of the airline canceling your flight, the cruise line is under no obligation to help you or return your cruise fare if you do not reach the ship on time. If you are joining a ship in a far-off country, allow some extra days (particularly in winter) just to cover the risk that your domestic airline connections do not work or are cancelled.

Because of the group-fare ticket basis by which cruise lines work, be aware that this can also mean that the airline routing to get you to your ship may not always be direct or nonstop. The airlines' use of this hub-and-spoke system can be extremely frustrating for passengers. Because of changes to air schedules, cruise and air tickets are often not sent to passengers until a few days before the cruise. A small number of upscale cruise lines include business-class air tickets.

In Europe, air/sea packages generally start at a major metropolitan airport, and some include first-class rail travel to the airport from outlying districts. In the United States, it is no longer necessary for passengers to depart from a major city, because many cruise lines will include connecting flights from small suburban airports as part of the whole package.

There are many variations on the air/sea theme, but all have the same advantage of offering passengers an all-inclusive price, even down to airport-to-ship transfers and port charges.

Most cruise lines offer the flexibility of jetting out to join a ship in one port and flying home from another. This is especially popular for Mediterranean, transcanal (Panama Canal), and long cruises. Cunard even has a transatlantic program that lets you cruise one way and then fly back the other. They have taken the idea even further by allowing you to return on specially selected, supersonic Concorde flights for a small additional charge.

Another advantage of almost every air/sea package is that you only have to check your baggage once—at the departure airport—for even the baggage transfer from plane to ship is handled for you. This does not, however, include intercontinental fly/cruises, where you must claim your baggage at the airport on arrival in order to clear it though customs.

You may be able to hold an open return air ticket, allowing you to make either a pre- or post-cruise stopover. This depends on the type of contract that exists between a cruise line and its airline partner. Usually, however, you have no stopovers en route, nor can you even change flights.

Whenever the price of an air/sea package is all-inclusive, it is often presented as "free air" in publicity material. Of course, there is no such thing as a free air ticket—the cost of the airfare is simply hidden in the overall cruise fare.

However, air tickets are not always included. Some cruise lines simply do not believe in increasing their rates to cover "free air," or they simply may wish to avoid subsidizing airline tickets. These are, for the most part, upmarket lines that operate long-distance cruises to some of the more exotic destinations. In some countries (such as Germany), the term "free air" cannot be stated in advertising, by law.

Pre- and post-cruise programs

To extend your cruise, it may be worth looking into the extra-stay programs that are offered by many cruise lines. These can be taken either before or after your cruise and can add another dimension to your cruise vacation. Hotel add-ons are well noted in most cruise brochures, but you will need to look deeper to find some of the more unusual add-ons.

These can include some of the world's most famous and luxurious trains, such as the famed Orient Express (which travels between Venice, London, or Paris), the Eastern and Oriental Express (which runs between Bangkok and Singapore), or The Royal Scotsman (which connects London and Edinburgh, with the possibility of additional train cruises around Scotland). Any of these can add a scenic land perspective to a luxury cruise.

CRUISE CUISINE

Food is still the single most talked- and written-about aspect of the cruise experience. One of the most sensual pleasures in life is eating; show me a person who is not aroused by the aroma of food being prepared, or who is not charmed by a delicious, satisfying meal in fine surroundings, with a correctly laid table.

There is a special thrill of anticipation that comes with dining out in a fine restaurant. It is the same on board a luxury cruise ship, where gracious dining in elegant, friendly, and comfortable surroundings stimulates an appetite already sharpened by the bracing sea air. Some passengers do carry shipboard dining to the limit, however. Indeed, I've seen plenty of people eat more in one meal than most others do in two or three days!

Attention to presentation, quality, and choice of menu in the honored tradition of the transatlantic luxury liners has made the cruise ships justly famous. Cruise lines know that you will spend more time eating on board than doing anything else, so their intention is to cater to your palate in every way possible, within the confines of a predetermined budget.

Aboard today's cruise ships, as in other areas of life ashore, YOU GET WHAT YOU PAY FOR. If you pay little for your cruise, you will get little, in the way of choice and quality. If you pay more, you will get more. On low-priced cruises, remember that you will get frozen food, which has been cooked or reheated. To get fresh food (particularly fresh fish and the best cuts and quality of meats), cruise lines must pay significantly more, which affects the cost of your cruise. Again, let me state, YOU GET WHAT YOU PAY FOR.

What is spent on food will range from about $8 to as much as $45 per person per day, depending on the cruise line and standard of cuisine required, although there are exceptions at the higher end, particularly in the Japanese market, where fresh fish and seafood costs are exorbitantly high, and food costs of $50-$75 per person per day are normal. Most cruise ships catering to the standard (mass) market spend between $8 and $17.50 per person per day.

The "intelligent standardization" of the food operation and menus translates to cost-effectiveness in the process of food budgeting for any cruise line. Being able to rationalize expenditures and provide maximum passenger satisfaction is almost a science today.

Courtesy Douglas Ward

Breakfast for two in your cabin is possible aboard many ships.

Did You Know...?

...that there is an unwritten rule, called "Ward's Third Law of Gluttony," which states that passengers will take precisely twice as much food as they need from breakfast and luncheon buffets, then add a lettuce leaf or two to justify the guilt complex brought about by overconsumption?

...that the liner *Amerika* in 1938 was the first ship to have an alternative restaurant open separately from the dining saloons? It was named the Ritz Carlton.

...that the first à la carte restaurant aboard a passenger ship was in the German ship *Amerika* of 1905?

...that the longest bar on any cruise ship is aboard *Aida*? It is 195 feet (59.5 meters) long.

...that a whole county in Iowa raises all its beef cattle for Carnival Cruise Lines?

...that *Legend of the Seas* was christened with the world's largest bottle of champagne? It had to be specially made, and was a "Sovereign-size" bottle (the equivalent of thirty-four bottles) of Moet & Chandon champagne.

...that the United States Line's *Manhattan* in 1931 was the first ship to have a cocktail named after it—perhaps the only ship with that distinction?

...that 2,000 Methuselah-sized bottles (the equivalent of twelve bottles) of Cristal champagne will be made specially for Crystal Cruises' passengers to purchase for the eve of the year 2000 (the millennium). The cost, of course, will be $2,000 each!

Cruise lines tend to put a maximum effort into convincing passengers how good their food is, often to the point of being unable to deliver what is shown in their brochures, and, thus, anticipated by passengers. Generally, however, the level of food provided is good, comparable to any family-style restaurant ashore. The best rule of thumb is to ask yourself what you would expect, relative to what you are paying, if you were to eat out in a good restaurant. Does the ship's dining experience meet or exceed your expectations? Would you come back again for the food? If you would, then that particular cruise line has met its promise to feed you with fine food. Although gourmet cuisine is enjoyed by a small percentage of people ashore, few ships have the facilities or availability of fresh foods to equal even those of a one-star Michelin-rated restaurant.

The cuisine will inevitably vary, and this will depend on the nationality and regional influence of the executive chef, his staff, and the ship's country of registry or ownership. Thus, choosing a cruise and ship also involves thinking about the kind of food that will be served on board, and how it is served.

There are perhaps as many different tastes as there are passengers. Some like plain food, some like spicy food. Some like nouvelle cuisine, some like meat and potatoes and lots of it. Some like to try new things, some stick with the same old stuff. It is all a matter of personal taste. So, what the "standard" market cruise lines do is to cater to general tastes. Upscale cruise lines can offer food cooked more or less individually to your liking, but, as in a good restaurant, you get what you pay for. This is why cruise ship standards are so different. Some people are accustomed to drinking coffee out of styrofoam cups and eating food off paper plates at home. Others wouldn't dream of doing that and expect fine dining, with food correctly served on fine china, just as they do at home.

Some ships have full place settings that include as many as ten pieces of cutlery; others provide the correct cutlery just before each course is served (this is more labor-intensive, but the time it takes to lay the cutlery gives the galley more time to get ready for the next course). If you find it bewildering or do not know which knife and fork to use for which course, the rule is always to start at the outermost pair and work toward the innermost pair. The knife and fork closest to where the plate is set will be for the entree (main course). Some ships have special knives for fish courses; others do not, requiring you to use a standard (flat) knife.

While on the subject of place settings, if you are left-handed, make sure you tell your waiter at your first meal exactly how you want your cutlery placed and to make sure that tea or coffee cup handles are turned in the correct direction (this is impossible with a fish knife, of course!). It would be even better if your right- or left-hand preferences were established at the time of booking and the cruise lines passed on the information to the ship.

Menus for luncheon and dinner are usually displayed outside the dining room each morning so that you can preview the day's meals. Aboard some of the more up-market ships, menus will be delivered to your suite or cabin each day, or placed on bar counters. When looking at the menu, one thing you will never have to do is to consider the price—it is all included.

Depending on the ship and cruise, you could sit down to various gourmet specialties, such as duck à l'orange, beef Wellington, lobster thermidor, or prime roast rib of Kansas beef. Or maybe châteaubriand, veal scaloppini, fresh sea bass in dill sauce, or rack of roast English lamb.

To top off the meal there could be crème brulée, chocolate mousse, kiwi tart, or that favorite standby, the massed meringue—Baked Alaska—not to mention the tableside flambé choices such as Cherries Jubilee or Crêpes Suzette. And you can always rely on your waiter to bring you a double portion, should you so wish! Of course, these specialties may not be available on all ships. But if you would prefer something that is not on the menu, see the maître d', give him 24 hours' notice (plus a small tip), and, if the galley can cope, it could well be all your own.

Despite what the glossy brochures say, however, not all meals on all cruise ships are gourmet affairs by any stretch of the imagination. In general, cruise cuisine can be compared favorably with the kind of "banquet" food served in a good hotel or family restaurant—in other words, tasteless. For a guide to the standard of cruise cuisine, service, and presentation on a particular ship, refer to The Ratings and Evaluations section in Part Two of this book, but remember that the rating of cruise cuisine is also determined in relation to the per diem cost averages paid by passengers.

Experienced passengers who "collect" cruises have seen it, smelled it, and tasted it all before on cruise ships: real rubber duck-foul (fowl) food, fit only to be stuffed, painted, and used as children's toys in their bathtubs! Talk about rock-hard lobster, leather fish, inedible month-old shrimp, "third-world" veterinarian-rejected chicken, and grenade-quality meats. And not to mention teary-eyed or hammer-proof cheese, soggy salty crackers, unripe fruits, and coffee that looks (and tastes) like army surplus paint! Or yellow-green leaves that could be either garnish or an excuse for salad! Sadly, it is all there, in the cruise industry's global cafeteria.

One reason that the food aboard ships cannot always be a gourmet experience is that the galley (ship's kitchen) may be striving to turn out hundreds of meals at the same time. What you will find is a very fine selection of highly palatable, pleasing, and complete meals served in very comfortable surroundings, in the company of good friends (and you do not have to do the cooking!). Add to this the possibility of a view from huge picture windows that overlook a shimmering sea, and perhaps even dining by candlelight. Dining in such a setting is a delightful and relaxed way to spend any evening.

Many cruise lines with large ships now feature buffets for breakfast and luncheon (they do not require as much staff, cutlery, linen, or cooked foods), one of the effects of discounted fares. Strangely, passengers do not seem to mind lining up for help-yourself food at the buffets. For the amount of money being paid, sitting down to a meal with service is surely better. Buffets look fine when they are fresh, but after a few minutes of hungry passengers serving themselves, they do not. And, one learns soon enough that the otherwise sweet little old ladies can become ruthlessly competitive when the buffet starting time comes round! Many cruise lines forget to put labels on food items, which slows down any buffet line. Particularly useful would be labels on salad dressings and sauces. Passengers should not have to play guessing games when it comes to food.

Plate service vs silver service

Most fine restaurants ashore now present what is termed "plate service" rather than "silver service." Plate service is when the food is presented as a complete dish, the chef's total concept of how the food should look; its color combinations, the size of the component parts, and its positioning on the plate—all of it representing the quality of his or her creativity.

In silver service, usually all component parts are brought to the table separately, so that the diner, not the chef, can make the choices regarding the food and what goes on the plate. Silver service works best when there is plenty of time to deliver the product. In most cruise ships, however, silver service is now all but impossible. What some cruise lines classify as silver service actually means silver service of vegetables only, with the main item, be it fish, fowl, or meat, already positioned on the plate.

In most cruise ships, plate service is now the norm. It works well and means that most people seated at a table will be served at the same time and can eat together, rather than let their food become cold, as is often the case in silver service, unless several waiters are available to serve one table.

Healthy eating

Nowadays, with more emphasis being placed on low-cholesterol and low-salt diets, many cruise ships feature "spa" menus where the heavy, calorie-filled sauces have been replaced by nouvelle cuisine and spa cuisine.

Some cruise lines now include basic nutritional information, such as the calorie count, fat, protein and carbohydrate content, on their "spa" or "alternative" menus, or for selected light items on their regular menus. However, this is mostly for dinner and very seldom for breakfast or luncheon.

If you are on any kind of restrictive diet, such as low-salt, low-fat, vegetarian, vegan, or macrobiotic, let your travel agent know at the time of booking, and get them to confirm that the ship can actually handle your dietary requirements.

The dining room

In many cruise ships, the running and staffing of dining rooms are contracted out to an outside catering organization specializing in cruise ships. Ships that are continually in waters away from their home country find that professional catering companies do an excellent job and provide a degree of relief from the operation and staffing of their dining rooms. The quality is generally to a very high standard. However, ships that control their own catering staff and food are often those that go to great lengths to ensure that their passengers are satisfied.

Here are a few examples of the principal maritime catering companies: Apollo Catering (U.S.), CFCS (Italy/U.S.), Century Catering (U.S.), I.C.H. (Switzerland), Ligabue Catering (Italy), and Zerbone Catering (Italy).

Dining room staff

The maître d' is an experienced host, with shrewd perceptions about compatibility; you can trust him when he gives you your table seating. If a table reservation has been arranged prior to boarding, you will find a table assignment/seating card in your cabin

A Sample Menu From Celebrity Cruises

Appetizers

Crab Cocktail Nautilus

Melon and Ham — Mozzarella in Carroza

Vegetable Terrine with Tomato Coulis

Soup

Cream of Chicken Bergerette — Consomme Sevigne — Chilled Avocado

Salads

Bermuda Garden Salad
Seasonal mixed Greenery with Tomatoes and Bermuda Onion Rings

Spinach Majestic
Spinach with Mushrooms, Egg and sliced Almonds

Roquefort, Thousand Island, Mustard Vinaigrette or Creamy Garlic Dressing

Entrees

* Scaloppine Di Vitello Al Limone
Thin slices of milk-fed Veal enhanced by a light Lemon Sauce

Mahi Mahi Amandine
Fillet of Mahi Mahi baked in Butter with flaked Almonds

Roast Turkey
A native American taste treat with the traditional trimmings, a Savory Dressing, Giblet Gravy and Cranberry Compote

Linguine Alla Gorgonzola
Pasta cooked al dente and served in a creamy Gorgonzola Sauce with Capocolla and Mushrooms

Steak Au Poivre
Grilled New York Steak with Peppercorn Sauce

Tiny Green Beans — Cauliflower Polonaise

Pear Potatoes — Maitre D'Hotel Potatoes — Sweet Potatoes

Desserts

Joconde Biscuit Alize — Tiramisu — Pineapple with Maraschino

Profiteroles with Sabayon and Cream

Pistachio, Vanilla or Black Walnut Ice Creams — Today's Sherbet

Fruit and Cheese
An assortment of fresh seasonal Fruit complemented by fine Cheese

Monterey Jack — Camembert — Danish Blue — Tomme des Pyrennees

* *Lean and Light*

The Chef Presents

We take pride in presenting Chef Michel Roux's recommendation for this evening's meal, foods especially designed to complement each other and provide a fine dining experience.

MELON AND HAM
Sweet seasonal Melon complemented by Parma Ham

CONSOMME SEVIGNE
A delicately seasoned Chicken Consomme offered with Chicken Quenelles

SPINACH MAJESTIC
Fresh Spinach tossed with Mushrooms, Hard-boiled Egg and sliced Almonds with a zesty Mustard Vinaigrette Dressing

STEAK AU POIVRE
Tender New York Steak grilled to your preference and presented with a Sauce of crushed Peppercorns

JOCONDE BISCUIT ALIZE
A Pastry Chef's triumph, Sponge Cake separated by layered Hazelnut Mousse, Raspberries and Chocolate

The Wine Steward Suggests

The following Wines are recommended to complement the Chef's Selection

Frascati Pallavicini, Estate Bottled, 1988, Latium $12.00

Lyeth Cabernet Sauvignon, Alexander Valley, 1985, California $30.00

Beverages

Freshly brewed Regular or Decaffeinated Coffee — Iced Coffee

Tea, Herbal Tea and Iced Tea — Hot Chocolate — Milk

Celebrity Cruises menus and service have been designed under the personal supervision of international chef, Michel Roux. He is unrivalled in Europe as one of the most innovative and exceptional of restauranteurs.

Courtesy Holland America Line

Dining at the captain's table is a special treat.

when you arrive. If this is not the case, you will need to make your reservations with the maître d' or one of his assistants. If you wish to reserve a special table or location in the dining room, do so as soon as possible after boarding.

Unless you are with your own group of friends, you will be seated next to strangers in the dining room. Tables for two are a rarity, except in some small ships and in some of the upmarket liners. Most tables seat six or eight people. It is a good idea to ask to be seated at a larger table, because if you are a couple seated at a table for four and you do not get along with your table partners, there is no one else to talk to. Remember, if the ship is full, it may be difficult to change tables once the cruise has started.

If you are unhappy with any aspect of the dining room operation, the earlier you complain the better. Do not wait until the cruise is over and then send a scathing letter to the cruise line, for then it is too late to do anything positive. See whoever is in charge—they are there to help you to enjoy your meals during the cruise. They want your comments—good or bad.

Each table has at least one waiter and one assistant waiter or busboy. In some ships, up to thirty nationalities may be represented among dining room staff, who are taught to be courteous, charming, and helpful.

Many ships like to organize special incentive programs, such as a "waiter of the month" competition. This sort of thing helps to keep the staff on their toes, especially if they want to reach the "best" tables. The result is that passengers really do get fine service.

The best waiters are without doubt those who have been trained in the exclusive European hotels or in hotel and catering schools such as the Maritime Catering Institute in Salzburg, Austria. These highly qualified individuals will excel in silver service and will always be ready with the next course when you want it. They will also know your likes and dislikes by the second night of the cruise. They normally work on the upmarket ships, where dignified professionalism is evident everywhere in the dining room.

Smoking/nonsmoking

Many cruise operators and their ships have totally nonsmoking dining rooms. These are mentioned in the ship descriptions in Part Two. Many cruise ships have dining rooms that provide smoking and nonsmoking sections, and most ask that passengers smoke only cigarettes and not cigars or pipes.

Nonsmokers who wish to sit in a nonsmoking area of the dining room should tell the maître d' or his assistants when reserving a table. Also, you should know that at open seating breakfasts and luncheons in the dining room (or informal buffet dining area), smokers and nonsmokers may be together. If you are bothered by smoke, request a table in a nonsmoking area.

The captain's table

The captain usually occupies a large table in or near the center of the dining room, the table seating eight or ten people picked from the passenger or "commend" list by the maître d'. Alternatively, the captain may ask personal friends or important company officials to dine with him. If you are invited to the captain's table for dinner, it is gracious to accept, and you will have the chance to ask all the questions you like about shipboard life.

The captain will not attend meals if he is required on the ship's bridge. When there are two seatings, the captain may have dinner at the first seating one night and at the second seating the next night. In some ships, the captain's guests are changed daily so that more people have a chance to enjoy the experience.

Generally, senior officers also host tables, and being seated with them can be a fascinating experience, especially as they tend to be less formal.

Which seating?

The best cruise ships feature "open" or "single" seating for meals, where you may dine in unhurried style. Open seating means that you can sit at any available table, with whom you wish, at whatever time you choose within dining room hours. Single seating means you can choose when you wish to eat, but have regularly assigned tables for the entire cruise. The majority of ships operate a two-seating arrangement.

The typical first-seating passengers include couples (those over fifty), families, groups, early risers, and those passengers who like to dine quickly and at their normal dining hours at home.

The typical late-seating passengers include couples (those under fifty), singles, honeymooners, late-risers, and those who like to dine in a leisurely and relaxed style over meals.

Those at the late seating may not be hungry enough to eat again at the midnight buffet, because it begins about two hours later.

Typical meal times for two-seating ships are:

Breakfast:	6:30 a.m./8:30 a.m.
Lunch:	12 noon/1:30 p.m.
Dinner:	6:30 p.m./8:30 p.m.

You should note that some ships that operate in Europe (the Mediterranean) or South America may have even later dinner seatings. Costa Cruises, for example, has its second dinner seating at 9 p.m. instead of the more usual 8:15 p.m. or 8:30 p.m. Dinner hours may vary when the ship is in port to allow for the timing of shore excursions.

You may also find that some of the better seats for the shows and at the movie theater have been taken by those who were on the first seating. Most ships resolve this problem by scheduling two performances for all the shows at night.

Most ships request that you enter the dining room within fifteen minutes after the meal has been announced. This is out of consideration for your fellow passengers, your table companions, and the dining room staff. This is especially true for those on the first seating, but it provides little time to sit and linger over cocktails or after-dinner drinks—one of the drawbacks of the two-seating arrangement.

Special requirements

If you are counting calories, vegetarian, or require a salt-free, sugar-restricted, macrobiotic or other diet, let the cruise line know when you first book. The line will then pass the information to the ship, so that your needs can be met. Some of the larger cruise lines, including Carnival Cruise Lines and Royal Caribbean International, now feature a vegetarian entree on all their dinner menus.

Because the food on all the cruises is regarded as "international" or French cuisine, be prepared for dishes that are liberally sprinkled with salt. The vegetables are often cooked with sauces containing dairy products, salt, and sugar. If you want food more to your taste, have a word with the maître d'.

First and second nights

For new and experienced passengers alike, the first evening at sea is exciting, much as the opening night at the theater is. Nowhere is there more a feeling of anticipation than at that first casual dinner when you get a foretaste of the feasting to come.

By contrast, the second night of a cruise tends to be formal, as this is usually the ship captain's welcome-aboard dinner. For this the chef will pull out all the stops to produce a gourmet meal. The dinner follows the captain's cocktail party, which takes place in one of the ship's larger lounges and is an excellent opportunity to meet your fellow passengers and the ship's officers. Toward the end of the party, the captain will give his welcome-aboard speech and may also introduce senior members of the staff.

Theme nights

Some of the nights on the cruise will be organized as special theme nights, when waiters dress up fittingly and the menu is planned to suit the occasion.

A typical day

From morning till night, food is on offer to the point of overkill, even on the most modest cruise ship. In fact, in some ships you can eat up to seven meals a day.

Early risers will discover piping hot coffee and tea on deck from about as early as 6 a.m. A full breakfast, of up to six courses and as many as sixty different items can be taken in the main dining room. For a more casual meal, you may wish to eat al fresco or buffet style at the outdoor deck café (ideal after an early swim or if you do not wish to dress for the more formal dining room). The choice is obviously more restricted than in the main dining room, but good nonetheless. Times of dining will be set out in your daily program.

A third possibility, especially for romantics, is to have breakfast in your cabin. There is something rather special about waking up and eating breakfast without getting out of bed. Some ships offer you a full choice of breakfast items, while others opt for the more simple, but usually well presented, Continental breakfast.

In many ships, the midmorning bouillon is an established favorite, often served up on one of the open decks—a legacy from the grand days of the transatlantic steamships. Bouillon aboard *Vistafjord* is served right at your chair-side from trolleys that parade around the promenade deck.

At lunch-time, there are at least two choices: a hot lunch with all the trimmings in the dining room, or a buffet-style luncheon in the outdoor café, featuring light meals, salads, and one or two hot dishes. On some days, this could well turn into a lavish spread, with enough food for a feast (special favorites are the seafood and tropical fruits). In some ships there will be a separate hot dog and hamburger stand or a pizzeria, where everything is cooked right in front of you but usually presented with less style than at a McDonald's restaurant.

At around 4 p.m. another throwback to the heyday of the great liners takes place: afternoon tea—of course in the best British tradition—complete with finger sandwiches and cakes. This is often served in one of the main lounges to the accompaniment of live music (it may even be a "tea-dance") or recorded classical music. Afternoon tea usually lasts about an hour (although in some ships it is only half an hour, in which case it is best to be on time so as not to miss out).

Dinner is, of course, the main event of the evening, and apart from the casualness of the first and last nights, it is formal in style.

If you enjoy wine with your dinner, you will find an excellent choice on board. Upmarket ships will carry a selection of wines far more extensive than you will find even in the better restaurants ashore, while other ships will provide some excellent inexpensive wines from the country of the ship's registry or ownership. It is wise to order your wine for the evening meal at lunch time, or at the very latest as soon as you are seated; the wine stewards tend to be extremely busy during the evening meal and need to draw their stock and possibly have it chilled. Note that if you sail aboard one of the smaller ships, the selection of half-bottles of wine will be very limited, as most small ships have little space and would rather stock full rather than half-bottles of wine.

A few hours after dinner, there is the Midnight Buffet, without doubt the most famous of all cruise ship meals. It really is at midnight (until 1 a.m.) and is a spread fit for royalty. Like dinner, it may be based around a different theme each night: a King Neptune seafood buffet one evening, an Oriental Buffet the next, a tropical fruit fantasy the third, and so on. The desserts at these buffets are out of this world.

On one night (usually the penultimate evening), there will be a magnificent gala midnight buffet, for which the chefs pull out all the stops. Beautifully sculpted ice carvings will be on display, each of them fashioned from a 300-lb. block of ice. Some of the ships also demonstrate ice carving.

Even if you are not hungry, stay up to see this display of culinary art—it is something most people never forget. In addition—or as an alternative—to the midnight buffet, pizza may be served for the late-night disco dancers or the casino crowd.

On a typical day at sea, the ship's bars will be open from about 10 a.m. to late into the night, depending on the bar, its location, and the number of patrons. The details of bar hours are given in the ship's Daily Program.

The executive chef

Each ship has its own executive chef, who is responsible for planning the menus, ordering enough food (in conjunction with the food manager), organizing his staff, and arranging all the meals on the menus.

When a cruise line finds a good executive chef, it is unlikely that they will part company. Many of the best ships employ European chefs who are members of the prestigious Confrérie de la Chaîne des Rôtisseurs, which is the world's oldest gourmet society. The top food and beverage experts work together with their executive chefs, striving for perfection.

One of the principal aims of any good executive chef will be to make sure that menus are never repeated, even on long cruises. He will be inventive enough to offer his passengers dishes that will be new gastronomic experiences for them. On long voyages, the executive chef will work with specially invited guest chefs to offer passengers a taste of the finest in regional cuisines. Sometimes, he may also purchase fish, seafood, fruit, and various other local produce in "wayside" ports and incorporate them into the menu with a "special of the day" announcement.

The galley

The galley ("kitchen" for landlubbers) is the very heart of all food preparation on board. At any time of the day or night, there is plenty of activity here—whether baking fresh bread at 2 a.m., making meals and snacks for passengers and crew around the clock, or decorating a special cake for a passenger's birthday celebration.

The staff, from executive chef to potwasher, must all work together as a team, each designated a specific role—and there is little room for error.

The galley and preparation areas consist of the following sections (the names in brackets are the French names given to the person who is the specialist in the area of expertise):

Fish Preparation Area (Poisonnier): This area contains freezers and a fully equipped preparation room, where fish is cleaned and cut to size before it is sent to the galley.

Meat Preparation Area (Butcher/Rotisseur): This area contains separate freezers for meat and poultry. These temperatures are kept at approximately 10°F. There are also defrosting areas (35°F to 40°F). Meat and poultry are sliced and portioned before being sent to the galley.

Vegetable Preparation Area (Entremetier): Vegetables are cleaned and prepared in this area.

Sauce Preparation Area (Saucier): This is where the sauces are prepared.

Soup Preparation Area (Potagier): Soups are made in huge tureens.

Cold Kitchen (Garde Manger): This is the area where all cold dishes and salads are prepared, from the simplest sandwich (for room service, for example) to the fine works of art that grace the most wonderful buffets. The area is well equipped with mixing machines, slicing machines, and refrigeration cabinets where prepared dishes are stored until required.

Bakery and Pastry Shop (Baker): This area provides the raw ingredients for preparing food and will contain dough mixers, refrigerators, proving ovens, ovens, and containers in all manner of shapes and sizes. Dessert items, pastries, sweets, and other confectionery are prepared and made here.

Pantry: This is where cheese and fruits are prepared and where sandwiches are made.

Dishwashing Area: This area contains huge conveyor-belt dishwashing machines. Wash and rinse temperatures are carefully controlled to comply with the relevant public health regulations. This is where all the special cooking utensils are scrubbed and cleaned and where the silverware is scrupulously polished.

Standards of hygiene

Galley equipment is in almost constant use. Regular inspections and maintenance help detect potential problems.

Hygiene and correct sanitation are also vital in the galley, and there is continual cleaning of equipment, utensils, bulkheads, floors, and hands. All the staff is required to wear rubber-soled shoes or boots, and the senior officers conduct regular inspections of galleys, equipment, and personnel.

Passenger cruise ships sailing from U.S. ports or visiting them are all subject to sanitation inspections by officials from the United States Public Health (USPH) Department of

Health and Human Services, under the auspices of the Centers for Disease Control and Prevention. This is a voluntary inspection, not a mandatory inspection (it is based on forty-two inspection items), and the cruise line pays for each ship inspection. A similar process takes place in Britain under the Port Health Authority, which has more stringent guidelines even than the USPH.

On board many ships, a hygiene officer oversees health and sanitation standards. A tour of the galley has proved to be a highlight for passengers in some smaller ships. On larger vessels, passengers are not usually allowed into the galley, due to constant activity and insurance restrictions. A Behind the Scenes video, for use on in-cabin television, may be provided.

In accordance with internationally accepted standards, the potable water brought on board or produced by distillation on cruise ships, should contain a free chlorine or bromine residual equal to or greater than 0.2 ppm (parts per million). This is why the drinking water served in the dining room often tastes of chlorine.

Environmental concerns

Cruise ships refine oil, treat human waste, and incinerate garbage, but that's not enough today, as pressures continue to mount for clean oceans. Cruise ships and their operating companies have a unique position among all shipping interests. They are not likely to damage the ocean environment as compared with oil tankers, although spillage of any kind is regrettable. Because of ever-increasing regulations and environmental concern, many cruise lines are replacing plastics with more biodegradable and recyclable materials. For example: plastic plates used in certain areas aboard general market ships should be replaced by china plates or washable and reusable hard plastics; the plastic laundry bags should be replaced by paper bags; plastic bottles used for in-cabin amenities should be replaced by containers made of recyclable or reusable materials. Cruise lines should make a greater effort to purchase products that have been produced from recycled paper.

Other environmental concerns involve the condition of the air aboard ships. Of particular note is the fact that a ship's air-conditioning system can provide an ideal site for mold growth such as that found in the aerospora group (including Cladosporium sp.). Thus, it is vitally important that cruise lines not skimp on maintenance and the replacement of filters and other items in the air-conditioning systems of today's ships.

Waste disposal

Today's cruise ships need to be capable of efficient handling of garbage and waste materials, as trash generated by passengers and crew must be managed, stored, and disposed of efficiently and economically. The larger the ship, the more waste will obviously be created, and the greater the need for efficient, reliable disposal systems.

Trash includes bottles, cans, corrugated cartons, fabrics, foodstuffs, paper products, and plastic containers, as well as medical waste, sludge oil, wet waste, and so on. The sheer magnitude of trash and waste materials can be highly problematic, especially on long cruises that have a large complement of passengers and crew. If solid waste is not burnable or cannot be disposed of overboard (this type of waste must be biodegradable), it must be stored aboard ship for later off-loading and disposal on land.

Although some of the latest breed of cruise ships are already equipped with "zero-discharge" facilities, other, older cruise ships still have a way to go when it comes to efficient and economical garbage handling. One method of dealing with food waste is to send it to a waste-pulping machine that has been partially filled with water. Cutting mechanisms reduce the waste and allow it to pass through a special sizing ring to be pumped directly overboard or into a holding tank or an incinerator when the ship is within three-mile limits.

Whichever method of waste disposal is chosen, it, as well as the ship, must meet the extremely stringent demands of Annex V of MARPOL 73/78 international regulations.

Sample Food and Beverage Consumption and Stores

Consumption and stores required for just one transatlantic crossing of *QE2* (six days):

Food Consumption

Beef	9,000 lbs.	Cereals	800 lbs.
Veal	8,000 lbs.	Rice/Other Grains	3,000 lbs.
Lamb	2,000 lbs.	Flour	5,000 lbs.
Pork	2,500 lbs.	Cream	250 gallons
Chicken	3,500 lbs.	Milk	1,150 gallons
Duck	1,000 lbs.	Ice Cream	450 gallons
Turkey	1,000 lbs.	Butter	2,500 lbs.
Bacon	2,000 lbs.	Eggs	43,000
Sausages	2,000 lbs.	Juices	3,000 gallons
Ham	8,000 lbs.	Jam/Marmalade	300 dozen jars
Caviar	75 lbs.	Jam/Marmalade (bulk)	700 lbs.
Foie Gras	15 lbs.	Pickles/Condiments	200 bottles
Fish	1,000 lbs.	Tea Bags	12,800
Lobsters	1,500 lbs.	Kosher Food	800 lbs.
Crabs	800 lbs.	Biscuits	2,000 lbs.
Tinned Fish	1,500 cans	Dog Biscuits	50 lbs.
Fresh Vegetables	12,000 lbs.	Baby Food	600 jars
Potatoes	3,000 lbs.		

Bar Consumption

Champagnes	780 bottles	Liqueurs	260 bottles
Assorted Wines*	1,560 bottles	Port	120 bottles
Whiskey	500 bottles	Sherry	240 bottles
Gin	600 bottles	Beer (passengers)	5,230 bottles
Rum	240 bottles	Beer (crew)	8,530 cans
Vodka	130 bottles	Fruit Juice	25,720 pints
Brandy	240 bottles	*the cellar contains 25,000 bottles	

The Laundry List

Tablecloths	2,932	Bath Mats	1,650
Blankets	4,300	Hand Towels	15,500
Oven Cloths	1,000	Bath/Other Towels	13,000
Sheets	11,600	Aprons	1,500
Pillow Cases	13,100	Deck Rugs	750
Laundry Bags	3,250		

CRUISING FOR THE PHYSICALLY CHALLENGED

The *advantages* of a cruise for the physically challenged are many:

- Good place for self-renewal.
- Pure air at sea (no smog, no pollen).
- No packing and unpacking.
- Spacious public rooms.
- Excellent medical facilities close by.
- Special dietary requirements can be catered to.
- The staff will generally be very helpful.
- Relaxation.
- Good entertainment.
- Gambling (but, as yet, no wheelchair-accessible gaming tables or slot machines).
- Security (no crime on board).
- Different ports of call.

The *disadvantages* of a cruise for the physically challenged are:

- No ships yet have installed access-help lifts into their swimming pools or thalassotherapy pools.
- Unless cabins are specifically designed for the physically challenged, problem areas include the entrance, configuration, closet hanging rails, and beds.
- Cabin bathrooms: doors that open inward are useless; the grab bars, wheel-in shower stall, and toiletries cabinet should be at an accessible height.
- Elevator doorways: the width of the door is important for wheelchair passengers; elevator controls are often not at a height suitable for operation from a wheelchair (except in the newer ships).
- Sometimes having to wait behind hordes of able-bodied passengers who really do not need to use the elevators.
- Access to outside decks is not often provided through electric-eye doors that open and close automatically; rather, it is provided through doorways that have to be opened manually.

Cruise lines, port authorities, airlines, and various allied services are slowly improving their facilities so that those who are wheelchair-bound or otherwise physically challenged can enjoy a cruise as fully as possible. At the last count, in the United States alone, some 43 million people—or one out of every five people over the age of fifteen—were registered as being physically challenged, while in the U.K. over 6 million persons were registered disabled. Not all are in wheelchairs, of course, but all have needs that the cruise industry is (slowly) working to accommodate. No cruise line has previously wanted to show a photograph of a passenger in a wheelchair, but Princess Cruises now does exactly that with a half-page photograph showing a passenger in a wheelchair in a wheelchair-accessible cabin.

The very design of ships has traditionally worked against physically challenged people. To keep out water or to prevent water escaping from a flooded cabin or public area, raised edges (known as "coamings" or "lips") are often placed in doorways and across exit pathways. Also, cabin doorways are often not wide enough to accommodate even a standard wheelchair. The standard cabin door is about 24 inches (60.9 cm) wide.

Cabins designed for the physically challenged have doors that are about 30 inches (76.2 cm) wide. Standard bathroom doors are normally only about 22 inches (55.8 cm) wide, whereas those designed for wheelchairs are about 28-30 inches (71.1-76.2 cm) wide. Do ask your travel agent to confirm the width of these two important access items, and do remember that, while the cabin door may be given as 30 inches (76.2 cm), you must allow for the fact that your knuckles on either side of a wheelchair can add three inches to the width of your wheelchair (the so-called industry standard size is 24 inches (62.2 cm) wide, while a junior adult size is 22 inches (67.1 cm) wide).

Royal Caribbean International's recent ships, *Legend of the Seas* and *Splendour of the Seas*, have cabin doorways that are 31 inches (78.7 cm) wide and elevator doorways of 43 inches (109.2 cm) wide. They also have cabins with private balconies for the disabled.

Bathroom doors are a particular problem in this regard, and the door itself, whether it opens outward into the cabin or inward into the bathroom, only compounds the problems of maneuvering a wheelchair within a cramped space. Four disabled cabins in *QE2* however, have electrically operated sliding doors into the bathroom, a completely level entrance into both cabin and bathroom, and remote controlled lights, curtains, and doors, as well as a door intercom and alarm. Remember also that bathrooms in most ships are normally small and are full of plumbing fixtures, often at odd angles—extremely awkward when you are trying to move about from the confines of a wheelchair. Bathrooms on newer ships are more accessible, except for the fact that their plumbing is often located beneath the complete prefabricated module, making the floor higher than that in the cabin, which means a ramp must be fitted in order to wheel in.

Some cruise lines, such as Holland America Line, will, if given advance notice, remove a bathroom door and hang a fabric curtain in its place. Many lines will provide ramps for the bathroom doorway, where a sill or lip is encountered. Beds in the cabins for the physically challenged aboard Carnival Cruise Lines' *Carnival Destiny* are equipped with a panic button adjacent to the bedside light switch.

It was once the policy of almost all cruise lines to discourage the physically challenged from taking a cruise or traveling anywhere by ship for reasons of safety, insurance, and legal liability. But it is now becoming clear that a cruise is the ideal holiday for a physically challenged person, as it provides a relaxed environment with plenty of social contact, organized entertainment, and activities. However, despite most cruise brochures declaring that they accept wheelchairs, few ships are well fitted to accommodate them. Some cruise lines, such as Carnival Cruise Lines, openly state that all public restrooms and cabin bathrooms are inaccessible to wheelchair-bound passengers.

The list at the end of this chapter pertains to all the ships presented in Part Two, and provides a guide as to their accessibility (the author personally wheels himself around each ship to check). Once you've decided on your ship and cruise, the next step is to select your accommodation. There are many grades of cabin, depending on size, facilities, and location. Choose a cruise line that permits you to choose a specific cabin, rather than one which merely allows you to select a price category, then assigns you a cabin immediately prior to your departure date or, worse still, actually at embarkation.

Cabins: What They Should Include:

- No lip or threshold at the cabin door, which should be a minimum of 35 inches wide (89.0 cm).
- Bedside panic button linked to the navigation bridge (which must be manned twenty-four hours a day)

- Enough space to maneuver a wheelchair between entrance, bed, closet, and bathroom.
- Closet with pull-down clothes rail.
- Telephone mounted at wheelchair height (not high up on wall).
- Mirrors that are usable when seated in a wheelchair.
- Safe or lockable drawer that is reachable at wheelchair height.

Bathrooms: What They Should Include:

- Outward opening door.
- No lip at bathroom door.
- No lip into shower stall
- Shower stall (with detachable showerhead located at head height when seated in a wheelchair).
- Shower chair that folds up when not in use, and grab rails.
- Grab rails for toilet.
- Toilet with electric automatic seat pad cleaner.
- Sink at low-enough height for wheelchair to move up close to it.
- Emergency (panic) button in or adjacent to shower (for falls).

The following tips will help you choose wisely:

- If the ship does not have any specially equipped cabins for the physically challenged, book the best outside cabin in your price range or find a ship that does have cabins specially constructed or adapted for the physically challenged. However, be careful as you may find that even those cruise brochures that state that a ship has "wheelchair accessible" cabins fail to say whether the wheelchair will fit through the bathroom door or whether there is a lip at the door. You should find out whether the wheelchair can fit into the shower area. Get your travel agent to check, and recheck these details. Do not take "I think so" as an answer. Get specific measurements.
- Choose a cabin that is close to an elevator. Remember that not all elevators go to all decks, so check the deck plan carefully. For example, the cabins for the physically challenged in *Radisson Diamond* are located as far away from the elevators as possible. Smaller and older vessels may not even have elevators, making the access to many areas, including the dining room, difficult and sometimes almost impossible.
- Avoid, at all costs, a cabin down a little alleyway shared by several other cabins, even if the price is attractive. The space along these alleyways is extremely limited, and entering one of these cabins in a wheelchair is likely to be a frustrating experience.
- Since cabins that are located amidships are less affected by the motion of the vessel, look for something in the middle of the ship if you are concerned about rough seas, no matter how infrequently they might occur.
- The larger (and therefore the more expensive) the cabin is, the more room you will have to maneuver in. Nowhere does this assume more importance than in the bathroom.
- If your budget allows, pick a cabin with a bath rather than just a shower, because there will be considerably more room, especially if you are unable to stand comfortably enough.

- Ships that exceed 20,000 grt will have more spacious alleyways and public rooms and (generally) bigger cabins. Ships under 20,000 grt tend to have cabins and passageways that are somewhat confining and therefore difficult to maneuver in, particularly past housekeeping carts.
- Meals in some ships may be served in your cabin, on special request—a decided advantage should you wish to avoid dressing for every meal. There are, however, few ships that have enough actual space in the cabin for dining tables.
- If you do want to join the other passengers in the dining room and your ship offers two fixed-time seatings for meals, choose the second rather than the first. Then you can linger over your dinner, secure in the knowledge that the waiter will not try to hurry you.
- Space at dining room tables can be somewhat limited in many ships. When making table reservations, therefore, tell the maître d' that you would like a table that leaves plenty of room for your wheelchair, so that it doesn't become an obstacle for the waiters and leaves plenty of room for them, or other passengers, to get past.
- Even if you do find a cruise/travel agent who knows your needs and understands your requirements, try and follow up on all aspects of the booking yourself so that there will be no slip-ups when the day arrives for you to travel.
- Take your own wheelchair with you, as ships carry a very limited number of wheelchairs; in any case, these are meant for emergency hospital use only. An alternative is to rent an electric wheelchair, which can be delivered to the ship on your sailing date.
- Hanging rails in the closets on most ships are positioned too high for someone who is wheelchair-bound to reach (even the latest ships seem to repeat this basic error). There are some cruise ships, however, which do have cabins specially fitted out to suit physically challenged passengers, in which this and similar problem areas have been dealt with. The cabins in *Queen Elizabeth 2* and *Royal Viking Sun*, for example, are fitted with walk-in closets (the four special cabins aboard *Queen Elizabeth 2* have a pull-down facility to bring your clothes down to any height you want). In Part Two of this book, the ships that have special cabins are marked with the number of cabins under "Wheelchair Cabins."
- Elevators aboard many ships are a constant source of difficulty for passengers in wheelchairs. Very often the control buttons are located far too high to reach, especially those for the upper decks.
- Doors on upper decks that open onto a Promenade or Lido Deck are very heavy, are difficult to handle, and have high sills. Unless you are ambulatory or can get out of your wheelchair, these doors can be a source of annoyance, even if there is help at hand, as they open inward or outward (they should ideally be electrically operated sliding doors).
- Advise any airline you might be traveling with of any special needs well ahead of time so that arrangements can be made to accommodate you without last-minute problems.
- Advise the cruise line repeatedly of the need for proper transfer facilities, in particular buses or vans with wheelchair ramps.

Embarkation

Even if you've alerted the airline and arranged your travel according to your needs, there is still one problem area that can remain when you arrive at the cruise embarkation port to join your ship: the actual boarding. If you embark at ground level, the gangway to the ship may be level or inclined. It will depend on the embarkation deck of the ship and/or the tide in the port.

Alternatively, you may be required to embark from an upper level of the terminal, in which case the gangway could well be of the floating loading-bridge type, such as those used at major airports. Some of these have floors that are totally flat, while others may have raised lips an inch or so in height, spaced every three feet. These are rather awkward to negotiate in a wheelchair, especially if the gangway is made steeper by a rising tide.

Tendering

I am constantly pressing the cruise lines to provide an anchor emblem in their brochures for those ports of call where ships will be at anchor instead of alongside. If the ship is at anchor, be prepared for an interesting but safe experience. The crew will lower you and your wheelchair into a waiting tender (ship-to-shore launch) and then, after a short boat ride, lift you out again onto a rigged gangway or integral platform. If the sea is calm, this maneuver proceeds uneventfully; if the sea is choppy, your embarkation could vary from exciting to harrowing. Fortunately (or not) this type of embarkation is rare unless you are leaving a busy port with several ships all sailing the same day.

No two cruise lines seem to have the same wording in their policies regarding tendering. In any case, you will find it in the fine print at the back of a cruise brochure.

Wheelchairs

Wheelchair passengers with limited mobility should use a collapsible wheelchair. By limited mobility, I mean a person able to get out of the wheelchair and step over a sill or walk with a cane, crutches, or other walking device.

The chart that follows indicates the best cruise ships for wheelchair accessibility. Finally, remember to ask questions before you make a reservation. Some of the most important to ask are:

- Does the cruise line's travel insurance (with a cancellation/trip interruption) cover you for any injuries while you are aboard ship?
- Are there any public rooms or public decks on board the ship that are inaccessible to wheelchairs (for instance, it is sometimes difficult to obtain access to the outdoor swimming pool deck)?
- Will you be guaranteed a good viewing place in the main show room from where you can see the shows if seated in a wheelchair?
- Will special transportation be provided to transfer you from airport to ship?
- If you need a collapsible wheelchair, can this be provided by the cruise line?
- Are passengers required to sign a medical release?
- Do passengers need a doctor's note to qualify for a handicapped cabin?
- Will crew members be on hand to help, or must the passengers rely on their own traveling companions for help?
- Are the ship's tenders accessible to wheelchairs?
- How do you get from your cabin to the lifeboats (which may be up or down several decks) in an emergency if the elevators are out of action and cannot be used?

Waivers

Passengers who do not require wheelchairs but are challenged in other ways, such as those who have impaired sight, hearing, or speech, present their own particular requirements. Many of these can be avoided if the person is accompanied by an able-bodied companion experienced in attending to their special needs. In any event, some cruise lines require physically challenged passengers to sign a waiver.

Sailing as one of the crew

For something different and adventurous, how about sailing yourself? The square-rigged *sts Lord Nelson*, constructed in 1988, is a specially built barque (sailing ship) with three masts and a total of eighteen sails. Designed for the physically challenged and able-bodied to share the challenge of crewing a ship at sea, the 141-foot-long ship is sailed in both the Caribbean and Mediterranean.

Aptly named after Britain's most famous sailor, the ship was built at Wivenhoe, England, at a cost of $5 million, for the Jubilee Sailing Trust, headquartered in Southampton, England. All decks are flat, without steps, and there are special lifts for you to get between them as well as up the ship's side to get aboard. There is even a lift seat to go up the main mast. Navigation aids do include an audio compass and bright track radar screen for the blind or partially sighted, and ship-to-shore radio and hydraulic-assist steering.

Down below, all accommodation is accessible to all the physically challenged or able-bodied crew, with specially fitted cabins and bathrooms. In addition, there is a saloon/bar, launderette, library, and workshop. Special yachting-type clothing is available on loan. Also, *Lord Nelson's* flat decks, powered lifts, wide companionways, and other facilities enable everyone on board to take part on equal terms as part of the ship's crew. On each voyage, under a professional captain and sailing master, six permanent crew, including a qualified medical purser and guide, instruct the 40-strong crew on each "cruise."

Hearing impaired

More than 6 million Americans suffer from hearing loss, and some 1.5 million Americans suffer from a hearing loss of more than 40 percent. Those affected should be aware of problems on board a ship:

- Hearing the announcements on the public address system
- Use of telephone
- Poor acoustics in key areas (for example, boarding shore tenders)

Remember to take a spare battery for your hearing aid. More and more new ships have cabins specially fitted with colored signs to help those who are hearing impaired. Norwegian Cruise Line's *Norwegian Dream* and *Norwegian Wind* provide special cabins for the hearing impaired. Four cabins in *Queen Elizabeth* 2 also have illuminated signs to help those who are hearing impaired. Crystal Cruises' *Crystal Harmony* and *Crystal Symphony* and Celebrity Cruises' *Century*, *Galaxy*, and *Mercury* are fitted with movie theaters that are equipped with special headsets for use by the hearing impaired.

Many ships, particularly those that carry more than 500 passengers, make life difficult for the hearing impaired, with constant, irritating, and repetitive announcements. It is often difficult for the hearing impaired to distinguish important or useful announcements from those that are of little or no importance.

Finally, when going ashore, particularly on organized excursions, be aware that most destinations are simply not equipped to handle the hearing impaired.

Ships Rated for Wheelchair Accessibility

Ship	Suitability Level	Ship	Suitability Level
Aegean I	D	*Elation*	C
Aida	B	*Emerald*	D
Albatros	D	*Enchanted Capri*	D
Americana	D	*Enchanted Isle*	D
Apollo	D	*Enchantment of the Seas*	B
Arcadia (Golden Sun Cruises)	D	*Europa* (Hapag-Lloyd Seetouristik)	B
Arcadia (P&O Cruises)	B	*Europa* (Hapag-Lloyd Seetouristik)	B
Arkona	C	*Explorer*	D
Astor	C	*Fair Princess*	D
Astra	D	*Fantasy*	C
Astra II	D	*Fascination*	C
Asuka	C	*Flamenco*	D
Atalante	D	*Fuji Maru*	D
Ausonia	D	*Funchal*	D
Bali Sea Dancer	D	*Galapagos Explorer*	D
Berlin	C	*Galaxy*	B
Black Prince	D	*Grande Caribe*	D
Black Watch	C	*Grand Princess*	A
Bolero	D	*Grandeur of the Seas*	B
Bremen	D	*Hanseatic*	D
Caledonian Star	D	*Hebridean Princess*	D
Calypso	D	*Holiday*	D
Carnival Destiny	B	*Horizon*	B
Carnival Triumph	B	*Imagination*	C
Carousel	D	*Independence*	D
Celebration	D	*Inspiration*	C
Century	B	*IslandBreeze*	D
Clelia II	D	*Island Princess*	C
Clipper Adventurer	D	*Italia Prima*	D
Club Med II	D	*Jason*	D
Columbus	C	*Jubilee*	D
CostaAllegra	D	*Kapitan Khlebnikov*	D
CostaClassica	B	*Kristina Regina*	D
CostaMarina	D	*Le Levant*	D
CostaRiviera	D	*Le Ponant*	D
CostaRomantica	B	*Leeward*	D
CostaVictoria	B	*Legend of the Seas*	B
Crown Princess	B	*Leisure World*	D
Crystal Harmony	A	*Lili Marleen*	D
Crystal Symphony	A	*Maasdam*	B
Dalmacija	D	*Majesty of the Seas*	C
Dawn Princess	A	*Marco Polo*	C
Delphin	D	*Maxim Gorkiy*	D
Deutschland	D	*MegaStar Aries*	D
Disney Magic	B	*MegaStar Taurus*	D
Disney Wonder	B	*Melia Don Juan*	D
Dolphin IV	D	*Melody*	C
Ecstasy	C	*Mercury*	B
Edinburgh Castle	D	*Mermoz*	D

Ships Rated for Wheelchair Accessibility (cont.)

Ship	Suitability Level
Minerva	C
Mistral	C
Monarch of the Seas	C
Monet	D
Monterey	D
Nantucket Clipper	D
Niagara Prince	D
Nieuw Amsterdam	C
Nippon Maru	D
Noordam	C
Nordic Empress	C
Norway	B
Norwegian Capricorn	B
Norwegian Crown	B
Norwegian Dream	C
Norwegian Dynasty	C
Norwegian Majesty	D
Norwegian Sea	D
Norwegian Sky	B
Norwegian Wind	C
OceanBreeze	D
Ocean Majesty	D
Ocean Princess	A
Oceanic	D
Oceanic Odyssey	D
Odysseus	D
Olympic Countess	D
Oriana	B
Orient Venus	D
Orpheus	D
Pacific Princess	C
Pacific Venus	C
Paradise	C
Paul Gauguin	C
Polaris	D
Princesa Amorosa	D
Princesa Marissa	D
Princesa Victoria	D
Princess Danae	D
Professor Khromov	D
Queen Elizabeth 2	B
R1	B
R2	B
Radisson Diamond	C
Regal Empress	D
Regal Princess	B
Rembrandt	C
Renaissance Six	D
Renaissance Seven	D
Renaissance Eight	D
Rhapsody	D
Rhapsody of the Seas	B
Rotterdam	A
Royal Clipper	D
Royal Princess	B
Royal Star	D
Royal Viking Sun	A
Ryndam	C
St. Helena	D
Saga Rose	C
Sapphire	D
Sea Cloud	D
Sea Goddess I	D
Sea Goddess II	D
Sea Princess	A
Seabourn Legend	D
Seabourn Pride	D
Seabourn Spirit	D
SeaBreeze	D
Seawind Crown	D
Seawing	D
Sensation	C
Shota Rustaveli	D
Silver Cloud	C
Silver Star	D
Silver Wind	C
Sir Francis Drake	D
Sky Princess	C
Song of America	D
Song of Flower	D
Sovereign of the Seas	C
Splendour of the Seas	B
Star Aquarius	D
Star Clipper	D
Star Flyer	D
Star Pisces	D
Statendam	C
Stella Oceanis	D
Stella Solaris	D
Sundream	D
Sun Princess	A
Sun Vista	D
SuperStar Capricorn	C
SuperStar Gemini	C
SuperStar Leo	B
SuperStar Sagittarius	D
SuperStar Virgo	B
Switzerland	D

Ships Rated for Wheelchair Accessibility (cont.)

Ship	Suitability Level
Symphony	D
Taras Shevchenko	D
The Azur	D
Topaz	D
Triton	D
Tropicale	D
Universe Explorer	D
Veendam	C
Victoria	C
Viking Serenade	D
Vision of the Seas	B
Vistafjord	C
Vistamar	D
Volendam	B
Voyager of the Seas	A
Walrus	D
Westerdam	C
Wilderness Adventurer	D
Wilderness Discoverer	D
Wind Song	D
Wind Spirit	D
Wind Star	D
Wind Surf	C
World Discoverer	D
World Renaissance	D
Yamal	D
Yorktown Clipper	D
Zaandam	B
Zenith	B

NOTES

A) Recommended as most suitable for wheelchair passengers

B) Good for wheelchair passengers

C) Acceptable for wheelchair passengers

D) Not suitable for wheelchair passengers

1) The following ships of Carnival Cruise Lines have double-width entertainment deck promenades that are good for wheelchair passengers, but the public restrooms are not accessible. In addition, although the cabin bathrooms are equipped with shower stalls and grab rails, the bathrooms have a steel "lip" and are, thus, neither suitable nor accessible when stepping out of a wheelchair: *Celebration, Ecstasy, Elation, Fantasy, Fascination, Holiday, Imagination, Inspiration, Jubilee, Paradise, Sensation.*

2) *Crystal Harmony* and *Crystal Symphony* (Crystal Cruises) are the only ships presently in operation that provide special access ramps from an accommodation deck directly to the ship's lifeboats.

3) *Crown Princess* and *Regal Princess* (Princess Cruises) both have large outside cabins for the disabled, but they have lifeboat-obstructed views.

CRUISING FOR ROMANTICS

TRAVELING SOLO OR SINGLE

Back in 1932, Warner Bros. released the film *One Way Passage*, a bittersweet story starring Kay Francis and William Powell. Then there was the shipboard affair kindled by Bette Davis and Paul Henried in *Now, Voyager*. Remember Irene Dunne and Charles Boyer in a film called *Love Affair*? Or the same characters in *An Affair to Remember*? All involved oceangoing passenger ships and romance. Then there was *Gentlemen Prefer Blondes*, in which Marilyn Monroe and Jane Russell starred.

Even in the early 1950s Howard Hughes presented Jane Russell in an RKO movie called *The French Line*, which depicted life on board one of the great ocean liners of the time—the *ss Liberté*—as being exciting, frivolous, promiscuous, and romantic. The movie was, in fact, made on board the great ship. Today that same romantic attraction is still very much in vogue.

In 1997, Kate Winslet and Leonardo DiCaprio showed young love and its great adventure aboard a stricken ocean liner on its maiden voyage across the North Atlantic, in the Hollywood blockbuster *Titanic*.

With more and more singles and solos (those who like to travel alone) in the world today, the possibility of a shipboard romance affords a special attraction. While you may not believe in mermaids, romance does happen—frequently. Almost 2 million cruise passengers (more than 25 percent of all cruise passengers) are singles. Cruise lines are only just waking up to this fact and are trying to help by providing special programs for single passengers, but they have not done a good job as yet. Unfortunately, many solos are turned off by cruising because they find it hard to understand why so many lines charge a single occupancy supplement to the fare of someone traveling alone.

The most precious commodity aboard any cruise ship is space. Every square foot must be used for essential facilities or revenue-earning areas. Since a single cabin is often as large as a double and uses the same electrical wiring, plumbing, and fixtures—and is, thus, just as expensive to build—cruise lines naturally feel justified in charging supplements or premiums for those who are occupying single cabins. Singles would probably not object to a smaller cabin but do not like being charged a supplement or given a poor location.

Where they do exist, single cabins are often among the most expensive, when compared with the per-person rates for double-occupancy cabins. They are also less flexible. From the point of view of the crew, it takes as much time to clean a single cabin as it does a double. And there is only one tip instead of two.

One answer would be to build double cabins only, and, whenever feasible, sell them as single-occupancy units—this is something that only a handful of cruise lines actually do. Guaranteed singles rates are offered by several cruise lines,

Courtesy Norwegian Cruise Line

There is plenty of room for your regular exercise regimen.

Did You Know...?

... that motion pictures' most famous on-screen odd couple, Jack Lemmon and Walter Matthau, teamed up to be gentlemen dance hosts aboard a Caribbean cruise ship, in a film released in the U.S. in July 1997? Called *Out to Sea*, the film also stars Gloria DeHaven, Dyan Cannon, Hal Linden, Alexander Powers, and Brent Spiner. The "cruise ship" interior was filmed at Raleigh Studios in Hollywood.

... that Epirotiki Line's *Jupiter* was used to carry the sixty-one finalists of the Miss Universe contest in 1976? (Epirotiki Line is now part of Royal Olympic Cruises)

... that on Valentine's Day, 1998, some 5,000 couples renewed their vows aboard the ships of Princess Cruises?

but the line and not the passenger picks the cabin. If the line does not find a roommate, the single passenger may get the cabin to himself or herself at no extra charge. Ideally, all lines would offer guaranteed singles rates, with no supplement.

Over one million North American passengers traveled as singles in 1997! Cruise lines are only now realizing that about a quarter of calls to travel agents are made by singles, single parents, and solos. Singles tend to test the waters by taking short cruises at first. There are lots of singles on the three- and four-day cruises from several U.S. ports (Los Angeles, Miami, Port Canaveral, San Juan) and from Piraeus (Greece). Some cruise lines or tour operators advertise special cruises for singles, but remember that the age range could be anything from seven to seventy.

Although there are some singles who travel with friends or family, many others like to travel alone. For this reason, cruise lines have established several programs to accommodate them. One is the "Guaranteed Single" rate, which provides a set price without having to be concerned about which cabin to choose.

A "Guaranteed Share" program is operated by some of the cruise lines. This allows you to pay the normal double-occupancy rate, but the cruise line will provide another passenger of the same sex to share the double cabin with you.

Some cruise lines do not advertise a guaranteed-share program in their brochures but will often try to accommodate such bookings, particularly when demand for space is light. Sometimes, you may end up booking a guaranteed share basis only to find that you end up with a cabin all to yourself. As cruise lines are apt to change such things on short notice, it is best to check with your travel agent for the latest rates, and read the fine print.

Those who want to travel alone and not share a cabin can pay either a flat rate for the cabin or a single supplement if they occupy a double cabin. Some lines charge a fixed amount—$250, for instance—as a supplement, no matter what cabin category, ship, itinerary, or length of cruise you require. Single supplements, or solo-occupancy rates, vary between lines, and sometimes between ships. Check with your travel agent for the latest rates.

Cruising for Single Women

Any single woman can take a cruise vacation knowing she is encapsulated in a safe, hassle-free environment. There is perhaps no better way to de-stress, and if you are seeking that special someone, cruising somehow brings people closer together.

There is always someone to talk to, whether it be couples or other singles, and cruising is not a "meat market" where you are always under observation. The easiest way to meet other singles, however, is to participate in scheduled activities. Be a little assertive, and get the cruise director or cruise staff to introduce you to other singles.

In the dining room, ask the maître d' to seat you with other singles, or a mix of singles and couples, as you wish. Single African-American women should note that there is often a dearth of single African-American men for dancing or socializing with (they simply have not discovered cruising yet).

If you are looking for romance, however, beware of the lure of the uniform, of an easy affair or fling with a ship's officer or member of the crew. They get to see new faces every week (or every cruise), and, thus, the possible risk of sexually transmitted diseases should be kept in mind.

Gentlemen cruise hosts

Because the female-to-male passenger ratio is high (as much as eight-to-one on world cruises and other long voyages), especially for passengers of middle to senior years, some lines feature gentlemen cruise hosts, generally about half a dozen of them, specially recruited to provide dance and bridge partners for passengers, and company during social functions. First used to good effect aboard Cunard's *QE2* in the late 1970s, gentlemen cruise hosts are now employed by a number of cruise lines.

They generally host a table in the dining room, appear as dance partners at all cocktail parties and dance classes, and accompany women on shore excursions. These gentlemen, usually over fifty-five years of age and/or retired, are outgoing, good minglers, well groomed, and enjoy cruise ships and traveling around the world free of charge.

If you think you would like such a job, do remember that you'll have to dance for several hours most nights, and dance just about every kind of dance well! Crystal Cruises, Cunard, Holland America Line, Ivaran Lines, and Silversea Cruises, among others, all provide gentlemen cruise hosts, especially on the longer voyages and world cruises.

The Love Boat connection

Two famous television shows, *The Love Boat* (U.S.) and *Traumschiff* (Germany), have given a tremendous boost to the concept of cruising as the ultimate romantic vacation, although what is shown on the screen does not quite correspond to reality. Indeed, the captain of one of the ships featured on television, after being asked the difference between his real-life job as captain and that of the master of *The Love Boat*, remarked: "On TV they can do a retake if things are not quite right [the] first time around, whereas I have to get it right [the] first time!"

Ships are indeed romantic places (watching the blockbuster Hollywood movie *Titanic*, released in 1997, should convince you). There is nothing quite like standing on the aft deck of a cruise ship with the object of your love—with hair blowing in the breeze—as you sail over the moonlit waters to yet another island paradise. Of course, a full moon only occurs once a month, so check the calendar to make sure the timing of your moonlit cruise is perfect.

But there is no doubt that cruises provide excellent opportunities for meeting people of similar interests. So if you are looking for romance, and if you choose the right ship, the odds are in your favor.

Getting married aboard ship

As in all those old black-and-white movies, a ship's captain can indeed marry you when at sea (unless the ship's country of registry prohibits, or does not recognize, such marriages), although in practice this service is rarely offered by cruise lines today. You would need to inquire in your country of domicile (or residence) whether such a marriage is legal, and ascertain what paperwork and blood tests are required. The onus to provide the validity of a marriage is yours. The captain could, in fact, be sued and perhaps held criminally liable if he marries a couple who are not legally entitled or able to be married (for example, an underage male or female who does not have the consent of a parent or guardian, or if one or both parties are not legally divorced).

It is a simple matter to arrange to get married aboard almost any cruise ship when the ship is alongside in port, provided you take along your own registered minister. Some companies, such as American Hawaii Cruises, Carnival Cruise Lines, Holland America Line, and Princess Cruises, for example, offer complete packages that include the services of a minister to marry you, wedding cake, champagne, bridal bouquet and matching boutonniere for the bridal party, a band to perform at the ceremony, and an album of wedding photos. Carnival Cruise Lines' program includes a marriage ceremony, on a beach in Grand Cayman or St. Thomas. Princess Cruises offers weddings on a beach in St. Thomas (price range $525-$1,175 per package).

Princess Cruises also features weddings aboard *Grand Princess*, in what is the first ocean-going wedding chapel aboard a present-day cruise vessel, performed by the ship's captain (the wedding is legal because of the ship's registry, Liberia, and no medical or blood tests are required). There are three packages, Pearl, Emerald, and Diamond; the cost is $1,400, $1,800, and $2,400, respectively). A Wedding Coordinator at the line handles all the details. And what better way than to be married aboard ship and have your honeymoon aboard, too!

Even if you can't get married aboard ship, you could have your wedding reception on one. Many cruise lines offer outstanding facilities and provide complete services to help you plan your reception. Contact the director of hotel services at the cruise line of your choice, and you will be pleased with the way cruise lines go out of their way to help, especially if you follow the reception with a honeymoon cruise.

U.K.-based passengers should know that P&O Cruises has a series of cruises called the "Red-Letter Anniversary Collection" especially for those celebrating ten, fifteen, twenty, twenty-five, thirty, thirty-five, forty, forty-five, fifty, fifty-five, or sixty years of marriage. Gifts you will receive with the compliments of P&O Cruises include a brass carriage clock, leather photograph album, free car parking at Southampton, or free first-class rail travel from anywhere in the U.K. (check with your travel agent for the latest details).

A cruise makes a fine, no-worry honeymoon vacation (perhaps that should read a "no worrymoon" vacation) but also a delightful belated honeymoon getaway if you had no time to spare when you were married. You will feel like you are in the middle of a movie set as you sail away to fairy-tale places, though actually the ship is a destination in itself.

Renewal of vows

There has recently been an upsurge in cruise lines performing the "renewal of vows" ceremony. A cruise is a wonderful setting for reaffirming to one's partner the strength of commitment. A handful of ships even have a small chapel where this ceremony can take place; otherwise, it can be anywhere aboard ship (a very romantic time is at sunrise or sunset on the open deck). The ceremony is conducted, usually by the ship's captain, in a nondenominational text that reaffirms the depth of the love and trust between "partners, lifetime friends, and companions."

Although some companies, such as Carnival Cruise Lines, Celebrity Cruises, and Holland America Line, have complete packages that you can purchase, which include music, champagne, hors d'oeuvres, a certificate, corsages for the women, and so on, other companies do not charge (yet). The ship's own photographer usually records the event (it is a revenue-generating photo opportunity) and will have special photo albums embossed with the cruise line's logo.

Cruising for honeymooners

There is no doubt that cruising is becoming ever more popular as a honeymoon vacation. The real advantages of a honeymoon cruise are obvious: you pack and unpack only once, it is a completely hassle-free and crime-free environment, and you get special attention,

Courtesy Douglas Ward

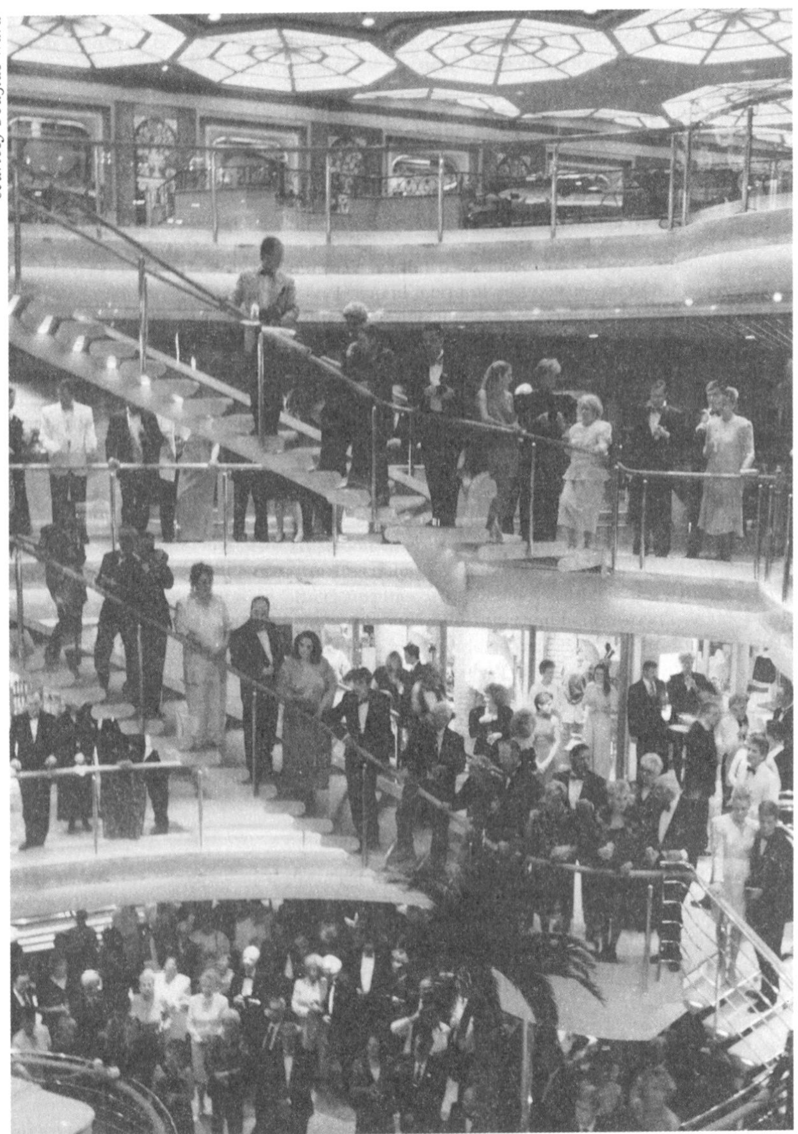

Captain's Welcome Aboard Party, held in the multilevel atrium aboard Sun Princess *(Princess Cruises).*

if you want it. What's more, it is also very easy to budget in advance, as one price often includes airfare, cruise, food, entertainment, several destinations, shore excursions, and pre- and post-cruise hotel stays and other arrangements. And, once you are married, some cruise lines often offer discounts to entice you to book a future anniversary cruise.

Just think, no cooking meals—everything will be done for you. You can think of the crew as your very own service and kitchen staff.

Although no ship as yet provides bridal suites (hint, hint), many ships do provide cabins with queen-sized or double beds. Some, but by no means all, also provide tables for two in the dining room.

Some cruise ships feature Sunday or Monday departures (from Miami, San Juan, Venice, and Singapore, for example), which allows couples to plan a Saturday wedding and reception, and a leisurely travel to the ship of choice. Pre- and post-cruise hotel accommodation can also be arranged by the cruise line.

Most large ships accommodate honeymoon couples really well; however, if you want to plan a more private, intimate honeymoon, then try one of the smaller, yachtlike cruise vessels, where you will feel like it is your own private ship and you have invited another fifty couples as guests. Highly recommended for a supremely elegant, utterly pampered honeymoon are the ships of Renaissance Cruises, the Sea Goddess ships of Cunard, the ships of Seabourn Cruise Line, Radisson Seven Seas Cruises, Silversea Cruises, and Windstar Cruises. All of these also have an open bridge policy, so you can join the captain on the bridge at almost any time.

Although most passengers like to socialize in the evenings, it might be more romantic for honeymooners to take a stroll by themselves on deck, to the forward part of the ship, above the ship's bridge. This will be the quietest (except perhaps for some wind noise), and most dimly lit part of the ship, an ideal spot for stargazing and romancing. Almost all ships are blessed with such places.

Cruise lines offer a variety of honeymoon packages, very much as hotels and resorts on land do. Here is a list of some of the things you can expect from them (note that not all cruise lines provide all services):

- Private captain's cocktail party for honeymooners.
- Tables for two in the dining room.
- Set of crystal champagne or wine glasses.
- Honeymoon photograph with the captain, and photo album.
- Complimentary champagne (imported or domestic) or wine.
- Honeymoon cruise certificate.
- Champagne and caviar for breakfast.
- Flowers in your suite or cabin.
- Complimentary cake.
- Special T-shirts.

Finally, before you go:

- Remember to bring a copy of your marriage license or certificate, for immigration (or marriage) purposes, as your passports will not yet have been amended.
- Remember to allow extra in your budget for things like shipboard gratuities (tips), shore excursions, and spending money ashore.
- If you want to sleep in a large bed next to your loved one, check with your travel agent and cruise line to make sure the cabin you have booked has such a bed. Better still, book a suite. But check and double check to avoid disappointment.
- If you need to take your wedding gown aboard for a planned wedding somewhere along the way—in Hawaii or Bermuda, for example—there is usually space to hang it in the dressing room next to the stage in the main show room, especially on larger ships.

CRUISING FOR FAMILIES

Yes, you can take children on a cruise. In fact, once you get them aboard, you will hardly see them at all, if you choose the right ship and cruise. Families can do different things on a cruise, and parents do not have to be concerned about the whereabouts of their children. Where else can you go out for a night on the town without having to drive, and be home in a moment should the babysitter need you?

Dad can sleep in, Mom can go swimming and join an aerobics class, the kids can join in the organized activities that go on all day long. Whether you share a cabin with them or whether they have their own separate but adjoining cabin, there will be plenty to keep them occupied. Aboard several ships that cruise in the Caribbean, you will even find favorite life-sized cartoon characters.

Some cruise lines have token family programs, with limited activities and only a couple of general staff allocated to look after children, even though their brochures might claim otherwise. But cruise lines that are really serious about family cruise programs dedicate complete teams of children's and "tweens and teens" counselors, who run special programs that are off-limits to adults. They also have facilities such as high chairs in the dining room, cots, and real playrooms. Most children's entertainment is designed to run simultaneously with adult programs. For those who cruise with very small children, babysitting services may also be available. Cunard's *QE2*, for example, has real children's nurses and even trained English nannies, while P&O Cruises' *Arcadia* and *Oriana* have a night nursery for children of two to five years of age, so parents can go "out on the town" while the staff takes care of their offspring.

Parents, of course, have long realized that children cost more as they age. For example, children under two years travel free on most cruise lines. But if they are over two, then they cost money. In case they have to fly, those over two also cost more, as they must take up an airline seat.

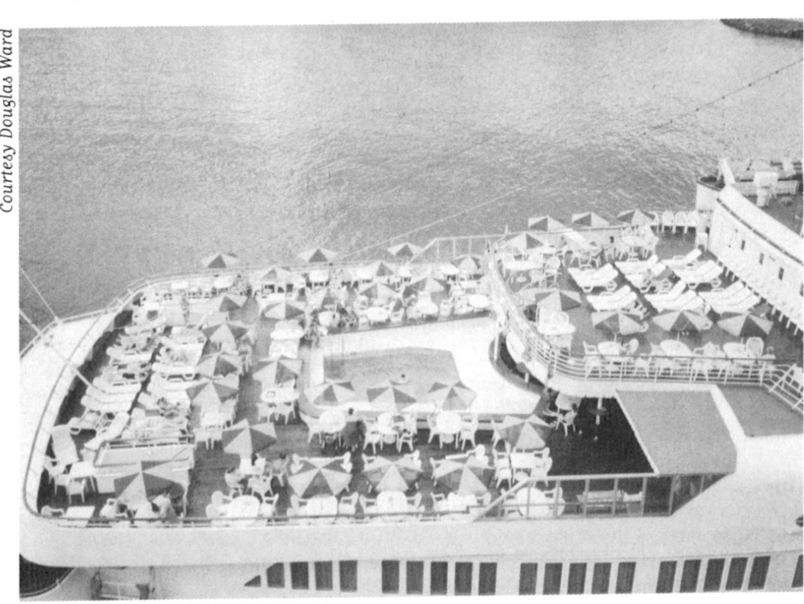

Courtesy Douglas Ward

Kids will love to swim above the natural water line.

Did You Know...?

...that the French liner *Ile de France* was the first—and only—ship to have a real carousel in the children's playroom? This was also the ship used in the movie *The Last Voyage.*

...that a fifteen-foot-high Goofy hangs upside down over the stern of *Disney Magic*? What is he doing? Why, painting the ship, of course!

...that Carnival Cruise Lines and Mattel have teamed up to produce and sell a nautical-themed Barbie doll? She can be found in the gift shops aboard all the company's ships.

But there is no doubt that families who cruise together stay together! There is no better vacation for families than a ship cruise—especially at holiday time—whether it is at Christmas and New Year's, Easter, or during the long summer vacation. Active parents can have the best of all worlds—family togetherness, social contact, and privacy. Cruise ships provide a very safe, crime-free, encapsulated environment, and give junior passengers a lot of freedom without parents having to be concerned about where their children are at all times. Cruising has never been more child-friendly or affordable, as the emergence of new lines catering specifically to families has proven. The range of destinations also provides a veritable palette of excursions for both parents and children to enjoy together.

A cruise also allows junior passengers a chance to meet and play with others in their own age group. And because days are quite long aboard, youngsters will also be able to spend time with their parents or grandparents, as well as with their peers.

A cruise for children is an educational experience. They will tour the ship's bridge, meet senior officers, learn about the navigation, radar, and communications equipment, and see how the ship operates. They will be exposed to different environments, experience many types of food, travel to and explore new places, and participate in any number of exciting activities.

Cruise ships can be full of kids, or they can provide quiet moments. But aboard the busiest ships, adults will rarely get to use the swimming pools alone—they will be overcome with children having a truly good time. One good thing about ship swimming pools for kids, however, is the fact that there is no sand to get in their eyes (or anywhere else)!

Many cruise lines, recognizing the needs of families, have added a whole variety of children's programs to their roster of daily activities. Some ships have separate swimming pools and play areas for children, as well as playrooms, junior discos, video rooms, and teen centers. Carnival Cruise Lines has created a "Camp Carnival" on its ships. Royal Caribbean International has junior counselors on almost all sailings. Other cruise lines generally have counselors sailing during the summer and other special holiday periods.

Cruise lines that are serious about children split them into five distinct age groups, with various names to match, according to cruise line and program: Toddlers (ages 2-4), Juniors (ages 5-7), Intermediate (ages 8-10), Tweens (ages 11-13), and Teens (ages 14-17). Notably, it often seems to be children under 12 who get the most from a cruise vacation.

The children and junior passengers are usually not permitted to participate in adult games, tournaments, quizzes, and so on, but have their own versions of them. Also, in compliance with international law, as well as with the policy of most cruise lines, casinos and bars are reserved strictly for passengers age eighteen and over.

One North American cruise company that has made a name for itself by catering to those with children is Premier Cruises (formerly Premier Cruise Lines), which carries an abundance of children's counselors on every cruise of its red-hulled ship, *Star/Ship Oceanic*, as well as some famous cartoon characters such as Daffy Duck and Sylvester. Meanwhile, Carnival Cruise Lines features a 114-ft.-long (34.7 m.) water slide at the swimming pool aboard all its ships; one even longer is aboard *Carnival Destiny*, at 214 ft. (65.2 m).

In Southeast Asia, Star Cruises, based in Singapore, has two new ships, *Superstar Leo* and *Superstar Virgo*, that have excellent facilities for families and children. There are also seven restaurants/dining places to choose from.

Disney's arrival

In late July 1998, Disney Cruise Line entered the family cruise market with a big splash. The giant entertainment company introduced the first of two mega-ships (each with two funnels) that will cater specifically to families with children. These two ships, designed to transit the Panama Canal, are the family cruise ships of the future. They are in the 85,000-tonne range, and cater to 1,750 adult passengers, plus up to 500 children, with the whole of the Disney organization to draw from for the shipboard entertainment program. The children's area measures 15,000 sq. ft. (1,393.5 m²), and there are more than thirty-five counselors on any given cruise. There is a separate family/children's pool, designated teen club, and game arcade. A drop-off service for children in the evenings has proven popular, and private babysitting services are available, as are character "tuck-ins" for children, and character breakfast and lunch. Strollers are also available at no charge. The cabins (880 of them) range in size from 220 sq. ft. (20.4 m²) to 960 sq. ft. (89.1 m²). Some 73 percent are outside, and 44 percent of those have private balconies. As for dining, there are three main restaurants and one alternative restaurant. Disney also has its own 1,000-acre private island, Castaway Cay (fully owned by Disney), which is an outstanding facility.

The first ship, *Disney Magic*, features three- and four-day cruises from Port Canaveral in Florida, combined with a three- or four-day stay at a Walt Disney World Resort. This project has all the signs of becoming the undisputed standard-bearer in the family cruise industry. The ships, each with three main dining rooms, have a stunning array of facilities for couples and single parents with children and couples without children. The activities and entertainment experiences will be really innovative, as will be the range of accommodation.

Courtesy Norwegian Cruise Line

A special character is always a delight for children.

General information

Parents with babies can rest assured that they will find selected baby foods on board ships that cater to children (along with cribs and high chairs—but ask your travel agent to check first). If you need something out of the ordinary, or that special brand of baby food, let your travel agent know well in advance. Most cruise lines are very accommodating and will do their best to obtain what is needed, provided enough notice is given, but parents using organic baby foods, such as those obtained from health food stores, should be aware that cruise lines buy their supplies from major general food suppliers and not the smaller, specialized food houses.

Although many ships have full programs for children during days at sea, these may be limited when the ship is in port. Ships expect you to take your children with you on organized excursions, and sometimes (though not always) there are special prices for children. If the ship has a playroom, it might be wise to find out if it is open and supervised on all days of the cruise. Do not expect your travel agent to know everything. Either ask the agent to find the answers to your questions, or do some research yourself.

When going ashore, remember that if you want to take your children swimming or to the beach, it is wise to phone ahead to a local hotel with a beach or pool. Whether it is in the Caribbean, the Mediterranean, or the Orient, most hotels will be delighted to show off their property, hoping for future business.

Some cruise ships in the Caribbean area have the use of a private island for a day—ideal for children. A lifeguard will be on duty, and there will be watersports and snorkeling equipment you can rent. Note, however, that the beaches on some private islands are fine for 200, but with 2,000 people they become crowded, and standing in line for beach barbecues and changing and toilet facilities becomes a necessary part of the experience.

Although the sun and sea might attract juniors to the warm waters of the Caribbean, children age seven and over will find a Baltic, Black Sea, or Mediterranean cruise a delight. They will also have a fine introduction to history, languages, and different cultures.

Children's rates

Most cruise lines offer special rates for children sharing their parents' cabin. The cost is often lower than third- and fourth-person share rates. To get the best possible rates, however, it is wise to book early. And do not overlook booking an inside cabin—you will rarely be in it anyway.

You should note that, although many adult cruise rates include airfare, most children's rates do not. Also, although some lines say children sail "free," they must in fact pay port taxes as well as airfare. The cruise line will get the airfare at the best rate, so there is no need to shop around for the lowest fare.

Unless they have plenty of things to keep them occupied, even the most placid and well-behaved children can become bored and restless. So try to choose a cruise where there are lots of other children, as these will be best equipped to provide the required entertainment.

Single parents

Single parents traveling with their child(ren) will have their own special needs, and need not feel left out, either. Female single parents can also feel safe on a cruise, free of the unwanted advances of single men.

They will feel more secure than in any hotel. In fact, a cruise provides a safe, convenient way for any single parent and child to be together but also have their own space and, in some cases, a guarantee of peer companionship for the child. Only a handful of cruise lines so far have introduced their own versions of the "Single Parent Plan." This offers an economical way for single parents to take their child(ren) on a cruise, with parent and child sharing a two-berth cabin, or parent and children sharing a three-berth cabin. Single parents will pay approximately one-third the normal single-person rate for their children, and there will be plenty of activities for both parent and child(ren) to enjoy.

Children-friendly cruise lines

These have been selected by the author for their excellent programs and care: Airtours Sun Cruises, American Hawaii Cruises, Carnival Cruise Lines, Celebrity Cruises, Cunard, Disney Cruise Line, Norwegian Cruise Line, P&O Cruises, Royal Caribbean International, Star Cruises, and Thomson Cruises.

Family Reunions

A cruise can provide the ideal place for a family reunion (either with or without children). Here are some tips to take into account when planning one:

- Let your travel agent do the planning and make all the arrangements (ask for a group discount if the total in your group adds up to more than fifteen). Make sure that together you choose the right cruise line, for the right reasons.
- Book twelve months in advance if possible, so that you can arrange cabins close to each other (remember to arrange for everyone to be at the same dinner seating, if the ship operates two seatings).
- If anyone in the group has a birthday or anniversary, tell your travel agent to arrange a special cake (most cruise lines do not charge extra for this). Special private parties can also be arranged, although there will be an additional cost. If the group is not too large, you may be able to request to dine at the captain's table.
- Arrange shore excursions as a group (in some ports, private arrangements may prove unbeatable).
- Finally, get everything in writing (particularly cabin assignments and locations).

BEFORE YOU GO

BAGGAGE

Cruise lines usually have no limit to the amount of personal baggage you take on your cruise ship, but as closet space is often quite limited, take only the things you will use. Allow extra space for purchases on the trip. Remember that towels, soap, shampoo, and shower caps are provided aboard most cruise ships.

It is important that you properly tag all your baggage with your name, ship, cabin number, sailing date, and port of embarkation. Tags are provided by the cruise line together with your ticket. Baggage transfers from airport to ship are generally smooth and problem-free when handled by the cruise line.

Liability for loss or damage to baggage is contained in the passenger contract. If you are not adequately covered for this, you should take out more insurance. The policy should extend from the date of departure until two or three days after your return home. Coverage can be obtained from your cruise/travel agent.

CLOTHING

If you think you might not wear it, do not take it: closet space on most ships is at a premium. Unless you are on an extended cruise, keep your luggage to a minimum. Most airlines have a limit of two suitcases at check-in (44 lbs or 20 kgs) per person, plus a tote bag or carryall for small items.

For cruises to tropical areas, where the weather is warm to hot with high humidity, casual wear should include plenty of lightweight cottons and other natural fibers. Synthetic materials do not "breathe" as well and often retain heat. Clothes should, however, be as opaque as possible to counteract the ultraviolet rays of the sun. Also, take a lightweight cotton sweater or windbreaker for the evenings, when the ship's air-conditioning will seem even more powerful after a day in the sun. Remember to pack sunglasses and a hat.

The same is true for cruises to the Mediterranean, Greek Isles, or North Africa, although there will be little or no humidity most of the year. Certain areas may be dusty as well as dry. In these latitudes, the weather can be changeable and cool in the evenings from October to March, so take extra sweaters and a windbreaker.

On cruises to Alaska, the North Cape, or the Norwegian fjords, take some warm comfortable clothing, plus a raincoat or parka for the northernmost port calls. Cruises to Alaska and the Land of the Midnight Sun only run during the peak summer months, when temperatures are pleasant and the weather is less likely to be inclement. Unless you are traveling to northern ports such as St. Petersburg during winter, you will not need thermal underwear. However, you will need it—and overcoats, too—if you are taking an adventure cruise to the Antarctic Peninsula or through the Northwest Passage.

In the Far East, what you wear will depend on the time of year. The information package that accompanies your tickets will give recommendations. For a cruise that sets off in winter from one of the northern ports (New York or Southampton, for example) and for cruises south to find the sun, take lightweight cottons plus a few sweaters.

Rainstorms in the tropics are infrequent and do not last long, but they can give you a good soaking, so take inexpensive, lightweight rainwear for excursions you go on.

In destinations with a strong religious tradition, like Venezuela, Haiti, Dominican Republic, Colombia, and countries in the Far East, note that shorts or bare shoulders may cause local offense, so cover up.

Aboard ship, dress rules are relaxed during the day, but in the evening what you wear should be tasteful. Men should take a blazer or sports jacket and ties for the dining room and for any informal occasions. Transatlantic crossings are normally more elegant.

If you are the athletic type, pack sportswear for the gymnasium or for aerobics classes.

For formal nights (usually two out of every seven), women should wear their best long evening gown, an elegant cocktail dress, or a smart pants suit. Gentlemen are expected to wear either a tuxedo or dark business suit. These "rules" are less rigid on short and moderately priced cruises.

Some cruise ships have a masquerade night, so you may wish to take a costume. Or you can create something on board out of materials that are provided. One of the staff may help, and there may be photographs of past entries. Prizes are awarded for the most creative costume.

No matter where in the world you are traveling, comfortable low- or flat-heeled shoes are a must for women, except for formal nights. Light, airy walking shoes are best for walking. If you are in the Caribbean or South Pacific and you are not used to heat and humidity, your ankles may swell, so, tight shoes are not recommended. Rubber soles are best for walking on the deck of a ship.

- **Formal:** Tuxedo or dinner jacket (alternatively a dark suit) for men; evening gown or other appropriate formal attire for women.
- **Informal:** Jacket and tie for men; cocktail dress, dressy pant suit, or the like for women.
- **Casual:** Slacks and jacket over sweater or open shirt for men; a blouse with skirt, slacks or similar comfortable attire for women.

On a typical seven-day cruise, the following is what you generally might expect as the dress code for each day:

Saturday	Casual
Sunday	Formal (captain's welcome aboard cocktail party)
Monday	Casual or informal
Tuesday	Casual or informal
Wednesday	Casual or informal
Thursday	Formal (captain's farewell cocktail party)
Friday	Casual

Documents

A passport is the most practical proof of your citizenship and identification. If you are a non-U.S. citizen taking a cruise from an American port, you must have a valid B-2 multiple-entry visitor's visa stamped in your passport in order to return to the United States at the end of your cruise. Note: British passport holders do not need a visa to enter the U.S., as the Visa Waiver Program presently applies.

If you are cruising to areas other than those of the Bahamas, Bermuda, the Caribbean, Alaska, Hawaii, or Canada, and most of Europe, you may need a tourist visa. Your cruise/travel agent will advise you.

On cruises to the Orient particularly, but also to the Middle East and Africa, you may have to hand in your passport to the purser prior to landing. This helps the customs and immigration officials to "clear" the ship more quickly, and is standard practice. Your passport will be returned when the ship departs, or prior to its arrival in the port of disembarkation.

Flying

For many people, flying to get to a port of embarkation has become the norm (although a survey in the U.S. revealed that 41 million Americans are afraid of flying). Most cruise lines now include "free air" as part of the cruise ticket. The effects of rampant discounting, however, have resulted in cruise lines negotiating contracts with airlines that involve passengers sometimes having to travel on flights with absurd connections, even when direct flights are available (these are more expensive).

In the case of the United States, deregulation has resulted in most airlines operating on a "hub and spoke" system, with flights feeding into major centers to connect with other flights. It is now more difficult to find nonstop coast-to-coast flights, as airlines prefer passengers to go through the system to ensure full domestic flights. This is not so prevalent in Europe, but distances are comparatively shorter given the size of each country.

Several cruise lines now have "air deviation" desks, so that you can change your air flights and connections, for an additional fee (about $25).

Medication

If you are planning a cruise that takes you away from your home country, make sure to take any medicine that you need, plus spare eyeglasses or contact lenses. In many countries it may be difficult to find certain medication. Others may be sold under quite different names. Those traveling on long cruises should ask their doctor for names of alternatives, in case the medicine they are taking is not available.

The ship pharmacy will stock certain standard remedies, but then again, do not expect a supply of the more unusual or obscure medicines. Remember to take along a doctor's prescription for any medication, especially when you are flying into foreign countries to join a ship, as customs may be difficult without documentation, particularly in the Far East.

Also, be advised that if you run out of your medication and you need to get a supply aboard ship, most ships will require that you see the doctor, even if you have a prescription. There is a minimum charge of $15 per visit, plus the cost of the medication.

Passengers who are diabetic should let spouses/companions carry a supply of insulin and syringes as well as a quick source of glucose. Make sure you carry a sufficient supply with you, and do not pack it in any luggage to be checked in when flying.

Money matters

Most cruise ships deal primarily in U.S. dollars but some take British pounds, German marks, Greek drachmas, Italian lire, Japanese yen, or even Australian dollars. Major credit cards and traveler's checks are widely accepted on board, but few lines take personal checks. Most ships now ask passengers to sign for drinks and other assorted services, as part of the "cashless cruising" policy. Some ships even have ATM cash machines.

Pets

Pets are not allowed aboard cruise ships, with two exceptions. One is on the regular scheduled transatlantic services of *QE2*, which has sixteen air-conditioned kennels (and even a genuine British lamppost), cat containers, and several special cages for birds. The second is on the regular scheduled South Atlantic service from England to Cape Town and the Ascension Islands aboard St. Helena. The quarantine and vaccination regulations should be obtained from the consulates of the country of intended entry.

Photography

It is hard to find any situation more ideal for photography than a cruise. Your photographs enable you to share your memories with others at home.

Think about where you are going when buying film. It is best to use low-speed film in tropical areas such as the Caribbean or South Pacific, as high-speed film is easily damaged by heat. Take plenty of film with you; standard sizes are available in the ship's shop, but the selection is limited. If you purchase film on a port visit, try to buy from an air-conditioned store, and check the expiration date.

Keep your film as cool as possible, as the latent image on exposed film is fragile and therefore easily affected by heat. There will be professional photographers on board who may develop film for you for a fee.

When taking photographs at the various ports of call, respect the wishes of the local inhabitants. Ask permission to photograph someone close-up. Most will smile and tell you to go ahead. But some people are superstitious or truly afraid of having their picture taken and will shy away from you. Do not press the point.

Work

If you need to work while on board, secretarial help and limited office facilities, including credit-card operated satellite-linked telephone and fax machines, and computers may be available (some ships, such as *Crystal Harmony*, *Crystal Symphony*, *Dawn Princess*, *Royal Viking Sun*, and *Sun Princess* have such business centers).

LIFE ABOARD

Air-conditioning

Aboard all modern cruise ships, cabin temperature is regulated by individually controlled thermostats, so you can adjust it to suit yourself. The temperature in the public rooms is controlled automatically. The air-conditioning is normally kept much cooler than you may be used to, so remember to take a sweater or scarf.

Baby-sitting

In some ships, stewards and other staff may be available as sitters for an hourly charge. You can make whatever arrangements you need at the purser's office.

Beauty salon/barbershop

It is advisable to make any appointments for the beauty salon or barbershop as soon after boarding as possible, especially on short cruises. Appointment times fill up rapidly, particularly before social events such as the captain's cocktail party. Charges are comparable to those ashore. The hours of opening will be posted at the salon, and also listed in the Daily Program or on the in-cabin television. African-American passengers should note that the Caucasian-run beauty salons simply do not know how to cater to them. Very few ships carry beauty products tailored to suit African-American hair and skin types.

Bridge visits

You should check the Daily Program for announcements of visits to the bridge, for which appointment cards can be picked up from the purser's office or cruise staff office. In some ships, bridge visits are not allowed for reasons of insurance and security. On others, although personal visits are forbidden, a Behind the Scenes video on how the ship is run may be shown on the in-cabin television system.

Cashless cruising

It is now the norm to cruise cash-free and settle your account with one easy payment. Often this is arranged by making an imprint of a credit card prior to departure, permitting you to sign for everything. Or you can pay by cash at the end of the cruise. In most ships, it is no longer possible to pay using cash at the bar, in the beauty salon, or in shops.

If your cruise ship includes a private island on its Bahamas/Caribbean itinerary, you will probably be asked to pay cash for all beverages, watersports/scuba diving gear, and other items purchased ashore.

Before the end of the cruise, a detailed statement will be delivered to your cabin. Avoid lines by using a credit card for express check-out. Some companies that use a "cashless" system may discontinue its use for the last day of the cruise, which can be most irritating.

Casino

A large number of cruise ships have a "full" casino, where a range of games are played, such as blackjack, roulette, craps, and baccarat. Playing chips and cash change are available.

Children under eighteen are not allowed in the casino. The casino is closed in port due to international customs regulations, and taking photographs in the casino is usually forbidden. You will find that German- and Japanese-registered ships are not permitted to operate casinos that give cash prizes.

Comment cards

On the last day of the cruise you are asked to fill out a company comment card. Some cruise lines offer incentives such as a bottle of champagne and even a free short cruise. Be honest when you fill out this important form, for it can serve as a way of communication between company and passenger. Note, however, that in some ships, dining room stewards present "sob" stories of how they will lose their station or section, or even their job, if you do not write "excellent" when you fill out your comment card. Some companies provide information on filling out the comment cards, inviting nothing short of an "excellent" rating.

If there have been problems with the service do not write or mark "excellent." Instead, be realistic and mark "good," "fair," or "poor" as the case may be. Otherwise, the cruise line will never know that there are problems and that the service needs improving.

Communications

Each cruise ship has been designated an internationally recognized call sign, which is made up of a combination of several letters and digits and can be obtained from the cruise line. To receive a call during your cruise, simply give the call sign and name of the ship to those concerned before you leave.

When the ship is at sea, you can call from your cabin (or the ship's radio room) to anywhere in the world:

- by radio-telephone (a slight to moderate background noise might be noticed);
- by satellite (which will be as clear as your own home phone).

Direct-dial satellite calls, a service started in 1986, are more expensive, but they are usually completed without delay. Many ships now also have credit card telephones located in public areas aboard ship, which connect instantly at any time of the day or night, via satellite. Satellite calls can still be made when the ship is in port, but radio-telephone calls cannot be made. You could, however, use the local telephones (often at the local post office). Satellite telephone calls cost between $5 and $15 per minute, depending on the type of communications equipment the ship carries (the latest system, called Inmarsat-M, is digital and offers lower-priced calls).

Calls will be charged to your cabin or onboard account. It is more difficult to pay cash for a satellite or cellular telephone call.

It is also comforting to know that you can be contacted during your cruise through shore-to-ship calling. Your relatives and friends can reach you by calling the High Seas Operator in almost any country (in the United States, dial 1-800-SEA-CALL). Vessels equipped with satellite telephone links can be reached by the caller phoning any local operator and asking for the Inmarsat operator. When connected, the name of the ship should be given, together with the ocean code (Atlantic is 871, Pacific is 872, and Indian Ocean is 873).

Telegrams, telexes, and faxes are all accepted at the purser's office or radio room for transmission when the ship is at sea. Your in-cabin phone can also be used to call any other part of the ship.

Cruisespeak

The following terminology is used aboard today's cruise ships. The correct nautical terminology is given, while the words in parentheses are what many of the contemporary ships use:

Cabin (Penthouse Suite, Junior Suite, Stateroom, Room)

Cabin Service (Room Service)

Passenger (Guest)

Purser's Office (Guest Relations Desk, Front Office)

Customs regulations

All countries vary in the allowances granted by their own customs service, but you will be informed aboard your cruise ship of the allowable amounts for your nationality and residency.

Daily program

The Daily Program contains a list of the day's activities, entertainment, and social events, and is normally delivered to your cabin the evening before the day that it covers. It is important to read it carefully, so that you know what, when, and where things are happening. If you lose your copy, you can obtain another from the purser's office or your cabin steward.

Death at sea

What happens if someone dies at sea? This seems to happen more on long cruises, where passengers are generally older. The cruise line can put a body in a special refrigeration unit for removal at the port of disembarkation, or the body can be flown home from a wayward port of call (more complicated, owing to the paperwork). Note that flying a body home usually involves a large expense (often twice the cost of a first-class airfare). A burial at sea can also be arranged aboard ship (some people have a body cremated at home, return to their favorite cruise ship, and have the ashes scattered at sea).

Deck chairs

Deck chairs and cushions are available from the duty deck steward and are free of charge on most ships. Specific locations cannot normally be reserved, except aboard the few ships where a charge is made, or by arrangement with the deck steward.

Departure tax

If you are disembarking in a foreign port and flying home, be advised that there may be a departure tax to pay at the airport. Cruise lines often neglect to advise passengers of this, with embarrassing results, especially when you are normally required to pay the departure tax in cash in the local currency of wherever you are.

Disembarkation

During the final part of your cruise, the cruise director will give an informal talk on customs, immigration, and disembarkation (sometimes called "debarkation") procedures. At least one member of each group or family should attend this important talk. This will help simplify and speed up the procedure and avoid confusion at arrival time.

The night before your ship reaches its final destination (in most cases this will be a return to the port you sailed from) you will be given a customs form to fill out. Any duty-free items bought from the shop on board must be included in your allowance, so save the receipts in case a customs officer wishes to see them.

The night before arrival, your main baggage should be packed and placed outside your cabin on retiring or before 4 a.m. It will be collected, put in a central baggage area, and off-loaded on arrival. Remember to leave out any fragile items and liquor, together with the clothes you intend to wear for disembarkation and onward travel (it is amazing just how many people have packed everything, only to find themselves in an embarrassing position on disembarkation day). Anything left in your cabin at this point will be considered carry-on baggage and has to be hand-carried off when you leave.

On disembarkation day, if you are on a two-seating ship, be aware that breakfast is usually brought forward by one hour. This means that first-seating breakfast could be as early as 5:30 a.m.! If you are flying home that same day, it is going to turn into a very long day. It might be better to miss breakfast and sleep later, providing that announcements on the ship's public address system do not wake you (it is possible aboard many ships to turn off such announcements).

Even worse than the early breakfast is the fact that you will be commanded (requested, if you are lucky) to leave your cabin early, only to wait for hours in the crowded public rooms. To add insult to injury, your cabin steward (after he has received his tip, of course) will knock on the door, saying he needs the sheets off the bed so the cabin can be made up for the incoming passengers. Cruise aboard a small "upscale" ship and this will not happen.

Before leaving the ship, remember to claim any items you have placed in the ship's safety deposit boxes and leave your cabin key in your cabin. Passengers cannot go ashore until all baggage has been off-loaded, and customs and/or immigration inspections or pre-inspections have been carried out on board.

In most ports, this takes two to three hours after arrival. Therefore, do not ask people to meet you at arrival time. They will not be allowed to board, and you cannot get off until all formalities have been completed.

Also, leave at least three hours from the time of arrival to catch a connecting flight or other transportation.

Listen for announcements about disembarkation procedures and try not to crowd the main disembarkation gangway or lobby areas. Once off the ship, you must identify your baggage at the pierside before going through any further customs (delays are usually minimal). Porters will be there to assist you.

Drugstore

In some ships, there may be a separate drugstore in which a fairly extensive range of standard items will be available, while on others the drugstore will be a small section of the ship's main gift shop. Opening hours will be posted at the store and given in the Daily Program.

Electric current

Most ships operating in U.S. waters have standard American 110-volt AC (alternating current) outlets. Newer and refurbished ships have 110- and 220-volt AC outlets. A few older vessels have 220-volt DC (direct current) outlets, but transformers/converters are available.

In general, electrical appliances may only be used if they operate on AC. Check with your cabin steward before plugging in anything more powerful than an electric razor (such as a high-wattage hair dryer), just to make sure that the cabin's circuitry can handle the load.

Engine room

In virtually all passenger ships, the engine room is off-limits to passengers, and visits are not allowed, for insurance and security reasons. In some ships, a technical information leaflet may be available from the purser's office. On others, a Behind the Scenes video may be shown on the in-cabin television system. For more specific or detailed information, contact a member of the ship's engineering staff via the purser's office.

Gift shops

The gift shop/boutique/drugstore will offer a selection of souvenirs, gifts, toiletries, and duty-free items, as well as a basic stock of essential items. You will find duty-free items, such as perfumes, watches, and so on, very competitively priced, and buying on board ship may save you the hassle of shopping ashore. Opening hours will be posted at the store and given in the Daily Program.

Health/fitness/spa facilities

Depending on the size of the ship, the health and fitness facilities may include one or more of the following: gymnasium, weight room, sauna, solarium, exercise classes, jogging track, exercise course, massage, swimming pool(s), whirlpool baths, nutrition lectures, herbal body wraps, and scuba and snorkel instruction. For information, check with your cruise/travel agent or, when on board, contact the cruise director or purser's office.

Some ships now have elaborate spas where (for an extra fee) whole days of treatments are on offer. Stress-reducing and relaxation treatments are practiced and combined with the use of seawater, which contains minerals, micronutrients, and vitamins. Personal massage can include Swedish remedial massage, shiatsu, and the Alexander method and aromatherapy treatments. Indeed, you can even get a massage on your private balcony aboard some ships.

Few ships today run their own spa facilities, as finding quality personnel to provide consistency of product is time-consuming and difficult. A small number of concessions now specialize in providing "turn-key" operations. The largest of these is Steiner, a company that resulted from the 1994 merger between Steiner of London and Coiffeur Transocean, also of London. Steiner operates the spa concession aboard more than 130 ships.

Launch (tender) services

Enclosed or open motor launches (called "tenders") are employed on those occasions when your cruise ship is unable to berth at a port or island. In these cases, a regular launch service is operated between ship and shore for the duration of the port call. Details of the launch service are provided in the Daily Program and announced over the ship's P.A. system. When stepping on or off a tender, remember to extend "forearm to forearm" to the person assisting you. Do not grip their hands because this simply has the effect of immobilizing the helper.

Launderette

Some ships are fitted with self-service launderettes, equipped with washers, dryers, and ironing facilities, often at no charge. Full-time supervisory staff may be available to assist you, as on *QE2*. Check the profile information for each individual ship in Part Two of this book.

Laundry and dry-cleaning

Most ships offer a full laundry and pressing service. Some ships may also offer dry-cleaning facilities. A detailed list of services (and prices) can be found in your cabin. Your steward will collect and deliver your laundry or dry-cleaning.

Library

Most cruise ships are equipped with a library offering a large selection of books, reference material, and periodicals. A small deposit (refundable on return of the book) is sometimes required should you wish to borrow a book. On the small luxury ships, the library is open twenty-four hours a day, and no deposit is required. On the larger ships, you will probably find that the library is open only a couple of hours each morning and afternoon.

The only ships with a full-time, fully qualified real librarian are *Oriana* and *QE2*. Sadly, some of the Carnival Cruise Lines ships have superb library rooms, luscious, overstuffed armchairs, and eclectic decor but, alas, few books! Aboard many ships, the library is also where you find board games like Scrabble, backgammon, and chess. Best library at sea: *QE2* (which also encompasses a maritime bookshop, where Cunard memorabilia is also sold).

Lifeboat drill

Safety at sea is the number one consideration of all members of the ship's crew. Standards are set by the Safety of Life at Sea (SOLAS) convention of the International Maritime Organization (IMO). For any evacuation procedure to be totally effective and efficient, passengers must know precisely where to go in the unlikely event that an emergency arises. For this reason, and to acquaint passengers with general safety procedures, a lifeboat drill is held at the start of the cruise. According to international maritime law, this must take place within twenty-four hours of embarkation. Some ships sensibly program the passenger lifeboat drill prior to sailing, so as not to take time away from passengers during the cruise (wise in case something should happen during the first night at sea).

There have been few recent incidents requiring the evacuation of passengers, although two cruise ships have been totally lost following collisions (*Jupiter*, 1988, and *Royal Pacific*, 1992). Travel by ship, however, remains one of the safest means of transportation. Even so, it cannot be stressed enough that attendance at lifeboat drill is not only required by the captain but also makes sense; participation is mandatory. You must, at the very least, know your boat station and how to get to it, in the event of an emergency requiring evacuation of the ship.

If others are lighthearted about the drill, do not let that affect your seriousness of purpose. Be sure to note your exit and escape pathways and learn how to put on your lifejacket correctly. The drill takes no more than fifteen minutes of your time and is a good investment in playing safe. (*Royal Pacific* sank in sixteen minutes following a collision.)

Lifejackets are found in your cabin. Instructions on how to get to your boat station are on the back of the cabin door.

Lost property

You should contact the purser's office immediately if you lose or find something on the ship. Notices regarding lost and found property may be posted on the bulletin boards.

Mail

You can buy stamps and post letters on most ships. Some ships use the postal privileges and stamps of their flag of registration, while others buy local stamps at ports of call. Mail is usually taken ashore by the ship's port agent just before the ship sails for the next port.

If you are sailing on an extended voyage (a world cruise, for example), the cruise line will send a list of all its agents and mailing addresses, together with your tickets and documents, before you leave for the cruise. In this way, you will be able to let your friends and family know where you may be contacted at certain times.

Massage

Make any appointments for massage as soon after embarkation as possible, in order to obtain the time and day of your choice. Larger ships have more staff and offer more flexibility in appointment times. The cost averages just over $1.00 per minute. In some ships, a massage service is available in your cabin, if it is large enough to accommodate a portable massage table.

Medical services

Except for ships registered in England or Norway, there are no mandatory international maritime requirements for cruise lines to carry a licensed physician or to have hospital facilities aboard. However, in general, all ships carrying over fifty passengers do have hospital facilities and carry at least one licensed doctor aboard ship (ships registered in England and Norway have both, without exception). Usually there is a reasonably equipped hospital in miniature, although the standard of medical practice and of the physicians themselves may vary from line to line. Most shipboard doctors are generalists; there are no cardiologists or neurosurgeons. The doctors are often employed as outside contractors and therefore charge for the use of their services. U.K. passengers should note that ships fall outside the U.K. National Health Service scheme.

Cunard's *QE2*, which carries up to 2,825 passengers and crew, has a fully equipped hospital with one surgeon, one doctor, and a staff of six nurses and two medical orderlies; contrast this with Carnival's *Sensation*, which carries up to 3,514 passengers and crew, with just one doctor and two nurses.

Regrettably, many cruise lines place a low priority on providing medical services (there are, however, some exceptions). Most shipboard physicians are not certified in trauma treatment or medical evacuation procedures, for example. Most ships that cater to North American passengers tend to carry doctors licensed in the United States, Canada, or Britain, but aboard many other ships, doctors come from a variety of countries and disciplines. Some medical organizations, such as the American College of Emergency Physicians, have created a special division for cruise medicine.

Although ships have some facilities, there is wide variation between standards and equipment. Obviously, any ship that features long-distance cruises, with several days at sea, should have better medical facilities, and a better qualified staff than one that is engaged in a standard seven-day Caribbean cruise, with a port of call to make almost every day.

There is, at present, no agreed industry-wide standard relating to the standard of medical certification that is required by cruise ships. Most ship doctors are necessarily of the general practice type, but often, short-term contracts can mean poor continuity and differing standards.

Ideally, a ship's medical staff should be certified in Advanced Cardiac Life Support. The minimal standard medical equipment should include:

- Examination room
- Isolation ward/bed
- X-ray machine (to verify the existence of broken or fractured bones)
- Cardiac monitor (EKG) and defibrillator
- Oxygen-saturation monitor (to determine a patient's blood-oxygen level)
- External pacemaker

- Oxygen, suction, and ventilators
- Hematology analyzer
- Culture incubator
- Mobile trolley intensive care unit

Any existing health problems that will require treatment on board must be reported at the time you are booking. Finally, the doctor is the only ship's officer who is actually an independent contractor. Aboard ship, that means that standard fees are charged for treatment, including for seasickness shots (except for Russian- and Ukrainian-registered vessels, where medical services are free).

Movies

In most cruise ships, a movie theater is an essential part of the ship's public-room facilities. The movies are recent, often selected by the cruise director or company entertainment director from a special film- or video-leasing service.

Some of the recently built or modified ships have replaced or supplemented the ship's movie theater with television sets and video players in each cabin. News and events filmed on board are shown, as are video movie features.

News and sports bulletins

The world's news and sports results are reported in the ship's newspaper or placed on the bulletin board, normally located near the purser's office or in the library. For sports results not listed, ask at the purser's office; it may be possible for the office to obtain the results for you.

Passenger lists

All ships of yesteryear provided passenger lists with each passenger's name and hometown or region. Few companies carry on the tradition (perhaps some passengers are traveling with someone they should not!).

Among the companies that still compile a cruise passenger list are Crystal Cruises, Cunard, Seabourn Cruise Line, Silversea Cruises, and Sun Line Cruises (part of Royal Olympic Cruises).

Photographs

Professional photographers travel on board to take pictures of passengers throughout the cruise, including their arrival on board. They also cover all main events and social functions, such as the captain's cocktail party.

All the photographs can be viewed without any obligation to purchase (the price is likely to be in excess of $6 for a postcard-sized color photograph). Photographs are usually displayed on photo boards either in the main foyer or in a separate photo gallery. The color and quality of these pictures are usually excellent.

Duplicates may be obtained even after your cruise from the shore-based headquarters of the photographic concessionaire.

Postcards and writing paper

These are available from the writing room, library, purser's office, or your room steward. Aboard many ships, they are available for a modest sum.

Purser's office

This is also known as the reception office, guest relations, or information desk. Centrally located, this is the nerve center of the ship for general on-board information and problems. Opening hours are posted outside the office and given in the Daily Program. In some ships, the purser's office is open twenty-four hours a day.

Religious services

Interdenominational services are conducted on board, usually by the captain or staff captain. A few older ships (and the new ships of Costa Cruises) have a small private chapel. Sometimes denominational services are also offered by specially invited or fellow-passenger members of the clergy.

Room service

Beverages and snacks are available at most hours. Liquor is normally limited to the hours when the ship's bars are open. Your room steward will advise you of the services that are offered. There is no charge for room service.

Safety aboard

Passenger safety is a high priority for all cruise lines. Crew members must attend frequent emergency drills, the lifeboat equipment is regularly tested, and the fire-detecting devices, alarm, and fire-fighting systems are checked throughout the ship. If you spot fire or smoke, use the nearest fire alarm box, alert a member of staff or contact the bridge. Cruise lines should insist on a common language for all crew members, but this is far from reality.

Be aware that slipping, tripping, and falling are the major sources of shipboard injury. This does not mean that ships are unsafe, but there are some things you can do to minimize the chance of injury. If you do suffer from an injury aboard a cruise ship, think it is the cruise line's fault, and want to take some kind of legal action against the cruise company, you should be aware of the following:

In the United States, Appendix 46, Section 183(b) of the U.S. Civil Code requires that "the injured passenger notify the cruise line in writing within six months from the date of the injury to file a claim and suit must be filed within one year from the date of injury." Thus, if you file a claim after the one-year period, the cruise line will probably seek a summary judgment for dismissal, which will invariably be granted.

It is imperative that you first read your ticket. The passenger ticket is a legal contract between passenger and cruise line. It will invariably state that you must file suit in the state (or country) designated on the ticket. For example, if a resident of California buys a cruise, and the cruise line is based in Florida, then the suit must be filed in Florida. If you reside in the U.S. and you purchase a cruise in the Mediterranean and the cruise line is based in Italy, for example, then you would have to file suit in Italy. This is known as the Forum Clause. There is usually a clause in the ticket that will read something like the following:

> "The Carrier's legal responsibility for death, injury, illness, damage, delay or other loss or detriment of person or property of whatever kind suffered by the Passenger will, in the first instance, be governed by the Athens Convention relating to the Carriage of Passengers and their Luggage by Sea, 1974, with protocols and amendments, together with the further provisions of the International Convention on Limitation of Liability for Maritime Claims, 1976, with revisions and amendments (hereinafter collectively referred to as the "Convention"). The Carrier shall not be liable for any such death, injury, illness, damage, delay, loss, or detriment caused by Act of God, war or warlike operations, civil commotions, labor trouble, interference by Authorities, perils of the

> sea, or any other cause beyond the control of the Carrier, fire, thefts, or any other crime, errors in the navigation or management of the Vessel, or defect in or unseaworthiness of hull, machinery, appurtenances, equipment, furnishing, or supplies of the Vessel, fault or neglect of pilot, tugs, agents, independent contractors, such as ship's Physician, Passengers, or other persons on board not in the Carrier's employ or for any other cause of whatsoever nature except and unless it is proven that such death, injury, illness, damage, delay, loss resulting from Carrier's act or omission was committed with the intent to cause such loss or with knowledge that such loss would probably result therefrom and in that event the Carrier's liability therefore shall not exceed the specified limitations per Passenger in Special Drawing Rights (S.D.R.) as defined in the applicable conventions or in any further revision and/or amendment thereto as shall become applicable."

One area in which passengers may not be able to sue the cruise line is in the event of injury or accident when they are on a shore excursion advertised and sold aboard ship. This is because the tour operators are usually independently contracted and do not belong to the cruise line. So, when you buy your shore excursion, ask if the ship's insurance fully covers you under the terms of the passenger ticket contract.

In Your Cabin

Note that aboard many ships, particularly older vessels, there are raised lips separating the bathroom from the sleeping area.

- Do not hang anything from the fire sprinkler heads located on most cabin ceilings.
- On older ships, it is wise to note how the door lock works—some require a key on the inside in order to unlock the door. Leave the key in the lock, so that in the event of a real emergency, you do not have to hunt for the key.

On Deck

- Aboard older ships, look out for raised lips in doorways leading to open deck areas. Be alert and do not trip over them.
- Wear sensible shoes with rubber soles (not crepe) when walking on deck or going to pool and lido areas. Do not wear high heels.
- Walk with caution when the outer decks are wet after being washed, or if they are wet after rain—this warning applies especially to metal decks. There is nothing more painful than falling onto a solid steel deck.
- Do not throw a lighted cigarette or cigar end, or knock out your pipe, over the ship's side. The sea might seem like a safe place to throw such items, but they can easily be sucked into an opening in the ship's side or onto an aft open deck area, only to cause a fire.

How to Survive a Shipboard Fire

Shipboard fires generate heat, smoke, and often panic. In the unlikely event that you are in one, try to remain calm and think logically and clearly.

When you board the ship and get to your cabin, check the way from there to the nearest emergency exits fore and aft. Count the number of cabin doorways and other distinguishing features to the exits in case you have to escape without the benefit of lighting, or in case the passageway is filled with smoke and you cannot see clearly. New ships will more and more make use of the "low location" lighting systems, which are either the electroluminescent or photoluminescent type.

- In many new ships, exit signs are located just above floor level, but on older vessels, exit signs may be above your head—virtually useless, as smoke and flames always rise.
- You should also note the nearest fire alarm location and know how to use it in case of dense smoke and/or no lighting. Indeed, all cabins should have pull-out flashlights, but as yet most do not.
- If you are in your cabin and there is fire in the passageway outside, first put on your lifejacket and feel for the cabin door. If the door handle is hot, soak a towel in water and use it to turn the handle of the door. If there is a raging fire in the passageway, cover yourself in wet towels and go through the flames—it may be your only means of escape, unless you have a balcony cabin.
- Check the passageway. If there are no flames, or if everything looks clear, walk to the nearest emergency exit or stairway. If there is smoke in the passageway, crawl to the nearest exit. If the exit is blocked, then go to an alternate one.
- It may take considerable effort to open a fire door to the exit, as they are very heavy. Never use the elevators, as they may stop at a deck that is on fire or full of smoke, and when the door opens you may not be able to escape.
- In the event of a fire beginning in your cabin, report it immediately by telephone. Then get out of your cabin if you can and close the door behind you to prevent any smoke or flames from entering the passageway. Finally, sound the alarm and alert your neighbors.

Sailing time

In each port of call, the ship's sailing and all-aboard times will be posted at the gangway where you leave from. The all-aboard time is usually half an hour before sailing (ships cannot wait for individual passengers who are delayed). In some ships, you will be given an identification card to be handed in at the gangway when you return from your visit ashore.

Sauna

Many ships offer a sauna, which is usually small and compact, and occasionally unisex. In some cases there will be a small charge for its use, especially when combined with a massage. Towels are available at the sauna, and there is also a small changing area. Opening times will be posted at the sauna and in the information material in your cabin. Reservations are not normally necessary.

Seasickness

Seasickness is rare these days, even in rough weather (less than 3 percent of all passengers become seasick). Ships have stabilizers—large underwater "fins" on each side of the hull—to counteract any rolling motion. Nevertheless, it is possible to develop some symptoms—anything from slight nausea to vomiting. The French term mal de mer may sound quaint, but the malady has been nauseating to seafarers since the Phoenicians. What do you do?

Seasickness occurs when the brain receives confusing messages from the body's sensory organs, causing an imbalance of a mechanism in the inner ear. The mind and brain are accustomed to our walking or riding on a nonmoving surface. If the surface itself moves in another direction, a signal is sent to the brain that something's wrong. Continuous mixed signals result in headaches, clammy skin, dizziness, paleness, and yawning, soon followed by nausea and vomiting. There is still no explanation for the great difference in individual susceptibility to seasickness.

Both old-time sailors and modern physicians have their own remedies, and you can take your choice or try them all (but not at the same time):

1. When you notice the first movement of a ship, go out on deck and walk back and forth. You will find that your knees, which are our own form of stabilizer, will start getting their feel of balance and counteraction. This is the sign that you are "getting your sea legs."

2. Get the fresh sea breeze into your face (this is the best antidote of all), and if nauseous, suck an orange or lemon.

3. When on deck, focus on a steady point, such as the horizon.

4. Eat lightly. Do not make the mistake of thinking a heavy meal will keep your stomach well anchored. It will not.

5. Dramamine (dimenhydrinate, a sedative, which was introduced just after World War II) will be available in tablet (chewable) form on board the ship.

6. Transderm Scop, known as "The Patch" (manufactured by Ciba-Geigy), has an ingredient known as scopolamine, which has proven an effective medication. Taken off the market for some time, it was reintroduced in 1997.

7. Also, if you are really distressed, the ship's doctor can give you an injection that will cure all discomfort. It may make you drowsy as well, but the last thing on your mind will be staying awake at the movie.

8. Try an aromatherapy oil, made by Borealis Healthcare in the U.K., called Travel Oil. It is a natural alternative to drug-based medications. Applied to the temples and across the forehead, there are no side effects.

9. Another natural preventive is ginger in powder form. (Mix half a teaspoon in a glass of warm water or milk, and drink it before sailing.) This is said to settle any stomach for a period of up to eight hours.

10. "Sea Bands" (called "Aquastraps" in the U.K.) are a drug-free method of controlling motion sickness. These are slim bands (often in varying colors) that are wrapped around the wrist, with a circular "button" that presses against an acupressure point (nei kuan) on the lower arm. They should be attached a few minutes before you step aboard and be worn on both wrists throughout the cruise.

All this being said, bear in mind that in addition to the stabilizers in the hull, most cruises are in warm, calm waters and most cruise ships spend much time along the coast or pull into port regularly. The odds are very much against being seasick.

Security

After the tragedy of the highjacking of *Achille Lauro* in 1985, the United States House of Representatives Committee on the Security of Ports and Vessels and the United Nations have suggested ways by which those traveling by cruise ship could expect to receive the same level of protection as those traveling by air. It is satisfying to report that we have seen the progressive formulation of a recognized standard of passenger ship protection. The cruise lines have reached this recognized standard as a result of several factors: a moral obligation which, like safety, is inherent in the industry; the expectation of passengers; and now the firmer and more formal pressures being applied across the world by governments and coast guards.

In spite of these pressures it is still true that the "recognized" standard can be interpreted widely by different companies and ports. The most conscientious cruise lines, ferry operators, and ports follow the standards laid down by International Maritime Security

(IMS), a British company that is acknowledged as the world leader in cruise ship, ferry, and port security.

Increasingly, passengers find that at embarkation, as well as at way ports, they are required to go through metal detection devices at the gangway, and baggage will be subject to more stringent inspection procedures. The question of security is now being taken into account during the final ratings and evaluation of the ships in Part Two.

All cabins are provided with keys of some kind, and it is recommended that you keep your cabin locked at all times when there is no one there. The usual keys are made of metal and operate a mechanical lock, whereas the newer and refurbished ships may have plastic "key cards," which operate electronically coded locks. Cruise lines do not accept responsibility for any money or valuables left in cabins and suggest that you store them in a safety deposit box at the purser's office, or, if one is supplied, in your in-cabin personal safe.

You will be issued a personal boarding pass when you embark (the latest high-tech passes will have your photo on them). This serves as identification and must be shown at the gangway each time you board (you will also be asked for a separate photo ID, such as a driver's license). If you misplace or lose it, let the purser's office know immediately. The system of boarding passes is one of many ways in which cruise lines ensure passenger safety.

Shipboard etiquette

Cruise lines want you to have a good vacation, but there are some rules that must be observed.

- In public rooms, smoking and nonsmoking sections are available. In the dining room, however, cigar and pipe smoking are not permitted at all.
- If you do have a video camera with you, you should be aware that you will not be allowed to tape any of the professional entertainment shows and cabarets because of the international copyright infringement regulations.
- It is all right to be casual when on vacation but not to enter the ship's dining room in just a bathing suit. Bare feet, likewise, are not permitted. If you are uncomfortable eating with the typical ten-piece dining room cutlery setting, do not fret. Some cruise lines even have etiquette classes to help you.

Sports facilities

The variety of sports facilities on board ship will depend on how large the ship is. The facilities will include some of the following: badminton, basketball practice area, golf driving cage, horseshoes, jogging track, miniature putting green, paddle tennis, quoits, ring toss, shuffleboard, skeet shooting, squash (rarely), table tennis, and volleyball. The sports director or the cruise staff arranges tournaments. Check the Daily Program for times of events.

Sun

If your cruise takes you to the sun, remember that the closer you get to the equator, the more potent and penetrating are the rays. These are most harmful from noon to 2 p.m., when the sun is directly overhead. If you are taking a short cruise to the Bahamas, Caribbean, or Mexico, be wary of trying to get the best possible tan in the shortest space of time. Be sure to use a protective sun cream (15–30 factor range), and reapply it every time you go for a swim or soak in the pool or ocean. If you overdo it, seek immediate help from the ship's doctor.

Swimming pools

Depending on the ship, it will have indoor or outdoor swimming pools, or both. They may be closed in port owing to local health regulations and/or cleaning. Hours of operation will be listed in the Daily Program.

Diving is not allowed, since pools are shallow. Parents should note that pools on most ships are not supervised. Be aware that some ships use excessive chlorine or bleaching agents for cleanliness, which could cause colors to run on your bathing attire.

Television

In most new and recently refurbished ships, in-cabin television is standard. Programming may be obtained by a mixture of satellite and onboard video channels. Some ships can lock on to live international news programs (such as those of CNN or BBC World News), or to text-only news services (like Oceansat News), for which cruise lines pay a subscription fee per cabin per month. Satellite television reception is sometimes poor, however, due to the fact that ships at sea are constantly moving out of an extremely narrow beam being downloaded from the satellite and they therefore cannot track the signal as accurately as a land-based facility.

Tipping (gratuities)

Many people find the whole question of tipping awkward and embarrassing. The information given here is meant as a guideline; you should then add your own good judgment.

In some ships, there are subtle suggestions made regarding tips, whereas on others, cruise directors, under the direction of the hotel manager, get carried away and are far too dictatorial as to the practice of tipping. Ships such as those of Princess Cruises offer hints on tipping via the in-cabin video system.

Some cruise brochures, such as those of Holland America Line, state that "tipping is not required." They may not be required, but they are most definitely expected by the ship's staff. The industry standard for cruises is roughly as follows:

- Dining room waiter: $3-$3.50 per person per day.
- Busboy: $1.50-$2 per day.
- Cabin steward: $3-$3.50 per person per day.
- Butler: $3-$3.50 per person per day.

Note: Passengers in accommodation designated as suites may have a butler to tip in addition to the steward. Suite and penthouse passengers aboard *QE2* should tip $5 per person per day to each of the dining room waiters and the suite stewards, as well as to the butler, if there is one (Cunard recommends $6 for the butler aboard *QE2*).

Any other gratuities should be given according to services rendered, just as you would tip in any good restaurant or hotel (for example to the maître d', wine waiter, and barman). Celebrity Cruises, for example, asks that you tip the restaurant manager $5 per person for a seven-day cruise. Aboard many ships (those that belong to Carnival Cruise Lines, Celebrity Cruises, Cunard, Norwegian Cruise Line, and Royal Caribbean International, for example), the tip for the barman or bar waiter is automatically added to your bar check, at 15 percent. On Celebrity Cruises, you are also expected to tip the chief housekeeper, at $3.50 per person for a seven-day cruise.

Gratuities are usually given on the last evening of a cruise of up to fourteen days' duration. For longer cruises, you normally extend half of the tip halfway through and the rest on your last evening. Note: In some Greek-staffed ships (Royal Olympic Cruises, for example), gratuities are pooled and given to the chief steward, who shares them at the end of each cruise. A daily amount of $8-$10 per person is the norm.

If you are traveling on a river cruise, you may even be asked to tip the cruise director (who is actually more of a cruise manager).

Envelopes for tipping are available from the purser's office, where you can also ask for advice on tipping, or may be placed in your cabin by your cabin steward on the last night of the cruise.

In some of the best-rated ships, gratuities can be prepaid, so that you do not have to tip at all on board. The ship's staff receives your tips directly from the company.

Gratuities are now included in the cruise fare on a number of ships (principally those in the luxury end of the market), in which no extra tipping is permitted (in theory). Some examples include *Asuka*, *Club Med II*, *QE2*, *Radisson Diamond*, *Royal Viking Sun*, *Sea Goddess I*, *Sea Goddess II*, *Seabourn Legend*, *Seabourn Pride*, *Seabourn Spirit*, *Silver Cloud*, *Silver Wind*, *Song of Flower*, *Topaz*, and *Vistafjord*. Ask your travel agent to check if you cannot find reference to "gratuities inclusive" statements in a cruise line brochure.

Origin of the Word "Tips"

Before the introduction of postage stamps, coachmen who carried passengers were often asked to carry a letter or other package. A small recompense was given for this service, called a "tip"—which stands for "to insure personal service." Hence, when in future some special service was provided, particularly in the hospitality industry, tips became an accepted way of saying thank you for services rendered.

Twenty-four-hour clock

Aboard many European-based ships, the twenty-four-hour clock is the standard way of referring to time, in keeping with the practicality of its use in international travel. In spite of the initial strangeness of this system of time telling, you will soon find it not only simple to use but far less likely to lead to confusion. Up to midday, the hours are shown as 0100 to 1200. Thereafter they proceed from 1300 to 2400. Thus, 1400 is 2 p.m., 1520 is 3:20 p.m., and so on.

Valuables

A small number of ships have a lock box built into each cabin. However, items of special value should be kept in a safety deposit box in the purser's office. You will then have simple and convenient access to your valuables during the cruise.

Visitors

Passes for visitors to see you on board your ship must always be arranged in advance, preferably at the time you make your booking. Announcements will be made when it is time for all visitors to go ashore.

Sadly, bon voyage parties, such as those you may have seen in the movies, are virtually a thing of the past. They are no longer possible aboard ship (with the exception of those ships operating around-the-world cruises) owing to greatly increased security concerns and insurance regulations.

Water Sports

Some of the small vessels, such as *Club Med II*, *Le Ponant*, *Sea Goddess I*, *Sea Goddess II*, *Seabourn Legend*, *Seabourn Pride*, *Seabourn Spirit*, *Silver Cloud*, *Silver Wind*, *Wind Song*, *Wind Spirit*, and *Wind Surf*, have a watersports platform that is lowered from the ship's stern or side. These ships carry windsurfers, waterski boats, jet skis, water skis, and scuba and snorkel equipment, usually at no extra charge. *Seabourn Legend, Seabourn Pride,* and *Seabourn Spirit* also feature an enclosed swimming "cage," which is needed for areas of the world where unpleasant fish might be lurking.

Although such facilities look good in the cruise brochures, in many cases ships seem reluctant to use them. This is because many itineraries have too few useful anchor ports. Also, the sea must be in an almost flat, calm condition, which is seldom the case. Another more prosaic reason is simply because of strict insurance regulations.

Wine and liquor

The cost of drinks on board is generally lower than on land, since ships have access to duty-free liquor. Drinks may be ordered in the dining room, at any of the ship's bars, or from the room service facility.

In the dining room, you can order wine with your meals from an extensive and reasonably priced wine list. If you want wine with your dinner, try to place your order at lunchtime, as waiters are always at their busiest at the evening meal.

In some ships, a duty-free sales point will allow you to purchase wine and liquor for personal consumption in your cabin. Passengers are not normally permitted to bring these purchases into the dining room or into other public rooms, nor indeed any duty-free wine or liquor purchased in port. These regulations are obviously made to protect bar sales, which are a substantial source of on-board revenue for the cruise line.

Indeed, some lines have even introduced a "corkage" fee as part of their policy to deter passengers from bringing their own wines with them into the dining room.

Top thirty pet peeves (mine and those of other passengers)

- Passengers who do not possess a credit card (particularly older Asian passengers) are made to feel inferior at the check-in/embarkation desks, particularly in the United States. Some cruise lines have the temerity to ask for a $500 deposit in cash, just for the "privilege" of securing an on-board charge card. No hotel on land does this. Simply refuse, and say that if you cannot trust me, then refund my cruise fare.
- Aboard the large, high-tech ships, getting Cabin Services, the "Guest Relations Desk," or the Operator to answer the telephone can be an exercise in frustration, patience, and gross irritation.
- Aboard many ships, 15 percent is automatically added to wine bills. This means that a wine waiter makes much more money on a more expensive bottle of wine, whether he knows anything about that wine (or how to decant and serve it, for example) or not. For doing just the same job for a wine costing $125 as for a wine costing $15 he makes a lot more. Therefore, insist on adding your own gratuity, and politely refuse to be told how much you have to tip.
- Cruise brochures that use models, and provide the anticipation of an onboard product that a ship cannot deliver; the result is disappointment for passengers.
- Cruise brochures that state that their ship has a "small ship feel, big ship choice" when it really caters to more than 1,000 passengers (often more than 2,000).
- Constant, irritating, and repetitive announcements for bingo, horse racing, and the latest gizmo sale in the shops.
- Any announcement that is repeated. Any announcement that is repeated.
- Flowers in one's cabin that are never watered or refreshed by the steward.
- Bathrobes provided but never changed for the duration of the cruise.
- Skimpy towels.

- Mini-bar/refrigerators that do not provide limes and lemons for drink mixes.
- Remote control units that need an instruction manual to understand their operation for turning on the television and getting a video player to work.
- In-cabin announcements at any time, except for emergencies (they are completely unnecessary for programmed events and shore excursions).
- Garnishes, when "parsley with everything" seems to be the rule of the seagoing entree experience.
- Baked Alaska parades.
- Paper, plastic, or Styrofoam cups for drinks of any kind.
- Paper napkins for meals or informal buffets (they should be linen or cotton).
- Plastic plates (often too small) for buffets.
- Buffets where only cold plates are available, even for hot food items.
- Repetitious breakfast and luncheon buffets and uncreative displays.
- "Elevator" music playing continuously in passageways and on open decks (even worse: rock music).
- Artwork placed aboard ships, but with the cruise line not caring or knowing enough about it to place the name of the artist and the year of creation alongside, whether it be a painting or a sculpture.
- Shopping lectures, shopping videos, art auctions, and carpet auctions.
- Shoreside porters who take your bags when you get off the bus or out of your car, then stand there until you tip them before they move your bags or drop them (worst ports: Ft. Lauderdale and Miami).
- Cabin stewards who place small folded pieces of paper in cabin doorframes to show when their passengers have left their cabins.
- Audio-visual technicians who think that the volume level of the show should equal that for a rock concert for 250,000 people.
- Bands that are scheduled to play in a lounge but do not start playing until passengers walk in and sit down.
- Private island days, when the tender ride to get to the island is longer than the flight to get to the ship.
- Ships that ask you to settle your shipboard account before the morning of disembarkation.
- Long lines and waiting periods for disembarkation.

Ten practical tips for a good cruise experience

What to do if...

1. **Your luggage does not arrive at the ship.** If you are traveling as part of the cruise line's air/sea package, the airline is wholly responsible for locating your luggage and delivering it to the next port. If you arranged your own air transportation it is wholly your problem. Always have easy-to-read name and address tags both inside as well as outside your luggage. Keep track of claim documents and give the airline a detailed itinerary and list of port agents (usually included with your documents).

2. **You miss the ship.** If you miss the ship's departure (due to late or nonperforming flight connections, etc.), and you are traveling on an air/sea package, the airline will arrange

to get you to the ship. If you are traveling "cruise-only," however, and have arranged your own air transportation, then you are responsible for onward flights, hotel stays, and transfers. Many cruise lines now have "deviation" desks where, for a small fee, you can adjust airline flights and dates to suit personal preferences. If you arrive at the port just as your ship is pulling away, contact the ship's port agent immediately.

3. **You don't like your dining room seating.** Most standard market ships operate two seatings for dinner (sometimes for all meals). When you book your cruise, you are asked whether you want first or second seating. The line will make every attempt to please you. But if you want second seating and are given first seating (perhaps there's a large group that's taken over the entire second seating, or the ship is full), there may be little the maître d' can do.

4. **A port of call is deleted from the itinerary.** If you only took the cruise because the ship goes to the place you have wanted to go for years, then before you go, read the fine print in the brochure. A cruise line is under no obligation to perform the stated itinerary which may be changed for whatever reason (political unrest, weather, mechanical problems, no berth space, safety, etc.). The ship's captain has the ultimate responsibility.

5. **You are unwell aboard ship.** Don't worry. All cruise ships carrying more than fifty passengers carry a fully qualified doctor (though perhaps not licensed in your own country) and medical facilities, which will include a small pharmacy. You will be well taken care of. You should be aware that the ship's medical doctor generally operates as a concession. So, although there are charges for medical services rendered, almost all cruise lines offer insurance packages that include medical coverage for most eventualities. It is wise to take out this insurance when you book.

6. **You have a problem with a crew member.** Go immediately to the hotel manager or purser and explain the problem (for single women this could be a persistent cabin steward with a master door key). No one will do anything unless you let him or her know. Cruise ships try to hire decent staff, but, with 60,000 crew members aboard the world's cruise fleet, there are bound to be a few bad apples. Insist on a full written report of the incident, which must be entered into the ship's daily log by the staff captain (or deputy captain).

7. **The cruise line's air arrangements have you flying from Los Angeles via Timbuktu to get to your cruise ship.** Well, it is fine if your cruise ship is in Timbuktu (it should not be, as Timbuktu is inland). Most cruise lines that have low rates also use the cheapest air routing to get you to your ship. That could mean charter flights from a central hub. It could also mean being dumped off the ship at the end of your cruise very early in the morning. Be warned that you get what you pay for. Ask questions before you book.

8. **You fly internationally to take a cruise.** If your cruise is a long distance away from your home, then it makes good sense to fly to your cruise embarkation point and stay for at least a day or two before the cruise. Why? You will be better rested. You will have time to adjust to any time changes. You will step aboard your ship already relaxed and ready for a real vacation.

9. **You have extra charges on your bill.** Check your itemized bill carefully. Then talk to the purser's office and ask them to show you the charge slips. Make sure you are given a copy of your bill after any modifications have been made.

10. **You are unhappy with your cruise experience.** You (or your travel agent) ultimately chose the ship and cruise. But if your ship does not meet your specific lifestyle and interests, or the ship performs less well than the brochure promises, then let your travel agent and the cruise line know as soon as possible. If your grievance is valid, many cruise lines will offer a credit, good toward a future cruise. But do read the fine print on the ticket.

ENTERTAINMENT

THAT'S ENTERTAINMENT!

After food, the most subjective (and talked about) part of any mainstream cruise experience is the entertainment program. Menus always present you with a choice of several foods, whereas the same is not often possible with cruise ship entertainment, which has to be diversified and innovative but never controversial. Ask 1,000 people what they would like to see as part of any evening entertainment program, and 1,000 different answers will ensue. It is all a matter of personal taste and choice. Whatever one expects, the days are gone when you would have been entertained by waiters doubling as singers, although a few bar waiters are still known to perform tray-spinning effects to boost their tips!

Many passengers (despite having paid so little for their cruise per passenger per day) expect to see top-notch entertainment, "headline" marquee-name cabaret artists, the world's most "popular" singers, and the most dazzling shows with slick special effects, just as one would find in the best venues in Las Vegas, London, or Paris. But there are many reasons why it is not exactly like that. International star acts invariably have an entourage that accompanies them to any venue: their personal manager, their musical director (often a pianist or conductor), a rhythm section (with bass player and drummer), even their hairdresser. On land, one-night shows are possible, but on a ship, an artist cannot always disembark after just one night, especially when it involves moving equipment, costumes, and baggage. They can also lose valuable moneymaking bookings and telephone contact. Although they can be contacted at sea, it is more difficult, and the telephone number is not theirs. This makes the whole matter logistically and financially unattractive for all but the very largest ships on fixed itineraries, where a marquee-name act might be considered a marketing draw.

When you are at home you can literally bring the world's top talent into your home via television. Cruise ships are a different matter altogether. Most entertainers do not like to be away from their "home base" for long periods, as they rely so much on the telephone for their work. Most do not like the long contracts that the majority of ships must offer in order to amortize the cost over several weeks.

So many acts working aboard cruise ships are interchangeable with so many other acts also working aboard cruise ships. Ever wonder why? Entertainers aboard ship must also live with their audiences for several days (sometimes weeks), something unheard of on land, as well as work on stages aboard older ships that were not designed for live performances. However, there is no question that cruise ships are the new location for vaudeville acts, where a guaranteed audience is a bonus for many former club-date acts, as well as fresh acts waiting to break in to the big time on land.

Many older (pre-1970) ships have extremely limited entertainment spaces, and very few ships provide proper dressing rooms and backstage facilities for the storage of costumes, props, or effects, not to mention the extensive sound and lighting equipment most live "name" artists demand or need. Only the latest ships provide the extensive facilities needed for presenting the kind of high-tech shows one would find in Las Vegas, London, or New York, for example. These feature elaborate electronic backdrops, revolving stages, orchestra pits, multislide projection, huge stageside video screens, pyrotechnic capabilities, and the latest light-mover and laser technology. Even the latest ships often lack enough dressing room and hanging space for the 150 costumes required in a single typical ship production show.

However, more emphasis has been placed on entertainment since the mid-1970s. Entertainment on today's large mainstream ships is market-driven. In other words, it is directed toward that segment of the industry that the cruise line's marketing department is specifically targeting (discounting notwithstanding). This is predominantly a family audience, so the entertainment must appeal to as broad an age range as possible—a tall order for any cruise line's director of entertainment.

Did You Know...?

...that Roy, of the famous Siegfried & Roy (Siegfried Fischbacher and Roy Uwe Ludwig Horn) illusion act, used to be a steward aboard the German liner *Bremen?*

...that the Cunard liner *Queen Mary* was the first ship to have a system of colored lights that varied according to music?

...that Verdi wrote an opera to commemorate the opening of the Suez Canal? Its name is *Aida.*

...that the 212-passenger *Seabourn Legend* was the star of the film *Speed 2: Cruise Control,* released in July 1997 in the U.S.? The film was shot on location in Marigot, the capital of the French side of the tiny two-nation Caribbean island of St. Martin/St. Maarten. The filming called for the building of almost a complete "town" at Marigot, into which the ship crashes.

...that *Titanic*—the stage musical—cost $10 million to mount in New York in 1997? That's $2.5 million more than it cost to build the original ship that debuted in 1912. The play debuted at the Lunt-Fontanne Theater in April 1997 (the ship sank on April 14, 1912).

...that the Hollywood film that cost the most money—but made the most—was based aboard a passenger liner? The film, *Titanic,* was released in 1997.

...that the cruise ship used in the movie *Juggernaut,* in which seven bombs in oil drums were placed aboard, was *Maxim Gorkiy?* The film starred Richard Harris, David Hemmings, and Anthony Hopkins.

A cruise line with several ships in its fleet will normally employ an entertainment department that is made up of an entertainment director and several assistants, and most cruise lines have contracts with one or more entertainment agencies that specialize in entertainment for cruise ships.

It is no use, for example, in a company booking a juggler who needs a floor-to-ceiling height of twelve feet, but finds that the ship has a show lounge with a height of just seven feet ("Couldn't he juggle sideways?" I have heard one cruise company executive ask!); or an acrobatic knife-throwing act (in a moving ship?); or a concert pianist when the ship only has an upright honky-tonk piano; or a singer who sings only in English when the passengers are German-speaking, and so on.

Indeed, the hardest audience to cater to is one of mixed nationalities (each of whom will expect entertainers to cater exclusively to their particular linguistic group). Given that cruise lines are now marketing to more international audiences in order to fill ships, the problem of finding the right entertainment is far more acute.

The more upscale cruise lines offer more classical music, even some light opera, and more fine guest lecturers and world-renowned authors than the seven-day package cruises heading for warm-weather destinations.

One area of entertainment that has become part of the experience and is expected—particularly on the larger, mainstream cruise ships—is that of the glamorous "production show." This is the kind of show one would expect to see in any good Las Vegas show palace, with a team of singers and dancers, a production manager, lavish backdrops, extravagant sets, grand lighting, special effects, and stunning custom-designed costumes. Unfortunately, many cruise line executives, who know little or nothing about entertainment, regard plumes and huge peacock feathers paraded by showgirls who step, but cannot dance, as being desirable. Some cruise ships have coarse shows that are not becoming to either dancer or passenger. Such things went out of vogue about twenty years ago. Shows that offer more creative costuming and real dancing win more votes today.

If you book back-to-back seven-day cruises (on alternating eastern and western Caribbean itineraries, for example), you should be aware that entertainment is generally geared to seven-day cruises. Thus, you will usually find the same two or three production shows and the same acts on the second week of your cruise. The way to avoid seeing everything twice is to pace yourself by just going to some events during the first week and saving the rest for the second week.

Regular passengers will notice that they seem to see the same acts time after time on various ships. For the reasons given above, plus a few more, the criteria narrows the field even though there are many fine land-based acts. In addition, ship entertainers need to love socializing. Successful cabaret acts tend to be good mixers, are presentable when in public, do not do drugs or take excess alcohol, are not womanizers (or man-izers?), are not late for rehearsals, and must cooperate with the cruise director and his staff as well as the band.

Sadly, with cruise lines forever looking for ways to cut costs, entertainment has of late been a major target for some companies (particularly the smaller ones). Cutting costs translates to bringing on, for example, lower-cost singers (who often turn out to be non-reading, vocally challenged persons) and bands that cannot read charts (musician-speak for musical arrangements) brought on board by cabaret acts.

One of the latest technical effects used is the laser light show, either out on deck and/or in the show lounge, where this lighting technique is programmed by a land-based company specializing in the latest high-tech wizardry. The German cruise vessel Aida is perhaps the best example of the use of laser light shows.

Other entertainment

Most cruise ships organize acts that, while perhaps not nationally recognized "names," can provide two or three different shows during a seven-day cruise. These will be singers, illusionists, puppeteers, hypnotists, and even circus acts, with wide age-range appeal.

There are comedians, comediennes, and comedy duos who perform "clean" material and who may find employment year-round on what is now known as the "cruise ship circuit." These popular comics enjoy good accommodation, are stars while on board, and often go from ship to ship on a standard rotation every few days. There are raunchy, late-night "adults only" comedy acts in some of the ships with younger, "hip" audiences, but few seem to have enough material for several shows.

The larger a ship, the larger the entertainment program. In some ships, the cruise director may "double" as an act, but most companies prefer him or her to be strictly an administrative and social director, allowing more time to be with passengers. Whichever ship and cruise you choose, you will find that being entertained "live" is an experience far superior to that of sitting at home in front of a television set watching its clinical presentation. That's show business!

NAUTICAL NOTES

The world of ships is a world of its own, and associated with it is a whole language and culture that can sometimes be confusing—but always fascinating—to the newcomer. Here are a few tidbits of nautical information for you, which may contribute to the pleasure of your cruise.

RULES OF THE ROAD

As the largest moving objects made by man, ships are subject to stringent international regulations. They must keep to the right in shipping lanes, and pass on the right (with certain exceptions). When circumstances raise some doubt or shipping lanes are crowded, ships often use their whistles, in the same way an automobile driver uses directional signals to show which way he will turn. When one ship passes another and gives a single blast on its whistle, this means it is turning to starboard (right). Two blasts mean a turn to port (left). The other ship acknowledges by repeating the same signal.

Ships switch on their navigational running lights at night—with green for starboard, red for port. Also, they have two white lights on the masts, the forward one lower than the aft one.

Flags and pennants form another part of a ship's communication facilities and are displayed for identification purposes. Each time a country is visited, its national flag is shown. While entering and leaving a port, the ship flies a blue and vertical striped flag to request a pilot, while a half-red, half-white flag (divided vertically) indicates that a pilot is on board. Cruise lines and other passenger shipping lines also display their own "house" flag, proudly fluttering from the mast.

A ship's funnel or smokestack is one other means of identification, each line having its own funnel design and color scheme. The size, height, and number of funnels were points worth advertising at the turn of the century. Most ocean liners of the time had four funnels and were called "four-stackers."

Today, perhaps the most distinctive funnel design belongs to ships of Royal Caribbean International; several of them actually have a nightclub or lounge perched partway up or set around the base of the stack itself. The view from one of these is spectacular, although in bad weather it is the room that will move most. There are numerous customs at sea, many of them older than any maritime law. Superstition has always been an important element, as in the following example quoted in the British Admiralty Manual of Seamanship:

"The custom of breaking a bottle of wine over the stem of a ship when it is being launched originates from the old practice of toasting prosperity to a ship with a silver goblet of wine, which was then cast into the sea in order to prevent a toast of ill intent being drunk from the same cup. This was a practice that proved too expensive, and it was replaced in 1690 by the breaking of a bottle of wine over the stem."

ON THE WATCH

A ship's working day is made up of six 4-hour time periods called "watches." In theory, a complement of officers and crew work the same watch round the clock: four hours on followed by eight hours off during any twenty-four-hour period.

> To avoid working identical hours day after day, one of the four-hour periods is split further into first and second "dog watches" of two hours each, as follows:
> 0000-0400 hours . . . . .midwatch
> 0400-0800 hours . . . . .morning watch

0800-1200 hours . . . . .forenoon watch
1200-1600 hours . . . . .afternoon watch
1600-1800 hours .first dog watch
1800-2000 hours . . . . .second dog watch
2000-2400 hours .evening watch

Aboard ship, the tradition is to record time by the striking of bells to indicate the state of the watch. Each bell represents a half-hour of time on watch, and the duty is ended when eight bells sound at midnight, 0400, 0800, 1200, etc.

Wind speeds

A navigational announcement to passengers is normally made once or twice a day, giving the ship's position, temperature, and weather information.

Various winds affect the world's weather patterns. Such well-known winds as the Bora, Mistral, Northwind, and Sirocco, among others, play an important part in the makeup of weather at and above sea level.

Wind velocity is measured on the Beaufort Scale, a method that was first devised in 1805 by Commodore Francis Beaufort, later Admiral and Knight Commander of the Bath, for measuring the force of wind at sea. Originally, it measured the effect of the wind on a fully rigged man-of-war (which was usually laden with cannons and heavy ammunition). It became the official way of recording wind velocity in 1874, when the International Meteorological Committee adopted it.

You might be confused by the numbering system for wind velocity. There are twelve velocities, known as "force" on the Beaufort Scale. They are as follows:

Force	Speed *(mph)*	Description/Ocean Surface
0	0-1	Calm; glassy (like a mirror)
1	1-3	Light wind; rippled surface
2	4-7	Light breeze; small wavelets
3	8-12	Gentle breeze; large wavelets, scattered whitecaps
4	13-18	Moderate breeze; small waves, frequent whitecaps
5	19-24	Fresh breeze; moderate waves, numerous whitecaps
6	25-31	Strong breeze; large waves, white foam crests
7	32-38	Moderate gale; streaky white foam
8	39-46	Fresh gale; moderately high waves
9	47-54	Strong gale; high waves
10	55-63	Whole gale, very high waves, curling crests
11	64-73	Storm; extremely high waves, froth and foam, poor visibility
12	73+	Hurricane; huge waves, thundering white spray, no visibility

Knots and logs

A knot is a unit of speed measuring one nautical mile. (A nautical mile is equal to one-sixtieth of a degree of the earth's circumference and measures exactly 6,080.2 ft. It is about 800 feet longer than a land mile. Thus, when a ship is traveling at a speed of 20

What is an island?

An island is defined as any land mass smaller than the smallest continent and completely surrounded by water.

The color of seawater

Seawater is colorless. We only see "color" in seawater because quantities of the water play with light. The deep blue of deep seawater is produced in part by the refraction of light particles in the water and by the reflection of the sky. Also, the color blue is absorbed least by seawater. "Green" seas are found closer to land and are the result of greater quantities of suspended matter carried in coastal waters. Thus, the color essentially results from the combination of the blue-looking ocean water and the yellow pigments that result from the decomposition of plant matter. The Red Sea was so named due to the periodic swarming of an alga that stains its surface.

Waves

Water waves are produced when the air-sea surface interface is distorted by a force such as the wind. Waves provide one of the most important mechanisms for transporting energy from one point to another on the surface of the sea. A restoring force such as gravity, surface tension, or the Coriolis force then acts to return the surface to equilibrium.

knots (note: this is never referred to as 20 knots per hour), she is traveling at 20 nautical miles per hour.

This unit of measurement has its origin in the days prior to the advent of modern aids. At that time, sailors used a log and a length of rope to measure the distance that their boat had covered, as well as the speed at which it was advancing.

A 1574 tract by William Bourne entitled "A Regiment for the Sea" recorded the method by which this was done. The log was weighted down at one end while the other end was affixed to a rope. The weighted end, when thrown over the stern, had the effect of making the log stand upright, thus being visible.

Sailors believed that the log remained stationary at the spot where it had been cast into the water, while the rope unraveled. By measuring the length of rope used, they could ascertain how far the ship had traveled and were thus able to calculate its speed.

Sailors first tied knots at regular intervals (eventually fixed at 47 feet 3 inches) along the rope and counted how many knots had passed through their hands in a specified time (later established as 28 seconds), which was measured by the amount of sand that had run out of an hourglass.

They then used simple multiplication to calculate the number of knots their ship was traveling at over the period of an hour.

The data gathered in this way were put into a record—called a logbook. Today, a logbook is used to record the day-to-day details of the life of a ship and its crew, as well as other pertinent information.

Latitude and longitude

Latitude signifies the distance north or south of the equator, while longitude signifies distance east or west of the 0 degree at Greenwich Observatory, London. Both are recorded in degrees, minutes, and seconds. At the equator, one minute of longitude is equal to one nautical mile, but as the meridians converge after leaving the equator (eventually meeting at the poles), the size of a degree becomes smaller.

Plimsoll mark

The safety of ships at sea and all those aboard owe much to the nineteenth-century social reformer Samuel Plimsoll, a member of the British Parliament.

He was especially concerned about the frequent loss of ships due to overloading. In those days there were certain shipowners who would load their vessels down to the gunwales so that they could squeeze every ounce of revenue out of them. They gambled on good weather, good fortune, and good seamanship to bring them safely into port. Consequently, many ships went to the bottom of the sea as a result of their buoyancy being seriously impaired by overloading.

Samuel Plimsoll helped to enact the legislation that came to be known as the Merchant Shipping Act of 1875. This required all shipowners to mark their vessels with a circular disc 12 inches (30.5 cm) long bisected by a line 18 inches (45.7 cm) long, which would be observed as a measure of their maximum draft, that is, the depth to which a ship's hull could be safely immersed at sea. However, the Merchant Shipping Act of 1890 was even stricter and required the Plimsoll mark (or line) to be positioned on the sides of vessels in accordance with tables that were drawn up by competent authorities.

The Plimsoll mark is now found on the ships of every nation. The Plimsoll mark indicates three different depths: the depth to which a vessel can be loaded in fresh water, which is less buoyant than salt water; the depth in summer, when seas are generally calmer; and the depth in winter, when seas are much rougher.

The challenge of the Blue Riband

No award has inspired as much rivalry between shipping lines as the coveted Blue Riband, given to the liner that makes the fastest transatlantic crossing in a particular year. Indeed, possession of the Blue Riband became a source of national pride.

By the late 1800s, references to the award were already being recorded, but the first real mention of it was made on August 1, 1900, when the Illustrated London News reported that the Blue Riband had been won by *Deutschland*, the Hamburg America Line passenger ship.

Although the great passenger liners of the North Atlantic raced to beat the speed record, there was no material award until 1935, when Harold K. Hales (1888–1942), a member of the British Parliament, donated a silver challenge trophy to be awarded each year to the steamship line that won the Blue Riband. Speed became so important that newspapers carried daily records of distance steamed by major ships, as well as the duration of each crossing. Average speeds, although not revealed, could be calculated from the figures provided.

Naturally, the distance covered can vary with each crossing of the Atlantic. Since 1900 the shortest distance recorded for Blue Riband purposes was the 2,807 nautical miles between Sandy Hook, New Jersey, and Queenstown (now Cobh) in Ireland, while the longest distance was 3,199 nautical miles, between Ambrose Light, New Jersey, and Cherbourg, France. Twelve ships have held the record westbound, and ten eastbound.

Some of the world's most illustrious passenger ships are listed among the holders of this prestigious award. For twenty-two years the Blue Riband was held by the U.K.'s *Mauretania*, passing briefly, in 1929, to Germany's *Bremen* and in 1930 to that country's *Europa*.

In 1933 Italy's *Rex* took over, only to lose it two years later to France's *Normandie*. Then arrived the U.K.'s *Queen Mary* to vie with *Normandie* for the award. Each kept the award for a year, in 1936 and 1937 respectively, until in 1938 Cunard firmly retrieved it with *Queen Mary*. In 1952, the prize was taken by the new U.S. liner, *United States*.

The liner *United States* has the distinction of being the fastest real liner ever to win the Blue Riband. Between July 3 and 7, 1952, during an eastbound crossing from Ambrose to Bishop Rock, the ship recorded an average speed of 35.59 knots, although it is claimed that in achieving such a speed, mechanical damage was caused to the extent that any attempt to repeat the performance was virtually out of the question.

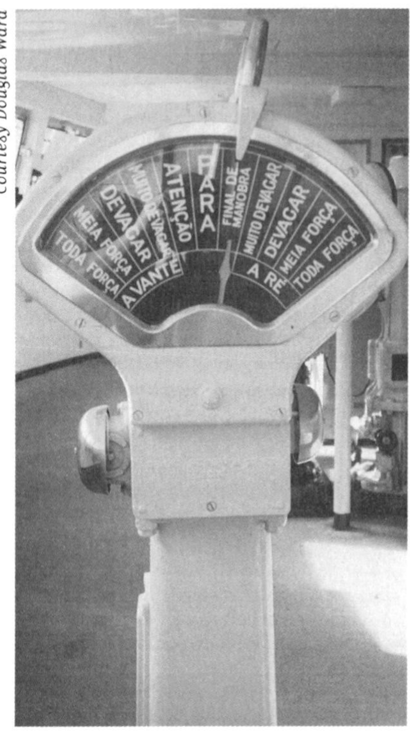

Courtesy Douglas Ward

On the navigation bridge of an older cruise ship.

No major passenger ship has been built since the early 1950s to challenge the liner *United States'* record, although with the re-engining of Cunard's *QE2*, it is conceivable that she could attempt a Blue Riband crossing, given that she achieved over 36 knots during her sea trials.

On June 22, 1990, a 243-foot-long, twin-hulled Sea Cat (catamaran-type) passenger ferry (and not a cruise ship) called *Hoverspeed Great Britain* made a successful, though somewhat unsporting, bid for the Blue Riband. The vessel, commissioned by Hoverspeed of England to bolster the company's fleet of hovercraft to counter the anticipated competition from the Channel Tunnel, carried only one passenger and had to refuel three times in midocean, something no genuine ocean-going passenger liner has ever had to do. The trophy was awarded despite this and is now back in England, the country where it first started.

Ship talk

Ships and the sea have their own special vocabulary. This list may be of use:

Abeam: off the side of the ship, at a right angle to its length

Aft: near, toward, or in the rear of the ship

Ahead: something that is ahead of the ship's bow

Alleyway: a passageway or corridor

Alongside: said of a ship when it is beside a pier or another vessel

Amidships: in or toward the middle of the ship; the longitudinal center portion of the ship

Anchor Ball: black ball hoisted above the bow to show that the vessel is anchored

Astern: the opposite of Ahead (i.e. meaning something behind the ship)

Backwash: motion in the water caused by the propeller(s) moving in a reverse (astern) direction

Bar: sandbar, usually caused by tidal or current conditions near the shore

Beam: width of the ship between its two sides at the widest point

Bearing: compass direction, expressed in degrees, from the ship to a particular objective or destination

Below: anything beneath the main deck

Berth: dock, pier, or quay. Also means bed on board ship

Bilge: lowermost spaces of the infrastructure of a ship

Boat Stations: allotted space for each person during a lifeboat drill or any emergency when lifeboats are lowered

Bow: the forwardmost part of the vessel

Bridge: navigational and command control center

Bulkhead: upright partition (wall) dividing the ship into compartments

Bunkers: the space where fuel is stored; "bunkering" means taking on fuel

Cable Length: a measured length equaling 100 fathoms or 600 feet

Chart: a nautical map used for navigating

Colors: refers to the national flag or emblem flown by the ship

Companionway: interior stairway

Course: direction in which the ship is headed, in degrees

Davit: a device for raising and lowering lifeboats

Deadlight: a ventilated porthole cover to prevent light from entering

Disembark/debark: to leave a ship

Dock: berth, pier, or quay

Draft/draught: measurement in feet from the ship's waterline to the lowest point of its keel

Embark: to join a ship

Fantail: the rear or overhang of the ship

Fathom: distance equal to 6 feet

Flagstaff: a pole at the stern of a ship where the flag of the ship's country of registry is flown

Free Port: port or place that is free of customs duty and regulations

Funnel: chimney from which the ship's combustion gases are propelled into the atmosphere

Galley: the ship's kitchen

Gangway: the stairway or ramp link between ship and shore

Gross Registered Tonnes (grt): not the weight of the ship but the total of all permanently enclosed spaces above and below decks, with certain exceptions, such as the bridge, radio room, galleys, washing facilities, and other specified areas. It is the basis for harbor dues. New international regulations introduced in 1982 required shipowners to remeasure the grt of their vessels (1 grt = 100 cubic feet of enclosed space/2.83 m^3) and not its weight. This unit of measure was invented in England centuries ago for taxation purposes. Wine that was shipped from France was stored in standard-size casks, called tonneaux. Thus a ship carrying twenty casks measured twenty tonnes, and taxes were applied accordingly.

Helm: the apparatus for steering a ship

House Flag: the flag denoting the company to which a ship belongs

Hull: the frame and body of the ship exclusive of masts or superstructure

Leeward: the side that is sheltered from the wind

Manifest: a list of the ship's passengers, crew, and cargo

Nautical Mile: one sixtieth of a degree of the circumference of the earth, which is equal to 6,080.2 feet. It is about 800 feet (or one-seventh) longer than a land mile

Pilot: a person licensed to navigate ships into or out of a harbor or through difficult waters, and to advise the captain on handling the ship during these procedures

Pitch: the rise and fall of a ship's bow that may occur when the ship is under way

Port: the left side of a ship when facing forward

Quay: berth, dock, or pier

Rudder: a finlike device astern and below the waterline, for steering the vessel

Screw: a ship's propeller

Stabilizer: a gyroscopically operated retractable "fin" extending from either or both sides of the ship below the waterline to provide a more stable ride

Starboard: the right side of the ship when facing forward

Stern: the aftmost part of the ship that is opposite the bow

Tender: a smaller vessel, often a lifeboat, which is used to transport passengers between the ship and shore when the vessel is at anchor

Wake: the track of agitated water left behind a ship when in motion

Waterline: the line along the side of a ship's hull that corresponds to the surface of the water

Windward: the side toward which the wind blows

Yaw: the erratic deviation from the ship's set course, usually caused by a heavy sea

The Bridge

A ship's navigation bridge is manned at all times, both at sea and in port. Besides the captain, who is master of the vessel, other senior officers take "watch" turns for four- or eight-hour periods. In addition, junior officers are continually honing their skills as experienced navigators, waiting for the day when they will be promoted to master of a luxury cruise ship.

In addition to the ship's captain, there is a qualified officer on duty at all times—even when the ship is docked in port. The captain is always in command at times of high risk, such as when the ship is entering or leaving a port, when the density of traffic is particularly high, or when visibility is severely restricted by poor weather.

Navigation has come a long way since the days of the ancient mariners, who used only the sun and the stars to calculate their course across the oceans. The space-age development of sophisticated navigation devices has enabled us to make giant strides from the less reliable techniques used long ago. Navigation satellites have allowed us to eliminate the guesswork of early navigation (the first global mobile satellite system came into being in 1979).

A ship's navigator today can establish accurately where the ship is in any weather and at any time. There follows a description of some of the navigation instruments, which will help you understand the complexities of seamanship today.

System Control

The most sophisticated state-of-the-art machinery and navigation systems are such technical marvels that sailors of yesteryear could not even conceive of their invention. The latest navigation and command system, which is known as the "Electronic Chart Precise Integrated Navigation System" (ECPINS), now combines the electronics of the latest satellite positioning methods (Global Positioning System) with automatic course plotting, video map displays of the oceans, gyrocompass, echo sounders, sonar doppler log, wind speed, and the various sensors to provide, in one compact computer unit, a comprehensive at-a-glance display of the ship in relation to the rest of the world, all in one "real-time" position on a single monitor's electronic chart.

The Compass

A compass is the instrument by which a ship may be steered on a preselected course, and by which bearings of visible objects can be taken in order to fix a ship's position on a navigation chart. There are two kinds of compass. The magnetic compass uses the inherent magnetic forces within and around the earth; the gyrocompass, a relatively recent invention, uses the properties of gyroscopic inertia and precession, ideally to align itself to a true north–south position.

Steering

There are two different methods that can be used to steer a ship:

1. Electrohydraulic steering uses automatic (telemotor-type) transmission from the wheel itself to the steering gear aft. This is generally used in conditions of heavy traffic, during maneuvers into and out of ports, or when there is poor visibility.

2. Automatic steering (gyropilot), which is used only in the open sea. This system does not require anyone at the wheel, because it is controlled by computer. However, on all ships, a quartermaster is always at the wheel as a backup to the system, for extra safety—and just in case a need should arise to switch from one steering system to another. This changeover from one to the other takes only a few seconds.

Satellite Navigator

Using this latest high-tech piece of equipment, ship's officers can read, on a small television screen, the ship's position in the open ocean anywhere in the world, any time, and in any weather with pinpoint accuracy (within plus or minus 600 feet).

The satellite navigator device uses the information transmitted by a constellation of up to six orbiting satellites. Each of these satellites is in a normal circular polar orbit at an altitude of 450 to 700 nautical miles, and orbits the Earth in about 108 minutes. Data from each gives its current orbital position every two minutes.

Apart from telling the ship where it is, it can continuously provide the distance from any given point, calculate the drift caused by currents and so on, and tell the ship when the next satellite will pass.

The basis of the satellite navigation is the U.S. Navy Satellite System (NNSS). This first became operational in January 1964 as the precision guidance system for the Polaris submarine fleet and was made available for commercial use in 1967.

The latest and more accurate system is the Global Positioning System (GPS), which is now fitted to an increasing number of ships. This uses twenty-four satellites (eighteen of which are on-line at any given time) that can provide an accuracy in estimating a ship's position of plus or minus 6 feet. Another variation, the Navigational Command System (NACOS), collects information from a variety of sources: satellites, radar, gyroscopic compass, speed log, and surface navigational systems as well as engines, thrusters, rudders, and human input. It then displays relevant computations and information on one screen controlled by a single keyboard.

Radar

Radar is one of the most important discoveries that has ever been made for the development of navigational aids, providing on screen a picture of all solid objects in a range selected by the navigator—which is from a half-mile to a seventy-two-mile radius. Its greatest asset is possibly as an invaluable aid to collision avoidance with other ships, although it has proven of value in finding a position at a distance when navigational marks or charted coastlines are within its range. Some ships have two or three radar sets with interswitch units.

Engine Telegraph

These automatic signaling devices are used to communicate orders between the bridge and the engine room. There may be three, one on the bridge and one on each bridgewing.

Bow Thruster Control

This small two-way handle is used to control the bow thrusters—powerful engines in the bow that push the ship away from the dockside without tugs. Some new ships may also have thrusters positioned at the stern.

Rudder Angle Indicator

This device is normally positioned in front of and above the quartermaster. It provides both the commanding officer and the quartermaster with a constant readout of the degrees of rudder angle, either to port (left) or starboard (right).

VHF Radio

This is a radio receiver and transmitter, operating on VHF (Very High Frequency) with a "line-of-sight" range. It is used for communicating with other ships, pilots, port authorities, and so on.

Radio Direction Finder

This operates on radio waves, enabling its operator to take bearings of shore radio stations. By crossing two or more bearings, you find the ship's position.

Depth Indicator

This equipment (which is an echo sounder) provides a ship with a constant digital monitor readout, together with a printed chart.

Course Recorder

This records and prints all courses followed by the ship at all times.

Clearview Screen

This device makes simple but effective use of centrifugal force, where instead of an automobile-type windshield wiper, a ship has circular screens that rotate at high speed to clear rain or sea spray away, providing those on the bridge with the best possible view in even the worst weather.

Engine Speed Indicators

These provide a reading of the number of revolutions per minute being generated by the engines. Each engine has a separate indicator, giving the speed in forward or reverse.

Facsimile Recorder

This is a special radio device that is designed to receive meteorological and oceanographic maps, satellite pictures, and other pertinent weather information that is transmitted by maritime broadcast stations that are located all over the world.

Emergency Controls

These include control boards, electric circuits, and other devices to control flooding and fires on board ship.

Fire Control

If anyone sounds the fire alarm, an alarm is automatically set off on the bridge. A red panel light will be illuminated on a large plan of the ship, indicating the section of the ship that has to be checked so that the crew can take immediate action.

In the event of a fire, a ship is sectioned into several distinct zones, each of which can be tightly closed off. In addition, most of the cruise ships have a water-fed sprinkler system that can be activated at the touch of a button or automatically activated when sprinkler vials are broken by fire-generated heat.

New electronic fire detection systems are being installed aboard ships in order to increase safety further.

Emergency Ventilation Control

This automatic fire damper system also has a manual switch that is activated to stop or control the flow of air to all areas of the ship, in this way reducing the fanning effect on flame and smoke via air-conditioning and fan systems.

Watertight Doors Control

Watertight doors throughout the ship can be closed off in order to contain the movement of water flooding the ship. A master switch activates all the doors in a matter of seconds.

All the ship's watertight doors can be operated electrically and manually, which means that nobody can be trapped in a watertight compartment.

Stabilizers Control

The ship's two stabilizing fins can be extended, housed, or controlled. They normally operate automatically under the command of a gyroscope located in the engine control room.

The Passenger's Prayer

"Heavenly Father, look down on us, Your humble, obedient passengers who are doomed to travel the seas and waterways of this earth, taking photographs, mailing postcards, buying useless souvenirs, and walking around in ill-fitting swimwear.

"We beseech You, oh Lord, to see that our plane is not hijacked, our luggage is not lost, and our oversized carry-ons go unnoticed.

"Protect us from surly and unscrupulous taxi drivers, avaricious porters, and unlicensed, English-speaking guides in foreign places.

"Give us this day Divine guidance in the selection of our cruise ships and our travel agents—so that we may find our bookings and dining room reservations honored, our cabins of generous proportions, that our luggage arrives before the first evening meal, and our beds are made up.

"We humbly ask that our shower curtains do not provoke us into meaningless frustration and destructive thoughts.

"We pray that our cabin telephones work, the operator (human or electrical) speaks our tongue, and that there are no phone calls from our children forcing us to abandon our cruise early.

"Lead us, dear Lord, to good, inexpensive restaurants in the world ashore—where the food is superb, the waiters friendly, and the wine included in the price of a meal.

"Please grant us a cruise director who does not "cream" excessively from the spoils of bingo or horse racing, or does not stress only those jewelry stores from which he accepts an offering.

"Grant us the strength to take shore excursions—to visit the museums, cathedrals, spice stalls, and gift shops listed in the guidebooks.

"And if on our return journey by non-air-conditioned buses we slip into slumber, have mercy on us, for our flesh is weak, hot, and tired.

"Give us the wisdom to tip correctly at the end of our voyage. Forgive us for under-tipping out of ignorance and over-tipping out of fear. Please make the chief purser and ship's staff love us for what we are and not for what we can contribute to their worldly goods or company comment forms.

"Dear God, keep our wives from shopping sprees and protect them from bargains they do not need or cannot afford. Lead them not into temptation in St. Thomas or Hong Kong, for they know not what they do.

"Almighty father, keep our husbands from looking at foreign women and comparing them to us. Save them from making fools of themselves in cafés and nightclubs. Above all, please do not forgive them their trespasses for they know exactly what they do.

"And when our voyage is over and we return home to our loved ones, grant us the favor of finding someone who will look at our home videos and listen to our stories, so our lives as tourists will not have been in vain. This we ask you in the name of our chosen cruise line, and in the name of American Express, Visa, Mastercard, and our banks. Amen."

Quips and quotes

Passengers cruising for the first time are the source of all the following questions to me when I worked aboard ships all those years ago:

"Do the crew sleep on board?"

"How far above sea level are we?"

"Is the island surrounded by water?"

"How does the captain know which port to go to?"

"Can we get off in the Panama Canal?"

"Does the ship generate its own electricity?"

"Does this elevator go up as well as down?"

"Will this elevator take me to my cabin?"

"Why is the sauna so hot?"

"What time's the midnight buffet?"

"Are there two seatings at the midnight buffet?"

"Is dinner in the dining room?"

"Can I please have some hot iced tea?"

"Why aren't there any no-smoking seats in the cigar club?"

"Do we have to stay up until midnight to change our clocks?"

"How many fjords to the dollar?"

"What time's the 2 o'clock tour?"

"Where's the bus for the walking tour?"

"Will we have time to take the shore excursion?"

"If I don't buy a shore excursion, am I allowed off in port?"

"Are the entertainers paid?"

"Why don't we have a Late Night Comedy Spot in the afternoon?"

"Why aren't the dancers fully dressed?"

"How do we know which photos are ours?"

"Will the ship wait for the tour buses to get back?"

"Will I get wet if I go snorkeling?"

"Do the Chinese do the laundry by hand?"

"Is the mail brought on by plane?"

"Does the ship dock in the middle of town?"

"Who's driving the ship if the captain is at the cocktail party?"

"Does the sun always rise on the left side of the ship?"

"Is the doctor qualified?"

"Is trapshooting held outside?"

"I'm married, but can I come to the Singles Party?"

"Should I put my luggage outside the cabin before or after I go to sleep?"

And here are some new ones:

"Can I have an inside cabin with a balcony?"

"Does an outside cabin mean it's outside the ship?"

In Alaska (Cunard *Princess*):

"Are the glaciers always here?"

In the dining room (*Stella Solaris*):

Me: "Do you have a decanter for this young red wine?"

Wine waiter: "Not unless it's on the wine list"

Overheard in the dining room (Cunard *Countess*):

"Waiter, this vichyssoise is cold."

"Was the fish caught this morning by the crew?"

Overheard on an Antarctic cruise (Hanseatic):

"Where are the shops?"

Overheard on a British islands cruise:

"Windsor Castle is terrific. But why did they build it so close to the airport?"

Overheard on a Greek islands cruise:

"Why did the Greeks build so many ruins?"

Overheard on a round-Japan cruise, in Kagoshima, with Mount Suribaya in the background (*QE2*):

"Can you tell me what time the volcano will erupt? I want to be sure to take a photograph."

Then there is the cruise brochure that describes cabin layout: "Cabins with a double bed can accommodate a third passenger!" (the now defunct Premier Cruise Lines)

And what about the saying, "He let the cat out of the bag"? On board a square-rigger 150 years ago, this would have sent shudders through one's spine—for it meant that a sailor had committed an offense serious enough to have the "cat o' nine tails" extracted from its bag. The "cat" was a whip made of nine lengths of cord, each being about 18 inches long with three knots at the end, all fixed to a rope handle. It could bring serious injuries, even death, upon the victim. It is no longer carried on today's tall ships, having been outlawed by the U.S. Congress in 1850, and then by Britain's Royal Navy in 1879.

WHO'S WHO ON BOARD

Think of a cruise ship as a highly structured floating hotel, in which each crew member fills a well-defined role. The highest authority is the captain, and the chain of command works down through the ranks.

All members of the ship's company wear a uniform by which their station and function are instantly identifiable. Rank is also designated by the colors and insignia worn on the sleeves and epaulets of the uniform itself, although the colors in conjunction with the gold braid can vary somewhat. For example, throughout most of the industry, red generally signifies the medical department, but aboard ships of Italian registry, red signifies the purser's department.

Captain

The captain is the master of the ship and has absolute dictatorial rights and control over his vessel, officers, crew, and passengers. He is a seaman first and manager of the ship second. He is also expected to be a generous and worthy host (the social aspect of a captain's job today requires an investment of about a quarter of his time spent with his passengers). When passenger ships are registered for insurance coverage (normally with Lloyd's of London), the captain's credentials and past record are reviewed together with the seaworthiness of the vessel itself.

Although on the bridge there may be several officers with a master's certificate, the captain still maintains unquestioned authority. He wears four gold bars on his sleeves and epaulets.

Every ship has a log, a daily record in which are noted all navigational and pertinent nautical data, details of reports from various department heads, and any relevant information on passengers or crew. Maritime law dictates that only the captain is allowed to sign that the daily entries in the log are correct. If a ship were to be abandoned, the log is the only record of the ship's operation, prevailing conditions, weather information, and geographical locations that could be reviewed. The captain normally attends numerous social functions during the course of a cruise, hosts a table in the dining room, and is often seen during the day on walkabout inspection tours.

Staff captain

The staff captain is second in command and can take over at any time if needed. As the title suggests, the staff captain is concerned not only with the navigation bridge but also concentrates on the day-to-day running of the ship, its staff and crew, and all discipline.

In some companies the staff captain takes over when the captain is on leave; in others, there is a "floating" captain who takes all the relief commands. The staff captain also wears four gold bars.

The captain and staff captain work closely together, dividing the duties according to company policy and/or personal interest. At all times, one of the two must be on call, and most cruise lines insist that one or the other remains on board in any port of call.

Although the captain earns a top salary, the staff captain is on almost the same scale. As a matter of interest, despite equal expertise and responsibility for a passenger count often three times as great, a ship's captain earns roughly half the salary of a jumbo jet pilot.

The airline captain has the added advantage of switching on an automatic pilot to handle almost every navigational task once aloft, and homes in on a runway through computer assistance and radar. His seagoing counterpart must be able to navigate manually and negotiate hidden reefs, sandbars, sunken vessels, and marker buoys—even hazards not recorded on any chart.

The seagoing captain also has the awesome responsibility of docking, maneuvering, and anchoring his ship, often in unfamiliar territory and sometimes in difficult weather conditions.

Bridge officers

Besides the captain and staff captain, other bridge officers include the chief officer, first officer, second officer, and several junior officers. Their job is the navigation and safe conduct of the vessel at all times. The bridge is manned twenty-four hours a day, even in port.

Also on the bridge are the fire detection systems and controls for the fire and watertight doors, which can be activated by compartments in the event of a problem on the ship.

Chief engineer

The chief engineer (almost always referred to as "Chief") has the ultimate responsibility for the mechanical well-being of a cruise ship. This includes overseeing not only the main and auxiliary engines but also the generators, electrical systems, air-conditioning, heating, plumbing, ventilation, refrigeration, and water desalinization systems.

He is trained in a multiplicity of on-board systems and is, in fact, the only person on board who talks to the captain as an equal. With regard to engineering, he is a mechanical master. He wears four gold bars.

Chief radio officer

The function of the chief radio officer is to keep the ship in constant touch with the outside world. The radio station is where all radio, telegraph, telex, and satellite communication equipment is found. The radio officer is also in charge of the automated telephone exchange and, on a large cruise ship, has a staff of at least three.

Today, however, the job has become much simpler with the new automated satellite uplink/downlink systems and is more concerned with the maintenance of this high-tech equipment.

Principal medical officer

Aboard large cruise ships, the medical department can be extremely busy, with up to 3,500 passengers and 1,200 crew to attend to. Hopefully, you will meet the doctor socially, not professionally.

The hospital aboard many cruise ships is a miniature version of a hospital ashore, and may be equipped with an operating theater, an X-ray room, examination rooms, several beds, and an isolation unit. There is at least one fully qualified doctor on board every cruise ship that is carrying fifty or more passengers, plus a small nursing staff. There may also be a physiotherapist, medical orderlies who may be petty officers, and maybe even a dentist.

Hotel manager (general manager)

As head of a "floating hotel" involving almost two-thirds of the entire crew, the hotel manager is in charge of overall passenger service, comfort, housekeeping, food, drink, and information services, plus entertainment—just as in any first-class hotel ashore.

There will also be several junior hotel officers and other staff to whom responsibility for the day-to-day running of various departments can be delegated.

The hotel manager's two most important associates and aides are the purser and the cruise director. At one time, the purser (called the chief purser in some ships) was responsible for the control of all passenger services. But due to the increasing emphasis placed on food, recreation, comfort, and entertainment, the new position of hotel manager has been developed. In some ships, hotel managers are simply former chief pursers with a new title and added responsibilities.

If at any time during your cruise you have any unresolved problems or a request that has not been satisfied, contact the hotel manager or deputy hotel manager through the purser's office.

Chief purser

The chief purser's office is the financial, business, accommodation, and information center of any ship and will be found in a convenient location in the main lobby area.

The purser's department handles all matters relating to money (including currency exchange), mail, telexes, telegrams, and telefaxes; accepts valuables for safekeeping; and provides a complete information service, sometimes around the clock. The purser is also responsible for all passenger and crew accounts, purchasing and requisitioning of supplies, shipboard concessions, the on-board printing of items such as the Daily Program and menus, and manning the telephone switchboard, if the ship does not have an automatic system. The purser's domain also includes relations with customs and immigration officials in all ports of call.

The purser has two main assistants: the hotel purser and the crew purser. The hotel purser is in charge of all passenger business, including accommodation (often under the direction of a berthing officer), while the crew purser handles all matters relating to the ship's personnel and contracts.

If the ship is based in foreign waters, the crew purser also oversees crew changeovers and requests, and arranges flights, baggage, and any other incidental crew matters. Many larger ships have two complete crews, one of which will be on leave while the other works the ship. Often, this works on a continuous rotation basis.

Deputy hotel manager

The deputy hotel manager can take over from the hotel manager at any time, while his special domain is the food and beverage operation. In some ships, this is run by a concessionaire, who supplies not only the food but also the dining room and bar staff, in which case the deputy hotel manager's role is that of an aide to both the hotel manager and the chief purser.

Concierge

In some luxury ships, such as those of Crystal Cruises and Cunard, the concierge acts as an invisible liaison officer between ship and passenger. The concierge's primary concern is the well-being and satisfaction of passengers, and duties may include setting up private parties, obtaining opera or theater tickets, arranging special transportation in ports of call, or simply obtaining items that passengers cannot find themselves.

Cruise director

Without a doubt, the most visible person on board, the cruise director, has the ultimate responsibility of planning and operating the passenger entertainment, activities, and sports programs, and acting as the master of ceremonies for shipboard functions and events. The cruise director oversees every area of leisure and recreation. The position is, thus, highly demanding—and well paid. However, the really good, experienced cruise directors in the industry can be counted on two hands; the rest are simply young puppets who copy others and use the same old spiel.

Before each cruise, the cruise director sketches in all projected activities, entertainment, and movies on a huge chart, showing the program in time slots throughout each day.

The cruise director has a number of helpers under his command, including the port lecturers; cruise staff and social hosts; "headliner" and lesser entertainers, bands, and musicians; other lecturers; recreation, sports, and health instructors; and children's counselors.

In some larger ships, there may be one or more assistant cruise directors or an entertainment manager, stage manager, and social director. Cruise lines label their staff positions in different ways.

The cruise director may be an officer (with two- or three-gold-stripe status), or he may be a "nonsailor" with a show biz background. Certainly one of the qualities required for the job is an ability to deal with difficult entertainers, crew, and, of course, passengers! A cruise director must plan entertainment, movies, and special theme nights with dexterity, taking care not to offend anyone in the process.

On the first day of the cruise, the cruise director will usually invite all passengers to the main lounge and explain the entertainment program to them, at the same time urging passengers to take advantage of the many events planned for the cruise. He may also introduce his staff and give a brief ship orientation soon after sailing.

At the start of each cruise, the cruise director usually gives a port lecture, often with audiovisual aids. In this, he will advise passengers what to do ashore, describe the excursions available, and even offer advice on where to shop. But beware of the cruise director who oversells certain stores, for he could well be on a healthy commission!

The cruise director has an office, together with members of his cruise staff, through which he can be reached for anything relating to the entertainment, activities, and sports programs on board. In Part Two of this book, you will find an evaluation of the cruise director and his staff for each ship rated.

In some ships, notably those operated by German companies, the cruise director is more of a cruise manager and also deals with matters such as immigration, port clearances, and travel arrangements for passengers. This position also occurs on Russian- or Ukrainian-registered ships chartered to German tour operators.

Social hostess

This position was created more for use on the larger cruise ships, where the cruise director needs a female counterpart to act as charming hostess at the various social functions and cocktail parties. The social hostess is not, however, the equivalent of being cruise director and is not an officer, nor is she required to fulfill lifeboat command roles. She is, however, an important part of the social fabric on larger ships and, in some, would be required to speak several languages.

She acts as hostess at the Captain's Welcome Aboard party, introducing passengers to the captain; writes invitations to the captain's table and officers' private parties; often holds "hostess corner" sessions; and may host other functions. She would be required to act as intermediary in the event of death or illness of passengers between the ship, passengers, and their family members ashore.

SHORE EXCURSIONS

For some, a cruise might simply be a means to get away from it all, and, no matter how many ports the ship visits, some never go ashore, preferring instead to revel in the complete shipboard aspect of cruising, the ship being the ultimate destination. For the majority, however, the ports offered on a cruise itinerary are an important draw, the ship providing the transportation—a means to link the destinations together. Shore excursions, both a challenge and a bane to cruise lines, are one of the most vital aspects of the total cruise experience. They are organized to be varied enough for everyone, from the young and active to the elderly and infirm.

Today you need not feel the least bit uncomfortable or hesitant in strange or unusual surroundings, or intimidated by languages other than your own. If you do not want to miss the major sightseeing attractions in each port, the organized shore excursions provide a good solution. Also, if you do not wish to be alone, they provide an ideal opportunity to get to know fellow passengers with similar interests.

Note: When you buy a shore excursion from the cruise line, you are fully covered by the ship's insurance; do it on your own and you are not covered when you step off the ship.

Cruise lines generally plan and oversee shore excursions assuming that you have not seen a place. They aim to show you the most attractive, striking, and fascinating aspects of a destination in a comfortable manner and at a reasonable price. Shore excursions are operated either by land, sea, or air, or a combination. They are of varying duration: half-day sightseeing; full-day sightseeing, including lunch; evening outings, such as nightclub tours, including admission charges and one or more drinks; and overland excursions that can last several days and involve overnight hotel stays.

On land, buses, rather than taxis or private cars, are usually provided. This cuts costs and allows the tour operator to narrow the selection of guides to only those most competent, knowledgeable, and fluent in English (or whatever language the majority of passengers speak), while providing some degree of security and control.

Courtesy Douglas Ward

A beautiful sight: Swan Hellenic Cruises' Minerva *passing through the open span of Tower Bridge in London.*

Did You Know...?

...that if you are not on one of the organized excursions, you are not covered by the ship's insurance?

...that often the local color and ambience of any destination are ruined by the fact that ship piers are usually surrounded by a gaggle of tourist junk that would never sell elsewhere?

...that hell on wheels is the tour to Kandy from Colombo, Sri Lanka? It consists of a three-hour tortuous bus drive to see the temple where Buddha's tooth is said to be enshrined. All bus drivers have been to the Bob Newhart kamikazi school of bus driving!

Shore excursions aboard most ships come under the heading of "additional on-board expenses" and are considered as sources of onboard revenue by cruise lines. Yet most of the money generated by the sale of shore excursions never reaches the cruise lines but goes to third parties—the tour operators in the ports of call. Only a handful of cruise products include shore excursions in the cruise fare, generally those lines specializing in "adventure" or "expedition" cruises to unusual and exotic destinations.

Passengers often consider shore excursion prices to be high, unaware of the tremendous behind-the-scenes organization required and the costs involved locally. A vast amount of time and money is spent in setting up suitable shore excursion programs. The ship's shore excursion office is the last link in the chain of operation of a successful shore excursion program.

Shore excursion brochures

The description of shore excursions often includes artistic license, with copy often written by head office personnel who have not visited the port of call or been on the excursion for sale. Often, the language used can lead to disappointment and confusion. Ideally, all cruise lines should adopt the following definitions in their descriptive literature and for their lectures and presentations: The term "visit" should be taken to mean actually entering the place or building concerned. The term "see" should be taken to mean viewing from the outside (as from a bus, for example).

Shore excursion manager

The ship's representative supervising the entire operation of the shore excursion program is the shore excursion manager. As the eyes and ears of the cruise line, he can recommend to the head office that any excursion be suspended if it is not to his or her satisfaction—which gives him or her a good deal of authority with local ground operators. The shore excursion manager and staff will be on the dockside dispatching the excursions in each port. Any last-minute problems or questions you have should be raised then.

Booking excursions

Early booking of excursions is recommended, especially those listed as "limited participation." This means that there are a restricted number of seats available, to be sold on a first come, first served basis. In some ships, where shore excursions can be booked prior to the sailing date, sellouts often occur. So, book as early as possible.

Courtesy Douglas Ward

See the whites of their size! Two large white cruise ships alongside in St. Thomas, U.S.V.I.

In some ships, prebooking forms for shore excursions will either be forwarded with your cruise tickets, or you may find them in your cabin on arrival. In some new ships, shore excursions can be booked via the in-cabin interactive television system.

Choosing the right shore excursion

Here are a few guidelines:

- Whether novice or repeat passenger, make an effort to attend the shore excursion briefing.
- Shore excursions are put together for general interest. If you want to see something that is not described in the excursion literature, do not take it. Go on your own or with friends.
- In the Caribbean, many sightseeing tours cover the same ground, regardless of the cruise line you sail with. Choose one and then do something different in the next port. (The same is true of the history/archaeology excursions operated in the Greek Isles.) It pays to avoid repeating a visit made already.
- If you are a history buff, remember that most excursions give very little in-depth history, and guides are often not acquainted with details beyond a superficial general knowledge. Pick up a pocket guidebook on the area or check the ship's library.
- City excursions are basically superficial. To get to know a city intimately, it is better to go alone or with a small group of friends. Travel by taxi or bus directly to the places that are of most interest to you, or simply walk.
- If you enjoy diving or snorkeling, many cruise ships operate dive-in excursions at a very reasonable price that includes flippers, mask, and snorkel. Instruction for novices is offered on board, and underwater cameras can often be rented, too.
- Departure times are listed in the descriptive literature and in the Daily Program, and may or may not be announced over the ship's public address system. Do not be late, or you may be too late. There are no refunds if you miss the excursion.

- If you are hearing-impaired, make arrangements with the shore excursion manager to assist you in departing for your excursions at the correct times.
- Only take along what is necessary; leave any valuables aboard ship, together with any money and credit cards you do not plan to use. Groups of people are often targets for pickpockets in major cities such as Barcelona, Caracas, and Rio de Janeiro. Beware of excursion guides who give you a colored disk to wear for "identification"—he may be marking you as a "rich" tourist for local shopkeepers.
- In foreign ports, convert a little money into local currency for minor expenses during any tour, or take a supply of U.S. one-dollar bills—useful if you wish to buy a soft drink, for example, or wish to take a taxi to the ship, if you prefer to shop rather than go back on the bus.

Going independently

You can, of course, go ashore on your own, and in most places it is generally safe. In most areas of the world there are no restrictions on independent travel ashore, with the exception of China and areas of military importance, together with countries that stipulate restrictions on individual visas, such as Myanmar (formerly Burma). Remember, however, that if you are not on one of the organized excursions, you are not covered by the ship's insurance.

Going ashore independently is ideal in the major cruise ports of Alaska, the Bahamas, Bermuda, the Caribbean, the Mexican Riviera, the Canary Islands, the Mediterranean, Aegean ports, and the islands of the South Pacific. In many South American ports, however, it is wise to go with a friend, especially if you are unfamiliar with the language. Do carry some identification (but not your passport), the name of your ship and the area in which it is docked. If the ship is anchored and you take a launch tender ashore, take note of exactly where the landing place is by observing nearby landmarks as well as writing down the location. This will be invaluable if you get lost and need to take a taxi back to the launch.

Going to a quiet secluded beach to swim? First check with the shore excursion manager; certain beaches may be off-limits because of a dangerous undertow, drug pushers, or persistent hawkers. And, if you are thinking of going diving alone, don't! Not anywhere, even if you know the area well. Always go diving with at least one companion (the "buddy" system).

Naturally, you do not have to go off the ship at all. Sometimes, after several days at sea, it just feels wonderful to stay aboard to enjoy the peace and calm, while everyone else, it seems, has deserted the ship.

Sightseeing by taxi

If you decide to hire a taxi for sightseeing, negotiate the price in advance, and do not pay until you get back to the ship. If you are with friends, hiring a taxi for a full- or half-day sightseeing trip can often work out cheaper than renting a car; you also avoid the hazards of driving. Naturally, prices vary according to where in the world you are, but if you can select a driver who speaks English, or whatever your national language is, and the taxi is comfortable, even air-conditioned, you are ahead.

Be wary of taxi drivers who wear a badge that claims, "I speak English," for it may be all the English they speak! To be certain, ask the driver a few questions, and make sure that the price you negotiate is clear to both of you. Better still, if your driver speaks only a little English, write down the agreed fare and show it to him. Make sure you know what currency the number represents.

Tips for successful shore excursions

- Take some ether to put the tour guide out in the bus on the way back from wherever it is you are visiting—you will have a much quieter time returning to the ship.

- Take some pliers or a pair of scissors to cut the wires to the microphone, then you will not have to be bothered by all that useless information that you do not really need, or cannot cope with on your "relaxing cruise" vacation.
- Take some pliers or a pair of scissors to cut the wires to the speakers, so that you will not go deaf when seated under them in the bus during the constant wail of the tour guide.
- Take some tools so that you can dismantle the horn unit in the bus. Then the driver will not be able to toot his air horns 773 times on the 45-minute shuttle bus ride to the center of town (not to mention the 773 times coming back).
- Do not take notice of tour descriptions that state that "a box lunch is included." Box lunch means that the box will be the most edible thing you'll have for lunch!
- Avoid flightseeing tours that take off in thick fog in Alaska, so as not to spend the rest of your time in that state rotting in some trees.
- Take your own bucket and spade if the cruise line says you are going to a "private" out-island. If you don't, they'll charge you for them, and anything else you might think should be included.

COASTAL CRUISES

EUROPE

There is year-round coastal cruising along the shores of Norway to the Land of the Midnight Sun aboard the ships of the Norwegian Coastal Express Line (formerly known as the Hurtig-Ruten). The fleet of eleven ships is composed of several new 450- to 490-passenger vessels that are mini-cruise ships, together with a range of older vessels that are small, yet comfortable, working express coastal packet steamers. Their principal job is the delivery of mail, small packaged goods, and foodstuffs, as well as passengers, to the communities that are spread along the shoreline on the route often called "Highway 1."

This 2,500-mile journey (from Bergen in Norway to Kirkenes, close to the Russian border), half of which is north of the Arctic Circle, takes twelve days, but you can join it at any of the thirty-four colorful ports of call and stay as long as you wish. Most seasoned travelers like to cruise for all of the twelve days. The ships sail every day of the year. In 1997, the company carried a total of 286,000 passengers.

The service started over 100 years ago, in 1893, and the three combined companies that run it have eleven ships. Each ship is of a different size and, with between 69 and 230 cabins, can accommodate between 144 and 490 passengers. The new ships in the fleet have an elevator that can accommodate a wheelchair passenger.

Archipelago hopping can be done on Sweden's eastern coast, too, by sailing in the daytime and staying overnight in one of the many small hotels on the way. One vessel sails from Norrtalje, north of Stockholm, to Oskarshamn, near the Baltic island of Oland, right through the spectacular Swedish archipelago. You can now cruise from the Finnish city of Lappeenranta to the Estonian city of Viborg without even a visa, thanks to perestroika.

Indeed, the point-to-point coastal transportation between neighboring countries, major cities, and commercial centers is big business in northern Europe. Some of the larger cruise ferries could easily rival major cruise ships in other regions now. They are designed to operate in all weather, and their facilities are virtually the same, but with much smaller cabins and an emphasis on duty-free shopping.

SCOTLAND

The fishing town of Oban, some two hours west of Glasgow by road, perhaps seems an unlikely point to start a cruise, but is the base for one of the world's very finest cruise

NORWEGIAN COASTAL EXPRESS SHIPS

SHIP	TONNAGE	BUILT	BERTHS
Harold Jarl	2,568	1960	165
Kong Harald	6,270	1993	490
Lofoten	2,597	1964	228
Midnatsol	4,200	1982	322
Narvik	4,073	1982	314
Nordkapp	11,204	1996	490
Nordlys	6,270	1994	490
Nordnorge	11,204	1997	490
Polarlys	11,204	1996	490
Richard With	6,270	1993	490
Vesteralen	4,073	1983	314

Did You Know...?

...that the whole disc of the sun is visible for twenty-four hours a day at some points north of the Arctic Circle? Points include North Cape (May 14–July 29), Hammerfest (May 16–July 27), Tromso (May 20–July 22), Harstad (May 26–July 19), and Bodo (June 4–July 8).

vacations. The former MacBrayne ferry *Hebridean Princess* is an absolute gem, with Laura Ashley-style interiors. This ship carries passengers around some of Scotland's most magnificent coastline and islands. Do remember to take lots of warm clothing, however (layers are ideal), as the weather can be somewhat unkind.

United States

In the United States, coastal vessels, flying the red, white, and blue flag, offer a change of style and pace from the big oceangoing cruise ships. On these cruises, informality is the order of the day. Accommodating up to 160 passengers, the ships tend to be more like a private party or club—there's no pretentiousness.

Unlike major cruise ships, these small vessels are rarely out of sight of land. Their operators seek out lesser-known cruise areas, offering in-depth visits to destinations inaccessible to larger ships, both along the eastern coast, and in Alaska.

During the last few years, there has been little growth in this segment of the cruise market. If you are the sort of person who prefers a small country inn to a larger resort, this type of cruise might appeal to you. The ships, each of which measures under 2,500 tonnes and each of which is classified as a "D"-class vessel, are subject neither to the bureaucratic regulations nor the union rules that sounded the death knell for large U.S.-registered ships. These vessels are restricted to cruising no more than twenty miles off shore, at a comfortable twelve knots. The public room facilities are limited, and because

Courtesy Douglas Ward

Yorktown Clipper *(Clipper Cruise Line) is an example of a small coastal cruise vessel.*

the vessels are of American registry, there is no casino on board. As far as entertainment goes, passengers are usually left to their own devices, although there may sometimes be a piano. Most of these vessels are in port during the evening, so you can go ashore for the local nightlife. Getting ashore is extremely easy; passengers can be off in a matter of minutes, with no waiting at the gangway.

Accommodation, though not elaborate, consists of all-outside cabins, each with its own large picture window and private bathroom. The cabins are small but quite cozy. Closet space is very limited, so take only what you absolutely need. There's no room service, and you will have to turn your own bed down at night. The only drawback to all-outside cabins is that some do open directly onto the deck—not convenient when it rains. And the fact that cabins are closer to the engines and generators means that noise is considerable throughout the night. The quietest cabins are at the bow, and most cruising is done during the day so that passengers will be able to sleep better at night. Tall passengers should note that the overall length of beds on most of these vessels does not exceed 6 feet (1.82 m).

The principal evening event on these cruises is dinner in the dining room, which accommodates all passengers at once. This can be a family-style affair, with passengers at long tables, and the food passed around. The cuisine is decidedly American, with fresh local specialties featured.

These vessels usually have three or four decks, and no elevators. Stairs can be on the steep side and are not recommended for people with walking difficulties. This kind of cruise is good for those who do enjoy a family-type cruise experience in pleasant surroundings. The maxim "You just relax, we'll move the scenery" is very appropriate in this case.

A small selection of the coastal and inland cruise vessels is featured in the profiles in Part Two, since they are small and specialized and have limited facilities. You should be aware that you may get a linen change only once or twice a week, and may not get a "turn-down" service. Typical cabin sizes range from 73 sq. ft. (6.7 m²) to 232 sq. ft. (21.5 m²).

COASTAL CRUISE SHIPS

SHIP	CRUISE LINE	CABINS
Ambassador I	Marco Polo Cruises	45
Dro Ki Cakau	Captain Cook Cruises	59
Executive Explorer	Glacier Bay Tours & Cruises	25
Grande Caribe	American Canadian Caribbean Line	48
Nantucket Clipper	Clipper Cruise Line	51
Niagara Prince	American Canadian Caribbean Line	42
Pacific Aurora	Inside Passage Cruises	35
Reef Endeavor	Captain Cook Cruises	75
Santa Cruz	Metropolitan Touring	43
Sea Bird	Special Expeditions	35
Sea Lion	Special Expeditions	35
Spirit of Alaska	Alaska Sightseeing/Cruise West	39
Spirit of Columbus	Alaska Sightseeing/Cruise West	39
Spirit of Discovery	Alaska Sightseeing/Cruise West	25
Spirit of Endeavor	Alaska Sightseeing/Cruise West	51
Spirit of Glacier Bay	Alaska Sightseeing/Cruise West	43
Temptress Explorer	Temptress Adventure Cruises	50
Temptress Voyager	Temptress Adventure Cruises	33
Terra Australis	Cruceros Australis	50
Wilderness Adventurer	Glacier Bay Tours & Cruises	38
Wilderness Discoverer	Glacier Bay Tours & Cruises	43
Wilderness Explorer	Glacier Bay Tours & Cruises	18
Yorktown Clipper	Clipper Cruise Line	69

RIVER AND BARGE CRUISES

Whether you want to cruise down the River Nile, along the mighty Amazon, or along the lesser Orinoco, the stately Volga, the primal Sepik, the magnificent Rhine, the "blue" Danube, the mystical Irrawaddy (which has been renamed the Ayeyarwady), or along the "yellow" Yangtze—to say nothing of the Don and the Dnieper, the Elbe, or Australia's Murray—there is a cruise and vessel ready for you.

What sort of person enjoys cruising aboard river vessels? Well, cruise ship passengers who survive very well without dressing up, bingo, casinos, discos, and entertainment, and those who like a totally unstructured lifestyle.

EUROPEAN RIVER CRUISING

Cruising down one of Europe's great waterways is an experience in itself—quite different from sailing on an open sea, where motion has to be taken into consideration (rivers are always calm). These cruises provide you with a constant change of scenery, often passing through several countries, each with their own history and architecture, in a weeklong journey. The river vessels are always close to land and offer you the chance to visit cities and areas that are inaccessible to large ships. Indeed, watching stunning scenery slip past your floating hotel is one of the most relaxing and refreshing ways to absorb the beauty that has inspired poets and artists through the centuries. A cruise on the Danube, for example, will take you through four countries and from the Black Forest to the Black Sea.

In 1840–41, the Marquess of Londonderry, a member of the British aristocracy, traveled across Europe along the Rhine and Danube rivers. He then wrote about these experiences, which were published in 1842, in a charming book entitled *A Steam Voyage to Constantinople*. And who could forget the romance implied by Johann Strauss's famous waltz "The Blue Danube." The new Rhine–Main–Danube waterway is now open, and at 2,175 miles it is the longest waterway in Europe. It connects fourteen countries from Rotterdam on the North Sea to Sulina and Izmail on the Black Sea, and offers river travelers some of the most fascinating sights anywhere.

River vessels are long and low in the water, and their masts must fold down in order to negotiate the low bridges found along most of Europe's rivers. Although they are small when compared to oceangoing cruise ships, these vessels do have a unique and friendly international atmosphere. The most modern of them do offer the discreet luxury of a small floating hotel, and some of them actually have several public rooms, including a large dining room. They typically have three or four decks. Most are air-conditioned, and the newest will also feature an observation lounge, bar, heated swimming pool (some of them may even have a heated indoor pool), sauna, solarium, whirlpool, gymnasium, massage, hairdresser, and shop kiosk.

Although the cabins may be small, with limited closet space, they will be mostly outside (facing the river), with a private bathroom, and will be very comfortable for a one-week journey. Cabins are largest aboard *Mozart*, at 205 sq. ft. (19 m^2), while most other river vessel cabins will be smaller. All of the cabins are generally clean and tidy as well as functional.

Many of the cabins on the most modern vessels feature a personal safe, a mini-bar, a television, and an alarm clock/radio. You will find that the ceilings are quite low, and that the beds are quite short, too. In general, shore excursions must be booked at the same time as you book your cabin, as only unsold space will be available on board the vessel.

In Europe, river cruising has now reached a very sophisticated level, and you can be assured of good service and meals of a consistently high European standard. The dining is quite pleasant, although not quite a gourmet experience (excepting those vessels that are catered by Austrian and Swiss companies). Lunch is normally a buffet affair. For dinner, a set menu, consisting of three or four courses, is the norm, except for the most upscale vessels. Without doubt the best cuisine and service can be found aboard *Danube Princess, Mozart, Prussian Princess,* and *River Cloud,* although reasonably decent cuisine is served aboard many other river vessels.

Typical rates for river cruises are from $800 to more than $3,000 per person for a one-week cruise (prices increase for the most popular periods), including meals, cabin with private facilities, side trips, and airport/railway transfers. If you are already in Europe, many cruises can be purchased "cruise-only" for greater flexibility.

Note: It is best to go for an outside cabin on a deck that does not have a promenade deck walkway outside it. Normally, cabins on the lowest deck have a four-berth configuration. It does not matter which side of the vessel you are on, as you will see a river bank, and scenery, on both sides. Informality is the order of the day, and, because rivers are calm by nature, you cannot get seasick.

River cruising: Russia

Perhaps the best way to get to know Russia is on a river/inland waterway cruise. Often referred to as the "Waterways of the Tsars," the country benefits as a cruise destination from a well-developed network of rivers, lakes, and canals. Geographically, the river routes for tourists are divided into three main areas: Central European Russia, Northwestern European Russia, and Asian Russia.

Rechtflot is the Russian government's management overlord. It consists of some twenty-one shipping companies, with the combined fleet made up of more than 5,000 vessels. The largest is the United Volga River Shipping Company, which alone has more than 2,000 river vessels. It carries more than fifty million passengers and about one hundred million tonnes of cargo each year. The Moscow River Shipping Company, the next largest, operates more than 1,000 vessels and transports as many as eleven million passengers and more than sixty million tonnes of cargo each year.

In the Central Basin, Moscow is the hub of river tourism, and the newly opened waterways between Moscow and St. Petersburg allow a seven-day cruise link between the present and former capitals.

The best-known Russian rivers are the Don, Moskva, Neva, and Volga, but the lesser known Belaya, Dvina (and North Dvina) Irtysh, Kama, Ob (longest river in Siberia), Oka, Svir, Tura, and Vyatka connect the great system of rivers and lakes in the vast Russian hinterland.

Many Russian vessels are chartered to foreign (non-Russian) cruise wholesalers and tour packagers. The vessels do vary somewhat; some are well equipped, air-conditioned, and are, for the most part, clean. I would advise you to choose one that has its food and hotel services (especially the food) catered by the Swiss company Flotel. *Kirov* is a good example.

One unusual Russian river vessel worth mentioning, *Rossiya,* is used for state visits and is extremely elegant and fitted throughout with exceptionally fine materials. Cruises include the services of a cruise manager and lecturers, and some companies also specialize in "home stays" before or after the cruise as part of an attractive cultural package. A Russian entry visa is required for all non-Russian visitors, which can be obtained for you by the cruise/tour company.

River cruising: The Nile

A journey along the Nile—the world's longest (and historically the greatest) river—is a journey back in time, to over 4,000 years before the birth of Christ when the Pharaohs thought they were immortal. Even though time proved them mistaken, the people who lived along the river banks formed one of the greatest civilizations the world has known. The scenery has changed little in over 2,000 years, and the best way to see it, of course, is by river boat.

Courtesy Douglas Ward

Sovyekskaya Russiya *alongside a port on Russia's Volga River.*

There are approximately 140 vessels featuring Nile cruises, many offering excellent standards of comfort, food, and service. Most have a swimming pool, lounge, piano bar, and disco. A specialist lecturer in Ancient Egyptian history accompanies almost all sailings, which cruise the 140 miles between Aswan and Luxor in four or five days. Extended cruises, typically of seven or eight days, cover about 295 miles and visit Dendera and Abydos. The longest cruises, which take ten to twelve days, cover 590 miles, and include visits to Sohag, El Amarna, Tuna El Gabal, and Ashmuneim, ending in Cairo. In all, there are over 7,000 departures every year! If you are worried about the recent spate of terrorist attacks on passengers, note that these have only occurred on the Cairo to Aswan cruise section. But the best and most fascinating Nile cruising is between Aswan and Luxor, and this is normally not touched by the terrorist groups.

Most Nile cruises include all sightseeing excursions, which are accompanied by experienced, trained guides who may reside on board, or who may meet the boat at each call. Multilingual guides also accompany each cruise.

River cruising: China

There are now several new river vessels featuring cruises along the Yangtze, the world's third-longest river, particularly through the area known as the Three Yangtze River Gorges, which is a 100-mile stretch between Nanjin Pass in the east and White King City in the west. The river Yangtze actually stretches 3,900 miles (6.276 km) from Shanghai through the very heartland of China. The Three Gorges are the 47-mile-long Xiling Gorge, the 25-mile-long Wu Gorge, and the 28-mile-long Qutang Gorge (known locally as "Wind Box Gorge"). Also, the Lesser Three Gorges (or Three Small Gorges) are, for many, a more impressive sight, sometimes part of the main cruise but also reached by small river vessels from Wushan. Take a cabin with a balcony—it is worth the extra money, and the view is better. Note that in China, rats and rivers often go together, so beware that rat poison may well be found under your bed.

Courtesy Delta Queen Steamboat Company

This view shows the stern paddle-wheel of Mississippi Queen *(Delta Queen Steamboat Company).*

Note: Standards of hygiene are generally far lower than you may be used to at home.

Arguably the best river vessels are the new *Elaine, Jeannie,* and *Sheena* (Regal China Cruises), a trio that cater superbly well to 258 passengers. The vessels have both Chinese- and Western-style restaurants, beauty salon, health club with sauna, and eight private mah-jongg and karaoke rooms. Fine Asian hospitality and service prevail, and cabins are always supplied with fresh towels and hot tea. There are several other operators, but do check on the facilities, meet-and-greet service, and the newness of the vessels before booking. The best time of the year to go is May–June and late August–October (July and early August are extremely hot and humid).

If you do want to cruise this area sometime in the future, you should know that a new $35-billion-plus hydroelectric Sanxia (Three Gorges) Dam, the world's largest (first envisioned by Sun Yat-Sen in 1919), is going to be constructed, essentially blocking off this major tourism attraction and making a 370-mile-long reservoir, scheduled for completion in 2009. Construction was scheduled to start after the winter of 1997/1998, which means that there will be no more river cruises after then if work goes ahead as scheduled.

Ayeyarwady (Irawaddy) River (Myanmar)

How about the *Road to Mandalay?* For those visiting Southeast Asia, Orient Express Hotels launched a new luxury river cruise vessel in Myanmar (formerly known as Burma), in January 1996. The vessel, named *Road to Mandalay,* operates weekly between Mandalay and Pagan, on the Ayeyarwady (formerly Irrawaddy) River.

River Murray (Australia)

The fifth-largest river in the world, the Murray was the lifeblood of the pioneers who lived on the driest continent on earth. Today the river flows for more than 1,250 miles (2,765 kilometers) across a third of Australia, her banks forming protected lagoons for an astonishing variety of bird and animal life. Paddlewheel boats such as *Murray Princess* offer all the amenities you will find on America's *Mississippi Queen*. There are even six cabins for the physically disabled.

Barge cruising: Europe

Smaller than river vessels, and more accurately called boats, "hotel barges" ply the inland waterways and canals of Europe from April to November, when the weather is generally good. Barge cruises are usually of three, six, or thirteen days' duration, and they offer a completely informal atmosphere for up to a dozen passengers. These barges cruise along slowly in the daytime, and moor early each evening, to give you time to pay a visit to a local village, and get a restful night's sleep.

Hotel barges are even more intimate than river vessels and offer a different experience. You go ashore on your own during the day and at night. Shopping opportunities are limited, and evening entertainment is always impromptu. Most of the barges carry between eight and twenty-four passengers.

Hotel barges tend to be beautifully fitted out with rich wood paneling, full carpeting, custom-built furniture, and tastefully chosen fabrics. Each barge has a dining room/lounge-bar and is equipped with the passengers' comfort in mind. Each barge captain takes pride in his vessel, often acquiring some rare memorabilia to be incorporated into the decor.

Locally grown fresh foods are usually purchased and prepared each day by a loving crew, allowing you to live well and feel like a house guest. Most of the barges can also be chartered exclusively so you can just take your family and friends, for example.

The waterways of France especially offer beauty, tranquillity, and a diversity of interests, and barge cruising is an excellent way of exploring an area not previously visited. Most cruises include a visit to a famous vineyard and wine cellar, as well as side trips to places of historic, architectural, or scenic interests. You will be accompanied by a crew member familiar with the surrounding countryside. You can even go hot air ballooning over the local countryside, and land to a welcome glass of champagne and your flight certificate. Although ballooning is an expensive extra, the experience of floating within earshot of chateaux and villages and over pastoral landscapes is something you can always treasure.

How you dine on board a barge will depend on which barge and area you choose: dining will range from home-style cooking to outstanding nouvelle cuisine, with all the trimmings. The hotel barges will have English or English-speaking French crews.

Barging on the canals often means going through a constant succession of locks. Nowhere is this more enjoyable and entertaining than in the Burgundy region of France where, between Dijon and Macon, for example, a barge can negotiate as many as fifty-four locks during a six-day cruise. Interestingly, all lock keepers in France are women!

Typical rates range from $600 to more than $3,000 per person for a six-day cruise. I do not recommend taking children. Rates include a cabin with private facilities, all meals, excellent wine with lunch and dinner, other beverages, use of bicycles, side trips, and airport/railway transfers. Some operators also provide a hotel the night before or after the cruise. Clothing, by the way, is totally casual at all times, but at the beginning and end of the season, the weather can be unreliable, so make sure you take sweaters and rain gear.

Steamboating: United States

The most famous of all river cruises in the United States are those aboard the steamboats of the mighty Mississippi River. Mark Twain, an outspoken fan of Mississippi cruising, at one time said: "When man can go 700 miles an hour, he'll want to go seven again."

The grand traditions of the steamboat era are maintained by the new *American Queen*, and by the older, smaller *Delta Queen* and *Mississippi Queen* (Delta Queen Steamboat

Company), all of which are powered by steam engines that drive huge wooden paddlewheels at the stern.

The smallest and oldest of the three boats, the 180-passenger *Delta Queen,* was built on Scotland's Clydeside in 1926 and is on the U.S. National Register of Historic Places. She gained the nation's attention when President Carter spent a week aboard in 1979.

Half a century younger, the 400-passenger *Mississippi Queen* was built at a cost of some $27 million in Jefferson, Indiana, the place where nearly 5,000 steamboats were built during the nineteenth century. *Mississippi Queen* itself was designed by the creator of Cunard's *QE2,* James Gardner of London. Each of the steamboats features one of the rarest of musical instruments—a calliope, or "steam piano," driven by the boat's engine.

The latest, a 222-cabin, 436-passenger American-built steamboat named *American Queen* (Delta Queen Steamboat Company), debuted in June 1995. Built at a cost of $60 million by McDermott Shipyard, Morgan City, Louisiana, the riverboat is fitted out with vintage tandem compound horizontal reciprocating steam engines (circa 1930) that originally drove a steam dredge called *Kennedy.* The engines are used to drive the 60-ton stern paddle wheel, with paddles made up of individual bucket boards that are 30 feet long and 2 feet wide. *American Queen* is the thirtieth steamboat built for the Delta Queen Steamboat Company.

Traveling aboard one of these steamboats makes you feel like you are stepping back into the past and into the world of American folklore. You will be surrounded by a certain charm and old-world graciousness, as well as by delightful woods, brass, and flowing staircases. And once every year, two boats challenge each other in the Great Steamboat Race—a ten-day extravaganza.

Steamboat cruises last from two to twelve days, and during the year there are several theme cruises, with big bands and lively entertainment. These boats cruise up and down the Mississippi and Ohio rivers.

As for food aboard the steamboats, it is generally very much "American" fare. That means steak, shrimp, Creole sauces, fried foods, and few fresh vegetables.

Traveling on the river is a great way of taking a vacation and avoiding the crush of congested roads and airports. And of course there are no immigration or customs procedures in the heartland of America.

EXPEDITION/NATURE CRUISES

The risk one runs in exploring a coast in these unknown and icy seas is so very great that I can be so bold to say no man will ever venture farther than I have done and that the lands to the south will never be explored.

So wrote Captain James Cook in 1774. His voyage was a feat of great courage, for not only did he take the risk of entering an unknown sea, but his ship, *Resolution*, was far too fragile a vessel (462 tonnes) to undertake such a trip. Yet there is no landscape quite so breathtaking and compelling as the polar regions of the south, and no experience so unforgettable as a visit there. Today, would-be Cooks have the curiosity and drive to move into adventure cruising.

With so many opportunities to cruise in Alaska and the Baltic, Caribbean, Mediterranean, and Mexican Riviera areas, you may be surprised to discover a small but growing group of enthusiasts heading out for strange and remote waters. But there are countless virtually untouched areas to be visited by the more adventurous, whose motto might be "see it before it is spoiled." Such passengers tend to be more self-reliant and more interested in doing or learning than in being entertained.

On expedition cruises, passengers take an active role in almost every aspect of the voyage, which is destination-, exploration-, and nature-intensive. Naturalists, historians, and lecturers (rather than entertainers) are aboard each ship to provide background information and observations about wildlife. Each participant receives his or her personal log book—illustrated and written by the renowned wildlife artists and writers who accompany each cruise. Such a logbook documents the entire expedition and serves as a great source of information as well as a complete memoire of the voyage. All companies that offer these adventure cruises provide expedition parka and waterproof boots, but you will need to take waterproof trousers (for Antarctica and the Arctic).

Imagine walking on pack ice in the Arctic Circle, exploring a penguin rookery on Antarctica or the Falkland Islands, searching for "lost" peoples in Melanesia, cruising close to the source of the Amazon, gazing at species of flora and fauna in the Galapagos Islands (Darwin's laboratory), or watching a genuine dragon (from a comfortable distance, of course). It is what expedition cruising is all about, and it is not really recommended for the novice passenger.

Because of the briefings, lectures, and laboratory at sea, there is a cultural and intellectual element to be found on expedition cruise vessels. There is no formal entertainment as such; passengers enjoy this type of cruise more for the camaraderie and learning experience. The ships themselves are designed and equipped to sail in ice-laden waters, and yet have a shallow enough draft to glide over coral reefs.

Expedition cruise vessels can, nevertheless, provide comfortable and even elegant surroundings for up to 200 passengers and a highly trained and knowledgeable staff, and offer first-class food and service. Without traditional cruise ports at which to stop, the ship must be self-sufficient, capable of long-range cruising, as well as environmentally friendly.

Expedition cruising came about as a result of people wanting to find out more about this remarkable planet of ours—its incredible animal, bird, and marine life. Lars-Eric Lindblad pioneered it in the late 1960s. He was a Swedish-American who was determined to turn travel into adventure by opening up parts of the world tourists had never visited.

After chartering several vessels for adventure cruises to Antarctica (which he started doing in 1966), he organized the design and construction of a ship capable of going almost anywhere in comfort and safety. In 1969, *Lindblad Explorer* was launched.

In the years that followed, the ship earned an enviable reputation in adventure travel. Lindblad's company sold the ship to Salen-Lindblad Cruising in 1982. They subsequently resold her to Society Expeditions, who renamed her *Society Explorer*. She is now operated by Abercrombie & Kent as *Explorer*. See Part Two, where details and ratings are provided.

Courtesy Douglas Ward

The luxurious Hanseatic *(Hapag-Lloyd Seetouristik) plowing through ice in Antarctica.*

Today there are but a handful of adventure/expedition cruise companies. They provide in-depth expertise and specially constructed vessels, usually with ice-hardened hulls that are capable of going into the vast reaches of the Arctic regions and Antarctica.

Expedition/nature cruise areas

Buddha was once asked to express verbally what life meant to him. He waited a moment—then, without speaking, held up a single rose. Several "destinations" on our planet cannot be adequately described by words—they instead have to be experienced, just as a single rose.

The principal adventure cruise areas of the world are Alaska and the Aleutians, Amazon and the Orinoco, Antarctica, Australasia and the Great Barrier Reef, the Chilean fjords, the Galapagos Archipelago, Indonesia, Melanesia, the Northwest Passage, Polynesia and the South Pacific. Other adventure cruise destinations growing in popularity are Baja California and the Sea of Cortez, Greenland, the Red Sea, East Africa, the Réunion Islands and the Seychelles, West Africa and the Ivory Coast, and the South China Seas and China Coast.

To put together their special cruise expeditions, the staff at the various companies turn to knowledgeable sources and advisors. Scientific institutions are consulted, experienced world explorers are questioned, and naturalists provide up-to-date reports on wildlife sightings, migrations, and other natural phenomena. Although some days are scheduled for relaxation or preparing for the days ahead, participants are kept active both physically and mentally. And speaking of physical activity, it is unwise to consider such an adventure cruise if you are not completely ambulatory.

Antarctica

Perhaps the most intriguing "destination" on earth is Antarctica, first sighted only in 1820 by the American sealer Nathaniel Palmer, British naval officer Edward Bransfield, and Russian captain Fabian Bellingshausen. For most, it is nothing but a wind-swept frozen wasteland (it has been calculated that the ice mass contains almost 90 percent of the snow

DID YOU KNOW...?

...that passengers once asked the operations director of a well-known expedition cruise ship where the best shops were in Antarctica? His reply: "On board, madam!"

...that in 1984, Salen Lindblad Cruising made maritime history by successfully negotiating a westbound voyage through the Northwest Passage, a forty-one-day epic that started from St. John's, Newfoundland, in Canada, and ended at Yokohama, Japan? The expedition cruise had taken two years of planning and was sold out just days after it was announced. The search for a Northwest Passage to the Orient attracted brave explorers for more than four centuries. Despite numerous attempts and loss of life, including Henry Hudson in 1610, a "white passage" to the East remained an elusive dream. Amundsen's forty-seven-ton ship *Gjoa* eventually navigated the route in 1906, taking three years to do so. It was not until 1943 that a Canadian ship, *St. Roch,* became the first vessel in history to make the passage in a single season. *Lindblad Explorer* became the thirty-fourth vessel, and the first cruise vessel, to complete the Northwest Passage.

...that Quark Expeditions had the good fortune of making maritime history in July/August 1991, when a Russian icebreaker, *Sovetskiy Soyuz,* made a spectacular twenty-one-day voyage to negotiate a passage from Murmansk, Russia, to Nome, Alaska, across the North Pole? The ship followed the trail that had been set in 1909 by Admiral Peary, who crossed the North Pole with fifty-six Eskimos, leaving by sled from Ellesmere Island. Although the polar ice cap had been navigated by the U.S. nuclear submarines *Skate* and *Nautilus*—as well as by dirigible and airplane—this was the first passenger ship to make the hazardous crossing. The planning for this expedition took over two years.

...that the most expensive expedition cruise excursion was a cruise/dive to visit the resting place of RMS *Titanic* aboard the two deep ocean submersibles *Mir I* and *Mir II* used in James Cameron's Hollywood blockbuster?

and ice in the world). For others, however, it represents the last pristine place on earth, empty of people, commerce, and pollution, yet offering awesome scenery and a truly wonderful abundance of marine and bird life. There are no germs, and not a single tree. Over 6,000 people visited the continent in 1997—the first and only smoke-free continent on earth—yet the first human to come here did so within a generation of man landing on the moon. There is not a single permanent inhabitant of the continent, whose ice is as much as two miles thick. Its total land mass equals more than all the rivers and lakes on earth and exceeds that of China and India combined. Indeed, icebergs can easily be the size of Belgium! The continent has a raw beauty and an ever-changing landscape.

Once part of the ancient land mass known as Gondwanaland (which also included Africa, South America, India, Australasia, and Madagascar), it is, perhaps, the closest thing on earth to another planet, and has an incredibly fragile ecosystem that needs international protection.

Although visited by "soft" expedition cruise ships and even "normal"-sized cruise ships with ice-hardened hulls (capable of carrying up to 800 passengers), you should know that the more remote "far side"—the Oates and Scott Coasts, McMurdo Sound, and the famous Ross Ice Shelf—can only be visited by real ice-breaker expedition ships such as *Kapitan Dranitsyn, Kapitan Khlebnikov,* and *Yamal* (vessels that carry 100 passengers or fewer), as the winds can easily reach more than 100 m.p.h. in this part of the continent.

As there are no docks in Antarctica, venturing "ashore" is done by Zodiac rubber inflatable craft, an integral part of the Antarctica experience.

Arctic

The Arctic is defined best as that region north of which no trees grow, and where water is the primary feature of the landscape. The Arctic is an ocean surrounded by continents, whereas Antarctica is a continent surrounded by ocean. The Arctic Circle is located at 66 degrees, 33 minutes, and 3 seconds north, although this really designates where twenty-four-hour days and nights begin. It is technically a desert (receiving less than 10 inches of rainfall a year) but actually teems with wildlife. It has short, cool summers, long, cold winters, and frequent high winds. Canada's Northwest Territories, which cover 1.3 million square miles, are part of the Arctic region.

Galapagos

A word of advice about the Galapagos Islands: you won't be able to take a cruise with a "foreign-flag" expedition ship. The Ecuadorians jealously guard their island and prohibit the movement of almost all non-Ecuadorian-registered cruise vessels within its boundaries. Thus, the best way to see the place that Darwin studied is to fly to Quito and cruise aboard an Ecuadorian-registered vessel such as Santa Cruz. The Galapagos National Park tax is presently about $80 per person.

Greenland

The world's largest island, Greenland, in the Northern Hemisphere's Arctic Circle, is technically a desert that is 82 percent covered with ice (actually compressed snow) that is up to 11,000 feet thick. Greenland's rocks are among the world's oldest (the 3.8 billion-year-old Isukasia formations), and its ecosystem is one of the newest. Forget Alaska—the glacier at Jacobshavn (also known as Ilulissat) is the fastest moving in the world, and creates a new iceberg every five minutes. Greenland is said to have more dogs than people, and these provide the principal means of transport for the Greenlanders.

The environment

Since the increase in environmental awareness, adventurers have banded together to protect the environment from further damage. In the future, only those ships that are capable of meeting new "zero discharge" standards, like those introduced in the Arctic by the Canadian Coast Guard, will be allowed to proceed through environmentally sensitive areas.

The expedition companies are deeply concerned about the environment, and they spend much time and money in educating both crews and passengers about safe environmental procedures.

In the course of the past two years, an "Antarctic traveler code" has been created, the rules of which are enforced by the expedition cruise companies, based on the Antarctic Conservation Act of 1978, and adopted by the U.S. Congress to protect and preserve the ecosystem, flora, and fauna of the Antarctic continent. By law, all U.S. citizens traveling to Antarctica must adhere to the Act.

Briefly, the Act makes it unlawful, unless authorized by regulation or permit issued under the Act, to take native animals or birds, to collect any special native plant or introduce species, to enter certain special areas (spas), or to discharge or dispose of any pollutants. To "take" means to remove, harass, molest, harm, pursue, hunt, shoot, kill, trap, capture, restrain, or tag any native mammal or bird, or to attempt to do so.

Under the Act, violators are subject to civil penalties, including a fine of up to $10,000 and one year of imprisonment for each violation. The Act is found in the library of each adventure/expedition ship that visits the continent.

Will large cruise ships ever cruise in Antarctica? Not in the foreseeable future, as ships are limited to a maximum of 400 passengers, so the likelihood of a mega-ship such as *Century* or *Sensation* zooming in on the penguins with 2,000-plus passengers is hardly likely, thank goodness.

The companies

Abercrombie & Kent

This well-known company operates the older but still highly suitable *Explorer* (ex-*Society Explorer*).

Hanseatic Tours

This company operates *Bremen* and *Hanseatic*, small, high-tech expedition cruise vessels, and features destination-intensive itineraries. Both ships have fine, quite luxurious appointments (*Bremen* is not as luxurious as *Hanseatic*) and are targeted at both English- and German-speaking passengers. Hanseatic Tours is a company wholly owned by Hapag-Lloyd Seetouristik.

Marine Expeditions

This Canadian company, which is in essence a Canadian version of Quark Expeditions, charters several Russian vessels for "soft" expedition/nature cruises to several popular areas, including Antarctica. The company applies its own ship names for the duration of the charter; for example, *Marine Discovery* (ex-*Maria Yermalova*) *Marine Adventurer* (ex-*Akademic Ioffe*), and *Marine Spirit* (*Akademik Shuleykin*).

Quark Expeditions

Quark Expeditions, formed by the former president of Salen Lindblad Cruising (which was purchased by NYK of Japan in October 1991), is the U.S. general sales agent for one or more of the Russian-owned nuclear- or diesel-powered icebreakers fitted with some outstanding amenities and decent creature comforts for up to 100 passengers. The operator specializes in intineraries to the Antarctic, Arctic, and North Polar regions. Among the vessels chartered are the superb *Kapitan Khlebnikov* and *Yamal*. In the U.K. the company is represented by Noble Caledonia Limited, London.

Society Expeditions

This company operates the more luxurious *World Discoverer*—a fine expedition cruise vessel featuring full creature comforts and a range of fascinating itineraries. The ship is often chartered to various societies and specialist tour operators.

Special Expeditions

This company operates *Polaris*, a small expedition vessel operating in the Galapagos Islands, which features fine appointments and full creature comforts (see profile section for details). In addition, two small vessels, *Sea Bird* and *Sea Lion* (ex-Exploration Cruise Lines vessels), operate "soft" expedition cruises in protected coastal areas in the United States, including Alaska.

SAIL-CRUISE SHIPS

Thinking of a cruise but really want to sail? Been cruising on a conventional Caribbean cruise ship that is more like an endurance test? Whatever happened to the romance of sailing? Think no more, for the answer, to quote a movie title, is "back to the future."

If you're active, think about cruising under sail, with towering masts and washing-powder-white sails to power you along. There is simply nothing that beats the thrill of being aboard a multimasted tall ship, sailing under thousands of square feet of canvas through waters that mariners have sailed for centuries.

This is what cruising in the old traditional manner is all about, on board authentic sailing ships, on contemporary copies of clipper ships, or on the very latest high-tech cruise-sail ships. Even the most jaded passengers will enjoy the exhilaration of being under sail.

Tall ships provide either a genuine sail-powered experience like those of the past (*Lili Marleen, Sea Cloud, Sir Francis Drake, Star Clipper*, and *Star Flyer*), or they are contemporary vessels built to emulate sail-powered vessels but are actually sail-assisted vessels in an ultra-chic form (*Club Med II, Le Ponant, Wind Song, Wind Spirit, Wind Star*, and *Wind Surf*).

Whichever you choose, there are no rigid schedules, and life aboard equates to a totally unstructured lifestyle, apart from meal times. Weather conditions may often dictate whether a scheduled port visit will be made or not, but passengers sailing on these vessels are usually unconcerned with being ashore anywhere. They would rather savor the thrill of being one with nature, albeit in a comfortable, civilized setting, and without having to do the work themselves.

Real tall ships

While we have all been dreaming of adventure, a pocketful of designers and yachtsmen have committed their pen to paper, hand in pocket and rigging to mast, and come up with a pot-pourri of stunning vessels to delight the eye and refresh the spirit.

Star Clippers' *Star Clipper* and *Star Flyer* are working four-masted clipper ships that rely on the wind about 80 percent of the time. Their diesel engines are used only as back-up in emergencies, for generating electrical power, and for desalinating approximately forty tonnes of seawater each day for shipboard needs. The crew performs almost every task aboard these ships, including hoisting, trimming, winching, and repairing the sails.

The whole cruise experience evokes the feeling of sailing aboard some famous private yacht at the turn of the century. Star Clippers' two modern clipper ships were born in the mind of a ship-loving owner, Mikaël Krafft.

When growing up, Krafft, himself a yachtsman (he actually sails a 128-foot schooner) in his native Sweden, was told tales of the four-masted clipper ships of yesteryear — the last one had been built 140 years ago. Krafft turned his boyhood dreams into reality in 1991, with the introduction of the tallest of the tall ships in the world, the Belgian-built *Star Flyer*. It has sails hoisted aloft on four masts, the tallest being 226 feet high. One year later, the almost identical *Star Clipper* emerged from the same shipyard as *Star Flyer*.

These are no ordinary clipper ships; they are built for passengers, who share in the experience of the trade winds of the Caribbean (and other areas). With accommodation for as many as 180 passengers, the new clipper ships are the only ones that are fully certified under the U.S. Coast Guard regulations. In addition to this, they also carry Lloyd's Register of Shipping's highest rating — a rating that has not been bestowed on any other sailing vessel since 1911.

Star Flyer, the first clipper sailing ship to be built for 140 years, became the first commercial sailing vessel to cross the North Atlantic in ninety years, and one of only a handful of sailing ships ever to be allowed into the port of Miami under full sail. It is no exaggeration to say that to be aboard the Star Clippers' ships is to seem to have died and gone to yachtsman's heaven.

Did You Know...?

...that "The Armada of the Century" for tall ships is being planned in Rouen, France, for July 9–18, 1999? There will be a parade down the length of the Seine from Rouen, which has a very extensive river frontage, to Le Havre. More than twenty tall ships have already booked their berth, and at least double that number are expected to take part in this unforgettable historic event.

While the rigging and sails above decks are totally traditional, the accommodation below decks is extremely well equipped, though not as lavish as that found aboard the *Club Med II* and the four Windstar vessels. Spacious cabins are each equipped with twin beds that convert into a double bed, individually controlled air-conditioning, two-channel audio, color television (they didn't have those in 1840), personal safe, and private bathroom with shower, toilet, sink, and even a hairdryer (the deluxe cabins also go to the extent of having a bathtub and a refrigerator).

Take minimal clothing, for these ships are the ultimate in casual dress. No jacket and tie are needed in the dining room, which can accommodate all the passengers at once in an open seating. Short-sleeved shirts and shorts for the men and very casual shorts and tops for the ladies are the order of the day (and night). The deck crew are real sailors, brought up with yachts and tall ships—and most would not set foot on a cruise ship.

Passengers gather each morning for "captain's story-time," a daily briefing of important events of the day. The captain also explains sailing maneuvers when changing the rigging or directing the ship as it sails into port. Passengers are encouraged to lend a hand, pulling on thick ropes to haul up the main sail. And they love it. At the end of the cruise, tipping (at a suggested $8 per passenger per day) is pooled and is distributed to all members of the crew. Passengers are provided with many of the amenities of large modern cruise vessels, such as air-conditioning, cashless cruising, occasional live music, a small shop, and a pool to swim in.

The Star Clippers' vessels also carry a range of watersports craft for the use of passengers—at no extra charge (except scuba diving). The equipment includes a water-ski boat, sailfish, and scuba diving and snorkeling gear.

While cuisine aboard the Star Clippers is perhaps less than the advertised excellence (as far as presentation and choice are concerned), one has to take into account the tiny galley and preparation space provided. Seating in the dining room is awkward for "correct" service and consists of six-seat tables set along the sides of the room. However, this is supposed to be a casual experience.

The above comments also apply in general to the beautiful, elegant *Sea Cloud*, an authentic 1930s three-masted barkentine whose masts are as high as a twenty-story building. She was the largest private yacht ever built when she was constructed in 1931 by E.F. Hutton for his wife, Marjorie Merriweather Post. Built for $1 million in the Krupp shipyard in Kiel, Germany, this steel-hulled yacht is immensely impressive. The cuisine is quite superb, although the choices are limited. This ship has some beautiful cabins, including two lavish owner's suites (both of them with fireplaces and a French canopy bed) left over from her private yacht days, and gorgeous handcrafted interiors.

In addition to her retained and refurbished original suites and cabins, with their paneling, antiques, and dressers, some newer, smaller cabins were also added when a consortium of German yachtsmen purchased the ship. Recent owners spent $7.5 million refurbishing her. Many original oil paintings adorn her interior walls. Now owned and operated under charter, *Sea Cloud* sails in both Caribbean and Mediterranean waters and is a tribute to elegant times past. The wood-paneled dining room is splendid.

Courtesy Douglas Ward

Windstar Cruises' Wind Spirit *under sail.*

A fine three-masted barkentine, a real working sailing ship owned and operated by German entrepreneur Peter Deilmann, *Lili Marleen* is the culmination of a lifelong dream. Built in 1994, this vessel cruises the Caribbean during the winter and the Mediterranean and Baltic during the summer and caters to both the English- and German-speaking market. Her rigging is actually even more authentic than that of the Star Clipper vessels, and was designed by Captain Immo Schnurbein, who was for many years captain of the German sail-training ship *Gorch Foch*. Life is comfortable aboard *Lili Marleen* (named after the famous song banned by Goebbels during the Second World War because it was unsuitable for marching to, but sung by soldiers on all fronts to express their longing for a time without war), with its teak decks, brass rails, and beds/berths made of tropical hardwoods. The cuisine is excellent, as is the service.

Meanwhile, a real vintage vessel, Sir Francis Drake, is another working tall ship experience. With carpeted cabins that each have a private bathroom, the ship caters to a more casual clientele than *Lili Marleen*, the two Star Clipper ships, or *Sea Cloud*. You will find that the cuisine is very basic fare, with no frills.

Contemporary Sail-Cruise Ships

At the other extreme, if you like sailing but want all your needs taken care of automatically (no energy needed), look no further than *Club Med II* (Club Mediterranée) and *Wind Surf* (Windstar Cruises)—with five tall aluminum masts the world's largest sail-cruise ships —and *Wind Song*, *Wind Spirit*, and *Wind Star* (Windstar Cruises), each with four masts. How so? Nary a hand touches the sails—they are controlled by computer from an ultra-high-tech bridge. These ships are the contemporary oceangoing robots.

From a yachtsman's point of view, the sail-to-power ratio is laughable. And that's why these cruise ships with sails have engine power to get them into and out of port. (The Star Clippers, by contrast, do it by sail alone, except when there is no wind—which is not often.) The Windstar ships were built first. You should be aware that on some itineraries, when there is little wind, you could well be under motor power for most of the cruise, with only a few hours spent under sail. The Windstar and Club Med ship would probably be under sail for no more than 40 percent of the time.

It was a Norwegian living in New York, Karl Andren, who first turned the concept of a cruise vessel with sails into reality. "Boyhood dream stuff," he said. The shipyard he chose, the Société Nouvelle des Ateliers et Chantiers du Havre (ACH, as it is known in Le Havre), enjoyed the challenge of building these most unusual vessels.

The shipyard had great experience in the design and construction of cable-laying ships using the hydraulic power of servomechanisms—a concept that was adopted for the Windstar automatic computer-controlled sail rig. Gilbert Fournier, the president of the shipyard and an expert computer programmer, was fascinated with this ship project. Three Windstar ships were delivered (a fourth was planned but never built). These ships carry mainly North American passengers, whereas the Club Med vessel caters primarily to French-speaking passengers.

The Windstar and Club Med ships offer quite luxurious accommodation, excellent full-service meals, and a fine-tuned service. These vessels also have some entertainment (however, the Gos—Gentils Organisateurs—aboard the Club Med ship provide amateurish holiday-camp-style entertainment) and several public rooms, all of which have contemporary sophisticated decor.

Another, slightly smaller but very chic vessel is the ultra-sleek *Le Ponant*. This three-masted ship caters to just sixty-four French-speaking passengers in elegant, yet casual, high-tech surroundings, developing the original Windstar concept to a very advanced state of 1990s technology.

Aboard the Club Meds, Star Clippers, Windstars, and *Le Ponant*, watersports take over in the Caribbean when you are not ashore sampling the delights of smaller islands like St. Barthélemy, St. Eustatius, or Les Isles du Saintes, where the huge "white-whale" cruise ships cannot go. The Club Med ship, Windstars, and *Le Ponant* feature an aft, fold-down watersports platform. On-board equipment includes scuba diving gear (you can take a full certification course), snorkeling equipment, water-ski boat, windsail boats, and rubber Zodiacs to whisk you off to private, unspoiled beaches.

CROSSINGS

By "crossings," I mean crossings of the North Atlantic, that is, 3,000 miles or so of it, from the Old World to the New World—or vice versa, although crossings might also include any other major ocean, such as the Pacific or the Indian Ocean.

Crossing the North Atlantic by ship is an adventure, when time seems to be totally suspended—it really is the most delicious way of enjoying life aboard ship. It actually takes little more than a long weekend. After the embarkation procedures have been completed, you will be shown to the gangway. Cross the gangway from pier to ship and you are in another world—a world that provides a complete antidote to the pressures of contemporary life ashore, and allows you to practice the fine art of doing nothing, if you so wish. After the exhilaration of a North Atlantic crossing, the anticipation of landfall among passengers is nothing short of electric.

Hemmed in by the polar ice caps, the Atlantic Ocean divides Europe and Africa from the Americas. It is three times the size of North America and contains the world's longest mountain range, which extends (undersea) over 7,000 miles and rises over 6,000 feet above the ocean floor. The only points of this ridge that rise to the surface are at St. Helena (Ascension), St. Paul's Rocks (the Azores), and Tristan da Cunha. The ocean's average width is 2,500 miles.

Although half the size of the Pacific Ocean, the Atlantic Ocean receives more than half of the water drainage of the world (four times that of the Pacific Ocean). Its average depth is 18,900 feet, and its greatest depth, which is known as the Milwaukee Depth, goes down beyond 30,240 feet.

Crossing the North Atlantic by passenger vessel should really be considered an art form. I have done it myself more than 140 times and always enjoy it immensely. As a former professional musician, I often consider crossings as rests in musical parlance, for both are described as "passages." Indeed, musicians do often "hear" rests in between notes. So if ports of call are the musical notes of a voyage, then the rests are the days at sea—a temporary interlude, when the indulgence of the person and psyche are of paramount importance.

Experienced mariners will tell you that a ship only behaves like a ship when it is on a crossing, for that's what a real ship is built for. Yet the days when ships were built specifically for crossings are almost gone. The only ship left offering a regularly scheduled transatlantic service (a "crossing") is Cunard's *QE2*, a 70,327-grt ship superbly designed to hold well against the very worst weather the Atlantic has to offer. Indeed, captains work harder on an Atlantic crossing than on regular cruising schedules.

The most unpredictable weather in the world, together with fog off the Grand Banks of Newfoundland, can mean that the captain will spend torturous hours on the bridge, with little time for socializing. And when it is foggy, the crew of *QE2* are often pestered by passengers wanting to know if the ship has yet approached latitude 41046' north, longitude 50014' west—where White Star Line's *Titanic* (43,326 tonnes) struck an Arctic iceberg on that fateful April night in 1912.

There is something magical in "doing a crossing." It takes you back to the days when hordes of passengers turned up at the piers of the ports of New York, Southampton, Cherbourg, or Hamburg, accompanied by chauffeurs and steamer trunks, jewels and finery ablaze in a show of what they thought was best in life. Movie stars of the 1920s, 1930s, and 1940s often traveled abroad on the largest liners of the day, to arrive refreshed and ready to dazzle European fans.

There is also the excitement and anticipation that precedes a crossing—the hubbub and bustle of check-in, of crossing the threshold of the gangway before being welcomed into the calmness aboard and then escorted to one's accommodation for the next several days. Once the umbilical cord of the gangway is severed, bow and stern mooring lines are cast off, and with three long blasts on the ship's deep whistle *QE2* is pried gently from

Did You Know...?

...that the first regular steamship service across the North Atlantic was inaugurated on March 28, 1838, when the 703-ton steamer *Sirius* left London for New York via Cork, Ireland?

...that the winter of 1970–1 was the first time since 1838 that there was no regular passenger service on the North Atlantic?

...that the first scheduled transatlantic advertisement appeared in the *New York Evening Post* on October 27, 1817, for the 424-ton sailing packet *James Monroe* to sail from New York to Liverpool on January 5, 1818, and for *Couvier* to sail from Liverpool to New York on January 1?

...that the following are just some of the personalities who have crossed in QE2? Carl Sagan, Joan Fontaine, Larry Hagman, Ben Lyon, Joan Rivers, Elaine Stritch, and Arthur Schlesinger, Jr.

...that QE2 is still the fastest passenger ship in service?

...that since the ship's maiden voyage in 1969, *QE2* has traveled more than four million nautical miles, and carried almost 2 million passengers?

...that the amount of paint used to cover *QE2*'s hull would completely cover one of the towers of New York's World Trade Center?

...that Cunard held the record from 1940 to 1996 for the largest passenger ship ever built (RMS *Queen Elizabeth*)?

her berth. She sails silently down the waterway, away from the world, as pretty as a picture, as serene as a Rolls-Royce and as sure as the Bank of England.

Passengers on deck observe a foolhardy yachtsman dangerously cutting under the raked bows of *QE2*, while numerous motorboats try to keep up with the giant liner as she edges down the Hudson River, past Battery Park, the Statue of Liberty, the restored Ellis Island, and then out toward the Verrazano-Narrows Bridge and out to the open sea. Coming the other way, arriving in New York by ship is one of the world's most thrilling travel experiences. Following a six-day westbound crossing aboard *QE2*, where five of the days are twenty-five hours long (they are twenty-three hours long on an eastbound crossing), everything else is an anticlimax.

QE2 can also accommodate up to forty cars per crossing, just in case you really do not want to be parted from your wheels. She also provides kennels, so you can even take your pet, although when crossing eastbound to Southampton, remember that they will have to be quarantined for up to six months. *QE2* is a distillation of over 150 years of transatlantic traditions, an oasis of creature comforts offered by no other ship.

QE2 is a very special ship—part liner, part cruise ship—a real legend in her own lifetime, and the only ship offering regularly scheduled crossings all year. Instead of allowing the ship to deteriorate, Cunard has spent a vast sum of money on refurbishments over time, including a $60 million refit in November/December 1994, and a further $15 million investment in 1996 that greatly improved the flow of passengers on and off the ship, and further enhanced and increased her already considerable facilities and amenities.

During the ship's initial planning stages, naval architect Dan Wallace and director of engineering Tom Kameen were responsible for the ship's design, which was to be for a high-speed, twin-screw ship capable of safely carrying out a six-day transatlantic crossing.

Cunard's chairman, Sir Basil Smallpiece, invited James Gardner and Dennis Lennon, well-known industrial designers, to be general design coordinators. Gardner concentrated on the exterior aesthetics, while Lennon, in addition to designing the restaurant interiors—the basic shape of which had already been determined by constructional and operational requirements—was also concerned with the introduction of a design signature that would be immediately apparent throughout the ship—for example, in staircases and corridors. The aim was that the interior design of *QE2* would emphasize the "classless" ship concept.

Apart from *QE2*'s regular crossings, a number of cruise lines feature transatlantic crossings. Although they do little more than repositioning cruises—a way of moving ships that cruise the Mediterranean in summer to the Caribbean in winter, and vice versa—they offer more chances to experience the romance and adventure of a crossing, usually in the spring and in the fall. Perhaps the most unusual transatlantic crossings—made twice a year—are aboard the sail-cruise vessel *Lili Marleen*, a three-masted barkentine that can carry fifty passengers, totally under sail.

Most cruise ships performing repositioning crossings actually cross the Atlantic using the "sunny southern route"—departing from southern ports such as Ft. Lauderdale, San Juan, or Barbados, and ending the journey in Lisbon, Genoa, or Copenhagen via the Azores or the Canary Islands off the coast of northern Africa. In this way they avoid the more difficult weather that is often encountered in the North Atlantic. The crossings take longer, however, and last between eight and twelve days.

WORLD CRUISES AND SEGMENTS

The ultimate classic voyage for any experienced traveler is an around-the-world cruise. This is usually defined as the complete circumnavigation of the earth in a continuous one-way voyage. The ports of call are carefully planned for their interest and diversity, and the entire trip can go on for as long as six months.

Voyages that go from cold to warm climates—almost always during January, February, and March, when the weather in the southern hemisphere is at its best—give you the experience of crisp, clear days, sparkling nights, delicious food, tasteful entertainment, superb accommodation, delightful company, and unforgettable memories. It is for some the cultural, social, and travel experience of a lifetime, and for the few who can afford it, an annual event!

The concept of the world sea cruise first became popular in the 1920s, although it has existed since the 1880s (the first round-the-world voyage was made by Ferdinand Magellan in 1519). A world cruise aboard a modern ship means experiencing stabilized, air-conditioned comfort in luxury cabins, and extraordinary sightseeing and excursions on shore and overland. In some ships, every passenger will get to dine with the captain at least once.

A world cruise gives you the opportunity to indulge yourself. Although at first the idea may sound totally extravagant, it need not be, and fares can be as low as $100 per day—to more than $3,000 per day. Alternatively, you can book just a segment of the cruise if that fits your pocket and interest.

How much a round-the-world cruise costs will depend on your choice of ship and accommodation. For 1999, a double-occupancy cruise fare will vary from about $12,000 to more than $100,000 per person. *QE2*'s split-level penthouse suites, for example, command more than $300,000 each (based on two persons occupying a suite). At the other end of the scale, a Russian/Ukrainian-registered vessel is the least expensive method of going round the world by ship. It almost pays not to stay home; the trip will cost less than $100 per person per day — including gratuities! There is a difference in what you get for your money, however. For example, aboard the more upscale ships, shuttle buses from your ship to the center of town (or attraction) will be included; not so aboard the less expensive ships.

Special features

Some of the special events planned for a world cruise will include such things as:

- Celebrity entertainers
- World-renowned lecturers
- Themed formal balls and parties
- Equator crossing ceremony
- International date line crossing ceremony
- Overnight and multi-day overland shore excursions
- Personalized stationery

Planning and preparation

Few enterprises can match the complexity of planning and preparing for a world cruise. More than 675,000 main meals will be prepared in the galleys during a *QE2* world cruise, for example. Several hundred professional entertainers, lecturers, bands, and musicians must all be booked about a year in advance of the trip. Crew changeovers during the cruise must be organized. A ship the size of Cunard's *QE2* requires two major crew changes during the three-month voyage. This normally involves chartering a jumbo jet to and from the relevant port of call. Airline tickets must be arranged for personnel flying in to join the ship—in the right port, and at the right time.

Because a modern world cruise ship has to be totally self-contained, a warehouse-full of spare parts (electrical, plumbing, and engineering supplies, for example) must be planned for, ordered, loaded, and stored somewhere aboard ship prior to sailing. For just about every shipboard department, the same basic consideration will apply: once at sea, it will be impossible to pick up a replacement projector bulb, air-conditioning belt, table tennis ball, saxophone reed, or anything else that the ship might run out of.

The cruise director will have his or her hands full planning entertainment and social events for a long voyage—not like the "old days" when an occasional game of bingo, horse racing, or the daily tote would satisfy passengers. Other preparations will include reserving fuel at various ports on the itinerary.

A cruise line must give advance notice of the date and time that pilots will be needed, together with requirements for tugs, docking services, customs and immigration authorities, or meetings with local dignitaries and the press. Then there is the organization of dockside labor and stevedoring services at each port of call, plus planning and contracting of bus or transportation services for shore excursions.

WORLD CRUISES: 1999-2000

The following list includes ships that are presently scheduled to operate a world cruise in 1999/2000:

SHIP	COMPANY	DAYS	FROM
Albatros	Phoenix Seereisen	100	Genoa
Arcadia	P&O Cruises	90	Southampton
Astor	Transocean Tours	132	Nice
Astor	Transocean Tours	111	Nice
Asuka	NYK Cruises	96	Yokohama
Columbus	Hapag-Lloyd Seetouristik	107	Miami
Crystal Symphony	Crystal Cruises	99	Los Angeles
Delphin *	Delphin Seereisen	118	Genoa
Deutschland	Deilmann Reederei	111	Tenerife
Europa	Hapag-Lloyd Seetouristik	111	Genoa
Island Princess **	Princess Cruises	65	San Francisco
Maxim Gorkiy	Phoenix Seereisen	115	Bremerhaven
Maxim Gorkiy	Phoenix Seereisen	120	Genoa
Nippon Maru	Mitsui OSK Passenger Line	92	Yokohama
Ocean Explorer I	The World Cruise Company	127	Athens
Ocean Majesty	The World Cruise Company	115	Athens
Oriana	P&O Cruises	92	Southampton
Queen Elizabeth 2	Cunard	104	New York
Rotterdam VI	Holland America Line	98	Los Angeles
Royal Viking Sun	Cunard	122	Miami
Saga Rose	Saga Holidays	102	Dover

NOTES

* This is an Africa/Caribbean/Latin America Cruise (not a complete around-the-world cruise)

** This is really a half-world cruise

The complexity of the preparations requires the concerted efforts of many departments and people on each continent to bring about, with precise timing, this ultimate cruising experience for travelers.

World cruise segments

Cruises to exotic destinations—China, the Orient, the South Pacific, around Africa and in the Indian Ocean, and around South America—offer all the delights associated with a world cruise. The cruise can be shorter and hence less expensive, yet offer the same elegance and comfort, splendid food, delightful ambience, and interesting, well-traveled fellow passengers.

An exotic voyage can be a totally self-contained cruise to a specific destination, lasting anywhere from thirty days to more than 100. Or you can book a segment of a world cruise to begin at one of its ports of call, getting off at another port. "Segmenting" is ideal for those who wish to be a part of a world cruise but have neither the time nor the money for the prolonged extravagance of a three- to six-month vacation.

The segment cruising idea necessarily involves flying either to or from your cruise, or both. You can travel to join your exotic cruise at principal ports such as Genoa, Rio de Janeiro, Acapulco, Honolulu, Sydney, Hong Kong, Singapore, Bangkok, Colombo, Mumbai (Bombay), Mombasa, or Athens, depending on the ship and itinerary.

DATE	DATE	WHERE
(Start)	(Finish)	(Finish)
7-Nov-99	15-Feb-00	Genoa
6-Jan-99	7-Apr-99	Southampton
18-Dec-98	28-Apr-99	Venice
13-Dec-99	1-Apr-00	Venice
3-Mar-99	7-Jun-99	Yokohama
21-Dec-98	4-Apr-99	Venice
18-Jan-99	28-Apr-99	Lisbon
21-Dec-98	17-Apr-99	Genoa
11-Nov-98	24-Apr-99	Lisbon
19-Dec-98	10-Apr-99	Venice
16-Sep-98	21-Nov-98	Rome
19-Dec-98	13-Apr-99	Genoa
8-Jan-00	7-May-00	Bremerhaven
20-Apr-99	20-Jul-99	Yokohama
19-Nov-99	25-Mar-00	Athens
19-Nov-99	12-Mar-00	Athens
4-Jan-99	5-Apr-99	Southampton
5-Jan-99	14-Apr-99	Southampton
20-Jan-99	28-Apr-99	New York
8-Jan-99	10-May-99	Miami
4-Jan-99	13-Apr-99	Dover

Did You Know...?

...that the Dollar Steamship Line featured a round-the-world cruise that started October 15, 1910 from New York, aboard the *ss Cleveland*? The cruise was advertised as "one-class, no overcrowding" voyage. The cost was "$650 and up," according to an advertisement placed by the Frank Clark Travel Agency, of the Times Building in New York.

...that an around-the-world cruise was made in 1922-23 by Cunard's *Laconia* (19,680 grt)—a three-class ship that sailed from New York? The itinerary included many of the ports of call that are still popular with world-cruise travelers today. The vessel accommodated 350 persons in each of its first two classes, and 1,500 in third class, giving a total capacity of 2,200 passengers—more than many ships of today.

...about the lady who went to her travel agent, who asked if she had enjoyed her cruise around the world? The lady replied, "Yes, but next year I want to go somewhere different!"

Ships that already cruise worldwide during the year offer the most experienced world cruises or segments. Most of these world cruise ships operate at about 75 percent capacity, thus providing their passengers with considerably more space than they would normally have.

Going P.O.S.H.

This colloquialism for "grand" or "first rate" has its origin in the days of ocean steamship travel between England and India. The wealthy passengers would, at some considerable extra cost, book their round-trip passage as "Port Outward, Starboard Home." In this way they would secure cabins on the cooler side of the ship while crossing the unbearably hot Indian Ocean under the sun. Abbreviated as P.O.S.H., the expression soon came to be applied to first-class passengers who could afford that luxury. (*Brewers Dictionary of Phrase & Fable*, Cassell Ltd.)

However, the reality is that the monsoon winds that blow in and out of the Asian area shift between winter and summer, so that the sheltered side of a ship would change according to the season. Further, in looking at deck plans of ships of the period, it appears that most cabins were located centrally, with indoor promenades or corridors along each side, so this explanation of the origin of P.O.S.H. may involve some artistic license.

Part Two:

THE CRUISE SHIPS AND RATINGS

Maasdam: *courtesy Holland America Line*

HOW SHIPS ARE EVALUATED

Ask 1,000 people how they would rate, or even design, a cruise ship, and you will get 1,000 answers (perhaps more)—all of them subjective. Professional ratings, however, are conducted with *total objectivity*, from a set of predetermined criteria and a modus operandi that works globally, not just regionally. I must stress that there is *no* "best cruise line in the world" or "best cruise ship," only the ship and cruise that is right for *you*.

I have been evaluating and rating cruise ships and the cruise product professionally since 1980. Most of the new ships are of similar dimensions, and basically only the decor is different. Thus, more and more emphasis is placed on the standard of the *dining experience*, and the *service and hospitality* aspects of the cruise than ever before. I also take into account the application of different criteria for ships of different size, style, and market segments throughout the world.

This section includes 225 oceangoing cruise ships (including some coastal cruise vessels, expedition ships, and sail-cruise ships) that were in service when this book was completed in July1998. Almost all except the new ships have been carefully evaluated, taking into account more than 400 separate inspection points based on personal cruises, visits, and revisits to ships. For the sake of clarity, the inspections are channeled into twenty major at-a-glance sections. With 100 points per section possible, the maximum possible score for any ship is, thus, 2,000 points.

Coastal cruise vessels, expeditionary cruise vessels, and sail-cruise ships cannot be judged according to the same criteria as "standard" cruise ships. They are purpose-built and many have unique features that reflect the type of expeditions or sailing experiences they offer, so the twenty major at-a-glance sections are, accordingly, slightly different.

I have also taken into consideration the fact that passengers of different nationalities expect different things from their cruise experiences. The expectations of European passengers aboard ships that operate in the Mediterranean, for example, vary considerably from those of North American passengers, who often seek the latest in high-tech interiors, facilities, and features, while their European counterparts enjoy older, smaller ships with more traditional fittings and fixtures, and less razzle-dazzle entertainment.

The Rating System

This was formulated and introduced by myself in 1980 and has been refined over the years (the same system is used by the United States Public Health Service for its vessel sanitation program). With an increasing number of ships in the marketplace and the building of ships for niche operations, tougher evaluations have become important.

Cruise lines, shipowners, and operators should note that ratings, like stocks and shares, can go down as well as up, even when things have supposedly been improved aboard their ships. This is explained by increased competition, the introduction of newer ships with more custom-designed facilities, and other market- or passenger-driven factors.

The ratings, therefore, more reflect the *standards* of the cruise product received by passengers (the software), and reflect less the physical plant (the hardware). Thus, although a ship may be the latest, most stunning vessel in the world in terms of design and decor, if the food, service, staff, and hospitality are not so good, the ratings will reflect these aspects more clearly.

When discounting was introduced to stimulate the demand for cruises in certain markets, so too were cost-cutting measures. As a result, cruise cuisine and service standards have suffered a downturn in the past few years, even though most operators constantly try to upgrade their ships. It is encouraging that cruise lines are now actively trying to catch up with those considered the best in their respective class (standard, premium, and luxury).

The stars beside the name of the ship at the top of each page relate directly to the Overall Rating. The highest number of stars awarded is five stars (☆☆☆☆☆), and the lowest is one star, which is the system universally recognized throughout the hospitality industry. A plus (+) indicates that a ship deserves just that little bit more than the number of stars attained. However, *it is the number of points achieved, rather than the number of stars,* that perhaps is more meaningful and useful to anyone wishing to compare ships.

SCORING METHOD: THE RATINGS

Overall Rating	Number of Stars
1851-2000	☆☆☆☆☆ +
1701-1850	☆☆☆☆☆
1551-1700	☆☆☆☆ +
1401-1550	☆☆☆☆
1251-1400	☆☆☆ +
1101-1250	☆☆☆
951-1100	☆☆ +
801-950	☆☆
651-800	☆ +
501-650	☆

It is assumed that all cruise products provide a packaged vacation of at least some tangible value and merit. A base of 500 points thus equals one star (most cruise ships are worthy of at least one star). Thus, for every rise of 300 points, the score is raised by one star. Every rise of 150 points raises the score by one-half star.

Cruise lines are in the business of creating and selling cruise products and vacation packages of (marketed and perceived) excellence. The common factor of all cruise ships is quality in return for the fare paid. Standards, however, have been going up in some areas, and down in other areas, and thus the need for this comprehensive analytical system that provides better ship comparisons.

Comments

The smaller details and my personal comments about each ship may help you determine what is best for you. These are divided into three distinct parts:

Accommodation

About the accommodation in general, including "penthouse apartments," suites, deluxe and standard outside cabins, and inside cabins.

Dining

About the cuisine, service, and the whole dining experience, including the main dining room and all dining options (informal cafés, bistros, buffets, pizzerias and other specialty food areas).

Other Comments

About the ship's exterior and interiors, and the "software" aspect, with both positive and less positive comments.

There is no such thing as a "one-size-fits-all" cruise ship. They come in all sizes and shapes, and feature a wide variety of internal layouts, facilities, appointments, and levels of service—as do hotels and resorts on land. The one thing all ships have in common is their gross registered tonnage, often abbreviated "grt," or given as tonnes (this is an international measurement used for ship classification and insurance purposes).

Since size plays an important part in the kind of facilities, level of comfort, and, of course, number of passengers on board, the ships are divided into three categories, according to the number of passengers carried (based on two passengers per cabin, plus or minus any single-occupancy cabins).

The results, comments, and ratings are strictly personal, based on over thirty-four years in the cruise industry, including eighteen years exclusively evaluating and rating ships, and are intended to guide you in formulating your own opinions and cruise plans. They are also intended to help travel agents differentiate between the many cruise ships and packaged products in today's marketplace, and to help you choose the *right ship* for the *right reasons*.

The Ratings and Evaluations cover five principal areas, each as important as the next:

A) **The Ship**

B) **Accommodation**

C) **Cuisine**

D) **Service**

E) **The Cruise Experience**

The Ship

This section forms 25 percent of the whole rating system.

1 **Ship: Hardware/Maintenance:** This score reflects the general profile and condition of the ship, both internally and externally. It takes into account the ship as physical hardware; its age and maintenance; the condition of the hull, exterior paint, decking materials, caulking, swimming pool surrounds, deck furniture, lifeboats, liferafts and life-preserving equipment, and other safety items; interior cleanliness with regard to the public restrooms, elevators, floor coverings, carpeting, wall coverings, stairways, passageways, doorways, other access points, crew stairways, alleyways, accommodations and galleys; food preparation areas, food storage rooms, and refrigeration units; and garbage handling, compacting, incineration, and waste disposal facilities.

2 **Ship: Outdoor Facilities/Space:** This score reflects the overall impression of space per passenger on open decks; crowding; swimming pools and whirlpools, surrounds, and adjacent lido areas; number and type of deck lounge chairs (with or without cushioned pads) and other outdoor deck furniture; outdoor sports facilities; availability, size, and quality of towels; shower stalls; changing facilities; and quiet areas (those without music).

3 **Ship: Interior Facilities/Space/Flow**: This score reflects the use of common interior passenger spaces, including enclosed promenades; passenger flow and points of congestion; ceiling height; lobby areas, stairways, and all passenger hallways; elevators and stairways; public restrooms and facilities; signs, lighting, and air-conditioning/ventilation flow; degree of comfort or crowding (passenger space ratio); and overall density.

4 **Ship: Decor/Furnishings/Artwork:** This score reflects the overall interior decor; the color scheme; hard and soft furnishings (including suitability and practicality); wood (and imitation wood) paneling, veneers, and use of glass and plastics; carpet material, tuft density, color and pattern practicality, and fit and finish (including seams and edging); chair comfort; ceiling treatments, bulkheads, and treatments; reflective surfaces; artwork (paintings, sculptures, and atrium centerpieces) quality and suitability; and color or definition and lighting.

5 **Ship: Spa/Fitness Facilities:** This score reflects any health spa facility, its location, accessibility, lighting, and flooring materials; the gymnasium and all muscle exercise equipment, aerobics exercise room, and fitness, sports, and games facilities; spa treatments and rejuvenation programs; indoor swimming pools, whirlpools, grand baths, aqua-spa pools, saunas, steam rooms, massage rooms (and the quality of massage), and changing facilities; and jogging and walking tracks.

Accommodation

This section forms 15 percent of the whole rating system.

6 **Cabins: Suites and Deluxe Grades:** This score reflects the design and layout of penthouse and other grand suites, suites, and deluxe grade cabins, private balconies (whether full floor-to-ceiling partitions or partial partitions, balcony lighting, balcony furniture), beds/berths, furniture (its placement and practicality), and other fittings; closets and other hanging space, drawer space, and bedside tables; vanity unit, bathroom facilities, washbasin, cabinets, and toiletries storage; lighting, air-conditioning, and ventilation; audiovisual facilities; quality and degree of luxury; artwork; and bulkhead insulation, noise, and vibration levels. Suites should not be so designated unless the sleeping room is completely separate from the living area. Note: some large cruise ships now have whole decks devoted to superior grade accommodation, and thus there is much difference between this accommodation and that of "standard" cabins.

This score also takes into account the soft furnishings and details in cabins, such as the information manual (list of services); paper and postcards (including personalized stationery); telephone directory; laundry lists; tea- and coffee-making equipment; flowers and/or fruit (if any); and bathroom amenities kits, bathrobes, slippers, and the size, thickness, quality, and material content of towels.

7 **Cabins: Standard Sizes:** This score reflects the design and layout of all standard cabins (whether outside or inside), beds/berths, furniture (its placement and practicality), and other fittings; closets and other hanging space, drawer space, and bedside tables; vanity unit, bathroom facilities, washbasin, cabinets, and toiletries storage; lighting, air-conditioning, and ventilation; audiovisual facilities; quality and degree of luxury; artwork; and bulkhead insulation, noise, and vibration levels.

The score also takes into account the soft furnishings and details in cabins, such as the information manual (list of services), paper and postcards (including personalized stationery); telephone directory; laundry lists; tea- and coffee-making equipment; flowers and/or fruit (if any); and bathroom amenities kits, bathrobes, slippers, and the size, thickness, quality, and material content of towels.

Cuisine

This section forms 15 percent of the whole rating system and is one of the most important, as food is often the main feature of today's cruise package. Cruise lines put maximum emphasis on telling passengers how good their food is, often to the point of being unable to deliver what is promised. Generally, however, the standard of food is good. The rule of thumb is: if you were to eat out in a good restaurant, what would you expect? Does the ship meet your expectations? Would you come back again for the food?

There are perhaps as many different tastes as there are passengers. The "standard" market cruise lines cater to a wide range of tastes. Upscale cruise lines can offer better-quality food, cooked individually to your taste. Generally, as with any good restaurant, you get what you pay for. Over the past two years, many cruise lines have been cutting back on their food quality (and service levels), and this has had a pronounced effect on the ratings.

8 **Food: Dining Room/Cuisine:** This score reflects the main dining room's physical structure, window treatments, seating (alcoves and individual chairs, with or without armrests), lighting and ambience, table set-ups, table centerpieces (flowers), and the quality and condition of linen, china, and cutlery; menus, food quality, presentation, food combinations, culinary creativity, variety, appeal, taste, palatability, freshness, color, balance, garnishes, and decorations; appetizers, soups, pastas, flambeaus, tableside cooking, and so on; fresh fruit and cakes; the principal wine list; the connoisseur wine list, the price range, and wine service.

9 **Food: Informal Dining/Buffets:** This score reflects the hardware (including the provision of hot and cold display units, sneeze guards, tongs, ice containers and ladles, and serving utensils); buffet displays (which have become extremely disappointing and institutionalized recently), presentation, trays and set-ups, correct food temperatures; food labeling; breakfast, luncheon, deck buffets, midnight buffets, and late-night snacks; decorative elements such as ice carvings; and staff attitude, service, and communication skills.

10 **Food: Quality of Ingredients**: This score reflects the overall quality of ingredients used, including consistency and portion size; grades of meat, fish, and fowl; and the price paid by the cruise line for its food product per passenger per day. It is the quality of ingredients that most dictates the eventual presentation and quality of the finished product as well as its taste. Also included is the quality of tea and coffee (better-quality ships are expected to provide better-quality tea and coffee).

11 **Food: Afternoon Tea/Bar Snacks:** This score reflects the quality of afternoon tea, including the teas available and their quality; whether mugs or cups and saucers are presented or available; whether milk is served in the correct open containers or in sealed packets; whether tea is self-service or graciously served; and cakes, scones, and pastries available. Also bar snacks, hot and cold canapes, hors d'oeuvres, and other bar/lounge snacks.

Service

This section forms 20 percent of the whole rating system.

12 **Service: Dining Room:** This score reflects the professionalism of the restaurant staff: Maitre d' hotel, dining room managers, head section waiters, waiters and assistant waiters (busboys), and sommeliers and wine waiters. It includes place settings and correct service (serving, removing from the correct side), communication skills, attitude, flair, dress sense (uniform), and finesse. Waiters should note whether passengers are right- or left-handed and, aboard ships with assigned table places, make sure that the cutlery and glasses are placed on the side of preference. Cutlery and wine glasses are also included in this score.

13 **Service: Bars:** This score reflects the lighting and ambience; overall service in bars and lounges; noise levels; the communication skills (between bartenders and bar staff and passengers in particular); staff attitude, personality, flair, and finesse; correct use of glasses (and correct size of glasses); correct billing, and the matter of attitude when presenting the bill (on those where a charge is made).

14 **Service: Cabins:** This score reflects the cleaning and housekeeping staff; butlers (for penthouse and suite passengers); cabin stewards/stewardesses and their supervisory staff; attention to detail and cleanliness; in-cabin food service; linen and bathrobe changes; and language and communication skills.

15 **Service: Open Decks:** This score reflects steward/stewardess service for beverages and food items around the open decks; service for placement and replacement of towels on chaise longues, replacement of self-help towels and emptying of used towel bins; general tidiness of all associated deck equipment; and availability of service at nonstandard times.

The Cruise Experience

This section forms 25 percent of the whole rating system.

16 **Cruise: Entertainment:** This score reflects the overall entertainment program and content as designed and targeted to specific passenger demographics. Cruise ship entertainment has to appeal to passengers of widely varying ages and types.

The rating includes the physical plant (stage/bandstand); technical support, lighting, follow spotlight operation, and set and backdrop design; sound and light systems (including laser shows), recorded click-tracks and cues, and all special effects; the variety and quality of large-scale production shows (including story and plot, content, cohesion, creativeness of costumes, relevancy, quality, choreography, and vocal content; cabaret; variety shows; singers; visual acts; and bands and solo musicians.

17 **Cruise: Activities Program:** This score reflects the variety, quality, and quantity of daytime activities and events. The rating includes the cruise director and cruise staff (including their visibility, availability, ability, and professionalism); sports programs; participation games; special interest programs; port and shopping lecturers; and mind-enrichment lecturers.

This score also reflects any watersports equipment carried (including banana boats, jet skis, scuba tanks, and snorkeling equipment); the water-ski boat; windsurfers; instruction programs and overall staff supervision; the marina (usually located aft) or side-retractable watersports platforms; and any enclosed swimming area (if applicable).

18 **Cruise: Movies/Television Programming:** This score reflects movies screened in onboard theaters, including screen, picture, and sound quality; videos screened on the in-cabin television system; other televised programming, including a ship's own television station programming, content, and entertainment value. Television audio channels are also included in this section.

19 **Cruise: Hospitality Standard:** This score reflects the level of hospitality of the crew and their attention to detail and personal satisfaction. It includes the professionalism of senior officers, middle management, supervisors, cruise staff, and general crew; social contact, appearance, and dress codes or uniforms; atmosphere and general ambience; motivation; communication skills (most important); and the attention to detail.

20 **Cruise: Overall Product Delivery:** This score reflects the quality of the overall cruise as a vacation experience; what the brochure states and promises (real or implied), which reflects on the level of expectation vs. the on-board product delivery.

THE RATINGS AND EVALUATIONS

Ship Profiles

Technical and specific information for each ship is given, followed by a point-by-point evaluation and a summary that includes positive and negative points.

Prefixes

The prefixes on the name of a ship are used to denote the type of propulsion system being used:

cs = "club ship" concept

ib = ice-breaker (diesel or nuclear)

ms = motor ship (diesel)

mts = motor twin screw (diesel) or motor turbine ship (steam)

mv = motor vessel (diesel)

msy = motor sailing yacht

my = motor yacht

mys = motor (assisted) sailing yacht

RMS = Royal Mail Ship

ss = steam ship

ssc = semi-submersible craft (swath)

sts = sail training ship

sy = sailing yacht

sv = sailing vessel

tes = turbo-electric ship (steam)

ts= turbine steamer (steam) or twin-screw vessel

tss = turbine steam ship

tsmv = twin-screw motor vessel

tts = turbine twin-screw ship

ys = yacht ship

Ship Size

A large letter, **S**, **M**, or **L**, denotes whether the entry is a small ship, medium ship, or large ship.

Lifestyle

After the name of each ship, the word LIFESTYLE is followed by STANDARD, PREMIUM, or LUXURY, according to a general classification into which segment of the market the ship best fits. It should thus further allow you to choose the right size of ship to fit your lifestyle.

→Those designated STANDARD will be the least expensive.

→Those designated PREMIUM will be more expensive and have generally better food, service, and facilities.

→Those designated LUXURY will be the most expensive, have the best facilities, food, and service, and provide the finest cruise experience possible.

Cruise Line

The cruise line and operator may be different if the company that owns the vessel does not market and operate it.

First Entered Service

Where two dates are given, the first is the ship's maiden passenger voyage when new and the second is the date it began service for the present operator.

Propulsion

The type of propulsion is given (i.e. diesel, diesel-electric, or steam turbine), together with the output (at 100 percent), expressed either as bhp = brake horsepower; kW = kilowatts generated; or shp = shaft horsepower

Propellers

Included is the type of propeller, where known, expressed as CP = controllable (or variable) pitch or FP = fixed (or direct) pitch.

Passenger Capacity

The number of passengers is based on:

a) Two beds/berths per cabin, plus all single cabins.

b) All available beds/berths filled (Note: this figure may not always be accurate, as cruise lines often make changes by adding or taking away third/fourth berths according to the demand).

Passenger Space Ratio (Tonnes per Passenger)

Achieved by dividing the *gross registered tonnage* by the *number of passengers*.

Cabin Size Range

From the smallest cabin to the largest suite (including private balconies), in square feet and square meters, rounded up to the nearest number.

Wheelchair Cabins

Cabins designed to accommodate passengers with mobility problems.

Note: In the Other Comments section at the bottom of each page, all gratuities are usually at extra cost unless specifically included in the price (extra gratuities are strictly prohibited). Likewise, insurance and port taxes are also at extra cost unless specifically stated as included.

mv Aegean I

☆☆☆

(M)

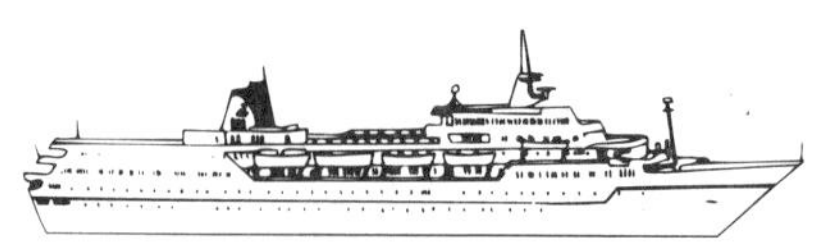

LIFESTYLE	**STANDARD**
Cruise Line:	Dolphin Hellas Shipping
Former Names:	*Aegean Dolphin/Narcis/Alkyon*
Gross Tonnage:	11,563
Builder:	Santierul N. Galatz (Romania)
Original Cost:	n/a
Entered Service:	1974/May 1988
Flag:	Greece
Tel No:	1130627
Fax No:	1130627
Length (ft./m.):	460.9/140.5
Beam (ft./m.):	67.2/20.5
Draft (ft./m.):	20.3/6.2
Propulsion/Propellers:	diesel (10,296kW)/2 (CP)
Decks:	8
Total Crew:	190
Pass. Capacity (basis 2):	576
Pass. Capacity (all berths):	670
Pass. Space Ratio (basis 2):	20.0
Pass. Space Ratio (all berths):	17.2
Officers:	Greek
Total Cabins:	288
Size Range (sq. ft./m.):	134.5–290.6/12.5–27.0
Cabins (outside view):	202
Cabins (inside):	86
Cabins (for one person):	0
Cabins (with private balcony):	0
Cabins (wheelchair accessible):	Yes
Cabin Current:	220 AC
Cabin TV:	Yes
Dining Rooms:	1
Seatings:	2
Elevators:	2
Casino:	Yes
Slot Machines:	Yes
Swimming Pools (outdoors):	1
Swimming Pools (inside):	0
Whirlpools:	0
Fitness Center:	Yes
Sauna/Steam Room:	Yes/No
Massage:	Yes
Self-Service Launderette:	Yes
Movie Theater/Seats:	Yes/176
Library:	Yes
Children's Facilities:	No
Classification Society:	Lloyd's Register

RATINGS	**SCORE**
Ship: Hardware/Maintenance	61
Ship: Outdoor Facilities/Space	58
Ship: Interior Facilities/Space/Flow	61
Ship: Decor/Furnishings/Artwork	60
Ship: Spa/Fitness Facilities	34
Cabins: Suites and Deluxe	58
Cabins: Standard Sizes	54
Food: Dining Room/Cuisine	57
Food: Informal Dining/Buffets	51
Food: Quality of Ingredients	56
Food: Afternoon Tea/Bar Snacks	48
Service: Dining Room	62
Service: Bars	61
Service: Cabins	63
Service: Open Decks	57
Cruise: Entertainment	49
Cruise: Activities Program	54
Cruise: Movies/Television Programming	42
Cruise: Hospitality Standard	57
Cruise: Overall Product Delivery	58
OVERALL SCORE	**1,101**

Accommodation: The cabins are mostly outside units, and all feature a refrigerator. They are reasonably spacious for the size of the ship, and are quite pleasantly decorated, but storage space is quite limited, and the walls and ceilings are very plain. Cabin soundproofing is poor. Closet, drawer, and luggage storage space for two is quite limited. The partly tiled bathrooms are small but adequate, although there is little space for personal toiletry items. Bathrobes are provided for all passengers.

Dining: The dining room, which is set low down in the ship, features restful colors, has mostly large tables (there are no tables for two), and is a totally nonsmoking room. There is plenty of space around each table, allowing waiters ample room to provide decent service. Features a mixed Continental/Greek cuisine, with a rather limited choice, particularly of breads, cheeses, and fruits, which tend to be very standard items.

For informal eating, small breakfast and lunch buffets are available on the Lido Deck aft, and a popular outdoor gyro and salad bar is set under a large canopy, which was added in 1996.

Other Comments: The profile of this ship looks quite smart, following an extensive $26-million conversion/stretch in 1988, although it is somewhat angular. The open deck space is generally good, but crowded when the ship is full, which means it could be difficult to find good sunbathing space.

Inside, the public rooms are quite tastefully decorated in soft, mostly pastel, colors although there is much use of mirrored surfaces. There is a good showroom, laid out amphitheater-style, with decent sight lines from most seats. The Belvedere Lounge, set high atop the ship and forward, features a smart piano bar and good ocean views.

A dialysis station is a bonus. In general, the service is quite friendly and attentive, although there is little finesse.

This ship really caters primarily to European passengers; it will provide a cruise in comfortable but densely populated surroundings, and at a fair price, but do not expect the spit and polish that other ships might have in this price range.

But: There are too many unnecessary and loud announcements (in several languages). The ship's narrow gangway is difficult to negotiate in some ports. There are no cushioned pads for the deck lounge chairs (lying on a towel on plastic ribbing is no fun for more than a few minutes!).

cs Aida

☆☆☆☆ +

(L)

Lifestyle	Standard
Cruise Line:	Arkona Touristik
Former Names:	-
Gross Tonnage:	38,600
Builder:	Kvaerner Masa-Yards (Finland)
Original Cost:	DM300 million
Entered Service:	June 1996
Flag:	Bahamas/Liberia
Tel No:	621858610
Fax No:	321813013
Length (ft./m.):	634.1/193.3
Beam (ft./m.):	90.5/27.6
Draft (ft./m.):	20.3/6.2
Propulsion/Propellers:	diesel (21,720kw)/2 (CP)
Decks:	9
Total Crew:	370
Pass. Capacity (basis 2):	1,186
Pass. Capacity (all berths):	1,230
Pass. Space Ratio (basis 2):	32.5
Pass. Space Ratio (all berths):	31.3
Officers:	German
Total Cabins:	593
Size Range (sq. ft./m.):	145.3–387.5/13.5–36.0
Cabins (outside view):	391
Cabins (inside):	202
Cabins (for one person):	0
Cabins (with private balcony):	4
Cabins (wheelchair accessible):	4
Cabin Current:	110/220 AC
Cabin TV:	Yes
Dining Rooms:	3
Seatings:	Open
Elevators:	5
Casino:	No
Slot Machines:	No
Swimming Pools (outdoors):	1
Swimming Pools (inside):	0
Whirlpools:	3
Fitness Center:	Yes
Sauna/Steam Room:	Yes/Yes
Massage:	Yes
Self-Service Launderette:	Yes
Movie Theater/Seats:	Yes/600
Library:	Yes
Children's Facilities:	Yes
Classification Society:	Germanischer Lloyd

Ratings	Score
Ship: Hardware/Maintenance	87
Ship: Outdoor Facilities/Space	83
Ship: Interior Facilities/Space/Flow	86
Ship: Decor/Furnishings/Artwork	87
Ship: Spa/Fitness Facilities	90
Cabins: Suites and Deluxe	83
Cabins: Standard Sizes	77
Food: Dining Room/Cuisine	77
Food: Informal Dining/Buffets	85
Food: Quality of Ingredients	80
Food: Afternoon Tea/Bar Snacks	68
Service: Dining Room	66
Service: Bars	76
Service: Cabins	76
Service: Open Decks	76
Cruise: Entertainment	78
Cruise: Activities Program	81
Cruise: Movies/Television Programming	78
Cruise: Hospitality Standard	82
Cruise: Overall Product Delivery	88
Overall Score	**1,604**

Accommodation: There are five grades: A-outside (17.0 m^2); B-outside (13.5 m^2); C-inside (14.5 m^2); Junior Suite (25.0 m^2); Suite (35.0 m^2). The accommodation features contemporary decor with a bright, youthful, contemporary look. All cabins are accented with multipatterned fabrics, wood-trimmed cabinetry (with nicely rounded edges), and rattan furniture. The twin beds have duvets and a fabric canopy from headboard to ceiling. Windows feature full pull-down blackout blinds.

Grades A, B, and C have just a small amount of drawer space, but, as you will not need many clothes, this is not really a drawback. Some cabins in grades A, B, and C have one bed and convertible daytime sofa bed. All cabin bathrooms, which are compact, but well designed and practical, feature showers, and wall-mounted soap/shampoo dispensers, so there is no wastage of throwaway plastic bottles (environmentally friendly), but you should bring your own conditioner, hand lotion, or any other personal toiletry items. Cotton bathrobes are also provided. Although bathrooms do not feature a hairdryer, one is located in the vanity unit in the cabin. Note: There is no toiletries cabinet.

Four Suites have a forward-facing private balcony (all four share the same, ship-wide balcony, as there are no partitions for privacy) and more luxurious furnishings and fittings. Seating in the cabin lounge area is in contemporary rattan chairs. There is a wall unit that houses a television that can be turned for viewing from either lounge or bedroom and a refrigerator.

Suites and Junior Suites have a generous amount of closet, drawer, and other storage space; a stocked minibar; and a VCR unit. Bathrooms feature a full-size bathtub and hairdryer.

The cabins are cleaned and beds are made each morning, but not in the evening. Note: For those who may be allergic to natural fibers, down-filled duvets and pillows can be replaced by synthetic ones.

Dining: There certainly are good dining options, with a wide range of food that is available almost 24 hours a day. There are two huge self-service buffet restaurants ("Caribbean" and "Market") and one à la carte restaurant (with waiter and sommelier service).

The standard of food offered at the buffets (which feature numerous food "islands" with the greatest variety in the cruise industry today) is good to excellent, with creative presentation and above average table-clearing service. There is no standing in the long lines so common aboard most other cruise ships today. There is always a fine selection of breads, cheeses, cold cuts, fruits, and make-your-own teas (with a choice of more than 30 types of loose-leaf regular and herbal teas, as well as coffee).

At peak times, the buffet restaurants do remind one of highway cafés (albeit fairly elegant ones), with all their attendant noise, but an excellent selection of foods is provided (there are over 1,200 items of food aboard this ship). You can sit where you want, when you want, and with whom you want, so dining really is a great social occasion. Highly entertaining are the comical, impromptu antics and theatrics performed by some of the entertainment staff (these take place in all restaurants during a typical cruise).

Because of the two large buffet rooms and self-serve dining concept, the actual crew to passenger ratio looks quite poor; but this is simply because there really are no waiters as such (except in the à la carte restaurant), only staff for clearing tables.

The Maritime Restaurant, which has 74 mostly high-back striped seats, set in an intimate dining atmosphere, is open for dinner only, and features a set five- or six-course menu, which is changed every two or three days. There is also an additional à la carte menu (featuring such things as sevruga caviar, smoked salmon, châteaubriand, rib-eye steak), and a decent wine list. Reservations are made each morning of the day you want to eat in the Maritime Restaurant, at the reception desk.

Other Comments: Aida has a sleek contemporary profile and is well proportioned, with a swept-back funnel and a large wedge-shaped stern. There is certainly no mistaking the red lips painted on her bows, as well as the blue eyes of Aida (from Verdi's opera of the same name).

Aida has diesel-mechanical propulsion and is a much larger, and more contemporary, half-sister to the company's traditional ship, *Arkona*, which is presently under a long-term charter to Seetours (which itself was purchased by Deutsche Seerederei in late 1997). Deutsche Seerederei is part of The Arkona Group, which has its own private island, Kirr, situated in the national park of Mecklenburg-Vorpommern off the coast of northern Germany (although it is not used by the cruise division); the company also operates hotels in five German cities: Eisenbach, Osnabruck, Potsdam, Stralsund, and Wismar.

Aida is a "Club Ship"—totally different to any traditional cruise ship and a breath of fresh air to the German cruise industry. The "Club Ship" concept (which stems from the famous Robinson Clubs) is a real fun ship that includes a whole army of "animateurs" (something like the GO's of Club Med, but much, much better) who enjoy doing varied activities by day (as well as acting as tour escorts) and are entertainers at night, acting in the colorful, often funny, shows alongside the professional entertainers. The "animateurs" (along with other staff) also interact with passengers throughout the ship, and can drink with them at the bars—something not allowed aboard any other ship.

The ship features an outdoor wraparound promenade deck, good for strolling or for sitting in a deck lounge chair and just taking in the sea air. Outside on deck, the swimming pool and surrounding area has several cascading levels at the forward end for deck chairs and sun lounging, plus a basketball court, although the pool itself is small.

Inside, there is no wasted space, and the public rooms flow into each other instead of being contained spaces. The "you are here" (deck plan) signs are excellent, and finding your way round is a simple matter. The decor is upbeat and trendy and will appeal to younger passengers, particularly those who may not have cruised before. A large observation lounge is set high atop the ship overlooking the bow. There is a wide array of intimate public rooms and spaces from which to choose.

The fitness, wellness, and sports programming is arguably the most extensive in the cruise industry today. There is an excellent "Wellness Center" located forward, which measures 1,100m^2 and contains two saunas (one seats more than 20 persons and has glass ocean-view walls), massage and other treatment rooms, and large lounging area. Adjoining the wellness center, forward and outside is an FKK nudist sunbathing deck. There is even a private meditation room. One really popular feature are 30 "Hit Bikes"—mountain bikes with tough front and rear suspension units—for conducted biking excursions in each port of call—the concept and concession of Austrian Downhill Champion Skier Erwin Resch.

Central to all social interactions is The Aida Lounge, which features novel "lollipop stick" decorations on the bar counter. The bar itself, at 185 feet (49.5 meters) long, is certainly the longest bar aboard any cruise ship. The feel is youthful, colorful, unpretentious, casual, relaxed, and sporting.

This really is a family-friendly ship, with plenty of activities for younger family members, from 9:00 a.m. to 6:00 p.m. every day (children are split into two age groups: Seepferdchen, from 4 to 7 years; Sharks, from 8 to 13 years). There is a diverse selection of children's and youth programs good for families. Children can make their own menus for the week (together with the chef) and get to go into the galley to make cookies and other items—a novel idea that more ships could adopt.

The ship caters particularly to first-time cruise passengers and youthful German-speaking couples. The dress code is simple: "casual" (no dinner jackets or ties) at all times.

Alternating seven-day itineraries can be combined for a fourteen-day cruise holiday. In addition, packages created by tour operators such as Jahn Reisen, Seetours, and TUI can add land stays for an even longer cruise and resort holiday experience. This presents a good amount of flexibility. During the summer, *Aida* sails in the Mediterranean from Antalya (Turkey), while in the winter, she sails on two alternating itineraries in the Caribbean from Santo Domingo (you are taken directly from plane to ship without the hassle of going through immigration or customs procedures; your luggage also goes directly to the ship. The reverse is also arranged upon disembarking the ship).

About 18 nationalities are represented among the crew, who are really upbeat and cheerful and want cruise passengers to have a great time. And they do, for this is definitely a young, vibrant, fun ship, with plenty of passenger participation in all kinds of events. The brochure accurately describes the lifestyle (only real passengers are used, not models), facilities, and activities aboard this truly refreshing and innovative ship.

All port taxes and gratuities (but not insurance) are included, and, with rates of approximately DM200-DM250 per day, it is almost cheaper than staying home, and a better value than almost any land-based vacation (flights are an additional cost). The airlines used in the various fly-cruise programs are Condor and Hapag-Lloyd. Currency aboard: Deutschmark.

But: There is a charge of DM1 for use of the washing machine and DM1 for the dryer in the self-service launderette.

ts Albatros

☆☆☆ +

(M)

Lifestyle	**Standard**
Cruise Line:	Phoenix Seereisen
Former Names:	*Dawn Princess/ FairWind/Sylvania*
Gross Tonnage:	24,803
Builder:	John Brown & Co. (UK)
Original Cost:	n/a
Entered Service:	June 1957/August 1993
Flag:	Bahamas
Tel No:	1306132
Fax No:	1306133
Length (ft./m.):	608.2/185.40
Beam (ft./m.):	80.3/24.49
Draft (ft./m.):	29.3/8.94
Propulsion/Propellers:	steam turbine (18,300kW)/2 (FP)
Decks:	11
Total Crew:	330
Pass. Capacity (basis 2):	940
Pass. Capacity (all berths):	1,100
Pass. Space Ratio (basis 2):	26.3
Pass. Space Ratio (all berths):	22.5
Officers:	German
Total Cabins:	470
Size Range (sq. ft./m.):	90–241/8.3–22.3
Cabins (outside view):	239
Cabins (inside):	231
Cabins (for one person):	0
Cabins (with private balcony):	0
Cabins (wheelchair accessible):	0
Cabin Current:	110 AC
Cabin TV:	Yes
Dining Rooms:	1
Seatings:	1
Elevators:	3
Casino:	Yes
Slot Machines:	Yes
Swimming Pools (outdoors):	3
Swimming Pools (inside):	0
Whirlpools:	0
Fitness Center:	Yes
Sauna/Steam Room:	Yes/No
Massage:	Yes
Self-Service Launderette:	Yes
Movie Theater/Seats:	Yes
Library:	No
Children's Facilities:	No
Classification Society:	Lloyd's Register

Ratings	**Score**
Ship: Hardware/Maintenance	55
Ship: Outdoor Facilities/Space	62
Ship: Interior Facilities/Space/Flow	54
Ship: Decor/Furnishings/Artwork	54
Ship: Spa/Fitness Facilities	51
Cabins: Suites and Deluxe	62
Cabins: Standard Sizes	55
Food: Dining Room/Cuisine	72
Food: Informal Dining/Buffets	70
Food: Quality of Ingredients	70
Food: Afternoon Tea/Bar Snacks	66
Service: Dining Room	67
Service: Bars	67
Service: Cabins	67
Service: Open Decks	61
Cruise: Entertainment	65
Cruise: Activities Program	63
Cruise: Movies/Television Programming	55
Cruise: Hospitality Standard	71
Cruise: Overall Product Delivery	68
Overall Score	**1,255**

Accommodation: There is a wide range of cabin sizes and configurations (28 categories), a throwback to the days when she was a ship operating transatlantic crossings, all of which feature really heavy-duty furniture, fittings, and strong doors. All of the cabins feature heavy-duty furniture and good storage space (many of the larger cabins have wood paneled walls), although closet and storage space could become limited for long voyages, particularly in the smaller, lower grade cabins.

The bathrooms are quite large, with cabinets and shelf space for toiletries in most. Bathrobes are provided for all passengers, as are some personal toiletry amenities.

Anyone booking a suite or one of the top five grades receives Phoenix VIP service, which includes flowers for the cabin, separate check-in desk, and priority disembarkation.

Dining: There are two dining rooms, both of which are quite charming and comfortable (with high ceilings), but the tables are very close together. This means they are also noisy dining rooms (although some would call this "ambience"). The menu is moderately creative, but the choice is quite limited, and the food is best described as "down-home basic."

The service is friendly and attentive, in true European style (the staff does speak German), although there is little finesse in their style of service. Still, it is quite unpretentious. Because there are two seatings for meals, one cannot dine leisurely.

Other Comments: This is a lovely vintage all-white classic ship with a forthright profile and large, single, centrally placed funnel. She is sturdily constructed, has a riveted hull that is virtually impossible to find today, and she has a deep draft that makes her very stable at sea, having been built as a two-class liner specifically for Cunard Line's transatlantic crossings in the 1950s.

She is an unpretentious ship that has an interesting old-world ambience and charm that somehow helps to make up for the lack of finesse associated with more upscale, newer (and thus more expensive) products.

There is plenty of open deck and sunbathing space. There is a second swimming pool (fitted into what was formerly a cargo hold) for the use of children, as Phoenix Seereisen appeals particularly well to families with children. Particularly popular are two decks of sheltered promenade decks, which are ideal for strolling or just sitting on one of the many decks' lounge chairs.

Inside the ship, a great deal of dark wood paneling and trim that was used in her original interiors has been retained. There are also many solid brass accents throughout her interiors and public rooms. There is a fine, serene library, with a good selection of both hardback and paperback books, as well as some reference material.

There are, however, relatively few public rooms from which to choose; they are usually quite crowded, and it is hard to get away from the smell of stale cigarette smoke. There are also a number of "thresholds" or high sills to step over at doorways, particularly to the outside decks and pool area, and so the ship cannot be recommended to anyone confined to a wheelchair under any circumstances.

Features extensive, interesting destination-intensive itineraries. Young, willing Phoenix Seereisen staff members are aboard every cruise to help with shore excursions. There is a very informal atmosphere and a relaxed, casual dress code.

Although the ship has been generally well maintained, remember that she is an old ship, having been designed for transatlantic service, so the layout is somewhat disjointed, and passageways are quite narrow. Because she is a steam ship, you should be aware of the possibility of black soot falling on the aft decks (in other words, do not wear white!) occasionally.

This ship will prove to be good for a first cruise experience with fellow German-speaking passengers and crew. Phoenix Seereisen always has a good on-board team of social staff to look after you, and the company's cruise directors are very experienced, fun loving people who really do go out of their way to help you enjoy your cruise experience. In other words, although this is not a new ship, she performs and behaves extremely well, and the resulting product is both entertaining and extremely reasonably priced for the popular market seeking an oceangoing holiday in totally relaxed, unstuffy, and unpretentious surroundings. It represents an excellent value for money cruise holiday. The currency aboard is the deutschmark.

mv Americana

☆☆☆☆

(S)

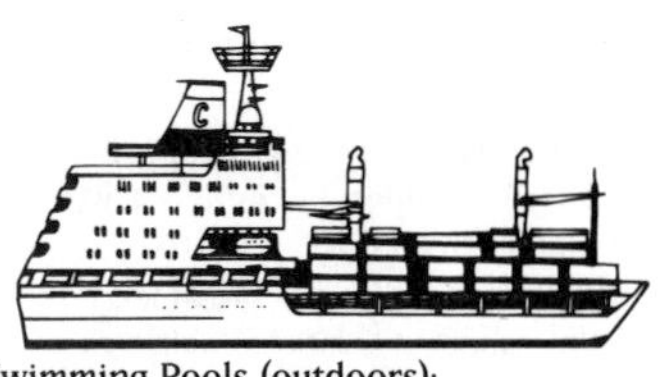

Lifestyle	Premium
Cruise Line:	Ivaran Lines
Former Names:	-
Gross Tonnage:	19,203
Builder: Hyundai Heavy Industries (South Korea)	
Original Cost:	$85 million
Entered Service:	March 1988
Flag:	Norway
Tel No:	1311131
Fax No:	1312714
Length (ft./m.):	579.7/176.70
Beam (ft./m.):	85.3/26.00
Draft (ft./m.):	28.8/8.80
Propulsion/Propellers:	diesel (18,564bhp)/1 (CP)
Decks:	6
Total Crew:	44
Pass. Capacity (basis 2):	88
Pass. Capacity (all berths):	108
Pass. Space Ratio (basis 2):	218.2
Pass. Space Ratio (all berths):	177.8
Officers:	Norwegian
Total Cabins:	52
Size Range (sq. ft./m.):	134–500/12.5–46.5
Cabins (outside view):	40
Cabins (inside):	12
Cabins (for one person):	20
Cabins (with private balcony):	4
Cabins (wheelchair accessible):	0
Cabin Current:	110/220 AC
Cabin TV:	Yes
Dining Rooms:	1
Seatings:	Open
Elevators:	2
Casino:	Yes
Slot Machines:	Yes
Swimming Pools (outdoors):	1
Swimming Pools (inside):	0
Whirlpools:	1
Fitness Center:	Yes
Sauna/Steam Room:	Yes/No
Massage:	Yes
Self-Service Launderette:	Yes
Movie Theater/Seats:	No
Library:	Yes
Children's Facilities:	No
Classification Society:	Det Norske Veritas

Ratings	Score
Ship: Hardware/Maintenance	80
Ship: Outdoor Facilities/Space	76
Ship: Interior Facilities/Space/Flow	74
Ship: Decor/Furnishings/Artwork	77
Ship: Spa/Fitness Facilities	50
Cabins: Suites and Deluxe	81
Cabins: Standard Sizes	77
Food: Dining Room/Cuisine	77
Food: Informal Dining/Buffets	74
Food: Quality of Ingredients	75
Food: Afternoon Tea/Bar Snacks	66
Service: Dining Room	77
Service: Bars	77
Service: Cabins	76
Service: Open Decks	65
Cruise: Entertainment	50
Cruise: Activities Program	55
Cruise: Movies/Television Programming	58
Cruise: Hospitality Standard	76
Cruise: Overall Product Delivery	77
Overall Score	**1,418**

Accommodation: The two owners' suites are quite lavish and feature separate bedroom and living rooms and large picture windows on two sides.

The standard-sized cabins are quite well designed and equipped and have warm, restful contemporary decor and fine soft furnishings. They come with a television, VCR, personal safe, and refrigerator. Unusual for a ship carrying this number of passengers, there are quite a number of cabins for single passengers.

Note that, unlike aboard most cruise ships, there is no room service (except on doctor's orders), even for morning beverages such as coffee or tea.

Dining: The dining room is quite elegant, has fine table settings, and overlooks the sea. The cuisine, while not elaborate, is quite appealing, well prepared, and features Norwegian and Continental fare.

Breakfast and lunch are presented buffet style. Elegant place settings and chinaware are featured. The service staff is Filipino.

Other Comments: This is certainly the best example of contemporary freighter-cruise travel. The incredible space ratio is the result of a well-designed ship, a freighter-cruise vessel that has passenger facilities located astern of a 1,120-capacity container section. The name of the line stems from the Norwegian owning company's founder, Ivar Anton Christensen (hence "Ivaran" Lines). Ivaran Lines was sold to Canadian Pacific in 1998.

Has an elegant (in a contemporary sense) and beautifully finished interior. There are many live tropical plants, soft leather chairs, and space everywhere—features that long-distance passengers appreciate. Features a rather neat double-spiral staircase. There is also a generous amount of both sheltered and open sunbathing space.

A well-stocked library assures one that there is plenty to read. Gentlemen "hosts" are carried on all voyages. Carrying a minimum of 50 passengers assures the ship of priority berthing rights in the ports of call. This ship will be good for those passengers with plenty time to spare—and who do not need entertainment in the evenings (dinner being the entertainment).

The ship operates out of Houston, Texas, and features twenty-two-day Caribbean/Gulf of Mexico cruises (her former trading route was from New York to Buenos Aires, but this was discontinued in early 1998). She is perhaps ideal for those wanting to take a cruise aboard a working vessel that also provides some of the amenities of a cruise ship. Port taxes are included.

But: There is a steep gangway in several ports of call. There is no wraparound promenade deck, and there are no cushioned pads for the outdoor deck lounge chairs.

tss Apollo

☆☆ +

(M)

LIFESTYLE	**STANDARD**
Cruise Line:	Royal Olympic Cruises/Direct Cruises
Former Names:	*Appollon/Star of Texas/ Mardi Gras/Empress of Canada*
Gross Tonnage:	28,574
Builder:	Vickers Armstrong (UK)
Original Cost:	UK8,250,000
Entered Service:	April 1962/April 1998
Flag:	Greece
Tel No:	761478975/76147896/323919310
Fax No:	761478977/323919313
Length (ft./m.):	650.0/198.13
Beam (ft./m.):	86.7/26.45
Draft (ft./m.):	29.0/8.83
Propulsion/Propellers:	steam turbine (22,400kw)/2 (FP)
Decks:	8
Total Crew:	408
Pass. Capacity (basis 2):	914
Pass. Capacity (all berths):	1,256
Pass. Space Ratio (basis 2):	31.2
Pass. Space Ratio (all berths):	23.0
Officers:	Greek
Total Cabins:	457
Size (sq. ft./m..):	n/a
Cabins (outside view):	193
Cabins (inside):	260
Cabins (for one person):	8
Cabins (with private balcony):	0
Cabins (wheelchair accessible):	0
Cabin Current:	110 AC
Cabin TV:	No
Dining Rooms:	2
Sittings:	2
Elevators:	4
Casino:	Yes
Slot Machines:	Yes
Swimming Pools (outdoors):	2
Swimming Pools (inside):	1
Whirlpools:	0
Fitness Center:	Yes
Sauna/Steam Room:	Yes/No
Massage:	Yes
Self-Service Launderette:	No (has ironing room)
Movie Theater/Seats:	Yes/200
Library:	Yes
Children's Facilities:	Yes
Classification Society:	Lloyd's Register

RATINGS	**SCORE**
Ship: Hardware/Maintenance	56
Ship: Outdoor Facilities/Space	53
Ship: Interior Facilities/Space/Flow	53
Ship: Decor/Furnishings/Artwork	53
Ship: Spa/Fitness Facilities	38
Cabins: Suites and Deluxe	58
Cabins: Standard Sizes	51
Food: Dining Room/Cuisine	57
Food: Informal Dining/Buffets	48
Food: Quality of Ingredients	55
Food: Afternoon Tea/Bar Snacks	40
Service: Dining Room	60
Service: Bars	61
Service: Cabins	61
Service: Open Decks	42
Cruise: Entertainment	48
Cruise: Activities Program	43
Cruise: Movies/Television Programming	40
Cruise: Hospitality Standard	55
Cruise: Overall Product Delivery	57
OVERALL SCORE	**1,029**

Accommodation: In general, the cabins are quite large, have good heavy-duty fittings, and there are many different configurations, a carry over from the days when the ship operated as a former liner; all have private facilities, and all have been refurbished. However, many cabins have upper and lower berths instead of lower beds (Direct Cruises' brochure uses the same terminology for beds or berths, so make sure you get what you want). Some of the upper grades feature several different woods. No cabins have televisions, but they all have a telephone, and a good amount of closet and drawer space.

Dining: The main dining room has an elegant entrance, portholes, reasonably contemporary decor, and tables for four, six, or eight. The cuisine is decidedly Continental in style, and reasonably tasty, but the choice is not extensive. Service, from an international staff, is quite friendly but frenzied. The wine list is rather limited, but the prices are quite reasonable. There is also the informal Seaview Buffet Restaurant for casual self-service buffet-style breakfast and lunch, although the fare here is really very basic, with little creativity.

Other Comments: This ship is presently chartered to Direct Cruises after having several varied former lives. Early in 1995, Carnival Cruise Lines sold this ship to Royal Olympic Cruises in a stock swap when both parted company, and companies. Originally, however, she was built for the now defunct Union Castle Line to perform line voyages between England and South Africa, hence she has a covered promenade deck. This is a well-constructed former ocean liner that has a large midships funnel; she has been well maintained by her former owners.

The open deck and sunbathing space is quite limited when the ship is full, as some of the space is taken by seating for the outdoor section of the buffet restaurant.

Inside, the numerous public rooms have high ceilings, a carry over from her original operators. You can also see some of the original woods and nicely polished brass fittings from the fifties, as well as some neat custom-made carpeting. Has an indoor swimming pool and good cinema—features not found aboard many new cruise vessels.

This ship provides a reasonable cruise experience in a comfortable mix of contemporary and real old-world surroundings, décor, and colors. Good for a first, no-frills cruise experience for families seeking a cruise vacation at a very modest price. For a large part of the year, the ship is under charter to Scotland-based Direct Cruises, in which case the cruise fare includes all gratuities, port charges, and travel insurance. For UK-based passengers, this means no flying, as the ship sails from Greenock on mostly fourteen-day cruises.

But: This high-density ship is really quite old and is quite well worn and tired in some areas. The gangway is narrow. There are a number of sills or "lips" at various doorways to negotiate.

mts Arcadia

☆☆

(S)

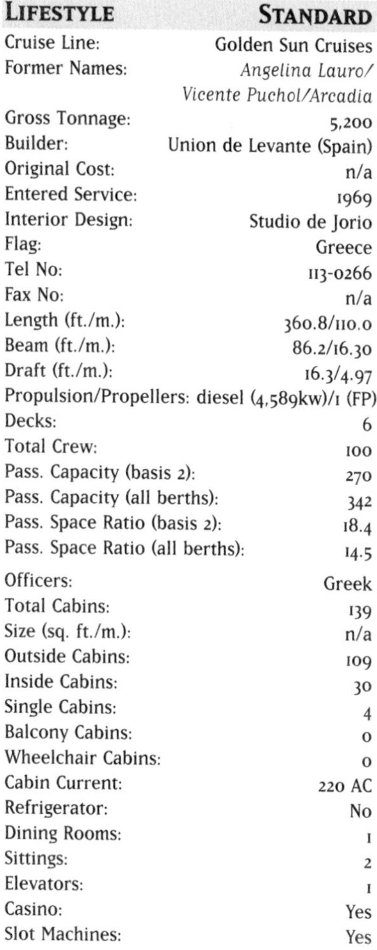

Lifestyle	Standard
Cruise Line:	Golden Sun Cruises
Former Names:	*Angelina Lauro/ Vicente Puchol/Arcadia*
Gross Tonnage:	5,200
Builder:	Union de Levante (Spain)
Original Cost:	n/a
Entered Service:	1969
Interior Design:	Studio de Jorio
Flag:	Greece
Tel No:	113-0266
Fax No:	n/a
Length (ft./m.):	360.8/110.0
Beam (ft./m.):	86.2/16.30
Draft (ft./m.):	16.3/4.97
Propulsion/Propellers:	diesel (4,589kw)/1 (FP)
Decks:	6
Total Crew:	100
Pass. Capacity (basis 2):	270
Pass. Capacity (all berths):	342
Pass. Space Ratio (basis 2):	18.4
Pass. Space Ratio (all berths):	14.5
Officers:	Greek
Total Cabins:	139
Size (sq. ft./m.):	n/a
Outside Cabins:	109
Inside Cabins:	30
Single Cabins:	4
Balcony Cabins:	0
Wheelchair Cabins:	0
Cabin Current:	220 AC
Refrigerator:	No
Dining Rooms:	1
Sittings:	2
Elevators:	1
Casino:	Yes
Slot Machines:	Yes

Swimming Pools (outdoors):	1
Swimming Pools (inside):	0
Whirlpools:	0
Fitness Center:	Yes
Sauna:	Yes
Massage:	No
Self-Service Laundry:	No
Cinema/Theatre:	No
Cabin TV:	No
Library:	No
Children's Facilities:	No
Classification Society:	Bureau Veritas

Ratings	Score
Ship: Hardware/Maintenance	42
Ship: Interior Facilities/Space/Flow	40
Ship: Decor/Furnishings/Artwork	39
Ship: Outdoor Facilities/Space	34
Ship: Spa/Fitness Facilities	21
Cabins: Suites and Deluxe	45
Cabins: Standard Sizes	40
Food: Dining Room/Cuisine	51
Food: Informal Dining/Buffets	42
Food: Quality of Ingredients	50
Food: Afternoon Tea/Bar Snacks	33
Service: Dining Room	52
Service: Bars	53
Service: Cabins	54
Service: Open Decks	45
Cruise: Entertainment	41
Cruise: Activities Program	33
Cruise: Movies/Television Programming	34
Cruise: Hospitality Standard	46
Cruise: Overall Product Delivery	51

Overall Score **846**

Accommodation: The cabins are very small, and just adequately equipped with the bare essentials. Closet, drawer, and storage space is very limited; the ceilings are plain; and the bathrooms really are tiny. Four cabins have double beds; all others are fixed twins or lower beds. Some cabins also have third/fourth person upper berths.

Dining: The dining room, although small, has large mirrors along both sides, making it appear double the size it actually is (there are no windows or portholes). Although noisy, it is somehow mildly charming, with its pastel pink color and a warm, very casual ambience. The cuisine is very basic fare (as is the price of a cruise) and so there is little choice in food, and the bread is poor. Adequate basic service, but it is hurried, and there's no finesse.

Other Comments: She is a small vessel (originally an ex-Spanish ferry) with an all-white hull, which divides superstructure and hull by a red line, and twin funnels, and was, for a short time operated by the now-defunct Lauro Cruises as *Angelina Lauro*. A recent refurbishment makes the vessel smarter in her new "whites."

The interior decor is "1980s contemporary" but dated, and is quite tastefully carried out, although there is too much use of reflective surfaces (mirrors). Chairs in the public lounges (there are only two) are of the low-back tub type, and not very comfortable. The tiny aft swimming pool is really only a "cool dip" pool.

This ship has been well worn and caters principally to European and Asian passengers seeking a small ship on which to cruise the Greek islands with minimum comfort and fuss. There is no finesse and the mixed crew displays only marginal hospitality.

But: Passengers who are tall should note that the ceilings are quite low everywhere. Vibration and engine noise are quite evident in several areas, however, particularly in the center and aft sections of the vessel. Entertainment is provided at deafening volumes.

ms Arcadia

☆☆☆☆

(L)

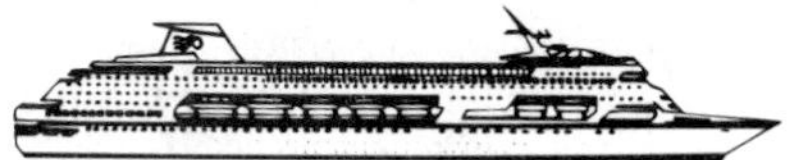

Lifestyle	Premium
Cruise Line:	P&O Cruises
Former Names:	*Star Princess/FairMajesty*
Gross Tonnage:	63,564
Builder:	Chantiers de L'Atlantique (France)
Original Cost:	$200 million
Entered Service:	March 1989/December 1997
Flag:	Great Britain
Tel No:	1240247
Fax No:	1240236
Length (ft./m.):	810.3/247.00
Beam (ft./m.):	105.6/32.20
Draft (ft./m.):	26.9/8.20
Propulsion/Propellers:	diesel-electric (39,000kW)/2 (CP)
Decks:	12
Total Crew:	650
Pass. Capacity (basis 2):	1,461
Pass. Capacity (all berths):	1,549
Pass. Space Ratio (basis 2):	43.5
Pass. Space Ratio (all berths):	41.0
Officers:	British
Total Cabins:	748
Size Range (sq. ft./m.):	180–530/16.7–49.2
Cabins (outside view):	583
Cabins (inside):	165
Cabins (for one person):	64
Cabins (with private balcony):	50
Cabins (wheelchair accessible):	8
Cabin Current:	110/220 AC
Cabin TV:	Yes
Dining Rooms:	1
Seatings:	2
Elevators:	9
Casino:	Yes
Slot Machines:	Yes
Swimming Pools (outdoors):	3
Swimming Pools (inside):	0
Whirlpools:	4
Fitness Center:	Yes
Sauna/Steam Room:	Yes/No
Massage:	Yes
Self-Service Launderette:	Yes
Movie Theater/Seats:	Yes/205
Library:	Yes
Children's Facilities:	Yes
Classification Society:	Lloyd's Register

Ratings	Score
Ship: Hardware/Maintenance	82
Ship: Outdoor Facilities/Space	75
Ship: Interior Facilities/Space/Flow	81
Ship: Decor/Furnishings/Artwork	77
Ship: Spa/Fitness Facilities	64
Cabins: Suites and Deluxe	78
Cabins: Standard Sizes	73
Food: Dining Room/Cuisine	68
Food: Informal Dining/Buffets	66
Food: Quality of Ingredients	67
Food: Afternoon Tea/Bar Snacks	64
Service: Dining Room	71
Service: Bars	70
Service: Cabins	71
Service: Open Decks	67
Cruise: Entertainment	73
Cruise: Activities Program	63
Cruise: Movies/Television Programming	72
Cruise: Hospitality Standard	76
Cruise: Overall Product Delivery	78
Overall Score	**1,436**

Accommodation: All of the inside- and outside-view standard-grade cabins are of good size and come well equipped, with an abundance of drawer and other storage space (plus some under-bed space for luggage), walk-in closets, and large, modular bathrooms with good showers. Bathrobes are provided for all passengers, as are toiletry amenity kits. However, you should know that the sound insulation between cabins is extremely poor (televisions late at night can be particularly irritating). A number of cabins also feature third and fourth person berths, and some cabins are designated for single occupancy.

There are 14 suites and 36 mini-suites (each thoughtfully named after historical P&O ships of the past), and each has a private balcony (the partitions are not of the full floor-to-ceiling type, however, so you will probably hear your neighbors—or smell their smoke). All suites and cabins have large walk-in closets, private safe, refrigerator, television, telephone, and hairdryer; all suite bathrooms have a bathtub as well as a shower stall. Room service for afternoon tea and snacks for suite accommodation occupants is quite basic, and could be further upgraded.

Dining: The multitiered Pacific Restaurant has a two-deck-high center ceiling, but dining in it can be quite a noisy affair as the sound seems to reverberate everywhere. There are tables for two, four, six, or eight, mostly in small sections that help give a cozy feel to the room. The food is typical of P&O, unpretentious and not memorable, and the presentation is quite straightforward, with little use of garnishes. The service is warm and friendly. The Great British Breakfast is always a popular and necessary feature of P&O ships, and Arcadia is no exception.

The indoor-outdoor "Conservatory" deck buffet restaurant (open for breakfast and lunch) is quite small, but there is also a pizzeria, an ice-cream bar, a patisserie, an in-pool bar, and a wine bar.

Other Comments: This ship is the third to bear the name *Arcadia* (the name was taken from a mythical region of Greece) for P&O. The first *Arcadia* was launched in 1887, the second, in 1954. This latest (and largest) one has good seagoing characteristics and provides a fine replacement for the company's much-loved *Canberra* (taken out of service in late 1997).

She was originally built for Sitmar Cruises, which was absorbed into Princess Cruises in 1988 (the ship's former operators prior to P&O Cruises). She was extensively refurbished in late 1997 at the Harland & Wolff shipyard in Belfast, and reconfigured specifically for British cruise passengers. The ship is well proportioned and has a decent amount of open deck space for sunbathing around her twin swimming pools (one has a swim-up bar, a first for P&O Cruises), as well as on her open decks aft of the funnel.

When P&O Cruises acquired the ship from sister company Princess Cruises, the company had to do a little "massaging" to her appointments and decor, as the ship would be used for anything from fourteen-day cruises to three-month-long around-the-world cruises—a far cry from her previous use operating standard seven-day Caribbean cruises.

Her interiors feature restrained contemporary styling mixed with traditional shipboard decor, including some pleasing art deco touches (chrome balustrades), so nothing jars the senses, is garish, or out of place. Her spacious public rooms, many of which have high ceilings, have tasteful decor. A good selection of artwork provides some warmth to what would otherwise be a rather clinical interior. Has a large, horseshoe-shaped balconied showroom, with adequate sight lines from most seats.

Little vignettes of the former P&O liner *Canberra* and the necessary cricket memorabilia are displayed resplendently in the wood paneled "The Oval" pub, which also has a dance floor. She provides a traditional large ship cruise ambience for the many British repeat passengers who enjoy such facilities and some degree of anonymity. Families with children will enjoy P&O's excellent children's programs; there are special rooms for children and teenagers (there is also a night nursery).

The focal point of a three-deck-high foyer is highlighted by a stainless steel kinetic sculpture that brings one's attention to the multideck staircases, and afternoon tea dances are a delight here. There is a domed observation lounge atop the ship; although it is a little out of the traffic flow, it is a restful spot for cocktails, although it turns into a nightspot/discotheque for night owls. The Canberra Room houses memorabilia from the famous ship. Aside from the memorabilia, most of *Canberra's* crew was transferred to *Arcadia*. Features an interesting assortment of worldwide cruise itineraries, and, incidentally, P&O's brochures are always logical in layout and easy to follow.

There is always a good mix of entertainment aboard the ships of P&O Cruises, and this includes the Theater at Sea, production shows, and cabaret acts suited to British taste. The children's playroom, called Peter Pan, is located aft, and also features an outdoor paddling pool and games area. There is no extra charge for use of the Night Nursery (6 p.m.–2 a.m.).

P&O Cruises puts together a fine program of special theme cruises (antiques, The Archers, art appreciation, classical music, comedy, cricket, gardening, jazz, motoring, popular fiction, Scottish dance, sequence dancing were among the themes in 1998); check with your travel agent to see what is available at the time you want to take your cruise.

<u>But:</u> For a ship of this size, it is a great shame that there is no wraparound outdoor promenade deck (port and starboard walking areas stretch only along part of the sides). The passageways and stairways are dull, as are the gray-painted cabin doors. The library is small and has poor lighting and few chairs. The Palladium show lounge has many pillars (on both balcony and main levels) that obstruct sight lines.

ms Arkona

☆☆☆☆ +

(M)

Lifestyle	**Premium**
Cruise Line:	Arkona Touristik
Former Names:	*Astor (I)*
Gross Tonnage:	18,591
Builder:	Howaldtswerke Deutsche Werft (Germany)
Original Cost:	$55 million
Entered Service:	December 1981/December 1985
Flag:	Liberia
Tel No:	n/a
Fax No:	n/a
Length (ft./m.):	539.2/164.35
Beam (ft./m.):	74.1/22.60
Draft (ft./m.):	20.0/6.11
Propulsion/Propellers:	diesel (13,200kW)/2 (CP)
Decks:	8
Total Crew:	243
Pass. Capacity (basis 2):	516
Pass. Capacity (all berths):	618
Pass. Space Ratio (basis 2):	36.0
Pass. Space Ratio (all berths):	30.0
Officers:	German
Total Cabins:	258
Size Range (sq. ft./m.):	150.0–725.0/13.4–65.3
Cabins (outside view):	176
Cabins (inside):	82
Cabins (for one person):	0
Cabins (with private balcony):	0
Cabins (wheelchair accessible):	0
Cabin Current:	220 AC
Cabin TV:	Yes
Dining Rooms:	1
Seatings:	2
Elevators:	3
Casino:	No
Slot Machines:	No
Swimming Pools (outdoors):	1
Swimming Pools (inside):	1
Whirlpools:	0
Fitness Center:	Yes
Sauna/Steam Room:	Yes/No
Massage:	Yes
Self-Service Launderette:	No
Movie Theater/Seats:	No
Library:	Yes
Children's Facilities:	No
Classification Society:	Germanischer Lloyd

Ratings	**Score**
Ship: Hardware/Maintenance	84
Ship: Outdoor Facilities/Space	78
Ship: Interior Facilities/Space/Flow	80
Ship: Decor/Furnishings/Artwork	78
Ship: Spa/Fitness Facilities	76
Cabins: Suites and Deluxe	80
Cabins: Standard Sizes	76
Food: Dining Room/Cuisine	81
Food: Informal Dining/Buffets	76
Food: Quality of Ingredients	79
Food: Afternoon Tea/Bar Snacks	76
Service: Dining Room	80
Service: Bars	78
Service: Cabins	80
Service: Open Decks	77
Cruise: Entertainment	77
Cruise: Activities Program	72
Cruise: Movies/Television Programming	74
Cruise: Hospitality Standard	78
Cruise: Overall Product Delivery	81
Overall Score	**1,561**

Accomodations: There are 14 categories of cabins from which to choose. Boat Deck suite rooms are simply lovely, and have just about everything one would need. Most of the other, more standard cabins are also well appointed and decorated, and all feature crisp, clean colors (some might find them plain, as are the ceilings).

The bathrooms are compact but fully tiled, with a good cabinet for toiletries. The ship features good traditional European hotel service, from a willing staff. All printed materials, including the brochure, are on recycled paper. Even the toilet paper is made from recycled paper. There is only a limited cabin service menu, however.

Dining: The Arkona Restaurant, located high in the ship, has big, ocean-view picture windows and is quite elegant, with dark wood paneling and restful decor. The food is adequate to very good, though choice is somewhat limited, but the service, by some charming waitresses, does help. The occasional formal candlelight dinners are romantic, and the daily outdoor deck buffets (for breakfast and luncheon) are quite varied.

Other Comments: This is a traditional cruise ship, originally constructed for the now defunct Astor Cruises, and has cruised under a long-term charter to Seetours (now owned by Deutsche Seerederei) since 1985.

She is a well-constructed modern vessel that has a handsome and well-balanced profile. There is a good amount of open deck and sunbathing space for her size, with some excellent teakwood decking and polished railings. Cushioned pads are provided for all deck lounge chairs. For the sports-minded there is a large volleyball court.

Has beautifully appointed interior fittings and decor, with much rosewood paneling and trim. Subdued lighting and soothing ambience, highlighted by good artwork throughout. Has good meetings facilities, a fine library, and, perhaps more important, an excellent pub with draught German beer from Rostock.

Subdued lighting and soothing ambience, highlighted by fine artwork throughout make for a pleasant, relaxing cruise experience.

There is an excellent indoor spa and fitness center, with a good range of facilities that include a swimming pool, fitness center, and three sunbed rooms for tanning sessions. In addition, sophisticated hospital facilities include oxygen multistep therapy.

The atmosphere is a little starchy. There are many cigarette and cigar smokers.

Features good traditional European hotel service, and mostly German (expensive, under the German flag) staff. The reception desk is open 24 hours daily. *Arkona* is under charter to the Seetours until the year 2000 (note that Seetours was purchased by Deutsche Seetouristik/Arkona Touristik in late 1997).

Arkona features good value for money cruising in contemporary comfort, and is best recommended for passengers who appreciate quality, fine surroundings, good food, and excellent destination-intensive itineraries, all packaged neatly in a relaxed, informal ambience. Many of the cruises have special themes. Port taxes are included. Seetours/TUI staff is available aboard every cruise and does go out of its way to make sure that you will have an excellent cruise experience in very comfortable surroundings. Has many repeat passengers, who enjoy an extremely friendly, mostly German crew (who provide a fun crew show). Port taxes are included. Gratuities are suggested at DM8-10 per person per day, and pooled.

<u>But:</u> There is no wraparound promenade deck. The show lounge has 10 pillars obstructing the sight lines, and the stage is also the dance floor and cannot be raised for shows; entertainment, therefore, is mostly cabaret-style. Finally, nonsmokers should note that there are many cigarette and cigar smokers, and it is often hard to get away from them.

ms Astor

☆☆☆☆ +

(M)

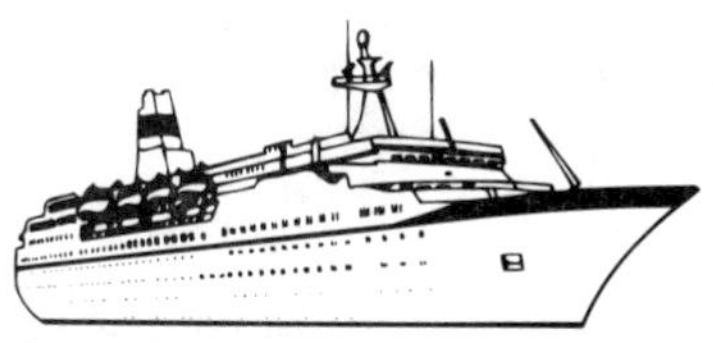

LIFESTYLE	**PREMIUM**
Cruise Line:	Transocean Tours
Former Names:	*Fedor Dostoyevskiy/Astor (II)*
Gross Tonnage:	20,158
Builder:	Howaldtswerke Deutsche Werft (Germany)
Original Cost:	$65 million
Entered Service:	February 1987/April 1997
Flag:	Bahamas
Tel No:	1402771/1402772
Fax No:	1400125
Length (ft./m.):	579.0/176.50
Beam (ft./m.):	74.1/22.61
Draft (ft./m.):	20.0/6.10
Propulsion/Propellers:	diesel (15,400kW)/2 (CP)
Decks:	7
Total Crew:	300
Pass. Capacity (basis 2):	590
Pass. Capacity (all berths):	650
Pass. Space Ratio (basis 2):	34.1
Pass. Space Ratio (all berths):	31.0
Officers:	Russian/Ukrainian
Total Cabins:	295
Size Range (sq. ft./m.):	140.0–280.0/13.0–26.0
Cabins (outside view):	199
Cabins (inside):	96
Cabins (for one person):	0
Cabins (with private balcony):	0
Cabins (wheelchair accessible):	0
Cabin Current:	220 AC
Cabin TV:	Yes
Dining Rooms:	1
Seatings:	2
Elevators:	3
Casino:	No
Slot Machines:	No
Swimming Pools (outdoors):	1
Swimming Pools (inside):	1
Whirlpools:	0
Fitness Center:	Yes
Sauna/Steam Room:	Yes/No
Massage:	Yes
Self-Service Launderette:	No (ironing room)
Movie Theater/Seats:	No
Library:	Yes
Children's Facilities:	Yes
Classification Society:	Germanischer Lloyd

RATINGS	**SCORE**
Ship: Hardware/Maintenance	81
Ship: Outdoor Facilities/Space	80
Ship: Interior Facilities/Space/Flow	81
Ship: Decor/Furnishings/Artwork	80
Ship: Spa/Fitness Facilities	80
Cabins: Suites and Deluxe	82
Cabins: Standard Sizes	78
Food: Dining Room/Cuisine	77
Food: Informal Dining/Buffets	76
Food: Quality of Ingredients	76
Food: Afternoon Tea/Bar Snacks	76
Service: Dining Room	78
Service: Bars	78
Service: Cabins	77
Service: Open Decks	75
Cruise: Entertainment	78
Cruise: Activities Program	76
Cruise: Movies/Television Programming	77
Cruise: Hospitality Standard	78
Cruise: Overall Product Delivery	80
OVERALL SCORE	**1,564**

Accommodation: The cabins (there are 18 categories) are all very nicely appointed and tastefully decorated in fresh pastel colors and have dark wood accents and cabinetry, so they are very restful. There is plenty of closet and drawer space in each cabin, as well as some under-bed storage space for luggage. The bathrooms are very practical, and each has a good sized toiletries cabinet, as well as all the necessary fittings, and 100 percent cotton towels, and a bathrobe for each passenger.

In addition, the suites, which have a completely separate bedroom, livingroom, and bathroom, have a refrigerator as well as a minibar-refrigerator, and large, boxed set of bathroom amenities.

However, the cabin service menu is poor and could be better (there is a charge for sandwiches, and little else is available). The bathroom towels are small and should be larger.

Dining: The dining room is really quite elegant, and well laid out. It also has two small wings (good for private parties or groups of up to 30). The service throughout is quite friendly, but unpretentious, and the food quality and presentation have received much attention and upgrading, with catering supplied by Zerbone of Italy. Menus are creative, and the quality and presentation are very good. In addition to the regular entrees (three for dinner), there is always a pasta dish and a vegetarian speciality dish.

The buffets are well presented, and constantly refreshed, although the choice of foods could still be improved.

Other Comments: *Astor* was the original name for this ship, the larger of two ships bearing this same name in the 1980s, originally built for the now-defunct Astor Cruises. Her previous owners, the now defunct AquaMarin Cruises, again brought back the name to *Astor* from her previous name *Fedor Dostoyevskiy*.

She is a very attractive modern ship with a raked bow, a large squarish funnel and a nicely balanced contemporary profile. The ship was constructed in the best German tradition (slightly larger than the first *Astor* (now called *Arkona*), and was extensively refurbished in late 1995 before commencing service for AquaMarin Cruises. She was then was taken over by Transocean Tours in 1996 (she is under charter to Transocean Tours until 2007) following the collapse of AquaMarin Cruises.

This ship represents an excellent mix of traditional and contemporary styling. Built to a high standard (in a German shipyard), fine teakwood decking and polished wooden rails are seen outside almost everywhere.

She has an excellent amount of open deck and sunbathing space, as well as padded cushions for the deck lounge chairs, a basketball court for active passengers, and there is a large deck chess game on an aft deck.

Her interior fittings are of extremely fine quality. There is a supremely comfortable and varied array of public rooms and conference facilities, most of which have high ceilings. A wood-paneled tavern (always with good German lager on draught) is a fine retreat, and is extremely popular. There is a well-designed interior fitness center and large swimming pool, but the charge of DM10 for use of the sauna is absurd (there should be no charge at any time).

The company features interesting, well-designed destination-intensive worldwide itineraries, and cruises are at a very attractive price. The Russian/Ukrainian hotel staff are friendly without being obtrusive and have been well trained.

This ship, which caters exclusively to German-speaking passengers, provides style, comfort, and elegance, and a fine leisurely cruise experience in a relaxed, spacious setting (there is no crowding anywhere) that is less formal than a ship such as *Europa*. Port taxes, insurance, and gratuities are included in the cruise price. The ship can be booked at any DERPART, Transmarin, or UDR travel agency, and represents a good choice for those seeking a well-packaged cruise in fine contemporary surroundings. Transocean Tours staff can be found aboard every cruise, some of which are designated as special-theme cruises. The currency aboard is the German deutschmark and U.S. dollar. Port taxes, insurance and all gratuities to staff are included.

But: The show lounge has pillars obstructing the sight lines, and the stage is also the dance floor and cannot be raised for shows; entertainment, therefore, is mostly cabaret-style.

ms Astra

☆☆

(S)

Lifestyle	Standard
Cruise Line:	Caravella Shipping
Former Names:	*Istra*
Gross Tonnage:	5,635
Builder:	Brodgradiliste (Yugoslavia)
Original Cost:	n/a
Entered Service:	1965/May 1993
Flag:	Russia
Tel No:	1403475
Fax No:	1403475
Length (ft./m.):	383.8/116.8
Beam (ft./m.):	54.1/16.5
Draft (ft./m.):	18.3/5.6
Propulsion/Propellers:	diesel (11,030kW)/2 (FP)
Decks:	5
Total Crew:	120
Pass. Capacity (basis 2):	282
Pass. Capacity (all berths):	282
Pass. Space Ratio (basis 2):	19.9
Pass. Space Ratio (all berths):	19.9
Officers:	Russian
Total Cabins:	141
Size Range (sq. ft./m.):	n/a
Cabins (outside view):	83
Cabins (inside):	58
Cabins (for one person):	0
Cabins (with private balcony):	0
Cabins (wheelchair accessible):	0
Cabin Current:	220 AC
Cabin TV:	No
Dining Rooms:	1
Seatings:	1
Elevators:	0
Casino:	No
Slot Machines:	No
Swimming Pools (outdoors):	1
Swimming Pools (inside):	0
Whirlpools:	0
Fitness Center:	No
Sauna/Steam Room:	No/No
Massage:	No
Self-Service Launderette:	No
Movie Theater/Seats:	No
Library:	Yes
Children's Facilities:	No
Classification Society:	Russian Survey

Ratings	Score
Ship: Hardware/Maintenance	41
Ship: Outdoor Facilities/Space	34
Ship: Interior Facilities/Space/Flow	40
Ship: Decor/Furnishings/Artwork	38
Ship: Spa/Fitness Facilities	21
Cabins: Suites and Deluxe	50
Cabins: Standard Sizes	41
Food: Dining Room/Cuisine	57
Food: Informal Dining/Buffets	47
Food: Quality of Ingredients	52
Food: Afternoon Tea/Bar Snacks	43
Service: Dining Room	56
Service: Bars	57
Service: Cabins	58
Service: Open Decks	57
Cruise: Entertainment	43
Cruise: Activities Program	40
Cruise: Movies/Television Programming	36
Cruise: Hospitality Standard	53
Cruise: Overall Product Delivery	55
Overall Score	**919**

Accommodation: The cabins are very modest in size and features, and one would not want to spend much time in them, particularly for those who have cruised aboard some of the more contemporary ships. There is little closet and storage space, and the bathrooms are tiny and quite basic. The upper berths in cabins do not have sufficient grab ("anti-fallout") protection.

Dining: Although the dining room is quite warm and mildly attractive, with decent place settings, there are no tables for two, and the tables are very close together (leaving very little room for waiters to serve properly). The food itself is limited in choice and variety. The selection of vegetables, fresh fruits, and breads could be better. The Ukrainian waitresses are quite friendly, attentive, and may occasionally smile, but there is no service finesse.

Other Comments: She is a small ship, originally built for close-in sailings of the Dalmatian coast, and has a typical low-built early sixties profile that is mildly attractive. At present the ship is cruising for both the German-speaking and Russian markets, with passengers cruising on a price-sensitive budget. There is very little open deck space, and what decks there are, are narrow. Maintenance and cleanliness need much more attention and money spent. The teakwood decking is in very poor condition.

She is particularly good for "nooks and crannies" ports of call, such as those found in the Mediterranean. There are few public rooms. Has an enclosed teak promenade deck.

The interior decor is attractive in general, though a little dark and somber (poor lighting does not help). A two-deck-high Lido Bar is attractive.

Features interesting itineraries, at very lowest prices, both of which attract many of her passengers. The dress code is extremely casual and there is a relaxed, unpretentious ambience. The service staff is quite friendly and attentive, although some of the crew tend to put themselves first, passengers second, when the reverse should be practiced.

But: Because she is a small ship, there are few public rooms, and little open deck space. The interior passageways are narrow and poorly lit. Maintenance, particularly of wooden outdoor decks, needs more attention, and particularly on the open deck areas (poor caulking is evident in many places, as are well-worn deck planking). Has a narrow gangway in most ports of call, and there is often a little wait before you can embark or disembark. Public rooms are always crowded and it is hard to get away from the cigarette smokers. Cannot be recommended for wheelchair or other disabled passengers, as the ship is simply too small and confined. There are no cushioned pads for the deck lounge chairs.

ms Astra II

☆☆☆

(S)

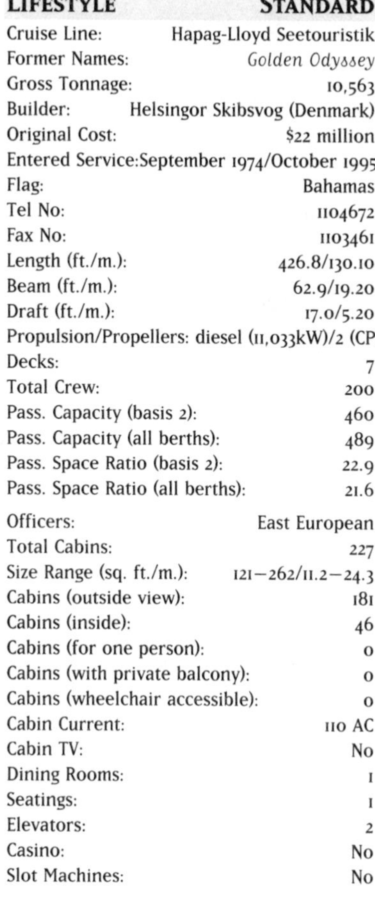

Lifestyle	Standard
Cruise Line:	Hapag-Lloyd Seetouristik
Former Names:	*Golden Odyssey*
Gross Tonnage:	10,563
Builder:	Helsingor Skibsvog (Denmark)
Original Cost:	$22 million
Entered Service:	September 1974/October 1995
Flag:	Bahamas
Tel No:	1104672
Fax No:	1103461
Length (ft./m.):	426.8/130.10
Beam (ft./m.):	62.9/19.20
Draft (ft./m.):	17.0/5.20
Propulsion/Propellers:	diesel (11,033kW)/2 (CP)
Decks:	7
Total Crew:	200
Pass. Capacity (basis 2):	460
Pass. Capacity (all berths):	489
Pass. Space Ratio (basis 2):	22.9
Pass. Space Ratio (all berths):	21.6
Officers:	East European
Total Cabins:	227
Size Range (sq. ft./m.):	121–262/11.2–24.3
Cabins (outside view):	181
Cabins (inside):	46
Cabins (for one person):	0
Cabins (with private balcony):	0
Cabins (wheelchair accessible):	0
Cabin Current:	110 AC
Cabin TV:	No
Dining Rooms:	1
Seatings:	1
Elevators:	2
Casino:	No
Slot Machines:	No
Swimming Pools (outdoors):	1
Swimming Pools (inside):	0
Whirlpools:	0
Fitness Center:	Yes
Sauna/Steam Room:	Yes/No
Massage:	Yes
Self-Service Launderette:	No
Movie Theater/Seats:	Yes/154
Library:	Yes
Children's Facilities:	No
Classification Society:	Lloyd's Register

Ratings	Score
Ship: Hardware/Maintenance	61
Ship: Outdoor Facilities/Space	60
Ship: Interior Facilities/Space/Flow	61
Ship: Decor/Furnishings/Artwork	63
Ship: Spa/Fitness Facilities	54
Cabins: Suites and Deluxe	62
Cabins: Standard Sizes	60
Food: Dining Room/Cuisine	61
Food: Informal Dining/Buffets	58
Food: Quality of Ingredients	60
Food: Afternoon Tea/Bar Snacks	56
Service: Dining Room	63
Service: Bars	64
Service: Cabins	63
Service: Open Decks	61
Cruise: Entertainment	61
Cruise: Activities Program	61
Cruise: Movies/Television Programming	56
Cruise: Hospitality Standard	67
Cruise: Overall Product Delivery	62
Overall Score	**1,214**

Accommodation: Most of the cabins, although quite small, are quite tastefully furnished and decorated and have a reasonable amount of closet and drawer space, and pleasant artwork (the ceilings are plain, however). The bathrooms really are quite small, as are the towels. There is little space for one's toiletries, and the plumbing is tired and can be troublesome at times.

Dining: There is a single, comfortable dining room that was enlarged a few years ago and features one seating for all meals, and good quality Continental food that is well presented. The menu choice is quite good (given the price of cruises), and the food is geared specifically to German tastes. There is a decent selection of cold cuts and cheeses at the buffets.

While there is not much finesse from the dining room staff, they are quite willing and eager to please. It is just that they have not been sent to the best culinary and hotel schools, so service tends to be basic but with a smile.

Other Comments: This is a fairly handsome looking compact ship that was well known in a previous life as Royal Cruise Line's *Golden Odyssey* and has a well-balanced, very compact, almost handsome profile that could be termed "cute." The ship has been fairly well maintained, although she is now more than twenty years old.

Originally constructed to accommodate the passenger load of a chartered Boeing 747 jet aircraft, this ship offers comfortable surroundings, at a moderate price, to a well-chosen palette of destinations.

This intimate little ship has already established a loyal following, and for good reason. The ship is clean and tidy throughout, and quite well maintained; she has a teakwood outdoor promenade deck, which is good for strolling, with several deck lounge chairs available for those who just like to sit, read, and watch the world go by. There is a good selection of public rooms for the size of the ship, with a couple of good bars (naturally, with German lager on draught).

An attentive staff offer fine-tuned personal service that is personable without being condescending, although a sense of tiredness prevails. Ideally suited to passengers who want a small ship atmosphere and who do not like big ships, *Astra II* is presently under a three-year charter to Hapag-Lloyd Seetouristik and is marketed to passengers seeking a decent cruise experience at a low price point.

The staff does a good job of keeping their passengers informed, entertained, and very grateful for their presence. Do remember when choosing a cruise that, as in many other areas of life, you get what you pay for. Having said that, this ship will provide a comfortable setting for a first cruise experience in surroundings that are cozy, intimate, and well run.

<u>But:</u> The gangway is quite steep and narrow in many ports, and may prove difficult for older passengers. There are no cushioned pads for the deck lounge chairs. The passenger hallways are quite narrow. Storage space for luggage in the cabins is very limited.

ms Asuka

☆☆☆☆ +

(M)

Lifestyle	**Premium**
Cruise Line:	NYK Cruises
Former Names:	-
Gross Tonnage:	28,717
Builder:	Mitsubishi Heavy Industries (Japan)
Original Cost:	$86 million
Entered Service:	December 1991
Flag:	Japan
Tel No:	1204654/1204660
Fax No:	1204662
Length (ft./m.):	632.5/192.81
Beam (ft./m.):	81.0/24.70
Draft (ft./m.):	20.3/6.20
Propulsion/Propellers:	diesel (17,300kW)/2 (CP)
Decks:	8
Total Crew:	243
Pass. Capacity (basis 2):	584
Pass. Capacity (all berths):	604
Pass. Space Ratio (basis 2):	49.1
Pass. Space Ratio (all berths):	47.5
Officers:	Japanese
Total Cabins:	292
Size Range (sq. ft./m.):	182–650/17.0–60.3
Cabins (outside view):	292
Cabins (inside):	0
Cabins (for one person):	0
Cabins (with private balcony):	100 (all have binoculars)
Cabins (wheelchair accessible):	2
Cabin Current:	110 AC
Cabin TV:	Yes
Dining Rooms:	1 (+ sushi restaurant)
Seatings:	2
Elevators:	5
Casino:	Yes
Slot Machines:	Yes
Swimming Pools (outdoors):	1
Swimming Pools (inside):	0
Whirlpools:	3
Fitness Center:	Yes
Sauna/Steam Room:	Yes/Yes
Massage:	Yes
Self-Service Launderette:	Yes
Movie Theater/Seats:	Yes/97
Library:	Yes
Children's Facilities:	No
Classification Society:	Nippon Kaiji Kyokai

Ratings	**Score**
Ship: Hardware/Maintenance	86
Ship: Outdoor Facilities/Space	84
Ship: Interior Facilities/Space/Flow	88
Ship: Decor/Furnishings/Artwork	87
Ship: Spa/Fitness Facilities	90
Cabins: Suites and Deluxe	90
Cabins: Standard Sizes	84
Food: Dining Room/Cuisine	86
Food: Informal Dining/Buffets	84
Food: Quality of Ingredients	87
Food: Afternoon Tea/Bar Snacks	84
Service: Dining Room	86
Service: Bars	86
Service: Cabins	86
Service: Open Decks	76
Cruise: Entertainment	81
Cruise: Activities Program	72
Cruise: Movies/Television Programming	78
Cruise: Hospitality Standard	85
Cruise: Overall Product Delivery	86
Overall Score	**1,686**

Accommodation: The "club" suites are excellent and are very well decorated. All cabinetry has rounded edges. Excellent insulation is provided between all cabins, as well as a good amount of closet and drawer space, including some lockable drawers. Tea-making unit, refrigerator, bathrobe, slippers, binoculars in "club" suites, and bathtubs in all cabins (while the "club" suite bathrooms are of generous proportions, the standard cabin bathrooms are rather small). There is no butler service in the "club" suites. The balcony door handles are awkward in all the suites.

Dining: The dining room, which is laid out so that it appears to be in two sections, with ocean-view windows along one side only, has a good amount of space around the tables, although there are very few tables for two. Features both Japanese and Western cuisine; traditional Japanese breakfast and luncheon, and mainly Western-style dinners. The Hotel Okura chain provides the menus and food. Although there are some good wines, the range of sake is limited.

There is also an à la carte sushi bar, which features fresh seafood, beautifully prepared and presented (at extra cost).

A traditional washitsu tatami room (the whole floor is covered in tatami mats, no shoes allowed) for special afternoon tea ceremonies.

Other Comments: She is the first all-new large ship specially designed for the slow-growing Japanese cruise market and the largest cruise ship constructed in Japan.

Has pleasing exterior styling and profile, with a large, squat funnel. There is a good amount of open deck space (Japanese passengers do not use it much, however). Provides good meetings facilities with some of the latest high-tech equipment available. There is a wraparound outdoor promenade deck, good for strolling.

The "cake-layer" stacking of public rooms hampers passenger flow and makes it a little disjointed, although the ship's Japanese passengers like the separation of public rooms. Has many intimate public rooms, and an excellent, spacious, and true Japanese grand bath. However, the massage room is located away from the grand bath area and should be integrated.

Features elegant interior decor and pleasing color combinations, fine quality fabrics, and soft furnishings. Fascinating Japanese artwork, including a multideck mural located on the wall of the main foyer staircase. Has cellular pay phones located in one of the deck foyers. Features a good mix of western and traditional Japanese entertainment.

There are formal and informal nights as far as the dress code goes, while during the day, it is quite casual. Gratuities are neither expected, nor allowed. Note that children under 10 are not allowed.

But: The forward staircase is rather utilitarian and plain. She now is in need of some refurbishment and upgrading in some areas.

ms Atalante

☆☆

(S)

LIFESTYLE	STANDARD
Cruise Line:	New Paradise Cruises
Former Names:	*Tahitien*
Gross Tonnage:	13,113
Builder:	Arsenal de la Marine Nationa Francaise (France)
Original Cost:	n/a
Entered Service:	May 1953/December 1992
Flag:	Cyprus
Tel No:	3579545600
Fax No:	3579370298
Length (ft./m.):	548.5/167.20
Beam (ft./m.):	67.9/20.70
Draft (ft./m.):	25.5/7.80
Propulsion/Propellers:	diesel (7,700kW)/2 (FP)
Decks:	5
Total Crew:	160
Pass. Capacity (basis 2):	484
Pass. Capacity (all berths):	635
Pass. Space Ratio (basis 2):	27.0
Pass. Space Ratio (all berths):	20.6
Officers:	Greek
Total Cabins:	242
Size Range (sq. ft./m.):	129.1–247.5/12.0–23.0
Cabins (outside view):	188
Cabins (inside):	54
Cabins (for one person):	2
Cabins (with private balcony):	0
Cabins (wheelchair accessible):	18
Cabin Current:	220 AC/200 DC
Cabin TV:	Yes
Dining Rooms:	1
Seatings:	2
Elevators:	0
Casino:	Yes
Slot Machines:	Yes
Swimming Pools (outdoors):	2
Swimming Pools (inside):	0
Whirlpools:	0
Fitness Center:	No
Sauna/Steam Room:	No/No
Massage:	No
Self-Service Launderette:	No
Movie Theater/Seats:	No
Library:	No
Children's Facilities:	No
Classification Society:	Bureau Veritas

RATINGS	SCORE
Ship: Hardware/Maintenance	50
Ship: Outdoor Facilities/Space	54
Ship: Interior Facilities/Space/Flow	40
Ship: Decor/Furnishings/Artwork	41
Ship: Spa/Fitness Facilities	30
Cabins: Suites and Deluxe	56
Cabins: Standard Sizes	47
Food: Dining Room/Cuisine	50
Food: Informal Dining/Buffets	42
Food: Quality of Ingredients	50
Food: Afternoon Tea/Bar Snacks	40
Service: Dining Room	60
Service: Bars	57
Service: Cabins	58
Service: Open Decks	57
Cruise: Entertainment	44
Cruise: Activities Program	44
Cruise: Movies/Television Programming	33
Cruise: Hospitality Standard	44
Cruise: Overall Product Delivery	46
OVERALL SCORE	**943**

Accommodation: The cabins are small and rather spartan, although most have been redecorated in pastel shades. There is limited closet space, but you do not need much clothing for this casual cruise environment. Note that the additional cabins installed in 1993 are subject to extreme squeaks and are noisy, which makes them quite difficult to sleep in. The top-grade cabins also have a refrigerator.

Dining: The dining room is low down in the ship and always seems to have a musty odor. The food is quite basic with little choice and unimaginative presentation. Poor selection of breads, fruits, and cheeses. The service is provided principally by Greek stewards. The buffets are minimal and could be more attractive.

Other Comments: Now well over forty years of age, the ship, a former passenger-car liner, is showing its age in a number of places, having gone through many changes. She has a small, squat funnel amidships and a long foredeck. She is a stable ship at sea, with a deep draft, and rides well. There is a generous amount of open deck and sunbathing space, but the outdoor decking is well worn in several places.

The number of public rooms is very limited, and the layout is very awkward. Recent decor changes are for the better, although still much of the interior decor is also dated and worn, yet adequate and comfortable for those who do not want the glitz of newer ships.

This ship is good for younger, budget-minded passengers wanting to party and travel with just the basics and without the need for much service.

But: The nightlife is disco-loud. There is no finesse anywhere, although the staff is reasonably enthusiastic. There is a steep gangway in some ports.

ts Ausonia

(M)

Lifestyle	Standard
Cruise Line:	Louis Cruise Lines/First Choice
Former Names:	-
Gross Tonnage:	12,609
Builder:	Cantieri Riuniti dell' Adriatico (Italy)
Original Cost:	n/a
Entered Service:	September 1957/May 1998
Flag:	Cyprus
Tel No:	n/a
Fax No:	n/a
Length (ft./m.):	522.5/159.26
Beam (ft./m.):	69.8/21.29
Draft (ft./m.):	21.4/6.54
Propulsion/Propellers:	steam turbine (12,799kW)/2 (FP)
Decks:	8
Total Crew:	280
Pass. Capacity (basis 2):	508
Pass. Capacity (all berths):	701
Pass. Space Ratio (basis 2):	24.8
Pass. Space Ratio (all berths):	17.9
Officers:	Greek/Cypriots
Total Cabins:	254
Size Range (sq. ft./m.):	69.9–269.1/6.5–25.0
Cabins (outside view):	152
Cabins (inside):	102
Cabins (for one person):	1
Cabins (with private balcony):	0
Cabins (wheelchair accessible):	0
Cabin Current:	220 AC
Cabin TV:	Upper grade cabins only
Dining Rooms:	1
Seatings:	2
Elevators:	1
Casino:	Yes
Slot Machines:	Yes
Swimming Pools (outdoors):	1
Swimming Pools (indoor):	0
Whirlpools:	1
Fitness Center:	Yes
Sauna/Steam Room:	Yes/No
Massage:	Yes
Self-Service Laundry:	No
Movie Theater/Seats:	Yes/125
Library:	Yes
Children's Facilities:	Yes
Classification Society:	RINA

Ratings	Score
Ship: Hardware/Maintenance	NYR
Ship: Outdoor Facilities/Space	NYR
Ship: Interior Facilities/Space/Flow	NYR
Ship: Decor/Furnishings/Artwork	NYR
Ship: Spa/Fitness Facilities	NYR
Cabins: Suites and Deluxe	NYR
Cabins: Standard Sizes	NYR
Food: Dining Room/Cuisine	NYR
Food: Informal Dining/Buffets	NYR
Food: Quality of Ingredients	NYR
Food: Afternoon Tea/Bar Snacks	NYR
Service: Dining Room	NYR
Service: Bars	NYR
Service: Cabins	NYR
Service: Open Decks	NYR
Cruise: Entertainment	NYR
Cruise: Activities Program	NYR
Cruise: Movies/Television Programming	NYR
Cruise: Hospitality Standard	NYR
Cruise: Overall Product Delivery	NYR

Expected Score Range
1,000-1,400

Accommodation: From suites to standard inside and outside cabins, all are quite small and compact, yet reasonably comfortable, in six cabin grades. They have all the basics, including a private bathroom and adequate closet space for frugal packers (drawer space is limited, however).

The uppermost cabin grades feature a full-sized bathtub (2 suites feature whirlpool baths), while all others have showers. There are several family cabins. Note that some inside and outside standard cabins have upper and lower berths.

Dining: The dining room (totally nonsmoking) is set high up in the vessel, has good ocean views from large picture windows, and features fine china and pleasant table settings. Tables are for four, six, or eight. Features friendly, efficient service with well programmed flair and attention. The cuisine is international in nature and provides a good mix of Continental fare, with some regional

Mediterranean specialities and British favorites. The selection of fruits and cheeses is perhaps limited. The wine list, while basic, provides an inexpensive range and a decent choice of wines.

Other Comments: This all-white ship has a somewhat classic steamship profile, with a large, single funnel placed amidships. There is a decent amount of open deck and sunning space although the swimming pool is tiny (it's really only a "dip" pool). She was purchased by Louis Cruise Lines in 1997 and underwent an extensive amount of refurbishing and upgrading in October 1998. She had not been well maintained under her previous owners during the past few years and is now still in need of a lot of attention to detail. There is a reasonable amount of open deck and sunning space. The ship has also undergone much mechanical and galley upgrading.

Inside the vessel, most of the public rooms are located on one deck (Corfu Deck), so it is easy to find one's way around. Most of the public areas have had upgraded decor and color changes and are now lighter and more cheerful, with new soft furnishings.

The number of public lounges and rooms is, however, limited. The Majorca Lounge (main show lounge) is pleasantly decorated, although the sight lines to the stage area are quite poor due to a large number of pillars obstructing the view; seats on the raised sections on the port and starboard sides are slightly better. There is also a small night club, a casino, a duty-free shop, an enclosed "winter garden" lounge/reading area on the starboard side, and a cinema.

This ship is presently under a long-term charter arrangement to First Choice Holidays of the U.K., and will provide a good, no-frills first cruise experience for those that choose to cruise on a limited budget, and will hopefully exceed your expectations.

But: There are few public rooms. Many passengers are heavy smokers and it is difficult to avoid them. Has a narrow gangway. You can book the deck you want your cabin to be on, but cabins are assigned by First Choice Cruises.

mv Bali Sea Dancer

☆☆ +

(S)

LIFESTYLE	STANDARD
Cruise Line:	Kleintours
Former Names:	*Illiria*
Gross Tonnage:	3,852
Builder:	Cantieri Navale Pellegrino (Italy)
Original Cost:	n/a
Entered Service:	1962
Flag:	Ecuador
Tel No:	1241440
Fax No:	1241441
Length (ft./m.):	332.6/101.40
Beam (ft./m.):	48.0/14.66
Draft (ft./m.):	16.4/5.02
Propulsion/Propellers:	diesel (4,281kW)/2 (FP)
Decks:	4
Total Crew:	90
Pass. Capacity (basis 2):	143
Pass. Capacity (all berths):	148
Pass. Space Ratio (basis 2):	26.9
Pass. Space Ratio (all berths):	26.0
Officers:	International
Total Cabins:	73
Size Range (sq. ft./m.):	77.0–261.0/7.1–24.2
Cabins (outside view):	64
Cabins (inside):	9
Cabins (for one person):	9
Cabins (with private balcony):	0
Cabins (wheelchair accessible):	0
Cabin Current:	220 AC
Cabin TV:	No
Dining Rooms:	1
Seatings:	Open
Elevators:	0
Casino:	No
Slot Machines:	No
Swimming Pools (outdoors):	1
Swimming Pools (inside):	0
Whirlpools:	0
Fitness Center:	No
Sauna/Steam Room:	No/No
Massage:	No
Self-Service Launderette:	No
Movie Theater/Seats:	No
Library:	Yes
Children's Facilities:	No
Classification Society:	American Bureau of Shipping

RATINGS	SCORE
Ship: Hardware/Maintenance	54
Ship: Outdoor Facilities/Space	54
Ship: Interior Facilities/Space/Flow	55
Ship: Decor/Furnishings/Artwork	57
Ship: Spa/Fitness Facilities	36
Cabins: Suites and Deluxe	60
Cabins: Standard Sizes	51
Food: Dining Room/Cuisine	61
Food: Informal Dining/Buffets	52
Food: Quality of Ingredients	58
Food: Afternoon Tea/Bar Snacks	40
Service: Dining Room	60
Service: Bars	60
Service: Cabins	61
Service: Open Decks	44
Cruise: Entertainment	45
Cruise: Activities Program	41
Cruise: Movies/Television Programming	38
Cruise: Hospitality Standard	58
Cruise: Overall Product Delivery	57
OVERALL SCORE	**1,042**

Accommodation: All of the cabins are a little on the small side, but they do have some wood accents and trim. All have private bathroom with shower, except for two deluxe cabins that have a full-sized bathtub. However, there really is little closet and drawer space, the bathrooms are small, and there is very little space for personal toiletry items.

Dining: The Dining Room is quite charming, but it is a little tight when the ship is full, although there is a good amount of space around each table. The cuisine is centered on international fare, with some local specialties, and should be quite adequate considering the cuising region. Features open seating dining (you may sit where and with whom you like). Has a limited wine list (wines are expensive).

Other Comments: This small, very pleasant, relaxed ship was originally constructed for charter cruises in the Greek islands, but presently operates year-round in the Galapagos Islands.

She will provide a comfortable destination-oriented cruise experience for those seeking to get close to the natural, ecologically interesting world off the coast of Ecuador. She is quite a clean ship throughout and has been well maintained, despite her age.

Inside appointments and the limited number of public rooms have pleasing decor and color-rich fabrics and soft furnishings. The main lounge has interesting box-fluted columns and oversized armchairs. There is a well-stocked reference library (and a nonworking fireplace). There are some interesting works of art in her public rooms. The ship now operates short cruises in the Galapagos Islands.

<u>But:</u> The ceilings are boringly plain aboard this ship (many cabins have old-fashioned "pegboard" ceilings).

mv Berlin

☆☆☆ +

(M)

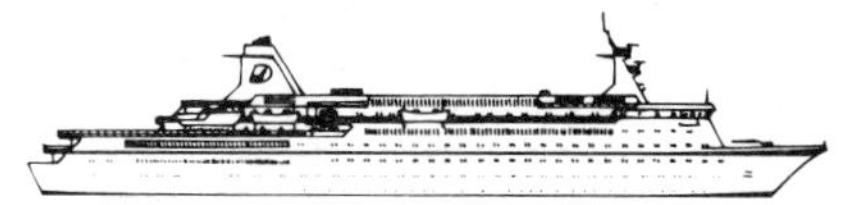

Lifestyle	**Standard**
Cruise Line:	Peter Deilmann Reederei
Former Names:	*Princess Mahsuri*
Gross Tonnage:	9,570
Builder:	Howaldtswerke Deutsche Werft (Germany)
Original Cost:	n/a
Entered Service:	June 1980
Flag:	Germany
Tel No:	1120251
Fax No:	1120264
Length (ft./m.):	457.0/139.30
Beam (ft./m.):	57.5/17.52
Draft (ft./m.):	15.7/4.80
Propulsion/Propellers:	diesel (7,060kW)/2 (CP)
Decks:	8
Total Crew:	180
Pass. Capacity (basis 2):	420
Pass. Capacity (all berths):	446
Pass. Space Ratio (basis 2):	22.6
Pass. Space Ratio (all berths):	21.3
Officers:	German
Total Cabins:	210
Size Range (sq. ft./m.):	93–192/8.6–17.8
Cabins (outside view):	157
Cabins (inside):	53
Cabins (for one person):	0
Cabins (with private balcony):	0
Cabins (wheelchair accessible):	0
Cabin Current:	220 AC
Cabin TV:	Yes
Dining Rooms:	2
Seatings:	2
Elevators:	2
Casino:	No
Slot Machines:	No
Swimming Pools (outdoors):	1
Swimming Pools (inside):	1
Whirlpools:	0
Fitness Center:	Yes
Sauna/Steam Room:	Yes/No
Massage:	Yes
Self-Service Launderette:	No
Movie Theater/Seats:	Yes/330
Library:	Yes
Children's Facilities:	On request
Classification Society:	Germanischer Lloyd

Ratings	**Score**
Ship: Hardware/Maintenance	74
Ship: Outdoor Facilities/Space	68
Ship: Interior Facilities/Space/Flow	72
Ship: Decor/Furnishings/Artwork	77
Ship: Spa/Fitness Facilities	68
Cabins: Suites and Deluxe	76
Cabins: Standard Sizes	66
Food: Dining Room/Cuisine	75
Food: Informal Dining/Buffets	68
Food: Quality of Ingredients	72
Food: Afternoon Tea/Bar Snacks	66
Service: Dining Room	71
Service: Bars	70
Service: Cabins	72
Service: Open Decks	71
Cruise: Entertainment	65
Cruise: Activities Program	63
Cruise: Movies/Television Programming	58
Cruise: Hospitality Standard	63
Cruise: Overall Product Delivery	71
Overall Score	**1,386**

Accommodation: The cabins are quite small, but they are quite comfortable and well appointed, with dark wood accents (most cabins have twin beds, however). The bathrooms have shower units but no bathtubs, and storage space for personal toiletries is best described as adequate, no more. Promenade and Main Deck cabins also have a refrigerator.

Dining: The dining room is really quite charming, and has large, ocean-view picture windows and dark wood accents, and there are tables for two, four, or six. Attentive, professional, European service, generally with a smile. The food caters strictly to German tastes, with rich cream sauces accompanying most entrees. Features a good selection of breads, cheeses, and cold cuts, and the desserts are extremely good. Service is by German-speaking staff.

Other Comments: She is a fairly handsome, though somewhat angular contemporary ship, with crisp, clean, all-white lines, a well-balanced profile, and an ice-strengthened hull (this does not mean that the ship is capable of cruising in Antarctic waters, however). The ship was in fact "stretched" in 1986, when a new midsection was inserted. *Berlin* has, for many years, been the star of the long-running German television show Traumschiff (Dream Ship), is well-known throughout the German-speaking market, and has generated an extremely loyal following, some of whom may not wish to change to the company's newest ship *Deutschland*.

Her interiors are crisp and tidy throughout, and she is a well-appointed ship with elegant, tasteful, and rather dark (restful) European decor and furnishings, accented by scroll work and gilt detailing. There is a splendid collection of original oil paintings that are part of the personal collection of the ship's owner, Peter Deilmann. There is a good indoor health spa and accompanying body treatments. An intimate, highly personable, and friendly atmosphere prevails. Sadly, there is no forward observation lounge.

This ship will provide a fairly exclusive destination-intensive cruise experience in quite elegant, well-maintained, intimate, but now somewhat dated surroundings for the discerning German-speaking passenger who does not need constant entertainment. Insurance and gratuities are included. Currency: Deutschmark.

But: The swimming pool is very small, the surrounding open-deck sunbathing space is very cramped, and the interior passageways are quite narrow.

ms Black Prince

☆☆☆

(S)

Lifestyle	Standard
Cruise Line:	Fred Olsen Cruise Lines
Former Names:	-
Gross Tonnage:	11,209
Builder:	Fender Werft (Germany)
Original Cost:	$20 million
Entered Service:	1966
Flag:	Norway
Tel No:	1313217
Fax No:	1313217
Length (ft./m.):	470.4/143.40
Beam (ft./m.):	66.6/20.30
Draft (ft./m.):	20.0/6.10
Propulsion/Propellers:	diesel (12,310kW)/2 (CP)
Decks:	7
Total Crew:	200
Pass. Capacity (basis 2):	446
Pass. Capacity (all berths):	517
Pass. Space Ratio (basis 2):	25.1
Pass. Space Ratio (all berths):	21.6
Officers:	European
Total Cabins:	238
Size Range (sq. ft./m.):	80–226/7.5–21.0
Cabins (outside view):	168
Cabins (inside):	70
Cabins (for one person):	30
Cabins (with private balcony):	0
Cabins (wheelchair accessible):	2
Cabin Current:	230 AC
Cabin TV:	Yes
Dining Rooms:	2
Seatings:	1
Elevators:	2
Casino:	Yes
Slot Machines:	No
Swimming Pools (outdoors):	1
Swimming Pools (inside):	1
Whirlpools:	2
Fitness Center:	Yes
Sauna/Steam Room:	Yes/No
Massage:	Yes
Self-Service Launderette:	No
Movie Theater/Seats:	No
Library:	Yes
Children's Facilities:	Yes
Classification Society:	Det Norske Veritas

Ratings	Score
Ship: Hardware/Maintenance	58
Ship: Outdoor Facilities/Space	56
Ship: Interior Facilities/Space/Flow	58
Ship: Decor/Furnishings/Artwork	57
Ship: Spa/Fitness Facilities	64
Cabins: Suites and Deluxe	60
Cabins: Standard Sizes	56
Food: Dining Room/Cuisine	61
Food: Informal Dining/Buffets	55
Food: Quality of Ingredients	58
Food: Afternoon Tea/Bar Snacks	41
Service: Dining Room	61
Service: Bars	62
Service: Cabins	62
Service: Open Decks	56
Cruise: Entertainment	55
Cruise: Activities Program	56
Cruise: Movies/Television Programming	47
Cruise: Hospitality Standard	61
Cruise: Overall Product Delivery	60
Overall Score	**1,144**

Accommodation: There is a wide range of cabin sizes and configurations, and a good percentage of cabins are for single passengers. Many cabins have poor air-conditioning, however, and hard beds. The outside suites are quite decent (particularly nice are the Gran Canaria and Lanzarote suites, with their wood-paneled walls). Other cabins are small, but quite nicely equipped and tastefully decorated, for a smaller ship. Note that there is a charge for room service. The upper grade cabins also have a refrigerator.

Dining: The two main dining rooms have big picture windows. Sometimes, first- and second-seating diners exchange seatings, a good arrangement. The food is generally of high quality, but there could be more menu choice, particularly at the buffet lunches. Has a very limited, basic wine list. Service is by Filipino stewards.

Other Comments: This is a solidly built ship that has been well maintained, but has a rather ungainly profile, and she does tend to pitch heavily in unkind seas.

Features a good indoor fitness/leisure center, complete with an indoor swimming pool (unusual for a small ship, added in 1996) and spa area.

Very homely restrained decor, feel, and ambience, with much of the soft furnishings hand-tailored on board. Good wooden stairways throughout, although the steps are a little steep. An ironing room is provided.

This small ship has a friendly feel, an almost totally Filipino staff, and is well suited to the informal, older, British passenger, but the standards of service are slipping. Still, there are many repeat passengers who would not dream of trying another ship.

But: It is often difficult to get away from smokers, and the service has become overly casual and sloppy of late. The company lists recommended gratuities of £4.00 per passenger per day.

ms Black Watch

☆☆☆☆

(M)

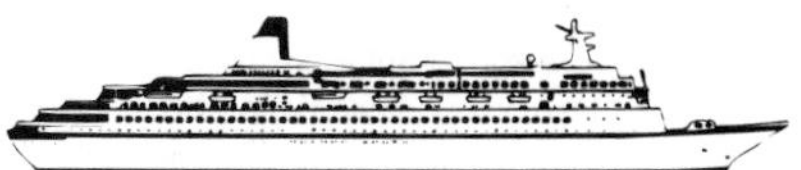

LIFESTYLE	**STANDARD**
Cruise Line:	Fred Olsen Cruise Lines
Former Names:	*Star Odyssey/Westward/ Royal Viking Star*
Gross Tonnage:	28,492
Builder:	Wartsila (Finland)
Original Cost:	$22.5 million
Entered Service:	June 1972/November 1996
Flag:	Bahamas
Tel No:	(47) 51848630
Fax No:	(47) 51848630
Length (ft./m.):	674.1/205.47
Beam (ft./m.):	82.6/25.20
Draft (ft./m.):	24.7/7.55
Propulsion/Propellers:	diesel (13,400kW)/2 (CP)
Decks:	8
Total Crew:	330
Pass. Capacity (basis 2):	801
Pass. Capacity (all berths):	892
Pass. Space Ratio (basis 2):	35.5
Pass. Space Ratio (all berths):	31.9
Officers:	European
Total Cabins:	422
Size Range (sq. ft./m.):	136–580/12.6–53.8
Cabins (outside view):	375
Cabins (inside):	47
Cabins (for one person):	37
Cabins (with private balcony):	9
Cabins (wheelchair accessible):	4
Cabin Current:	110/220 AC
Cabin TV:	Yes
Dining Rooms:	1
Seatings:	2
Elevators:	5
Casino:	Yes
Slot Machines:	Yes
Swimming Pools (outdoors):	2
Swimming Pools (inside):	0
Whirlpools:	3
Fitness Center:	Yes
Sauna/Steam Room:	Yes/Yes
Massage:	Yes
Self-Service Launderette:	Yes
Movie Theater/Seats:	Yes/156
Library:	Yes
Children's Facilities:	Yes
Classification Society:	Det Norske Veritas

RATINGS	**SCORE**
Ship: Hardware/Maintenance	79
Ship: Outdoor Facilities/Space	77
Ship: Interior Facilities/Space/Flow	79
Ship: Decor/Furnishings/Artwork	77
Ship: Spa/Fitness Facilities	71
Cabins: Suites and Deluxe	81
Cabins: Standard Sizes	76
Food: Dining Room/Cuisine	72
Food: Informal Dining/Buffets	63
Food: Quality of Ingredients	64
Food: Afternoon Tea/Bar Snacks	61
Service: Dining Room	72
Service: Bars	70
Service: Cabins	73
Service: Open Decks	63
Cruise: Entertainment	75
Cruise: Activities Program	64
Cruise: Movies/Television Programming	61
Cruise: Hospitality Standard	70
Cruise: Overall Product Delivery	76
OVERALL SCORE	**1,424**

Accommodation: A wide range of cabins provides something for everyone, from spacious suites with real separate bedrooms, to small cabins (inside). All are nicely equipped, and there is plenty of good closet, drawer, and storage space (drawers are metal and tinny, however, and in some closets they are of the wire-basket type. Nonsmoking cabins are also available. Note that some cabin bathrooms have awkward access, and that the insulation between cabins is quite poor. The towels are of substandard quality and are just too small. The room service menu could be improved.

Dining: The dining room has a high ceiling and provides plenty of space at each table. Features good cuisine, attractively presented, with an emphasis on seafood. The food is generally of good quality, although the menu variety is somewhat limited, particularly at the buffet lunches (best described as a Scandinavian Smorgasbord). The breakfast buffets are repetitious, however. Communication with the Filipino waiters can prove frustrating at times. The self-service beverage station needs improvement. There is a good range of wines. The room service (in-cabin) menu is quite limited.

Other Comments: Acquired by Fred Olsen Cruise Lines in late 1996, this handsome ship, originally built for long-distance cruising for the now-defunct Royal Viking Line, has a sharply raked bow and quite a sleek appearance, and was "stretched" in 1981. There is an excellent amount of open deck and sunbathing space, and a good health-fitness spa high atop ship.

The interior decor is restful, having been made more attractive in a recent refit (the artwork is drab, however). Good materials, fabrics (including the use of the Black Watch tartan), and soft furnishings add to a pleasant ambience and warmth. The spacious public rooms have high ceilings, and the staircases are wide and well lit.

There is a good cinema with a steeply tiered floor, and a very pleasant library and lounge for card players. The observation lounge high atop ship has commanding views and is very comfortable as a relaxing lounge.

This ship will provide a good cruise experience, at a modest price, in true Fred Olsen style, but do remember that she is now quite an old ship and that means little problems like plumbing and other ideosyncracies will occur from time to time.

ms Bolero

☆☆☆ +

(M)

Lifestyle	Standard
Cruise Line:	Festival Cruises/First Choice
Former Names:	*Starward*
Gross Tonnage:	16,107
Builder:	A.G. Weser (Germany)
Original Cost:	n/a
Entered Service:	December 1968/December 1995
Flag:	Panama
Tel No:	1354502
Fax No:	1354502
Length (ft./m.):	525.3/160.13
Beam (ft./m.):	74.9/22.84
Draft (ft./m.):	20.4/6.22
Propulsion/Propellers:	diesel (12,950kW)/2 (CP)
Decks:	7
Total Crew:	330
Pass. Capacity (basis 2):	802
Pass. Capacity (all berths):	984
Pass. Space Ratio (basis 2):	20.1
Pass. Space Ratio (all berths):	16.3
Officers:	Greek
Total Cabins:	401
Size Range (sq. ft./m.):	111.9–324.0/10.4–30.1
Cabins (outside view):	237
Cabins (inside):	164
Cabins (for one person):	0
Cabins (with private balcony):	0
Cabins (wheelchair accessible):	2
Cabin Current:	110/220 AC
Cabin TV:	No
Dining Rooms:	1
Seatings:	2
Elevators:	4
Casino:	Yes
Slot Machines:	Yes
Swimming Pools (outdoors):	2
Swimming Pools (inside):	0
Whirlpools:	0
Fitness Center:	Yes
Sauna/Steam Room:	Yes/No
Massage:	Yes
Self-Service Launderette:	No
Movie Theater/Seats:	Yes/210
Library:	Yes
Children's Facilities:	No
Classification Society:	Det Norske Veritas

Ratings	Score
Ship: Hardware/Maintenance	64
Ship: Outdoor Facilities/Space	57
Ship: Interior Facilities/Space/Flow	60
Ship: Decor/Furnishings/Artwork	60
Ship: Spa/Fitness Facilities	52
Cabins: Suites and Deluxe	62
Cabins: Standard Sizes	51
Food: Dining Room/Cuisine	73
Food: Informal Dining/Buffets	66
Food: Quality of Ingredients	67
Food: Afternoon Tea/Bar Snacks	62
Service: Dining Room	75
Service: Bars	74
Service: Cabins	74
Service: Open Decks	62
Cruise: Entertainment	64
Cruise: Activities Program	56
Cruise: Movies/Television Programming	42
Cruise: Hospitality Standard	67
Cruise: Overall Product Delivery	69
Overall Score	**1,257**

Accommodation: Except for five good-sized suites, the cabins are very compact units that are moderately comfortable and are decorated in clean, bright, contemporary colors. They are, however, quite adequate, particularly as this company specializes in destination-intensive seven-day cruises. The cabin closet and drawer space is limited in size, and the metal drawers are quite tinny. The bathrooms are quite small, and the towels are not large, although they are made of 100 percent cotton; the insulation between cabins could be better.

Dining: This ship has a dining room that is quite cheerful and charming, with some prime tables (most are for four, six, or eight) overlooking the stern. The company provides good food and a wide menu choice, as in sister ships *Flamenco* and *The Azur*. Service is cheerful, friendly, and comes with a smile, but there is not much finesse (remember, this is an inexpensive, informal cruise experience). There is a good selection of standard breads, cold cuts of meat, fresh fruits, and cheeses at the buffets, which are nicely laid out and presented quite well, given the space limitations. The wine list is quite acceptable, but the wines, for the most part, are very young.

Other Comments: This ship has a smart looking, contemporary upper profile with dual swept-back funnels, and is an ideal size for cruising in the Mediterranean region. There is a reasonable amount of open deck and sunbathing space, and there are plenty of white, plastic deck lounge chairs, and blue/yellow sun umbrellas for shade at the aft outdoor decks. Just forward of her twin blue funnels is an enclosed basketball/volleyball court.

A neat bar and indoor/outdoor sitting area is located just behind the mast, in a solarium-style shielded housing that has three levels. What spoils her exterior, however, is a less than handsome duck-tailed sponson stern.

Bolero was formerly a Caribbean-based ship owned and operated by Norwegian Cruise Line. She was acquired in late 1995 by Festival Cruises, the Genoa-based cruise line "for Europeans." The ship has a warm, friendly upbeat ambience.

Inside the ship, there is a good choice of public rooms for this size of vessel, and they feature clean, contemporary furnishings and upbeat, cheerful fabric colors and decor throughout. Has a good, steeply tiered movie theater, with excellent sight lines.

This is a very comfortably sized vessel that is ideal for Mediterranean cruises. This ship is attractive and is a good choice for first-time passengers. For seven months each in 1999 and 2000, the ship is being operated during the summer season under charter to U.K. tour operator First Choice, specifically for British passengers (First Choice also operates its own airline, Air 2000).

During the winter (Caribbean) season the ship may operate under charter to tour operators such as Regent Holidays of Canada. Festival Cruises provides a well-tuned European-style cruise experience in comfortable, although certainly not elegant or glitzy, surroundings, at a modest price. The staff is friendly and tries hard to make you feel comfortable.

But: Do remember that this is a fairly high-density vessel that really feels a little crowded when full (it is called "ambience"). There are no cushioned pads for the deck lounge chairs. The diesel engines are somewhat noisy and tend to "throb" in some parts of the vessel, including those cabins on lower decks. There are simply too many repetitive announcements in several languages.

ms Bremen

☆☆☆☆

(S)

Lifestyle	**Premium**
Cruise Line:	Hapag-Lloyd Seetouristik
Former Names:	*Frontier Spirit*
Gross Tonnage:	6,752
Builder:	Mitsubishi Heavy Industries (Japan)
Original Cost:	$42 million
Entered Service:	November 1990/November 1993
Flag:	Bahamas
Tel No:	1103404
Fax No:	1103405
Length (ft./m.):	365.8/111.51
Beam (ft./m.):	55.7/17.00
Draft (ft./m.):	15.7/4.80
Propulsion/Propellers:	diesel (4,855kW)/2 (CP)
Decks:	6
Total Crew:	94
Pass. Capacity (basis 2):	164
Pass. Capacity (all berths):	184
Pass. Space Ratio (basis 2):	41.1
Pass. Space Ratio (all berths):	36.6
Officers:	European
Total Cabins:	82
Size Range (sq. ft./m.):	175–322/16.2–30.0
Cabins (outside view):	82
Cabins (inside):	0
Cabins (for one person):	0
Cabins (with private balcony):	18
Cabins (wheelchair accessible):	2
Cabin Current:	110 AC
Cabin TV:	Yes
Dining Rooms:	1 (open seating)
Elevators:	2
Casino:	No
Slot Machines:	No
Swimming Pools (outdoors):	1
Swimming Pools (inside):	0
Whirlpools:	0
Fitness Center:	Yes
Sauna/Steam Room:	Yes/No
Massage:	No
Self-Service Launderette:	Yes
Lecture/Film Room:	Yes (seats 164)
Library:	Yes
Zodiacs:	12
Helicopter Pad:	Yes
Classification Society:	Lloyd's Register

Ratings	**Score**
Ship: Hardware/Maintenance	78
Ship: Expedition Equipment	80
Ship: Interior Facilities/Space/Flow	78
Ship: Decor/Furnishings/Artwork	76
Ship: Spa/Fitness Facilities	42
Cabins: Suites and Deluxe	80
Cabins: Standard Sizes	72
Food: Dining Room/Cuisine	77
Food: Informal Dining/Buffets	72
Food: Quality of Ingredients	75
Food: Afternoon Tea/Bar Snacks	74
Service: Dining Room	80
Service: Bars	80
Service: Cabins	81
Service: Open Decks	70
Cruise: Library/Lecture Programs	73
Cruise: Movies/Television Programming	64
Cruise: Hospitality Standard	74
Cruise: Expedition Experience	73
Cruise: Overall Product Delivery	80
Overall Score	**1,479**

Accommodation: The cabins, which come in only three different configurations, are all outside and are quite spacious and very well equipped for the size of the vessel (all of them even have a wall clock) and feature a VCR unit. Each has moderate closet space, although there is little drawer space or storage space for your luggage. Some cabins also have very small balconies, a first for any expedition cruise vessel. Soft drinks in refrigerators are replenished daily, at no charge.

Dining: The dining room is quite charming, with elegant, sophisticated decor, and has big picture windows. The food is excellent, with high-quality ingredients, although it is quite highly salted. Good choice of breads, pastries, cheeses, and fruits. The service is very good, with bilingual (German- and English-speaking) waiters and waitresses immaculately dressed. In addition, breakfast and luncheon buffets are available on deck.

Other Comments: This purpose-built expedition cruise vessel (formerly *Frontier Spirit*, for U.S.-based Frontier Cruises) has a handsome, though wide, squat contemporary profile and fairly decent, although not the latest, high-tech equipment. Its wide beam provides good general stability, and the long cruising range and ice-hardened hull provides the ship with access to the most remote destinations. She therefore has the highest ice classification.

Zero-discharge of waste matter is practiced; this means that absolutely nothing is discharged into the oceans that does not meet with the international conventions on ocean pollution (MARPOL). All the equipment for in-depth marine and shore excursions is provided. When the ship goes to cold weather/ice areas such as the Arctic or Antarctic, red parks (waterproof outdoor jackets) are supplied, as are high waterproof boots (you will need to take are some waterproof trousers and several pairs of thick socks, plus "thermal" underwear).

Fine, well-planned destination-intensive itineraries, good documentation, and port information. High degree of comfort (though not quite as luxurious as the slightly larger Hanseatic). 24-hour reception desk. The fleet of Zodiacs is a real plus for this kind of operation.

This is one of the most comfortable and practical expedition cruise vessels today. It will provide you with an outstanding learning and expedition experience. The ship underwent an extensive upgrading of her interiors and debuted in late 1993 for Hanseatic Tours and Hapag-Lloyd Tours, catering principally to German-speaking passengers. Insurance, port taxes, and all staff gratuities are all included.

But: The ship has a steep gangway in some ports of call. The swimming pool is tiny, as is the open deck space, although there are both shaded and open areas. The sauna is really tiny. Plastic chairs on deck should have cushions.

mv Caledonian Star

☆☆☆ +

(S)

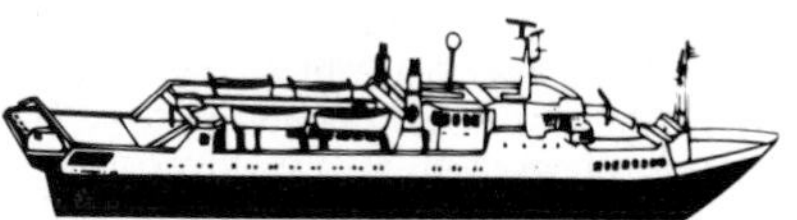

Lifestyle	Standard
Cruise Line:	Noble Caledonia/ Special Expeditions
Former Names:	*North Star/Marburg/Lindmar*
Gross Tonnage:	3,095
Builder:	A.G. Weser Seebeckwerft (Germany)
Original Cost:	n/a
Entered Service:	1966/1984
Flag:	Bahamas
Tel No:	1104706
Fax No:	1104766
Length (ft./m.):	292.6/89.20
Beam (ft./m.):	45.9/14.00
Draft (f//m):	20.3/6.20
Propulsion/Propellers:	diesel (3,236kW)/1 (FP)
Decks:	6
Total Crew:	60
Pass. Capacity (basis 2):	120
Pass. Capacity (all berths):	150
Pass. Space Ratio (basis 2):	25.7
Pass. Space Ratio (all berths):	20.6
Officers:	Scandinavian
Total Cabins:	61
Size Range (sq. ft./m.):	192–269/17.8–25.0
Cabins (outside view):	68
Cabins (inside):	0
Cabins (for one person):	2
Cabins (with private balcony):	0
Cabins (wheelchair accessible):	0
Cabin Current:	110/220 AC
Cabin TV:	Yes
Dining Rooms:	1 (open seating)
Elevators:	0
Casino:	Yes
Slot Machines:	Yes
Swimming Pools (outdoors):	1
Whirlpools:	0
Fitness Center:	No
Sauna/Steam Room:	No/No
Massage:	No
Self-Service Launderette:	No
Lecture/Film Room:	No
Library:	Yes
Zodiacs:	4
Helicopter Pad:	No
Classification Society:	Det Norske Veritas

Ratings	Score
Ship: Hardware/Maintenance	63
Ship: Expedition Equipment	61
Ship: Interior Facilities/Space/Flow	54
Ship: Decor/Furnishings/Artwork	62
Ship: Spa/Fitness Facilities	30
Cabins: Suites and Deluxe	62
Cabins: Standard Sizes	54
Food: Dining Room/Cuisine	72
Food: Informal Dining/Buffets	61
Food: Quality of Ingredients	72
Food: Afternoon Tea/Bar Snacks	62
Service: Dining Room	74
Service: Bars	73
Service: Cabins	75
Service: Open Decks	60
Cruise: Library/Lecture Programs	64
Cruise: Movies/Television Programming	55
Cruise: Hospitality Standard	73
Cruise: Expedition Experience	62
Cruise: Overall Product Delivery	74
Overall Score	**1,263**

Accommodation: The all-outside-view cabins are very compact, but quite comfortable units and they are decorated in warm, muted tones. All cabins feature a minibar-refrigerator, VCR, good closet and drawer space, and a clock. The cabin ceilings are rather plain, however, and bathrooms are tight, with little space for the storage of personal toiletry items.

Dining: The dining room is small and quite charming, but the low-back chairs are quite small. The cuisine is European in style with high quality, very fresh ingredients, but not a lot of menu choice. Attentive and friendly service is provided.

Other Comments: She is a reasonably handsome ship that is extremely tidy and has been well cared for. Has an open bridge policy. Carries Zodiac landing craft for in-depth excursions, and there is also an enclosed shore tender. An aft stairway (it is quite steep) leads down to the landing craft platform.

This ship (known as CalStar by her regulars) is very comfortable and unpretentious, with a warm, intimate ambience, and a casual dress code that helps make her feel quite homey.

For such a small ship there is a good range of public rooms and facilities (all refurbished in mid-1998) that includes a good lecture lounge/bar/library, where a selection of videos is stocked for in-cabin use. An excellent set of lecturers that are placed aboard for each cruise make this a real life-enrichment and learning experience for an intellectual (mainly North American and British) clientele wanting to travel and learn, while enveloped in comfortable, unpretentious surroundings.

This very likable little ship provides a well-tuned destination-intensive, soft expedition-style cruise experience, at a very reasonable price. Attracts a lot of loyal repeat passengers who do not want to sail aboard ships that look like apartment blocks. Itineraries now include Antarctica (starting December 1998).

But: The interior stairways are a little steep. The exterior stairway to the zodiac embarkation points is steep. Noise from the diesel engines (generators) is irksome. Communication can sometimes prove frustrating.

mv Calypso

☆☆☆

(M)

Lifestyle	**Standard**
Cruise Line:	Transocean Tours
Former Names:	*Sun Fiesta/Canguro Verde, Durr*
Gross Tonnage:	11,162
Builder:	Fincantieri (Italy)
Original Cost:	n/a
Entered Service:	1968/June 1994
Flag:	Bahamas
Tel No:	1306564
Fax No:	1306565
Length (ft./m.):	444.2/135.4
Beam (ft./m.):	62.9/19.2
Draft (ft./m.):	20.6/6.3
Propulsion/Propellers:	diesel (9,000kW)/2 (CP)
Decks:	8
Total Crew:	220
Pass. Capacity (basis 2):	486
Pass. Capacity (all berths):	593
Pass. Space Ratio (basis 2):	22.9
Pass. Space Ratio (all berths):	18.8
Officers:	European
Total Cabins:	243
Size Range (sq. ft./m.):	135–244/12.5–22.6
Cabins (outside view):	158
Cabins (inside):	85
Cabins (for one person):	0
Cabins (with private balcony):	0
Cabins (wheelchair accessible):	2
Cabin Current:	110 AC
Cabin TV:	Yes
Dining Rooms:	1
Seatings:	2
Elevators:	2
Casino:	Yes
Slot Machines:	Yes
Swimming Pools (outdoors):	1
Swimming Pools (inside):	0
Whirlpools:	0
Fitness Center:	Yes
Sauna/Steam Room:	Yes/No
Massage:	Yes
Self-Service Launderette:	No
Movie Theater/Seats:	No
Library:	Yes
Children's Facilities:	No
Classification Society:	Lloyd's Register

Ratings	**Score**
Ship: Hardware/Maintenance	51
Ship: Outdoor Facilities/Space	44
Ship: Interior Facilities/Space/Flow	51
Ship: Decor/Furnishings/Artwork	50
Ship: Spa/Fitness Facilities	40
Cabins: Suites and Deluxe	58
Cabins: Standard Sizes	51
Food: Dining Room/Cuisine	76
Food: Informal Dining/Buffets	73
Food: Quality of Ingredients	76
Food: Afternoon Tea/Bar Snacks	60
Service: Dining Room	73
Service: Bars	73
Service: Cabins	71
Service: Open Decks	65
Cruise: Entertainment	62
Cruise: Activities Program	60
Cruise: Movies/Television Programming	53
Cruise: Hospitality Standard	71
Cruise: Overall Product Delivery	62
Overall Score	**1,220**

Accommodation: The ship features mostly outside cabins, which are quite attractive, with warm, pastel colors, although the fabrics and soft furnishings could be of better quality. The cabin bathrooms all have showers, but none have bathtubs.

The cabins really are quite small and barely adequate, so take only the minimum amount of clothing. Some 66 cabins have double beds, while others are twins, with many featuring third and fourth berths. Has a limited cabin service menu.

Dining: The dining room, located aft, is attractive and well decorated, although its layout is somewhat awkward, as it is on two slightly different levels. Good general cuisine and service standards are provided, and attractive buffets feature plenty of cheeses and cold cuts of meat, while are essential to German-speaking passengers.

Other Comments: This former Strintzis Line ferry was reconstructed in Greece (although her resulting profile is certainly not an attractive one) and then operated by the now-defunct Regency Cruises before being placed under a five-year bare-boat charter to Transocean Tours.

The ship carries a predominantly German-speaking clientele who strictly seek to travel to interesting and somewhat off-beat destinations in modest surroundings, at a very modest price, and with very friendly and helpful Transocean Tours staff aboard each cruise.

One really practical feature is the ship's enclosed wooden promenade deck, good for strolling. There are plenty of public rooms, bars, and lounges to use for the size of the ship. The fit and finish of the vessel is disappointingly poor, as is the quality of some of the interior decoration.

A cozy, relaxed, and unpretentious ambience is what many passengers want, and get, aboard this ship. The dress code is very relaxed, and formal attire is definitely not required. So, for those seeking a casual cruise experience in unstuffy surroundings should be comfortable aboard this ship, which caters well to first-time passengers.

Transocean Tours has earned itself a well-known and trusted name for delivering a well-balanced cruise product, and the company's on-board managers and staff do an excellent job of making sure passengers have a good cruise experience at very modest rates. The company also provides a number of special "cruise combination" rates, as well as various reductions for children based on ages. All gratuities are included on many cruises. All gratuities to staff are included in the cruise fare.

But: This really is a high-density ship, which means that it is very crowded when full, so expect some lines to form for shore excursions and buffets. Expect a large number of smokers. Has very steep, narrow stairways on the outer decks.

ms Carnival Destiny

☆☆☆☆

(L)

LIFESTYLE	**STANDARD**
Cruise Line:	Carnival Cruise Lines
Former Names:	-
Gross Tonnage:	101,353
Builder:	Fincantieri (Italy)
Original Cost:	$400 million
Entered Service:	November 1996
Flag:	Panama
Tel No:	335655710
Fax No:	335655715
Length (ft./m.):	892.3/272.0
Beam (ft./m.):	116.0/35.3
Draft (ft./m.):	27.0/8.2
Propulsion/Propellers:	diesel-electric (63,400kW)/2 (CP)
Decks:	12
Total Crew:	1,000
Pass. Capacity (basis 2):	2,642
Pass. Capacity (all berths):	3,400
Pass. Space Ratio (basis 2):	38.3
Pass. Space Ratio (all berths):	29.8
Officers:	Italian
Total Cabins:	1,321
Size Range (sq. ft./m.):	180–483/16.7–44.8
Cabins (outside view):	740
Cabins (inside):	519
Cabins (for one person):	0
Cabins (with private balcony):	418
Cabins (wheelchair accessible):	25
Cabin Current:	110 AC
Cabin TV:	Yes
Dining Rooms:	2
Seatings:	2
Elevators:	18
Casino:	Yes
Slot Machines:	Yes
Swimming Pools (outdoors):	3 (+1 with magrodome)
Swimming Pools (inside):	0
Whirlpools:	7
Fitness Center:	Yes
Sauna/Steam Room:	Yes/Yes
Massage:	Yes
Self-Service Launderette:	No
Movie Theater/Seats:	1/1,040 (show lounge)
Library:	Yes
Children's Facilities:	Yes
Classification Society:	Lloyd's Register

RATINGS	**SCORE**
Ship: Hardware/Maintenance	90
Ship: Outdoor Facilities/Space	82
Ship: Interior Facilities/Space/Flow	86
Ship: Decor/Furnishings/Artwork	86
Ship: Spa/Fitness Facilities	86
Cabins: Suites and Deluxe	85
Cabins: Standard Sizes	80
Food: Dining Room/Cuisine	67
Food: Informal Dining/Buffets	64
Food: Quality of Ingredients	62
Food: Afternoon Tea/Bar Snacks	51
Service: Dining Room	72
Service: Bars	71
Service: Cabins	71
Service: Open Decks	68
Cruise: Entertainment	87
Cruise: Activities Program	75
Cruise: Movies/Television Programming	77
Cruise: Hospitality Standard	66
Cruise: Overall Product Delivery	78
OVERALL SCORE	**1,504**

Accommodation: Over half of all cabins are outside (and at 225 sq. ft./21 m² they are the largest in the standard market). They are spread over four decks and have private balconies (with glass rather than steel balustrades, for better, unobstructed ocean views), with balconies extending from the ship's side. The balconies also feature bright fluorescent lighting.

The standard cabins are of good size and come equipped with all the basics, although the furniture is rather square and angular, with no rounded edges. Three decks of cabins (eight on each deck, each with private balcony) overlook the stern (with three days at sea on each of two alternating itineraries, vibration is kept to a minimum).

Eight penthouse suites, each with a large balcony, are quite lavish in their appointments, although, at only 483 sq. ft. (44.8 m²) are small when compared to the best suites in many smaller ships. There are also 40 other suites, each of which features a decent sized bathroom, and a good amount of lounge space.

In those cabins with balconies (more cabins have balconies aboard this ship than those that do not), the partition between each balcony is open at top and bottom, so you can hear noise from neighbors (or smell their cigarette/cigar smoke). Now that we approach a new century, it is disappointing to see three categories of cabins (both outside and inside) with upper and lower bunk beds (lower beds are far more preferable, but this is how the ship accommodates an extra 600 over and above the lower bed capacity).

The cabins feature soft color schemes and more soft furnishings in more attractive fabrics than any other ship in the fleet. Interactive "Fun Vision" technology lets you choose movies on demand (and for a fee). Bathrooms, which have good-sized showers, feature good storage space in the toiletries cabinet. Take your own shampoo, conditioner, hand cream, shower cap, or other personal toiletry items as these are not supplied in the cabins (the line believes that passengers like to take their own).

Dining: The ship's two dining rooms (the Galaxy, forward, with windows on two sides, has 706 seats; the Universe, aft, with windows on three sides, has 1,090 seats); both are nonsmoking. Each spans two decks (a first for any Carnival ship), and incorporate a dozen pyramid-shaped domes and chandeliers, and a soft, mellow peachy color scheme. The Universe dining room features a two-deck-high wall of glass overlooking the stern. There are tables for four, six, and eight (and even a few tables for two that the line tries to keep for honeymooners).

The menus, which have been upgraded somewhat recently, feature a better selection than before, with more choices, and improved quality entree items. Although there is a decent wine list, there are no wine waiters. However, the waiters do sing and dance and there are always the expected waiter parades; the dining room is show business—all done in the name of gratuities at the end of your cruise.

The dining room entrances have comfortable drinking areas for pre-dinner cocktails. There are also many options for casual dining, particularly during the daytime. Two decks high is the Sun and Sea Restaurant, the ship's informal international food court-style eatery, which is adjacent to the aft pool and can be covered by a magrodome glass cover in inclement weather. Included in this eating mall are a trattoria (Italian cuisine, with made-to-order pasta dishes), Happy Valley (Chinese cuisine, with wok preparation), a 24-hour pizzeria, and a patisserie (extra charge for pastries), as well as a grill (for fast foods such as hamburgers and hot dogs).

Other Comments: This is Carnival's 11th brand new ship in the past fifteen success-filled years, and the first ship to be built that is unable to transit the Panama Canal due to her size.

She is a stunning ship, built to impress at every turn, has the most balanced profile of all the ships in the Carnival Cruise Lines fleet, although the bow itself is extremely short. Amidships on the open deck is the longest water slide at sea (200 feet in length), as well as tiered sunbathing decks positioned between two swimming pools and several hot tubs. As aboard all Carnival ships, there is a "topless" sunbathing area set around the funnel base (can't be seen from the pool deck below).

Inside the ship, Joe Farcus, the interior designer who has designed all of the ship interiors for Carnival Cruise Lines, has outdone himself, but tastefully so. The ship is simply superb, and a fantasy land for the senses (though nowhere near as glitzy as some of the Fantasy-class ships). The layout is logical, so finding your way around is a fairly simple matter.

There are three decks full of lounges, 10 bars, and lots of rooms to play in. Like her smaller (though still large) predecessors, this ship features a double-wide indoor promenade, a nine-deck-high glass-domed rotunda atrium lobby, and a huge (15,000 sq. ft./1,393.5 m^2) Nautica Spa. The three-level (nonsmoking) Palladium show lounge is quite stunning, and features a revolving stage, hydraulic orchestra pit, superb sound, and seating on three levels (the upper levels being tiered through two decks) as well as a proscenium over the stage that acts as a scenery loft (there are two large-scaled Vegas-like razzle-dazzle production shows each cruise). For those who like to gamble, the Millionaire's Club Casino is certainly the largest (and noisiest) at sea; there are also more than 320 slot machines.

An additional feature that this ship has which the Fantasy-class ships do not have is the Flagship bar, located in the Rotunda (atrium), which faces forward to the glass-walled elevators. Another new (for Carnival) feature is a sports bar (All Star Bar), with tables that feature (naturally) sports memorabilia.

Children are provided with good facilities, including their own two-level Children's Club (including an outdoor pool), and are well cared for with "Camp Carnival," the line's extensive children's program.

From the viewpoint of safety, passengers will be able to embark directly into the lifeboats from their secured position without having to wait for them to be lowered, thus saving time in the event of a real emergency. Well done.

However, this certainly is a big ship, with lots of people everywhere, and that means some waiting in line, particularly for shore excursions, buffets, embarkation, and disembarkation (although the port of Miami has greatly improved terminal facilities specifically for this ship, with some 90 check-in desks). It also means a very impersonal cruise experience. For such a large ship, there really is not much open deck space per passenger.

Finally, this ship has quickly become one of the ultimate floating Caribbean playgrounds for young, active adults who enjoy constant stimulation and close contact with lots and lots of others—a live board game with every move executed in typically grand, colorful, fun-filled Carnival Cruise Lines style. And what a fine vessel for large incentive groups! Potential passengers of other nationalities should note that this is definitely an all-American experience and product, with all its attendant glitz and jazzy/rock sounds—a real "life on the ocean rave."

But: The terraced pool deck is really cluttered, and there are no cushioned pads for the deck chairs. Getting away from people and noise is difficult.

ms Carnival Triumph
(L)

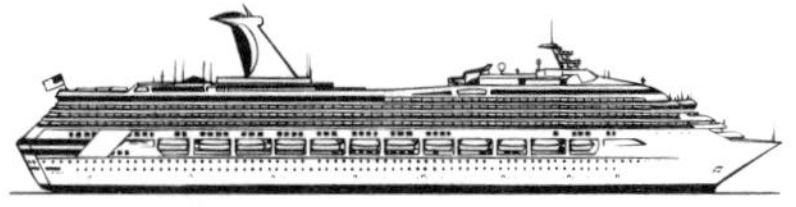

Lifestyle	**Standard**
Cruise Line:	Carnival Cruise Lines
Former Names:	-
Gross Tonnage:	101,353
Builder:	Fincantieri (Italy)
Original Cost:	$415 million
Entered Service:	February 1999
Flag:	Panama
Tel No:	n/a
Fax No:	n/a
Length (ft./m.):	892.3/272.0
Beam (ft./m.):	116.0/35.3
Draft (ft./m.):	27.0/8.2
Propulsion/Propellers:	diesel-electric (63,400kW)/2 (CP)
Decks:	12
Total Crew:	1,000
Pass. Capacity (basis 2):	2,642
Pass. Capacity (all berths):	3,400
Pass. Space Ratio (basis 2):	37.8
Pass. Space Ratio (all berths):	29.4
Officers:	Italian
Total Cabins:	1,321
Size Range (sq. ft./m.):	180–483/16.7–44.8
Cabins (outside view):	740
Cabins (inside):	519
Cabins (for one person):	0
Cabins (with private balcony):	418
Cabins (wheelchair accessible):	25
Cabin Current:	110 AC
Cabin TV:	Yes
Dining Rooms:	2
Seatings:	2
Elevators:	18
Casino:	Yes
Slot Machines:	Yes
Swimming Pools (outdoors):	3 (+1 with magrodome)
Swimming Pools (inside):	0
Whirlpools:	7
Fitness Center:	Yes
Sauna/Steam Room:	Yes/Yes
Massage:	Yes
Self-Service Launderette:	No
Movie Theater/Seats:	Yes/1,040 (show lounge)
Library:	Yes
Children's Facilities:	Yes
Classification Society:	Lloyd's Register

Ratings	**Score**
Ship: Hardware/Maintenance	NYR
Ship: Outdoor Facilities/Space	NYR
Ship: Interior Facilities/Space/Flow	NYR
Ship: Decor/Furnishings/Artwork	NYR
Ship: Spa/Fitness Facilities	NYR
Cabins: Suites and Deluxe	NYR
Cabins: Standard Sizes	NYR
Food: Dining Room/Cuisine	NYR
Food: Informal Dining/Buffets	NYR
Food: Quality of Ingredients	NYR
Food: Afternoon Tea/Bar Snacks	NYR
Service: Dining Room	NYR
Service: Bars	NYR
Service: Cabins	NYR
Service: Open Decks	NYR
Cruise: Entertainment	NYR
Cruise: Activities Program	NYR
Cruise: Movies/Television Programming	NYR
Cruise: Hospitality Standard	NYR
Cruise: Overall Product Delivery	NYR

Expected Score Range:

Similar to Carnival Destiny

For general comments, see *Carnival Destiny* (although the names of public rooms will be different, most other comments apply).

ms Carousel

☆☆☆ +

(L)

Lifestyle	Standard
Cruise Line:	Airtours Sun Cruises
Former Names:	Nordic Prince
Gross Tonnage:	23,200
Builder:	Wartsila (Finland)
Original Cost:	$13.5 million
Entered Service:	July 1971/May 1995
Flag:	Norway
Tel No:	1310547
Fax No:	1310547
Length (ft./m.):	637.5/194.32
Beam (ft./m.):	78.8/24.03
Draft (ft./m.):	21.9/6.70
Propulsion/Propellers:	diesel (13,400kW)/2 (CP)
Decks:	7
Total Crew:	434
Pass. Capacity (basis 2):	1,062
Pass. Capacity (all berths):	1,200
Pass. Space Ratio (basis 2):	21.8
Pass. Space Ratio (all berths):	19.3
Officers:	European
Total Cabins:	531
Size Range (sq. ft./m.):	120–483/11.1–44.8
Cabins (outside view):	345
Cabins (inside):	186
Cabins (for one person):	0
Cabins (with private balcony):	0
Cabins (wheelchair accessible):	0
Cabin Current:	110 AC
Cabin TV:	No
Dining Rooms:	1
Seatings:	2
Elevators:	4
Casino:	Yes
Slot Machines:	Yes
Swimming Pools (outdoors):	1
Swimming Pools (inside):	0
Whirlpools:	0
Fitness Center:	Yes
Sauna/Steam Room:	Yes/No
Massage:	Yes
Self-Service Launderette:	No
Movie Theater/Seats:	No
Library:	No
Children's Facilities:	No
Classification Society:	Det Norske Veritas

Ratings	Score
Ship: Hardware/Maintenance	75
Ship: Outdoor Facilities/Space	68
Ship: Interior Facilities/Space/Flow	67
Ship: Decor/Furnishings/Artwork	66
Ship: Spa/Fitness Facilities	56
Cabins: Suites and Deluxe	66
Cabins: Standard Sizes	57
Food: Dining Room/Cuisine	64
Food: Informal Dining/Buffets	62
Food: Quality of Ingredients	63
Food: Afternoon Tea/Bar Snacks	57
Service: Dining Room	66
Service: Bars	66
Service: Cabins	67
Service: Open Decks	61
Cruise: Entertainment	68
Cruise: Activities Program	64
Cruise: Movies/Television Programming	62
Cruise: Hospitality Standard	80
Cruise: Overall Product Delivery	76
Overall Score	**1,311**

Accommodation: The cabins are provided in just four grades (Standard, Superior, Promenade, and Deluxe) and six types, making it an easy matter to select your accommodation. Most cabins are of a similar size (which is small) and the insulation between them is quite poor. The cabins also have mediocre closets and very little storage space, yet somehow everyone seems to manage (the ship was built originally for Caribbean cruising). The best advice is therefore to take only casual clothing and only the things you really need. Do note that cabin voltage is 110 volts, so you will need to take adapters for electrical appliances such as a hairdryer. Note that cabins are not assigned until you arrive at the ship. The cabin hallways are also quite narrow. Only the owner's suite features a refrigerator.

Dining: The dining room is quite large, but noisy, and tables (for four, six, or eight) are close together. The catering operation is good, however, although all the food seems to taste alike. There is a limited selection of breads, cheeses, and fruits. Attentive, friendly but rather hurried service. The wine list is fairly basic, but the prices are very modest, as are the prices for most alcoholic beverages.

Other Comments: This ship, originally built for and operated by Royal Caribbean International, has a fairly handsome, contemporary look with good lines, a nicely raked bow, and large blue funnel (complete with sunburst logo). This ship was acquired by Airtours Sun Cruises (one of Britain's Big Three tour companies) in 1995. Airtours is now part-owned by Carnival Corporation, who also own Carnival Cruise Lines (and others), and provides an activity-filled cruise product in comfortable, but fairly busy surroundings. The ship underwent a $7-million refit in late 1997. While most of the work was below decks, with the fitting of new, better, more powerful generators, some cosmetic work was completed in her interiors.

There is a good, polished, outdoor wraparound promenade deck (it can be slippery when wet) and wooden railings. The open deck space for sunbathing is very crowded and noisy when the ship is full (which is most of the time), but makes for a good party ambience.

The interior layout and passenger flow is quite good, with clean, bright decor, and some good wooden paneling and trim. The dress code is very casual, good for unstuffy, unpretentious cruising. This is a very affordable cruise, particularly for families with children, and Airtours also features a wide selection of pre- and post-cruise hotel programs.

Airtours is known for packaging its products really well, and this ship represents an excellent buy for families who want to cruise, but on a limited budget. The company flies you to and from the ship in one of its own modern jets, and transfers to/from the ship are included for good measure. The company really does go out of its way to provide a fine "no-nonsense" good value-for-money vacation, as long as your expectations are not too high. This is not the ship if you are looking for a quiet, relaxing vacation. If you have been on a land-based Airtours vacation, you'll know what to expect. The currency is the U.K. pound sterling. Tipping is recommended at £5.00 per day. Insurance is included (but you will be charged for it) unless declined.

But: There are too many repetitious announcements. Blue-coated social staff provide the lively entertainment, but, although they try hard, it is rather amateurish.

ms Celebration

☆☆☆ +

(L)

Lifestyle	Standard
Cruise Line:	Carnival Cruise Lines
Former Names:	-
Gross Tonnage:	47,262
Builder:	Kockums (Sweden)
Original Cost:	$135 million
Entered Service:	March 1987
Flag:	Liberia
Tel No:	1240526
Fax No:	1240526
Length (ft./m.):	732.6/223.30
Beam (ft./m.):	92.5/28.20
Draft (ft./m.):	25.5/7.80
Propulsion/Propellers:	diesel (23,520kW)/2 (CP)
Decks:	10
Total Crew:	670
Pass. Capacity (basis 2):	1,486
Pass. Capacity (all berths):	1,896
Pass. Space Ratio (basis 2):	31.8
Pass. Space Ratio (all berths):	24.9
Officers:	Italian
Total Cabins:	743
Size Range (sq. ft./m.):	185/17.1
Cabins (outside view):	453
Cabins (inside):	290
Cabins (for one person):	0
Cabins (with private balcony):	10
Cabins (wheelchair accessible):	14
Cabin Current:	110 AC
Cabin TV:	Yes
Dining Rooms:	2
Seatings:	2
Elevators:	8
Casino:	Yes
Slot Machines:	Yes
Swimming Pools (outdoors):	3
Swimming Pools (inside):	0
Whirlpools:	2
Fitness Center:	Yes
Sauna/Steam Room:	Yes/No
Massage:	Yes
Self-Service Launderette:	Yes
Movie Theater/Seats:	No
Library:	Yes
Children's Facilities:	Yes
Classification Society:	Lloyd's Register

Ratings	Score
Ship: Hardware/Maintenance	76
Ship: Outdoor Facilities/Space	71
Ship: Interior Facilities/Space/Flow	73
Ship: Decor/Furnishings/Artwork	74
Ship: Spa/Fitness Facilities	61
Cabins: Suites and Deluxe	76
Cabins: Standard Sizes	67
Food: Dining Room/Cuisine	66
Food: Informal Dining/Buffets	62
Food: Quality of Ingredients	61
Food: Afternoon Tea/Bar Snacks	51
Service: Dining Room	71
Service: Bars	71
Service: Cabins	70
Service: Open Decks	63
Cruise: Entertainment	74
Cruise: Activities Program	61
Cruise: Movies/Television Programming	63
Cruise: Hospitality Standard	61
Cruise: Overall Product Delivery	73
Overall Score	**1,345**

Accommodation: The cabins, most of which are identical in terms of layout and decor (which means they are good for large groups who generally like to have identical cabins for their participants), are of quite generous proportions (except for the inside cabins, which are small). Cabins are comfortable and well equipped, although only soap and ice water are supplied in the bathroom (no shampoo, conditioner or shower cap).

The best accommodation can be found in the 10 suites, each of which has its own private balcony, larger bathroom, and more closet, drawer, and storage space.

Dining: The two dining rooms are cramped when full and extremely noisy (both are nonsmoking), with low ceilings in the center (raised) sections. The decor is colorful, to say the least. Do not even think about this ship if you like good food. The meals stress quantity, not quality, and the line does not spend as much on food as some other companies. The buffets are quite disappointing, although there has been an attempt to improve their variety of late. Although there is a wine list, there are no wine waiters (the waiters are expected to serve both food and wine).

Other Comments: The ship's exterior is rather boxy, but typical of the space-conscious designs that were introduced in the early eighties. The swimming pools are smaller than one would expect, but the open deck space is good, provided the ship is not full, when, like most ships, the deck always seems crowded.

Inside, this ship has double-width indoor promenades and a very good selection of public rooms in which to play. The flamboyant interior decor in public rooms is stimulating instead of relaxing, as is the colorful artwork. Features New Orleans-themed decor throughout the public rooms, except for some nautical-themed decor in the Wheelhouse Bar/Grill. Huge, very active, noisy casino. The party atmosphere is good for anyone wanting a stimulating cruise experience. Features a wide range of entertainment and activities.

Carnival Cruise Lines excels at providing plenty of entertainment venues and passenger participation activities to keep you occupied.

This ship should prove a good choice for families with children (there are so many places for them to explore). There are good dazzle and sizzle shows on stage, which are good for the whole family. This ship is good if you are taking your first cruise, providing that you like lots of people, noise, and lively action.

But: There are too many loud announcements. There really is nowhere to go for privacy, peace, and quiet, but then you should choose another ship for that.

ms Century

☆☆☆☆☆

(L)

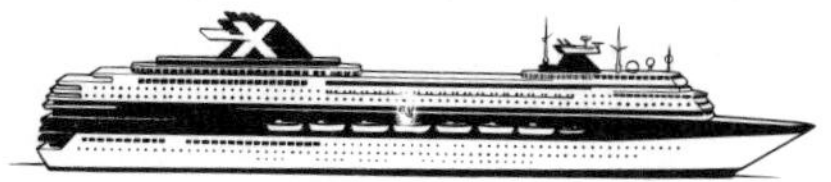

Lifestyle	**Premium**
Cruise Line:	Celebrity Cruises
Former Names:	-
Gross Tonnage:	70,606
Builder:	Meyer Werft (Germany)
Original Cost:	$320 million
Entered Service:	December 1995
Flag:	Liberia
Tel No:	363633911
Fax No:	363633920
Length (ft./m.):	807.1/246.00
Beam (ft./m.):	105.6/32.20
Draft (ft./m.):	24.6/7.50
Propulsion/Propellers:	diesel (29,250kW)/2 (CP)
Decks:	10
Total Crew:	843
Pass. Capacity (basis 2):	1,750
Pass. Capacity (all berths):	2,150
Pass. Space Ratio (basis 2):	40.3
Pass. Space Ratio (all berths):	32.8
Officers:	Greek
Total Cabins:	875
Size Range (sq. ft./m.):	172–1,515/15.7–140.7
Cabins (outside view):	571
Cabins (inside):	304
Cabins (for one person):	0
Cabins (with private balcony):	61
Cabins (wheelchair accessible):	8
Cabin Current:	110/220 AC
Cabin TV:	Yes
Dining Rooms:	2
Seatings:	2
Elevators:	9
Casino:	Yes
Slot Machines:	Yes
Swimming Pools (outdoors):	2
Swimming Pools (inside):	1 hydropool
Whirlpools:	4
Fitness Center:	Yes
Sauna/Steam Room:	Yes
Massage:	Yes
Self-Service Launderette:	No
Movie Theater/Seats:	Yes/190
Library:	Yes
Children's Facilities:	Yes
Classification Society:	Lloyd's Register

Ratings	**Score**
Ship: Hardware/Maintenance	91
Ship: Outdoor Facilities/Space	90
Ship: Interior Facilities/Space/Flow	90
Ship: Decor/Furnishings/Artwork	91
Ship: Spa/Fitness Facilities	88
Cabins: Suites and Deluxe	91
Cabins: Standard Sizes	87
Food: Dining Room/Cuisine	85
Food: Informal Dining/Buffets	82
Food: Quality of Ingredients	86
Food: Afternoon Tea/Bar Snacks	73
Service: Dining Room	85
Service: Bars	80
Service: Cabins	82
Service: Open Decks	77
Cruise: Entertainment	82
Cruise: Activities Program	80
Cruise: Movies/Television Programming	85
Cruise: Hospitality Standard	85
Cruise: Overall Product Delivery	91
Overall Score	**1,701**

Accommodation: The wide variety of cabin types includes 18 family cabins, each with two lower beds, two foldaway beds, and one upper berth. All cabins have interactive television and entertainment systems (you can go shopping, or play casino games, interactively), as well as hairdryers in the bathrooms, and 100 percent cotton towels. However, the standard twenty-four-hour cabin menu is disappointing, and very limited. Sadly, there are no cabins for singles.

All cabins have a personal safe, minibar-refrigerator (extra cost), and hairdryer and are nicely equipped and decorated, with warm wood-finish furniture, and none of the boxy feel of cabins on many ships, due to the angled placement of vanity and audio-video consoles at an angle. In addition, all suites on Deck 10 (and the Sky deck suites) feature butler service and in-cabin dining facilities. Suites that have private balconies also have floor-to-ceiling windows and sliding doors to balconies (a few have outward opening doors).

For the ultimate in accommodation aboard this ship choose one of two beautifully decorated Presidential Suites of 1,173 sq. ft. (109 m²), each, located amidships in the most desirable position (each can be combined with the adjacent mini-suite via an inter-connecting door, to provide a total of 1,515 sq. ft. (140.7 m²) of living space. Each has a marble-floor foyer, a living room with mahogany wood floor and hand-woven rug. Features include a separate dining area with six-seat dining table; butler's pantry with wet bar, wine bar with private label stock, refrigerator and microwave; huge private balcony with dining table for two, chaise lounge chairs with cushioned pads, hot tub and dimmer-controlled lighting; master bedroom dressed with fine fabrics and draperies, Egyptian cotton bed linen, king-sized bed; all-marble bathroom with jet-spray shower and whirlpool bath; walk-in closet with abundant storage space.

Features interactive Sony audio and video facilities for booking shore excursions, ordering room service, and purchasing goods from the ship's boutiques, so you do not have to leave your quarters if you do not wish to, especially if you do not like the ports of call. The interactive system is available in English, French, German, Italian, and Spanish.

All accommodation designated as suites have duvets on the beds instead of sheets/blankets, fresh flowers, use of the AquaSpa without charge, and butler service. Electrically operated blinds and other goodies are standard, with everything controlled from a special unit. The larger suites have three remotes for television/audio equipment (one would be better) and VCR units.

Dining: A grand staircase connects the upper and lower levels of the two-level dining room, each level with its own finishing galley. The design of the two galleys is excellent, and is such that food that should be hot does arrive hot at the table. Three different decorative panels, changed according to theme nights, adorn the huge aft windows. The dining room chairs, which are heavy, should, but do not, have armrests.

There is also a huge indoor/outdoor Lido café, called Islands, with four well-designed serving stations, as well as two grill serving stations located adjacent to the swimming pools. An in-suite dining alternative (for all meals, including full dinners, served course by course) is featured for the 2 Presidential and 48 Century suites. For those that cannot live without them, freshly baked pizzas (boxed) can be delivered, in an insulated pouch, to your cabin.

Celebrity Cruises has established an enviable reputation for fine dining aboard its ships, and this tradition is being continued. Michel Roux designs Celebrity Cruises' menus and exerts tight personal control over their correct cooking and delivery to assure consistency of product. All meals are made from scratch, with nothing pre-cooked or pre-packaged ashore. However, the food served as room-service items is decidedly below the standard of food featured in the dining room.

Other Comments: This ship, which looks externally like a larger version of the company's popular *Horizon/Zenith*, is well balanced despite its squared-off stern and has the distinctive Celebrity Cruises' "X" funnel ("X" being the Greek letter "C" which stands for Chandris, the former owning company). With a high passenger space ratio for such a large ship, there is no real sense of crowding, and passenger flow has been well thought out. A high crew/passenger ratio of 1 to 9 provides excellent passenger service throughout.

The interior decor is quite elegant. Technical and engineering excellence prevail, and there is an overindulgence of fire and safety equipment. Overall, she is a fine vessel for a big-ship cruise vacation. She is a contemporary ship, with fine public rooms, and an array of television and video screens in many of them, all provided by Sony electronics. The medical facilities are excellent.

There is a three-quarter, two-level teakwood promenade deck, and, for joggers, a wraparound jogging track atop the ship. A stunning, two-level, 1,000-seat show lounge/theater with side balconies features a huge stage, a split orchestra pit (hydraulic), and the latest in high-tech lighting and sound equipment.

A three-deck-high main foyer (atrium) is not ostentatious, and its walls are covered with nine large television screens that provide constantly changing scenery. It is not glitzy, but its decor somehow does not closely match the rest of the ship.

There are 4.5 acres of open deck space, together with a stunning array of other public rooms and enhanced passenger facilities. An outstanding AquaSpa (9,340 sq. ft./867.6 m^2), set forward and high, has some of the more unusual wellness treatments anywhere, with huge panoramic windows and the latest high-tech equipment, all set in a Japanese environment, complete with shoji screens and Japanese rock garden.

Wide passageways provide plenty of indoor space for strolling, so there is no feeling of being crowded, and passenger flow is excellent. There is also a small, dedicated movie theater, which doubles as a conference and meeting center with all the latest audio-visual technology that includes three-language simultaneous translation and headsets for the hearing-impaired.

Cigar smokers will love Michael's Club—a cigar and cognac room of superb taste; it is a lovely triangular-shaped room that has become a favorite watering place for those who smoke, with decor reminiscent of a real English gentlemen's club. Features include a cigar humidor, and several sizes of Cuban cigars are hand-rolled each day by a cigar maker. The club has a satellite-linked ATM machine.

Outstanding are the 500 pieces of art that adorn the ship—a $3.8 million art collection that includes many Warhol favorites and some fascinating contemporary sculptures. In fact, the "Century Collection" includes a comprehensive survey of the most important artists and the major developments in art since the 1960s, and embraces Abstract Expressionism, Pop, Conceptualism, Minimalism, and Neo-Expressionism.

Century operates Caribbean and Mediterranean cruises (1999 is the first year that Celebrity Cruises has featured cruises in Europe).

But: The shore excursion operation, embarkation and disembarkation are still the weak links in the Celebrity operation, and the cruise staff unpolished. The room-service menu is poor, and room service food items are decidedly below the standard of food featured in the dining room. The interactive television system is frustrating to use.

ms Clelia II

☆☆☆☆ +

(S)

LIFESTYLE	**PREMIUM**
Cruise Line:	Golden Sea Cruises
Former Names:	*Renaissance Four*
Gross Tonnage:	4,077
Builder:	Cantieri Navale Ferrari (Italy)
Original Cost:	$20 million
Entered Service:	January 1991/March 1998
Flag:	Bahamas
Tel No:	1307526
Fax No:	1307527
Length (ft./m.):	289.0/88.1
Beam (ft./m.):	50.1/15.3
Draft (ft./m.):	13.4/4.1
Propulsion/Propellers:	diesel (3,514kW)/2 (CP)
Decks:	5
Total Crew:	55
Pass. Capacity (basis 2):	84
Pass. Capacity (all berths):	84
Pass. Space Ratio (basis 2):	48.5
Pass. Space Ratio (all berths):	48.5
Officers:	French
Total Cabins:	42
Size Range (sq. ft./m.):	210.0–538.2/19.5–50.0
Cabins (outside view):	42
Cabins (inside):	0
Cabins (for one person):	0
Cabins (with private balcony):	4
Cabins (wheelchair accessible):	0
Cabin Current:	110 AC
Cabin TV:	Yes
Dining Rooms:	1
Seatings:	1
Elevators:	1
Casino:	No
Slot Machines:	No
Swimming Pools (outdoors):	1
Swimming Pools (inside):	0
Whirlpools:	1
Fitness Center:	Yes
Sauna/Steam Room:	No/Yes
Massage:	No
Self-Service Launderette:	No
Movie Theater/Seats:	No
Library:	Yes
Children's Facilities:	No
Classification Society:	Lloyd's Register

RATINGS	**SCORE**
Ship: Hardware/Maintenance	80
Ship: Outdoor Facilities/Space	80
Ship: Interior Facilities/Space/Flow	78
Ship: Decor/Furnishings/Artwork	84
Ship: Spa/Fitness Facilities	77
Cabins: Suites and Deluxe	89
Cabins: Standard Sizes	83
Food: Dining Room/Cuisine	84
Food: Informal Dining/Buffets	81
Food: Quality of Ingredients	83
Food: Afternoon Tea/Bar Snacks	76
Service: Dining Room	86
Service: Bars	86
Service: Cabins	85
Service: Open Decks	82
Cruise: Entertainment	80
Cruise: Activities Program	80
Cruise: Movies/Television Programming	60
Cruise: Hospitality Standard	88
Cruise: Overall Product Delivery	86
OVERALL SCORE	**1,628**

Accommodation: Excellent all-outside cabins (called "suites" in the brochure) combine highly polished imitation rosewood paneling with lots of mirrors and fine, hand-crafted Italian furniture. All suites have twin beds that can convert to a queen-sized bed, a sitting area with three-person sofa, one individual chair, coffee table, minibar-refrigerator (all drinks are at extra cost), color television and VCR unit, and direct-dial satellite telephone. Note that while closet space is quite good, space for stowing luggage is tight, and there is little drawer space (each cabin has three drawers, two of which are lockable, plus several open shelves in a separate closet). Also note that there are no music channels in the cabins, and there is no switch to turn announcements off in your cabin.

The number of cabins was cut from 50 to 42 when the present owners acquired the vessel in 1997; thus providing more space per passenger. Outside each cabin are two brass porthole-shaped lights, which provide a stately, nautical feel to the dark wood-paneled hallways.

The marble bathrooms are compact units that have showers (no bathrooms have a bathtub) with fold-down (plastic) seat, real teakwood floor, marble vanity, large mirror, recessed towel rail (good for storing personal toiletries), and built-in hairdryer. Note: there is a high "lip" into the bathroom.

There are also four VIP "apartments," each consisting of two consecutive adjoining "suites," thus providing a bedroom, large lounge (with red-leather topped office desk), and two bathrooms (his 'n' hers).

There is one Presidential Apartment (owner's suite) with an en-suite office, two full separate bedrooms and living room (each with three windows), two bathrooms, and private, though narrow, balcony.

Dining: The Golden Star Restaurant, which has an open seating policy (it can seat up to 100), is bright, elegant, and welcoming (nonsmoking). It is on the lowest deck and has portholes rather than windows, due to maritime regulations. There are tables for two, four, six, or eight, and you can sit where you like, with whom you like, when you like. Dinners are normally sit-down affairs, although, depending on the itinerary and length of cruise, there could be an occasional buffet. Breakfast and lunch are usually buffets and can be taken at the poolside (weather permitting), in your suite, or in the restaurant.

The cuisine consists of continental dishes complemented by local (regional) delicacies. The food quality, choice, and presentation are all good. While the food is very well presented, the choice of entrees is limited to three for dinner.

Other Comments: This ship, with its royal blue hull and white superstructure, has the look and feel of a contemporary mega-yacht, with handsome styling throughout, although the exterior profile is not particularly handsome. Has two teakwood outdoor wraparound promenade decks. There is a small water sports platform at the stern, and a "Baby Clelia" water jet-propelled shore tender hangs over the stern. The ship also carries jet skis, waterski boat, and sailfish for use when cruising in warm weather areas.

The accommodation is located forward, with public rooms aft. Features pleasing colors and refined and attractive interior decor, with some accent on Greek design. There is a small library, which also houses the video library, a lounge that can accommodate all passengers (good for use as a lecture room), and a piano bar/lounge.

Originally one of a fleet of eight similar-sized ships operated by Renaissance Cruises, this ship was very nicely refurbished for service in early 1998. Greek artists are featured in many pieces of art around the ship, courtesy of the new owners. With her name change (the new name is also the name of the ship's owner), this charming little ship operates Greek Island cruises during most of the year. She is very comfortable and inviting, and is close, but not quite the equal of some of the other small premium ships (but neither is the price). This ship provides a destination-intensive, refined, quiet, relaxed cruise for passengers who do not like crowds, dressing up, scheduled activities, or entertainment.

Presently under charter to New York-based Travel Dynamics for much of the year, and operated by Le Ponant (a small French ship management company), the ship is also available for charter to other operators. The officers and crew are almost all French; all provide a certain "savoire faire" and warmth and are youthful and very creative. No smoking is allowed anywhere inside the ship, only on open decks.

But: The tiny "dip" pool is not a swimming pool. The open deck and sunbathing space is quite limited. The decor consists of plastic woods instead of real woods (it looks almost too perfect in places). There are many slim pillars in the public rooms in odd places. The constant music played throughout the public spaces (including accommodation hallways) is irritating and unnecessary.

ms Clipper Adventurer

☆☆☆

(S)

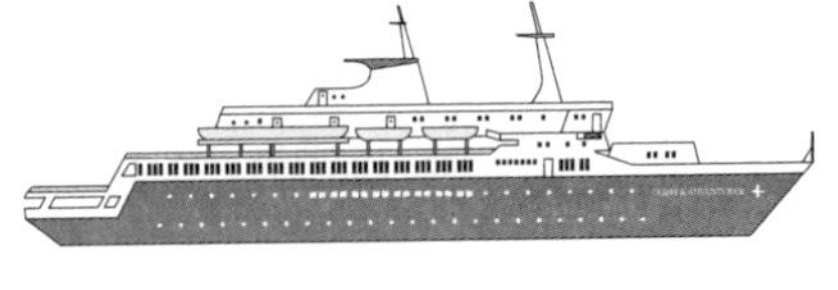

Lifestyle	**Standard**
Cruise Line:	Clipper Cruise line
Former Names:	*Alla Tarasova*
Gross Tonnage:	5,750
Builder:	Brodgradiliste Uljanik (Yugoslavia)
Original Cost:	n/a
Entered Service:	1976/May 1998
Flag:	Bahamas
Tel No:	n/a
Fax No:	n/a
Length (ft./m.):	328.1/100.01
Beam (ft./m.):	53.2/16.24
Draft (ft./m.):	15.2/4.65
Propulsion/Propellers:	diesel (3,884kW)/2 (CP)
Decks:	3
Total Crew:	84
Pass. Capacity (basis 2):	122
Pass. Capacity (all berths):	122
Pass. Space Ratio (basis 2):	47.1
Pass. Space Ratio (all berths):	47.1
Officers:	Scandinavian
Total Cabins:	61
Size Range (sq. ft./m.):	n/a
Cabins (outside view):	61
Cabins (inside):	0
Cabins (for one person):	0
Cabins (with private balcony):	0
Cabins (wheelchair accessible):	0
Cabin Current:	220 AC
Cabin TV:	No
Dining Rooms:	1
Seatings:	1
Elevators:	0
Casino:	No
Slot Machines:	No
Swimming Pools (outdoors):	No
Swimming Pools (inside):	No
Whirlpools:	No
Fitness Center:	No
Sauna/Steam Room:	No/No
Massage:	No
Self-Service Launderette:	No
Movie Theater/Seats:	No
Library:	Yes
Children's Facilities:	No
Classification Society:	RS

Ratings	**Score**
Ship: Hardware/Maintenance	73
Ship: Outdoor Facilities/Space	53
Ship: Interior Facilities/Space/Flow	51
Ship: Decor/Furnishings/Artwork	75
Ship: Spa/Fitness Facilities	40
Cabins: Suites and Deluxe	63
Cabins: Standard Sizes	57
Food: Dining Room/Cuisine	72
Food: Informal Dining/Buffets	60
Food: Quality of Ingredients	61
Food: Afternoon Tea/Bar Snacks	54
Service: Dining Room	67
Service: Bars	63
Service: Cabins	64
Service: Open Decks	48
Cruise: Entertainment	40
Cruise: Activities Program	44
Cruise: Movies/Television Programming	50
Cruise: Hospitality Standard	67
Cruise: Overall Product Delivery	73
Overall Score	**1,175**

Accommodation: All of the cabins (there are seven grades, including a dedicated price for single cabin occupancy) have outside views and have twin lower beds, with private bathroom with shower, and toilet. The bathrooms are really tiny (of the "me first, you next" variety), however, although they are tiled, and come with all the basics. Several of the double-occupancy cabins can be booked at special rates by passengers traveling alone.

All cabins feature a private lockable drawer for valuables, telephone, and individual temperature control. Some cabins have picture windows, while others have portholes. Two larger cabins (called suites in the brochure, which they really are not) are quite well equipped for the size of the vessel.

Dining: Pleasant, though with somewhat dark decor, the dining room seats all passengers at a single seating. The food consists of a combination of American and Continental cuisine, prepared freshly by chefs trained at some of America's finest culinary institutions. There are limited menu choices, but the food is wholesome, and quite simply, but attractively presented. Dining room service is provided by young American waitresses whose bubbly enthusiasm makes up for the lack of training in service finesse.

Other Comments: This ship has an ice-strengthened (classified A-1 ice class), royal blue hull complete with bow-thruster and stabilizers. Although the ship is not new, she went through a $6-million refit/conversion in the winter of 1997–1998, and meets the latest international safety codes and requirements. She specializes in operating close-in expedition-style cruising. She carries ten Zodiac rubber inflatable landing craft for in-depth excursions and wet landings, and has a covered promenade deck of Oregon pine.

She is a tidy, neat, and clean ship throughout, with attractive, warm decor, lots of polished dark wood paneling and numerous real brass fixtures (like a "real" ship). She is quite cozy and caters to travelers rather than mere passengers.

The public spaces, however, are limited, with just one main lounge and bar. There is a small library but it is poor and needs a more contemporary selection of books. There is no forward observation lounge, although there is an outdoor observation area directly below the bridge. The dress code is casual and on all cruises, Clipper Cruise Line provides its own cruise staff and experienced historians and naturalist lecturers.

She is now quite a smart looking vessel, and features cruises to unusual destinations not frequented by the flood of larger vessels. A no-smoking policy throughout all interior areas is in effect, although smoking is permitted on the outside decks. Travel insurance is included in the cruise fare.

<u>But:</u> The passageways are quite narrow (it is difficult to pass housekeeping carts), and the stairs are steep on the outer decks.

mys Club Med II

☆☆☆☆

(S)

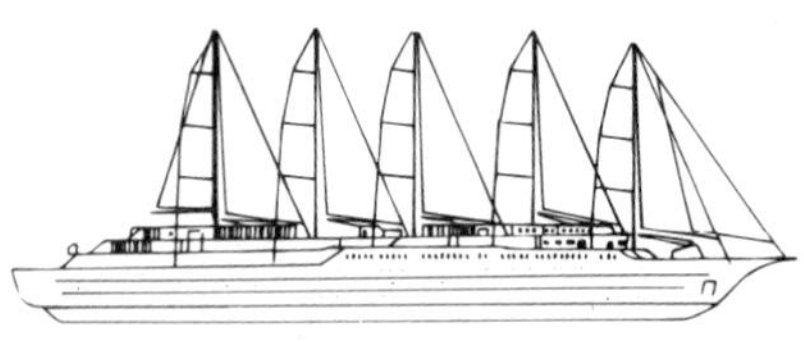

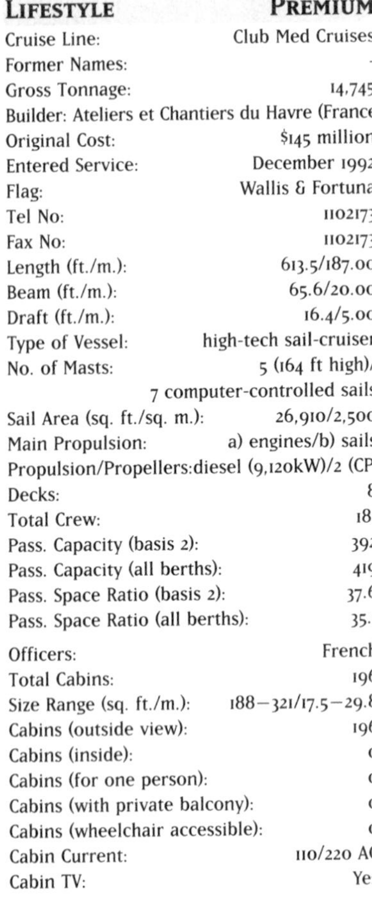

Lifestyle	Premium
Cruise Line:	Club Med Cruises
Former Names:	-
Gross Tonnage:	14,745
Builder: Ateliers et Chantiers du Havre (France)	
Original Cost:	$145 million
Entered Service:	December 1992
Flag:	Wallis & Fortuna
Tel No:	1102173
Fax No:	1102173
Length (ft./m.):	613.5/187.00
Beam (ft./m.):	65.6/20.00
Draft (ft./m.):	16.4/5.00
Type of Vessel:	high-tech sail-cruiser
No. of Masts:	5 (164 ft high)/ 7 computer-controlled sails
Sail Area (sq. ft./sq. m.):	26,910/2,500
Main Propulsion:	a) engines/b) sails
Propulsion/Propellers:	diesel (9,120kW)/2 (CP)
Decks:	8
Total Crew:	181
Pass. Capacity (basis 2):	392
Pass. Capacity (all berths):	419
Pass. Space Ratio (basis 2):	37.6
Pass. Space Ratio (all berths):	35.1
Officers:	French
Total Cabins:	196
Size Range (sq. ft./m.):	188–321/17.5–29.8
Cabins (outside view):	196
Cabins (inside):	0
Cabins (for one person):	0
Cabins (with private balcony):	0
Cabins (wheelchair accessible):	0
Cabin Current:	110/220 AC
Cabin TV:	Yes

Dining Rooms:	2 (open seating)
Elevators:	2
Casino:	Yes
Slot Machines:	Yes
Swimming Pools (outdoors):	2
Whirlpools:	0
Fitness Center:	No
Sauna/Steam Room:	Yes/No
Massage:	Yes
Self-Service Launderette:	No
Library:	Yes
Classification Society:	Bureau Veritas

Ratings	Score
Ship: Hardware/Maintenance	86
Ship: Sails and Equipment	86
Ship: Interior Facilities/Space/Flow	82
Ship: Decor/Furnishings/Artwork	84
Ship: Spa/Fitness Facilities	74
Cabins: Suites and Deluxe	83
Cabins: Standard Sizes	81
Food: Dining Room/Cuisine	78
Food: Informal Dining/Buffets	67
Food: Quality of Ingredients	75
Food: Afternoon Tea/Bar Snacks	73
Service: Dining Room	75
Service: Bars	73
Service: Cabins	73
Service: Open Decks	71
Cruise: The Sailing Experience	82
Cruise: Lecturers/Entertainment	76
Cruise: Movies/Television Programming	76
Cruise: Hospitality Standard	74
Cruise: Overall Product Delivery	79
Overall Score	**1,548**

Accommodation: The cabins are very nicely equipped, have an inviting decor, and feature a mini-bar-refrigerator, 24-hour room service (but you pay for food), personal safe, television, plenty of storage space, bathrobes, and hairdryers. There are six 4-person cabins, and some 35 doubles are fitted with an extra pullman berth—good for young families, although this makes them a little more cramped when occupied.

Dining: There are two lovely dining rooms, each of which has tables for one, two, or more. Open seating is featured for all meals, so you can sit with whom you wish. The Odyssey Restaurant has a delightful open terrace for informal meals. Complimentary wines and beers are available with lunch and dinner. Afternoon tea is a delight. The cuisine itself provides French, continental, and Japanese specialties, and the presentation is good.

Other Comments: She is one of a pair of the world's largest sail-cruisers. Her sister ship, formerly *Club Med I* (now *Wind Surf*), is operated by Windstar Cruises. This vessel is part cruise ship, part yacht, and is rather like a larger version of the earlier Windstar vessels. Five huge masts provide seven computer-controlled sails with a total area of 2,500 m^2.

There are extensive water sports facilities and an aft marina platform. Water sports equipment includes 12 windsurfers, 3 sailboats, 2 water-ski boats, 20 single scuba tanks, snorkels, and 4 motorized watersport boats.

Inside the ship, other facilities include a computer workshop and a golf simulator (for which there is an extra charge) instead of a fitness center. Your cruise can also be combined with a Club Med Village Vacation.

Activities come under the direction of a large team of young, energetic GOs (Gentile Ordinaires), who, like their compatriots on land, have the full run of the ship. Entertainment is rather clown-like and very amateurish, although everyone seems to have fun.

This vessel is excellent for the more upscale active singles and couples who might like casual elegance rather than the wilder vacation experience one might find at some Club Med resorts. No gratuities are expected or accepted, as at all Club Med resorts.

Note: This ship is expected to join her sister ship in 1999 and will probably be renamed and operated by Windstar Cruises.

ms Columbus

☆☆☆☆

(S)

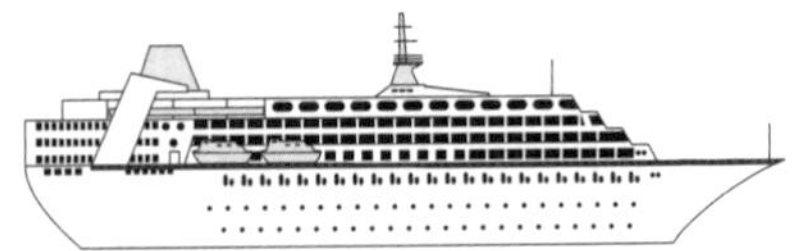

Lifestyle	Standard
Cruise Line:	Hapag-Lloyd Tours
Former Names:	-
Gross Tonnage:	14,903
Builder:	MTW Schiffswerft (Germany)
Original Cost:	$69 million
Entered Service:	July 1997
Flag:	Bahamas
Tel No:	330990810/630990810
Fax No:	330990812/330990815
Length (ft./m.):	472.8/144.13
Beam (ft./m.):	70.5/21.50
Draft (ft./m.):	16.8/5.15
Propulsion/Propellers:	diesel (10,560kW)/2 (CP)
Decks:	8
Total Crew:	170
Pass. Capacity (basis 2):	410
Pass. Capacity (all berths):	423
Pass. Space Ratio (basis 2):	36.3
Pass. Space Ratio (all berths):	35.2
Officers:	German
Total Cabins:	205
Size Range (sq. ft./m.):	129.1–322.9/12.0–30.0
Cabins (outside view):	158
Cabins (inside):	47
Cabins (for one person):	0
Cabins (with private balcony):	0
Cabins (wheelchair accessible):	0
Cabin Current:	110 AC
Cabin TV:	Yes
Dining Rooms:	1
Seatings:	2
Elevators:	3
Casino:	No
Slot Machines:	No
Swimming Pools (outdoors):	1
Swimming Pools (inside):	0
Whirlpools:	0
Fitness Center:	Yes
Sauna/Steam Room:	Yes/Yes
Massage:	Yes
Self-Service Launderette:	No
Movie Theater/Seats:	No
Library:	Yes
Children's Facilities:	No
Classification Society:	Germanischer Lloyd

Ratings	Score
Ship: Hardware/Maintenance	86
Ship: Outdoor Facilities/Space	74
Ship: Interior Facilities/Space/Flow	76
Ship: Decor/Furnishings/Artwork	81
Ship: Spa/Fitness Facilities	61
Cabins: Suites and Deluxe	79
Cabins: Standard Sizes	71
Food: Dining Room/Cuisine	73
Food: Informal Dining/Buffets	66
Food: Quality of Ingredients	72
Food: Afternoon Tea/Bar Snacks	65
Service: Dining Room	75
Service: Bars	76
Service: Cabins	78
Service: Open Decks	66
Cruise: Entertainment	64
Cruise: Activities Program	61
Cruise: Movies/Television Programming	72
Cruise: Hospitality Standard	73
Cruise: Overall Product Delivery	78
Overall Score	**1,447**

Accommodation: The standard cabins are quite small, and many of them are inside. All but 10 cabins feature lower berths, but the 16 categories established are really too many for such a small ship. Sadly, there are no balcony cabins. The decor is bright and upbeat, and the fully tiled bathrooms have showers (none have bathtubs).

There are eight suites (each is at least double the size of a standard cabin), and each has a curtained partition between the lounge and sleeping areas, with a wall unit that houses a television that can be turned 360 degrees for viewing from either the lounge or the bedroom.

Dining: There is one main dining room located at the stern, with large ocean-view windows on three sides. There are tables for four, six, or eight (there are no tables for two). There is even a table for 16—good for family reunions. The cuisine is moderate, and the menu selection is quite limited (there is generally a choice of two entrees for dinner).

Other Comments: This ship has a smart, contemporary profile, with twin funnels placed aft. Under long-term charter to Hapag-Lloyd Seetouristik from owner Conti Reederei, this ship will provide a good cruise experience, but the level of "luxury" is well below that of Hapag-Lloyd's *Europa*.

The ship also features an ice-hardened hull (Class E2), useful for cold-weather cruise areas. In addition, the bridge "wings" also fold inward (as do the overhang lights) so that the vessel can enter the locks in the U.S. Great Lakes region.

Has a good passenger space ratio. There is a good range of public rooms to choose from, all located in a "cake-layer" vertical stacking aft of the accommodation, but the ceilings in the public rooms are plain and unimaginative.

She is a brand new ship for the more standard market German-speaking traveler, and, as such, she offers good value for the money. First-time cruise passengers in particular will find this a handsome ship in which to take a cruise vacation. Of particular note are the Great Lakes cruises (the last oceangoing cruise vessel to operate Great Lakes cruises was *World Discoverer* in 1974), which was only possible because of the ship's pencil-slim design.

But: The swimming pool is small, more like a "dip" pool. The cabins are very small. Sadly, there is no wraparound outdoor promenade deck, and outdoor space is very limited.

mv CostaAllegra

☆☆☆

(M)

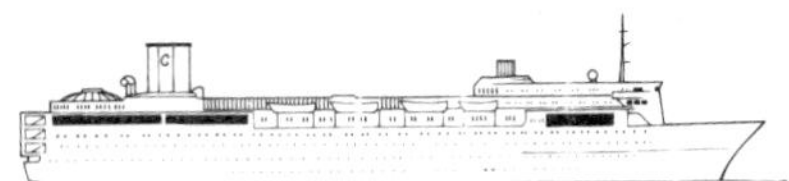

Lifestyle	**Standard**
Cruise Line:	Costa Cruises
Former Names:	*Annie Johnson*
Gross Tonnage:	28,430
Builder:	Mariotti Shipyards (Italy)
Original Cost:	$175 million
Entered Service:	December 1992
Flag:	Liberia
Tel No:	1252216
Fax No:	1252217
Length (ft./m.):	616.7/187.94
Beam (ft./m.):	84.6/25.75
Draft (ft./m.):	27.1/8.22
Propulsion/Propellers:	diesel (19,200kW)/2 (CP)
Decks:	8
Total Crew:	405
Pass. Capacity (basis 2):	810
Pass. Capacity (all berths):	1,066
Pass. Space Ratio (basis 2):	35.1
Pass. Space Ratio (all berths):	26.6
Officers:	Italian
Total Cabins:	405
Size Range (sq. ft./m.):	105–266/9.8–24.7
Cabins (outside view):	218
Cabins (inside):	187
Cabins (for one person):	0
Cabins (with private balcony):	10
Cabins (wheelchair accessible):	8 (inside)
Cabin Current:	110 AC
Cabin TV:	Yes
Dining Rooms:	1
Seatings:	2
Elevators:	4
Casino:	Yes
Slot Machines:	Yes
Swimming Pools (outdoors):	1
Swimming Pools (inside):	0
Whirlpools:	3
Fitness Center:	Yes
Sauna/Steam Room:	Yes/Yes
Massage:	No
Self-Service Launderette:	No
Movie Theater/Seats:	Yes/370
Library:	Yes
Children's Facilities:	Yes
Classification Society:	RINA

Ratings	**Score**
Ship: Hardware/Maintenance	63
Ship: Outdoor Facilities/Space	61
Ship: Interior Facilities/Space/Flow	62
Ship: Decor/Furnishings/Artwork	64
Ship: Spa/Fitness Facilities	61
Cabins: Suites and Deluxe	66
Cabins: Standard Sizes	64
Food: Dining Room/Cuisine	62
Food: Informal Dining/Buffets	58
Food: Quality of Ingredients	63
Food: Afternoon Tea/Bar Snacks	48
Service: Dining Room	63
Service: Bars	64
Service: Cabins	65
Service: Open Decks	57
Cruise: Entertainment	62
Cruise: Activities Program	57
Cruise: Movies/Television Programming	58
Cruise: Hospitality Standard	61
Cruise: Overall Product Delivery	64
Overall Score	**1,223**

Accommodation: The standard cabins are light and airy, with splashes of fabric colors. However, they are small, and there is little closet and drawer space, so take only casual clothing. The bathrooms are compact, although they do feature good shower stalls. There are, however, many small inside cabins, and all cabins suffer from poor soundproofing. The cabin service menu is poor.

On Rousseau Deck there are three forward-facing suites, each of which features a living room, dinette, and wet bar. Another 10 slightly smaller mini-suites feature a small balcony, but it is really not very private, as it can be seen from the walking track on the deck above.

Dining: The dining room is quite spacious and has large glass window views to the stern, while the port side and starboard side feature large portholes. It is a very noisy room, and has tables for four, six, or eight (there are no tables for two). Dinner is later when the ship operates in Europe. The cuisine is mostly continental, with many Italian dishes featured, and the service from a bubbly staff is generally excellent. Good, fresh pasta dishes are served daily. The wine list is modest, but there are no wine waiters; instead, the waiters serve the wine (when they have time).

As far as breakfast and lunch buffets are concerned, Costa Cruises comes way down the list; they are rather plain, repetitive, and unimaginative, and fruit and cheese selections are poor. For ice-cream lovers, a gelati cart provides welcome relief at least once each day.

Other Comments: This is a jazzy, rather angular-looking ship with a low-slung appearance, complemented by three bolt upright yellow funnels that take a little getting used to. Slightly longer and larger than her sister ship *CostaMarina,* this ship enjoys better quality interior fit and finish.

Has a high glass-to-steel ratio, with numerous glass domes and walls admitting light. Good outdoor deck and sunbathing space, although there is no forward observation lounge. Cushioned pads are provided for outdoor lounge chairs. Interesting glass-enclosed stern.

The decks are named after famous Italian painters. This ship features surprisingly fine interior decor, with restful colors and soft furnishings, as well as nice domed ceilings. In the Folies Bergeres show lounge, some 14 pillars obstruct the sight lines to the semicircular stage from many seats.

This ship will provide a decent first cruise experience for young adults who enjoy European service and a real upbeat, almost elegant atmosphere with a loud Italian accent, although not many of the officers and crew are actually Italian, as one would expect.

But: There are few public restrooms. The children's room is too small, and the ship is simply not equipped to handle large numbers of children, which are aboard in the summer and at peak holiday periods. There are simply far too many loud announcements, in several languages. Tipping envelopes state the amount you are expected to give.

mv CostaClassica

☆☆☆ +

(L)

Lifestyle	**Standard**
Cruise Line:	Costa Cruises
Former Names:	-
Gross Tonnage:	52,950
Builder:	Fincantieri (Italy)
Original Cost:	$325 million
Entered Service:	January 1992
Flag:	Liberia
Tel No:	1252243
Fax No:	1252244
Length (ft./m.):	718.5/220.61
Beam (ft./m.):	98.4/30.8
Draft (ft./m.):	25.0/7.60
Propulsion/Propellers:	diesel (22,800kW)/2 (CP)
Decks:	10
Total Crew:	590
Pass. Capacity (basis 2):	1,308
Pass. Capacity (all berths):	1,766
Pass. Space Ratio (basis 2):	40.4
Pass. Space Ratio (all berths):	29.9
Officers:	Italian
Total Cabins:	654
Size Range (sq. ft./m.):	185–430/17.2–40.0
Cabins (outside view):	438
Cabins (inside):	216
Cabins (for one person):	0
Cabins (with private balcony):	10
Cabins (wheelchair accessible):	6 (inside)
Cabin Current:	110 AC
Cabin TV:	Yes
Dining Rooms:	1
Seatings:	2
Elevators:	8
Casino:	Yes
Slot Machines:	Yes
Swimming Pools (outdoors):	2
Swimming Pools (inside):	0
Whirlpools:	4
Fitness Center:	Yes
Sauna/Steam Room:	Yes/Yes
Massage:	Yes
Self-Service Launderette:	No
Movie Theater/Seats:	Yes/577
Library:	Yes
Children's Facilities:	Yes
Classification Society:	RINA

Ratings	**Score**
Ship: Hardware/Maintenance	77
Ship: Outdoor Facilities/Space	75
Ship: Interior Facilities/Space/Flow	80
Ship: Decor/Furnishings/Artwork	80
Ship: Spa/Fitness Facilities	76
Cabins: Suites and Deluxe	81
Cabins: Standard Sizes	73
Food: Dining Room/Cuisine	63
Food: Informal Dining/Buffets	58
Food: Quality of Ingredients	64
Food: Afternoon Tea/Bar Snacks	48
Service: Dining Room	72
Service: Bars	72
Service: Cabins	74
Service: Open Decks	64
Cruise: Entertainment	64
Cruise: Activities Program	60
Cruise: Movies/Television Programming	60
Cruise: Hospitality Standard	70
Cruise: Overall Product Delivery	72
Overall Score	**1,383**

Accommodation: The cabins are of quite a generous size. They have cherry wood veneered cabinetry and include a vanity desk unit with a large mirror. There are useful sliding doors to bathroom and closets, and good soundproofing. The soft furnishings are of good quality, but the room service menu is quite disappointing. The suites feature more space (although they are not large), and hand-woven bedspreads.

Dining: The dining room has a lovely indented clean white ceiling, but is extremely noisy. Has a good number of tables for two. Changeable wall panels help create a European Renaissance atmosphere, albeit at the expense of blocking off windows. Dinner on European cruises is late. Reasonable continental cuisine, with many Italian (salty) dishes, but presentation, quality, and service are poor and quite basic. There is a wine list, but there are no wine waiters.

The outdoors Alfresco Café is quite good. Unfortunately, breakfast and luncheon buffets are quite poor and unimaginative, with little variety, and long lines are typical. The selection of bread, rolls, fruits, and cheeses is disappointing.

Other Comments: This all-white ship has a slab-sided profile, which is topped by Costa Cruises' unmistakable trio of tall yellow funnels. This ship has brought Costa into the mainstream, Italian-style.

Inside, she features contemporary, innovative Italian design and styling that is best described as befitting European tastes. There is an excellent range of public rooms, lounges, and bars from which to choose. A number of specially designed good business and meeting facilities can be found; the rooms provide multiflexible configurations.

Has some fascinating artwork, including six hermaphrodite statues in one lounge. There is a fine, if unconventional multitiered amphitheater-style showroom, but the seats are bolt upright and downright uncomfortable for more than a few minutes. The multilevel atrium is stark and angular, and quite cold.

The marble-covered staircases look pleasant, but are uncarpeted and really do not work well aboard a cruise ship, and are institutional (not to mention just a little dangerous if water or drinks are spilled on them when the ship is moving).

Perhaps the interior is best described as an innovative design project that almost works. A forward observation lounge/night club sits atop ship like a lump of cheese, and, unfortunately, fails to work well as a night club.

The staff is quite friendly, and, although "spit and polish" of fine service is definitely missing, they will help you to have an enjoyable cruise (especially when pushing for gratuities). Sadly, the dress code has become quite casual throughout, even on formal nights. Most passengers will be Italian, with a generous sprinkling of other European nationalities. One night is reserved for Roman Bacchanal, which means that passengers dress up toga-style.

<u>But:</u> There is no wraparound outdoor promenade deck. There are too many loud, repetitious, and irritating announcements. Shore excursions are very expensive. Tipping envelopes provided in your cabin state the amount you are expected to give.

mv CostaMarina

☆☆☆

(M)

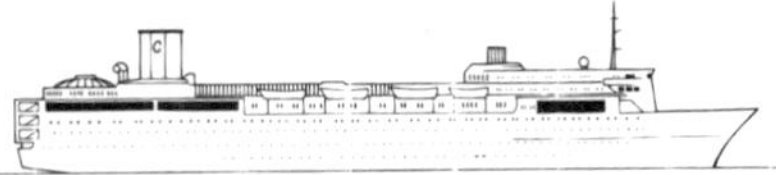

Lifestyle	Standard
Cruise Line:	Costa Cruises
Former Names:	*Axel Johnson*
Gross Tonnage:	25,441
Builder:	Marriotti Shipyards (Italy)
Original Cost:	$130 million
Entered Service:	July 1990
Flag:	Liberia
Tel No:	1252245
Fax No:	1252246
Length (ft./m.):	571.8/174.25
Beam (ft./m.):	84.6/25.75
Draft (ft./m.):	26.1/8.20
Propulsion/Propellers:	diesel (19,152kW)/2 (CP)
Decks:	8
Total Crew:	390
Pass. Capacity (basis 2):	772
Pass. Capacity (all berths):	1,025
Pass. Space Ratio (basis 2):	31.8
Pass. Space Ratio (all berths):	24.0
Officers:	Italian
Total Cabins:	386
Size Range (sq. ft./m.):	104–258/9.7–24.6
Cabins (outside view):	183
Cabins (inside):	203
Cabins (for one person):	14
Cabins (with private balcony):	0
Cabins (wheelchair accessible):	8 (inside)
Cabin Current:	110 AC
Cabin TV:	Yes
Dining Rooms:	1
Seatings:	2
Elevators:	4
Casino:	Yes
Slot Machines:	Yes
Swimming Pools (outdoors):	1
Swimming Pools (inside):	0
Whirlpools:	3
Fitness Center:	Yes
Sauna/Steam Room:	Yes/Yes
Massage:	Yes
Self-Service Launderette:	No
Movie Theater/Seats:	Yes/442
Library:	Yes
Children's Facilities:	Yes
Classification Society:	RINA

Ratings	Score
Ship: Hardware/Maintenance	63
Ship: Outdoor Facilities/Space	61
Ship: Interior Facilities/Space/Flow	62
Ship: Decor/Furnishings/Artwork	63
Ship: Spa/Fitness Facilities	61
Cabins: Suites and Deluxe	66
Cabins: Standard Sizes	64
Food: Dining Room/Cuisine	63
Food: Informal Dining/Buffets	58
Food: Quality of Ingredients	62
Food: Afternoon Tea/Bar Snacks	48
Service: Dining Room	63
Service: Bars	64
Service: Cabins	65
Service: Open Decks	57
Cruise: Entertainment	62
Cruise: Activities Program	57
Cruise: Movies/Television Programming	58
Cruise: Hospitality Standard	61
Cruise: Overall Product Delivery	64
Overall Score	**1,222**

Accommodation: Both outside and inside cabins are quite comfortable, yet with very plain, almost clinical, decor and no warmth. In other words, they really are quite basic units. Bathrooms are functional, but there is little space for personal toiletry items. The illuminated cabin numbers outside each cabin are quite novel. The room service menu is very poor.

Dining: The dining room, which is located at the stern, has excellent ocean views on three sides, is reasonably spacious, and is reached by escalator. The awful lime green color, however, is less than attractive; in fact it is rather institutional. There are only two tables for two. The table candlelights are of poor quality. The ship serves good commercial pasta and features mainly continental cuisine. The service is adequate, but there are few Italians in the dining room, as one might expect.

Other Comments: She is an interesting, though very angular-looking, mid-sized ship, the first of two such ships (her almost identically designed, though slightly longer sister ship is

CostaAllegra). There is a high glass-to-steel ratio, with numerous glass domes and walls. Has a cutaway stern that is virtually replaced by a glass wall (which are in fact the dining room windows), and a stark upright cluster of three yellow funnels.

There is generally good passenger flow throughout her public room spaces. Most public rooms are located above the accommodation decks and feature several bars and lounges useful for social meetings. This very Italian ship will provide a good first cruise experience for young adults, although it is much better suited to European passengers.

But: The fit and finish of this vessel is below the standard of competing ships in the same price category. There is a very limited amount of open deck and sunbathing space. There is no forward observation lounge. Has a tiny swimming pool. There are simply too many cabins (inside). There are poor sight lines in the showroom, with too many pillars (14 of them). The library is really poor. Tipping envelopes provided in your cabin state the amount you are expected to give.

ss CostaRiviera

☆☆☆

(M)

LIFESTYLE	STANDARD
Cruise Line:	Costa Cruises
Former Names:	*American Adventure/ CostaRiviera/Guglielmo Marconi*
Gross Tonnage:	31,500
Builder:	Cantieri Riuniti dell' Adriatico (Italy)
Original Cost:	$33.7 million (reconstruction)
Entered Service:	November 1963/May 1995
Flag:	Liberia
Tel No:	1252212/1252214
Fax No:	1252215
Length (ft./m.):	700.9/213.65
Beam (ft./m.):	94.1/28.71
Draft (ft./m.):	28.3/8.65
Propulsion/Propellers:	steam turbine (32,800kW)/2 (FP)
Decks:	8
Total Crew:	654
Pass. Capacity (basis 2):	924
Pass. Capacity (all berths):	1,500
Pass. Space Ratio (basis 2):	34.0
Pass. Space Ratio (all berths):	21.0
Officers:	Italian
Total Cabins:	462
Size Range (sq. ft./m.):	150–210/14.0–19.5
Cabins (outside view):	286
Cabins (inside):	176
Cabins (for one person):	0
Cabins (with private balcony):	0
Cabins (wheelchair accessible):	0
Cabin Current:	110/220 AC
Cabin TV:	No
Dining Rooms:	1
Seatings:	2
Elevators:	7
Casino:	Yes
Slot Machines:	Yes
Swimming Pools (outdoors):	3
Swimming Pools (inside):	0
Whirlpools:	3
Fitness Center:	Yes
Sauna/Steam Room:	Yes/No
Massage:	Yes
Self-Service Launderette:	Yes
Movie Theater/Seats:	Yes/186
Library:	Yes
Children's Facilities:	No
Classification Society:	RINA

RATINGS	SCORE
Ship: Hardware/Maintenance	60
Ship: Outdoor Facilities/Space	62
Ship: Interior Facilities/Space/Flow	69
Ship: Decor/Furnishings/Artwork	64
Ship: Spa/Fitness Facilities	46
Cabins: Suites and Deluxe	61
Cabins: Standard Sizes	54
Food: Dining Room/Cuisine	62
Food: Informal Dining/Buffets	58
Food: Quality of Ingredients	62
Food: Afternoon Tea/Bar Snacks	48
Service: Dining Room	65
Service: Bars	63
Service: Cabins	64
Service: Open Decks	63
Cruise: Entertainment	60
Cruise: Activities Program	53
Cruise: Movies/Television Programming	52
Cruise: Hospitality Standard	56
Cruise: Overall Product Delivery	61
OVERALL SCORE	**1,183**

Accommodation: There is a wide variety of cabin sizes, styles, and configurations from which to choose. Many cabins are large enough for families of five or six, while many others will accommodate three or four persons. The cabin insulation is not good, however, and the bathrooms are small compact units, with little space to place or store personal toiletry items.

Dining: The dining room, which has portholes, is large and bubbly (noisy), although it is quite plain and unattractive, especially the ceiling. Reasonable continental food is provided; this includes plenty of pasta, pizza, and buffets. Good service with a smile from an international staff (you won't find many Italians in this dining room), although it is not for those who like a quiet dining experience.

Other Comments: This reconstructed former three-class ocean liner was completely refurbished in 1993 in theme-park style for families, then refurbished again in 1994 for Italian family cruising.

She is a solidly built ship that is stable at sea and rides well, due to her deep draft. Built-up fore and aft decks provide a good amount of open deck and sunbathing space.

The interior decor and styling, colors, appointments, and everything else are geared principally to families. There is a good array of public rooms, although what is missing is a forward observation lounge. Has a very casual, bubbly ambience and relaxed dress code.

This ship will provide a cruise vacation in relatively comfortable, family-filled surroundings for a modest price, with activities designed for participation. Think of her as a colorful, activity-filled ship, particularly catering to an Italian family clientele.

But: Do expect lines for embarkation, disembarkation, buffets, and shore excursions. There are too many announcements. Everywhere there is noise, and a lot of cigarette smoke. Tipping envelopes provided in your cabin state the amount you are expected to give.

mv CostaRomantica

☆☆☆ +

(L)

Lifestyle	**Standard**
Cruise Line:	Costa Cruises
Former Names:	-
Gross Tonnage:	53,049
Builder:	Fincantieri (Italy)
Original Cost:	$325 million
Entered Service:	November 1993
Flag:	Liberia
Tel No:	1252227/1252232
Fax No:	1252231
Length (ft./m.):	718.5/220.61
Beam (ft./m.):	98.4/30.89
Draft (ft./m.):	25.0/7.60
Propulsion/Propellers:	diesel (22,800kW)/2 (CP)
Decks:	10
Total Crew:	600
Pass. Capacity (basis 2):	1,356
Pass. Capacity (all berths):	1,782
Pass. Space Ratio (basis 2):	39.1
Pass. Space Ratio (all berths):	29.7
Officers:	Italian
Total Cabins:	678
Size Range (sq. ft./m.):	185–430/17.2–40.0
Cabins (outside view):	462
Cabins (inside):	216
Cabins (for one person):	0
Cabins (with private balcony):	10
Cabins (wheelchair accessible):	6 (inside)
Cabin Current:	110 AC
Cabin TV:	Yes
Dining Rooms:	1
Seatings:	2
Elevators:	8
Casino:	Yes
Slot Machines:	Yes
Swimming Pools (outdoors):	2
Swimming Pools (inside):	0
Whirlpools:	4
Fitness Center:	Yes
Sauna/Steam Room:	Yes/No
Massage:	Yes
Self-Service Launderette:	No
Movie Theater/Seats:	Yes/626
Library:	Yes
Children's Facilities:	Yes
Classification Society:	RINA

Ratings	**Score**
Ship: Hardware/Maintenance	77
Ship: Outdoor Facilities/Space	75
Ship: Interior Facilities/Space/Flow	80
Ship: Decor/Furnishings/Artwork	81
Ship: Spa/Fitness Facilities	76
Cabins: Suites and Deluxe	81
Cabins: Standard Sizes	73
Food: Dining Room/Cuisine	63
Food: Informal Dining/Buffets	58
Food: Quality of Ingredients	64
Food: Afternoon Tea/Bar Snacks	48
Service: Dining Room	72
Service: Bars	72
Service: Cabins	74
Service: Open Decks	64
Cruise: Entertainment	64
Cruise: Activities Program	60
Cruise: Movies/Television Programming	60
Cruise: Hospitality Standard	70
Cruise: Overall Product Delivery	72
Overall Score	**1,384**

Accommodation: The 16 suites (with floor-to-ceiling windows) and 18 minisuites are quite lovely (except for the balconies of the 10 suites on Madrid Deck, where a solid steel half-wall blocks the view; a glass half-wall and polished wood rail wood be better). A sliding door separates the bedroom from the living room, and bathrooms are of a decent size. Cherry wood walls and cabinetry help make these suites warm and very attractive. The six suites at the forward section of Monte Carlo Deck are the largest, and have huge glass windows with superb forward views, but no balconies.

All other cabins are of a standard, quite generous size, and all have nicely finished cherry wood cabinetry and walls (the ceilings are quite plain). However, the cabin bathrooms and showers are small. There are a good number of triple and quad cabins that are ideal for families with children. The company's in-cabin food service menu is very basic.

Dining: The dining room is better designed and a little less noisy than in sister ship of the same size *CostaClassica*, and there are several tables for two. Features reasonable continental cuisine, but the presentation, quality, and service need improving. There is a poor selection of bread, rolls, fruits, and cheeses. The pasta dishes and cream sauces, however, are very good. Although there is a wine list, there are no wine waiters.

For informal dining there is a much improved and more practical buffet layout than in her sister ship, but it is far too small, and buffets are very much standard fare, quite unimaginative and noncreative, with the exception of some good commercial pasta dishes. One would expect Italian waiters, but, sadly, this is not the case now, with most of the waiters coming from countries other than Italy (many are from the Philippines).

Other Comments: This bold, contemporary ship has an upright yellow funnel cluster of three typical of Italian styling today. Costa is well established in Europe, and its Italian-style cruising is something it does well. Sadly, there is no wraparound promenade deck, and so contact with the sea is minimal, although there is some good open space on several of the upper levels.

She has a much nicer interior design than her sister ship, *CostaClassica*, and the decor is decidedly warmer. The layout and flow are somewhat disjointed, however. Has a good number of business and conference facilities, with several flexible meeting rooms for groups of different sizes. The decor is decidedly Italian, chic, and very tasteful, and should appeal to both Europeans and sophisticated North Americans.

The multilevel atrium is open and spacious and features a revolving mobile sculpture. The amphitheater-style, two-deck high, multitiered showroom is good, and has interesting artwork, but the stark upright seating is really quite uncomfortable and the sight lines are interrupted by 10 large pillars. There is also a small chapel (in a different location to that in her sister ship) and several small public rooms, lounges and bars.

Costa Cruises does a good job of providing first-time cruise passengers with a well-packaged vacation that is a mix of sophistication and basic fare, albeit accompanied by rather loud music and an international staff that seem to have lost direction. During the summer, this ship cruises in the Mediterranean region, while during the winter she cruises in the Caribbean (when there are more American passengers than Europeans).

<u>But:</u> Announcements are many and loud. The reception desk staff is very poor and impersonal, like in a bad hotel, and cigarette smoke is everywhere. Tipping envelopes provided in your cabin state the amount you are expected to give.

ms CostaVictoria

☆☆☆☆

(L)

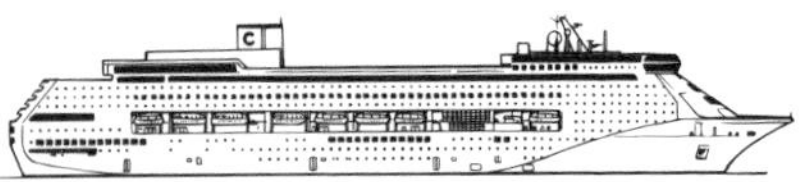

LIFESTYLE	**STANDARD**
Cruise Line:	Costa Cruises
Former Names:	-
Gross Tonnage:	75,200
Builder:	Bremer Vulkan (Germany)
Original Cost:	$388 million
Entered Service:	July 1996
Flag:	Liberia
Tel No:	363653510
Fax No:	363653520
Length (ft./m.):	823.0/251.00
Beam (ft./m.):	105.5/32.25
Draft (ft./m.):	25.6/7.80
Propulsion/Propellers:	diesel (30,000kW)/2 (CP)
Decks:	14
Total Crew:	800
Pass. Capacity (basis 2):	1,928
Pass. Capacity (all berths):	2,424
Pass. Space Ratio (basis 2):	39.0
Pass. Space Ratio (all berths):	31.0
Officers:	Italian
Total Cabins:	964
Size Range (sq. ft./m.):	120.0–430.5/11.1–40.0
Cabins (outside view):	573
Cabins (inside):	391
Cabins (for one person):	0
Cabins (with private balcony):	6
Cabins (wheelchair accessible):	6
Cabin Current:	110/220 AC
Cabin TV:	Yes
Dining Rooms:	2
Seatings:	2
Elevators:	12
Casino:	Yes
Slot Machines:	Yes
Swimming Pools (outdoors):	2
Swimming Pools (inside):	1
Whirlpools:	8
Fitness Center:	Yes
Sauna/Steam Room:	Yes/Yes
Massage:	Yes
Self-Service Launderette:	Yes
Movie Theater/Seats:	Yes/950 (show lounge)
Library:	Yes
Children's Facilities:	Yes
Classification Society:	RINA

RATINGS	**SCORE**
Ship: Hardware/Maintenance	86
Ship: Outdoor Facilities/Space	85
Ship: Interior Facilities/Space/Flow	84
Ship: Decor/Furnishings/Artwork	84
Ship: Spa/Fitness Facilities	79
Cabins: Suites and Deluxe	84
Cabins: Standard Sizes	74
Food: Dining Room/Cuisine	65
Food: Informal Dining/Buffets	53
Food: Quality of Ingredients	64
Food: Afternoon Tea/Bar Snacks	50
Service: Dining Room	71
Service: Bars	69
Service: Cabins	72
Service: Open Decks	61
Cruise: Entertainment	73
Cruise: Activities Program	64
Cruise: Movies/Television Programming	64
Cruise: Hospitality Standard	62
Cruise: Overall Product Delivery	74
OVERALL SCORE	**1,418**

Accommodation: There are six large Panorama suites (each has third/fourth pullman berths in a separate, tiny, train-like compartment) and 14 mini-suites (the six suites feature Laura Ashley-style fabrics), all with butler service. Sixty-five percent of all other cabins are outside, but they are small (for two). While the suites are not large, all other cabins are of rather mean dimensions. Some (only 16) of the cabins (inside) accommodate four, while all other cabins are for two or three persons.

All cabins feature wood cabinetry, with a fair amount of closet and drawer space for two for a one-week cruise, excellent air-conditioning, minibar-refrigerator, and electric blackout window blind (there are no curtains). The ocean-view cabins have large picture windows. The cabin bathrooms are small but well appointed and (sensibly) have a sliding door. There are six cabins for the physically handicapped (each has two bathrooms); all are well located and adjacent to elevators in the center of the ship.

Note that the personal safe is difficult to reach, and cabin stewards simply have too many cabins to clean, and no help, which means that service is less than desirable.

Dining: The two main dining rooms are the Fantasia and Sinfonia, separated by the main galley. They are expansive (there are a few tables for two, most being for four, six, or eight) and feature marble and pine walls. The cuisine is good basic fare, and so the presentation is adequate. Perhaps somewhat lacking is the use of garnishes to dress the plates. As you would expect, there is always plenty of pasta. Sadly, there are no wine waiters (table waiters are expected to serve both food and wine). Aboard an Italian ship, one would expect a dining room full of Italian waiters, but, sadly, this is not so, for there are none. Romantic candlelight dining featured on formal nights.

The ship also features casual breakfast and lunch buffets with indoor/outdoor seating (under a canvas sailcloth canopy for the outdoor section), although the buffet displays are very disappointing. There is also a pizzeria (it is open afternoons and evenings), good for casual fast-food devotees who may be used to frozen/reheated commercial pizzas.

Other Comments: The ship's exterior profile is similar to that of an enlarged version of the popular and very successful *CostaClassica* and *CostaRomantica*, with huge upright yellow funnels. A sister ship, *CostaOlympia* was scheduled for delivery in 1998, but was not completed due to shipyard bankruptcy. Having replaced all its older tonnage in the past few years, Costa Cruises now has a good contemporary fleet, operating in the Caribbean, Mediterranean, and South America.

Has a fully enclosed bridge. There is an outdoor wraparound promenade deck (but it is full of deck lounge chairs) as well as a wraparound jogging track.

Inside the ship is a lovely four-deck-high forward-facing observation lounge (Concorde Plaza) with a "beam-me-up" glass elevator; in the center is a cone-shaped waterfall (huge video screens flank the walls), while "pod" balconies overlook the room's center; it is a stunning space and has its own bar. Sadly, thick floor-to-ceiling pillars obstruct sight lines from most seats.

A seven-deck-high "planetarium" atrium (a novel, but somewhat impractical, design) has four glass elevators that go up to a clear crystal dome (you can see the weather outside through it), set on the deck where two outside swimming pools are located, together with four blocks of showers, and an ice-cream bar and grill. There is a large forward shopping area, adjacent to the atrium. Ship lovers should look in the Tavernetta Lounge (aft) for ten paintings of past and present Costa Cruises ships. There is also a small chapel.

Unusual for a new ship (and welcomed by European passengers) is a pleasant but small indoor swimming pool, sauna (it is tiny, and there are no adjacent changing or locker facilities), steam room, and gymnasium (limited assortment of equipment), as well as an adjacent covered walking/jogging track. There is also a tennis court. Sunbathers on the forward deck close to the mast have their own showers (excellent) and no music (good).

Where this ship differs from most large ships is in her distinct European interior decor, with decidedly Italian styling. The ship is modern without being glitzy, and bold without being brash.

But, when inside, there is absolutely no feeling that this is a ship. There are not enough seats in the show lounge. There are no fresh flowers in evidence anywhere. The service is decidedly loud and casual (make that sloppy and inconsistent) and there is little real hospitality. The telephone numbering system is incredibly complicated (try remembering 05313 for the information desk, or 06718 to book a massage).

But: The live music everywhere is loud, very loud, and there are too many repetitive announcements. Tipping envelopes provided in your cabin state the amount you are expected to give.

mv Crown Princess

☆☆☆☆

(L)

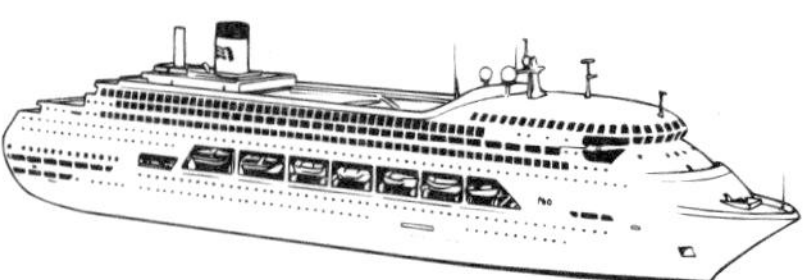

Lifestyle	**Premium**
Cruise Line:	Princess Cruises
Former Names:	-
Gross Tonnage:	69,845
Builder:	Fincantieri Navali (Italy)
Original Cost:	$276.8 million
Entered Service:	July 1990
Flag:	Liberia
Tel No:	1150543
Fax No:	1150544
Length (ft./m.):	804.7/245.30
Beam (ft./m.):	105.8/32.26
Draft (ft./m.):	26.5/8.10
Propulsion/Propellers:	diesel-electric (24,000kW)/2 (CP)
Decks:	11
Total Crew:	696
Pass. Capacity (basis 2):	1,590
Pass. Capacity (all berths):	1,910
Pass. Space Ratio (basis 2):	43.9
Pass. Space Ratio (all berths):	36.5
Officers:	Italian
Total Cabins:	795
Size Range (sq. ft./m.):	190–575/17.6–53.4
Cabins (outside view):	624
Cabins (inside):	171
Cabins (for one person):	0
Cabins (with private balcony):	184
Cabins (wheelchair accessible):	10
Cabin Current:	110/220 AC
Cabin TV:	Yes
Dining Rooms:	1
Seatings:	2
Elevators:	9
Casino:	Yes
Slot Machines:	Yes
Swimming Pools (outdoors):	2
Swimming Pools (inside):	0
Whirlpools:	4
Fitness Center:	Yes
Sauna/Steam Room:	Yes/No
Massage:	Yes
Self-Service Launderette:	Yes
Movie Theater/Seats:	Yes/169
Library:	Yes
Children's Facilities:	No
Classification Society:	Lloyd's Register

Ratings	**Score**
Ship: Hardware/Maintenance	81
Ship: Outdoor Facilities/Space	73
Ship: Interior Facilities/Space/Flow	82
Ship: Decor/Furnishings/Artwork	80
Ship: Spa/Fitness Facilities	76
Cabins: Suites and Deluxe	83
Cabins: Standard Sizes	79
Food: Dining Room/Cuisine	73
Food: Informal Dining/Buffets	68
Food: Quality of Ingredients	70
Food: Afternoon Tea/Bar Snacks	63
Service: Dining Room	78
Service: Bars	76
Service: Cabins	76
Service: Open Decks	74
Cruise: Entertainment	84
Cruise: Activities Program	77
Cruise: Movies/Television Programming	82
Cruise: Hospitality Standard	78
Cruise: Overall Product Delivery	83
Overall Score	**1,536**

Accommodation: In general, the cabins are well designed and have large bathrooms as well as good soundproofing. Walk-in closets, refrigerator, personal safe, and an interactive video system are provided in all cabins. Twin beds convert to queen-size beds in standard cabins. Bathrobes and personal toiletry amenities are standard, too. Note that the handicapped cabins have obstructed views.

The 14 top suites (each has a large private balcony) are very well laid out, with a practical design that positions most things in just the right place. The bedroom is separated from the living room by a wooden door (there are televisions in both rooms). Closet and drawer space is very generous, good enough even for long cruises.

Dining: The dining room (all Princess Cruises' dining rooms are nonsmoking) is large but lacks tables for two. Some of the most desirable tables are those that overlook the stern. The cuisine is disappointing (it is quite stodgy, with poor creativity and presentation) although there has been some improvement and better creativity of late. The pasta dishes are good, however, usually served by section headwaiters. The general service level is quite reasonable, but it always seems hurried, particularly for those on the first seating. There is an excellent pizzeria, however, for informal meals. The wine list is average, with a heavy emphasis on Californian wines.

Themed late-night buffets are provided, but afternoon teas are poor. For sweet snacks during the day, a Patisserie (items are at extra charge) is located in the spacious lobby.

Other Comments: This was the first ship in the 70,000-tonne range for Princess Cruises, and provided a foretaste of ever-larger ships for this company. The ship has an interesting, jumbo-airplane look to it when viewed from the front, with a dolphin-like upper structure, and a large upright funnel placed aft.

The open deck space is very limited for the size of the ship and the number of passengers carried. There is no wraparound outdoor promenade deck (the only walking space being along the sides of the ship). When full, there is simply not enough outdoor space (there is little real connection with the outside), apart from a good, though small, swimming pool deck.

Inside, however, innovative, elegant styling is mixed with traditional features and a spacious interior layout. The interior spaces are well designed, although the layout is somewhat disjointed. An understated decor of soft pastel shades is highlighted by some very colorful artwork.

An observation dome, set high atop the ship like the head of a dolphin, features a large casino, numerous rubber trees, a dance floor, and live music. The ship has good health spa facilities. A striking, elegant three-deck-high atrium features grand staircase with fountain sculpture (real, stand-up cocktail parties are held here). Characters Bar has wonderful drink concoctions and unusual glasses.

Finally, this ship provides a very pleasant cruise in elegant and very comfortable surroundings, and fine-tuned staff will make you feel welcome. Princess Cruises provides white-gloved stewards to take you to your cabin when you embark, another nice touch.

But: There are too many support pillars in the public rooms that obstruct the sight lines and flow. The outdoor sunbathing space is quite limited when the ship is full. Inside, the layout is quite disjointed and takes getting used to. There is no wraparound outdoor promenade deck. Galley fumes seem to waft constantly over the aft open decks.

mv Crystal Harmony

☆☆☆☆☆

(M)

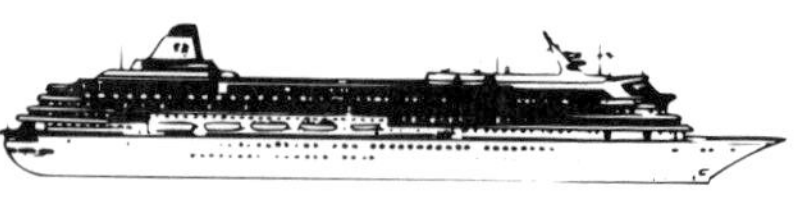

Lifestyle	**Luxury**
Cruise Line:	Crystal Cruises
Former Names:	-
Gross Tonnage:	48,621
Builder:	Mitsubishi Heavy Industries (Japan)
Original Cost:	$240 million
Entered Service:	July 1990
Flag:	Bahamas
Tel No:	1103237
Fax No:	1103234
Length (ft./m.):	790.5/240.96
Beam (ft./m.):	97.1/29.60
Draft (ft./m.):	24.6/7.50
Propulsion/Propellers:	diesel-electric (32,800kW)/2 (CP)
Decks:	8
Total Crew:	545
Pass. Capacity (basis 2):	960
Pass. Capacity (all berths):	1,010
Pass. Space Ratio (basis 2):	50.6
Pass. Space Ratio (all berths):	48.9
Officers:	Scandinavian/Japanese
Total Cabins:	480
Size Range (sq. ft./m.):	183–948/17.0–88.0
Cabins (outside view):	461
Cabins (inside):	19
Cabins (for one person):	0
Cabins (with private balcony):	260
Cabins (wheelchair accessible):	4
Cabin Current:	115/220 AC
Cabin TV:	Yes
Dining Rooms:	3 (2 alternative restaurants)
Seatings:	2 (dinner only, main restaurant)
Elevators:	8
Casino:	Yes
Slot Machines:	Yes
Swimming Pools (outdoors):	2 (1 with magrodome)
Swimming Pools (inside):	0
Whirlpools:	2
Fitness Center:	Yes
Sauna/Steam Room:	Yes/Yes
Massage:	Yes
Self-Service Launderette:	Yes
Movie Theater/Seats:	Yes/270
Library:	Yes
Children's Facilities:	Yes
Classification Society:	Lloyd's Register/Nippon Kaiji Kyokai

Ratings	**Score**
Ship: Hardware/Maintenance	90
Ship: Outdoor Facilities/Space	91
Ship: Interior Facilities/Space/Flow	93
Ship: Decor/Furnishings/Artwork	92
Ship: Spa/Fitness Facilities	86
Cabins: Suites and Deluxe	92
Cabins: Standard Sizes	83
Food: Dining Room/Cuisine	86
Food: Informal Dining/Buffets	86
Food: Quality of Ingredients	87
Food: Afternoon Tea/Bar Snacks	86
Service: Dining Room	87
Service: Bars	86
Service: Cabins	87
Service: Open Decks	86
Cruise: Entertainment	88
Cruise: Activities Program	86
Cruise: Movies/Television Programming	88
Cruise: Hospitality Standard	89
Cruise: Overall Product Delivery	92
Overall Score	**1,761**

Accommodation: This ship features spacious, well-designed accommodation, including four spectacular Crystal penthouses that feature a huge private balcony and lounge, bedroom with queen-sized bed and electric curtains, and stunning ocean-view bathroom. Five butlers feature the best in personal service in the top category suites (Penthouse Deck 10 with a total of 132 beds), where all room service food arrives on sterling silver trays, and all laundry is included. More than 50 percent of all cabins have private balconies and are supremely comfortable. Even in standard cabins, there is plenty of drawer space, some recently added to lower grade cabins, although closet hanging space is somewhat limited for long voyages. All cabins have VCR units and excellent soundproofing. Generously sized personal bathroom amenities are featured.

Except for the penthouse suites and all other accommodation on Deck 10, the cabin bathrooms are somewhat compact, and closet space is quite limited, particularly on longer voyages. Some cabins (grades G and I), although no public rooms, have obstructed views.

Dining: There are plenty of dining choices aboard this lovely ship.

The dining room is quite elegant, with plenty of space around each table, well-placed waiter service stations, and a good number of tables for two. It is noisy at times, making it difficult to carry on a conversation at the larger tables in the center (raised) section. The food is attractively presented and well served in a friendly but correct manner. It is of a high standard, with good quality ingredients used throughout (meat quality could be improved, however). Features a mixture of European specialties and North American favorites. The menus are extremely varied, and special orders are available (including caviar and other niceties). All in all, the food is most acceptable and, with the choice of the two alternative dining spots, provides consistently high marks from passengers.

Sadly, dinner in the main dining room is in two seatings (the early seating is simply too rushed), although with two alternative restaurants, off-menu choices, a fine hand-picked European staff, and excellent service, dining is often memorable.

Pasta specialties are made each day on request to the head waiters. For those who enjoy caviar, it is available, although it is sevruga (malossol) and not beluga. The wine list is superb.

Afternoon tea (and coffee) in the Palm Court is good. The choice of sandwiches, cakes, and pastries is good (although I am concerned about cutbacks). Needless to say, service is generally excellent.

The two alternative dining spots, Prego (features fine pasta dishes) and Kyoto, with pseudo-Japanese specialties (there is no extra charge, other than a recommended $5 waiter gratuity per meal that should be included in the cruise fare) are intimate, have great views, and feature fine food. There should be separate entrances for these two alternative restaurants (at present one entrance serves both).

Other Comments: She is a handsome, contemporary ship with raked clipper bow and well-balanced, sleek flowing lines. Excellent open deck, sunbathing space, and sports facilities that include a paddle tennis court. One of two outdoor swimming pools has a swim-up bar and can be covered by a magrodome. There is almost no sense of crowding anywhere, a superb example of comfort by design, quality construction, and engineering. There is a wraparound teakwood deck for walking and an abundance of open deck and sunbathing space.

Inside, the design shows that form follows function superbly well. There is a fine assortment of public entertainment lounges and small intimate rooms (except for a night club/lounge that is simply too large for the number of late-night passengers frequenting it), and passenger flow is excellent. Outstanding are the Vista (observation) Lounge and the supremely tranquil, elegant Palm Court, one of the nicest rooms afloat. A Business Center features laptop computers, printers, satellite faxes, and phones.

Has an excellent book and video library. The theater features high-definition video projection and special headsets for the hearing impaired. Useful self-service launderette on each deck. Fine-quality fabrics and soft furnishings, china, flatware, and silver are used. Fine in-cabin television programming, and close-captioned videos for the hearing impaired.

Smokers will enjoy a fine range of cigars available in the Vista Lounge. The decorations on the Christmas cruise are simply stunning.

This very friendly, well-trained, highly professional staff and excellent teamwork (with one of the lowest turnover of staff in the industry) is under the direction of a solid, all-European middle management. It is the extra attention to detail that makes a cruise aboard this ship so special, such as few announcements, and no background music anywhere. The company pays attention to its fine base of repeat passengers, and makes subtle changes in operations in order to constantly fine-tune its product.

This ship has just about everything for the discerning seasoned traveler who wants and is prepared to pay for good style, space, and the comfort and the facilities of a large vessel capable of longer voyages. She is, without doubt, an outstanding example of the latest style in contemporary grand hotels afloat and provides abundant choices and flexibility. Following a refit in 1997, some of the public rooms have been expanded (most notably the casino). You will be surrounded by a cocoon of fine comfort and pampering to the highest degree, although it is let down by the two seatings for dinner. Insurance and gratuities are extra, although they should be included at this price level.

ms Crystal Symphony
☆☆☆☆☆
(M)

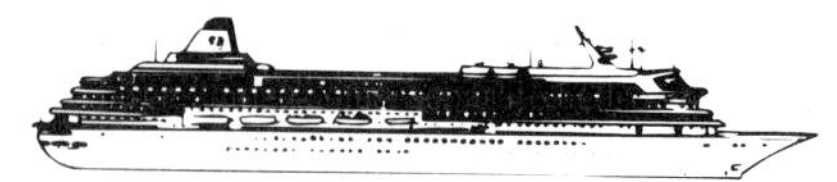

LIFESTYLE	**LUXURY**
Cruise Line:	Crystal Cruises
Former Names:	-
Gross Tonnage:	50,202
Builder:	Masa-Yards (Finland)
Original Cost:	$300 million
Entered Service:	May 1995
Flag:	Bahamas
Tel No:	630916820/30/40/50/60
Fax No:	1306716
Length (ft./m.):	777.8/237.10
Beam (ft./m.):	98.0/30.20
Draft (ft./m.):	24.9/7.60
Propulsion/Propellers:	diesel-electric (33,880kW)/2 (CP)
Decks:	8
Total Crew:	530
Pass. Capacity (basis 2):	960
Pass. Capacity (all berths):	1,010
Pass. Space Ratio (basis 2):	52.2
Pass. Space Ratio (all berths):	49.7
Officers:	Scandinavian
Total Cabins:	480
Size Range (sq. ft./m.):	202–982/18.7–91.2
Cabins (outside view):	480
Cabins (inside):	0
Cabins (for one person):	0
Cabins (with private balcony):	276
Cabins (wheelchair accessible):	7
Cabin Current:	110/220 AC
Cabin TV:	Yes
Dining Rooms:	3
Seatings:	2 (dinner only, main dining room)
Elevators:	8
Casino:	Yes
Slot Machines:	Yes
Swimming Pools (outdoors):	2 (1 with magrodome)
Swimming Pools (inside):	0
Whirlpools:	2
Fitness Center:	Yes
Sauna/Steam Room:	Yes/Yes
Self-Service Launderette:	Yes
Massage:	Yes
Movie Theater/Seats:	Yes/143
Library:	Yes
Children's Facilities:	Yes
Classification Society:	Lloyd's Register

RATINGS	**SCORE**
Ship: Hardware/Maintenance	92
Ship: Outdoor Facilities/Space	91
Ship: Interior Facilities/Space/Flow	93
Ship: Decor/Furnishings/Artwork	93
Ship: Spa/Fitness Facilities	88
Cabins: Suites and Deluxe	93
Cabins: Standard Sizes	85
Food: Dining Room/Cuisine	86
Food: Informal Dining/Buffets	86
Food: Quality of Ingredients	87
Food: Afternoon Tea/Bar Snacks	86
Service: Dining Room	86
Service: Bars	86
Service: Cabins	87
Service: Open Decks	86
Cruise: Entertainment	88
Cruise: Activities Program	86
Cruise: Movies/Television Programming	88
Cruise: Hospitality Standard	90
Cruise: Overall Product Delivery	92
OVERALL SCORE	**1,769**

Accommodation: The spacious, well-designed accommodation includes two spectacular 982 sq. ft. (91.2 m^2) Crystal penthouses with a huge balcony and lounge, bedroom with queen-sized bed, and stunning ocean-view bathroom with large whirlpool bath. Butlers feature the best in personal service in the top category suites on Penthouse Deck 10, where all room service food arrives on sterling silver trays, and lots of extra goodies are provided for occupants. All other cabins (called "penthouses" by Crystal Cruises) on Deck 10 are worth the asking price, being extremely spacious, supremely comfortable, and quiet units equipped with everything necessary for refined, private living at sea, including VCR units.

More than 50 percent of all cabins have private balconies, are very well equipped, and are extremely comfortable, with excellent sound insulation. The balcony partitions, however, do not go from floor to ceiling, so you can hear your neighbors. Even in the lowest category of standard cabins, there is plenty of drawer space, but the closet hanging space may prove somewhat limited for long voyages. Has generously sized personal bathroom amenities, duvets, and down pillows. European stewardesses provide excellent service and attention.

Some cabins (grades G and I), although no public rooms, have obstructed views. Except for the penthouse suites, cabin bathrooms are somewhat compact. A privacy curtain should be placed between entrance and sleeping area in all non-Penthouse Deck cabins.

Dining: The main dining room is quite elegant, with crisp design and plenty of space around each table, well-placed waiter service stations, and ample tables for two. The main dining room is well laid out, and features a raised, circular central section, although it is somewhat noisy at times, and not conducive to a fine dining experience. There are tables for two (many of them positioned adjacent to large windows), four, six, or eight.

The food is attractively presented and well served (mix of plate and silver service). It is of a high standard, with fine quality ingredients used. European dishes are predominant. Menus are extremely varied and feature a good selection of meat, fish, and vegetarian dishes. Special (off-menu) orders are available, as are caviar and other culinary niceties.

Overall, the food is most acceptable for a large ship and, with the choice of the two alternative dining spots, receives high passenger praise. Dinner in the main dining room is in two seatings, although with two alternative restaurants, off-menu choices, a fine European staff, and excellent service, dining can be quite memorable.

Fresh pasta and dessert flambeau specialties are made each day by the head waiters at table-side.

Afternoon tea in the Palm Court is a delightful daily event. The Lido provides breakfast and luncheon buffets that are fairly standard fare.

Two alternative dining rooms, the 75-seat Prego (serving Italian cuisine) and the 84-seat Jade Garden (serving contemporary Chinese dishes), are appreciably larger and set on a lower deck (Deck 6) than those aboard her sister ship, and each restaurant has a separate entrance and theme decor. They both provide an excellent standard of culinary fare, with food cooked to order at no extra charge (but the recommended $5 waiter gratuity per meal should be included in the cruise fare).

In addition, The Bistro provides a fine array of snacks, cakes, coffees, and teas throughout the day, with unusual, Crystal Cruises-logo china that can also be purchased in one of the ship's boutiques.

Other Comments: This is a contemporary ship that has a nicely raked clipper bow and well-balanced lines. While some might not like the "apartment block" look of the ship's exterior, it is the look of the future, as balconies become the norm. Has excellent open deck, sunbathing space, and sports facilities. The aft of two outdoor swimming pools can be covered by a magrodome in inclement weather. No sense of crowding anywhere, a superb example of comfort by design, high-quality construction and engineering. Has a wide wraparound teakwood deck for walking, uncluttered by lounge chairs.

The interior decor is restful, with color combinations that do not jar the senses. Has a good mixture of public entertainment lounges and small intimate rooms. Outstanding is the Palm Court, a forward observation lounge that is tranquil and one of the nicest rooms afloat (it is larger than aboard the sister ship). There is an excellent book, video, and CD-ROM library (combined with a Business Center). The theater (smaller than aboard the sister ship) features high-definition video projection and headsets for the hearing impaired. Useful self-service launderette on each deck. Fine-quality fabrics and soft furnishings, china, flatware, and silver are used. Excellent in-cabin television programming (including CNN and ESPN) and close-captioned videos for the hearing impaired.

Highly professional and attentive staff. It is the extra attention to detail that makes a cruise with this ship so special, such as very few announcements.

This ship has just about everything for the discerning seasoned traveler who wants and is prepared to pay good money for fine style, abundant space, and the comfort and the facilities of a large vessel capable of extended voyages. The one thing that lets the product down is the dining room operation in two seatings.

It is the staff that make this cruise experience really special. They are a fine-tuned, well-trained group who stress hospitality at all times. The ship achieves a high rating because of her fine facilities, service, and crew. Gratuities should be included on a ship so highly rated (they can, however, be pre-paid).

ms Dalmacija

☆☆ +

(S)

Lifestyle	Standard
Cruise Line:	Jadrolinija/TUI
Former Names:	-
Gross Tonnage:	5,650
Builder:	Brodogradiliste Uljanik (Yugoslavia)
Original Cost:	n/a
Entered Service:	1965
Flag:	Croatia
Tel No:	n/a
Fax No:	n/a
Length (ft./m.):	383.4/116.87
Beam (ft./m.):	54.1/16.51
Draft (ft./m.):	17.3/5.28
Propulsion/Propellers:	diesels (11,030kw)/2 (FP)
Decks:	5
Total Crew:	112
Pass. Capacity (basis 2):	284
Pass. Capacity (all berths):	300
Pass. Space Ratio (basis 2):	19.8
Pass. Space Ratio (all berths):	18.8
Officers:	Croatian
Cabins:	142
Size (sq. ft./m.):	n/a
Cabins (outside view):	93
Cabins (inside):	55
Cabins (for one person):	0
Cabins (with private balcony):	0
Cabins (wheelchair accessible):	0
Cabin Current:	220 AC
Dining Rooms:	1
Seatings:	1
Elevators:	0
Casino:	No
Slot Machines:	No
Swimming Pools (outdoors):	1
Swimming Pools (inside):	0
Whirlpools:	0
Fitness Center:	No
Sauna/Steam Room:	No
Massage	No
Cinema/Theatre:	No
Cabin TV:	No
Library:	Yes
Children's Facilities:	No
Classification Society:	n/a

Ratings	Score
Ship: Hardware/Maintenance	58
Ship: Outdoor Facilities/Space	51
Ship: Interior Facilities/Space/Flow	52
Ship: Decor/Furnishings/Artwork	46
Ship: Spa/Fitness Facilities	30
Cabins: Suites and Deluxe	64
Cabins: Standard Sizes	57
Food: Dining Room/Cuisine	59
Food: Informal Dining/Buffets	49
Food: Quality of Ingredients	58
Food: Afternoon Tea/Bar Snacks	44
Service: Dining Room	58
Service: Bars	57
Service: Cabins	63
Service: Open Decks	55
Cruise: Entertainment	41
Cruise: Activities Program	45
Cruise: Movies/Television Programming	33
Cruise: Hospitality Standard	52
Cruise: Overall Product Delivery	54
Overall Score	**1,026**

Accommodation: The cabins really are very small and most have only a limited amount of drawer space, although the closet space is reasonably adequate (for short cruises). Each cabin has its own private bathroom, which is very small and utilitarian, with a tiny shower stall in which you will be invited to dance with the shower curtain.

Dining: This ship has a dining room that is quite pleasant, with cheerful decor and service. The service staff is friendly and attentive, although the service is quite basic. The choice of meals is very limited, and the food is generally overcooked. There is little choice of fresh fruits, cheeses, and breads. The wine list is poor.

Other Comments: This ship has an all-white exterior and presents a reasonably clean-looking small ship profile. She is a cozy, very high-density ship that does not pretend to be glamorous. She is clean and tidy throughout, however, having undergone a refurbishment in 1997. Her limited number of public rooms feature wood accenting, which helps warm the otherwise plain decor.

There is a small outdoor swimming pool (which is really a "dip" pool), an entertainment lounge, photo shop, a small fitness center, and two bars.

She caters primarily to European passengers looking for a destination-intensive cruise in comfortable, but not elegant, surroundings, at a modest price, without the finesse and fuss of a lost of other ships.

But: There is a limited amount of open deck and sunbathing space. Passenger hallways are quite dark and dreary, and lighting throughout is inconsistent.

ms Dawn Princess

☆☆☆☆ +

(L)

Lifestyle	**Premium**
Cruise Line:	Princess Cruises
Former Names:	-
Gross Tonnage:	77,000
Builder:	Fincantieri (Italy)
Original Cost:	$300 million
Entered Service:	May 1997
Flag:	Liberia
Tel No:	363657010
Fax No:	363657020
Length (ft./m.):	856.2/261.0
Beam (ft./m.):	105.8/32.25
Draft (ft./m.):	26.0/7.95
Propulsion/Propellers:	diesel-elec/2 (FP)
Decks:	14
Total Crew:	900
Pass. Capacity (basis 2):	1,950
Pass. Capacity (all berths):	2,250
Pass. Space Ratio (basis 2):	39.4
Pass. Space Ratio (all berths):	34.2
Officers:	Italian
Total Cabins:	1,050
Size Range (sq. ft./m.):	159–611/14.7–56.7
Cabins (outside view):	652
Cabins (inside):	398
Cabins (for one person):	0
Cabins (with private balcony):	446
Cabins (wheelchair accessible):	20
Cabin Current:	110/220 AC
Cabin TV:	Yes
Dining Rooms:	2 main/3 others
Seatings:	2 (main dining rooms)
Elevators:	11
Casino:	Yes
Slot Machines:	Yes
Swimming Pools (outdoors):	3
Swimming Pools (inside):	0
Whirlpools:	5
Fitness Center:	Yes
Sauna/Steam Room:	Yes
Massage:	Yes
Self-Service Launderette:	Yes
Movie Theater/Seats:	Yes
Library:	Yes
Children's Facilities:	Yes
Classification Society:	Lloyd's Register

Ratings	**Score**
Ship: Hardware/Maintenance	90
Ship: Outdoor Facilities/Space	87
Ship: Interior Facilities/Space/Flow	91
Ship: Decor/Furnishings/Artwork	90
Ship: Spa/Fitness Facilities	85
Cabins: Suites and Deluxe	86
Cabins: Standard Sizes	84
Food: Dining Room/Cuisine	73
Food: Informal Dining/Buffets	69
Food: Quality of Ingredients	70
Food: Afternoon Tea/Bar Snacks	63
Service: Dining Room	76
Service: Bars	76
Service: Cabins	77
Service: Open Decks	73
Cruise: Entertainment	87
Cruise: Activities Program	78
Cruise: Movies/Television Programming	84
Cruise: Hospitality Standard	81
Cruise: Overall Product Delivery	85
Overall Score	**1,605**

Accommodation: The cabins are well designed and functional in layout, although they are a little on the small side. Many of the outside cabins have private balconies (more than any other Princess Cruises ship to date except *Grand Princess*), and all seem to be quite well soundproofed, although the balcony partition is not floor to ceiling type, so you can hear your next door neighbors clearly. Good closet and drawer space is provided in all cabins—plenty for a seven-day cruise. The cabin bathrooms are quite practical, and come complete with all the little details one needs. Real glasses are provided in cabin bathrooms. Proportionately, there are quite a lot of inside cabins.

The suites and minisuites are very well laid out, with larger bathrooms (Jacuzzi bathtubs and separate large shower) and separate bedroom.

Dining: There are two main dining rooms; each of which has its own galley and each is split into multitier sections, which help create a feeling of intimacy, although there is a lot of noise from the waiter stations, which are adjacent to many tables. Breakfast and lunch are provided in open seating, while dinner is in two seatings. The food, its presentation, and its delivery are disappointing, but adequate (this is banquet catering, after all), and let this otherwise beautifully decorated ship down.

There is also a patisserie (for cappuccino/espresso coffees and pastries), a wine/caviar bar, and a pizzeria (complete with cobblestone floors and wrought iron decorative features). The pizzas (there are six to choose from) are excellent.

The Horizon Buffet is open almost 24 hours a day, and, at night, features an informal dinner setting with sit-down waiter service and a small bistro menu (available from 6 p.m. to 2 a.m.). Buffet displays are, for the most part, unappetizing and could be improved. The cabin service menu is limited, and presentation of food items is poor.

Other Comments: Although large, this ship has a good profile, and is well balanced by its large funnel, which contains a deck tennis/basketball/volleyball court in its aft base. There is a wide, teak wood-decked outdoor, wraparound promenade deck, some real teak wood steamer-style deck chairs, and 93,000 sq. ft. (8,640 m^2) of outdoor space. A great amount of glass area on the upper decks provides plenty of light and connection with the outside world. The swimming pools are small for so many passengers, and the pool deck is cluttered with deck lounge chairs (plastic).

The ship, while large, almost has an intimate feel to her, which is just what the designers intended. Her interiors are very pretty and warm, with attractive colors and welcoming decor that includes some stunning wall murals and other artwork. The signs around the ship could be improved, however.

There is a wide range of public rooms to choose from, with several intimate rooms and spaces so that you do not feel overwhelmed by large spaces. Features tasteful decor throughout, with attractive color combinations that are warm and do not clash. The interior focal point is a huge four-deck-high atrium lobby, complete with two panoramic glass-walled elevators.

The main public entertainment rooms are located under three cabin decks. There is plenty of space, the traffic flow is good, and the ship absorbs people well. There are two showrooms, one at each end of the ship; one is a superb 550-seat theater-style show lounge (movies are also shown here) and the other is a 480-seat cabaret-style lounge, complete with bar.

The health spa complex, located aft, surrounds a swimming pool suspended between two decks (there are two other pools, although they are not large for the size of the ship). There is a conference center for up to 300, as well as a business center, with computers, copy, and fax machines. The collection of artwork is outstanding, particularly on the stairways and helps make the ship feel smaller than it is.

This ship was, for almost a year, the largest ship (in terms of gross tonnage, but not length) in the cruise industry, superseded by *Grand Princess*. At the end of the day, as is the case in most large ships today, if you live in the top suites, you will be well attended; if you do not, you will merely be one of a very large number of passengers.

But: There is no escape from the many unnecessary and repetitious announcements that intrude constantly. Waiting for tenders in anchor ports is irritating, but typical of large ship operations.

ms Delphin

☆☆☆ +

(S)

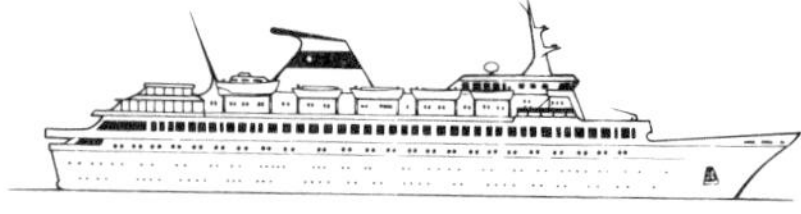

Lifestyle	Standard
Cruise Line:	Delphin Seereisen
Former Names:	*Kazakhstan II/Belorussiya*
Gross Tonnage:	16,214
Builder:	Wartsila (Finland)
Original Cost:	$25 million
Entered Service:	January 1975/December 1993
Flag:	Malta
Tel No:	1257506/624945111
Fax No:	1257507/624945115
Length (ft./m.):	512.5/156.24
Beam (ft./m.):	71.8/21.90
Draft (ft./m.):	20.3/6.20
Propulsion/Propellers:	diesel (13,250kW)/2 (CP)
Decks:	8
Total Crew:	234
Pass. Capacity (basis 2):	466
Pass. Capacity (all berths):	556
Pass. Space Ratio (basis 2):	35.6
Pass. Space Ratio (all berths):	29.8
Officers:	Ukrainian
Total Cabins:	233
Size Range (sq. ft./m.):	150.0–492.0/14.0–45.7
Cabins (outside view):	128
Cabins (inside):	105
Cabins (for one person):	0
Cabins (with private balcony):	0
Cabins (wheelchair accessible):	0
Cabin Current:	220 AC
Cabin TV:	Yes
Dining Rooms:	1
Seatings:	1
Elevators:	2
Casino:	No
Slot Machines:	No
Swimming Pools (outdoors):	1
Swimming Pools (inside):	0
Whirlpools:	0
Fitness Center:	Yes
Sauna/Steam Room:	Yes/Yes
Massage:	Yes
Self-Service Launderette:	Yes
Movie Theater/Seats:	No
Library:	Yes
Children's Facilities:	No
Classification Society:	Germanischer Lloyd

Ratings	Score
Ship: Hardware/Maintenance	74
Ship: Outdoor Facilities/Space	76
Ship: Interior Facilities/Space/Flow	76
Ship: Decor/Furnishings/Artwork	76
Ship: Spa/Fitness Facilities	58
Cabins: Suites and Deluxe	74
Cabins: Standard Sizes	62
Food: Dining Room/Cuisine	67
Food: Informal Dining/Buffets	66
Food: Quality of Ingredients	65
Food: Afternoon Tea/Bar Snacks	65
Service: Dining Room	76
Service: Bars	72
Service: Cabins	72
Service: Open Decks	68
Cruise: Entertainment	65
Cruise: Activities Program	62
Cruise: Movies/Television Programming	60
Cruise: Hospitality Standard	76
Cruise: Overall Product Delivery	80
Overall Score	**1,390**

Accommodation: The Boat Deck suites (located forward) are extremely large and well equipped, with an absolute abundance of drawers and good closet space, and all feature blond wood furniture, and refrigerator. The bathrooms are very spacious, and come with full-sized bathtubs and large toiletries cabinet; bathrobes are also provided.

All other cabins are compact, yet adequate, although there is little drawer space, making storage quite tight on long cruises, which this ship often features. All of the beds have duvets, and all cabins receive fresh flowers each cruise. The bathrooms are small, but there is good space for toiletry items.

Dining: Has a single, large dining room, with a high ceiling, big picture windows and pleasing, elegant decor; seats all passengers in a single seating. The catering remains a weak point, but is improving constantly.

The food, while attractively presented and quite reasonable, is of a limited choice and quality. While white and red table wines are included for lunch and dinner, there is also an additional wine list with a reasonably decent selection. The breakfast and lunch buffets, available in the Lido, are quite decent, while the gala buffet is excellent. Service comes with a smile from very attractive Ukrainian waitresses.

Other Comments: This smart-looking modern ship has a rather square funnel and was very well refitted and refurbished throughout following a shipyard roll-over incident (when she was named *Belorussiya*).

New facilities were added, which improved almost all the public areas and added new health/fitness and spa facilities and an improved outdoor pool/lido deck (the circular pool is small, however). Has good outdoor promenade decks (but there are "lips" to step over in the forward section). The interior decor is very tasteful, and enhanced by several flower bouquets and colorful artwork throughout.

This ship will provide a comfortable cruise experience for German-speaking passengers at an extremely attractive price. It is not a luxury product, nor does it pretend to be, but she is a very comfortable and friendly ship in which to cruise. She attracts many repeat passengers because of the excellent itineraries and very good service levels. Finally, Delphin Seereisen's own onboard cruise director and staff are excellent. Port taxes and insurance are included.

ms Deutschland

☆☆☆☆ +

(M)

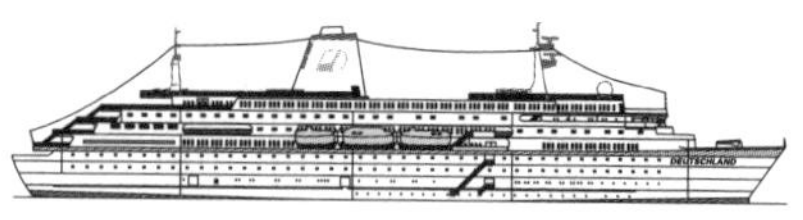

Lifestyle	Premium
Cruise Line:	Peter Deilmann Reederei
Former Names:	-
Gross Tonnage:	22,400
Builder:	Howaldtswerke Deutsche Werft (Germany)
Original Cost:	DM250 million
Entered Service:	May 1998
Flag:	Germany
Tel No:	321837010
Fax No:	321837011
Length (ft./m.):	573.4/174.8
Beam (ft./m.):	75.4/23.0
Draft (ft./m.):	19.0/5.8
Propulsion/Propellers:	diesel (12,300kW)/2 (CP)
Decks:	7
Total Crew:	270
Pass. Capacity (basis 2):	604
Pass. Capacity (all berths):	650
Pass. Space Ratio (basis 2):	37.0
Pass. Space Ratio (all berths):	34.4
Officers:	German
Total Cabins:	302
Size Range (sq. ft./m.):	161.4–365.9/15.0–34.0
Cabins (outside view):	224
Cabins (inside):	78
Cabins (for one person):	0
Cabins (with private balcony):	0
Cabins (wheelchair accessible):	2
Cabin Current:	220 AC
Cabin TV:	Yes
Dining Rooms:	2 (+ Lido Cafe)
Seatings:	Open
Elevators:	3
Casino:	No
Slot Machines:	No
Swimming Pools (outdoors):	1
Swimming Pools (inside):	1
Whirlpools:	0
Fitness Center:	Yes
Sauna/Steam Room:	Yes/No
Massage:	Yes
Self-Service Launderette:	Yes
Movie Theater/Seats:	Yes/83
Library:	Yes
Children's Facilities:	No
Classification Society:	Norddeutscher Lloyd

Ratings	Score
Ship: Hardware/Maintenance	94
Ship: Outdoor Facilities/Space	92
Ship: Interior Facilities/Space/Flow	91
Ship: Decor/Furnishings/Artwork	95
Ship: Spa/Fitness Facilities	89
Cabins: Suites and Deluxe	88
Cabins: Standard Sizes	84
Food: Dining Room/Cuisine	84
Food: Informal Dining/Buffets	80
Food: Quality of Ingredients	79
Food: Afternoon Tea/Bar Snacks	81
Service: Dining Room	81
Service: Bars	77
Service: Cabins	77
Service: Open Decks	74
Cruise: Entertainment	77
Cruise: Activities Program	76
Cruise: Movies/Television Programming	76
Cruise: Hospitality Standard	74
Cruise: Overall Product Delivery	87
Overall Score	**1,656**

Accommodation: There are 10 cabin grades (the higher the deck, the more you pay).

All cabins are furnished in beautiful bird's-eye maple wood throughout, and the ceilings are all one-piece units, unlike the metal strip ceilings of most contemporary cruise vessels, and come with molded coving and ornamentation. The closet and drawer space is generous. The bathrooms are also generously appointed and feature pink marble sink, gold anodized fittings, and plenty of space for personal toiletry items.

The suites (of which there are two grades) are reasonably large, with a living area that contains a large sofa, coffee table, and two chairs, while the bathroom features full-size bathtubs, while all other cabins have showers. Thick cotton bathrobes are provided for all passengers.

Dining: There are several dining options aboard this lovely ship.

The main restaurant (Berlin), with 300 seats, is quite lovely, intimate, and all the chairs have armrests, although space for serving at the window-side tables is tight. There are tables for two, four, six, or eight. Two self-service (or waiter service) cold buffet bars are featured for breakfast and lunch.

The Restaurant Vierjahreszeiten (Four Seasons), with 104 seats, is an intimate dining room (for suite occupants and for à la carte dining). There is much detailing and ornamentation in the decor, and the ornate ceiling lamps and indented ceiling coving create an unmistakable intimate and elegant ambience. There are tables for two, four, or six, plus a private dining room with large oval table that seats 10 for special occasions.

The Lido Restaurant, with 152 seats, is the informal dining spot, with large ocean-view windows on two sides and a central, circular, multisection help-yourself buffet station.

In addition, the Lido Terrasse, set at the stern, has windows on three sides, is set on two levels, and houses the ship's library, complete with statuary and a garden-like setting. This room also has a bar, and elegant tea (and coffee) service is featured.

Other Comments: This is an important, and fine, new cruise ship for the German-speaking market. Looking like a larger version of the company's successful, but older Berlin, she has a contemporary, although fairly low-in-the-water profile, and a large, single squat, traditional funnel.

There is a good amount of open deck and sunbathing space, including three aft decks for open-air lovers, and real teakwood deck chairs, complete with thick royal blue cushioned pads (with *ms Deutschland* tastefully set in white). The Lido Deck has sides covered by canvas shading and white turn-of-the century support pillars (like the one's you would find on seaside piers in England) as a setting for the outdoor swimming pool. The Lido Deck really is a delightful, self-contained deck that features not only the pool, but the casual Lido Buffet restaurant and Lido Terrasse café, which means you could spend all day outdoors on this deck without having to dress to go indoors to eat. There is also a small waterfall aft of the pool.

Inside the ship, what is fascinating is that the interior decor has been designed to re-create and reproduce the atmosphere of the ocean liners of the 1920s, and this has been very successfully achieved. She is beautifully and tastefully decorated throughout (some might say overdecorated), with rich woods and intricate brass and wrought iron staircases that remind one of what would have been called "gentlemen's clubs" in former days. There is so much detail in the decoration work aboard this ship, and especially in the ornate ceilings.

A galleried show lounge with red velveteen chairs is reminiscent of a small opera house, complete with a huge central chandelier.

Unusual for a ship of this size is an indoor swimming pool surrounded by a health center with thalassotherapy, sauna and massage, and a dialysis station. Close by is the ship's hospital.

The ship is also a showcase gallery for the extensive art collection belonging to her rightfully proud owner, Peter Deilmann, himself an avid art collector. There is also an incredible amount of statuary aboard this ship. Deilmann's hand in the detailed interiors is evident everywhere. *Deutschland* is registered under the German flag, which means an expensive, single-nationality crew dedicated to serving German-speaking passengers (although English-speaking passengers are welcome). This is a ship for discriminating passengers to enjoy to the full, particularly for the destination-rich itineraries featured by this company. The currency aboard is the deutschmark.

Besides two oceangoing cruise ships (*Berlin, Deutschland*) and a lovely three-masted tall ship (*Lili Marleen*), Peter Deilmann Reederei owns and operates a fleet of handsome, contemporary river vessels (*DonauPrinzessin, Mozart, Princess de Provence, Prinzessin von Preussen*).

But: There is no wraparound outdoor promenade deck (there are, however, port and starboard midship walking decks under the inboard lifeboats), and no cabins with private balconies.

ms Disney Magic

☆☆☆☆
(L)

LIFESTYLE	PREMIUM
Cruise Line:	Disney Cruise Line
Former Names:	-
Gross Tonnage:	83,338
Builder:	Fincantieri (Italy)
Original Cost:	$350 million
Entered Service:	July 1998
Flag:	Bahamas
Tel No:	330851612/13/17/18
Fax No:	330851611/330851616
Length (ft./m.):	964.5/294.00
Beam (ft./m.):	105.7/32.22
Draft (ft./m.):	26.2/8.0
Propulsion/Propellers:	diesel-electric (38,000kW)/2 (FP)
Decks:	12
Total Crew:	945
Pass. Capacity (basis 2):	1,760
Pass. Capacity (all berths):	3,325
Pass. Space Ratio (basis 2):	48.2
Pass. Space Ratio (all berths):	25.0
Officers:	European/Norwegian
Total Cabins:	880
Size Range (sq. ft./m.):	180.8–968.7/16.8–90.0
Cabins (outside view):	640
Cabins (inside):	240
Family Cabins:	80
Cabins (with private balcony):	280
Cabins (wheelchair accessible):	20
Cabin Current:	110 AC
Cabin TV:	Yes
Dining Rooms:	3 main (+1 Alternative +1 Cafe)
Seatings:	2
Elevators:	12
Casino:	No
Slot Machines:	0
Swimming Pools (outdoors):	3
Swimming Pools (inside):	0
Whirlpools:	6
Fitness Center:	Yes
Sauna/Steam Room:	Yes/Yes
Massage:	Yes
Self-Service Launderette:	Yes (3)
Movie Theater/Seats:	Yes/270
Library:	No
Children's Facilities:	Yes
Classification Society:	Lloyd's Register

RATINGS	SCORE
Ship: Hardware/Maintenance	90
Ship: Outdoor Facilities/Space	88
Ship: Interior Facilities/Space/Flow	92
Ship: Decor/Furnishings/Artwork	90
Ship: Spa/Fitness Facilities	86
Cabins: Suites and Deluxe	88
Cabins: Standard Sizes	84
Food: Dining Room/Cuisine	61
Food: Informal Dining/Buffets	42
Food: Quality of Ingredients	60
Food: Afternoon Tea/Bar Snacks	40
Service: Dining Room	74
Service: Bars	80
Service: Cabins	77
Service: Open Decks	74
Cruise: Entertainment	95
Cruise: Activities Program	88
Cruise: Movies/Television Programming	84
Cruise: Hospitality Standard	74
Cruise: Overall Product Delivery	79
OVERALL SCORE	**1,546**

Accommodation: Spread over six decks, there are several types of suites and cabins from which to choose; all have been designed for practicality and have space-efficient layouts. Most cabins have common features such as a neat vertical steamer trunk used for clothes storage, a hairdryer located at a vanity desk (not in the bathroom), and bathrobes for all passengers. Many cabins have third- and fourth pull-down berths that can be raised totally into the ceiling when not in use, but standard inside and outside cabins, while acceptable for two, are tight with three or four. The decor is practical and very colorful, with lots of neat styling touches.

The bathrooms, although quite compact (due to the fact that the toilet is separate from the rest of the bathroom), are really functional units, designed with split-use facilities so that more than one person can use them at the same time (good for families); many have bathtubs (really shower tubs).

Suites naturally offer much more space and goodies such as VCR units, CD players, large screen televisions, and extra beds that are useful for larger families; some of the suites are, however, underneath the pool deck, teen lounge, or informal cafe, so there could be lots of noise as the ceiling insulation is poor (but cabin-to-cabin insulation is good).

Wheelchair-bound passengers have a variety of cabin sizes and configurations to choose from, including suites with private balcony and large bathrooms with excellent roll-in showers .

A twenty-four-hour room service is available (suite occupants also get concierge service); the room service menu is very limited, as are the cabin breakfast menu and delivery service.

Dining: There are three main dining rooms, each with 442 seats and a unique theme: Lumiere has *Beauty and the Beast*, Parrot Cay has a pseudo-***Caribbean*** theme, and Animator's Palate (the most visual of the three) features food and electronic art to make the evening repast and décor change from black and white to a full-color dining experience during the meal. This is "rotation" dining—you move together with your waiter to each dining room in turn, thus providing a different dining experience (each has a different decor, different menus). Parrot Cay and Lumiere have open seating for breakfast and lunch (the lunch menu is awful).

In addition, Palo is an elegant 140-seat reservations-only alternative restaurant (there is a cover/gratuity charge of $5). It has a 270-degree view and is for adults only; the a la carte cuisine is cooked to order, and the wine list is good (prices are high). Make your reservations as soon as you board or miss out on the only decent food aboard this ship.

For casual munching there is an indoor/outdoor cafe featuring low-class breakfast and lunch buffets with incredibly poor choice and presentation, a buffet dinner for children (mostly fried foods), and an ice cream and frozen yogurt bar (Scoops) that is open infrequently; there are other fast food outlets for hamburgers, hot dogs, inedible pizzas, and sandwiches (Pinocchios) open at varying times throughout the day (but not in the evening).

Overall, the food is extremely disappointing and non-memorable, with too much concentration on fried foods, few green vegetables, and little thought of nutritional content. Vegetarians will be totally underwhelmed, as will those who want spa (light) cuisine.

Other Comments: This ship's profile has tried to combine streamlining with tradition and nostalgia, and has two large red and black funnels designed to remind you of the ocean liners of the past. One of the funnels is a dummy, but contains a variety of public spaces, including a neat ESPN sports bar and a broadcast center. The ship's whistle even plays "When You Wish Upon A Star" (sort of). The bow features handsome gold scrollwork that is more often seen adorning the tall ships of yesteryear. There is a wrap-around outdoor promenade deck for strolling.

Those who thought that Disney Cruise Line would add ostentatious decoration to the ship's exterior were wrong (well, somewhat wrong). Mickey's ears are painted on the funnels; there is also a special 85-feet-long (25.9 m) paint stripe that cleverly incorporates Disney characters into the somewhat whimsical yellow paintwork along each side of the hull at the bow. Cute: the ship's exterior colors are also those of Mickey Mouse himself (call it a well-planned coincidence). Also of note is a 15-feet-tall (4.5 m) Goofy hanging upside down in a bosun's chair, painting the stern of the vessel.

Inside, the ship is quite stunning, although hurriedly (poorly) finished in places. The Art Deco theme of the old ocean liners has been tastefully carried out (check out the stainless steel/pewter Disney detailing on the handrails and balustrades in the three-deck-high lobby). Most public rooms have high ceilings. Actually, the decor is more reminiscent of New York's Radio City Music Hall. The interior detailing is stunning, much of it whimsical—pure Disney. The lobby provides a real photo opportunity that should not be missed: a 6-foot-high (1.8 m) bronze statue of Mickey in the role of a ship's helmsman. Mickey is also visible in many other areas, albeit somewhat subtly (for Disney). If you can't sleep, try counting the number of times Mickey's logo appears—it's an impossible task!

There are two large shops and an abundance of Disney Cruise Line-themed clothing, soft toys, collectibles, and specialty items. Features a superb 1,040-seat Walt Disney Theatre (spread over four decks but without a balcony), piano bar, adults-only nightclub/disco, family lounge, and a dedicated cinema (where classic Disney films will be shown, as well as first-run movies).

On deck, a sports deck features a paddle tennis court, table tennis, basketball court, and shuffleboard, as well as a golf driving range. The ESPN Skybox features twelve televisions of differing sizes for live sports events and noisy conversation. There are three outdoor pools; one pool is for adults only, one is for children, and one is for families. However, there's music everywhere, and it's hard to find any quiet spots. The children's pool features a long yellow water slide, held up by

Mickey's hand. For fitness devotees, there is also an ocean-view fitness spa measuring 8,500 sq. ft. (789.6 m^2) with windows that overlook the navigation bridge below.

The children's entertainment areas measure 13,000 sq. ft. (1,207.7 m^2), and more than thirty counselors are aboard for any given cruise. There is also a separate teen club and video game arcade. A child drop-off service works in the evenings, private babysitting services are available ($11 per hour), as are character "tuck-ins" for children, and character breakfast and lunch. Strollers are available, at no charge, and parents can be provided with beepers, so that they can also enjoy their time alone, away from the kids for much of the day.

Entertainment and activities programming for families and children is outstanding. Stage shows feature the Disney theme; "Hercules—A Muse-ical Comedy," "Voyage of the Ghost Ship" (a lighthearted look at cruising), "Disney Dreams" (featuring a bedtime story with Peter Pan, Aladdin, the Little Mermaid and others); sadly, all are performed without a hint of a live orchestra, although lighting and staging are excellent. A show called "Island Magic," which features only Disney characters, is performed the day before reaching Castaway Cay; it is the only show featuring a live orchestra. On the four-day cruise, an additional (local Bahamian) show called "Junkanoo" takes place outdoors at one of the swimming pools.

"Beat Street" is a great idea; it is an adult entertainment area that includes a wacky Hollywood-style street, and incorporates three entertainment rooms: "Sessions" (a piano lounge, complete with private headphones for listening to music of all types when no live music is scheduled); "Rockin' Bar D" (for rock 'n roll and country music); and "Off-Beat" (for improvisational comedy involving the audience).

Although Nassau is decidedly unappealing and not very tourist-friendly, the highlight of the itinerary is undoubtedly Disney's private island, Castaway Cay. It is an outstanding private island, with its own pier so that the ship can dock alongside—a cruise industry first. There is a post office with its own special Bahamas/Disney stamp, and a whole host of dedicated, well thought-out attractions and amenities for all ages (including a large adults-only beach, complete with massage cabanas).

Disney characters are aboard for all cruises and lots of photo opportunities; they come out to play mainly when children's activities are scheduled. All the artwork throughout the ship's public areas comes from Disney films or animation features, with many original drawings dating from the early thirties. One neat onboard service is that any photographs taken by the ship's photographers are automatically delivered to your cabin - no more searching on endless boards.

This ship should appeal to couples, single-parents and families alike (there are few activities for couples during the daytime, but plenty of entertainment at night). Whether cruising with 500 (or more) kids aboard will make for a relaxing vacation for those without kids depends on how much noise one can take.

At Port Canaveral, a special terminal has been constructed (a copy of the original Ocean terminal used by the transatlantic liners *Queen Elizabeth* and *Queen Mary* in Southampton, England). Embarkation and disembarkation is an entertainment event rather than the hassle-laden affair that it has become for many cruise lines with large ships (if all the buses do not arrive together).

Disney Magic features year-round three- and four-day cruises to the Bahamas—part of a seven-day vacation package that includes a three- or four-day stay at a Walt Disney World resort hotel in Orlando (the cruise forms the second half of the vacation). It's all tied up in one encapsulated, well-controlled, seamless, and crime-free environment that promises escape and adventure. American Express cardholders get special treatment and extra goodies. Transfers between Walt Disney World resorts in Orlando and the ship are included. Special buses feature vintage 1930s/1940s style interior decor (thirty sets of Mickey's face and ears can be found in the blue fabric of each seat); five of the forty-five custom-made buses are outfitted to carry wheelchair passengers.

This ship, the cruise industry's only floating theme park, has been rated on its own, in common with all other ships in this book: that is *not including* the additional three- or four-day stay at a Disney World resort, which forms part of the total Disney Cruise Line vacation (although it is possible to book just a cruise on its own). You should be aware that this is a highly programmed, strictly timed and regimented onboard experience, with tickets, lines, and reservations necessary for almost everything. Disney may know how to operate theme parks, but when it comes to cruise ships it is obvious the company knows little.

But: The elevators are very small. It is very expensive for a short cruise (but then so is a week at any Disney resort), gratuities are extra, and 15 percent is added to all bar/beverage/wine accounts. Don't even think about it if you don't like Disney, kids, and lining up and registering for activities. Lines at the Guest Relations Desk are intolerably long at any hour of the day or night. Most disappointing of all is the food product and delivery—it is seriously lacking and of woefully lower quality than less expensive cruise products.

ms Disney Wonder
(L)

Lifestyle	**Premium**
Cruise Line:	Disney Cruise Lines
Former Names:	-
Gross Tonnage:	85,000
Builder:	Fincantieri (Italy)
Original Cost:	$350 million
Entered Service:	July 1999
Flag:	Bahamas
Tel No:	n/a
Fax No:	n/a
Length (ft./m.):	964.5/294.00
Beam (ft./m.):	105.7/32.22
Draft (ft./m.):	26.2/8.0
Propulsion/Propellers:	diesel-electric (38,000kW)/2 (FP)
Decks:	n/a
Total Crew:	945
Pass. Capacity (basis 2):	1,760
Pass. Capacity (all berths):	2,800
Pass. Space Ratio (basis 2):	48.2
Pass. Space Ratio (all berths):	30.3
Officers:	European/Norwegian
Total Cabins:	880
Size Range (sq. ft./m.):	180.8–968.7/10.8–90.0
Cabins (outside view):	640
Cabins (inside):	240
Family Cabins:	80
Cabins (with private balcony):	280
Cabins (wheelchair accessible):	20
Cabin Current:	110 AC
Cabin TV:	Yes
Dining Rooms:	3 main (+1 Alternative +1 Cafe)
Seatings:	2
Elevators:	12
Casino:	No
Slot Machines:	0
Swimming Pools (outdoors):	3
Swimming Pools (inside):	0
Whirlpools:	6
Fitness Center:	Yes
Sauna/Steam Room:	Yes/Yes
Massage:	Yes
Self-Service Launderette:	Yes (3)
Movie Theater/Seats:	Yes/270
Library:	Yes
Children's Facilities:	Yes
Classification Society:	Lloyd's Register

Ratings	**Score**
Ship: Hardware/Maintenance	NYR
Ship: Outdoor Facilities/Space	NYR
Ship: Interior Facilities/Space/Flow	NYR
Ship: Decor/Furnishings/Artwork	NYR
Ship: Spa/Fitness Facilities	NYR
Cabins: Suites and Deluxe	NYR
Cabins: Standard Sizes	NYR
Food: Dining Room/Cuisine	NYR
Food: Informal Dining/Buffets	NYR
Food: Quality of Ingredients	NYR
Food: Afternoon Tea/Bar Snacks	NYR
Service: Dining Room	NYR
Service: Bars	NYR
Service: Cabins	NYR
Service: Open Decks	NYR
Cruise: Entertainment	NYR
Cruise: Activities Program	NYR
Cruise: Movies/Television Programming	NYR
Cruise: Hospitality Standard	NYR
Cruise: Overall Product Delivery	NYR

Expected Score Range
1,400-1,750

For comments, see *Disney Magic*.

ss Dolphin IV

☆☆ +

(M)

Lifestyle	**Standard**
Cruise Line:	Cape Canaveral Cruise Line
Former Names:	*Ithaca/Amelia De Melo/Zion*
Gross Tonnage:	13,000
Builder:	Howaldtswerke Deutsche Werft (Germany)
Original Cost:	n/a
Entered Service:	March 1956/January 1996
Flag:	Bahamas
Tel No:	n/a
Fax No:	n/a
Length (ft./m.):	501.2/152.77
Beam (ft./m.):	65.1/19.87
Draft (ft./m.):	27.5/8.40
Propulsion/Propellers:	steam turbine (7,723kW)/1 (FP)
Decks:	7
Total Crew:	290
Pass. Capacity (basis 2):	588
Pass. Capacity (all berths):	684
Pass. Space Ratio (basis 2):	22.1
Pass. Space Ratio (all berths):	19.0
Officers:	Greek
Total Cabins:	281
Size Range (sq. ft./m.):	73–258/6.7–24.0
Cabins (outside view):	206
Cabins (inside):	75
Cabins (for one person):	0
Cabins (with private balcony):	0
Cabins (wheelchair accessible):	0
Cabin Current:	110/220 AC
Cabin TV:	No
Dining Rooms:	1
Seatings:	2
Elevators:	1
Casino:	Yes
Slot Machines:	Yes
Swimming Pools (outdoors):	1
Swimming Pools (inside):	0
Whirlpools:	1
Fitness Center:	Yes
Sauna/Steam Room:	No/No
Massage:	No
Self-Service Launderette:	No
Movie Theater/Seats:	No
Library:	No
Children's Facilities:	Yes
Classification Society:	Lloyd's Register

Ratings	**Score**
Ship: Hardware/Maintenance	53
Ship: Outdoor Facilities/Space	51
Ship: Interior Facilities/Space/Flow	47
Ship: Decor/Furnishings/Artwork	51
Ship: Spa/Fitness Facilities	33
Cabins: Suites and Deluxe	57
Cabins: Standard Sizes	51
Food: Dining Room/Cuisine	56
Food: Informal Dining/Buffets	48
Food: Quality of Ingredients	50
Food: Afternoon Tea/Bar Snacks	41
Service: Dining Room	59
Service: Bars	58
Service: Cabins	58
Service: Open Decks	47
Cruise: Entertainment	58
Cruise: Activities Program	51
Cruise: Movies/Television Programming	41
Cruise: Hospitality Standard	47
Cruise: Overall Product Delivery	51
Overall Score	**1,008**

Accommodation: The cabins are very small and have very plain, basic decor. However, they may be judged almost comfortable and adequate for the short cruises made by this ship. Cabins on the lower decks suffer from noise (and the smell of diesel fuel) from the engineroom.

Dining: The dining room is quite an attractive room and has a warm ambience, but it is narrow and has a low ceiling. The food is indifferent, and the ingredients are not the best, but it is good value for the budget-minded. The service is hurried and lacks any finesse, although the staff is quite friendly and tries to please. Fairly attractive buffet displays, but there could be more creativity.

Other Comments: She is a fairly attractive older ship, with pleasing lines, even with its now very noticeable center-sag. The open deck and sunbathing areas are very cramped due to high passenger density, and the plastic chairs and tables are in need of help.

The ship's public rooms are quite nicely decorated in clean, crisp, contemporary colors, albeit with much use of reflective surfaces (mirrors). There is a good shopping area, although it really is full of tacky items, more for souvenirs and gifts than anything else.

The showroom is really quite poor, and the stage would be better at the opposite end (the seating is also uncomfortable for long periods). Also, the discotheque is rather small and claustrophobic. Has a moderately friendly staff and ambience, but the entertainment is weak and decidedly low budget, typical of what you would find in a poor night club ashore in southern Florida.

This ship has a lively atmosphere for short, fun cruises for the young and active set, but I wonder how much longer can she compete with the bright new ships that offer more space and better facilities, and indeed more of everything. Operates two- and four-night Bahamas cruises.

<u>But:</u> This is a high-density ship, and it is difficult to find a quiet corner anywhere. Some of the staff (particularly those at the Purser's Office/Reception Desk) need to be sent to charm school.

ms Ecstasy

☆☆☆☆

(L)

Lifestyle	Standard
Cruise Line:	Carnival Cruise Lines
Former Names:	-
Gross Tonnage:	70,367
Builder:	Kvaerner Masa-Yards (Finland)
Original Cost:	$275 million
Entered Service:	June 1991
Flag:	Liberia
Tel No:	1244233
Fax No:	1244234
Length (ft./m.):	855.8/260.60
Beam (ft./m.):	104.0/31.40
Draft (ft./m.):	25.9/7.89
Propulsion/Propellers:	diesel-electric (42,240kW)/2 (CP)
Decks:	10
Total Crew:	920
Pass. Capacity (basis 2):	2,040
Pass. Capacity (all berths):	2,594
Pass. Space Ratio (basis 2):	34.4
Pass. Space Ratio (all berths):	27.1
Officers:	Italian
Total Cabins:	1,020
Size Range (sq. ft./m.):	173.2–409.7/16.0–38.0
Cabins (outside view):	618
Cabins (inside):	402
Cabins (for one person):	0
Cabins (with private balcony):	26
Cabins (wheelchair accessible):	20
Cabin Current:	110 AC
Cabin TV:	Yes
Dining Rooms:	2
Seatings:	2
Elevators:	14
Casino:	Yes
Slot Machines:	Yes
Swimming Pools (outdoors):	3
Swimming Pools (inside):	0
Whirlpools:	6
Fitness Center:	Yes
Sauna/Steam Room:	Yes/Yes
Massage:	Yes
Self-Service Launderette:	Yes
Movie Theater/Seats::	No
Library:	Yes
Children's Facilities:	Yes
Classification Society:	Lloyd's Register

Ratings	Score
Ship: Hardware/Maintenance	81
Ship: Outdoor Facilities/Space	74
Ship: Interior Facilities/Space/Flow	81
Ship: Decor/Furnishings/Artwork	82
Ship: Spa/Fitness Facilities	77
Cabins: Suites and Deluxe	78
Cabins: Standard Sizes	73
Food: Dining Room/Cuisine	66
Food: Informal Dining/Buffets	62
Food: Quality of Ingredients	61
Food: Afternoon Tea/Bar Snacks	51
Service: Dining Room	68
Service: Bars	70
Service: Cabins	68
Service: Open Decks	64
Cruise: Entertainment	81
Cruise: Activities Program	67
Cruise: Movies/Television Programming	65
Cruise: Hospitality Standard	63
Cruise: Overall Product Delivery	77
Overall Score	**1,409**

Accommodation: The plain but comfortable cabins are quite roomy and practical (most are of the same size and appointments), with good storage space and well-designed bathrooms. The suites are attractive, but nothing special, being much smaller than those on several competing companies' ships of a similar size.

Dining: The two dining rooms have attractive decor and colors, but are large, crowded, and very noisy. The food is adequate, but no more, although Carnival Cruise Lines has made several improvements. The service is a little robotic, closely timed, and inflexible, although waiters are willing and quite friendly. The wine list is quite decent, although there are no wine waiters.

Other Comments: This is one of the most successful Fantasy-class of ships for Carnival Cruise Lines. Although the exterior displays a bold profile, the large funnel, with its familiar wing tips and red, white, and blue colors, offsets it.

This ship has very good general passenger flow, and the interior design is clever, functional, and very colorful. The neon lighting in the interior decor takes a little getting used to at first, as the color combinations are vivid, to say the least. There is a vintage Rolls Royce motor car located on the principal, double-width indoor promenade. The health spa and fitness facilities are quite decent. A stunning, 10-ton sculpture graces marble and glass atrium that spans seven decks. The library is quite lovely, but there are few books. The Chinatown Lounge comes complete with Oriental decor and features hanging lanterns and smoking dragon. The balconied show lounge is large, but 20 pillars do obstruct the views from several seats.

This ship will provide a great introduction to cruising for the novice passenger seeking an action-packed short cruise experience in contemporary surroundings, with a real swinging party atmosphere, and minimum fuss and finesse. You will have a fine time if you like nightlife and lots of silly participation games. Like life in the fast lane, this is cruising in theme-park fantasyland, and the dress code is casual. The staff helps you have fun, and that is what Carnival does best. Want to party? Then this should prove to be a great ship for you. Features three- and four-day cruises to the Bahamas year-round.

But: This ship is not for those who want a quiet, relaxing cruise. There are simply too many annoying announcements and a great deal of hustling for drinks.

ss Edinburgh Castle

☆☆☆

(L)

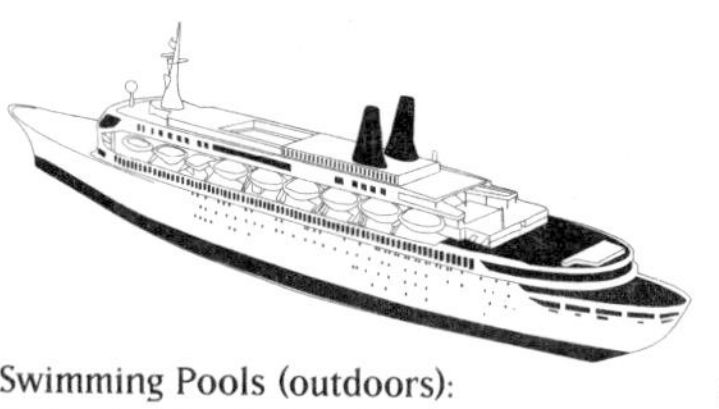

Lifestyle	Standard
Cruise Line:	Castle Shipping/Direct Cruises
Former Names:	*EugenioCosta/Eugenio C*
Gross Tonnage:	32,753
Builder:	Cantieri Riuniti dell' Adriatico (Italy)
Original Cost:	$24.5 million
Entered Service:	August 1966/November 1997
Flag:	Great Britain
Tel No:	2014008945
Fax No:	323472811
Length (ft./m.):	713.2/217.39
Beam (ft./m.):	96.1/29.39
Draft (ft./m.):	28.3/8.63
Propulsion/Propellers:	steam turbine (40,456kW)/2 (FP)
Decks:	10
Total Crew:	480
Pass. Capacity (basis 2):	1,012
Pass. Capacity (all berths):	1,418
Pass. Space Ratio (basis 2):	32.3
Pass. Space Ratio (all berths):	23.0
Officers:	British
Total Cabins:	506 (8 without facilities)
Size Range (sq. ft./m.):	93–236/8.7–22.0
Cabins (outside view):	271
Cabins (inside):	235
Cabins (for one person):	0
Cabins (with private balcony):	0
Cabins (wheelchair accessible):	0
Cabin Current:	127 AC
Cabin TV:	No
Dining Rooms:	3
Seatings:	2
Elevators:	5
Casino:	Yes
Slot Machines:	Yes
Swimming Pools (outdoors):	2
Swimming Pools (inside):	0
Whirlpools:	1
Fitness Center:	Yes
Sauna/Steam Room:	Yes/No
Massage:	Yes
Self-Service Launderette:	Yes
Movie Theater/Seats:	Yes/230
Library:	Yes
Children's Facilities:	Yes
Classification Society:	RINA

Ratings	Score
Ship: Hardware/Maintenance	60
Ship: Outdoor Facilities/Space	62
Ship: Interior Facilities/Space/Flow	63
Ship: Decor/Furnishings/Artwork	60
Ship: Spa/Fitness Facilities	47
Cabins: Suites and Deluxe	65
Cabins: Standard Sizes	52
Food: Dining Room/Cuisine	61
Food: Informal Dining/Buffets	56
Food: Quality of Ingredients	60
Food: Afternoon Tea/Bar Snacks	48
Service: Dining Room	61
Service: Bars	61
Service: Cabins	61
Service: Open Decks	51
Cruise: Entertainment	57
Cruise: Activities Program	52
Cruise: Movies/Television Programming	40
Cruise: Hospitality Standard	60
Cruise: Overall Product Delivery	66
Overall Score	**1,143**

Accommodation: Most of the accommodation is located on lower decks, with most of the public rooms located above, with the exception of the largest suites, located in what was formerly the first class section of the ship. The suites feature large living rooms; separate bedroom; abundant closet, drawer, and cupboard space for a large family; and bathroom with full-sized bathtub and bidet.

There is a wide range of general accommodation (in 13 categories), with many different styles, sizes, and configurations to choose from. Many cabins feature third and fourth berths (good for families); bathrooms are generally quite small, except for those in the uppermost grades (many of which also feature a bidet and full-sized bathtub). The towels are small, but they are changed daily, while bed linen is changed every second day.

Dining: The principal dining room is large and quite noisy. There is no assigned seating however, so you can dine with whomever you wish. The catering is good, and menus feature a reasonable range of items (typically including three dinner entrees), although you should remember that catering is done according to the price paid. The standard is basically sound, and, although not really memorable, it is more than adequate, with special themed meals featuring popular spices (as in Indian/Thai/South-East Asian foods). There is a decent selection of breads, cheeses, and fruits. For those wanting superior food or to celebrate a special occasion, a plainly decorated but spacious reservation-only alternative dining spot called the Princess Grill provides a fine a la carte menu, which adds an extra charge of £10 per person.

Casual meals can be found at a self-service buffet available for breakfast, lunch, and dinner, at no extra charge.

Other Comments: *Edinburgh Castle* is a well-proportioned ex-ocean liner that was originally built for Costa Cruises for transatlantic crossings, and was operated for many years on the southern transatlantic trade between Italy and South America. The ship has the graceful, flowing lines of a sixties ocean liner and twin slender funnels that are located aft.

Her new owners, Castle Shipping, who purchased the ship in 1997, intended to recreate the feeling of the old Union Castle days and to bring back the gracious ambience that prevailed in the late fifties and early sixties aboard the mauve-hulled ships that sailed between England and South Africa. She has carpeted promenade decks, twin funnels, and a reasonable amount of open deck and sunbathing space. She has good teak decking outdoors.

Inside, there is a good array of spacious public rooms, mostly laid out on one deck. These all have high (pegboard) ceilings, and were scheduled for refurbishment in late 1998. There is a large full-screen cinema, complete with an upper (balcony) level, and, for those who like to dance, at least two of the lounges sport good-sized wooden dance floors.

This ship is quite comfortable throughout, and provides good value cruising for couples and families in an informal setting. The ship is under charter to package holiday companies such as UK-based Direct Cruises. Provides good value cruises for its UK-based clientele, but remember that she is a well-worn ship and not a new ship, despite having undergone much refurbishment, and therefore some idiosyncrasies must be accepted. What is good for UK-based passengers is the fact that they will not have to fly to join the ship, as she sails from UK ports during the summer season. Travel insurance, port charges, and all gratuities are included in the cruise fare.

But: This is a cruise ship operated to strict no-frills prices; some staff leave much to be desired. The entertainment is decidedly of the "end-of-pier" variety and needs upgrading, although most passengers are happy with it.

ms Elation

☆☆☆☆

(L)

Lifestyle	Standard
Cruise Line:	Carnival Cruise Lines
Former Names:	-
Gross Tonnage:	70,367
Builder:	Kvaerner Masa-Yards (Finland)
Original Cost:	$315 million
Entered Service:	April 1998
Flag:	Liberia
Tel No:	n/a
Fax No:	n/a
Length (ft./m.):	855.0/260.60
Beam (ft./m.):	104.0/31.40
Draft (ft./m.):	25.9/7.90
Propulsion/Propellers:	diesel-electric (57,430bhp)/2 (Azipod)
Decks:	10
Total Crew:	920
Pass. Capacity (basis 2):	2,040
Pass. Capacity (all berths):	2,594
Pass. Space Ratio (basis 2):	34.4
Pass. Space Ratio (all berths):	26.7
Officers:	Italian
Total Cabins:	1,020
Size Range (sq. ft./m.):	173.2–409.7/16.0–38.0
Cabins (outside view):	618
Cabins (inside):	402
Cabins (for one person):	0
Cabins (with private balcony):	26
Cabins (wheelchair accessible):	20
Cabin Current:	110 AC
Cabin TV:	Yes
Dining Rooms:	2
Seatings:	2
Elevators:	14
Casino:	Yes
Slot Machines:	Yes
Swimming Pools (outdoors):	3
Swimming Pools (inside):	0
Whirlpools:	6
Fitness Center:	Yes
Sauna/Steam Room:	Yes/Yes
Massage:	Yes
Self-Service Launderette:	Yes
Movie Theater/Seats:	No
Library:	Yes
Children's Facilities:	Yes
Classification Society:	Lloyd's Register

Ratings	Score
Ship: Hardware/Maintenance	81
Ship: Outdoor Facilities/Space	74
Ship: Interior Facilities/Space/Flow	81
Ship: Decor/Furnishings/Artwork	82
Ship: Spa/Fitness Facilities	77
Cabins: Suites and Deluxe	78
Cabins: Standard Sizes	73
Food: Dining Room/Cuisine	66
Food: Informal Dining/Buffets	65
Food: Quality of Ingredients	61
Food: Afternoon Tea/Bar Snacks	51
Service: Dining Room	68
Service: Bars	70
Service: Cabins	68
Service: Open Decks	64
Cruise: Entertainment	81
Cruise: Activities Program	67
Cruise: Movies/Television Programming	65
Cruise: Hospitality Standard	63
Cruise: Overall Product Delivery	77
Overall Score	**1,412**

Accommodation: As in her sister ships in the same (Fantasy-class) series, the cabins are almost all identical in size, shape, fittings, and decoration. The 28 outside suites have whirlpool bathtubs and some fascinating, eclectic decor and furniture. Standard cabin ceilings are very plain, and amenities consist only of ice water and soap, so bring shampoo and conditioner (shower cap for ladies) and other personal toiletry items.

Dining: There are two large, rather boisterous dining rooms (both are nonsmoking) with Carnival's usual efficient (fast), programmed, well-practiced service and delivery. The improved cuisine is acceptable, but it still is not the company's strong point (you get what you pay for, remember). There is a wine list, but there are no wine waiters.

For casual meals, there's The Lido, which, aboard this ship, has some improvements and additions worthy of note, such as an orange juice machine, where you put in oranges and out comes fresh juice (better than the concentrate stuff supplied in the dining room). There's also a sushi bar. Things are looking up, which means more choices.

Other Comments: This is the seventh in a series of eight mega-ships of the same series and identical internal configuration. It is a very successful design for this successful company that targets the mass market, and particularly the first-time cruise passenger. Elation has a bold, forthright, angular appearance that is typical of today's space-creative designs. What is new, however, is the Azipod propulsion system, which gives the ship more maneuverability, while reducing required machinery space and vibration at the stern. There is a banked outdoor jogging track.

The theme of the interior decor is composers and their compositions (most of the public rooms have musical names), and the colors, while bright, are less so than aboard previous ships in this series. As in her sister ships, there is a dramatic six-deck-high atrium, appropriately dressed to impress, topped by a large glass dome, and featuring a fascinating, entertaining artistic centerpiece. Has expansive open deck areas and a good, expansive health spa. There are public entertainment lounges, bars and clubs galore, with something for everyone, including a children's playroom, larger than aboard the previous ships in this series. Some busy colors and design themes abound in the handsome public rooms—these are connected by wide indoor boulevards and beg your attention and indulgence. There is also a good art collection, much of it bright and vocal. The library is a fine room, as aboard most Carnival ships (but there are few books). One neat feature (not found aboard previous ships in this series) is an atrium bar, complete with live classical music—something new for this company.

Features a lavish, yet almost elegant multitiered 1,010-seat showroom and the line's fine, loud, high-energy razzle-dazzle shows. A large, three-deck-high glass-enclosed health spa is always a busy place, including a gymnasium full of the latest high-tech muscle-pumping machinery. A large casino invites almost nonstop action. Good for those who like big city life ashore and want it on their cruise vacation. Operates seven-day Mexican Riviera cruises year-round from the port of Los Angeles.

But: This is another ship that provides a rather impersonal cruise experience, as the ship is large and there are so many other passengers. There are many repetitive announcements.

ss Emerald

☆☆☆

(M)

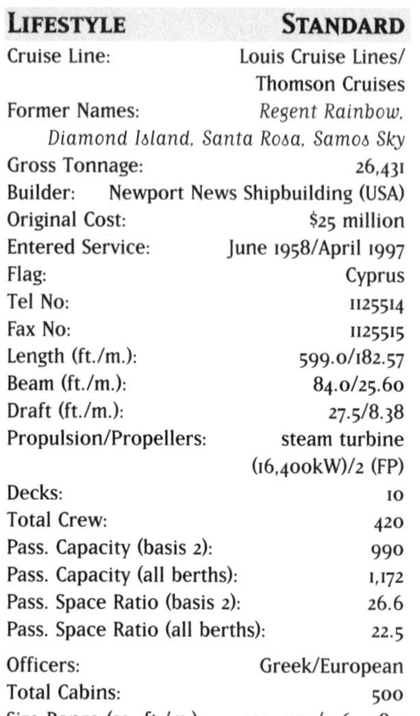

LIFESTYLE	STANDARD
Cruise Line:	Louis Cruise Lines/ Thomson Cruises
Former Names:	*Regent Rainbow, Diamond Island, Santa Rosa, Samos Sky*
Gross Tonnage:	26,431
Builder:	Newport News Shipbuilding (USA)
Original Cost:	$25 million
Entered Service:	June 1958/April 1997
Flag:	Cyprus
Tel No:	1125514
Fax No:	1125515
Length (ft./m.):	599.0/182.57
Beam (ft./m.):	84.0/25.60
Draft (ft./m.):	27.5/8.38
Propulsion/Propellers:	steam turbine (16,400kW)/2 (FP)
Decks:	10
Total Crew:	420
Pass. Capacity (basis 2):	990
Pass. Capacity (all berths):	1,172
Pass. Space Ratio (basis 2):	26.6
Pass. Space Ratio (all berths):	22.5
Officers:	Greek/European
Total Cabins:	500
Size Range (sq. ft./m.):	125–305/11.6–28.3

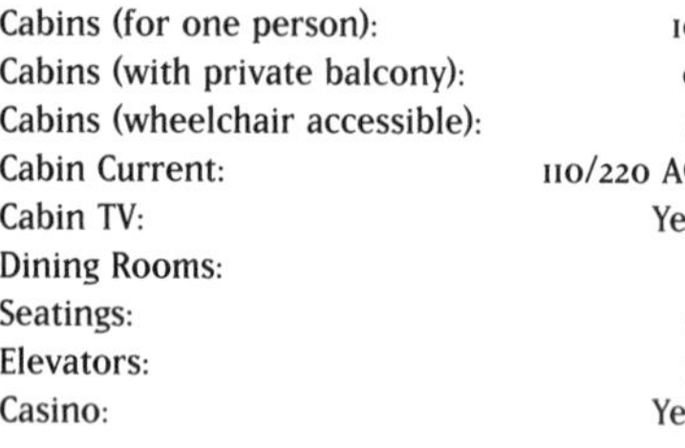

Cabins (outside view):	338
Cabins (inside):	162
Cabins (for one person):	10
Cabins (with private balcony):	0
Cabins (wheelchair accessible):	2
Cabin Current:	110/220 AC
Cabin TV:	Yes
Dining Rooms:	1
Seatings:	2
Elevators:	3
Casino:	Yes
Slot Machines:	Yes
Swimming Pools (outdoors):	1
Swimming Pools (inside):	0
Whirlpools:	2
Fitness Center:	Yes
Sauna/Steam Room:	Yes/No
Massage:	Yes
Self-Service Launderette:	No
Movie Theater/Seats:	No
Library:	Yes
Children's Facilities:	Yes
Classification Society:	American Bureau of Shipping

RATINGS	SCORE
Ship: Hardware/Maintenance	62
Ship: Outdoor Facilities/Space	61
Ship: Interior Facilities/Space/Flow	62
Ship: Decor/Furnishings/Artwork	62
Ship: Spa/Fitness Facilities	45
Cabins: Suites and Deluxe	63
Cabins: Standard Sizes	57
Food: Dining Room/Cuisine	60
Food: Informal Dining/Buffets	54
Food: Quality of Ingredients	58
Food: Afternoon Tea/Bar Snacks	48
Service: Dining Room	66
Service: Bars	64
Service: Cabins	67
Service: Open Decks	58
Cruise: Entertainment	61
Cruise: Activities Program	53
Cruise: Movies/Television Programming	51
Cruise: Hospitality Standard	60
Cruise: Overall Product Delivery	65
OVERALL SCORE	**1,177**

Accommodation: This ship has a varied mix of cabins both old and new that offer a wide range of configurations from which to choose, presented in just three main categories: premier, superior, and standard (although there are, in effect, seven price levels). You should note that cabins are not assigned until you are at the embarkation port for check-in. This ad-hoc method of assigning cabins means that those who arrive first probably will get the best cabins, in the best locations.

Many of the original cabins are quite spacious, with good closet and drawer space, while newer ones are a little more compact, and have poor insulation. Continental breakfast in your cabin will cost about $7.50 (£4.50) per person extra (each time). There is also a 24-hour cabin service menu for snacks, all at extra cost.

Dining: The dining room has large picture windows and an interesting, neat orchestra balcony. The food quality and presentation are good for the cost of a cruise. The service is friendly and quite attentive, although you should not expect grand hotel-style service.

Other Comments: After being laid up for over 10 years, this American-built former liner underwent a great amount of reconstruction (costing $72 million) in 1992 in Greece, and more again in 1997, when she was purchased by Louis Cruise Lines. With new upper decks added, her new profile is not exactly handsome, and the open deck and sunbathing space is limited when the ship is full. However, there is a large number of deck lounge chairs and a good wraparound outdoor promenade deck.

The ship's interiors are very pleasant, surprisingly comfortable and feature warm decor that is contemporary without being brash. Many public rooms have high ceilings, which provides a spacious ocean liner feel to the ship, and some lovely wrought iron railings on the stairways. The artwork, unfortunately, looks cheap.

The entertainment is generally of typical low-budget quality, and the sight lines in the show lounge are poor, particularly from port and starboard side seating, with obstruction from 12 thick pillars. For short cruises, however, the ship provides a range of public spaces that, in turn, promotes a good party ambience. Has a large casino with a high ceiling. During the summer, the ship is based on *Palma Majorca*, under charter to Thomson Cruises. She cruises the Mediterranean, and is well-suited for this task. Gratuities are included. Thomson's wholly-owned airline company is Britannia Airways, which will probably fly you to your port of embarkation.

But: She is somewhat of a high-sided ship, with a narrow beam, and is inclined to roll in poor weather. The high density of this vessel means little room to move about when full.

ms Enchanted Capri

☆☆ +

(S)

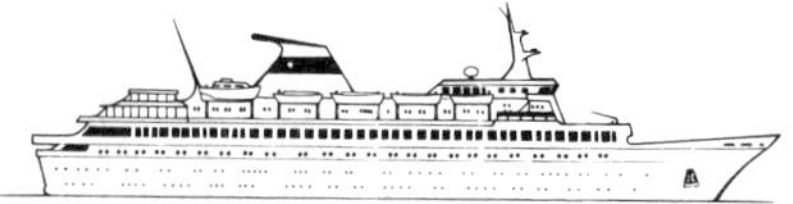

Lifestyle	Standard
Cruise Line:	Black Sea Shipping Company
Former Names:	*Island Holiday/Arkadiya/ Azerbaydzhan*
Gross Tonnage:	15,410
Builder:	Wartsila (Finland)
Original Cost:	$25 million
Entered Service:	January 1976/June 1998
Flag:	Bahamas
Tel No:	n/a
Fax No:	n/a
Length (ft./m.):	512.5/156.24
Beam (ft./m.):	72.3/22.05
Draft (ft./m.):	19.4/5.92
Propulsion/Propellers:	diesel (13,430kW)/2 (CP)
Decks:	8
Total Crew:	300
Pass. Capacity (basis 2):	460
Pass. Capacity (all berths):	637
Pass. Space Ratio (basis 2):	33.5
Pass. Space Ratio (all berths):	24.2
Officers:	American/European
Total Cabins:	230
Size Range (sq. ft./m.):	150–428/14.0–39.7
Cabins (outside view):	112
Cabins (inside):	118
Cabins (for one person):	0
Cabins (with private balcony):	0
Cabins (wheelchair accessible):	0
Cabin Current:	220 AC
Cabin TV:	Boat Deck cabins only
Dining Rooms:	1
Seatings:	2
Elevators:	1
Casino:	Yes
Slot Machines:	Yes
Swimming Pools (outdoors):	1
Swimming Pools (inside):	0
Whirlpools:	0
Fitness Center:	Yes
Sauna/Steam Room:	Yes/No
Massage:	Yes
Self-Service Launderette:	Yes
Movie Theater/Seats:	Yes/145
Library:	Yes
Children's Facilities:	Yes
Classification Society:	Ukraine Register of Shipping

Ratings	Score
Ship: Hardware/Maintenance	57
Ship: Interior Facilities/Space/Flow	59
Ship: Decor/Furnishings/Artwork	54
Ship: Outdoor Facilities/Space	55
Ship: Spa/Fitness Facilities	40
Cabins: Suites and Deluxe	60
Cabins: Standard Sizes	53
Food: Dining Room/Cuisine	61
Food: Informal Dining/Buffets	53
Food: Quality of Ingredients	54
Food: Afternoon Tea/Bar Snacks	40
Service: Dining Room	62
Service: Bars	62
Service: Cabins	62
Service: Open Decks	46
Cruise: Entertainment	56
Cruise: Activities Program	47
Cruise: Movies/Television Programming	42
Cruise: Hospitality Standard	57
Cruise: Overall Product Delivery	64
Overall Score	**1,084**

Accommodation: The suites and deluxe cabins are quite large and very nicely furnished (particularly those in the front of the vessel), and have wood-paneled walls and cabinetry, and an abundance of closet and drawer space. Boat Deck cabins also have a refrigerator. Other cabins are small, have clean lines and are quite simply furnished, without much closet and drawer space, but they are quite adequate and comfortable. There are really too many inside cabins. The cabin insulation in general is quite poor, so you can hear your neighbors.

Dining: There is one rather plain, but brightly decorated dining room. The service is provided by waiters of mixed nationality, who are reasonably friendly. The cuisine is so-so, with limited choice, and it is presented in a very basic meat and potatoes fashion, although it does have good taste. The wine list is also basic, with mostly California wines represented.

Other Comments: She is a smart looking ship, originally one of a series of five almost identical vessels built for the Black Sea Shipping Company, and has a large, square funnel housing. This ship is quite basic, has an informal, unpretentious ambience, and was operated for many years by the now-defunct CTC Cruise Lines. She is now under a five-year charter to the south Florida-based Commodore Cruise Line, until 2003.

There is a reasonable amount of open deck and sunbathing space for the size of the ship, although it does tend to be quite tight and cluttered. Much used, however, are the sports facilities, which include a basketball court. The outdoor swimming pool is located aft, and is circular and quite deep, but very small, and so it is really more of a "dip" pool.

Inside, there is just a handful of public rooms, lounges and bars from which to spend time in, but there is a good-sized casino (created in a 1998 makeover from what used to be the ship's second dining room).

She now operates two- and five-night cruises from New Orleans, and provides a good way for novice cruise passengers to test the waters before trying a longer cruise. The company also operates the older *Enchanted Isle.* The crew is quite friendly and attentive.

But: The ship has a steep, narrow gangway in ports of call. There is no wraparound outdoor promenade deck, no observation lounge, and a poor library.

ss Enchanted Isle

☆☆☆

(M)

Lifestyle	Standard
Cruise Line:	Commodore Cruise Line
Former Names	*Commodore Hotel/ Enchanted Isle/ Bermuda Star/ Veendam/Monarch Star/Argentina*
Gross Tonnage:	23,395
Builder:	Ingalls Shipbuilding (USA)
Original Cost:	$26 million
Entered Service:	December 1958/February 1995
Flag:	Panama
Tel No:	1333171
Fax No:	1333201
Length (ft./m.):	617.5/188.22
Beam (ft./m.):	88.1/26.88
Draft (ft./m.):	27.2/8.30
Propulsion/Propellers:	steam turbine (19,000kW)/2 (FP)
Decks:	9
Total Crew:	350
Pass. Capacity (basis 2):	729
Pass. Capacity (all berths):	729
Pass. Space Ratio (basis 2):	32.0
Pass. Space Ratio (all berths):	32.0
Officers:	European
Total Cabins:	366
Size Range (sq. ft./m.):	104–293/9.6–27.2
Cabins (outside view):	290
Cabins (inside):	76
Cabins (for one person):	3
Cabins (with private balcony):	0
Cabins (wheelchair accessible):	0
Cabin Current:	110 AC
Cabin TV:	No
Dining Rooms:	1
Seatings:	2
Elevators:	3
Casino:	Yes
Slot Machines:	Yes
Swimming Pools (outdoors):	1
Swimming Pools (inside):	0
Whirlpools:	0
Fitness Center:	Yes
Sauna/Steam Room:	Yes/No
Massage:	Yes
Self-Service Launderette:	No
Movie Theater/Seats:	Yes/200
Library:	No
Children's Facilities:	Yes
Classification Society:	Lloyd's Register

Ratings	Score
Ship: Hardware/Maintenance	60
Ship: Outdoor Facilities/Space	62
Ship: Interior Facilities/Space/Flow	60
Ship: Decor/Furnishings/Artwork	52
Ship: Spa/Fitness Facilities	42
Cabins: Suites and Deluxe	57
Cabins: Standard Sizes	53
Food: Dining Room/Cuisine	60
Food: Informal Dining/Buffets	54
Food: Quality of Ingredients	58
Food: Afternoon Tea/Bar Snacks	48
Service: Dining Room	66
Service: Bars	64
Service: Cabins	67
Service: Open Decks	58
Cruise: Entertainment	59
Cruise: Activities Program	53
Cruise: Movies/Television Programming	51
Cruise: Hospitality Standard	57
Cruise: Overall Product Delivery	61
Overall Score	**1,142**

Accommodation: The cabins are quite spacious, with solid, heavy-duty furniture and fittings and a good amount of closet and drawer space, depending on the cabin grade chosen. The bathrooms are of a decent size, for the most part, but the old plumbing fittings often prove frustrating.

Dining: The dining room is located on a lower deck and really needs more light. The food is very standard fare, but the menu choice is rather limited, and the wine list is downright poor. The buffets are minimal, and presentation needs some more creativity. The service is attentive and friendly, but there is certainly no finesse.

Other Comments: This ship, originally built for and operated by Holland America Line, has a pleasing profile, typical of a small ocean liner. Has a large, but false funnel. Thanks to her deep draft, she is a stable ship at sea. *Enchanted Isle* has been quite well looked after over the years (she has had a great number of name changes), and now has a rather homey, matronly look and ambience. Has good exterior teakwood decking and plenty of open deck space.

There is a good choice of public rooms, and passenger flow is quite good, as the ship seems to absorb people well. The interior is by no means glamorous, but provides unpretentious surroundings and decor reminiscent of quiet ocean liners, although it is somewhat dated and worn. Has poor sight lines in the show lounge. The casino is not particularly inviting, but is well used.

This ship will provide a basic, but fairly decent first-time cruise experience, in a fun atmosphere, at a down-to-earth price, providing you do not expect too much.

ms Enchantment of the Seas

☆☆☆☆

(L)

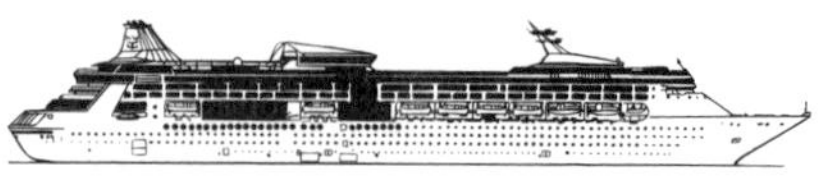

Lifestyle	Standard
Cruise Line:	Royal Caribbean International
Former Names:	-
Gross Tonnage:	74,137
Builder:	Kvaerner Masa Yards (Finland)
Original Cost:	$300 million
Entered Service:	September 1997
Flag:	Liberia
Tel No:	325790-011
Fax No:	325790-012
Length (ft./m.):	917.3/279.6
Beam (ft./m.):	105.6/32.2
Draft (ft./m.):	25.5/7.8
Propulsion/Propellers:	diesel-electric (50,400kw)/2 (FP)
Decks:	11
Total Crew:	760
Pass. Capacity (basis 2):	1,954
Pass. Capacity (all berths):	2,440
Pass. Space Ratio (basis 2):	38.0
Pass. Space Ratio (all berths):	30.3
Officers:	International
Total Cabins:	977
Size Range (sq. ft./m.):	158–1,033/14.7–96.0
Cabins (outside view):	578
Cabins (inside):	399
Cabins (for one person):	0
Cabins (with private balcony):	212
Cabins (wheelchair accessible):	14
Cabin Current:	110/220 AC
Cabin TV:	Yes
Dining Rooms:	1
Seatings:	2
Elevators:	9
Casino:	Yes
Slot Machines:	Yes
Swimming Pools (outdoors):	1
Swimming Pools (inside):	1 (indoor/outdoor w/glass roof)
Whirlpools:	6
Fitness Center:	Yes
Sauna/Steam Room:	Yes/Yes
Massage:	Yes
Self-Service Launderette:	No
Movie Theater/Seats:	No
Library:	Yes
Children's Facilities:	Yes
Classification Society:	Det Norske Veritas

Ratings	Score
Ship: Hardware/Maintenance	89
Ship: Outdoor Facilities/Space	86
Ship: Interior Facilities/Space/Flow	86
Ship: Decor/Furnishings/Artwork	87
Ship: Spa/Fitness Facilities	86
Cabins: Suites and Deluxe	88
Cabins: Standard Sizes	81
Food: Dining Room/Cuisine	71
Food: Informal Dining/Buffets	63
Food: Quality of Ingredients	66
Food: Afternoon Tea/Bar Snacks	52
Service: Dining Room	78
Service: Bars	76
Service: Cabins	77
Service: Open Decks	71
Cruise: Entertainment	81
Cruise: Activities Program	76
Cruise: Movies/Television Programming	76
Cruise: Hospitality Standard	73
Cruise: Overall Product Delivery	77
Overall Score	**1,540**

Accommodation: All of the standard cabins have twin beds that convert to a queen-size bed. There is a reasonably good amount of closet space for a one-week cruise, and an adequate amount of drawer space, although under-bed storage for luggage is limited. The bathrooms are practical, but the decor is plain. Category A/B cabins also have VCR units.

Dining: The 1,195-seat dining room is spread over two decks, with both levels connected by a grand, sweeping staircase. General comments regarding the food operation aboard the company's now well-established *Legend of the Seas* and *Splendour of the Seas* apply, but some further options have been introduced to provide a little more flexibility.

A large, informal Windjammer Café, which features a great expanse of ocean-view glass windows, is where breakfast and lunch buffets are available as an alternative to the dining room.

There is an intimate terrace Champagne Bar located forward of the lower level of the two-deck-high dining room and just off the atrium for those who might like to taste something a little out of the ordinary, in a setting that is bright and contemporary. There is a good use of tropical plants throughout the public rooms, which helps to counteract the clinical pastel wall colors.

Other Comments: This is one of two of a recent breed of ships for this popular cruise line (her sister ship is *Grandeur of the Seas*), introduced in December 1996. She looks long, with her single funnel located well aft, has a nicely rounded stern (rather like the *Sovereign of the Seas*-class ships), and a Viking Crown Lounge set amidships. This, together with the forward mast, provides three distinct focal points in her exterior profile. There is a wraparound outdoor promenade deck (there are no cushioned pads for the deck lounge chairs, however).

A large Viking Crown Lounge (a trademark of all Royal Caribbean International ships) sits between funnel and mast and overlooks the forward section of the swimming pool deck, as aboard *Legend of the Seas/Splendour of the Seas*, with access provided from stairway off the central atrium.

Inside is a seven-deck-high Centrum (atrium), which provides a central focal and meeting point (the Purser's Desk and Shore Excursion Desk are located on one level). Many public entertainment rooms and facilities can be located off the atrium.

There are two showrooms; one (the principal show lounge, 875 seats), for big production shows; the other (the secondary show lounge, 575 seats), for smaller shows and adult cabarets. The children's and teens' facilities are good, much expanded from previous ships in the fleet.

This ship is quite pretty, and will provide a good cruise vacation, particularly for first-time passengers seeking comfortable surroundings typical of what would be found in a Hyatt Hotel-type of setting, with fabrics and soft furnishings that blend together to provide a contemporary resort environment. The food is typical of what one would find in a big-city brasserie—adequate in quantity and nicely presented, but made from premixed ingredients. This is provides a rather homogeneous cruise experience, with the same old passenger participation activities and events that have been provided for the past 20 years.

<u>But:</u> There are too many announcements and constant contemporary pop music played around the swimming pool throughout the day and night (difficult to get away from).

ms Europa

☆☆☆☆☆

(M)

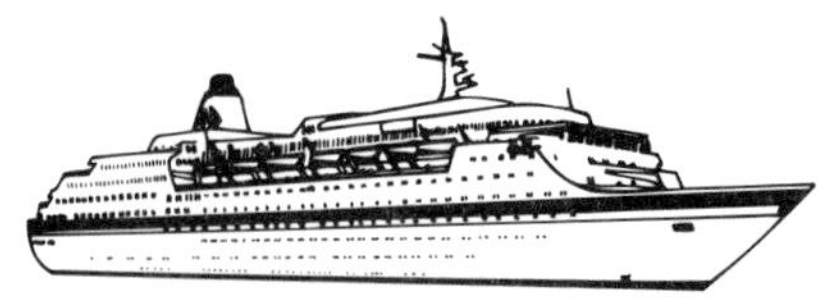

Lifestyle	**Luxury**
Cruise Line:	Hapag-Lloyd Seetouristik
Former Names:	*Europa*
Gross Tonnage:	37,012
Builder:	Bremer Vulkan (Germany)
Original Cost:	$120 million
Entered Service:	January 1982
Flag:	Bahamas
Tel No:	1320211/1320213
Fax No:	1320212
Length (ft./m.):	654.9/199.63
Beam (ft./m.):	93.8/28.60
Draft (ft./m.):	27.6/8.42
Propulsion/Propellers:	diesel (21,270kW)/2 (FP)
Decks:	10
Total Crew:	300
Pass. Capacity (basis 2):	600
Pass. Capacity (all berths):	600
Pass. Space Ratio (basis 2):	61.6
Pass. Space Ratio (all berths):	61.6
Officers:	European
Total Cabins:	316
Size Range (sq. ft./m.):	150–420/14.0–39.0
Cabins (outside view):	260
Cabins (inside):	56
Cabins (for one person):	32
Cabins (with private balcony):	0
Cabins (wheelchair accessible):	1
Cabin Current:	110/220 AC
Cabin TV:	Yes
Dining Rooms:	1
Seatings:	1
Elevators:	4
Casino:	No
Slot Machines:	No
Swimming Pools (outdoors):	2 (1 magrodome)
Swimming Pools (inside):	1 (fresh water)
Whirlpools:	0
Fitness Center:	Yes
Sauna/Steam Room:	Yes/No
Massage:	Yes
Self-Service Launderette:	Yes
Movie Theater/Seats:	Yes/238
Library:	Yes
Children's Facilities:	No
Classification Society:	Germanischer Lloyd

Ratings	**Score**
Ship: Hardware/Maintenance	86
Ship: Outdoor Facilities/Space	88
Ship: Interior Facilities/Space/Flow	93
Ship: Decor/Furnishings/Artwork	90
Ship: Spa/Fitness Facilities	90
Cabins: Suites and Deluxe	87
Cabins: Standard Sizes	84
Food: Dining Room/Cuisine	88
Food: Informal Dining/Buffets	84
Food: Quality of Ingredients	87
Food: Afternoon Tea/Bar Snacks	85
Service: Dining Room	87
Service: Bars	87
Service: Cabins	87
Service: Open Decks	86
Cruise: Entertainment	85
Cruise: Activities Program	83
Cruise: Movies/Television Programming	86
Cruise: Hospitality Standard	85
Cruise: Overall Product Delivery	87
Overall Score	**1,735**

Accommodation: All cabins aboard this ship are very good, and all were completely refurbished in 1995. All feature lighted closets, dark wood cabinetry with rounded edges, several full-length mirrors, color television and VCR player, minibar-refrigerator with complimentary soft drinks and beer, and personal safe, hairdryer, and superior cabin insulation. The bathrooms have deep bathtubs (some cabins have shower only), a three-head shower unit, large toiletries cabinet and handsome-sized amenities, but the bath towels are a little small. Unlike newer ships, there are no cabins with private balconies.

Dining: The dining room is extremely spacious, and, with single seating for all meals, dining is unhurried. Traditional silver service and plenty of space between tables help to provide an elegant dining experience. There is also a large, extremely varied cold table for breakfast and luncheon. A "gala night" buffet is held in the dining room once each cruise.

Menus are not repeated, even on long voyages, and excellent-quality fresh food ingredients are used (all meats are American). Caviar (both Iranian and Russian) is always available, as are special orders, as well as some tableside flambeau items. The food and cuisine are, of course, geared to German (including Austrian and Swiss-German) tastes, which means a wide variety of meat and fish dishes, as well as many breads and cheeses.

Other Comments: This well-designed, handsome contemporary ship presents a really well balanced profile. She is a fine, stable, well-behaved ship at sea, and looks like a ship, not a floating hotel. Excellent maintenance and care are evident throughout. Has excellent outdoor deck and sunbathing space, including a private (FKK) nudist deck just aft of the funnel. There is no wraparound outdoor promenade deck (only a half-length port and starboard promenade).

An indoor swimming pool is larger than most outdoor pools aboard new, much larger ships, and there are excellent personal care clinic and spa facilities. Many rejuvenation facilities and treatments not available in other ships can be found here, provided by what is arguably the most professional and dedicated spa staff afloat.

There is an incredible amount of space per passenger, even when the ship is full. Some fine artwork and sculptures are featured. Dark, restful colors are applied in most public rooms and cabins, and subtle, hidden lighting is used throughout. The Belvedere Lounge, the ship's forward observation lounge, is still one of the most elegant rooms afloat.

Refreshingly there is not a trace of horse racing, gambling tables, or slot machines anywhere. The entertainment is varied, with classical and chamber concerts, some light opera, as well as lighter show fare, and a "conferenciere" (master of ceremonies).

A friendly European staff provides classic service that ranges from formal to informal. There are virtually no announcements. This ship deserves praise for providing an elegant cruise experience in supremely luxurious and quiet, spacious surroundings. This company provides fascinating itineraries that are well-planned, with several overnight stays and late-night departures as standard.

It is the food, service, and quiet, refined ambience that are generally excellent. If you seek a restful, restorative cruise, with high quality European entertainment, seldom repeated worldwide itineraries, good food, and first-class service, then this German-language ship still provides it. Passengers are almost entirely German-speaking, so do not book unless you understand this language (many staff also speak English). It is a very relaxing cruise experience, to be enjoyed particularly on long cruises with plenty of days at sea. However, with the discounting in the marketplace, the standards aboard this ship have sadly been allowed to slip in the past year.

Many repeat passengers know that there is nothing finer for the German-speaking market until the new *Europa* is introduced in August 1999, when this ship is scheduled to become *Megastar Asia* for Singapore-based Star Cruises. Port taxes and insurance are included.

But: There are no balcony cabins or a wraparound promenade deck.

ms Europa

(S)

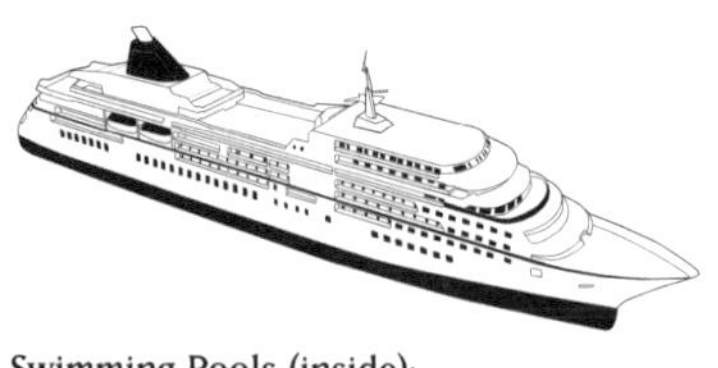

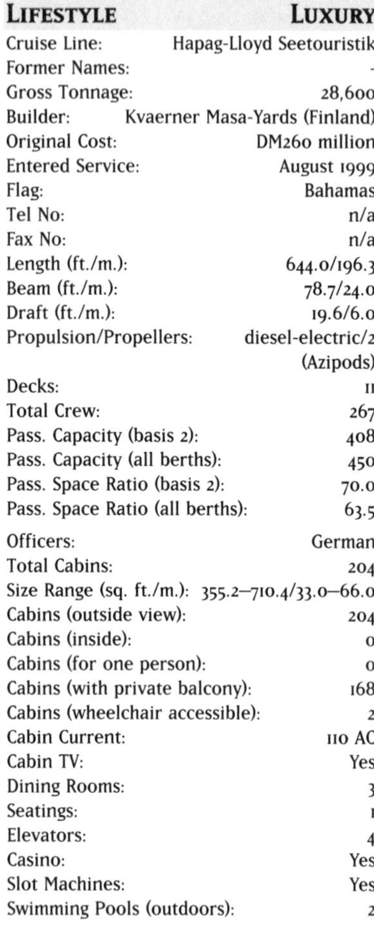

Lifestyle	Luxury
Cruise Line:	Hapag-Lloyd Seetouristik
Former Names:	-
Gross Tonnage:	28,600
Builder:	Kvaerner Masa-Yards (Finland)
Original Cost:	DM260 million
Entered Service:	August 1999
Flag:	Bahamas
Tel No:	n/a
Fax No:	n/a
Length (ft./m.):	644.0/196.3
Beam (ft./m.):	78.7/24.0
Draft (ft./m.):	19.6/6.0
Propulsion/Propellers:	diesel-electric/2 (Azipods)
Decks:	11
Total Crew:	267
Pass. Capacity (basis 2):	408
Pass. Capacity (all berths):	450
Pass. Space Ratio (basis 2):	70.0
Pass. Space Ratio (all berths):	63.5
Officers:	German
Total Cabins:	204
Size Range (sq. ft./m.):	355.2–710.4/33.0–66.0
Cabins (outside view):	204
Cabins (inside):	0
Cabins (for one person):	0
Cabins (with private balcony):	168
Cabins (wheelchair accessible):	2
Cabin Current:	110 AC
Cabin TV:	Yes
Dining Rooms:	3
Seatings:	1
Elevators:	4
Casino:	Yes
Slot Machines:	Yes
Swimming Pools (outdoors):	2
Swimming Pools (inside):	1
Whirlpools:	2
Fitness Center:	Yes
Sauna/Steam Room:	Yes/Yes
Massage:	Yes
Self-Service Launderette:	Yes (2)
Movie Theater/Seats:	Yes/60
Library:	Yes
Children's Facilities:	Yes
Classification Society:	Germanischer Lloyd

Ratings	Score
Ship: Hardware/Maintenance	NYR
Ship: Outdoor Facilities/Space	NYR
Ship: Interior Facilities/Space/Flow	NYR
Ship: Decor/Furnishings/Artwork	NYR
Ship: Spa/Fitness Facilities	NYR
Cabins: Suites and Deluxe	NYR
Cabins: Standard Sizes	NYR
Food: Dining Room/Cuisine	NYR
Food: Informal Dining/Buffets	NYR
Food: Quality of Ingredients	NYR
Food: Afternoon Tea/Bar Snacks	NYR
Service: Dining Room	NYR
Service: Bars	NYR
Service: Cabins	NYR
Service: Open Decks	NYR
Cruise: Entertainment	NYR
Cruise: Activities Program	NYR
Cruise: Movies/Television Programming	NYR
Cruise: Hospitality Standard	NYR
Cruise: Overall Product Delivery	NYR

Expected Score Range
1,600-1,900

Accommodation: The accommodation consists of all-outside suites, each of which has a large private balcony, refrigerator, television, and VCR unit. There is a generous amount of closet and drawer space for long voyages. The bathrooms are extremely well designed and have a large cabinet for personal toiletry items. Thick 100 percent cotton bathrobes are provided, as are slippers.

Dining: There is one main, formal dining room, with seats for all passengers, in an assigned seating arrangement. Full silver service will be featured. There are also two alternative restaurants, one Chinese, one Italian, for more casual dining. These will be available by reservation, at no extra charge.

Other Comments: Her sleek appearance should please even the most critical among passengers, with her sweeping lines and graceful profile. The ship will carry as many as seven Zodiac landing craft for use on close-up shore excursions.

She is certainly the most spacious cruise ship in the world, and is the company's (smaller) replacement for the previous *Europa*, which, during her seventeen-year history, amassed a fine clutch of loyal devotees and a high rating for her service standards. Reducing the size of the vessel and the number of passengers should enable Hapag-Lloyd to once again reach and maintain the high standards for which the company has become known, and which passengers expect. Features a full teakwood wraparound outside promenade deck.

Besides being the most spacious, she promises to be the most luxuriously appointed cruise ship in the world, with the finest of soft furnishings chosen for her interiors, which will blend traditional with modern in a subtle manner.

Although little was known of her interior design when this book went to press, it is known that her interiors include a three-deck-high atrium—a first for any modern Hapag-Lloyd cruise ship.

mv Explorer

☆☆☆

(S)

Lifestyle	**Standard**
Cruise Line:	Abercrombie & Kent
Former Names:	*Society Explorer/ Lindblad Explorer/World Explorer*
Gross Tonnage:	2,398
Builder:	Nystad Varv Shipyard (Finland)
Original Cost:	$2.5 million
Entered Service:	1969/March 1993
Flag:	Liberia
Tel No:	1241223
Fax No:	1241223
Length (ft./m.):	239.1/72.88
Beam (ft./m.):	46.0/14.03
Draft (ft./m.):	13.7/4.20
Propulsion/Propellers:	diesel (2,795kW)/1 (FP)
Decks:	6
Total Crew:	71
Pass. Capacity (basis 2):	100
Pass. Capacity (all berths):	114
Pass. Space Ratio (basis 2):	23.9
Pass. Space Ratio (all berths):	21.0
Officers:	European
Total Cabins:	50
Size Range (sq. ft./m.):	68.9–162.0/6.41–15.05
Cabins (outside view):	50
Cabins (inside):	0
Cabins (for one person):	8
Cabins (with private balcony):	0
Cabins (wheelchair accessible):	0
Cabin Current:	220 AC
Cabin TV:	No
Dining Rooms:	1 (open seating)
Elevators:	0
Casino:	No
Slot Machines:	No
Swimming Pools (outdoors):	1
Whirlpools:	0
Exercise Room:	Yes
Sauna/Steam Room:	Yes/No
Massage:	Yes
Self-Service Launderette:	No
Lecture/Film Room:	Yes
Library:	Yes
Zodiacs:	Yes
Helicopter Pad:	No
Classification Society:	Det Norske Veritas

Ratings	**Score**
Ship: Hardware/Maintenance	60
Ship: Expedition Equipment	62
Ship: Interior Facilities/Space/Flow	56
Ship: Decor/Furnishings/Artwork	57
Ship: Spa/Fitness Facilities	30
Cabins: Suites and Deluxe	58
Cabins: Standard Sizes	50
Food: Dining Room/Cuisine	70
Food: Informal Dining/Buffets	60
Food: Quality of Ingredients	66
Food: Afternoon Tea/Bar Snacks	54
Service: Dining Room	70
Service: Bars	70
Service: Cabins	71
Service: Open Decks	53
Cruise: Library/Lecture Programs	61
Cruise: Movies/Television Programming	48
Cruise: Hospitality Standard	65
Cruise: Expedition Experience	63
Cruise: Overall Product Delivery	73
Overall Score	**1,197**

Accommodation: The cabins are extremely small and utilitarian, and there is very little closet, drawer, and storage space. Even so, they are just about adequate for this type of cruising, where you need only very casual clothing. The bathrooms (and the towels) are really tiny, however, and there is little room even for your toiletries. National Geographic maps are provided in all cabins.

Dining: The dining room is cheerful and intimate, although somewhat noisy, but it does seat all passengers in one seating. Good, creatively presented food (but there is little choice) and wine list. Smiling, attentive, and genuinely friendly service, but it is quite casual.

Other Comments: Although she is a small vessel, she is well fitted out with all the necessary equipment for successful in-depth exploration cruising, including a fleet of Zodiac rubber landing craft. She is now aging and showing many signs of wear and tear, however, and cannot compete effectively with the newer expedition-style ships, despite recent refurbishment. She does, however, have an ice-hardened hull and a well-balanced profile, and she is extremely maneuverable.

There are few public rooms, but the interior decor is quite tasteful and cheerful. There is a large reference library of books associated with nature and wildlife. Good lecturers and nature specialists are on board for each cruise, provided by specialists Abercrombie & Kent.

This is cruising for the serious adventurer who wants to explore specialized areas of the world yet have some of the basic creature comforts of home within reach. All shore excursions and gratuities are included.

tss Fair Princess

☆☆ +

(M)

LIFESTYLE	STANDARD
Cruise Line:	P&O Holidays
Former Names:	*Fair Princess/Fairsea/ Fairland/Carinthia*
Gross Tonnage:	24,724
Builder:	John Brown & Co. (UK)
Original Cost:	£21 million
Entered Service:	June 1956/1997
Flag:	Bahamas
Tel No:	n/a
Fax No:	n/a
Length (ft./m.):	608.2/185.40
Beam (ft./m.):	80.3/24.49
Draft (ft./m.):	28.5/8.71
Propulsion/Propellers:	steam turbine (18,300kW)/2 (FP)
Decks:	11
Total Crew:	450
Pass. Capacity (basis 2):	890
Pass. Capacity (all berths):	1,100
Pass. Space Ratio (basis 2):	27.7
Pass. Space Ratio (all berths):	22.4
Officers:	International
Total Cabins:	464
Size Range (sq. ft./m.):	90–241/8.3–22.3
Cabins (outside view):	230
Cabins (inside):	234
Cabins (for one person):	0
Cabins (with private balcony):	0
Cabins (wheelchair accessible):	0
Cabin Current:	110 AC
Cabin TV:	Yes
Dining Rooms:	2
Seatings:	2
Elevators:	3
Casino:	Yes
Slot Machines:	Yes
Swimming Pools (outdoors):	3
Swimming Pools (inside):	0
Whirlpools:	0
Fitness Center:	Yes
Sauna/Steam Room:	Yes/No
Massage:	Yes
Self-Service Launderette:	No
Movie Theater/Seats:	Yes (with balcony)/330
Library:	Yes
Children's Facilities:	Yes
Classification Society:	Lloyd's Register

RATINGS	SCORE
Ship: Hardware/Maintenance	50
Ship: Outdoor Facilities/Space	56
Ship: Interior Facilities/Space/Flow	62
Ship: Decor/Furnishings/Artwork	61
Ship: Spa/Fitness Facilities	51
Cabins: Suites and Deluxe	58
Cabins: Standard Sizes	55
Food: Dining Room/Cuisine	57
Food: Informal Dining/Buffets	52
Food: Quality of Ingredients	53
Food: Afternoon Tea/Bar Snacks	50
Service: Dining Room	60
Service: Bars	60
Service: Cabins	60
Service: Open Decks	53
Cruise: Entertainment	55
Cruise: Activities Program	50
Cruise: Movies/Television Programming	41
Cruise: Hospitality Standard	52
Cruise: Overall Product Delivery	61
OVERALL SCORE	**1,097**

Accommodation: The cabins are generally quite spacious for an older ship and have heavy-duty furnishings and fittings. The cabin bathrooms are now quite antiquated, with much exposed plumbing in some of them. There are many cabins with third and fourth berths, and there are many more inside cabins than ocean-view cabins.

Dining: The dining rooms, although crowded and noisy, have tables for two, for, six, or eight. The cuisine is low-budget banquet food, and quantity, not quality, prevails. Fairly attentive service, but there is little finesse. There is also a busy pizzeria for quick meals.

Other Comments: This solidly constructed former ocean liner has classic, but dated, lines and profile, which translates to good seaworthiness. However, down in the engine room, some parts are definitely well worn and create occasional problems; in other words, there are breakdowns. The open deck and sunbathing space are quite good, unless the ship is full. There is a jogging track.

Inside, the art-deco interiors on Promenade Deck are quite elegant, but otherwise the interior decor and color scheme are mundane. Has an adequate old-style library, and there are good facilities for families with children.

This high-density ship represents good value if you do not expect much. She really is old and tired (and has been breaking down regularly over the past two years), and is very crowded when full. Actually, she replaced a ship *(Fairstar)* that was only one year older (she was retired on 31 January 1997). Do expect lines for embarkation, disembarkation, and shore tenders.

There is not much sophistication anywhere. The public rooms are reasonably comfortable, but barely adequate for the number of passengers carried, and it is difficult to get away from smokers. There are too many announcements.

ms Fantasy

☆☆☆☆

(L)

Lifestyle	**Standard**
Cruise Line:	Carnival Cruise Lines
Former Names:	-
Gross Tonnage:	70,367
Builder:	Kvaerner Masa-Yards (Finland)
Original Cost:	$225 million
Entered Service:	March 1990
Flag:	Liberia
Tel No:	1242660
Fax No:	1242661
Length (ft./m.):	855.8/263.60
Beam (ft./m.):	104.0/31.40
Draft (ft./m.):	25.9/7.90
Propulsion/Propellers:	diesel-electric (42,240kW)/2 (CP)
Decks:	10
Total Crew:	920
Pass. Capacity (basis 2):	2,044
Pass. Capacity (all berths):	2,634
Pass. Space Ratio (basis 2):	34.4
Pass. Space Ratio (all berths):	26.7
Officers:	Italian
Total Cabins:	1,022
Size Range (sq. ft./m.):	173.2–409.7/16.0–38.0
Cabins (outside view):	620
Cabins (inside):	402
Cabins (for one person):	0
Cabins (with private balcony):	54
Cabins (wheelchair accessible):	20
Cabin Current:	110 AC
Cabin TV:	Yes
Dining Rooms:	2
Seatings:	2
Elevators:	14
Casino:	Yes
Slot Machines:	Yes
Swimming Pools (outdoors):	3
Swimming Pools (inside):	0
Whirlpools:	6
Fitness Center:	Yes
Sauna/Steam Room:	Yes/Yes
Massage:	Yes
Self-Service Launderette:	Yes
Movie Theater/Seats:	No
Library:	Yes
Children's Facilities:	Yes
Classification Society:	Lloyd's Register

Ratings	**Score**
Ship: Hardware/Maintenance	81
Ship: Outdoor Facilities/Space	74
Ship: Interior Facilities/Space/Flow	81
Ship: Decor/Furnishings/Artwork	82
Ship: Spa/Fitness Facilities	77
Cabins: Suites and Deluxe	78
Cabins: Standard Sizes	73
Food: Dining Room/Cuisine	66
Food: Informal Dining/Buffets	62
Food: Quality of Ingredients	61
Food: Afternoon Tea/Bar Snacks	51
Service: Dining Room	68
Service: Bars	70
Service: Cabins	68
Service: Open Decks	64
Cruise: Entertainment	81
Cruise: Activities Program	67
Cruise: Movies/Television Programming	65
Cruise: Hospitality Standard	63
Cruise: Overall Product Delivery	77
Overall Score	**1,409**

Accommodation: All of the standard cabins are alike, fairly spacious, and have enough storage space for a one-week cruise, and, although the decor is bright it is also rather spartan. Only the 28 outside suites have whirlpool bathtubs, and a decor that is more pleasant for being less plain.

Dining: The two large dining rooms, both with ocean-view windows (both nonsmoking), are noisy, but the decor is attractive, but rather vivid. The food is very disappointing even though it has been upgraded steadily over the past couple of years. The service is basic, and pushy, with absolutely no finesse. Although there is a wine list, there are no wine waiters.

Other Comments: Although externally angular and not handsome, this is one of a series of eight identical (and very successful) mega-ships built for Carnival Cruise Lines. Features vibrant colors and extensive use of neon lighting for sensory stimulation. Almost vibration-free service is provided by the diesel electric propulsion system. Has a six-deck-high atrium, topped by a large glass dome, features spectacular artistic centerpiece. Has expansive open deck areas, but they quickly become inadequate when the ship is full and everyone wants to be out on deck.

Inside, this ship has public entertainment lounges, bars, and clubs galore, with something for everyone (except quiet space). Has a fine library and reading room, but few books. Her handsome public rooms connected by wide indoor boulevards, beat a futuristic theme, and are painted in dazzling colors that beg your indulgence. The multitiered showroom is quite lavish, but 20 pillars do obstruct the views from several seats. Dramatic three-deck-high glass enclosed health spa. Banked jogging track. The large casino has almost nonstop action, as one would expect aboard any Carnival Cruise Lines ship.

The cuisine is just so-so but the real fun begins at sundown, when Carnival really excels in lights, razzle-dazzle shows, and late-night sounds. From the futuristic Electricity Disco to the ancient Cleopatra's Bar, this ship will entertain you well. The ship features three- and four-day Bahamas cruises year-round, and is based on Port Canaveral.

What should be of great interest to families, however, is a special partnership with Universal Studios' travel company, which packages a cruise together with a land stay and choice of three different theme parks: Universal Studios, Wet 'n Wild, and Sea World. The pricing is competitive with that of the Disneyland-cruise product.

<u>But:</u> There are simply too many annoying, and loud, intrusive announcements.

ms Fascination

☆☆☆☆

(L)

Lifestyle	Standard
Cruise Line:	Carnival Cruise Lines
Former Names:	-
Gross Tonnage:	70,367
Builder:	Kvaerner Masa-Yards (Finland)
Original Cost:	$315 million
Entered Service:	July 1994
Flag:	Liberia
Tel No:	1346374
Fax No:	1346375
Length (ft./m.):	855.0/260.60
Beam (ft./m.):	104.9/31.69
Draft (ft./m.):	25.7/7.86
Propulsion/Propellers:	diesel-electric (42,240kW)/2 (CP)
Decks:	10
Total Crew:	920
Pass. Capacity (basis 2):	2,040
Pass. Capacity (all berths):	2,594
Pass. Space Ratio (basis 2):	34.4
Pass. Space Ratio (all berths):	26.7
Officers:	Italian
Total Cabins:	1,020
Size Range (sq. ft./m.):	173.2–409.7/16.0–38.0
Cabins (outside view):	618
Cabins (inside):	402
Cabins (for one person):	0
Cabins (with private balcony):	26
Cabins (wheelchair accessible):	0
Cabin Current:	110 AC
Cabin TV:	Yes
Dining Rooms:	2
Seatings:	2
Elevators:	14
Casino:	Yes
Slot Machines:	Yes
Swimming Pools (outdoors):	3
Swimming Pools (inside):	0
Whirlpools:	6
Fitness Center:	Yes
Sauna/Steam Room:	Yes/Yes
Massage:	Yes
Self-Service Launderette:	Yes
Movie Theater/Seats:	No
Library:	Yes
Children's Facilities:	Yes
Classification Society:	Lloyd's Register

Ratings	Score
Ship: Hardware/Maintenance	81
Ship: Outdoor Facilities/Space	74
Ship: Interior Facilities/Space/Flow	81
Ship: Decor/Furnishings/Artwork	82
Ship: Spa/Fitness Facilities	77
Cabins: Suites and Deluxe	78
Cabins: Standard Sizes	73
Food: Dining Room/Cuisine	66
Food: Informal Dining/Buffets	62
Food: Quality of Ingredients	61
Food: Afternoon Tea/Bar Snacks	51
Service: Dining Room	68
Service: Bars	70
Service: Cabins	68
Service: Open Decks	64
Cruise: Entertainment	81
Cruise: Activities Program	67
Cruise: Movies/Television Programming	65
Cruise: Hospitality Standard	63
Cruise: Overall Product Delivery	77
Overall Score	**1,409**

Accommodation: The standard cabins are quite functional and of a good size. The decor is bright but somewhat plain and uninspiring; each features a small vanity desk, twin beds that convert to a queen-size bed (some of the lower grade cabins have upper/lower berths), and a fairly decent amount of closet and drawer space.

There are 28 outside suites, each with a king-size bed, whirlpool tub, and more elegant decor, fittings, and soft furnishings. Take your own shampoo and conditioner (none is provided, although soap is).

Dining: The two large, noisy dining rooms (both are nonsmoking) come with Carnival's typically usual efficient, assertive, fast service. Improved cuisine is so-so, but first-time cruise passengers seem to accept it. The buffets are rather run-of-the-mill, with little creativity. Although there is a wine list (with some good California whites and reds), there are no wine waiters.

Other Comments: This is one of a series of eight identical mega-ships built for Carnival that reflects the fine creative interior design work of Joe Farcus. Features a somewhat ungainly exterior profile, but the space created has been well used. Has expansive open deck areas, but never enough when the ship is full (the aft decks tend to be less noisy, whereas all the activities are focused around the main pool). A well-defined "topless" sunbathing area can be found around the funnel base on Verandah Deck.

Inside, a dramatic atrium lobby spans six decks and features cool marble and hot neon topped by a large glass dome and a spectacular artistic centerpiece called "Nucleus," which illustrates the kleig lights of a Hollywood premiere. The ship offers public entertainment lounges, bars, and clubs galore, with something for everyone.

The interior decor aboard all Carnival ships is themed; this one sports a sophisticated Hollywood theme that begs your indulgence. The principal public rooms are all connected by a double-width indoor boulevard, and there are some excellent photo opportunities with some superb life-like figures from the movies—look for Marilyn Monroe and James Dean outside the casino at Stars Bar, and Humphrey Bogart and Ingrid Bergman at the piano at Bogart's Cafe. Sophia Loren and Paul Newman are also close by. Meanwhile, John Wayne is at the entrance to the Passage to India Lounge, while Edward G. Robinson is inside. Vivien Leigh and Clark Gable are in Tara's Library. Outside the Diamonds Are Forever discotheque are none other than Elizabeth Taylor and Elvis Presley. Anyone else? Why yes, there's Lena Horne and Sydney Poitier outside the Beverly Hills Bar, while inside are Katherine Hepburn and Spencer Tracy. Just in case you want to gamble, you'll find Lucille Ball outside the casino. Incidentally, all the slot machines aboard all Carnival ships are linked into a big prize, called, naturally, Megacash.

The multitiered showroom is quite lavish, and features good, raucus, razzle-dazzle shows (sight lines are obscured from seats behind or adjacent to 20 pillars). Has a dramatic, well-segmented three-deck-high glass-enclosed health spa and gymnasium with the latest muscle-pump equipment. There is a large shop, but it is stuffed to the gills with low-quality merchandise.

However, the real fun begins at sundown, when Carnival excels in decibels. This ship will entertain you in timely fashion. With such an enormous ship to play on, you will never be bored and even may forget to get off in port! There's no doubt that Carnival does "fun" better than anyone else, and if you want to party and live it up, then this ship should do it.

But: I've heard less announcements at a military training camp—it's time to cut them out.

mv Flamenco

☆☆☆+
(M)

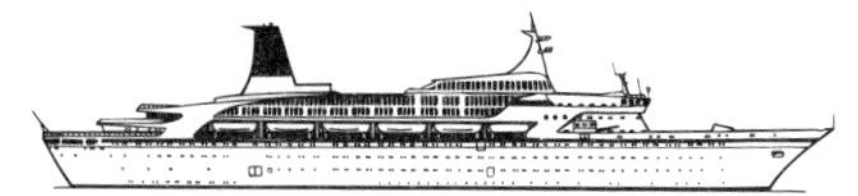

LIFESTYLE	STANDARD
Cruise Line:	Festival Cruises
Former Names:	*Southern Cross, Star/Ship Majestic, Sun Princess, Spirit of London*
Gross Tonnage:	17,042
Builder:	Cantieri Navale Del Tirreno & Riuniti (Italy)
Original Cost:	n/a
Entered Service:	November 1972/December 1997
Flag:	Bahamas
Tel No:	1104553
Fax No:	1104553
Length (ft./m.):	536.0/163.40
Beam (ft./m.):	81.4/24.82
Draft (ft./m.):	21.3/6.52
Propulsion/Propellers:	diesel (13,450kW)/2 (CP)
Decks:	7
Total Crew:	350
Pass. Capacity (basis 2):	720
Pass. Capacity (all berths):	987
Pass. Space Ratio (basis 2):	23.6
Pass. Space Ratio (all berths):	17.2
Officers:	Greek
Total Cabins:	377
Size Range (sq. ft./m.):	99–237/9.0–22.0
Cabins (outside view):	255
Cabins (inside):	122
Cabins (for one person):	29
Cabins (with private balcony):	0
Cabins (wheelchair accessible):	2
Cabin Current:	110/220 AC
Cabin TV:	Yes
Dining Rooms:	1
Seatings:	2
Elevators:	4
Casino:	Yes
Slot Machines:	Yes
Swimming Pools (outdoors):	1 (+children's wading pool)
Swimming Pools (inside):	0
Whirlpools:	0
Fitness Center:	Yes
Sauna/Steam Room:	No/No
Massage:	Yes
Self-Service Launderette:	No
Movie Theater/Seats:	Yes/186
Library:	Yes
Children's Facilities:	Yes
Classification Society:	Lloyd's Register

RATINGS	SCORE
Ship: Hardware/Maintenance	76
Ship: Outdoor Facilities/Space	66
Ship: Interior Facilities/Space/Flow	65
Ship: Decor/Furnishings/Artwork	67
Ship: Spa/Fitness Facilities	61
Cabins: Suites and Deluxe	64
Cabins: Standard Sizes	60
Food: Dining Room/Cuisine	74
Food: Informal Dining/Buffets	67
Food: Quality of Ingredients	67
Food: Afternoon Tea/Bar Snacks	63
Service: Dining Room	75
Service: Bars	74
Service: Cabins	74
Service: Open Decks	63
Cruise: Entertainment	59
Cruise: Activities Program	55
Cruise: Movies/Television Programming	46
Cruise: Hospitality Standard	71
Cruise: Overall Product Delivery	76
OVERALL SCORE	**1,324**

Accommodation: There are twelve cabin grades. Those designated as deluxe suites are reasonably spacious, while all other inside and outside cabins are on the small side, but quite well equipped, and with colorful soft furnishings. However, the cabin walls are really thin, which means you will be able to hear your next-door neighbors brushing their teeth. There is very little drawer space. The cabin telephone system is rather antiquated and needs updating. The bathrooms are compact units, but adequate.

Dining: The dining room is quite charming, and with its high ceiling provides a light and airy space, but it can be extremely noisy. The tables are quite close together (as aboard Festival Cruises' other ships). The service standards are good, and being fine-tuned constantly. The quality of food and its presentation are reasonably good. There is a limited choice of breads, rolls, cheeses, and fruits, which all tend to be quite standard. Informal self-service buffets for breakfast and lunch are quite good, however, and well presented.

Other Comments: This ship has a fairly handsome contemporary profile, with a rakish superstructure and an all-white hull (under her previous owners, the hull was painted scarlet red), and twin blue funnels. She underwent a $9-million refurbishment in late 1997, after acquiring her from her former owners, CTC Cruise Lines. Just aft of the mast is a large conservatory-like pod that encloses lounges on two levels, overlooking the swimming pool. There is a reasonable amount of open deck and sunbathing space for a ship of this size, but it is cramped when full, and there are no cushioned pads for the deck lounge chairs.

Inside the ship, the layout makes it easy to find your way around. The public rooms received a good facelift during a 1997 refurbishment by her new owners. All of the public rooms are quite comfortable, now with pleasing, attractive decor and soft furnishings. The interior decor features tasteful colors mixed with the extensive use of reflective surfaces to provide an upbeat, contemporary feel.

This ship provides good value for the money, and a comfortable cruise experience in relaxed surroundings. Festival Cruises (called First European Cruises in the U.S.) specializes in cruising for Europeans. Languages (and announcements) used throughout ship: English, French, German, Italian, and Spanish. The itineraries are well designed and include several sea days on longer voyages.

But: She is a rather high-density vessel, and so there will be some lines during embarkation and disembarkation, as well as for tenders and buffets. There are too many loud announcements, in several languages.

mv Fuji Maru

☆☆☆☆

(S)

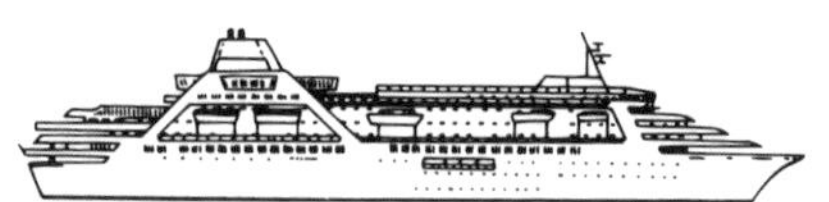

Lifestyle	Standard
Cruise Line:	Mitsui OSK Passenger Line
Former Names:	-
Gross Tonnage:	23,340
Builder:	Mitsubishi (Japan)
Original Cost:	$55 million
Entered Service:	April 1989
Flag:	Japan
Tel No:	1200467
Fax No:	1200470
Length (ft./m.):	547.9/167.00
Beam (ft./m.):	78.7/24.00
Draft (ft./m.):	21.4/6.55
Propulsion/Propellers:	diesel (15,740kW)/2 (CP)
Decks:	8
Total Crew:	190
Pass. Capacity (basis 2):	328
Pass. Capacity (all berths):	603
Pass. Space Ratio (basis 2):	71.1
Pass. Space Ratio (all berths):	38.7
Officers:	Japanese
Total Cabins:	164
Size Range (sq. ft./m.):	182–376/17.0–35.0
Cabins (outside view):	164
Cabins (inside):	0
Cabins (for one person):	0
Cabins (with private balcony):	0
Cabins (wheelchair accessible):	2
Cabin Current:	100 AC
Cabin TV:	Yes
Dining Rooms:	1
Seatings:	1
Elevators:	5
Casino:	Yes (K)
Slot Machines:	No
Swimming Pools (outdoors):	1
Swimming Pools (inside):	0
Whirlpools:	0 (4 Japanese Baths)
Fitness Center:	Yes
Sauna/Steam Room:	Yes/No
Massage:	Yes (*)
Self-Service Launderette:	Yes
Movie Theater/Seats:	Yes/142
Library:	Yes
Children's Facilities:	Yes (*)
Classification Society:	Nippon Kaiji Kyokai

(*) = On leisure cruises only

Ratings	Score
Ship: Hardware/Maintenance	76
Ship: Outdoor Facilities/Space	75
Ship: Interior Facilities/Space/Flow	76
Ship: Decor/Furnishings/Artwork	76
Ship: Spa/Fitness Facilities	79
Cabins: Suites and Deluxe	78
Cabins: Standard Sizes	67
Food: Dining Room/Cuisine	74
Food: Informal Dining/Buffets	71
Food: Quality of Ingredients	74
Food: Afternoon Tea/Bar Snacks	68
Service: Dining Room	77
Service: Bars	76
Service: Cabins	76
Service: Open Decks	66
Cruise: Entertainment	67
Cruise: Activities Program	66
Cruise: Movies/Television Programming	66
Cruise: Hospitality Standard	71
Cruise: Overall Product Delivery	76
Overall Score	**1,455**

Accommodation: There are two suites that are quite lovely, and the deluxe cabins are of a high standard, with a full-sized bathtub and refrigerator. Other cabins are simply furnished but ideal for seminar and school usage (very small for long voyages). The cabin insulation is reasonable. Folded blankets, a MOPAS tradition, are lovely.

Dining: The large dining room is attractive, has a high ceiling, but rather bright lighting. Features Japanese or Western cuisine for all meals. The food itself is of a good standard, with simple but colorful presentation. There are several beverage machines around the ship for those who are used to them ashore.

Other Comments: Well-thought-out and flexible multifunctional design, principally for incentives, conventions, a seminar and training ship, and individual passengers. The outdoor decks are spartan and little used.

Her interiors are plain and a little clinical, although there is some good artwork throughout. Has extensive lecture and conference rooms, the largest of which is two decks high, seats 600, and converts into a sports stadium or hall for industrial product introductions. The lobby is elegant and is part of a two-level atrium. Has a classic wood-paneled library. Has two Japanese-style grand baths and traditional Washitsu tatami mat room. Hanaguruma owner's room is elegant for small formal functions. Sakura Salon is soothing, with a blend of Western and traditional Japanese design. High-tech media and television system throughout (bilingual multiplex televisions in crew cabins).

This fascinating exhibition, training, and educational charter cruise ship has up-to-date facilities, although not ideally designed for individual passengers. No tipping is allowed.

ms Funchal

☆☆ +

(S)

Lifestyle	Standard
Cruise Line:	Classic International Cruises
Former Names:	-
Gross Tonnage:	9,563
Builder:	Helsingor Skibsvog (Denmark)
Original Cost:	n/a
Entered Service:	October 1961/May 1986
Flag:	Panama
Tel No:	1330320
Fax No:	1336716
Length (ft./m.):	503.6/153.51
Beam (ft./m.):	62.5/19.08
Draft (ft./m.):	20.3/6.20
Propulsion/Propellers:	diesel (7,356kW)/2 (FP)
Decks:	6
Total Crew:	155
Pass. Capacity (basis 2):	439
Pass. Capacity (all berths):	548
Pass. Space Ratio (basis 2):	22.2
Pass. Space Ratio (all berths):	18.2
Officers:	Greek/Portuguese
Total Cabins:	222
Size Range (sq. ft./m.):	102.2–252.9/9.5–23.5
Cabins (outside view):	151
Cabins (inside):	71
Cabins (for one person):	14
Cabins (with private balcony):	0
Cabins (wheelchair accessible):	0
Cabin Current:	220 AC
Cabin TV:	No
Dining Rooms:	2
Seatings:	1
Elevators:	3
Casino:	Yes
Slot Machines:	Yes
Swimming Pools (outdoors):	1
Swimming Pools (inside):	0
Whirlpools:	0
Fitness Center:	Yes
Sauna/Steam Room:	Yes/No
Massage:	No
Self-Service Launderette:	No
Movie Theater/Seats:	No
Library:	Yes
Children's Facilities:	No
Classification Society:	Rinave Portuguesa

Ratings	Score
Ship: Hardware/Maintenance	47
Ship: Outdoor Facilities/Space	46
Ship: Interior Facilities/Space/Flow	51
Ship: Decor/Furnishings/Artwork	48
Ship: Spa/Fitness Facilities	44
Cabins: Suites and Deluxe	53
Cabins: Standard Sizes	48
Food: Dining Room/Cuisine	57
Food: Informal Dining/Buffets	53
Food: Quality of Ingredients	54
Food: Afternoon Tea/Bar Snacks	46
Service: Dining Room	61
Service: Bars	63
Service: Cabins	61
Service: Open Decks	52
Cruise: Entertainment	54
Cruise: Activities Program	44
Cruise: Movies/Television Programming	32
Cruise: Hospitality Standard	57
Cruise: Overall Product Delivery	56
Overall Score	**1,027**

Accommodation: The cabins are compact yet tastefully appointed units and come in both twin- and double-bedded configurations. Each now has a private bathroom (all were refurbished in 1997/8), and there is just enough closet and drawer space, provided you don't pack too many clothes. The cabins are decorated in very plain colors, accented with colorful soft furnishings. All cabin bathrooms have soap, shampoo, shower cap, shoeshine and sewing kits, and bathrobe.

Dining: There are two dining rooms, Coimbra (which also doubles as a video screening room after dinner) and Lisboa; both have large ocean-view picture windows, are tastefully decorated, and have a very homey and cozy old-world atmosphere. The food is European in style (and includes plenty of fresh fish) and is surprisingly good, as is the service from friendly Portuguese waiters. There is a decent selection of breads, cheeses, and fruits, and the wine list, while not extensive, includes a good selection of Portuguese wines at very modest prices.

Other Comments: This ship has a real classic 1960s profile with well-balanced, rounded lines and pleasing real wooden decks (not a hint of astroturf anywhere), including one outdoor deck with two sheltered promenades, although they do not completely encircle the ship.

Inside, one deck houses all the main public rooms, the most appealing of which is the Porto Bar, which is reminiscent of a late nineteenth century drinking club with its wood paneled walls, furniture, and lovely bar. A highly polished wooden spiral stairway is a beautiful, classic piece of decoration not found today's ships and is reminiscent of the days of the transatlantic steamers of the early twentieth century.

The mostly Portuguese staff is friendly, caring, and quite attentive, although a little reserved at first. This ship is popular with Europeans and Scandinavians during the summer and Brazilians during the winter (anyone used to new cruise ships would probably find the ship too eclectic). She features destination-intensive cruises in a comfortable, old-world atmosphere, ideally suited to couples and solo passengers seeking good value for money and a good balance of sea days and port days.

She attracts a great number of loyal repeat passengers, who sail again and again because of the charming, mostly Portuguese crew and Greek captains. Good if you enjoy small, older ships with their accompanying eccentricities. Often operates under charter to various tour packagers and operators.

<u>But:</u> Much of the ship's exterior paintwork is quite sloppy. Poor maintenance in her early life means that some of the exterior plating is well worn, but the feeling of camaraderie and friendliness from her loyal crew (many of whom have been aboard the ship for many years) offsets some of the hardware negatives.

ms Galapagos Explorer

☆☆☆☆

(S)

Lifestyle	Premium
Cruise Line:	Galapagos Cruises
Former Names:	*Renaissance Three*
Gross Tonnage:	3,990
Builder:	Cantieri Navale Ferrari (Italy)
Original Cost:	$20 million
Entered Service:	August 1990/January 1998
Flag:	Liberia
Tel No:	1250166
Fax No:	1250167
Length (ft./m.):	289.6/88.30
Beam (ft./m.):	50.1/15.30
Draft (ft./m.):	11.9/3.65
Propulsion/Propellers:	diesel (3,514kW)/2 (CP)
Decks:	5
Total Crew:	72
Pass. Capacity (basis 2):	100
Pass. Capacity (all berths):	111
Pass. Space Ratio (basis 2):	39.9
Pass. Space Ratio (all berths):	35.9
Officers:	International
Total Cabins:	50
Size Range (sq. ft./m.):	231–282/21.5–26.2
Cabins (outside view):	50
Cabins (inside):	0
Cabins (for one person):	0
Cabins (with private balcony):	4
Cabins (wheelchair accessible):	0
Cabin Current:	110 AC
Cabin TV:	Yes
Dining Rooms:	1
Seatings:	1
Elevators:	1
Casino:	Yes
Slot Machines:	Yes
Swimming Pools (outdoors):	1
Swimming Pools (inside):	0
Whirlpools:	1
Fitness Center:	No
Sauna/Steam Room:	Yes/No
Massage:	No
Self-Service Launderette:	No
Movie Theater/Seats:	No
Library:	No
Children's Facilities:	No
Classification Society:	RINA

Ratings	Score
Ship: Hardware/Maintenance	76
Ship: Outdoor Facilities/Space	77
Ship: Interior Facilities/Space/Flow	79
Ship: Decor/Furnishings/Artwork	80
Ship: Spa/Fitness Facilities	71
Cabins: Suites and Deluxe	81
Cabins: Standard Sizes	76
Food: Dining Room/Cuisine	73
Food: Informal Dining/Buffets	61
Food: Quality of Ingredients	66
Food: Afternoon Tea/Bar Snacks	51
Service: Dining Room	77
Service: Bars	77
Service: Cabins	76
Service: Open Decks	75
Cruise: Entertainment	60
Cruise: Activities Program	62
Cruise: Movies/Television Programming	67
Cruise: Hospitality Standard	71
Cruise: Overall Product Delivery	77
Overall Score	**1,433**

Accommodation: Accommodation is located forward, with public rooms aft. All cabins have queen-sized bed, a sitting area, and feature most things you need, including a refrigerator and VCR unit. The bathrooms, which are small, have showers with a fold-down seat, real teakwood floors and marble vanities.

The cabins have small closets. Space for luggage is tight, and there is not really enough drawer space. The bathrooms, which are very small, are equipped with showers (no bathtubs). All cabins have a stocked mini-bar (all items are chargeable).

Dining: The dining room, which has open seating, is small and elegant. It is on lowest deck and has portholes (construction regulations requirement) and is quite cozy and welcoming. There are tables for two, four, six, and even eight. Sit where you like, with whom you like, when you like. Meals are self-service buffet-style cold foods for breakfast and lunch, with hot foods chosen from a table menu and served properly. The dining room operation works well. Food quality, choice, and presentation are all fairly decent, but not at all memorable. While the food is reasonably presented, it is quite limited in choice, particularly the entrees.

Other Comments: Originally constructed as one of a fleet of four small, identical and intimate cruise vessels for Renaissance Cruises. Smaller than the second series of four ships, this ship does not sail well in inclement weather. Similar in concept to the *Sea Goddess* ships, though more casual, and less expensive. This vessel is comfortable and inviting, but has not been particularly well maintained. Water sports facilities include an aft platform, sailfish, snorkel equipment, and several zodiacs.

Has contemporary mega-yacht looks and handsome styling throughout. Exquisite all-outside suites combine gorgeous, highly polished imitation rosewood paneling with lots of mirrors, handcrafted Italian furniture, wet bar (pre-stocked when you book, at extra cost). Has wooden outside promenade deck. Not the equal of other small luxury ships, but neither is the price. This ship will provide a destination-intensive, refined, quiet, and very relaxed cruising for passengers who do not like crowds, dressing up, scheduled activities, or entertainment. Naturalist guides who have been trained at the Darwin Station lead the guided shore excursions, which are included in the fare. Operates three-, four-, and seven-night Galapagos cruises year-round from San Cristobal, which are sold through various tour operators. Liquor, beer, cocktails, and soft drinks are included in the fare, but wine and champagne are not.

But: The tiny "dip" pool is not a swimming pool. The open deck and sunbathing space is quite cramped. Plastic woods instead of real woods everywhere (looks too perfect). Small library is attractive, but book selection is poor. The brochure rates do not include Galapagos Islands visitor tax (to be paid at Guayaquil or Quito airport or in the islands).

ms Galaxy

☆☆☆☆☆

(L)

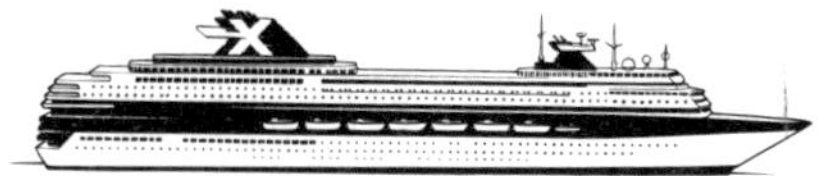

LIFESTYLE	**PREMIUM**
Cruise Line:	Celebrity Cruises
Former Names:	-
Gross Tonnage:	76,522
Builder:	Meyer Werft (Germany)
Original Cost:	$320 million
Entered Service:	December 1996
Flag:	Liberia
Tel No:	363653411/663653410
Fax No:	363753420
Length (ft./m.):	865.8/263.9
Beam (ft./m.):	105.6/32.20
Draft (ft./m.):	25.2/7.70
Propulsion/Propellers:	diesel 31,500kW (29,250kw)/2 (CP)
Decks:	10
Total Crew:	900
Pass. Capacity (basis 2):	1,896
Pass. Capacity (all berths):	2,681
Pass. Space Ratio (basis 2):	40.3
Pass. Space Ratio (all berths):	28.5
Officers:	Greek
Total Cabins:	948
Size Range (sq. ft./m.):	172–1,515/15.7–140.7
Cabins (outside view):	639
Cabins (inside):	309
Cabins (for one person):	0
Cabins (with private balcony):	220
Cabins (wheelchair accessible):	8
Cabin Current:	110/220 AC
Cabin TV:	Yes
Dining Rooms:	2
Seatings:	2
Elevators:	10
Casino:	Yes
Slot Machines:	Yes
Swimming Pools (outdoors):	2
Swimming Pools (inside):	1 indoor/outdoor (magrodome)
Whirlpools:	3
Fitness Center:	Yes
Sauna/Steam Room:	Yes/No
Massage:	Yes
Self-Service Launderette:	No
Movie Theater/Seats:	Yes
Library:	Yes
Children's Facilities:	Yes
Classification Society:	Lloyd's Register

RATINGS	**SCORE**
Ship: Hardware/Maintenance	91
Ship: Outdoor Facilities/Space	91
Ship: Interior Facilities/Space/Flow	91
Ship: Decor/Furnishings/Artwork	92
Ship: Spa/Fitness Facilities	90
Cabins: Suites and Deluxe	93
Cabins: Standard Sizes	89
Food: Dining Room/Cuisine	85
Food: Informal Dining/Buffets	82
Food: Quality of Ingredients	86
Food: Afternoon Tea/Bar Snacks	73
Service: Dining Room	85
Service: Bars	80
Service: Cabins	81
Service: Open Decks	78
Cruise: Entertainment	84
Cruise: Activities Program	73
Cruise: Movies/Television Programming	85
Cruise: Hospitality Standard	83
Cruise: Overall Product Delivery	90
OVERALL SCORE	**1,702**

Accommodation: The largest suites are the two Presidential Suites, located amidships. Each is a 1,173 sq. ft. (108.9 m²) penthouse with its own butler's pantry and has an inter-connecting door (when joined with the next-door suite it becomes an impressive 1,515 sq. ft. (140.7 m²) apartment suite).

Most of the Deck 10 suites and cabins are of generous proportions, are beautifully equipped, and have balconies with full floor-to-ceiling partitions, as well as VCR units. The Sky Deck suites are also excellent, with huge balconies (the partitions are not quite of the floor-to-ceiling type), wall clock, large floor-to-ceiling mirrors, marble-topped vanity/writing desk, excellent closet and drawer space, and even dimmer-controlled ceiling lights.

All of the standard inside and outside cabins are of a good size and come nicely furnished with twin beds that can convert to a queen-sized unit. The bathrooms, in particular, are spacious and come well equipped (with generous-size showers, hairdryers, and space for personal toiletry items). Sadly, there are no cabins for singles. Baby-monitoring telephones are also in all cabins.

All cabins feature interactive television for booking shore excursions, ordering room service, playing electronic casino games, and purchasing goods from the ship's boutiques. So, you do not have to leave your quarters if you do not wish to, especially if you do not like the ports of call (available in English, French, German, Italian, and Spanish).

Most of the suites with private balconies have floor-to-ceiling windows and sliding doors to balconies (a few have outward opening doors). All accommodation designated as suites feature duvets on the beds instead of sheets/blankets. In-suite massage service is available (with the right balcony, such as those in the Sky Suites, this is an excellent service).

Dining: There is a huge two-level dining room reminiscent of the dining halls aboard the ocean liners of the 1930s, with a grand staircase between both levels and perimeter alcoves that provide more intimate dining spaces. Each level of the dining room has its own separate galley, and the noise level in the two sections is quite acceptable (more noise is noticeable on the larger, lower level, however). The cuisine is based on menus created by Michel Roux, and executed by the chefs and cooks on board. The food has lots of taste (in particular the sauces that accompany many of the main dishes) and has fine color balance.

Just outside the lower-level entrance, a champagne and caviar bar serves ossetra and sevruga caviar nicely presented with all the trimmings.

For informal breakfasts and lunches, there is the two-level lido café with several serving lines (features warm wood-accented decor), and eight bay windows provide some really prime seating spots. There are also two poolside grills; one located adjacent to the midships pools, the other wedged into the aft pool.

In addition, Tasting's is a coffee lounge and bar for specialty coffees and pastries. For passengers in the 2 Presidential and 48 other suites, in-cabin dining is an option. However, the food served as room-service items is decidedly below the standard of food featured in the dining room. For those that cannot live without them, freshly baked pizzas (in a box) can be delivered, in an insulated pouch, to your cabin.

Celebrity Cruises is known for its excellent cuisine and presentation, and, although it is more difficult to deliver aboard the new, larger ships, Celebrity Cruises seems to have got it just right.

Other Comments: Slightly longer than sister ship *Century* (by 14 meters), the extra length provides room for a third swimming pool, which is covered by a large glass magrodome. Although there are over 4.5 acres of space on the open deck, it seems small when the ship is full.

Inside, there are two foyers (atriums); one is a four-deck-high main foyer, and the second is a three-deck-high atrium. There is a 1,000-seat show lounge with large side balconies and good sight lines from just about every seat. There is also a small, dedicated movie theater, which doubles as a conference and meeting center with all the latest audio-visual technology that includes three-language simultaneous translation and headsets for the hearing-impaired.

The AquaSpa, which has proved extremely popular aboard *Century*, contains 9,040 sq. ft. (839.8 m^2) of space dedicated to well-being and body treatments, and includes a large fitness/exercise area, complete with all the latest high-tech muscle machines and video cycles.

The ship has a superb, somewhat whimsical collection of artwork, which casts an eclectic look at life in some of its many forms. The collection is the result of the personal work of Christina Chandris, wife of the company's chairman.

Although improved, shore excursions are still a weak point of this operation. A "zero announcement" policy is much appreciated by passengers.

Apart from the "front of house" aspects of this ship, it is the "back of house" facilities, the design and flow of the main galley (2,200 m^2), where the ship really shines. The consideration for safety is second to none. Also has excellent tender loading platforms.

Stratosphere, the ship's large combination observation lounge and discotheque, provides what is probably the best viewing room when the ship operates Alaska cruises.

For a big-ship cruise experience, this one has it all. *Galaxy* delivers an outstanding product that is worth much more than the cruise fare charged.

<u>But:</u>The one are of congestion is the Photo Gallery, when passenger flow at peak evening times is poor.

mv Grande Caribe

(S)

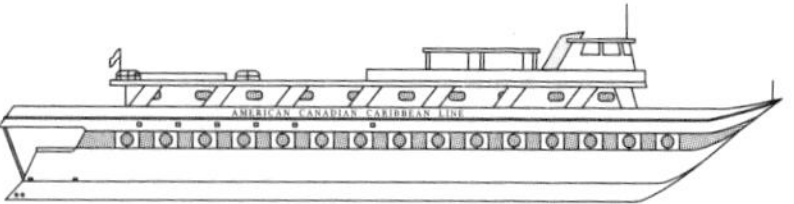

Lifestyle	Standard
Cruise Line:	American Canadian Caribbean Line
Former Names:	-
Gross Tonnage:	99
Builder:	Blount industries (USA)
Original Cost:	$8 million
Entered Service:	June 1997
Flag:	USA
Tel No:	n/a
Fax No:	n/a
Length (ft./m.):	177.0/53.9
Beam (ft./m.):	40.0/12.1
Draft (ft./m.):	6.7/2.0
Propulsion/Propellers:	diesel (1,400hp)/2
Decks:	3
Total Crew:	17
Pass. Capacity (basis 2):	100
Pass. Capacity (all berths):	100
Pass. Space Ratio (basis 2):	0.99
Pass. Space Ratio (all berths):	0.99
Officers:	American
Total Cabins:	50
Size Range (sq. ft./m.):	72.0–96.0/6.6–8.9
Cabins (outside view):	41
Cabins (inside):	9
Cabins (for one person):	0
Cabins (with private balcony):	0
Cabins (wheelchair accessible):	0
Cabin Current:	110 AC
Cabin TV:	No
Dining Rooms:	1
Seatings:	1
Elevators:	0
Casino:	0
Slot Machines:	0
Swimming Pools (outdoors):	0
Swimming Pools (inside):	0
Whirlpools:	0
Fitness Center:	0
Sauna/Steam Room:	0/0
Massage:	0
Self-Service Launderette:	No
Movie Theater/Seats:	0
Library:	Yes
Children's Facilities:	No
Classification Society:	American Bureau of Shipping

Ratings	Score
Ship: Hardware/Maintenance	68
Ship: Outdoor Facilities/Space	54
Ship: Interior Facilities/Space/Flow	60
Ship: Decor/Furnishings/Artwork	60
Ship: Public Rooms	50
Cabins: Suites and Deluxe	61
Cabins: Standard Sizes	53
Food: Dining Room/Cuisine	66
Food: Informal Dining/Buffets	62
Food: Quality of Ingredients	70
Food: Afternoon Tea/Bar Snacks	43
Service: Dining Room	65
Service: Bars	68
Service: Cabins	65
Service: Open Decks	46
Cruise: Port Information	50
Cruise: Shore Programs	60
Cruise: Movies/Television Programming	42
Cruise: Hospitality Standard	66
Cruise: Overall Product Delivery	73
Overall Score	**1,182**

Accommodation: This vessel has the largest number of cabins of all the ACCL ships, but they are still extremely small, relatively spartan units, with very little closet space (but enough drawers) and small (very small) bathrooms. There are 48 cabins, each with twin beds convertible to queen-sized beds (there is good storage space under the beds). There is no room service menu, and only soap is supplied (bring your own shampoo and other toiletries). Each cabin has its own air conditioner, so passengers do not have to share air with the rest of the ship (and other passengers). Refreshingly, there are no cabin keys.

Dining: The dining room seats all passengers in an open seating, so you dine with whomever you wish. The advantage of this is that you can make new friends and enjoy different conversation each day (it is also good for small groups). Dining tables convert to card tables for use between meals.

Passengers are welcome to bring their own alcohol, as the company does not sell it aboard ship. The service is provided by young, effervescent American waitresses, although there is no finesse.

Other Comments: This is the largest and the most contemporary of the Blount-built vessels. During passenger emergency drill, passengers are taught how to use fire extinguishers, a very useful piece of training.

This vessel has a shallow draft, which enables it to cruise into off-the-beaten-path destinations well out of reach of larger ships, and also features a retractable navigation bridge—good for those low bridges along the inland waterways. She is the only ship in the fleet that has stabilizers. The style is unpretentious and very casual (no jackets or ties) both day and night. There are two 24-passenger launches, a glass bottom boat, and some snorkeling equipment.

There is one lounge/bar, now thankfully located on a different deck to the dining room—a departure for ACCL from the company's former vessels. Water sports facilities include a glass-bottom boat and sunfish sailboat.

This ship will be good for anyone who does not want crowds or entertainment of any kind, or a high standard of service. All gratuities are pooled by all the staff (although you should note that the suggested daily rate is high for the product delivered).

ms Grand Princess

☆☆☆☆ +

(L)

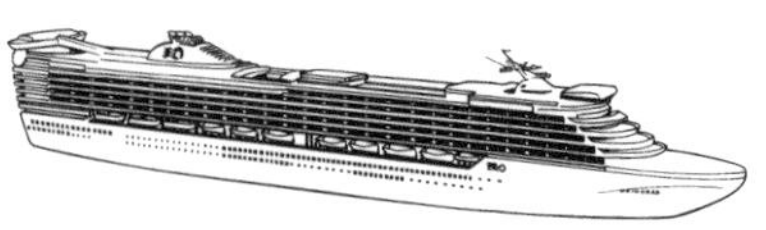

Lifestyle	Premium
Cruise Line:	Princess Cruises
Former Names:	-
Gross Tonnage:	108,806
Builder:	Fincantieri (Italy)
Original Cost:	$430 million
Entered Service:	May 1998
Flag:	Liberia
Tel No:	363677211
Fax No:	363677220/363677320
Length (ft./m.):	951.4/290.0
Beam (ft./m.):	118.1/36.0
Draft (ft./m.):	26.2/8.0
Propulsion/Propellers:	diesel-electric (42,000kW)/2 (FP)
Decks:	12
Total Crew:	1,100
Pass. Capacity (basis 2):	2,600
Pass. Capacity (all berths):	3,100
Pass. Space Ratio (basis 2):	41.8
Pass. Space Ratio (all berths):	35.0
Officers:	British
Total Cabins:	1,300
Size Range (sq. ft./m.):	161.4–764.2/15.0–71.0
Cabins (outside view):	938
Cabins (inside):	362
Cabins (for one person):	0
Cabins (with private balcony):	712
Cabins (wheelchair accessible):	28 (18 outside/10 inside)
Cabin Current:	110/220 AC
Cabin TV:	Yes
Dining Rooms:	3
Seatings:	2
Elevators:	16
Casino:	Yes
Slot Machines:	Yes
Swimming Pools (outdoors):	4
Swimming Pools (inside):	0
Whirlpools:	9
Fitness Center:	Yes
Sauna/Steam Room:	Yes/Yes
Massage:	Yes
Self-Service Launderette:	Yes
Movie Theater/Seats:	Yes
Library:	Yes
Children's Facilities:	Yes
Classification Society:	Lloyd's Register

Ratings	Score
Ship: Hardware/Maintenance	92
Ship: Outdoor Facilities/Space	81
Ship: Interior Facilities/Space/Flow	92
Ship: Decor/Furnishings/Artwork	92
Ship: Spa/Fitness Facilities	90
Cabins: Suites and Deluxe	91
Cabins: Standard Sizes	85
Food: Dining Room/Cuisine	77
Food: Informal Dining/Buffets	76
Food: Quality of Ingredients	71
Food: Afternoon Tea/Bar Snacks	66
Service: Dining Room	77
Service: Bars	76
Service: Cabins	76
Service: Open Decks	75
Cruise: Entertainment	87
Cruise: Activities Program	77
Cruise: Movies/Television Programming	86
Cruise: Hospitality Standard	86
Cruise: Overall Product Delivery	91
Overall Score	**1,644**

Accommodation: There are six types of cabins and configurations: (a) grand suite, (b) suite, (c) mini-suite, (d) outside double with balcony, (e) outside double, and (f) inside double. There are, however, 35 different brochure price categories; the choice is bewildering for both travel agents and passengers. Pricing depends on two things, size and location.

(a) The plushest suite is the Grand Suite, which has a hot tub accessible from both the private balcony and from the bedroom, two bedrooms, a lounge, two bathrooms, and a huge walk-in closet.

(b/c) Suites (with private balcony) have a separate living room (with sofa bed) and bedroom (with a television in each). The bathroom is quite large and features both a bathtub and shower stall. The mini-suites also have a private balcony and feature a separate living and sleeping area (with a television in each). The bathroom is also quite spacious and features both a bathtub and shower stall. The differences between the suites and mini-suites are basically in the size and appointments, the suite being more of a square shape while mini-suites are more rectangular, and have few drawers. Both suites and mini-suites feature butler service (known in Princess Cruises' language as Grand Class Gold), and really plush bathrobes, fully tiled bathrooms with ample open shelf storage space. Passengers in suites and mini-suites have priority attention, including speedy embarkation and disembarkation privileges.

(d/e/f) Both inside and outside-view (the outsides come either with or without private balcony) cabins are of a functional, practical, design, although almost no drawers are provided. They are very attractive, with warm, pleasing decor and fine soft furnishing fabrics; 80 percent of the outside cabins have private balconies. The tiled bathrooms have a good amount of open shelf storage space for personal toiletries.

Additionally, two family suites consist of two suites with an interconnecting door, plus a large balcony), and can sleep up to 10 (if at least four are children, or up to 8 if all are adults).

All accommodation occupants receive turndown service and chocolates on pillows, as well as bathrobes and toiletry amenity kits (larger, naturally, for suite/mini-suite occupants). You should note that the majority of the outside cabins on Emerald Deck have views obstructed by the lifeboats. Sadly, there are no cabins for singles.

In-cabin television programming includes BBC World Service, CNNfn, ESPN, and TNT.

Dining: As befits the size of the ship, there is a wide variety of informal dining options, more than aboard any other Princess Cruises ship to date. For formal meals there are three principal dining rooms (named Botticelli, Da Vinci, and Michelangelo), assigned according to the location of your cabin: Botticelli (504 seats), Da Vinci (486 seats), and Michelangelo (486 seats). All three are nonsmoking and split into multitier sections in a nonsymmetrical design similar to those seen in *Dawn Princess* and *Sun Princess*, breaking what are quite large spaces into many smaller sections, for better ambience. Each dining room has its own galley.

Several other dining areas are provided: a Trattoria (for pizzas and other Italian fare; reservation only, cover charge $3.50 per person), as well as the Painted Desert (southwestern American food; by reservation only, cover charge $3.50 per person). A coffee bar/patisserie (extra charge), wine/caviar bar (extra charge), a poolside hamburger grill and pizza bar are additional dining spots for casual bites.

Specially designed dinnerware and high-quality linens and silverware are featured; by Dudson of England (dinnerware), Frette Egyptian (cotton table linens), and Hepp of Germany (silverware).

Other Comments: The design for this large vessel, presently the world's largest (though not longest) cruise ship, is indicative of what is to come in the future for the big players in this industry. She presents a surprisingly bold, forthright profile, with a racy "spoiler" effect at her galleon-like transom stern (this acts as a stern observation lounge by day, and a stunning discotheque by night). She really is quite a ship—too wide to transit the Panama Canal with many balcony cabins overhanging the hull.

There is a good sheltered teakwood promenade deck, which almost wraps around and a walkway which goes right to the enclosed bow of the ship. The outdoor pools have various beach-like surroundings. One lap pool has a pumped "current" to swim against.

Unlike the outside decks, there is plenty of space inside the ship (but there are also plenty of passengers), and a wide array of public rooms to choose from, with many "intimate" (this is a relative word) spaces and places to play. The passenger flow has been well thought out, and works with little congestion. The decor is very attractive, with lots of beiges and earth tones (well suited to both American and European tastes). In fact, she is the culmination of the best of all that Princess Cruises has to offer from its many years of operating a fine quality product.

Four areas center on swimming pools, one of which is two decks high and is covered by a magrodome, itself an extension of the funnel housing. A large health spa complex surrounds one of the swimming pools (you can have a massage or other spa treatment in an ocean-view treatment room). High atop the stern of the ship is a ship-wide glass-walled disco pod (I have nicknamed it the ETR: energy transfer room). It looks like an aerodynamic "spoiler" and is positioned some 150.1 feet (45.75 meters) above the waterline, with spectacular views from the extreme port and starboard side windows (you can look along the ship's side and onto lots of "private" balconies).

An extensive collection of artwork has been chosen, and this complements the interior design and colors well. If you see something you like, you will be able to purchase it on board—it's almost all for sale.

This ship features the first oceangoing Wedding Chapel. The ship's captain can legally marry couples (due to the ship's Liberian registry and a special dispensation, although this should be verified when in the planning stage, according to where you reside). So, what better way to be married and have your honeymoon in one location that moves with you. Princess Cruises offers three wedding packages: Pearl, Emerald, and Diamond. Fees include registration and official marriage certificate. However, to get married and take your close family members and entourage with you on your honeymoon is going to cost a lot of money (do you really want our family with you on your honeymoon!). The "Hearts & Minds" chapel is also useful for "renewal of vows" ceremonies.

Another neat feature is the "virtual reality" room with its enclosed motion-based rides, and a "blue screen" studio, where passengers can star in their own videos. Features an excellent library/CD-ROM computer room, and a separate card room. For children there is a two-deck-high playroom, teen's room, and a host of specially trained counselors.

For entertainment, Princess Cruises prides itself on its glamorous all-American production shows, and the shows aboard this ship ("Gotta Sing, Gotta Dance," "Glamour," and "Swing Time") will not disappoint. Neither will the comfortable show lounges (the largest features $3 million in sound and light equipment, as well as a nine-piece orchestra, and a scenery loading bay that connects directly from stage to a hull door for direct transfer to the dockside). Two other entertainment lounges help spread things around. Casino lovers should enjoy what is presently the largest casino at sea, with more than 260 slot machines (all with dolphin-shaped handles). There are blackjack, craps, and roulette tables, plus newer games such as Let It Ride Bonus, Spanish 21, and Caribbean Draw Progressive. But the highlight could well be Neptune's Lair, a multimedia gaming extravaganza.

Ship lovers should enjoy the wood-paneled Wheelhouse Bar, finely decorated with memorabilia and ship models tracing part of parent company P&O's history. Princess Cays, Princess Cruises' own "private island" in the Caribbean, is "yours" (along with a couple of thousand other passengers) for a day (but you need to take a shore tender to get to and from it, and this can take some time). A high-tech hospital is provided, with live SeaMed tele-medicine link-ups with specialists at the Cedars-Sinai Medical Center in Los Angeles available for emergency help; it's the first such seagoing system in the world.

The ship operates seven-day Caribbean cruises during the winter, and twelve-day Mediterranean cruises during the summer, and provides you with a stunning, grand playground in which to roam when you are not ashore. Princess Cruises delivers a fine, well-packaged vacation product, with a good sense of style, at an attractive, highly competitive price, and this ship will appeal to those that really enjoy a big city to play in, with all the trimmings and lots of fellow passengers. The ship is full of revenue centers, however, which are designed to help you part with even more money than what is paid for in the price of your cruise ticket.

Whether this really can be considered a relaxing vacation is a moot point, but with so many choices and "small" rooms to enjoy, the ship has been extremely well designed, and the odds are that you'll have a fine cruise vacation. If you choose a Mediterranean cruise, it is wise to add a post-cruise stay option, as the disembarkation is rudely early.

<u>But:</u> If you are not used to large ships, it will take you some time to find your way around (take good walking shoes), despite the company's claim that this vessel offers passengers a "small ship feel, big ship choice." The cabin bath towels are small, and drawer space is very limited, particularly for the 12-day Mediterranean cruises. The automated telephone system is utterly frustrating, and luggage delivery needs to be more efficient. Lines form for many things, but particularly for the purser's office and for open seating breakfast and lunch in the three main dining rooms. Long lines for shore excursions are also a fact of life aboard large ships such as this, as is waiting for elevators at peak times.

ms Grandeur of the Seas

☆☆☆☆

(L)

Lifestyle	**Standard**
Cruise Line:	Royal Caribbean International
Former Names:	-
Gross Tonnage:	74,137
Builder:	Kvaerner Masa Yards (Finland)
Original Cost:	$300 million
Entered Service:	December 1996
Flag:	Liberia
Tel No:	1260734/363654710
Fax No:	1260735/363654720
Length (ft./m.):	917.3/279.6
Beam (ft./m.):	105.6/32.2
Draft (ft./m.):	25.5/7.8
Propulsion/Propellers:	diesel-electric (50,400kw)/2 (FP)
Decks:	11
Total Crew:	760
Pass. Capacity (basis 2):	1,950
Pass. Capacity (all berths):	2,440
Pass. Space Ratio (basis 2):	38.0
Pass. Space Ratio (all berths):	30.3
Officers:	International
Total Cabins:	975
Size Range (sq. ft./m.):	158–1,033/14.7–96.0
Cabins (outside view):	576
Cabins (inside):	399
Cabins (for one person):	0
Cabins (with private balcony):	212
Cabins (wheelchair accessible):	14
Cabin Current:	110/220 AC
Cabin TV:	Yes
Dining Rooms:	1
Seatings:	2
Elevators:	9
Casino:	Yes
Slot Machines:	Yes
Swimming Pools (outdoors):	1
Swimming Pools (inside):	1 (indoor/outdoor w/glass roof)
Whirlpools:	6
Fitness Center:	Yes
Sauna/Steam Room:	Yes/Yes
Massage:	Yes
Self-Service Launderette:	No
Movie Theater/Seats:	No
Library:	Yes
Children's Facilities:	Yes
Classification Society:	Det Norske Veritas

Ratings	**Score**
Ship: Hardware/Maintenance	87
Ship: Outdoor Facilities/Space	86
Ship: Interior Facilities/Space/Flow	86
Ship: Decor/Furnishings/Artwork	87
Ship: Spa/Fitness Facilities	86
Cabins: Suites and Deluxe	88
Cabins: Standard Sizes	81
Food: Dining Room/Cuisine	71
Food: Informal Dining/Buffets	63
Food: Quality of Ingredients	66
Food: Afternoon Tea/Bar Snacks	52
Service: Dining Room	78
Service: Bars	76
Service: Cabins	77
Service: Open Decks	71
Cruise: Entertainment	81
Cruise: Activities Program	76
Cruise: Movies/Television Programming	76
Cruise: Hospitality Standard	73
Cruise: Overall Product Delivery	77
Overall Score	**1,538**

Accommodation: The suites are very well appointed and have very pleasing decor, with good wood and color accenting (the largest suite even has a baby grand piano). Category A and B cabins also have VCR units. All standard cabins have twin beds that convert to a queen-size bed, ample closet space for a one-week cruise, and a good amount of drawer space, although under-bed storage space is not good for large suitcases. Bathrooms have nine mirrors. The plastic buckets for champagne/wine are really shoddy.

Dining: The dining room, which seats 1,195, is a huge, two-deck-high banquet room. General comments regarding the food operation aboard *Legend of the Seas* and *Splendour of the Seas* apply, but some innovative options are also included (even fish knives are available in this ship), although presentation is inconsistent. There is an intimate Champagne Bar, and the popular, informal Windjammer Café is better, with more food islands.

Other Comments: The ships in the Royal Caribbean International fleet are always evolving, and this ship is no exception. It presents a nice long profile with a funnel placed well aft (almost a throwback to some ship designs used in the 1950s). She has a well-rounded stern (as have the *Sovereign of the Seas*-class ships) and a Viking Crown Lounge in the center, just forward of the funnel. This lounge, together with the forward mast and aft funnel, provides three distinct focal points in her exterior profile. The Viking Crown Lounge sits between funnel and mast and overlooks the forward section of the swimming pool deck, as aboard *Legend of the Seas/Splendour of the Seas*, with access provided by a multi-deck atrium. No cushioned pads are provided for the plastic-webbed deck lounge chairs.

There is a wraparound outdoor promenade deck, with a seven-deck-high atrium inside. A delightful champagne terrace bar sits forward of the lower level of the two-deck-high dining room.

There are two showrooms. One is the principal show lounge, for the big production shows, and has excellent sight lines from 98 percent of the 875 seats; the other is the secondary show lounge, for smaller shows and adult cabaret, with 575 seats. Good children's and teens' facilities, much expanded from previous ships in the fleet.

This is another new ship design for Royal Caribbean International (her sister ship is *Enchantment of the Seas*), with what, inside, has proven to be a good passenger flow. The vessel has a good, varied collection of artwork (including several sculptures), principally by British artists, with classical music, ballet, and theater themes. The casino has a fascinating, somewhat theatrical glass-covered, underfloor exhibit.

This ship will be good for first-time cruise passengers who want fine, very comfortable surroundings and all the very latest in facilities, entertainment lounges, and high-tech sophistication in one neat, well-packaged, and fine-tuned cruise vacation, with plenty of music and entertainment.

ms Hanseatic

☆☆☆☆☆

(S)

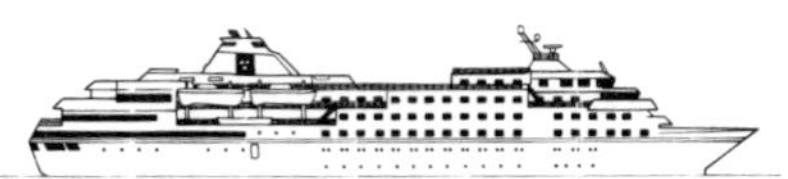

Lifestyle	Luxury
Cruise Line:	Hanseatic Tours
Former Names:	-
Gross Tonnage:	8,378
Builder:	Rauma Yards (Finland)
Original Cost:	$68 million
Entered Service:	March 1993
Flag:	Bahamas
Tel No:	1103730
Fax No:	1103726
Length (ft./m.):	402.9/122.80
Beam (ft./m.):	59.1/18.00
Draft (ft./m.):	15.5/4.71
Propulsion/Propellers:	diesel (5,880kW)/2 (CP)
Decks:	6
Total Crew:	122
Pass. Capacity (basis 2):	184
Pass. Capacity (all berths):	194
Pass. Space Ratio (basis 2):	45.5
Pass. Space Ratio (all berths):	43.1
Officers:	German
Total Cabins:	92
Size Range (sq. ft./m.):	231.4–470.3/21.5–43.7
Cabins (outside view):	92
Cabins (inside):	0
Cabins (for one person):	0
Cabins (with private balcony):	0
Cabins (wheelchair accessible):	2
Cabin Current:	220 AC
Cabin TV:	Yes
Dining Rooms:	1
Seatings:	1
Elevators:	2
Swimming Pools (outdoors):	1
Whirlpools:	1
Exercise Room:	Yes
Sauna/Steam Room:	Yes/No
Massage:	Yes
Self-Service Launderette:	No
Lecture/Film Room:	Yes (seats 160)
Library:	Yes
Zodiacs:	14
Helicopter Pad:	Yes
Classification Society:	Det Norske Veritas

Ratings	Score
Ship: Hardware/Maintenance	91
Ship: Expedition Equipment	90
Ship: Interior Facilities/Space/Flow	88
Ship: Decor/Furnishings/Artwork	88
Ship: Spa/Fitness Facilities	77
Cabins: Suites and Deluxe	88
Cabins: Standard Sizes	84
Food: Dining Room/Cuisine	88
Food: Informal Dining/Buffets	86
Food: Quality of Ingredients	86
Food: Afternoon Tea/Bar Snacks	85
Service: Dining Room	87
Service: Bars	86
Service: Cabins	86
Service: Open Decks	84
Cruise: Library/Lecture Programs	88
Cruise: Movies/Television Programming	86
Cruise: Hospitality Standard	88
Cruise: Expedition Experience	93
Cruise: Overall Product Delivery	91
Overall Score	**1,740**

Accommodation: The all-outside cabins, located in the forward section of the ship, are large and very well equipped and include a separate lounge area next to a large picture window (which has a pull-down blackout blind as well as curtains) and refrigerator. All furniture is in warm woods and everything has rounded edges. Wood trim accents the ceiling perimeter and acts as a divider between bed and lounge areas. Each cabin has a mini-bar, television, VCR unit, two locking drawers, and plenty of closet and drawer space, as well as two separate cupboards and hooks for all-weather gear.

All cabin bathrooms have a large bathtub, two toiletries cabinets, wall-mounted hairdryer, and bathrobe. There are only two types of cabins; 34 have double beds, others have twin beds. Towels, bed linens, and pillowcases are of 100 percent cotton, and individual cotton-filled duvet covers are provided.

The suites and cabins on Bridge Deck have impeccable butler service and full in-cabin dining privileges, as well as personalized stationery. Soft drinks are supplied in the cabin refrigerator and replenished daily, at no charge (all liquor is at extra cost, however). A very relaxed ambience prevails on board.

Dining: The dining room is very elegant, warm and welcoming, and features large picture windows on two sides as well as aft, and table settings are graced with fine Rosenthal china and silverware. The cuisine and service are first rate, but are more informal than, for example, aboard the larger *Europa* (which is at or around the same price level). Top quality ingredients are always used, and many items are purchased fresh when available.

The meals are very creative and nicely presented, and each is appealing to the eye as well as to the palate. There is always an excellent selection of breads, cheeses, desserts, and pastry items. Note that when operating in the Arctic or Antarctic, table set-ups are often minimal, due to the possible movement of the ship (stabilizers cannot be used in much of the Antarctic region), so cutlery is provided and changed for each course.

The ship added an alternative dining room in March 1996. The Columbus Lounge now changes into an Oriental dining room at night. Reservations are required (you make them in the morning of the day you want to dine there), but there is no extra charge and no tipping at any time. Also, on each cruise a full Viennese tea-time is featured, as well as a regular daily tea-time.

Other Comments: *Hanseatic* was designed and constructed specifically to provide worldwide exploration-style cruises in luxurious contemporary surroundings. As such, she looks like the practical vessel she was designed to be. The ship is extremely environmentally-friendly and features the latest, "zero-discharge," nonpolluting waste disposal system, including a pollution-filtered incinerator, full biological sewage treatment plant, and large storage capacity.

She is an outstanding ship for the best in destination-intensive exploration voyages and is under long-term charter to specialist operator Hanseatic Tours (part of the Hapag-Lloyd group). Features a fully enclosed bridge (with an open bridge policy, so that passengers can visit the bridge at almost any time) and an ice-hardened hull with the highest passenger vessel classification of 1A1 Super. The ship also features the very latest in high-tech navigation equipment.

A fleet of 14 Zodiac inflatable craft (all are named after famous explorers) is used for in-depth shore landings. These craft provide the ship with tremendous flexibility in itineraries and provide excellent possibilities for up-close wildlife viewing in natural habitats, with small numbers of passengers. Rubber boots, parkas, and a boot-washing and storage room are provided for passengers, particularly useful for Arctic and Antarctic cruises.

Inside, the ship is equipped with fine quality luxury fittings and soft furnishings. There is a choice of several public rooms, all of them well furnished and decorated, and all of them have high ceilings, which helps to provide an impression of space; the result is that the ship feels much larger than her actual size. The library/observation lounge provides a good selection of hardback books and videos in both the English and German languages.

This ship provides destination-intensive, nature, and life-enrichment cruises and expeditions in elegant but unstuffy surroundings, to some of the world's most fascinating destinations, at a suitable price. Hanseatic Tours keeps the passenger maximum generally to about 150, which means plenty of comfort, and lots of space for everyone. Competes directly with *Europa*, in terms of the rates per day per passenger, but this is a very different, more hands-on travel experience (small ship as opposed to large ship).

The ship really is at her best when operating in Arctic and Antarctic regions. The ship always operates in two languages, English and German, and caters well to both sets of passengers. All port taxes, insurance, gratuities, Zodiac trips, and most shore excursions (except for those in Europe) are included.

Outstanding, fascinating lecturers and naturalists accompany each cruise. Some other ship staff are very willing and helpful and speak several languages.

Hanseatic Tours specializes in providing outstanding, well-planned itineraries. Where this ship really scores, however, is in her Antarctic sailings, where the experience of her captain and cruise director and the crew really shine. The lectures, briefings, and the amount of information provided for passengers about the itinerary and ports of call is outstanding.

<ins>But:</ins> She is principally marketed to German-speaking and English-speaking passengers, so other nationalities may find it hard to integrate. There are no marine quality telescopes mounted outdoors (there should be). There is, at present, no privacy curtain between cabin door and the sleeping area (there should be).

mv Hebridean Princess

☆☆☆☆ +

(S)

Lifestyle	**Luxury**
Cruise Line:	Hebridean Island Cruises
Former Names:	*Columba*
Gross Tonnage:	2,112
Builder:	Hall Russell (Scotland)
Original Cost:	n/a
Entered Service:	1964/April 1989
Flag:	Scotland
Tel No:	1440772
Fax No:	1440772
Length (ft./m.):	235.0/71.6
Beam (ft./m.):	46.0/14.0
Draft (ft./m.):	10.0/3.0
Propulsion/Propellers:	diesel (1,790kW)/2 (FP)
Decks:	5
Total Crew:	35
Pass. Capacity (basis 2):	48
Pass. Capacity (all berths):	55
Pass. Space Ratio (basis 2):	44.0
Pass. Space Ratio (all berths):	38.4
Officers:	British
Total Cabins:	29
Size Range (sq. ft./m.):	112–367/10.4–34.0
Cabins (outside view):	23
Cabins (inside):	6
Cabins (for one person):	11
Cabins (with private balcony):	4
Cabins (wheelchair accessible):	0
Cabin Current:	240 AC
Cabin TV:	Yes
Dining Rooms:	1
Seatings:	1
Elevators:	0
Casino:	No
Slot Machines:	No
Swimming Pools (outdoors):	0
Swimming Pools (inside):	0
Whirlpools:	0
Fitness Center:	Yes
Sauna/Steam Room:	No/No
Massage:	No
Self-Service Launderette:	No
Movie Theater/Seats:	No
Library:	Yes
Children's Facilities:	No
Classification Society:	Lloyd's Register

Ratings	**Score**
Ship: Hardware/Maintenance	86
Ship: Outdoor Facilities/Space	82
Ship: Interior Facilities/Space/Flow	85
Ship: Decor/Furnishings/Artwork	90
Ship: Public Rooms	82
Cabins: Suites and Deluxe	91
Cabins: Standard Sizes	86
Food: Dining Room/Cuisine	89
Food: Informal Dining/Buffets	87
Food: Quality of Ingredients	88
Food: Afternoon Tea/Bar Snacks	86
Service: Dining Room	87
Service: Bars	86
Service: Cabins	87
Service: Open Decks	81
Cruise: Port Information	83
Cruise: Shore Programs	80
Cruise: Movies/Television Programming	70
Cruise: Hospitality Standard	86
Cruise: Overall Product Delivery	87
Overall Score	**1,699**

Accommodation: All cabins have different color schemes and names (there are no numbers, and, refreshingly, no door locks, so don't ask for the door key). All are individually designed (no two cabins are identical) and created, with sweeping chintz curtains and drapes over the beds. They really are quite delightful and come in a range of configurations (some with single, some with double, some with twin beds), including four that have a private balcony (lovely). All feature a refrigerator. All except two cabins have a private bathroom with bath or shower; all have real Victorian bathroom fittings (some are even gold-plated, and brass cabin portholes that actually open. Three of the newest cabins added are outfitted in Scottish Baronial style. Some cabins also have a VCR unit.

Dining: Features a totally nonsmoking dining room, with tables laid with lace overlays. Some chairs have armrests, some do not. The outstanding cuisine is about the same quality and presentation as the Sea Goddess ships. Fresh produce is purchased locally, a welcome change from the mass catering of most ships. Although there are no flambe items (the galley has electric, not gas, cookers), what is created is beautifully presented and of the very highest standard. And the desserts are simply out of this world!

Breakfast menus alternate every two days and feature special dishes in addition to the traditional Scottish fare (try the "porridge and a wee dram"—it sets you up for the whole day). Although there is waiter service for most things, there is also a delightful buffet table display for breakfast and luncheon. This little ship features a very decent wine list, with extremely moderate prices. There are also many wonderful whiskeys (more than 45 of them) and vintage cognacs available (try the 50-year-old Remy Martin Louis XIII). Highly personal and attentive service from British/Scottish staff.

Other Comments: Small is beautiful! This utterly charming little ship has stately home service and a warm, totally cosseted, traditional country house ambience. The Tiree Lounge has a real brick-walled fireplace, and a very cozy bar with a wide variety of whiskeys (the selection of single malts is wonderful) and cognacs for real connoisseurs. Use of the ship's small boats, speedboat, bicycles, and fishing gear is included in the price, as are entrance fees to gardens, castles, and other attractions. The destination-intensive cruises have very creative itineraries. Specialist guides accompany all cruises.

Inspector Hercules Poirot would be very much at home here. Who needs mega-ships when you can take a retro-cruise aboard this absolute gem of a ship. Sheer pleasure is a week (or more) aboard *Hebridean Princess*—a superb Scottish Island Fling. Direct bookings are accepted. Presently the only cruise vessel in the world with an all-U.K. crew, she is one of the world's most well-kept travel secrets. A polished gem, she is especially popular with single passengers, and more than 50 percent of her passengers are repeaters. If you cruise from Oban, you will be met at Glasgow station (or airport) and taken to/from the ship in a private motor coach.

But: Although this vessel is strong, she does have structural limitations and noisy engines that cause some vibration (however, the engines do not run at night, and the ship anchors before bedtime, providing soul-renewing peace and tranquility). Drinks are not, but should at this price, be included. It is often cold (and very wet) in the Scottish islands, so take plenty of warm clothing for layering.

ms Holiday

☆☆☆ +

(L)

Lifestyle	Standard
Cruise Line:	Carnival Cruise Lines
Former Names:	-
Gross Tonnage:	46,052
Builder:	Aalborg Vaerft (Denmark)
Original Cost:	$170 million
Entered Service:	July 1985
Flag:	Bahamas
Tel No:	1103216
Fax No:	1103216
Length (ft./m.):	726.9/221.57
Beam (ft./m.):	92.4/28.17
Draft (ft./m.):	25.5/7.77
Propulsion/Propellers:	diesel (22,360kW)/2 (CP)
Decks:	9
Total Crew:	660
Pass. Capacity (basis 2):	1,452
Pass. Capacity (all berths):	1,800
Pass. Space Ratio (basis 2):	31.7
Pass. Space Ratio (all berths):	25.5
Officers:	Italian
Total Cabins:	726
Size Range (sq. ft./m.):	185–190/17.0–17.6
Cabins (outside view):	447
Cabins (inside):	279
Cabins (for one person):	0
Cabins (with private balcony):	10
Cabins (wheelchair accessible):	15
Cabin Current:	110 AC
Cabin TV:	Yes
Dining Rooms:	2
Seatings:	2
Elevators:	8
Casino:	Yes
Slot Machines:	Yes
Swimming Pools (outdoors):	3
Swimming Pools (inside):	0
Whirlpools:	2
Fitness Center:	Yes
Sauna/Steam Room:	Yes/No
Massage:	Yes
Self-Service Launderette:	Yes
Movie Theater/Seats:	No
Library:	Yes
Children's Facilities:	Yes
Classification Society:	Lloyd's Register

Ratings	Score
Ship: Hardware/Maintenance	76
Ship: Outdoor Facilities/Space	71
Ship: Interior Facilities/Space/Flow	73
Ship: Decor/Furnishings/Artwork	74
Ship: Spa/Fitness Facilities	61
Cabins: Suites and Deluxe	76
Cabins: Standard Sizes	67
Food: Dining Room/Cuisine	66
Food: Informal Dining/Buffets	62
Food: Quality of Ingredients	61
Food: Afternoon Tea/Bar Snacks	51
Service: Dining Room	71
Service: Bars	71
Service: Cabins	70
Service: Open Decks	63
Cruise: Entertainment	74
Cruise: Activities Program	61
Cruise: Movies/Television Programming	63
Cruise: Hospitality Standard	61
Cruise: Overall Product Delivery	73
Overall Score	**1,345**

Accommodation: Carnival Cruise Lines has always tried to provide an adequate amount of space in passenger cabins, and the cabins aboard Holiday are no exception. They are quite functional and provide all the basics; bathrooms are practical units, with decent-sized shower stalls. The only toiletry amenities provided, however, are soap and ice water, so you should take your own shampoo (ladies may also need to take a shower cap).

Dining: There are two dining rooms; both are large and have low ceilings, making the raised center sections seem crowded and very noisy because they are always full. The food is characterized by quantity, not quality, with little taste. The service is quite average, robotic, and hurried.

The buffets are very basic, as is the selection of breads, rolls, fruit, and cheeses. There are no wine waiters, although there is a surprisingly decent wine list.

Other Comments: This is a bold, high-sided, all-white contemporary ship with short, rakish bow and stubby stern typical of so many recently built ships. Has a distinctive, large, swept-back wing-tipped funnel in Carnival Cruise Lines colors of red, white and blue.

Inside, the passenger flow is quite good. There are numerous public rooms on two entertainment decks to choose from and play in, and these flow from a double-width indoor promenade. A real red-and-cream bus is located right in the middle of one of the two promenades, and this is used as a snack café.

There is a stunning, multitiered showroom, although the sight lines are restricted from some seats that are located behind the several pillars.

The very bright interior decor has a distinct Broadway theme. The Carnegie Library (which has very few books) is the only public room that is not bright. Excellent casino with round-the-clock action. Plenty of dazzle-and-sizzle entertainment. "Camp Carnival" takes care of junior cruisers, and facilities include virtual-reality machines.

This ship, now over 10 years old, is ideal for a first cruise experience in glitzy, very lively surroundings, and for the active set who enjoy constant stimulation, loud music, and a fun-filled atmosphere, at an attractive price. The line does not provide finesse, nor does it claim to. There is no doubt that Carnival does a great job of providing a fun venue, but many passengers say that once is enough, and after you will want to move to a more upscale experience.

But: There is almost constant hustling for drinks, but at least it is done with a knowing smile. A cruise aboard this ship is a noisy affair, and not relaxing at all (good if you want big-city nightlife).

mv Horizon

☆☆☆☆ +

(L)

LIFESTYLE	**PREMIUM**
Cruise Line:	Celebrity Cruises
Former Names:	-
Gross Tonnage:	46,811
Builder:	Meyer Werft (Germany)
Original Cost:	$185 million
Entered Service:	May 1990
Flag:	Liberia
Tel No:	1243527
Fax No:	1243532
Length (ft./m.):	680.7/207.49
Beam (ft./m.):	95.1/29.00
Draft (ft./m.):	23.6/7.20
Propulsion/Propellers:	diesel (19,960kW)/2 (CP)
Decks:	9
Total Crew:	645
Pass. Capacity (basis 2):	1,354
Pass. Capacity (all berths):	1,660
Pass. Space Ratio (basis 2):	34.5
Pass. Space Ratio (all berths):	28.1
Officers:	Greek
Total Cabins:	677
Size Range (sq. ft./m.):	185–334/17.0–31.0
Cabins (outside view):	529
Cabins (inside):	148
Cabins (for one person):	0
Cabins (with private balcony):	0
Cabins (wheelchair accessible):	4
Cabin Current:	110 AC
Cabin TV:	Yes
Dining Rooms:	1
Seatings:	2
Elevators:	7
Casino:	Yes
Slot Machines:	Yes
Swimming Pools (outdoors):	2
Swimming Pools (inside):	0
Whirlpools:	3
Fitness Center:	Yes
Sauna/Steam Room:	Yes/No
Massage:	Yes
Self-Service Launderette:	No
Movie Theater/Seats:	Yes/850
Library:	Yes
Children's Facilities:	Yes
Classification Society:	Lloyd's Register

RATINGS	**SCORE**
Ship: Hardware/Maintenance	85
Ship: Outdoor Facilities/Space	86
Ship: Interior Facilities/Space/Flow	87
Ship: Decor/Furnishings/Artwork	86
Ship: Spa/Fitness Facilities	75
Cabins: Suites and Deluxe	82
Cabins: Standard Sizes	79
Food: Dining Room/Cuisine	85
Food: Informal Dining/Buffets	76
Food: Quality of Ingredients	86
Food: Afternoon Tea/Bar Snacks	72
Service: Dining Room	85
Service: Bars	80
Service: Cabins	81
Service: Open Decks	76
Cruise: Entertainment	80
Cruise: Activities Program	76
Cruise: Movies/Television Programming	77
Cruise: Hospitality Standard	81
Cruise: Overall Product Delivery	88
OVERALL SCORE	**1,623**

Accommodation: The standard inside and outside cabins have good quality fittings, are tastefully decorated and of an above-average size, with an excellent amount of closet and drawer space and reasonable insulation between cabins. The bathrooms have a very generous shower area, and a small range of toiletries is provided, although the bathroom towels are a little small.

The largest cabins are the suites on Deck 10, which feature butler service and have a separate bedroom and lounge and larger bathroom complete with whirlpool bathtub. All accommodation designated as suites feature European duvets on the beds instead of sheets/blankets. However, no cabins have private balconies (they were not yet in vogue when this ship was constructed).

Dining: Celebrity Cruises has achieved an enviable reputation for providing outstanding quality food, fine presentation, and service. The dining room, set on a single level with raised central section, is large, yet feels almost intimate. It is quite elegant, and there are several tables for two. Two wings are good for small groups. The chairs do not have armrests, however, due to space limitations. There are separate menus for vegetarians and children. The wine list is quite extensive, and the prices are very reasonable.

An informal café features decent buffets for breakfast (including an omelet station) and lunch (including a pasta station and vegetarian salad bar); waiters take your trays of food and escort you to tables. At night, the informal café changes into an alternative dining venue for passengers who want good food but in a more casual setting than the main restaurant, with items such as grilled salmon, steaks, and rotisserie chicken, as well as specialties that change frequently (ideal for families with children).

An outdoor grill serves fast-food items. Caviar, at extra cost, is available in the America's Cup Club. For those that cannot live without them, freshly baked pizzas (in a box) can be delivered, in an insulated pouch, to your cabin.

Other Comments: This is quite a handsome, contemporary ship (the first in a series of newbuilds for Celebrity Cruises), with any sharp angles softened by clever exterior paint work and styling (blue striping along the ship's hull break up the monotonous all-white exterior of so many of today's ships). There is a good amount of open deck space and cushioned pads for poolside deck lounge chairs.

Inside, the public rooms are quite spacious, feature high ceilings, and provide very good passenger flow throughout. Elegant furnishings and appointments are the norm, with fine quality fabrics used throughout. Soothing pastel colors are relaxing, but not boring. The wood-paneled casino has a stately look (outside is a satellite-linked BankAtlantic ATM machine, with a $5 access charge).

The two-level show lounge has excellent sight lines from most seats, including the balcony level. There is nothing brash or glitzy about this ship anywhere, although the decor is a little clinical in places. The two-deck-high lobby is unusual, with its peachy Miami Beach art-deco hotel look. A self-service launderette would have proven useful for longer cruises. A good feature is the "zero announcement" policy.

A refurbishment in October 1998 saw the addition of a "Michael's Club" cigar smoking lounge in what was formerly an underused discotheque, as well as an enlarged library, and small business center. Also added were a martini bar, a room dedicated to the display of art (for art auctions), and an expanded health spa that now includes a rasul treatment room and beauty salon. This ship delivers a well-defined North American cruise experience at a very modest price. Note that the rating score was given in 1998 before the new additions were put in place.

But: Room-service food items are below the standard of food featured in the dining room. Unlike the company's larger *Century*, *Galaxy*, and *Mercury*, there is no AquaSpa thalassotherapy pool. Prticipation activities are verging on the mindless and should be upgraded.

ms Imagination

☆☆☆☆

(L)

Lifestyle	**Standard**
Cruise Line:	Carnival Cruise Lines
Former Names:	-
Gross Tonnage:	70,367
Builder:	Kvaerner Masa-Yards (Finland)
Original Cost:	$330 million
Entered Service:	July 1995
Flag:	Panama
Tel No:	1347673
Fax No:	1347674
Length (ft./m.):	855.0/260.60
Beam (ft./m.):	104.0/31.40
Draft (ft./m.):	25.9/7.90
Propulsion/Propellers:	diesel-electric (42,240kW)/2 (CP)
Decks:	10
Total Crew:	920
Pass. Capacity (basis 2):	2,040
Pass. Capacity (all berths):	2,594
Pass. Space Ratio (basis 2):	34.4
Pass. Space Ratio (all berths):	26.7
Officers:	Italian
Total Cabins:	1,020
Size Range (sq. ft./m.):	173.2–409.7/16.0–38.0
Cabins (outside view):	618
Cabins (inside):	402
Cabins (for one person):	0
Cabins (with private balcony):	26
Cabins (wheelchair accessible):	20
Cabin Current:	110 AC
Cabin TV:	Yes
Dining Rooms:	2
Seatings:	2
Elevators:	14
Casino:	Yes
Slot Machines:	Yes
Swimming Pools (outdoors):	3
Swimming Pools (inside):	0
Whirlpools:	6
Fitness Center:	Yes
Sauna/Steam Room:	Yes/Yes
Massage:	Yes
Self-Service Launderette:	Yes
Movie Theater/Seats:	No
Library:	Yes
Children's Facilities:	Yes
Classification Society:	Lloyd's Register

Ratings	**Score**
Ship: Hardware/Maintenance	81
Ship: Outdoor Facilities/Space	74
Ship: Interior Facilities/Space/Flow	81
Ship: Decor/Furnishings/Artwork	82
Ship: Spa/Fitness Facilities	77
Cabins: Suites and Deluxe	78
Cabins: Standard Sizes	73
Food: Dining Room/Cuisine	66
Food: Informal Dining/Buffets	61
Food: Quality of Ingredients	62
Food: Afternoon Tea/Bar Snacks	51
Service: Dining Room	68
Service: Bars	70
Service: Cabins	68
Service: Open Decks	64
Cruise: Entertainment	81
Cruise: Activities Program	67
Cruise: Movies/Television Programming	65
Cruise: Hospitality Standard	63
Cruise: Overall Product Delivery	77
Overall Score	**1,409**

Accommodation: The Verandah Suites have rather eclectic colors and designs, but they are very comfortable (although the balconies are very narrow). Standard cabins are just that—standard cabins. They are functional, of cookie-cutter likeness, but have a reasonably good amount of closet and drawer space. The bathrooms are practical, as are the large, functional shower units. You will get soap and ice water, so bring your own shampoo or other toiletries you might have expected the line to supply (ladies should bring a shower cap, if needed).

Dining: There are two large, colorful, noisy dining rooms. Each has the usual efficient, programmed, assertive service. The improved cuisine is fair, but certainly not memorable. There are no wine waiters. One plus is a 24-hour pizzeria. Shorts are permitted in the dining room for one dinner each cruise.

Other Comments: Has a forthright, angular appearance typical of today's space-creative designs. This is the fifth in a series of eight identically-sized Carnival ships that reflects the talents of interior designer Joe Farcus, whose philosophy is that the cruise ship environment should provide fantasy and an escape from routine.

Like all Carnival ships, this one has themed decor for her interiors; for this ship classical mythology and ethereal decor can be found throughout the public rooms, which are connected by a double-width indoor boulevard. The ship has expansive open deck areas and a good, well segmented health spa, and there is also a $1 million art collection, with many items in public areas featuring some timeless mosaics.

Ship buffs will enjoy six Stephen Card paintings of clipper ships, positioned in the Grand Bar. The Victorian-era–style library is a curious room, with intentionally mismatched furnishings (reminds one of Alice-in-Wonderland), fine oriental rugs, and even a few books. The lavish, yet somehow elegant multitiered showroom (but with 20 pillars obstructing sight lines) is the setting for fine, colorful, frenetic razzle-dazzle shows. Has an ATM machine located outside the large casino (all the slot machines aboard all Carnival ships are linked into a Megacash give-away).

But: Some may well complain of sensory overload. There are many loud, rather repetitive announcements. There are virtually no quiet spaces aboard to get away from crowds. Aggressive hustling for drinks means there is plenty of service everywhere.

However, this ship will entertain those who are young at heart in fine fashion and make them forget about solid ground for a while.

ss Independence

(M)

Lifestyle	**Standard**
Cruise Line:	American Hawaii Cruises
Former Names:	*Oceanic Independence/ Sea Luck I*
Gross Tonnage:	30,090
Builder:	Bethlehem Shipbuilders (USA)
Original Cost:	$25 million
Entered Service:	February 1951/June 1980
Flag:	USA
Tel No:	808-847-3172
Fax No:	808-848-0406
Length (ft./m.):	682.4/208.01
Beam (ft./m.):	89.1/27.18
Draft (ft./m.):	30.1/9.19
Propulsion/Propellers:	steam turbine (40,456kW)/2 (FP)
Decks:	9
Total Crew:	315
Pass. Capacity (basis 2):	809
Pass. Capacity (all berths):	1,025
Pass. Space Ratio (basis 2):	37.1
Pass. Space Ratio (all berths):	29.3
Officers:	American
Total Cabins:	414
Size Range (sq. ft./m.):	70–375/6.5–34.8
Cabins (outside view):	203
Cabins (inside):	211
Cabins (for one person):	19
Cabins (with private balcony):	0
Cabins (wheelchair accessible):	3
Cabin Current:	110 AC
Cabin TV:	No
Dining Rooms:	1
Seatings:	2
Elevators:	4
Casino:	No
Slot Machines:	No
Swimming Pools (outdoors):	2
Swimming Pools (inside):	0
Whirlpools:	0
Fitness Center:	Yes
Sauna/Steam Room:	Yes/No
Massage:	Yes
Self-Service Launderette:	Yes
Movie Theater/Seats:	Yes/144
Library:	Yes
Children's Facilities:	Yes
Classification Society:	American Bureau of Shipping

Ratings	**Score**
Ship: Hardware/Maintenance	59
Ship: Outdoor Facilities/Space	64
Ship: Interior Facilities/Space/Flow	60
Ship: Decor/Furnishings/Artwork	62
Ship: Spa/Fitness Facilities	38
Cabins: Suites and Deluxe	62
Cabins: Standard Sizes	54
Food: Dining Room/Cuisine	59
Food: Informal Dining/Buffets	51
Food: Quality of Ingredients	57
Food: Afternoon Tea/Bar Snacks	53
Service: Dining Room	62
Service: Bars	61
Service: Cabins	62
Service: Open Decks	58
Cruise: Entertainment	58
Cruise: Activities Program	52
Cruise: Movies/Television Programming	56
Cruise: Hospitality Standard	65
Cruise: Overall Product Delivery	71
Overall Score	**1,164**

Accommodation: There is a wide range of cabin types, with more than 50 different configurations to choose from (a carry-over from her nights as a three-class liner), all of which offer ample room to move in. There is adequate closet and drawer space and fairly bright decor, with Hawaii-themed soft furnishings. However, all cabinetry is steel, and so there is little warmth to it (the metal drawers are particularly tinny). Also, the cabin bathrooms are small. Overall, the cabins are adequate, but they do reflect the age of the vessel.

Six large "solarium suites," with skylights, are located without inside access, which means you must go up the forward stairs and out on deck to get to them.

Dining: The dining rooms are set low down, and without the benefit of an ocean view (the bi-level forward section is more elegant), but it is fairly cheerful, and has tables for two to ten persons. The cuisine is American, with the norm being quantity, not quality. The first evening's dinner is buffet-style. The informal buffet area is good, but buffets are predictable, not creative. Fresh local fruits are plentiful, as are snacks and hors d'oeuvres.

Other Comments: American-built, crewed, and registered (originally constructed for the 1950s transatlantic trade between New York and the Mediterranean) she, together with her now-scuttled sister ship Constitution, were among the first ships to have air-conditioning. This all white ship has expansive open deck space for sun-worshippers, particularly on her aft, tiered sections, and features a wraparound outdoor teakwood promenade deck.

This ship features spacious public rooms with high ceilings (not as attractive as aboard sister ship Constitution, now laid up). Has good facilities for meetings.

Inside, the public areas are quite spacious. The Hawaii-themed decor is a natural for the ship's operating area. Has heavy-duty, "neo-art deco" furniture and fittings, designed for unkind oceans. Hardwood floors, ceiling fans, and large plants add up to a tropical 1950s ambience. Local Hawaiian artists have their artwork featured on board.

The dress code is very casual, and entertainment is regional. Fortunately, such things as bingo and horse-racing are low-key, and not daily. Those intending to marry should look into the company's Nani Kai (Bountiful Seas) wedding package.

A laid-back atmosphere prevails, with Aloha smiles from the friendly staff. This is a destination-intensive operation aboard a ship that is quite tired, despite a $30 million refurbishment in 1994. On top of the fares, there is a Hawaii State Tax of 4.166 percent in addition to port charges and, for singles, a single supplement (plus gratuities). Airfare is also an additional cost, and 15 percent is added to all drinks and wine purchases. Having said all the above, there is something utterly magical about seeing the Hawaiian islands by ship, and this ship provides the means in a modicum of comfort. Complimentary shuttles to nearby shopping areas are provided at each port of call.

But: The ship is now over forty years old, and although she has been through some refurbishment, she is looking decidedly sad and tired in many places. The show lounge is not large enough and is always crowded. Drink prices are high. There are no stabilizers, so the ship can roll in inclement weather.

ms Inspiration

☆☆☆☆

(L)

Lifestyle	Standard
Cruise Line:	Carnival Cruise Lines
Former Names:	-
Gross Tonnage:	70,367
Builder:	Kvaerner Masa-Yards (Finland)
Original Cost:	$270 million
Entered Service:	April 1996
Flag:	Panama
Tel No:	1354562
Fax No:	1354563
Length (ft./m.):	855.0/260.60
Beam (ft./m.):	104.0/31.40
Draft (ft./m.):	25.9/7.90
Propulsion/Propellers:	diesel-electric (42,240kW)/2 (CP)
Decks:	10
Total Crew:	920
Pass. Capacity (basis 2):	2,040
Pass. Capacity (all berths):	2,594
Pass. Space Ratio (basis 2):	34.4
Pass. Space Ratio (all berths):	26.7
Officers:	Italian
Total Cabins:	1,020
Size Range (sq. ft./m.):	173.2–409.7/16.0–38.0
Cabins (outside view):	618
Cabins (inside):	402
Cabins (for one person):	0
Cabins (with private balcony):	26
Cabins (wheelchair accessible):	20
Cabin Current:	110 AC
Cabin TV:	Yes
Dining Rooms:	2
Seatings:	2
Elevators:	14
Casino:	Yes
Slot Machines:	Yes
Swimming Pools (outdoors):	3
Swimming Pools (inside):	0
Whirlpools:	6
Fitness Center:	Yes
Sauna/Steam Room:	Yes/Yes
Massage:	Yes
Self-Service Launderette:	Yes
Movie Theater/Seats:	No
Library:	Yes
Children's Facilities:	Yes
Classification Society:	Lloyd's Register

Ratings	Score
Ship: Hardware/Maintenance	81
Ship: Outdoor Facilities/Space	74
Ship: Interior Facilities/Space/Flow	81
Ship: Decor/Furnishings/Artwork	82
Ship: Spa/Fitness Facilities	77
Cabins: Suites and Deluxe	78
Cabins: Standard Sizes	73
Food: Dining Room/Cuisine	66
Food: Informal Dining/Buffets	61
Food: Quality of Ingredients	62
Food: Afternoon Tea/Bar Snacks	51
Service: Dining Room	68
Service: Bars	70
Service: Cabins	68
Service: Open Decks	64
Cruise: Entertainment	81
Cruise: Activities Program	67
Cruise: Movies/Television Programming	65
Cruise: Hospitality Standard	63
Cruise: Overall Product Delivery	77
Overall Score	**1,409**

Accommodation: The outside suites are decorated in a jazzy style and have whirlpool tubs, although they are not large. The standard cabins provide a comfortable home away from home, are of good size, but are also quite plainly decorated. Take your own shampoo and shower cap, however, as the company provides only ice water and soap in the cabins.

Dining: There are two large (rather noisy, or perhaps that should be translated better as "lively") dining rooms. The cuisine has been improved somewhat by this cruise line during the past two years, but it is definitely not Carnival's strong point (it is, for example, difficult to ask for anything remotely unusual or off-menu). Service is attentive, but too fast and assertive, and does not have any finesse. The wine list is definitely not for lovers of fine wines, and there are no wine waiters.

What has noticeably improved is the quality of food available at the informal food outlets such as the Brasserie Bar and Grill, which also includes a pizzeria (open 24 hours).

Other Comments: Bold and forthright all-white ship has a large wing-tipped funnel in red, white and blue; at its base is a "topless" area for sunbathing.

Like her seven sister ships of the same size, this ship also features a seven-deck-high atrium topped by a glass dome. The atrium features scrolled shapes resembling the necks and heads of violins, and a marble staircase. There are expansive open-deck areas and an excellent, three-deck-high glass-enclosed health spa. There are public entertainment lounges, bars and clubs galore, with something for just about everyone. The public rooms are connected by wide indoor boulevards.

Various colors and design themes have been used throughout, although the ship does feature somewhat softer decor than on some of Carnival's ships. Includes a $1 million art collection. Particularly fascinating is the avant-garde rendition of the famed Mona Lisa, in Pablo's Lounge. The decor itself is themed after the arts (in an art nouveau style) and literature.

The Shakespeare Library is a stunning, stately room (25 of his quotations adorn the oak veneer). Another dazzling room is the Rock and Roll Discotheque, with its guitar-shaped dance floor and video dance club and dozens of video monitors around the room. The ship also features a lavish, multitiered showroom (although some 20 pillars cause some seats to have obstructed sight lines) and high-energy razzle-dazzle shows. The casino is large, but always humming with hopeful action.

But: There are no cushioned pads for the deck lounge chairs, which are plastic and hard to sit on with just a towel for any length of time. There is constant, aggressive hustling for drinks. There are many announcements. There is too much use of plastic on board, particularly in the informal food service areas.

Finally, the company's brochure tells it exactly like it is, providing a good look at the unpretentious lifestyle of its passengers. This ship provides a fine adult playground for those that like to party. It will entertain you well, but do not go for the food, go for the fun, the almost non-stop, all-too-predictable action and participation activities, and for a way to visit the Caribbean in a well-packaged manner that is best described as a compact Las Vegas afloat.

ss IslandBreeze

☆☆☆

(L)

Lifestyle	**Standard**
Cruise Line:	Premier Cruises/Thomson Cruises
Former Names:	*Festivale/ TransVaal Castle/S.A. Vaal*
Gross Tonnage:	31,793
Builder:	John Brown & Co. (UK)
Original Cost:	n/a
Entered Service:	January 1962/May 1996
Flag:	Bahamas
Tel No:	1103150
Fax No:	1103150
Length (ft./m.):	760.1/231.70
Beam (ft./m.):	90.1/27.49
Draft (ft./m.):	31.9/9.75
Propulsion/Propellers:	steam turbine (32,800kW)/2 (FP)
Decks:	9
Total Crew:	612
Pass. Capacity (basis 2):	1,146
Pass. Capacity (all berths):	1,464
Pass. Space Ratio (basis 2):	27.7
Pass. Space Ratio (all berths):	21.7
Officers:	Greek
Total Cabins:	583
Size Range (sq. ft./m.):	50–167/4.6–15.5
Cabins (outside view):	273
Cabins (inside):	310
Cabins (for one person):	0
Cabins (with private balcony):	10
Cabins (wheelchair accessible):	0
Cabin Current:	110 AC
Cabin TV:	No
Dining Rooms:	1
Seatings:	2
Elevators:	4
Casino:	Yes
Slot Machines:	Yes
Swimming Pools (outdoors):	3
Swimming Pools (inside):	0
Whirlpools:	0
Fitness Center:	Yes
Sauna/Steam Room:	Yes/No
Massage:	Yes
Self-Service Launderette:	No (has ironing room)
Movie Theater/Seats:	Yes/202
Library:	Yes
Children's Facilities:	Yes
Classification Society:	Lloyd's Register

Ratings	**Score**
Ship: Hardware/Maintenance	67
Ship: Outdoor Facilities/Space	55
Ship: Interior Facilities/Space/Flow	60
Ship: Decor/Furnishings/Artwork	54
Ship: Spa/Fitness Facilities	38
Cabins: Suites and Deluxe	60
Cabins: Standard Sizes	51
Food: Dining Room/Cuisine	63
Food: Informal Dining/Buffets	54
Food: Quality of Ingredients	57
Food: Afternoon Tea/Bar Snacks	42
Service: Dining Room	60
Service: Bars	61
Service: Cabins	64
Service: Open Decks	50
Cruise: Entertainment	56
Cruise: Activities Program	51
Cruise: Movies/Television Programming	44
Cruise: Hospitality Standard	57
Cruise: Overall Product Delivery	62
Overall Score	**1,106**

Accommodation: In general, the cabins are small when compared to those of ships of a similar size. There are a large number of bunk beds (third and fourth berths), but there is only just enough closet and drawer space for this style of informal cruising. Heavy-duty fittings were standard aboard older ships such as this. In general, the bathrooms are of a good size, although the lighting is poor. Some of the large cabins are especially good for families. Note that the outside cabins on Veranda Deck have obstructed views.

Note that when operated for Thomson Cruises, there are four principal cabin categories; suites, premier, superior, and standard (although there are eight price levels). Note that specific cabins are not assigned until you arrive at the embarkation port for check-in. When operated under the

Thomson Cruises banner, Continental breakfast in your cabin will cost about $7.50 (£4.50) per person extra (each time). There is also a twenty-four-hour cabin service menu for snacks, all at extra cost.

Dining: The dining room, located low down, is bright, cheerful, and noisy (and it is nonsmoking, although smokers gather outside, so smoke can be smelled in the dining room anyway). There are no tables for two. The food quality is quite adequate, with a good variety. The service is quite reasonable, but is hurried and lacks polish.

An informal café is suited to self-service buffets for those that do not want to bother with the dining room, but the selection of food presented here is very standardized and not very creative.

Other Comments: This is one of the real classic former ocean liners, with a well-balanced profile and long, tiered foredeck. She looks like a real ship, and has a fine amount of open deck space. She is also being well maintained.

Her interiors retain much of the original wood and brass fittings intact from her former days as a Union Castle ocean liner (Union Castle disbanded in the seventies). There is a good array of public rooms, including a 5,000 sq. ft. casino. Has a fascinating steel art deco staircase. The officers are well dressed and visible in public areas.

But: The layout is not easy to master. The strange color schemes are eclectic, a leftover from her days as a Carnival Cruise Lines ship. The signs are confusing (it is difficult to find the "you are here" spots, or what deck you are on when exiting elevators, for example). The staff is not overly friendly, hustle for drinks, and English is a problem for some. You should expect low-budget entertainment. In addition, the Piccadilly show lounge is poor and has very limited sight lines. The public address system is as poor as the cruise staff.

This ship now does dual-duty, being operated by Premier Cruises during the winter and by Thomson Cruises (based on Naples) during the summer months (gratuities are included for Thomson's British passengers, and air travel will probably be provided by Britannia Airways, owned by Thomson). Adequate older-ship experience for the young at heart who want a low-budget cruise in comfortable, unstuffy surroundings, with lively casino action, no finesse, and lots of atmosphere.

ms Island Princess

☆☆☆ +

(M)

LIFESTYLE	**PREMIUM**
Cruise Line:	Princess Cruises
Former Names:	*Island Venture*
Gross Tonnage:	19,907
Builder: Rheinstahl Nordseewerke (Germany)	
Original Cost:	$25 million
Entered Service:	February 1972/August 1974
Flag:	Great Britain
Tel No:	1440214
Fax No:	1440214
Length (ft./m.):	553.6/168.74
Beam (ft./m.):	80.8/24.64
Draft (ft./m.):	24.5/7.49
Propulsion/Propellers: diesel (13,400kW)/2 (CP)	
Decks:	7
Total Crew:	350
Pass. Capacity (basis 2):	610
Pass. Capacity (all berths):	717
Pass. Space Ratio (basis 2):	32.6
Pass. Space Ratio (all berths):	27.7
Officers:	British
Total Cabins:	305
Size Range (sq. ft./m.):	126–443/11.7–41.0
Cabins (outside view):	238
Cabins (inside):	67
Cabins (for one person):	2
Cabins (with private balcony):	0
Cabins (wheelchair accessible):	2
Cabin Current:	110/220 AC
Cabin TV:	Yes
Dining Rooms:	1
Seatings:	2
Elevators:	4
Casino:	Yes
Slot Machines:	Yes
Swimming Pools (outdoors):	2
Swimming Pools (inside):	0
Whirlpools:	0
Fitness Center:	Yes
Sauna/Steam Room:	Yes/No
Massage:	Yes
Self-Service Launderette:	No
Movie Theater/Seats:	Yes/250
Library:	Yes
Children's Facilities:	No
Classification Society:	Lloyd's Register

RATINGS	**SCORE**
Ship: Hardware/Maintenance	68
Ship: Outdoor Facilities/Space	67
Ship: Interior Facilities/Space/Flow	71
Ship: Decor/Furnishings/Artwork	70
Ship: Spa/Fitness Facilities	51
Cabins: Suites and Deluxe	66
Cabins: Standard Sizes	61
Food: Dining Room/Cuisine	73
Food: Informal Dining/Buffets	68
Food: Quality of Ingredients	70
Food: Afternoon Tea/Bar Snacks	63
Service: Dining Room	74
Service: Bars	75
Service: Cabins	76
Service: Open Decks	68
Cruise: Entertainment	76
Cruise: Activities Program	65
Cruise: Movies/Television Programming	66
Cruise: Hospitality Standard	71
Cruise: Overall Product Delivery	77
OVERALL SCORE	**1,376**

Accommodation: The suites are quite large and well designed, with plenty of space to move around in. Other cabins have ample room, are well appointed, and there is plenty of closet and drawer space. Bathrobes and adequate amenities are provided in all cabins.

Dining: Features a lovely dining room (nonsmoking) with satisfactory service from an attentive staff. The food quality is basically sound, if uncreative, and standards that had slipped for a couple of years are now a little better. Good pasta dishes are presented by friendly Italian headwaiters. Poor bread rolls, pastry items, and fruits, however.

Other Comments: This twenty-four-year-old ship (sold to Princess Cruises in 1972) has a very attractive profile and exterior styling. Has very pleasing lines, and, not too long ago underwent a dramatic facelift and refurbishment program. Sadly, there is no wraparound outdoor promenade deck.

Has sharply dressed officers and crew. Extremely spacious public areas, with wide passageways and high ceilings in public rooms. Pleasant two-deck-high lobby. Tasteful decor throughout, with pastel colors and fine artwork that is pleasing to the eye. Forward observation lounge also acts as an indoor buffet dining area.

Quality prevails aboard this ship, which is aging well, is quite elegant, and provides a good cruise experience in comfortable surroundings for the older passenger who wants plenty of space and does not want to be part of the larger, more impersonal ships.

mv Italia Prima

☆☆☆ +

(M)

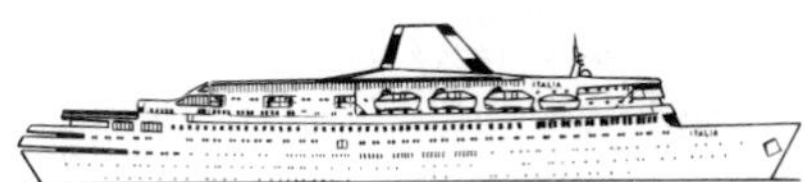

LIFESTYLE	**STANDARD**
Cruise Line:	Nina Cruise Line
Former Names:	*Volkerfreundschaft/ Stockholm/Fridtjof Nansen*
Gross Tonnage:	15,000
Builder:	Varco Chiapella (Italy)
Original Cost:	$150 million (reconstruction)
Entered Service:	February 1948/May 1994
Flag:	Italy
Tel No:	115-2210/115-2214
Fax No:	115-2211/115-2215
Length (ft./m.):	525.2/160.10
Beam (ft./m.):	68.8/21.04
Draft (ft./m.):	24.6/7.5
Propulsion/Propellers:	diesel (11,200kW)/2 (CP)
Decks:	7
Total Crew:	260
Pass. Capacity (basis 2):	540
Pass. Capacity (all berths):	600
Pass. Space Ratio (basis 2):	27.7
Pass. Space Ratio (all berths):	25.0
Officers:	Italian
Total Cabins:	260
Size Range (sq. ft./m.):	129–376/12.0–35.0
Outside Cabins:	221
Inside Cabins:	39
Single Cabins:	0
Balcony Cabins:	0
Wheelchair Cabins:	0
Cabin Current:	110/220 AC
Cabin TV:	Yes
Dining Rooms:	1
Seatings:	1
Elevators:	2
Casino:	Yes
Slot Machines:	Yes
Swimming Pools (outdoors):	1
Swimming Pools (inside):	0
Whirlpools:	1
Gymnasium:	Yes
Sauna/Steam Room:	Yes/Yes (Turkish Bath)
Massage:	Yes
Self-Service Launderette:	No
Movie Theater/Seats:	Yes/400
Library:	Yes
Children's Facilities:	No
Classification Society:	RINA

RATINGS	**SCORE**
Ship: Hardware/Maintenance	71
Ship: Outdoor Facilities/Space	70
Ship: Interior Facilities/Space/Flow	76
Ship: Decor/Furnishings/Artwork	75
Ship: Spa/Fitness Facilities	61
Cabins: Suites and Deluxe	77
Cabins: Standard Sizes	70
Food: Dining Room/Cuisine	71
Food: Informal Dining/Buffets	60
Food: Quality of Ingredients	62
Food: Afternoon Tea/Bar Snacks	50
Service: Dining Room	71
Service: Bars	68
Service: Cabins	70
Service: Open Decks	60
Cruise: Entertainment	60
Cruise: Activities Program	51
Cruise: Movies/Television Programming	50
Cruise: Hospitality Standard	57
Cruise: Overall Product Delivery	71
OVERALL SCORE	**1,301**

Accommodation: All cabins have mini-bars, and there are 38 suites that feature Jacuzzi bathtubs (all cabin bathrooms feature a bathtub, and good, indented space for toiletries). Each cabin has a large Italian fresco above the bed, although the ceilings are very plain. Note that the cabins on Sole Deck forward have lifeboat-obstructed views.

Dining: The single, large dining room, set low down in the vessel, is attractive, and has tables for two, four, six, and eight. As you might expect, Italian cuisine is featured, with good pasta dishes. There is a good selection of Italian wines. Standard house wines are included for lunch and dinner (depending on the charterer/operator). Also has a pizzeria. There is a limited selection of breads, fruits, and cheeses, and the cabin service menu is poor.

Other Comments: This ex-ocean liner made history when she rammed and sank the Andrea Doria in 1956. Reconstructed as a cruise ship in 1994 using her old, riveted hull, but with completely new superstructure. There is a wraparound teakwood outdoor promenade deck, and wooden "steamer" deck chairs are provided, although there are no cushioned pads for them.

Her interiors are decorated in contemporary Italian style. There is a good selection of public rooms to choose from, including a good 400-seat auditorium for meetings, and smart boutiques. The contemporary decor is upbeat and fresh, and is complemented by a good selection of colorful artwork. There is also a Turkish bath, which is quite unusual aboard cruise vessels today.

This really is a high-density ship, and the hallways on the accommodation decks are a little on the narrow side. This ship is often under charter to various tour operators.

But: The deck plans are not easy to read. The small swimming pool is really only a "dip" pool. There is no forward observation lounge, and sight lines in the single-level show lounge are poor. In the cinema, the seats are not staggered and so the sight lines are poor. The steep gangway is designed for European, not Caribbean, ports.

mts Jason

☆☆ +

(S)

LIFESTYLE	STANDARD
Cruise Line:	Royal Olympic Cruises
Former Names:	*Eros*
Gross Tonnage:	5,250
Builder:	Cantieri Riuniti dell' Adriatico (Italy)
Original Cost:	n/a
Entered Service:	April 1967
Flag:	Greece
Tel No:	1130175
Fax No:	1130175
Length (ft./m.):	333.0/101.50
Beam (ft./m.):	52.6/16.06
Draft (ft./m.):	17.5/5.34
Propulsion/Propellers:	diesel (8,090kw)/2 (FP)
Decks:	6
Total Crew:	139
Pass. Capacity (basis 2):	272
Pass. Capacity (all berths):	302
Pass. Space Ratio (basis 2):	19.3
Pass. Space Ratio (all berths):	17.3
Officers:	Greek
Total Cabins:	136
Size Range (sq. ft./m.):	73–182/6.7–17.0
Cabins (outside view):	100
Cabins (inside):	36
Cabins (for one person):	0
Cabins (with private balcony):	0
Cabins (wheelchair accessible):	0
Cabin Current:	220 AC
Cabin TV:	No
Dining Rooms:	1
Seatings:	2
Elevators:	1
Casino:	Yes
Slot Machines:	Yes
Swimming Pools (outdoors):	1
Swimming Pools (inside):	0
Whirlpools:	0
Fitness Center:	No
Sauna/Steam Room:	No/No
Massage:	No
Self-Service Launderette:	No
Movie Theater/Seats:	No
Library:	Yes
Children's Facilities:	No
Classification Society:	Lloyd's Register

RATINGS	SCORE
Ship: Hardware/Maintenance	58
Ship: Outdoor Facilities/Space	46
Ship: Interior Facilities/Space/Flow	48
Ship: Decor/Furnishings/Artwork	58
Ship: Spa/Fitness Facilities	23
Cabins: Suites and Deluxe	57
Cabins: Standard Sizes	50
Food: Dining Room/Cuisine	61
Food: Informal Dining/Buffets	52
Food: Quality of Ingredients	58
Food: Afternoon Tea/Bar Snacks	47
Service: Dining Room	65
Service: Bars	64
Service: Cabins	67
Service: Open Decks	54
Cruise: Entertainment	44
Cruise: Activities Program	48
Cruise: Movies/Television Programming	38
Cruise: Hospitality Standard	60
Cruise: Overall Product Delivery	63
OVERALL SCORE	**1,061**

Accommodation: The cabins are very small, yet they are quite cozy and inviting, and most come with a sofa bed that converts to a daytime sitting area. The bathrooms are extremely small, with little room for storage of toiletries, but manageable for short cruises.

Dining: The charming dining room has big picture windows, comfortable seating, and some precious tapestries. The cuisine is Continental, with some excellent Greek dishes. The service, provided by Greek waiters, is warm, friendly, and quite attentive throughout, but lacks any degree of polish. Dining room seating and table assignments are done by the maitre d' upon embarkation.

Other Comments: This charming little ship has a traditional, rather low, profile. Her simple layout provides good outdoor deck and sunbathing space. Warm ambience filters from officers and crew through to passengers. Tasteful interior decor reflects warmth and intimacy. There is a small fortune in artworks aboard this vessel, as well as a well-stocked library.

This ship will provide a pleasant, intimate cruise experience in some degree of comfort and classical style, without the crowds, at a very fair price, but she is a high-density ship. Operates mostly under charter to various tour operators, and so the onboard product often changes to accommodate the requests of the charterers.

Gratuities (suggested at $9 per person per day) are pooled among the crew.

ms Jubilee

☆☆☆ +

(L)

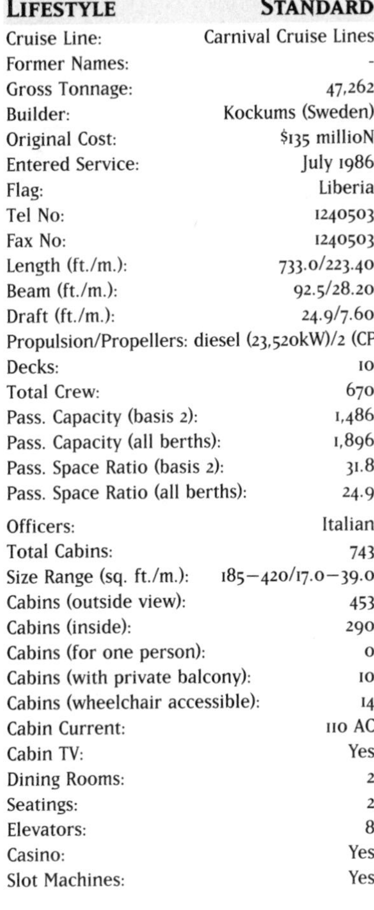

Lifestyle	**Standard**
Cruise Line:	Carnival Cruise Lines
Former Names:	-
Gross Tonnage:	47,262
Builder:	Kockums (Sweden)
Original Cost:	$135 millioN
Entered Service:	July 1986
Flag:	Liberia
Tel No:	1240503
Fax No:	1240503
Length (ft./m.):	733.0/223.40
Beam (ft./m.):	92.5/28.20
Draft (ft./m.):	24.9/7.60
Propulsion/Propellers:	diesel (23,520kW)/2 (CP)
Decks:	10
Total Crew:	670
Pass. Capacity (basis 2):	1,486
Pass. Capacity (all berths):	1,896
Pass. Space Ratio (basis 2):	31.8
Pass. Space Ratio (all berths):	24.9
Officers:	Italian
Total Cabins:	743
Size Range (sq. ft./m.):	185–420/17.0–39.0
Cabins (outside view):	453
Cabins (inside):	290
Cabins (for one person):	0
Cabins (with private balcony):	10
Cabins (wheelchair accessible):	14
Cabin Current:	110 AC
Cabin TV:	Yes
Dining Rooms:	2
Seatings:	2
Elevators:	8
Casino:	Yes
Slot Machines:	Yes
Swimming Pools (outdoors):	3
Swimming Pools (inside):	0
Whirlpools:	2
Fitness Center:	Yes
Sauna/Steam Room:	Yes/No
Massage:	Yes
Self-Service Launderette:	Yes
Movie Theater/Seats:	No
Library:	Yes
Children's Facilities:	Yes
Classification Society:	Lloyd's Register

Ratings	**Score**
Ship: Hardware/Maintenance	76
Ship: Outdoor Facilities/Space	70
Ship: Interior Facilities/Space/Flow	72
Ship: Decor/Furnishings/Artwork	73
Ship: Spa/Fitness Facilities	60
Cabins: Suites and Deluxe	76
Cabins: Standard Sizes	67
Food: Dining Room/Cuisine	66
Food: Informal Dining/Buffets	62
Food: Quality of Ingredients	61
Food: Afternoon Tea/Bar Snacks	51
Service: Dining Room	71
Service: Bars	71
Service: Cabins	70
Service: Open Decks	63
Cruise: Entertainment	74
Cruise: Activities Program	61
Cruise: Movies/Television Programming	63
Cruise: Hospitality Standard	60
Cruise: Overall Product Delivery	72
Overall Score	**1,339**

Accommodation: The cabins are quite spacious, neatly appointed, and have attractive, though spartan, decor. Especially nice are the ten large suites on Veranda Deck. The outside cabins feature large picture windows. The company provides only soap and ice water, so take your own shampoo (ladies should take a shower cap) and other needed toiletry items.

Dining: There are two dining rooms (both are nonsmoking). They are quite attractive, but have low ceilings, and a raised center section is somewhat cramped. The food, although upgraded, is still very much a low-budget affair. Poor selection of breads, rolls, and fruit (too much canned fruit). The service is hurried, there being little time for attention to detail or anything out of the ordinary. There are no wine waiters, although there is a reasonably good wine list.

Other Comments: She has a bold, forthright all-white profile, but a very short, rakish bow. Sports Carnival's distinctive swept-back wing-tipped, red, white, and blue funnel.

Inside, there are flamboyant, vivid colors in all the public rooms except for the somewhat elegant Churchill's Library, which, sadly, is almost devoid of books. A large casino has almost round-the-clock action. Numerous public rooms are spread throughout two entertainment decks. Excellent double width promenade deck features a white gazebo. Stimulating multitiered Atlantis Lounge showroom has huge theater stage. This ship provides constant entertainment and activities designed for passenger participation in a party-like setting.

This ship, now ten years old, provides novice cruisers with an excellent first cruise experience in comfortable surroundings. Fun-filled, noisy, almost non-stop action provides a stimulating vacation, targeted particularly to those who like to party and have fun. Excellent for families with children, and especially good for singles who want constant action (sleep before you cruise). Provides very good value, with plenty of dazzle and sizzle entertainment and constant activities, which Carnival does so well, particularly for first-time cruise passengers.

But: There are many annoying and unnecessarily loud announcements. Constant hustling for drinks is the norm.

mv Kapitan Khlebnikov

☆☆☆ +

(S)

Lifestyle	**Standard**
Cruise Line:	Murmansk Shipping/ Quark Expeditions
Former Names:	-
Gross Tonnage:	12,288
Builder:	Wartsila (Finland)
Original Cost:	n/a
Entered Service:	1981
Flag:	Russia
Tel No:	1400676
Fax No:	1400676
Length (ft./m.):	434.6/132.49
Beam (ft./m.):	87.7/26.75
Draft (ft./m.):	27.8/8.50
Propulsion/Propellers:	diesel-electric (22,000hp)/3 (CP)
Decks:	4
Total Crew:	60
Pass. Capacity (basis 2):	100
Pass. Capacity (all berths):	116
Pass. Space Ratio (basis 2):	122.8
Pass. Space Ratio (all berths):	105.9
Officers:	Russian
Total Cabins:	54
Size Range (sq. ft./m.):	150.6–269/14.0–25.0
Cabins (outside view):	54
Cabins (inside):	0
Cabins (for one person):	0
Cabins (with private balcony):	0
Cabins (wheelchair accessible):	0
Cabin Current:	220 AC
Cabin TV:	No
Dining Rooms:	1
Seatings:	1
Elevators:	0
Casino:	No
Slot Machines:	No
Swimming Pools (outdoors):	0
Swimming Pools (inside):	1
Whirlpools:	0
Fitness Center:	Yes
Sauna/Steam Room:	Yes-2/No
Massage:	No
Lecture/Film Room:	No
Library:	Yes
Zodiacs:	4
Helicopter Pad:	Yes (1 helicopter)
Classification Society:	RS

Ratings	**Score**
Ship: Hardware/Maintenance	74
Ship: Expedition Equipment	83
Ship: Interior Facilities/Space/Flow	62
Ship: Decor/Furnishings/Artwork	58
Ship: Spa/Fitness Facilities	38
Cabins: Suites and Deluxe	71
Cabins: Standard Sizes	64
Food: Dining Room/Cuisine	66
Food: Informal Dining/Buffets	61
Food: Quality of Ingredients	65
Food: Afternoon Tea/Bar Snacks	52
Service: Dining Room	64
Service: Bars	65
Service: Cabins	63
Service: Open Decks	58
Cruise: Library/Lecture Programs	72
Cruise: Movies/Television Programming	58
Cruise: Hospitality Standard	70
Cruise: Expedition Experience	68
Cruise: Overall Product Delivery	75
Overall Score	**1,287**

Accommodation: The cabins are spread over four decks, and all have private facilities and plenty of storage space. Although nothing special, they are quite comfortable, with two lower berths, large closets, and portholes that actually open. The bathrooms are practical units.

Dining: The dining room is plain and unpretentious, and is totally nonsmoking. Hearty food and generous portions with an emphasis on fish are served in a dining room that is comfortable and practical without being the slightest bit pretentious. The food production and presentation is supervised by Scandinavian advisors, who import Western foods specifically for these chartered voyages.

Other Comments: This is a real, working icebreaker, one of a fleet of ten that are available for various charters. The ship has an incredibly thick hull, forthright profile, and a bow like an inverted whale head. The funnel is placed amidships, and the accommodation block is placed forward. An open bridge policy allows passengers to visit the bridge at almost any time. Strong diesel-electric engines allow her to plow through ice several feet thick. There is plenty of open deck and observation space. Has a heated indoor swimming pool. There is always a team of excellent naturalists and lecturers aboard. Heavy parka and boots are provided for passengers, who really become participants in this kind of hands-on expedition cruising. A helicopter is usually carried and can be used by all passengers for sightseeing forays.

This vessel is particularly good for tough expedition cruising, and will provide practical surroundings, a friendly, experienced, and dedicated crew, and excellent value for the money in true expeditionary style.

But: The ship offers only basic cruise amenities and a very spartan, no-frills decor. Also, you should be prepared for the tremendous roaring noise when the ship breaks through pack ice.

ms Kristina Regina

☆☆ +

(S)

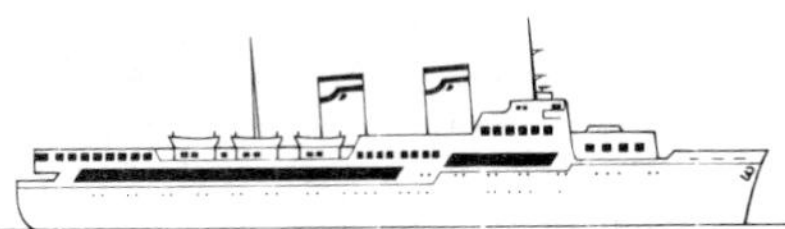

Lifestyle	**Standard**
Cruise Line:	Kristina Cruises
Former Names:	*Borea/Bore*
Gross Tonnage:	3,878
Builder:	Oskarshamn Shipyard (Sweden)
Original Cost:	n/a
Entered Service:	1960/1987
Flag:	Finland
Tel No:	1623154
Fax No:	1623154
Length (ft./m.):	327.4/99.80
Beam (ft./m.):	50.1/15.30
Draft (ft./m.):	17.3/5.30
Propulsion/Propellers:	diesel (3,223kw)/2
Decks:	6
Total Crew:	55
Pass. Capacity (basis 2):	276
Pass. Capacity (all berths):	350
Pass. Space Ratio (basis 2):	14.0
Pass. Space Ratio (all berths):	11.0
Officers:	Finnish
Total Cabins:	141
Size Range (sq. ft./m.):	65–125/6–11.6
Cabins (outside view):	108
Cabins (inside):	33
Cabins (for one person):	0
Cabins (with private balcony):	0
Cabins (wheelchair accessible):	0
Cabin Current:	220 AC
Cabin TV:	Deluxe cabins only
Dining Rooms:	2 (1 for buffets/1 a la carte)
Seatings:	1
Elevators:	0
Casino:	No
Slot Machines:	No
Swimming Pools (outdoors):	0
Swimming Pools (inside):	0
Whirlpools:	0
Fitness Center:	No
Sauna/Steam Room:	Yes/No
Massage:	No
Self-Service Launderette:	No
Movie Theater/Seats:	No
Library:	Yes
Children's Facilities:	Yes
Classification Society:	Lloyd's Register

Ratings	**Score**
Ship: Hardware/Maintenance	54
Ship: Outdoor Facilities/Space	40
Ship: Interior Facilities/Space/Flow	51
Ship: Decor/Furnishings/Artwork	54
Ship: Spa/Fitness Facilities	34
Cabins: Suites and Deluxe	57
Cabins: Standard Sizes	53
Food: Dining Room/Cuisine	62
Food: Informal Dining/Buffets	60
Food: Quality of Ingredients	61
Food: Afternoon Tea/Bar Snacks	55
Service: Dining Room	63
Service: Bars	61
Service: Cabins	62
Service: Open Decks	47
Cruise: Entertainment	42
Cruise: Activities Program	40
Cruise: Movies/Television Programming	33
Cruise: Hospitality Standard	60
Cruise: Overall Product Delivery	63
Overall Score	**1,052**

Accommodation: All cabins have shower and toilet, radio, telephone, but not much else, and they are really tiny, as are the bathrooms. As the cabins have very little closet and drawer space, do take only what's really necessary. There are also five allergy-free cabins.

Dining: The dining room is charming and features Continental (European) cuisine, with a distinct accent on fish, seafood, and fresh berries. The breads and cheeses are also good. Fine, hearty, and friendly service comes with a smile.

Other Comments: This lovely old-world ship was built specifically for close-in northern European coastal and archipelago cruises, and was extensively refurbished in 1990. She is one of very few ships left today that has two funnels, and is owned by a single family concern. Currency: U.S. dollars/Finnish marks.

Features include an outdoor wraparound wooden promenade deck. There are few public rooms, but she does have some beautiful hardwoods and lots of brass featured throughout her interior decor. The Scandinavian artwork is also quite fascinating. She exudes old-world charm. Has a well-designed auditorium that doubles as a movie theater.

But: This is a high density ship, so there is little room to move about inside when full.

mv Le Levant
(S)

Lifestyle	**Premium**
Cruise Line:	Compagnie des Isles du Ponant/Classical Cruises
Former Names:	-
Gross Tonnage:	3,500
Builder:	Leroux & Lotz (France)
Original Cost:	$35 million
Entered Service:	January 1999
Flag:	France
Tel No:	n/a
Fax No:	n/a
Length (ft./m.):	328.0/100.0
Beam (ft./m.):	45.9/14.00
Draft (ft./m.):	11.4/3.5
Propulsion/Propellers:	diesel/2 (CP)
Decks:	5
Total Crew:	50
Pass. Capacity (basis 2):	95
Pass. Capacity (all berths):	95
Pass. Space Ratio (basis 2):	36.8
Pass. Space Ratio (all berths):	36.8
Officers:	French
Total Cabins:	45
Size Range (sq. ft./m.):	199.1/18.5
Cabins (outside view):	45
Cabins (inside—no view):	0
Cabins (single occupancy):	0
Cabins (with private balcony):	0
Cabins (wheelchair accessible):	0
Cabin Current:	110/220 AC
Cabin TV:	Yes
Dining Rooms:	2
Seatings:	Open
Elevators:	1
Casino:	No
Slot Machines:	No
Swimming Pools (outdoors):	1
Swimming Pools (inside):	0
Whirlpools:	0
Fitness Center:	Yes
Sauna/Steam Room:	No/Yes
Massage:	No
Self-Service Launderette:	No
Movie Theater/Seats:	No
Library:	Yes
Children's Facilities:	No
Classification Society:	Bureau Veritas

Ratings	**Score**
Ship: Hardware/Maintenance	NYR
Ship: Outdoor Facilities/Space	NYR
Ship: Interior Facilities/Space/Flow	NYR
Ship: Decor/Furnishings/Artwork	NYR
Ship: Spa/Fitness Facilities	NYR
Cabins: Suites and Deluxe	NYR
Cabins: Standard Sizes	NYR
Food: Dining Room/Cuisine	NYR
Food: Informal Dining/Buffets	NYR
Food: Quality of Ingredients	NYR
Food: Afternoon Tea/Bar Snacks	NYR
Service: Dining Room	NYR
Service: Bars	NYR
Service: Cabins	NYR
Service: Open Decks	NYR
Cruise: Entertainment	NYR
Cruise: Activities Program	NYR
Cruise: Movies/Television Programming	NYR
Cruise: Hospitality Standard	NYR
Cruise: Overall Product Deliver	NYR

Expected Score Range
1,600-1,800

Accommodation: The 45 ocean-view cabins (the brochure says "suites") are all located midships and forward, but there are five different price categories. Each cabin features a large ocean-view window, inlaid wood furniture and accenting, designer fabrics, two beds that convert to a queen-size bed, a television, VCR, refrigerator, personal safe, and personal amenity kits in the marble-appointed bathrooms, all of which feature a shower (no bathtubs).

Dining: There are two dining rooms; the first is a wood paneled main Dining Room, which has round and oval tables; the second is the more informal Veranda Restaurant, with a panoramic view overlooking the stern. Dining is in open seating, with unassigned seats, so you can dine with whomever you wish. Complimentary wines are included for lunch and dinner, and the cuisine is, naturally, classic French.

Other Comments: This new high-class vessel looks like a streamlined private mega-yacht, and has quite a stunning low profile appearance with its royal blue (ice-hardened) hull and blue/white superstructure. She sports two slim funnels that carry any soot away from the vessel. Built in a yacht shipyard in St. Malo, France. An "open bridge" policy is featured, so that passengers may visit the bridge whenever they wish (except when maneuvering in difficult conditions). She sports a stern "marina" platform for scuba diving, snorkeling, or swimming. Two special landing craft are carried for shore visits, hidden in the stern, as well as six inflatable Zodiac runabouts for landings in "soft" expedition areas such as the Amazon.

Inside, the vessel features contemporary, clean, and uncluttered decor. The public rooms are elegant and refined, with much use of wood trim and accenting throughout. Particularly pleasing is the wood-paneled library, a feature so often lacking aboard many ships today. There is also one grand salon, which accommodates all passengers, and is used by day as a lecture room, and by night as the main lounge/bar. A resident scuba divemaster is aboard for all Caribbean sailings. In addition, Classical Cruises features life-enrichment lecturers aboard each cruise, as well as tour leaders.

This ship, under charter to New York-based Classical Cruises, will operate cruises in the Great Lakes (between Toronto and Chicago) during the summer of 1999 (her pencil-slim beam allows her to navigate the locks). During the fall of 1999 she heads to Canada/New England, and even as far north as Hudson Bay and the Northern Territories of Canada. During the winter months she heads to the Caribbean and South America.

The company also owns and operates *Le Ponant,* a chic ultra-sleek sailing vessel. This is all-inclusive cruising, with all port charges, gratuities, shore excursions, and port charges included in the cruise fare. The crew is almost entirely French.

But: Although you can walk around the uppermost accommodation deck, there really is no wrap-around promenade deck. No cabins have balconies.

mys Le Ponant

☆☆☆☆

(S)

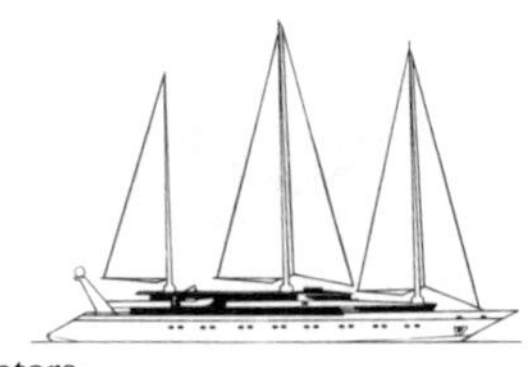

LIFESTYLE	**PREMIUM**
Cruise Line:	Compagnie des Isles du Ponant
Former Names:	-
Gross Tonnage:	1,489
Builder:	SFCN (France)
Original Cost:	n/a
Entered Service:	1991
Flag:	France
Tel No:	1111406
Fax No:	1111406
Length (ft./m.):	288.7/88.00
Beam (ft./m.):	39.3/12.00
Draft (ft./m.):	13.1/4.00
Type of Vessel:	high tech sail-cruiser
No. of Masts:	3
Sail Area (sq. ft./sq. m.):	16,150/1,500
Main Propulsion:	a) engine/b) sails
Propulsion/Propellers:	diesel/sail power/1 (CP)
Decks:	3
Total Crew:	30
Pass. Capacity (basis 2):	56
Pass. Capacity (all berths):	67
Pass. Space Ratio (basis 2):	26.5
Pass. Space Ratio (all berths):	22.2
Officers:	French
Total Cabins:	32
Size Range (sq. ft./m.):	140/13.0
Cabins (outside view):	32
Cabins (inside):	0
Cabins (for one person):	0
Cabins (with private balcony):	0
Cabins (wheelchair accessible):	0
Cabin Current:	220 AC
Cabin TV:	No
Dining Rooms:	1 (open seating)
Elevators:	No
Casino:	No
Slot Machines:	No
Swimming Pools (outdoors):	0
Whirlpools:	0
Fitness Center:	Yes
Sauna/Steam Room:	No/No
Massage:	No
Self-Service Launderette:	No
Library:	Yes
Classification Society:	Lloyd's Register

RATINGS	**SCORE**
Ship: Hardware/Maintenance	86
Ship: Sails and Equipment	86
Ship: Interior Facilities/Space/Flow	84
Ship: Decor/Furnishings/Artwork	86
Ship: Spa/Fitness Facilities	57
Cabins: Suites and Deluxe	85
Cabins: Standard Sizes	81
Food: Dining Room/Cuisine	81
Food: Informal Dining/Buffets	76
Food: Quality of Ingredients	77
Food: Afternoon Tea/Bar Snacks	76
Service: Dining Room	81
Service: Bars	80
Service: Cabins	80
Service: Open Decks	78
Cruise: The Sailing Experience	83
Cruise: Lecturers/Entertainment	62
Cruise: Movies/Television Programming	36
Cruise: Hospitality Standard	81
Cruise: Overall Product Delivery	84
OVERALL SCORE	**1,540**

Accommodation: Crisp, clean blond woods and pristine white provide the decor in cabins that feature double or twin beds, minibar, personal safe, and private bathroom. All cabins feature portholes, crisp artwork, and a refrigerator. There is a limited amount of storage space, however, and few drawers. The cabin bathrooms are quite small, but efficiently designed.

Dining: The lovely Karukera dining room features complimentary wines and good food. There is fresh fish every day, and meals are true "affaires gastonomiques." There is also a charming outdoor café under canvas sailcloth awning.

Other Comments: Ultra-sleek and very efficient, this latest generation of sail-cruise ship has three masts that rise 16.7 meters above the water line. This captivating ship has plenty of room on her open decks for sunbathing. Water sports facilities include an aft marina platform, windsurfers, water-ski boat, scuba, and snorkel equipment.

Very elegant, no-glitz interior design is clean, stylish, and functional, and ultra-high-tech throughout. Three public lounges have pastel decor, soft colors, and great European flair.

One price fits all. Marketed mainly to young, sophisticated French-speaking passengers who love yachting and the sea. Tres French, and tres chic. The company also has a stunning mega-yacht cruise vessel, *Le Levant.* Gratuities are not "required," but they are expected.

ms Leeward

☆☆☆ +

(M)

Lifestyle	**Standard**
Cruise Line:	Norwegian Cruise Line
Former Names:	*Sally Albatros/Viking Saga*
Gross Tonnage:	25,000
Builder:	Wartsila (Finland)
Original Cost:	n/a
Entered Service:	1980/October 1995
Flag:	Liberia
Tel No:	1335547010
Fax No:	1335547011
Length (ft./m.):	492.1/150.0
Beam (ft./m.):	82.6/25.2
Draft (ft./m.):	18.0/5.5
Propulsion/Propellers:	diesel (19,120kW)/2 (CP)
Decks:	7
Total Crew:	400
Pass. Capacity (basis 2):	950
Pass. Capacity (all berths):	1,150
Pass. Space Ratio (basis 2):	26.3
Pass. Space Ratio (all berths):	21.7
Officers:	Norwegian
Total Cabins:	475 (548)
Size Range (sq. ft./m.):	53–387/5.0–36.0
Cabins (outside view):	219
Cabins (inside):	256
Cabins (for one person):	0
Cabins (with private balcony):	10
Cabins (wheelchair accessible):	6
Cabin Current:	110/220 AC
Cabin TV:	Yes
Dining Rooms:	2
Seatings:	2
Elevators:	4
Casino:	Yes
Slot Machines:	Yes
Swimming Pools (outdoors):	1
Swimming Pools (inside):	0
Whirlpools:	1
Fitness Center:	Yes
Sauna/Steam Room:	Yes/No
Massage:	Yes
Self-Service Launderette:	No
Movie Theater/Seats:	No
Library:	No
Children's Facilities:	Yes
Classification Society:	Bureau Veritas

Ratings	**Score**
Ship: Hardware/Maintenance	75
Ship: Outdoor Facilities/Space	64
Ship: Interior Facilities/Space/Flow	75
Ship: Decor/Furnishings/Artwork	74
Ship: Spa/Fitness Facilities	62
Cabins: Suites and Deluxe	74
Cabins: Standard Sizes	71
Food: Dining Room/Cuisine	63
Food: Informal Dining/Buffets	60
Food: Quality of Ingredients	63
Food: Afternoon Tea/Bar Snacks	58
Service: Dining Room	61
Service: Bars	61
Service: Cabins	64
Service: Open Decks	65
Cruise: Entertainment	76
Cruise: Activities Program	63
Cruise: Movies/Television Programming	76
Cruise: Hospitality Standard	65
Cruise: Overall Product Delivery	71
Overall Score	**1,341**

Accommodation: Some of the top-grade cabins have neatly angled private balconies. Six cabins are specially designed for allergy sufferers. However, most of the standard cabins are very small, bathrooms are tiny (expect to dance with the shower curtain), and there is little room for personal toiletry items. Note that many outside cabins on Deck 6 have obstructed views.

Dining: There are two principal dining rooms, located aft. The service is generally good, but hurried. Menu choice is good, and presentation is reasonable, but there is no finesse. Like other NCL ships, this ship has a limited selection of breads, cheeses, and fruits, all standard fare that you would find ashore in family restaurants.

However, there is also Le Bistro, an attractive and popular 80-seat informal (alternative) dining spot for pasta and other lighter fare.

Other Comments: This ship has undergone a number of changes during her lifetime, from passenger ferry to cruise ship. She now has a sleek, swept-back, wedge-shaped design with steeply tiered aft decks, although there is hardly any bow. The bridge is of the fully enclosed type. There is a teakwood wraparound outdoor promenade deck, and a large spa and recreation center, but an awful, cramped pool deck. What this ship really needs is a forward observation lounge.

There is a warm, friendly ambience aboard. Glitzy but pleasant lobby that features contemporary, bright decor, with modern artworks and splashes of color everywhere. There is a good show lounge, which has tiered seating, and fairly good sight lines. Sports fans will like the Sports Bar and Grill, an informal television-filled long bar and adjacent fast food joint. This is, however, a high-density ship with many low ceilings.

A 1995 refit cost $60 million. Has a flat, squared-off stern, with car deck ramps (ideal for a future Miami-Cuba run). Presently under a four-year charter to Norwegian Cruise Line for short cruises, for which she is well suited.

ms Legend of the Seas

☆☆☆☆

(L)

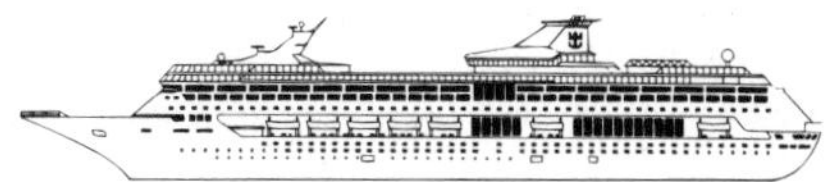

LIFESTYLE	**STANDARD**
Cruise Line:	Royal Caribbean International
Former Names:	-
Gross Tonnage:	70,950
Builder:	Chantiers de l'Atlantique (France)
Original Cost:	$325 million
Entered Service:	May 1995
Flag:	Norway/Panama
Tel No:	363600710
Fax No:	363600712
Length (ft./m.):	867.0/264.20
Beam (ft./m.):	105.0/32.00
Draft (ft./m.):	24.5/7.46
Propulsion/Propellers:	diesel (40,200kW)/2 (CP)
Decks:	11
Total Crew:	732
Pass. Capacity (basis 2):	1,804
Pass. Capacity (all berths):	2,064
Pass. Space Ratio (basis 2):	39.3
Pass. Space Ratio (all berths):	34.3
Officers:	Norwegian
Total Cabins:	902
Size Range (sq. ft./m.):	138–1,148/12.8–106.6
Cabins (outside view):	575
Cabins (inside):	327
Cabins (for one person):	0
Cabins (with private balcony):	231
Cabins (wheelchair accessible):	17
Cabin Current:	110/220 AC
Cabin TV:	Yes
Dining Rooms:	1
Seatings:	2
Elevators:	11
Casino:	Yes
Slot Machines:	Yes
Swimming Pools (outdoors):	2 (1 with sliding roof)
Swimming Pools (inside):	0
Whirlpools:	4
Fitness Center:	Yes
Sauna/Steam Room:	Yes/Yes
Massage:	Yes
Self-Service Launderette:	No
Movie Theater/Seats:	No
Library:	Yes
Children's Facilities:	Yes
Classification Society:	Det Norske Veritas

RATINGS	**SCORE**
Ship: Hardware/Maintenance	88
Ship: Outdoor Facilities/Space	83
Ship: Interior Facilities/Space/Flow	88
Ship: Decor/Furnishings/Artwork	87
Ship: Spa/Fitness Facilities	86
Cabins: Suites and Deluxe	87
Cabins: Standard Sizes	82
Food: Dining Room/Cuisine	71
Food: Informal Dining/Buffets	61
Food: Quality of Ingredients	66
Food: Afternoon Tea/Bar Snacks	52
Service: Dining Room	78
Service: Bars	74
Service: Cabins	76
Service: Open Decks	67
Cruise: Entertainment	82
Cruise: Activities Program	76
Cruise: Movies/Television Programming	80
Cruise: Hospitality Standard	71
Cruise: Overall Product Delivery	78
OVERALL SCORE	**1,533**

Accommodation: Royal Caribbean International has realized that small cabins do not happy passengers make. The company therefore set about designing a ship with much larger standard cabins than in any of the company's previous vessels (except sister ship *Splendour of the Seas*). Some cabins on Deck 8 also have a larger door for wheelchair access in addition to the 17 cabins for the physically handicapped, and the ship is very accessible, with ample ramped areas and sloping decks. All cabins have a sitting area and beds that convert to double configuration, and there is ample closet and drawer space, although there is not much space around the bed (and the showers could have been better).

Cabins with balconies have glass railings rather than steel/wood to provide less intrusive sight lines. The largest accommodation, named the Royal Suite, is a superb living space for those who can afford the best. It is beautifully designed, finely decorated, and features a baby grand piano, whirlpool bathtub, and other fine amenities. Several sitting areas are located adjacent to the best cabins amidships. Seventeen cabin categories is really too many. Sadly, there are no cabins for singles.

Dining: The two-deck-high dining room has dramatic two-deck-high glass side walls, so many passengers both upstairs and downstairs can see both the ocean and each other in reflection (it would, perhaps, have been even better located at the stern), but it is quite noisy when full (call it atmosphere). There is also a cavernous indoor-outdoor café, located towards the bow and above the bridge, as well as a good-sized snack area, which provide more informal dining choices.

Meals, choices, and presentation were much improved of late. In addition, full vegetarian menus were also introduced. Royal Caribbean International delivers generally good food and service, with waiters that are smartly dressed and very attentive. Special orders are seldom possible, however, and there is neither good caviar nor tableside carving or flambeau items.

Other Comments: This ship's contemporary profile looks somewhat unbalanced (but it soon grows on you), and she does have a nicely tiered stern. The pool deck amidships overhangs the hull to provide an extremely wide deck, while still allowing the ship to navigate the Panama Canal. With engines placed midships, there is little noise and no noticeable vibration, and the ship has an operating speed of up to 24 knots.

The interior decor is quite colorful but too glitzy for European tastes. The outside light is brought inside in many places, with an extensive amount of glass area that provides contact with sea and air (there are, in fact, over two acres of glass). Features an innovative single-level sliding glass roof (not a magrodome) over the more formal setting of one of two swimming pools, thus providing a multi-activity, all-weather indoor-outdoor area, called Solarium. The glass roof provides shelter for the Roman-style pool and adjacent health and fitness facilities (which are superb) and slides aft to cover the miniature golf course when required (both cannot be covered at the same time, however).

Golfers might enjoy the eighteen-hole, 6,000 sq. ft. (557.5 m^2) miniature golf course, aptly named Legend of the Links (it is the first of its kind in any cruise ship). It has the topography of a real championship course, complete with trees, foliage, grass, bridges, water hazards, and lighting for play at night.

Inside, there are two full entertainment decks sandwiched between five decks full of cabins. The tiered and balconied show lounge, which covers two decks, is expansive and has excellent sight lines, and very comfortable seats. Several large-scale production shows are provided here, and there is an orchestra pit that can be raised or lowered as required. A multitiered seven-deck-high atrium lobby, complete with a huge stainless steel sculpture, connects with the impressive Viking Crown Lounge via glass-walled elevators. The casino is really expansive, overly glitzy, and absolutely packed. The library, outside of which is a bust of Shakespeare, is a fine facility, with over 2,000 books.

There is, sadly, no separate cinema. The casino could be somewhat disorienting, with its mirrored walls and lights flashing everywhere, although it is no different to those found in Las Vegas fantasy gaming halls. As with any large ship, you can expect to find yourself standing in lines for embarkation, disembarkation, buffets and shore excursions, although the company does its best to minimize such lines.

Representing natural evolution, this ship is an outstanding new cruise vessel for the many repeat passengers who enjoy Royal Caribbean International's consistent delivery of a well-integrated, fine-tuned, very comfortable and well-liked product. With larger cabins, excellent décor, and contemporary style, *Legend of the Seas* has taken Royal Caribbean International passengers, most of whom are typically from middle-America, into a much upgraded cruise experience from that of the company's other ships. The ship provides a very cost-effective cruise for all ages. Similar comments apply to sister ship *Splendour of the Seas*.

ms Leisure World

☆☆ +

(M)

Lifestyle	**Standard**
Cruise Line:	New Century Tours
Former Names:	*Fantasy World/Asean World/Shangri-La World/Skyward*
Gross Tonnage:	16,254
Builder:	Seebeckwerft (Germany)
Original Cost:	n/a
Entered Service:	December 1969/1990
Flag:	BVI
Tel No:	1104164
Fax No:	1104164
Length (ft./m.):	525.3/160.13
Beam (ft./m.):	74.9/22.84
Draft (ft./m.):	20.6/6.29
Propulsion/Propellers:	diesel (12,950kW)/2 (CP)
Decks:	8
Total Crew:	250
Pass. Capacity (basis 2):	730
Pass. Capacity (all berths):	1,071
Pass. Space Ratio (basis 2):	22.2
Pass. Space Ratio (all berths):	15.1
Officers:	International
Total Cabins:	365
Size Range (sq. ft./m.):	90–330/8.3–30.5
Cabins (outside view):	219
Cabins (inside):	145
Cabins (for one person):	0
Cabins (with private balcony):	0
Cabins (wheelchair accessible):	0
Cabin Current:	110/220 AC
Refrigerator:	No
Cabin TV:	No
Dining Rooms:	1
Seatings:	2
Elevators:	4
Casino:	Yes
Slot Machines:	Yes
Swimming Pools (outdoors):	1
Swimming Pools (inside):	0
Whirlpools:	0
Fitness Center:	Yes
Sauna/Steam Room:	Yes/No
Massage:	Yes
Self-Service Launderette:	No
Movie Theater/Seats:	Yes/180
Library:	Yes
Children's Facilities:	Yes
Classification Society:	Det Norske Veritas

Ratings	**Score**
Ship: Hardware/Maintenance	48
Ship: Outdoor Facilities/Space	51
Ship: Interior Facilities/Space/Flow	52
Ship: Decor/Furnishings/Artwork	50
Ship: Spa/Fitness Facilities	29
Cabins: Suites and Deluxe	56
Cabins: Standard Sizes	47
Food: Dining Room/Cuisine	63
Food: Informal Dining/Buffets	55
Food: Quality of Ingredients	62
Food: Afternoon Tea/Bar Snacks	52
Service: Dining Room	67
Service: Bars	70
Service: Cabins	68
Service: Open Decks	54
Cruise: Entertainment	52
Cruise: Activities Program	44
Cruise: Movies/Television Programming	40
Cruise: Hospitality Standard	58
Cruise: Overall Product Delivery	53
Overall Score	**1,071**

Accommodation: Except for 10 suites, the cabins are small, have very limited closet and drawer space and tinny metal furniture, as well as very poor soundproofing (yes, you can hear your neighbors brushing their hair). Bathrooms are also small, with little storage space for toiletries.

Dining: The dining room is cramped and extremely noisy, and food service is fast and without finesse. There is a choice of a la carte menu or Asian/Western buffet. However, the quality of the food is only moderately good, but then the price of the cruise is low. Cheerful, rather hurried service from a staff that lacks refinement, and wine service that is poor (so is the wine list, although the prices are high).

Other Comments: She is a mildly attractive, but somewhat dated-looking seventies ship with a distinctive daytime sun lounge set high and forward around the ship's mast.

The refurbished interior features light, airy decor in clean, crisp colors. Lounge and bar atop ship has plenty of light. Pleasant balconied theater. Good karaoke lounge for those inevitable sing-alongs, and the casino action is constant and noisy.

Being a very high-density ship means crowded public areas, lots of noise, and lines for buffets and elevators. Despite what company brochures and advertising claim, this is not a luxury liner, by any stretch of the imagination. It attracts many gamblers, who like the fast-paced action. Adequate for short cruises (one-, two- and three-day cruises are featured, some in conjunction with the Rakyat Express train to Tampin) for active passengers wanting an upbeat cruise experience in comfortable, friendly, and casual surroundings.

sy Lili Marleen

☆☆☆☆

(S)

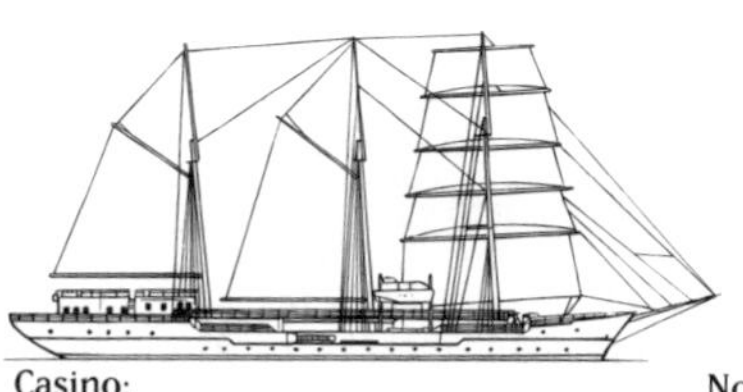

Lifestyle	**Premium**
Cruise Line:	Peter Deilmann Reederei
Former Names:	-
Gross Tonnage:	750
Builder:	Elsflether Werft (Germany)
Original Cost:	DM16 million
Entered Service:	July 1994
Flag:	Germany
Tel No:	1123465
Fax No:	1123466
Length (ft./m.):	249.3/76.0
Beam (ft./m.):	31.6/9.5
Draft (ft./m.):	12.7/3.9
Type of Vessel:	barkentine schooner
No. of Masts:	3/16 manually furled sails
Sail Area (sq. ft./sq. m.):	12,917/1,200
Main Propulsion:	sail power
Propulsion/Propellers:	diesel (660kW)/1 (CP)
Decks:	3
Total Crew:	26
Pass. Capacity (basis 2):	50
Pass. Capacity (all berths):	50
Pass. Space Ratio (basis 2):	15.0
Pass. Space Ratio (all berths):	15.0
Officers:	German
Total Cabins:	25
Size Range (sq. ft./m.):	96.8–129.1/9.0–12.0
Cabins (outside view):	25
Cabins (inside):	0
Cabins (for one person):	0
Cabins (with private balcony):	0
Cabins (wheelchair accessible):	0
Cabin Current:	220 AC
Cabin TV:	No
Dining Rooms:	1
Seatings:	1
Elevators:	0
Casino:	No
Slot Machines:	No
Swimming Pools (outdoors):	0
Swimming Pools (inside):	0
Whirlpools:	0
Fitness Center:	No
Sauna/Steam Room:	No
Massage:	No
Self-Service Launderette:	No
Movie Theater/Seats:	No
Library:	Yes
Children's Facilities:	No
Classification Society:	Germanischer Lloyd

Ratings	**Score**
Ship: Hardware/Maintenance	87
Ship: Sails and Equipment	90
Ship: Interior Facilities/Space/Flow	87
Ship: Decor/Furnishings/Artwork	86
Ship: Spa/Fitness Facilities	31
Cabins: Suites and Deluxe	86
Cabins: Standard Sizes	83
Food: Dining Room/Cuisine	86
Food: Informal Dining/Buffets	78
Food: Quality of Ingredients	79
Food: Afternoon Tea/Bar Snacks	76
Service: Dining Room	83
Service: Bars	81
Service: Cabins	81
Service: Open Decks	78
Cruise: The Sailing Experience	92
Cruise: Lecturers/Entertainment	58
Cruise: Movies/Television Programming	35
Cruise: Hospitality Standard	83
Cruise Overall Product Delivery	86
Overall Score	**1,546**

Accommodation: The twin-bedded and double-bedded cabins are very comfortable, although they are quite compact units (three "suites" located around the navigation bridge have a little more space), but you should note that most cabins feature upper and lower berths. All furniture is of bird's-eye maple, set against white walls, and there are one-piece ceilings.

The white, fully tiled bathrooms are well equipped and have gold-anodized fittings. The high-pressure showers are very good. Bathrobes are provided for all, and there is a good range of personal toiletry amenities. Note that there is no cabin service for food or beverages.

Dining: Has a really charming dining room, and on some evenings dinner is accompanied by candlelight dining at assigned tables. Single seating dining is featured, with a good mix of buffets (for appetizers, cheeses, and fruits) and sit-down meals. Features fine quality china and silverware. The cuisine is international, with some regional specialties, and both the creativity and presentation are excellent. Wines and liquor are extra, but soft drinks are included in the fare.

Other Comments: She is a fine three-masted barkentine (with one square-rigged and two gaff- or schooner-rigged masts), the tallest of which is 118 feet high (36 m). This is a timeless design that relies on the power of nature most of the time. However, note that there is little room on the open decks, as aboard any true sailing vessel (due to the rigging and ropes); there is no swimming pool. When under motor power (for going into and coming out of ports), there are no stabilizers, so she can roll.

This is first and foremost a sailing ship, where everything is done by a crew of professional sailors, many of whom have served aboard the best naval sail-training ships in the world. You should not, therefore, expect to take an active part with the sails, although you may be allowed to go up the rigging (at the captain's discretion). The captain conducts voyage and sailing seminars and recaps for his passengers every couple of days. Although there are some scheduled ports of call (the schedules are always subject to the prevailing weather conditions, and arrival/departure times constantly change), this kind of sail-cruising really is for those who do not really care whether the ship calls at any ports or not. She is also for those who do not need entertainment of any kind.

The oneness with the elements can be quite exhilarating (speed under sail is about nine knots). Features some good facilities for passenger comfort considering the size of the vessel. She is a good ship for those seeking beach and swim itineraries to the more out of the way places where the big cruise ships cannot go.

Note that only casual clothing will be needed on this kind of cruise (except for one night where jacket and tie are needed in the dining room), which provides a really relaxing way to travel. Remember, however, that she is a sailing ship, and not a cruise ship, and she should not be compared with Sea Cloud, which is a much grander vessel. *Lili Marleen*, however, is a lovely ship nonetheless, and very intimate. No one who is physically challenged should consider this vessel. She is, however, one of the best-kept secrets in the cruise industry. The deutsche mark is the currency used on board, and, quite naturally, German is the language used throughout. Gratuities and insurance are not included.

ms Maasdam

☆☆☆☆ +

(L)

Lifestyle	Premium
Cruise Line:	Holland America Line
Former Names:	-
Gross Tonnage:	55,451
Builder:	Fincantieri (Italy)
Original Cost:	$215 million
Entered Service:	December 1993
Flag:	Netherlands
Tel No:	624295813
Fax No:	1302514
Length (ft./m.):	719.3/219.30
Beam (ft./m.):	101.0/30.80
Draft (ft./m.):	24.6/7.50
Propulsion/Propellers:	diesel-electric (34,560kW)/2 (CP)
Decks:	10
Total Crew:	588
Pass. Capacity (basis 2):	1,266
Pass. Capacity (all berths):	1,627
Pass. Space Ratio (basis 2):	43.8
Pass. Space Ratio (all berths):	34.0
Officers:	Dutch
Total Cabins:	632
Size Range (sq. ft./m.):	187–1,126/17.3–104.5
Cabins (outside view):	502
Cabins (inside):	131
Cabins (for one person):	0
Cabins (with private balcony):	150
Cabins (wheelchair accessible):	6
Cabin Current:	110/220 AC
Cabin TV:	Yes
Dining Rooms:	1
Seatings:	2
Elevators:	12
Casino:	Yes
Slot Machines:	Yes
Swimming Pools (outdoors):	1
Swimming Pools (inside):	1 (magrodome)
Whirlpools:	2
Fitness Center:	Yes
Sauna/Steam Room:	Yes/No
Massage:	Yes
Self-Service Launderette:	Yes
Movie Theater/Seats:	Yes/249
Library:	Yes
Children's Facilities:	No
Classification Society:	Lloyd's Register

Ratings	Score
Ship: Hardware/Maintenance	87
Ship: Outdoor Facilities/Space	82
Ship: Interior Facilities/Space/Flow	86
Ship: Decor/Furnishings/Artwork	85
Ship: Spa/Fitness Facilities	78
Cabins: Suites and Deluxe	83
Cabins: Standard Sizes	79
Food: Dining Room/Cuisine	77
Food: Informal Dining/Buffets	74
Food: Quality of Ingredients	73
Food: Afternoon Tea/Bar Snacks	65
Service: Dining Room	76
Service: Bars	76
Service: Cabins	76
Service: Open Decks	71
Cruise: Entertainment	77
Cruise: Activities Program	76
Cruise: Movies/Television Programming	76
Cruise: Hospitality Standard	76
Cruise: Overall Product Delivery	82
Overall Score	**1,555**

Accommodation: There are 28 suites with accommodation for four that also feature in-suite dining as an alternative to the dining room. They are very spacious, tastefully decorated and well laid out, with separate living room and bedroom, and plenty of closet and drawer space. Marble bathroom with Jacuzzi tub.

The standard cabins feature twin beds that convert to a queen-size unit, and a separate living space with sofa and coffee table. The closet and drawer space, although tight, is adequate for a seven-day cruise. The tiled bathrooms are compact but practical, and come with a good range of personal toiletry amenities. Bathrobes are also provided, as are hairdryers.

Dining: The two-level dining room, located at the stern (upper level for smokers, lower level for nonsmokers) is quite dramatic, and has a grand staircase (although few seem to use it), panoramic views on three sides, and music balcony. Open seating for breakfast and lunch, two seatings for dinner. The food and service have improved somewhat, but dinner is still not a memorable experience. This is mass catering, after all. There is too much use of canned fruits and the choice of cheeses is very limited.

Other Comments: The decor is softer, more sophisticated, and far less eclectic than in her sister ship, Statendam, the first in this series of ships. Antiques and artwork are stunning, and beautifully displayed. This line always has some fine flower arrangements in public areas. The ship has a dramatic three-deck high atrium foyer. A hydraulic magrodome roof covers the large indoor-outdoor swimming pool/whirlpools and central Lido area so that this can be used in fine or inclement weather.

The two-deck-high showroom is well thought out, but the ceiling is low and balcony sight lines are not good. Has a lovely, relaxing reference library. The ship is kept very clean and tidy throughout, and there is good passenger flow.

This is a well-built, quality ship, and Holland America Line is constantly fine-tuning its performance. Note: The line does not add an automatic 15 percent for beverage purchases, unlike many other cruise lines.

But: Communication with staff is often frustrating. There is no division of smoking and no-smoking areas at the outdoor Lido Cafe. There is an extra charge for the self-service laundry machines ($1.50).

ms Majesty of the Seas

☆☆☆☆

(L)

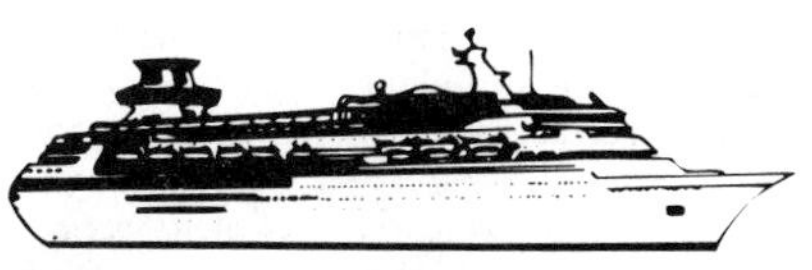

LIFESTYLE	**STANDARD**
Cruise Line:	Royal Caribbean International
Former Names:	-
Gross Tonnage:	73,941
Builder:	Chantiers de l'Atlantique
Original Cost:	$300 million
Entered Service:	April 1992
Flag:	Norway
Tel No:	1313370
Fax No:	1313370
Length (ft./m.):	873.6/266.30
Beam (ft./m.):	105.9/32.30
Draft (ft./m.):	24.9/7.60
Propulsion/Propellers:	diesel (21,844kW)/2 (CP)
Decks:	12
Total Crew:	822
Pass. Capacity (basis 2):	2,354
Pass. Capacity (all berths):	2,744
Pass. Space Ratio (basis 2):	31.4
Pass. Space Ratio (all berths):	26.9
Officers:	Norwegian
Total Cabins:	1,177
Size Range (sq. ft./m.):	120–446/11.0–41.5
Cabins (outside view):	732
Cabins (inside):	445
Cabins (for one person):	0
Cabins (with private balcony):	62
Cabins (wheelchair accessible):	4
Cabin Current:	110 AC
Cabin TV:	Yes
Dining Rooms:	2
Seatings:	2
Elevators:	18
Casino:	Yes
Slot Machines:	Yes
Swimming Pools (outdoors):	2
Swimming Pools (inside):	0
Whirlpools:	2
Fitness Center:	Yes
Sauna/Steam Room:	Yes/No
Massage:	Yes
Self-Service Launderette:	No
Movie Theater/Seats:	Yes/200
Library:	Yes
Children's Facilities:	Yes
Classification Society:	Det Norske Veritas

RATINGS	**SCORE**
Ship: Hardware/Maintenance	78
Ship: Outdoor Facilities/Space	79
Ship: Interior Facilities/Space/Flow	80
Ship: Decor/Furnishings/Artwork	78
Ship: Spa/Fitness Facilities	72
Cabins: Suites and Deluxe	76
Cabins: Standard Sizes	70
Food: Dining Room/Cuisine	70
Food: Informal Dining/Buffets	60
Food: Quality of Ingredients	66
Food: Afternoon Tea/Bar Snacks	52
Service: Dining Room	75
Service: Bars	72
Service: Cabins	73
Service: Open Decks	66
Cruise: Entertainment	76
Cruise: Activities Program	70
Cruise: Movies/Television Programming	72
Cruise: Hospitality Standard	68
Cruise: Overall Product Delivery	77
OVERALL SCORE	**1,430**

Accommodation: Except for a few suites, all cabins are small because the company's policy is one of getting passengers out in the public areas. They are attractive in a basic way, but the bathrooms are small and utilitarian. There is no doubt that cabins are the weak point of a cruise aboard this ship.

Dining: The two musical-themed dining rooms are large, attractive, and colorful (there are no tables for two). The dining operation is well orchestrated, with emphasis on highly programmed (insensitive) hurried service.

Food is consistently good, but not memorable. Features French, Oriental, Italian, Caribbean, American theme nights, with waiters/busboys in appropriate costumes. Extensive wine list. The staff is overly friendly, even intrusive.

Other Comments: Royal Caribbean International's trademark Viking Crown lounge and bar surrounds the funnel and provides a stunning view. The open deck space is very cramped when full, as aboard any large ship, although there seems to be plenty of it.

This ship has a spacious, well-designed interior, with excellent signs. Beautiful, well-stocked library adds class. Five-deck-high Centrum is a focal point. While suites are more spacious, most cabins are small, but attractively decorated. Special "family suites," located amidships, sleep four. The entertainment program is very good, and includes good children's/teens' programs and cheerful youth counselors.

In the final analysis, you will probably be overwhelmed by the public spaces, and underwhelmed by the size of the cabins. However, this is basically a well run, fine-tuned, highly programmed cruise product geared particularly to those seeking an action-packed cruise vacation in seven days, at a moderately good price, with around 2,500 fellow passengers.

But: There are too many loud, intrusive announcements. The officers, junior officers, and staff often forget that hospitality is the key to happy passengers.

mv Marco Polo

☆☆☆☆

(M)

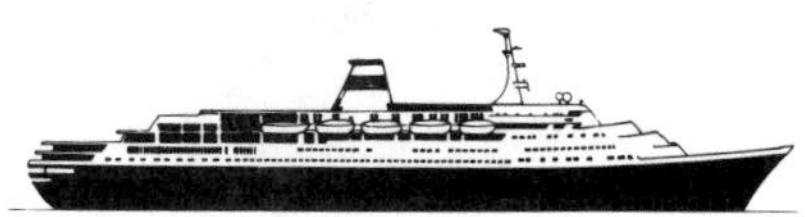

Lifestyle	**Premium**
Cruise Line:	Orient Lines
Former Names:	*Aleksandr Pushkin*
Gross Tonnage:	20,502
Builder:	VEB Mathias Thesen (Germany)
Original Cost:	n/a
Entered Service:	April 1966/October 1993
Flag:	Bahamas
Tel No:	630869310
Fax No:	1306216
Length (ft./m.):	578.4/176.28
Beam (ft./m.):	77.4/23.60
Draft (ft./m.):	26.8/8.17
Propulsion/Propellers:	diesel (14,444kW)/2 (CP)
Decks:	8
Total Crew:	356
Pass. Capacity (basis 2):	848
Pass. Capacity (all berths):	915
Pass. Space Ratio (basis 2):	24.1
Pass. Space Ratio (all berths):	22.4
Officers:	European
Total Cabins:	425
Size Range (sq. ft./m.):	120–480/11.0–44.5
Cabins (outside view):	294
Cabins (inside):	131
Cabins (for one person):	(many doubles sold for single occupancy)
Cabins (with private balcony):	0
Cabins (wheelchair accessible):	2
Cabin Current:	110/220 AC
Cabin TV:	Yes
Dining Rooms:	2
Seatings:	2
Elevators:	4
Casino:	Yes
Slot Machines:	Yes
Swimming Pools (outdoors):	1
Swimming Pools (inside):	0
Whirlpools:	3
Fitness Center:	Yes
Sauna/Steam Room:	Yes/No
Massage:	Yes
Self-Service Launderette:	No
Movie Theater/Seats:	No
Library:	Yes
Children's Facilities:	No
Classification Society:	Bureau Veritas

Ratings	**Score**
Ship: Hardware/Maintenance	83
Ship: Outdoor Facilities/Space	79
Ship: Interior Facilities/Space/Flow	81
Ship: Decor/Furnishings/Artwork	81
Ship: Spa/Fitness Facilities	76
Cabins: Suites and Deluxe	75
Cabins: Standard Sizes	72
Food: Dining Room/Cuisine	84
Food: Informal Dining/Buffets	81
Food: Quality of Ingredients	83
Food: Afternoon Tea/Bar Snacks	77
Service: Dining Room	80
Service: Bars	78
Service: Cabins	81
Service: Open Decks	76
Cruise: Entertainment	73
Cruise: Activities Program	65
Cruise: Movies/Television Programming	64
Cruise: Hospitality Standard	75
Cruise: Overall Product Delivery	81
Overall Score	**1,545**

Accommodation: The cabins, which come in a profusion of different sizes and configurations, are pleasantly decorated and adequate in size, but nothing special, except for the rich wood accenting. The weak point of each is the bathroom, which is very small, with little space for anything. Although cabin furnishings and details are not the high point of this ship, the overall effect is quite cheerful. Note that some Upper Deck and Sky Deck cabins have lifeboat-obstructed views. There should be (but there isn't) twenty-four-hour room service, particularly in light of the fact that many passengers are of senior years.

Dining: The main dining room is nicely decorated, practical in design, and functions well, but it is noisy, and the tables are very close together. There are tables for two to ten. Fine place settings and china. The food itself is of a very high standard, with good presentation. The wine list is very limited. A 10 percent service charge is added to bar bills.

For informal breakfasts and lunches, Raffles is the place; it also becomes an alternative dining spot, for about 75 persons (reservations required, but there is no extra charge) on several evenings each cruise.

Other Comments: Originally constructed as one of five almost identical sister ships for the Russian/Ukrainian fleet, this vessel has a fine "real-ship" profile, a strong ice-strengthened hull, and huge storage spaces for long voyages. After being completely refitted and refurbished, she now features well-designed, destination-intensive cruises, at very realistic prices. She is fitted with the latest navigational aids and biological waste treatment center, and carries 10 Zodiac landing craft for in-depth shore trips in eco-sensitive areas. This is a very comfortable vessel throughout and she rides well. There is a helicopter landing pad atop ship.

There is a wide range of public rooms, and a sense of spaciousness pervades, as most have high ceilings. Features very tasteful interior decor, with careful use of mirrored surfaces, and colors that do not clash but are relaxing without being boring.

This ship features well-planned destination-intensive cruises, and offers extremely fine value for money in very comfortable surroundings, and a friendly and accommodating Filipino crew help make a cruise aboard her a very pleasant experience. The ship was purchased by Norwegian Cruise Line in May 1998.

But: There are not enough elevators. Expect lines for the small shore tenders, when operated at anchor ports.

ts Maxim Gorkiy

☆☆☆ +

(M)

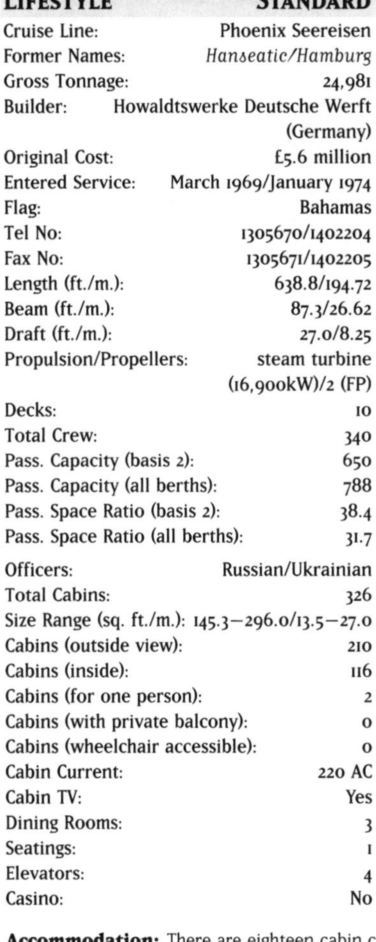

Lifestyle	**Standard**
Cruise Line:	Phoenix Seereisen
Former Names:	*Hanseatic/Hamburg*
Gross Tonnage:	24,981
Builder:	Howaldtswerke Deutsche Werft (Germany)
Original Cost:	£5.6 million
Entered Service:	March 1969/January 1974
Flag:	Bahamas
Tel No:	1305670/1402204
Fax No:	1305671/1402205
Length (ft./m.):	638.8/194.72
Beam (ft./m.):	87.3/26.62
Draft (ft./m.):	27.0/8.25
Propulsion/Propellers:	steam turbine (16,900kW)/2 (FP)
Decks:	10
Total Crew:	340
Pass. Capacity (basis 2):	650
Pass. Capacity (all berths):	788
Pass. Space Ratio (basis 2):	38.4
Pass. Space Ratio (all berths):	31.7
Officers:	Russian/Ukrainian
Total Cabins:	326
Size Range (sq. ft./m.):	145.3–296.0/13.5–27.0
Cabins (outside view):	210
Cabins (inside):	116
Cabins (for one person):	2
Cabins (with private balcony):	0
Cabins (wheelchair accessible):	0
Cabin Current:	220 AC
Cabin TV:	Yes
Dining Rooms:	3
Seatings:	1
Elevators:	4
Casino:	No
Slot Machines:	No
Swimming Pools (outdoors):	1
Swimming Pools (inside):	1
Whirlpools:	0
Fitness Center:	Yes
Sauna/Steam Room:	Yes/No
Massage:	Yes
Self-Service Launderette:	Yes
Movie Theater/Seats:	Yes/290
Library:	Yes
Children's Facilities:	No
Classification Society:	Det Norske Veritas

Ratings	**Score**
Ship: Hardware/Maintenance	68
Ship: Outdoor Facilities/Space	68
Ship: Interior Facilities/Space/Flow	71
Ship: Decor/Furnishings/Artwork	65
Ship: Spa/Fitness Facilities	62
Cabins: Suites and Deluxe	72
Cabins: Standard Sizes	65
Food: Dining Room/Cuisine	76
Food: Informal Dining/Buffets	73
Food: Quality of Ingredients	75
Food: Afternoon Tea/Bar Snacks	64
Service: Dining Room	76
Service: Bars	74
Service: Cabins	76
Service: Open Decks	73
Cruise: Entertainment	62
Cruise: Activities Program	60
Cruise: Movies/Television Programming	60
Cruise: Hospitality Standard	70
Cruise: Overall Product Delivery	75
Overall Score	**1,385**

Accommodation: There are eighteen cabin categories. Most cabins are generally quite spacious, and many have wood paneling and trim. The bathrooms are large and have full-sized bathtubs in all except 20 cabins; there is plenty of room for toiletries. The deluxe cabins are very good, come fully equipped, and have huge picture windows, while most others have portholes. In-cabin Russian and German satellite TV programs.

Anyone booking a suite or one of the top five grades receives Phoenix VIP service, which includes flowers for the cabin, a separate check-in desk, and priority disembarkation.

Dining: There are three restaurants, all located low down in the ship, but they are cheerfully decorated, and were modernized in a 1993 refurbishment. There is always excellent lager on draught.

Moderately good food is served, and wine at lunch and dinner is included in the cruise fare, but more choice and better presentation would be welcome.

The service is quite attentive and courteous from the well-meaning staff, although it is somewhat hurried even though there is only one seating for all meals, and all passengers have assigned tables. Cushions would be a welcome addition to some of the banquette seating.

Other Comments: This all-white ship was originally built for the transatlantic service of the now defunct Deutsche Atlantik Linie, and has long, pleasing lines and outer styling. The ship is easily identified by its odd-looking, platform-topped funnel (designed to disperse smoke away from the aft, tiered, open decks. Generally well maintained, with more facilities added during her last refurbishment. There is a generous amount of open deck and sunbathing space, and deck lounge chairs have cushioned pads.

Inside, there are some handsome, well-designed public rooms, and passenger flow is good. A generous amount of wood paneling was used in her construction, most of which still looks good, although some refinishing is needed in some areas. The decor, while restful, is dark and dull. The show lounge, an important room, is pleasant, but does not hold enough passengers, and the stage and lighting facilities could be much better. The gymnasium is small, and much of the equipment is old and should be updated. Has two relaxing winter gardens with large ocean-view windows.

This ship provides an excellent cruise experience in very comfortable, almost elegant, surroundings, at a modest price, although you should remember that this is an older ship that does not have the latest in facilities. Particularly targeted to German-speaking passengers who appreciate good value. The friendly, attentive service staff are Russian and Ukrainain. Port taxes, insurance, and gratuities are included.

Phoenix Seereisen has, over the years, attained almost a cult status among her passengers, in that the company provides a consistently fine popular product for those passengers who seek a casual cruise experience and lifestyle among friendly people who enjoy life. Where passengers are required to fly to join their cruises, the airline most used by Phoenix Seereisen is LTU. The currency on board is the deutsche mark.

ms MegaStar Aries

☆☆☆☆ +

(S)

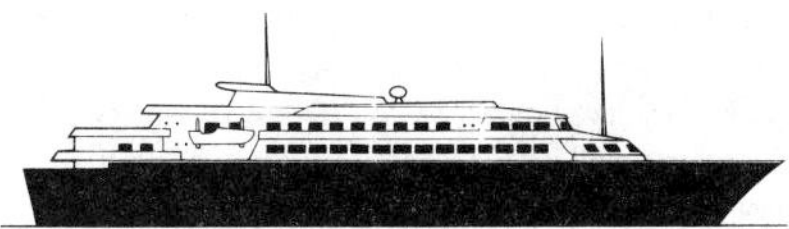

Lifestyle	**Luxury**
Cruise Line:	Star Cruises
Former Names:	*Aurora I/Lady Diana*
Gross Tonnage:	3,300
Builder:	Flender Werft (Germany)
Original Cost:	$35 million
Entered Service:	January 1992/November 1994
Flag:	Bahamas
Tel No:	1305141
Fax No:	1305144
Length (ft./m.):	269.6/82.2
Beam (ft./m.):	45.9/14.0
Draft (ft./m.):	10.9/3.3
Propulsion/Propellers:	diesel (3,356kW)/2 (CP)
Decks:	4
Total Crew:	59
Pass. Capacity (basis 2):	80
Pass. Capacity (all berths):	80
Pass. Space Ratio (basis 2):	41.2
Pass. Space Ratio (all berths):	41.2
Officers:	Scandinavian
Total Cabins:	44
Size Range (sq. ft./m.):	250–430/23.0–40.0
Cabins (outside view):	44
Cabins (inside):	0
Cabins (for one person):	6
Cabins (with private balcony):	0
Cabins (wheelchair accessible):	0
Cabin Current:	110/220 AC
Cabin TV:	Yes
Dining Rooms:	1
Seatings:	Open
Elevators:	0
Casino:	No
Slot Machines:	No
Swimming Pools (outdoors):	1
Swimming Pools (inside):	0
Whirlpools:	0
Fitness Center:	No
Sauna/Steam Room:	No/No
Massage:	No
Self-Service Launderette:	No
Movie Theater/Seats:	No
Library:	Yes
Children's Facilities:	No
Classification Society:	Germanischer Lloyd

Ratings	**Score**
Ship: Hardware/Maintenance	80
Ship: Outdoor Facilities/Space	78
Ship: Interior Facilities/Space/Flow	81
Ship: Decor/Furnishings/Artwork	82
Ship: Spa/Fitness Facilities	70
Cabins: Suites and Deluxe	86
Cabins: Standard Sizes	84
Food: Dining Room/Cuisine	84
Food: Informal Dining/Buffets	80
Food: Quality of Ingredients	81
Food: Afternoon Tea/Bar Snacks	80
Service: Dining Room	83
Service: Bars	83
Service: Cabins	84
Service: Open Decks	81
Cruise: Entertainment	76
Cruise: Activities Program	75
Cruise: Movies/Television Programming	82
Cruise: Hospitality Standard	80
Cruise: Overall Product Delivery	82
Overall Score	**1,612**

Accommodation: Has large cabins for ship size, and most are very comfortable, with big picture windows and VCR units. The bathrooms, which are enormous for the size of the ship, have clean, crisp colors. All cabins have unobstructed views, as well as a personal fax machine and refrigerator.

Dining: The dining room is charming, intimate, and very comfortable, with smart contemporary decor. The cuisine is Asian and International in style, and food is well prepared and nicely presented, although there is not a great deal of menu choice. Fine china and flatware.

Other Comments: This ship was built originally for the defunct Windsor Line and is a little like the Sea Goddess ships in style. Being small, she does roll in strong seas, however. Although there is no wraparound outdoor promenade deck, there are teakwood decks for strolling and real wooden "steamer" chairs. The swimming pool is tiny, however, as it is really a "dip" pool.

Inside, public room space is limited, but there is a warm friendly ambience. Wood-accented trim and fine soft furnishings, plush chairs and couches, and fresh flowers. Fine library, and karaoke room. This is strictly a private club at sea, for VIPs.

Rather like having the privileges of a private yacht, without the burden of ownership. This ship is ideal for small corporate charters and for high-roller gamblers, and operates year-round only on short cruises, based on Port Kelang, Malaysia. Port taxes are included.

ms MegaStar Taurus

☆☆☆☆ +

(S)

LIFESTYLE	**LUXURY**
Cruise Line:	Star Cruises
Former Names:	*Aurora II/Lady Sarah*
Gross Tonnage:	3,300
Builder:	Flender Werft (Germany)
Original Cost:	$35 million
Entered Service:	February 1992/January 1995
Flag:	Bahamas
Tel No:	1305151
Fax No:	1305154
Length (ft./m.):	269.6/82.2
Beam (ft./m.):	45.9/14.0
Draft (ft./m.):	10.9/3.3
Propulsion/Propellers:	diesel (3,356kW)/2 (CP)
Decks:	4
Total Crew:	59
Pass. Capacity (basis 2):	80
Pass. Capacity (all berths):	80
Pass. Space Ratio (basis 2):	41.2
Pass. Space Ratio (all berths):	41.2
Officers:	Scandinavian
Total Cabins:	44
Size Range (sq. ft./m.):	250–430/23.0–40.0
Cabins (outside view):	44
Cabins (inside):	0
Cabins (for one person):	6
Cabins (with private balcony):	0
Cabins (wheelchair accessible):	0
Cabin Current:	110/220 AC
Cabin TV:	Yes
Dining Rooms:	1
Seatings:	Open
Elevators:	0
Casino:	No
Slot Machines:	No
Swimming Pools (outdoors):	1
Swimming Pools (inside):	0
Whirlpools:	0
Fitness Center:	No
Sauna/Steam Room:	No/No
Massage:	No
Self-Service Launderette:	No
Movie Theater/Seats:	No
Library:	Yes
Children's Facilities:	No
Classification Society:	Germanischer Lloyd

RATINGS	**SCORE**
Ship: Hardware/Maintenance	80
Ship: Outdoor Facilities/Space	78
Ship: Interior Facilities/Space/Flow	81
Ship: Decor/Furnishings/Artwork	82
Ship: Spa/Fitness Facilities	70
Cabins: Suites and Deluxe	86
Cabins: Standard Sizes	84
Food: Dining Room/Cuisine	84
Food: Informal Dining/Buffets	80
Food: Quality of Ingredients	81
Food: Afternoon Tea/Bar Snacks	80
Service: Dining Room	83
Service: Bars	83
Service: Cabins	84
Service: Open Decks	81
Cruise: Entertainment	76
Cruise: Activities Program	75
Cruise: Movies/Television Programming	82
Cruise: Hospitality Standard	80
Cruise: Overall Product Delivery	82
OVERALL SCORE	**1,612**

Accommodation: The cabins really are quite large, have big picture windows, and are superbly equipped with fine woods, writing desk, fax machine, VCR player, and refrigerator. All cabins have unobstructed views, and bathrooms are large.

Dining: The dining room is charming, intimate, with smart contemporary decor. Asian/International cuisine. Food is well prepared and nicely presented.

Other Comments: This smart-looking ship has a low, sleek profile and royal blue hull. Designed for highly personal cruising. There is no wraparound outdoor promenade deck, although there are teakwood outdoor decks and real wooden "steamer" chairs.

There are limited public spaces, but good for VIPs seeking a private club ambience in new and highly sophisticated surroundings, with a small number of fellow high-rollers. Has a karaoke room.

She is one of a pair of exclusive identical ships (originally created for the defunct Windsor Line), comes with great style and fine personal service. Ideal for small corporate and incentive charters, and honeymoon groups, the ship operates only on short cruises, year-round, based on Port Kelang, Malaysia.

mv Melia Don Juan

☆☆☆

(S)

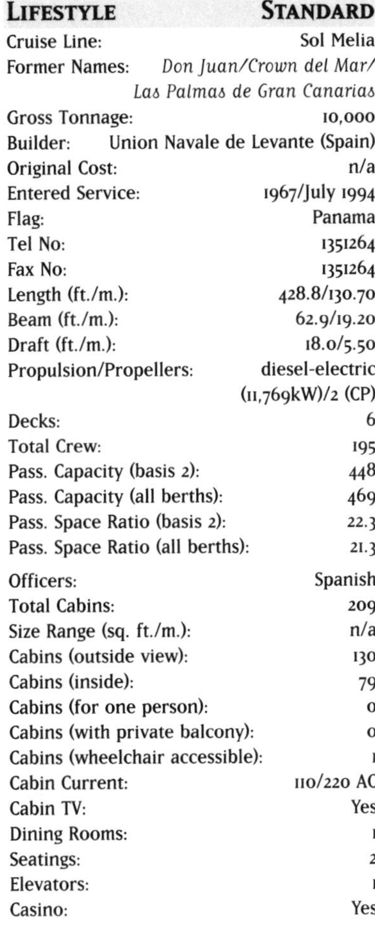

Lifestyle	Standard
Cruise Line:	Sol Melia
Former Names:	*Don Juan/Crown del Mar/ Las Palmas de Gran Canarias*
Gross Tonnage:	10,000
Builder:	Union Navale de Levante (Spain)
Original Cost:	n/a
Entered Service:	1967/July 1994
Flag:	Panama
Tel No:	1351264
Fax No:	1351264
Length (ft./m.):	428.8/130.70
Beam (ft./m.):	62.9/19.20
Draft (ft./m.):	18.0/5.50
Propulsion/Propellers:	diesel-electric (11,769kW)/2 (CP)
Decks:	6
Total Crew:	195
Pass. Capacity (basis 2):	448
Pass. Capacity (all berths):	469
Pass. Space Ratio (basis 2):	22.3
Pass. Space Ratio (all berths):	21.3
Officers:	Spanish
Total Cabins:	209
Size Range (sq. ft./m.):	n/a
Cabins (outside view):	130
Cabins (inside):	79
Cabins (for one person):	0
Cabins (with private balcony):	0
Cabins (wheelchair accessible):	1
Cabin Current:	110/220 AC
Cabin TV:	Yes
Dining Rooms:	1
Seatings:	2
Elevators:	1
Casino:	Yes
Slot Machines:	Yes
Swimming Pools (outdoors):	1
Swimming Pools (inside):	0
Whirlpools:	2
Fitness Center:	No
Sauna/Steam Room:	Yes/No
Massage:	Yes
Self-Service Launderette:	No
Movie Theater/Seats:	No
Library:	No
Children's Facilities:	Yes
Classification Society:	Lloyd's Register

Ratings	Score
Ship: Hardware/Maintenance	54
Ship: Outdoor Facilities/Space	51
Ship: Interior Facilities/Space/Flow	56
Ship: Decor/Furnishings/Artwork	54
Ship: Spa/Fitness Facilities	44
Cabins: Suites and Deluxe	62
Cabins: Standard Sizes	48
Food: Dining Room/Cuisine	62
Food: Informal Dining/Buffets	51
Food: Quality of Ingredients	56
Food: Afternoon Tea/Bar Snacks	44
Service: Dining Room	66
Service: Bars	65
Service: Cabins	65
Service: Open Decks	62
Cruise: Entertainment	53
Cruise: Activities Program	50
Cruise: Movies/Television Programming	42
Cruise: Hospitality Standard	57
Cruise: Overall Product Delivery	61
Overall Score	**1,103**

Accommodation: Five suites, located just below the navigation bridge, command forward views, are well furnished, and have full bathtubs (most other cabins have showers), but no balconies. The standard cabins are just about adequate at best, and have almost no drawer space, little closet space, and very small bathrooms.

Dining: The dining room is set low down and has ocean views, but it is a little dark and somber. There are no tables for two. The cuisine is barely adequate, and menu choice is limited. Reasonably attentive service staff throughout, but there is no finesse, and it is hard to communicate. Dining times are late (typically at 8 p.m. and 10 p.m.), but not late enough for the Spanish passengers.

Other Comments: Refurbished in 1994, this former Spanish ferry sports a more modern, though somewhat angular look. There is a decent amount of open deck space, but there are no cushioned pads for deck lounge chairs.

Inside, soft earth tones are used in the decor. There is a three-deck high atrium, with a circular staircase, but it is small. Most of the public rooms are set below accommodation decks, except for one forward observation lounge. The showroom is set between accommodation decks, which makes it noisy at night for some passenger cabins. Some flower bouquets would add warmth to the ambience.

This ship will provide a comfortable cruise experience, but forget the word "luxury," for this is quite basic. It represents good value, for Spanish-speaking passengers only who are not used to cruise ships. Based in Havana, Cuba.

mv Melody

☆☆☆ +

(L)

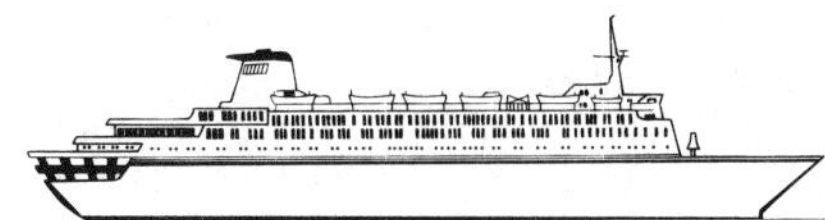

Lifestyle	**Standard**
Cruise Line:	Mediterranean Shipping Cruises
Former Names:	*Star/Ship Atlantic/Atlantic*
Gross Tonnage:	36,500
Builder:	C.N.I.M. (France)
Original Cost:	$100 million
Entered Service:	April 1982/June 1997
Flag:	Liberia
Tel No:	335315710/635315710
Fax No:	335315712/635315713
Length (ft./m.):	671.9/204.81
Beam (ft./m.):	89.7/27.36
Draft (ft./m.):	25.5/7.80
Propulsion/Propellers:	diesel (22,070kW)/2 (CP)
Decks:	9
Total Crew:	535
Pass. Capacity (basis 2):	1,098
Pass. Capacity (all berths):	1,600
Pass. Space Ratio (basis 2):	33.2
Pass. Space Ratio (all berths):	22.8
Officers:	Italian
Total Cabins:	549
Size Range (sq. ft./m.):	137.0–427.0/12.7–39.5
Cabins (outside view):	380
Cabins (inside):	169
Cabins (for one person):	0
Cabins (with private balcony):	0
Cabins (wheelchair accessible):	Yes
Cabin Current:	110 AC
Cabin TV:	No
Dining Rooms:	1
Seatings:	2
Elevators:	4
Casino:	Yes
Slot Machines:	Yes
Swimming Pools (outdoors):	1
Swimming Pools (inside):	1
Whirlpools:	3
Fitness Center:	Yes
Sauna/Steam Room:	Yes/No
Massage:	Yes
Self-Service Launderette:	No
Movie Theater/Seats:	Yes/251
Library:	Yes (2 book racks)
Children's Facilities:	Yes
Classification Society:	American Bureau of Shipping

Ratings	**Score**
Ship: Hardware/Maintenance	75
Ship: Outdoor Facilities/Space	69
Ship: Interior Facilities/Space/Flow	69
Ship: Decor/Furnishings/Artwork	68
Ship: Spa/Fitness Facilities	73
Cabins: Suites and Deluxe	77
Cabins: Standard Sizes	73
Food: Dining Room/Cuisine	60
Food: Informal Dining/Buffets	55
Food: Quality of Ingredients	57
Food: Afternoon Tea/Bar Snacks	43
Service: Dining Room	63
Service: Bars	61
Service: Cabins	62
Service: Open Decks	55
Cruise: Entertainment	62
Cruise: Activities Program	57
Cruise: Movies/Television Programming	54
Cruise: Hospitality Standard	60
Cruise: Overall Product Delivery	66
Overall Score	**1,259**

Accommodation: Six suites have plenty of space for families of four, and feature a decent walk-in closet. The bathroom is large and has a full-size bathtub, oversize sink (large enough to bathe twins in), and an uncomfortable square toilet.

Other cabins (both outside and inside) are of a good size, and have ample closet and drawer space. Many cabins have upper berths—good for families, although with four persons there would be little space for anything else, such as luggage. The cabin insulation is extremely poor, however, and the room service menu is quite basic.

Dining: The dining room, located on a lower deck, is large and quite attractive, but the tables are much too close together, and it is difficult for waiters to serve properly. Also, the chairs do not have armrests, and the noise level is extremely high. The cuisine is Italian and the food quality generally is adequate for the price paid, but do not expect much finesse. There is a limited wine list.

There is good basic service provided by an attentive multi-national staff. The buffets are quite poor, however, in comparison with many other ships in this standard category.

Other Comments: This ship (originally built for the now defunct Home Lines, then operated by Premier Cruise Line) has a short, stubby bow and squat funnel. Her hull is all in white.

There is a good amount of outdoor deck space, but noise levels can be high when the ship is full, and there are many families with children.

The interior is quite spacious, with plenty of public rooms, most of which have high ceilings. The decor is somewhat somber in places, and lighting is very subdued. There is a generous amount of stainless steel and teak wood trim. A large observation lounge is wasted as an informal eating area. There is a good indoor-outdoor pool area (covered by a magrodome in inclement weather).

For families, there is a reasonable children's program during the peak periods, and several children's (and teens) counselors. In any event, this ship (the largest in the MSC fleet so far) will provide a good basic cruise experience for families, at a fair price, in comfortable, modern surroundings, in typical MSC style, and that means lots of extra charges. Typically about 60 percent of passengers will be Italian, while the rest may be a mix of other Europeans.

<u>But:</u> The almost constant, loud, and repetitive announcements are annoying and intrusive, particularly when the ship is in port. There is no wraparound outdoor promenade deck, nor are cushioned pads provided for the deck lounge chairs. Just four elevators for this number of passengers is simply not enough.

ms Mercury

☆☆☆☆☆

(L)

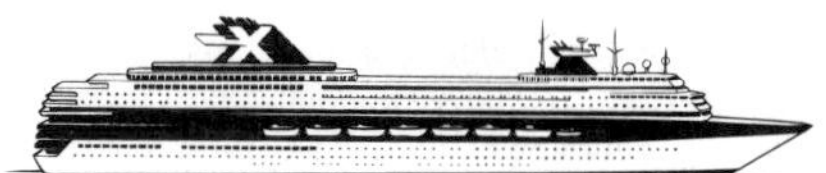

Lifestyle	**Premium**
Cruise Line:	Celebrity Cruises
Former Names:	-
Gross Tonnage:	76,522
Builder:	Meyer Werft (Germany)
Original Cost:	$320 million
Entered Service:	November 1997
Flag:	Liberia
Tel No:	335151711/335151721
Fax No:	335151712/335151722
Length (ft./m.):	865.8/263.90
Beam (ft./m.):	105.6/32.20
Draft (ft./m.):	25.2/7.70 (24.2/7.40)
Propulsion/Propellers:	diesel 31,500kW/2 (CP)
Decks:	10
Total Crew:	900
Pass. Capacity (basis 2):	1,896 (1,908)
Pass. Capacity (all berths):	2,681 (2,262)
Pass. Space Ratio (basis 2):	40.3 (38.7)
Pass. Space Ratio (all berths):	28.5 (32.6)
Officers:	Greek
Total Cabins:	948 (954)
Size Range (sq. ft./m.):	172–1,515/15.7–140.7
Cabins (outside view):	639 (650)
Cabins (inside):	309 (304)
Cabins (for one person):	0
Cabins (with private balcony):	220
Cabins (wheelchair accessible):	8
Cabin Current:	110/220 AC
Cabin TV:	Yes
Dining Rooms:	2
Seatings:	2
Elevators:	10
Casino:	Yes
Slot Machines:	Yes
Swimming Pools (outdoors):	2
Swimming Pools (inside):	1 indoor/outdoor (magrodome)
Whirlpools:	3
Fitness Center:	Yes
Sauna/Steam Room:	Yes
Massage:	Yes
Self-Service Launderette:	No
Movie Theater/Seats:	Yes/
Library:	Yes
Children's Facilities:	Yes
Classification Society:	Lloyd's Register

Ratings	**Score**
Ship: Hardware/Maintenance	91
Ship: Outdoor Facilities/Space	91
Ship: Interior Facilities/Space/Flow	91
Ship: Decor/Furnishings/Artwork	91
Ship: Spa/Fitness Facilities	90
Cabins: Suites and Deluxe	93
Cabins: Standard Sizes	89
Food: Dining Room/Cuisine	85
Food: Informal Dining/Buffets	82
Food: Quality of Ingredients	86
Food: Afternoon Tea/Bar Snacks	73
Service: Dining Room	85
Service: Bars	80
Service: Cabins	82
Service: Open Decks	78
Cruise: Entertainment	84
Cruise: Activities Program	73
Cruise: Movies/Television Programming	85
Cruise: Hospitality Standard	83
Cruise: Overall Product Delivery	90
Overall Score	**1,702**

Accommodation: The accommodation is extremely comfortable throughout this ship, regardless of which cabin grade you choose. Naturally, if you choose a suite you will find more space, butler service (whether you want it or not), more and better amenities and more personal service than if you choose any of the standard cabin grades.

Occupants of all accommodation designated as suites (Deck 12, Deck 10) get gold cards to open their doors (these also help to get you priority service throughout the ship, free cappuccino/espresso coffees served by a butler, welcome champagne, flowers, VCR unit, and use of the AquaSpa thalassotherapy pool); all occupants of standard (inside and outside) cabins have white cards. Suites that have private balconies also have floor-to-ceiling windows and sliding doors to balconies (a few suites have outward opening doors).

There are 2 Presidential Suites, located amidships. These provide spectacular living spaces, perhaps even better than those in *Century* and *Galaxy*, depending on your personal taste. There is a separate bedroom (with high-tech Sony multimedia entertainment center), large lounge (complete with dining table), huge walk-in closet with mountains of drawers, and king-sized marble-tiled bathroom.

There is in-suite dining for the 2 Presidential and 12 Century Suites, as well as for the 24 Sky Suites (1202/1203/1236/1237 have enormous fully private balconies, while the others are only semi-private). All suites feature full butler service, personalized stationery, and business cards. If you choose one of the forwardmost Sky Deck suites, however, be warned that you may well be subject to constant music and noise from the pool deck (one deck below) between 8 a.m. and 6 p.m. (not good if you want to relax). The closet and drawer space provided in these suites is superb. In the bathrooms of the Sky Suites, the shaving mirror is positioned too high, and the television cannot be viewed from the bed. Push-button bell and privacy curtains should be, but are not, provided. In-suite massage is available (this really is pleasant when provided on the balcony of the Sky Suites).

The standard (inside and outside) cabins are quite spacious and nicely decorated with cheerful fabrics, and marble-topped vanity unit. The bathrooms are generous with space, tiled from floor to ceiling, and the power showers are extremely practical units.

All grades of accommodation feature interactive television for booking shore excursions, ordering cabin service items and purchasing goods from the ship's boutiques, so you do not have to leave your quarters if you do not wish to, especially if you do not like the ports of call (the system works in English, French, German, Italian, and Spanish). There are five channels of music, all available from the television, therefore you cannot have music without having a picture). All cabins are also equipped with a "baby monitoring telephone system" which allows you to telephone your cabin whilst you are elsewhere aboard ship, and to have a two-way intercom to "listen in." Automatic "wake-up" calls can also be dialed in. All accommodation designated as suites have duvets on the beds instead of sheets/blankets.

Dining: The two-level formal dining room, located at the ship's stern, is really grand and elegant (each level has its own full galley); a grand staircase connects the two levels. Large picture windows look out to sea on three sides; at night, large blinds (with scenes of Manhattan, the name of the dining room) roll down electronically to cover the stern-facing windows. The same excellent cuisine that has made Celebrity Cruises the shining star of the contemporary cruise industry is directed by three-star Michelin chef, Michel Roux. The menus are creative, and the food is very attractively presented. There is also an excellent wine list, and real wine waiters (unlike so many other large ship companies), although prices are high (particularly for good champagne), and the wine vintages are young—very young.

There are also several informal dining spots as an alternative to the main dining room: a Lido Café, with four main serving lines; a poolside grill, and another indoor/outdoor grill located b the aft swimming pool. The Lido Café has fine wood paneling and is much more elegant than the informal dining areas found aboard most ships today, and has some seating in bay window areas with great ocean views.

In the center of the ship is Tastings, a delightful coffee/tea lounge; in one corner is a presentation of goodies made by COVA, the chocolatier from Milan—an exclusive to Celebrity Cruises.

Finally, for those that cannot live without them, freshly baked pizzas (in a box) can be ordered and delivered, in an insulated pouch, to your cabin.

Other Comments: She is quite a stunning ship, both inside and outside. As aboard her identical sister, *Galaxy*, there is an excellent 1,000-seat show lounge, with side balconies, and no pillars to obstruct views (there are three high-tech "dazzle and sizzle" production shows per seven-day cruise, although they consist mainly of running, jumping, smoke, colored laser lighting, and little story line intelligence); a three-deck-high main foyer with marble floored lobby and waterfall; over 4.5 acres of open deck space (poolside lounge chairs have cushioned pads, those on other decks do not); a magrodome-covered indoor-outdoor pool; AquaSpa thalassotherapy pool (with several "active" water jet stations), and assorted treatment rooms, including a "rasul" mud treatment room; "Michael's Club" cigar/cognac room overlooking the atrium; a small but luxurious cinema; a large casino (this is extremely glitzy, and the layout is confusing and congested); and excellent children's facilities (open until 10:00 p.m., it is called the "Fun Factory") as well as an outdoor play area and paddling pool.

The decor includes plenty of wood (or wood-look) paneling and accenting throughout, and many refinements have been made during the three-ship "Century Series" that Celebrity Cruises has introduced in the past few years. The ship also houses a $3.5-million living art collection with true, museum-quality pieces. The health/fitness facilities are among the nicest aboard any ship, and has been well thought out and designed for quiet, efficient operation, with everything in just the right place.

This ship will provide you with a finely packaged cruise vacation in elegant surroundings. The ship is efficiently run. There are many more staff per passengers than would be found aboard other ships of the same size in the premium category, and hence service in general is very good indeed.

But: Trying to get Cabin Service, or the Guest Relations Desk to answer the phone (to order breakfast, for example, if you don't want to do so via the interactive television) is a matter of luck, timing and patience (a sad reminder of the automated age, and lack of personal contact). The library is disappointingly small, and poorly located away from the main flow of passengers. There is a charge for using the Aquaspa/sauna/steam room complex. The room-service menu is poor, and food items are decidedly below the standard of food featured in the dining room.

While under the direction of its former owner John Chandris, Celebrity Cruises managed to create a superb quality cruise vacation product virtually unbeatable at the prices charged in the Alaska and Caribbean markets, representing outstanding value for money. However, given the subtle changes that have occurred since Celebrity Cruises was integrated into the Royal Caribbean International family in late 1997, it has become evident that slippage of product delivery standards has occurred, and the latest score reflects these changes.

ms Mermoz

☆☆ +

(M)

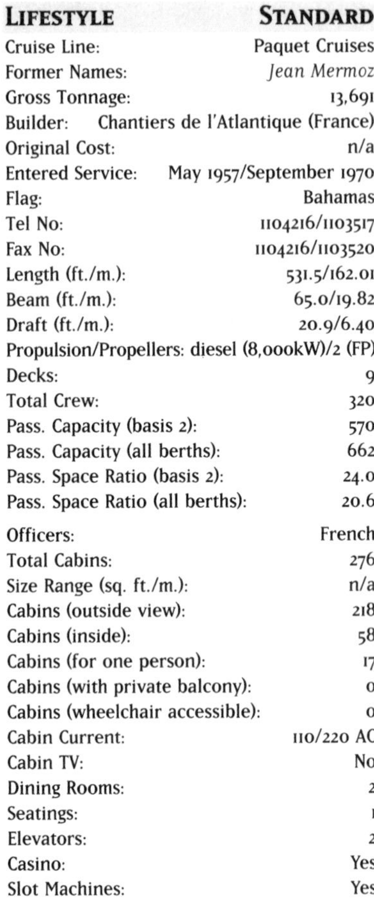

Lifestyle	Standard
Cruise Line:	Paquet Cruises
Former Names:	*Jean Mermoz*
Gross Tonnage:	13,691
Builder:	Chantiers de l'Atlantique (France)
Original Cost:	n/a
Entered Service:	May 1957/September 1970
Flag:	Bahamas
Tel No:	1104216/1103517
Fax No:	1104216/1103520
Length (ft./m.):	531.5/162.01
Beam (ft./m.):	65.0/19.82
Draft (ft./m.):	20.9/6.40
Propulsion/Propellers:	diesel (8,000kW)/2 (FP)
Decks:	9
Total Crew:	320
Pass. Capacity (basis 2):	570
Pass. Capacity (all berths):	662
Pass. Space Ratio (basis 2):	24.0
Pass. Space Ratio (all berths):	20.6
Officers:	French
Total Cabins:	276
Size Range (sq. ft./m.):	n/a
Cabins (outside view):	218
Cabins (inside):	58
Cabins (for one person):	17
Cabins (with private balcony):	0
Cabins (wheelchair accessible):	0
Cabin Current:	110/220 AC
Cabin TV:	No
Dining Rooms:	2
Seatings:	1
Elevators:	2
Casino:	Yes
Slot Machines:	Yes
Swimming Pools (outdoors):	2
Swimming Pools (inside):	0
Whirlpools:	Yes
Fitness Center:	No
Sauna/Steam Room:	Yes/No
Massage:	Yes
Self-Service Launderette:	No
Movie Theater/Seats:	Yes/240
Library:	Yes
Children's Facilities:	No
Classification Society:	Bureau Veritas

Ratings	Score
Ship: Hardware/Maintenance	44
Ship: Outdoor Facilities/Space	53
Ship: Interior Facilities/Space/Flow	52
Ship: Decor/Furnishings/Artwork	54
Ship: Spa/Fitness Facilities	48
Cabins: Suites and Deluxe	57
Cabins: Standard Sizes	48
Food: Dining Room/Cuisine	68
Food: Informal Dining/Buffets	55
Food: Quality of Ingredients	61
Food: Afternoon Tea/Bar Snacks	51
Service: Dining Room	64
Service: Bars	61
Service: Cabins	62
Service: Open Decks	50
Cruise: Entertainment	56
Cruise: Activities Program	37
Cruise: Movies/Television Programming	35
Cruise: Hospitality Standard	56
Cruise: Overall Product Delivery	58
Overall Score	**1,070**

Accommodation: The cabins are quite small and only equipped with basic facilities, but they are tastefully furnished, cozy and comfortable, with solid fixtures and lots of wood everywhere, and all have lower beds. There is a fair amount of closet and drawer space, but the cabin bathrooms are very small (and there is little room for storage of toiletry items). Bathrobes are provided for all passengers.

Dining: The cuisine has changed a little since its Paquet Cruises days (pre-1994). There is a fine grill room (Renaissance Grill), with wicker furniture, as well as the regular dining room (named Massalia after one of Paquet Cruises' former ships). The food is very creatively presented. There is also a very extensive wine cellar containing many thousands of bottles, and wine is complimentary with dinner.

Other Comments: The ship has traditional 1950s lines, and a now very dated profile. There is a reasonable amount of open deck and sunbathing space, however, for sun-loving French passengers.

Delightfully chic art deco-style interior decor, which is rather eclectic, with a pastel color scheme throughout and a real "colonial" ambience feel. Quaint and typically French in atmosphere and fine service. The spa and solarium are good spaces, with a main emphasis on hydrotherapy treatments.

The annual Classical Music Festival At Sea is a real cultural delight for classical music and opera buffs, but it is extremely hard to get tickets for this special cruise. Much of the artwork and ship models are of interest to ship lovers. Sadly, there is no forward observation lounge.

This ship has a fine, perhaps somewhat eclectic French character, and is for those who enjoy being aboard an older ship, with all its quirks and idiosyncracies, albeit for a moderate price. Dress is casual during the day, but very dressy at night. Sadly she is getting a bit long in the tooth and should be replaced soon. However, she is still one of the only French-flag ships still operating, so French passengers continue to sail aboard her. The currency on board is French francs.

mv Minerva

☆☆☆☆ +

(S)

Lifestyle	**Premium**
Cruise Line:	Swan Hellenic Cruises
Former Names:	-
Gross Tonnage:	12,500
Builder:	Marriotti (Italy)
Original Cost:	n/a
Entered Service:	April 1996
Flag:	Bahamas
Tel No:	630947710
Fax No:	630947711
Length (ft./m.):	436.3/133.0
Beam (ft./m.):	65.6/20.0
Draft (ft./m.):	19.6/6.0
Propulsion/Propellers:	2 x diesels/2 (CP)
Decks:	6
Total Crew:	157
Pass. Capacity (basis 2):	344
Pass. Capacity (all berths):	474
Pass. Space Ratio (basis 2):	36.3
Pass. Space Ratio (all berths):	26.3
Officers:	European
Total Cabins:	170
Size Range (sq. ft./m.):	140.1–277.0/ 13.02–25.74
Cabins (outside view):	136
Cabins (inside):	34
Cabins (for one person):	4
Cabins (with private balcony):	12
Cabins (wheelchair accessible):	4
Cabin Current:	220 AC
Cabin TV:	Yes
Dining Rooms:	1
Seatings:	Open seating
Elevators:	2
Casino:	No
Slot Machines:	No
Swimming Pools (outdoors):	1
Swimming Pools (inside):	0
Whirlpools:	0
Fitness Center:	Yes
Sauna/Steam Room:	Yes/No
Massage:	Yes
Self-Service Launderette:	Yes
Movie Theater/Seats:	Yes/300
Library:	Yes
Children's Facilities:	No
Classification Society:	Lloyds Register

Ratings	**Score**
Ship: Hardware/Maintenance	90
Ship: Outdoor Facilities/Space	87
Ship: Interior Facilities/Space/Flow	90
Ship: Decor/Furnishings/Artwork	93
Ship: Spa/Fitness Facilities	78
Cabins: Suites and Deluxe	85
Cabins: Standard Sizes	82
Food: Dining Room/Cuisine	80
Food: Informal Dining/Buffets	76
Food: Quality of Ingredients	75
Food: Afternoon Tea/Bar Snacks	75
Service: Dining Room	78
Service: Bars	77
Service: Cabins	77
Service: Open Decks	76
Cruise: Entertainment	80
Cruise: Activities Program	78
Cruise: Movies/Television Programming	76
Cruise: Hospitality Standard	85
Cruise: Overall Product Delivery	88
Overall Score	**1,626**

Accommodation: The range of accommodation is well thought out, and all have excellent closet and storage space; the suites and deluxe cabins also feature a refrigerator. The cabin bathrooms are totally white, and have showers (except for the suites, which have bathtubs and green/black marble floors), but the plumbing fixtures were poorly installed. Cabin electrical sockets are of the standard English, square, three-pin type. Hair dryers are provided in all suites, and are available on request in all other cabins. All suite occupants are provided with high-powered binoculars. However, there is no "privacy curtain" between entryway and sleeping area in the suites.

Dining: Features open seating dining (dine with whomever you wish) in both the main restaurant and the informal indoor/outdoor cafe. The menus are quite simple, but the food is attractively presented and has good taste. Service is provided by an East European and Filippino staff. Some "quiet tables" are provided for breakfast for those who like to eat without talking—a welcome touch. Coffee and tea are available twenty-four hours a day in the self-service Bridge Cafe.

Other Comments: Originally intended to be a spy ship for the Soviet navy, the keel was purchased by V-Ships (the ship's present owners), who then took the hull to Italy, where she was converted into a ship specifically tailored to the requirements of Swan Hellenic Cruises as charterer. She replaced Orpheus, which Swan Hellenic had chartered for the previous 21 years. She has a well-balanced profile, with a single, central funnel. There is ample open and shaded deck space for this size ship, and a teakwood wraparound promenade deck.

Inside, there is an excellent selection of public rooms that includes a vast, well-stocked library, with its classical themed decor. The decor generally is contemporary, yet restrained (for European passengers with good taste). Cigar smokers will appreciate the special smoking room and humidor service; the high back leather chairs provide an air of exclusivity.

The ship has fine wool carpets throughout, with an Oriental motif running through the passageways and public rooms. Perhaps the most used public room in the ship is the library, with its fine range of reference books (many of university standard). Passengers take delight in the multitude of puzzles and games, and jigsaw puzzles galore. The reception desk is manned 24 hours a day.

Perhaps the most striking detail of interior decoration is the outstanding array of artwork aboard this ship. It is everywhere, in all passageways, on stairwells, in all public rooms, and cabins. Most of it has been provided by Swan Hellenic passengers, and more is being added all the time. The one disappointment is in the plain white ceilings in the public rooms.

This really is cruising for the intelligent who yearns to learn more about life and times in civilizations past and present, albeit in a refined, comfortable setting. Features well-planned, in-depth itineraries and shore excursions (the majority of which are included in the cruise fare) accompanied by some fine lecturers, and all gratuities and shore excursions are included (these are carried out with almost military precision). Note that this ship is not for children.

ms Mistral

(L)

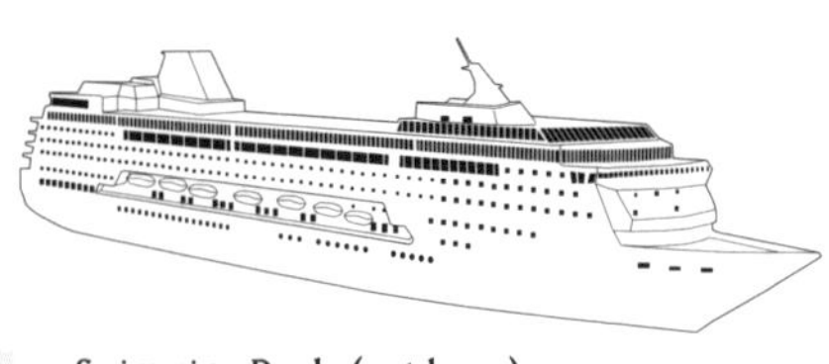

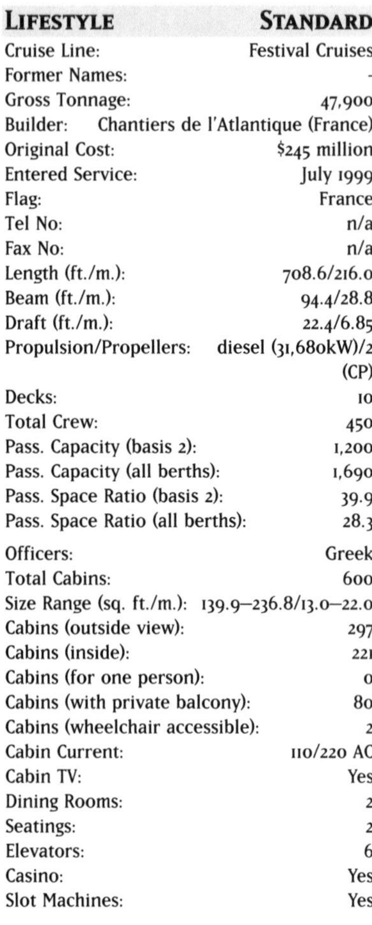

LIFESTYLE	**STANDARD**
Cruise Line:	Festival Cruises
Former Names:	-
Gross Tonnage:	47,900
Builder:	Chantiers de l'Atlantique (France)
Original Cost:	$245 million
Entered Service:	July 1999
Flag:	France
Tel No:	n/a
Fax No:	n/a
Length (ft./m.):	708.6/216.0
Beam (ft./m.):	94.4/28.8
Draft (ft./m.):	22.4/6.85
Propulsion/Propellers:	diesel (31,680kW)/2 (CP)
Decks:	10
Total Crew:	450
Pass. Capacity (basis 2):	1,200
Pass. Capacity (all berths):	1,690
Pass. Space Ratio (basis 2):	39.9
Pass. Space Ratio (all berths):	28.3
Officers:	Greek
Total Cabins:	600
Size Range (sq. ft./m.):	139.9–236.8/13.0–22.0
Cabins (outside view):	297
Cabins (inside):	221
Cabins (for one person):	0
Cabins (with private balcony):	80
Cabins (wheelchair accessible):	2
Cabin Current:	110/220 AC
Cabin TV:	Yes
Dining Rooms:	2
Seatings:	2
Elevators:	6
Casino:	Yes
Slot Machines:	Yes

Swimming Pools (outdoors):	1
Swimming Pools (inside):	0
Whirlpools:	1 (thalassotherapy)
Fitness Center:	Yes
Sauna/Steam Room:	Yes/Yes
Massage:	Yes
Self-Service Launderette:	No
Movie Theater/Seats:	No
Library:	Yes
Children's Facilities:	Yes
Classification Society:	Bureau Veritas

RATINGS	**SCORE**
Ship: Hardware/Maintenance	NYR
Ship: Outdoor Facilities/Space	NYR
Ship: Interior Facilities/Space/Flow	NYR
Ship: Decor/Furnishings/Artwork	NYR
Ship: Spa/Fitness Facilities	NYR
Cabins: Suites and Deluxe	NYR
Cabins: Standard Sizes	NYR
Food: Dining Room/Cuisine	NYR
Food: Informal Dining/Buffets	NYR
Food: Quality of Ingredients	NYR
Food: Afternoon Tea/Bar Snacks	NYR
Service: Dining Room	NYR
Service: Bars	NYR
Service: Cabins	NYR
Service: Open Decks	NYR
Cruise: Entertainment	NYR
Cruise: Activities Program	NYR
Cruise: Movies/Television Programming	NYR
Cruise: Hospitality Standard	NYR
Cruise: Overall Product Delivery	NYR

EXPECTED SCORE RANGE
1,400-1,700

Accommodation: There are three basic cabin types: suites (there are 80 of these, each of which has a private balcony), ocean-view standard cabins, and inside standard cabins. In addition, there are 2 ocean-view wheelchair accessible cabins for the handicapped.

All of the cabins feature twin beds that convert to a queen-sized unit, personal safe, color television/VCR combination, and telephone, and a good amount of closet and drawer space for a one-week cruise. The bathrooms, although not large, do have a good-sized shower stall, and storage space for personal toiletry items.

Dining: There are two dining rooms, which can be configured in any of several different ways. The principal dining room, which seats 600, has tables for two, four, six or eight. The second dining room, with seats for 300, will be used for both informal meals and as an alternative restaurant, and has tables for two, four or six. The food offered by Festival Cruises is surprisingly good, and, with varied menus and extremely fine presentation, should prove a highlight for most passengers. The wine list is quite good, and features a wide variety of wines at reasonable prices.

Other Comments: This is an all-white ship, with a single blue funnel, and is the first newbuild for this growing Greece-based cruise line, which caters almost exclusively to European passengers. While the ship is actually owned by a consortium of French investors, she is being operated under a long-term charter agreement by Festival Cruises, a young company that is growing rapidly. She is now the largest ship sailing under the French flag. The ship's profile is similar to that of an enlarged version of the Silversea Cruises' vessels.

The lido deck surrounding the outdoor swimming pool also features Jacuzzi whirlpool tubs and a large bandstand set in raised canvas-covered pods. All the deck lounge chairs have cushioned pads.

Inside, the layout and passenger flow is generally very sound, as are the deck ("you are here") signs. The interior décor is light and cheerful without being glitzy in any way, with much use of blond wood paneling and rich, textured soft furnishings. The deck names are those of European capitals. There is also a smoking room, which has all the hallmarks of a gentleman's club. The library has real writing desks (something many ships seem to omit today). High atop the ship is a forward-view observation lounge, which also doubles as a discotheque for the late at night set.

The ship operates seven-day Mediterranean cruises from Italy during the summer and fall, and seven-day Caribbean cruises during the winter. As the ship will operate in several languages (remember that this means all announcements will be in several languages also), a good number of multi-lingual cruise staff will be featured.

But: There is no wraparound outdoor promenade deck, although there is a partial walking deck under the lifeboats, as well as an oval jogging track atop ship.

ms Monarch of the Seas

☆☆☆☆

(L)

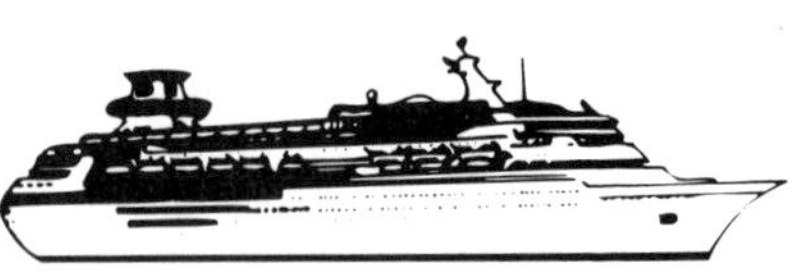

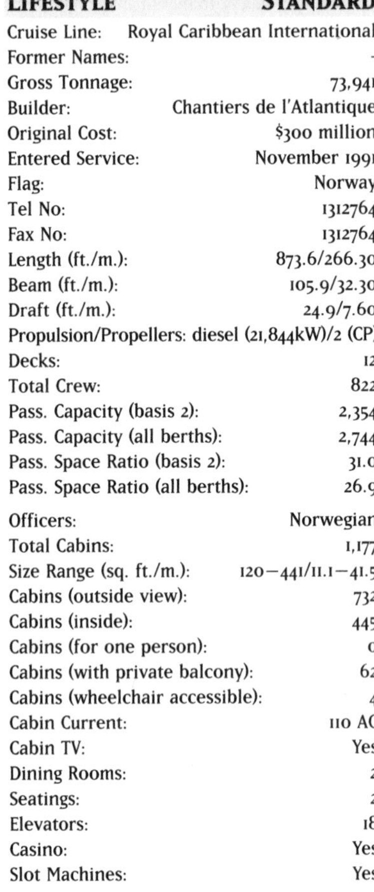

Lifestyle	**Standard**
Cruise Line:	Royal Caribbean International
Former Names:	-
Gross Tonnage:	73,941
Builder:	Chantiers de l'Atlantique
Original Cost:	$300 million
Entered Service:	November 1991
Flag:	Norway
Tel No:	1312764
Fax No:	1312764
Length (ft./m.):	873.6/266.30
Beam (ft./m.):	105.9/32.30
Draft (ft./m.):	24.9/7.60
Propulsion/Propellers:	diesel (21,844kW)/2 (CP)
Decks:	12
Total Crew:	822
Pass. Capacity (basis 2):	2,354
Pass. Capacity (all berths):	2,744
Pass. Space Ratio (basis 2):	31.0
Pass. Space Ratio (all berths):	26.9
Officers:	Norwegian
Total Cabins:	1,177
Size Range (sq. ft./m.):	120–441/11.1–41.5
Cabins (outside view):	732
Cabins (inside):	445
Cabins (for one person):	0
Cabins (with private balcony):	62
Cabins (wheelchair accessible):	4
Cabin Current:	110 AC
Cabin TV:	Yes
Dining Rooms:	2
Seatings:	2
Elevators:	18
Casino:	Yes
Slot Machines:	Yes
Swimming Pools (outdoors):	2
Swimming Pools (inside):	0
Whirlpools:	2
Fitness Center:	Yes
Sauna/Steam Room:	Yes/No
Massage:	Yes
Self-Service Launderette:	No
Movie Theater/Seats:	Yes-2/146 each
Library:	Yes
Children's Facilities:	Yes
Classification Society:	Det Norske Veritas

Ratings	**Score**
Ship: Hardware/Maintenance	77
Ship: Outdoor Facilities/Space	78
Ship: Interior Facilities/Space/Flow	80
Ship: Decor/Furnishings/Artwork	78
Ship: Spa/Fitness Facilities	72
Cabins: Suites and Deluxe	76
Cabins: Standard Sizes	70
Food: Dining Room/Cuisine	70
Food: Informal Dining/Buffets	60
Food: Quality of Ingredients	66
Food: Afternoon Tea/Bar Snacks	52
Service: Dining Room	75
Service: Bars	72
Service: Cabins	73
Service: Open Decks	66
Cruise: Entertainment	76
Cruise: Activities Program	70
Cruise: Movies/Television Programming	72
Cruise: Hospitality Standard	68
Cruise: Overall Product Delivery	77
Overall Score	**1,428**

Accommodation: This ship has small cabins, but the company's philosophy is that you will not spend much time in your cabin. The suites are quite spacious, but most cabins are small, comfortable and attractively decorated, except for the very plain ceilings. Special "family suites," located amidships, sleep four. The in-cabin food service menu is quite poor (too much standardization).

Dining: The two musical-themed dining rooms are large (sadly, there are no tables for two), but have consistently good (but fast) service and reasonable banquet food (nothing is memorable). Most nights are themed (French, Oriental, Italian, Caribbean, American), as they have been for years, with waiters and busboys in appropriate costumes. Features dessert parades. The wine list is average.

Other Comments: Almost identical in size and appearance to sister *Sovereign of the Seas*, but with improved internal layout, public room features, passenger flow, and signs. Surprisingly stable and smooth sailing. Many public rooms to choose from. RCI's trademark Viking Crown lounge and bar surrounds funnel and provides a stunning view. A five-deck-high atrium is the interior focal point, as well as the glass elevators. Exceptionally fine library. Has good children's and teens' programs and counselors, and a busy but good entertainment program.

Monarch of the Seas provides excellent facilities, with consistently good, well operated but highly programmed service from an attentive, though rather insensitive staff.

But: There are too many announcements.

my Monet
(S)

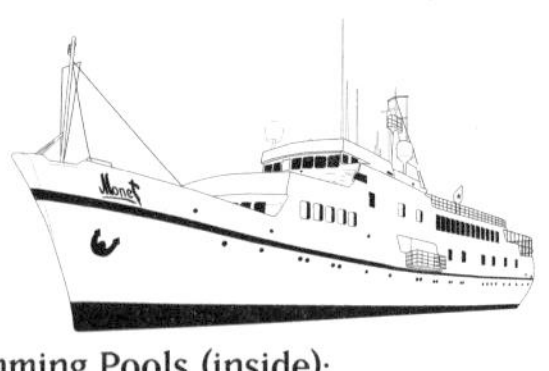

Lifestyle	**Premium**
Cruise Line:	Leisure Cruises
Former Names:	-
Gross Tonnage:	1,395
Builder:	Brodoremont Shipyard (Croatia)
Original Cost:	n/a
Entered Service:	May 1998
Flag:	Malta
Tel No:	n/a
Fax No:	n/a
Length (ft./m.):	223.4/68.1
Beam (ft./m.):	33.1/10.1
Draft (ft./m.):	11.5/3.5
Propulsion/Propellers:	diesel (1,000kW)/1 (CP)
Decks:	4
Total Crew:	29
Pass. Capacity (basis 2):	56
Pass. Capacity (all berths):	58
Pass. Space Ratio (basis 2):	24.9
Pass. Space Ratio (all berths):	24.0
Officers:	Croatian
Total Cabins:	26
Size Range (sq. ft./m.):	92.0–151.0/8.5–14.0
Cabins (outside view):	26
Cabins (inside—no view):	0
Cabins (single occupancy):	0
Cabins (with private balcony):	0
Cabins (wheelchair accessible):	0
Cabin Current:	220 AC
Cabin TV:	Yes
Dining Rooms:	1
Seatings:	1
Elevators:	0
Casino:	No
Slot Machines:	No
Swimming Pools (outdoors):	1 (splash pool)
Swimming Pools (inside):	0
Whirlpools:	2
Fitness Center:	Yes
Sauna/Steam Room:	No/No
Massage:	No
Self-Service Launderette:	No
Movie Theater/Seats:	No
Library:	Yes
Children's Facilities:	No
Classification Society:	Bureau Veritas

Ratings	**Score**
Ship: Hardware/Maintenance	NYR
Ship: Outdoor Facilities/Space	NYR
Ship: Interior Facilities/Space/Flow	NYR
Ship: Decor/Furnishings/Artwork	NYR
Ship: Spa/Fitness Facilities	NYR
Cabins: Suites and Deluxe	NYR
Cabins: Standard Sizes	NYR
Food: Dining Room/Cuisine	NYR
Food: Informal Dining/Buffets	NYR
Food: Quality of Ingredients	NYR
Food: Afternoon Tea/Bar Snacks	NYR
Service: Dining Room	NYR
Service: Bars	NYR
Service: Cabins	NYR
Service: Open Decks	NYR
Cruise: Entertainment	NYR
Cruise: Activities Program	NYR
Cruise: Movies/Television Programming	NYR
Cruise: Hospitality Standard	NYR
Cruise: Overall Product Deliver	NYR

Expected Score Range: 1,100-1,500

Accommodation: The all-outside cabins come in four size categories. All of them feature hardwood cabinetry and fine soft furnishings, television and VCR unit, multiple music channels, telephone, hairdryer, and vanity desk with lighted mirror. All have lower beds, in either a twin bed or double bed arrangement (two cabins can accommodate three persons) and a tiny bathroom with shower. There is also one owner's suite.

Dining: The dining room, which has large square ocean-view picture windows, is intimate and quite charming, although the decor and colors are a light and contemporary. Meals are cooked individually to order—no mass catering here.

Other Comments: *Monet* (how different having a ship named after an immortal French artist) is a new, small, all-white vessel, and is good for for up-close, in-depth coastal cruising. Carries one Zodiac inflatable landing craft.

Her interior decor is quite charming, with warm colors used throughout her limited public spaces, and brass and chrome on her stairways. The housekeeping staff is from the Philippines.

She is presently being operated on behalf of Leisure Cruises, a Switzerland-based company that also operates the larger ms Switzerland. She operates Mediterranean cruises during the summer months. The dress code is totally relaxed, and informality rules. Nice little ship for those who do not like lines, hubbub, or crowds.

ss *Monterey*

☆☆ +

(M)

Lifestyle	**Standard**
Cruise Line:	Mediterranean Shipping Cruises
Former Names:	*Free State Mariner*
Gross Tonnage:	21,051
Builder:	Bethlehem Steel Corp. (USA)
Original Cost:	n/a
Entered Service:	December 1952/August 1988
Flag:	Panama
Tel No:	1333517
Fax No:	1333522
Length (ft./m.):	563.6/171.81
Beam (ft./m.):	76.3/23.27
Draft (ft./m.):	29.3/8.95
Propulsion/Propellers:	steam turbine (14,400kW)/1 (FP)
Decks:	4
Total Crew:	280
Pass. Capacity (basis 2):	600
Pass. Capacity (all berths):	638
Pass. Space Ratio (basis 2):	35.0
Pass. Space Ratio (all berths):	32.9
Officers:	Italian
Total Cabins:	300
Size Range (sq. ft./m.):	64.5–344.4/6.5–32.0
Cabins (outside view):	171
Cabins (inside):	129
Cabins (for one person):	0
Cabins (with private balcony):	0
Cabins (wheelchair accessible):	0
Cabin Current:	110 AC
Cabin TV:	Suites only
Dining Rooms:	1
Seatings:	2
Elevators:	2
Casino:	Yes
Slot Machines:	Yes
Swimming Pools (outdoors):	1
Swimming Pools (inside):	0
Whirlpools:	2
Fitness Center:	Yes
Sauna/Steam Room:	Yes/No
Massage:	Yes
Self-Service Launderette:	No
Movie Theater/Seats:	Yes/107
Library:	Yes
Children's Facilities:	No
Classification Society:	American Bureau of Shipping

Ratings	**Score**
Ship: Hardware/Maintenance	55
Ship: Outdoor Facilities/Space	61
Ship: Interior Facilities/Space/Flow	58
Ship: Decor/Furnishings/Artwork	58
Ship: Spa/Fitness Facilities	30
Cabins: Suites and Deluxe	62
Cabins: Standard Sizes	52
Food: Dining Room/Cuisine	60
Food: Informal Dining/Buffets	54
Food: Quality of Ingredients	57
Food: Afternoon Tea/Bar Snacks	43
Service: Dining Room	62
Service: Bars	60
Service: Cabins	60
Service: Open Decks	52
Cruise: Entertainment	53
Cruise: Activities Program	51
Cruise: Movies/Television Programming	44
Cruise: Hospitality Standard	54
Cruise: Overall Product Delivery	61
Overall Score	**1,087**

Accommodation: There is a wide choice of cabin sizes and configurations, but only the top three categories have full bathtubs. Has extremely spacious suites; other cabins are very quite roomy, well-appointed units, but most have tinny metal drawers (a carry-over from her former years as a Matson Line ship).

The cabins located forward on Boat Deck have lifeboat-obstructed views, but other cabins on this deck are quite large; all have a window, plenty of closet and drawer space, together with a vanity desk, coffee table, sofa, and chair. Bathrobes are provided for all passengers.

Dining: The charming two-level dining room is set low down, and decorated in soft earth tones, so the ambience is quite cozy, although it is noisy when full. Features continental cuisine, with some excellent pasta dishes. Limited selection of breads, cheeses, and fruits. Service is friendly and attentive, in typical Italian style, but it is somewhat hurried.

There is also a casual café, with fine views over the aft pool deck and stern, for breakfast and lunch buffets, and an Italian gelato cart.

Other Comments: This ship has a traditional 1950s (now somewhat dated) liner profile. She was built originally for the United States Maritime Commission as a C-4 cargo vessel before becoming a Matson Lines ship in 1956, with a name change to *Monterey*. She is very stable at sea, with an almost vertical bow and an overhanging aircraft-carrier-like stern that is not at all handsome when viewed from ashore, but provides a good amount of open deck space around the white-tiled swimming pool and Jacuzzis. There are also partly enclosed port and starboard walking promenades, although, sadly, they do not wrap around the vessel. On the navigation bridge is a neat, original spirit level!

The ship was refurbished in a moderate art deco style, and a new sports deck was added several years ago. Has a good amount of sheltered and open deck space, and some forward open observation deck space atop some suites which were added in the late 1980s.

Inside, there are a reasonable number of public rooms to choose from. All of them have high ceilings, but little elegance. There is too much cold steel and not enough warmth in the interior decoration, although this is being addressed as décor changes are made. Rising through three decks is a large, slim totem pole, a carry-over from her limited days as a ship operating under the banner of Aloha Pacific Cruises.

The crew features a number of Italians, and they provide a friendly atmosphere, but there is really little finesse in service.

This ship will cruise you in reasonable style and surroundings, with mainly European, and particularly Italian-speaking passengers (about 60 percent). Currency aboard: lire. Port taxes are included.

But: There is no forward observation lounge. There are far too many loud, repetitive, and unnecessary announcements, often in five languages. There is a charge for the sauna, which is located inside the beauty salon and operated by the concession.

mv Nantucket Clipper

☆☆☆ +

(S)

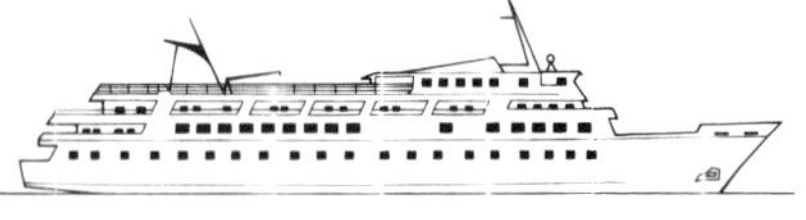

Lifestyle	**Standard**
Cruise Line:	Clipper Cruise Line
Former Names:	-
Gross Tonnage:	1,471
Builder:	Jeffboat (USA)
Original Cost:	$9 million
Entered Service:	December 1984
Flag:	USA
Tel No:	n/a
Fax No:	n/a
Length (ft./m.):	207.0/63.00
Beam (ft./m.):	37.0/11.20
Draft (ft./m.):	8.0/2.40
Propulsion/Propellers:	diesel (700kW)/2 (FP)
Decks:	4
Total Crew:	37
Pass. Capacity (basis 2):	102
Pass. Capacity (all berths):	102
Pass. Space Ratio (basis 2):	14.4
Pass. Space Ratio (all berths):	14.4
Officers:	American
Total Cabins:	51
Size Range (sq. ft./m.):	121–138/11.2–12.8
Cabins (outside view):	51
Cabins (inside):	0
Cabins (for one person):	0
Cabins (with private balcony):	0
Cabins (wheelchair accessible):	0
Cabin Current:	110 AC
Cabin TV:	No
Dining Rooms:	1
Seatings:	1
Elevators:	0
Casino:	No
Slot Machines:	No
Swimming Pools (outdoors):	0
Swimming Pools (inside):	0
Whirlpools:	0
Fitness Center:	No
Sauna/Steam Room:	No/No
Massage:	No
Self-Service Launderette:	No
Movie Theater/Seats:	No
Library:	Yes
Children's Facilities:	No
Classification Society:	American Bureau of Shipping

Ratings	**Score**
Ship: Hardware/Maintenance	66
Ship: Outdoor Facilities/Space	65
Ship: Interior Facilities/Space/Flow	66
Ship: Decor/Furnishings/Artwork	64
Ship: Public Rooms	65
Cabins: Suites and Deluxe	66
Cabins: Standard Sizes	62
Food: Dining Room/Cuisine	79
Food: Informal Dining/Buffets	73
Food: Quality of Ingredients	78
Food: Afternoon Tea/Bar Snacks	66
Service: Dining Room	76
Service: Bars	75
Service: Cabins	74
Service: Open Decks	64
Cruise: Port Information	71
Cruise: Shore Programs	72
Cruise: Movies/Television Programming	53
Cruise: Hospitality Standard	73
Cruise: Overall Product Delivery	79
Overall Score	**1,387**

Accommodation: The all-outside cabins (in four categories) are very small, but somehow comfortable if you do not expect much. They are relatively tastefully furnished, with wood-accented trim and good sound insulation. Honeymooners and lovers be advised that the beds are twins, however, and are bolted to the deck and wall. The bathrooms are tight, but, thoughtfully, a night-light is provided, although there's little space for your toiletries.

Dining: The dining room is warm and inviting, and has large picture windows. There is a single seating, and you can sit with whomever you wish, although meals are at fixed times. There are no tables for two. Features simple and plain American cuisine that is quite tasty, although the menu choice is limited, and the portions are small. The chefs are from the Culinary Institute of America, and all ingredients are fresh. The chocolate chip cookies are popular and are served at various times, usually in the lounge.

Other Comments: This small, shallow draft vessel is specially built for coastal and inland cruises and is very maneuverable. Well maintained, although now showing signs of aging. There is a narrow wraparound open teakwood walking deck.

Note that this extremely high-density ship has only two public rooms—the dining room and an observation lounge—where most passengers congregate in the evening. Passengers can visit the bridge at any time. Not recommended for night owls, and passengers should be over 50 years of age.

The service is by young, friendly, all-American college-age types. This is most definitely an "Americana" experience for those seeking particularly to learn more about the coastal ports around the U.S. Casual and unstructured lifestyle, rather like a small (but certainly not luxurious) country club afloat, with some attention to detail. This should not be compared with big ship ocean cruising. Thankfully, there are no mindless activities or corny games.

There are always one or two lecturers aboard each sailing, which highlights the learning experience that is an essential part of cruising with Clipper Cruise Lines. Now, if only the ship would carry a few bicycles! A no-smoking policy throughout all interior areas was put into effect December 1996.

But: There is high engine noise level when underway. The per diem price is high for what you get, and airfare is extra.

mv Niagara Prince

☆☆ +

(S)

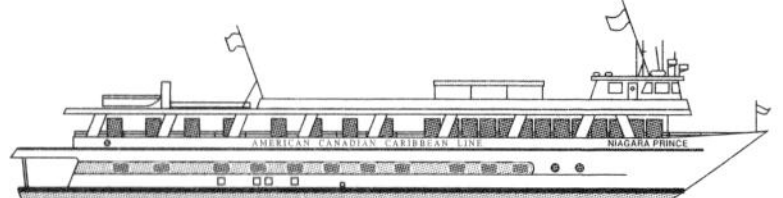

LIFESTYLE	STANDARD
Cruise Line:	American Canadian Caribbean Line
Former Names:	-
Gross Tonnage:	99
Builder:	Blount Industries (USA)
Original Cost:	$7.5 million
Entered Service:	November 1994
Flag:	USA
Tel No:	n/a
Fax No:	n/a
Length (ft./m.):	177.0/53.9
Beam (ft./m.):	40.0/12.1
Draft (ft./m.):	6.7/2.0
Propulsion/Propellers:	diesel/1
Decks:	3
Total Crew:	17
Pass. Capacity (basis 2):	84
Pass. Capacity (all berths):	94
Pass. Space Ratio (basis 2):	1.1
Pass. Space Ratio (all berths):	1.0
Officers:	American
Total Cabins:	48
Size Range (sq. ft./m.):	72.0–96.0/6.6–8.9
Cabins (outside view):	40
Cabins (inside):	2
Cabins (for one person):	6
Cabins (with private balcony):	0
Cabins (wheelchair accessible):	0
Cabin Current:	110 AC
Cabin TV:	No
Dining Rooms:	1
Seatings:	1
Elevators:	0
Casino:	0
Slot Machines:	0
Swimming Pools (outdoors):	0
Swimming Pools (inside):	0
Whirlpools:	0
Fitness Center:	0
Sauna/Steam Room:	0/0
Massage:	0
Self-Service Launderette:	No
Movie Theater/Seats:	0
Library:	Yes
Children's Facilities:	No
Classification Society:	American Bureau of Shipping

RATINGS	SCORE
Ship: Hardware/Maintenance	58
Ship: Outdoor Facilities/Space	41
Ship: Interior Facilities/Space/Flow	49
Ship: Decor/Furnishings/Artwork	50
Ship: Public Rooms	34
Cabins: Suites and Deluxe	54
Cabins: Standard Sizes	41
Food: Dining Room/Cuisine	65
Food: Informal Dining/Buffets	60
Food: Quality of Ingredients	67
Food: Afternoon Tea/Bar Snacks	43
Service: Dining Room	64
Service: Bars	67
Service: Cabins	65
Service: Open Decks	45
Cruise: Port Information	44
Cruise: Shore Programs	58
Cruise: Movies/Television Programming	42
Cruise: Hospitality Standard	66
Cruise: Overall Product Delivery	74
OVERALL SCORE	**1,087**

Accommodation: No smoking is allowed in any cabin aboard this vessel. The air conditioning consists of re-circulated air. Beds in 75 percent of the cabins can be made up as two singles or a queen size bed (10 cabins have a third berth).

Dining: The dining room is an open seating affair, with tables for four, six, eight, or ten. Meals are served "family-style." The cuisine features good, wholesome Americana fare, with fresh-baked breads and regional dishes. There are, perhaps, too many high-cholesterol, fatty foods for older passengers. A "bring your own bottle" policy exists for those who want wine with dinner, or any alcoholic beverages (mixers are available).

Other Comments: Cruising aboard this company's vessels is for those who do not want or need pampering, much service, or entertainment. There is a high rate of repeat passengers who want a simple, unpretentious lifestyle. Take only casual clothing. All gratuities are pooled by all the staff.

The vessel is also equipped with a unique, retractable wheelhouse for passage under low bridges on island waterway itineraries, and there is also a small platform for those who want to swim off the stern. There is also a glass-bottom boat and a sunfish sailboat.

ms Nieuw Amsterdam

☆☆☆☆

(L)

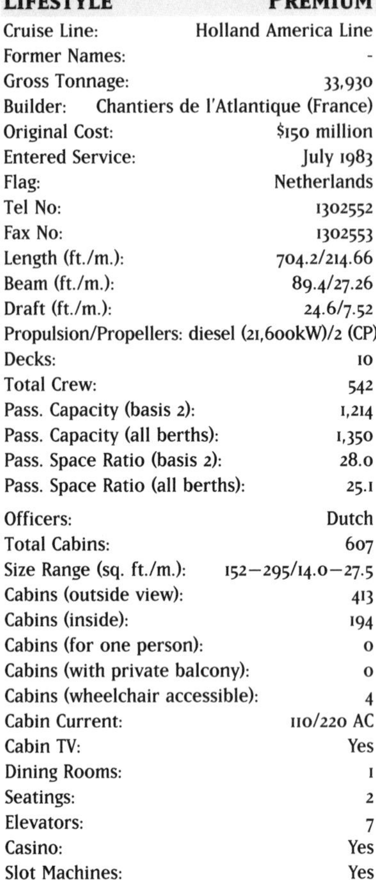

Lifestyle	**Premium**
Cruise Line:	Holland America Line
Former Names:	-
Gross Tonnage:	33,930
Builder:	Chantiers de l'Atlantique (France)
Original Cost:	$150 million
Entered Service:	July 1983
Flag:	Netherlands
Tel No:	1302552
Fax No:	1302553
Length (ft./m.):	704.2/214.66
Beam (ft./m.):	89.4/27.26
Draft (ft./m.):	24.6/7.52
Propulsion/Propellers:	diesel (21,600kW)/2 (CP)
Decks:	10
Total Crew:	542
Pass. Capacity (basis 2):	1,214
Pass. Capacity (all berths):	1,350
Pass. Space Ratio (basis 2):	28.0
Pass. Space Ratio (all berths):	25.1
Officers:	Dutch
Total Cabins:	607
Size Range (sq. ft./m.):	152–295/14.0–27.5
Cabins (outside view):	413
Cabins (inside):	194
Cabins (for one person):	0
Cabins (with private balcony):	0
Cabins (wheelchair accessible):	4
Cabin Current:	110/220 AC
Cabin TV:	Yes
Dining Rooms:	1
Seatings:	2
Elevators:	7
Casino:	Yes
Slot Machines:	Yes
Swimming Pools (outdoors):	2
Swimming Pools (inside):	0
Whirlpools:	1
Fitness Center:	Yes
Sauna/Steam Room:	Yes/No
Massage:	Yes
Self-Service Launderette:	Yes
Movie Theater/Seats:	Yes/230
Library:	Yes
Children's Facilities:	No
Classification Society:	Lloyd's Register

Ratings	**Score**
Ship: Hardware/Maintenance	84
Ship: Outdoor Facilities/Space	78
Ship: Interior Facilities/Space/Flow	83
Ship: Decor/Furnishings/Artwork	83
Ship: Spa/Fitness Facilities	72
Cabins: Suites and Deluxe	82
Cabins: Standard Sizes	77
Food: Dining Room/Cuisine	77
Food: Informal Dining/Buffets	74
Food: Quality of Ingredients	73
Food: Afternoon Tea/Bar Snacks	65
Service: Dining Room	77
Service: Bars	76
Service: Cabins	76
Service: Open Decks	71
Cruise: Entertainment	77
Cruise: Activities Program	76
Cruise: Movies/Television Programming	73
Cruise: Hospitality Standard	76
Cruise: Overall Product Delivery	81
Overall Score	**1,531**

Accommodation: The spacious and well-appointed cabins have quality furniture and fittings, nice wood paneling, good counter and storage space, and good-sized bathrooms. The top three categories of cabins have full bathtubs while all others have showers. Several cabins have king- or queen-sized beds, and cabin insulation is good. Some cabins on Boat and Navigation Decks have obstructed views.

Dining: The dining room is quite large and attractive, with warm decor, and ample space. Breakfast and lunch are served in an open seating (so you may get a different table and different waiters for each meal), and in two seatings for dinner (where you do have the same table each evening). Presentable but not memorable food, although the quality has improved somewhat. The waiters try hard, but sometimes it is difficult to communicate with them.

Other Comments: This ship has a nicely-raked bow. There is plenty of open deck space. Traditional teak wood outdoor decks, including a wraparound promenade deck.

She has a spacious interior design and layout, with soothing color combinations that do not jar the senses. There is much polished teak and rosewood paneling throughout. Features some stunning antiques and artwork. The Explorers' Lounge is relaxing for after-meal coffee and live chamber music. The main lounge, which has a balcony level, is reminiscent of the former ocean liners era.

Recommended for older passengers wanting pleasant surroundings and fairly bland food. Note: The line does not add an automatic 15 percent for beverage purchases, unlike many others.

But: There is considerable vibration at the stern. Charge of $1.50 for self-service washing machines in the launderette.

ms Nippon Maru

☆☆☆☆

(S)

Lifestyle	**Standard**
Cruise Line:	Mitsui OSK Passenger Line
Former Names:	-
Gross Tonnage:	21,903
Builder:	Mitsubishi Heavy Industries (Japan)
Original Cost:	$59.4 million
Entered Service:	September 1990
Flag:	Japan
Tel No:	1200462
Fax No:	1200462
Length (ft./m.):	546.7/166.65
Beam (ft./m.):	78.7/24.00
Draft (ft./m.):	21.4/6.55
Propulsion/Propellers:	diesel (15,740kW)/2 (CP)
Decks:	7
Total Crew:	160
Pass. Capacity (basis 2):	408
Pass. Capacity (all berths):	607
Pass. Space Ratio (basis 2):	53.6
Pass. Space Ratio (all berths):	36.0
Officers:	Japanese
Total Cabins:	204
Size Range (sq. ft./m.):	150–430/14.0–40.0
Cabins (outside view):	189
Cabins (inside):	15
Cabins (for one person):	0
Cabins (with private balcony):	0
Cabins (wheelchair accessible):	2
Cabin Current:	100 AC
Cabin TV:	Yes
Dining Rooms:	1
Seatings:	1
Elevators:	5
Casino:	Yes (*)
Slot Machines:	No
Swimming Pools (outdoors):	1
Swimming Pools (inside):	0
Whirlpools:	4 (Japanese baths)
Fitness Center:	Yes
Sauna/Steam Room:	Yes/No
Massage:	Yes (*)
Self-Service Launderette:	Yes
Movie Theater/Seats:	Yes/135
Library:	Yes
Children's Facilities:	Yes (*)
Classification Society:	Nippon Kaiji Kyokai

(*) = On leisure cruises only

Ratings	**Score**
Ship: Hardware/Maintenance	77
Ship: Outdoor Facilities/Space	76
Ship: Interior Facilities/Space/Flow	77
Ship: Decor/Furnishings/Artwork	77
Ship: Spa/Fitness Facilities	80
Cabins: Suites and Deluxe	78
Cabins: Standard Sizes	67
Food: Dining Room/Cuisine	74
Food: Informal Dining/Buffets	71
Food: Quality of Ingredients	74
Food: Afternoon Tea/Bar Snacks	68
Service: Dining Room	77
Service: Bars	76
Service: Cabins	76
Service: Open Decks	66
Cruise: Entertainment	67
Cruise: Activities Program	66
Cruise: Movies/Television Programming	66
Cruise: Hospitality Standard	73
Cruise: Overall Product Delivery	77
Overall Score	**1,463**

Accommodation: Most cabins are located forward, with public rooms positioned aft. The suites and deluxe cabins are quite nicely decorated, but the standard cabins are spartan and utilitarian (good for convention and seminar cruise passengers).

Dining: The dining room is quite basic and features both traditional Japanese cuisine and some Western dishes. Features one seating for leisure cruises and two seatings for ship charter cruises. The food presentation is quite decent, but rather plain, and menu choice is limited, although quite welcome by most passengers.

Other Comments: Has a traditional profile and a single, large, orange funnel aft of midships. Inside, the public rooms have very high ceilings. The interior decor, however, including the ceilings in public areas, is plain and unexciting. There is an elegant, dramatic six-deck-high atrium.

Specifically built and outfitted for Japanese passengers and the Japanese seminar/lecture marketplace. Excellent teakwood decking. Well-designed public rooms have high quality furnishings and soothing color combinations. Features true Japanese baths, and washitsu tatami room.

This ship is principally for Japanese passengers who want to cruise at moderate rates. No tipping allowed.

ms Noordam

☆☆☆☆

(L)

Lifestyle	**Premium**
Cruise Line:	Holland America Line
Former Names:	-
Gross Tonnage:	33,930
Builder:	Chantiers de l'Atlantique (France)
Original Cost:	$160 million
Entered Service:	April 1984
Flag:	Netherlands
Tel No:	1302541
Fax No:	1302537
Length (ft./m.):	704.2/214.66
Beam (ft./m.):	89.4/27.26
Draft (ft./m.):	24.2/7.40
Propulsion/Propellers:	diesel (21,600kW)/2 (CP)
Decks:	10
Total Crew:	530
Pass. Capacity (basis 2):	1,214
Pass. Capacity (all berths):	1,350
Pass. Space Ratio (basis 2):	28.0
Pass. Space Ratio (all berths):	25.1
Officers:	Dutch
Total Cabins:	607
Size Range (sq. ft./m.):	152–295/14.0–27.5
Cabins (outside view):	413
Cabins (inside):	194
Cabins (for one person):	0
Cabins (with private balcony):	0
Cabins (wheelchair accessible):	4
Cabin Current:	110/220 AC
Cabin TV:	Yes
Dining Rooms:	1
Seatings:	2
Elevators:	7
Casino:	Yes
Slot Machines:	Yes
Swimming Pools (outdoors):	2
Swimming Pools (inside):	0
Whirlpools:	1
Fitness Center:	Yes
Sauna/Steam Room:	Yes/No
Massage:	Yes
Self-Service Laundry:	Yes
Movie Theater/Seats:	Yes/230
Library:	Yes
Children's Facilities:	No
Classification Society:	Lloyd's Register

Ratings	**Score**
Ship: Hardware/Maintenance	84
Ship: Outdoor Facilities/Space	78
Ship: Interior Facilities/Space/Flow	83
Ship: Decor/Furnishings/Artwork	83
Ship: Spa/Fitness Facilities	72
Cabins: Suites and Deluxe	82
Cabins: Standard Sizes	77
Food: Dining Room/Cuisine	77
Food: Informal Dining/Buffets	74
Food: Quality of Ingredients	73
Food: Afternoon Tea/Bar Snacks	65
Service: Dining Room	77
Service: Bars	76
Service: Cabins	76
Service: Open Decks	71
Cruise: Entertainment	77
Cruise: Activities Program	76
Cruise: Movies/Television Programming	73
Cruise: Hospitality Standard	76
Cruise: Overall Product Delivery	81
Overall Score	**1,531**

Accommodation: These are spacious, practical cabins that have plenty of storage space, good closets and counter space, and adequate bathrooms (the top three categories have full bathtubs, while all others have showers). All of the cabins are well equipped and have good insulation. Some of the cabins on Boat and Navigation Decks have obstructed views.

Dining: Charming, spacious dining room. Features open seating for breakfast and lunch, two seatings for dinner. The Indonesian staff provides generally good service. Features international cuisine with an American flavor, but the ingredients are not the best quality. Limited selection of breads, cheeses, and fruits.

Other Comments: Features fine, traditional teak wood outdoor decks, including a wraparound promenade deck, and good deck lounge chairs.

Outstanding and well-displayed seventeenth- and eighteenth-century artwork and Dutch artifacts. Flower bouquets throughout the ship are lovely. The Crow's Nest observation lounge, located atop the ship, is a good retreat. The Explorers' Lounge is fine for after-dinner coffees with live, relaxing chamber music. Good indoor/outdoor dining area.

This ship provides older passengers with a pleasant cruise in comfortable surroundings, at a fair price. Note: The line does not add an automatic 15 percent for beverage purchases, unlike many others.

But: Has only average, low-budget entertainment. It is frustrating trying to communicate with newer staff. Charge of $1.50 for self-service launderette washing machines.

ms Nordic Empress

☆☆☆ +

(L)

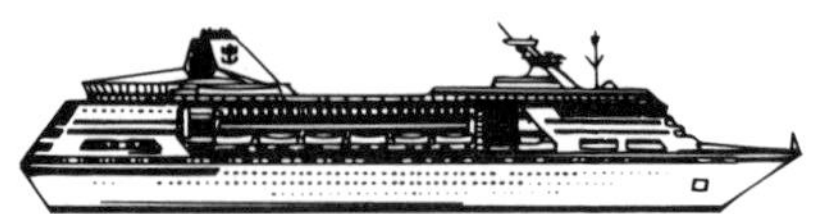

Lifestyle	Standard
Cruise Line:	Royal Caribbean International
Former Names:	-
Gross Tonnage:	48,563
Builder:	Chantiers de l'Atlantique (France)
Original Cost:	$170 million
Entered Service:	June 1990
Flag:	Liberia
Tel No:	1243540
Fax No:	1243547
Length (ft./m.):	692.2/211.00
Beam (ft./m.):	100.7/30.70
Draft (ft./m.):	23.2/7.10
Propulsion/Propellers:	diesel (16,200kW)/2 (CP)
Decks:	12
Total Crew:	671
Pass. Capacity (basis 2):	1,600
Pass. Capacity (all berths):	2,020
Pass. Space Ratio (basis 2):	30.2
Pass. Space Ratio (all berths):	24.0
Officers:	Scandinavian
Total Cabins:	800
Size Range (sq. ft./m.):	117–269/10.8–25.0
Cabins (outside view):	471
Cabins (inside):	329
Cabins (for one person):	0
Cabins (with private balcony):	69
Cabins (wheelchair accessible):	4
Cabin Current:	110 AC
Cabin TV:	Yes
Dining Rooms:	1
Seatings:	2
Elevators:	7
Casino:	Yes
Slot Machines:	Yes-220
Swimming Pools (outdoors):	2
Swimming Pools (inside):	0
Whirlpools:	4
Fitness Center:	Yes
Sauna/Steam Room:	Yes/No
Massage:	Yes
Self-Service Launderette:	No
Movie Theater/Seats:	No
Library:	No
Children's Facilities:	Yes
Classification Society:	Det Norske Veritas

Ratings	Score
Ship: Hardware/Maintenance	81
Ship: Outdoor Facilities/Space	66
Ship: Interior Facilities/Space/Flow	76
Ship: Decor/Furnishings/Artwork	75
Ship: Spa/Fitness Facilities	66
Cabins: Suites and Deluxe	67
Cabins: Standard Sizes	61
Food: Dining Room/Cuisine	71
Food: Informal Dining/Buffets	62
Food: Quality of Ingredients	66
Food: Afternoon Tea/Bar Snacks	52
Service: Dining Room	77
Service: Bars	74
Service: Cabins	76
Service: Open Decks	66
Cruise: Entertainment	77
Cruise: Activities Program	67
Cruise: Movies/Television Programming	66
Cruise: Hospitality Standard	66
Cruise: Overall Product Delivery	76
Overall Score	**1,388**

Accommodation: Nine cabins have private balconies overlooking the stern. All cabins are very small, though reasonably comfortable for the short cruises this ship operates. Cabins have twin beds that convert to a queen-size configuration.

Dining: Two-level, musical-themed dining room is delightful, though noisy, and has huge windows overlooking the stern. The entire dining room operation is well orchestrated, with emphasis on highly programmed service but with some finesse. The food is consistently fair, but certainly not memorable (it is hotel banquette food, after all).

Other Comments: This is a fine contemporary ship with short bow and squared-off stern that looks quite stunning. *Nordic Empress* was designed specifically for the short-cruise market, for which the ship is well suited. Has an outdoor polished wraparound wooden promenade deck, and there is a dramatic use of glass-enclosed viewing spaces that provide good contact from the upper, open decks to the sea.

Inside, a stunning nine-deck-high atrium is the focal point. Passenger flow is generally good, although at show time some congestion is inevitable adjacent to the entrance foyer. Lots of crystal and brass are used to good effect to reflect light. An ingenious use of lighting effects provides illuminating interiors that make you feel warm. The three-level casino has a sailcloth ceiling. There is a superb outdoor pool deck designed for evenings under the stars. The Viking Crown Lounge, aft of the funnel, is a two-level night club/disco for the late-night set.

This is a glamorous ship with high passenger density, but the ship features an adequate array of activities for all ages. Will operate New York to Bermuda cruises in the summer of 1999.

But: The two-level showroom has poor sight lines in the upper lateral balconies. The constant, loud announcements are irritating.

ss Norway

☆☆☆☆

(L)

Lifestyle	**Standard**
Cruise Line:	Norwegian Cruise Line
Former Names:	*France*
Gross Tonnage:	76,049
Builder:	Chantiers de l'Atlantique (France)
Original Cost:	$80 million
Entered Service:	February 1962/June 1980
Flag:	Bahamas
Tel No:	1104603
Fax No:	1104604
Length (ft./m.):	1035.1/315.50
Beam (ft./m.):	109.9/33.50
Draft (ft./m.):	35.4/10.80
Propulsion/Propellers:	steam turbine (29,850kW)/4 (FP)
Decks:	12
Total Crew:	875
Pass. Capacity (basis 2):	2,032
Pass. Capacity (all berths):	2,370
Pass. Space Ratio (basis 2):	37.4
Pass. Space Ratio (all berths):	32.8
Officers:	Norwegian
Total Cabins:	1,016
Size Range (sq. ft./m.):	100–957/9.2–89.0
Cabins (outside view):	649
Cabins (inside):	367
Cabins (for one person):	20
Cabins (with private balcony):	56
Cabins (wheelchair accessible):	11
Cabin Current:	110 AC
Cabin TV:	Yes
Dining Rooms:	2
Seatings:	2
Elevators:	13
Casino:	Yes
Slot Machines:	Yes
Swimming Pools (outdoors):	2
Swimming Pools (inside):	1 (plus Aquacize Pool)
Whirlpools:	2
Fitness Center:	Yes
Sauna/Steam Room:	Yes/No
Massage:	Yes
Self-Service Launderette:	No
Movie Theater/Seats:	Yes/840
Library:	Yes
Children's Facilities:	Yes
Classification Society:	Bureau Veritas

Ratings	**Score**
Ship: Hardware/Maintenance	77
Ship: Outdoor Facilities/Space	75
Ship: Interior Facilities/Space/Flow	77
Ship: Decor/Furnishings/Artwork	74
Ship: Spa/Fitness Facilities	83
Cabins: Suites and Deluxe	83
Cabins: Standard Sizes	68
Food: Dining Room/Cuisine	67
Food: Informal Dining/Buffets	63
Food: Quality of Ingredients	67
Food: Afternoon Tea/Bar Snacks	58
Service: Dining Room	72
Service: Bars	71
Service: Cabins	72
Service: Open Decks	67
Cruise: Entertainment	79
Cruise: Activities Program	76
Cruise: Movies/Television Programming	76
Cruise: Hospitality Standard	67
Cruise: Overall Product Delivery	74
Overall Score	**1,446**

Accommodation: There is a really wide range of suites and cabins from really luxurious and spacious outside suites to tiny inside cabins. All have high ceilings, long beds, good closet and drawer space, and full amenities.

Outstanding owner's suites are extremely lavish, and new suites on two decks atop the ship are very comfortable (however, all suite occupants should have had a private dining room). There are many cabins suitable for families of four or five, even six.

Dining: There are two large dining rooms. The nicest is the Windward, with its fine domed ceiling, and wall murals retained from her former days as the first-class dining room, while the Leeward (the former tourist-class restaurant) has a fine balcony. There are few tables for two, however, and tables are close together. The food is not memorable and the menus are often uninspiring and quite disappointing. Limited selection of breads, rolls, and fruit. The service ranges from poor to good. The cuisine in general can be said to be reasonable American hotel banquet food, no more, although it has become better in the past year or so. Good, moderately priced wine list, but there is almost nothing for good wine lovers.

Le Bistro is an informal alternative dining spot that provides for a change from the two restaurants (and the attendant noise). It offers a taste of Italy in a contemporary "South Miami Beach" style, at no extra charge (it always seems difficult to get a table, however).

The casual, outdoor buffet area is useful for those out on deck, but it is always crowded, with long lines to get to what can best be described as "food as it shouldn't be presented." It never looks good, despite staff efforts to restock the displays.

Other Comments: She is a majestic-looking ship, with two large funnels, despite major structural alterations that added two complete new glass-enclosed decks atop the ship a few years ago. The new decks provide 135 outside suites and junior suites, and lower the profile of the two wing-tip funnels considerably, but the balconies are not very private. Two large landing craft provide fast, efficient transportation ashore.

A 1996 refurbishment also refreshed her interiors. Some rooms feature art deco touches reminiscent of the former ocean liner she once was. Has two different color schemes in the forward and aft sections, which help first-time passengers to find their way around.

The public rooms are, for the most part, quite pleasing, and many have high ceilings. Soft furnishings and much marble freshened the ship's interior recently. Has well-varnished outdoor decks, but the astroturf on the ship's top deck just is not right. Features a good indoor Roman Spa, set low down in the ship, and a range of spa programs. There is an extensive jogging track (but it cannot be used before 8:00 a.m. as it is located above some of the most expensive cabins). The Club Internationale is an elegant carryover from her former days, and still the perfect meeting place for cocktails and sophisticated evenings. There is an excellent proscenium theater for dazzle and sizzle production shows. Large active casino invites you to spend your money, and it is noisy. Sadly, the former library has been changed into a perfume shop. To keep up-to-date, a new Sports Illustrated Bar replaced Checkers Lounge in her winter 1998 refit.

Take the family, as children and teens will have a fine time aboard this ship. She is so large, there are plenty of places to play.

This ship, formerly the grand classic transatlantic liner *France*, was for many years the world's largest cruise ship (she is still the longest). Like Cunard's *QE2*, *Norway* is a floating contemporary resort, and should prove fascinating for active passengers and families with children of all ages. She provides an action-packed, sun-filled cruise in comfortable, but rather overpopulated surroundings, for an adequate price. British passengers should note that all onboard gratuities are included, as are port taxes. In the summer of 1998 she sailed in the Mediterranean area during the summer, going back to the future by again taking her former name, *France* as the lure and romance of ocean liners continues.

<u>But:</u> The open deck and sunbathing space is now quite poor, particularly when the ship is full. *Norway* does not dock anywhere because of its size and deep draft (a problem for the non-ambulatory). The Roman Spa fitness facilities incur a hefty extra charge, plus an added 12 percent tip. There are just too many loud announcements, making for too much of a holiday camp atmosphere.

ms Norwegian Capricorn

☆☆☆☆

(M)

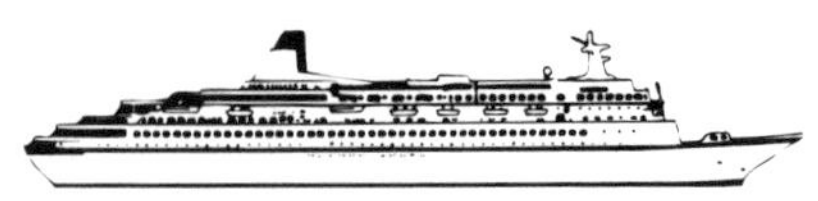

LIFESTYLE	**STANDARD**
Cruise Line:	Norwegian Capricorn Line
Former Names:	*Norwegian Star, Royal Odyssey, Royal Viking Sea*
Gross Tonnage:	28,078
Builder:	Wartsila (Finland)
Original Cost:	$22.5 million
Entered Service:	November 1973/December 1998
Flag:	Bahamas
Tel No:	1104504
Fax No:	1104511
Length (ft./m.):	674.2/205.50
Beam (ft./m.):	83.6/25.50
Draft (ft./m.):	23.6/7.20
Propulsion/Propellers:	diesel (13,400kW)/2 (CP)
Decks:	8
Total Crew:	380
Pass. Capacity (basis 2):	800
Pass. Capacity (all berths):	1,150
Pass. Space Ratio (basis 2):	35.0
Pass. Space Ratio (all berths):	24.4
Officers:	Norwegian
Total Cabins:	400
Size Range (sq. ft./m.):	136.0–580.0/12.6–53.8
Cabins (outside view):	360
Cabins (inside):	40
Cabins (for one person):	0
Cabins (with private balcony):	9
Cabins (wheelchair accessible):	0
Cabin Current:	110/220 AC
Cabin TV:	Yes
Dining Rooms:	1
Seatings:	2
Elevators:	5
Casino:	Yes
Slot Machines:	Yes
Swimming Pools (outdoors):	1
Swimming Pools (inside):	0
Whirlpools:	3
Fitness Center:	Yes
Sauna/Steam Room:	Yes/No
Massage:	Yes
Self-Service Launderette:	No
Movie Theater/Seats:	Yes/156
Library:	No
Children's Facilities:	Yes
Classification Society:	Det Norske Veritas

RATINGS	**SCORE**
Ship: Hardware/Maintenance	76
Ship: Outdoor Facilities/Space	75
Ship: Interior Facilities/Space/Flow	80
Ship: Decor/Furnishings/Artwork	76
Ship: Spa/Fitness Facilities	72
Cabins: Suites and Deluxe	81
Cabins: Standard Sizes	75
Food: Dining Room/Cuisine	67
Food: Informal Dining/Buffets	62
Food: Quality of Ingredients	66
Food: Afternoon Tea/Bar Snacks	54
Service: Dining Room	73
Service: Bars	73
Service: Cabins	74
Service: Open Decks	67
Cruise: Entertainment	74
Cruise: Activities Program	64
Cruise: Movies/Television Programming	66
Cruise: Hospitality Standard	76
Cruise: Overall Product Delivery	76
OVERALL SCORE	**1,427**

Accommodation: There are nine penthouse suites (those on the port side are larger); each is named after destinations (one of them has lifeboat-obstructed views). All other cabins (most of which are outside) are well appointed, with good closet, drawer and storage space, although some bathrooms in the lower categories have awkward access. Some of the newer cabins have whirlpool bathtubs. Bathrobes are provided for suite passengers only. Nonsmoking cabins are available. Note that tinny drawers in the cabins remain from her former days as a Royal Viking Line ship.

Dining: The dining room has a high ceiling, and is quite spacious. Dining is in two seatings, with assigned tables for two, four, six, or eight. Breakfast and luncheon can also be taken outdoors by the swimming pool. There is too much use of canned fruits at the breakfast buffets. Good choice of breads and tropical fruits. The hot food choice is quite good, and the presentation of entrees has been beefed up to cater to the tastes of Australasian passengers.

There is also an informal dining spot called Le Bistro, where casual dining makes for an alternative to the dining room. For those who do not wish to dress for dinner. In addition, there is a sports bar and grill. Pizza is available each afternoon.

Other Comments: This ship has a smart, almost contemporary profile, with well-balanced lines and a delightful, sharply raked bow, something not found on the newest cruise ships today. She also has a decent draft, which makes her eminently suitable for the (sometimes) unkind waters around Australia and New Zealand, her principal cruising regions. The ship has been well maintained (she started life as one of three original Royal Viking Line sister ships in the 1970s operating worldwide cruises), and has a wide expanse of open deck, sunbathing, and several sports areas, including a large paddle tennis court.

Inside, the public rooms are quite elegant and have high ceilings. The spa and fitness facilities are generally good. The casino has tasteful decor.

This ship was "stretched" in 1983, and a major multimillion dollar reconstruction took place in 1997, when more cabins were added (sadly, the library was taken away). Also added was a "Kids Korner" playroom, and a video arcade (although there really are few other facilities for children, the ship being better suited to older adults).

This ship is presently under charter to Norwegian Capricorn Line, a new joint venture between The Australian Cruise Project and Norwegian Cruise Line. She provides a well programmed cruise experience for those passengers who do not want to cruise aboard the megaships. The ship is based in Sydney, Australia, and operates seven- and fourteen-day cruises. Summer cruises feature New Zealand and Tasmania, while winter cruises feature the Coral Sea and Australia's Queensland coast. Most passengers are from Australasia, but the ship is also marketed to North Americans and British passengers.

But: Although very smart-looking, the ship is getting old, and her design has been superceded by more trendy ships in other markets.

ms Norwegian Crown

☆☆☆☆

(L)

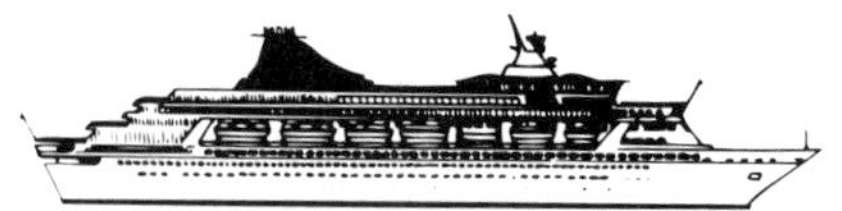

Lifestyle	**Standard**
Cruise Line:	Norwegian Cruise Line
Former Names:	*Crown Odyssey*
Gross Tonnage:	34,242
Builder:	Meyer Werft (Germany)
Original Cost:	$178 million
Entered Service:	June 1988/March 1996
Flag:	Bahamas
Tel No:	1104673
Fax No:	1104674
Length (ft./m.):	615.9/187.75
Beam (ft./m.):	92.5/28.20
Draft (ft./m.):	23.8/7.26
Propulsion/Propellers:	diesel (21,330kW)/2 (CP)
Decks:	10
Total Crew:	470
Pass. Capacity (basis 2):	1,052
Pass. Capacity (all berths):	1,221
Pass. Space Ratio (basis 2):	32.5
Pass. Space Ratio (all berths):	28.0
Officers:	Norwegian
Total Cabins:	526
Size Range (sq. ft./m.):	154–615/14.3–57.0
Cabins (outside view):	412
Cabins (inside):	114
Cabins (for one person):	0
Cabins (with private balcony):	16
Cabins (wheelchair accessible):	4
Cabin Current:	110 AC
Cabin TV:	No
Dining Rooms:	1
Seatings:	2
Elevators:	4
Casino:	Yes
Slot Machines:	Yes
Swimming Pools (outdoors):	1
Swimming Pools (inside):	1
Whirlpools:	4
Fitness Center:	Yes
Sauna/Steam Room:	Yes/No
Massage:	Yes
Self-Service Launderette:	Yes
Movie Theater/Seats:	Yes/215
Library:	Yes
Children's Facilities:	No
Classification Society:	Lloyd's Register

Ratings	**Score**
Ship: Hardware/Maintenance	78
Ship: Outdoor Facilities/Space	81
Ship: Interior Facilities/Space/Flow	85
Ship: Decor/Furnishings/Artwork	85
Ship: Spa/Fitness Facilities	78
Cabins: Suites and Deluxe	83
Cabins: Standard Sizes	74
Food: Dining Room/Cuisine	67
Food: Informal Dining/Buffets	62
Food: Quality of Ingredients	66
Food: Afternoon Tea/Bar Snacks	54
Service: Dining Room	74
Service: Bars	72
Service: Cabins	74
Service: Open Decks	67
Cruise: Entertainment	76
Cruise: Activities Program	61
Cruise: Movies/Television Programming	66
Cruise: Hospitality Standard	73
Cruise: Overall Product Delivery	76
Overall Score	**1,452**

Accommodation: The suites are quite spacious, and each is decorated in a different style. Most other cabins have good closet and drawer space and come well equipped, although almost all cabins are showing signs of wear and tear. Cabin soundproofing is good. Nonsmoking cabins are available.

Dining: Large, noisy dining room features a stained-glass ceiling and comfortable seating. The cuisine is not gourmet either in quality or presentation, yet is more than adequate for the expectations of Norwegian Cruise Line's passengers. The waiters are generally good, and quite attentive. Decent, well-priced wine list, although the wines are quite young.

Other Comments: This well designed and built ship has quite a handsome exterior profile, with generally good passenger flow, ample space and fine-quality interiors. However, these interiors are now showing signs of hard wear in many places, and more maintenance is needed.

Features a full teak wood wraparound outdoor promenade deck. There are, however, no padded mattresses for the deck lounge chairs.

Inside, the ship has a spacious layout and a good array of public rooms. Generous amounts of warm woods and marble used in the decor, but there are lots of mirrored surfaces. Excellent Roman-style indoor spa, pool, and facilities, unusual for a Caribbean ship, but excellent for cruises to Alaska. There is a good theater-style showroom, but the sight lines could be better.

This ship, for many years a favorite of passengers of the now defunct Royal Cruise Line, is excellent particularly for the young-at-heart passenger, and it exudes quality, style, and charm, for a really moderate cruise price.

British passengers should note that all onboard gratuities are included, as are port taxes.

ms Norwegian Dream

☆☆☆☆

(L)

Lifestyle	**Standard**
Cruise Line:	Norwegian Cruise Line
Former Names:	*Dreamward*
Gross Tonnage:	50,760
Builder:	Chantiers de l'Atlantique (France)
Original Cost:	$240 million
Entered Service:	December 1992
Flag:	Bahamas
Tel No:	1305510
Fax No:	1305507
Length (ft./m.):	754.0/229.80
Beam (ft./m.):	93.5/28.50
Draft (ft./m.):	22.3/6.80
Propulsion/Propellers:	diesel (18,480kW)/2 (CP)
Decks:	11
Total Crew:	614
Pass. Capacity (basis 2):	1,748
Pass. Capacity (all berths):	2,159
Pass. Space Ratio (basis 2):	29.0
Pass. Space Ratio (all berths):	23.5
Officers:	Norwegian
Total Cabins:	874
Size Range (sq. ft./m.):	140–350/13.0–32.5
Cabins (outside view):	716
Cabins (inside):	158
Cabins (for one person):	0
Cabins (with private balcony):	48
Cabins (wheelchair accessible):	6 (+ 30 for hearing-impaired)
Cabin Current:	110 AC
Cabin TV:	Yes
Dining Rooms:	4
Seatings:	2
Elevators:	10
Casino:	Yes
Slot Machines:	Yes
Swimming Pools (outdoors):	2
Swimming Pools (inside):	0
Whirlpools:	4
Fitness Center:	Yes
Sauna/Steam Room:	Yes/No
Massage:	Yes
Self-Service Launderette:	No
Movie Theater/Seats:	No
Library:	Yes
Children's Facilities:	Yes
Classification Society:	Det Norske Veritas

Ratings	**Score**
Ship: Hardware/Maintenance	81
Ship: Outdoor Facilities/Space	78
Ship: Interior Facilities/Space/Flow	82
Ship: Decor/Furnishings/Artwork	81
Ship: Spa/Fitness Facilities	76
Cabins: Suites and Deluxe	79
Cabins: Standard Sizes	76
Food: Dining Room/Cuisine	67
Food: Informal Dining/Buffets	62
Food: Quality of Ingredients	66
Food: Afternoon Tea/Bar Snacks	54
Service: Dining Room	74
Service: Bars	73
Service: Cabins	74
Service: Open Decks	67
Cruise: Entertainment	74
Cruise: Activities Program	64
Cruise: Movies/Television Programming	66
Cruise: Hospitality Standard	76
Cruise: Overall Product Delivery	75
Overall Score	**1,445**

Accommodation: There are fifteen grades of cabins. The majority of cabins are outside and feature wood-trimmed cabinetry and warm decor, with multicolored soft furnishings, but there is almost no drawer space (the closets have open shelves, however), so take minimal clothing. All cabins have a sitting area, but this takes away any free space, making movement pretty tight. The bathrooms are small but practical, although there is little space for storage of personal toiletry items.

There are 18 suites (12 of which have a private entance and private balcony), each with separate living room and bedroom, fine quality cabinetry, and lots of closet and drawer space. Occupants of suites receive "concierge" service, which provides extra personal attention. In addition, 16 suites and 70 cabins have inter-connecting doors—good for families, or perhaps those that want separate "his and hers" living spaces. There are several cabins specially equipped for the hearing-impaired. Note that all cabins on the port side of the ship are designated nonsmoking.

Dining: There are three main dining rooms: The Sun Terrace, The Terraces (the nicest), which look out over the ship's tiered aft decks, and the enlarged, midships-located Four Seasons (now with 452 seats, but no nearby rest rooms). All have the same menu and food). The Four Seasons is now the largest, and has some prime tables at ocean-view window seats in a section that extends from the ship's side in a half-moon.

In addition, The Bistro features casual evening dining at no extra charge, a Sports Bar features breakfast, luncheon and teatime buffets (this is a small space for this number of passengers, and the offerings are quite poor), and there's also a poolside pizzeria. Newly added is a small coffee lounge.

The food is adequate, but not memorable, like the service. The wine list is quite good, and well put together, with moderate prices. There are many types of beer (including some on draught in the popular Sports Bar & Grill) to choose from. The cutlery is standard (there are no fish knives). There is no afternoon tea.

Other Comments: Built first, this sister ship to Norwegian Wind has a handsome, well-balanced profile, despite a large, square funnel. Has inboard lifeboats and a rubber-covered promenade deck. The tiered pool deck is neat, as are the multi-deck aft sun terraces.

In the spring of 1998, the ship underwent a "chop and stretch" operation, which, together with sister ship Norwegian Wind, cost $138 million. This added a completely new mid-section. Included in the 131.2 ft. (40 m) section were 251 new passengers cabins, and 50 crew cabins, together with several new or enlarged public rooms, including a new 60-seat conference center.

Some innovative features were incorporated in the original design, and these have been kept and enhanced. The passenger flow is generally good, with the ship absorbing them quite well even when full. The design provides a good number of intimate rooms rather than large hangers. The pastel interior color scheme is soothing, and she is considered to be a pretty ship inside. The entrance lobby could be warmer (more flowers would help).

This ship has proven highly successful for Norwegian Cruise Line's young sports-minded passengers, providing a good alternative to the larger mega-ships and their mega-crowds, although there are plenty of other passengers to keep you company. British passengers should note that all onboard gratuities are included, as are port taxes.

<u>But:</u> The room service menu is poor and needs improvement. The outdoor stairways are numerous and confusing. The carpeted steel interior stairwell steps are quite tinny. When the ship was 'stretched' it reduced the amount of outdoor space per passenger, and this is reflected in more density around the pools. There simply are not enough public rooms to absorb the increase in passengers.

ms Norwegian Dynasty

☆☆☆☆

(M)

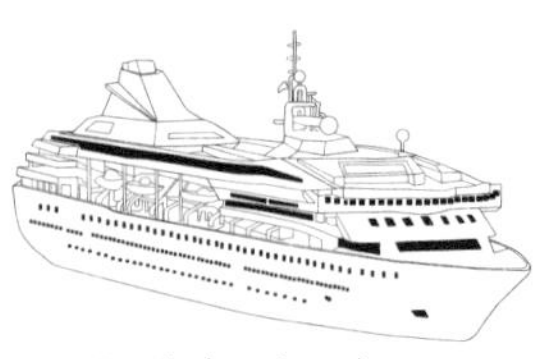

Lifestyle	**Standard**
Cruise Line:	Norwegian Cruise Line
Former Names:	*Crown Majesty/Cunard Dynasty/Crown Dynasty*
Gross Tonnage:	19,089
Builder:	Union Navale de Levante (Spain)
Original Cost:	$100 million
Entered Service:	July 1993/September 1997
Flag:	Panama
Tel No:	1337757
Fax No:	1337761
Length (ft./m.):	537.4/163.81
Beam (ft./m.):	73.8/22.5
Draft (ft./m.):	17.7/5.40
Propulsion/Propellers:	diesel (13,200kW)/2 (CP)
Decks:	7
Total Crew:	320
Pass. Capacity (basis 2):	800
Pass. Capacity (all berths):	916
Pass. Space Ratio (basis 2):	23.8
Pass. Space Ratio (all berths):	20.8
Officers:	European/Scandinavian
Total Cabins:	401
Size Range (sq. ft./m.):	140–350/13.0–32.5
Cabins (outside view):	277
Cabins (inside):	124
Cabins (for one person):	0
Cabins (with private balcony):	10
Cabins (wheelchair accessible):	4
Cabin Current:	110/220 AC
Cabin TV:	Yes
Dining Rooms:	1
Seatings:	2 (open seating breakfast/lunch)
Elevators:	4
Casino:	Yes
Slot Machines:	Yes
Swimming Pools (outdoors):	1
Swimming Pools (inside):	0
Whirlpools:	3
Fitness Center:	Yes
Sauna/Steam Room:	Yes/No
Massage:	Yes
Self-Service Launderette:	No
Movie Theater/Seats:	No
Library:	No
Children's Facilities:	No
Classification Society:	Det Norske Veritas

Ratings	**Score**
Ship: Hardware/Maintenance	81
Ship: Outdoor Facilities/Space	78
Ship: Interior Facilities/Space/Flow	80
Ship: Decor/Furnishings/Artwork	78
Ship: Spa/Fitness Facilities	74
Cabins: Suites and Deluxe	78
Cabins: Standard Sizes	75
Food: Dining Room/Cuisine	76
Food: Informal Dining/Buffets	74
Food: Quality of Ingredients	70
Food: Afternoon Tea/Bar Snacks	73
Service: Dining Room	76
Service: Bars	75
Service: Cabins	76
Service: Open Decks	71
Cruise: Entertainment	71
Cruise: Activities Program	62
Cruise: Movies/Television Programming	65
Cruise: Hospitality Standard	74
Cruise: Overall Product Delivery	78
Overall Score	**1,485**

Accommodation: The cabins are nicely furnished, trimmed with wood and feature large picture windows. They come quite well equipped, complete with vanity desk unit, a good amount of drawer space, curtained windows, and personal safe. Bathrooms are somewhat compact, but are nicely fitted out and have an excellent shower stall. However, the cabins unfortunately have very poor soundproofing; passengers in cabins on Deck 4 in particular are disturbed by anyone running or jogging on the deck above.

Dining: The dining room is pleasing and attractive, with large ocean-view windows on three sides. However, it is rather cramped, and there are no tables for two. The ambience, however, is warm. The cuisine is disappointing, and lacking in presentation. A varied menu is provided, but food arrives invariably overcooked (a problem of distance from the galley). While not up to the standard of the small deluxe ships, creativity is generally good, but inconsistent.

Other Comments: This really is a sleek, mid-sized ship that has handsome exterior styling, and is a refreshing change for those who do not want to cruise on larger ships. Fairly good open deck and sunbathing space, but there is no getting away from the constant music.

Has a well designed five-deck-high, glass-walled atrium. The off-center stairways in her interiors add a sense of spaciousness. Clever interior design surrounds passengers with sea and light. Pleasant, but not outstanding, artwork is colorful.

The interior decor in public spaces is warm and inviting, with contemporary, but not brash, art-deco color combinations. However, the health spa is very compact, and the show lounge has congestion problems and is poorly designed for passenger movement.

This company provide a consistent cruise product in clean, decent surroundings, and the staff try hard to please.

But: Do expect lines for buffets, tenders, and the few elevators.

ms Norwegian Majesty

☆☆☆ +

(L)

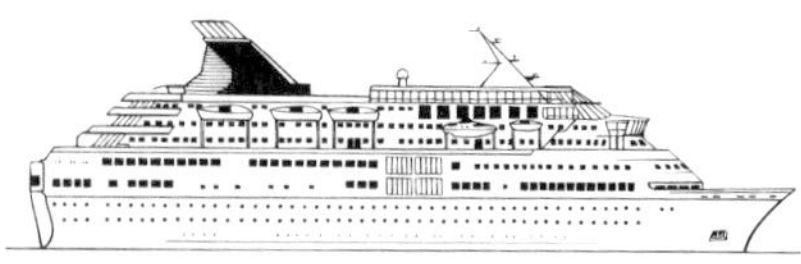

Lifestyle	**Standard**
Cruise Line:	Norwegian Cruise Line
Former Names:	*Royal Majesty*
Gross Tonnage:	32,396
Builder:	Kvaerner Masa Yards (Finland)
Original Cost:	$229 million
Entered Service:	September 1992/ November 1997
Flag:	Panama
Tel No:	1336557
Fax No:	1336563
Length (ft./m.):	567.9/173.10
Beam (ft./m.):	90.5/27.60
Draft (ft./m.):	20.3/6.20
Propulsion/Propellers:	diesel (21,120kW)/2 (CP)
Decks:	9
Total Crew:	438
Pass. Capacity (basis 2):	1,056
Pass. Capacity (all berths):	1,501
Pass. Space Ratio (basis 2):	31.3
Pass. Space Ratio (all berths):	21.5
Officers:	Norwegian
Total Cabins:	528 (132 no-smoking)
Size Range (sq. ft./m.):	118–375/11.0–34.8
Cabins (outside view):	343
Cabins (inside):	185
Cabins (for one person):	0
Cabins (with private balcony):	0
Cabins (wheelchair accessible):	4
Cabin Current:	110/220 AC
Cabin TV:	Yes
Dining Rooms:	1
Seatings:	2
Elevators:	4
Casino:	Yes
Slot Machines:	Yes
Swimming Pools (outdoors):	1
Swimming Pools (inside):	0
Whirlpools:	2
Fitness Center:	Yes
Sauna/Steam Room:	Yes/No
Massage:	Yes
Self-Service Launderette:	No
Movie Theater/Seats:	Yes/100
Library:	Yes
Children's Facilities:	Yes (also children's pool)
Classification Society:	Lloyd's Register

Ratings	**Score**
Ship: Hardware/Maintenance	81
Ship: Outdoor Facilities/Space	73
Ship: Interior Facilities/Space/Flow	81
Ship: Decor/Furnishings/Artwork	82
Ship: Spa/Fitness Facilities	76
Cabins: Suites and Deluxe	83
Cabins: Standard Sizes	75
Food: Dining Room/Cuisine	67
Food: Informal Dining/Buffets	62
Food: Quality of Ingredients	66
Food: Afternoon Tea/Bar Snacks	54
Service: Dining Room	67
Service: Bars	65
Service: Cabins	67
Service: Open Decks	56
Cruise: Entertainment	69
Cruise: Activities Program	61
Cruise: Movies/Television Programming	58
Cruise: Hospitality Standard	67
Cruise: Overall Product Delivery	76
Overall Score	**1,386**

Accommodation: The suites feature butler service and are well equipped (they also have VCR units), though they are not really large. Most other cabins are on the small side, but very comfortable, and with excellent bathroom showers. There are 132 cabins designated for nonsmokers. All cabins are provided with ironing boards (but no irons). Some cabins have obstructed views (check the deck plans carefully).

Dining: The dining room is quite intimate and totally nonsmoking. However, it is very noisy and the tables are rather close together, which means that correct service is difficult. In addition, the service is too fast. The food, menu, creativity, and service are basically sound, but bread rolls, cheese, and fruits could be better. Dinners are "themed" each evening.

Other Comments: This smart, stylish, contemporary cruise ship has a good profile and is generally a well-designed vessel. However, the open deck and sunbathing space is very limited, and there are no cushioned pads for the plastic deck chairs. NCL intends to "stretch" this ship in mid-1999; this will add 190 cabins, and bring the ship's double occupancy to 1,436.

Inside she is a pretty ship, tastefully appointed, with lots of teak and brass accents, discreet lighting, soothing colors, and no glitz. Wide passageways provide a feeling of inner spaciousness. The circular lobby is bright and classical in appearance. Has three good conference/group meeting rooms. In the Observation Lounge, models and plans of nineteenth-century sailing ships provide a nautical ambience. The ship has a nice touch of elegance and open walking areas provide a fine feel to it. The showroom, however, is poorly designed, with 14 pillars obstructing the sight lines.

This ship will provide you with a very comfortable cruise experience in warm, quite elegant surroundings, with generally good food, and a modicum of hospitality. The ship is based on Boston during the summer season for seven-day cruises to Bermuda (the crew even wear Bermuda shorts), while during the winter she is based on Miami for seven-day Caribbean cruises. British passengers should note that all onboard gratuities are included, as are port taxes.

<u>But:</u> There are many repetitive, loud announcements, and the increased amount of squeezing for onboard revenue makes a cruise aboard her less enjoyable than it should be.

ms Norwegian Sea

☆☆☆☆

(L)

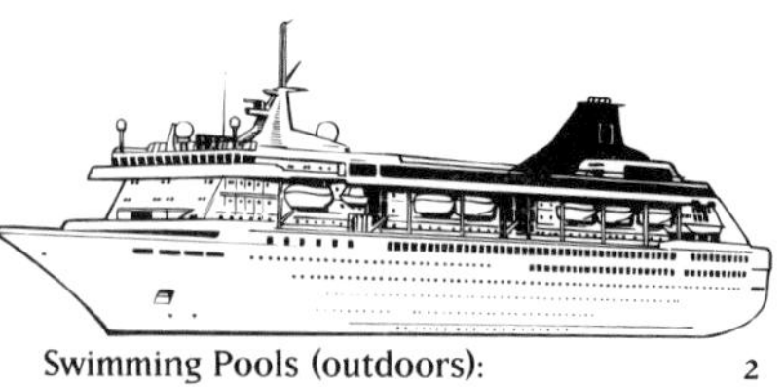

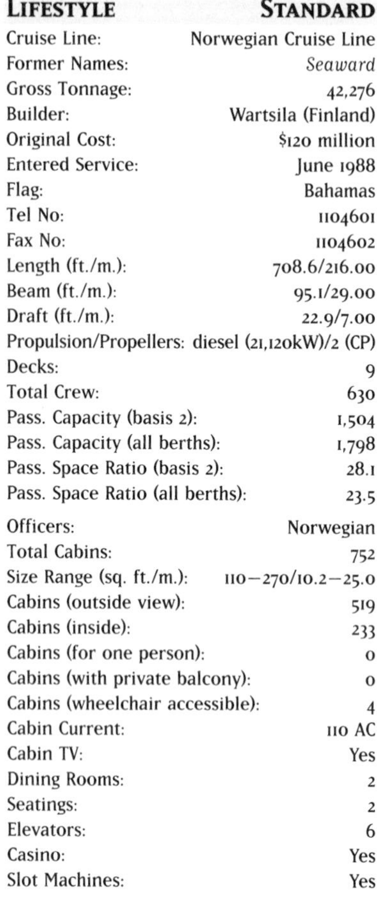

LIFESTYLE	STANDARD
Cruise Line:	Norwegian Cruise Line
Former Names:	*Seaward*
Gross Tonnage:	42,276
Builder:	Wartsila (Finland)
Original Cost:	$120 million
Entered Service:	June 1988
Flag:	Bahamas
Tel No:	1104601
Fax No:	1104602
Length (ft./m.):	708.6/216.00
Beam (ft./m.):	95.1/29.00
Draft (ft./m.):	22.9/7.00
Propulsion/Propellers:	diesel (21,120kW)/2 (CP)
Decks:	9
Total Crew:	630
Pass. Capacity (basis 2):	1,504
Pass. Capacity (all berths):	1,798
Pass. Space Ratio (basis 2):	28.1
Pass. Space Ratio (all berths):	23.5
Officers:	Norwegian
Total Cabins:	752
Size Range (sq. ft./m.):	110–270/10.2–25.0
Cabins (outside view):	519
Cabins (inside):	233
Cabins (for one person):	0
Cabins (with private balcony):	0
Cabins (wheelchair accessible):	4
Cabin Current:	110 AC
Cabin TV:	Yes
Dining Rooms:	2
Seatings:	2
Elevators:	6
Casino:	Yes
Slot Machines:	Yes
Swimming Pools (outdoors):	2
Swimming Pools (inside):	0
Whirlpools:	2
Fitness Center:	Yes
Sauna/Steam Room:	Yes/No
Massage:	Yes
Self-Service Launderette:	No
Movie Theater/Seats:	No
Library:	No
Children's Facilities:	No
Classification Society:	Det Norske Veritas

RATINGS	SCORE
Ship: Hardware/Maintenance	77
Ship: Outdoor Facilities/Space	78
Ship: Interior Facilities/Space/Flow	80
Ship: Decor/Furnishings/Artwork	80
Ship: Spa/Fitness Facilities	74
Cabins: Suites and Deluxe	81
Cabins: Standard Sizes	74
Food: Dining Room/Cuisine	67
Food: Informal Dining/Buffets	62
Food: Quality of Ingredients	66
Food: Afternoon Tea/Bar Snacks	54
Service: Dining Room	73
Service: Bars	72
Service: Cabins	74
Service: Open Decks	65
Cruise: Entertainment	74
Cruise: Activities Program	64
Cruise: Movies/Television Programming	66
Cruise: Hospitality Standard	76
Cruise: Overall Product Delivery	76
OVERALL SCORE	**1,433**

Accommodation: The cabins are of average size for a seven-day cruise ship (which translates to "somewhat cramped for two") but they are tastefully appointed and comfortable, with pastel colors, and bright soft furnishings, although the walls and ceilings are quite plain and simple. The bathrooms are efficient units that are quite well designed, though quite basic; hairdryers are included in all bathrooms.

Dining: The two main dining rooms (Four Seasons and Seven Seas) are quite homey, with pastel decor; which dining room you get depends on which accommodation you choose. The cuisine, for a mass-market ship, ranges from adequate to quite good. There is a major emphasis on meat dishes, with heavy sauces, and overcooked vegetables. However, fish and fowl are good. The emphasis is on Tex-Mex cuisine, with lots of spicy sauses. The service is, on the whole, adequate, nothing more, and proves that good staff who can communicate well are getting hard to find.

In addition to the dining room, this ship also features several alternative dining spots. For breakfast and lunch there's the Big Apple Grill, which has indoor and outdoor seating. There's also Le Bistro, open for casual dinners; and Gatsby's is a popular wine bar that features a good wine and champagne list.

The selection of wines is excellent, but breakfast and luncheon buffets are not.

Other Comments: This angular, yet attractive ship has a contemporary European cruise-ferry profile with a well-raked bow and sleek mast and funnel. This ship is well designed, with good passenger flow, and is among the best in the Caribbean mass-market. Fine teak wood outdoor wraparound promenade deck.

The interior decor is designed to remind you of sea and sky by stressing coral, blue, and mauve colors. Has tinny steps on stairways, and the hallways and stairways are quite plain. There is an excellent gymnasium/fitness center. The striking two-deck-high lobby has a crystal and water sculpture. Has two glass-walled stairways. Two-deck-high Crystal Court lobby is pleasing. A fine theater-showroom provides large-scale dazzle and sizzle shows with lots of energy and volume. The most intimate place is the mahogany-paneled Oscar's Lounge.

This ship provides a cruise in good taste for first-time cruise passengers, at a sensible, competitive price. However, the weak spot is the food operation, which still needs upgrading, with better food quality and higher levels of presentation, supervision, and service. British passengers booking through Thomson Cruises should note that all onboard gratuities and port taxes are included; you will join the ship in the Dominican Republic, having been flown by Britannia Airways, which is owned by Thomson.

But: There are too many unnecessary repetitive announcements, and outdoor deck space is tight.

ms Norwegian Sky

(L)

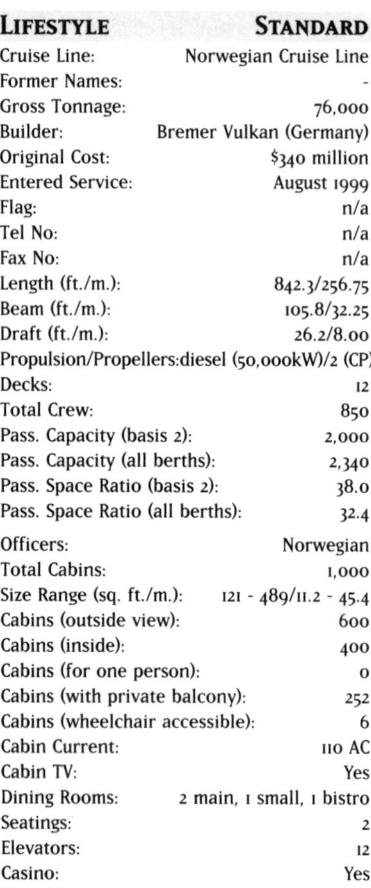

LIFESTYLE	**STANDARD**
Cruise Line:	Norwegian Cruise Line
Former Names:	-
Gross Tonnage:	76,000
Builder:	Bremer Vulkan (Germany)
Original Cost:	$340 million
Entered Service:	August 1999
Flag:	n/a
Tel No:	n/a
Fax No:	n/a
Length (ft./m.):	842.3/256.75
Beam (ft./m.):	105.8/32.25
Draft (ft./m.):	26.2/8.00
Propulsion/Propellers:	diesel (50,000kW)/2 (CP)
Decks:	12
Total Crew:	850
Pass. Capacity (basis 2):	2,000
Pass. Capacity (all berths):	2,340
Pass. Space Ratio (basis 2):	38.0
Pass. Space Ratio (all berths):	32.4
Officers:	Norwegian
Total Cabins:	1,000
Size Range (sq. ft./m.):	121 - 489/11.2 - 45.4
Cabins (outside view):	600
Cabins (inside):	400
Cabins (for one person):	0
Cabins (with private balcony):	252
Cabins (wheelchair accessible):	6
Cabin Current:	110 AC
Cabin TV:	Yes
Dining Rooms:	2 main, 1 small, 1 bistro
Seatings:	2
Elevators:	12
Casino:	Yes
Slot Machines:	Yes
Swimming Pools (outdoors):	2
Swimming Pools (inside):	0
Whirlpools:	6
Fitness Center:	Yes
Sauna/Steam Room:	Yes/Yes
Massage:	Yes
Self-Service Launderette:	No
Movie Theater/Seats:	No
Library:	Yes
Children's Facilities:	Yes
Classification Society:	RINA

RATINGS	**SCORE**
Ship: Hardware/Maintenance	NYR
Ship: Outdoor Facilities/Space	NYR
Ship: Interior Facilities/Space/Flow	NYR
Ship: Decor/Furnishings/Artwork	NYR
Ship: Spa/Fitness Facilities	NYR
Cabins: Suites and Deluxe	NYR
Cabins: Standard Sizes	NYR
Food: Dining Room/Cuisine	NYR
Food: Informal Dining/Buffets	NYR
Food: Quality of Ingredients	NYR
Food: Afternoon Tea/Bar Snacks	NYR
Service: Dining Room	NYR
Service: Bars	NYR
Service: Cabins	NYR
Service: Open Decks	NYR
Cruise: Entertainment	NYR
Cruise: Activities Program	NYR
Cruise: Movies/Television Programming	NYR
Cruise: Hospitality Standard	NYR
Cruise: Overall Product Delivery	NYR

EXPECTED SCORE RANGE
1,400-1,800

Accommodation: All standard outside-view cabins feature two lower beds that can convert to a queen-sized bed, a lounge area with sofa and table, and large, circular windows.

There are eight suites that feature a Jacuzzi tub outside on their private, teakwood floor balconies, slightly better bathrooms, and more space. The 21 junior suites also feature a private teakwood balcony.

Dining: There are two main dining rooms plus a small, connecting dining room. There is also a 50-seat "Le Bistro" alternative dining spot for alternative dining. In addition, there is also a sports bar, wine bar, champagne bar, ice-cream bar, and a cigar club.

Other Comments: This ship was created from the hull of what was to be *CostaOlympia*, which was purchased for $40 million and not completed when the shipyard went into bankruptcy. Norwegian

Cruise Line thus was able to build this ship in about 20 months, almost half of the time it would normally have taken.

There is a two-level show lounge, with large proscenium stage for the high-energy dazzle and sizzle shows that NCL passengers enjoy.

The cabaret lounge is equipped with what NCL states is the longest bar at sea (at present, however, this honor goes to *Aida,* owned by NCL but under charter to Arkona Reisen of Germany). Other features include a large casino, shopping arcade, children's playroom (there is also a splash pool atop ship), video arcade, large health/fitness spa (including an aerobics room and separate gymnasiums. There is a also a conference room, library, and beauty salon.

ms Norwegian Wind

☆☆☆☆

(L)

Lifestyle	**Standard**
Cruise Line:	Norwegian Cruise Line
Former Names:	*Windward*
Gross Tonnage:	50,760
Builder:	Chantiers de l'Atlantique (France)
Original Cost:	$240 million
Entered Service:	June 1993
Flag:	Bahamas
Tel No:	1305713/1305715
Fax No:	1305714/1305716
Length (ft./m.):	754.0/229.8
Beam (ft./m.):	93.5/28.5
Draft (ft./m.):	22.3/6.8
Propulsion/Propellers:	diesel (18,480kW)/2 (CP)
Decks:	10
Total Crew:	614
Pass. Capacity (basis 2):	1,748
Pass. Capacity (all berths):	2,156
Pass. Space Ratio (basis 2):	29.0
Pass. Space Ratio (all berths):	23.5
Officers:	Norwegian
Total Cabins:	874
Size Range (sq. ft./m.):	140–350/13.0–32.5
Cabins (outside view):	716
Cabins (inside):	158
Cabins (for one person):	0
Cabins (with private balcony):	48
Cabins (wheelchair accessible):	6 (+ 30 for hearing impaired)
Cabin Current:	110 AC
Cabin TV:	Yes
Dining Rooms:	2
Seatings:	2
Elevators:	10
Casino:	Yes
Slot Machines:	Yes
Swimming Pools (outdoors):	2
Swimming Pools (inside):	0
Whirlpools:	2
Fitness Center:	Yes
Sauna/Steam Room:	Yes/No
Massage:	Yes
Self-Service Launderette:	No
Movie Theater/Seats:	No
Library:	Yes
Children's Facilities:	Yes
Classification Society:	Det Norske Veritas

Ratings	**Score**
Ship: Hardware/Maintenance	81
Ship: Outdoor Facilities/Space	78
Ship: Interior Facilities/Space/Flow	82
Ship: Decor/Furnishings/Artwork	81
Ship: Spa/Fitness Facilities	76
Cabins: Suites and Deluxe	79
Cabins: Standard Sizes	76
Food: Dining Room/Cuisine	67
Food: Informal Dining/Buffets	62
Food: Quality of Ingredients	66
Food: Afternoon Tea/Bar Snacks	54
Service: Dining Room	74
Service: Bars	73
Service: Cabins	74
Service: Open Decks	67
Cruise: Entertainment	74
Cruise: Activities Program	64
Cruise: Movies/Television Programming	66
Cruise: Hospitality Standard	76
Cruise: Overall Product Delivery	75
Overall Score	**1,445**

For comments, see *Norwegian Dream*.

ss OceanBreeze

☆☆☆

(L)

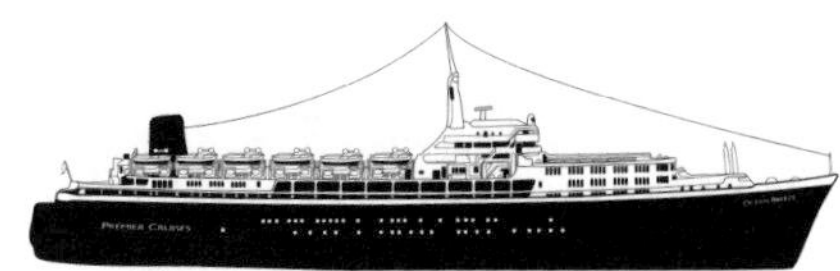

Lifestyle	Standard
Cruise Line:	Premier Cruises
Former Names:	*Azure Seas/Calypso/ Monarch Star/Southern Cross*
Gross Tonnage:	21,486
Builder:	Harland & Wolff (UK)
Original Cost:	n/a
Entered Service:	March 1955/May 1992
Flag:	Liberia
Tel No:	1246254
Fax No:	1246255
Length (ft./m.):	603.8/184.06
Beam (ft./m.):	80.0/24.41
Draft (ft./m.):	26.1/7.97
Propulsion/Propellers:	steam turbine (14,900kW)/2 (FP)
Decks:	9
Total Crew:	380
Pass. Capacity (basis 2):	776
Pass. Capacity (all berths):	1,012
Pass. Space Ratio (basis 2):	27.6
Pass. Space Ratio (all berths):	21.2
Officers:	Greek
Total Cabins:	388
Size Range (sq. ft./m.):	99–400/90.0–37.0
Cabins (outside view):	298
Cabins (inside–no view):	90
Cabins (single occupancy):	0
Cabins (with private balcony):	0
Cabins (wheelchair accessible):	0
Cabin Current:	110/220 AC
Cabin TV:	Suites only
Dining Rooms:	1
Seatings:	2
Elevators:	2
Casino:	Yes
Slot Machines:	Yes
Swimming Pools (outdoors):	1
Swimming Pools (inside):	0
Whirlpools:	1
Fitness Center:	Yes
Sauna/Steam Room:	Yes/No
Massage:	No
Self-Service Launderette:	No
Movie Theater/Seats:	Yes/55
Library:	Yes
Children's Facilities:	No
Classification Society:	Bureau Veritas

Ratings	Score
Ship: Hardware/Maintenance	62
Ship: Outdoor Facilities/Space	60
Ship: Interior Facilities/Space/Flow	55
Ship: Decor/Furnishings/Artwork	57
Ship: Spa/Fitness Facilities	40
Cabins: Suites and Deluxe	61
Cabins: Standard Sizes	52
Food: Dining Room/Cuisine	62
Food: Informal Dining/Buffets	54
Food: Quality of Ingredients	57
Food: Afternoon Tea/Bar Snacks	44
Service: Dining Room	64
Service: Bars	61
Service: Cabins	65
Service: Open Decks	54
Cruise: Entertainment	54
Cruise: Activities Program	53
Cruise: Movies/Television Programming	41
Cruise: Hospitality Standard	56
Cruise: Overall Product Delivery	62
Overall Score	**1,114**

Accommodation: The cabins are reasonably comfortable and nicely decorated in earth tones, and, though not large, are well appointed and have heavy-duty fittings (she is an old ship). There are 12 larger suites, some with forward view and with a separate bedroom and living area.

Dining: The Caravelle Restaurant is located low down in the ship, but has a warm, cheerful ambience (the chairs do not have armrests). The food is generally quite sound, and there is plenty of it, but it is not gourmet, despite what the brochure claims. The service is reasonable and quite attentive, but somewhat rushed. There is a limited choice of cheeses and fresh fruits.

Other Comments: This older ship, which used to operate liner voyages from England to Australia in the 1950s, has a long, low profile, and is easily identified by its single funnel astern. She has been maintained quite well, although now she is showing her age in several areas—she is, after all, over 40 years old! Vast amount of wooden open decks is in good condition, while a 1997 refurbishment has revitalized some of the public rooms.

The ship has some interesting art deco features. There is a generous amount of open deck and sunbathing space. The two-level casino is beautifully decorated in art deco style, in what used to be the cinema. Has a decent children's program for families with youngsters. This is a good ship for those wanting a pleasant cruise vacation for a modest price, in casual surroundings. Carries both North American/Canadian and South American passengers.

She is one of few ships to operate a seven-day year-round cruise from Jamaica, with an itinerary that includes a trip through part of the Panama Canal.

But: Do expect lines for embarkation, disembarkation, shore excursions and buffets. There are lots of smokers among the passengers. Many crew members do not speak English well.

ms Ocean Majesty

☆☆☆ +

(M)

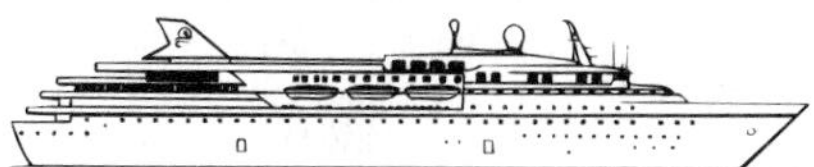

LIFESTYLE	STANDARD
Cruise Line:	Majestic International Cruises
Former Names:	*Homeric/Olympic/ Ocean Majesty/Kypros Star/Juan March*
Gross Tonnage:	10,417
Builder:	Union de Levante (Spain)
Original Cost:	$65 million
Entered Service:	1966/April 1994
Flag:	Greece
Tel No:	1132141
Fax No:	1132142
Length (ft./m.):	443.8/135.30
Beam (ft./m.):	62.9/19.20
Draft (ft./m.):	19.5/5.95
Propulsion/Propellers:	diesel (12,200kW)/2 (CP)
Decks:	8
Total Crew:	235
Pass. Capacity (basis 2):	535
Pass. Capacity (all berths):	621
Pass. Space Ratio (basis 2):	19.4
Pass. Space Ratio (all berths):	16.7
Officers:	Greek
Total Cabins:	273
Size Range (sq. ft./m.):	96–182/9.0–17.0
Cabins (outside view):	186
Cabins (inside–no view):	87
Cabins (single occupancy):	11
Cabins (with private balcony):	8
Cabins (wheelchair accessible):	2
Cabin Current:	110/220 AC
Cabin TV:	Suites only
Dining Rooms:	1
Seatings:	2
Elevators:	3
Casino:	Yes
Slot Machines:	Yes
Swimming Pools (outdoors):	1
Swimming Pools (inside):	0
Whirlpools:	1
Fitness Center:	Yes
Sauna/Steam Room:	Yes/No
Massage:	Yes
Self-Service Launderette:	No
Movie Theater/Seats:	No
Library:	Yes
Children's Facilities:	Yes
Classification Society:	American Bureau of Shipping

RATINGS	SCORE
Ship: Hardware/Maintenance	71
Ship: Outdoor Facilities/Space	63
Ship: Interior Facilities/Space/Flow	68
Ship: Decor/Furnishings/Artwork	73
Ship: Spa/Fitness Facilities	56
Cabins: Suites and Deluxe	76
Cabins: Standard Sizes	72
Food: Dining Room/Cuisine	71
Food: Informal Dining/Buffets	64
Food: Quality of Ingredients	64
Food: Afternoon Tea/Bar Snacks	50
Service: Dining Room	67
Service: Bars	64
Service: Cabins	66
Service: Open Decks	62
Cruise: Entertainment	63
Cruise: Activities Program	57
Cruise: Movies/Television Programming	51
Cruise: Hospitality Standard	62
Cruise: Overall Product Delivery	71
OVERALL SCORE	**1,291**

Accommodation: Most of the cabins (twelve cabin categories are too many for a ship of this size) are small and functional, and, because they have little closet and drawer space, you really should not take many clothes. The ceilings are plain and unimaginative, and soundproofing could be better. The bathrooms are bright and functional, with good lighting, but lack space for putting one's toiletry items.

Dining: The dining room is set low down and, although it is quite attractive, it is also extremely noisy (particularly at the tables adjacent to the waiter stations). There are no tables for two. The cuisine is continental in style, with the emphasis on Greek preparation and presentation. There is a limited selection of breads, fruits, and cheeses, and the buffets are generally simple, unimaginative and repetitive affairs that need some serious attention and more creativity.

Other Comments: This ship has a pleasing, balanced, almost handsome profile, with an aft funnel. A former Spanish ro-ro vessel (sister vessel to the present *Melia Don Juan*), this ship underwent an extensive transformation into a fairly smart cruise vessel, with the exception of hull, shaft, and propellers (all of which was completed in 1994). Her conversion was well done, although her built-up stern is not particularly handsome.

There are several good, practical public rooms, bars, and lounges, furnished with good quality materials and soft furnishing fabrics. The decor includes an abundance of highly polished mirrored surfaces.

Cruising aboard this ship will provide a busy, destination-oriented experience in surroundings that are very casual, comfortable, but nothing special. The ship is under charter to Orient Lines for Mediterranean cruises.

But: This is a high-density vessel, so expect lines for embarkation, disembarkation, shore excursions and buffets. Open deck and sunbathing space is very limited. Has a somewhat awkward interior layout and steep interior stairways with short steps.

ms Ocean Princess
(L)

LIFESTYLE	**PREMIUM**
Cruise Line:	Princess Cruises
Former Names:	-
Gross Tonnage:	77,000
Builder:	Fincantieri (Italy)
Original Cost:	$300 million
Entered Service:	November 1999
Flag:	Liberia
Tel No:	n/a
Fax No:	n/a
Length (ft./m.):	856.2/261.00
Beam (ft./m.):	105.8/32.25
Draft (ft./m.):	26.0/7.95
Propulsion/Propellers:	diesel-elec/2 (FP)
Decks:	14
Total Crew:	900
Pass. Capacity (basis 2):	1,950
Pass. Capacity (all berths):	2,250
Pass. Space Ratio (basis 2):	39.4
Pass. Space Ratio (all berths):	34.2
Officers:	Italian
Total Cabins:	1,050
Size Range (sq. ft./m.):	159–611/14.7–56.7
Cabins (outside view):	652
Cabins (inside–no view):	398
Cabins (single occupancy):	0
Cabins (with private balcony):	446
Cabins (wheelchair accessible):	20
Cabin Current:	110/220 AC
Cabin TV:	Yes
Dining Rooms:	2 main/3 others
Seatings:	2 (main dining rooms)
Elevators:	11
Casino:	Yes
Slot Machines:	Yes
Swimming Pools (outdoors):	3
Swimming Pools (inside):	0
Whirlpools:	5
Fitness Center:	Yes
Sauna/Steam Room:	Yes
Massage:	Yes
Self-Service Launderette:	Yes
Movie Theater/Seats:	Yes
Library:	Yes
Children's Facilities:	Yes
Classification Society:	Lloyd's Register

RATINGS	**SCORE**
Ship: Hardware/Maintenance	NYR
Ship: Outdoor Facilities/Space	NYR
Ship: Interior Facilities/Space/Flow	NYR
Ship: Decor/Furnishings/Artwork	NYR
Ship: Spa/Fitness Facilities	NYR
Cabins: Suites and Deluxe	NYR
Cabins: Standard Sizes	NYR
Food: Dining Room/Cuisine	NYR
Food: Informal Dining/Buffets	NYR
Food: Quality of Ingredients	NYR
Food: Afternoon Tea/Bar Snacks	NYR
Service: Dining Room	NYR
Service: Bars	NYR
Service: Cabins	NYR
Service: Open Decks	NYR
Cruise: Entertainment	NYR
Cruise: Activities Program	NYR
Cruise: Movies/Television Programming	NYR
Cruise: Hospitality Standard	NYR
Cruise: Overall Product Delivery	NYR

EXPECTED SCORE RANGE
1,400-1,700

For comments, see *Dawn Princess*.

ss Oceanic

☆☆☆

(L)

Lifestyle	**Standard**
Cruise Line:	Premier Cruises
Former Names:	*Oceanic*
Gross Tonnage:	38,772
Builder:	Cantieri Riuniti dell' Adriatico (Italy)
Original Cost:	$40 million
Entered Service:	April 1965/April 1986
Flag:	Bahamas
Tel No:	1120520
Fax No:	1120520
Length (ft./m.):	782.1/238.40
Beam (ft./m.):	96.5/29.44
Draft (ft./m.):	28.2/8.60
Propulsion/Propellers:	steam turbine (45,100kW)/2 (FP)
Decks:	10
Total Crew:	565
Pass. Capacity (basis 2):	1,116
Pass. Capacity (all berths):	1,898
Pass. Space Ratio (basis 2):	34.7
Pass. Space Ratio (all berths):	20.4
Officers:	Greek
Total Cabins:	574
Size Range (sq. ft./m.):	139–455/13.0–42.2
Cabins (outside view):	261
Cabins (inside–no view):	313
Cabins (single occupancy):	0
Cabins (with private balcony):	21
Cabins (wheelchair accessible):	0
Cabin Current:	110 AC
Cabin TV:	No
Dining Rooms:	1
Seatings:	2
Elevators:	5
Casino:	Yes
Slot Machines:	Yes
Swimming Pools (outdoors):	2
Swimming Pools (inside):	0
Whirlpools:	3
Fitness Center:	Yes
Sauna/Steam Room:	No/No
Massage:	Yes
Self-Service Launderette:	No
Movie Theater/Seats:	Yes/420
Library:	No
Children's Facilities:	Yes
Classification Society:	American Bureau of Shipping

Ratings	**Score**
Ship: Hardware/Maintenance	63
Ship: Outdoor Facilities/Space	64
Ship: Interior Facilities/Space/Flow	63
Ship: Decor/Furnishings/Artwork	60
Ship: Spa/Fitness Facilities	61
Cabins: Suites and Deluxe	77
Cabins: Standard Sizes	72
Food: Dining Room/Cuisine	74
Food: Informal Dining/Buffets	61
Food: Quality of Ingredients	58
Food: Afternoon Tea/Bar Snacks	40
Service: Dining Room	63
Service: Bars	62
Service: Cabins	63
Service: Open Decks	51
Cruise: Entertainment	56
Cruise: Activities Program	60
Cruise: Movies/Television Programming	58
Cruise: Hospitality Standard	57
Cruise: Overall Product Delivery	64
Overall Score	**1,227**

Accommodation: There are 8 deluxe suites with private balcony; 65 suites (13 of which have a private balcony), while the rest is a mixture of inside and outside cabins. There is a wide choice of cabin grades, sizes, and shapes. All cabins have heavy-duty furniture and are well equipped, although some need refurbishing. Many cabins feature double beds.

Dining: The dining room (nonsmoking for both seatings) is cheerful, but very noisy when full. Features good food and service (it was upgraded somewhat in 1998) considering the cruise fare, but there is a limited selection of breads, cheeses, and fruits.

Other Comments: Built originally as an ocean liner (now owned by Cruise Holdings, of Miami, and operated by Premier Cruises), the ship has undergone a successful conversion to provide cheap and cheerful family cruises. Also known as the Big Red Boat. There is a reasonable amount of open deck space for sunbathing, but it becomes quite cramped (and noisy) when the ship is full, and there are no cushioned pads for the deck lounge chairs. The swimming pool atop the ship has a magrodome roof for inclement weather.

Her interiors feature reasonably contemporary decor, and cheerful, bright, soft furnishing colors and fabrics. Has good enclosed promenades for strolling or sitting. This ship provides a good cruise experience for families with children by featuring many youth counselors. The cruise-and-stay packages are well designed.

Provides a family-oriented (much less expensive than the Disney Cruise Line product), fun-filled cruise aboard a classic ship setting, but it does tend to remind one of a summer camp at sea.

But: The constant repetitive announcements are quite irritating. The interiors need more attention to detail and cleanliness.

ms Oceanic Odyssey

☆☆☆☆ +

(S)

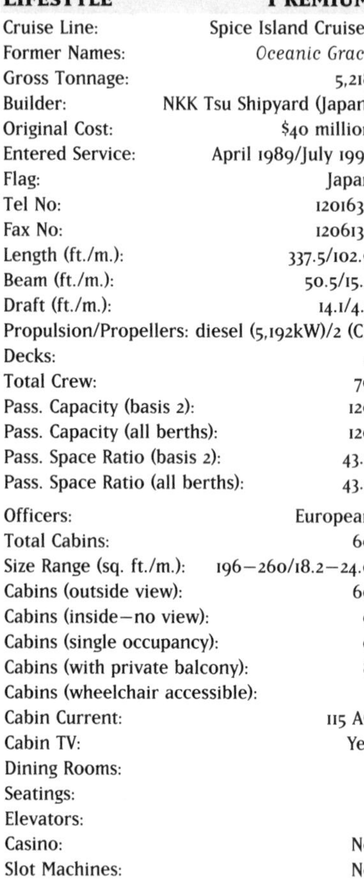

Lifestyle	Premium
Cruise Line:	Spice Island Cruises
Former Names:	*Oceanic Grace*
Gross Tonnage:	5,218
Builder:	NKK Tsu Shipyard (Japan)
Original Cost:	$40 million
Entered Service:	April 1989/July 1997
Flag:	Japan
Tel No:	1201634
Fax No:	1206134
Length (ft./m.):	337.5/102.9
Beam (ft./m.):	50.5/15.4
Draft (ft./m.):	14.1/4.3
Propulsion/Propellers:	diesel (5,192kW)/2 (CP)
Decks:	4
Total Crew:	70
Pass. Capacity (basis 2):	120
Pass. Capacity (all berths):	120
Pass. Space Ratio (basis 2):	43.4
Pass. Space Ratio (all berths):	43.4
Officers:	European
Total Cabins:	60
Size Range (sq. ft./m.):	196–260/18.2–24.0
Cabins (outside view):	60
Cabins (inside—no view):	0
Cabins (single occupancy):	0
Cabins (with private balcony):	8
Cabins (wheelchair accessible):	1
Cabin Current:	115 AC
Cabin TV:	Yes
Dining Rooms:	1
Seatings:	1
Elevators:	1
Casino:	No
Slot Machines:	No

Swimming Pools (outdoors):	1
Swimming Pools (inside):	0
Whirlpools:	1
Fitness Center:	Yes
Sauna/Steam Room:	Yes/Yes
Massage:	Yes
Self-Service Launderette:	No
Movie Theater/Seats:	No
Library:	Yes
Children's Facilities:	No
Classification Society:	Nippon Kaiji Kyokai

Ratings	Score
Ship: Hardware/Maintenance	86
Ship: Outdoor Facilities/Space	87
Ship: Interior Facilities/Space/Flow	88
Ship: Decor/Furnishings/Artwork	87
Ship: Spa/Fitness Facilities	84
Cabins: Suites and Deluxe	86
Cabins: Standard Sizes	82
Food: Dining Room/Cuisine	91
Food: Informal Dining/Buffets	86
Food: Quality of Ingredients	90
Food: Afternoon Tea/Bar Snacks	78
Service: Dining Room	86
Service: Bars	85
Service: Cabins	86
Service: Open Decks	83
Cruise: Entertainment	78
Cruise: Activities Program	67
Cruise: Movies/Television Programming	78
Cruise: Hospitality Standard	82
Cruise: Overall Product Delivery	88
Overall Score	**1,678**

Accommodation: The all-outside cabins are tastefully furnished and feature blond wood cabinetry, twin- or queen-sized beds, three-sided mirrors, personal safe, minibar-refrigerator, safe, television and VCR player, tea-making unit, cotton bathrobes. Bathrooms feature a deep, full-sized bathtub. Cabins with balconies (they are very small balconies) have awkward door handles. The bathroom toilet seats are high, particularly for South East Asian passengers.

Dining: A very inviting dining room features fresh foods from local ports, in a mix of regional and some Western cuisine. Service is provided by friendly, smiling Indonesian staff.

Other Comments: This ship features impressive, if somewhat square-ish, contemporary looks and sports twin outboard funnels. She was built originally as a Japanese attempt to copy the *Sea Goddesses*, but specifically outfitted for the Japanese market.

There is a decompression chamber for scuba divers, and water sports equipment is carried, as is a fleet of Zodiacs (inflatable landing craft for "soft" expedition use). Water sports facilities include an aft platform, scuba, snorkel, water-ski boat. There is plenty of open deck and sunbathing space. The small swimming pool is just a "dip" pool, however. Has a wide teakwood outdoor jogging track. Maintenance is still good, but noted to be slipping somewhat.

Nothing jars the senses, as the interior design concept successfully balances East-West color combinations with some Indonesian accents.

Under her new owners, the ship operates three- and four-day cruises from November through April, and ten- to twelve-day cruises from April to November (Eastern Indonesia, South Pacific, New Zealand, and Australia's Great Barrier Reef) from Bali.

mts Odysseus

☆☆☆

(S)

Lifestyle	Standard
Cruise Line:	Royal Olympic Cruises
Former Names:	*Aquamarine/Marco Polo/ Princesa Isabel*
Gross Tonnage:	12,000
Builder:	Society Espanola Shipyard (Spain)
Original Cost:	n/a
Entered Service:	1962/Spring 1987
Flag:	Greece
Tel No:	1130652/623703510
Fax No:	1130252/623703511
Length (ft./m.):	483.1/147.30
Beam (ft./m.):	61.2/18.67
Draft (ft./m.):	24.1/7.35
Propulsion/Propellers:	diesel (6,766kW)/2 (CP)
Decks:	7
Total Crew:	194
Pass. Capacity (basis 2):	454
Pass. Capacity (all berths):	484
Pass. Space Ratio (basis 2):	26.4
Pass. Space Ratio (all berths):	24.7
Officers:	Greek
Total Cabins:	226
Size Range (sq. ft./m.):	102–280/9.5–26.0
Cabins (outside view):	183
Cabins (inside–no view):	43
Cabins (single occupancy):	0
Cabins (with private balcony):	0
Cabins (wheelchair accessible):	0
Cabin Current:	110 AC
Cabin TV:	No
Dining Rooms:	2
Seatings:	2
Elevators:	1
Casino:	Yes
Slot Machines:	Yes
Swimming Pools (outdoors):	1
Swimming Pools (inside):	0
Whirlpools:	4
Fitness Center:	Yes
Sauna/Steam Room:	Yes/No
Massage:	Yes
Self-Service Launderette:	No
Movie Theater/Seats:	Yes/145
Library:	Yes
Children's Facilities:	No
Classification Society:	Lloyd's Register

Ratings	Score
Ship: Hardware/Maintenance	73
Ship: Outdoor Facilities/Space	70
Ship: Interior Facilities/Space/Flow	61
Ship: Decor/Furnishings/Artwork	75
Ship: Spa/Fitness Facilities	46
Cabins: Suites and Deluxe	72
Cabins: Standard Sizes	64
Food: Dining Room/Cuisine	61
Food: Informal Dining/Buffets	52
Food: Quality of Ingredients	58
Food: Afternoon Tea/Bar Snacks	47
Service: Dining Room	66
Service: Bars	62
Service: Cabins	66
Service: Open Decks	51
Cruise: Entertainment	53
Cruise: Activities Program	52
Cruise: Movies/Television Programming	49
Cruise: Hospitality Standard	58
Cruise: Overall Product Delivery	64
Overall Score	**1,200**

Accommodation: The attractive, quite roomy, mostly outside cabins have convertible sofabeds which convert from a sofa during the day into a bed by night (a few cabins have real double beds). There is a decent amount of closet and drawer space, and tasteful wood trim adorns the cabinetry. The cabin bathrooms, however, are small (particularly the shower stalls).

Any in-cabin food/beverage service tends to be quite basic, without the finesse found aboard more expensive vessels.

Dining: The dining room is quite charming, though it tends to be noisy due to the ceiling height and the location of waiter stations. The food is typically Continental, and features several Greek dishes. Warm, attentive service is provided in typical Greek fashion, but the menu choice is rather limited. The quality and selection of breads, cheeses, and fruits could be better. Note that dining room seating and table assignments are done by the maître d' upon embarkation. An informal dining spot (Marine Club) is available for casual breakfast and lunch.

Other Comments: This attractive-looking vessel has a balanced profile, and was acquired and completely reconstructed by Epirotiki Cruise Line (now part of Royal Olympic Cruises) in 1987. There is ample open deck and sunbathing space. Has twin teak-decked sheltered promenade walking areas.

There is a good range of public rooms, which feature pleasing Mediterranean decor, warm colors, and some decent artwork throughout. Almost all of the public rooms are located on one deck, so finding them is easy. The Taverna is especially popular with the younger set.

This ship, now part of the joint Epirotiki/Sun Line fleet called Royal Olympic Cruises, is really for those who want to cruise at a modest cost, in warm surroundings, aboard a comfortable smaller vessel which features destination-intensive itineraries in the Aegean and Mediterranean areas. The ship is often placed under charter to tour operators specializing in "learning enrichment" vacations, and the cruises are sold by a number of cruise-tour companies in various countries. This means that passengers are likely to consist of a wide mix of nationalities, and daily programs and announcements, therefore, will probably be in several languages.

Gratuities (suggested at $9 per person per day) are pooled among the crew (you give them to the Chief Steward).

But: The company provides little port information for passengers wishing to go ashore individually, but heavily sells its shore excursion programs.

mv Olympic Countess

☆☆☆ +

(M)

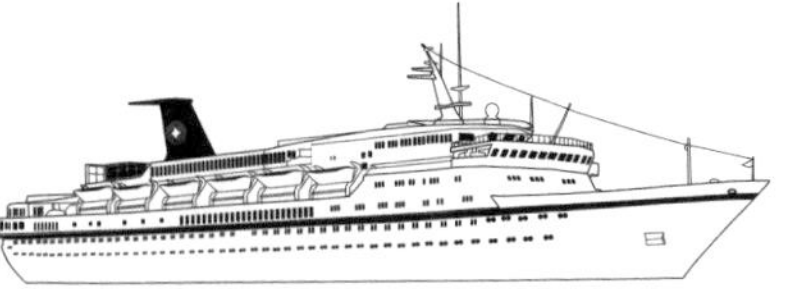

Lifestyle	**Standard**
Cruise Line:	Royal Olympic Cruises
Former Names:	*Awani Dream II/ Cunard Countess*
Gross Tonnage:	17,593
Builder:	Burmeister & Wein (Denmark)
Original Cost:	£12 million
Entered Service:	August 1976/1998
Flag:	Panama
Tel No:	1104676
Fax No:	1104676
Length (ft./m.):	536.6/163.56
Beam (ft./m.):	74.9/22.84
Draft (ft./m.):	19.0/5.82
Propulsion/Propellers:	diesel (15,670kW)/2 (CP)
Decks:	8
Total Crew:	350
Pass. Capacity (basis 2):	846
Pass. Capacity (all berths):	959
Pass. Space Ratio (basis 2):	20.7
Pass. Space Ratio (all berths):	18.3
Officers:	Greek
Total Cabins:	423
Size Range (sq. ft./m.):	88–265/8.1–24.6
Cabins (outside view):	281
Cabins (inside—no view):	142
Cabins (single occupancy):	0
Cabins (with private balcony):	0
Cabins (wheelchair accessible):	0
Cabin Current:	110/220 AC
Cabin TV:	No
Dining Rooms:	1
Seatings:	2
Elevators:	2
Casino:	Yes
Slot Machines:	Yes
Swimming Pools (outdoors):	1
Swimming Pools (inside):	0
Whirlpools:	2
Fitness Center:	Yes
Sauna/Steam Room:	Yes/No
Massage:	No
Self-Service Launderette:	No
Movie Theater/Seats:	Yes/126
Library:	Yes
Children's Facilities:	No
Classification Society:	Lloyd's Register

Ratings	**Score**
Ship: Hardware/Maintenance	67
Ship: Outdoor Facilities/Space	66
Ship: Interior Facilities/Space/Flow	63
Ship: Decor/Furnishings/Artwork	65
Ship: Spa/Fitness Facilities	65
Cabins: Suites and Deluxe	65
Cabins: Standard Sizes	56
Food: Dining Room/Cuisine	66
Food: Informal Dining/Buffets	62
Food: Quality of Ingredients	63
Food: Afternoon Tea/Bar Snacks	56
Service: Dining Room	66
Service: Bars	64
Service: Cabins	67
Service: Open Decks	54
Cruise: Entertainment	56
Cruise: Activities Program	57
Cruise: Movies/Television Programming	52
Cruise: Hospitality Standard	68
Cruise: Overall Product Delivery	73
Overall Score	**1,251**

Accommodation: The cabins are mostly of a standard (small) size, and come in very light colors and nice decor. They are space-efficient units with metal fixtures and poor insulation, which means you hear your neighbors brushing their hair. The cabins on the lowest deck (2 Deck) suffer from vibration and the odor of diesel fuel. Cabin bathrooms are small modular units, good for one, impossible for two.

Dining: The large, pleasant dining room has ocean-view picture windows on two sides. Reasonable banquet food standard, tailored for American and European passengers. Out-of-the-ordinary requests are difficult. Limited fresh fruit and cheese selection. Good, cheerful service from an attentive Greek staff.

Other Comments: Originally built for Cunard as an informal Caribbean cruise vessel, she was purchased in late 1997 by Royal Olympic Cruises from her former operators, the now defunct Awani Dream Cruises of Indonesia, who purchased the vessel from Cunard.

The ship still displays a contemporary profile, with crisp, clean lines and a distinctive swept-back funnel (her almost identical sister presently operates as *Rhapsody* for Mediterranean Shipping Cruises).

Inside the ship, there is a good selection of public rooms to choose from, and most of them have attractive, light colors and cheerful decor.

Aft of the show lounge, which is a single-level room with raised seating on its port and starboard sides (although several pillars obstruct sight lines), there is a good indoor-outdoor entertainment lounge/night club that incorporates a large aft open deck area.

Passengers seeking a casual, destination-intensive cruise will probably like this comfortable vessel, which is a change from the newer, larger ships of today, and is very well suited to cruising in the Aegean/Mediterranean region.

<u>But:</u> This is a very high-density ship. The outside decks still need attention.

ms Oriana

☆☆☆☆ +

(L)

Lifestyle	Premium
Cruise Line:	P&O Cruises
Former Names:	-
Gross Tonnage:	69,153
Builder:	Meyer Werft (Germany)
Original Cost:	£200 million
Entered Service:	April 1995
Flag:	Great Britain
Tel No:	1453403
Fax No:	1453404
Length (ft./m.):	853.0/260.0
Beam (ft./m.):	105.6/32.2
Draft (ft./m.):	25.9/7.9
Propulsion/Propellers:	diesel (47,750kW)/2 (CP)
Decks:	10
Total Crew:	760
Pass. Capacity (basis 2):	1,828
Pass. Capacity (all berths):	1,975
Pass. Space Ratio (basis 2):	37.8
Pass. Space Ratio (all berths):	35.0
Officers:	British
Total Cabins:	914
Size Range (sq. ft./m.):	151–501/14.0–46.5
Cabins (outside view):	594
Cabins (inside–no view):	320
Cabins (single occupancy):	112
Cabins (with private balcony):	118
Cabins (wheelchair accessible):	8
Cabin Current:	110/220 AC
Cabin TV:	Yes
Dining Rooms:	2
Seatings:	2
Elevators:	10
Casino:	Yes
Slot Machines:	Yes
Swimming Pools (outdoors):	3
Swimming Pools (inside):	0
Whirlpools:	5
Fitness Center:	Yes
Sauna/Steam Room:	Yes/Yes
Massage:	Yes
Self-Service Launderette:	Yes
Movie Theater/Seats:	Yes/189
Library:	Yes
Children's Facilities:	Yes
Classification Society:	Lloyd's Register

Ratings	Score
Ship: Hardware/Maintenance	90
Ship: Outdoor Facilities/Space	87
Ship: Interior Facilities/Space/Flow	90
Ship: Decor/Furnishings/Artwork	91
Ship: Spa/Fitness Facilities	87
Cabins: Suites and Deluxe	90
Cabins: Standard Sizes	86
Food: Dining Room/Cuisine	81
Food: Informal Dining/Buffets	76
Food: Quality of Ingredients	78
Food: Afternoon Tea/Bar Snacks	67
Service: Dining Room	82
Service: Bars	82
Service: Cabins	83
Service: Open Decks	80
Cruise: Entertainment	88
Cruise: Activities Program	77
Cruise: Movies/Television Programming	81
Cruise: Hospitality Standard	78
Cruise: Overall Product Delivery	84
Overall Score	**1,658**

Accommodation: There is a wide range of well-equipped cabin configurations and categories, including family cabins with extra beds (110 cabins can accommodate four persons). Some suites and cabins with balconies have an inter-connecting door, and include a trouser press, ironing board, and iron (neatly tucked into a cupboard), binoculars, umbrella, a large atlas, and a second television as well as a sliding glazed panel between bedroom and sitting room. The bathrooms are somewhat disappointing, with an ordinary sink (I expected a marble unit). The whirlpool bathtubs are good, however, although they have high sides to step over. All in all, the suites, and particularly the bathrooms, are disappointing when compared with similar sized suites on other ships (they do, however, have a VCR player).

There is much use of rich, warm limed oak or cherry wood in the cabins, which makes even the least expensive four-berth cabin seem inviting. There is also a good number of cabins for single passengers. Standard cabin bathrooms are compact, but they do have art deco-style cabinets and lighting.

Dining: The two restaurants, Peninsular and Oriental, allocated according to the cabin grade and cabin chosen, are midships and aft. Both are quite handsome (each has tables for two, four, six, or eight). Both have interesting ceilings, chandeliers, and decor. Oriental Restaurant has windows on three sides, including the stern.

"Eat and run" instead of "dining" tends to be the norm. Besides the Anton Mosimann-designed signature dishes, the meals are fairly non-memorable, "Middle-England" standard fare, and presentation lacks creativity.

The Conservatory Café offers breakfast and lunch buffets, and twenty-four-hour self-service beverage stands. An alternative restaurant featuring Indian food would be a useful addition.

Other Comments: The ship is, thankfully, quite conventional: evolutionary rather than revolutionary. Capable of speedy long-distance cruising, it has the largest stabilizers of any ship, covering an area of 231 sq. ft. (21.5 m^2). She is a ship that takes Canberra's traditional appointments and public rooms and adds more up-to-date touches, together with better facilities and passenger flow, and a feeling of timeless elegance.

Her interiors are gentle, welcoming, and restrained. Splendid amount of open deck and sunbathing space, an important plus for her outdoors-loving British passengers. Has an extra-wide wraparound outdoor promenade deck. Features inboard lifeboats, as do so many ships today. The stern superstructure is nicely rounded and has several tiers that overlook an aft deck, pool, and children's outdoor facilities. Inside, the well laid-out design provides good horizontal passenger flow and wide passageways. Noticeable are the fine detailed ceiling treatments. Being a ship for all types of people, specific areas have been designed to attract different age groups and lifestyles.

There is a four-deck-high atrium and waterfall; it is elegant but not glitzy, topped by a dome of Tiffany glass. The large number of public entertainment rooms provides plenty of choice. The Theatre Royal, designed by John Wyckham, is decorated in rich reds and created specifically for drama and light theatrical presentations. It has individually air-conditioned seats, an orchestra pit, revolving stage and excellent acoustics. The theater seats would provide better stage sight lines if they were staggered. A night club, the Pacific Lounge, has too many pillars that obstruct the view. Anderson's Lounge (named after the founder of the Peninsular Steam Navigation Company in the 1830s) features a series of nineteenth-century marine paintings, and is decorated in the manner of a British gentlemen's club. Although there is no fireplace, it is the most popular lounge.

The fine, restful library has a well-chosen selection of hardback books (and a real librarian), skillfully crafted tables, and some extremely comfortable chairs. Lord's Tavern is, without doubt, the most sporting place to pitch a beverage or two, decorated as it is in cricket memorabilia (indeed, the house of the ship's interior designer, John McNeece, stands on the site of the original Lord's cricket ground in London). Thackeray's (a writing room) is named after William Makepeace Thackeray, a P&O passenger in 1844. Carpeting throughout the ship is of excellent quality, much of it custom designed and made (100 percent wool). There are some outstanding pieces of sculpture that add a touch of a floating museum, and original artworks by all-British artists that include tapestries and sculptures.

The health spa is located forward and atop ship, is quite large, and provides all the latest alternative therapy treatment. The co-ed sauna is a large facility (most ships have separate saunas for men and women). The aerobic exercise room and health spa are not connected, however (you first must go out of the spa, into a foyer, and then into the exercise room).

Children and teens have "Club Oriana" programs with their own rooms ("Peter Pan" and "Decibels"), and their own outdoor pool. There is also a special night nursery for small children (ages two to five). The cabins also have a baby-listening device.

There is always a good variety of entertainment aboard the ships of P&O Cruises, as well as fine program of special theme cruises (antiques, The Archers, art appreciation, classical music, comedy, cricket, gardening, jazz, motoring, popular fiction, Scottish dance, and sequence dancing were among the themes in 1998); check with your travel agent to see what is available at the time you want to take your cruise.

Oriana provides a fine cruise experience for British passengers (of all dialects) who do not want to fly to get to a cruise ship. A fine British brass band send-off accompanies all sailings. Port taxes and insurance included for UK passengers. For gratuities, allow £3.00 per person, per day.

mv Orient Venus

(S)

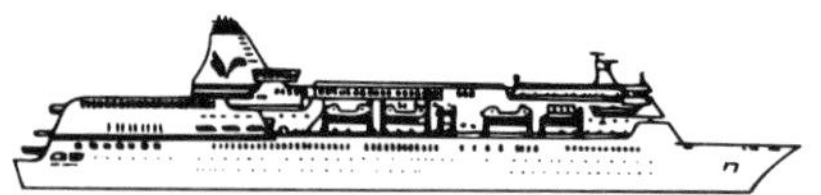

LIFESTYLE	**STANDARD**
Cruise Line:	Venus Cruise (Nippon Cruise Kyakusen)
Former Names:	-
Gross Tonnage:	21,884
Builder:	Ishikawajima Heavy Industries (Japan)
Original Cost:	$150 million
Entered Service:	July 1990
Flag:	Japan
Tel No:	1201731
Fax No:	1201731
Length (ft./m.):	570.8/174.00
Beam (ft./m.):	78.7/24.00
Draft (ft./m.):	21.3/6.52
Propulsion/Propellers:	diesel (18,540bhp)/2 (CP)
Decks:	8
Total Crew:	120
Pass. Capacity (basis 2):	390
Pass. Capacity (all berths):	606
Pass. Space Ratio (basis 2):	56.1
Pass. Space Ratio (all berths):	36.1
Officers:	Japanese
Total Cabins:	195
Size Range (sq. ft./m.):	182.9–592.0/17.0–55.0
Cabins (outside view):	195
Cabins (inside—no view):	0
Cabins (single occupancy):	0
Cabins (with private balcony):	2
Cabins (wheelchair accessible):	0
Cabin Current:	110 AC
Cabin TV:	Yes
Dining Rooms:	2
Seatings:	1
Elevators:	3
Casino:	No
Slot Machines:	No
Swimming Pools (outdoors):	1
Swimming Pools (inside):	0
Whirlpools:	0
Fitness Center:	Yes
Sauna/Steam Room:	No/No
Massage:	No
Self-Service Launderette:	Yes
Movie Theater/Seats:	Yes/606
Library:	Yes
Children's Facilities:	No
Classification Society:	Nippon Kaiji Kyokai

RATINGS	**SCORE**
Ship: Hardware/Maintenance	78
Ship: Outdoor Facilities/Space	81
Ship: Interior Facilities/Space/Flow	81
Ship: Decor/Furnishings/Artwork	80
Ship: Spa/Fitness Facilities	82
Cabins: Suites and Deluxe	81
Cabins: Standard Sizes	74
Food: Dining Room/Cuisine	77
Food: Informal Dining/Buffets	72
Food: Quality of Ingredients	76
Food: Afternoon Tea/Bar Snacks	69
Service: Dining Room	76
Service: Bars	74
Service: Cabins	76
Service: Open Decks	66
Cruise: Entertainment	64
Cruise: Activities Program	66
Cruise: Movies/Television Programming	76
Cruise: Hospitality Standard	75
Cruise: Overall Product Delivery	81
OVERALL SCORE	**1,505**

Accommodation: There are just four cabin grades (royal, deluxe, state, and standard). The all-outside standard cabins, many of which have upper berths for third/fourth passengers, have decor that is best described as plain, with reasonable closet space, but little drawer space.

The largest suites (there are two) have an expansive lounge area with large, plush armchairs, coffee table, and window-side chairs and drinks table, floor-to-ceiling windows, and large private balcony; there is a separate sleeping room (curtained off from the living room) with twin- or queen-sized bed, vanity/office desk, and large bathroom.

All grades of accommodation feature a tea drinking set (with electric hot water kettle), color television, telephone, and stocked refrigerator.

Dining: The main dining room is very attractive, and there is plenty of space around the dining tables. In addition, the alternative Romanesque Grill is quite unusual, with classic period Roman decor and a high, elegant ceiling. Features reasonably good, but rather commercial, Japanese cuisine exclusively.

Other Comments: This conventional-shaped ship has quite a graceful profile. Has an expansive amount of open deck and sunbathing space, which is not often used. There is also an expansive amount of open deck space for sunbathing, aft of funnel.

Inside the ship, the Night and Day Lounge set at funnel base looks forward over the swimming pool. Windows of the Orient is a small, attractive, peaceful forward observation lounge. The conference facilities are excellent, and consist of both main and small conference rooms with 620 movable seats. There is a fine array of public rooms with tasteful and very inviting decor. The horseshoe-shaped main lounge has very good sight lines to the platform stage.

This cruise ship, with its western-style decor, will provide its mostly Japanese corporate passengers with extremely comfortable surroundings, and provides a superb cruise and seminar/learning environment and experience. She was joined by a new, slightly larger sister ship, *Pacific Venus* in spring 1998.

But: The ship does not really cater to individual passengers well. The decor is rather plain in many public rooms. The crew-to-passenger ratio is poor, but typical of seminar-intensive ships.

mts Orpheus

☆☆ +

(S)

Lifestyle	Standard
Cruise Line:	Royal Olympic Cruises
Former Names:	*Thesus/Munster I/Munster*
Gross Tonnage:	5,092
Builder:	Harland & Wolff (UK)
Original Cost:	n/a
Entered Service:	1952/1969
Flag:	Greece
Tel No:	1133165
Fax No:	1131336
Length (ft./m.):	374.8/114.26
Beam (ft./m.):	50.1/15.30
Draft (ft./m.):	16.0/4.88
Propulsion/Propellers:	diesel (4,119kW)/2 (FP)
Decks:	6
Total Crew:	140
Pass. Capacity (basis 2):	304
Pass. Capacity (all berths):	310
Pass. Space Ratio (basis 2):	16.7
Pass. Space Ratio (all berths):	16.4
Officers:	Greek
Total Cabins:	152
Size Range (sq. ft./m.):	99.8–226.0/9.28–21.00
Cabins (outside view):	117
Cabins (inside—no view):	35
Cabins (single occupancy):	7
Cabins (with private balcony):	0
Cabins (wheelchair accessible):	0
Cabin Current:	220 AC
Cabin TV:	No
Dining Rooms:	1
Seatings:	Open
Elevators:	0
Casino:	No
Slot Machines:	No
Swimming Pools (outdoors):	1
Swimming Pools (inside):	0
Whirlpools:	0
Fitness Center:	No
Sauna/Steam Room:	No/No
Massage:	No
Self-Service Launderette:	No
Movie Theater/Seats:	No
Library:	Yes
Children's Facilities:	No
Classification Society:	Lloyd's Register

Ratings	Score
Ship: Hardware/Maintenance	51
Ship: Outdoor Facilities/Space	44
Ship: Interior Facilities/Space/Flow	54
Ship: Decor/Furnishings/Artwork	59
Ship: Spa/Fitness Facilities	33
Cabins: Suites and Deluxe	52
Cabins: Standard Sizes	48
Food: Dining Room/Cuisine	60
Food: Informal Dining/Buffets	56
Food: Quality of Ingredients	60
Food: Afternoon Tea/Bar Snacks	54
Service: Dining Room	63
Service: Bars	62
Service: Cabins	65
Service: Open Decks	51
Cruise: Entertainment	52
Cruise: Activities Program	50
Cruise: Movies/Television Programming	51
Cruise: Hospitality Standard	63
Cruise: Overall Product Delivery	70
Overall Score	**1,098**

Accommodation: The cabins (in six grades) are very compact but quite nicely appointed for an older ship, and thus quite adequate for short cruises. There is a limited amount of closet, drawer, and under-bed storage space, so take only minimal clothing. The bathrooms, however, are really short on space.

Dining: The dining room is quite attractive and features an open seating policy. Features attentive, friendly service from the Greek waiters, but they are very casual. The food itself is quite reasonable, but certainly not memorable, and the selection of breads, cheeses, and fruits is limited. Dining room seating and table assignments are done by the maître d' upon embarkation.

Other Comments: Has a traditional small ship profile, with a small, squat funnel. She is a charming older ship that has been reasonably well maintained. There is ample open deck and sunbathing space for a ship of this size, including a wraparound outdoor promenade deck, and there is also a small outdoor pool and bar, as well as a forward observation area outside on Apollo Deck.

There are few public rooms, but they are comfortable, and have Mediterranean decor, good fabrics, and interesting regional artwork. Informality is the order of the day throughout, and dress codes are very casual (no formal nights).

The company features a number of guest lecturers who provide informed, yet informal presentations aboard all cruises. During the summer, the ship typically operates three- and four-day cruises from Piraeus. Gratuities (suggested at $9 per person per day) are pooled among the crew (you give them to the Chief Steward).

But: The high density of this vessel means that public rooms are always crowded when the ship is full.

mv Pacific Princess

☆☆☆ +

(M)

LIFESTYLE	PREMIUM
Cruise Line:	Princess Cruises
Former Names:	*Sea Venture*
Gross Tonnage:	20,636
Builder: Rheinstahl Nordseewerke (Germany)	
Original Cost:	$25 million
Entered Service:	May 1971/April 1975
Flag:	Great Britain
Tel No:	1440212
Fax No:	1440212
Length (ft./m.):	553.6/168.74
Beam (ft./m.):	80.8/24.64
Draft (ft./m.):	25.2/7.70
Propulsion/Propellers: diesel (13,240kW)/2 (CP)	
Decks:	7
Total Crew:	350
Pass. Capacity (basis 2):	610
Pass. Capacity (all berths):	717
Pass. Space Ratio (basis 2):	33.8
Pass. Space Ratio (all berths):	28.7
Officers:	British
Total Cabins:	305
Size Range (sq. ft./m.):	126–443/11.7–41.0
Cabins (outside view):	238
Cabins (inside–no view):	67
Cabins (single occupancy):	2
Cabins (with private balcony):	0
Cabins (wheelchair accessible):	2
Cabin Current:	110/220 AC
Cabin TV:	Yes
Dining Rooms:	1
Seatings:	2
Elevators:	4
Casino:	Yes
Slot Machines:	Yes
Swimming Pools (outdoors):	2
Swimming Pools (inside):	0
Whirlpools:	0
Fitness Center:	Yes
Sauna/Steam Room:	Yes/No
Massage:	Yes
Self-Service Launderette:	No
Movie Theater/Seats:	Yes/250
Library:	Yes
Children's Facilities:	No
Classification Society:	Lloyd's Register

RATINGS	SCORE
Ship: Hardware/Maintenance	68
Ship: Outdoor Facilities/Space	67
Ship: Interior Facilities/Space/Flow	71
Ship: Decor/Furnishings/Artwork	70
Ship: Spa/Fitness Facilities	51
Cabins: Suites and Deluxe	66
Cabins: Standard Sizes	61
Food: Dining Room/Cuisine	73
Food: Informal Dining/Buffets	68
Food: Quality of Ingredients	70
Food: Afternoon Tea/Bar Snacks	63
Service: Dining Room	74
Service: Bars	75
Service: Cabins	76
Service: Open Decks	68
Cruise: Entertainment	76
Cruise: Activities Program	65
Cruise: Movies/Television Programming	66
Cruise: Hospitality Standard	71
Cruise: Overall Product Delivery	77
OVERALL SCORE	**1,376**

Accommodation: The suites and all other (non-suite) cabins are quite roomy and well appointed, functional and comfortable without being overdone. The decor, however, now seems a little dated and rather plain, and could do with brightening. The bathrooms are practical, and bathrobes are provided for all passengers.

Dining: The dining room (nonsmoking) is located on a lower deck, but has nice, light decor and feels comfortable and spacious. Good service and fairly good food, although standards have been slipping as a result of discounted fares.

Other Comments: This ship was originally built for the now-defunct Sea Venture Cruises, and was sold to Princess Cruises in 1975. She is a well-proportioned, handsome medium-size ship with a relatively high superstructure and quite graceful lines. Princess Cruises has spent a considerable sum of money in upgrading her, and she has been quite well maintained. There is plenty of good open deck space and several sunbathing areas, but, sadly, there is no wraparound outdoor promenade deck. One swimming pool has a magrodome roof for use in inclement weather.

Inside, the spacious public areas have wide passageways and high ceilings. Tasteful earth-toned decor throughout, with complementary artwork. There is a decent movie theater. As for entertainment, the production shows and general entertainment is adequate. Smartly-dressed officers and crew help to add a feeling of passenger care.

Finally, this ship is definitely for the older passenger. Quite elegant and moderately expensive, it offers a stylish cruise in very comfortable and elegant surroundings.

ms Pacific Venus

☆☆☆☆ +

(M)

LIFESTYLE	**STANDARD**
Cruise Line:	Venus Cruise (Nippon Cruise Kyakusen)
Former Names:	-
Gross Tonnage:	26,518
Builder:	Ishikawajima Heavy Industries (Japan)
Original Cost:	114 million (Yen13 billion)
Entered Service:	April 1998
Flag:	Japan
Tel No:	n/a
Fax No:	n/a
Length (ft./m.):	601.7/183.4
Beam (ft./m.):	82.0/25.0
Draft (ft./m.):	21.3/6.5
Propulsion/Propellers:	diesel/2 (CP)
Decks:	9
Total Crew:	180
Pass. Capacity (basis 2):	532
Pass. Capacity (all berths):	720
Pass. Space Ratio (basis 2):	49.8
Pass. Space Ratio (all berths):	36.8
Officers:	Japanese
Total Cabins:	266
Size Range (sq. ft./m.):	164.6–699.6/15.3–65.0
Cabins (outside view):	250
Cabins (inside–no view):	16
Cabins (single occupancy):	0
Cabins (with private balcony):	20
Cabins (wheelchair accessible):	1
Cabin Current:	110 AC
Cabin TV:	Yes
Dining Rooms:	2
Seatings:	1
Elevators:	4
Casino:	Yes
Slot Machines:	No
Swimming Pools (outdoors):	1 (+ 1 for children)
Swimming Pools (inside):	0
Whirlpools:	1
Fitness Center:	Yes
Sauna/Steam Room:	No/Yes
Massage:	Yes
Self-Service Launderette:	Yes (2)
Movie Theater/Seats:	Yes/94
Library:	Yes
Children's Facilities:	Yes
Classification Society:	Nippon Kaiji Kyokai

RATINGS	**SCORE**
Ship: Hardware/Maintenance	87
Ship: Outdoor Facilities/Space	88
Ship: Interior Facilities/Space/Flow	90
Ship: Decor/Furnishings/Artwork	87
Ship: Spa/Fitness Facilities	87
Cabins: Suites and Deluxe	91
Cabins: Standard Sizes	84
Food: Dining Room/Cuisine	86
Food: Informal Dining/Buffets	83
Food: Quality of Ingredients	82
Food: Afternoon Tea/Bar Snacks	81
Service: Dining Room	81
Service: Bars	83
Service: Cabins	85
Service: Open Decks	80
Cruise: Entertainment	85
Cruise: Activities Program	76
Cruise: Movies/Television Programming	85
Cruise: Hospitality Standard	89
Cruise: Overall Product Delivery	86
OVERALL SCORE	**1,696**

Accommodation: There are five different types of accommodation: royal suites, suites, deluxe cabin, state cabin (four grades), and standard cabin, all located from the uppermost to lowermost decks, respectively.

Four royal suites are decorated in two different styles—one contemporary, one more traditional Japanese style. Each has a private balcony with sliding door (teakwood table and two chairs), an expansive lounge area with large sofa and plush armchairs, coffee table, window-side chairs and drinks table, floor-to-ceiling windows, VCR unit, separate bedroom, with twin- or queen-sized bed, vanity/office desk, large walk-in closet with private safe, large bathroom with Jacuzzi bathtub (tiny) with ocean-view windows, separate shower, and his/hers sinks.

Sixteen suites also feature a private balcony (with teakwood table and two chairs), living area with vanity desk, dining table, chair and curved sofa, separate sleeping area, and bathroom with deep bathtub that is slightly larger than the royal suites, and single large sink. There is ample lighted closet and drawer space (two locking drawers instead of a personal safe), and VCR unit.

The 20 deluxe cabins have large picture windows fronted by a large, curtained arch, sleeping area with twin (or queen) beds, plus a daytime sofa that converts into a third bed.

The 210 state cabins (172 of which have upper berths for third passengers) have decor that is best described as basic, with a reasonable closet, but little drawer space.

The 16 standard cabins are quite plain, but accommodate three persons, although drawer and storage space is tight.

All grades of cabin feature a tea drinking set (with electric hot water kettle), color television, telephone, fully stocked minibar-refrigerator (all items are included), hairdryer, and extensive array of personal toiletry items (particularly in the suites). All room service menu items are available at extra charge. All passengers get a yukata; in addition, suite occupants get a plush bathrobe.

Dining: The main dining room (Primavera) is located aft, and has ocean views on three sides. The tables are for six, ten, or twelve. The food consists of both Japanese and Western items; the menu is varied and the food is attractively presented.

A second, intimate, yet stately 42-seat alternative dining room called Grand Siecle features an à la carte (extra charge) menu; it is decorated in Regency-style; it has lovely wood paneling and a nicely indented ceiling.

Other Comments: Venus Cruise is part of Japan Cruise Line, which is itself a joint venture between Shin Nohonakai, Hankyu and Kanpu ferry companies, and the company owns and operates the slightly smaller *Orient Venus*, which is operated principally for the charter and incentive group market. *Pacific Venus*, which is being operated for individual cruises (no charters) is one deck higher than her sister ship, and also is slightly longer and beamier, and is, in fact, the second-largest cruise vessel built by a Japanese shipyard.

There is a good amount of open deck space aft of the funnel, good for deck sports, while protected sunbathing space is provided around the small swimming pool (all deck lounge chairs have cushioned pads). The base of the funnel itself is the site of a day/night lounge, which overlooks the swimming pool (it is slightly reminiscent of the lounges that Royal Caribbean International features aboard its vessels). There is an outdoor wraparound (rubber coated) promenade deck.

Inside the ship, the high passenger space ratio means that there is plenty of space per passenger. The decor is clean and fresh, with much use of pastel colors and blond woods. One deck (Deck 7) features a double-width indoor promenade off which the dining rooms are located. The three-deck-high atrium is topped by a fine crystal chandelier.

Facilities include male and female Grand Baths, which include bathing pool and health/cleansing facilities. Other facilities include special rooms for meetings/conference organizers, piano salon with colorful low-back chairs, a large main hall (with nicely sculptured high ceiling and 720 moveable seats—production shows are performed here), a 350-seat main lounge for cabaret shows, small theater, library and card room, casino, two private karaoke rooms, Japanese chashitsu (tatami) room for tea ceremonies, and beauty salon. There is also a twenty-four-hour vending machine corner (juice, beer, camera film, and other items), self-service launderette (no charge), and several (credit card/coin) public telephone booths.

Overall, this company provides a well-packaged cruise in a ship which presents a very comfortable, serene environment. The dress code is relaxed and no tipping is allowed.

ms Paradise

(L)

Lifestyle	Standard
Cruise Line:	Carnival Cruise Lines
Former Names:	-
Gross Tonnage:	70,367
Builder:	Kvaerner Masa-Yards (Finland)
Original Cost:	$315 million
Entered Service:	November 1998
Flag:	Liberia
Tel No:	n/a
Fax No:	n/a
Length (ft./m.):	855.0/260.60
Beam (ft./m.):	104.0/31.40
Draft (ft./m.):	25.9/7.90
Propulsion/Propellers:	diesel-electric (57,430bhp)/2 (Azipod)
Decks:	10
Total Crew:	920
Pass. Capacity (basis 2):	2,040
Pass. Capacity (all berths):	2,594
Pass. Space Ratio (basis 2):	34.4
Pass. Space Ratio (all berths):	26.7
Officers:	Italian
Total Cabins:	1,020
Size Range (sq. ft./m.):	173.2–409.7/16.0–38.0
Cabins (outside view):	618
Cabins (inside):	402
Cabins (for one person):	0
Cabins (with private balcony):	26
Cabins (wheelchair accessible):	20
Cabin Current:	110 AC
Cabin TV:	Yes
Dining Rooms:	2
Seatings:	2
Elevators:	14
Casino:	Yes
Slot Machines:	Yes
Swimming Pools (outdoors):	3
Swimming Pools (inside):	0
Whirlpools:	6
Fitness Center:	Yes
Sauna/Steam Room:	Yes/Yes
Massage:	Yes
Self-Service Launderette:	Yes
Movie Theater/Seats:	No
Library:	Yes
Children's Facilities:	Yes
Classification Society:	Lloyd's Register

Ratings	Score
Ship: Hardware/Maintenance	NYR
Ship: Outdoor Facilities/Space	NYR
Ship: Interior Facilities/Space/Flow	NYR
Ship: Decor/Furnishings/Artwork	NYR
Ship: Spa/Fitness Facilities	NYR
Cabins: Suites and Deluxe	NYR
Cabins: Standard Sizes	NYR
Food: Dining Room/Cuisine	NYR
Food: Informal Dining/Buffets	NYR
Food: Quality of Ingredients	NYR
Food: Afternoon Tea/Bar Snacks	NYR
Service: Dining Room	NYR
Service: Bars	NYR
Service: Cabins	NYR
Service: Open Decks	NYR
Cruise: Entertainment	NYR
Cruise: Activities Program	NYR
Cruise: Movies/Television Programming	NYR
Cruise: Hospitality Standard	NYR
Cruise: Overall Product Delivery	NYR

Expected Score Range
1,400-1,600

For comments, see *Elation*.

ms Paul Gauguin

☆☆☆☆ +

(S)

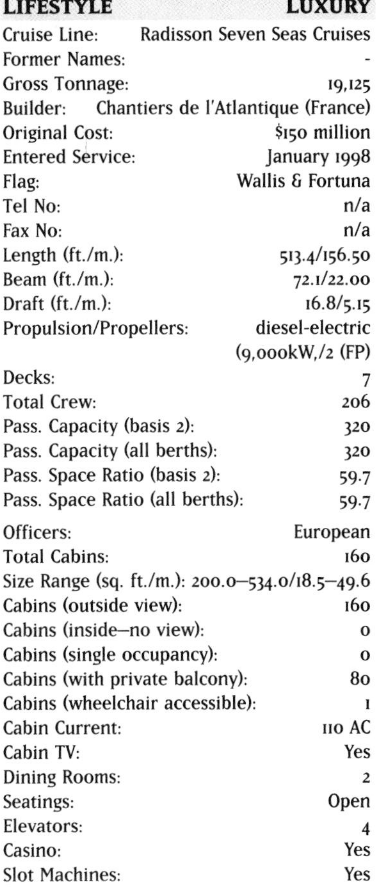

Lifestyle	Luxury
Cruise Line:	Radisson Seven Seas Cruises
Former Names:	-
Gross Tonnage:	19,125
Builder:	Chantiers de l'Atlantique (France)
Original Cost:	$150 million
Entered Service:	January 1998
Flag:	Wallis & Fortuna
Tel No:	n/a
Fax No:	n/a
Length (ft./m.):	513.4/156.50
Beam (ft./m.):	72.1/22.00
Draft (ft./m.):	16.8/5.15
Propulsion/Propellers:	diesel-electric (9,000kW,/2 (FP)
Decks:	7
Total Crew:	206
Pass. Capacity (basis 2):	320
Pass. Capacity (all berths):	320
Pass. Space Ratio (basis 2):	59.7
Pass. Space Ratio (all berths):	59.7
Officers:	European
Total Cabins:	160
Size Range (sq. ft./m.):	200.0–534.0/18.5–49.6
Cabins (outside view):	160
Cabins (inside–no view):	0
Cabins (single occupancy):	0
Cabins (with private balcony):	80
Cabins (wheelchair accessible):	1
Cabin Current:	110 AC
Cabin TV:	Yes
Dining Rooms:	2
Seatings:	Open
Elevators:	4
Casino:	Yes
Slot Machines:	Yes

Swimming Pools (outdoors):	1
Swimming Pools (inside):	0
Whirlpools:	0
Fitness Center:	Yes
Sauna/Steam Room:	No/Yes
Massage:	Yes
Self-Service Launderette:	No
Movie Theater/Seats:	No
Library:	Yes
Children's Facilities:	No
Classification Society:	Bureau Veritas

Ratings	Score
Ship: Hardware/Maintenance	90
Ship: Outdoor Facilities/Space	88
Ship: Interior Facilities/Space/Flow	87
Ship: Decor/Furnishings/Artwork	87
Ship: Spa/Fitness Facilities	73
Cabins: Suites and Deluxe	87
Cabins: Standard Sizes	82
Food: Dining Room/Cuisine	86
Food: Informal Dining/Buffets	83
Food: Quality of Ingredients	81
Food: Afternoon Tea/Bar Snacks	76
Service: Dining Room	83
Service: Bars	80
Service: Cabins	80
Service: Open Decks	77
Cruise: Entertainment	77
Cruise: Activities Program	76
Cruise: Movies/Television Programming	78
Cruise: Hospitality Standard	86
Cruise: Overall Product Delivery	88
Overall Score	**1,645**

Accommodation: The outside-view cabins, half of which boast private balconies, are very nicely equipped, although they are strictly rectangular (none have more interesting shapes). Most have large windows, except those on the lowest accommodation deck, which have portholes. Each has queen- or twin-sized beds (convertible to queen) and wood-accented cabinetry with rounded edges. A mini-bar/refrigerator (stocked with complimentary soft drinks), VCR unit, personal safe, and hairdryer are standard. The marble-look appointed bathrooms have a bathtub and a shower. Bathrobes are provided for all passengers.

The two largest suites have a private balcony at the front and side of the vessel. Although there is a decent amount of in-cabin space, with a beautiful long vanity unit (and plenty of drawer space), the bathrooms are disappointingly small and plain, and too similar to all other standard cabin bathrooms.

Dining: The main dining room, L'Etoile, features lunch and dinner, while La Veranda, an alternative dining spot, is open for breakfast, lunch, and dinner. Both dining rooms provide "open seating" which means that passengers can choose when they want to dine and with whom. This provides a good opportunity to meet new people for dinner each evening. La Veranda provides dinner by reservation, with French and Italian menus; the French menus are provided by Chef Jean-Pierre Vigato, a two-star Michelin chef with his own restaurant in Paris called Apicius.

The dining operation is well orchestrated, with cuisine and service of a high standard. Complimentary standard table wines are served with dinner (although a connoisseur selection is also available, at extra cost, for real wine lovers), and mineral water, fruit juices, and soft drinks are complimentary throughout the ship—a nice touch.

In addition, an outdoor bistro provides informal cafe fare on deck aft of the pool, while the Connoisseur Club offers a luxurious retreat for cigars and cognacs.

Other Comments: This smart looking vessel also has a retractable aft marina platform, and carries two water skiing boats and two inflatable craft for water sports, as well as scuba and snorkeling gear. Built by a French company, managed and operated by the U.S.-based Radisson Seven Seas Cruises, this ship is extremely spacious. While she could carry more passengers, under French law operating in the Polynesian islands, she is unable to do so.

Inside the ship, both the artwork and the decor have a real French Polynesia look and feel. However, the interior colors are quite bland. Expert lecturers on Tahiti and Gauguin will accompany each cruise, and a Fare Tahiti Gallery will offer books, videos, and other materials on the unique art, history, and culture of the islands; three original Gauguin sketches are displayed under glass. There is a good health spa program with treatment services by Carita of Paris, although the changing facilities are very limited, there is no sauna, and use of the steam room incurs an extra charge (it should be free). Water sports facilities include a marina (retractable), water skiing, windsurfers, kayaks, scuba and snorkeling.

The library is quite pleasant but it could be larger. This ship (a more deluxe version of the company's popular *Song of Flower*) will present Radisson Seven Seas Cruises with the opportunity to score very high marks with her passengers, as the company is known for its attention to detail and passenger care. A no-tie policy means the dress code is very relaxed. The ship's high crew-to-passenger ratio means highly personalized service. Gratuities are included.

But:: Although it sounds exotic, the itinerary is only marginally interesting to the well travelled, the best island experience being in Bora Bora. The ship's shallow draft means that you can expect some movement, as she is quite high-sided for her size. Minimum purchase rule in ship's boutique is irritating (due to local government rules). The spa is very small, and the fitness room is window-less.

ms Polaris

☆☆☆

(S)

Lifestyle	**Standard**
Cruise Line:	Special Expeditions/ Metropolitan Touring
Former Names:	*Lindblad Polaris/Oresund*
Gross Tonnage:	2,214
Builder:	Aalborg Vaerft (Denmark)
Original Cost:	n/a
Entered Service:	1960/May 1987
Flag:	Bahamas
Tel No:	1104424
Fax No:	1103276
Length (ft./m.):	236.6/72.12
Beam (ft./m.):	42.7/13.03
Draft (ft./m.):	13.7/4.30
Propulsion/Propellers:	diesel (2,354kW)/2 (CP)
Decks:	4
Total Crew:	43
Pass. Capacity (basis 2):	80
Pass. Capacity (all berths):	84
Pass. Space Ratio (basis 2):	27.6
Pass. Space Ratio (all berths):	26.3
Officers:	Swedish
Total Cabins:	41
Size Range (sq. ft./m.):	100–230/9.2–21.3
Cabins (outside view):	41
Cabins (inside—no view):	0
Cabins (single occupancy):	0
Cabins (with private balcony):	0
Cabins (wheelchair accessible):	0
Cabin Current:	220 AC
Cabin TV:	No
Dining Rooms:	1 (open seating)
Elevators:	0
Casino:	No
Slot Machines:	No
Swimming Pools (outdoors):	0
Whirlpools:	0
Exercise Room:	No
Sauna/Steam Room:	Yes/No
Massage:	No
Self-Service Launderette:	No
Lecture/Film Room:	No
Library:	Yes
Zodiacs:	8
Helicopter Pad:	No
Classification Society:	Bureau Veritas

Ratings	**Score**
Ship: Hardware/Maintenance	64
Ship: Expedition Equipment	60
Ship: Interior Facilities/Space/Flow	60
Ship: Decor/Furnishings/Artwork	57
Ship: Spa/Fitness Facilities	30
Cabins: Suites and Deluxe	60
Cabins: Standard Sizes	53
Food: Dining Room/Cuisine	71
Food: Informal Dining/Buffets	61
Food: Quality of Ingredients	70
Food: Afternoon Tea/Bar Snacks	56
Service: Dining Room	71
Service: Bars	70
Service: Cabins	70
Service: Open Decks	47
Cruise: Library/Lecture Programs	65
Cruise: Movies/Television Programming	40
Cruise: Hospitality Standard	71
Cruise: Expedition Experience	61
Cruise: Overall Product Delivery	73
Overall Score	**1,210**

Accommodation: The cabins, all of which are above the waterline, are quite roomy and nicely appointed, but there is little drawer space. Some have been refurbished, and feature large (lower) beds. Each has a hair dryer. Refreshingly, cabin keys are not used. The cabin bathrooms are really tiny, so take only what you need. Note that there is no cabin service menu.

Dining: The dining room has big picture windows and a wraparound view. Seating is now at individual tables (formerly family style) in an unhurried single seating. Has good food, with a major emphasis on local fish and seafood dishes. There is also a fine wine list. Breakfast and lunch are buffet-style. Has friendly service from an attentive staff.

Other Comments: This "soft" expedition cruise vessel, of modest proportions, sports a dark blue hull and white superstructure. She has been well maintained and operated. Sports a fantail and improved aft outdoor lounge area. Carries several Zodiac inflatable rubber landing craft, as well as a glass bottom boat.

Inside, although there are few public rooms, the Scandinavian-style interior furnishings and decor are very tidy and welcoming, accented by lots of wood trim. Has a friendly, very intimate atmosphere on board, with Filipino service staff. Features a good team of lecturers and nature observers, whose daily recaps are a vital part of the experience. A restful, well-stocked library helps passengers learn more about the region and the natural world.

This is a good small vessel, which now operates year-round nature-intensive "soft" expedition cruises around the Galapagos Islands. This is an area to which the ship is well suited (only 90 passengers from any one ship are allowed at any one time in the Galapagos Islands, where tourism is managed well by Ecuador). In fact, this ship is among the best suited to this region. All port charges are included in this product, which is marketed by Special Expeditions and Noble Caledonia, together with other specialist packagers.

mts Princesa Amorosa

☆☆ +

(S)

Lifestyle	**Standard**
Cruise Line:	Louis Cruise Lines
Former Names:	*Galaxias/Galaxy/Scottish Coast*
Gross Tonnage:	5,026
Builder:	Harland & Wolff (UK)
Original Cost:	n/a
Entered Service:	1957/July 1990
Flag:	Cyprus
Tel No:	n/a
Fax No:	n/a
Length (ft./m.):	342.2/104.32
Beam (ft./m.):	52.6/16.06
Draft (ft./m.):	15.7/4.81
Propulsion/Propellers:	diesel (4,781kW)/2 (FP)
Decks:	6
Total Crew:	130
Pass. Capacity (basis 2):	284
Pass. Capacity (all berths):	327
Pass. Space Ratio (basis 2):	17.6
Pass. Space Ratio (all berths):	15.3
Officers:	Cypriot/Greek
Total Cabins:	142
Size Range (sq. ft./m.):	107.6–172.2/10.0–16.0
Cabins (outside view):	115
Cabins (inside—no view):	27
Cabins (single occupancy):	0
Cabins (with private balcony):	0
Cabins (wheelchair accessible):	0
Cabin Current:	220 AC
Cabin TV:	No
Dining Rooms:	1
Seatings:	2
Elevators:	0
Casino:	Yes
Slot Machines:	Yes
Swimming Pools (outdoors):	1
Swimming Pools (inside):	0
Whirlpools:	0
Fitness Center:	No
Sauna/Steam Room:	No/No
Massage:	No
Self-Service Launderette:	No
Movie Theater/Seats:	No
Library:	Yes
Children's Facilities:	No
Classification Society:	Lloyd's Register

Ratings	**Score**
Ship: Hardware/Maintenance	59
Ship: Outdoor Facilities/Space	52
Ship: Interior Facilities/Space/Flow	56
Ship: Decor/Furnishings/Artwork	58
Ship: Spa/Fitness Facilities	33
Cabins: Suites and Deluxe	58
Cabins: Standard Sizes	54
Food: Dining Room/Cuisine	62
Food: Informal Dining/Buffets	56
Food: Quality of Ingredients	62
Food: Afternoon Tea/Bar Snacks	51
Service: Dining Room	61
Service: Bars	60
Service: Cabins	61
Service: Open Decks	52
Cruise: Entertainment	47
Cruise: Activities Program	46
Cruise: Movies/Television Programming	40
Cruise: Hospitality Standard	56
Cruise: Overall Product Delivery	62
Overall Score	**1,086**

Accommodation: Most cabins are outside and are quite comfortable, with crisp Mediterranean colors and some wood trim, but they are small, and bathrooms do show their age. The cabins and bathrooms are very small. Note that cabins located above the disco are very noisy late at night.

Dining: The dining room has portholes and is quite cheerful. The food is decidedly Mediterranean, with some reasonable choice, and excellent presentation. In addition, a full vegetarian menu is available. Service is quite cheerful, and the staff try hard. Both a la carte and buffet meals are featured.

Other Comments: This is an older vessel that has fairly spacious open decks for her size. Seeing the bridge is like stepping back in time, with many shiny brass instruments. The swimming pool is really only a "dip" pool.

Inside the ship, the limited number of public rooms has been nicely refurbished. There is an interesting maroon wrought iron staircase whose balustrades show the ship's former British heritage.

Earth-tone colors have been used to good effect in the interior decor, creating a mild sense of spaciousness. There is a pleasant lounge and bar for socializing, with comfortable seating and warm decor. The ambience aboard is delightfully warm and friendly.

Purchased by Louis Cruise Lines in 1989, she offers good "no frills" seven-day Greek Isles/Mediterranean cruises for those without high expectations, particularly well suited to the local Cypriot market, where the ship has a loyal following.

But: There is a steep, narrow gangway in some ports. Too many announcements.

mv Princesa Marissa

☆☆ +

(M)

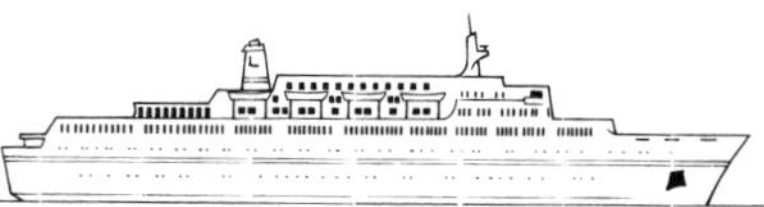

Lifestyle	**Standard**
Cruise Line:	Louis Cruise Lines
Former Names:	*Finnhansa/Princessan*
Gross Tonnage:	10,487
Builder:	Wartsila (Finland)
Original Cost:	n/a
Entered Service:	1966/June 1987
Flag:	Cyprus
Tel No:	none
Fax No:	none
Length (ft./m.):	440.6/134.30
Beam (ft./m.):	65.2/19.90
Draft (ft./m.):	18.7/5.70
Propulsion/Propellers:	diesel (10,300kW)/2 (CP)
Decks:	9
Total Crew:	185
Pass. Capacity (basis 2):	628
Pass. Capacity (all berths):	839
Pass. Space Ratio (basis 2):	16.6
Pass. Space Ratio (all berths):	12.4
Officers:	Cypriot/Greek
Total Cabins:	314
Size Range (sq. ft./m.):	75.3–226.0/7.0–21.0
Cabins (outside view):	148
Cabins (inside–no view):	166
Cabins (single occupancy):	0
Cabins (with private balcony):	0
Cabins (wheelchair accessible):	0
Cabin Current:	220 AC
Cabin TV:	No
Dining Rooms:	2
Seatings:	2
Elevators:	1
Casino:	Yes
Slot Machines:	Yes
Swimming Pools (outdoors):	0
Swimming Pools (inside):	0
Whirlpools:	0
Fitness Center:	No
Sauna/Steam Room:	Yes/No
Massage:	No
Self-Service Launderette:	No
Movie Theater/Seats:	No
Library:	No
Children's Facilities:	Yes
Classification Society:	Det Norske Veritas

Ratings	**Score**
Ship: Hardware/Maintenance	51
Ship: Outdoor Facilities/Space	40
Ship: Interior Facilities/Space/Flow	54
Ship: Decor/Furnishings/Artwork	53
Ship: Spa/Fitness Facilities	30
Cabins: Suites and Deluxe	55
Cabins: Standard Sizes	48
Food: Dining Room/Cuisine	60
Food: Informal Dining/Buffets	54
Food: Quality of Ingredients	60
Food: Afternoon Tea/Bar Snacks	45
Service: Dining Room	61
Service: Bars	59
Service: Cabins	60
Service: Open Decks	46
Cruise: Entertainment	43
Cruise: Activities Program	36
Cruise: Movies/Television Programming	35
Cruise: Hospitality Standard	55
Cruise: Overall Product Delivery	57
Overall Score	**1,002**

Accommodation: The standard cabins are quite smart and functional. A whole section of new cabins, added in 1995, are of good size, have picture windows, and decor is bright and cheerful (they also have good, practical bathrooms).

Dining: The two dining rooms are quite attractive (the forward one is more intimate). Both à la carte and buffet style meals are featured, and the menu choice includes three entrees. There is also a full vegetarian menu. Comfortable dining room chairs. Good breads and selection of ice cream sundaes.

Other Comments: This former ferry has a square stern, twin funnels, and a short, stubby bow. There is a very limited amount of open deck and sunbathing space.

Her interiors are very smart and tidy, and the ship is quite well maintained. The public room decor is attractive, with warm, fairly bright contemporary colors, well-designed fabrics, and soft furnishings. Has some facilities for meetings/small conferences.

The ship provides low fare transportation in unstuffy surroundings and year-round short cruises to Egypt and Israel (principally for Cyprus residents and British passengers) that include shore excursions.

But: High passenger density. Also, the ceilings are quite low, typical of ferry construction. There are few crew members for so many passengers. Passengers must board through the aft car deck, but this is no real hardship.

mv Princesa Victoria

☆☆ +

(M)

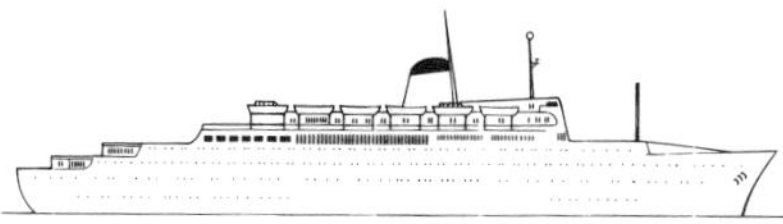

Lifestyle	**Standard**
Cruise Line:	Louis Cruise Lines
Former Names:	*The Victoria/Victoria/ Dunottar Castle*
Gross Tonnage:	15,007
Builder:	Harland & Wolff (UK)
Original Cost:	n/a
Entered Service:	July 1936/January 1993
Flag:	Cyprus
Tel No:	1101627
Fax No:	1101630
Length (ft./m.):	572.8/174.60
Beam (ft./m.):	71.9/21.92
Draft (ft./m.):	27.8/8.50
Propulsion/Propellers:	diesel (10,450kW)/2 (FP)
Decks:	7
Total Crew:	230
Pass. Capacity (basis 2):	566
Pass. Capacity (all berths):	750
Pass. Space Ratio (basis 2):	26.5
Pass. Space Ratio (all berths):	20.0
Officers:	Cypriot/Greek
Total Cabins:	287
Size Range (sq. ft./m.):	156.0–258.3/14.5–24.0
Cabins (outside view):	216
Cabins (inside–no view):	71
Cabins (single occupancy):	8
Cabins (with private balcony):	0
Cabins (wheelchair accessible):	0
Cabin Current:	115 AC
Cabin TV:	Yes
Dining Rooms:	1
Seatings:	2
Elevators:	3
Casino:	Yes
Slot Machines:	Yes
Swimming Pools (outdoors):	2
Swimming Pools (inside):	0
Whirlpools:	0
Fitness Center:	Yes
Sauna/Steam Room:	Yes/No
Massage:	No
Self-Service Launderette:	No
Movie Theater/Seats:	Yes/250
Library:	Yes
Children's Facilities:	Yes
Classification Society:	Lloyd's Register

Ratings	**Score**
Ship: Interior Facilities/Space/Flow	53
Ship: Decor/Furnishings/Artwork	54
Ship: Outdoor Facilities/Space	54
Ship: Hardware/Maintenance	55
Ship: Spa/Fitness Facilities	48
Cabins: Suites and Deluxe	61
Cabins: Standard Sizes	52
Food: Dining Room/Cuisine	62
Food: Informal Dining/Buffets	56
Food: Quality of Ingredients	60
Food: Afternoon Tea/Bar Snacks	51
Service: Dining Room	63
Service: Bars	60
Service: Cabins	61
Cruise: Entertainment	53
Cruise: Activities Program	50
Cruise: Movies/Television Programming	36
Cruise: Hospitality Standard	60
Cruise: Overall Product Delivery	62
Overall Score	**1,051**

Accommodation: The standard cabins are quite spacious, and feature heavy-duty furniture and fittings. The suite rooms are cavernous, and the large bathrooms come with deep, full bathtubs, something not seen on today's cruise vessels.

Dining: The dining room is set low down, but is comfortable and has a fine two-deck high center section with barrel-shaped ceiling, music balcony, and lots of wood paneling. The standard of cuisine is good, particularly bearing in mind the price you pay. There are three entrees, as well as a complete vegetarian menu. Salads, bakery items and fruits are reasonable.

Other Comments: This ship, originally built for Union Castle Line, and then Chandris Cruises, has been quite well maintained, despite her age. There is generous amount of open deck space. There are no showers at the twin swimming pools.

Inside, the center stairway is built in true art deco style. There is a friendly, old-world ambience on board. The Riviera Club is a contemporary room that is totally out of keeping with the rest of ship.

Provides a good cruise experience for first-time cruisers and for those seeking to optimize their hotel vacation in Cyprus. She really is an old ship, however, and so does not have the kind of ultra-contemporary facilities that most modern ships feature.

But: The repetitive announcements are annoying. There is little separation of smokers and non-smokers, and the ship is old and worn in many places.

mts Princess Danae

☆☆☆

(M)

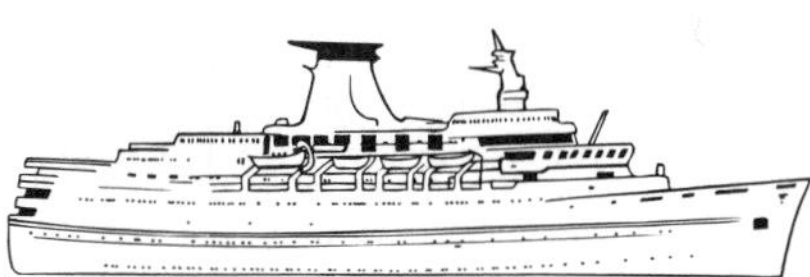

LIFESTYLE	**STANDARD**
Cruise Line:	Arcalia Shipping/ Classic International Cruises
Former Names:	*Baltica/Danae/ Therisos Express/Port Melbourne*
Gross Tonnage:	17,074
Builder:	Swan, Hunter (UK)
Original Cost:	n/a
Entered Service:	July 1955/1997
Flag:	Panama
Tel No:	1346425
Fax No:	1346425
Length (ft./m.):	532.7/162.39
Beam (ft./m.):	70.0/21.34
Draft (ft./m.):	41.9/12.80
Propulsion/Propellers:	diesel (9,850kW)/2 (FP)
Decks:	7
Total Crew:	240
Pass. Capacity (basis 2):	560
Pass. Capacity (all berths):	670
Pass. Space Ratio (basis 2):	30.4
Pass. Space Ratio (all berths):	25.4
Officers:	European
Total Cabins:	280
Size Range (sq. ft./m.):	200.0–270.0/18.5–25.0
Cabins (outside view):	215
Cabins (inside–no view):	65
Cabins (single occupancy):	0
Cabins (with private balcony):	6
Cabins (wheelchair accessible):	0
Cabin Current:	220 AC
Cabin TV:	No
Dining Rooms:	1
Seatings:	2
Elevators:	2
Casino:	Yes
Slot Machines:	Yes
Swimming Pools (outdoors):	1
Swimming Pools (inside):	0
Whirlpools:	2
Fitness Center:	Yes
Sauna/Steam Room:	Yes/No
Massage:	Yes
Self-Service Launderette:	No
Movie Theatre/Seats:	Yes/275
Library:	Yes
Children's Facilities:	No
Classification Society:	American Bureau of Shipping

RATINGS	**SCORE**
Ship: Hardware/Maintenance	72
Ship: Outdoor Facilities/Space	67
Ship: Interior Facilities/Space/Flow	71
Ship: Decor/Furnishings/Artwork	70
Ship: Spa/Fitness Facilities	46
Cabins: Suites and Deluxe	75
Cabins: Standard Sizes	71
Food: Dining Room/Cuisine	71
Food: Informal Dining/Buffets	64
Food: Quality of Ingredients	64
Food: Afternoon Tea/Bar Snacks	53
Service: Dining Room	62
Service: Bars	63
Service: Cabins	63
Service: Open Decks	54
Cruise: Entertainment	58
Cruise: Activities Program	54
Cruise: Movies/Television Programming	44
Cruise: Hospitality Standard	60
Cruise: Overall Product Delivery	66
OVERALL SCORE	**1,248**

Accommodation: Most cabins are of good size (in eight categories) and feature heavy-duty furniture and fittings with ample closet and drawer space. Note that the cabins located under the disco can suffer from thumping noise late at night. The lower-grade cabins are quite plain. Some 210 cabin bathrooms have a bathtub and shower, while 70 have a shower only.

Dining: The dining room is decorated quite nicely and has a high ceiling. Features open seating dining (dine with whoever you wish). Features Continental/European cuisine and service that is quite attentive.

Other Comments: She is a solidly built ship with good lines. Has a good amount of open deck space for sunbathing. Sadly, there is no forward observation lounge. There is a pleasing traditional shipboard ambience aboard her, combined with more contemporary features and good quality interior appointments. Features a number of spacious public rooms, although the decor is somewhat conservative. A new bar amidships was recently added. There is a roomy, traditional movie theater.

This ship, which underwent a refurbishment early in 1996, provides a comfortable, though by no means glamorous, cruise experience for her passengers, many of whom are from South America. Provides Caribbean cruises from Santo Domingo in winter, from Brazil during the summer, and Mediterranean cruises during some summer months.

mv Professor Khromov

☆☆

(S)

Lifestyle	**Standard**
Cruise Line:	Quark Expeditions/ Murmansk Shipping
Former Names:	-
Gross Tonnage:	2,142
Builder:	Wartsila (Finland)
Original Cost:	n/a
Entered Service:	1983
Flag:	Russia
Tel No:	n/a
Fax No:	n/a
Length (ft./m.):	234.9/71.6
Beam (ft./m.):	42/12.8
Draft (ft./m.):	15.0/4.6
Propulsion/Propellers:	diesel (3,120shp)/2 (CP)
Decks:	3
Total Crew:	25
Pass. Capacity (basis 2):	36
Pass. Capacity (all berths):	36
Pass. Space Ratio (basis 2):	59.5
Pass. Space Ratio (all berths):	59.5
Officers:	Russian
Total Cabins:	19
Size Range (sq. ft./m.):	n/a
Cabins (outside view):	18
Cabins (inside—no view):	0
Cabins (single occupancy):	0
Cabins (with private balcony):	0
Cabins (wheelchair accessible):	0
Cabin Current:	220 V
Cabin TV:	No
Dining Rooms:	1
Seatings:	1
Elevators:	0
Casino:	0
Slot Machines:	0
Swimming Pools (outdoors):	0
Swimming Pools (inside):	0
Whirlpools:	0
Fitness Center:	No
Sauna/Steam Room:	Yes/No
Massage:	No
Self-Service Launderette:	No
Movie Theater/Seats:	0
Library:	Yes
Children's Facilities:	0
Classification Society:	Russian KMLI

Ratings	**Score**
Ship: Hardware/Maintenance	56
Ship: Expedition Equipment	56
Ship: Interior Facilities/Space/Flow	42
Ship: Decor/Furnishings/Artwork	43
Ship: Spa/Fitness Facilities	30
Cabins: Suites and Deluxe	47
Cabins: Standard Sizes	40
Food: Dining Room/Cuisine	56
Food: Informal Dining/Buffets	47
Food: Quality of Ingredients	56
Food: Afternoon Tea/Bar Snacks	44
Service: Dining Room	51
Service: Bars	54
Service: Cabins	53
Service: Open Decks	30
Cruise: Library/Lecture Programs	44
Cruise: Movies/Television Programming	37
Cruise: Hospitality Standard	51
Cruise: Expedition Experience	52
Cruise: Overall Product Delivery	58
Overall Score	**947**

Accommodation: With the exception of a single "suite," almost all other cabins are very small, spartan, and rather clinical. Those on the lowest deck share a bathroom.

Dining: There are two dining rooms, and all passengers are accommodated in one seating. The meals are hearty international fare, with no frills. When under charter to Quark Expedition/Noble Caledonia, a western chef oversees the food operation. The cuisine itself is best described as hearty fare.

Other Comments: This vessel was specially constructed for polar and oceanographic research and is not to be taken as a cruise ship, although it was converted and refurbished in 1992 to carry passengers. Has an ice-hardened, steel hull, which is good for Arctic and Antarctic cruising. All passengers have access to the navigation bridge. Has several Zodiac landing craft. Public rooms consist of a library and lounge/bar. The dining rooms also serve as a lecture room. Has good medical facilities.

This is cruising expedition style. It provides a somewhat primitive, but genuine adventure experience to places others only dream about. The bigger ships cannot get this close to Antarctica. The same comments apply to sister ship *Professor Molchanov.*

tsmv Queen Elizabeth 2

☆☆☆☆☆ to ☆☆☆☆

(L)

Lifestyle	**Luxury/Premium**
Cruise Line:	Cunard
Former Names:	-
Gross Tonnage:	70,327
Builder:	Upper Clyde Shipbuilders (UK)
Original Cost:	£29 million
Entered Service:	May 1969
Flag:	Great Britain
Tel No:	1440412
Fax No:	1441331
Length (ft./m.):	963.0/293.50
Beam (ft./m.):	105.1/32.03
Draft (ft./m.):	32.4/9.87
Propulsion/Propellers:	diesel-electric (99,900kW)/2 (CP)
Decks:	13
Total Crew:	1,004
Pass. Capacity (basis 2):	1,741
Pass. Capacity (all berths):	1,890
Pass. Space Ratio (basis 2):	40.3
Pass. Space Ratio (all berths):	37.2
Officers:	British
Total Cabins:	931
Size Range (sq. ft./m.):	107.0–785.0/10.0–73.0
Cabins (outside view):	625
Cabins (inside–no view):	185
Cabins (single occupancy):	121
Cabins (with private balcony):	33
Cabins (wheelchair accessible):	4
Cabin Current:	110/220 AC
Cabin TV:	Yes
Dining Rooms:	5
Seatings:	1
Elevators:	13
Casino:	Yes
Slot Machines:	Yes
Swimming Pools (outdoors):	1
Swimming Pools (inside):	1 (+ AquaSpa pool)
Whirlpools:	4
Fitness Center:	Yes
Sauna/Steam Room:	Yes/Yes
Massage:	Yes
Self-Service Launderette:	Yes
Movie Theater/Seats:	Yes/531
Library:	Yes
Children's Facilities:	Yes
Classification Society:	Lloyd's Register

Ratings	**Score** (a)	**Score** (b)	**Score** (c)
Ship: Hardware/Maintenance	90	86	75
Ship: Outdoor Facilities/Space	90	80	71
Ship: Interior Facilities/Space/Flow	92	85	77
Ship: Decor/Furnishings/Artwork	91	85	76
Ship: Spa/Fitness Facilities	92	90	83
Cabins: Suites and Deluxe	92	85	64
Cabins: Standard Sizes	90	78	57
Food: Dining Room/Cuisine	98	85	77
Food: Informal Dining/Buffets	86	81	75
Food: Quality of Ingredients	95	87	77
Food: Afternoon Tea/Bar Snacks	91	83	72
Service: Dining Room	92	82	73
Service: Bars	90	84	77
Service: Cabins	92	82	72
Service: Open Decks	88	80	70
Cruise: Entertainment	84	84	84
Cruise: Activities Program	86	85	85
Cruise: Movies/Television Programming	88	86	83
Cruise: Hospitality Standard	89	81	74
Cruise: Overall Product Delivery	92	84	76
Overall Score	**1,808**	**1,673**	**1,498**

Ratings Key (a)-Grill Class; (b)-Caronia Class; (c)-Mauretania Class

Accommodation: There is a wide range of accommodation from which to choose, most of which features fine wood-paneled walls; generous closet and drawer space; thick, real wood furniture; and large, marble bathrooms. From two-level suites with private balconies, walk-in closets, refrigerators and mini-bars, and bathrooms large enough for four, to modest inside cabins that are compact but well equipped, you pay for the amount of space and grade you want. The accommodation you choose will determine in which of the ship's five restaurants you will dine.

Dining: There are five principal restaurants (all of which include many tables for two, unlike so many other ships today) and one informal dining spot: The Lido, and The Grill. In order of excellence they are: Queens Grill, Britannia Grill and Princess Grill, Caronia Restaurant, and Mauretania Restaurant. The menus are always varied and well balanced, and include a good choice of spa/light cuisine items. Alternative dining (for buffet-style dinners) was also introduced in April 1997 in The Lido, with smart casual dress called for. The luncheon and midnight buffets provide a good range of foods, although at peak times there will be lines.

A la carte dining (with everything cooked to order a la minute) was introduced in the Queens Grill in early 1997, under the direction of Cunard's corporate executive chef Rudi Sodamin, to great acclaim. Indeed, with the a la carte menus (featured only on transatlantic crossings) the Queens Grill in *QE2* is arguably the finest dining experience at sea, and is comparable to the very best shoreside gourmet restaurants anywhere, with tableside carvings, flambeaus and outstanding presentation by utterly dedicated British head waiters.

Other Comments: *Queen Elizabeth 2* is a world-renowned dual-purpose true ocean liner, with a dark blue hull, that performs a regular schedule of transatlantic crossings as well as several cruises each year, together with an annual round-the-world cruise from January to April. She is still the fastest, as well as the most integrated ocean liner in the world (it is important to think of this ship as an ocean liner rather than as a cruise ship in the more contemporary sense of the word). An excellent range of joint travel programs and tour configurations is integrated into the marketing of this ship. It is also pleasing to note that the dress code is mostly formal, a change from so many ships where the dress codes have all but disappeared.

Sadly, there is no forward observation lounge (there was when the ship was first constructed). Following recent refurbishments, small, intimate hideaway bars are fewer in number, and one cannot have just a sauna or use of the steam room without paying a $10 charge for a "Spa Experience" package.

Originally constructed as a steam turbine ship, she underwent a $160 million refit in Bremen, Germany, in 1986. Her original steam turbines were extracted and exchanged for a diesel-electric propulsion system, resulting in greater speed, better economy and more reliability. A new, fatter funnel was constructed, designed to better keep any soot off her expansive open decks.

In late 1994, the ship underwent a $45-million interior refurbishment that included numerous structural changes designed to facilitate better passenger flow and greater dining space. Her interiors were changed to provide a more cohesive and coordinated color scheme, with the use of fine wood paneling and more traditional furnishings reminiscent of the ocean liners of yesteryear—just what passengers expect of this ship.

All bathrooms in all accommodation grades have been entirely replaced; they now sport marble fixtures and jazzy art deco-style toiletries cabinets. Several new suites were added, as well as an enlarged library, with a multimedia CD-ROM center and a fine, memorabilia/book shop, and dedicated florist. The Club Lido magrodome-covered pool was replaced with an informal buffet bistro-like dining area (The Lido) complete with its own galley, bar, and separate poolside grill. The new enhancements have provided grace, pace, and space.

In 1997, the Caronia Restaurant was relocated to Quarter Deck, while the Mauretania Restaurant was relocated to Upper Deck. The Queens Grill has been completely redecorated and refurbished, and is now better than ever.

Other Comments: Transatlantic Crossings: She is still the fastest passenger ship presently in service, but even at a speed of close to 30 knots there is little vibration at the stern. Features the most extensive range of facilities of any passenger ship afloat, including a garage for up to 40 cars.

She is a city at sea, and, like any city, there are several parts of town. There are three distinct classes: Grill Class, Caronia Class and Mauretania Class. Grill Class accommodation consists of outstanding penthouse suites (with true butler service only in the Sun Deck and Sports Deck suites), and large outside-view cabins (with standard cabin service in One Deck and Two Deck cabins). Dining is in one of three grill rooms: Queens Grill (named after the former transatlantic liner pair *Queen Elizabeth* and *Queen Mary*), Britannia Grill, or Princess Grill, according to cabin grade chosen. Caronia Class accommodation consists of outside-view double cabins, and inside and outside single cabins, with dining in the Caronia Restaurant (high noise level). Mauretania Class accommodation features lower-priced cabin grades, but dining is in two seatings in the Mauretania Restaurant (a fine restaurant with many dining alcoves) when the ship is full, and one seating when the ship is not full.

All passengers enjoy the use of all public rooms, except for the Queens Grill Lounge (reserved exclusively for Grill Class passengers). The Queens Grill has its own separate galley, the best waiters and service, a fine, formal atmosphere for dinner, and food that can be best described as memorable (you can also order from the à la carte menu, as well as "off-menu"). The Britannia Grill, Princess Grill and Mauretania Restaurant share the same galley, but the service and setting in the intimate Britannia Grill, and Princess Grill is far superior. The Caronia and Mauretania Restaurants have good, creative and varied menus, but service is provided by the least experienced waiters.

Grill Class and Caronia Class passengers have separate open deck space and assigned chairs, but join all other passengers for major shows, other entertainment events and social functions. Grill Class is the most sophisticated way to cross the Atlantic; Caronia Class (formerly known as first class) is good but not quite what it used to be, while Mauretania Class (formerly known as transatlantic class) provides comfortable travel in a price-sensitive setting.

In the final analysis, *Queen Elizabeth 2* is the last of the transatlantic liners and a truly civilized experience (ideal for the many people who do not like to fly, who enjoy the grace and pace of this ship). The enormous amount of personal luggage one is allowed is also useful especially for relocating between continents (or for extended vacations). Arriving in either New York or Southampton after six days of not having to lift a finger is actually a bittersweet anti-climax for most passengers, a disquieting reminder that life ashore has to be faced after the calming, quieting effect of *QE2* on one's innermost being. Indeed, I can think of nothing more pleasing to the soul than a transatlantic crossing, cosseted in the finery of dining in either of the three grill restaurants with their superb cuisine and dining experiences. All gratuities are included.

Other Comments: Cruises: After refits in 1994 and 1996, the public rooms and passenger facilities have been refreshed and color-coordinated for the better. The Penthouse Suites are truly superb and quiet, and are among the most refined living spaces at sea (all bathrooms were replaced in 1996). The Heritage Trail, a ship-wide display consisting of 26 exhibits of Cunard ocean liner history and ship models that ship buffs will find fascinating, includes a stunning 16-foot-long illuminated model of the company's 1907 Mauretania. There is a great abundance of memorabilia items (some are for sale in the memorabilia bookshop/library).

The extensive facilities include a Grand Lounge (a dedicated show lounge with thrust stage, three seating tiers, and high-tech sound system); a Tour and Travel Center (for shore excursions, theater tickets, and other concierge services); a Shopping Concourse which features good brand name merchandise at high European prices; a Cunard Collection shop (which replaced Harrods, and features high-quality clothing and special Cunard logo items). The Yacht Club is a delightfully nautical, practical, and popular aft-facing room that becomes a night club (afternoon recorded classical concerts here are a bonus). There is an extensive indoor spa which includes a ten-station AquaSpa and treatment rooms (treatments are at extra cost); fitness center and beauty salons for men and women; a safety deposit center and passenger accounts office; a large Computer Learning Center; an automated telephone system.

More facilities: The Queens Room is a real ballroom, with a large dance floor, for real society dancing to a big band, whereas during the day it is a stately "quiet" room with comfortable chairs. The Midships Lobby, the ship's embarkation point, has a distinctive, ocean liner image and feel, with fine birds-eye maple woodwork and wrap-around murals of the former and present Cunard Queens. A large computer center (with daily lectures) is a real bonus. There is a large self-service launderette (no charge). The Lido, a large, informal bistro dining spot with twenty-four-hour hot beverage stations, is also a bonus on cruises (espresso and cappuccino coffees are free). The elegant Chart Room Bar (formerly the Midships Bar) is a charming, quiet drinking spot (it contains a piano from the liner *Queen Mary*).

And more facilities: There is also a large movie theater/concert hall, with balcony level; the Golden Lion Pub comes complete with Victorian decor and selection of over twenty beers (both bottled and draught). There is also a superb library, much loved by passengers (it is without doubt the best at sea, with over 7,000 books, in several languages, which, combined with a memorabilia bookshop, has doubled in size and features professional librarians. The Player's Club Casino features fitting art deco and blond wood decor.

QE2 has British officers, although the hotel staff is a very international mix, quite attentive and service-oriented, though many do not speak English well, as is the case aboard so many ships today. Features good quality entertainment and fine lecture programs. Has an excellent laundry and dry-cleaning facilities. Fine English nannies and children's facilities. This ship offers refined living at sea for those in upper grade accommodation, otherwise she is just a large ship, albeit with some superb facilities. Tender ports should be avoided whenever possible, however, although the double-deck shore tenders used are fine, practical units.

MORE ABOUT ***QE2:*** Physically challenged passengers will appreciate four cabins specially equipped for wheelchair-bound passengers, created using the guidelines of the American Disabled Association (ADA). The cabin door is wide enough for a wheelchair (no "lip"); the bathroom door slides open electronically at the touch of a button (located at wheelchair height), and the floor is flat. The full bath has special assist handles, and the toilet has grab bars. Closets have hanging rails with hydraulically balanced lever that lowers them towards the outside of the closet, to the right height. There is an intercom, alarm, and remote controls for lighting, curtains, and doors. These cabins are also good for the hearing-impaired, with three brightly colored, lighted signs on the cabin bulkhead, as well as a telephone system for the deaf. While these cabins are specially designed for the physically challenged, their ingenious design would not upset a regular passenger.

The famous Ocean Liner Express, which runs between London's Waterloo Station and Southampton Docks, pulls right up alongside the Ocean Terminal to connect with all transatlantic sailings of the ship. This special train consists of beautifully refurbished, carpeted 1950s first-class carriages, richly paneled and fitted with individual deep-upholstery seats. Complimentary hot canapés and champagne are served. Passengers traveling from London to Southampton are able to complete all formalities and ship check-in procedures on the train, so they simply walk directly on board *QE2* on arrival. Baggage loaded onto the train's baggage carriage in Waterloo is delivered directly to your cabin.

The Cunard/British Airways Concorde program is also something worth experiencing. Combining a *QE2* transatlantic crossing with a one-way British Airways Concorde flight is, without doubt, the ultimate way to go. Six days one way, and three hours, fifteen minutes the other is one of the great travel experiences available today. And, with special, Cunard-subsidized fares, there is no excuse for not indulging, at least once in your life. All gratuities are now included. In 1997 *QE2* became the first cruise ship to have an e-mail address: QE2@cruisemail.com.

She is the last of the great ocean liners, and features the best of high-tech facilities blended with traditional ocean liner facilities. She is rather like a well-worn shoe—comfortable, but a little tired and frayed around the edges in places, which makes her a difficult ship to evaluate. Sadly, there seem to be fewer British crew aboard her than her passengers expect, and less crew speak English when in passenger areas. However, she has a wonderful, loyal following, and provides the only civilized way to cross the North Atlantic Ocean with the space, pace, and grace of a real Cunard-White Star liner. Will she survive the onslaught of the mega-ships? Yes, simply because she isn't one of them.

<u>But:</u>What's missing are the grand, flowing staircases, the air of romance, the high standard of maintenance and hotel service personnel of the ocean liners of former years. Art Auctions are tacky and do not belong aboard a ship such as this stately, aging lady. Five Deck cabins should be taken out of service. There should be no charge for use of the sauna and steam rooms.

mv R1

(M)

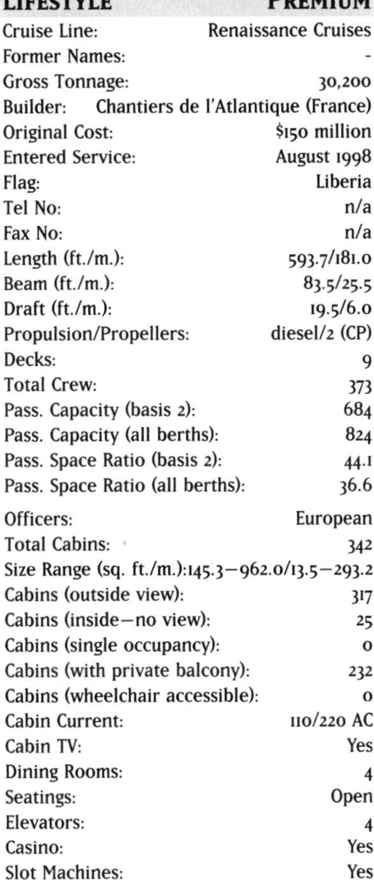

Lifestyle	Premium
Cruise Line:	Renaissance Cruises
Former Names:	-
Gross Tonnage:	30,200
Builder:	Chantiers de l'Atlantique (France)
Original Cost:	$150 million
Entered Service:	August 1998
Flag:	Liberia
Tel No:	n/a
Fax No:	n/a
Length (ft./m.):	593.7/181.0
Beam (ft./m.):	83.5/25.5
Draft (ft./m.):	19.5/6.0
Propulsion/Propellers:	diesel/2 (CP)
Decks:	9
Total Crew:	373
Pass. Capacity (basis 2):	684
Pass. Capacity (all berths):	824
Pass. Space Ratio (basis 2):	44.1
Pass. Space Ratio (all berths):	36.6
Officers:	European
Total Cabins:	342
Size Range (sq. ft./m.):	145.3–962.0/13.5–293.2
Cabins (outside view):	317
Cabins (inside—no view):	25
Cabins (single occupancy):	0
Cabins (with private balcony):	232
Cabins (wheelchair accessible):	0
Cabin Current:	110/220 AC
Cabin TV:	Yes
Dining Rooms:	4
Seatings:	Open
Elevators:	4
Casino:	Yes
Slot Machines:	Yes

Swimming Pools (outdoors):	1
Swimming Pools (inside):	0
Whirlpools:	3
Fitness Center:	Yes
Sauna/Steam Room:	Yes/Yes (2)
Massage:	Yes
Self-Service Launderette:	Yes
Movie Theater/Seats:	No
Library:	Yes
Children's Facilities:	No
Classification Society:	Bureau Veritas

Ratings	Score
Ship: Hardware/Maintenance	NYR
Ship: Outdoor Facilities/Space	NYR
Ship: Interior Facilities/Space/Flow	NYR
Ship: Decor/Furnishings/Artwork	NYR
Ship: Spa/Fitness Facilities	NYR
Cabins: Suites and Deluxe	NYR
Cabins: Standard Sizes	NYR
Food: Dining Room/Cuisine	NYR
Food: Informal Dining/Buffets	NYR
Food: Quality of Ingredients	NYR
Food: Afternoon Tea/Bar Snacks	NYR
Service: Dining Room	NYR
Service: Bars	NYR
Service: Cabins	NYR
Service: Open Decks	NYR
Cruise: Entertainment	NYR
Cruise: Activities Program	NYR
Cruise: Movies/Television Programming	NYR
Cruise: Hospitality Standard	NYR
Cruise: Overall Product Delivery	NYR

Expected Score Range
1,400 – 1,800

Accommodation: All cabins have twin beds (or queen-size bed), with good under-bed storage areas, personal safe, vanity desk with large mirror, good closet and drawer space (all in rich, dark woods), bathrobes and slippers, and VCR unit. The bathrooms are quite compact, fairly standard units, and include a shower stall with removable hand-held shower unit, hairdryer, and toiletries storage shelves and retractable laundry line.

Cabins with private balconies have partial balcony partitions, not full ones, and 14 cabins on Deck 6 have lifeboat-obstructed views.

The most spacious suites (there are 10 of them, all called Owner's Suites) are beautiful living spaces located at the very forward and aft sections of the accommodation decks. They have extensive private balconies that really are private and cannot be overlooked by anyone on the decks above. All have an entrance foyer, living room, bedroom (the bed faces the sea, which can be seen through the floor-to-ceiling windows and sliding glass door), bathroom, and small guest bathroom.

The 52 mini-suites are not overly large, but they do feature a good-sized bathtub (suites have Jacuzzi tub), refrigerated mini-bar, and lounge area with breakfast table. Some 66 percent of all cabins have private balconies, while all feature interactive televisions, and carry CNN, plus a sports channel.

It is due to good design that only 14 cabins have views almost totally obstructed by lifeboats.

Dining: Flexibility is what this ship's dining facilities are all about. There are four different themed restaurants (one main restaurant, with 154 indoor and 186 outdoor seats; an Italian restaurant, with 96 seats; an American steak house with 98 seats; and The Club, the most formal, for fine dining and dinner dance music, with 354 seats). All feature open seating dining. In addition, there is a Poolside Grill Bar, and a patisserie called Sweets. You really can dine whenever you want, twenty-four-hours a day.

Other Comments: This ship is the first in a planned series of six such ships, and a real departure for Renaissance Cruises, who have traditionally operated smaller vessels. This ship has been well designed, and presents a balanced exterior profile, and, with her deep blue hull and white superstructure, she looks very good.

The interior decor is really stunning and elegant, with detailed ceiling cornices, wrought iron staircase railings, leather paneled walls, tromp l'oeil ceilings, rich regal red carpeting, and many other interesting (and expensive) decorative touches throughout the vessel. There is no doubt that the overall feel is of an exclusive country club. Regular Renaissance Cruises passengers will probably be quite stunned at the fine taste with which her interiors have been designed and executed. The company's brochure is most definitely understated.

The public rooms are basically spread over three decks, while outside on deck is a jogging track. This is the first totally nonsmoking ship (there is no smoking anywhere, including cabins, dining room, public rooms, or on the open decks—whether the crew will be smoke-free remains to be seen).

The reception hall (lobby) features a staircase with intricate wrought iron railings. The main lounge has an inviting marble fireplace (in fact there are three such fireplaces aboard this ship). A Sports Bar, located high atop ship (which is also an observation lounge), features a long bar, two giant-screen televisions, forward views, and an array of slot machines and bar counter-top electronic gaming machines (so the room is good not only for men, but also for women, even though they may not be sports-minded). There are plenty of bars aboard this ship, including in the restaurant entrances, but the nicest is the casino bar/lounge, a really beautiful room reminiscent of London's grand hotels.

What this company provides is a seamless cruise and tour package, principally geared toward North American passengers, at a price that is hard to beat considering the destination-rich itineraries that are featured, together with pre- and post-cruise land stays at high quality hotels, and all transfers. At the end of the day, this company provides an excellent, hassle-free cruise vacation package for cruising in the Mediterranean, together with sister ship *R2*. Prices are kept low due to the fact that the company pays low rates of commission to travel agents.While both *R1* and *R2* will feature Mediterranean cruises, the next two ships in the series, *R3* and *R4*, will feature cruises in French Polynesia, and the operating regions and itineraries of the final two ships in the series had not yet been determined at press time.

But: There is no wraparound outdoor promenade deck (there is a small jogging track).

mv R2
(M)

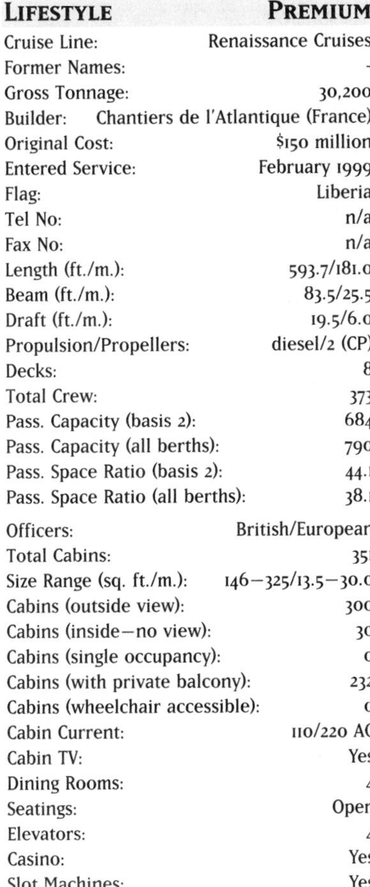

Lifestyle	**Premium**
Cruise Line:	Renaissance Cruises
Former Names:	-
Gross Tonnage:	30,200
Builder:	Chantiers de l'Atlantique (France)
Original Cost:	$150 million
Entered Service:	February 1999
Flag:	Liberia
Tel No:	n/a
Fax No:	n/a
Length (ft./m.):	593.7/181.0
Beam (ft./m.):	83.5/25.5
Draft (ft./m.):	19.5/6.0
Propulsion/Propellers:	diesel/2 (CP)
Decks:	8
Total Crew:	373
Pass. Capacity (basis 2):	684
Pass. Capacity (all berths):	790
Pass. Space Ratio (basis 2):	44.1
Pass. Space Ratio (all berths):	38.1
Officers:	British/European
Total Cabins:	351
Size Range (sq. ft./m.):	146–325/13.5–30.0
Cabins (outside view):	300
Cabins (inside—no view):	30
Cabins (single occupancy):	0
Cabins (with private balcony):	232
Cabins (wheelchair accessible):	0
Cabin Current:	110/220 AC
Cabin TV:	Yes
Dining Rooms:	4
Seatings:	Open
Elevators:	4
Casino:	Yes
Slot Machines:	Yes

For comments, see *R1*.

Swimming Pools (outdoors):	1
Swimming Pools (inside):	0
Whirlpools:	2
Fitness Center:	Yes
Sauna/Steam Room:	Yes/Yes (2)
Massage:	Yes
Self-Service Launderette:	Yes
Movie Theater/Seats:	No
Library:	Yes
Children's Facilities:	No
Classification Society:	Bureau Veritas

Ratings	**Score**
Ship: Hardware/Maintenance	NYR
Ship: Outdoor Facilities/Space	NYR
Ship: Interior Facilities/Space/Flow	NYR
Ship: Decor/Furnishings/Artwork	NYR
Ship: Spa/Fitness Facilities	NYR
Cabins: Suites and Deluxe	NYR
Cabins: Standard Sizes	NYR
Food: Dining Room/Cuisine	NYR
Food: Informal Dining/Buffets	NYR
Food: Quality of Ingredients	NYR
Food: Afternoon Tea/Bar Snacks	NYR
Service: Dining Room	NYR
Service: Bars	NYR
Service: Cabins	NYR
Service: Open Decks	NYR
Cruise: Entertainment	NYR
Cruise: Activities Program	NYR
Cruise: Movies/Television Programming	NYR
Cruise: Hospitality Standard	NYR
Cruise: Overall Product Delivery	NYR

Expected Score Range
1,400-1,700

ssc Radisson Diamond

☆☆☆☆ +

(S)

Lifestyle	Luxury
Cruise Line:	Radisson Seven Seas Cruises
Former Names:	-
Gross Tonnage:	20,295
Builder:	Rauma Yards (Finland)
Original Cost:	$125 million
Entered Service:	May 1992
Flag:	Finland
Tel No:	1623243
Fax No:	1623252
Length (ft./m.):	430.4/131.2
Beam (ft./m.):	104.9/32.0
Draft (ft./m.):	26.2/8.0
Propulsion/Propellers:	diesel (11,340kW)/ 2 nozzles
Decks:	6
Total Crew:	200
Pass. Capacity (basis 2):	354
Pass. Capacity (all berths):	354
Pass. Space Ratio (basis 2):	57.3
Pass. Space Ratio (all berths):	57.3
Officers:	Scandinavian/European
Total Cabins:	177
Size Range (sq. ft./m.):	220.0/20.5
Cabins (outside view):	177
Cabins (inside—no view):	0
Cabins (single occupancy):	0
Cabins (with private balcony):	123
Cabins (wheelchair accessible):	2
Cabin Current:	110/220 AC
Cabin TV:	Yes
Dining Rooms:	1 (+1 Grill Restaurant)
Seatings:	Open
Elevators:	3
Casino:	Yes
Slot Machines:	Yes
Swimming Pools (outdoors):	1
Swimming Pools (inside):	0
Whirlpools:	1
Fitness Center:	Yes
Sauna/Steam Room:	Yes/Yes
Massage:	Yes
Self-Service Launderette:	No
Movie Theater/Seats:	No
Library:	Yes
Children's Facilities:	No
Classification Society:	Det Norske Veritas

Ratings	Score
Ship: Hardware/Maintenance	83
Ship: Outdoor Facilities/Space	81
Ship: Interior Facilities/Space/Flow	82
Ship: Decor/Furnishings/Artwork	84
Ship: Spa/Fitness Facilities	83
Cabins: Suites and Deluxe	88
Cabins: Standard Sizes	84
Food: Dining Room/Cuisine	87
Food: Informal Dining/Buffets	86
Food: Quality of Ingredients	83
Food: Afternoon Tea/Bar Snacks	78
Service: Dining Room	84
Service: Bars	84
Service: Cabins	84
Service: Open Decks	80
Cruise: Entertainment	81
Cruise: Activities Program	68
Cruise: Movies/Television Programming	77
Cruise: Hospitality Standard	81
Cruise: Overall Product Delivery	82
Overall Score	**1,640**

Accommodation: All cabins are nicely designed, spacious, and well-equipped. There are outside-view cabins, most of which have private balconies with outdoor lights. All are furnished in blond woods, with marble bathroom vanities and a tiny bathtub. There are bay windows in 47 suites.

All cabins are of the same dimensions, with the exception of two "VIP" master suites with private balconies. Each cabin has an oversized window or floor-to-ceiling balcony windows/door. Features include a spacious sitting area with sofa and chairs, dressing table with hair dryer, minibar and refrigerator, telephone, color remote-control TV with integral VCR player, twin beds that convert to a queen-sized unit, two good, adjustable reading lamps that are bright, a personal safe (somewhat hidden and difficult for older passengers to reach and operate), full-length mirror, and excellent drawer space. The closet space, however, is really minimal, adequate for short cruises, but tight for two on a seven-day cruise, worse for longer cruises. The cabin bathrooms have very small tubs (they are really shower tubs).

Each cabin has a minibar that is stocked with beer and soft drinks; half-liter bottles of four liquors are provided. Bottled mineral water is provided.

Dining: The two-deck-high dining room is quite elegant, has a 270-degree view over the stern and open seating, so you can dine with whomever you wish, when you wish. The cuisine quality and food presentation are European in style, and quite outstanding in both quality, choice, and presentation. Also features health foods and dietary specials. The waitresses are quite charming, supervised superbly by experienced Italian headwaiters. As far as wines go, although basic whites and reds are included for lunch and dinner, a separate wine list is available for those who appreciate better wines (at extra cost). Dining, in fact, is the vessel's strongest point.

The Grill is a 50-seat alternative Italian casual indoor/outdoor dining spot (there is no extra charge). Run like a real restaurant ashore (make your reservations early each day you want to eat there), this informal dining spot features superb homemade pasta dishes daily, has a fine menu, including cream sauces and exotic garnishes. Each day is different and food is presented in small portions, course by course. It is lovingly prepared and exquisite to taste, although somewhat rich. Seating is at sturdy, practical glass-topped wooden tables for two, four, or six. Tableside dessert flambeaus are often featured. Dining at The Grill is a pleasant experience.

Other Comments: This ship features an innovative design based on SWATH (Small Waterplane Area Twin Hull) technology. She is thus very stable when at sea (except, of course, in rough seas), with four stabilizing fins (two on the inner side of each pontoon), so that motion is really minimized when compared with conventional (monohull) vessels. The wide beam of this design also provides outstanding passenger space, although the public rooms are stacked vertically and are contained mostly on the inside of the ship, which is like a seagoing version of a Radisson hotel ashore.

The casino has gaming tables on one side of the passageway, slot machines on the other (good for serious game players who do not want the sound of slot machines to intrude).

A five-deck-high atrium has glass-enclosed elevators (which, together with the staircase), take up most of the space). There is also a little-used underwater viewing area (it actually consists of just two portholes). There is a good outdoor jogging track.

Has a well-stocked library and video center, and a sophisticated business center with facilities that are ideal for small groups and conventions. For groups and meetings, the high-tech audio and video conference facilities, and a high-tech security system that uses approximately 50 cameras to monitor just about everywhere, provide a good feeling of exclusivity.

There is also a retractable, free-floating water sports marina platform, but it is really only useful in dead calm sea conditions. There are jet-skis, and a water ski boat.

However, the design means that many public rooms are inside, with little or no connection with the sea. Flowers would help a lot. The ship has a maximum speed of 12.5 knots, which means it is fine for leisurely island cruising, but is slow going on longer itineraries. The awkward one-way (contra-flow) interior staircase is frustrating. The spaciousness of the ship, while providing flexibility of the several individual public rooms, actually detracts from the overall flow. Also awkward is the multi-level entertainment room (show lounge). Has excellent health spa facilities, but they cannot be reached by elevator. Still has some uncomfortable chairs in the main dining room. The meet-and-greet service is quite inconsistent and is the subject of passenger complaints.

This semi-submersible, twin-hulled cruise vessel, which some have said looks like a white-caped "Batman" from the stern, certainly has the most unusual and distinctive looks of any cruise ship, although its design has not been as successful as hoped. This ship will appeal to those seeking extremely high standards of service in sophisticated and personable, somewhat "hotel-style" surroundings, and unstructured daytime activities. One nice plus is the fact that all gratuities are included. The standard of onboard service is high, which helps to make up for the design and structural shortcomings of the vessel.

ms Regal Empress

☆☆ +

(M)

Lifestyle	**Standard**
Cruise Line:	Regal Cruises
Former Names:	*Caribe I/Olympia*
Gross Tonnage:	22,979
Builder:	Alex Stephen & Son (UK)
Original Cost:	n/a
Entered Service:	October 1953/May 1993
Flag:	Bahamas
Tel No:	n/a
Fax No:	n/a
Length (ft./m.):	611.8/186.5
Beam (ft./m.):	79.0/24.1
Draft (ft./m.):	28.2/8.6
Propulsion/Propellers:	diesel (14,400bhp)/2 (FP)
Decks:	8
Total Crew:	345
Pass. Capacity (basis 2):	893
Pass. Capacity (all berths):	1,148
Pass. Space Ratio (basis 2):	25.7
Pass. Space Ratio (all berths):	20.0
Officers:	European
Total Cabins:	451
Size Range (sq. ft./m.):	105–295/9.7–27.5
Cabins (outside view):	226
Cabins (inside–no view):	225
Cabins (single occupancy):	9
Cabins (with private balcony):	0
Cabins (wheelchair accessible):	1
Cabin Current:	110 AC
Cabin TV:	No
Dining Rooms:	1
Seatings:	2
Elevators:	3
Casino:	Yes
Slot Machines:	Yes
Swimming Pools (outdoors):	1
Swimming Pools (inside):	0
Whirlpools:	2
Fitness Center:	Yes
Sauna/Steam Room:	No/No
Massage:	No
Self-Service Launderette:	No
Movie Theater/Seats:	Yes/166
Library:	Yes
Children's Facilities:	Yes
Classification Society:	Lloyd's Register

Ratings	**Score**
Ship: Hardware/Maintenance	58
Ship: Outdoor Facilities/Space	56
Ship: Interior Facilities/Space/Flow	52
Ship: Decor/Furnishings/Artwork	55
Ship: Spa/Fitness Facilities	44
Cabins: Suites and Deluxe	65
Cabins: Standard Sizes	58
Food: Dining Room/Cuisine	57
Food: Informal Dining/Buffets	51
Food: Quality of Ingredients	53
Food: Afternoon Tea/Bar Snacks	44
Service: Dining Room	60
Service: Bars	57
Service: Cabins	62
Service: Open Decks	51
Cruise: Entertainment	54
Cruise: Activities Program	48
Cruise: Movies/Television Programming	46
Cruise: Hospitality Standard	52
Cruise: Overall Product Delivery	55
Overall Score	**1,078**

Accommodation: There is a wide range of cabin sizes and configurations, in twelve suite/cabin grades. Most are quite roomy, with good closet and reasonable drawer space, and heavy-duty fittings. Largest are the four "penthouse suites" on Upper Deck, with views over the bow.

Dining: Lovely old-world dining room is a step back in time to a more gracious era, with its original oil paintings on burnished wood paneling, ornate lighting fixtures and etched glass panels, and original murals depicting New York and Rio. Most tables are for groups of six or more, with a few tables for four. Smoking and nonsmoking sections are provided on the starboard and port sides respectively. The food is plentiful and of a reasonably high standard considering the price, with the exception of the buffets, which are really basic and unimaginative.

Other Comments: This forty-year-old ship has a traditional ocean liner profile. There is a good amount of open deck space for sun worshippers, although this can become very crowded when the ship is full. Features good, polished teak decking and handrails.

The enclosed (air-conditioned) promenade deck is popular with strollers and for those who like to sit and read.

Inside the ship you'll find plenty of real woods and heavy brass detailing throughout many of her public rooms, with fine satin woods and brass featured on her interior staircases. There really are few public rooms except for a large casino, single-level show lounge (with slightly raised port and starboard sections), and night club/disco and piano lounge.

There is, however, a superb, old-fashioned library with untouched, original paneling, although the book selection is poor and out of date, the dog-eared paperbacks just do not look right, and no magazines are provided.

Features four- to ten-day Gulf of Mexico/Panama Canal cruises from Port Manatee (Florida) during the winter; a fifty-three-day around South America cruise in October; and short cruises from New York during the summer. This ship provides a basic cruise in adequate surroundings, but do remember that the ship is old and service is perfunctory, at best.

But: Do expect lines for embarkation, disembarkation, and buffets. The ship has an awkward layout, and many passageways do not extend for the length of the ship. Finally, the tipping glasses stationed around the ship are particularly insulting.

mv Regal Princess

☆☆☆☆

(L)

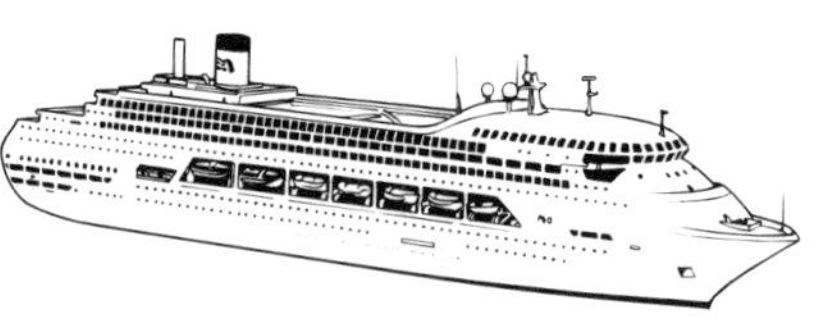

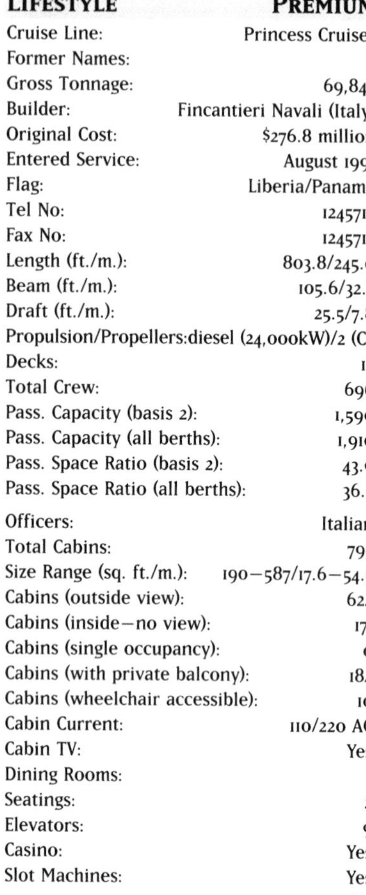

LIFESTYLE	**PREMIUM**
Cruise Line:	Princess Cruises
Former Names:	-
Gross Tonnage:	69,845
Builder:	Fincantieri Navali (Italy)
Original Cost:	$276.8 million
Entered Service:	August 1991
Flag:	Liberia/Panama
Tel No:	1245712
Fax No:	1245712
Length (ft./m.):	803.8/245.0
Beam (ft./m.):	105.6/32.2
Draft (ft./m.):	25.5/7.8
Propulsion/Propellers:	diesel (24,000kW)/2 (CP)
Decks:	12
Total Crew:	696
Pass. Capacity (basis 2):	1,590
Pass. Capacity (all berths):	1,910
Pass. Space Ratio (basis 2):	43.9
Pass. Space Ratio (all berths):	36.5
Officers:	Italian
Total Cabins:	795
Size Range (sq. ft./m.):	190–587/17.6–54.5
Cabins (outside view):	624
Cabins (inside–no view):	171
Cabins (single occupancy):	0
Cabins (with private balcony):	184
Cabins (wheelchair accessible):	10
Cabin Current:	110/220 AC
Cabin TV:	Yes
Dining Rooms:	1
Seatings:	2
Elevators:	9
Casino:	Yes
Slot Machines:	Yes

Swimming Pools (outdoors):	2
Swimming Pools (inside):	0
Whirlpools:	4
Fitness Center:	Yes
Sauna/Steam Room:	Yes/No
Massage:	Yes
Self-Service Launderette:	Yes
Movie Theater/Seats:	Yes/169
Library:	Yes
Children's Facilities:	No
Classification Society:	Lloyd's Register

RATINGS	**SCORE**
Ship: Hardware/Maintenance	81
Ship: Outdoor Facilities/Space	73
Ship: Interior Facilities/Space/Flow	82
Ship: Decor/Furnishings/Artwork	80
Ship: Spa/Fitness Facilities	76
Cabins: Suites and Deluxe	83
Cabins: Standard Sizes	79
Food: Dining Room/Cuisine	73
Food: Informal Dining/Buffets	68
Food: Quality of Ingredients	70
Food: Afternoon Tea/Bar Snacks	63
Service: Dining Room	78
Service: Bars	76
Service: Cabins	76
Service: Open Decks	74
Cruise: Entertainment	84
Cruise: Activities Program	77
Cruise: Movies/Television Programming	82
Cruise: Hospitality Standard	79
Cruise: Overall Product Delivery	83
OVERALL SCORE	**1,537**

For comments, see *Crown Princess*.

ss Rembrandt

☆☆☆ +

(L)

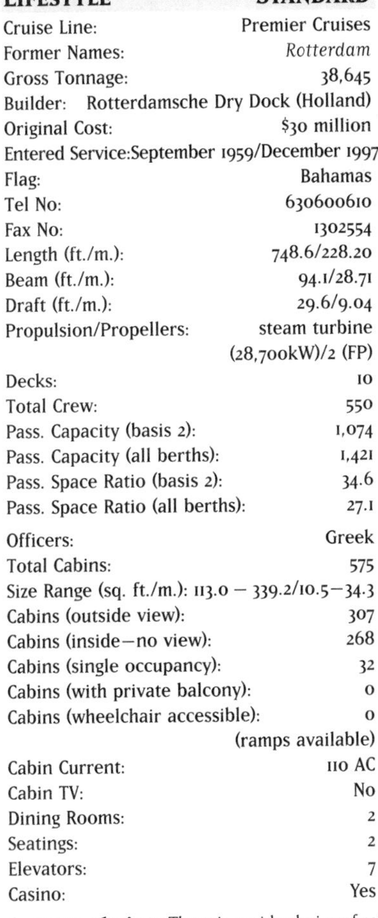

Lifestyle	**Standard**
Cruise Line:	Premier Cruises
Former Names:	*Rotterdam*
Gross Tonnage:	38,645
Builder:	Rotterdamsche Dry Dock (Holland)
Original Cost:	$30 million
Entered Service:	September 1959/December 1997
Flag:	Bahamas
Tel No:	630600610
Fax No:	1302554
Length (ft./m.):	748.6/228.20
Beam (ft./m.):	94.1/28.71
Draft (ft./m.):	29.6/9.04
Propulsion/Propellers:	steam turbine (28,700kW)/2 (FP)
Decks:	10
Total Crew:	550
Pass. Capacity (basis 2):	1,074
Pass. Capacity (all berths):	1,421
Pass. Space Ratio (basis 2):	34.6
Pass. Space Ratio (all berths):	27.1
Officers:	Greek
Total Cabins:	575
Size Range (sq. ft./m.):	113.0 – 339.2/10.5–34.3
Cabins (outside view):	307
Cabins (inside–no view):	268
Cabins (single occupancy):	32
Cabins (with private balcony):	0
Cabins (wheelchair accessible):	0 (ramps available)
Cabin Current:	110 AC
Cabin TV:	No
Dining Rooms:	2
Seatings:	2
Elevators:	7
Casino:	Yes
Slot Machines:	Yes
Swimming Pools (outdoors):	1
Swimming Pools (inside):	1
Whirlpools:	0
Fitness Center:	Yes
Sauna/Steam Room:	Yes/No
Massage:	Yes
Self-Service Launderette:	Yes
Movie Theater/Seats:	Yes/620
Library:	Yes
Children's Facilities:	Yes
Classification Society:	Lloyd's Register

Ratings	**Score**
Ship: Hardware/Maintenance	71
Ship: Outdoor Facilities/Space	71
Ship: Interior Facilities/Space/Flow	67
Ship: Decor/Furnishings/Artwork	57
Ship: Spa/Fitness Facilities	40
Cabins: Suites and Deluxe	72
Cabins: Standard Sizes	56
Food: Dining Room/Cuisine	76
Food: Informal Dining/Buffets	67
Food: Quality of Ingredients	65
Food: Afternoon Tea/Bar Snacks	64
Service: Dining Room	76
Service: Bars	72
Service: Cabins	68
Service: Open Decks	59
Cruise: Entertainment	59
Cruise: Activities Program	56
Cruise: Movies/Television Programming	51
Cruise: Hospitality Standard	64
Cruise: Overall Product Delivery	73
Overall Score	**1,284**

Accommodation: There is a wide choice of cabin sizes and configurations (she was built before the days of modular cabins), but all of them are quite comfortable and come well equipped with solid wood cabinetry, solid fittings, and good quality furnishings, plenty of drawer space, and all cabins have illuminated closets. Some cabins have upper and lower berths rather than beds. There are plenty of cabins for single passengers—a welcome touch. All cabin bathrooms have exposed plumbing, however, a throwback to her former days as a transatlantic liner, but all have a personal toiletries cabinet, glass shelves, and just enough mirror facing.

There are also 12 deluxe suites (these even have wall clock built into the vanity desk mirror front) and 24 suites. Some have large walk-in closets, while others have regular (illuminated) closets, vanity desks, an abundance of drawers and other storage spaces, and a sleeping area and lounge with sofa, table, and chairs befitting a Miami Beach art deco hotel. Passengers in accommodation designated as suites receive amenity kits (if booked at brochure rates), champagne and chocolate truffles, late afternoon canapes, and fruit basket.

All cabins have good soundproofing. The cabin service menu consists of five items (available twenty-four hours).

Dining: There are two dining rooms, both of which are set low down, have high domed ceilings, neat wall artwork (with fish logo) and offer good basic fare, with reasonable banquet food and somewhat robotic, rushed service. For breakfast and lunch open seating is generally featured, and there are two seatings for dinner (both smoking and nonsmoking areas are provided, so non-smokers should be aware that they may sit adjacent to smokers).

In the main dining roon the food is attractively presented, but the meals are not memorable, and standards are still spotty. When the ship is in Europe, the vegetables have taste; when she is in South America, this is not quite the case. There is a rather limited selection of breads, cheese, and fruit. Self-service buffets are featured in the Lido Café, with seating both indoors and outdoors (but it is difficult to get away from smokers), while an outdoor grill provides the requisite hamburgers.

Other Comments: *Rembrandt*—such a fitting name for this sturdily built steamship, and distinguished ocean liner! She has handsome, rounded lines, and a thick, royal blue, riveted hull (they don't build ships this way today). This grand dame is still lovely, and indeed she is well loved by her many followers. Gracious and graceful, she was well cared for by her previous owners, Holland America Line. She is being extremely well maintained (even improved) under her new owners, Premier Cruises, who want, quite rightly, to bring back the utter romance of cruising by operating a collection of carefully maintained, former ocean liners. Has expansive open deck and sunbathing space, with real teakwood promenade decks and wooden deck lounge chairs (with good cushioned pads that make them a pleasure to relax on).

Inside the ship, there are numerous public rooms to play in, but the decor is somewhat a mismatch of color combinations and, at times, might seem a little dark. However, the acres of beautiful wood paneling and wood trim throughout provide a real solid ship feel (almost impossible to find aboard today's new ships) and she has a most interesting wrought iron staircase, a carry-over from her former transatlantic days when she was first operated as a two-class ship. The dance floors feature lovely inlaid marquetry and parquet patterns, and her heavy-duty fittings and fixtures makes her a floating study in solidly crafted art deco workmanship. There is a decent (but now dated) collection of artwork throughout the ship.

The two-level Ritz Carlton lounge (complete with a gorgeous chandelier and wide, curved staircase) is still one of the most elegant art deco rooms afloat. There is a lovely theater, complete with a mezzanine balcony, in the old tradition (although the seats are not staggered). The one room not to be missed is the Ambassador Lounge, with its bordello-red and black chairs and pink spotted light fixtures—a fascinating place.

A cruise aboard this stately old ship fits quite comfortably—rather like a well-worn shoe—and the price is right. However, do remember that she is an old lady, and cannot compete with all the latest contemporary ships with their high-tech facilities (but then, it's the old-world charm of a well-proportioned ocean liner that passengers enjoy). She is, however, an extremely comfortable steamship.

She was acquired by Premier Cruises in September 1997 from her former owners, Holland America Line, and operates seven-day South America cruises during the winter and seven-day Mediterranean cruises during the summer, with a American, Brazilian, British, and Scandinavian passenger mix.

Choose this ship if you want to experience the thrill of sailing aboard a real (former) ocean liner, with high-ceilinged public rooms, expansive stairways and wide promenade deck. All port charges are included.

<u>But:</u> The fireplace in the casino seems out of place (so does the casino). Has poor (low-budget) entertainment. Communication between service staff and passengers remains the single most important thing for Premier Cruises to concentrate on—many of the crew speak or understand very little English.

ms Renaissance Six/Seven/Eight

☆☆☆☆

(S)

Lifestyle	**Premium**
Cruise Line:	Renaissance Cruises
Former Names:	-
Gross Tonnage:	4,280
Builder:	Nuovi Cantieri Apuania (Italy)
Original Cost:	$25 million each
Entered Service:	October 1991 (6) December 1991 (7) May 1992 (8)
Flag:	Liberia
Tel No:	(6) 1250142 (7) 1151322 (8) 1151375
Fax No:	(6) 1250141 (7) 1250146 (8) 1250145
Length (ft./m.):	297.2/90.60
Beam (ft./m.):	50.1/15.30
Draft (ft./m.):	12.9/3.95
Propulsion/Propellers:	diesel (5,000kW)/2 (CP)
Decks:	5
Total Crew:	72
Pass. Capacity (basis 2):	114
Pass. Capacity (all berths):	114
Pass. Space Ratio (basis 2):	37.5
Pass. Space Ratio (all berths):	37.5
Officers:	Italian
Total Cabins:	50
Size Range (sq. ft./m.):	215.0–312.0/20.0–29.0
Cabins (outside view):	50
Cabins (inside–no view):	0
Cabins (single occupancy):	0
Cabins (with private balcony):	4
Cabins (wheelchair accessible):	0
Cabin Current:	110 AC
Cabin TV:	Yes
Dining Rooms:	1
Seatings:	1
Elevators:	1
Casino:	Yes
Slot Machines:	Yes
Swimming Pools (outdoors):	1
Swimming Pools (inside):	0
Whirlpools:	1
Fitness Center:	No
Sauna/Steam Room:	Yes/No
Massage:	Yes
Self-Service Launderette:	No
Movie Theater/Seats:	No
Library:	Yes
Children's Facilities:	No
Classification Society:	RINA

Ratings	**Score**
Ship: Hardware/Maintenance	79
Ship: Outdoor Facilities/Space	80
Ship: Interior Facilities/Space/Flow	80
Ship: Decor/Furnishings/Artwork	82
Ship: Spa/Fitness Facilities	77
Cabins: Suites and Deluxe	84
Cabins: Standard Sizes	80
Food: Dining Room/Cuisine	76
Food: Informal Dining/Buffets	72
Food: Quality of Ingredients	72
Food: Afternoon Tea/Bar Snacks	63
Service: Dining Room	81
Service: Bars	80
Service: Cabins	81
Service: Open Decks	77
Cruise: Entertainment	70
Cruise: Activities Program	70
Cruise: Movies/Television Programming	78
Cruise: Hospitality Standard	77
Cruise: Overall Product Delivery	79
Overall Score	**1,538**

Accommodation: The spacious cabins combine highly polished imitation rosewood paneling with lots of mirrors and hand-crafted Italian furniture, lighted walk-in closets, three-sided vanity mirrors, and just about everything you need, including a television and VCR unit, refrigerator (pre-stocked when you book, but at extra cost). The bathrooms, however, are small; they have real teakwood floors and marble vanities, but no bathtubs.

Dining: The dining room (open seating for all meals) is small and elegant, with several tables for two, four, six, and even eight. Sit where you like, with whom you like, and at what time you like. Better dining room layout than on the "first four" is more intimate. Meals are self-service, buffet-style cold foods for breakfast and lunch, with hot foods chosen from a table menu and served properly. The dining room operation works well. The food quality, choice, and presentation are all fairly decent, and close to California "lean cuisine," but there is no flair at all.

Other Comments: Contemporary mega-yacht looks and handsome styling, with twin flared funnels. There are four identical vessels, similar in design to the Sea Goddess vessels. Increased length, duck-tail stern, and redesigned layout makes this second set of four vessels superior to the first four in the series, especially for stability and comfort (the first four have been withdrawn and sold). There is one outside promenade deck, and a reasonable amount of open deck and sunbathing space. Water sports facilities include an aft platform, sailfish, snorkel equipment, and Zodiacs.

Inside the ship, one finds an elegant interior design. The main lounge, the focal point for all social activities, has six pillars which destroy sight lines to the small stage area. Has a very small book and video library.

These vessels are very comfortable and totally inviting, offering destination-intensive cruising for the privileged passenger who appreciates the finer things in life and is prepared to pay accordingly. Although neither ship nor product delivery is anywhere near the standard of a Sea Goddess or Seabourn vessel, these intimate ships can still provide a good cruise experience for a moderate sum of money. Note that *Renaissance Seven* is chartered to the New York based travel organization Raymond and Whitcomb and is named *Regina Renaissance* for the period of the charter.

mv Rhapsody

☆☆☆

(M)

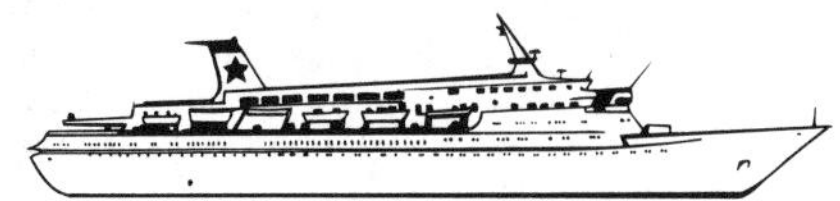

Lifestyle	**Standard**
Cruise Line:	Mediterranean Shipping Cruises
Former Names:	*Cunard Princess/ Cunard Conquest*
Gross Tonnage:	17,495
Builder:	Burmeister & Wein (Denmark)
Original Cost:	£12 million
Entered Service:	March 1977/May 1995
Flag:	Bahamas
Tel No:	1104111
Fax No:	1104111
Length (ft./m.):	536.6/163.56
Beam (ft./m.):	74.9/22.84
Draft (ft./m.):	19.0/5.82
Propulsion/Propellers:	diesel (15,670kW)/2 (CP)
Decks:	8
Total Crew:	350
Pass. Capacity (basis 2):	804
Pass. Capacity (all berths):	959
Pass. Space Ratio (basis 2):	21.7
Pass. Space Ratio (all berths):	18.1
Officers:	Italian
Total Cabins:	402
Size Range (sq. ft./m.):	88–265/8.1–24.6
Cabins (outside view):	266
Cabins (inside—no view):	136
Cabins (single occupancy):	1
Cabins (with private balcony):	0
Cabins (wheelchair accessible):	0
Cabin Current:	110/220 AC
Cabin TV:	No
Dining Rooms:	1
Seatings:	2
Elevators:	2
Casino:	Yes
Slot Machines:	Yes
Swimming Pools (outdoors):	1
Swimming Pools (inside):	0
Whirlpools:	2
Fitness Center:	Yes
Sauna/Steam Room:	Yes/No
Massage:	No
Self-Service Launderette:	No
Movie Theater/Seats:	Yes/130
Library:	Yes
Children's Facilities:	No
Classification Society:	Lloyd's Register

Ratings	**Score**
Ship: Hardware/Maintenance	68
Ship: Outdoor Facilities/Space	65
Ship: Interior Facilities/Space/Flow	63
Ship: Decor/Furnishings/Artwork	67
Ship: Spa/Fitness Facilities	60
Cabins: Suites and Deluxe	67
Cabins: Standard Sizes	58
Food: Dining Room/Cuisine	61
Food: Informal Dining/Buffets	55
Food: Quality of Ingredients	56
Food: Afternoon Tea/Bar Snacks	44
Service: Dining Room	60
Service: Bars	61
Service: Cabins	59
Service: Open Decks	58
Cruise: Entertainment	62
Cruise: Activities Program	55
Cruise: Movies/Television Programming	52
Cruise: Hospitality Standard	61
Cruise: Overall Product Delivery	66
Overall Score	**1,198**

Accommodation: Although the cabins are small and compact, with somewhat tinny (noisy) metal fixtures and very thin walls that provide extremely poor cabin insulation, they are adequate for short cruises. The soft furnishings are pleasing, and the closet and drawer space is reasonable. The bathrooms are adequate, if a little tight, with little storage space for toiletries.

Dining: Features a pleasant, bubbly dining room that has sea views from large picture windows, but it is quite noisy due to its open design. The standard "banquet" food is reasonable, and tailored mainly to Italian passengers, with typical Italian dishes including plenty of pasta (but sadly there is no tableside cooking). The service is quite bubbly, cheerful, attentive, and comes with a smile, but lacks finesse. There is a limited selection of breads and fruits. The cabin service menu is very limited.

Other Comments: This ship is almost identical to its sister, the former *Cunard Countess*, with the same contemporary profile and good looks. She was acquired in 1995 by StarLauro Cruises (now called Mediterranean Shipping Cruises) as a replacement for its *Achille Lauro,* which caught fire and sank in 1995. There is a good amount of open deck space for sun-worshippers, although there is no outdoor wraparound outdoor promenade deck.

There is a good selection of public rooms with attractive decor, in light, bright colors, including an observation lounge above the bridge, overlooking the bow. Has an excellent indoor-outdoor entertainment night club and bar, which incorporates the occasional use of an aft open deck area.

This ship will provide a very comfortable first cruise experience, featuring destination-intensive itineraries, in a pleasing, casual, but high-density environment.

This ship is now marketed mostly to Europeans, and to Italian passengers in particular, who form about 60 percent of the passengers. While the ship still looks sharp following an extensive refit and refurbishment in 1997, the standard of food and service offered are disappointing.

ms Rhapsody of the Seas

☆☆☆☆

(L)

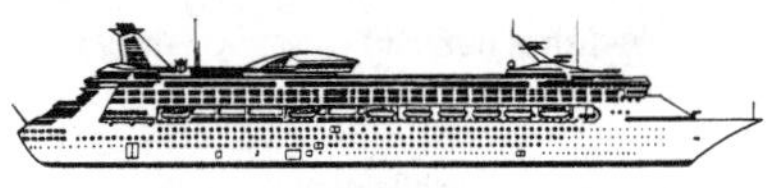

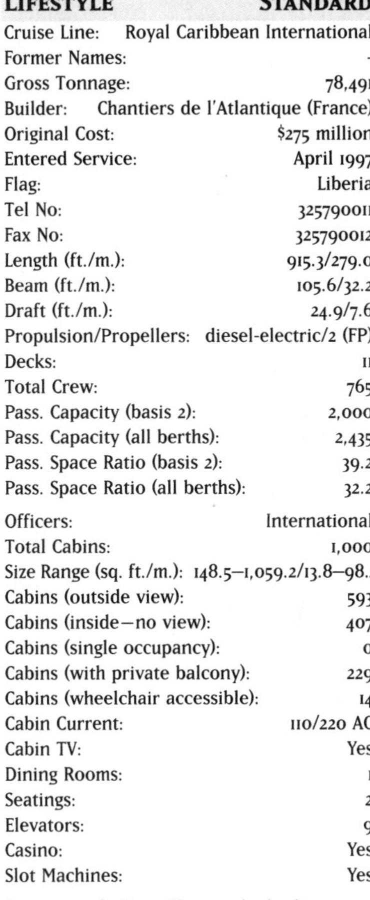

Lifestyle	Standard
Cruise Line:	Royal Caribbean International
Former Names:	-
Gross Tonnage:	78,491
Builder:	Chantiers de l'Atlantique (France)
Original Cost:	$275 million
Entered Service:	April 1997
Flag:	Liberia
Tel No:	325790011
Fax No:	325790012
Length (ft./m.):	915.3/279.0
Beam (ft./m.):	105.6/32.2
Draft (ft./m.):	24.9/7.6
Propulsion/Propellers:	diesel-electric/2 (FP)
Decks:	11
Total Crew:	765
Pass. Capacity (basis 2):	2,000
Pass. Capacity (all berths):	2,435
Pass. Space Ratio (basis 2):	39.2
Pass. Space Ratio (all berths):	32.2
Officers:	International
Total Cabins:	1,000
Size Range (sq. ft./m.):	148.5–1,059.2/13.8–98.4
Cabins (outside view):	593
Cabins (inside–no view):	407
Cabins (single occupancy):	0
Cabins (with private balcony):	229
Cabins (wheelchair accessible):	14
Cabin Current:	110/220 AC
Cabin TV:	Yes
Dining Rooms:	1
Seatings:	2
Elevators:	9
Casino:	Yes
Slot Machines:	Yes
Swimming Pools (outdoors):	1
Swimming Pools (inside):	1 (inside/outside)
Whirlpools:	6
Fitness Center:	Yes
Sauna/Steam Room:	Yes/Yes
Massage:	Yes
Self-Service Launderette:	No
Movie Theater/Seats:	No
Library:	Yes
Children's Facilities:	Yes
Classification Society:	Det Norske Veritas

Ratings	Score
Ship: Hardware/Maintenance	89
Ship: Outdoor Facilities/Space	86
Ship: Interior Facilities/Space/Flow	88
Ship: Decor/Furnishings/Artwork	88
Ship: Spa/Fitness Facilities	88
Cabins: Suites and Deluxe	88
Cabins: Standard Sizes	81
Food: Dining Room/Cuisine	71
Food: Informal Dining/Buffets	63
Food: Quality of Ingredients	66
Food: Afternoon Tea/Bar Snacks	52
Service: Dining Room	78
Service: Bars	76
Service: Cabins	77
Service: Open Decks	71
Cruise: Entertainment	81
Cruise: Activities Program	76
Cruise: Movies/Television Programming	76
Cruise: Hospitality Standard	73
Cruise: Overall Product Delivery	78
Overall Score	**1,546**

Accommodation: The standard cabins are of an adequate size, and have just enough functional facilities to make them comfortable for a one-week cruise, but longer might prove confining. The decor is bright and cheerful, although the ceilings are plain. Twin lower beds convert to queen-sized beds, and there is a reasonable amount of closet and drawer space (there is little room to maneuver between the bed and desk/television unit). The bathrooms are functional, although the shower units themselves are small. The towels could be larger and thicker. In the passageways, upbeat artwork depicts musical themes, from classical to jazz and popular.

The ultimate accommodation aboard this ship is the Royal Suite, which resembles a Palm Beach apartment, complete with white baby grand (player) piano. The decor is simple and elegant, with pastel colors and wood-accented ceiling treatments.

Dining: The two-level main dining room (called Edelweiss) is attractive and works well, although the noise level can be quite high. The quality and serving of meals aboard RCI ships has become very mechanized over the past few years. It can best be described as good, but rather basic, hotel banquet food, but, as is typical aboard so many ships today, there is little taste. While meats are reasonable quality, the fish is not, and most vegetables taste the same. In other words, the meals are basically sound, but certainly not memorable. There is also a limited selection of breads and cheeses. There is a decent but fairly basic wine list, and the prices are high. The dining room features open seating for breakfast and lunch, while dinner is at 6 p.m. (main seating) and 8:30 p.m. (second seating).

The informal dining spots are designed quite well with contemporary decor and colors, but the food is really quite basic fare and disappointing. The four-sided self-service buffet area is small for the number of passengers that use it. More money needs to be spent for better-quality ingredients. Each evening, buffets feature a different theme, something this company has been doing for more than 25 years—perhaps it's time for more creativity. One thing this company does once each cruise is to feature "Galley Buffet" whereby passengers go through a section of the galley picking up food for a midnight buffet.

Other Comments: This striking ship shares design features that make all Royal Caribbean International ships identifiable, including a Viking Crown Lounge, which is a terrific multi-level night spot (the music can be loud and overbearing, however, and so can the cigarette smoke around the bar). However, the Viking Crown Lounge (which is also the ship's disco) aboard this ship (and sister ship *Vision of the Seas*, which debuted in 1998) is positioned just forward of the center of the ship, while the funnel located well aft, a departure from all other RCI ships to date, which have the lounge positioned around or at the base of the funnel. The ship's stern is beautifully rounded. There is a reasonable amount of open-air walking space, although this can become cluttered with deck lounge chairs.

There is a wide range of interesting public rooms, lounges, and bars to play in, and the interiors have been cleverly designed to avoid congestion and aid passenger flow into revenue areas. Speaking of which, for those who enjoy gambling, the astrologically-themed casino is large and quite glitzy (although not as bold as aboard some of the company's other ships), again typical of most of the new large ships; a couple of pieces of "electrostatic" art in globe form provide fascinating relief.

There is, as one might expect, a large shopping area, although the merchandise is consistently tacky. Much improved over previous new ships in the fleet is the theater, with more entrances, less bottlenecks; there are still pillars obstructing sight lines from many seats, however. Also improved are the facilities for children and teens.

This ship has good health spa facilities, set in a spacious environment on one of the uppermost decks. The decor here has Egypt as its theme, with pharaohs lining the pool.

Ship lovers will enjoy the chair fabric in the Shall We Dance lounge, with its large aft-facing windows, and the glass case-enclosed mechanical sculptures.

Royal Caribbean International provides a consistently good, highly programmed cruise vacation for those seeking to travel in a large ship, with a large number of other lively passengers. What, in particular, makes this ship feel warm and cozy are the use of fine, light wood surfaces throughout her public rooms, as well as the large array of potted plants everywhere.

But: The daily program is so full of the day's events, in small type size, is that it is extremely difficult to read, particularly for older passengers. The light colored carpeting used on the stairwells is impractical.

ms Rotterdam

☆☆☆☆ +

(L)

Lifestyle	**Premium**
Cruise Line:	Holland America Line
Former Names:	-
Gross Tonnage:	59,652
Builder:	Fincantieri (Italy)
Original Cost:	$250 million
Entered Service:	October 1997
Flag:	The Netherlands
Tel No:	n/a
Fax No:	n/a
Length (ft./m.):	777.5/237.00
Beam (ft./m.):	105.8/32.25
Draft (ft./m.):	25.5/7.80
Propulsion/Propellers:	diesel-electric (37,500kW)/2 (CP)
Decks:	12
Total Crew:	644
Pass. Capacity (basis 2):	1,320
Pass. Capacity (all berths):	1,668
Pass. Space Ratio (basis 2):	45.1
Pass. Space Ratio (all berths):	35.7
Officers:	Dutch
Total Cabins:	660
Size Range (sq. ft./m.):	185-1,126/17.1-104.5
Cabins (outside view):	542
Cabins (inside—no view):	118
Cabins (single occupancy):	0
Cabins (with private balcony):	160
Cabins (wheelchair accessible):	20
Cabin Current:	110/220 AC
Cabin TV:	Yes
Dining Rooms:	2
Seatings:	2
Elevators:	16
Casino:	Yes
Slot Machines:	Yes
Swimming Pools (outdoors):	1
Swimming Pools (inside):	1 (magrodome cover)
Whirlpools:	2
Fitness Center:	Yes
Sauna/Steam Room:	Yes/Yes
Massage:	Yes
Self-Service Launderette:	Yes
Movie Theater/Seats:	Yes/235
Library:	Yes
Children's Facilities:	Yes
Classification Society:	Lloyd's Register

Ratings	**Score**
Ship: Hardware/Maintenance	92
Ship: Outdoor Facilities/Space	90
Ship: Interior Facilities/Space/Flow	89
Ship: Decor/Furnishings/Artwork	90
Ship: Spa/Fitness Facilities	85
Cabins: Suites and Deluxe	92
Cabins: Standard Sizes	83
Food: Dining Room/Cuisine	75
Food: Informal Dining/Buffets	72
Food: Quality of Ingredients	76
Food: Afternoon Tea/Bar Snacks	65
Service: Dining Room	63
Service: Bars	68
Service: Cabins	74
Service: Open Decks	66
Cruise: Entertainment	86
Cruise: Activities Program	83
Cruise: Movies/Television Programming	88
Cruise: Hospitality Standard	87
Cruise: Overall Product Delivery	91
Overall Score	**1,615**

Accommodation: The accommodation is spread over five decks (a number of cabins have full or partially obstructed views). Interestingly, no cabin is more than 144 ft. (44 m.) from a stairway, which makes it easier to get from cabins to public rooms. All cabin doors feature a birds-eye maple look, and hallways feature framed fabric panels to make them warmer and less clinical.

All standard inside and outside cabins are tastefully furnished, and have twin beds that convert to a queen-sized bed (space is tight for walking between beds and vanity unit). There is a decent amount of closet and drawer space, although this will prove tight for the longer voyages featured. The bathrooms, which are fully tiled, are disappointingly small (particularly for long cruises) and have small shower tubs, utilitarian personal toiletries cupboards, and exposed under-sink plumbing. There is no detailing to distinguish them from bathrooms aboard the Statendam-class ships, given that this is claimed by Holland America Line as the "flagship" of the fleet.

There are 36 full verandah suites (Navigation Deck), including four penthouse suites, which share a private Concierge Lounge with a concierge to handle such things as special dining arrangements, shore excursions, and special requests, although strangely there are no butlers for these suites, as aboard ships with similar facilities. Each suite has a separate steward's entrance, and separate bedroom, dressing, and living areas. The concierge lounge, with its latticework teak detailing and private library, is accessible only by private key-card.

Handicapped passengers have 20 cabins to choose from, including two of the large "penthouse" suites (which include concierge services). However, there are different cabin configurations, and it is wise to check.

Dining: There is one principal, large two-level dining room (La Fontaine), with tables for four, six, or eight, similar to the Statendam-class ships (there are just nine tables for two). Open seating is featured for breakfast and lunch, with two seatings for dinner (with both smoking and nonsmoking sections on both upper and lower levels). Fine Rosenthal china and good cutlery is featured (although there are no fish knives).

The food is marginally better than that presently served aboard the other HAL ships, with better buffets and more attention to detail, although it does not come up to the standard of other ships in the premium segment of the industry. What is definitely not luxurious are the packets (not glass jars) of breakfast jam, marmalade, and honey.

There is also an 88-seat alternative restaurant called Odyssey Italian, decorated in the manner of an opulent baroque Italian villa, and available to all passengers on a reservation basis. This alternative restaurant is a first on any Holland America Line ship (there's no extra charge). The room, whose basic color is black with gold accenting, is divided into three sections. The cuisines from the Perugia, Tuscany, and Umbria regions of Italy are featured, although the portions are quite small.

Other Comments: She has been constructed to look like a slightly larger (longer and beamier), but certainly much sleeker version of the Statendam-class ships, while retaining the graceful lines of the former *Rotterdam*, including a nicely-raked bow, as well as the familiar interior flow and design style. Also retained is the twin-funnel feature well recognized by former Holland America Line passengers, though somewhat streamlined. The new *Rotterdam* (the sixth Holland America Line ship to bear the name) is capable of 25 knots, which is useful for the longer distance itineraries she features.

The focal interior point is a three-deck high atrium, in an oval, instead of circular, shape. The atrium's focal point is a huge "one-of-a-kind" clock, which includes an astrolabe, an astrological clock and 14 other clocks in a structure that takes up three decks. Instead of just the two staircases aboard the Statendam-class ships, Rotterdam features three (better from the viewpoint of safety) and passenger accessibility. There is a magrodome-covered pool on the Lido Deck between the mast and the ship's twin funnels, as aboard the company's Statendam-class ships, which have only one large, very square funnel.

The interior public spaces also carry on the same layout and flow as found aboard the Statendam-class ships. Interior decor is quite restrained, with much use of wood accenting. One room features a glass ceiling similar to that found aboard a former Statendam. As a whole, the decor of this ship is extremely refined, with much of the traditional ocean liner detailing so loved by frequent Holland America Line passengers. Additions are children's and teens' play areas, although these really are token gestures by a company that traditionally does not cater well to children. Popcorn is available at the Wajang Theatre for moviegoers, while adjacent is the popular Java Café. The casino, which is located in the middle of a major passenger flow, now features blackjack, roulette, poker, and dice tables alongside the requisite rows of slot machines.

The artwork consists of a collection of seventeenth-century Dutch and Japanese artifacts together with contemporary works specially created for the ship, although there seems little linkage between some of the items.

Holland America Line's new flagship replaced the former ship of the same name when she was retired in September 1997, just in time for the start of the company's 125th anniversary in 1998. She is the most contemporary ship for Holland America Line, with lighter, brighter decor. She is an extremely comfortable ship in which to cruise, with some fine, elegant and quite luxurious decorative features. However, these are marred by the poor quality of dining room service and the lack of understanding of what it takes to make a "luxury" cruise experience, despite what is touted in the company's brochures. Refreshingly, the company does not add an automatic 15 percent for beverage purchases.

But: With one whole deck of suites (with a dedicated, private concierge lounge, and preferential passenger treatment), the company has in effect created a two-class ship. The charge ($1) to use the washing machines and dryers in the self-service launderette really is irritating and petty, particularly for suite passengers who pay high prices for long cruises. Communication (in English) with many of the staff, particularly in the dining room, can prove quite frustrating (example: I asked for salt for the table, and the waiter brought toast!). Nonsmokers should avoid this ship, as smokers are everywhere.

ys Royal Clipper
(S)

Lifestyle	Premium
Cruise Line:	Star Clippers
Former Names:	-
Gross Tonnage:	5,000
Builder:	Gdansk Shipyard (Poland)
Original Cost:	$75 million
Entered Service:	Late 1999
Flag:	Luxembourg
Tel No:	n/a
Fax No:	n/a
Length (ft./m.):	439.6/134.0
Beam (ft./m.):	54.1/16.5
Draft (ft./m.):	18.5/5.6
Type of Vessel:	sail-cruise (square rigger)
No. of Masts:	5
Sail Area (sq. ft. /sq. m.):	560,00/5,204.5
Main Propulsion:	42 sails
Propulsion/Propellers:	diesel/1 (CP)
Decks:	5
Total Crew:	100
Pass. Capacity (basis 2):	224
Pass. Capacity (all berths):	246
Pass. Space Ratio (basis 2):	22.3
Pass. Space Ratio (all berths):	20.3
Officers:	International
Total Cabins:	112
Size Range (sq. ft./m.):	100.0 – 320.0/9.3 – 29.7
Cabins (outside view):	112
Cabins (inside—no view):	0
Cabins (single occupancy):	0
Cabins (with private balcony):	14
Cabins (wheelchair accessible):	0
Cabin Current:	110/220 AC
Cabin TV:	Yes
Dining Rooms:	1
Seatings:	1
Elevators:	0
Casino:	No
Slot Machines:	No
Swimming Pools (outdoors):	3
Whirlpools:	0
Fitness Center:	No
Sauna/Steam Room:	No/No
Massage:	Yes
Self-Service Launderette:	No
Library:	Yes
Classification Society:	Lloyd's Register

Ratings	Score
Ship: Hardware/Maintenance	NYR
Ship: Outdoor Facilities/Space	NYR
Ship: Interior Facilities/Space/Flow	NYR
Ship: Decor/Furnishings/Artwork	NYR
Ship: Spa/Fitness Facilities	NYR
Cabins: Suites and Deluxe	NYR
Cabins: Standard Sizes	NYR
Food: Dining Room/Cuisine	NYR
Food: Informal Dining/Buffets	NYR
Food: Quality of Ingredients	NYR
Food: Afternoon Tea/Bar Snacks	NYR
Service: Dining Room	NYR
Service: Bars	NYR
Service: Cabins	NYR
Service: Open Decks	NYR
Cruise: Entertainment	NYR
Cruise: Activities Program	NYR
Cruise: Movies/Television Programming	NYR
Cruise: Hospitality Standard	NYR
Cruise: Overall Product Delivery	NYR

Expected Score Range
1,400-1,700

Accommodation: There are two owner's suites; these are to be the most lavish accommodation, while another 14 deck suites also promise luxurious appointments, plenty of space, and a private balcony; all have Jacuzzi bathtubs.

All other standard cabins have twin beds that can convert into a queen-sized bed, and a VCR unit.

Dining: The dining room, which seats 250, is constructed on several connecting levels, and seats all passengers at a single seating under a three-deck-high atrium dome. One corner can be closed off for private parties.

Other Comments: This will be the largest true sailing ship in the world, and an extension of the company's two other (smaller) tall ships. She is a copy of the only other five-masted sailing ship to be built—the *Preussen*, built in 1902—and has the same dimensions (much larger than the famous

Cutty Sark, for example). With five masts that reach as high as 197 feet/60.0 meters above the waterline, and up to 42 sails, she will look magnificent when under full sail. She is being constructed in a very short time due to the fact that the hull was almost completed for another owner but became available to Star Clippers for completion and fitting out. The ship is instantly recognizable due to her geometric black and white hull markings.

The sail handling system is such that she can be converted from a full rigger to a schooner in an incredibly short amount of time.

Inside, a three-deck-high midships atrium sits under one of the ship's three swimming pools, and funnels sunlight down through a piano lounge, a deck of cabins and into the dining room. A forward observation lounge is a real plus, and is connected to the piano lounge via a central corridor. The Edwardian library/card room is decorated with a belle epoque fireplace. The female massage staff will be from Thailand.

The Captain Nemo Club is a lounge where passengers can observe fish and sea life when the ship is at anchor, through thick glass portholes. Snorkeling gear is available at no cost, while scuba diving is available at an extra charge, and an aft platform will be used to access the shore tenders and for swimming.

This new spectacular tall ship will operate seven-day and fourteen-day cruises in the Grenadines and Lower Windward Islands of the Caribbean during the winter and in the Mediterranean during the summer. Her officers will navigate using both traditional (sextant) and contemporary methods (advanced electronic positioning system).

mv Royal Princess

☆☆☆☆ +

(L)

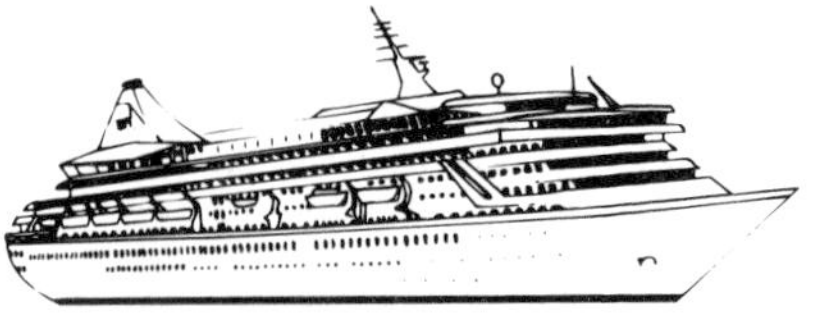

Lifestyle	**Premium**
Cruise Line:	Princess Cruises
Former Names:	-
Gross Tonnage:	44,348
Builder:	Wartsila (Finland)
Original Cost:	$165 million
Entered Service:	November 1984
Flag:	Great Britain
Tel No:	1440211
Fax No:	1440215
Length (ft./m.):	754.5/230.0
Beam (ft./m.):	95.8/29.2
Draft (ft./m.):	25.5/7.8
Propulsion/Propellers:	diesel (29,160kW)/2 (CP)
Decks:	9
Total Crew:	520
Pass. Capacity (basis 2):	1,200
Pass. Capacity (all berths):	1,275
Pass. Space Ratio (basis 2):	36.9
Pass. Space Ratio (all berths):	34.7
Officers:	British
Total Cabins:	600
Size Range (sq. ft./m.):	68–806/6.3–74.8
Cabins (outside view):	600
Cabins (inside–no view):	0
Cabins (single occupancy):	0
Cabins (with private balcony):	150
Cabins (wheelchair accessible):	10
Cabin Current:	110/220 AC
Cabin TV:	Yes
Dining Rooms:	1
Seatings:	2
Elevators:	6
Casino:	Yes
Slot Machines:	Yes
Swimming Pools (outdoors):	2 (+2 splash pools)
Swimming Pools (inside):	0
Whirlpools:	2
Fitness Center:	Yes
Sauna/Steam Room:	Yes/No
Massage:	Yes
Self-Service Launderette:	Yes
Movie Theater/Seats:	Yes/150
Library:	Yes
Children's Facilities:	No
Classification Society:	Lloyd's Register

Ratings	**Score**
Ship: Hardware/Maintenance	83
Ship: Outdoor Facilities/Space	85
Ship: Interior Facilities/Space/Flow	86
Ship: Decor/Furnishings/Artwork	85
Ship: Spa/Fitness Facilities	82
Cabins: Suites and Deluxe	87
Cabins: Standard Sizes	83
Food: Dining Room/Cuisine	73
Food: Informal Dining/Buffets	69
Food: Quality of Ingredients	70
Food: Afternoon Tea/Bar Snacks	63
Service: Dining Room	78
Service: Bars	76
Service: Cabins	76
Service: Open Decks	74
Cruise: Entertainment	84
Cruise: Activities Program	76
Cruise: Movies/Television Programming	82
Cruise: Hospitality Standard	80
Cruise: Overall Product Delivery	84
Overall Score	**1,576**

Accommodation: The all-outside cabins (152 have private balconies and there are only four suite and cabin types) are well thought out, very comfortable and well-appointed. The suites are extremely attractive, and feature excellent personal toiletry amenity kits.

All cabins have a full bathtub and shower, and three-sided mirrors. Bathrobes are provided for all passengers. Prompt, attentive room service is available twenty-four hours a day. Note that some cabins on Baja and Caribe decks have lifeboat-obstructed views. The cabin numbering system remains illogical, with numbers going through several hundred series on the same deck.

Dining: The elegant dining room (nonsmoking) is set low down, adjacent to the lobby. Food and service are moderately good, having been improved recently, and the standard of service is good. The cuisine is improving with the introduction of new menus, but most food is overcooked and the selection of vegetables with luncheon and dinner entrees is limited. The quality of fish is poor, with most covered by gravy-based sauces, and little or no garnish (the meat quality is good, however). There is always a pasta dish on the menu, and table captains are willing to make something special for you. The portions are quite generous, and presentation is improving, albeit slowly.

The in-cabin service menu is quite basic and could include more items. The indoor-outdoor Lido Café was expanded dramatically in a refit not long ago and now features twenty-four-hour food availability for casual dining, and better beverage stations that mean less lines.

Other Comments: This ship has handsome, contemporary outer styling, with a short, well-raked bow. Quality construction and materials were used throughout. Has an excellent amount of outdoor deck and sunbathing space, and traditional wraparound promenade deck outdoors.

Well-designed, though slightly unconventional interior layout and passenger flow provides passenger cabins that are located above the public room decks. Features include large, beautifully appointed and spacious public rooms rather than the smaller, more intimate public rooms and lounges found aboard many ships today. There are spacious passageways and delightful, imposing staircases. Contemporary without being the least bit garish, the decor reflects the feeling of space, openness and light.

The signs throughout the ship are adequate at best, and some of them are quite difficult to read.

The Horizon Lounge, set around the funnel base, has fine views, and makes for a peaceful environment during the day. This ship will provide a fine cruise experience in spacious, quite elegant surroundings, at the appropriate price, although attention to the small details of service finesse is often missing.

mv Royal Star

☆☆☆ +

(S)

LIFESTYLE	STANDARD
Cruise Line:	Star Line Cruises
Former Names:	*Ocean Islander/San Giorgio/ City of Andros*
Gross Tonnage:	5,360
Builder:	Cantieri Riuniti dell' Adriatico (Italy)
Original Cost:	n/a
Entered Service:	1956/December 1990
Flag:	Bahamas
Tel No:	1104407
Fax No:	1103460
Length (ft./m.):	367.4/112.00
Beam (ft./m.):	51.0/15.55
Draft (ft./m.):	18.2/5.56
Propulsion/Propellers:	diesel (4,817kW)/2 (FP)
Decks:	5
Total Crew:	130
Pass. Capacity (basis 2):	222
Pass. Capacity (all berths):	255
Pass. Space Ratio (basis 2):	24.1
Pass. Space Ratio (all berths):	21.0
Officers:	Greek
Total Cabins:	111
Size Range (sq. ft./m.):	107.0–398.0/10.0–37.0
Cabins (outside view):	97
Cabins (inside–no view):	14
Cabins (single occupancy):	0
Cabins (with private balcony):	1
Cabins (wheelchair accessible):	0
Cabin Current:	110/220 AC
Cabin TV:	No
Dining Rooms:	1
Seatings:	2
Elevators:	1
Casino:	Yes
Slot Machines:	Yes
Swimming Pools (outdoors):	1
Swimming Pools (inside):	0
Whirlpools:	0
Fitness Center:	Yes
Sauna/Steam Room:	Yes/No
Massage:	Yes
Self-Service Launderette:	No
Movie Theater/Seats:	No
Library:	Yes
Children's Facilities:	No
Classification Society:	American Bureau of Shipping

RATINGS	SCORE
Ship: Hardware/Maintenance	72
Ship: Outdoor Facilities/Space	58
Ship: Interior Facilities/Space/Flow	66
Ship: Decor/Furnishings/Artwork	66
Ship: Spa/Fitness Facilities	48
Cabins: Suites and Deluxe	76
Cabins: Standard Sizes	68
Food: Dining Room/Cuisine	68
Food: Informal Dining/Buffets	63
Food: Quality of Ingredients	65
Food: Afternoon Tea/Bar Snacks	57
Service: Dining Room	68
Service: Bars	64
Service: Cabins	68
Service: Open Decks	56
Cruise: Entertainment	57
Cruise: Activities Program	51
Cruise: Movies/Television Programming	44
Cruise: Hospitality Standard	65
Cruise: Overall Product Delivery	71
OVERALL SCORE	**1,251**

Accommodation: The cabins, although not large, are pleasantly decorated with good-quality furnishings and ample closet and drawer space. The cabin bathrooms, however, are really tiny, although the suites have two bathrooms (and a hair dryer) and a refrigerator. There is a limited cabin service menu.

Dining: The Belvedere Restaurant is a charming dining room, with reasonably good service and an international cuisine, although the standards are variable. Table wines are included with meals for lunch and dinner. There is a limited selection of breads, cheeses, and fruits, and the choice of teas is poor.

Other Comments: African Safari Club is a thirty-two-year-old Swiss hotel and tour company that specializes in land-based safaris and East African resort stays. The company, which has six hotels in

Mombasa, has been operating the ship for several years in conjunction with these land-based safaris. Royal Star is a charming little vessel (she was formerly operated by the now defunct Ocean Cruise Lines), with a well-balanced profile. There is an open bridge policy for all passengers while the ship is at sea (weather permitting). Has reasonable open deck space for sunbathing (but remember this operates for much of the year close to the equator, so the sun is incredibly strong).

This small vessel is well suited to cruising in sheltered areas. Clean and tidy throughout, the ship provides a warm, intimate, friendly, relaxed and highly personable ambience throughout. Has attractive contemporary interior decor, with lots of brass railings and solid wood doors. Has a newly improved fitness center. Entertainment is very low-key, and the Filipino crew provides much of it.

Well-packaged and operated, with excellent itineraries, this little ship will provide a most enjoyable cruise and safari experience in very comfortable, small-ship surroundings, at an extremely realistic price (port taxes are included). The African Safari Club has its own DC10 aircraft to transport you from Frankfurt to Mombasa (check with your travel agent in case a visa is needed). The currency is the deutsche mark.

ms Royal Viking Sun

☆☆☆☆☆

(M)

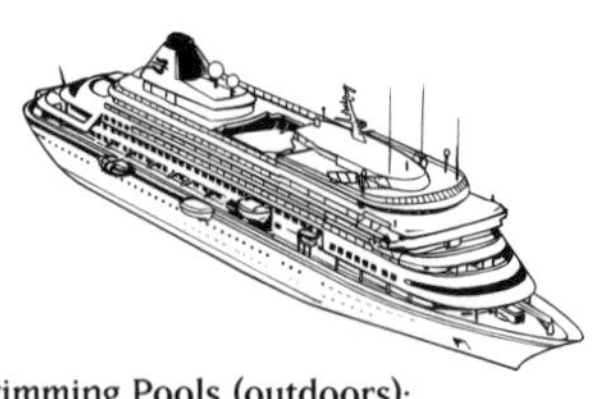

Lifestyle	**Luxury**
Cruise Line:	Cunard
Former Names:	-
Gross Tonnage:	37,845
Builder:	Wartsila (Finland)
Original Cost:	$125 million
Entered Service:	December 1988/June 1993
Flag:	Bahamas
Tel No:	1104515/1104517
Fax No:	1104514/1104516
Length (ft./m.):	674.2/205.5
Beam (ft./m.):	91.8/28.0
Draft (ft./m.):	23.6/7.2
Propulsion/Propellers:	diesel (21,120kW)/2 (CP)
Decks:	8
Total Crew:	460
Pass. Capacity (basis 2):	740
Pass. Capacity (all berths):	814
Pass. Space Ratio (basis 2):	51.1
Pass. Space Ratio (all berths):	46.4
Officers:	European/Norwegian
Total Cabins:	370
Size Range (sq. ft./m.):	138–724/12.8–67.2
Cabins (outside view):	350
Cabins (inside–no view):	20
Cabins (single occupancy):	2
Cabins (with private balcony):	145
Cabins (wheelchair accessible):	4
Cabin Current:	110 AC
Cabin TV:	Yes
Dining Rooms:	1
Seatings:	1
Elevators:	4
Casino:	Yes
Slot Machines:	Yes
Swimming Pools (outdoors):	2
Swimming Pools (inside):	0
Whirlpools:	2
Fitness Center:	Yes
Sauna/Steam Room:	Yes/No
Massage:	Yes
Self-Service Launderette:	Yes
Movie Theater/Seats:	Yes/101
Library:	Yes
Children's Facilities:	No
Classification Society:	Det Norske Veritas

Ratings	**Score**
Ship: Hardware/Maintenance	88
Ship: Outdoor Facilities/Space	90
Ship: Interior Facilities/Space/Flow	91
Ship: Decor/Furnishings/Artwork	88
Ship: Spa/Fitness Facilities	77
Cabins: Suites and Deluxe	92
Cabins: Standard Sizes	86
Food: Dining Room/Cuisine	90
Food: Informal Dining/Buffets	87
Food: Quality of Ingredients	87
Food: Afternoon Tea/Bar Snacks	85
Service: Dining Room	88
Service: Bars	86
Service: Cabins	88
Service: Open Decks	86
Cruise: Entertainment	84
Cruise: Activities Program	86
Cruise: Movies/Television Programming	87
Cruise: Hospitality Standard	87
Cruise: Overall Product Delivery	90
Overall Score	**1,743**

Accommodation: The Owner's Suite, at 723 sq. ft. (67.2 m^2), is one of the most desirable living spaces at sea. It is light and airy, and features two bathrooms, one of which has a large whirlpool bathtub with ocean views, and anodized gold bathroom fittings. The living room contains a large dining table and chairs, large sofas, and plenty of space to spread out.

Eighteen penthouse suites have large balconies and gracious butler service, as well as two leather sofas and a large bar/entertainment center (minibar-refrigerator, color television, VCR, and CD player). Bathrooms have separate toilet, sink, and toiletries cabinets, connecting sliding door into the bathroom, which has a large mirror, two toiletries cabinets, plenty of storage space, full bathtub, and anodized gold fittings. Each evening the butler brings different goodies—hot and cold hors d'oeuvres and other niceties.

If you choose one of the penthouses on Sky Deck, it might be best on the starboard side where they are located in a private hallway, while those on the port side (including the owner's suite) are positioned along a public hallway. All of the penthouse suites on Bridge Deck are positioned along private hallways.

Most of the other cabins (spread over 5 other decks) are of generous proportions and are well appointed, with just about everything you would need (including a VCR unit). Some 38 percent of all cabins have a private balcony. All cabins, however, have walk-in closets, lockable drawers, full-length mirrors, hairdryers, large fluffy cotton bathrobes and ample cotton towels. Good mix of Scandinavian and Filipino stewardesses provide excellent, unobtrusive service. Four well-equipped, L-shaped cabins for the handicapped are well designed, quite large, and feature special wheel-in bathrooms with shower facilities and closets. The only disappointment is with the rather plain cabin ceilings.

All cabins underwent complete refurbishment in 1997.

Dining: Excellent cuisine and good service are provided in a completely unhurried, caring atmosphere, with menus that are not repeated, no matter how long the voyage. Crystal glasses, finest quality flatware and cutlery are provided. The food is very creative and well presented, with good use of color combinations and garnishes. There is a fine, well-chosen wine list from distinguished vintners from around the world. There is also a separate, but somewhat underused wine bar. Although the dining room wine list is extensive, the wine prices are quite high. Mineral water, however, should be served for all meals in the dining room, instead of the standard chlorinated ship water provided.

There is also a fine, well utilized indoor-outdoor lido buffet area (Garden Café), with a fine variety and creative presentation (particularly of the many special themed buffets provided), as well as "Venezia," a separate a la carte Italian restaurant that is an elegant, lavish alternative dining spot, with a great view. For those wanting a light dinner alternative in a casual setting, The Bistro is also available at night. Finally, if you want total privacy, you can also dine, course by course, in your suite or cabin.

Other Comments: This contemporary, well-designed ship (now ten years old) has sleek, flowing lines, a sharply raked bow and a well-rounded profile, with lots of floor-to-ceiling glass. The ship's tenders are thoughtfully air-conditioned and even have radar and a toilet. The maintenance of the ship is excellent. Wide outdoor teakwood decks provide excellent walking areas, including a wraparound promenade deck. Sadly, there is no way to get from the uppermost pool, which has a swim-up/sit-in bar, to the second pool, located adjacent to the small health spa and gymnasium, without first going inside the vessel (there always seem to be compromises when ships are designed and built).

Inside the ship there are two glass-walled elevators. Separate baggage elevators mean passengers never have to wait for luggage. This vessel has an extremely spacious interior layout (it is ideal when a maximum of 600 passengers are aboard). Impressive public rooms and tasteful decor reign inside. Two handrails, one wooden, one chrome, are provided on all stairways, a thoughtful extra touch. The Stella Polaris Lounge, the ship's forward observation lounge, is simply one of the most elegant lounges at sea. Pebble Beach is the name of the ship's own golf club, complete with wet bar and electronic golf simulator. The Dickens Library is well-organized, although it is not large enough. Distinguished male guest hosts are provided on all cruises. The Oak Room features a fine marble fireplace, but sadly it cannot be used due to United States Coast Guard regulations (the ship operates principally out of U.S. ports); it would, however, make a fine library.

This fine vessel operates mainly long-distance cruises (including an annual complete world cruise) in great comfort (free shuttle buses are provided in almost all ports of call). Her beauty is the result of three designers: Njal R. Eide (ship design); Finn G. Nilsson (accommodation); and Frank Mingis (Owner's Suite and Penthouse Suites, who also assisted in selecting the interior color scheme, china, glass, and silverware). There are two outdoor swimming pools. The gymnasium is good, although the sauna and massage treatment areas could be larger. An excellent lecture program presents subjects of cultural interest, while gentlemen "dance hosts" provide fine partners for ladies traveling alone.

Whether by intention or not, the ship has created a two-class feeling, with passengers in "upstairs" penthouse suites and "A" grade staterooms gravitating to the somewhat quieter Stella Polaris lounge (particularly at night), while other passengers (the participants) go to the main entertainment deck.

This ship has a wide range of facilities, including a concierge, self-service launderettes (useful when on long voyages), excellent guest lecture program, twenty-four-hour information office, and true twenty-four-hour cabin service, for the discriminating passenger who demands the finest in spacious personal surroundings, food, and service, regardless of price. Absolutely first class, this Sun is set to shine for a long time.

Committed to the pursuit of gracious living at sea, she is one of the finest breed of contemporary grand floating hotels, with a warm ambience. The ship's direct competitors are *Crystal Harmony/Crystal Symphony* (arguably more elegant ships, with larger suites, but with two seatings for dinner) and the excellent, soon to be replaced *Europa* (principally for German-speaking passengers). While *Royal Viking Sun* is not perfect (the perfect ship has still not yet been delivered), the few design flaws that are evident (for example: poorly designed bar service counters; odd signs in elevators) are minor points. Even though the hardware is not perfect, the software (personnel and service) are generally very good.

She is being well maintained by Cunard, who purchased her along with the brand name Royal Viking Line in 1993, but she is now losing a little of her former shine and finesse. First-class air transportation is provided to passengers on long, exotic voyages. Cunard seems committed to keep up the standards aboard this ship, and this is good for passengers. A long cruise aboard Royal Viking Sun is arguably one of the world's most civilized travel experiences (although, as with any ship, the larger the cabin the better), with plenty of space, uncluttered surroundings, and no lines anywhere. Port taxes and gratuities are included. Perhaps the ship's best asset is her friendly and personable, mostly European crew.

But: The cabin ceilings are plain. All drinks should be, but are not, included (but then prices would need to be stable and totally non-discounted, something for Cunard to ponder for the future). She is a very spacious ship, but is showing signs of wear and tear, and, in certain areas, has been subject to some cost-cutting exercises, which are reflected in her slightly lower rating scores.

ms Ryndam

☆☆☆☆ +

(L)

LIFESTYLE	**PREMIUM**
Cruise Line:	Holland America Line
Former Names:	-
Gross Tonnage:	55,451
Builder:	Fincantieri (Italy)
Original Cost:	$215 million
Entered Service:	November 1994
Flag:	Netherlands
Tel No:	624506613
Fax No:	1306563
Length (ft./m.):	719.3/219.3
Beam (ft./m.):	101.0/30.8
Draft (ft./m.):	24.6/7.5
Propulsion/Propellers:	diesel-electric (34,560kW)/2 (CP)
Decks:	10
Total Crew:	588
Pass. Capacity (basis 2):	1,266
Pass. Capacity (all berths):	1,627
Pass. Space Ratio (basis 2):	43.8
Pass. Space Ratio (all berths):	34.0
Officers:	Dutch
Total Cabins:	633
Size Range (sq. ft./m.):	187–1,126/17.3–104.5
Cabins (outside view):	502
Cabins (inside–no view):	131
Cabins (single occupancy):	0
Cabins (with private balcony):	150
Cabins (wheelchair accessible):	6
Cabin Current:	110/220 AC
Cabin TV:	Yes
Dining Rooms:	1
Seatings:	2
Elevators:	12
Casino:	Yes
Slot Machines:	Yes
Swimming Pools (outdoors):	1
Swimming Pools (inside):	1 (magrodome)
Whirlpools:	2
Fitness Center:	Yes
Sauna/Steam Room:	Yes/No
Massage:	Yes
Self-Service Launderette:	Yes
Movie Theater/Seats:	Yes/249
Library:	Yes
Children's Facilities:	No
Classification Society:	Lloyd's Register

RATINGS	**SCORE**
Ship: Hardware/Maintenance	87
Ship: Outdoor Facilities/Space	82
Ship: Interior Facilities/Space/Flow	86
Ship: Decor/Furnishings/Artwork	85
Ship: Spa/Fitness Facilities	78
Cabins: Suites and Deluxe	83
Cabins: Standard Sizes	79
Food: Dining Room/Cuisine	77
Food: Informal Dining/Buffets	74
Food: Quality of Ingredients	72
Food: Afternoon Tea/Bar Snacks	65
Service: Dining Room	76
Service: Bars	76
Service: Cabins	76
Service: Open Decks	71
Cruise: Entertainment	77
Cruise: Activities Program	76
Cruise: Movies/Television Programming	76
Cruise: Hospitality Standard	77
Cruise: Overall Product Delivery	82
OVERALL SCORE	**1,555**

Accommodation: The standard cabins are quite spacious units, tastefully decorated, and well laid out, although some are a little cramped for two. The largest suites, however, are incredibly spacious and provide luxurious living at sea for the few.

Dining: Two-deck-high dining room with dramatic grand staircase located at stern is very elegant and has panoramic windows on three sides (lower level). There is open seating for breakfast and lunch, and two seatings for dinner. Food and service are of typical Holland America Line standards (extremely disappointing and completely non-memorable meals), with much use of fine china. The waiter stations in the dining room are very noisy, however, for anyone seated adjacent to them. In-suite dining is available in 28 suites, each of which can accommodate four.

Other Comments: She is a well-built, quality ship, the third in a series of four of the new breed of contemporary yet sophisticated ships specifically built for the nineties. Features excellent teakwood decking, and no astroturf anywhere.

Inside, there is an asymmetrical layout that breaks up her interiors and reduces bottlenecks and congestion. A three-deck high atrium foyer is quite stunning, with a central sculpture as focal point. A magrodome roof covers the indoor-outdoor pool and central Lido area. The art collection is outstanding, with a fine display of Dutch antiques. Subdued and tasteful interior decor. Flowers everywhere.

The two-deck-high showroom is well thought out, but the ceiling is low and sight lines are not as good as they should be in the upper (balcony) level.

The ship continues the company's strong maritime traditions, but present food and service components let the rest of the ship and cruise experience down badly. Note: The line does not add an automatic 15 percent for beverage purchases.

But: The single escalator is virtually useless. Extra charge for washers ($1.50) at the self-service launderettes. There is no bell-push outside the suites.

RMS St. Helena

☆☆☆ +

(S)

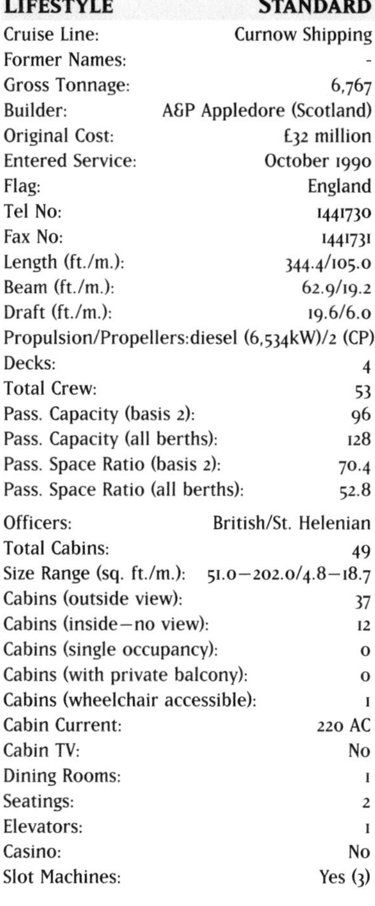

Lifestyle	**Standard**
Cruise Line:	Curnow Shipping
Former Names:	-
Gross Tonnage:	6,767
Builder:	A&P Appledore (Scotland)
Original Cost:	£32 million
Entered Service:	October 1990
Flag:	England
Tel No:	1441730
Fax No:	1441731
Length (ft./m.):	344.4/105.0
Beam (ft./m.):	62.9/19.2
Draft (ft./m.):	19.6/6.0
Propulsion/Propellers:	diesel (6,534kW)/2 (CP)
Decks:	4
Total Crew:	53
Pass. Capacity (basis 2):	96
Pass. Capacity (all berths):	128
Pass. Space Ratio (basis 2):	70.4
Pass. Space Ratio (all berths):	52.8
Officers:	British/St. Helenian
Total Cabins:	49
Size Range (sq. ft./m.):	51.0–202.0/4.8–18.7
Cabins (outside view):	37
Cabins (inside–no view):	12
Cabins (single occupancy):	0
Cabins (with private balcony):	0
Cabins (wheelchair accessible):	1
Cabin Current:	220 AC
Cabin TV:	No
Dining Rooms:	1
Seatings:	2
Elevators:	1
Casino:	No
Slot Machines:	Yes (3)

Swimming Pools (outdoors):	1
Swimming Pools (inside):	0
Whirlpools:	0
Fitness Center:	No
Sauna/Steam Room:	No/No
Massage:	No
Self-Service Launderette:	Yes
Movie Theater/Seats:	No
Library:	Yes
Children's Facilities:	Yes
Classification Society:	Lloyd's Register

Ratings	**Score**
Ship: Hardware/Maintenance	77
Ship: Outdoor Facilities/Space	52
Ship: Interior Facilities/Space/Flow	62
Ship: Decor/Furnishings/Artwork	67
Ship: Spa/Fitness Facilities	31
Cabins: Suites and Deluxe	70
Cabins: Standard Sizes	62
Food: Dining Room/Cuisine	75
Food: Informal Dining/Buffets	63
Food: Quality of Ingredients	67
Food: Afternoon Tea/Bar Snacks	71
Service: Dining Room	75
Service: Bars	76
Service: Cabins	77
Service: Open Decks	53
Cruise: Entertainment	41
Cruise: Activities Program	42
Cruise: Movies/Television Programming	50
Cruise: Hospitality Standard	66
Cruise: Overall Product Delivery	75
Overall Score	**1,252**

Accommodation: The accommodation is in two-, three-, or four-berth cabins, which are quite simply furnished, yet comfortable. There are 9 cabins that do not have private facilities.

Dining: The dining room is totally nonsmoking. It has two seatings, which, on such a small ship, is rather disruptive. The food is very British, with hearty breakfasts and a relatively simple menu, attractively presented on fine china. Afternoon tea, complete with freshly baked cakes, is a must.

Other Comments: This amazing little combination of contemporary cargo-passenger has all modern conveniences, including stabilizers and air-conditioning. Passengers can even take their pets. Operates just like a full-size cruise vessel, and has an open bridge policy. The swimming pool, however, is really a "dip" pool only, and is tiny.

Inside, the decor is tasteful and homey. There is a pleasant library/reading lounge. There is a free self-service laundry.

The brochure states that landing at Ascension is at times "a hazardous process" due to slippery and steep wharf steps—now that's telling it like it is. The staff is warm, welcoming, eager to see you enjoying the journey, and delightful to sail with.

The ship operates a regular Cardiff-Tenerife-St. Helena-Ascension Island-Tristan Da Cunha-Capetown line service, which is like a mini-cruise, or long voyage, with lots of days at sea. There are, at present, six round-trip sailings a year.

ms Saga Rose

☆☆☆ +

(M)

LIFESTYLE	PREMIUM
Cruise Line:	Saga Shipping
Former Names:	*Gripsholm/Sagafjord*
Gross Tonnage:	24,474
Builder:	Forges et Chantiers de la Mediteranee (France)
Original Cost:	$30 million
Entered Service:	October 1965/May 1997
Flag:	Bahamas
Tel No:	1104115
Fax No:	1103564
Length (ft./m.):	619.6/188.88
Beam (ft./m.):	80.3/24.49
Draft (ft./m.):	27.0/8.25
Propulsion/Propellers:	diesel (20,150kW)/2 (FP)
Decks:	7
Total Crew:	350
Pass. Capacity (basis 2):	589
Pass. Capacity (all berths):	620
Pass. Space Ratio (basis 2):	41.5
Pass. Space Ratio (all berths):	39.4
Officers:	British
Total Cabins:	321
Size Range (sq. ft./m.):	96.8–387.5/9.0–36.0
Cabins (outside view):	298
Cabins (inside—no view):	23
Cabins (single occupancy):	43
Cabins (with private balcony):	26
Cabins (wheelchair accessible):	8
Cabin Current:	110 AC
Cabin TV:	Yes
Dining Rooms:	1
Seatings:	1
Elevators:	4
Casino:	Yes
Slot Machines:	Yes
Swimming Pools (outdoors):	1
Swimming Pools (inside):	1
Whirlpools:	0
Fitness Center:	Yes
Sauna/Steam Room:	Yes/No
Massage:	Yes
Self-Service Launderette:	Yes
Movie Theater/Seats:	Yes/181
Library:	Yes
Children's Facilities:	No
Classification Society:	Det Norske Veritas

RATINGS	SCORE
Ship: Hardware/Maintenance	65
Ship: Outdoor Facilities/Space	78
Ship: Interior Facilities/Space/Flow	80
Ship: Decor/Furnishings/Artwork	77
Ship: Spa/Fitness Facilities	73
Cabins: Suites and Deluxe	81
Cabins: Standard Sizes	76
Food: Dining Room/Cuisine	74
Food: Informal Dining/Buffets	68
Food: Quality of Ingredients	71
Food: Afternoon Tea/Bar Snacks	68
Service: Dining Room	73
Service: Bars	74
Service: Cabins	73
Service: Open Decks	62
Cruise: Entertainment	48
Cruise: Activities Program	61
Cruise: Movies/Television Programming	60
Cruise: Hospitality Standard	66
Cruise: Overall Product Delivery	69
OVERALL SCORE	**1,397**

Accommodation: Has large, very spacious suites and cabins (in 18 categories), with superb appointments, all with excellent insulation, and all completely refurbished in 1997. There is also a large number of single cabins (excellent for the over-fifties traveler who enjoys privacy). There is generous drawer, under-bed storage, and lighted closet space. Good service is provided by the cabin stewardesses. Soft 100-percent cotton bathrobes and towels provided for all.

Dining: The dining room is superb in the classic sense, with a two-deck-high central ceiling and a grand entrance staircase. Features fine chinaware and flatware. Creative cuisine uses good-quality ingredients. The food is quite well presented, and garnishes are consistent with nouvelle cuisine. Pastries and dessert items are of a good standard, and there are reasonable choices of cheeses and fruits. Also features a good wine list with moderate prices. Classic service in the style of a grand hotel from thoughtful and attentive waiters.

Other Comments: She is still one of the most beautifully proportioned ships afloat, with a sweeping profile and well-placed funnel amidships. Like an aging Bentley, she will never go out of style. Built for long-distance cruising, she has a very spacious interior, with high-ceilinged public rooms and tasteful decor (but there are too many low-back chairs).

Quiet as a fine watch, this classic ship provides a refined life at sea for the discriminating over-50 passenger. Note: those under 50 are not allowed. Clean and graceful, with well-rounded lines, her grey hull contrasts against the large single red and black funnel. Built to a high standard, this ship has been well maintained and is operated with pride by her new owners.

Features fine quality furnishings and fittings, including hardwoods, brass and stainless steel. In fact, it is difficult to find any plastic in her. Has wide, open promenade decks, and a large, classic cinema. Her ballroom/main lounge is among the best afloat for real cocktail parties, with furniture that can be moved for almost any configuration, and a good wooden dance floor.

Saga Rose fits like an old shoe—so comfortable that you do not want to discard it. It is made from the best materials, and fits well as soon as you put it on. She attracts passengers that appreciate quality and decent service. Designed and created for long-distance cruising, the ship excels in quiet, refined living, featuring numerous nights at sea and extended itineraries in surroundings of high comfort. Her high repeat passenger base confirms that there is a place for a ship such as this. Indeed, a voyage aboard this ship proves to be a most pleasurable travel experience. This is classic cruising for her mainly British passengers (the ship is based at Dover), under the banner of Saga Holiday International whose staff have a reputation for being attentive (note that the cabin voltage is 110 AC, so take adapters if you have any electrical appliances). She is a gracious old lady (now more than thirty years old), having seen some fine service throughout the world. All port taxes, insurance, and tips are included.

But: The entertainment is a real weak link (end-of-pier style). The food is disappointing, and service needs improvement. The hospitality and general standard of product delivery are not as good as when Cunard operated the ship.

ms Sapphire

☆☆☆

(S)

Lifestyle	**Standard**
Cruise Line:	Thomson Cruises
Former Names:	*Princesa Oceanica/Sea Prince/ Ocean Princess/Italia/Princess Italia*
Gross Tonnage:	12,183
Builder:	Cantieri Navale Felszegi (Italy)
Original Cost:	n/a
Entered Service:	August 1967/April 1996
Flag:	Cyprus
Tel No:	n/a
Fax No:	n/a
Length (ft./m.):	491.7/149.8
Beam (ft./m.):	70.9/21.5
Draft (ft./m.):	21.6/6.6
Propulsion/Propellers:	diesel (11,050kW)/2 (CP)
Decks:	8
Total Crew:	225
Pass. Capacity (basis 2):	540
Pass. Capacity (all berths):	650
Pass. Space Ratio (basis 2):	22.5
Pass. Space Ratio (all berths):	18.7
Officers:	Greek
Total Cabins:	270
Size Range (sq. ft./m.):	75.3–226.0/7.0–21.0
Cabins (outside view):	125
Cabins (inside–no view):	125
Cabins (single occupancy):	0
Cabins (with private balcony):	0
Cabins (wheelchair accessible):	0
Cabin Current:	110 AC
Cabin TV:	No
Dining Rooms:	1
Seatings:	2
Elevators:	5
Casino:	Yes
Slot Machines:	Yes
Swimming Pools (outdoors):	1
Swimming Pools (inside):	0
Whirlpools:	0
Fitness Center:	No
Sauna/Steam Room:	No/No
Massage:	Yes
Self-Service Launderette:	No
Movie Theater/Seats:	Yes/170
Library:	Yes
Children's Facilities:	Yes
Classification Society:	RINA

Ratings	**Score**
Ship: Hardware/Maintenance	63
Ship: Outdoor Facilities/Space	64
Ship: Interior Facilities/Space/Flow	67
Ship: Decor/Furnishings/Artwork	66
Ship: Spa/Fitness Facilities	46
Cabins: Suites and Deluxe	71
Cabins: Standard Sizes	66
Food: Dining Room/Cuisine	64
Food: Informal Dining/Buffets	57
Food: Quality of Ingredients	61
Food: Afternoon Tea/Bar Snacks	57
Service: Dining Room	66
Service: Bars	66
Service: Cabins	67
Service: Open Decks	58
Cruise: Entertainment	61
Cruise: Activities Program	55
Cruise: Movies/Television Programming	44
Cruise: Hospitality Standard	58
Cruise: Overall Product Delivery	63
Overall Score	**1,220**

Accommodation: There are seven cabin grades, but you should note that cabins are not assigned until you arrive at the port of embarkation. The cabin closet and drawer space is very limited. Reasonable-sized cabins have pleasing, though plain, decor, furnishings, and fittings. All have tiled bathrooms, but they are small. Continental breakfast in your cabin will cost you about $7.50 (£4.50) per person extra (each time). There is also a twenty-four-hour cabin service menu for snacks, all at extra cost.

Dining: The dining room is charming and has an art deco feel, a raised-center ceiling, and lovely etched glass dividers, but the noise level is high from the waiter stations. You'll find that service is reasonably attentive from a willing, friendly staff. There is a good general standard of international cuisine, although do remember that this is a low-cost cruise, and so you should not expect high-class cuisine.

For casual breakfast and luncheon, the Café de Paris (located indoors but looking out onto the pool deck) is the place (it also has a bar).

Other Comments: The ship's long, low, handsome lines and swept-back aft-placed funnel provide a very attractive profile for this small ship. Has inboard lifeboats. Has good open deck and sunbathing space, but the heated outdoor pool is small.

Inside, contemporary interior decor is featured; a mix of attractive colors, together with much use of mirrored surfaces, add warmth in the public rooms. Some public rooms have a fairly low ceiling height. Harry's Bar is perhaps the most popular gathering place, although there are few seats (the gaming tables are adjacent). There is also a cinema with comfortable seating.

Cyprus-based Louis Cruise Lines purchased the ship in August 1995 and, following an extensive refurbishment, placed her into service in April 1996 on behalf of Thomson, the U.K. tour operator. This ship will take its mainly British passengers to some decent destinations in good, contemporary surroundings, and in a relaxed casual style (you will probably fly to/from the ship on Britannia Airways, a Thomson-owned company). The realistic, inexpensive price of this product is a real bonus, and gratuities are included.

sy Sea Cloud

☆☆☆☆ +

(S)

Lifestyle	**Luxury**
Cruise Line:	Sea Cloud Cruises
Former Names:	*Antaria/Patria/ Angelita/Hussar*
Gross Tonnage:	2,532
Builder:	Krupp Werft (Germany)
Entered Service:	1931/1978 (restored)
Flag:	Malta
Tel No:	1256105
Fax No:	1256173
Length (ft./m.):	315.9/96.30
Beam (ft./m.):	49.0/14.94
Draft (ft./m.):	16.8/5.13
Type of Vessel:	4-masted barque
No. of Masts:	4 (17.7 meters)/(29 sails)
Sail Area (sq. ft. /sq. m.):	32,292/3,000
Main Propulsion:	sail power
Propulsion/Propellers:	diesel (6,000bhp)/1 (FP)
Decks:	3
Total Crew:	60
Pass. Capacity (basis 2):	69
Pass. Capacity (all berths):	69
Pass. Space Ratio (basis 2):	37.2
Pass. Space Ratio (all berths):	37.2
Officers:	European
Total Cabins:	34
Size Range (sq. ft./m.):	102.2–409.0/9.5–38.0
Cabins (outside view):	34
Cabins (inside–no view):	0
Cabins (single occupancy):	0
Cabins (with private balcony):	0
Cabins (wheelchair accessible):	0
Cabin Current:	110/220 AC
Cabin TV:	No
Dining Rooms:	1 (open seating)
Elevators:	0
Casino:	No
Slot Machines:	No
Swimming Pools (outdoors):	0
Whirlpools:	0
Fitness Center:	No
Sauna/Steam Room:	No/No
Massage:	No
Self-Service Launderette:	No
Library:	Yes
Classification Society:	Germanischer Lloyd

Ratings	**Score**
Ship: Hardware/Maintenance	84
Ship: Sails and Equipment	88
Ship: Interior Facilities/Space/Flow	86
Ship: Decor/Furnishings/Artwork	86
Ship: Spa/Fitness Facilities	66
Cabins: Suites and Deluxe	90
Cabins: Standard Sizes	81
Food: Dining Room/Cuisine	87
Food: Informal Dining/Buffets	78
Food: Quality of Ingredients	81
Food: Afternoon Tea/Bar Snacks	76
Service: Dining Room	82
Service: Bars	78
Service: Cabins	77
Service: Open Decks	74
Cruise: The Sailing Experience	88
Cruise: Lecturers/Entertainment	67
Cruise: Movies/Television Programming	58
Cruise: Hospitality Standard	82
Cruise: Overall Product Delivery	83
Overall Score	**1,592**

Accommodation: All of the accommodation is very comfortable, but the two owner's suites (Cabins 1 and 2) are really extravagant, and feature real, original Chippendale furniture, fine gilt detailing, a real fireplace, and large Italian marble bathrooms.

Owner's Cabin 1 is decorated in white throughout, and has a fireplace and Louis Phillippe chairs. Owner's Cabin 2 is completely paneled in rich woods, and retains the mahogany secretary used sixty years ago by Mr. Edward F. Hutton, husband of American cereal heiress Marjorie Merriweather Post.

Other cabins (both the original ones, and some newer additions) are all beautifully furnished, and all were refurbished in 1993. The cabin bathrooms, too, are extremely good, and equipped with really everything you will need. There is plenty of closet and drawer space, and bathrobes are provided for all. Note that there is no cabin food or beverage service.

Dining: The dining room, located in the center of the vessel, is very elegant (it also houses the ship's library) and has beautiful wood paneled walls and a wood beam ceiling. There is ample space at each table, so there is never a crowded feeling. German chefs are in charge, and the cuisine is international, with some regional dishes according to where the ship is sailing. Wines are usually provided for lunch and dinner.

Excellent quality food and cuisine are featured, although the choice is a little limited. There are always some excellent seafood and fish, which are purchased fresh when available, as are many of the ingredients. Breakfast and lunch buffets are really good, and beautifully presented. Wines are included with lunch and dinner.

Other Comments: The oldest and most beautiful tall ship sailing, and the largest private yacht ever built (she is three times the size of Captain Cook's *Endeavour*), she is constructed of the best materials. Her masts reach as high as a 20-floor building (actually 191.5 ft./58.3 m. above the main deck). Originally built for Marjorie Merriweather Post, this lovely working sailing ship is now owned by a consortium of nine German yachtsmen and is chartered to various operators.

Sea Cloud is, without doubt, the ultimate, most romantic sailing ship afloat today. Although there are many imitations, there still is none better than this vintage vessel. She is still kept close to her original state when built. There is plenty of deck space available, even under the vast expanse of white sail, and the outdoor promenade deck still has wonderful varnished sea chests. The original engine room (with diesel engines) is still in operation for the rare occasions when sail power cannot be used.

The interior exudes warmth, and is finely hand crafted. There is much antique furniture, fine original oil paintings, gorgeous carved oak paneling everywhere, and some finely detailed ceilings.

The largest private yacht ever built, it is constructed of the very best materials. During World War II, the vessel saw action as a weather observation ship, under the code name *IX-99*. You can still see five chevrons on the bridge, one for each half-year of duty, serving as a reminder of those important years. The crew are dedicated to the fine art of sailing, and service is excellent.

A cruise aboard *Sea Cloud* is, today, in three words, a truly exhilarating experience, and is still much today as it was when she was first launched. She really is a special ship like no other, for the discerning few to relish the uncompromising comfort and elegance of a bygone era. Truly a stately home afloat, this ship remains one of the world's finest travel and holiday experiences, and a wonderful escape from the stress and strain of life ashore. The U.S. dollar is used as onboard currency. The owning company, which is German, also operates the new river vessel *River Cloud*, introduced in May 1996, for cruises on the Danube, Main, Mosel, and Rhine areas.

<u>But:</u> The interior staircase is quite steep, as it is on most sailing vessels. Remember that a sailing ship sails, and even a big sailing vessel such as this can heel to one side occasionally. Somehow the plastic chairs on deck just do not go with this ship's romantic, very exclusive image.

mv Sea Goddess I

☆☆☆☆☆

(S)

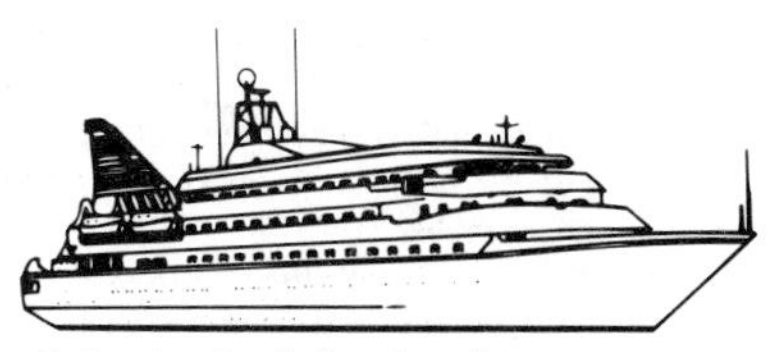

LIFESTYLE	**LUXURY**
Cruise Line:	Cunard
Former Names:	-
Gross Tonnage:	4,260
Builder:	Wartsila (Finland)
Original Cost:	$34 million
Entered Service:	April 1984
Flag:	Isle of Man
Tel No:	1454141/1454143
Fax No:	1454142
Length (ft./m.):	343.8/104.81
Beam (ft./m.):	47.9/14.60
Draft (ft./m.):	13.6/4.17
Propulsion/Propellers:	diesel (3,540kW)/2 (CP)
Decks:	5
Total Crew:	90
Pass. Capacity (basis 2):	116
Pass. Capacity (all berths):	116
Pass. Space Ratio (basis 2):	36.7
Pass. Space Ratio (all berths):	36.7
Officers:	British/Norwegian
Total Cabins:	58
Size Range (sq. ft./m.):	179.0–410.0/16.7–38.0
Cabins (outside view):	58
Cabins (inside—no view):	0
Cabins (single occupancy):	0
Cabins (with private balcony):	0
Cabins (wheelchair accessible):	0
Cabin Current:	110/220 AC
Cabin TV:	Yes
Dining Rooms:	1
Seatings:	Open (+in-cabin dining)
Elevators:	1
Casino:	Yes
Slot Machines:	Yes
Swimming Pools (outdoors):	1
Swimming Pools (inside):	0
Whirlpools:	1
Fitness Center:	Yes
Sauna/Steam Room:	Yes/No
Massage:	Yes
Self-Service Launderette:	No
Movie Theater/Seats:	No
Library:	Yes
Children's Facilities:	No
Classification Society:	Lloyd's Register

RATINGS	**SCORE**
Ship: Hardware/Maintenance	90
Ship: Outdoor Facilities/Space	91
Ship: Interior Facilities/Space/Flow	90
Ship: Decor/Furnishings/Artwork	92
Ship: Spa/Fitness Facilities	86
Cabins: Suites and Deluxe	89
Cabins: Standard Sizes	86
Food: Dining Room/Cuisine	96
Food: Informal Dining/Buffets	90
Food: Quality of Ingredients	93
Food: Afternoon Tea/Bar Snacks	93
Service: Dining Room	93
Service: Bars	92
Service: Cabins	93
Service: Open Decks	92
Cruise: Entertainment	85
Cruise: Activities Program	85
Cruise: Movies/Television Programming	86
Cruise: Hospitality Standard	92
Cruise: Overall Product Delivery	91
OVERALL SCORE	**1,805**

Accommodation: The cabins are fully equipped all-outside "suites." Beds are positioned next to the window so that you can entertain in the living area without going past the sleeping area (as one must aboard the Seabourn Cruise Line and Silversea Cruises ships, for example). All cabinetry and furniture is of thick blond wood, with beautifully rounded edges. A long vanity desk in the sleeping area has a large mirror above it (but no three-sided mirror) and two small drawers for cosmetic items; there is also a brass clock located on one wall. A long desk in the lounge area has six drawers, plus a vertical cupboard unit that houses a sensible safe, refrigerator, and drinks cabinet. There is also a VCR unit.

The beds have thick cotton duvets, and non-allergenic pillows (and duvets) are also available. The bathrooms, which now urgently need updating, are very tight (particularly for those who are of larger than average build), and doors open inward, so space inside really is at a premium. There is a glass shelf for personal toiletry items, while an under-sink drawer and cupboard provides space for larger items. Plush, thick 100-percent cotton bathrobes and towels are supplied.

For the ultimate accommodation aboard this ship, choose a double suite (there are eight of them), each with interconnecting doors, which provide two bathrooms (his and hers), with one suite acting as a lounge/dining room, the other for use as a bedroom.

One drawback is the fact that the insulation between cabins is not as good as it could be, although rarely does this present problems, as most passengers aboard the Sea Goddesses are generally extremely quiet, considerate types who are allergic to noise.

Dining: The dining salon is bright, warm, and inviting in its new primrose yellow decor. It is cozy, yet with plenty of space around each table for fine service, and the ship provides a floating culinary celebration.

Tables for two, four, six, or eight are immaculately laid with settings of real silver base plates, pristine white table linen, and fresh flowers (there are also fresh flowers in several wall sconces). Hutschenreuther, Villeroy and Boch, and Tiffany are the appointments. There is even a box full of spare spectacles for menu reading in case you forget your own. You get leather-bound menus, and supremely attentive, close to impeccable personalized European service. Open seating means you can dine wherever, whenever, and with whomever you want (for dinner, generally between 8 p.m. and 10 p.m.).

The *Sea Goddess* experience really is all about dining, and is the height of culinary excellence at sea. Only the very freshest and finest quality ingredients are used in the best culinary artistry. Fine European service is provided.

Live (electric) piano music is provided for dinner each evening. The ship features exquisite, creative cuisine, with everything prepared individually to order. Special orders are welcomed, and flaming desserts are cooked at your table. You can also dine course by course in your suite for any meals, at any time (you can also eat à la carte twnty-four-hours a day if you wish). There is plenty of fine quality caviar, at any time of the day or night. And, thankfully, never a hint of baked Alaska!

A selection of decent wines accompanies each meal, while real connoisseurs will appreciate the availability of an extra wine list of really special vintages and premier crus (at extra cost). If you want to do something different with a loved one, you can also arrange to dine one evening on the open (but covered) deck, overlooking the swimming pool and stern—it is a magical and very romantic setting.

There is also an informal outdoor Café, where excellent buffets are provided for breakfast and luncheon, and you never have to get, or carry, your food (the waiters will do that for you). Teakwood tables and chairs add an additional, essential, air of luxury.

Other Comments: This is a small ship with an ultra-sleek profile and the ambience of a private club. She has been well maintained, although, at fifteen years old, there are signs of wear and tear. The ship was refurbished in late 1997, when new teakwood deck furniture was added. At her stern is a small water sports platform; water-ski boats, windsurfers, jet skis, scuba, and snorkeling equipment are provided at no extra charge. However, the sea conditions have to be just right (minimal swell) for these items to be used, which, on average is once or twice during a seven-day cruise. You may also be allowed to swim off the stern platform.

Inside, there is a delightful feeling of unabashed but discreet sophistication. Elegant, chic public rooms and flowers and pot-pourri everywhere. There is even a small gymnasium and sauna, hidden around the funnel base. Oriental rugs can be found in the lobby. Fine quality furnishings and fabrics are used throughout, with marble and blond wood accents. Everything, including beverages and wines, is included.

Unadulterated indulgence and refined, unstructured, and langorous private living at sea is the hallmark of life aboard this vessel. This is for the experienced, independent traveler who does not like cruise ships, and especially for those who do not like large ships, glitzy lounges, platoons of people, or kids running around. No one under the age of sixteen is allowed aboard without exception, a new rule brought into effect in 1998 to the cheers of many repeat passengers.

This really is the ultimate boutique ship—like having your own private island where hospitality and anticipation are art forms practiced to the highest degree. The staff is delightful and accommodating ("no" is not in this ship's vocabulary); if there is anything special you want, you have only to ask, and the staff will be only too happy to oblige in the style of the best European hotels.

The dress code is resort casual by day (one could almost live in one's bathrobe), dressy by night (gentlemen must wear jacket and tie to the dining room). Hospitality is an art form practiced to the highest degree aboard this ship.

Port charges and insurance are not included. However, one shore excursion in each port of call (even in the Mediterranean, where shore excursions are very expensive) and all gratuities are included (no further tipping is allowed). Life could hardly be better at sea—so, as many regular *Sea Goddess* passengers say, why bother with ports of call? Embarkation always starts at 3 p.m., never before, in case you are eager to get aboard.

But: Although this was the first of the mega-yacht-style ships, no cabins have private balconies (they arrived just a couple of years later aboard other, newer ships). The company has sadly seen fit to decrease the standard of personal amenities supplied for the bathroom, and some other little special touches and details have disappeared lately, and thus are reflected in the ratings. Two new mahogany shore tenders should replace the present (aging) ones.

mv Sea Goddess II

☆☆☆☆☆

(S)

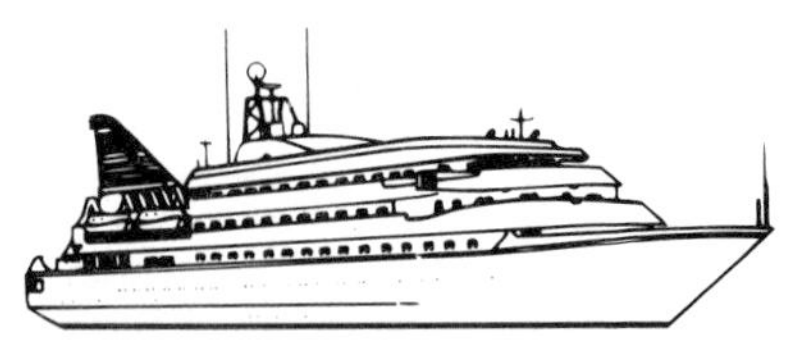

LIFESTYLE	**LUXURY**
Cruise Line:	Cunard
Former Names:	-
Gross Tonnage:	4,260
Builder:	Wartsila (Finland)
Original Cost:	$34 million
Flag:	Isle of Man
Tel No:	1453752/623373710
Fax No:	1310644/623373713
Length (ft./m.):	343.8/104.81
Beam (ft./m.):	47.9/14.60
Draft (ft./m.):	13.6/4.17
Propulsion/Propellers:	diesel (3,540kW)/2 (CP)
Decks:	5
Total Crew:	90
Pass. Capacity (basis 2):	115
Pass. Capacity (all berths):	115
Pass. Space Ratio (basis 2):	36.7
Pass. Space Ratio (all berths):	36.7
Officers:	British/Norwegian
Total Cabins:	58
Size Range (sq. ft./m.):	179.0–410.0/16.7–38.0
Cabins (outside view):	58
Cabins (inside–no view):	0
Cabins (single occupancy):	1
Cabins (with private balcony):	0
Cabins (wheelchair accessible):	0
Cabin Current:	110/220 AC
Cabin TV:	Yes
Dining Rooms:	1
Seatings:	Open (+in-cabin dining)
Elevators:	1
Casino:	Yes
Slot Machines:	Yes
Swimming Pools (outdoors):	1
Swimming Pools (inside):	0
Whirlpools:	1
Fitness Center:	Yes
Sauna/Steam Room:	Yes/No
Massage:	Yes
Self-Service Launderette:	No
Movie Theater/Seats:	No
Library:	Yes
Children's Facilities:	No
Classification Society:	Lloyd's Register

RATINGS	**SCORE**
Ship: Hardware/Maintenance	90
Ship: Outdoor Facilities/Space	91
Ship: Interior Facilities/Space/Flow	90
Ship: Decor/Furnishings/Artwork	92
Ship: Spa/Fitness Facilities	86
Cabins: Suites and Deluxe	89
Cabins: Standard Sizes	86
Food: Dining Room/Cuisine	96
Food: Informal Dining/Buffets	90
Food: Quality of Ingredients	93
Food: Afternoon Tea/Bar Snacks	93
Service: Dining Room	93
Service: Bars	92
Service: Cabins	93
Service: Open Decks	92
Cruise: Entertainment	85
Cruise: Activities Program	85
Cruise: Movies/Television Programming	86
Cruise: Hospitality Standard	92
Cruise: Overall Product Delivery	91
OVERALL SCORE	**1,805**

For comments, see *Sea Goddess I*.

ms Sea Princess
(L)

Lifestyle	**Premium**
Cruise Line:	Princess Cruises
Former Names:	-
Gross Tonnage:	77,000
Builder:	Fincantieri (Italy)
Original Cost:	$300 million
Entered Service:	November 1998
Flag:	Liberia
Tel No:	n/a
Fax No:	n/a
Length (ft./m.):	856.2/261.00
Beam (ft./m.):	105.8/32.25
Draft (ft./m.):	26.0/7.95
Propulsion/Propellers:	diesel-elec/2 (FP)
Decks:	14
Total Crew:	900
Pass. Capacity (basis 2):	1,950
Pass. Capacity (all berths):	2,250
Pass. Space Ratio (basis 2):	39.4
Pass. Space Ratio (all berths):	34.2
Officers:	Italian
Total Cabins:	1,050
Size Range (sq. ft./m.):	159–611/14.7–56.7
Cabins (outside view):	652
Cabins (inside–no view):	398
Cabins (single occupancy):	0
Cabins (with private balcony):	446
Cabins (wheelchair accessible):	20
Cabin Current:	110/220 AC
Cabin TV:	Yes
Dining Rooms:	2 main/3 others
Seatings:	2 (main dining rooms)
Elevators:	11
Casino:	Yes
Slot Machines:	Yes
Swimming Pools (outdoors):	3
Swimming Pools (inside):	0
Whirlpools:	5
Fitness Center:	Yes
Sauna/Steam Room:	Yes
Massage:	Yes
Self-Service Launderette:	Yes
Movie Theater/Seats:	Yes
Library:	Yes
Children's Facilities:	Yes
Classification Society:	Lloyd's Register

Ratings	**Score**
Ship: Hardware/Maintenance	NYR
Ship: Outdoor Facilities/Space	NYR
Ship: Interior Facilities/Space/Flow	NYR
Ship: Decor/Furnishings/Artwork	NYR
Ship: Spa/Fitness Facilities	NYR
Cabins: Suites and Deluxe	NYR
Cabins: Standard Sizes	NYR
Food: Dining Room/Cuisine	NYR
Food: Informal Dining/Buffets	NYR
Food: Quality of Ingredients	NYR
Food: Afternoon Tea/Bar Snacks	NYR
Service: Dining Room	NYR
Service: Bars	NYR
Service: Cabins	NYR
Service: Open Decks	NYR
Cruise: Entertainment	NYR
Cruise: Activities Program	NYR
Cruise: Movies/Television Programming	NYR
Cruise: Hospitality Standard	NYR
Cruise: Overall Product Delivery	NYR

Overall Score	**NYR**

For comments, see *Dawn Princess*.

ms Seabourn Legend

☆☆☆☆☆

(S)

Lifestyle	**Luxury**
Cruise Line:	Seabourn Cruise Line
Former Names:	*Queen Odyssey/ Royal Viking Queen*
Gross Tonnage:	9,975
Builder:	Schichau Seebeckwerft (Germany)
Original Cost:	$87 million
Entered Service:	March 1992/July 1996
Flag:	Norway
Tel No:	1316175
Fax No:	1316176
Length (ft./m.):	439.9/134.10
Beam (ft./m.):	62.9/19.20
Draft (ft./m.):	16.7/5.10
Propulsion/Propellers:	diesel (7,280kW)/2 (CP)
Decks:	6
Total Crew:	150
Pass. Capacity (basis 2):	204
Pass. Capacity (all berths):	204
Pass. Space Ratio (basis 2):	48.8
Pass. Space Ratio (all berths):	48.8
Officers:	Norwegian
Total Cabins:	102
Size Range (sq. ft./m.):	277.0–590.0/25.7–54.8
Cabins (outside view):	102
Cabins (inside–no view):	0
Cabins (single occupancy):	0
Cabins (with private balcony):	6
Cabins (wheelchair accessible):	4
Cabin Current:	110/220 AC
Cabin TV:	Yes
Dining Rooms:	1
Seatings:	Open
Elevators:	3
Casino:	Yes
Slot Machines:	Yes
Swimming Pools (outdoors):	1
Swimming Pools (inside):	0
Whirlpools:	3
Fitness Center:	Yes
Sauna/Steam Room:	Yes/Yes
Massage:	Yes
Self-Service Launderette:	Yes
Movie Theater/Seats:	No
Library:	Yes
Children's Facilities:	No
Classification Society:	Det Norske Veritas

Ratings	**Score**
Ship: Hardware/Maintenance	92
Ship: Outdoor Facilities/Space	93
Ship: Interior Facilities/Space/Flow	95
Ship: Decor/Furnishings/Artwork	93
Ship: Spa/Fitness Facilities	90
Cabins: Suites and Deluxe	94
Cabins: Standard Sizes	92
Food: Dining Room/Cuisine	90
Food: Informal Dining/Buffets	88
Food: Quality of Ingredients	88
Food: Afternoon Tea/Bar Snacks	86
Service: Dining Room	87
Service: Bars	88
Service: Cabins	90
Service: Open Decks	88
Cruise: Entertainment	87
Cruise: Activities Program	86
Cruise: Movies/Television Programming	88
Cruise: Hospitality Standard	90
Cruise: Overall Product Delivery	91
Overall Score	**1,796**

Accommodation: All the suites are comfortably large and beautifully equipped with everything one could need (they are larger than those aboard the company's smaller *Sea Goddesses*, but the ship is also larger, and carries almost double the number of passengers). They have a large walk-in closet, 100-percent thick cotton towels and plush terrycloth bathrobes, VCR unit, personalized stationery, and leather ticket wallet, which arrives suitably boxed and nicely packaged. Nonsmoking cabins are also available. Course-by-course in-cabin dinners are also available (during restaurant dinner hours); twenty-four-hour room service is also provided.

For the ultimate in privacy the two Owner's Suites (001/002) located forward on Deck 6 offer a superbly private living environment at sea. Each has a walk-in closet, second closet, one full bathroom, and a second room with toilet and washbasin (for guests). There is also a forward-facing balcony, complete with sun lounge chairs and wooden drinks table. These are secluded, and good for nude sunbathing. The living area has ample bookshelf space (included is a complete edition of Encyclopedia Britannica), large refrigerator and drinks cabinet, television and VCR (plus a second television in the bedroom). All windows, as well as the door to the balcony, have electric blinds, and a complete blackout is possible in both bedroom and living room. On the Christmas cruise, each Owner's Suite has its own decorated and illuminated Christmas tree, a nice touch.

Dining: In-suite, course-by-course dining is available at any time. Elegant decor prevails in the formal dining room, which has a mixture of marble and carpeted floor. Seabourn's fine, extremely creative cuisine is artfully presented, with almost all items cooked to order. The menu is not repeated, no matter how long the voyage. Special orders are available whenever you want them, and caviar is always available on request. Tableside flambeaus are presented, as are flaming desserts cooked at your table. There is always a good selection of exotic fruits and cheeses. The wine list is quite extensive with prices ranging from quite moderate to high, many wines coming from smaller, exclusive vineyards. The European dining room staff is hand-picked and provide impeccable service.

In addition, breakfast (available until at least 11 a.m.—civilized enough for late-risers) and lunch buffets and informal alternative, casual candlelight dinners (except on formal nights) can be taken in the popular Veranda Café adjacent to the swimming pool.

Other Comments: This is a strikingly sleek ship with a handsome profile, almost identical in looks to *Seabourn Pride* and *Seabourn Spirit,* but built to an even higher standard, with streamline "decorator" bars located along the side of the upper superstructure. The ship features two fine mahogany water taxis for use as shore tenders. There is also an aft water sports platform and marina, which can be used in suitably calm warm-water areas. Water sports facilities include a small, enclosed "dip" pool, sea kayaks, snorkel equipment, windsurfers, water ski boat, Zodiac inflatable boats.

Inside, there is a wide central passageway throughout the accommodation areas. The finest quality interior fixtures, fittings, and fabrics have been combined in her sumptuous public areas to present an outstanding, elegant decor, with warm color combinations (there is no glitz anywhere) and some fine artwork. Wonderful, 360-degree mural in the reception lobby (the ship's interior designer is painted into the mural). Relaxed by day, a more formal dress code applies at night. All beverages are now included in the cruise fare.

This ship provides discerning passengers with an outstanding level of personal service and a superb, utterly civilized cruise experience. For a grand, small ship cruise experience in the finest surroundings, with only just over 100 other couples as neighbors, this ship is very difficult to beat. All gratuities are included, and no further tipping is allowed (the hotel staff receive a fixed gratuity per day).

<u>But:</u> The plastic chairs on the open decks really are unacceptable for this type of ship and should be changed to teakwood. Sadly, there is no wraparound outdoor promenade deck, however, and there is little shade adjacent to the swimming pool.

ms Seabourn Pride

☆☆☆☆☆

(S)

LIFESTYLE	LUXURY
Cruise Line:	Seabourn Cruise Line
Former Names:	-
Gross Tonnage:	9,975
Builder:	Seebeckwerft (Germany)
Original Cost:	$50 million
Entered Service:	December 1988
Flag:	Norway
Tel No:	1311351
Fax No:	1311352
Length (ft./m.):	439.9/134.10
Beam (ft./m.):	62.9/19.20
Draft (ft./m.):	16.8/5.15
Propulsion/Propellers:	diesel (5,355kW)/2 (CP)
Decks:	6
Total Crew:	150
Pass. Capacity (basis 2):	204
Pass. Capacity (all berths):	204
Pass. Space Ratio (basis 2):	48.8
Pass. Space Ratio (all berths):	48.8
Officers:	Norwegian
Total Cabins:	102
Size Range (sq. ft./m.):	277.0–575.0/25.7–53.4
Cabins (outside view):	102
Cabins (inside–no view):	0
Cabins (single occupancy):	0
Cabins (with private balcony):	6
Cabins (wheelchair accessible):	4
Cabin Current:	110/220 AC
Cabin TV:	Yes
Dining Rooms:	1
Seatings:	Open (+in-cabin dining)
Elevators:	3
Casino:	Yes
Slot Machines:	Yes
Swimming Pools (outdoors):	1 (plus 1 aft marina-pool)
Swimming Pools (inside):	0
Whirlpools:	3
Fitness Center:	Yes
Sauna/Steam Room:	Yes/Yes
Massage:	Yes
Self-Service Launderette:	Yes
Movie Theater/Seats:	No
Library:	Yes
Children's Facilities:	No
Classification Society:	Det Norske Veritas

RATINGS	SCORE
Ship: Hardware/Maintenance	91
Ship: Outdoor Facilities/Space	93
Ship: Interior Facilities/Space/Flow	95
Ship: Decor/Furnishings/Artwork	93
Ship: Spa/Fitness Facilities	90
Cabins: Suites and Deluxe	94
Cabins: Standard Sizes	92
Food: Dining Room/Cuisine	90
Food: Informal Dining/Buffets	88
Food: Quality of Ingredients	88
Food: Afternoon Tea/Bar Snacks	86
Service: Dining Room	87
Service: Bars	88
Service: Cabins	90
Service: Open Decks	88
Cruise: Entertainment	87
Cruise: Activities Program	86
Cruise: Movies/Television Programming	88
Cruise: Hospitality Standard	90
Cruise: Overall Product Delivery	91
OVERALL SCORE	**1,795**

Accommodation: The all-outside cabins (called suites in brochure-speak) are comfortably large and beautifully equipped with everything, including refrigerator, personal safe, VCR unit, personalized stationery, and large walk-in illuminated closet with wooden hangers. Electric blackout blinds are provided for the large windows as well as curtains. The beautiful blond wood cabinetry has softly rounded edges. The cabin doors are neatly angled away from passageway. The cabin ceilings are very plain. Large, marble bathrooms have two wash basins, decent sized bathtub, plenty of storage areas, 100-percent thick cotton towels and plush terrycloth bathrobe. Course-by-course in-cabin dining is available during dinner hours; there is also twenty-four-hour room service.

For the ultimate in privacy the two Owner's Suites (001/002) located forward on Deck 6 offer a superbly private living environment. Each has a walk-in closet plus a second closet, one full bathroom, and a second room with toilet and washbasin (for guests), and butler service. There is also a forward-facing balcony, complete with sun lounge chairs and wooden drinks table. These are secluded, and good for nude sunbathing. The living area has ample bookshelf space (included is a complete edition of Encyclopedia Britannica), refrigerator and drinks cabinet, television and VCR (there is a second television in the bedroom), four-person dining table, and large circular glass coffee table. All windows, as well as the door, to the balcony have electric blinds, and a complete blackout is possible in both bedroom and living room. On the Christmas cruise, each Owner's Suite has its own decorated and illuminated Christmas tree. However, the telephone system to call the butler is archaic and quite difficult to master.

Dining: The part marble, part carpeted dining room features portholes and elegant decor but is not as intimate as that found aboard the *Sea Goddesses*. Culinary excellence prevails, however, and both food quality and presentation are outstanding. The menus are extremely creative, and not repeated, even on long cruises. Special orders are welcome, and caviar is always available (on request). The service is close to impeccable, although with a full ship it can prove a little inconsistent at times (but shouldn't be).

Relaxed breakfast and lunch buffets and candlelight dinners (except on formal nights) can be taken in the informal Veranda Cafe instead of the dining room.

All drinks are included in the cruise fare. The wine list is quite extensive, with prices ranging from quite moderate to high, with many wines coming from smaller, exclusive vineyards.

Other Comments: Beautiful, contemporary outer styling for this lovely, luxuriously appointed cruise vessel, identical sister to *Seabourn Spirit*. She is a strikingly sleek ship with a handsome profile with swept-back, rounded lines. Has two superb mahogany water taxis. Note that there is no wraparound outdoor promenade deck.

There is also an aft water sports platform and marina, which is used in suitably calm, warm-water areas. Water sports facilities include an aft platform, enclosed marina pool, banana boat, pedalos, scuba, sea kayaks, snorkel, windsurfers, water-ski boat.

Has a wide central passageway throughout the accommodation areas. Inviting, sumptuous public areas have warm colors. Fine quality interior fixtures, fittings, fabrics, color combinations, and artwork combine to present an outstanding, elegant decor. Wonderful, 360-degree mural by Richard Haas in the reception lobby (the ship's interior designer is painted into the mural, which is a deck scene from the ocean liners of the 1920s).

Not for the budget-minded, this ship is for those desiring the utmost in supremely elegant, stylish, small-ship surroundings, but she is perhaps too small for long voyages in open waters. Presents an utterly civilized cruise vacation. Gratuities are included, and no further tipping is allowed (hotel staff receive a fixed daily gratuity).

<u>But:</u> The deck lounge chairs are plastic (although light and easy to store, they are second class, and should be made of wood). There are no seat cushions on the wooden chairs at the indoor/outdoor cafe. There is only one dryer in the self-service launderette.

ms Seabourn Spirit

☆☆☆☆☆

(S)

LIFESTYLE	LUXURY
Cruise Line:	Seabourn Cruise Line
Former Names:	-
Gross Tonnage:	9,975
Builder:	Seebeckwerft (Germany)
Original Cost:	$50 million
Entered Service:	November 1989
Flag:	Norway
Tel No:	1310464
Fax No:	1310527
Length (ft./m.):	439.9/134.10
Beam (ft./m.):	62.9/19.20
Draft (ft./m.):	16.8/5.15
Propulsion/Propellers:	diesel (5,355kW)/2 (CP)
Decks:	6
Total Crew:	150
Pass. Capacity (basis 2):	204
Pass. Capacity (all berths):	204
Pass. Space Ratio (basis 2):	48.8
Pass. Space Ratio (all berths):	48.8
Officers:	Norwegian
Total Cabins:	102
Size Range (sq. ft./m.):	277.0–575.0/25.7–53.4
Cabins (outside view):	102
Cabins (inside–no view):	0
Cabins (single occupancy):	0
Cabins (with private balcony):	6
Cabins (wheelchair accessible):	4
Cabin Current:	110/220 AC
Cabin TV:	Yes
Dining Rooms:	1
Seatings:	Open (+in-cabin dining)
Elevators:	3
Casino:	Yes
Slot Machines:	Yes
Swimming Pools (outdoors):	1 (plus aft marina-pool)
Swimming Pools (inside):	0
Whirlpools:	3
Fitness Center:	Yes
Sauna/Steam Room:	Yes/Yes
Massage:	Yes
Self-Service Launderette:	Yes
Movie Theater/Seats:	No
Library:	Yes
Children's Facilities:	No
Classification Society:	Det Norske Veritas

RATINGS	SCORE
Ship: Hardware/Maintenance	91
Ship: Outdoor Facilities/Space	93
Ship: Interior Facilities/Space/Flow	95
Ship: Decor/Furnishings/Artwork	93
Ship: Spa/Fitness Facilities	90
Cabins: Suites and Deluxe	94
Cabins: Standard Sizes	92
Food: Dining Room/Cuisine	90
Food: Informal Dining/Buffets	88
Food: Quality of Ingredients	88
Food: Afternoon Tea/Bar Snacks	86
Service: Dining Room	87
Service: Bars	88
Service: Cabins	90
Service: Open Decks	88
Cruise: Entertainment	87
Cruise: Activities Program	86
Cruise: Movies/Television Programming	88
Cruise: Hospitality Standard	90
Cruise: Overall Product Delivery	91
OVERALL SCORE	**1,795**

For comments, see *Seabourn Pride*.

ss SeaBreeze

☆☆ +

(M)

Lifestyle	**Standard**
Cruise Line:	Premier Cruises
Former Names:	*Federico "C"/Royale*
Gross Tonnage:	21,900
Builder:	Ansaldo Sestri-Ponente (Italy)
Original Cost:	n/a
Entered Service:	March 1958/March 1989
Flag:	Panama
Tel No:	1336354
Fax No:	1336355
Length (ft./m.):	605.6/184.61
Beam (ft./m.):	78.9/24.06
Draft (ft./m.):	29.0/8.84
Propulsion/Propellers:	steam turbine (21,350kW)/2 (FP)
Decks:	8
Total Crew:	400
Pass. Capacity (basis 2):	842
Pass. Capacity (all berths):	1,367
Pass. Space Ratio (basis 2):	26.0
Pass. Space Ratio (all berths):	16.0
Officers:	Greek
Total Cabins:	421
Size Range (sq. ft./m.):	64.5 – 258.3/6.0–24.0
Cabins (outside view):	263
Cabins (inside–no view):	158
Cabins (single occupancy):	2
Cabins (with private balcony):	0
Cabins (wheelchair accessible):	0
Cabin Current:	110/220 AC
Cabin TV:	No
Dining Rooms:	1
Seatings:	2
Elevators:	4
Casino:	Yes
Slot Machines:	Yes
Swimming Pools (outdoors):	1
Swimming Pools (inside):	0
Whirlpools:	3
Fitness Center:	Yes
Sauna/Steam Room:	No/No
Massage:	Yes
Self-Service Launderette:	No
Movie Theater/Seats:	Yes/110
Library:	No
Children's Facilities:	Yes
Classification Society:	Lloyd's Register

Ratings	**Score**
Ship: Hardware/Maintenance	60
Ship: Outdoor Facilities/Space	49
Ship: Interior Facilities/Space/Flow	52
Ship: Decor/Furnishings/Artwork	51
Ship: Spa/Fitness Facilities	40
Cabins: Suites and Deluxe	60
Cabins: Standard Sizes	51
Food: Dining Room/Cuisine	62
Food: Informal Dining/Buffets	55
Food: Quality of Ingredients	58
Food: Afternoon Tea/Bar Snacks	43
Service: Dining Room	62
Service: Bars	61
Service: Cabins	65
Service: Open Decks	47
Cruise: Entertainment	54
Cruise: Activities Program	52
Cruise: Movies/Television Programming	40
Cruise: Hospitality Standard	56
Cruise: Overall Product Delivery	62
Overall Score	**1,080**

Accommodation: There is a wide variety of cabin sizes, with many different configurations to choose from. Many cabins can accommodate five, which is good for families with children. The drawer space is limited but closet space is good. Note: As these cruises provide a very casual atmosphere you will not need many clothes.

Dining: The dining room has bright, cheerful decor, but it is quite noisy, and the tables are rather close together for serving comfort (however, there are several tables for two). The dining room operation is well run, and the meals are attractively presented. The buffets are also colorful and well presented. Premier Cruises provides birthday and other celebration cakes at no charge, unlike some lines.

Other Comments: This ship's classic 1950s ocean liner styling still looks quite attractive, with a forthright blue hull/white superstructure and stripes in the center of her hull. Sports a neat sailcloth canopy over the aft outdoor area. The open deck and sunbathing space aboard this high-density ship are very limited, and thus the ship feels extremely crowded when full (some would call it ambience).

Inside, she has a rather awkward interior layout, which is a carry-over from her former ocean liner days as a three-class ship, and this hinders passenger flow and makes it difficult to find one's way around at first. However, the public rooms are bright and cheerful, and tastefully decorated, although there are lots of mirrored and chromed surfaces. There is no real finesse, but the staff is very willing to please, and is quite attentive. The ship is well maintained, and still sparkles despite her age.

This ship has plenty of life and atmosphere, is quite comfortable, caters well to families and remains very good value for a first cruise experience, but she is getting old and perhaps should be retired soon. Having said that, she provides a feeling of the ships of yesteryear, and could be said to provide a more romantic setting than some of the latest ships.

tss Seawind Crown

☆☆☆

(M)

Lifestyle	Standard
Cruise Line:	Premier Cruises
Former Names:	*Vasco da Gama/ Infante Dom Henrique*
Gross Tonnage:	24,568
Builder:	Cockerill-Ougree (Belgium)
Original Cost:	n/a
Entered Service:	September 1961/October 1991
Flag:	Panama
Tel No:	1331251
Fax No:	1331252
Length (ft./m.):	641.6/195.59
Beam (ft./m.):	84.4/25.73
Draft (ft./m.):	26.9/8.20
Propulsion/Propellers:	steam turbine (16,180kW)/2 (FP)
Decks:	8
Total Crew:	362
Pass. Capacity (basis 2):	764
Pass. Capacity (all berths):	931
Pass. Space Ratio (basis 2):	33.4
Pass. Space Ratio (all berths):	26.3
Officers:	Greek
Total Cabins:	387
Size Range (sq. ft./m.):	118–560/11.0–52.0
Cabins (outside view):	266
Cabins (inside–no view):	121
Cabins (single occupancy):	6
Cabins (with private balcony):	2
Cabins (wheelchair accessible):	2
Cabin Current:	220 AC
Cabin TV:	Yes
Dining Rooms:	2
Seatings:	2
Elevators:	4
Casino:	Yes
Slot Machines:	Yes
Swimming Pools (outdoors):	2
Swimming Pools (inside):	0
Whirlpools:	0
Fitness Center:	Yes
Sauna/Steam Room:	Yes/No
Massage:	Yes
Self-Service Launderette:	No
Movie Theater/Seats:	Yes/208
Library:	Yes
Children's Facilities:	Yes
Classification Society:	Lloyd's Register

Ratings	Score
Ship: Hardware/Maintenance	67
Ship: Outdoor Facilities/Space	67
Ship: Interior Facilities/Space/Flow	73
Ship: Decor/Furnishings/Artwork	64
Ship: Spa/Fitness Facilities	60
Cabins: Suites and Deluxe	79
Cabins: Standard Sizes	73
Food: Dining Room/Cuisine	67
Food: Informal Dining/Buffets	56
Food: Quality of Ingredients	57
Food: Afternoon Tea/Bar Snacks	47
Service: Dining Room	62
Service: Bars	58
Service: Cabins	62
Service: Open Decks	55
Cruise: Entertainment	53
Cruise: Activities Program	46
Cruise: Movies/Television Programming	44
Cruise: Hospitality Standard	57
Cruise: Overall Product Delivery	63
Overall Score	**1,210**

Accommodation: Has a wide assortment of cabins; some with queen-, double- or twin beds, some with upper/lower berths. All cabins have excellent closet and drawer space, refrigerator, hairdryer, cotton bathrobes and towels. The suites (they really are suites) are huge; occupants get nice little extras.

Dining: The two dining rooms are quite comfortable, and both food and service are good, considering the cruise fare charged. There are few tables for two. Remember, you get what you pay for, and the food budget is quite low. There is a limited selection of breads, cheeses, and fruits, and the dining room breakfast and lunch buffets are repetitive.

Other Comments: This former long-distance liner has been extensively refurbished. She has a handsome profile, classic lines, deep draft (keeps her stable), and is being well maintained. Has a long foredeck, rakish bow, and teak promenade decks (one outdoor, one covered).

Inside, she is a surprisingly spacious, classic cruise vessel. There is a mix of old-world elegance and contemporary features. A host of intimate public rooms feature tasteful decor and pastel tones, but generally, the eclectic decor has little color coordination. However, new original oil paintings grace her interiors, including some Guy Buffet dining scenes (as aboard the ships of Crystal Cruises).

There is a delightful chapel, and a well equipped hospital. Features lots of fine wood paneling and trim throughout her interiors, spacious foyers and wide stairways so typical of the more classic ships. Has a good-sized cinema, but the seats should be staggered for better viewing. Sports facilities include paddle-tennis and indoor squash court. Has a very poor library.

There is a multinational passenger mix on each cruise, but the principal nationalities are Brazilian and North American. All port charges are included.

But: The emergency drill is conducted in six languages. Nonsmokers be warned—smokers are everywhere. Has a steep gangway in main embarkation port. Announcements in several languages are irritating. Disorganized disembarkation.

☆☆☆ +

(M)

LIFESTYLE	**STANDARD**
Cruise Line:	Airtours Sun Cruises
Former Names:	*Southward*
Gross Tonnage:	16,607
Builder:	Cantieri Navale del Tirreno et Riuniti (Italy)
Original Cost:	n/a
Entered Service:	November 1971/March 1995
Flag:	Bahamas
Tel No:	1104165
Fax No:	1104165
Length (ft./m.):	535.7/163.30
Beam (ft./m.):	74.7/22.79
Draft (ft./m.):	21.3/6.50
Propulsion/Propellers:	diesel (13,400kW)/2 (CP)
Decks:	7
Total Crew:	320
Pass. Capacity (basis 2):	754
Pass. Capacity (all berths):	976
Pass. Space Ratio (basis 2):	22.0
Pass. Space Ratio (all berths):	17.0
Officers:	Norwegian
Total Cabins:	377
Size Range (sq. ft./m.):	90–256/8.3–23.7
Cabins (outside view):	262
Cabins (inside–no view):	115
Cabins (single occupancy):	0
Cabins (with private balcony):	0
Cabins (wheelchair accessible):	0
Cabin Current:	110 AC
Cabin TV:	No
Dining Rooms:	1
Seatings:	2
Elevators:	4
Casino:	Yes
Slot Machines:	Yes
Swimming Pools (outdoors):	1
Swimming Pools (inside):	0
Whirlpools:	0
Fitness Center:	Yes
Sauna/Steam Room:	Yes/No
Massage:	Yes
Self-Service Launderette:	No
Movie Theater/Seats:	Yes/198
Library:	Yes
Children's Facilities:	No
Classification Society:	Det Norske Veritas

RATINGS	**SCORE**
Ship: Hardware/Maintenance	75
Ship: Outdoor Facilities/Space	68
Ship: Interior Facilities/Space/Flow	67
Ship: Decor/Furnishings/Artwork	66
Ship: Spa/Fitness Facilities	56
Cabins: Suites and Deluxe	66
Cabins: Standard Sizes	57
Food: Dining Room/Cuisine	64
Food: Informal Dining/Buffets	62
Food: Quality of Ingredients	63
Food: Afternoon Tea/Bar Snacks	57
Service: Dining Room	66
Service: Bars	66
Service: Cabins	67
Service: Open Decks	61
Cruise: Entertainment	68
Cruise: Activities Program	64
Cruise: Movies/Television Programming	62
Cruise: Hospitality Standard	78
Cruise: Overall Product Delivery	68
OVERALL SCORE	**1,301**

Accommodation: Ten suites are quite spacious (for the size of the vessel), come well equipped, and have full bathtubs; other cabins are compact but clean and tidy, with adequate closet space for one-week cruises, but not for longer ones. There are three cabin grades (Standard, Superior, and Deluxe) and five price categories. Note: Your cabin is not assigned until you actually reach the ship at the embarkation port. Room service food items incur an extra charge.

Dining: The dining room is quite charming, with warm colors. The food is quite adequate (for the price), but not memorable, so do not expect gourmet fare. Bread and fruit selections are poor. Service and ambience are both informal. There is an extra charge for room service menu items. The wine list is acceptable, and the prices are very reasonable.

Other Comments: This ship, which was formerly operated by Norwegian Cruise Line, was the first ship with which Airtours entered the cruise marketplace. She has a crisp, clean profile with rakish superstructure, dual funnels and inboard lifeboats. The open deck and sunbathing space is quite limited, and the swimming pool is small.

Inside, there is a good selection of comfortable public rooms with bright, contemporary decor. Perhaps the favorite is the night club, set high atop the forward mast. Also has a balconied theater. The sight lines in the showroom are poor. Families with children will find lots to do. Airtours provides good value for money with these cruises, designed for the young at heart.

This ship provides all the right ingredients for an active, fun-filled short cruise vacation for sun loving couples and families at the right price, but the ship shows her age in places. This is basic, but quite sound, cruising for those wanting a no-frills vacation in pleasant surroundings at a really modest price level. Onboard drinks prices are very reasonable.

Insurance is included (at an extra charge, unless you decline same). Formerly operated by Norwegian Cruise Line, the ship is now owned and operated by Airtours Sun Cruises and tailored specifically to the UK family cruise market (on-board currency is the pound sterling).

But: Do remember that this is a high-density ship, which means lines for buffets, embarkation, and disembarkation. There are too many repetitive (holiday-camp style) announcements. The ship can be rowdy at times when there are lots of children running around, particularly during holiday sailings. There is little professional entertainment, operating as it does with "blue coat" social staff/entertainers.

ms Sensation

☆☆☆☆

(L)

Lifestyle	**Standard**
Cruise Line:	Carnival Cruise Lines
Former Names:	-
Gross Tonnage:	70,367
Builder:	Kvaerner Masa-Yards (Finland)
Original Cost:	$300 million
Entered Service:	November 1993
Flag:	Liberia
Tel No:	1341372
Fax No:	1341373
Length (ft./m.):	855.0/260.6
Beam (ft./m.):	104.0/31.4
Draft (ft./m.):	25.9/7.9
Propulsion/Propellers:	diesel-electric (42,240kW)/2 (CP)
Decks:	10
Total Crew:	920
Pass. Capacity (basis 2):	2,040
Pass. Capacity (all berths):	2,594
Pass. Space Ratio (basis 2):	34.4
Pass. Space Ratio (all berths):	26.7
Officers:	Italian
Total Cabins:	1,020
Size Range (sq. ft./m.):	173.2–409.7/16.0–38.0
Cabins (outside view):	618
Cabins (inside–no view):	402
Cabins (single occupancy):	0
Cabins (with private balcony):	26
Cabins (wheelchair accessible):	20
Cabin Current:	110 AC
Cabin TV:	Yes
Dining Rooms:	2
Seatings:	2
Elevators:	14
Casino:	Yes
Slot Machines:	Yes
Swimming Pools (outdoors):	3
Swimming Pools (inside):	0
Whirlpools:	6
Fitness Center:	Yes
Sauna/Steam Room:	Yes/Yes
Massage:	Yes
Self-Service Launderette:	Yes
Movie Theater/Seats:	No
Library:	Yes
Children's Facilities:	Yes
Classification Society:	Lloyd's Register

Ratings	**Score**
Ship: Hardware/Maintenance	81
Ship: Outdoor Facilities/Space	74
Ship: Interior Facilities/Space/Flow	81
Ship: Decor/Furnishings/Artwork	82
Ship: Spa/Fitness Facilities	77
Cabins: Suites and Deluxe	78
Cabins: Standard Sizes	73
Food: Dining Room/Cuisine	66
Food: Informal Dining/Buffets	62
Food: Quality of Ingredients	61
Food: Afternoon Tea/Bar Snacks	51
Service: Dining Room	68
Service: Bars	70
Service: Cabins	68
Service: Open Decks	64
Cruise: Entertainment	81
Cruise: Activities Program	67
Cruise: Movies/Television Programming	65
Cruise: Hospitality Standard	63
Cruise: Overall Product Delivery	77
Overall Score	**1,409**

Accommodation: The standard cabins are of a decent size, and although plainly decorated, they have ample closet and drawer space for a one-week cruise. Remember to take shampoo and other toiletries (shower cap for ladies, for example), as the company provides only soap and ice water in cabins. There are 28 outside suites, all with better decor, nicer soft furnishings, and whirlpool tubs in their larger bathrooms.

Dining: Has two huge, noisy dining rooms (both nonsmoking) with the usual efficient, assertive service. Improved cuisine is still mediocre, and not Carnival's strong point, now or ever. Service is attentive, but completely programmed and inflexible. There are no wine waiters, although the wine list is quite good.

Other Comments: The ship features almost vibration-free service from diesel-electric propulsion system. Has a dramatic six-deck-high atrium, with cool marble and hot neon, topped by a large colored glass dome and featuring a spectacular artistic centerpiece. Features expansive open-deck areas and an excellent health spa with a large gymnasium and the latest high-tech muscle machines. There are public entertainment lounges, bars, and clubs galore, with something for everyone. Dazzling colors and design themes in handsome public rooms connected by wide indoor boulevards.

There is also a $1-million art collection, much of it bright and vocal. The library is a lovely room, but there are almost no books (Carnival thinks its passengers do not read.) The Michelangelo Lounge is a creative thinker's delight, while Fingers Lounge is sheer sensory stimulation. Lavish, but elegant multitiered showroom (there are 20 pillars to obstruct some sight lines) and high-energy razzle-dazzle shows. Dramatic three-deck-high glass enclosed health spa. Banked jogging track. Gigantic casino has non-stop action. This ship will entertain you well. (See also comments for *Imagination* and other Carnival ships.) The ship now operates seven-day cruises year-round from the Port of Tampa, Florida, as from December 1998.

But: As in most Carnival ships, there is a sense of overwhelming sensory indulgence, like in a video game parlor. There are too many loud, repetitive announcements. The constant, aggressive hustling for drinks by bar waiters is irritating, as are drinks in plastic glasses.

ms Shota Rustaveli

☆☆ +

(M)

Lifestyle	Standard
Cruise Line:	Ukrainian Passenger Fleet
Former Names:	-
Gross Tonnage:	20,499
Builder:	VEB Mathias Thesen (Germany)
Original Cost:	n/a
Entered Service:	June 1968
Flag:	Ukraine
Tel No:	1400253
Fax No:	1400253
Length (ft./m.):	576.6/175.77
Beam (ft./m.):	77.4/23.60
Draft (ft./m.):	26.5/8.09
Propulsion/Propellers:	diesel (15,700kW)/2 (CP)
Decks:	8
Total Crew:	350
Pass. Capacity (basis 2):	493
Pass. Capacity (all berths):	602
Pass. Space Ratio (basis 2):	41.4
Pass. Space Ratio (all berths):	34.0
Officers:	Russian/Ukrainian
Total Cabins:	249
Size Range (sq. ft./m.):	n/a
Cabins (outside view):	244
Cabins (inside—no view):	5
Cabins (single occupancy):	0
Cabins (with private balcony):	0
Cabins (wheelchair accessible):	0
Cabin Current:	220 AC
Cabin TV:	No
Dining Rooms:	3
Seatings:	2
Elevators:	3
Casino:	No
Slot Machines:	No
Swimming Pools (outdoors):	2
Swimming Pools (inside):	0
Whirlpools:	0
Fitness Center:	Yes
Sauna/Steam Room:	Yes/No
Massage:	Yes
Self-Service Launderette:	Yes
Movie Theater/Seats:	Yes/130
Library:	Yes
Children's Facilities:	Yes
Classification Society:	RS

Ratings	Score
Ship: Hardware/Maintenance	47
Ship: Outdoor Facilities/Space	61
Ship: Interior Facilities/Space/Flow	61
Ship: Decor/Furnishings/Artwork	51
Ship: Spa/Fitness Facilities	42
Cabins: Suites and Deluxe	60
Cabins: Standard Sizes	51
Food: Dining Room/Cuisine	57
Food: Informal Dining/Buffets	51
Food: Quality of Ingredients	52
Food: Afternoon Tea/Bar Snacks	42
Service: Dining Room	56
Service: Bars	55
Service: Cabins	58
Service: Open Decks	47
Cruise: Entertainment	43
Cruise: Activities Program	44
Cruise: Movies/Television Programming	42
Cruise: Hospitality Standard	53
Cruise: Overall Product Delivery	55
Overall Score	**1,028**

Accommodation: Apart from two De-Luxe grade cabins with private balconies, this ship has small but very comfortable outside cabins, with attractive wood accents, solid fixtures, and pleasing decor. Many portholes actually open, which is quite unusual in today's world of air-conditioned ships.

Dining: The dining room is quite comfortable. With both French and Russian chefs, the food is acceptable (although it is quite stodgy), but there is little choice. Limited selection of breads and fruits. Free carafes of wine for lunch and dinner. Service is attentive but somewhat inflexible.

Other Comments: She has good-looking, well-built traditional styling, with an all-white profile, but the general ship maintenance is not good in some areas. Built as one of five sister ships, she has good teakwood decks and wraparound open promenade. There is a good amount of open deck space for sunbathing, with real wooden deck chairs.

Spacious interior with quite pleasing decor, although somewhat spartan and dated. The colors are a little somber, and the ceilings are plain. There is a good amount of wood paneling and trim used in accenting the decor. Decent inside swimming pool.

This ship was renovated in 1991, and is often chartered to European cruise-tour companies. European cruise staff cater well to principally French- and Italian-speaking passengers. Good for the passenger on a low budget who does not expect any degree of luxury or finesse.

But: This ship has a steep, narrow gangway in some ports. Do expect to stand in some lines for embarkation, disembarkation, buffets, and shore tenders. Unfortunately, the aroma inside the vessel is one of well worn socks (very stale).

ms Silver Cloud

☆☆☆☆☆

(S)

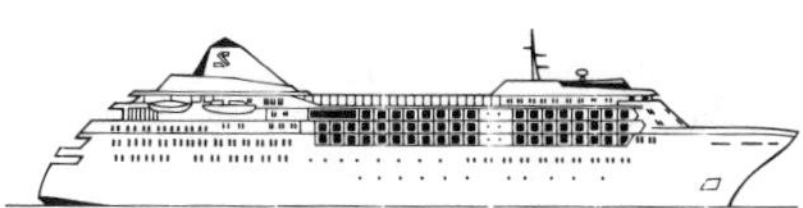

Lifestyle	Luxury
Cruise Line:	Silversea Cruises
Former Names:	-
Gross Tonnage:	16,800
Builder:	SEC/T. Mariotti (Italy)
Original Cost:	$125 million
Entered Service:	April 1994
Flag:	Bahamas
Tel No:	1306601
Fax No:	1306602
Length (ft./m.):	514.4/155.8
Beam (ft./m.):	70.62/21.4
Draft (ft./m.):	17.3/5.3
Propulsion/Propellers:	diesel (11,700kW)/2 (CP)
Decks:	8
Total Crew:	198
Pass. Capacity (basis 2):	296
Pass. Capacity (all berths):	315
Pass. Space Ratio (basis 2):	56.7
Pass. Space Ratio (all berths):	53.3
Officers:	Italian
Total Cabins:	148
Size Range (sq. ft./m.):	240.0–1,314.0/22.–122.0
Cabins (outside view):	148
Cabins (inside–no view):	0
Cabins (single occupancy):	0
Cabins (with private balcony):	110
Cabins (wheelchair accessible):	0
Cabin Current:	110/220 AC
Cabin TV:	Yes
Dining Rooms:	1 (open seating+in-cabin dining)
Elevators:	4
Casino:	Yes
Slot Machines:	Yes
Swimming Pools (outdoors):	1
Swimming Pools (inside):	0
Whirlpools:	2
Fitness Center:	Yes
Sauna/Steam Room:	Yes/Yes
Massage:	Yes
Self-Service Launderette:	Yes
Movie Theater/Seats:	Yes/306
Library:	Yes
Children's Facilities:	No
Classification Society:	RINA

Ratings	Score
Ship: Hardware/Maintenance	89
Ship: Outdoor Facilities/Space	87
Ship: Interior Facilities/Space/Flow	93
Ship: Decor/Furnishings/Artwork	88
Ship: Spa/Fitness Facilities	85
Cabins: Suites and Deluxe	93
Cabins: Standard Sizes	88
Food: Dining Room/Cuisine	88
Food: Informal Dining/Buffets	86
Food: Quality of Ingredients	87
Food: Afternoon Tea/Bar Snacks	83
Service: Dining Room	84
Service: Bars	87
Service: Cabins	87
Service: Open Decks	82
Cruise: Entertainment	77
Cruise: Activities Program	84
Cruise: Movies/Television Programming	86
Cruise: Hospitality Standard	87
Cruise: Overall Product Delivery	88
Overall Score	**1,729**

Accommodation: The all-outside suites (75 percent of which have private teakwood balconies) have convertible queen-to-twin beds and are beautifully fitted out with just about everything one needs, including huge floor-to-ceiling windows, large walk-in closets, dressing table, writing desk, stocked minibar-refrigerator (no charge), and fresh flowers. Marble floor bathrooms have bathtub and plenty of towels. Personalized stationery, bathrobes, and good amenities kit in all cabins. The top suites also have CD-players.

All cabins have VCRs, but they are PAL (European) system and not VHS (U.S. system). However, the walk-in closets do not actually provide much hanging space (particularly for such items as full-length dresses), and the door should open outward instead of inward (the drawers are poorly positioned, too). Although the cabin insulation above and below each cabin is good, the insulation between cabins is still poor (a privacy curtain should also be installed), and light from the passageway leaks into the cabin, making it hard to achieve a dark room.

Note that the cabins with balconies on the lowest deck often suffer from sticky salt spray when the ship is moving, so the balconies require lots of cleaning.

Each evening, the stewardesses bring plates of canapes to your suite—just right for a light bite with cocktails.

Dining: The contemporary dining room has an attractive arched gazebo center and wavy ceiling as its focal point, and is set with fine Limoges china and well-balanced flatware. Features twenty-four-hour in-suite dining service, but the balcony tables are too low for outdoor dining. Good dining throughout the ship, with choice of formal and informal areas, although the cuisine and presentation was still not up to the standards of products such as the smaller *Sea Goddesses* or *Seabourn* ships. Standard table wines are included for lunch and dinner, but there is also a "connoisseur list" of premium wines at extra charge.

Very popular is the alternative Italian restaurant at night, called Cucina Italiana, which, by day, acts as an informal cafe, but by night turns into a lovely intimate dining spot, complete with candlelight and print tablecloths.

The ship also provides twenty-four-hour in-cabin dining service (full course-by-course dinners are available).

Other Comments: Sleek, handsome profile, rather like a small version of *Crystal Harmony*, or larger version of the *Seabourn* ships. Vertical cake-layer stacking of public rooms aft and accommodation forward ensures quiet cabins. Features a teakwood wraparound outdoor promenade deck, and an excellent, spacious outdoor pool deck. Good water sports facilities for use in warm weather areas, including a side platform, two kayaks, two Zodiacs, two sailfish, snorkel, two windsurfers, two water-ski boats.

The spacious interior is well planned, and with elegant decor and fine quality soft furnishings, is accented by the gentle use of brass and fine woods and very creative ceilings throughout. The spa areas need improvement, and the tiled decor is bland and uninviting.

There is a useful business center as well as a CD-ROM and hardback book library, open twenty-four hours a day. There is an excellent two-level showroom with tiered seating, but the entertainment is disappointing and not as as good as when the ship first debuted.

There is an outstanding amount of space per passenger, and no hint of a line anywhere. Excellent documentation is provided.

Managed and operated by "V" Ships, the company that created Sitmar Cruises some years ago. An elegant onboard ambience prevails, and there is no pressure, no hype, and a good staff to pamper you, with a high ratio of Europeans. Insurance is extra (although it was included when Silversea Cruises first started), but all drinks, gratuities and port taxes are included, and, refreshingly, no further tipping anywhere on board is allowed. This ship is perhaps ideal for those former Royal Viking Line devotees, who like to have spacious surroundings, excellent food, and some entertainment. It would be difficult not to have good cruise vacation aboard this ship, albeit at a fairly high price.

But: Officers should, but rarely do, host dining room tables. Some strong vibration is evident when the ship uses bow thrusters or the anchor, particularly in the forwardmost cabins. The self-service launderette is poor and simply not large enough for longer cruises, when passengers like to be able to do their own small items. Sadly, the crew facilities are minimal, and so keeping consistency is difficult, as high crew turnover is a fact of life.

mv Silver Star

☆☆ +

(S)

Lifestyle	Standard
Cruise Line:	Mano Cruises
Former Names:	*Royal Dream, Odessa Song, Bashkiriya*
Gross Tonnage:	5,092
Builder:	VEB Mathias-Thesen (Germany)
Original Cost:	n/a
Entered Service:	1964/1998
Flag:	Malta
Tel No:	1257176
Fax No:	1257177
Length (ft./m.):	400.5/122.1
Beam (ft./m.):	52.4/16.0
Draft (ft./m.):	18.3/5.59
Propulsion/Propellers:	diesel/2
Decks:	6
Total Crew:	130
Pass. Capacity (basis 2):	286
Pass. Capacity (all berths):	425
Pass. Space Ratio (basis 2):	17.8
Pass. Space Ratio (all berths):	11.9
Officers:	Ukrainian
Total Cabins:	157
Size Range (sq. ft./m.):	4.35 x 2.9/// 3.07 x 2.9 + 2.97 x 2.71
Cabins (outside view):	124
Cabins (inside—no view):	23
Cabins (single occupancy):	0
Cabins (with private balcony):	0
Cabins (wheelchair accessible):	0
Cabin Current:	220 AC
Cabin TV:	No
Dining Rooms:	1
Seatings:	2
Elevators:	0
Casino:	Yes
Slot Machines:	Yes
Swimming Pools (outdoors):	1
Swimming Pools (inside):	0
Whirlpools:	0
Fitness Center:	No
Sauna/Steam Room:	Yes/No
Massage:	No
Self-Service Launderette:	No
Movie Theater/Seats:	No
Library:	Yes
Children's Facilities:	Yes
Classification Society:	Hellenic Register

Ratings	Score
Ship: Hardware/Maintenance	46
Ship: Outdoor Facilities/Space	47
Ship: Interior Facilities/Space/Flow	48
Ship: Decor/Furnishings/Artwork	47
Ship: Spa/Fitness Facilities	30
Cabins: Suites and Deluxe	52
Cabins: Standard Sizes	46
Food: Dining Room/Cuisine	64
Food: Informal Dining/Buffets	62
Food: Quality of Ingredients	66
Food: Afternoon Tea/Bar Snacks	56
Service: Dining Room	62
Service: Bars	57
Service: Cabins	61
Service: Open Decks	55
Cruise: Entertainment	53
Cruise: Activities Program	45
Cruise: Movies/Television Programming	44
Cruise: Hospitality Standard	62
Cruise: Overall Product Delivery	61
Overall Score	**1,064**

Accommodation: The 2 suites, Silver Iris and Silver Jasmine, are the largest of the seven cabin grades, which is a lot for this small ship. They have a separate living room and bedroom, plus a bathroom with full-sized bathtub.

Other cabins are small and basic, yet quite comfortable, and the few inside cabins are actually quite large. Most cabins have beds in an L-shaped configuration; some cabins have third and fourth upper berths, although the closet and drawer space is extremely limited when all are occupied; all have a private bathroom with shower (soap and shampoo are provided). The cabin insulation is quite poor, and drawer space is modest.

Dining: The dining room, which is set low down and has portholes, is decorated in a typical Middle Eastern style. The food is surprisingly good, with lots of fresh salads and vegetables, as well as good meats and local fish. There is certainly plenty of variety. Kosher food can also be supplied for a surcharge, per passenger, per cruise.

Other Comments: This former Russian vessel has a large square funnel, and is now operated under a fifteen-year charter to Mano Cruises of Haifa, Israel. There is little outdoor walking space, although there is a decent amount of open deck and sunbathing space. The swimming pool is really just a "dip" pool, however, and the painted steel decks forward of the pool really should be covered with wood or other heat-absorbing materials.

There is really only one main public room, and that is the main lounge/showroom, which has a bar on the port side adjacent to the entrance. The seating is arranged around the circular wooden dance floor.

There is one other lounge, which acts as the ship's disco at night, and a small room that is usually used for children.

Silver Star (nothing to do with Silversea Cruises) is an older vessel that has received the benefit of extensive refit and refurbishment work, and is now operating seven-day Medterranean cruises almost exclusively for the local Israeli market.

But: She really is quite a high-density ship, with little space per person. There is a charge for use of the sauna.

ms Silver Wind

☆☆☆☆☆

(S)

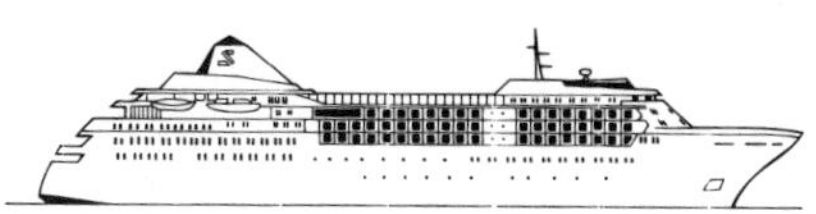

Lifestyle	**Luxury**
Cruise Line:	Silversea Cruises
Former Names:	-
Gross Tonnage:	16,927
Builder:	Societa Esercizio Cantieri (Italy)
Original Cost:	$125 million
Entered Service:	January 1995
Flag:	Italy
Tel No:	1152245
Fax No:	1152250
Length (ft./m.):	514.4/155.8
Beam (ft./m.):	70.62/21.4
Draft (ft./m.):	17.3/5.3
Propulsion/Propellers:	diesel (11,700kW)/2 (CP)
Decks:	6
Total Crew:	197
Pass. Capacity (basis 2):	296
Pass. Capacity (all berths):	315
Pass. Space Ratio (basis 2):	57.1
Pass. Space Ratio (all berths):	53.7
Officers:	Italian
Total Cabins:	148
Size Range (sq. ft./m.):	240.0–1,314.0/22.2–122.0
Cabins (outside view):	148
Cabins (inside–no view):	0
Cabins (single occupancy):	0
Cabins (with private balcony):	110
Cabins (wheelchair accessible):	2
Cabin Current:	110/220 AC
Cabin TV:	Yes
Dining Rooms:	1 (open seating+in-cabin dining)
Elevators:	4
Casino:	Yes
Slot Machines:	Yes
Swimming Pools (outdoors):	1
Swimming Pools (inside):	0
Whirlpools:	2
Fitness Center:	Yes
Sauna/Steam Room:	Yes/Yes
Massage:	Yes
Self-Service Launderette:	Yes
Movie Theater/Seats:	Yes/306
Library:	Yes
Children's Facilities:	No
Classification Society:	RINA

Ratings	**Score**
Ship: Hardware/Maintenance	89
Ship: Outdoor Facilities/Space	87
Ship: Interior Facilities/Space/Flow	93
Ship: Decor/Furnishings/Artwork	88
Ship: Spa/Fitness Facilities	85
Cabins: Suites and Deluxe	93
Cabins: Standard Sizes	88
Food: Dining Room/Cuisine	88
Food: Informal Dining/Buffets	86
Food: Quality of Ingredients	87
Food: Afternoon Tea/Bar Snacks	83
Service: Dining Room	84
Service: Bars	87
Service: Cabins	87
Service: Open Decks	82
Cruise: Entertainment	77
Cruise: Activities Program	84
Cruise: Movies/Television Programming	86
Cruise: Hospitality Standard	87
Cruise: Overall Product Delivery	88
Overall Score	**1,729**

For comments, see *Silver Cloud*.

sy Sir Francis Drake

☆☆ +

(S)

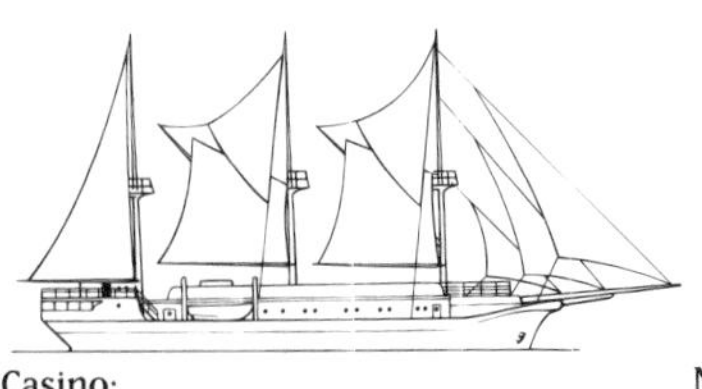

Lifestyle	Standard
Cruise Line:	Tall Ship Adventures
Former Names:	*Godewind/Landkirchen*
Gross Tonnage:	450 DWT
Builder:	(Germany)
Original Cost:	n/a
Entered Service:	1917/1988
Flag:	Honduras
Tel No:	809-496-0914 (cellular)
Fax No:	n/a
Length (ft./m.):	162.4/49.5
Beam (ft./m.):	22.9/7.0
Draft (ft./m.):	9.1/2.8
Type of Vessel:	topsail schooner
No. of Masts:	3 (9 manually-furled sails)
Sail Area (sq ft /sq m):	1,968/600
Main Propulsion:	sail power
Propulsion/Propellers:	diesel/1 (FP)
Decks:	2
Total Crew:	14
Pass. Capacity (basis 2):	28
Pass. Capacity (all berths):	30
Pass. Space Ratio (basis 2):	16.0
Pass. Space Ratio (all berths):	15.0
Officers:	British
Total Cabins:	14
Size Range (sq. ft./m.):	80.0–120.0/7.4–11.1
Cabins (outside view):	14
Cabins (inside–no view):	0
Cabins (single occupancy):	0
Cabins (with private balcony):	0
Cabins (wheelchair accessible):	0
Cabin Current:	110/220 AC
Cabin TV:	No
Dining Rooms:	1 (open seating)
Casino:	No
Slot Machines:	No
Swimming Pools (outdoors):	0
Whirlpools:	0
Fitness Center:	No
Sauna/Steam Room:	No/No
Massage:	No
Self-Service Launderette:	No
Library:	No
Classification Society:	Germanischer Lloyd

Ratings	Score
Ship: Hardware/Maintenance	52
Ship: Sails and Equipment	57
Ship: Interior Facilities/Space/Flow	56
Ship: Decor/Furnishings/Artwork	51
Ship: Spa/Fitness Facilities	30
Cabins: Suites and Deluxe	51
Cabins: Standard Sizes	46
Food: Dining Room/Cuisine	50
Food: Informal Dining/Buffets	43
Food: Quality of Ingredients	50
Food: Afternoon Tea/Bar Snacks	41
Service: Dining Room	56
Service: Bars	61
Service: Cabins	50
Service: Open Decks	50
Cruise: The Sailing Experience	60
Cruise: Lecturers/Entertainment	47
Cruise: Movies/Television Programming	34
Cruise: Hospitality Standard	60
Cruise: Overall Product Delivery	58
Overall Score	**1,003**

Accommodation: The cabins come in a variety of configurations, with a mixture of beds and upper bunks that are small but reasonably comfortable for a sailing vessel.

Dining: Charming dark-wood paneled dining room with wood-trimmed chairs and picture windows. Cuisine is decidedly casual Americana fare. Little choice for non-meat eaters, although the chef will try to accommodate requests. Food quality is barely adequate, although most passengers seem happy with it.

Other Comments: This is an authentic topsail schooner, restored to her original condition, and well appointed. Has cozy chairs and benches on deck. More than a windjammer, this tall ship is a treasure for those who do not expect the service finesse offered aboard more contemporary ships.

Inside, there is much wood paneling, brass fittings, and solid furniture. Carries snorkeling equipment. Passengers can, and often do, participate in hoisting the sails, but otherwise, there is little to do but relax, and let her crew help you unwind totally. This is unhurried hands-on cruising in fairly comfortable, but basic surroundings, combined with plenty of beaches and water sports. Pack very lightly. Tipping, at about $10 per person per day, is expected.

But: The ship has steep interior stairways, as aboard most true sailing vessels. The constant music on deck is irritating.

tss Sky Princess

☆☆☆☆

(L)

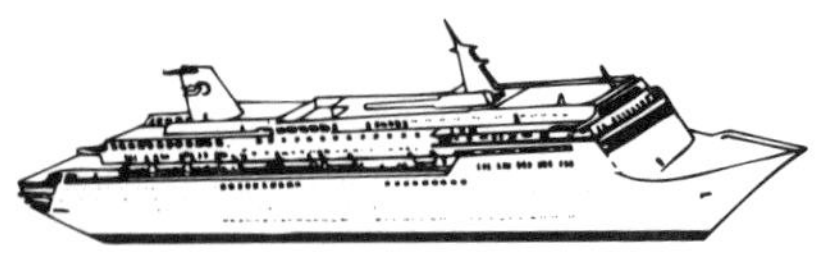

Lifestyle	Premium
Cruise Line:	Princess Cruises
Former Names:	*Fairsky*
Gross Tonnage:	43,692
Builder:	C.N.I.M. (France)
Original Cost:	$156 million
Entered Service:	May 1984
Flag:	Great Britain
Tel No:	1442264
Fax No:	1442266
Length (ft./m.):	788.6/240.39
Beam (ft./m.):	91.3/27.84
Draft (ft./m.):	26.7/8.15
Propulsion/Propellers:	steam turbine (21,700kW)/2 (CP)
Decks:	11
Total Crew:	550
Pass. Capacity (basis 2):	1,200
Pass. Capacity (all berths):	1,350
Pass. Space Ratio (basis 2):	36.4
Pass. Space Ratio (all berths):	32.3
Officers:	British
Total Cabins:	600
Size Range (sq. ft./m.):	169–520/15.7–48.3
Cabins (outside view):	385
Cabins (inside–no view):	215
Cabins (single occupancy):	0
Cabins (with private balcony):	10
Cabins (wheelchair accessible):	10
Cabin Current:	110 AC
Cabin TV:	Yes
Dining Rooms:	2
Seatings:	2
Elevators:	6
Casino:	Yes
Slot Machines:	Yes
Swimming Pools (outdoors):	3
Swimming Pools (inside):	0
Whirlpools:	1
Fitness Center:	Yes
Sauna/Steam Room:	Yes/No
Massage:	Yes
Self-Service Launderette:	Yes
Movie Theater/Seats:	Yes/237
Library:	Yes
Children's Facilities:	Yes
Classification Society:	Lloyd's Register

Ratings	Score
Ship: Hardware/Maintenance	81
Ship: Outdoor Facilities/Space	73
Ship: Interior Facilities/Space/Flow	81
Ship: Decor/Furnishings/Artwork	78
Ship: Spa/Fitness Facilities	73
Cabins: Suites and Deluxe	83
Cabins: Standard Sizes	78
Food: Dining Room/Cuisine	73
Food: Informal Dining/Buffets	68
Food: Quality of Ingredients	70
Food: Afternoon Tea/Bar Snacks	62
Service: Dining Room	78
Service: Bars	76
Service: Cabins	76
Service: Open Decks	74
Cruise: Entertainment	84
Cruise: Activities Program	77
Cruise: Movies/Television Programming	82
Cruise: Hospitality Standard	78
Cruise: Overall Product Delivery	83
Overall Score	**1,528**

Accommodation: Features spacious and very comfortable, well-appointed cabins, with all the essentials and good-sized rectangular showers. There are, however, many inside cabins. The cabin walls and ceilings are plain and unappealing, however, and need some color to brighten them. The large Lido Deck suites are really very lovely units, and provide good living space. As aboard all ships in the Princess Cruises fleet, bathrobes are supplied for all passengers.

Many cabins have one or two upper berths, which make them extremely cramped when occupied, but they are useful for families with children. As in all Princess Cruises ships, cabin service is very good. A room service menu is available twenty-four hours a day.

Dining: The dining rooms are brightly lit and decor is pleasant, although there are no tables for two. Pasta dishes, created by the headwaiters, are good, but other food lacks quality, flair and presentation. Service, while quite attentive, is somewhat impersonal and superficial.

The Veranda Café, a popular outdoor buffet area for breakfast and lunch, is poorly designed and always congested, although some improvements have been made recently.

Other Comments: Well-designed contemporary vessel has a short, sharply raked bow and swept-back funnel. She is the first cruise ship to have steam turbine machinery since Cunard's *Queen Elizabeth 2* debuted in 1969, which means virtually no vibration (she was originally ordered by Sitar Cruises, acquired by Princess Cruises in 1988). Sadly, there is no wraparound promenade deck outdoors, although there is a good enclosed promenade deck.

Inside the ship, the layout is comfortable and it is easy to find one's way around—good signs also help. The clean, bland, clinical, yet oddly tasteful minimalist interior decor lacks warmth—more flowers and greenery are needed. There is a fine array of public rooms, including expansive shops. Improved showroom, with good visibility from all seats. The Horizon Lounge, set atop the ship, is restful at night. Has a popular pizzeria. Split casino configuration. Features decent health spa/fitness facilities.

This ship provides a well-balanced, pleasing cruise experience for the mature passenger, with plenty of space and little crowding. British officers and a European dining crew help to create a friendly ambience aboard this ship.

ms Song of America

☆☆☆☆

(L)

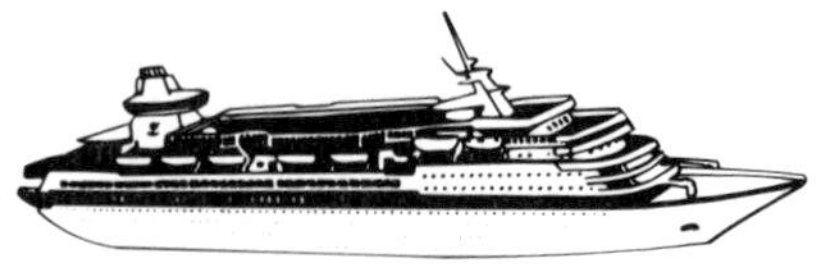

Lifestyle	Standard
Cruise Line:	Airtours Sun Cruises
Former Names:	-
Gross Tonnage:	37,584
Builder:	Wartsila (Finland)
Original Cost:	$140 million
Entered Service:	December 1982/1998
Flag:	Norway
Tel No:	1313507
Fax No:	1313507
Length (ft./m.):	705.0/214.88
Beam (ft./m.):	93.1/28.40
Draft (ft./m.):	22.3/6.80
Propulsion/Propellers:	diesel (16,480kW)/2 (CP)
Decks:	11
Total Crew:	535
Pass. Capacity (basis 2):	1,402
Pass. Capacity (all berths):	1,552
Pass. Space Ratio (basis 2):	26.8
Pass. Space Ratio (all berths):	24.2
Officers:	Norwegian
Total Cabins:	701
Size Range (sq. ft./m.):	120–425/11.0–39.5
Cabins (outside view):	406
Cabins (inside—no view):	295
Cabins (single occupancy):	0
Cabins (with private balcony):	0
Cabins (wheelchair accessible):	0
Cabin Current:	110 AC
Cabin TV:	Yes
Dining Rooms:	1
Seatings:	2
Elevators:	7
Casino:	Yes
Slot Machines:	Yes
Swimming Pools (outdoors):	2
Swimming Pools (inside):	0
Whirlpools:	0
Fitness Center:	Yes
Sauna/Steam Room:	Yes/No
Massage:	Yes
Self-Service Launderette:	No
Movie Theater/Seats:	No
Library:	Yes
Children's Facilities:	No
Classification Society:	Det Norske Veritas

Ratings	Score
Ship: Hardware/Maintenance	78
Ship: Outdoor Facilities/Space	80
Ship: Interior Facilities/Space/Flow	81
Ship: Decor/Furnishings/Artwork	77
Ship: Spa/Fitness Facilities	61
Cabins: Suites and Deluxe	75
Cabins: Standard Sizes	61
Food: Dining Room/Cuisine	71
Food: Informal Dining/Buffets	63
Food: Quality of Ingredients	67
Food: Afternoon Tea/Bar Snacks	58
Service: Dining Room	77
Service: Bars	73
Service: Cabins	74
Service: Open Decks	68
Cruise: Entertainment	80
Cruise: Activities Program	71
Cruise: Movies/Television Programming	73
Cruise: Hospitality Standard	72
Cruise: Overall Product Delivery	80
Overall Score	**1,440**

Accommodation: The cabins, and particularly the bathrooms, with shower curtains that wrap-around, are very, very small, yet most passengers seem happy with them, mainly as they spend little time in them on these destination-intensive cruises. Unquestionably, those who have cruised aboard other ships with larger cabins will be disappointed. There is very little closet and drawer space, and almost nowhere to stow your luggage (in other words, take as little as possible).

Dining: The Madame Butterfly Dining Room is a large room, but the low ceiling creates a high level of ambient noise. There are tables for four to eight (but, sadly, there are no tables for two). The service is consistently average in this efficient dining room operation. French, Italian, Oriental, Caribbean, or American are the menu themes on different nights. The food is of a generally high quality and portions are reasonable. Bottled water (extra cost) is offered (pushed);

drinking water not provided unless requested. The Veranda Café, an informal place for breakfast and lunch, has good flow.

Other Comments: This smart-looking, contemporary ship has rounded lines and sharply raked bow. The striking Viking Crown Lounge wrapped around the funnel is the line's trademark, and incorporates a bar. Good open deck and sunbathing space. Has beautifully polished wooden decks and rails.

Inside, there is a good array of public rooms, mostly with musical-themed decor. There is also a conference center for meetings and group business. Attentive, quite good service throughout. There are, however, too many irritating announcements.

This ship will prove a good choice for first-time passengers. Provides a consistent, well-tuned product in very comfortable surroundings. Note that *Song of America* has been sold to the British company Airtours, who will operate the ship from May 1999.

ms Song of Flower

☆☆☆☆ +

(S)

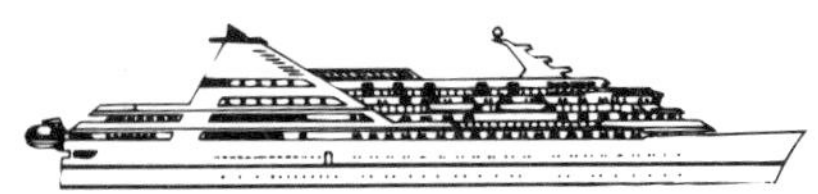

Lifestyle	Luxury
Cruise Line:	Radisson Seven Seas Cruises
Former Names:	*Explorer Starship*
Gross Tonnage:	8,282
Builder:	KMV (Norway)/Lloyd Werft (Germany)
Original Cost:	n/a
Entered Service:	1986/February 1990
Flag:	Norway
Tel No:	1310152
Fax No:	1310153
Length (ft./m.):	407.4/124.2
Beam (ft./m.):	52.4/16.0
Draft (ft./m.):	16.0/4.9
Propulsion/Propellers:	diesel (5,500kW)/2 (CP)
Decks:	6
Total Crew:	144
Pass. Capacity (basis 2):	200
Pass. Capacity (all berths):	200
Pass. Space Ratio (basis 2):	41.4
Pass. Space Ratio (all berths):	41.4
Officers:	Norwegian
Total Cabins:	100
Size Range (sq. ft./m.):	183.0–398.0/17.0–37.0
Cabins (outside view):	107
Cabins (inside–no view):	0
Cabins (single occupancy):	0
Cabins (with private balcony):	10
Cabins (wheelchair accessible):	0
Cabin Current:	220 AC
Cabin TV:	Yes
Dining Rooms:	1
Seatings:	Open
Elevators:	2
Casino:	Yes
Slot Machines:	Yes
Swimming Pools (outdoors):	1
Swimming Pools (inside):	0
Whirlpools:	1
Fitness Center:	Yes
Sauna/Steam Room:	Yes/No
Massage:	Yes
Self-Service Launderette:	No
Movie Theater/Seats:	No
Library:	Yes
Children's Facilities:	No
Classification Society:	Det Norske Veritas

Ratings	Score
Ship: Hardware/Maintenance	82
Ship: Outdoor Facilities/Space	83
Ship: Interior Facilities/Space/Flow	86
Ship: Decor/Furnishings/Artwork	88
Ship: Spa/Fitness Facilities	81
Cabins: Suites and Deluxe	86
Cabins: Standard Sizes	81
Food: Dining Room/Cuisine	90
Food: Informal Dining/Buffets	86
Food: Quality of Ingredients	87
Food: Afternoon Tea/Bar Snacks	81
Service: Dining Room	86
Service: Bars	86
Service: Cabins	87
Service: Open Decks	86
Cruise: Entertainment	78
Cruise: Activities Program	77
Cruise: Movies/Television Programming	81
Cruise: Hospitality Standard	84
Cruise: Overall Product Delivery	87
Overall Score	**1,683**

Accommodation: There are 10 elegant suites; 10 cabins are strictly nonsmoking. All others are well equipped, complete with bathrobes and slippers, refrigerator, and VCR unit. All come with excellent closet and drawer space. Many have bathtubs, but they are tiny (shower tubs would be a better description). Disabled passengers should choose a cabin with a shower instead of a bath. Sadly, there are no in-cabin dining facilities for dinner. When compared with the *Sea Goddesses*, *Seabourn* and *Silversea* ships, the cabins are somewhat lacking and plain.

Dining: The dining room is really quite charming and has warm colors and a welcoming ambience. Very creative food and presentation, with small portions attractively presented. All alcoholic and nonalcoholic beverages included with the exception of some premium wines. Outstanding personal service from a warm, highly personable, and attentive staff. There are also several tables for two.

Hand-scripted menus look like those one would find in an English country hotel. A new addition is an Italian alternative dining spot called A Taste of Italy, created in what was formerly the casino.

Other Comments: This is an excellent small cruise ship (originally built as the ro-ro vessel *Begonia* in 1974 and fully converted in 1986), with tall, twin funnels that give a somewhat squat profile. The bow could be a little longer to give a sleeker appearance! She has been well maintained and cared for and is spotlessly clean throughout. There is a good amount of sheltered open deck and sunbathing space. Water sports facilities include snorkel equipment.

Inside, the interior decor is warm, with many pastel colors used. High-quality soft furnishings and fabrics are used throughout, to good effect. The health spa facility is very compact. The tiered show-room is good, quite comfortable, and has good sight lines. Has a wonderful, warm, caring staff who really do anticipate your needs. Totally understated elegance and warm, informal lifestyle. This ship will provide a fine, destination-intensive, yet relaxing cruise experience, delivered with style and panache. Gratuities are included, and no further tipping is allowed, but port charges are extra.

But: Announcements for the day's activities are completely unnecessary when everything is listed in the daily program. Vibration, particularly at the stern, is a problem that continues to undermine the fine hospitality experienced in the overall cruise product.

ms Sovereign of the Seas

☆☆☆☆

(L)

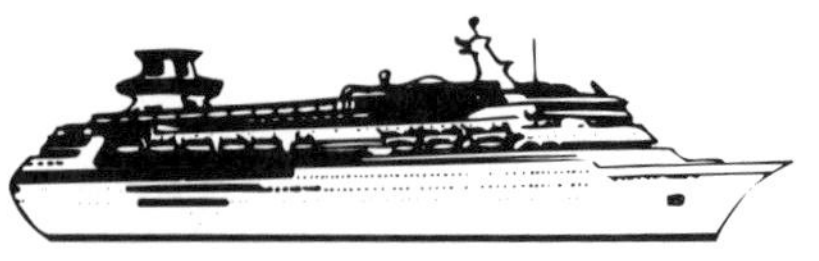

Lifestyle	Standard
Cruise Line:	Royal Caribbean International
Former Names:	-
Gross Tonnage:	73,192
Builder:	Chantiers de l'Atlantique (France)
Original Cost:	$183.5 million
Entered Service:	January 1988
Flag:	Norway
Tel No:	1310711
Fax No:	1310711
Length (ft./m.):	873.6/266.30
Beam (ft./m.):	105.6/32.20
Draft (ft./m.):	24.7/7.55
Propulsion/Propellers:	diesel (21,844kW)/2 (CP)
Decks:	12
Total Crew:	808
Pass. Capacity (basis 2):	2,276
Pass. Capacity (all berths):	2,744
Pass. Space Ratio (basis 2):	32.1
Pass. Space Ratio (all berths):	26.6
Officers:	Norwegian
Total Cabins:	1,138
Size Range (sq. ft./m.):	120–446/11.0–41.5
Cabins (outside view):	722
Cabins (inside–no view):	416
Cabins (single occupancy):	0
Cabins (with private balcony):	0
Cabins (wheelchair accessible):	16
Cabin Current:	110 AC
Cabin TV:	Yes
Dining Rooms:	2
Seatings:	2
Elevators:	18
Casino:	Yes
Slot Machines:	Yes
Swimming Pools (outdoors):	2
Swimming Pools (inside):	0
Whirlpools:	1
Fitness Center:	Yes
Sauna/Steam Room:	Yes/No
Massage:	Yes
Self-Service Launderette:	No
Movie Theater/Seats:	Yes-2/146 each
Library:	Yes
Children's Facilities:	Yes
Classification Society:	Det Norske Veritas

Ratings	Score
Ship: Hardware/Maintenance	77
Ship: Outdoor Facilities/Space	78
Ship: Interior Facilities/Space/Flow	80
Ship: Decor/Furnishings/Artwork	78
Ship: Spa/Fitness Facilities	72
Cabins: Suites and Deluxe	76
Cabins: Standard Sizes	70
Food: Dining Room/Cuisine	70
Food: Informal Dining/Buffets	60
Food: Quality of Ingredients	66
Food: Afternoon Tea/Bar Snacks	52
Service: Dining Room	75
Service: Bars	72
Service: Cabins	73
Service: Open Decks	66
Cruise: Entertainment	76
Cruise: Activities Program	70
Cruise: Movies/Television Programming	72
Cruise: Hospitality Standard	68
Cruise: Overall Product Delivery	77
Overall Score	**1,428**

Accommodation: Twelve suites on Bridge Deck are quite large and nicely furnished. The standard (inside and outside) cabins are very small, however, although an arched window treatment give the illusion of more space. Almost all cabins have twin beds that convert to a double bed configuration, with moveable bedside tables. All of the standard cabins have very little closet and drawer space (you will need some luggage engineering to stow your cases). You should, therefore, think of packing only minimal clothing.

Dining: Two dining rooms provide well-presented food and service, but there are no tables for two, and food varies little in taste. Poor breads, rolls, and fruit selection, but a good selection of light meals, and a vegetarian menu is available. Adequate wine list and prices. The staff is perhaps overly friendly for some tastes.

Other Comments: This is a handsome mega-ship with well-balanced profile, nicely rounded lines, and high superstructure, but the open deck space is adequate, no more. A Viking Crown Lounge is built around the funnel and has superb views. Has wraparound outdoor polished wood deck.

While the interior layout is awkward (being designed in a vertical stack), the ship has an impressive array of spacious and elegant public rooms. A stunning five-deck-high Centrum lobby has cascading stairways and two glass-walled elevators. Good two-level showroom and fine array of shops. The line provides a good range of children's and teens' programs and counselors. The dress code is very casual.

This floating resort provides a well-tuned, yet impersonal short cruise experience, for a lot of passengers. The ship was extensively refurbished in 1997, when some 220 new third and fourth berths were added to increase capacity to over 2,700, and the shopping area was increased. Also added were more seats in the dining rooms. Features short cruises to the Bahamas year-round, from Miami.

But: There is congested passenger flow in some areas. There are too many announcements.

ms Splendour of the Seas

☆☆☆☆

(L)

Lifestyle	Standard
Cruise Line:	Royal Caribbean International
Former Names:	-
Gross Tonnage:	69,130
Builder:	Chantiers de l'Atlantique (France)
Original Cost:	$325 million
Entered Service:	March 1996
Flag:	Norway
Tel No:	1316155
Fax No:	1316156
Length (ft./m.):	867.0/264.20
Beam (ft./m.):	105.0/32.00
Draft (ft./m.):	24.5/7.46
Propulsion/Propellers:	diesel (40,200kW)/2 (CP)
Decks:	11
Total Crew:	732
Pass. Capacity (basis 2):	1,804
Pass. Capacity (all berths):	2,064
Pass. Space Ratio (basis 2):	38.3
Pass. Space Ratio (all berths):	33.4
Officers:	Norwegian
Total Cabins:	902
Size Range (sq. ft./m.):	138–1,148/12.8–106.6
Cabins (outside view):	575
Cabins (inside–no view):	327
Cabins (single occupancy):	0
Cabins (with private balcony):	231
Cabins (wheelchair accessible):	17
Cabin Current:	110/220 AC
Cabin TV:	Yes
Dining Rooms:	1
Seatings:	2
Elevators:	11
Casino:	Yes
Slot Machines:	Yes
Swimming Pools (outdoors):	2 (1 with sliding roof)
Swimming Pools (inside):	0
Whirlpools:	4
Fitness Center:	Yes
Sauna/Steam Room:	Yes/Yes
Massage:	Yes
Self-Service Launderette:	No
Movie Theater/Seats:	No
Library:	Yes
Children's Facilities:	Yes
Classification Society:	Det Norske Veritas

Ratings	Score
Ship: Hardware/Maintenance	88
Ship: Outdoor Facilities/Space	83
Ship: Interior Facilities/Space/Flow	88
Ship: Decor/Furnishings/Artwork	87
Ship: Spa/Fitness Facilities	86
Cabins: Suites and Deluxe	87
Cabins: Standard Sizes	82
Food: Dining Room/Cuisine	71
Food: Informal Dining/Buffets	61
Food: Quality of Ingredients	66
Food: Afternoon Tea/Bar Snacks	52
Service: Dining Room	78
Service: Bars	74
Service: Cabins	76
Service: Open Decks	67
Cruise: Entertainment	82
Cruise: Activities Program	76
Cruise: Movies/Television Programming	80
Cruise: Hospitality Standard	71
Cruise: Overall Product Delivery	78
Overall Score	**1,533**

Accommodation: The seventeen cabin categories really are far too many to deal with, but in this ship even the standard cabins are of a good size. All cabins have a sitting area and beds that convert to double configuration, and there is ample closet and drawer space, although there is not much space around the bed (bathroom showers are disappointing). There are sadly no cabins for singles.

Dining: Dramatic 20-foot-high glass side walls in two-deck-high dining room. There is also a large indoor-outdoor café, and a good-sized snack area, providing more informal dining choices. Menus presentation and food choices were much improved in the last couple of years. Full vegetarian menus. Consistently adequate food and service, with smartly dressed, attentive waiters. There is no good caviar; special orders, table-side carving, and flambeau items are not offered.

Other Comments: This large ship has a nicely raked bow. With engines midships, vibration and noise are kept low, and the ship's maximum 24-knot speed means she is well equipped for long-distance itineraries. There is an expansive use of glass throughout the ship's uppermost decks, which provides passengers with some contact with the sea. Passengers who enjoy golf should enjoy the (extra charge) 18-hole, 6,000-sq. ft. (557.5 m^2) miniature golf; the course itself is 155-230 sq. ft. (14.3-21.4 m^2).

Stunning, contemporary, very colorful interior decor. There are two entertainment decks to play on. Excellent tiered and balconied two-deck-high show lounge has excellent sight lines and comfortable seats; several large-scale production shows are provided, and an orchestra pit can be raised or lowered as required. Dazzling casino (lots of mirrored surfaces and colored lights).

A seven-deck-high atrium connects with the impressive Viking Crown Lounge via glass-walled elevators. The library is a fine facility, with over 2,000 books. There is a fine collection of artworks, some 2,000 pieces of it, created by some 50 artists, with a common nautical/solar theme throughout.

See in-depth comments for sister ship *Legend of the Seas*. This is a well-integrated, fine-tuned, comfortable and well-liked product, for first-time passengers.

mv Star Aquarius

☆☆☆☆

(L)

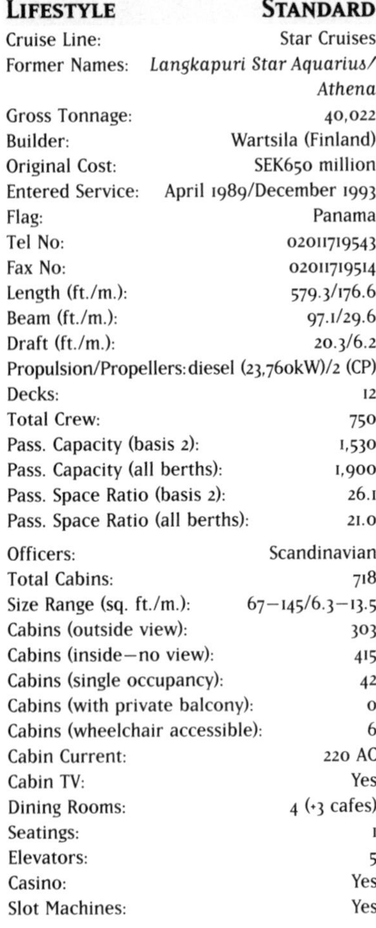

Lifestyle	Standard
Cruise Line:	Star Cruises
Former Names:	*Langkapuri Star Aquarius/ Athena*
Gross Tonnage:	40,022
Builder:	Wartsila (Finland)
Original Cost:	SEK650 million
Entered Service:	April 1989/December 1993
Flag:	Panama
Tel No:	02011719543
Fax No:	02011719514
Length (ft./m.):	579.3/176.6
Beam (ft./m.):	97.1/29.6
Draft (ft./m.):	20.3/6.2
Propulsion/Propellers:	diesel (23,760kW)/2 (CP)
Decks:	12
Total Crew:	750
Pass. Capacity (basis 2):	1,530
Pass. Capacity (all berths):	1,900
Pass. Space Ratio (basis 2):	26.1
Pass. Space Ratio (all berths):	21.0
Officers:	Scandinavian
Total Cabins:	718
Size Range (sq. ft./m.):	67–145/6.3–13.5
Cabins (outside view):	303
Cabins (inside—no view):	415
Cabins (single occupancy):	42
Cabins (with private balcony):	0
Cabins (wheelchair accessible):	6
Cabin Current:	220 AC
Cabin TV:	Yes
Dining Rooms:	4 (+3 cafes)
Seatings:	1
Elevators:	5
Casino:	Yes
Slot Machines:	Yes
Swimming Pools (outdoors):	1
Swimming Pools (inside):	1
Whirlpools:	6
Fitness Center:	Yes
Sauna/Steam Room:	Yes/Yes
Massage:	Yes
Self-Service Launderette:	No
Movie Theater/Seats:	Yes (2)/210 each
Library:	Yes
Children's Facilities:	Yes
Classification Society:	Det Norske Veritas

Ratings	Score
Ship: Hardware/Maintenance	72
Ship: Outdoor Facilities/Space	58
Ship: Interior Facilities/Space/Flow	73
Ship: Decor/Furnishings/Artwork	73
Ship: Spa/Fitness Facilities	75
Cabins: Suites and Deluxe	82
Cabins: Standard Sizes	60
Food: Dining Room/Cuisine	76
Food: Informal Dining/Buffets	77
Food: Quality of Ingredients	70
Food: Afternoon Tea/Bar Snacks	66
Service: Dining Room	78
Service: Bars	76
Service: Cabins	77
Service: Open Decks	74
Cruise: Entertainment	78
Cruise: Activities Program	76
Cruise: Movies/Television Programming	77
Cruise: Hospitality Standard	80
Cruise: Overall Product Delivery	81
Overall Score	**1,479**

Accommodation: Except for some very large suites for top-paying passengers, the cabins are very small (the ship was originally built as a Baltic ferry), and come with just basic facilities (some are for families, with quad occupancy), and very little drawer space. The standard cabin bathrooms are very small.

The top suites, each of which is decorated in luxurious materials, feature two bathrooms, butler service, a private club meeting room, private sun deck, and spa.

Dining: With seven restaurants to choose from, there is a wide choice of cuisine and dining styles. The Ocean Palace Chinese restaurant (Cantonese and Sechuan cuisine) has a Hong Kong chef and live fish tanks from which to select your seafood, as well as private dining rooms; Kamogawa Japanese restaurant includes a sushi bar and waitresses in kimonos, as well as private tatami rooms; Marco

Polo Italian restaurant features candlelight dining; Spice Island buffet restaurant is for laksa, satay, and hawker delights; Mariner buffet has food to choose from large open-concept kitchen stalls and a children's buffet; Castaway Café features afternoon teas and coffees; and Blue Lagoon offers fast-food snacks (open twenty-four hours a day).

There are more choices for food and dining options aboard this ship than most other current cruise ships, and the choice is particularly good for families with children. Note: Your cruise fare includes only basic buffet meals—all other restaurants are a la carte, and quite expensive).

Other Comments: This ex-Viking Line ferry was skillfully converted into a cruise vessel specifically for the Asian family market, with a reduction in berths to 1,900 (from 2,200). The ship sports a stunning deep-blue hull and a blue band around the funnel base. Scandinavian design is combined with a touch of the Orient. This ship even has a helipad. She features a large duty-free shopping center and supermarket, and there is an imperial casino for gambling VIPs, with a 13-feet-high, finely detailed ceiling and regal decor (there is also a second casino for general passenger use). Has a karaoke lounge and eight private karaoke rooms.

Besides a general Universe Fitness and Health Bar (with juice bar and low-calorie items), there is also a superb health club for men (King Neptune), offering an extensive range of features and facilities, including a gymnasium, indoor pool and two whirlpools, plus all massage, steam, and sauna facilities.

There are eleven meeting rooms (all have audio-visual facilities), two conference auditoriums, and a business center, with full secretarial support, computers, fax, telex, and copy machines. Has outstanding family facilities for children and teens, with a wide assortment of computers and video game machines in the huge children's entertainment and play center. Where this ship really scores is in its programing, with a wide range and variety of activities for the whole family, so its Asian passengers will never be bored. There is also free ice cream for kids.

However, such a high-density ship means very crowded public rooms, lots of noise, and long lines for shore visits, buffets, embarkation, and disembarkation. The amount of open deck space is quite limited.

Finally, with a low, very attractive ticket price, everything on board (including food, except for the buffet restaurant) costs extra, so a cruise for the family can end up being quite expensive. The ship does, however, offer a tremendous number of choices for the whole family, and the service and hospitality is superb (better than any ship sailing from any U.S. port) and really fine-tuned. Without a doubt, Star Cruises is the Carnival Cruise Lines of Southeast Asia, and is set to go far. Gratuities are strictly forbidden aboard this ship.

sv Star Clipper

☆☆☆☆

(S)

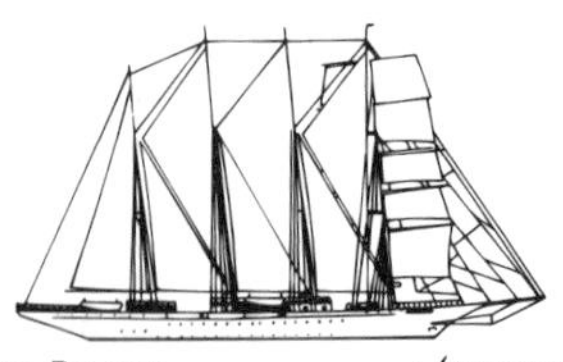

LIFESTYLE	STANDARD
Cruise Line:	Star Clippers
Former Names:	-
Gross Tonnage:	3,025
Builder:	Scheepswerven van Langerbrugge (Belgium)
Original Cost:	$30 million
Entered Service:	May 1992
Flag:	Luxembourg
Tel No:	1253210
Fax No:	1253206
Length (ft./m.):	366.1/111.6
Beam (ft./m.):	49.2/15.0
Draft (ft./m.):	17.7/5.6
Type of Vessel:	barkentine schooner
No. of Masts:	4 (208 ft)
Sail Area (sq ft /sq m):	36,221/3,365/16 manually furled sails
Main Propulsion:	sail power
Propulsion/Propellers:	diesel (1,030kW)/1 (CP)
Decks:	4
Total Crew:	72
Pass. Capacity (basis 2):	168
Pass. Capacity (all berths):	180
Pass. Space Ratio (basis 2):	18.0
Pass. Space Ratio (all berths):	16.8
Officers:	European
Total Cabins:	84
Size Range (sq. ft./m.):	95.0–150.0/8.8–14.0
Cabins (outside view):	78
Cabins (inside–no view):	6
Cabins (single occupancy):	0
Cabins (with private balcony):	0
Cabins (wheelchair accessible):	0
Cabin Current:	110 AC
Cabin TV:	Yes
Dining Rooms:	1 (open seating)
Elevators:	0
Casino:	No
Slot Machines:	No
Swimming Pools (outdoors):	2
Whirlpools:	0
Fitness Center:	No
Sauna/Steam Room:	No/No
Massage:	No
Self-Service Launderette:	No
Library:	Yes
Classification Society:	Lloyd's Register

RATINGS	SCORE
Ship: Hardware/Maintenance	85
Ship: Sails and Equipment	84
Ship: Interior Facilities/Space/Flow	78
Ship: Decor/Furnishings/Artwork	82
Ship: Spa/Fitness Facilities	67
Cabins: Suites and Deluxe	80
Cabins: Standard Sizes	77
Food: Dining Room/Cuisine	76
Food: Informal Dining/Buffets	72
Food: Quality of Ingredients	74
Food: Afternoon Tea/Bar Snacks	66
Service: Dining Room	72
Service: Bars	75
Service: Cabins	74
Service: Open Decks	75
Cruise: The Sailing Experience	87
Cruise: Lecturers/Entertainment	76
Cruise: Movies/Television Programming	66
Cruise: Hospitality Standard	81
Cruise: Overall Product Delivery	83
OVERALL SCORE	**1,530**

Accommodation: Has well-equipped, comfortable, contemporary cabins, with wood-trimmed cabinetry. The bathrooms are compact units, and the shower is a push-button affair, timed for a short shower (that this can prove frustrating when trying to wash your hair, but is typical of vessels built as true sailing ships). Note that there is no cabin food or beverage service.

Dining: The dining room is quite charming, and features lots of wood accenting and nautical decor. Buffet breakfasts and lunches are featured, together with a mix of buffet and a la carte dinners (generally a choice of two entrées). The seating arrangement (mostly with tables of six) makes it difficult for waiters to serve properly. However, it is in an open seating arrangement, so you can dine with whomever you wish. While the cuisine is not gourmet it is nevertheless quite creative given the very small space allotted to the galley.

Perhaps fewer passenger cabins and more room in the galley would have enabled the chefs to provide a better dining experience than the present arrangement. There is a limited choice of bread rolls, pastry items, and fruits.

Tea and coffee should be, but is not, available twenty-four hours a day, particularly in view of the fact that there is no cabin food service at all. When it is available, paper cups are provided (real china would be better).

Other Comments: This is the second of a pair of tall ships. This sailing vessel with cruise accommodation evokes memories of the nineteenth-century clipper sailing ships. Accurate four-masted barkentine-rigged vessel with graceful lines, finely-shaped hull and 19.3-meter-high masts. Quite breathtaking when under full sail! Good for water sports lovers, this vessel has excellent sea manners. Water sports facilities include a water ski boat, sunfish, scuba and snorkel equipment, and eight Zodiacs. Sports directors provide basic dive instruction (for a fee).

Inside, the classic Edwardian nautical decor throughout is clean, warm, intimate, and inviting. The paneled library has a fireplace, and chairs that are supremely comfortable. A cruise aboard her means no lines, no hassle, and "Sailing a Square Rigger" classes are now part of every cruise.

The staff is quite informal, however, and often mixes in areas that should be reserved for passengers. This vessel provides a carefree and casual (no jacket or tie needed at all) sailing cruise experience in a totally unstructured setting at a modest price. Take only casual clothes. No jackets, ties, high-heeled shoes, cocktail dresses, or the slightest hint of formal wear. *Star Clipper* and *Star Flyer* promote total informality. They are really fine experiences, and very highly recommended for even the most jaded cruise passenger. Operates seven-day Caribbean cruises year-round.

But: This ship is not for the physically impaired or children. The internal stairs are steep, as in most sailing vessels. The tipping system, where all tips are pooled, causes concern for many passengers.

sv Star Flyer

☆☆☆☆

(S)

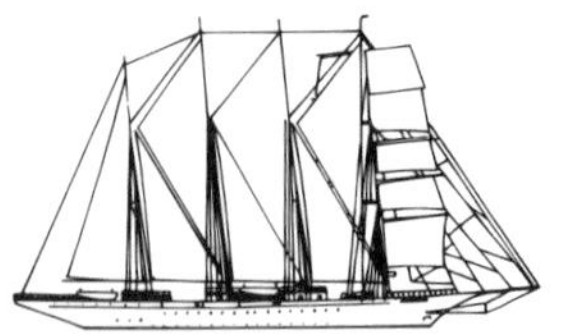

Lifestyle	**Standard**
Cruise Line:	Star Clippers
Former Names:	-
Gross Tonnage:	3,025
Builder:	Sheepswerven van Langerbrugge (Belgium)
Original Cost:	$25 million
Entered Service:	July 1991
Flag:	Luxembourg
Tel No:	1546232
Fax No:	1546231
Length (ft./m.):	366.1/111.6
Beam (ft./m.):	49.2/15.0
Draft (ft./m.):	17.7/5.6
Type of Vessel:	barkentine schooner
No. of Masts:	4 (208 ft)
Sail Area (sq ft /sq m):	36,221/3,365/16 manually furled sails
Main Propulsion:	sail power
Propulsion/Propellers:	diesel (1,030kW)/1 (CP)
Decks:	4
Total Crew:	72
Pass. Capacity (basis 2):	168
Pass. Capacity (all berths):	180
Pass. Space Ratio (basis 2):	18.0
Pass. Space Ratio (all berths):	16.8
Officers:	European
Total Cabins:	84
Size Range (sq. ft./m.):	95.0–150.0/8.8–14.0
Cabins (outside view):	78
Cabins (inside–no view):	6
Cabins (single occupancy):	0
Cabins (with private balcony):	0
Cabins (wheelchair accessible):	0
Cabin Current:	110 AC
Cabin TV:	Yes
Dining Rooms:	1 (open seating)
Elevators:	0
Casino:	No
Slot Machines:	No
Swimming Pools (outdoors):	2
Whirlpools:	0
Fitness Center:	No
Sauna/Steam Room:	No/No
Massage:	No
Self-Service Launderette:	No
Library:	Yes
Classification Society:	Lloyd's Register

Ratings	**Score**
Ship: Hardware/Maintenance	85
Ship: Sails and Equipment	84
Ship: Interior Facilities/Space/Flow	78
Ship: Decor/Furnishings/Artwork	82
Ship: Spa/Fitness Facilities	67
Cabins: Suites and Deluxe	80
Cabins: Standard Sizes	77
Food: Dining Room/Cuisine	76
Food: Informal Dining/Buffets	72
Food: Quality of Ingredients	74
Food: Afternoon Tea/Bar Snacks	66
Service: Dining Room	72
Service: Bars	75
Service: Cabins	74
Service: Open Decks	75
Cruise: The Sailing Experience	87
Cruise: Lecturers/Entertainment	76
Cruise: Movies/Television Programming	66
Cruise: Hospitality Standard	81
Cruise: Overall Product Delivery	83
Overall Score	**1,530**

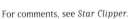

For comments, see *Star Clipper*.

mv Star Pisces

☆☆☆☆

(L)

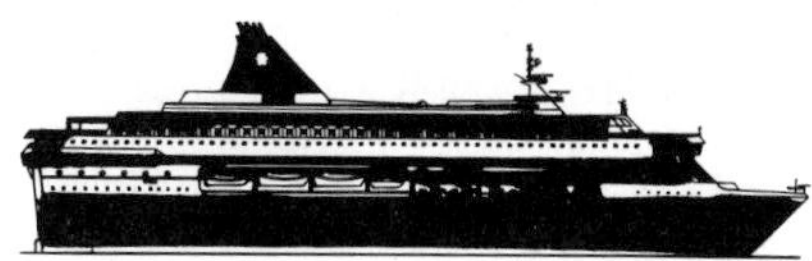

LIFESTYLE	**STANDARD**
Cruise Line:	Star Cruises
Former Names:	*Kalypso*
Gross Tonnage:	40,012
Builder:	Wartsila (Finland)
Original Cost:	SEK650 million
Flag:	Panama
Tel No:	635286122
Fax No:	635286111
Length (ft./m.):	579.3/176.6
Beam (ft./m.):	97.1/29.6
Draft (ft./m.):	20.3/6.2
Propulsion/Propellers:	diesel (23,760kW)/2 (CP)
Decks:	12
Total Crew:	750
Pass. Capacity (basis 2):	1,530
Pass. Capacity (all berths):	1,900
Pass. Space Ratio (basis 2):	26.1
Pass. Space Ratio (all berths):	21.0
Officers:	Scandinavian
Total Cabins:	598
Size Range (sq. ft./m.):	67–145/6.3–13.5
Cabins (outside view):	258
Cabins (inside—no view):	340
Cabins (single occupancy):	0
Cabins (with private balcony):	0
Cabins (wheelchair accessible):	0
Cabin Current:	220 AC
Cabin TV:	Yes
Dining Rooms:	3 (+2 cafes)
Seatings:	1
Elevators:	5
Casino:	Yes
Slot Machines:	Yes
Swimming Pools (outdoors):	1
Swimming Pools (inside):	1
Whirlpools:	3
Fitness Center:	Yes
Sauna/Steam Room:	Yes/Yes
Massage:	Yes
Self-Service Launderette:	No
Movie Theater/Seats:	Yes (2)/210 each
Library:	Yes
Children's Facilities:	Yes
Classification Society:	Det Norske Veritas

RATINGS	**SCORE**
Ship: Hardware/Maintenance	76
Ship: Outdoor Facilities/Space	60
Ship: Interior Facilities/Space/Flow	76
Ship: Decor/Furnishings/Artwork	77
Ship: Spa/Fitness Facilities	76
Cabins: Suites and Deluxe	83
Cabins: Standard Sizes	62
Food: Dining Room/Cuisine	76
Food: Informal Dining/Buffets	76
Food: Quality of Ingredients	70
Food: Afternoon Tea/Bar Snacks	67
Service: Dining Room	77
Service: Bars	76
Service: Cabins	78
Service: Open Decks	75
Cruise: Entertainment	80
Cruise: Activities Program	77
Cruise: Movies/Television Programming	78
Cruise: Hospitality Standard	81
Cruise: Overall Product Delivery	82
OVERALL SCORE	**1,503**

Accommodation: Except for some large imperial suites, almost all cabins are very small, and come with just the basic facilities. The cabin insulation is poor, and the bathrooms are really tiny.

Dining: Seven restaurants provide a wide choice of cuisine and dining styles: A Chinese restaurant has live fish tanks from which to select your fish and seafood; a Japanese restaurant includes a sushi bar, waitresses in kimonos, and private tatami rooms; an Italian restaurant features candlelight dining; a Spice Island buffet restaurant features items such as laksa, satay, and hawker delights; and three other snack cafés (your cruise fare includes only the basic buffets restaurants—all other restaurants are à la carte, and quite expensive).

Other Comments: This ship has Scandinavian design combined with a touch of the Orient. Also has a helipad, huge duty-free shopping center and supermarket. Regal casino for VIPs is large and has a high, detailed ceiling (there is also a second casino for general use). Has a fine health club for men (with many "extra" services). There are many meeting rooms, conference auditoriums and a business center. Children's facilities are extensive and include computers and educational rooms, play areas and a huge video machine section. Free ice cream for kids. Excellent Asian hospitality, and there are lots of activities for the whole family.

Skillfully converted into a cruise vessel for the Asian family market. Has a low ticket price, but everything costs extra. Gratuities are prohibited.

But: This high-density ship means that many of the public rooms will be crowded. Poor open deck space.

ms Statendam

☆☆☆☆ +

(L)

Lifestyle	**Premium**
Cruise Line:	Holland America Line
Former Names:	-
Gross Tonnage:	55,451
Builder:	Fincantieri (Italy)
Original Cost:	$215 million
Flag:	Netherlands
Tel No:	1302515
Fax No:	1302516
Length (ft./m.):	719.4/219.3
Beam (ft./m.):	101.0/30.8
Draft (ft./m.):	24.6/7.5
Propulsion/Propellers:	diesel-electric (34,560kW)/2 (CP)
Decks:	10
Total Crew:	588
Pass. Capacity (basis 2):	1,266
Pass. Capacity (all berths):	1,627
Pass. Space Ratio (basis 2):	43.8
Pass. Space Ratio (all berths):	34.0
Officers:	Dutch
Total Cabins:	633
Size Range (sq. ft./m.):	187–1,126/17.3–104.5
Cabins (outside view):	502
Cabins (inside–no view):	131
Cabins (single occupancy):	0
Cabins (with private balcony):	150
Cabins (wheelchair accessible):	6
Cabin Current:	110/220 AC
Cabin TV:	Yes
Dining Rooms:	1
Seatings:	2
Elevators:	12
Casino:	Yes
Slot Machines:	Yes
Swimming Pools (outdoors):	1
Swimming Pools (inside):	1 (magrodome)
Whirlpools:	2
Fitness Center:	Yes
Sauna/Steam Room:	Yes/No
Massage:	Yes
Self-Service Launderette:	Yes
Movie Theater/Seats:	Yes/249
Library:	Yes
Children's Facilities:	No
Classification Society:	Lloyd's Register

Ratings	**Score**
Ship: Hardware/Maintenance	86
Ship: Outdoor Facilities/Space	82
Ship: Interior Facilities/Space/Flow	86
Ship: Decor/Furnishings/Artwork	85
Ship: Spa/Fitness Facilities	78
Cabins: Suites and Deluxe	83
Cabins: Standard Sizes	79
Food: Dining Room/Cuisine	76
Food: Informal Dining/Buffets	74
Food: Quality of Ingredients	72
Food: Afternoon Tea/Bar Snacks	65
Service: Dining Room	76
Service: Bars	76
Service: Cabins	76
Service: Open Decks	71
Cruise: Entertainment	77
Cruise: Activities Program	76
Cruise: Movies/Television Programming	76
Cruise: Hospitality Standard	77
Cruise: Overall Product Delivery	82
Overall Score	**1,553**

Accommodation: There are 28 suites (each can accommodate four) featuring an in-suite dining alternative and free laundry/dry-cleaning. Other cabins are spacious, tastefully decorated and well laid out, and most feature a daytime sitting area. The standard cabins have little closet space for long cruises, and space around the beds is tight, but they are nicely appointed.

Dining: The two-level dining room has a grand staircase and a music balcony. There is an open seating for breakfast and lunch, and two seatings for dinner. Fine china and silverware. Food and service standards, unfortunately, are going down, and the tasteless, bland food is disappointing (particularly in the Lido).

Other Comments: This square-looking ship has a bold exterior profile. Has teakwood outdoor decks and a wraparound promenade deck. Magrodome roof covers indoor-outdoor pool, whirlpools and central Lido area, whose focal point is a huge dolphin sculpture. Elegant, yet eclectic interior design and decor feature traditional styling and use of classic materials—woods and ceramics—providing a restrained approach to interior styling and very little glitz.

A three-deck high atrium foyer with statue is lovely, but space is tight. Good reference library and card room. The art collection adds much color. Excellent large flower displays throughout. Note: The line does not add an automatic 15 percent for beverage purchases, unlike many others.

But: The Crows Nest Lounge has awful decor. The showroom has glitzy decor and poor sight lines. Entertainment has improved, but is still below the standard of that provided on many ships of a similar size. The extra charge for launderette washing machines ($1.50) is petty.

ms Stella Oceanis

☆☆ +

(S)

Lifestyle	**Standard**
Cruise Line:	Royal Olympic Cruises
Former Names:	*Aphrodite*
Gross Tonnage:	6,000
Builder: Cantieri Riuniti dell' Adriatico (Italy)	
Original Cost:	n/a
Entered Service:	1965/1967
Flag:	Greece
Tel No:	1130471
Fax No:	1130471
Length (ft./m.):	344.9/105.14
Beam (ft./m.):	55.5/16.92
Draft (ft./m.):	14.9/4.56
Propulsion/Propellers:	diesel (8,090kW)/1 (CP)
Decks:	6
Total Crew:	140
Pass. Capacity (basis 2):	300
Pass. Capacity (all berths):	369
Pass. Space Ratio (basis 2):	20.0
Pass. Space Ratio (all berths):	16.2
Officers:	Greek
Total Cabins:	159
Size Range (sq. ft./m.):	96.0–208.0/9.0–19.3
Cabins (outside view):	113
Cabins (inside–no view):	46
Cabins (single occupancy):	0
Cabins (with private balcony):	0
Cabins (wheelchair accessible):	0
Cabin Current:	220 AC
Cabin TV:	No
Dining Rooms:	1
Seatings:	2
Elevators:	1
Casino:	No
Slot Machines:	No
Swimming Pools (outdoors):	1
Swimming Pools (inside):	0
Whirlpools:	0
Fitness Center:	No
Sauna/Steam Room:	No/No
Massage:	No
Self-Service Launderette:	No
Movie Theater/Seats:	No
Library:	Yes
Children's Facilities:	No
Classification Society:	Lloyd's Register

Ratings	**Score**
Ship: Hardware/Maintenance	60
Ship: Outdoor Facilities/Space	49
Ship: Interior Facilities/Space/Flow	57
Ship: Decor/Furnishings/Artwork	61
Ship: Spa/Fitness Facilities	38
Cabins: Suites and Deluxe	61
Cabins: Standard Sizes	49
Food: Dining Room/Cuisine	61
Food: Informal Dining/Buffets	52
Food: Quality of Ingredients	58
Food: Afternoon Tea/Bar Snacks	47
Service: Dining Room	65
Service: Bars	63
Service: Cabins	66
Service: Open Decks	53
Cruise: Entertainment	42
Cruise: Activities Program	40
Cruise: Movies/Television Programming	40
Cruise: Hospitality Standard	55
Cruise: Overall Product Delivery	62
Overall Score	**1,079**

Accommodation: The cabins (there are eight categories) are small and quite plain and have limited closet and drawer space, but those on Lido and Stella decks have interconnecting doors. Some cabins have a full bathtub, while others have a shower only. All cabins have private bathrooms, but there is little space for personal toiletries.

Dining: The dining room is tastefully decorated and quite charming, although the ceiling is plain. Good food, but there is really little choice, although the salads are good. Dining room seating and table assignments are done by the maître d' upon embarkation.

Other Comments: She is a tidy-looking, well-maintained ship with clean, rounded lines. Outside on deck, there is only a limited amount of open deck and sunbathing space.

The number of public rooms is limited, but this is a small ship, and the rooms are all nicely decorated, although in dated 1970s style. Perhaps the most popular room is the Plaka Taverna, which is decorated in rich woods. An intimate, casual, and friendly atmosphere prevails. Has a narrow, steep gangway in some ports of call, as do many ships that are many years old.

This ship lacks the sophistication of some of the other ships in the fleet, but is nonetheless quite charming. Royal Olympic Cruises (a combination of the Greek companies Epirotiki Lines and Sun Line Cruises) provides a good destination-intensive cruise experience, made better by the charming, friendly officers and crew.

The dress code is casual throughout (no formal nights). Gratuities (suggested at $9 per person per day) are pooled among the crew.

ss Stella Solaris

☆☆☆

(M)

Lifestyle	Standard
Cruise Line:	Royal Olympic Cruises
Former Names:	Stella V/Camboge
Gross Tonnage:	17,832
Builder:	Ateliers et Chantiers de France (France)
Original Cost:	n/a
Entered Service:	July 1953/June 1973
Flag:	Greece
Tel No:	1130403/1130226
Fax No:	1130227/1130733
Length (ft./m.):	545.1/166.15
Beam (ft./m.):	72.4/22.08
Draft (ft./m.):	25.8/7.88
Propulsion/Propellers:	steam turbine (17,900kW)/2 (FP)
Decks:	8
Total Crew:	320
Pass. Capacity (basis 2):	620
Pass. Capacity (all berths):	700
Pass. Space Ratio (basis 2):	28.7
Pass. Space Ratio (all berths):	25.4
Officers:	Greek
Total Cabins:	329
Size Range (sq. ft./m.):	96–225/9.0–21.0
Cabins (outside view):	250
Cabins (inside—no view):	79
Cabins (single occupancy):	0
Cabins (with private balcony):	0
Cabins (wheelchair accessible):	0
Cabin Current:	110/220 AC
Cabin TV:	Yes
Dining Rooms:	1
Seatings:	2
Elevators:	3
Casino:	Yes
Slot Machines:	Yes (in separate room)
Swimming Pools (outdoors):	1
Swimming Pools (inside):	0
Whirlpools:	0
Fitness Center:	Yes
Sauna/Steam Room:	No/Yes
Massage:	Yes
Self-Service Launderette:	No
Movie Theater/Seats:	Yes/275
Library:	Yes
Children's Facilities:	No
Classification Society:	Lloyd's Register

Ratings	Score
Ship: Hardware/Maintenance	57
Ship: Outdoor Facilities/Space	70
Ship: Interior Facilities/Space/Flow	67
Ship: Decor/Furnishings/Artwork	61
Ship: Spa/Fitness Facilities	74
Cabins: Suites and Deluxe	73
Cabins: Standard Sizes	63
Food: Dining Room/Cuisine	58
Food: Informal Dining/Buffets	51
Food: Quality of Ingredients	57
Food: Afternoon Tea/Bar Snacks	47
Service: Dining Room	66
Service: Bars	62
Service: Cabins	66
Service: Open Decks	54
Cruise: Entertainment	57
Cruise: Activities Program	54
Cruise: Movies/Television Programming	47
Cruise: Hospitality Standard	49
Cruise: Overall Product Delivery	60
Overall Score	**1,193**

Accommodation: There are 11 cabin grades (166 suites and deluxe; 163 standard inside and outside cabins). The outside cabins can best de described as adequate (particularly those on Sapphire, Ruby, and Emerald Decks), although many have what amounts to almost a full bathtub (inside cabins have very small bathrooms, however). All bathrooms have mosaic tiled floors.

The cabin decor has been only slightly changed over the years, but presently features slightly brighter fabrics and colors than previously, although the old pegboard ceilings remain as a reminder that the ship was built in the 1950s. Note that the insulation between cabins, and between decks, is extremely poor. The accommodation passageways are reasonably wide, however.

The suites on Boat Deck (all have names of Greek islands) overlook the outdoor promenade deck —a feature not found aboard many ships today—and many of them have windows that can be opened. However, those located in the aft third of the ship are subject to the irritating noise of deck lounge chairs being moved on the pool deck above. There is an abundance of closet and drawer space, a vanity unit, television (cannot be seen from the bed, only in the lounge area), telephone. The bathrooms come with a decent-sized bathtub, small toiletries cabinet, and hairdryer. Bathrobes may be obtained upon request (suite passengers only).

Note that many cabins located on aft on Sapphire Deck and amidships on Emerald Deck are subject to throbbing engine noise. The towels are thin, although they are of 100 percent cotton. Personal amenities provided are soap, shampoo (doubles as bath foam), and body lotion.

A room service menu with limited items such as sandwiches, cookies, and beverages is available 24 hours a day (better selection available 7 a.m. to 11 p.m.).

Dining: The large, high-ceilinged dining room (totally nonsmoking) has tables for four or six (although when the ship is not full tables for two can be arranged). The room's focal point is a huge mural in shades of bronze, copper, and gold that depicts scenes from Greek mythology. Features a wide variety of food, with spa and vegetarian dishes on each lunch and dinner menu. However, the food has very little taste. Open seating for breakfast and lunch (a breakfast buffet is set up in the dining room, but a regular breakfast menu is also available). Dining room seating and table assignments are done by the maître d' upon embarkation.

The wine list is a mixture of a couple of good wines (but poor vintages) and a selection of reasonably priced wines, including many from Greece.

The old-world service from Greek dining room stewards adds to the experience, although it is not nearly as good as it was in former years and is far too hurried.

Informal breakfast and lunch buffets are available in the Lido Café (inside) adjacent to the pool, although the room is very small. The selection really is very limited, as is the food display. Breakfast features too many tinned fruits and packaged items.

The ship makes its own potato chips, revered by repeat passengers, and available in all bars on many days.

Other Comments: Has a traditional ship profile, with a royal blue hull and a large, attractive funnel amidships, and was originally built to carry cargo and passengers to Indonesia during the war the French waged in that area in the 1950s and was then successfully converted into a cruise vessel in the early 1970s.

Although she is now one of the oldest cruise ships still in existence, she is reasonably clean and tidy, although maintenance is fighting a losing battle. There is an expansive amount of open deck space, and this includes an outdoor wraparound promenade deck. Much of the teakwood decking and caulking are now well worn, but the well-polished railings are good. Has an attractive figure-eight pool and sunbathing area. The mostly Greek staff is friendly, and some of them have been with the company for many years.

Inside, the public rooms have good quality, solid furniture and fixtures, although everything has that well-worn look (sagging seats, broken springs). Sadly, there is no forward observation lounge, although there is a feeling of space and old-world grace. The elevators are large and can even accommodate wheelchairs (although access to most of the ship is awful).

There are also plenty of public restrooms, although, for some reason, many seem to be permanently locked. The fresh flowers that were formerly everywhere, are now sadly missing. The show lounge, which is combined with a bar (which itself is home to three blackjack tables), is large, with old-style chairs and banquet seating; all the shows feature cabaret-style entertainers. A "health spa" added a few years ago provides some much needed facilities, although the $10 per-person charge to use the steam room (wrongly called a "Turkish Bath") is absurd.

This ship is for the much older passenger who seeks a relaxed, unhurried, and old-world cruise experience in decent, though very tired, surroundings, at reasonable cost, with reasonably friendly service, but without the hype of the more contemporary ships.

Features well-planned, interesting itineraries. There are always a number of lecturers aboard for each cruise, as well as one or two gentlemen dance "hosts." Gratuities ("suggested" at $9 per person, per day) are given to the Chief Steward, then pooled and shared among the crew.

But: This ship really is very tired and worn (and needs considerable financial investment to improve her interiors), and so are many of the crew, who seem to have lost the art of hospitality (unless they know you well). Gone is the grace of yesteryear. The seats in the movie theater are not staggered so sight lines are poor. Port information literature is very limited for those who want to go ashore independently. The in-cabin audio channels are not available at night. There is no enforcement of smoking and nonsmoking areas. Vibration at the stern is irritating.

ms Sundream

☆☆☆ +

(L)

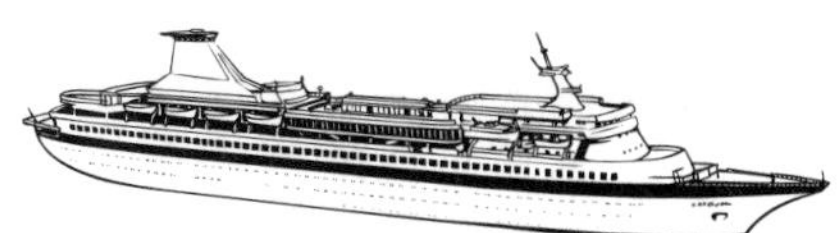

LIFESTYLE	**STANDARD**
Cruise Line:	Airtours Sun Cruises
Former Names:	*Song of Norway*
Gross Tonnage:	22,945
Builder:	Wartsila (Finland)
Original Cost:	$13.5 million
Entered Service:	November 1970/May 1997
Flag:	Bahamas
Tel No:	1310562
Fax No:	1310562
Length (ft./m.):	637.5/194.32
Beam (ft./m.):	78.8/24.03
Draft (ft./m.):	21.9/6.70
Propulsion/Propellers:	diesel (13,400kW)/2 (CP)
Decks:	8
Total Crew:	423
Pass. Capacity (basis 2):	1,004
Pass. Capacity (all berths):	1,138
Pass. Space Ratio (basis 2):	22.8
Pass. Space Ratio (all berths):	20.1
Officers:	European
Total Cabins:	502
Size Range (sq. ft./m.):	120–266/11.0–24.7
Cabins (outside view):	325
Cabins (inside—no view):	177
Cabins (single occupancy):	0
Cabins (with private balcony):	0
Cabins (wheelchair accessible):	0
Cabin Current:	110 AC
Cabin TV:	No
Dining Rooms:	1
Seatings:	2
Elevators:	4
Casino:	Yes
Slot Machines:	Yes
Swimming Pools (outdoors):	1
Swimming Pools (inside):	0
Whirlpools:	0
Fitness Center:	Yes
Sauna/Steam Room:	No/No
Massage:	No
Self-Service Launderette:	No
Movie Theater/Seats:	No
Library:	No
Children's Facilities:	No
Classification Society:	Det Norske Veritas

RATINGS	**SCORE**
Ship: Hardware/Maintenance	75
Ship: Outdoor Facilities/Space	68
Ship: Interior Facilities/Space/Flow	67
Ship: Decor/Furnishings/Artwork	66
Ship: Spa/Fitness Facilities	56
Cabins: Suites and Deluxe	66
Cabins: Standard Sizes	57
Food: Dining Room/Cuisine	64
Food: Informal Dining/Buffets	62
Food: Quality of Ingredients	63
Food: Afternoon Tea/Bar Snacks	57
Service: Dining Room	66
Service: Bars	66
Service: Cabins	67
Service: Open Decks	61
Cruise: Entertainment	68
Cruise: Activities Program	64
Cruise: Movies/Television Programming	62
Cruise: Hospitality Standard	80
Cruise: Overall Product Delivery	76
OVERALL SCORE	**1,311**

Accommodation: The cabins are provided in just four grades (Standard, Superior, Promenade, and Deluxe) and six types, making it an easy matter to select your accommodation. Most cabins are of a similar size (small by today's standards) and the insulation between them is quite poor. The cabins also have mediocre closets and very little storage space, yet somehow everyone seems to manage (the ship was built originally for Caribbean cruising). However, they really are adequate for a one-week cruise, as you will need only casual clothes and, with these destination-intensive cruises, you really will not need many clothes anyway (shoes can always go under the bed). The largest cabins are named after famous explorers of the world.

The best advice is therefore to take only casual clothing and only the things you really need. Do note that cabin voltage is 110 volts AC, so British passengers will need to take adapters for electrical appliances such as a hairdryer. Note that although cabin grades are chosen when you book your cruise, the actual cabins are not assigned until you arrive at the ship. The accommodation deck hallways are also quite narrow.

Dining: The large King and I dining room is quite attractive, but noisy. It is a good operation but the food, while consistent in quality and presentation, is not memorable. The service is generally quite good, performed by friendly Filipino waiters and wine waiters. There is an adequate, but limited, wine list, and the wines are almost all very young.

Other Comments: This smart ship, built originally for many years by Royal Caribbean International (then Royal Caribbean Cruise Line), has sleek modern lines, with a sharply-raked bow and a single blue funnel, aft of which is a large amount of open deck space for sports. Has a polished wraparound wooden deck outdoors. There is a reasonable amount of open deck space, but it does get crowded when the ship is full (which is almost always), particularly around the small swimming pool.

Inside the ship, the layout is quite logical, which makes it easy to find one's way around. The decor is based on themed Broadway musicals, with fairly bright, crisp, clean colors. The passageways are not wide, but they do contain lots of artwork and wood trim. In fact, there is quite an abundance of artwork throughout this ship. There are several lounges and bars to choose from, most of which are located on one deck.

She is the sister ship to ***Carousel,*** and was "stretched" in 1978 when she was operated by Royal Caribbean International. Airtours is now partly owned by Carnival Corporation, who also own Carnival Cruise Lines (and others). ***Sundream,*** which commenced operations for Airtours Sun Cruises (one of Britain's Big Three tour companies) in May 1997, caters efficiently to novice passengers with well-programmed flair and provides an activity-filled cruise product in comfortable, but fairly busy surroundings, at very modest cruise rates for its mainly British and Canadian passengers. Features seven-day Caribbean (winter) and seven-day Mediterranean (summer) cruises.

But: There are many announcements. Many seats in the "My Fair Lady" show lounge have poor sight lines obstructed by several pillars. The cruise staff remind one of holiday camp "blue coats" with their well-meaning participation activities.

ms Sun Princess

☆☆☆☆ +

(L)

Lifestyle	**Premium**
Cruise Line:	Princess Cruises
Former Names:	-
Gross Tonnage:	77,000
Builder:	Fincantieri (Italy)
Original Cost:	$300 million
Entered Service:	December 1995
Flag:	Liberia
Tel No:	1260136/363633451
Fax No:	1260137/363633420
Length (ft./m.):	856.2/261.00
Beam (ft./m.):	105.8/32.25
Draft (ft./m.):	26.0/7.95
Propulsion/Propellers:	diesel-electric (28,000kW)/2 (FP)
Decks:	14
Total Crew:	900
Pass. Capacity (basis 2):	1,950
Pass. Capacity (all berths):	2,250
Pass. Space Ratio (basis 2):	39.4
Pass. Space Ratio (all berths):	34.2
Officers:	Italian
Total Cabins:	975
Size Range (sq. ft./m.):	135–754/12.5–70.0
Cabins (outside view):	603
Cabins (inside–no view):	372
Cabins (single occupancy):	0
Cabins (with private balcony):	410
Cabins (wheelchair accessible):	19
Cabin Current:	110/220 AC
Cabin TV:	Yes
Dining Rooms:	2 main/3 others
Seatings:	2 (main dining rooms)
Elevators:	11
Casino:	Yes
Slot Machines:	Yes
Swimming Pools (outdoors):	3
Swimming Pools (inside):	0
Whirlpools:	5
Fitness Center:	Yes
Sauna/Steam Room:	Yes/Yes
Massage:	Yes
Self-Service Launderette:	Yes
Movie Theater/Seats:	Yes/550
Library:	Yes
Children's Facilities:	Yes
Classification Society:	Lloyd's Register

Ratings	**Score**
Ship: Hardware/Maintenance	90
Ship: Outdoor Facilities/Space	87
Ship: Interior Facilities/Space/Flow	91
Ship: Decor/Furnishings/Artwork	90
Ship: Spa/Fitness Facilities	85
Cabins: Suites and Deluxe	86
Cabins: Standard Sizes	84
Food: Dining Room/Cuisine	73
Food: Informal Dining/Buffets	68
Food: Quality of Ingredients	70
Food: Afternoon Tea/Bar Snacks	63
Service: Dining Room	76
Service: Bars	76
Service: Cabins	77
Service: Open Decks	73
Cruise: Entertainment	87
Cruise: Activities Program	78
Cruise: Movies/Television Programming	84
Cruise: Hospitality Standard	81
Cruise: Overall Product Delivery	85
Overall Score	**1,604**

For comments, see *Dawn Princess*.

ss Sun Vista

☆☆☆ +

(L)

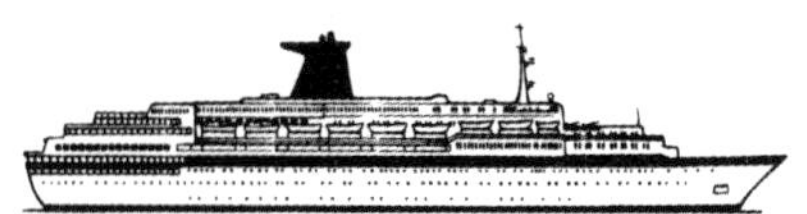

Lifestyle	**Standard**
Cruise Line:	Sun Cruises
Former Names:	*Meridian/Galileo/ Galileo Galilei*
Gross Tonnage:	30,440
Builder:	Cantieri Riuniti dell' Adriatico (Italy)
Original Cost:	n/a
Entered Service:	April 1963/November 1997
Flag:	Bahamas
Tel No:	1103143
Fax No:	1103145
Length (ft./m.):	700.9/213.65
Beam (ft./m.):	94.1/28.71
Draft (ft./m.):	28.3/8.64
Propulsion/Propellers:	steam turbine (32,800kW)/2 (FP)
Decks:	8
Total Crew:	770
Pass. Capacity (basis 2):	1,106
Pass. Capacity (all berths):	1,398
Pass. Space Ratio (basis 2):	27.5
Pass. Space Ratio (all berths):	21.7
Officers:	International
Total Cabins:	553
Size Range (sq. ft./m.):	n/a
Cabins (outside view):	295
Cabins (inside—no view):	258
Cabins (single occupancy):	0
Cabins (with private balcony):	0
Cabins (wheelchair accessible):	2
Cabin Current:	110/220 AC
Cabin TV:	No
Dining Rooms:	1
Seatings:	2
Elevators:	3
Casino:	No
Slot Machines:	No
Swimming Pools (outdoors):	1
Swimming Pools (inside):	0
Whirlpools:	3
Fitness Center:	Yes
Sauna/Steam Room:	Yes/Yes
Massage:	Yes
Self-Service Launderette:	No
Movie Theater/Seats:	Yes/218
Library:	Yes
Children's Facilities:	Yes
Classification Society:	Lloyd's Register

Ratings	**Score**
Ship: Hardware/Maintenance	73
Ship: Outdoor Facilities/Space	63
Ship: Interior Facilities/Space/Flow	61
Ship: Decor/Furnishings/Artwork	64
Ship: Spa/Fitness Facilities	51
Cabins: Suites and Deluxe	80
Cabins: Standard Sizes	71
Food: Dining Room/Cuisine	71
Food: Informal Dining/Buffets	64
Food: Quality of Ingredients	60
Food: Afternoon Tea/Bar Snacks	51
Service: Dining Room	75
Service: Bars	72
Service: Cabins	70
Service: Open Decks	64
Cruise: Entertainment	60
Cruise: Activities Program	51
Cruise: Movies/Television Programming	68
Cruise: Hospitality Standard	62
Cruise: Overall Product Delivery	66
Overall Score	**1,297**

Accommodation: There is a wide selection of cabin sizes and configurations and all are quite well equipped. The cabin bathrooms are disappointingly small, however, and there is little space for stowage of personal toiletry items. The best cabins are the Sports deck suites, which have large skylights, are large, comfortable, and well appointed.

Dining: The Four Seasons dining room is warm and inviting (there are tables for two, three, four, six, eight, and ten). A mix of Chinese and European foods is provided. There is a good selection of pastries and popular dessert items. The service, provided mainly by a Filipino staff, is friendly, attentive, and quite polished. The brochure states you can "have whatever you like, whenever you feel like it," although this is really not the case in practice. Buffets are provided (from dawn till dusk) in the Marina Café, which is small and quite cramped. Poolside barbecues are featured at the Oasis Bar and Grill.

Other Comments: She has a nicely balanced classic ocean liner profile (she was extensively reconfigured and refurbished as a cruise vessel by Celebrity Cruises, who operated her from early 1990 until October 1997). She has a nicely raked bow, a well-rounded stern, and a single, large funnel. As she is powered by steam turbines, there is little vibration. The sheltered deck areas and open deck sun bathing space is quite good, and there is an indoor/outdoor wraparound promenade deck, as well as an undercover Palm Garden walking deck. Sadly, there is no forward observation lounge.

Inside, her many public rooms have generally high ceilings and soft, elegant pastel decor and color tones throughout, with extensive use of mirrored surfaces. There is a large, single-level, gently sloped show lounge, but several pillars obstruct sight lines from some seats. Churchill's Wine Bar is where imported cigars can be found. The dress code is casual, as it is throughout South East Asia.

The company provides lots of activities for children, but they do tend to make a lot of noise around the ship. There is also a video arcade, next door to the karaoke lounge (private karaoke rooms are also available). Operates six-day and two-day (weekend) cruises. All of the staff is English-speaking, although they are multilingual. The currency is the Singapore dollar. A "no-tipping" policy is featured, although 10 percent is added to all beverage purchases.

But: Do expect lines for embarkation (Level 2, Singapore Cruise Terminal), disembarkation (waiting in public lounges is an uncivilized pain), shore tenders, and buffets. There are no cushioned pads for the deck lounge chairs.

Under her new Singaporean, owners Sun Cruises (who compete directly with Malaysian-owned Star Cruises and are no relation to the U.K.-based Sun Cruises), this ship delivers a lively, friendly, family-oriented cruise product, and represents good value for money for South East Asian passengers.

ms SuperStar Capricorn

☆☆☆☆

(M)

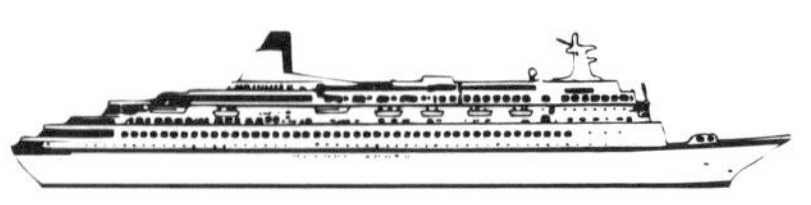

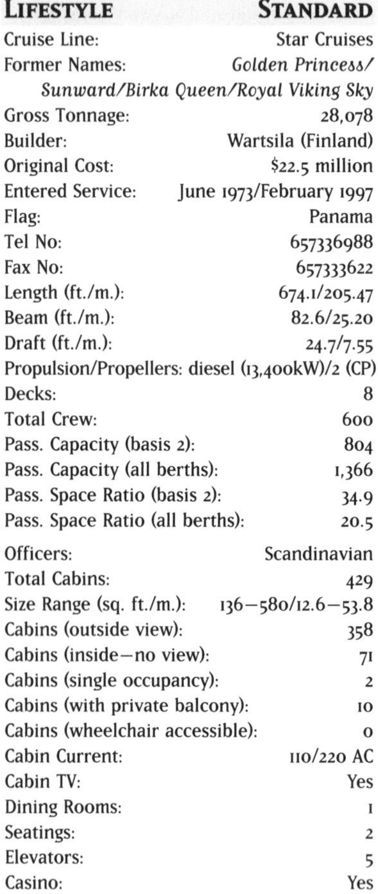

LIFESTYLE	STANDARD
Cruise Line:	Star Cruises
Former Names:	*Golden Princess/ Sunward/Birka Queen/Royal Viking Sky*
Gross Tonnage:	28,078
Builder:	Wartsila (Finland)
Original Cost:	$22.5 million
Entered Service:	June 1973/February 1997
Flag:	Panama
Tel No:	657336988
Fax No:	657333622
Length (ft./m.):	674.1/205.47
Beam (ft./m.):	82.6/25.20
Draft (ft./m.):	24.7/7.55
Propulsion/Propellers:	diesel (13,400kW)/2 (CP)
Decks:	8
Total Crew:	600
Pass. Capacity (basis 2):	804
Pass. Capacity (all berths):	1,366
Pass. Space Ratio (basis 2):	34.9
Pass. Space Ratio (all berths):	20.5
Officers:	Scandinavian
Total Cabins:	429
Size Range (sq. ft./m.):	136–580/12.6–53.8
Cabins (outside view):	358
Cabins (inside—no view):	71
Cabins (single occupancy):	2
Cabins (with private balcony):	10
Cabins (wheelchair accessible):	0
Cabin Current:	110/220 AC
Cabin TV:	Yes
Dining Rooms:	1
Seatings:	2
Elevators:	5
Casino:	Yes
Slot Machines:	Yes
Swimming Pools (outdoors):	2
Swimming Pools (inside):	1
Whirlpools:	1
Fitness Center:	Yes
Sauna/Steam Room:	Yes/Yes
Massage:	Yes
Self-Service Launderette:	Yes
Movie Theater/Seats:	No
Library:	Yes
Children's Facilities:	Yes
Classification Society:	Det Norske Veritas

RATINGS	SCORE
Ship: Hardware/Maintenance	74
Ship: Outdoor Facilities/Space	78
Ship: Interior Facilities/Space/Flow	80
Ship: Decor/Furnishings/Artwork	77
Ship: Spa/Fitness Facilities	73
Cabins: Suites and Deluxe	81
Cabins: Standard Sizes	74
Food: Dining Room/Cuisine	76
Food: Informal Dining/Buffets	76
Food: Quality of Ingredients	70
Food: Afternoon Tea/Bar Snacks	66
Service: Dining Room	77
Service: Bars	75
Service: Cabins	77
Service: Open Decks	73
Cruise: Entertainment	74
Cruise: Activities Program	65
Cruise: Movies/Television Programming	71
Cruise: Hospitality Standard	80
Cruise: Overall Product Delivery	81
OVERALL SCORE	**1,498**

Accommodation: There are 9 suites that are spacious and nicely equipped, and each has a separate bedroom and a large living area, with private balcony.

All other cabins are quite well appointed and have good closet, drawer, and reasonable storage space (although the metal drawers are tinny and noisy). Most bathrooms are sound, although some, on the lower decks, have awkward access.

Dining: The spacious dining room has a high ceiling, is quiet, and provides a reasonably elegant setting for cuisine that is now centered on Asian specialties. The overall food quality is in line with that of other similarly priced cruises, and the company does a good job at catering to several Asian nationalities, as well as Australian passengers (some Western foods are also featured). The wine list is generally quite sound.

Other Comments: Has handsome outer styling, a benefit from her former life as a Royal Viking Line ship, although she has gone through a series of other owners in the past few years. Has a nicely balanced profile and lines, with a sharply raked bow. There is a good amount of open deck and sunbathing space; in fact, there is plenty of space everywhere. Has a good outdoor wraparound promenade deck, as well as some good fitness and sports facilities.

Inside, the ship features decor that is quite tasteful, with splashes of bright colors throughout. There are lots of public rooms to choose from, including a karaoke lounge and private karaoke rooms. The casino action is lively.

This ship, which was stretched in 1982, provides a good cruise experience in spacious, nicely furnished surroundings. She was purchased by Star Cruises in 1996 and went through an extensive $5-million refit that added an indoor swimming pool and a video arcade. There are a great number of Chinese among the hotel service crew. Onboard currency are Taiwanese or U.S. dollars or Japanese Yen. Although announcements are made in Japanese and Mandarin, the principal language used on board is English; daily programs are printed in English, Japanese, and Mandarin.

ms SuperStar Gemini

☆☆☆ +

(M)

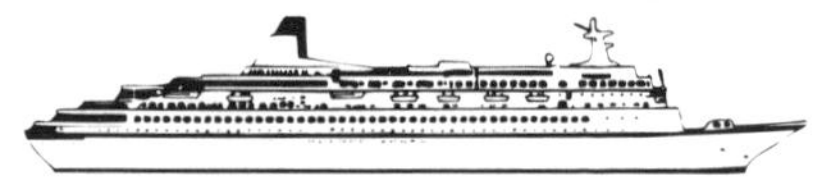

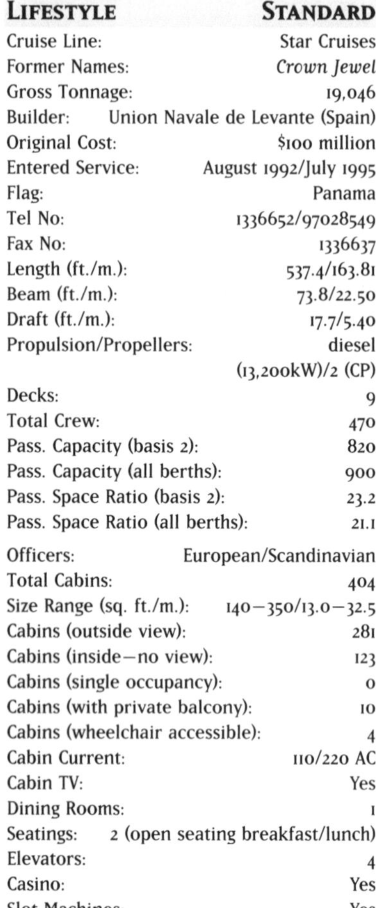

Lifestyle	Standard
Cruise Line:	Star Cruises
Former Names:	*Crown Jewel*
Gross Tonnage:	19,046
Builder:	Union Navale de Levante (Spain)
Original Cost:	$100 million
Entered Service:	August 1992/July 1995
Flag:	Panama
Tel No:	1336652/97028549
Fax No:	1336637
Length (ft./m.):	537.4/163.81
Beam (ft./m.):	73.8/22.50
Draft (ft./m.):	17.7/5.40
Propulsion/Propellers:	diesel (13,200kW)/2 (CP)
Decks:	9
Total Crew:	470
Pass. Capacity (basis 2):	820
Pass. Capacity (all berths):	900
Pass. Space Ratio (basis 2):	23.2
Pass. Space Ratio (all berths):	21.1
Officers:	European/Scandinavian
Total Cabins:	404
Size Range (sq. ft./m.):	140–350/13.0–32.5
Cabins (outside view):	281
Cabins (inside–no view):	123
Cabins (single occupancy):	0
Cabins (with private balcony):	10
Cabins (wheelchair accessible):	4
Cabin Current:	110/220 AC
Cabin TV:	Yes
Dining Rooms:	1
Seatings:	2 (open seating breakfast/lunch)
Elevators:	4
Casino:	Yes
Slot Machines:	Yes
Swimming Pools (outdoors):	1
Swimming Pools (inside):	0
Whirlpools:	3 (2 outside/1 inside)
Fitness Center:	Yes
Sauna/Steam Room:	Yes/Yes
Massage:	Yes
Self-Service Launderette:	No
Movie Theater/Seats:	No
Library:	Yes
Children's Facilities:	Yes
Classification Society:	Det Norske Veritas

Ratings	Score
Ship: Hardware/Maintenance	77
Ship: Outdoor Facilities/Space	75
Ship: Interior Facilities/Space/Flow	76
Ship: Decor/Furnishings/Artwork	74
Ship: Spa/Fitness Facilities	64
Cabins: Suites and Deluxe	77
Cabins: Standard Sizes	71
Food: Dining Room/Cuisine	71
Food: Informal Dining/Buffets	64
Food: Quality of Ingredients	72
Food: Afternoon Tea/Bar Snacks	64
Service: Dining Room	73
Service: Bars	71
Service: Cabins	73
Service: Open Decks	66
Cruise: Entertainment	61
Cruise: Activities Program	61
Cruise: Movies/Television Programming	64
Cruise: Hospitality Standard	71
Cruise: Overall Product Delivery	73
Overall Score	**1,398**

Accommodation: The standard (inside and outside) and deluxe grade cabins are small but nicely furnished, and most feature broad picture windows (note that some deluxe cabins on Deck 6 have lifeboat-obstructed views). They are practical and comfortable, with wood-trimmed accents and multicolored soft furnishings, but there is little drawer space, and the closet space is also very tight. The bathrooms are decent for the size of the ship, and each features two small toiletries cabinets, although the shower cubicle is quite small. However, note the cabin soundproofing is very poor; the 100 percent cotton towels are thin; there is little room for luggage, so take only what is really necessary (casual clothing only, no formal attire needed, even the captain's gala dinner night asks for "smart casual" attire).

The Executive Suites (eight of them have a private balcony, but the partitions are not of the floor-to-ceiling type and so you can hear your neighbors clearly—or smell their smoke) and Junior Suites (they are really little larger than standard and deluxe cabins, although there is more closet space) are nicely furnished, and the sleeping area can be curtained off. A tea/coffee making set, and laser disc player is provided (Executive Suites only).

Bathrobes, slippers, and toiletry amenities are provided in all cabins, as well as a small color television, telephone, and bottled water.

Note: No cabins have a bathtub. Hairdryers are not supplied for any cabin category, so take your own if you need to use one. Also, there is no room service for such items as coffee or tea, nor is there a menu for snacks. The cabin numbering system and signage is confusing.

Dining: The attractive Ocean Palace dining room is located aft and has large picture windows on three sides (although the center ceiling accenting makes the room appear round). However, it is not open for dinner each night, but is dependent on the itinerary (some nights only the casual Mariner's Buffet is available).

The ambience is good, but there are few tables for two (most tables are for four, six, or eight). Features international cuisine with an Oriental touch, and there is open seating for all meals, except for dinner on the single "formal" night. On the six-day cruise, one night includes a barbecue outside on the pool deck (the main dining room is closed on this night). The wine list itself is reasonable, but the wines are all young and prices are high (the cost of wines and spirits in South East Asia is high) and champagne is incredibly expensive.

There is also an informal cafe, called Mariner's Buffet (a pork-free eatery). Breakfast here always includes some South East Asian dishes such as nasi lemak and fried noodles, as well as Western favorites. Lunch and dinner are also provided in this eatery. Australian passengers will appreciate the ample supply of Vegemite.

There is a good selection of beers, including some regional varieties, and some draft lager.

Other Comments: This is a handsome mid-sized cruise ship with smart exterior styling (the largest ever built in Spain). Although the fit and finish was originally poor, Star Cruises has made the ship's interiors much more colorful and warm.

Has a traditional layout that provides reasonable horizontal passenger flow, althought he passageways are narrow. Has picture windows in almost all public rooms that connect passengers with the sea and the outside light. There is a fair amount of open deck and sunbathing space, including a neat area high atop the ship in front of a glass windbreak area —lovely for those balmy evenings outdoors—away from the crowds inside. Cushioned pads are provided for the deck lounge chairs. There is also a wraparound walking area. Features a five-deck-high glass-walled atrium, and there is a karaoke/disco lounge. Has attractive decor, with upbeat art deco color combinations and splashy, colorful soft furnishings. The artwork is fairly plain and simple and could be improved. The fitness center/spa area is good but cramped.

Communication at the Reception Desk is often frustrating, and the staff has little finesse, but is slowly improving. Also, there are simply too many unnecessary announcements, and music plays constantly in public spaces, in hallways, and on open decks, making a relaxing cruise experience impossible.

This very informal ship caters specifically to Australian, European (mainly British and German), and Singaporean passengers (all announcements are in English only). While most passengers will embark/disembark in Singapore, you can also arrange to do so in any of the way ports as well as do pre- and post-cruise stays in those ports (on the six-day cruise). The ship presently operates seven-day cruises year-round.

All in all, the company provides really good value for money cruising in a ship that is bright and very informal, although the staff is young and fresh, and needs more experience in hospitality and flexibility. Gratuities are included and no further tipping is allowed.

ms SuperStar Leo

(L)

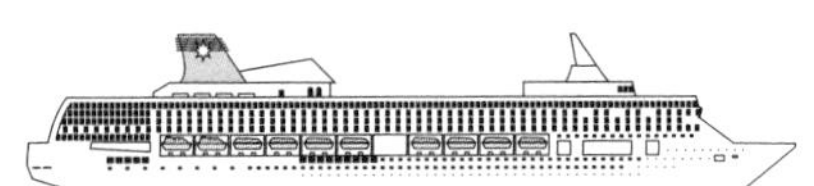

Lifestyle	Standard
Cruise Line:	Star Cruises
Former Names:	-
Gross Tonnage:	74,500
Builder:	Meyer Werft (Germany)
Original Cost:	$350 million
Entered Service:	October 1998
Flag:	Panama
Tel No:	n/a
Fax No:	n/a
Length (ft./m.):	879.2/268.0
Beam (ft./m.):	105.6/32.2
Draft (ft./m.):	25.9/7.9
Propulsion/Propellers:	2 diesels (50,400kW)/2(CP)
Decks:	10
Total Crew:	1,000
Pass. Capacity (basis 2):	1,974
Pass. Capacity (all berths):	3,500
Pass. Space Ratio (basis 2):	37.7
Pass. Space Ratio (all berths):	21.2
Officers:	International
Total Cabins:	1,385
Size Range (sq. ft./m.):	150.6–638.3/14.0–59.3
Cabins (outside view):	608
Cabins (inside–no view):	379
Cabins (single occupancy):	0
Cabins (with private balcony):	391
Cabins (wheelchair accessible):	4
Cabin Current:	240 AC
Cabin TV:	Yes
Dining Rooms:	6
Seatings:	2
Elevators:	9
Casino:	Yes
Slot Machines:	Yes
Swimming Pools (outdoors):	2
Swimming Pools (inside):	0
Whirlpools:	4
Fitness Center:	Yes
Sauna/Steam Room:	Yes/Yes
Massage:	Yes
Self-Service Launderette:	No
Movie Theater/Seats:	Yes/tba
Library:	Yes
Children's Facilities:	Yes
Classification Society:	Det Norske Veritas

Ratings	Score
Ship: Hardware/Maintenance	NYR
Ship: Outdoor Facilities/Space	NYR
Ship: Interior Facilities/Space/Flow	NYR
Ship: Decor/Furnishings/Artwork	NYR
Ship: Spa/Fitness Facilities	NYR
Cabins: Suites and Deluxe	NYR
Cabins: Standard Sizes	NYR
Food: Dining Room/Cuisine	NYR
Food: Informal Dining/Buffets	NYR
Food: Quality of Ingredients	NYR
Food: Afternoon Tea/Bar Snacks	NYR
Service: Dining Room	NYR
Service: Bars	NYR
Service: Cabins	NYR
Service: Open Decks	NYR
Cruise: Entertainment	NYR
Cruise: Activities Program	NYR
Cruise: Movies/Television Programming	NYR
Cruise: Hospitality Standard	NYR
Cruise: Overall Product Delivery	NYR

Expected Score Range
1,400-1,700

Accommodation: Three complete decks of cabins have private balconies, while two-thirds of all cabins have an outside view, although most cabins really are quite small. Accommodation designated as suites have sea-facing Jacuzzis and exotic (possibly erotic) artwork and wood-paneled walls.

Dining: The principal (two-level) dining room seats 1,000. There is also a 400-seat Lido Café. This is presently the only ship in the world to have both an authentic Chinese restaurant (Taipan, with its Hong Kong hey-day-themed decor) and a Japanese restaurant (Shogun, for sashimi, sushi, tempura and teppanyaki); both restaurants seat 120. Another restaurant features Southeast Asian cuisine, while a 400-seat Raffles Lido Café is yet another feature.

Other Comments: *SuperStar Leo* is the first new ship ordered specifically for the Asian market, and will soon be joined by ***SuperStar Virgo***. There is a wraparound outdoor promenade deck. There are two indoor boulevards (as in Carnival Cruise Lines' Fantasy-class ships).

Inside the ship is a six-deck-high central atrium, with three glass-walled elevators and ample space to peruse the shops and cafes that line its inner sanctum. The design theme revolves around art, architecture, history, and literature. The ship has a mix of both eastern and western design and decor details, and public room names have been chosen to appeal to a mixture of American, European, and Asian passengers.

There is a 973-seat, two-deck-high show lounge (Moulin Rouge) with almost no support columns to obstruct sight lines, and a revolving stage for Broadway-style reviews. A 450-seat room atop the ship is an observation lounge during the day and becomes the ship's disco at night. Another two-deck-high show lounge seats 1,000. There is a business center (complete with 167-seat conference center—good for small groups) and writing room, as well as private mahjongg and karaoke rooms.

Sports facilities include a jogging track, golf driving range, basketball and tennis courts, as well as four levels of sunbathing decks. Fitness devotees will enjoy Caesar's Bath and the Nero Fitness Center.

Families with children should note that they have their own video arcade, and hamburger, spaghetti, and ice cream outlets. There is also has a helicopter landing pad and a shopping plaza. This ship operates under a no-tipping policy. She is expected to operate a round-the-world cruise in 2000.

Star Cruises has established a good local area cruise audience for its diverse fleet of ships. *SuperStar Leo* and soon to be sister ship *SuperStar Virgo* are the first pair of newbuilds for this growing company, but several more ships are expected to be ordered fro this growing market area. Passengers include many Europeans, Australians, Singaporeans, Chinese, Japanese and those of other Southeast Asian nations, which makes for a fascinating mix of cultures and dietary requirements.

ms SuperStar Sagittarius

☆☆☆ +

(M)

Lifestyle	Standard
Cruise Line:	Star Cruises
Former Names:	*Sun Viking*
Gross Tonnage:	18,556
Builder:	Wartsila (Finland)
Original Cost:	$17.5 million
Entered Service:	December 1972/January 1998
Flag:	Norway
Tel No:	1312151
Fax No:	1312151
Length (ft./m.):	563.2/171.69
Beam (ft./m.):	78.8/24.03
Draft (ft./m.):	20.6/6.30
Propulsion/Propellers:	diesel (13,400kW)/2 (CP)
Decks:	8
Total Crew:	341
Pass. Capacity (basis 2):	714
Pass. Capacity (all berths):	818
Pass. Space Ratio (basis 2):	25.9
Pass. Space Ratio (all berths):	22.6
Officers:	Scandinavian
Total Cabins:	357
Size Range (sq. ft./m.):	120–237/11.0–22.0
Cabins (outside view):	240
Cabins (inside–no view):	117
Cabins (single occupancy):	0
Cabins (with private balcony):	0
Cabins (wheelchair accessible):	0
Cabin Current:	110 AC
Cabin TV:	No
Dining Rooms:	1
Seatings:	2
Elevators:	4
Casino:	Yes
Slot Machines:	Yes
Swimming Pools (outdoors):	1
Swimming Pools (inside):	0
Whirlpools:	0
Fitness Center:	Yes
Sauna/Steam Room:	Yes/No
Massage:	Yes
Self-Service Launderette:	No
Movie Theater/Seats:	No
Library:	Yes
Children's Facilities:	No
Classification Society:	Det Norske Veritas

Ratings	Score
Ship: Hardware/Maintenance	74
Ship: Outdoor Facilities/Space	63
Ship: Interior Facilities/Space/Flow	62
Ship: Decor/Furnishings/Artwork	62
Ship: Spa/Fitness Facilities	57
Cabins: Suites and Deluxe	65
Cabins: Standard Sizes	56
Food: Dining Room/Cuisine	71
Food: Informal Dining/Buffets	67
Food: Quality of Ingredients	70
Food: Afternoon Tea/Bar Snacks	62
Service: Dining Room	66
Service: Bars	64
Service: Cabins	67
Service: Open Decks	63
Cruise: Entertainment	64
Cruise: Activities Program	61
Cruise: Movies/Television Programming	61
Cruise: Hospitality Standard	73
Cruise: Overall Product Delivery	72
Overall Score	**1,300**

Accommodation: Almost all the cabins aboard this ship are extremely small (in fact they are among the smallest in the cruise industry), and can best be described as only moderately comfortable. They have very little closet, drawer, and storage space, so do take only the absolutely minimal in casual clothing (no ties or formal wear are needed anyway). While they are small, they have pleasant colors for the soft furnishings. The bathrooms, too, are very small and utilitarian, with little space for personal toiletries.

Dining: The single dining room has pleasing decor and is quite attractive, with its large picture ocean-view windows. There are tables for four, six, or eight (there are no tables for two). The food is a mix of western and Asian cuisine and features considerable buffet displays.

Other Comments: She is a well-proportioned medium-size ship with fairly contemporary styling that is typical of the 1970s. She was built for Royal Caribbean Cruise Line, who operated her for more than twenty years. The ship retains the lounge located part way up the funnel.

There is a decent amount of open deck and sunbathing space (this becomes very tight when the ship is full) and a wraparound outdoor polished wood deck. The public rooms are decorated in modern style and colors.

Star Cruises acquired this ship from Royal Caribbean International and placed her in service in January 1998. This company wants the passengers to be out and about the public rooms, not in their small cabins, and caters to passengers who want a more intimate cruise, with all the Star Cruises trimmings at a fair price. Has a charming, friendly ambience throughout.

Tailored specifically to the Southeast Asian market, the ship is based at Star Cruises' own terminal in Port Klang (the port for Kuala Lumpur).

But: This really is a high-density ship, which means that public rooms are always busy. Long wait for elevators, in buffet lines, and for disembarkation in ports.

ms SuperStar Virgo
(L)

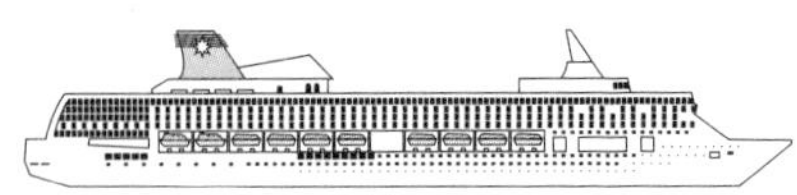

LIFESTYLE	STANDARD
Cruise Line:	Star Cruises
Former Names:	-
Gross Tonnage:	74,500
Builder:	Meyer Werft (Germany)
Original Cost:	$350 million
Entered Service:	March 1999
Flag:	Panama
Tel No:	n/a
Fax No:	n/a
Length (ft./m.):	879.2/268.0
Beam (ft./m.):	105.6/32.2
Draft (ft./m.):	25.9/7.9
Propulsion/Propellers:	diesel (50,400kW)/2 CP
Decks:	10
Total Crew:	1,000
Pass. Capacity (basis 2):	1,974
Pass. Capacity (all berths):	3,500
Pass. Space Ratio (basis 2):	37.7
Pass. Space Ratio (all berths):	21.2
Officers:	European
Total Cabins:	1,385
Size Range (sq. ft./m.):	150.6–638.3/14.0–59.3
Cabins (outside view):	608
Cabins (inside–no view):	379
Cabins (single occupancy):	0
Cabins (with private balcony):	391
Cabins (wheelchair accessible):	4
Cabin Current:	240 AC
Cabin TV:	Yes
Dining Rooms:	6
Seatings:	2
Elevators:	9
Casino:	Yes
Slot Machines:	Yes
Swimming Pools (outdoors):	2
Swimming Pools (inside):	0
Whirlpools:	4
Fitness Center:	Yes
Sauna/Steam Room:	Yes/Yes
Massage:	Yes
Self-Service Launderette:	No
Movie Theater/Seats:	Yes/tba
Library:	Yes
Children's Facilities:	Yes
Classification Society:	Det Norske Veritas

RATINGS	SCORE
Ship: Hardware/Maintenance	NYR
Ship: Outdoor Facilities/Space	NYR
Ship: Interior Facilities/Space/Flow	NYR
Ship: Decor/Furnishings/Artwork	NYR
Ship: Spa/Fitness Facilities	NYR
Cabins: Suites and Deluxe	NYR
Cabins: Standard Sizes	NYR
Food: Dining Room/Cuisine	NYR
Food: Informal Dining/Buffets	NYR
Food: Quality of Ingredients	NYR
Food: Afternoon Tea/Bar Snacks	NYR
Service: Dining Room	NYR
Service: Bars	NYR
Service: Cabins	NYR
Service: Open Decks	NYR
Cruise: Entertainment	NYR
Cruise: Activities Program	NYR
Cruise: Movies/Television Programming	NYR
Cruise: Hospitality Standard	NYR
Cruise: Overall Product Delivery	NYR

EXPECTED SCORE RANGE
1,400-1,700

For comments, see *SuperStar Leo*.

mts Switzerland

☆☆☆ +

(S)

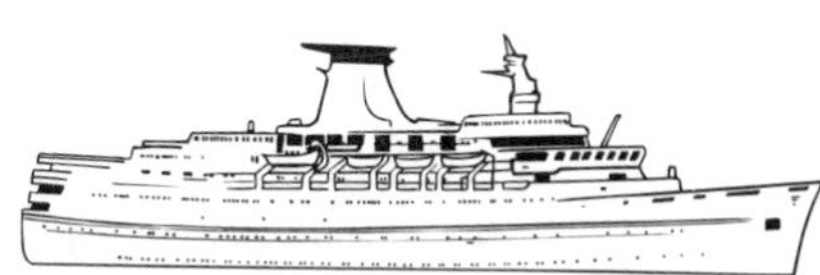

Lifestyle	**Standard**
Cruise Line:	Leisure Cruises
Former Names:	*Daphne/Therisos Express/Port Sydney*
Gross Tonnage:	15,739
Builder:	Swan, Hunter (UK)
Original Cost:	n/a
Entered Service:	March 1955/March 1997
Flag:	Liberia
Tel No:	1243127/663601714
Fax No:	66361715
Length (ft./m.):	532.7/162.39
Beam (ft./m.):	70.2/21.42
Draft (ft./m.):	28.4/8.66
Propulsion/Propellers:	diesel (9,850kW)/2 (FP)
Decks:	7
Total Crew:	210
Pass. Capacity (basis 2):	424
Pass. Capacity (all berths):	486
Pass. Space Ratio (basis 2):	37.1
Pass. Space Ratio (all berths):	32.3
Officers:	International
Total Cabins:	212
Size Range (sq. ft./m.):	150.0–398.2/14.0–37.0
Cabins (outside view):	190
Cabins (inside—no view):	22
Cabins (single occupancy):	0
Cabins (with private balcony):	0
Cabins (wheelchair accessible):	0
Cabin Current:	220 AC
Cabin TV:	Suites only
Dining Rooms:	1
Seatings:	1
Elevators:	2
Casino:	Yes
Slot Machines:	Yes
Swimming Pools (outdoors):	1
Swimming Pools (inside):	0
Whirlpools:	2
Fitness Center:	Yes
Sauna/Steam Room:	Yes/No
Massage:	Yes
Self-Service Launderette:	Yes
Movie Theater/Seats:	Yes/200
Library:	Yes
Children's Facilities:	No
Classification Society:	RINA

Ratings	**Score**
Ship: Hardware/Maintenance	73
Ship: Outdoor Facilities/Space	71
Ship: Interior Facilities/Space/Flow	70
Ship: Decor/Furnishings/Artwork	72
Ship: Spa/Fitness Facilities	64
Cabins: Suites and Deluxe	76
Cabins: Standard Sizes	62
Food: Dining Room/Cuisine	71
Food: Informal Dining/Buffets	63
Food: Quality of Ingredients	68
Food: Afternoon Tea/Bar Snacks	63
Service: Dining Room	73
Service: Bars	71
Service: Cabins	72
Service: Open Decks	66
Cruise: Entertainment	58
Cruise: Activities Program	62
Cruise: Movies/Television Programming	60
Cruise: Hospitality Standard	72
Cruise: Overall Product Delivery	76
Overall Score	**1,363**

Accommodation: This ship has some very spacious forward-facing suites (incorrectly called penthouses) as well as the more standard cabins. All have good solid fittings and heavy-duty doors. There really is plenty of closet and drawer space, as well as good insulation between each cabin. The cabin bathrooms are of a generous size and fitted out well, but there is no pull-out clothes line (needed for long cruises), and walls are plain. Tea and coffee provided as room service items are at extra cost.

The penthouse suites have a completely separate bedroom and living room, plus a balcony (passengers are brought complimentary cocktails on days at sea and have a butler service). A minibar-refrigerator is provided, but all items are at extra cost. The bathroom has a full-sized bathtub and glazed tile floor, but no pull-out clothes line (useful for long cruises or on an around-the-world voyage). Bathrobes and a good range of toiletry amenities are provided.

Dining: The dining room is quite charming, and has an uncluttered seating arrangement, with several tables for two located by large picture windows. Features friendly, attentive service by Russian and Ukrainian staff. The food is not very creatively presented, but is of a good general standard, provided by a respected Swiss maritime catering company. Dinners consist of only one or two appetizers and entrees, but there is always a good choice of cheeses. At all meals (except formal days) a salad buffet table, complete with cheese selection, is provided for lunch and dinner. Breakfast buffet is also provided in the dining room. There is also a separate informal café (Neptune Bar) for breakfast and lunch buffets. There is also a neat wine bar (Piazzo Vino) with a decent selection.

Other Comments: This ship (originally built for Port Line and converted into a cruise ship at a cost of $37 million in 1975) has expansive outdoor decks and plenty of sunbathing space. She was refitted and completely refurbished in early 1997 for her present owners. There is no forward-looking observation lounge and no wraparound promenade deck.

Features bright, contemporary decor in the public rooms. Has a large, fine theater, which is especially good for meetings and groups. Other public rooms have fairly high ceilings.

Almost identical in outward appearance to sister ship *Princess Danae*. Originally constructed as a general cargo vessel, she was rebuilt as a cruise ship, and operated for many years for Costa Cruises as *Daphne*. Now owned and operated by the new Swiss-based company, Leisure Cruises, she is a very comfortable vessel. There is much emphasis on health and fitness, with a wellness program that includes Ayurvedic treatments in the Aqua Vitalis spa and yoga and tai-chi as part of the exercise program.

The use of mobile phones aboard ship is not permitted. This ship maintains an air of intimacy, has a fine range of public rooms, and should represent good value when cruising on her itineraries. The onboard currency is the U.S. dollar, a 15 percent gratuity is added to all bar bills, and other gratuities are not included in the fare ($8 per day per person is recommended). Operated by Leisure Cruises, the ship is chartered at various times of the year by other organizations.

ts Symphony

☆☆ +

(M)

LIFESTYLE	**STANDARD**
Cruise Line:	Mediterranean Shipping Cruises
Former Names:	*EnricoCosta/ Enrico "C"/Provence*
Gross Tonnage:	16,495
Builder:	Swan, Hunter (UK)
Original Cost:	n/a
Entered Service:	March 1951/1995
Flag:	Italy
Tel No:	1150561
Fax No:	1150561
Length (ft./m.):	579.0/176.49
Beam (ft./m.):	73.1/22.31
Draft (ft./m.):	24.6/7.52
Propulsion/Propellers:	diesel (11,768kW)/2 (FP)
Decks:	7
Total Crew:	330
Pass. Capacity (basis 2):	664
Pass. Capacity (all berths):	845
Pass. Space Ratio (basis 2):	24.8
Pass. Space Ratio (all berths):	19.5
Officers:	Italian
Total Cabins:	332
Size Range (sq. ft./m.):	86–216/8.0–20.1
Cabins (outside view):	159
Cabins (inside–no view):	173
Cabins (single occupancy):	0
Cabins (with private balcony):	0
Cabins (wheelchair accessible):	0
Cabin Current:	220 DC
Cabin TV:	No
Dining Rooms:	1
Seatings:	2
Elevators:	2
Casino:	No
Slot Machines:	No
Swimming Pools (outdoors):	3
Swimming Pools (inside):	0
Whirlpools:	0
Fitness Center:	No
Sauna/Steam Room:	No/No
Massage:	No
Self-Service Launderette:	Yes
Movie Theater/Seats:	Yes/85
Library:	No
Children's Facilities:	Yes
Classification Society:	RINA

RATINGS	**SCORE**
Ship: Hardware/Maintenance	52
Ship: Outdoor Facilities/Space	53
Ship: Interior Facilities/Space/Flow	57
Ship: Decor/Furnishings/Artwork	53
Ship: Spa/Fitness Facilities	42
Cabins: Suites and Deluxe	61
Cabins: Standard Sizes	51
Food: Dining Room/Cuisine	61
Food: Informal Dining/Buffets	55
Food: Quality of Ingredients	56
Food: Afternoon Tea/Bar Snacks	42
Service: Dining Room	59
Service: Bars	60
Service: Cabins	59
Service: Open Decks	57
Cruise: Entertainment	56
Cruise: Activities Program	54
Cruise: Movies/Television Programming	42
Cruise: Hospitality Standard	54
Cruise: Overall Product Delivery	61
OVERALL SCORE	**1,085**

Accommodation: There is a wide variety of cabin sizes and configurations to choose from. Most of the cabins are compact but comfortable units, with tasteful pastel decor and soft furnishings to match. They have real chrome locks and keys, a throwback to her former life as an ocean liner. The accommodation passageways have wooden handrails, but inconsistent lighting quality.

Dining: The dining room is comfortable, though very noisy, but does have wooden porthole surrounds. The painted pegboard ceiling in many areas looks old and shabby and should be replaced. Good bubbly Italian service and food, with good pasta, but other dishes lack quality and have poor presentation and consistency.

Other Comments: Has traditional ocean liner styling, preserved from her former life as a cargo-passenger liner. Has a large, single funnel. This solidly built vessel received an extensive refurbishment in 1996. She has a deep draft, and so is reasonably stable at sea. Although there are fairly decent open deck promenade areas, there is no wraparound promenade deck.

Inside, a great amount of fine old wood paneling and brass trim throughout the ship adds some warmth and old-world elegance often lacking in many of the new breed of glitzy ships. The newer facilities added during various refurbishments are fine, while others have been much upgraded. The public rooms feature what is best described as "Belle Epoque" decor and are very smart, but they are crowded when full.

This ship caters primarily to budget-minded European passengers looking for a Mediterranean cruise without the trimmings and carries principally Italian passengers (at least 60 percent). It offers a basic, no-frills cruise experience.

But: The ship does not have stabilizers. The ceilings are very plain and uninteresting. The entertainment is loud and of very poor quality. There are too many loud, unnecessary, and repetitious announcements.

ms Taras Shevchenko

☆☆ +

(M)

Lifestyle	**Standard**
Cruise Line:	Ukrainian Passenger Fleet
Former Names:	-
Gross Tonnage:	20,027
Builder:	VEB Mathias Thesen (Germany)
Original Cost:	n/a
Entered Service:	April 1967/1994
Flag:	Ukraine
Tel No:	1400266
Fax No:	1400266
Length (ft./m.):	577.4/176.00
Beam (ft./m.):	77.4/23.60
Draft (ft./m.):	26.7/8.16
Propulsion/Propellers:	diesel (15,700kW)/2 (CP)
Decks:	8
Total Crew:	370
Pass. Capacity (basis 2):	574
Pass. Capacity (all berths):	712
Pass. Space Ratio (basis 2):	34.8
Pass. Space Ratio (all berths):	28.1
Officers:	Ukrainian
Total Cabins:	287
Size Range (sq. ft./m.):	n/a
Cabins (outside view):	287
Cabins (inside—no view):	0
Cabins (single occupancy):	0
Cabins (with private balcony):	0
Cabins (wheelchair accessible):	0
Cabin Current:	220 AC
Cabin TV:	No
Dining Rooms:	3
Seatings:	1
Elevators:	3
Casino:	Yes
Slot Machines:	Yes
Swimming Pools (outdoors):	2
Swimming Pools (inside):	1
Whirlpools:	1
Fitness Center:	Yes
Sauna/Steam Room:	Yes/No
Massage:	No
Self-Service Launderette:	Yes
Movie Theater/Seats:	Yes/130
Library:	Yes
Children's Facilities:	Yes
Classification Society:	RS

Ratings	**Score**
Ship: Hardware/Maintenance	46
Ship: Outdoor Facilities/Space	58
Ship: Interior Facilities/Space/Flow	57
Ship: Decor/Furnishings/Artwork	48
Ship: Spa/Fitness Facilities	32
Cabins: Suites and Deluxe	57
Cabins: Standard Sizes	48
Food: Dining Room/Cuisine	56
Food: Informal Dining/Buffets	48
Food: Quality of Ingredients	50
Food: Afternoon Tea/Bar Snacks	41
Service: Dining Room	56
Service: Bars	56
Service: Cabins	58
Service: Open Decks	48
Cruise: Entertainment	47
Cruise: Activities Program	41
Cruise: Movies/Television Programming	40
Cruise: Hospitality Standard	52
Cruise: Overall Product Delivery	55
Overall Score	**994**

Accommodation: Has all-outside cabins that are reasonably comfortable, although the storage space for luggage is limited and drawer space is minimal. Each cabin has private facilities, although there is little space for personal toiletry items, and some of the plumbing is exposed.

There are 10 suites, which, for the size of the ship, are very spacious and are quite tastefully appointed, with plenty of closet and drawer space and large bathrooms.

Dining: The single seating dining room is functional, nothing more, and the decor needs to be upgraded. The food is very basic, yet seemingly adequate for the ship's clientele, but there is little menu choice. Service is attentively provided by attractive Ukrainian waitresses. There is a poor selection of bread rolls, cheeses, and fruits and little in the way of bar snacks.

Other Comments: She is a solidly constructed vessel with nicely rounded lines and a classic profile, with an all-white ice-hardened hull. There is a good open deck and sunbathing space. Has a complete wraparound outdoor promenade deck, but there are no cushioned pads for the deck chairs, and the decks are well worn.

Inside, the ship, which has a number of public rooms, has very plain decor that could do with more tropical greenery to enhance them. The layout is disjointed and signage is quite poor. The ceilings in public areas are also plain and boring. Some refurbishment has upgraded the vessel somewhat and added more color. There is a spacious music salon.

This ship simply is not up to Western standards. The ship was renovated in 1988 and now needs further significant refurbishing. The ship provides a very basic cruise experience at a modest rate, for a mostly French and Italian clientele. Often operates under charter, but there is absolutely no finesse either in service or in hospitality. In 1998 the ship was chartered by the Japanese organization Peace Boat, and undertook a bare-bones around-the-world cruise.

But: A musty (old potatoes) kind of odor permeates throughout the ship. The (fixed) gangway is narrow and can be steep in many ports. It's like something out of the 1950s that has been left to rot.

mv The Azur

☆☆☆

(M)

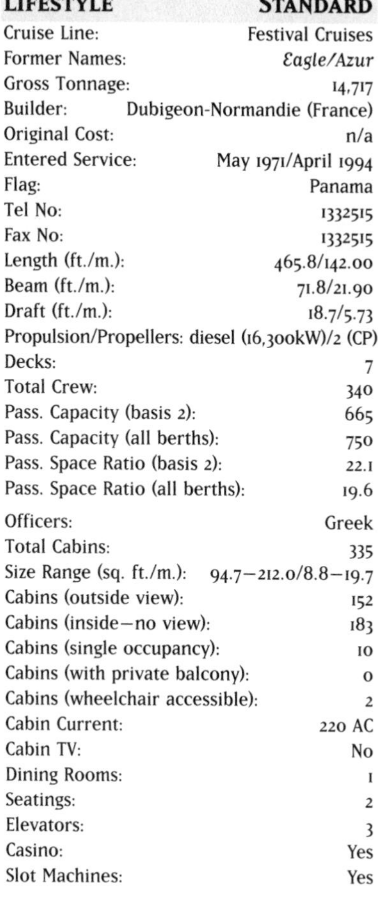

Lifestyle	**Standard**
Cruise Line:	Festival Cruises
Former Names:	*Eagle/Azur*
Gross Tonnage:	14,717
Builder:	Dubigeon-Normandie (France)
Original Cost:	n/a
Entered Service:	May 1971/April 1994
Flag:	Panama
Tel No:	1332515
Fax No:	1332515
Length (ft./m.):	465.8/142.00
Beam (ft./m.):	71.8/21.90
Draft (ft./m.):	18.7/5.73
Propulsion/Propellers:	diesel (16,300kW)/2 (CP)
Decks:	7
Total Crew:	340
Pass. Capacity (basis 2):	665
Pass. Capacity (all berths):	750
Pass. Space Ratio (basis 2):	22.1
Pass. Space Ratio (all berths):	19.6
Officers:	Greek
Total Cabins:	335
Size Range (sq. ft./m.):	94.7–212.0/8.8–19.7
Cabins (outside view):	152
Cabins (inside—no view):	183
Cabins (single occupancy):	10
Cabins (with private balcony):	0
Cabins (wheelchair accessible):	2
Cabin Current:	220 AC
Cabin TV:	No
Dining Rooms:	1
Seatings:	2
Elevators:	3
Casino:	Yes
Slot Machines:	Yes

Swimming Pools (outdoors):	2
Swimming Pools (inside):	0
Whirlpools:	0
Fitness Center:	Yes
Sauna/Steam Room:	No/No
Massage:	No
Self-Service Launderette:	No
Movie Theater/Seats:	Yes/175
Library:	Yes
Children's Facilities:	Yes
Classification Society:	Bureau Veritas

Ratings	**Score**
Ship: Hardware/Maintenance	62
Ship: Outdoor Facilities/Space	54
Ship: Interior Facilities/Space/Flow	53
Ship: Decor/Furnishings/Artwork	54
Ship: Spa/Fitness Facilities	50
Cabins: Suites and Deluxe	62
Cabins: Standard Sizes	52
Food: Dining Room/Cuisine	74
Food: Informal Dining/Buffets	64
Food: Quality of Ingredients	68
Food: Afternoon Tea/Bar Snacks	53
Service: Dining Room	74
Service: Bars	72
Service: Cabins	74
Service: Open Decks	65
Cruise: Entertainment	71
Cruise: Activities Program	60
Cruise: Movies/Television Programming	38
Cruise: Hospitality Standard	70
Cruise: Overall Product Delivery	70
Overall Score	**1,240**

Accommodation: Most of the cabins are quite small, and many of them have upper berths, thus accommodating three or four persons. Most cabins are quite plain, but nicely furnished and decorated in earth tones. All have private bathroom, with tiled floor and shower, with retractable clothesline. Note that there are many inside cabins (there are more inside than outside). These are, naturally, the least expensive, but they have very little storage space. A number of deluxe cabins have a full bathtub/shower combination and plenty of closet, drawer, and under-bed storage space.

There are two outside cabins for the physically challenged, but the ship really cannot be recommended for anyone in a wheelchair, as access to most of it is difficult at best.

The cabin insulation is poor throughout the ship. Features friendly Goanese cabin staff, many of whom formerly worked for the now-defunct Chandris Cruises and Chandris Lines.

Dining: The low-ceilinged dining room is quite charming and has large ocean-view windows on three sides, but the chairs are uncomfortable. The food is actually quite good, and its presentation is attractive, as are the menus. There is a rather limited selection of breads, fruits, and cheeses. Courteous staff and service.

The informal breakfast and lunch buffets are adequate but never seem to look very attractive, the result of a food concession that is used to the repetition and routine of doing things the same way all the time.

Other Comments: This smart though somewhat stubby-looking ship (the first ship for this fairly new cruise line) has a short bow and twin tall funnels set well aft and was originally constructed as a cruise-ferry. There is a reasonable amount of open deck space for sunbathing, although this becomes very tight when the ship is full (which is almost all of the time). There are no cushioned pads for the plastic deck lounge chairs. The two swimming pools (located on different decks, one atop the ship, the other aft) are very small (more like "dip" pools).

Inside, the layout is quite awkward to get used to at first, with many stairways aft that have short, steep steps (typical of her original cruise-ferry construction). There is a reasonable selection of public rooms and several bars, with light, well-chosen, upbeat decor, and the use of many mirrored surfaces. The showroom has extremely poor sight lines and a low ceiling (but it is good for meetings). A two-level cinema (unusual for a ship of this size) is used for movies and lectures. Has lively action in the casino, although the room is out of the main passenger flow. The ship has quite a large amount of indoor space devoted to sports, including an indoor volleyball court.

Festival Cruises (whose owners come from a long line of shipowners) has done an excellent job of creating a totally European product in a short space of time, and garnered a good name for honest, value-for-money cruising.

Festival Cruises, which is known in the U.S. as First European Cruises, provides destination-intensive cruises principally aimed at European passengers. The ship should appeal to the young active set looking for a good first cruise experience to a host of destinations at a reasonable price and with very friendly service and unpretentious, but tasty, food, and a mix of international passengers speaking many different languages.

The ship operates very successfully in several languages for its European passengers and is usually chartered during the winter months to one of the German tour operators who know how well the ship performs. Languages (and announcements) used throughout ship: English, French, German, Italian, Spanish. The currency used aboard is Italian lire.

But: It is difficult to find any quiet space, as music is playing constantly in all public rooms and open spaces (for ambience). Constant announcements in several languages are irritating, but typical of European operations that try to cater to everyone. The poolside towels are small and thin.

tts Topaz

☆☆☆

(L)

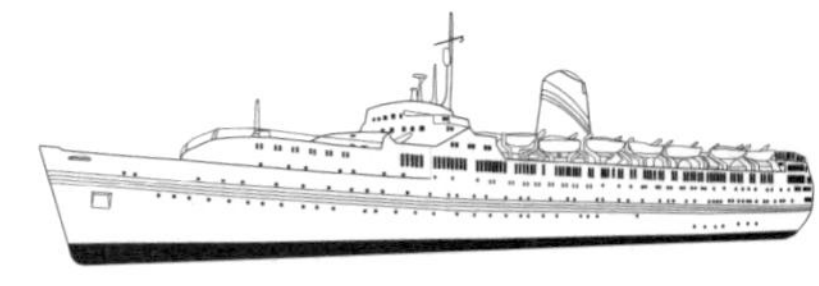

Lifestyle	**Standard**
Cruise Line:	Thomson Cruises
Former Names:	*Olympic/FiestaMarina/ Carnivale/Empress of Britain/ Queen Anna Maria*
Gross Tonnage:	31,500
Builder:	Fairfield Shipbuilding (UK)
Original Cost:	£7.5 million
Entered Service:	April 1956/1994
Flag:	Greece
Tel No:	1132333
Fax No:	1132334
Length (ft./m.):	640.0/195.08
Beam (ft./m.):	87.0/26.51
Draft (ft./m.):	29.0/8.84
Propulsion/Propellers:	steam turbine (22,400kW)/2 (FP)
Decks:	9
Total Crew:	550
Pass. Capacity (basis 2):	976
Pass. Capacity (all berths):	1,386
Pass. Space Ratio (basis 2):	32.2
Pass. Space Ratio (all berths):	22.7
Officers:	Greek
Total Cabins:	488
Size Range (sq. ft./m.):	100.7–301.3/9.36–28.0
Cabins (outside view):	221
Cabins (inside—no view):	267
Cabins (single occupancy):	0
Cabins (with private balcony):	0
Cabins (wheelchair accessible):	0
Cabin Current:	110 AC
Cabin TV:	No
Dining Rooms:	1
Seatings:	2
Elevators:	4
Casino:	Yes
Slot Machines:	Yes
Swimming Pools (outdoors):	2
Swimming Pools (inside):	1
Whirlpools:	1
Fitness Center:	Yes
Sauna/Steam Room:	Yes/No
Massage:	Yes
Self-Service Launderette:	No (has ironing room)
Movie Theater/Seats:	Yes/180
Library:	No
Children's Facilities:	Yes
Classification Society:	Lloyd's Register

Ratings	**Score**
Ship: Hardware/Maintenance	64
Ship: Outdoor Facilities/Space	55
Ship: Interior Facilities/Space/Flow	61
Ship: Decor/Furnishings/Artwork	54
Ship: Spa/Fitness Facilities	45
Cabins: Suites and Deluxe	67
Cabins: Standard Sizes	54
Food: Dining Room/Cuisine	61
Food: Informal Dining/Buffets	52
Food: Quality of Ingredients	58
Food: Afternoon Tea/Bar Snacks	47
Service: Dining Room	64
Service: Bars	61
Service: Cabins	64
Service: Open Decks	52
Cruise: Entertainment	55
Cruise: Activities Program	52
Cruise: Movies/Television Programming	42
Cruise: Hospitality Standard	60
Cruise: Overall Product Delivery	71
Overall Score	**1,139**

Accommodation: There is a big range of cabins and many different configurations (a carry-over from her former days as a transatlantic liner), although they are assigned in only three categories: superior outside, standard outside, and standard inside. Most of them are reasonably spacious, some with rich wood furniture, all of them redecorated recently. Many of the cabins have third and fourth berths, good for families with children. She is an old ship, however, and the cabin bathrooms are small, even in the five "suites." The smallest cabins are very small (particularly the bathrooms). The cabins are not assigned until the day of embarkation, so you cannot choose when you book, except for the grade of cabin you pay for.

Dining: The dining room is large, but crowded and noisy, although it has been quite pleasingly redecorated. The food, be aware, is certainly not for gourmets, being quantity instead of quality. Dining room seating and table assignments are done by the maître d' upon embarkation.

Other Comments: This solidly built former ocean liner has a large funnel amidships and the "sheer" of a real classic fifties ship and has had many lives. The ship has had many refurbishments over the years (she is now over 40 years old, but has been well maintained), and spent a great deal of her former life operated by Carnival Cruise Lines. All of the lifeboats are of the open-air type and could well be updated. Teak outdoor and glass-enclosed indoor promenade decks encircle the ship.

The interior colors are quite stimulating, and the public rooms have rather jazzy decor. The casino is large for a ship that is catering principally to Europeans. Has some delightful original woods and polished brass throughout her public spaces, a large whirlpool has been added, and there is a colorful tiled outdoor deck.

This ship is presently under charter to Thomson Cruises, a British company that provides a good basic cruise vacation in a very casual setting. This could be the right ship for a first cruise, at a very modest price, to some fascinating destinations. Do remember, however, that she is an old lady, and does not have the latest high-tech facilities and features. This ship also features Thomson's first foray into "all-inclusive" pricing, whereby all drinks and wines are included in the cruise fare.

But: The announcements are irritating. Expect some lines (queues in English) for embarkation, disembarkation, buffets, and shore excursions.

ms Triton

☆☆☆

(M)

Lifestyle	**Standard**
Cruise Line:	Royal Olympic Cruises
Former Names:	*Cunard Adventurer/Sunward II*
Gross Tonnage:	14,155
Builder:	Rotterdamsche Dry Dock (Holland)
Original Cost:	n/a
Entered Service:	October 1971/May 1992
Flag:	Greece
Tel No:	1131266
Fax No:	1131266
Length (ft./m.):	491.1/149.70
Beam (ft./m.):	70.5/21.50
Draft (ft./m.):	19.22/5.86
Propulsion/Propellers:	diesel (19,860kW)/2 (CP)
Decks:	7
Total Crew:	265
Pass. Capacity (basis 2):	756
Pass. Capacity (all berths):	945
Pass. Space Ratio (basis 2):	18.7
Pass. Space Ratio (all berths):	14.9
Officers:	Greek
Total Cabins:	378
Size Range (sq. ft./m.):	118–132/11.0–12.2
Cabins (outside view):	236
Cabins (inside–no view):	142
Cabins (single occupancy):	0
Cabins (with private balcony):	0
Cabins (wheelchair accessible):	0
Cabin Current:	110 AC
Cabin TV:	No
Dining Rooms:	1
Seatings:	2
Elevators:	2
Casino:	Yes
Slot Machines:	Yes
Swimming Pools (outdoors):	1
Swimming Pools (inside):	0
Whirlpools:	0
Fitness Center:	Yes
Sauna/Steam Room:	Yes/No
Massage:	Yes
Self-Service Launderette:	No
Movie Theater/Seats:	Yes/96
Library:	No
Children's Facilities:	Yes
Classification Society:	Lloyd's Register

Ratings	**Score**
Ship: Hardware/Maintenance	74
Ship: Outdoor Facilities/Space	65
Ship: Interior Facilities/Space/Flow	71
Ship: Decor/Furnishings/Artwork	72
Ship: Spa/Fitness Facilities	51
Cabins: Suites and Deluxe	62
Cabins: Standard Sizes	56
Food: Dining Room/Cuisine	61
Food: Informal Dining/Buffets	52
Food: Quality of Ingredients	58
Food: Afternoon Tea/Bar Snacks	47
Service: Dining Room	65
Service: Bars	62
Service: Cabins	66
Service: Open Decks	55
Cruise: Entertainment	58
Cruise: Activities Program	53
Cruise: Movies/Television Programming	46
Cruise: Hospitality Standard	59
Cruise: Overall Product Delivery	66
Overall Score	**1,199**

Accommodation: Features cabins (there are eight grades) that are small, but quite well appointed for the size of the ship, although storage space and soundproofing are quite poor. The cabin bathrooms have very small shower units, and little space for personal toiletry items.

Dining: While the dining room is quite attractive and has contemporary colors and ambience, it is also very noisy. The cuisine is continental, which means much use of oils. Choice is adequate, but presentation is inconsistent. Poor bread, rolls, and fruits. The Greek dining room staff provides friendly service, but it is too hurried. Dining room seating and table assignments are done by the maître d' upon embarkation.

Other Comments: This ship, originally built for Cunard/Overseas National Airways for informal cruises, has a handsome, fairly sleek profile, deep clipper bow, and is one of the most contemporary ships in the present Royal Olympic Cruises fleet. The ship has been quite well maintained, although she is now showing her age. There is a wraparound outdoor promenade deck, as well as a decent amount of open deck space for sunbathing and a small "kidney-shaped" swimming pool.

Inside, there is good layout and passenger flow, with ample public rooms and delightful, contemporary decor that is bright, cheerful, and warm, and some interesting regional artwork. Has a good night club with forward observation views. Pity there is no library.

The destination-intensive itineraries (typically from April to November) are excellent for those who want to see many places in a short time, but they are very busy, and there are no days at sea. This is a good ship for short cruises. Triton is a decent ship for short cruises around the Greek islands and Mediterranean.

The dress code is casual (there are no formal nights). Gratuities (suggested at $9 per person per day) are pooled among the crew.

<u>But:</u> This really is a high-density ship with crowded public areas. Expect lines for buffets and shore excursions. There are too many announcements for tours, in many languages, when in ports of call.

ms Tropicale

☆☆☆ +

(L)

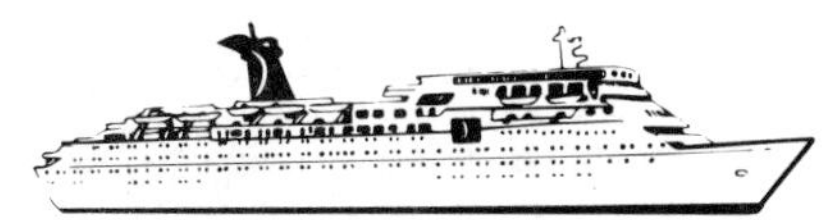

Lifestyle	**Standard**
Cruise Line:	Carnival Cruise Lines
Former Names:	-
Gross Tonnage:	36,674
Builder:	Aalborg Vaerft (Denmark)
Original Cost:	$100 million
Entered Service:	January 1982/Spring 1998
Flag:	Liberia
Tel No:	1240561
Fax No:	1240561
Length (ft./m.):	671.7/204.76
Beam (ft./m.):	86.7/26.45
Draft (ft./m.):	23.3/7.11
Propulsion/Propellers:	diesel (19,566kW)/2 (CP)
Decks:	10
Total Crew:	550
Pass. Capacity (basis 2):	1,022
Pass. Capacity (all berths):	1,400
Pass. Space Ratio (basis 2):	35.8
Pass. Space Ratio (all berths):	26.1
Officers:	Italian
Total Cabins:	511
Size Range (sq. ft./m.):	180/9.2
Cabins (outside view):	324
Cabins (inside—no view):	187
Cabins (single occupancy):	0
Cabins (with private balcony):	12
Cabins (wheelchair accessible):	11
Cabin Current:	110 AC
Cabin TV:	Yes
Dining Rooms:	1
Seatings:	2
Elevators:	8
Casino:	Yes
Slot Machines:	Yes
Swimming Pools (outdoors):	3
Swimming Pools (inside):	0
Whirlpools:	0
Fitness Center:	Yes
Sauna/Steam Room:	Yes/No
Massage:	Yes
Self-Service Launderette:	Yes
Movie Theater/Seats:	No
Library:	Yes
Children's Facilities:	Yes
Classification Society:	Lloyd's Register

Ratings	**Score**
Ship: Hardware/Maintenance	73
Ship: Outdoor Facilities/Space	68
Ship: Interior Facilities/Space/Flow	66
Ship: Decor/Furnishings/Artwork	62
Ship: Spa/Fitness Facilities	56
Cabins: Suites and Deluxe	63
Cabins: Standard Sizes	58
Food: Dining Room/Cuisine	66
Food: Informal Dining/Buffets	62
Food: Quality of Ingredients	62
Food: Afternoon Tea/Bar Snacks	51
Service: Dining Room	67
Service: Bars	70
Service: Cabins	70
Service: Open Decks	61
Cruise: Entertainment	72
Cruise: Activities Program	58
Cruise: Movies/Television Programming	60
Cruise: Hospitality Standard	61
Cruise: Overall Product Delivery	73
Overall Score	**1,279**

Accommodation: Most of the inside and outside cabins are of the standard cookie-cutter variety, with little imaginative decor, and just enough closet and drawer space for passengers to manage for a week.

Dining: The dining room is located on a lower deck. It is colorful, cheerful, brightly lit, but very noisy and cramped, and there are no tables for two. The cuisine is reasonably adequate fare, with emphasis on quantity but not quality (it looks better than it tastes). Service is very hurried and without finesse, but it is quite cheerful. The buffets are nothing special. The wine list is quite decent, although there are no wine waiters.

Other Comments: This ship, the first new build for Carnival Cruise Lines, has a fairly distinctive contemporary look, with a single large, wing-tipped funnel in Carnival's red, white, and blue colors.

The interior design is well laid out, and the ship has good passenger flow. The public rooms are decorated in stimulating colors, designed to make everyone excited and thus head for the casino, where the action is always lively.

Good ship for families with children, as the company goes out of its way to entertain young cruisers as well as their parents.

This ship was operated by Carnival Cruise Lines in the Caribbean for many years (she also offered Alaska cruises during the summer). This is not a luxury cruise product, nor does it pretend to be. But you will have fun, and there are plenty of almost round-the-clock gambling opportunities.

ss Universe Explorer

☆☆☆

(M)

Lifestyle	**Standard**
Cruise Line:	World Explorer Cruises
Former Names:	*Enchanted Seas/ Queen of Bermuda/Canada Star/Liberte/ Island Sun/Volendam/Monarch Sun/Brazil*
Gross Tonnage:	23,879
Builder:	Ingalls Shipbuilding (USA)
Original Cost:	$26 million
Entered Service:	September 1958/ November 1990
Flag:	Bahamas
Tel No:	1131605
Fax No:	1331605
Length (ft./m.):	617.4/188.2
Beam (ft./m.):	84.3/25.7
Draft (ft./m.):	27.2/8.3
Propulsion/Propellers:	steam turbine (19,000kW)/2 (FP)
Decks:	8
Total Crew:	365
Pass. Capacity (basis 2):	740
Pass. Capacity (all berths):	846
Pass. Space Ratio (basis 2):	32.2
Pass. Space Ratio (all berths):	28.2
Officers:	European
Total Cabins:	371
Size Range (sq. ft./m.):	104–293/9.6–27.2
Cabins (outside view):	290
Cabins (inside–no view):	79
Cabins (single occupancy):	2
Cabins (with private balcony):	0
Cabins (wheelchair accessible):	0
Cabin Current:	110 AC
Cabin TV:	Yes
Dining Rooms:	1
Seatings:	2
Elevators:	3
Casino:	Yes
Slot Machines:	Yes
Swimming Pools (outdoors):	2
Swimming Pools (inside):	0
Whirlpools:	0
Fitness Center:	Yes
Sauna/Steam Room:	No/No
Massage:	Yes
Self-Service Launderette:	No
Movie Theater/Seats:	Yes/200
Library:	Yes
Children's Facilities:	Yes
Classification Society:	American Bureau of Shipping

Ratings	**Score**
Ship: Hardware/Maintenance	60
Ship: Outdoor Facilities/Space	62
Ship: Interior Facilities/Space/Flow	61
Ship: Decor/Furnishings/Artwork	54
Ship: Spa/Fitness Facilities	42
Cabins: Suites and Deluxe	57
Cabins: Standard Sizes	54
Food: Dining Room/Cuisine	63
Food: Informal Dining/Buffets	55
Food: Quality of Ingredients	58
Food: Afternoon Tea/Bar Snacks	50
Service: Dining Room	67
Service: Bars	65
Service: Cabins	67
Service: Open Decks	59
Cruise: Entertainment	59
Cruise: Activities Program	53
Cruise: Movies/Television Programming	50
Cruise: Hospitality Standard	60
Cruise: Overall Product Delivery	63
Overall Score	**1,159**

Accommodation: The cabins, of which there are many different sizes and configurations, are of a generous size, with heavy-duty furniture and fittings and a good amount of closet and drawer space. The bathrooms are old fashioned, and a bit utilitarian, but practical.

Dining: Has a dining room that is quite charming and warm and that has large windows that provide plenty of light and a nice ambience. The menu choice is somewhat limited, but service is attentive and comes with a smile, even if it is without finesse. Limited selection of bread rolls, cheeses (very standard processed items), and fruits.

Other Comments: Classic 1960s traditional ocean liner profile. Extensively refurbished. Beautifully finished outdoor teakwood decks. Being an older ship, she has spacious outdoor promenade areas for walking.

Inside, the public rooms are quite spacious and well appointed, with high ceilings, pleasing decor, and colors that do not jar the senses. The showroom is quite good, but cannot compare with those on larger, more modern ships, and the sight lines are poor. Has a large casino. There is plenty of sheltered and open sunbathing space.

This ship will provide you with an enjoyable cruise experience in comfortable surroundings reminiscent of old-world style. Now under long-term charter to World Explorer Cruises, renamed *Universe Explorer* at the press time. The ship offers a mixture of Alaska cruises in the summer, with cruises to the Western Caribbean and Yucatan Peninsula in the winter, as well as a world cruise under the "Semester at Sea" banner.

ms Veendam

☆☆☆☆ +

(L)

Lifestyle	**Premium**
Cruise Line:	Holland America Line
Former Names:	-
Gross Tonnage:	55,451
Builder:	Fincantieri (Italy)
Original Cost:	$215 million
Entered Service:	May 1996
Flag:	Bahamas
Tel No:	330943511
Fax No:	330943512
Length (ft./m.):	719.3/219.3
Beam (ft./m.):	101.0/30.8
Draft (ft./m.):	24.6/7.5
Propulsion/Propellers:	diesel-electric (34,560kW)/2 (CP)
Decks:	10
Total Crew:	588
Pass. Capacity (basis 2):	1,266
Pass. Capacity (all berths):	1,627
Pass. Space Ratio (basis 2):	43.8
Pass. Space Ratio (all berths):	34.0
Officers:	Dutch
Total Cabins:	633
Size Range (sq. ft./m.):	187–1,126/17.3–104.5
Cabins (outside view):	502
Cabins (inside—no view):	131
Cabins (single occupancy):	0
Cabins (with private balcony):	150
Cabins (wheelchair accessible):	6
Cabin Current:	110/220 AC
Cabin TV:	Yes
Dining Rooms:	1
Seatings:	2
Elevators:	12
Casino:	Yes
Slot Machines:	Yes
Swimming Pools (outdoors):	1
Swimming Pools (inside):	1 (magrodome)
Whirlpools:	2
Fitness Center:	Yes
Sauna/Steam Room:	Yes/No
Massage:	Yes
Self-Service Launderette:	Yes
Movie Theater/Seats:	Yes/249
Library:	Yes
Children's Facilities:	No
Classification Society:	Lloyd's Register

Ratings	**Score**
Ship: Hardware/Maintenance	87
Ship: Outdoor Facilities/Space	82
Ship: Interior Facilities/Space/Flow	86
Ship: Decor/Furnishings/Artwork	86
Ship: Spa/Fitness Facilities	78
Cabins: Suites and Deluxe	83
Cabins: Standard Sizes	79
Food: Dining Room/Cuisine	77
Food: Informal Dining/Buffets	74
Food: Quality of Ingredients	72
Food: Afternoon Tea/Bar Snacks	65
Service: Dining Room	76
Service: Bars	77
Service: Cabins	76
Service: Open Decks	71
Cruise: Entertainment	77
Cruise: Activities Program	76
Cruise: Movies/Television Programming	76
Cruise: Hospitality Standard	76
Cruise: Overall Product Delivery	82
Overall Score	**1,556**

Accommodation: There is a wide range of cabins and suites to choose from, many of which have private balconies (most also have floor-to-ceiling windows, while others have large picture windows). Most cabins use their space well, are tastefully decorated, and also quite well laid out. However, although drawer space is generally good, closet space is very tight, particularly for long cruises. The bathrooms are good, but bathtubs are small units best described as shower tubs.

Dining: The two-deck-high dining room (located at the stern) has a dramatic grand staircase (the lower level has windows on three sides) and is an elegant setting. There are tables for two, four, six, and eight, but as in most large dining rooms, the noise level can be high at times, particularly for those passengers seated adjacent to the waiter stations. There are two seatings for dinner, and an open seating for breakfast and lunch. A total of 28 suites feature an in-suite dining alternative for those who want a change from the noise and business of the main dining room.

There is also an extensive, dual-line Lido Buffet (one side is smoking, the other nonsmoking). The beverage station, however, lets it down, for it is no better than those found in family outlets ashore in the United States.

The food and service are typical of HAL standards of late, which means nonmemorable, but both presentation and cuisine were seen to be improving last year.

Other Comments: She is a well-built ship, and the fourth in the Statendam class. Has a somewhat bold and forthright exterior appearance, but inside the decor, color coordination, and soft furnishings have all evolved since the first ship in the series (*Statendam*).

It is very good to see that the outside decks have lots of teakwood decking and no sign of astroturf anywhere. A magrodome roof covers an indoor-outdoor pool and central Lido area, with a sculpture as the focal point.

Inside the ship, there is good passenger flow throughout the main entertainment deck, and there are plenty of nooks and crannies that are located off a winding passageway. The library is quite lovely and has an extensive range of reference books. What is outstanding and very noticeable is the array of artworks throughout the ship, assembled to represent the fine Dutch heritage of Holland America Line and to present a balance between standard itineraries and onboard creature comforts. The two-deck-high showroom is a good room, but the ceiling is low and sight lines are not good from the upper level, although there is some improvement compared to *Maasdam*, *Ryndam*, and *Statendam*.

The ship continues the company's strong maritime traditions, but the food and dining room service are still somewhat disappointing, although improvements are being made (one must remember that the cruise prices, however, are very modest). Where Holland America Line scores with passengers is in the friendly attitude and smiling faces of the Filipino and Indonesian service staff. Unlike many others, the line does not add an automatic 15 percent for beverage purchases.

But: The cabin service, by Indonesian stewards, is generally good, but is spotty and inconsistent, and communication can prove frustrating. The $1.50 charge for washing machines in the self-service launderette is petty.

mv Victoria

☆☆☆ +

(M)

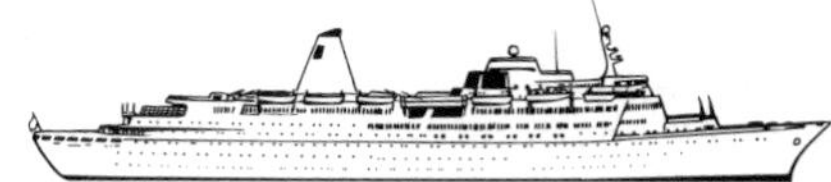

LIFESTYLE	**PREMIUM**
Cruise Line:	P&O Cruises
Former Names:	*Sea Princess/Kungsholm*
Gross Tonnage:	27,670
Builder:	John Brown & Co. (UK)
Original Cost:	$22 million
Entered Service:	April 1966/February 1979
Flag:	Great Britain
Tel No:	1440320
Fax No:	1440320
Length (ft./m.):	660.2/201.23
Beam (ft./m.):	87.1/26.57
Draft (ft./m.):	28.0/8.56
Propulsion/Propellers:	diesel (18,800kW)/2 (CP)
Decks:	8
Total Crew:	417
Pass. Capacity (basis 2):	726
Pass. Capacity (all berths):	778
Pass. Space Ratio (basis 2):	38.1
Pass. Space Ratio (all berths):	35.5
Officers:	British
Total Cabins:	370
Size Range (sq. ft./m.):	138–467/12.8–43.3
Cabins (outside view):	286
Cabins (inside–no view):	84
Cabins (single occupancy):	14
Cabins (with private balcony):	0
Cabins (wheelchair accessible):	10
Cabin Current:	220 AC
Cabin TV:	Yes (higher grade cabins only)
Dining Rooms:	1
Seatings:	2
Elevators:	4
Casino:	Yes
Slot Machines:	Yes
Swimming Pools (outdoors):	2
Swimming Pools (inside):	1
Whirlpools:	1
Fitness Center:	Yes
Sauna/Steam Room:	Yes/No
Massage:	Yes
Self-Service Launderette:	Yes
Movie Theater/Seats:	Yes/289
Library:	Yes
Children's Facilities:	Yes
Classification Society:	Lloyd's Register

RATINGS	**SCORE**
Ship: Hardware/Maintenance	76
Ship: Outdoor Facilities/Space	75
Ship: Interior Facilities/Space/Flow	76
Ship: Decor/Furnishings/Artwork	77
Ship: Spa/Fitness Facilities	67
Cabins: Suites and Deluxe	76
Cabins: Standard Sizes	72
Food: Dining Room/Cuisine	74
Food: Informal Dining/Buffets	66
Food: Quality of Ingredients	67
Food: Afternoon Tea/Bar Snacks	65
Service: Dining Room	67
Service: Bars	66
Service: Cabins	67
Service: Open Decks	65
Cruise: Entertainment	68
Cruise: Activities Program	64
Cruise: Movies/Television Programming	63
Cruise: Hospitality Standard	71
Cruise: Overall Product Delivery	73
OVERALL SCORE	**1,395**

Accommodation: There is a wide range of cabins to choose from, including 6 suites. Most of them are quite roomy, and many of them feature some fine wood-paneled walls, and most have been nicely refurbished over the years. In the latest refurbishment, all new soft furnishings were changed, televisions replaced, and bathrooms revamped.

Most cabins have excellent closet and drawer space, and fine wood-paneled walls. Generous-sized bathrooms have solid fixtures and storage space for toiletries. Some cabins have upper and lower berths. The bathroom towels are small, however.

Dining: The tiered European-style dining room is quite elegant, with old-world traditions and charm, and display of eighteenth-century Chinese porcelain (has some nice etched glass panels with nautical themes). There are tables for two, four, six, and eight (more tables for two were added during the 1997 refurbishment). Good general food and selection that is tailored for British tastes and excellent service from the Goanese staff. Buffets are very basic and disappointing in both display and food quality, as is the selection of breads and fruits. The wine list, also, is quite limited.

The casual outdoor Lido Buffet was remodeled in the last refit and now is less congested owing to a redesign of the area, more temperature-controlled display space, and better serving lines. However, the plastic chairs at the Lido Buffet should at least have cushions.

Other Comments: This solidly built ex-ocean liner (originally built for the now-defunct Swedish America Line) has flowing, rounded lines and a well-balanced profile, with that "sheer" that makes her look like a "real" ship. She has been nicely refurbished and well maintained since becoming a P&O Cruises ship in the late seventies. The open deck and sunbathing space is good.

Inside, there are numerous spacious public rooms trimmed with fine woods and with fine furnishings and fabrics. One nice feature is an indoor (sea water) swimming pool, together with the usual associated saunas and gymnasium.

There is always a good variety of entertainment aboard the ships of P&O Cruises, as well as fine program of special theme cruises (antiques, The Archers, art appreciation, classical music, comedy, cricket, gardening, jazz, motoring, popular fiction, Scottish dance, and sequence dancing were among the themes in 1998); check with your travel agent to see what is available at the time you want to take your cruise.

This ship will provide an enjoyable, very traditional, and conservative British cruise experience, but with thirty years afloat she does look a little worn in places, although she underwent a $9-million refurbishment in late 1997. Port taxes and insurance are included for British passengers.

ms Viking Serenade

☆☆☆ +

(L)

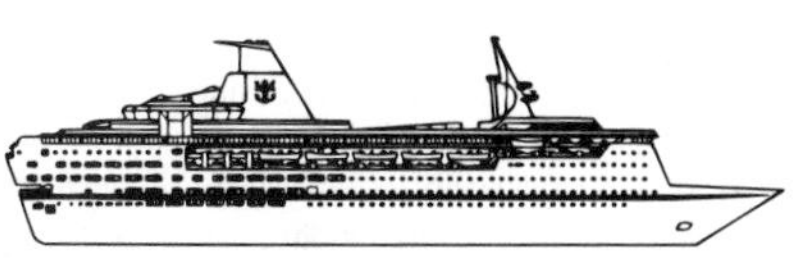

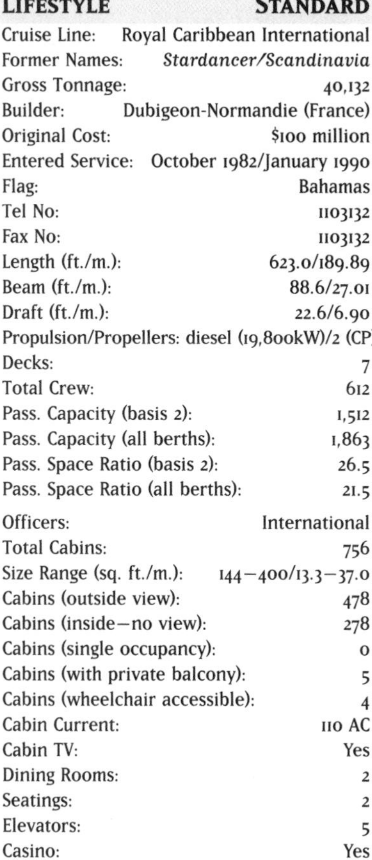

LIFESTYLE	STANDARD
Cruise Line:	Royal Caribbean International
Former Names:	*Stardancer/Scandinavia*
Gross Tonnage:	40,132
Builder:	Dubigeon-Normandie (France)
Original Cost:	$100 million
Entered Service:	October 1982/January 1990
Flag:	Bahamas
Tel No:	1103132
Fax No:	1103132
Length (ft./m.):	623.0/189.89
Beam (ft./m.):	88.6/27.01
Draft (ft./m.):	22.6/6.90
Propulsion/Propellers:	diesel (19,800kW)/2 (CP)
Decks:	7
Total Crew:	612
Pass. Capacity (basis 2):	1,512
Pass. Capacity (all berths):	1,863
Pass. Space Ratio (basis 2):	26.5
Pass. Space Ratio (all berths):	21.5
Officers:	International
Total Cabins:	756
Size Range (sq. ft./m.):	144–400/13.3–37.0
Cabins (outside view):	478
Cabins (inside–no view):	278
Cabins (single occupancy):	0
Cabins (with private balcony):	5
Cabins (wheelchair accessible):	4
Cabin Current:	110 AC
Cabin TV:	Yes
Dining Rooms:	2
Seatings:	2
Elevators:	5
Casino:	Yes
Slot Machines:	Yes
Swimming Pools (outdoors):	1 (magrodome)
Swimming Pools (inside):	0
Whirlpools:	0
Fitness Center:	Yes
Sauna/Steam Room:	Yes/No
Massage:	Yes
Self-Service Launderette:	No
Movie Theater/Seats:	No
Library:	Yes
Children's Facilities:	Yes
Classification Society:	Det Norske Veritas

RATINGS	SCORE
Ship: Hardware/Maintenance	71
Ship: Outdoor Facilities/Space	62
Ship: Interior Facilities/Space/Flow	65
Ship: Decor/Furnishings/Artwork	66
Ship: Spa/Fitness Facilities	75
Cabins: Suites and Deluxe	71
Cabins: Standard Sizes	60
Food: Dining Room/Cuisine	71
Food: Informal Dining/Buffets	63
Food: Quality of Ingredients	66
Food: Afternoon Tea/Bar Snacks	52
Service: Dining Room	74
Service: Bars	73
Service: Cabins	74
Service: Open Decks	65
Cruise: Entertainment	74
Cruise: Activities Program	70
Cruise: Movies/Television Programming	71
Cruise: Hospitality Standard	65
Cruise: Overall Product Delivery	73
OVERALL SCORE	**1,361**

Accommodation: The small, rather compact cabins are quite well appointed and have reasonable closet space for short cruises. There are too many inside cabins and drawer space is poor. The cabin bathrooms are tiny, so you should expect to dance with the shower curtain, particularly if you have a larger-than-average-sized body.

Dining: There are two large dining rooms that are quite attractive and well laid out (romantic passengers should note that there are no tables for two, however). Typical standard hotel banquet food, perfectly portioned, with rather robotic presentation. Poor bread rolls and fruits, but what is really disappointing is the fact that there is little taste in the food.

Other Comments: This ship has a good amount of open deck and sunbathing space, and there is a magrodome-covered pool for use in inclement weather.

Inside, there is a wide array of public rooms and facilities, including a conference center and the Viking Crown Lounge cantilevered around the funnel. Public rooms have contemporary decor, tasteful colors, and good quality furnishings. Fine health spa facilities. Attentive service from Caribbean staff. This ship should provide a decent short cruise experience for families with children.

The ship underwent a $75-million reconstruction in 1991. Provides a well-programmed cruise experience in upbeat surroundings. Has operated from Los Angeles to Mexico for several years.

But: There are too many loud, irritating announcements, and the passenger participation events tend to be quite juvenile.

ms Vision of the Seas

☆☆☆☆

(L)

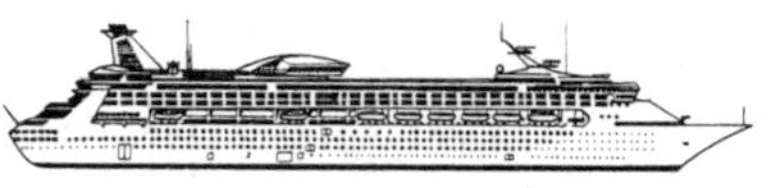

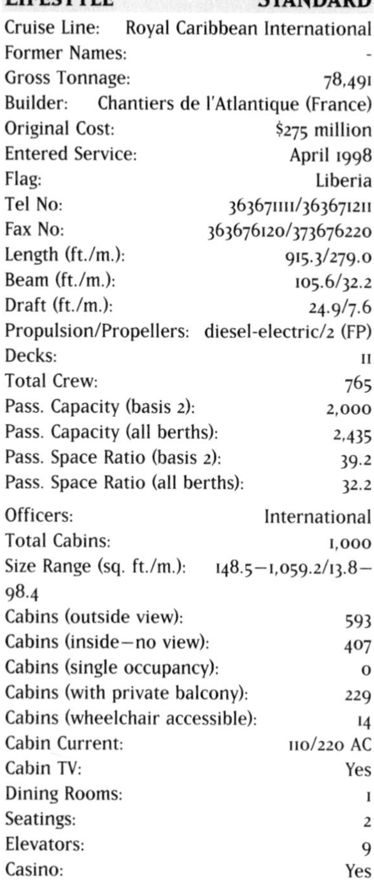

LIFESTYLE	STANDARD
Cruise Line:	Royal Caribbean International
Former Names:	-
Gross Tonnage:	78,491
Builder:	Chantiers de l'Atlantique (France)
Original Cost:	$275 million
Entered Service:	April 1998
Flag:	Liberia
Tel No:	363671111/363671211
Fax No:	363676120/373676220
Length (ft./m.):	915.3/279.0
Beam (ft./m.):	105.6/32.2
Draft (ft./m.):	24.9/7.6
Propulsion/Propellers:	diesel-electric/2 (FP)
Decks:	11
Total Crew:	765
Pass. Capacity (basis 2):	2,000
Pass. Capacity (all berths):	2,435
Pass. Space Ratio (basis 2):	39.2
Pass. Space Ratio (all berths):	32.2
Officers:	International
Total Cabins:	1,000
Size Range (sq. ft./m.):	148.5–1,059.2/13.8–98.4
Cabins (outside view):	593
Cabins (inside—no view):	407
Cabins (single occupancy):	0
Cabins (with private balcony):	229
Cabins (wheelchair accessible):	14
Cabin Current:	110/220 AC
Cabin TV:	Yes
Dining Rooms:	1
Seatings:	2
Elevators:	9
Casino:	Yes
Slot Machines:	Yes
Swimming Pools (outdoors):	1
Swimming Pools (inside):	1 (inside/outside)
Whirlpools:	6
Fitness Center:	Yes
Sauna/Steam Room:	Yes/Yes
Massage:	Yes
Self-Service Launderette:	No
Movie Theater/Seats:	No
Library:	Yes
Children's Facilities:	Yes
Classification Society:	Det Norske Veritas

RATINGS	SCORE
Ship: Hardware/Maintenance	90
Ship: Outdoor Facilities/Space	86
Ship: Interior Facilities/Space/Flow	88
Ship: Decor/Furnishings/Artwork	88
Ship: Spa/Fitness Facilities	88
Cabins: Suites and Deluxe	88
Cabins: Standard Sizes	81
Food: Dining Room/Cuisine	71
Food: Informal Dining/Buffets	63
Food: Quality of Ingredients	66
Food: Afternoon Tea/Bar Snacks	52
Service: Dining Room	78
Service: Bars	76
Service: Cabins	77
Service: Open Decks	71
Cruise: Entertainment	81
Cruise: Activities Program	76
Cruise: Movies/Television Programming	76
Cruise: Hospitality Standard	73
Cruise: Overall Product Delivery	78
OVERALL SCORE	**1,547**

Accommodation: The accommodation ranges from large suites, each of which has its own private balcony, to standard inside and outside cabins. All are quite tastefully furnished and come equipped with all the necessary amenities needed for a one-week cruise. The company provides colorful soft furnishings that make one's home away from home look like the inside of a modern Scandinavian hotel—minimalist, yet colorful.

Choose a "C" grade suite if you want spacious accommodation that includes a separate (curtained off) sleeping area, good-sized outside balcony (with part, not full, partition), lounge with sofa, two chairs, and coffee table; three closets, plenty of drawer and storage space; VCR unit; large bathroom with full-size bathtub, integral shower, and two washbasins/two toiletries cabinets.

All other standard inside and outside cabins have colorful soft furnishings, twin beds convert to a queen-sized bed, sofa, coffee table, vanity desk unit with drawers and cupboards, and television on swivel base so that it can be seen from both bed and sitting area (sofa). The bathroom is small, but has a toilet, shower cubicle, and sink, but no toiletries cabinet.

Dining: The dining room is set on two levels with large ocean-view picture windows on two sides (rectangular windows on the upper level, large circular windows on the lower level), and a large connecting stairway and is nonsmoking. RCI's standard of dining room food and service has always been consistent in presentation, although the food generally has little taste, the result of controlled food costs as well as the use of many mixes and preprepared items. Whilst most passengers seem to enjoy it, it has become very standard, nonmemorable fare, and really needs more attention and creativity. Vegetarian dishes are available for lunch and dinner. The wine list features only standard wines, none of any decent vintage.

The Windjammer Café is the ship's informal dining spot and offers more choice for for those who enjoy casual meals in a contemporary setting, with attractive colors and decor and large ocean-view windows that provide plenty of light. However, only the basics are available at the beverage stations.

Other Comments: This striking ship, sixth in the Vision-class of vessels, shares design features that make all Royal Caribbean International ships identifiable, including a Viking Crown Lounge (which is also the ship's disco). Aboard this ship (and sister ship *Rhapsody of the Seas*, which debuted in 1998) the Viking Crown Lounge is located just forward of the center of the ship, with the funnel located well aft, a departure from all other RCI ships to date. The ship's stern is beautifully rounded. There is a reasonable amount of open-air walking space, although this can become cluttered with deck lounge chairs (which do not have cushioned pads).

Inside, the ship provides the latest incarnation of RCI's interpretation of a floating contemporary hotel, and presents the nicest mix of colors and decor of any of the Vision-class ships, with lots of warm beige and pink tones (particularly in the expansive atrium).

The artwork (which cost $6 million) is plentiful, colorful, and very creative (much seems to have been inspired by that aboard Galaxy, which belongs to sister company Celebrity Cruises), with more previously blank wall space covered with interesting artworks of differing shapes and sizes. Most noticeable is the extensive use of glass (two beautiful glass sculptures stand out—one in the atrium (at the entrance to a Champagne Bar) and one on the upper level of the Viking Crown Lounge). There are plenty of public rooms, bars, and lounges to play in, as well as a large, well-lit casino.

The spa, with its solarium and indoor/outdoor dome-covered pool, Inca- and Mayan-theme decor, sauna/steam rooms, and gymnasium, provides a haven for the health-conscious and fitness buff (although there is a pizza bar forward of the pool area). There is a lovely "Mayan Serpent" sculpture in the solarium.

The Viking Crown Lounge is a multilevel night spot (the music can be loud and overbearing, however, and so can cigarette smoke around the bar, one of few places where smokers can light up). Perhaps the best atmosphere can be found in the nautical-theme Schooner Bar. The Library features an excellent array of hardback books, as well as a neat wooden sculpture of something that looks like the Tin Man (from The Wizard of Oz).

The entertainment throughout is upbeat (in fact, it is difficult to get away from music and noise), but is typical of the kind of resort hotel found ashore in Las Vegas. There is even background music in all corridors and elevators and constant music outdoors on the pool deck. If you want a quiet relaxing vacation, this is the wrong ship. If you enjoy big-city life, with a fine array of sounds and entertainment around you, this could be just right.

But: The staff is mildly accommodating, and only a small percentage say hello when passing you in the corridors (including officers). In other words, the hospitality factor is below average. The elevators talk to you ("going up/going down" is informative, but monotonous, although the illuminated picture displays of decks is good).

ms Vistafjord

☆☆☆☆ +

(M)

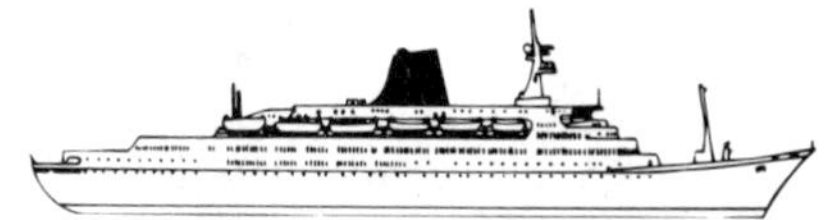

LIFESTYLE	**LUXURY**
Cruise Line:	Cunard Line
Former Names:	-
Gross Tonnage:	24,492
Builder:	Swan, Hunter (UK)
Original Cost:	$35 million
Entered Service:	May 1973/May 1984
Flag:	Bahamas
Tel No:	1104114
Fax No:	1305630
Length (ft./m.):	626.9/191.09
Beam (ft./m.):	82.1/25.05
Draft (ft./m.):	27.0/8.23
Propulsion/Propellers:	diesel (17,900kW)/2 (FP)
Decks:	9
Total Crew:	400
Pass. Capacity (basis 2):	677
Pass. Capacity (all berths):	732
Pass. Space Ratio (basis 2):	36.1
Pass. Space Ratio (all berths):	33.4
Officers:	European/Norwegian
Total Cabins:	376
Size Range (sq. ft./m.):	67–872.0/6.2–81.0
Cabins (outside view):	324
Cabins (inside–no view):	52
Cabins (single occupancy):	73
Cabins (with private balcony):	25
Cabins (wheelchair accessible):	4
Cabin Current:	110 AC
Cabin TV:	Yes
Dining Rooms:	1
Seatings:	1
Elevators:	6
Casino:	Yes
Slot Machines:	Yes
Swimming Pools (outdoors):	1
Swimming Pools (inside):	1
Whirlpools:	2
Fitness Center:	Yes
Sauna/Steam Room:	Yes/No
Massage:	Yes
Self-Service Launderette:	Yes
Movie Theater/Seats:	Yes/190
Library:	Yes
Children's Facilities:	No
Classification Society:	Lloyd's Register

RATINGS	**SCORE**
Ship: Hardware/Maintenance	86
Ship: Outdoor Facilities/Space	86
Ship: Interior Facilities/Space/Flow	85
Ship: Decor/Furnishings/Artwork	86
Ship: Spa/Fitness Facilities	81
Cabins: Suites and Deluxe	93
Cabins: Standard Sizes	84
Food: Dining Room/Cuisine	89
Food: Informal Dining/Buffets	86
Food: Quality of Ingredients	86
Food: Afternoon Tea/Bar Snacks	85
Service: Dining Room	86
Service: Bars	86
Service: Cabins	86
Service: Open Decks	81
Cruise: Entertainment	82
Cruise: Activities Program	78
Cruise: Movies/Television Programming	81
Cruise: Hospitality Standard	84
Cruise: Overall Product Delivery	86
OVERALL SCORE	**1,697**

Accommodation: The suites with private balconies are superbly equipped, and have ample space. All cabins are extremely well appointed and tastefully redecorated (all cabins had new bathrooms installed in the 1994 refit), and all feature a refrigerator, minibar, personal safe, and European duvets (in two thicknesses). All the wooden furniture has rounded edges.

All cabins also have excellent closet and drawer space (illuminated closets), VCR unit, and bathrooms feature whisper-quiet (nonvacuum) toilets. There is also an excellent range of cabins for single travelers. Thick cotton bathrobes are provided for all passengers. Some Sun Deck and Promenade Deck suites have obstructed views.

Really outstanding are two duplex apartments—the lower level contains a large bedroom and bathroom with Jacuzzi bathtub; the upper level has an expansive living room, with Bang & Olufsen sound system, treadmill, private bar, another bathroom (with Jacuzzi bathtub), and separate private sauna, while outdoors is a large private balcony with two-person whirlpool.

Dining: The dining room is a grand, elegant room, recently expanded, for single-seating dining. There are tables for two, four, six, or eight (there are more tables for two in the dining room than in any other cruise ship afloat). This is because the company has recognized that a great number of its passengers are single and enjoy traveling alone.

Senior officers host tables for dinner each evening. A main feature is single-waiter service in the best European tradition. The tables are a little close together, making it somewhat difficult for waiters to serve in some areas.

Features international cuisine offering the highest quality and variety of ingredients (there is an excellent variety of breads and cheeses at every meal, which are particularly liked by the ship's 40 percent German-speaking clientele). At all dining room meals, a cold table is set for such things as breads and cheeses at lunch time, and passengers can either help themselves or be served by a waiter. Salad items, salad dressings (ten varieties), juices (nine varieties), and cheeses (a fine selection of more than forty international cheeses) are always set on the cold table.

Plate service is the standard procedure (where vegetables and entrees are set artistically on the main course plate). Extra vegetables can be obtained at any time. This is European-style service in the classic seagoing tradition. Waiters are well trained through a good on-board management structure.

Table-side flambeaus cannot be done at individual tables, but they are done in several central locations, and the waiters collect the finished product to take to their respective tables.

Although the chef has his favorites, the menus are not repeated, even on the longest voyages. Also, one of the good points about this and other ships in her class is that, while the menus are extremely creative, you can order "off-menu" at any time and create your own delightful cuisine. Little touches in presentation, such as paper doilies under teacups, soup bowls, and towel-wrapped water jugs, make a difference in product delivery.

Apart from the regular menu (several appetizers, three soups, sorbet, five entrees, two salads, several desserts, and a superb selection of international cheeses at every dinner meal), there is always a Cunard Spa menu, a vegetarian menu, as well as diabetic desserts every day.

Different color tablecloths and napkins are featured daily for luncheon and dinner. There is an outstanding, extensive wine list, with prices ranging from $13 to almost $400. Cappuccino and espresso coffees are available at any time in the dining room (or at the Lido Deck Café), without charge. There is an excellent selection of breads, fruits, and cheeses.

Tivoli, a completely separate 40-seat Italian à la carte restaurant (an alternative dining spot added in the ship's 1994 refit) is intimate and elegant, and the food is quite outstanding, from a varied menu that features many special dishes daily. It has the feel of a small, exclusive bistro.

The Lido Deck Café is an informal dining area that is extremely popular for a wide range of theme buffets, as well as for breakfast and lunch. Each day, different foods and themed buffets are presented,

Other Comments: This ship has classic liner styling and profile, and looks like a ship. She is a finely proportioned vessel with beautiful, rounded, flowing lines and a sleek profile (with midships funnel) from any angle. Grandly refurbished in late 1994, she has been well maintained and is kept very clean. At sea she is stable, smooth, and quiet as a swan.

Has expansive open decks and ample sunbathing space. Built with fine quality materials throughout. Features a teakwood outdoor wraparound promenade deck, and deck lounge chairs have cushioned pads. Ship's bell sounded at noon in fine maritime tradition.

Inside, the spacious and elegant public rooms have high ceilings. Has tasteful decor throughout, improved in her latest refit. Real ballroom/show lounge has a fine, large, wooden dance floor, and big band for real ballroom dancing. Features excellent European and Filipino stewardesses. Conservative, sophisticated, classically-oriented entertainment. Has wide interior stairwells. There are refreshingly few announcements and interruptions. Operates in two languages, English and German.

This ship caters especially well to discerning passengers in an elegant, refined, yet friendly style and very comfortable surroundings for adults (children do not fit, nor are there any facilities for them). Although not shiny and new, she has been well refurbished and now provides one of the world's most pleasant and civilized travel experiences (all gratuities are included).

Few international long-distance ships can compete with *Vistafjord* for her ambience and fine-tuned service from a well-organized and happy crew, most of whom speak German. With a mix of about 40 percent German-speaking and 60 percent English-speaking passengers, this is a fine ship for those that want to mingle in a more international setting.

ms Vistamar

☆☆☆ +

(S)

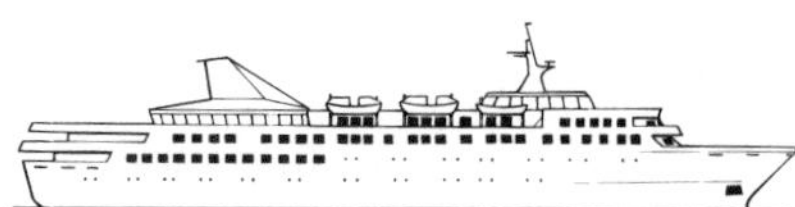

Lifestyle	Standard
Cruise Line:	Plantours
Former Names:	-
Gross Tonnage:	7,478
Builder:	Union Navale de Levante (Spain)
Original Cost:	$45 million
Entered Service:	September 1989
Flag:	Liberia
Tel No:	1332275
Fax No:	1332275
Length (ft./m.):	385.1/117.40
Beam (ft./m.):	55.1/16.82
Draft (ft./m.):	14.9/4.55
Propulsion/Propellers:	diesel (3,900kW)/2 (CP)
Decks:	6
Total Crew:	100
Pass. Capacity (basis 2):	295
Pass. Capacity (all berths):	340
Pass. Space Ratio (basis 2):	25.3
Pass. Space Ratio (all berths):	21.9
Officers:	Spanish
Total Cabins:	150
Size Range (sq. ft./m.):	129.1–150.6/12.0-14.0
Cabins (outside view):	126
Cabins (inside–no view):	24
Cabins (single occupancy):	5
Cabins (with private balcony):	0
Cabins (wheelchair accessible):	0
Cabin Current:	220 AC
Cabin TV:	Yes
Dining Rooms:	1
Seatings:	1
Elevators:	3
Casino:	No
Slot Machines:	Yes
Swimming Pools (outdoors):	1
Swimming Pools (inside):	0
Whirlpools:	0
Fitness Center:	Yes
Sauna/Steam Room:	Yes/No
Massage:	Yes
Self-Service Launderette:	No
Movie Theater/Seats:	No
Library:	Yes
Children's Facilities:	No
Classification Society:	Det Norske Veritas

Ratings	Score
Ship: Hardware/Maintenance	76
Ship: Outdoor Facilities/Space	75
Ship: Interior Facilities/Space/Flow	76
Ship: Decor/Furnishings/Artwork	75
Ship: Spa/Fitness Facilities	62
Cabins: Suites and Deluxe	77
Cabins: Standard Sizes	71
Food: Dining Room/Cuisine	76
Food: Informal Dining/Buffets	71
Food: Quality of Ingredients	65
Food: Afternoon Tea/Bar Snacks	61
Service: Dining Room	71
Service: Bars	72
Service: Cabins	73
Service: Open Decks	66
Cruise: Entertainment	66
Cruise: Activities Program	61
Cruise: Movies/Television Programming	60
Cruise: Hospitality Standard	63
Cruise: Overall Product Delivery	75
Overall Score	**1,392**

Accommodation: The passenger accommodation areas are forward, while public rooms are located aft, which means there is a minimal amount of noise in the cabins. The cabins are extremely comfortable and come well equipped, although bathrooms are small, and both closet and drawer space is limited.

Dining: The dining is charming, with warm contemporary colors and decor. The food is moderate, but the selection of breads, cheeses, and fruits is limited.

Other Comments: Has a small, rather smart but squat ship profile. The tiny "dip" swimming pool is almost useless.

Inside, there is a single central staircase. Wood-trimmed interior decor, which is attractive and warm, but mirrored metallic ceilings are irritating. Outdoor pool has splash surround and neat water fountain. A jazzy night club/disco, with acres of glass, is set around the funnel base. Four-deck-high atrium with "sky dome" has a glass-walled elevator and wraparound staircase.

This ship has been chartered principally by Plantours for German-speaking passengers since 1991. In late 1996, all suites were refurbished and all cabin bathrooms updated somewhat.

ms Volendam

(L)

Lifestyle	**Premium**
Cruise Line:	Holland America Line
Former Names:	-
Gross Tonnage:	63,000
Builder:	Fincantieri (Italy)
Original Cost:	$300 million
Entered Service:	July 1999
Flag:	The Netherlands
Tel No:	n/a
Fax No:	n/a
Length (ft./m.):	777.5/237.00
Beam (ft./m.):	105.8/32.25
Draft (ft./m.):	25.5/7.80
Propulsion/Propellers:	diesel-electric (37,500kW)/2 (CP)
Decks:	12
Total Crew:	647
Pass. Capacity (basis 2):	1,440
Pass. Capacity (all berths):	1,440
Pass. Space Ratio (basis 2):	43.7
Pass. Space Ratio (all berths):	43.7
Officers:	Dutch
Total Cabins:	770
Size Range (sq. ft./m.):	113.0–339.2/10.5–34.3
Cabins (outside view):	581
Cabins (inside—no view):	139
Cabins (single occupancy):	0
Cabins (with private balcony):	197
Cabins (wheelchair accessible):	23
Cabin Current:	110 AC
Cabin TV:	Yes
Dining Rooms:	1 main (+1 alternative)
Seatings:	2
Elevators:	16
Casino:	Yes
Slot Machines:	Yes
Swimming Pools (outdoors):	2
Swimming Pools (inside):	1 (magrodome cover)
Whirlpools:	2
Fitness Center:	Yes
Sauna/Steam Room:	Yes/Yes
Massage:	Yes
Self-Service Launderette:	Yes
Movie Theater/Seats:	Yes/205
Library:	Yes
Children's Facilities:	Yes
Classification Society:	Lloyds Register

Ratings	**Score**
Ship: Hardware/Maintenance	NYR
Ship: Outdoor Facilities/Space	NYR
Ship: Interior Facilities/Space/Flow	NYR
Ship: Decor/Furnishings/Artwork	NYR
Ship: Spa/Fitness Facilities	NYR
Cabins: Suites and Deluxe	NYR
Cabins: Standard Sizes	NYR
Food: Dining Room/Cuisine	NYR
Food: Informal Dining/Buffets	NYR
Food: Quality of Ingredients	NYR
Food: Afternoon Tea/Bar Snacks	NYR
Service: Dining Room	NYR
Service: Bars	NYR
Service: Cabins	NYR
Service: Open Decks	NYR
Cruise: Entertainment	NYR
Cruise: Activities Program	NYR
Cruise: Movies/Television Programming	NYR
Cruise: Hospitality Standard	NYR
Cruise: Overall Product Delivery	NYR

Expected Score Range
1,500-1,800

Accommodation: The range of accommodation will be similar to that found aboard the similarly sized *Rotterdam*. There is 1 penthouse suite, and 28 suites, while the rest comprises a mix of outside-view and inside (no-view) cabins. There are more balcony cabins aboard this ship than found aboard the slightly smaller Statendam-class ships. With the exception of the one penthouse suite, the bathrooms in the other suites are really disappointing.

Dining: There is one main restaurant, and one alternative dining spot (for dinner). The main restaurant is a grand room, spread over two decks, with ocean views on three sides and a grand staircase connecting the upper and lower levels.

An alternative, casual-dress restaurant (seating 88) created in the style of a California artists' bistro, provides Italian cuisine (comprising a set menu together with nightly specials). Passengers thus have more choice, and an occasional change of venue (those booking suite-grade accommodation always have priority reservations).

In addition, there is the Lido Buffet, a casual, self-serve café that has proved popular aboard all HAL ships, as well as an outdoor grill for those who enjoy hamburgers, hot dogs, and other grilled fast-food items.

Other Comments: This is the third ship of the same name for Holland America Line, and the first of the evolving generation of *Statendam*-class ships. The name is derived from the fishing village of the same name, located north of Amsterdam, Holland. Her full is dark blue, in keeping with all Holland America Line ships. Although similar in size to the line's flagship *Rotterdam*, this ship has a single funnel, not unlike those found aboard *Nieuw Amsterdam* and *Noordam*.

Having been built to approximately the same size as the company's newest *Rotterdam*, the same layout and public rooms have been incorporated into her interiors, carrying on the same flow and feeling, so that passengers will immediately feel at home aboard all ships in the fleet. The principal design theme for the ship's interiors is flowers, from the seventeenth to the twenty-first centuries.

The interior focal point is a crystal sculpture, located in the three-deck-high atrium, by one of Italy's leading contemporary glass artists, Luciano Vistosi.

In the casino bar, also known as the ship's sports bar, a cinematic theme presents visions of Hollywood, and includes a collection of costumes, props, photos, and posters of movies and the stars who made them.

At the Lido Deck swimming pool, leaping dolphins are the focal point, but in a different design to that seen aboard the *Statendam*-class ships. The pool itself is also one deck higher than the S-class ships, permitting direct access between the aft and midships pools.

This ship is scheduled to operate seven to thirteen day cruises in the Caribbean during her inaugural season.

ms Voyager of the Seas
(L)

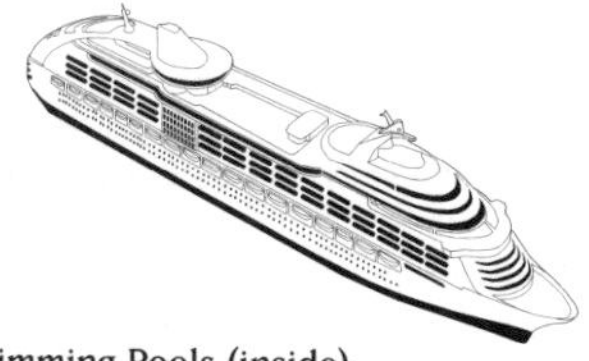

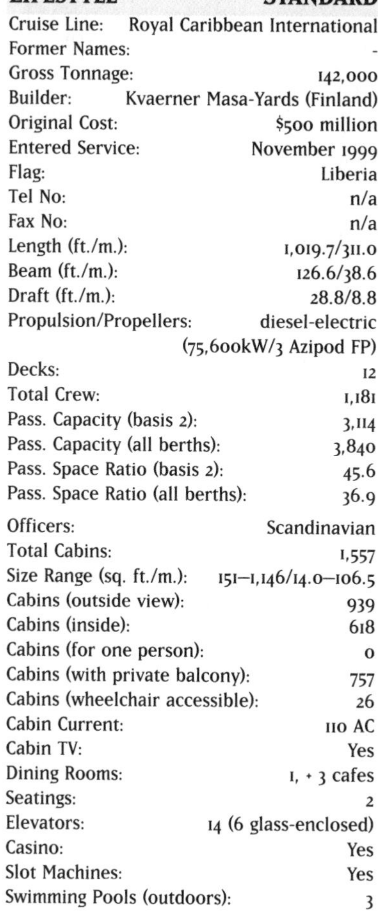

Lifestyle	**Standard**
Cruise Line:	Royal Caribbean International
Former Names:	-
Gross Tonnage:	142,000
Builder:	Kvaerner Masa-Yards (Finland)
Original Cost:	$500 million
Entered Service:	November 1999
Flag:	Liberia
Tel No:	n/a
Fax No:	n/a
Length (ft./m.):	1,019.7/311.0
Beam (ft./m.):	126.6/38.6
Draft (ft./m.):	28.8/8.8
Propulsion/Propellers:	diesel-electric (75,600kW/3 Azipod FP)
Decks:	12
Total Crew:	1,181
Pass. Capacity (basis 2):	3,114
Pass. Capacity (all berths):	3,840
Pass. Space Ratio (basis 2):	45.6
Pass. Space Ratio (all berths):	36.9
Officers:	Scandinavian
Total Cabins:	1,557
Size Range (sq. ft./m.):	151–1,146/14.0–106.5
Cabins (outside view):	939
Cabins (inside):	618
Cabins (for one person):	0
Cabins (with private balcony):	757
Cabins (wheelchair accessible):	26
Cabin Current:	110 AC
Cabin TV:	Yes
Dining Rooms:	1, + 3 cafes
Seatings:	2
Elevators:	14 (6 glass-enclosed)
Casino:	Yes
Slot Machines:	Yes
Swimming Pools (outdoors):	3
Swimming Pools (inside):	0
Whirlpools:	6
Fitness Center:	Yes
Sauna/Steam Room:	Yes/Yes
Massage:	Yes
Self-Service Launderette:	No
Movie Theater/Seats:	No
Library:	Yes
Children's Facilities:	Yes
Classification Society:	Det Norske Veritas

Ratings	**Score**
Ship: Hardware/Maintenance	NYR
Ship: Outdoor Facilities/Space	NYR
Ship: Interior Facilities/Space/Flow	NYR
Ship: Decor/Furnishings/Artwork	NYR
Ship: Spa/Fitness Facilities	NYR
Cabins: Suites and Deluxe	NYR
Cabins: Standard Sizes	NYR
Food: Dining Room/Cuisine	NYR
Food: Informal Dining/Buffets	NYR
Food: Quality of Ingredients	NYR
Food: Afternoon Tea/Bar Snacks	NYR
Service: Dining Room	NYR
Service: Bars	NYR
Service: Cabins	NYR
Service: Open Decks	NYR
Cruise: Entertainment	NYR
Cruise: Activities Program	NYR
Cruise: Movies/Television Programming	NYR
Cruise: Hospitality Standard	NYR
Cruise: Overall Product Delivery	NYR

Expected Score Range

1,400-1,800

Accommodation: There will be a whole range of cabin categories, from large luxuriously appointed penthouse suites to the more modest inside and outside cabins, although many of the cabins will be of a similar size. Some of the inside cabins look into the atrium (rather like the inside cabins aboard some Baltic ferries with inside cabins that look into the shopping plaza).

Dining: The main dining room is very large, and is set on three levels. A number of other dining options will be incorporated for casual and informal meals at all hours, including a pizzeria. The cuisine is expected to be similar in nature to that offered aboard the company's present ships. In other words, we are talking about mass banquet catering that offers standard fare comparable to that found in American family-style restaurants ashore. Anything such as caviar (once a standard menu item) will incur a hefty extra charge.

Other Comments: This will be a stunning mega-ship (one of two on order, with an option for a third) and has a design not unlike a very much enlarged version of the company's *Vision*-class ships. When the ship debuts, she will be the largest cruise vessel in the world. With her increase in size, this new vessel will provide more options, and cater to more passengers than any other Royal Caribbean International ship has in the past. This ship is too large to go through the Panama Canal, thus limiting her itineraries exclusively to the Caribbean.

The ship's propulsion is derived from three Azipod, 14-megawatt motors (two outboard units and one fixed at the centerline) instead of conventional rudders and propellers. Passengers will be able to stand right at the bow of this ship, arms spread in an "eagle-like" position, just like the stars in the film *Titanic*. Just imagine the photographs, although for the best ones, like in the film, you'll need to bring a helicopter!

Embarkation and disembarkation will take place through two stations/access points in order to minimize the inevitable lines at the start and end of the cruise. Once inside the ship, you'll need good walking shoes, particularly when you need to go from one end to the other – it really is a long way.

Just some of the many public rooms and facilities featured include a large television studio, located adjacent to rooms that can be used for trade show exhibit space. For the more sporting, youthful passengers, there will be a rock-climbing wall, an inline skating track, and an ice rink located under the show lounge floor (this will feature real, not fake, ice).

More sedate, but no less important facilities will include a stunning two-deck library (the first aboard any ship), and a whopping $10.1 million has been spent on the artwork for this huge ship.

For water lovers, a long water slide is featured at one of the aft outdoor pools; all of the swimming pools provide a resort-like environment, with the latest in high-tech everything.

Royal Caribbean International has, since its inception, always been an innovator in the cruise industry, and will remain so with this new vessel, the first of three such "floating resort" vessels to be placed into service by the company. *Voyager of the Seas* will operate seven-day Western Caribbean cruises from Miami.

ms Walrus

☆☆☆ +

(M)

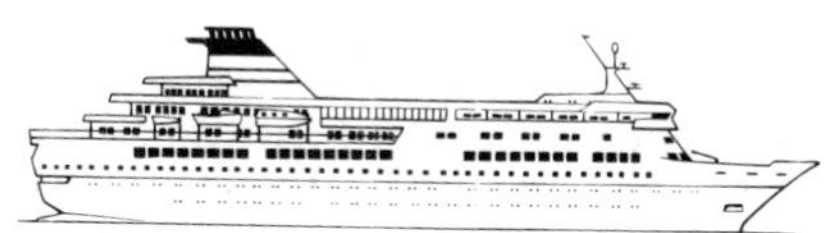

Lifestyle	**Standard**
Cruise Line:	Ki Development Corp
Former Names:	*Nautican/Crown Monarch*
Gross Tonnage:	15,271
Builder:	Union Navale de Levante (Spain)
Original Cost:	$95 million
Entered Service:	December 1990/October 1994
Flag:	Panama
Tel No:	1333627
Fax No:	1333630
Length (ft./m.):	494.4/150.72
Beam (ft./m.):	67.6/20.62
Draft (ft./m.):	17.7/5.40
Propulsion/Propellers:	diesel (13,680kW)/2 (CP)
Decks:	7
Total Crew:	215
Pass. Capacity (basis 2):	510
Pass. Capacity (all berths):	556
Pass. Space Ratio (basis 2):	29.9
Pass. Space Ratio (all berths):	27.4
Officers:	International
Total Cabins:	255
Size Range (sq. ft./m.):	145–398/13.5–37.0
Cabins (outside view):	225
Cabins (inside–no view):	30
Cabins (single occupancy):	0
Cabins (with private balcony):	10
Cabins (wheelchair accessible):	5
Cabin Current:	110 AC
Cabin TV:	Yes
Dining Rooms:	1
Seatings:	2
Elevators:	4
Casino:	Yes
Slot Machines:	Yes
Swimming Pools (outdoors):	1
Swimming Pools (inside):	0
Whirlpools:	2
Fitness Center:	Yes
Sauna/Steam Room:	Yes/No
Massage:	Yes
Self-Service Launderette:	No
Movie Theater/Seats:	No
Library:	Yes
Children's Facilities:	No
Classification Society:	Det Norske Veritas

Ratings	**Score**
Ship: Hardware/Maintenance	71
Ship: Outdoor Facilities/Space	67
Ship: Interior Facilities/Space/Flow	72
Ship: Decor/Furnishings/Artwork	66
Ship: Spa/Fitness Facilities	56
Cabins: Suites and Deluxe	71
Cabins: Standard Sizes	66
Food: Dining Room/Cuisine	70
Food: Informal Dining/Buffets	65
Food: Quality of Ingredients	65
Food: Afternoon Tea/Bar Snacks	54
Service: Dining Room	71
Service: Bars	70
Service: Cabins	73
Service: Open Decks	63
Cruise: Entertainment	63
Cruise: Activities Program	55
Cruise: Movies/Television Programming	62
Cruise: Hospitality Standard	65
Cruise: Overall Product Delivery	75
Overall Score	**1,320**

Accommodation: The suites with private balconies are well designed. All other cabins are nicely appointed and have elegant, pleasing decor and wood accents and double-to-twin convertible beds, with floral patterned bedspreads. Most cabins are quite spacious for the size of the ship. Unfortunately, the cabin soundproofing is very poor.

Dining: The dining room is quite charming, is elegantly appointed, and has real wood chairs with armrests, warm decor, and an informal atmosphere. The food is generally good, with generous portions, but choice is limited. Service is good to excellent, from a friendly and attentive staff. There is also an indoor/outdoor café, but it is poorly designed and has limited seating and poor traffic flow.

Other Comments: This is a moderately handsome, highly maneuverable small ship with swept back funnel and fine, well-balanced profile. Has reasonably good open deck and sunbathing space. The lifeboats are well located to avoid obstructed views. Numerous public rooms to choose from, all tastefully decorated and very comfortable. Well-designed interior has an excellent layout and good passenger flow.

This ship provides Asian passengers with a reasonably good cruise experience in pleasant, quite comfortable, and contemporary surroundings, at a modest price. Presently under a three-year charter to Ki Development Corporation.

ms Westerdam

☆☆☆☆

(L)

Lifestyle	**Premium**
Cruise Line:	Holland America Line
Former Names:	*Homeric*
Gross Tonnage:	53,872
Builder:	Meyer Werft (Germany)
Original Cost:	$150 million
Entered Service:	May 1986/November 1988
Flag:	Netherlands
Tel No:	1302534
Fax No:	1302532
Length (ft./m.):	797.9/243.23
Beam (ft./m.):	95.1/29.00
Draft (ft./m.):	23.6/7.20
Propulsion/Propellers:	diesel (23,830kW)/2 (VP)
Decks:	9
Total Crew:	642
Pass. Capacity (basis 2):	1,494
Pass. Capacity (all berths):	1,773
Pass. Space Ratio (basis 2):	36.0
Pass. Space Ratio (all berths):	30.3
Officers:	Dutch
Total Cabins:	747
Size Range (sq. ft./m.):	131–425/12.0–39.5
Cabins (outside view):	495
Cabins (inside—no view):	252
Cabins (single occupancy):	0
Cabins (with private balcony):	0
Cabins (wheelchair accessible):	4
Cabin Current:	110 AC
Cabin TV:	Yes
Dining Rooms:	1
Seatings:	2
Elevators:	7
Casino:	Yes
Slot Machines:	Yes
Swimming Pools (outdoors):	2 (1 with magrodome)
Swimming Pools (inside):	0
Whirlpools:	2
Fitness Center:	Yes
Sauna/Steam Room:	Yes/No
Massage:	Yes
Self-Service Launderette:	Yes-5
Movie Theater/Seats:	Yes/237
Library:	Yes
Children's Facilities:	Yes
Classification Society:	Lloyd's Register

Ratings	**Score**
Ship: Hardware/Maintenance	81
Ship: Outdoor Facilities/Space	80
Ship: Interior Facilities/Space/Flow	82
Ship: Decor/Furnishings/Artwork	76
Ship: Spa/Fitness Facilities	75
Cabins: Suites and Deluxe	80
Cabins: Standard Sizes	75
Food: Dining Room/Cuisine	77
Food: Informal Dining/Buffets	74
Food: Quality of Ingredients	72
Food: Afternoon Tea/Bar Snacks	65
Service: Dining Room	76
Service: Bars	76
Service: Cabins	77
Service: Open Decks	71
Cruise: Entertainment	78
Cruise: Activities Program	75
Cruise: Movies/Television Programming	74
Cruise: Hospitality Standard	73
Cruise: Overall Product Delivery	81
Overall Score	**1,518**

Accommodation: The cabins are generously proportioned, well appointed, and equipped with almost everything, including ample closet, drawer, and storage space, and good-sized bathrooms (towels are scratchy and small). There are, however, far too many inside cabins, and the cabin insulation is quite poor.

Dining: The traditional dining room has a raised central dome, and the portholes are highlighted at night by lighting. Features two seatings for dinner and open seating for breakfast and lunch. Attractive Rosenthal china and place settings. The food is attractive, but somewhat tasteless. The selection of cheeses and fresh fruits is quite disappointing. The service is reasonable, but communication can prove frustrating sometimes, and smiles from the Indonesian waiters and assistants can only do so much. The Verandah Café and Lido Café provide two buffets for breakfast and lunch, but the long lines are not enjoyable.

Other Comments: This second-largest passenger ship in the Holland America fleet has good teakwood outside decks and a wraparound promenade deck with real wooden deck lounge chairs. There is also a good amount of open deck space for sunbathing. The magrodome-covered swimming pool deck is, however, too small for the number of passengers. There is some noticeable vibration in some areas.

The ship has elegant, functional, and restful interior decor. The public rooms are decorated in pastel tones, although some decor looks dated. She absorbs passengers well and has good passenger flow, but the layout is awkward to learn at first. Good quality furnishings and fabrics are used throughout. The expanded health and fitness center is an improvement.

She is a well-run, modern ship that underwent an $84-million stretch in 1990, and now provides a satisfactory cruise experience, generally for the older passenger, but increasingly for families with kids. Has a "no-tipping-required" (but staff do expect them) policy and a friendly Filipino and Indonesian crew. The product has some nice extras, like chocolates and classical music at night in the Explorer's Lounge, hot hors d'oeuvres at cocktail times, and good dance music. The line does not add an automatic 15 percent for beverage purchases, unlike many other cruise lines.

But: The entertainment is fairly mediocre, even though better production shows are now presented. A $1.50 charge for the washing machines in the self-service launderettes is petty.

mv Wilderness Adventurer

☆☆ +

(S)

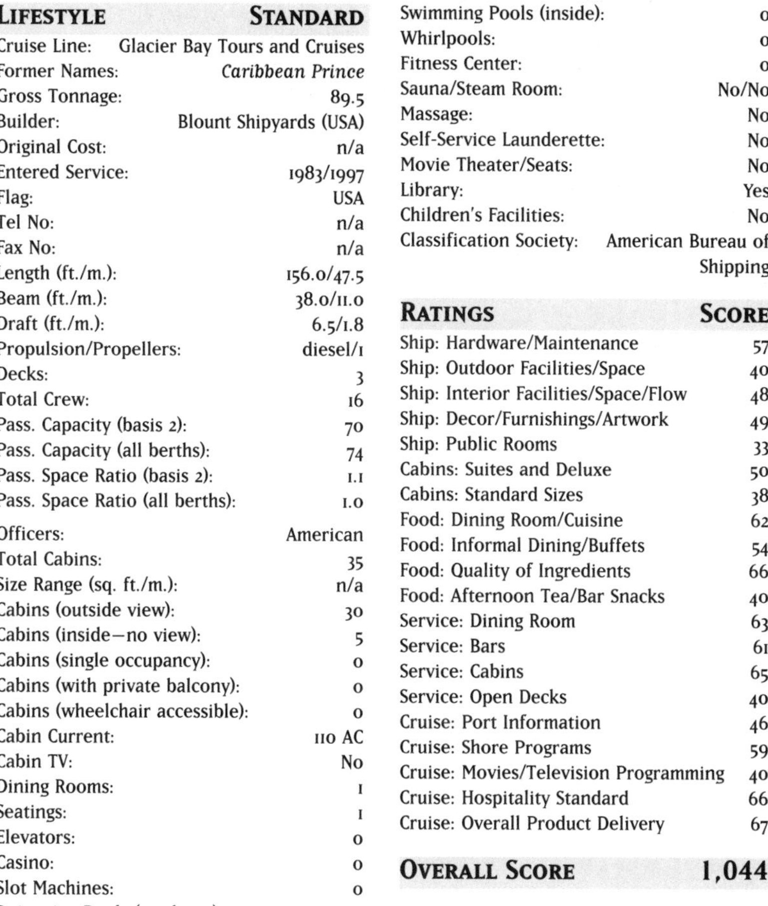

Lifestyle	**Standard**
Cruise Line:	Glacier Bay Tours and Cruises
Former Names:	*Caribbean Prince*
Gross Tonnage:	89.5
Builder:	Blount Shipyards (USA)
Original Cost:	n/a
Entered Service:	1983/1997
Flag:	USA
Tel No:	n/a
Fax No:	n/a
Length (ft./m.):	156.0/47.5
Beam (ft./m.):	38.0/11.0
Draft (ft./m.):	6.5/1.8
Propulsion/Propellers:	diesel/1
Decks:	3
Total Crew:	16
Pass. Capacity (basis 2):	70
Pass. Capacity (all berths):	74
Pass. Space Ratio (basis 2):	1.1
Pass. Space Ratio (all berths):	1.0
Officers:	American
Total Cabins:	35
Size Range (sq. ft./m.):	n/a
Cabins (outside view):	30
Cabins (inside—no view):	5
Cabins (single occupancy):	0
Cabins (with private balcony):	0
Cabins (wheelchair accessible):	0
Cabin Current:	110 AC
Cabin TV:	No
Dining Rooms:	1
Seatings:	1
Elevators:	0
Casino:	0
Slot Machines:	0
Swimming Pools (outdoors):	0
Swimming Pools (inside):	0
Whirlpools:	0
Fitness Center:	0
Sauna/Steam Room:	No/No
Massage:	No
Self-Service Launderette:	No
Movie Theater/Seats:	No
Library:	Yes
Children's Facilities:	No
Classification Society:	American Bureau of Shipping

Ratings	**Score**
Ship: Hardware/Maintenance	57
Ship: Outdoor Facilities/Space	40
Ship: Interior Facilities/Space/Flow	48
Ship: Decor/Furnishings/Artwork	49
Ship: Public Rooms	33
Cabins: Suites and Deluxe	50
Cabins: Standard Sizes	38
Food: Dining Room/Cuisine	62
Food: Informal Dining/Buffets	54
Food: Quality of Ingredients	66
Food: Afternoon Tea/Bar Snacks	40
Service: Dining Room	63
Service: Bars	61
Service: Cabins	65
Service: Open Decks	40
Cruise: Port Information	46
Cruise: Shore Programs	59
Cruise: Movies/Television Programming	40
Cruise: Hospitality Standard	66
Cruise: Overall Product Delivery	67
Overall Score	**1,044**

Accommodation: The cabins really are spartan, ultra-tiny, no-frills units that are just about adequate if you are not used to or do not want anything better. There is no room service for food or snack items.

Dining: The dining room has minimal decor, but the open seating policy means that you can dine with whomever you wish, in a single seating. The cuisine is decidedly plain and simple Americana fare, as is the cutlery (no fish knifes are used, for example), it is quite tasty. This is due to the fact that the ingredients are all fresh. If you want wine or other drinks, you must bring your own.

Other Comments: This vessel is good for real in-depth, up-close cruising along the coastline of the U.S. and upper Caribbean regions. One bonus is the fact that at the bow of the vessel, a "bow gangway" comes into its own for landing passengers. The ship is also equipped with a unique, retractable wheelhouse for passenger under low bridges on island waterways, and also has a platform for those who want to swim off the stern. Water sports facilities include a glass-bottom boat/sunfish sailboat.

The dress code is absolutely casual (not even a jacket for men is needed, and no ties, please). There is an ample supply of snorkeling gear aboard the vessel, so there is really no need to take your own. However, do make sure you take comfortable walking shoes, as well as photographic materials for wildlife spotting. All tips are pooled by all staff, using the amounts recommended in the cruise line's brochure of $8–$12 per passenger, per day, which is high for the services offered.

But: There is an almost constant throbbing from the diesel engines/generator. Remember that there is no doctor on board, and so anyone with medical problems should really not consider this vessel.

mv Wilderness Discoverer

☆☆ +

(S)

LIFESTYLE	STANDARD
Cruise Line:	Glacier Bay Tours and Cruises
Former Names:	*Mayan Prince*
Gross Tonnage:	98.4
Builder:	Blount Industries (USA)
Original Cost:	$7.5 million
Entered Service:	June 1992/1998
Flag:	USA
Tel No:	n/a
Fax No:	n/a
Length (ft./m.):	169.0/51.5
Beam (ft./m.):	38.0/11.5
Draft (ft./m.):	6.7/2.0
Propulsion/Propellers:	diesel/1 (FP)
Decks:	3
Total Crew:	18
Pass. Capacity (basis 2):	90
Pass. Capacity (all berths):	92
Pass. Space Ratio (basis 2):	1.0
Pass. Space Ratio (all berths):	1.0
Officers:	American
Total Cabins:	43
Size Range (sq. ft./m.):	70.0–80.0/6.5–7.4
Cabins (outside view):	37
Cabins (inside–no view):	0
Cabins (single occupancy):	0
Cabins (with private balcony):	0
Cabins (wheelchair accessible):	0
Cabin Current:	110 AC
Cabin TV:	No
Dining Rooms:	1
Seatings:	1
Elevators:	0
Casino:	0
Slot Machines:	0
Swimming Pools (outdoors):	0
Swimming Pools (inside):	0
Whirlpools:	0
Fitness Center:	No
Sauna/Steam Room:	No/No
Massage:	No
Self-Service Launderette:	No
Movie Theater/Seats:	No
Library:	Yes
Children's Facilities:	No
Classification Society:	American Bureau of Shipping

RATINGS	SCORE
Ship: Hardware/Maintenance	57
Ship: Outdoor Facilities/Space	41
Ship: Interior Facilities/Space/Flow	49
Ship: Decor/Furnishings/Artwork	50
Ship: Public Rooms	34
Cabins: Suites and Deluxe	50
Cabins: Standard Sizes	38
Food: Dining Room/Cuisine	62
Food: Informal Dining/Buffets	54
Food: Quality of Ingredients	66
Food: Afternoon Tea/Bar Snacks	40
Service: Dining Room	63
Service: Bars	61
Service: Cabins	65
Service: Open Decks	40
Cruise: Port Information	46
Cruise: Shore Programs	59
Cruise: Movies/Television Programming	40
Cruise: Hospitality Standard	66
Cruise: Overall Product Delivery	67
OVERALL SCORE	**1,048**

Accommodation: There are four cabin grades spread over three decks, and all are dimensionally challenged, so take only the most minimal amount of clothing and personal effects you possible can. There are 6 cabins on the lowest deck that do not have a window, and they are really tiny. The air-conditioning consists of recirculated air, much like that found aboard aircraft, and is, therefore, not very fresh. There is no room service for snack items or beverages.

Dining: The dining room is mildly attractive and has a single, open seating policy (so you can dine with whomever you wish). There is a "bring your own bottle" policy aboard this ship, whether you want wine with dinner or indeed any alcoholic beverages at all. The food is reasonably sound Americana fare, with good presentation and decent creativity.

Other Comments: This vessel, originally built for American Canadian Caribbean Line, is small and squat, has a shallow draft, and is designed specifically for in-depth coastal cruising. There is even a glass-bottom boat/sunfish sailboat.

A cruise aboard her is for those who really enjoy the camaraderie of others, there is little service and no entertainment. Indeed, unless you go to your cabin, there is no getting away from other passengers. Take only very casual clothing, as the attire is strictly non-dressy.

The ship is also equipped with a unique, retractable wheelhouse for passage under low bridges on island waterway itineraries, and there is a small platform for those who want to swim off the stern.

The vessel was acquired in early 1998 by the Tlingit Indian-owned company and presently operates five-night roundtrip cruises from Juneau to Haines, Skagway, Sitka, Glacier Bay, and Tracy Arm, Alaska during the summer, and Baja, California, cruises during the winter. The cruises are very expensive (particularly when compared with other ships operating in the same areas) and are for those who want to be up close to nature and wildlife in a small environment. Gratuities are expected, at about $8 per person, per day.

mys Wind Song

☆☆☆☆ +

(S)

Lifestyle	**Premium**
Cruise Line:	Windstar Cruises
Former Names:	-
Gross Tonnage:	5,703
Builder: Ateliers et Chantiers du Havre (France)	
Original Cost:	$34.2 million
Entered Service:	July 1987
Flag:	Bahamas
Tel No:	1104270
Fax No:	1104271
Length (ft./m.):	439.6/134.0
Beam (ft./m.):	51.8/15.8
Draft (ft./m.):	13.4/4.1
Type of Vessel:computer-controlled sail-cruiser	
No. of Masts:	4/6 self-furling sails
Sail Area (sq ft /sq m):	21,489/1,996.4
Main Propulsion:	a) engines/b) sails
Propulsion/Propellers:	diesel-electric (1,400kW)/1 (CP)
Decks:	5
Total Crew:	91
Pass. Capacity (basis 2):	148
Pass. Capacity (all berths):	159
Pass. Space Ratio (basis 2):	38.5
Pass. Space Ratio (all berths):	34.1
Officers:	British
Total Cabins:	74
Size Range (sq. ft./m.): 185.0–220.0/17.0–20.5	
Cabins (outside view):	74
Cabins (inside—no view):	0
Cabins (single occupancy):	0
Cabins (with private balcony):	0
Cabins (wheelchair accessible):	0
Cabin Current:	110 AC
Cabin TV:	Yes
Dining Rooms:	1 (open seating)
Casino:	Yes
Slot Machines:	Yes
Swimming Pools (outdoors):	1 (dip pool)
Whirlpools:	1
Fitness Center:	Yes
Sauna/Steam Room:	Yes/No
Massage:	Yes
Self-Service Launderette:	No
Library:	Yes
Classification Society:	Bureau Veritas

Ratings	**Score**
Ship: Hardware/Maintenance	77
Ship: Sails and Equipment	85
Ship: Interior Facilities/Space/Flow	82
Ship: Decor/Furnishings/Artwork	84
Ship: Spa/Fitness Facilities	73
Cabins: Suites and Deluxe	84
Cabins: Standard Sizes	82
Food: Dining Room/Cuisine	81
Food: Informal Dining/Buffets	73
Food: Quality of Ingredients	75
Food: Afternoon Tea/Bar Snacks	67
Service: Dining Room	80
Service: Bars	73
Service: Cabins	75
Service: Open Decks	73
Cruise: The Sailing Experience	77
Cruise: Lecturers/Entertainment	78
Cruise: Movies/Television Programming	73
Cruise: Hospitality Standard	77
Cruise: Overall Product Delivery	82
Overall Score	**1,551**

Accommodation: The cabins are all outside one-price units (except for one owner's suite) and come completely equipped with everything you really need; most have two portholes with deadlights (steel covers that provide a complete blackout at night). There is even a CD player (there is a small selection aboard ship, so it may be a good idea to take your own CDs), as well as a mini-bar-refrigerator (all drinks are at extra cost), television, and VCR and twenty-four-hour room service with a limited menu. The decor is a pleasant mix of rich woods, natural fabrics, and colorful soft furnishings and hi-tech yacht-style amenities. When watching a movie in your cabin, you can also order popcorn to be delivered.

The bathrooms are a neat figure-eight shape and, although a little tight, are well equipped, efficiently designed units, complete with a teakwood floor. Each has an excellent shower (no cabin bathrooms have bathtubs) and two toiletries cabinets with plenty of space. Bathrobes, of 100 percent cotton, are provided, and so are fragrant soap, shampoo, body lotion, shower cap, and mouthwash.

Dining: There is one chic, quite elegant dining room, with ocean views from large, picture windows. Features nouvelle cuisine, which is creative and attractively presented (including some signature dishes created by Joachim Splichal), and almost up to the standard of the small luxury ships.

When the company first started, European waiters provided service with practiced European finesse. However, those waiters have been replaced by Indonesians, whose communication skills at times can prove frustrating, although the service is pleasant enough. The selection of breads, cheeses, and fruits could be better.

There is a big push to sell wines, although the prices are extremely high, as they are for most alcoholic drinks (even bottled water is the highest in the industry, at $7 per liter bottle).

In addition, there is often casual dinner on the open deck under the stars, with grilled seafood and steaks. At the bars, hot and cold hors d'oeuvres appear at cocktail times.

Other Comments: This is a long, sleek-looking craft that is part yacht/part cruise ship, with four giant masts that tower 169.5 feet (51.66 meters) above the deck (they are actually 204 feet, or 62.1 meters) and fitted with computer-controlled sails; the masts, sails, and rigging alone cost $5 million. One of three identical vessels (a fourth, *Wind Saga*, was never built). When the masts for *Wind Star* (first of the three original Windstar vessels) were lowered into position, a U.S. silver dollar, dated 1889, was placed under mast number two (the main mast).

There is little open deck space when the ship is full, due to the amount of complex sail machinery. There is a tiny dip pool. At the stern is a small water sports platform for those who enjoy all the goodies the ship offers (but only when at anchor, and only in really calm sea conditions). Water sports facilities include a banana boat kayaks, sunfish sailboats, windsurf boards, water ski boat, scuba and snorkel equipment, and four Zodiacs. You will be asked to sign a waiver if you wish to use the water sports equipment.

Features a finely crafted interior with pleasing, blond woods, together with soft, complementary colors and decor that is chic, even elegant, but a little cold. Note that the main lounge aboard *Wind Star* is of a different design than *Wind Song* and *Wind Spirit*.

No scheduled activities help to make this a real relaxing, unregimented "get away from it all" vacation. The Windstar ships will cruise you in extremely comfortable surroundings that are bordering on contemporary luxury, yet in an unstructured environment.

Windstar Cruises' ships will provide a very relaxing, virtually unstructured cruise experience that is just right for seven idyllic nights in sheltered areas (but can be disturbing when a Windstar vessel is in small ports with several huge cruise ships). Ideal for couples who do not like large ships. This ship provides a delightful way to unwind in a stress-free environment. The dress code is casual (no jackets and ties required), even for dinner (the brochure states casual elegance). There are no formal nights or theme nights.

Wind Song sails seven-day Costa Rica cruises year-round. *Wind Spirit* sails Caribbean and Mediterranean itineraries. *Wind Star* sails seven-day Caribbean (from Barbados) cruises, and ten- and eleven-day South East Asia cruises (from Singapore) starting December 1998.

You will probably be under sail for under 40 percent of the time (conditions and cruise area winds permitting). Gratuities are "not required" by the friendly, smiling staff, according to the brochure, but passengers find they are always accepted! Finally, this is cruising with no worries, no hassles, and no wanna go back home!

<u>But:</u> Be prepared for the "whine" of the vessel's generators, which are needed to run the air-conditioning and lighting systems 24 hours a day. That means you will also hear it at night in your cabin (any cabin), and takes most passengers a day or two to get used to. The swimming pool is a tiny "dip" pool. Beverage prices are high. The library is small and needs more hardback fiction. The staff, though friendly, is casual and a little sloppy in the finer points of service at times.

mys Wind Spirit

☆☆☆☆ +

(S)

Lifestyle	**Premium**
Cruise Line:	Windstar Cruises
Former Names:	-
Gross Tonnage:	5,736
Builder: Ateliers et Chantiers du Havre (France)	
Original Cost:	$34.2 million
Entered Service:	April 1988
Flag:	Bahamas
Tel No:	1104434
Fax No:	1104435
Length (ft./m.):	439.6/134.0
Beam (ft./m.):	51.8/15.8
Draft (ft./m.):	13.4/4.1
Type of Vessel:computer-controlled sail-cruiser	
No. of Masts:	4/6 self-furling sails
Sail Area (sq ft /sq m):	21,489/1,996.4
Main Propulsion:	a) engines/b) sails
Propulsion/Propellers:	diesel-electric (1,400kW)/1 (CP)
Decks:	5
Total Crew:	91
Pass. Capacity (basis 2):	148
Pass. Capacity (all berths):	159
Pass. Space Ratio (basis 2):	38.7
Pass. Space Ratio (all berths):	36.0
Officers:	British/Dutch
Total Cabins:	74
Size Range (sq. ft./m.): 185.0–220.0/17.0–22.5	
Cabins (outside view):	74
Cabins (inside–no view):	0
Cabins (single occupancy):	0
Cabins (with private balcony):	0
Cabins (wheelchair accessible):	0
Cabin Current:	110 AC
Cabin TV:	Yes
Dining Rooms:	1 (open seating)
Casino:	Yes
Slot Machines:	Yes
Swimming Pools (outdoors):	1 (dip pool)
Whirlpools:	1
Fitness Center:	Yes
Sauna/Steam Room:	Yes/No
Massage:	Yes
Self-Service Launderette:	No
Library:	Yes
Classification Society:	Bureau Veritas

Ratings	**Score**
Ship: Hardware/Maintenance	85
Ship: Sails and Equipment	86
Ship: Interior Facilities/Space/Flow	82
Ship: Decor/Furnishings/Artwork	84
Ship: Spa/Fitness Facilities	75
Cabins: Suites and Deluxe	84
Cabins: Standard Sizes	82
Food: Dining Room/Cuisine	81
Food: Informal Dining/Buffets	69
Food: Quality of Ingredients	75
Food: Afternoon Tea/Bar Snacks	68
Service: Dining Room	77
Service: Bars	74
Service: Cabins	74
Service: Open Decks	72
Cruise: The Sailing Experience	78
Cruise: Lecturers/Entertainment	80
Cruise: Movies/Television Programming	73
Cruise: Hospitality Standard	74
Cruise: Overall Product Delivery	81
Overall Score	**1,554**

For comments, see *Wind Song*.

mys Wind Star

☆☆☆☆ +

(S)

Lifestyle	Premium
Cruise Line:	Windstar Cruises
Former Names:	-
Gross Tonnage:	5,703
Builder:	Ateliers et Chantiers du Havre (France)
Original Cost:	$34.2 million
Entered Service:	December 1986
Flag:	Bahamas
Tel No:	1104266
Fax No:	1104267
Length (ft./m.):	439.6/134.0
Beam (ft./m.):	51.8/15.8
Draft (ft./m.):	13.4/4.1
Type of Vessel:	computer-controlled sail-cruiser
No. of Masts:	4/6 self-furling sails
Sail Area (sq ft /sq m):	21,489/1,996.4
Main Propulsion:	a) engines/b) sails
Propulsion/Propellers:	diesel-electric (1,400kW)/1 (CP)
Decks:	5
Total Crew:	91
Pass. Capacity (basis 2):	148
Pass. Capacity (all berths):	168
Pass. Space Ratio (basis 2):	38.5
Pass. Space Ratio (all berths):	34.1
Officers:	British
Total Cabins:	74
Size Range (sq. ft./m.):	185.0–220.0/17.0–22.5
Cabins (outside view):	74
Cabins (inside–no view):	0
Cabins (single occupancy):	0
Cabins (with private balcony):	0
Cabins (wheelchair accessible):	0
Cabin Current:	110 AC
Cabin TV:	Yes
Dining Rooms:	1 (open seating)
Casino:	Yes
Slot Machines:	Yes
Swimming Pools (outdoors):	1 (dip pool)
Whirlpools:	1
Fitness Center:	Yes
Sauna/Steam Room:	Yes/No
Massage:	Yes
Self-Service Launderette:	No
Library:	Yes
Classification Society:	Bureau Veritas

Ratings	Score
Ship: Hardware/Maintenance	85
Ship: Sails and Equipment	86
Ship: Interior Facilities/Space/Flow	82
Ship: Decor/Furnishings/Artwork	84
Ship: Spa/Fitness Facilities	75
Cabins: Suites and Deluxe	84
Cabins: Standard Sizes	82
Food: Dining Room/Cuisine	81
Food: Informal Dining/Buffets	69
Food: Quality of Ingredients	75
Food: Afternoon Tea/Bar Snacks	68
Service: Dining Room	77
Service: Bars	74
Service: Cabins	74
Service: Open Decks	72
Cruise: The Sailing Experience	78
Cruise: Lecturers/Entertainment	80
Cruise: Movies/Television Programming	73
Cruise: Hospitality Standard	74
Cruise: Overall Product Delivery	81
Overall Score	**1,554**

For comments, see *Wind Song*.

Water sports facilities include an aft marina platform, kayaks, windsurf boards (two), sunfish sailboats (two), water ski boat, scuba and snorkeling equipment, and Zodiacs (four).

mys Wind Surf

☆☆☆☆ +

(S)

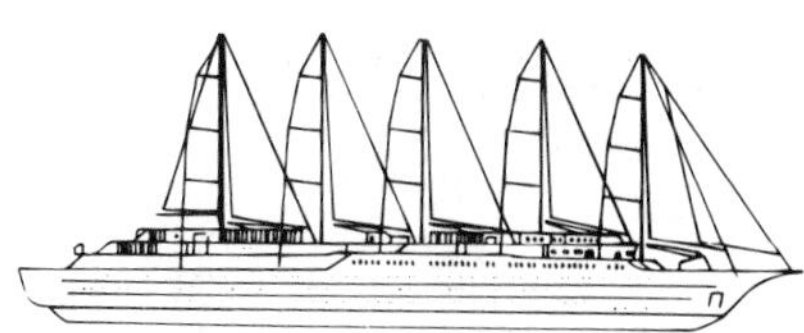

Lifestyle	Premium
Cruise Line:	Windstar Cruises
Former Names:	*Club Med I*
Gross Tonnage:	14,745
Builder: Ateliers et Chantiers du Havre (France)	
Original Cost:	$140 million
Entered Service:	February 1990/May 1998
Flag:	Bahamas
Tel No:	1103117
Fax No:	1103117
Length (ft./m.):	613.5/187.0
Beam (ft./m.):	65.6/20.0
Draft (ft./m.):	16.4/5.0
Type of Vessel:	high-tech sail-cruiser
No. of Masts:	5/7 computer-controlled sails
Sail Area (sq.ft/sq.m):	26,910/2,500
Main Propulsion:	a) engines/b) sails
Propulsion/Propellers:	diesel (9,120kW)/2 (CP)
Decks:	8
Total Crew:	163
Pass. Capacity (basis 2):	312
Pass. Capacity (all berths):	312
Pass. Space Ratio (basis 2):	47.2
Pass. Space Ratio (all berths):	47.2
Officers:	European
Total Cabins:	156
Size Range (sq. ft./m.):	188.0–375.6/57.3–114.5
Cabins (outside view):	156
Cabins (inside–no view):	0
Cabins (single occupancy):	0
Cabins (with private balcony):	0
Cabins (wheelchair accessible):	0
Cabin Current:	110/220 AC
Cabin TV:	Yes
Dining Rooms:	2 (open seating)
Elevators:	2
Casino:	Yes
Slot Machines:	Yes
Swimming Pools (outdoors):	2
Whirlpools:	2
Fitness Center:	Yes
Sauna/Steam Room:	Yes/No
Massage:	Yes
Self-Service Launderette:	No
Library:	Yes
Classification Society:	Bureau Veritas

Ratings	Score
Ship: Hardware/Maintenance	87
Ship: Sails and Equipment	86
Ship: Interior Facilities/Space/Flow	82
Ship: Decor/Furnishings/Artwork	83
Ship: Spa/Fitness Facilities	86
Cabins: Suites and Deluxe	84
Cabins: Standard Sizes	82
Food: Dining Room/Cuisine	82
Food: Informal Dining/Buffets	74
Food: Quality of Ingredients	75
Food: Afternoon Tea/Bar Snacks	68
Service: Dining Room	76
Service: Bars	72
Service: Cabins	73
Service: Open Decks	72
Cruise: The Sailing Experience	82
Cruise: Lecturers/Entertainment	80
Cruise: Movies/Television Programming	74
Cruise: Hospitality Standard	77
Cruise: Overall Product Delivery	82
Overall Score	**1,577**

Accommodation: All of the standard cabins are very nicely equipped, have crisp inviting decor, and feature minibar-refrigerator, 24-hour room service, safe, TV, plenty of storage space, bathrobes, hairdryers, and two portholes. There are 6 four-person cabins; 35 doubles are fitted with an extra Pullman berth, and several cabins have an interconnecting door (good for families).

Some 31 new suites (double the size of the former standard cabins) were added to Deck 3 during an extensive refit in 1998, resulting in a decrease of passenger capacity from that of the ship's former owners (Club Mediterranee). All except one of the new suites feature two bathrooms, and a separate living/dining area and bedroom (you can even have in-suite massage).

Dining: The Restaurant (with 272 seats) has tables for two, four, or six, and open seating is featured for all meals, so you can sit with whom you wish, when you like. The ship provides a mixture of

California and Continental cuisine. Signature dishes created by master chefs Joachim Splichal and Jeanne Jones are featured daily.

Apart from the main dining room, there is also the Veranda Bistro, with its open terrace for informal (buffet) meals, including dinner (it really is lovely to be outside, eating an informal meal on a balmy night).

Other Comments: One of a pair of the world's largest sail-cruisers is part cruise ship, part yacht. She is a larger, grander sister to the original three Windstar vessels. Five huge masts of 164.0/50.0 meters provide seven sails with a total surface area of 26,881 sq. ft. (2,497 m^2). No human hands touch the sails, as everything is handled electronically by computer control from the bridge.

Features a large, hydraulic water sports platform at the stern and extensive water sports facilities that include twelve windsurfers; three sailboats; two water-ski boats; twenty single scuba tanks, snorkels, fins, and masks; and four motorized water sport boats (for water-skiing, etc.), all at no extra charge.

The principal new facility aboard this ship is a totally new, expanded health spa, with some excellent facilities and treatment rooms, and a staff of twelve (there are special spa packages that can be prebooked through your travel agent) and a good fitness center. The ship also has small meeting rooms.

This vessel should be superb for the more upscale active singles and couples who might like the informality found aboard this vessel.

This ship was acquired by Windstar Cruises in March 1998. Her passenger capacity was reduced from 386 to 312, and 31 new larger suites were created from former smaller (standard) cabins.

She now features cruises from Barbados (November through March) and from Nice (May through October). However, note that the European itineraries are really port-intensive, which means you sail each night and are in port each day. With such itineraries, there seems little point to having the sails. More balanced itineraries would be much better (on three out of four Caribbean itineraries there is one day at sea).

This ship has become a larger, more upscale partner for the three original Windstar Cruises vessels presently operating (*Wind Song, Wind Spirit, Wind Star*). All gratuities and port taxes are included in the brochure price (no additional gratuities are expected), which itself is considerably higher than those of the three smaller vessels in the fleet.

ms World Discoverer

☆☆☆☆

(S)

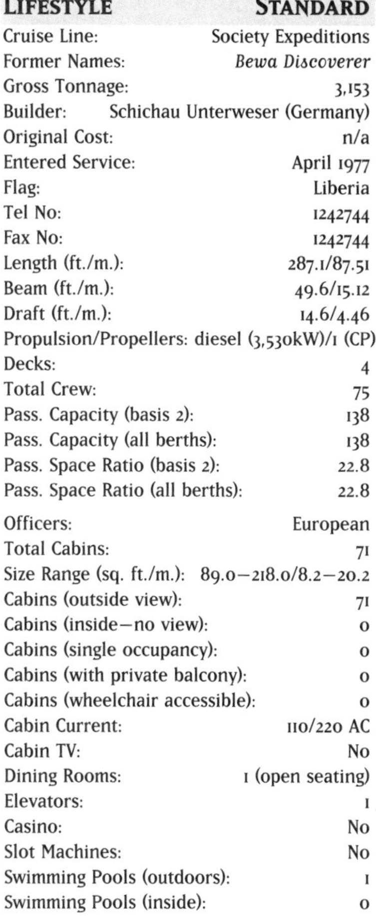

Lifestyle	Standard
Cruise Line:	Society Expeditions
Former Names:	*Bewa Discoverer*
Gross Tonnage:	3,153
Builder:	Schichau Unterweser (Germany)
Original Cost:	n/a
Entered Service:	April 1977
Flag:	Liberia
Tel No:	1242744
Fax No:	1242744
Length (ft./m.):	287.1/87.51
Beam (ft./m.):	49.6/15.12
Draft (ft./m.):	14.6/4.46
Propulsion/Propellers:	diesel (3,530kW)/1 (CP)
Decks:	4
Total Crew:	75
Pass. Capacity (basis 2):	138
Pass. Capacity (all berths):	138
Pass. Space Ratio (basis 2):	22.8
Pass. Space Ratio (all berths):	22.8
Officers:	European
Total Cabins:	71
Size Range (sq. ft./m.):	89.0–218.0/8.2–20.2
Cabins (outside view):	71
Cabins (inside—no view):	0
Cabins (single occupancy):	0
Cabins (with private balcony):	0
Cabins (wheelchair accessible):	0
Cabin Current:	110/220 AC
Cabin TV:	No
Dining Rooms:	1 (open seating)
Elevators:	1
Casino:	No
Slot Machines:	No
Swimming Pools (outdoors):	1
Swimming Pools (inside):	0
Whirlpools:	0
Fitness Center:	Yes
Sauna/Steam Room:	No/No
Massage:	Yes
Self-Service Launderette:	No
Lecture Room/Theater:	No
Library:	Yes
Zodiacs:	Yes
Helicopter Pad:	No
Classification Society:	American Bureau of Shipping

Ratings	Score
Ship: Hardware/Maintenance	81
Ship: Expedition Equipment	81
Ship: Interior Facilities/Space/Flow	79
Ship: Decor/Furnishings/Artwork	77
Ship: Spa/Fitness Facilities	43
Cabins: Suites and Deluxe	81
Cabins: Standard Sizes	76
Food: Dining Room/Cuisine	77
Food: Informal Dining/Buffets	71
Food: Quality of Ingredients	75
Food: Afternoon Tea/Bar Snacks	72
Service: Dining Room	80
Service: Bars	79
Service: Cabins	81
Service: Open Decks	71
Cruise: Library/Lecture Programs	73
Cruise: Movies/Television Programming	64
Cruise: Hospitality Standard	76
Cruise: Expedition Experience	74
Cruise: Overall Product Delivery	83
Overall Score	**1,494**

Accommodation: The cabins are of good proportions given the size of the ship; they are quite comfortable and very tastefully furnished. The cabin closet space is rather limited, however, and the bathrooms are small, with little space for toiletry items.

Dining: Has a very attractive and cozy dining room (there are even a few tables for two). Big picture windows and comfortable chairs make for an elegant setting. Features excellent cuisine and service, although it relies heavily on dairy products. Limited selection of breads and fruits.

Other Comments: This sophisticated, small, but very comfortable vessel was built expressly for expedition and adventure cruising and has a well-proportioned profile with a contemporary, swept-back funnel. Features an ice-hardened hull, is extremely maneuverable, and is well maintained. Well-equipped for in-depth expedition cruising in comfort. Water sports facilities include scuba diving and snorkeling equipment, fishing, water-ski boat, and windsurfing equipment.

Inside the ship, the decor is quite elegant, with warm colors and fine soft fabrics throughout. Naturalists and expert lecturers and nature specialists escort every expedition. She is one of the nicest of the expedition cruise vessels of this type in service today. The passenger gangway is rather narrow, and quite steep, however.

This ship provides a fine setting for expedition cruising to some of the most remote destinations in the world. It is quite expensive, but well worth it for discerning, well-traveled passengers yearning for a sense of adventure and for those who enjoy learning about the world around us and its fascinating peoples.

ms World Renaissance

☆☆ +

(S)

Lifestyle	**Standard**
Cruise Line:	Royal Olympic Cruises
Former Names:	*Awani Dream/ World Renaissance/Renaissance/ Homeric Renaissance*
Gross Tonnage:	11,724
Builder:	Chantiers de l'Atlantique (France)
Original Cost:	n/a
Entered Service:	May 1966/January 1996
Flag:	Greece
Tel No:	1130440
Fax No:	1130440
Length (ft./m.):	492.1/150.02
Beam (ft./m.):	69.0/21.06
Draft (ft./m.):	22.9/7.00
Propulsion/Propellers:	diesel (10,060kW)/2 (FP)
Decks:	8
Total Crew:	204
Pass. Capacity (basis 2):	457
Pass. Capacity (all berths):	599
Pass. Space Ratio (basis 2):	25.6
Pass. Space Ratio (all berths):	19.5
Officers:	Greek
Total Cabins:	242
Size Range (sq. ft./m.):	110–270/10.2–25.0
Cabins (outside view):	178
Cabins (inside–no view):	63
Cabins (single occupancy):	1
Cabins (with private balcony):	0
Cabins (wheelchair accessible):	0
Cabin Current:	110 AC
Cabin TV:	No
Dining Rooms:	1
Seatings:	2
Elevators:	1
Casino:	Yes
Slot Machines:	Yes
Swimming Pools (outdoors):	2
Swimming Pools (inside):	0
Whirlpools:	0
Fitness Center:	Yes
Sauna/Steam Room:	Yes/No
Massage:	Yes
Self-Service Launderette:	No
Movie Theater/Seats:	Yes/110
Library:	Yes
Children's Facilities:	No
Classification Society:	Lloyd's Register

Ratings	**Score**
Ship: Hardware/Maintenance	51
Ship: Outdoor Facilities/Space	56
Ship: Interior Facilities/Space/Flow	51
Ship: Decor/Furnishings/Artwork	52
Ship: Spa/Fitness Facilities	34
Cabins: Suites and Deluxe	57
Cabins: Standard Sizes	48
Food: Dining Room/Cuisine	65
Food: Informal Dining/Buffets	59
Food: Quality of Ingredients	62
Food: Afternoon Tea/Bar Snacks	52
Service: Dining Room	64
Service: Bars	63
Service: Cabins	65
Service: Open Decks	51
Cruise: Entertainment	50
Cruise: Activities Program	50
Cruise: Movies/Television Programming	42
Cruise: Hospitality Standard	60
Cruise: Overall Product Delivery	64
Overall Score	**1,096**

Accommodation: Some of the cabins have some fine wood paneling. They are homey and reasonably spacious, though certainly not luxurious. The cabin bathrooms are tiled, but are quite small, with little space for toiletries.

Dining: The dining room is quite pleasant, although there are no tables for two, and the tables are close together. The cuisine is now predominantly Indonesian, with plenty of spicy foods. There is thus a limited selection of breads, pastry, fruit, and cheeses. The service is very basic and there is really no finesse.

Other Comments: This ship has traditional 1960s styling and profile topped by a slender funnel. She was operated for many years by Epirotiki Lines (now part of Royal Olympic Cruises), and is now back with ROC after a short sojourn in Indonesia with Awani Dream Cruises, who ceased operations in late 1997. She has a pencil-slim funnel and white superstructure atop a royal blue hull.

The ship has a generous amount of open deck and sunbathing space for its size. The interior layout, however, is disjointed and awkward, and signage could be better.

Inside the ship, the decor can be said to be both "colonial" and eclectic, with some touches that still remind one of her original days as a French ship. Although the main lounge is comfortable, there are few other public rooms and therefore the ship always feels busy (crowded). The library is a restful place to relax. Has a friendly Greek staff and good basic service, although there is little refinement.

But: The ship has a steep passenger gangway in most ports of call. There is no wraparound outdoor promenade deck, and there are no cushioned pads for the deck lounge chairs.

ib Yamal

☆☆☆ +

(S)

Lifestyle	**Standard**
Cruise Line:	Murmansk Shipping
Former Names:	-
Gross Tonnage:	20,646
Builder:	Baltic Shipyard, Murmansk (Russia)
Original Cost:	$150 million
Entered Service:	November 1992
Flag:	Russia
Tel No:	1405744
Fax No:	1405745
Length (ft./m.):	492.1/150.0
Beam (ft./m.):	98.4/30.0
Draft (ft./m.):	36.0/11.0
Propulsion/Propellers:	nuclear-powered turbo-electric (75,000shp)/3
Decks:	4
Total Crew:	130
Pass. Capacity (basis 2):	100
Pass. Capacity (all berths):	100
Pass. Space Ratio (basis 2):	206.4
Pass. Space Ratio (all berths):	206.4
Officers:	Russian/Ukrainian
Total Cabins:	50
Size Range (sq. ft./m.):	130.0–300.0/14.3–27.8
Cabins (outside view):	50
Cabins (inside—no view):	0
Cabins (single occupancy):	0
Cabins (with private balcony):	0
Cabins (wheelchair accessible):	0
Cabin Current:	220 AC
Cabin TV:	Yes
Dining Rooms:	1
Seatings:	open seating
Elevators:	0
Casino:	No
Slot Machines:	No
Swimming Pools (inside):	1
Whirlpools:	0
Fitness Center:	Yes
Sauna/Steam Room:	Yes-2/No
Massage:	No
Self-Service Launderette:	Yes
Lecture/Film Room:	Yes (seats 100)
Library:	Yes
Zodiacs:	4
Helicopter Pad:	2 helicopters for passenger use
Classification Society:	RS

Ratings	**Score**
Ship: Hardware/Maintenance	74
Ship: Expedition Equipment	83
Ship: Interior Facilities/Space/Flow	64
Ship: Decor/Furnishings/Artwork	60
Ship: Spa/Fitness Facilities	38
Cabins: Suites and Deluxe	71
Cabins: Standard Sizes	64
Food: Dining Room/Cuisine	66
Food: Informal Dining/Buffets	61
Food: Quality of Ingredients	65
Food: Afternoon Tea/Bar Snacks	52
Service: Dining Room	64
Service: Bars	65
Service: Cabins	63
Service: Open Decks	58
Cruise: Library/Lecture Programs	73
Cruise: Movies/Television Programming	58
Cruise: Hospitality Standard	70
Cruise: Expedition Experience	68
Cruise: Overall Product Delivery	75
Overall Score	**1,292**

Accommodation: All of the cabins are generously sized (considering the type of specialized vessel this is), and all are outside, with private facilities, VCR, and refrigerator. There is, however, a limited amount of closet and drawer space in most cabins. The bathrooms are small and utilitarian, and you will need to take your own favorite toiletry items.

Dining: Has a nicely appointed dining room. When the ship is under charter to Quark Expeditions, the catering is provided by a Swedish company, and the cuisine is surprisingly hearty, with plenty of meat and potato dishes, but little fruit and cheese. Remember, these are not meant to be gourmet cruises, but the food is actually quite decent, and there is plenty of it.

Other Comments: The ultimate in technology accompanies this special ship, one of a fleet of the world's most powerful ice breakers. Two helicopters are carried for reconnaissance and passenger sightseeing use (their use is included in the expedition cruise fare).

Rugged, unpretentious, yet surprisingly comfortable surroundings prevail inside. There are two lounges to choose from. A tiered lecture theater with stage is the setting for a team of biologists, scientists, geologists, and other lecturers. There is also a heated indoor pool. Attentive and friendly Russian service is provided. Passengers are also allowed on the bridge at all times.

This really is an incredible vessel, with a three-inch-thick reinforced bow for negotiating tough ice conditions. Carries enough fuel for four years without refueling! This is undoubtedly one of the most exciting expedition cruise experiences available today.

mv Yorktown Clipper

☆☆☆ +

(S)

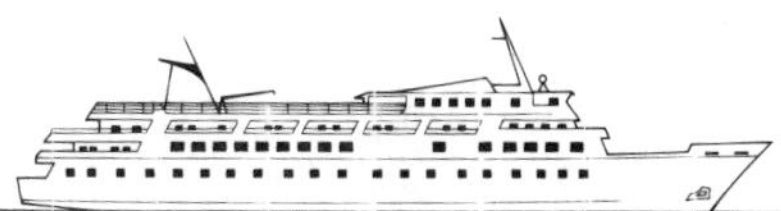

LIFESTYLE	STANDARD
Cruise Line:	Clipper Cruise Line
Former Names:	-
Gross Tonnage:	2,354
Builder:	First Coast Shipbuilding (USA)
Original Cost:	$12 million
Entered Service:	April 1988
Flag:	USA
Tel No:	n/a
Fax No:	n/a
Length (ft./m.):	257.0/78.30
Beam (ft./m.):	43.0/13.10
Draft (ft./m.):	8.0/2.43
Propulsion/Propellers:	diesel (1,400shp)/2 (FP)
Decks:	4
Total Crew:	37
Pass. Capacity (basis 2):	138
Pass. Capacity (all berths):	149
Pass. Space Ratio (basis 2):	17.0
Pass. Space Ratio (all berths):	15.7
Officers:	American
Total Cabins:	69
Size Range (sq. ft./m.):	121.0–138.0/11.2–12.8
Cabins (outside view):	69
Cabins (inside–no view):	0
Cabins (single occupancy):	0
Cabins (with private balcony):	0
Cabins (wheelchair accessible):	0
Cabin Current:	110 AC
Cabin TV:	No
Dining Rooms:	1
Seatings:	1
Elevators:	0
Casino:	No
Slot Machines:	No
Swimming Pools (outdoors):	0
Swimming Pools (inside):	0
Whirlpools:	0
Fitness Center:	No
Sauna/Steam Room:	No/No
Massage:	No
Self-Service Launderette:	No
Movie Theater/Seats:	No
Library:	Yes
Children's Facilities:	No
Classification Society:	American Bureau of Shipping

RATINGS	SCORE
Ship: Hardware/Maintenance	66
Ship: Outdoor Facilities/Space	65
Ship: Interior Facilities/Space/Flow	66
Ship: Decor/Furnishings/Artwork	65
Ship: Public Rooms	65
Cabins: Suites and Deluxe	66
Cabins: Standard Sizes	63
Food: Dining Room/Cuisine	78
Food: Informal Dining/Buffets	73
Food: Quality of Ingredients	78
Food: Afternoon Tea/Bar Snacks	66
Service: Dining Room	77
Service: Bars	76
Service: Cabins	75
Service: Open Decks	64
Cruise: Port Information	69
Cruise: Shore Programs	72
Cruise: Movies/Television Programming	50
Cruise: Hospitality Standard	74
Cruise: Overall Product Delivery	80
OVERALL SCORE	**1,388**

Accommodation: The all-outside cabins are small, but, with lots of wood-accented trim and restful colors, are quite comfortable and tastefully furnished. The bathrooms, likewise, are small, with little space for toiletry items (but a nightlight is provided, so you don't have to turn on bright lights in the middle of the night—a thoughtful touch). There is no room service for food and beverage items, as found aboard larger ships.

Dining: The dining room is warm and quite inviting and has large picture windows, but there are no tables for two. The service is provided by young, all-American, Midwestern college types, who smile a lot and are quite friendly, although the finesse of European service is simply not there. The food, however, is of a good quality, and made from locally purchased fresh ingredients. There is little menu choice, but the food provided is nicely presented. There is an adequate but very limited selection of breads and fruits.

Other Comments: This small vessel was built specifically to operate coastal and inland waterway cruises. She has a shallow draft and good maneuverability, and has been well maintained. There is a teakwood outdoor sun deck. Inflatable rubber Zodiac craft are used for for close-in shore excursions.

Inside, there is a glass-walled observation lounge. This ship offers an "Americana" experience for those seeking to learn more about the coastal ports around the U.S. during the summer months, while Caribbean cruises are featured during the winter months.

A casual, completely nonregimented lifestyle is featured aboard, and it is rather like a small, congenial country club without any of the pretentiousness. There are no mindless activities or corny games, and no entertainment as such, except for an occasional movie after dinner (the movie screen is located in the dining room). However, there are always one or two lecturers aboard each sailing, which highlights the learning experience that is an essential part of cruising with Clipper Cruise Line.

This really should not be compared with big ship ocean cruising. The price, however, is quite high for what you get, and airfare is extra. A nonsmoking policy throughout all interior areas was put into effect December 1996.

But: She really is a high-density ship, with only two public rooms: a dining room and a lounge. High engine and generator noise are a irritating when the ship is underway and need getting used to (not so irritating for those who may be hard of hearing).

ms Zaandam
(L)

LIFESTYLE	**PREMIUM**
Cruise Line:	Holland America Line
Former Names:	-
Gross Tonnage:	63,000
Builder:	Fincantieri (Italy)
Original Cost:	$300 million
Entered Service:	January 2000
Flag:	The Netherlands
Tel No:	n/a
Fax No:	n/a
Length (ft./m.):	777.5/237.00
Beam (ft./m.):	105.8/32.25
Draft (ft./m.):	25.5/7.80
Propulsion/Propellers:	diesel-electric (37,500kW)/2 (CP)
Decks:	12
Total Crew:	647
Pass. Capacity (basis 2):	1,440
Pass. Capacity (all berths):	1,440
Pass. Space Ratio (basis 2):	43.7
Pass. Space Ratio (all berths):	43.7
Officers:	Dutch
Total Cabins:	770
Size Range (sq. ft./m.):	113.0–339.2/10.5–34.3
Cabins (outside view):	581
Cabins (inside–no view):	139
Cabins (single occupancy):	0
Cabins (with private balcony):	197
Cabins (wheelchair accessible):	23
Cabin Current:	110 AC
Cabin TV:	Yes
Dining Rooms:	1 main (+1 alternative)
Seatings:	2
Elevators:	16
Casino:	Yes
Slot Machines:	Yes
Swimming Pools (outdoors):	2
Swimming Pools (inside):	1 (magrodome cover)
Whirlpools:	2
Fitness Center:	Yes
Sauna/Steam Room:	Yes/Yes
Massage:	Yes
Self-Service Launderette:	Yes
Movie Theater/Seats:	Yes/205
Library:	Yes
Children's Facilities:	Yes
Classification Society:	Lloyds Register

For comments, see *Volendam*.

RATINGS	**SCORE**
Ship: Hardware/Maintenance	NYR
Ship: Outdoor Facilities/Space	NYR
Ship: Interior Facilities/Space/Flow	NYR
Ship: Decor/Furnishings/Artwork	NYR
Ship: Spa/Fitness Facilities	NYR
Cabins: Suites and Deluxe	NYR
Cabins: Standard Sizes	NYR
Food: Dining Room/Cuisine	NYR
Food: Informal Dining/Buffets	NYR
Food: Quality of Ingredients	NYR
Food: Afternoon Tea/Bar Snacks	NYR
Service: Dining Room	NYR
Service: Bars	NYR
Service: Cabins	NYR
Service: Open Decks	NYR
Cruise: Entertainment	NYR
Cruise: Activities Program	NYR
Cruise: Movies/Television Programming	NYR
Cruise: Hospitality Standard	NYR
Cruise: Overall Product Delivery	NYR

EXPECTED SCORE RANGE
1,500-1,800

mv Zenith

☆☆☆☆ +

(L)

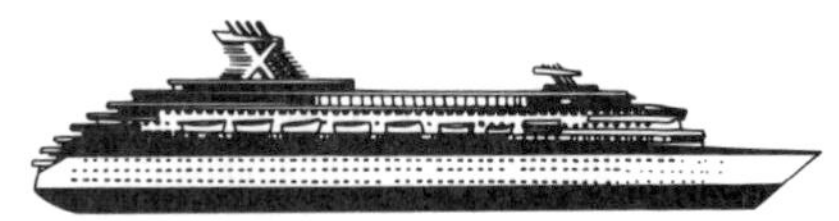

Lifestyle	**Premium**
Cruise Line:	Celebrity Cruises
Former Names:	-
Gross Tonnage:	47,255
Builder:	Meyer Werft (Germany)
Original Cost:	$210 million
Entered Service:	April 1992
Flag:	Liberia
Tel No:	1245564
Fax No:	1245567
Length (ft./m.):	681.0/207.59
Beam (ft./m.):	95.1/29.00
Draft (ft./m.):	23.6/7.20
Propulsion/Propellers:	diesel (19,960kW)/2 (CP)
Decks:	9
Total Crew:	628
Pass. Capacity (basis 2):	1,374
Pass. Capacity (all berths):	1,796
Pass. Space Ratio (basis 2):	34.3
Pass. Space Ratio (all berths):	26.3
Officers:	Greek
Total Cabins:	687
Size Range (sq. ft./m.):	185–334/17.0–31.0
Cabins (outside view):	541
Cabins (inside–no view):	146
Cabins (single occupancy):	0
Cabins (with private balcony):	0
Cabins (wheelchair accessible):	4
Cabin Current:	110 AC
Cabin TV:	Yes
Dining Rooms:	1
Seatings:	2
Elevators:	7
Casino:	Yes
Slot Machines:	Yes
Swimming Pools (outdoors):	2
Swimming Pools (inside):	0
Whirlpools:	3
Fitness Center:	Yes
Sauna/Steam Room:	Yes/No
Massage:	Yes
Self-Service Launderette:	No
Movie Theater/Seats:	Yes/850
Library:	Yes
Children's Facilities:	Yes
Classification Society:	Lloyd's Register

Ratings	**Score**
Ship: Hardware/Maintenance	86
Ship: Outdoor Facilities/Space	86
Ship: Interior Facilities/Space/Flow	87
Ship: Decor/Furnishings/Artwork	86
Ship: Spa/Fitness Facilities	75
Cabins: Suites and Deluxe	82
Cabins: Standard Sizes	79
Food: Dining Room/Cuisine	85
Food: Informal Dining/Buffets	76
Food: Quality of Ingredients	86
Food: Afternoon Tea/Bar Snacks	73
Service: Dining Room	85
Service: Bars	80
Service: Cabins	82
Service: Open Decks	76
Cruise: Entertainment	86
Cruise: Activities Program	76
Cruise: Movies/Television Programming	78
Cruise: Hospitality Standard	83
Cruise: Overall Product Delivery	90
Overall Score	**1,637**

Accommodation: The suites are very tastefully furnished (although they are not as large as the suites aboard the company's three larger vessels: *Century, Galaxy, Mercury*). They do, however, have excellent bathrooms, as well as butler service.

The standard-sized inside and outside cabins are well insulated, have a good amount of closet and drawer space, and are nicely appointed and spacious enough for seven-day cruises. The bathrooms are very practical and well laid out, with large shower areas, and various toiletries are provided (soap, shampoo/conditioner, body lotion, and shower cap). Note that most outside cabins on Bermuda Deck have lifeboat-obstructed views. Cabin soundproofing is quite good to very good, depending on location. All accommodation designated as suites have duvets on the beds instead of sheets/blankets. For light meals and snacks, the in-cabin service menu is now quite varied, having been improved.

Dining: The cuisine and its presentation and service are really very good. The large dining room, which features a raised section in its center, has several tables for two, as well as for four, six, or eight (in banquettes), although the chairs do not have armrests. There is a separate menu for vegetarians and children.

For informal meals, the Windsurf Café features good buffets for breakfast (including an omelet station) and lunch (including a pasta station). At night, this changes into an alternative dining spot for passengers who want good food but in a more casual setting than the main restaurant, with items such as grilled salmon, steaks, and rotisserie chicken, as well as specialties that change frequently.

The Grill, located outdoors adjacent to (but aft of) the Windsurf Café, serves typical fast-food items. And for those that cannot live without them, freshly baked pizzas (in a box) can be delivered, in an insulated pouch, to your cabin.

Other Comments: This ship has a smart, contemporary profile with a powerful thrust, like her sister *Horizon* (which is two years older), similar interior layout and elegant but warmer decor, and an enlarged and enhanced forward observation lounge with a larger dance floor.

Inside, the principal deck that houses public entertainment rooms features a double-width indoor promenade. The feeling is one of uncluttered surroundings. Features well-chosen art works throughout. An art deco-style hotel-like lobby (reminiscent of hotels in Miami Beach) has a two-deck-high ceiling and a spacious feel to it. Soothing pastel colors and high-quality soft furnishings have been used throughout this ship.

There is also an excellent show lounge (with better shows than *Horizon*), with main and balcony levels, and good sight lines from almost all seats (however, the railing in the balcony level impedes viewing). Has a good (seasonal) program for children and teenagers, with specially trained youth counselors. There is a large, elegantly appointed casino with its own bar, while outside is a satellite-linked BankAtlantic ATM machine (there is a $5 access charge) in case you didn't bring enough cash.

A refurbishment in mid-1999 will add a "Michael's Club" cigar smoking lounge in what is at present an underused discotheque, as well as an enlarged library and small business center. Also added will be a martini bar, a room dedicated to the display of art (for art auctions), and an expanded health spa that now includes a rasul treatment room and beauty salon.

This ship will provide you with a well-packaged cruise vacation in elegant, calming surroundings, with finely presented food in a formal dining room setting, and service by a well-trained service staff that includes a large percentage of Europeans. Almost all passengers feel that the company exceeds their expectations from a seven-day cruise experience.

But: The doors to public restrooms and the outdoor decks are quite heavy. Public restrooms are still quite clinical. There are cushioned pads for poolside deck lounge chairs only, but not for chairs on other outside decks. The food on the room service menu is very basic. Unlike the company's larger *Century*, *Galaxy*, and *Mercury*, there is no AquaSpa thalassotherapy pool.

THE CRUISE INDUSTRY: MILESTONES (1960–1998)

1960

→Passenger shipping directories listed more than thirty ships operating transatlantic voyages for the better part of each year. Many ships were laid up in the ten-year period 1960–1970, and most were sold for a fraction of their value (or building cost). Most passenger lines simply went out of business or tried to survive by mixing transatlantic crossings with voyages south in search of the sun, which proved difficult for those without sufficient air-conditioning systems.

→The last passenger ship to wear the White Star colors, *Britannic*, was withdrawn from service and sent to Inverkeithing, Scotland, to be scrapped.

1961

→Sun Line Cruises was founded by the late Charalambos A. Keusseouglou, who began his career at Home Lines, the immigrant passenger carrier. He died in 1984, aged 64, after a thirty-seven-year cruise industry career.

1962

→The Compagnie Generale Transatlantique's *ss France*, at 1,035 feet the world's longest passenger ship ever built, entered service between Le Havre and New York despite growing competition from the airlines.

1963

→Cunard Line's RMS *Queen Elizabeth* made an experimental cruise from New York to the West Indies, with great success. This led to her being fitted with full air-conditioning in a 1965/66 refit, and more extensive cruising activities.

→Home Lines ceased regularly scheduled transatlantic services.

1965

→P&O obtained the remaining shares of the Orient Steam Navigation Company. Orient Line was absorbed into the P&O Group, and the name P&O-Orient Line disappeared forever. The new company became known as the Peninsular & Oriental Steam Navigation Company.

→Princess Cruises was founded by Seattle entrepreneur and industrialist Stanley B. McDonald.

→Sitmar Cruises started cruise operations from Sydney, Australia.

→American President Lines ceased passenger-carrying operations.

1966

→Soviet transatlantic service was reopened with *Aleksandr Pushkin*, owned by the Black Sea Shipping Company, inaugurating service between Montreal and Leningrad (now St. Petersburg) for the first time since 1949.

→The Norwegian company Klosters Reederei formed a partnership with Miami businessman Ted Arison to market Caribbean cruises from Miami. Klosters provided the ship and Arison provided the passengers.

→Commodore Cruise Line was founded by Sanford Chobol, with a single ship, *Boheme* (now *Freewinds*).

1967

→Cunard announced the imminent withdrawal of the liners *Queen Mary* and *Queen Elizabeth*. *Queen Mary* was withdrawn from service on September 26 after completing 1,001 transatlantic crossings. She was sold to the city of Long Beach, California. She left Southampton on October 31, 1967, and has been in Long Beach ever since.

1968

→American Export Lines ceased its transatlantic passenger service.

→Cunard's *Queen Elizabeth* (at 83,673 grt, the world's largest passenger ship ever) was withdrawn from service in October. She had steamed a total of 3,472,672 miles and carried a total of 2,311,324 passengers (1,500,000 peacetime passengers and 811,324 wartime passengers) during her career. She was sold to a Ft. Lauderdale consortium, "Queens, Inc.," which quickly failed. She was then sold to the Hong Kong-based shipping tycoon, C. Y. Tung (now deceased) in September, 1970. He had the ship towed from Southampton via Cape Horn to Hong Kong on February 10, 1971. The ship then underwent an extensive refit and was renamed *Seawise University*.

→Cunard Line ceased its regularly scheduled transatlantic service to Canada.

→Zim Lines ceased its transatlantic passenger service.

→Cunard Line refused delivery of the new *Queen Elizabeth 2* from her builders, John Brown, in December, owing to unacceptable turbine vibration levels. Repairs led to a five-month delay on her maiden transatlantic sailing to New York.

→Boise Cascade purchased Princess Cruises from its founder, Stanley B. McDonald, who repurchased the line two years later.

1969

→Lars-Eric Lindblad's *Lindblad Explorer* was launched, expressly designed for close-in expedition cruising.

→Royal Caribbean Cruise Line was founded January 31 by a consortium of Norwegian shipping companies, Gotaas-Larsen (actually it was American-owned), I. M. Skaugen, and Anders Wilhelmsen, and formally incorporated as Royal Caribbean Cruise Line A/S in Oslo. Edwin Stephan, who provided the initial concept and wisdom, was made president and set up the Miami marketing arm of the company, which ordered two new sister ships for delivery in 1970 and 1971.

→The liner *United States* was laid up in November following a strike against the ship by the militant seamen's union and the fact that the U.S. government no longer wanted to subsidize the loss-making ship (which cost $118.8 million between 1955 and 1969). She was subsequently laid up for twenty-three years on November 7, 1969, until sold to Marmara Marine, Inc., on April 27, 1992.

1970

→Royal Viking Line was founded by a consortium of three partners (Bergen Line, A. F. Klaveness, and Nordenfjeldske) who each contributed one ship (*Royal Viking Sea*, *Royal Viking Sky*, and *Royal Viking Star*).

→Germany's Norddeutscher Lloyd and Hapag (Hamburg American Line) merged on September 1. They chose the new name Hapag-Lloyd.

1971

→Cunard Line was sold to Trafalgar House Investments.

→Holland America Line ceased transatlantic passenger service.

→Canadian Pacific ceased all passenger-carrying operations.

1972

→American President Lines ceased passenger operations.

→Carnival Cruise Lines was formed by Ted Arison, following a disagreement with Knut Kloster when both worked for Kloster's Norwegian Cruise Lines. After unsuccessfully trying to purchase Cunard's *Carmania* and *Franconia*, he learned of the availability of the *Empress of Canada*. The new company, funded by and operated as a subsidiary of the Boston-based American International Travel Service, Inc. (AITS), started with just one ship, *Mardi Gras* (ex-*Empress of Canada*). After a poor start (*Mardi Gras* ran aground on its first voyage, and ships from competing companies even named a drink after her called "Mardi Gras on the Rocks"), the company went from strength to strength. Under Arison's aggressive direction it has become the biggest success story of the contemporary cruise industry.

1973

→Holland America Line withdrew sisters *Veendam* and *Volendam* from service and laid them up, owing to the abundance of other cruise ships, combined with high operating costs, a fall in the value of the U.S. dollar, and a dramatic rise in fuel costs. The ships were placed under charter to Monarch Cruise Lines in 1976 for the sum of $5,000 each per day (*Veendam* became *Monarch Star* and *Volendam* became *Monarch Sun*). The Dutch-flag ships were re-registered in Panama and staffed by a multinational crew.

→Sitmar Cruises began operations from the Port of Sydney, Australia, with a single ship, *Fairstar*, a converted troop carrier formerly operated by Bibby Line.

→Deutsche Atlantik Line suspended operations following financial difficulty. The company's *Hanseatic*, in service for only four years, was laid up at Hamburg. In December, the intended sale of the ship to Ryutsu Kaiun KK of Japan for $25 million failed to materialize. She was instead sold to Robin International Corporation, New York, acting as buyers for the Black Sea Shipping Company of Odessa. The ship was

Courtesy Douglas Ward

The eyes of Aida *are upon you.*

renamed *Maksim Gorkiy* and is still in service for Phoenix Seereisen, catering to German-speaking passengers.

1974

- P&O purchased Princess Cruises from its founder, Stanley B. McDonald, during the summer.
- Sitmar Line ceased scheduled line voyages and concentrated on its cruising activities.
- In July, the Compagnie Generale Transatlantique announced that after only twelve years of service, the *ss France* was to be withdrawn from service on October 25. She was losing money and was being subsidized by the French government to the tune of $12 million a year. As the ship was about to berth in Le Havre on September 12, angry French trade unionists took over the ship from its officers and anchored her in the entrance channel, in protest of the impending loss of jobs. Passengers disembarked by tender. The ship was able to dock on October 9 and was laid up.
- The Port Authority of New York and New Jersey opened its new Passenger Ship Terminal in November. It included six berths at three piers (formerly Piers 88, 90, and 92) and cost $35 million.
- The Union Castle Steamship Company ceased operations as a passenger line, leaving Cape Town without a regular steamship service between England and South Africa.
- Royal Cruise Lines' first ship, *Golden Odyssey*, purpose-built to accommodate the equivalent passenger load of a Boeing 747 aircraft (425 passengers), was introduced. The company, founded by Pericles S. Panagopoulos in 1971, attracted a loyal U.S. West Coast following, gained mainly through direct marketing methods.

1975

- Princess Cruises' *Island Princess* and *Pacific Princess* become the "stars" of the American television show *The Love Boat*.
- The Greek Line, Shaw Savill, and Swedish America Line all ceased passenger operations. Carnival Cruise Lines purchased the former Greek Line ship *Queen Anna Maria* for $3.2 million.

1976

- The Italian Line and Lloyd Triestino ceased transatlantic passenger operations.

1977

- World Explorer Cruises was founded and entered the cruise industry with a single ship, *Universe*.
- Princess Grace of Monaco christened *Cunard Princess* at the Passenger Ship Terminal in March, the first time a passenger ship christening had taken place in the Port of New York.
- Union-Castle/Safmarine, the South Africa-based shipping company, ceased passenger operations when its last vessel, S.A. *Vaal*, was sold to Carnival Cruise Lines in April.
- Holland America Line announced it would take over the entire operation of Monarch Cruise Lines Inc. The two Monarch ships were handed to Holland America Line in January 1978.

1978

- United States Cruises was formed by Richard Hadley, who paid $5 million for the liner *United States*.

→After sailing on an unsuccessful June 30 cruise from New York for new owners Venture Cruise Lines (also called America Cruise Lines), *America* (ex-*Australis*) was arrested for debt and auctioned on August 28. Her previous owners, the Chandris Group, repurchased the ship and renamed her *Italis*.

→Royal Caribbean Cruise Line's *Song of Norway* and *Nordic Prince* were lengthened at the Wartsila shipyard in Helsinki (March–June 1980).

1979

→American Hawaii Cruises was formed. Jimmy Carter, then president of the United States, signed a bill redocumenting *Independence* under the U.S.flag. The new company began cruise operations on June 21, 1980, with *Independence*, joined by sister ship *Constitution* in 1982.

→Special Expeditions was founded by Sven-Olof Lindblad to provide expedition cruise vacations to seldom-visited destinations.

→Society Expeditions was formed by a group of German investors under the direction of sole stockholder T. C. Schwartz expressly to manage and operate the adventure/expedition cruises of the purpose-built *World Discoverer*.

→The liner *France* was purchased by Lauritz Kloster in June. The ship was taken to Bremerhaven and rebuilt for the Caribbean cruise trade by Hapag-Lloyd. She was renamed *Norway* and transferred to the ownership of Norwegian Caribbean Lines in September 1984.

→President Jimmy Carter spent a week aboard the river steamboat *Delta Queen*, whose life began on Clydeside in 1926. The steamboat is now on the U.S. National Register of Historic Places.

1980

→Sea Goddess Cruises was founded by Helge Naarstad. The first of two twin vessels, *Sea Goddess I*, was delivered four years later, in 1984.

→Denmark's DFDS (United Steamship Company) founded Scandinavian World Cruises to operate one-day cruises from Miami (the company subsequently became SeaEscape).

→The International Organization of Masters, Mates and Pilots formed a joint venture company with Aloha Pacific Cruises. The company purchased *Monterey* (the last U.S. flag ship that qualified under the Jones Act to operate between American ports) for intended cruise service in Tahiti. The purchase went through in 1981. The union poured $5.7 million into the ship, for upkeep alone, between 1981 and 1986.

→After a planned merger with Royal Viking Line failed in May, Norwegian America Cruises (formerly Norwegian America Line) was formed to manage *Sagafjord* and *Vistafjord*.

1981

→Transatlantic service provided by Soviet-registered ships was discontinued due to the U.S. government embargo instituted in the "cold war."

→Astor Cruises was formed in the U.K. and began operations with a single ship, the brand-new *Astor*.

→*Royal Viking Star* was lengthened in the A. G. Weser shipyard in Bremerhaven, Germany. Sister ships *Sky* and *Sea* were lengthened by the same shipyard (in 1982 and 1983, respectively).

1982

→The British government chartered Cunard's *Queen Elizabeth 2* for use as a troop carrier for the famous Ghurka Regiment, among others, during the Falklands War between Argentina and Britain, at a rate of $225,000 per day. The ship eluded an Argentinean submarine sent to destroy it, due to the submarine's ineffectiveness in the icebergs close to the Falklands and the speed of *QE2*. The government also chartered P&O Cruises' *Canberra* for use as a troopship (sailed from Southampton on April 9, returned to Southampton on July 11, and went back to passenger service in September), as well as B&I Line's *Uganda*, used as a hospital ship. All three ships performed well.

→Lindblad Travel, the company founded by Lars-Eric Lindblad in 1969, sold its *Lindblad Explorer*, and the rights to the Lindblad name, to Salen-Lindblad Cruising.

1983

→Holland America Line ceased operating its lucrative New York-Bermuda sailings. The company moved its headquarters from New York to Seattle.

→Ocean Cruise Lines was founded by British entrepreneur Gerry Herrod as an offshoot of Travellers, Europe's largest tour operator for Americans abroad.

→P&O appointed Jeffrey Sterling chairman in order to fend off an unwanted takeover bid by Trafalgar House Investments, owners of Cunard Line.

→Premier Cruise Lines was cofounded by Bruce Nierenburg and Bjornar Hermansen, both former executives of Norwegian Cruise Lines.

→B&I's *Uganda* was taken over by the British Ministry of Defense in January for two years for service between Ascension and the Falkland Islands. This marked the end of passenger service for the British and India Steam Navigation Company (B&I).

→Cunard's parent company, Trafalgar House, purchased Norwegian America Cruises (NAC) in May, together with *Sagafjord* and *Vistafjord*.

→Salen-Lindblad Cruising's *Lindblad Explorer* became the first passenger ship to navigate the Northwest Passage successfully (in September), sailing 4,790 miles from Saint John's, Newfoundland, to Point Barrow, Alaska. The entire forty-one-day cruise, which started on August 20, finished in Yokohama, Japan, on September 29. When the ship reached Point Barrow, the champagne flowed and beards were shaved off (the crew had all vowed not to shave until that point). Lars Wikander provided the idea and planning expertise.

1984

→Sundance Cruises, founded by Stanley B. McDonald, entered the cruise business with a single ship, *Sundancer*.

→Carnival Cruise Line launched a $10 million television advertising campaign, the largest ever seen in the cruise industry. Two different thirty-second spots were aired a total of 133 times in the U.S.

→An American investor group headed by J. H. Whitney & Company signed an agreement in principle in May for the purchase of Royal Viking Line and its three ships for $240 million. The sale did not go through. Instead, Royal Viking Line was purchased by Kloster Cruise Limited, Oslo.

→Delta Steamship Lines ceased passenger-carrying operations. Its four ships (*Santa Magdalena, Santa Maria, Santa Mariana,* and *Santa Mercedes*) were sold.

→Regency Cruises was founded by Anastassios Kiriakidis, Fred Mayer, and William Schanz. The new company completed its initial public stock offering in June and commenced operations with a single ship, *Regent Sea*, in November.

→Windstar Sail Cruises was founded in December by Karl Andren and Jacob Stolt-Nielsen to build and operate a fleet of three sail-cruise ships originally designed by Kai Levander, then of Wartsila shipyard in Helsinki, Finland. Andren intended to re-launch the age of commercial sail.

→Dolphin Cruise Line was founded by Peter Bulgarides and Paris Katsoufis (but actually owned by Ulysses Shipping, Piraeus).

→Premier Cruise Lines, owned by the Greyhound-Dial Corporation, entered the cruise industry with its first ship.

1985

→The Chandris Group of Companies acquired Fantasy Cruises from GoGo Tours. Fantasy Cruises became known as Chandris Fantasy Cruises in the U.S. and Chandris Cruises in the U.K.

→The first-ever sailing ship designed for crewing by physically disabled passengers was launched at Wivenhoe, Essex, on October 15. The sts *Lord Nelson* was owned by the Jubilee Sailing Trust, whose patron, His Royal Highness Prince Andrew, officially named the vessel at Southampton, England, on May 9, 1986.

1986

→Signet Cruise Line was founded in Norway by an investment group headed by Atle Brynestad. Owing to a lawsuit brought by an American who claimed the right to the name Signet, the company changed its name to Seabourn Cruise Line. The company's first ship, *Seabourn Pride*, entered service in December 1988, one cruise later than the planned maiden voyage, which was canceled due to a major storm front encountered during the transatlantic delivery voyage.

→Eastern Cruise Lines, Western Cruise Lines, and Sundance Cruises were merged into one unit, called Admiral Cruises.

→Diamond Cruise Ltd. was founded in Helsinki, Finland, by the late Captain Offe Nyblin and his partner Christian Aspegren. They were to take delivery of *Radisson Diamond*, a semi-submersible twin-hulled vessel.

→Cunard acquired Sea Goddess Cruises, together with *Sea Goddess I* and *Sea Goddess II*, through a complex financial and management package negotiated with Norske Cruise A/S, whose 138 shareholders provided the funding for the construction and introduction of the new luxury yacht-ship concept.

1987

→Carnival Cruise Lines made its first public stock offering.

→Cunard's *QE2* was converted from steam turbine to diesel-electric power. It was the largest ever conversion in maritime history.

→Society Expeditions was purchased by German businessman Heiko Klein, chairman of Discoverer Reederei, the company that owns the vessels marketed and operated by Society Expeditions.

→Kockums, the Swedish shipyard, ceased shipbuilding operations following the delivery of twin cruise ships for Carnival Cruise Lines, *Celebration* (1987) and *Jubilee* (1986).

→Bahama Cruise Line changed its name to Bermuda Star Line.

AquaSpa aboard Mercury; *Courtesy of Celebrity Cruises*

Relax in a spa aboard ship.

- Ocean Cruise Lines merged with Pearl Cruises.
- Princess Cruises replaced almost 500 unionized British hotel and catering staff on the company's five ships.
- The United States Public Health Service (USPH) resumed ship inspections January 1 (after being halted in May 1986) due to public interest, and cooperation of the cruise lines.
- Holland America Line acquired a 50 percent share in Windstar Sail Cruises in March.
- Norwegian Caribbean Lines changed its name and logo (though not its initials: NCL) to Norwegian Cruise Line.

1988

- Commodore Cruise Lines sold its *Boheme* to the Church of Scientology. The ship was renamed *Freewinds*.
- Crystal Cruises was formed as a wholly owned company of Nippon Yusen Kaisha (NYK) of Japan, the world's largest shipping company. The company's first ship, *Crystal Harmony*, entered service in July 1990.
- The three owning partners of Royal Caribbean Cruise Line (the Norwegian consortium Gotaas-Larsen, I. M. Skaugen, and Anders Wilhelmsen) decided in March to merge RCCL with the Gataas-Larsen-dominated Admiral Cruises (the Swedish company Axel Johnson group and the Finnish EFFOA group held 49 percent). Named Royal Admiral Cruises (later renamed Royal Caribbean Cruises), the new group was owned 36 percent by Gotaas-Larsen and 28 percent each by Skaugen and Wilhelmsen, while Johnson/EFFOA held the remaining 8 percent of stock.
- Home Lines ceased operations in April. Its two ships, *Atlantic* (1984) and *Homeric* (1986) were purchased by Holland America Line. *Atlantic* was subsequently placed under long-term charter to Premier Cruise Lines.
- Effjohn International purchased Bermuda Star Line in May for $17 million. Included in the deal were *Bermuda Star*, *Queen of Bermuda*, and *Veracruz I*. The company was renamed BSL Cruises, Inc.

→Sitmar Cruises (Societa Italiana Trasporti Marittimi), founded in 1938 by Alexandre Vlasov, was purchased by Princess Cruises (part of the P&O Group) for $210 million. The two companies merged their North American operations.

→Carnival Cruise Lines' negotiations with Gotaas-Larsen to purchase its share in Royal Caribbean Cruise Line for $260 million came to light in August, following RCCL's administration move from Oslo to Miami. At first, Skaugen and Wilhelmsen tried to preempt the Carnival offer. Later, Skaugen accepted a similar offer from Carnival. Wilhelmsen, the remaining partner in RCCL (28 percent), found the financing to preempt the Carnival offer of $567 million by going 50/50 with the Hyatt Hotel group of companies, owned by the Pritzker family of Chicago. The new joint owners paid the agreed amount five days before the deadline date of October 5.

→Holland America Line completed the purchase of Windstar Sail Cruises. Carnival Cruise Lines acquired Holland America Line in November, including its land-based hotel/transport operations and Windstar Cruises, for a total of $625 million, plus liabilities that pushed the purchase price effectively to $900 million.

1989

→The Chandris Group of Companies announced the creation of a new company, Celebrity Cruises, which promptly ordered two new cruise ships, to be named *Horizon* and *Zenith*, from Meyer Werft shipyard in Papenburg, Germany. The company also announced plans for the conversion of *Galileo* into *Meridian*, at the Lloyd Werft shipyard in Bremerhaven, Germany.

→Ocean Quest International was formed to provide seven-day cruises for scuba diving enthusiasts and entered the industry with a single ship, *Ocean Spirit* (ex-*Sunward*).

→Meyer Werft, Papenburg, Germany, became the first shipyard to conduct a "chop and stretch" operation on a major cruise vessel in drydock (all other ships being previously lengthened while afloat), when *Westerdam* (ex-*Homeric*) was lengthened in the same covered building shed as *Horizon*, under construction for Celebrity Cruises.

→Renaissance Cruises was formed by Fearnley & Eger, the 120-year-old Oslo-based shipping concern. The company would build and market eight small luxury cruise vessels. The first, *Renaissance I*, commenced service in December 1989. The last built, *Renaissance VIII*, commenced service in 1992.

→Showa Line entered the cruise passenger market in Japan for the first time in sixty years with the introduction of its new *Oceanic Grace* (sold in 1997 to Spice Island Cruises).

→Mitsui OSK Line entered the cruise market in Japan for the first time in fifty years with its 23,340-grt, 600-passenger *Fuji Maru*, specially built for the charter and incentive market for Japanese companies.

→The Panama Canal is now seventy-five years old. The canal, cutting a 75-mile swath through the isthmus of Panama, which joins the North and South American continents, is the only place in the world where it is possible to cruise over the Continental Divide.

→Lars-Eric Lindblad's Lindblad Travel Company went into bankruptcy.

→Aloha Pacific Cruises went into bankruptcy just six months after start-up. The company's single ship, *Monterey*, was put up for sale.

→Wartsila Industries, Helsinki, Finland, one of the most famous and prestigious builders of cruise ships, collapsed in a tangle of financial problems. It was reorganized as Masa-Yards and is presently owned by Kvaerner of Norway.

1990

- Starlite Cruises (part of the Piraeus-based Lelakis Group) was formed to provide ships for one-day and seven-day cruises.
- Ocean Cruise Lines was acquired by Croisieres Paquet, itself owned by the French giant Accor Leisure Company.
- Japan Cruise Line entered the cruise passenger market in Japan with its new 21,906-grt, 606-passenger *Orient Venus*. This company specializes in charters and incentive cruises for Japanese companies.
- Two intimate sixty-eight-passenger cruise vessels, named *Lady Diana* and *Lady Sarah*, were refused delivery in March by the newly formed Windsor Line, whose owner, Nicolopoulos, is a Greek anthropologist. The line was wound up and the two ships were later sold.
- Aloha Pacific Cruises' *Monterey* was put up for auction by the Connecticut Bank & Trust Company on March 15. It was purchased by the Mediterranean Shipping Company, which chartered it to StarLauro Cruises.
- Chandris Cruises introduced its new premium-grade Celebrity Cruises company in April with the debut of the reconstructed *Meridian* and the brand-new *Horizon*.
- Delfin Cruises, established only one year earlier with two small ships for cruise service in the Baltic Sea, ceased operations.
- At the start of the Persian Gulf War, the U.S. government chartered *Cunard Princess* for six months for use as a rest and relaxation center for U.S. service personnel in the Persian Gulf. The ship was docked in Bahrain for the $31-million charter.

1991

- Carnival Cruise Lines acquired a 25 percent stake in Seabourn Cruise Line.
- With the Soviet Union dissolved, the Soviet cruise fleet was converted into its constituent parts: Baltic Shipping Company (Russia), Black Sea Shipping Company (Ukraine), Estonian Shipping Company (Estonia), and Far East Shipping Company (Russia).
- In March, Fearnley & Eger, owner of Renaissance Cruises, announced voluntary liquidation and protection from its creditors under Chapter 11 of the U.S. Bankruptcy Code. Renaissance Cruises was sold to a new investment group consisting of the Cameli Group, controlled by Sebastiano Cameli (Italy), and Luxury Liners, Ltd., a holding company involving Norwegian shipowner Jorgen Jahre and controlled by Edward B. Rudner in the U.S.
- In April, Carnival Cruise Lines announced it would buy Premier Cruise Lines, but later backed out of the $220-million deal with the Dial Corporation after Carnival inspected Premier's books and insisted it should pay less for the company following a dispute over Premier's short-term earnings potential.
- Effjohn International purchased the rights to the name Crown Cruise Line together with the rights to operate its fleet of eight small ships.
- Seawind Cruise Line commenced cruise operations with its single ship, *Seawind Crown* (ex-*Vasco da Gama*), following a 70/30 percent interest purchase in the company by Swedish concern Nordisk and Arcalia Shipping, Lisbon.
- Nippon Yusen Kaisha (NYK) purchased the expedition cruise company Salen Lindblad Cruising.
- Nippon Yusen Kaisha (NYK) Cruises introduced *Asuka*, the first cruise vessel specifically designed for Japanese passengers.

→New York-based Overseas Shipholding Group agreed to lend Kloster Cruise $175 million in exchange for a 50 percent stake in the company. The offer was withdrawn after OSG reviewed Kloster's financial structure and profitability.

1992

→Society Expeditions ceased operation. Its two expedition vessels, *Society Explorer* and *World Discoverer*, were placed on the sale/charter books. The company also refused to take delivery of the brand-new *Society Adventurer*, built at the Rauma Shipyards in Finland (now Hanseatic). In January, Society Expeditions filed a Chapter 11 reorganization plan.

→Costa Cruise Lines introduced its new Euro-Luxe cruise concept with the debut of *CostaClassica*.

→Admiral Cruises ceased operations. The company's two vessels, *Azure Seas* and *Emerald Seas*, were sold to other interests (Dolphin Cruise Line and SunFest Cruises, respectively), at $3.9 million for both.

→Some sixteen cruise ships were chartered for use as accommodation vessels in Barcelona for the 1992 Olympic Games (July 24–August 9), due to lack of hotel space in the city. The ships provided about 44,000 beds for the Games. The ships:

Berlin, Club Med I, Crown Jewel, Crystal Harmony, Cunard Princess, Daphne, Golden Odyssey, Royal Majesty, Royal Viking Sun, Sally Albatross, Sea Cloud, Sea Goddess II, Seabourn Spirit, Star Clipper, Star Flyer, and *Vistafjord*.

→Hurricane Andrew hit the south Miami area and rendered several hundred cruise line executives and employees homeless. Carnival Cruise Lines, with 600 of its staff without living quarters, deployed *Mardi Gras* for use as an accommodation ship.

→The cruise division of the Chandris Group of Companies and Overseas Shipholding Group (OSG) signed an agreement in Paris on October 21 to form a joint venture company, to be called Celebrity Cruise Lines, Inc. The deal involved Chandris supplying the three ships of Celebrity Cruises, plus the three ships of Fantasy Cruises, while OSG supplied $220 million cash in funding, with Chandris holding a 51 percent interest.

→Chargeurs and Accor, the French property and leisure industries group that owned Paquet Cruises and Ocean Cruise Lines, purchased a 23 percent stake in Costa Crociere, the parent company of Costa Cruises, through a rights issue worth 80 billion lire ($60 million). The agreement signaled the first cross-border venture in Europe. The buy-in by the French company reduced the Costa family's stake in Costa Crociere from 40 percent to 31 percent.

1993

→In January, Carnival Cruise Lines announced a new subsidiary, Fiesta Marina Cruises, specifically for the Spanish-speaking Latin American marketplace. The company's ship, *FiestaMarina* (ex-*Carnivale*), would commence operations October 22 from San Juan. Everything aboard ship would be in the Spanish language.

→Cunard and Effjohn announced a joint venture, good for ten years, and created Cunard Crown Cruises.

→American Family Cruises was announced by Bruce Nierenberg. The new company would target American families and would initially use two Costa ships (*CostaRiviera* and *EugenioCosta*). *CostaRiviera* was converted into *American Adventure*.

→ In May, Rainbow Cruises purchased all the stock of Regency Cruises. Both companies were merged under the name Regency Cruises.

→ American Hawaii Cruises' secured lenders forced the line into involuntary bankruptcy in federal court in Honolulu. The company was subsequently purchased by the Delta Queen Steamboat Company.

→ Festival Cruises was founded by George Poulides, who reacquired *The Azur*, then on charter to Chandris Fantasy Cruises.

→ SeaQuest Cruises closed its doors and ceased trading. The company's *Frontier Spirit* was returned to its Japanese owners, which was chartered to Hanseatic Cruises, Germany, and renamed *Bremen*.

→ Kloster Cruise Ltd. signed a letter of intent to sell Royal Cruise Line and Royal Viking Line to ASA Investors, Inc., a consortium of 60 chief executives and former chief executives of American companies. The purchase price for the two lines was to be $565 million. Royal Cruise Line ships were *Crown Odyssey*, *Royal Odyssey* and *Star Odyssey* (*Golden Odyssey*, which was being sold separately, was not included in the deal). Royal Viking Line ships were *Royal Viking Queen* and *Royal Viking Sun*. This meant that AEA Investors Inc. paid $565 million, less $60 million for advance bookings, thus making $505 million for a total of 3,887 beds, or $129,920 per bed. The deal was expected to be finalized in the spring of 1994 but did not go through, the investment group concluding that there was not sufficient profit potential.

1994

→ Delta Queen Steamboat Company changed its corporate name to American Classic Voyages Company, effective at the end of the month. The company owns American Hawaii Cruises and Delta Queen Steamboat Company.

→ Festival Cruises started operations with one ship, designated for the European passenger.

→ Trafalgar House, Cunard's parent company, signed an agreement to purchase for $170 million the rights to the name Royal Viking Line, together with *Royal Viking Sun*. *Royal Viking Queen*, not part of the agreement, would go to Royal Cruise Line, to be renamed *Queen Odyssey*, on January 1, 1995.

→ In September, American Family Cruises ceased operations. The company's single ship, *American Adventure*, was returned to the Costa Cruises fleet, to be renamed *CostaRiviera*.

→ In September, FiestaMarina Cruises, a division of the Carnival Corporation, ceased operations.

→ Cycladic Cruises, based in Greece, ceased operations. Its two vessels were subsequently sold to other companies.

1995

→ British company Airtours Sun Cruises purchased *Southward* from Norwegian Cruise Line and *Nordic Prince* from Royal Caribbean Cruises in late 1994, and commenced operations in March 1995.

→ Commodore Cruise Line was sold to International Cruise Finance, Ltd.

→ Regency Cruises ceased operations abruptly at the end of October. Several vessels were impounded, subsequently to be put up for auction.

Ryndam; Courtesy Holland America Line

Cruising into port is a wonderful experience.

1996

→ Royal Venture Cruise Line started operations in March with a single ship, *Sun Venture* (ex-*Ukraine*), then ceased operations abruptly. The company was then restarted as Royal Seas Cruise Line, using the same ship but renamed *Royal Seas*.

→ Kloster Cruise (parent company of Norwegian Cruise Line and Royal Cruise Line) announced the closure of its Royal Cruise Line division. Two of the company's ships (*Crown Odyssey* and *Royal Odyssey*) went to sister company Norwegian Cruise Line as *Norwegian Crown* and *Norwegian Star*, respectively; a third (*Star Odyssey*) went to Fred Olsen Cruise Lines to become *Black Watch*; the fourth, and smaller, vessel (*Queen Odyssey*) went to Seabourn Cruise Line as *Seabourn Legend*.

→ Baltic Line ceased operations. The company's ships were acquired by other cruise lines.

→ Sunshine Cruise Lines ceased operations. The company's *Baltica* was acquired by Arcalia Shipping (renamed *Princess Danae*).

→ Carnival Corporation, parent company of Carnival Cruise Lines, Holland America Line, Seabourn Cruise Line, and Windstar Cruises, purchased 29.6 percent share in Airtours Plc, for approximately $310 million.

→ Cunard (together with parent company Trafalgar House) was purchased by Kvaerner.

1997

→ Carnival Corporation, jointly with Airtours, purchased the shares of Costa Cruises for $300 million. The deal was completed in June. Costa Cruises remains a wholly owned subsidiary of Carnival Corporation.

→ Germany's AquaMarin Cruises ceased operations following insolvency. Its single ship, *Astor*, was chartered to Transocean Tours, for ten years.

→ Dolphin Cruise Line, Premier Cruise Lines, and Seawind Cruise Line were purchased by Cruise Holdings, Inc., of Miami.

→ Carnival Corporation purchased the sail-cruise vessel *Club Med I*. The ship was added to the three ships already in the Windstar Cruises fleet.

→ Majesty Cruise Line ceased operations. Its single ship, *Crown Majesty*, was traded to Norwegian Cruise Line for $110 million.

→ Showa Line sold its only ship, *Oceanic Grace*, to Spice Island Cruises and ceased to operate in the cruise business. The ship's new name is *Oceanic Odyssey*.

→ Celebrity Cruises was purchased by Royal Caribbean International for $1.3 billion—the largest deal in the cruise industry. Celebrity Cruises continues to operate as a separate brand.

→ Miami-based Cruise Holdings Ltd. merged its three cruise companies (Dolphin Cruise Lines, Premier Cruise Lines, and Seawind Cruise Line) into one company: Premier Cruises. The company also purchased the former Holland America Line ship *Rotterdam*, now renamed *Rembrandt*.

→ Hapag-Lloyd Seetouristik's *Europa* was sold to Star Cruises for $75 million. The ship was leased back to Hapag-Lloyd until mid-1999, when a new ship is due to be completed for the company.

→ Star Cruises purchased *Europa* (ex-Hapag-Lloyd Seetouristik), to be renamed *MegaStar Asia*, for $75 million, and *Sun Viking* (ex-Royal Caribbean International), now renamed *SuperStar Sagittarius*, for $30 million.

→ P&O Cruises' *Canberra* was withdrawn from service and sent to Pakistan for scrap. During her career, the ship carried 6,500 troops to the South Atlantic in the 1982 Falkland Islands War, and held 3,200 Argentine prisoners of war aboard the ship.

→ CTC Cruises (UK) ceased operations. The company's chartered vessel, *Kareliya*, was put up for auction after being arrested in Haifa.

→ Awani Dream Cruises ceased operations. The company's two ships (*Awanu Dream* and *Awani Dream II*) were purchased by Royal Olympic Cruises.

1998

→ Costa Cruises celebrated its fiftieth year of cruise operations.

→ Holland America Line celebrated its 125th year of passenger operations.

→ Australia repealed its cabotage, which means that international cruise ships can dock and operate from Australian ports without restrictions.

→ A new company, Norwegian Capricorn Line, began operations from Sydney, Australia.

→ Hebridean Island Cruises was sold to Altnamara Shipping and Gallic Shipping, a joint venture company.

→ Cunard was sold for $500 million by owning company Kvaerner to a consortium that includes Carnival Corporation as majority shareholder together with a group led by Christiana Markets. Cunard and Seabourn Cruise Line will continue to operate as separate brands under the umbrella name of Cunard Line.

→ Royal Caribbean International sold its *Song of America* for $95 million. The British company Airtours will operate the vessel.

→ Ivaran Lines, operator of the hybrid container-cruise vessel *Americana*, was sold to Canadian Pacific.

→ Orient Lines, together with its single ship *Marco Polo*, was purchased by Norwegian Cruise Line for $54 million ($8 million in cash plus shares).

NEW OCEANGOING CRUISE SHIPS TO DEBUT: 1999/2000/2001/2002/2003

DEBUT DATE	CRUISE LINE	NAME OF SHIP	TONNAGE
1999			
January	Compagnie des Isles du Ponant	*Le Levant*	3,500
April	Carnival Cruise Lines	*Carnival Triumph*	101,353
July	Disney Cruise Line	*Disney Wonder*	85,000
July	Holland America Line	*Volendam*	65,000
July	Radisson Seven Seas Cruises	tba	25,000
July	Renaissance Cruises	*R3*	30,200
August	Hapag-Lloyd Seetouristik	tba	28,000
August	Norwegian Cruise Line	*Norwegian Sky*	76,000
September	Star Cruises	*Superstar Virgo*	74,500
October	Renaissance Cruises	*R4*	30,200
November	Royal Caribbean International	*Voyager of the Seas*	142,000
November	Princess Cruises	*Ocean Princess*	77,000
December	Festival Cruises	*Mistral*	47,900
Late	Norwegian Cruise Line	*Norwegian Sky*	76,000
Late	Star Clippers	*Royal Clipper*	5,000
2000			
January	Holland America Line	*Zaandam*	65,000
February	Renaissance Cruises	*R5*	30,200
Spring	Royal Olympic Cruises	tba	25,000
Spring	P&O Cruises	tba	76,000
May	Renaissance Cruises	*R6*	30,200
June	Celebrity Cruises	tba	85,000
July	Silversea Cruises	tba	25,000
Summer	Norwegian Cruise Line	tba	76,000
Fall	Carnival Cruise Lines	*Carnival Victory*	101,353
Late	Carnival Cruise Lines	tba	82,000
Late	Costa Cruises	tba	82,000
Late	Holland America Line	tba	63,000
Late	Royal Caribbean International	tba	142,000

NOTE: tba = to be announced

* = letter of intent, not firm contract (at press time)

COST	LENGTH (FEET)	LENGTH (METERS)	CABINS	BUILDER
$35 million	321.5	98	45	Leroux et Lotz (France)
$400 million	882.6	269	1,321	Fincantieri (Italy)
$350 million	964.5	294	880	Fincantieri (Italy)
$300 million	777.5	237	770	Fincantieri (Italy)
$200 million	559.7	170.6	245	T. Marriotti (Italy)
$169 million	593.7	181	342	Chantiers de l'Atlantique (France)
$150 million	643.0	196	205	Kvaerner Masa-Yards (Finland)
$300 million	842.0	256.6	1,000	Lloyd Werft (Germany)
$350 million	879.2	268	1,385	Meyer Werft (Germany)
$168.5 million	593.7	181	342	Chantiers de l'Atlantique (France)
$500 million	1019.7	311	1,557	Kvaerner Masa-Yards (Finland)
$300 million	856.2	261	975	Fincantieri (Italy)
$250 million	708.6	216	600	Chantiers de l'Atlantique (France)
$340 million	753.0	251	1,000	Kvaerner Masa-Yards (Finland)
$75 million	439.0	133.8	112	Gdansk Shipyard (Poland)
$300 million	777.5	237	770	Fincantieri (Italy)
$168.5 million	593.7	181	342	Chantiers de l'Atlantique (France)
$165 million	590.5	180	400	Blohm & Voss (Germany)
$320 million	885.8	270	900	Meyer Werft (Germany)
$168.5 million	593.7	181	351	Chantiers de l'Atlantique (France)
$350 million	964.5	294	975	Chantiers de l'Atlantique (France)
$150 million	597.1	182	198	Marriotti/Visentini (Italy)
$340 million	753.0	251	1,000	Chantiers de l'Atlantique (France)
$430 million	882.6	269	1,321	Fincantieri (Italy)
$375 million	957.0	297.1	1,050	Kvaerner Masa-Yards (Finland)
$390 million	n/a	n/a	1,050	Kvaerner Masa-Yards (Finland)
$300 million	777.5	237	690	Fincantieri (Italy)
$500 million	1019.7	311	1,557	Kvaerner Masa-Yards (Finland)

NEW OCEANGOING CRUISE SHIPS TO DEBUT: 1999/2000/2001/2002/2003

(cont.)

DEBUT DATE	CRUISE LINE	NAME OF SHIP	TONNAGE
2001			
January	Celebrity Cruises	tba	85,000
February	Royal Caribbean International	tba	85,000
April	ResidenSea	*The World of ResidenSea*	86,000
Spring	Royal Olympic Cruises	tba	25,000
Spring	Princess Cruises	tba	109,000
Spring	Royal Caribbean International	tba	142,000
May	Silversea Cruises	tba	25,000
Summer	Norwegian Cruise Line	tba (*)	76,000
Fall	Princess Cruises	tba	109,000
Late	Carnival Cruise Lines	tba	82,000
Late	Celebrity Cruises	tba	85,000
Late	Star Cruises	tba	85,000
2002			
Summer	Norwegian Cruise Line	tba (*)	76,000
Late	Carnival Cruise Lines	tba	82,000
Late	Celebrity Cruises	tba	85,000
Late	Star Cruises	tba	85,000
2003			
Summer	Norwegian Cruise Line	tba (*)	76,000

NOTE: tba = to be announced

* = letter of intent, not firm contract (at press time)

COST	LENGTH (FEET)	LENGTH (METERS)	CABINS	BUILDER
$350 million	964.5	294	975	Chantiers de l'Atlantique (France)
$350 million	n/a	n/a	1,000	Meyer Werft (Germany)
$545 million	958.0	292	469	Howaldtswerke-Deutsche Werft (Germany)
$165 million	590.5	180	400	Blohm & Voss (Germany)
$425 million	935.0	285	1,300	Fincantieri (Italy)
$500 million	1019.7	311	1,557	Kvaerner Masa-Yards (Finland)
$150 million	597.1	182	198	Marriotti/Visentini (Italy)
$332 million	753.0	229.5	1,000	Lloyd Werft (Germany)
$425 million	935.0	285	1,300	Fincantieri (Italy)
$375 million	957.0	297.1	1,050	Kvaerner Masa-Yards (Finland)
$350 million	964.5	294	975	Chantiers de l'Atlantique (France)
$380 million	n/a	n/a	1,150	Chantiers de l'Atlantique (France)
$332 million	753.0	229.5	1,000	Lloyd Werft (Germany)
$375 million	n/a	n/a	1,050	Kvaerner Masa-Yards (Finland)
$350 million	964.5	294	975	Chantiers de l'Atlantique (France)
$380 million	n/a	n/a	1,150	Chantiers de l'Atlantique (France)
$332 million	753.0	229.5	1,000	Lloyd Werft (Germany)

Index to Ships' Ratings

SMALL SHIPS (LESS THAN 500 PASSENGERS): 78 SHIPS/74 RATED

Ship	Score	Rating
Sea Goddess I	1805	5
Sea Goddess II	1805	5
Seabourn Legend	1796	5
Seabourn Pride	1795	5
Seabourn Spirit	1795	5
Hanseatic	1740	5
Silver Cloud	1729	5
Silver Wind	1729	5
Hebridean Princess	1699	4+
Song of Flower	1683	4+
Oceanic Odyssey	1678	4+
Paul Gauguin	1645	4+
Radisson Diamond	1640	4+
Clelia II	1628	4+
Minerva	1626	4+
MegaStar Aries	1612	4+
MegaStar Taurus	1612	4+
Sea Cloud	1592	4+
Wind Surf	1577	4+
Wind Spirit	1554	4+
Wind Star	1554	4+
Wind Song	1551	4+
Club Med II	1548	4
Lili Marleen	1546	4
Le Ponant	1540	4
Renaissance Six/Seven/Eight	1538	4
Star Clipper	1530	4
Star Flyer	1530	4
Orient Venus	1505	4
World Discoverer	1494	4
Bremen	1479	4
Nippon Maru	1463	4
Fuji Maru	1455	4
Columbus	1447	4
Galapagos Explorer	1433	4
Americana	1418	4
Vistamar	1392	3+
Delphin	1390	3+
Yorktown Clipper	1388	3+
Nantucket Clipper	1387	3+
Switzerland	1363	3+
Yamal	1292	3+
Kapitan Khlebnikov	1287	3+
Caledonian Star	1263	3+

SMALL SHIPS (LESS THAN 500 PASSENGERS): 78 SHIPS/74 RATED

Ship	Score	Rating
St. Helena	1252	3+
Royal Star	1251	3+
Sapphire	1220	3
Astra II	1214	3
Polaris	1210	3
Odysseus	1200	3
Explorer	1197	3
Grand Caribe	1182	3
Clipper Adventurer	1175	3
Black Prince	1144	3
Melia Don Juan	1103	3
Orpheus	1098	2+
World Renaissance	1096	2+
Niagara Prince	1087	2+
Princesa Amorosa	1086	2+
Enchanted Capri	1084	2+
Stella Oceanis	1079	2+
Silver Star	1064	2+
Jason	1061	2+
Kristina Regina	1052	2+
Wilderness Discoverer	1048	2+
Wilderness Adventurer	1044	2+
Bali Sea Dancer	1042	2+
Funchal	1027	2+
Dalmacija	1026	2+
Sir Francis Drake	1003	2+
Professor Khromov	947	2
Atalante	943	2
Astra	919	2
Arcadia	846	2
Europa	NYR	NYR
Le Levant	NYR	NYR
Monet	NYR	NYR
Royal Clipper	NYR	NYR

MEDIUM SHIPS (500-1,000 PASSENGERS): 63 SHIPS/60 RATED

Ship	Score	Rating
Crystal Symphony	1769	5
Crystal Harmony	1761	5
Royal Viking Sun	1743	5
Europa	1735	5
Vistafjord	1697	4+
Pacific Venus	1696	4+
Asuka	1686	4+
Deutschland	1656	4+
Astor	1564	4+
Arkona	1561	4+
Marco Polo	1545	4
SuperStar Capricorn	1498	4
Norwegian Dynasty	1485	4
Norwegian Capricorn	1427	4
Black Watch	1424	4
SuperStar Gemini	1398	3+
Saga Rose	1397	3+
Victoria	1395	3+
Berlin	1386	3+
Maxim Gorkiy	1385	3+
Island Princess	1376	3+
Pacific Princess	1376	3+
Leeward	1341	3+
Flamenco	1324	3+
Walrus	1320	3+
Italia Prima	1301	3+
Seawing	1301	3+
SuperStar Sagittarius	1300	3+
Ocean Majesty	1291	3+
Bolero	1257	3+
Albatros	1255	3+
Olympic Countess	1251	3+
Princess Danae	1248	3
The Azur	1240	3
CostaAllegra	1223	3
CostaMarina	1222	3
Calypso	1220	3
Seawind Crown	1210	3
Triton	1199	3
Rhapsody	1198	3
Stella Solaris	1193	3
CostaRiviera	1183	3
Emerald	1177	3
Independence	1164	3

Medium Ships (500-1,000 passengers): 63 Ships/60 Rated

Ship	Score	Rating
Universe Explorer	1159	3
Enchanted Isle	1142	3
Aegean I	1101	3
Fair Princess	1097	2+
Monterey	1087	2+
Symphony	1085	2+
SeaBreeze	1080	2+
Regal Empress	1078	2+
Leisure World	1071	2+
Mermoz	1070	2+
Princesa Victoria	1051	2+
Apollo	1029	2+
Shota Rustaveli	1028	2+
Dolphin IV	1008	2+
Princesa Marissa	1002	2+
Taras Shevchenko	994	2+
Ausonia	NYR	NYR
R1	NYR	NYR
R2	NYR	NYR

LARGE SHIPS (OVER 1,000 PASSENGERS): 84 SHIPS/72 RATED

Ship	Score	Rating
Queen Elizabeth 2 (Grill Class)	1808	5
Galaxy	1702	5
Mercury	1702	5
Century	1701	5
Queen Elizabeth 2 (Caronia Class)	1673	4+
Oriana	1658	4+
Grand Princess	1644	4+
Zenith	1637	4+
Horizon	1623	4+
Rotterdam	1615	4+
Dawn Princess	1605	4+
Aida	1604	4+
Sun Princess	1604	4+
Royal Princess	1576	4+
Veendam	1556	4+
Maasdam	1555	4+
Ryndam	1555	4+
Statendam	1553	4+
Vision of the Seas	1547	4
Disney Magic	1546	4
Rhapsody of the Seas	1546	4
Enchantment of the Seas	1540	4
Grandeur of the Seas	1538	4
Regal Princess	1537	4
Crown Princess	1536	4
Legend of the Seas	1533	4
Splendour of the Seas	1533	4
Nieuw Amsterdam	1531	4
Noordam	1531	4
Sky Princess	1528	4
Westerdam	1518	4
Carnival Destiny	1504	4
Star Pisces	1503	4
Queen Elizabeth 2 (Mauretania Class)	1498	4
Star Aquarius	1479	4
Norwegian Crown	1452	4
Norway	1446	4
Norwegian Dream	1445	4
Norwegian Wind	1445	4
Song of America	1440	4
Arcadia	1436	4
Norwegian Sea	1433	4
Majesty of the Seas	1430	4
Monarch of the Seas	1428	4

LARGE SHIPS (OVER 1,000 PASSENGERS): 84 SHIPS/72 RATED

Ship	Score	Rating
Sovereign of the Seas	1428	4
CostaVictoria	1418	4
Elation	1412	4
Ecstasy	1409	4
Fantasy	1409	4
Fascination	1409	4
Imagination	1409	4
Inspiration	1409	4
Sensation	1409	4
Nordic Empress	1388	3+
Norwegian Majesty	1386	3+
CostaRomantica	1384	3+
CostaClassica	1383	3+
Viking Serenade	1361	3+
Celebration	1345	3+
Holiday	1345	3+
Jubilee	1339	3+
Carousel	1311	3+
Sundream	1311	3+
Sun Vista	1297	3+
Rembrandt	1284	3+
Tropicale	1279	3+
Melody	1259	3+
Oceanic	1227	3
Topaz	1139	3
Edinburgh Castle	1120	3
OceanBreeze	1114	3
IslandBreeze	1106	3
Carnival Triumph	NYR	NYR
Disney Wonder	NYR	NYR
Mistral	NYR	NYR
Norwegian Sky	NYR	NYR
Ocean Princess	NYR	NYR
Paradise	NYR	NYR
Sea Princess	NYR	NYR
SuperStar Leo	NYR	NYR
SuperStar Virgo	NYR	NYR
Volendam	NYR	NYR
Voyager of the Seas	NYR	NYR
Zaandam	NYR	NYR

CRUISE LINE ADDRESSES

Major cruise line head office addresses

USA

Abercrombie & Kent
1520 Kensington Road
Oak Brook, IL 60523-2141
USA

Alaska Sightseeing/Cruise West
4th & Battery Building, Suite 700
Seattle, WA 98121
USA

American Canadian
Caribbean Line
461 Water Street
Warren, RI 02885
USA

American Hawaii Cruises
1380 Port of New Orleans Place
New Orleans, LA 70130-1890
USA

Bergen Line
405 Park Avenue
New York, NY 10022
USA

Cape Canaveral Cruise Line
7099 North Atlantic Avenue
Cape Canaveral, FL 32920
USA

Carnival Cruise Lines
3655 NW 87 Avenue
Miami, FL 33178-2428
USA

Celebrity Cruises
1050 Port Boulevard
Miami, FL 33124
USA

Classical Cruises/ Travel Dynamics
132 East 70 Street
New York, NY 10021
USA

Clipper Cruise Line
7711 Bonhomme Avenue
St. Louis, MO 63105
USA

Commodore Cruise Line
4000 Hollywood Blvd, Suite 385
Hollywood, FL 33021
USA

Costa Cruises
World Trade Center
80 SW 8 Street
Miami, FL 33130-3097
USA

Crystal Cruises
2121 Avenue of the Stars
Los Angeles, CA 90067
USA

Cunard
6100 Blue Lagoon Drive, Suite 400
Miami, FL 33126
USA

Deilmann EuropAmerica Cruises
1800 Diagonal Road
Alexandria, VA 22314
USA

Delta Queen Steamboat Company
30 Robin Street Wharf
New Orleans, LA 70130
USA

Disney Cruise Line
210 Celebration Place, Suite 400
Celebration, FL 33747-4600
USA

First European Cruises
95 Madison Avenue, Suite 1203
New York, NY 10016
USA

Holland America Line
300 Elliott Avenue West
Seattle, WA 98119
USA

Ivaran Lines
Ivaran Agencies
Newport Financial Center
111 Pavonia Avenue
Jersey City, NJ 07310
USA

Norwegian Cruise Line
7665 Corporate Center Drive
Miami, FL 33126
USA

Orient Lines
1510 S.E. 17th Street
Ft. Lauderdale, FL 33316
USA

Princess Cruises
10100 Santa Monica Blvd
Los Angeles, CA 90067-4189
USA

Quark Expeditions
980 Post Road
Darien, CT 06820
USA

Radisson Seven Seas Cruises
600 Corporate Drive, Suite 410
Ft. Lauderdale, FL 33180
USA

Raymond & Whitcomb
400 Madison Avenue
New York, NY 10017
USA

Regal Cruises
4199 34 Street South
St. Petersburg, FL 33711
USA

Renaissance Cruises
1800 Eller Drive, Suite 300
Ft. Lauderdale, FL 33335-0307
USA

Royal Caribbean International
1050 Caribbean Way
Miami, FL 33132-2096
USA

Seabourn Cruise Line
55 Francisco Street, Suite 210
San Francisco, CA 94133
USA

Silversea Cruises
110 E. Broward Boulevard, Suite 300
Ft. Lauderdale, FL 33301
USA

Special Expeditions
720 Fifth Avenue, Suite 605
New York, NY 10019
USA

Star Clippers
4101 Salzedo Avenue
Coral Gables, FL 33146
USA

Tall Ship Adventures
1010 South Joliet Street, Suite 200
Aurora, CO 80012
USA

Windjammer Barefoot Cruises
P.O. Box 120
Miami Beach, FL 33119
USA

Windstar Cruises
300 Elliott Avenue West
Seattle, WA 98119
USA

World Explorer Cruises
555 Montgomery Avenue
San Francisco, CA 94111
USA

REST OF THE WORLD

Airtours Sun Cruises
Wavell House
Holcombe Road
Helmshore
Rossendale
Lancs BB4 4NB
UK

Club Mediterranee, SA
25, Rue Vivienne
F-75088 Paris
FRANCE

Compagnie Les Isles des Ponent Cruises
60 Boulebard Marchal Juin
44100 Nantes
FRANCE

Costa Crociere
Via Gabriele D'Annunzio, 2/80
16121 Genoa
ITALY

Curnow Shipping Ltd
The Shipyard
Porthleven
Helston
Cornwall TR13 9JA
ENGLAND

Deilmann Reederei
Am Hafensteig 17-19
D-23730 Neustadt in Holstein
GERMANY

Delphin Seereisen GmbH
Blumenstrasse 20
63004 Offenbach/Main
GERMANY

Deutsche Seereederei GmbH
Am Seehafen 1
Postfach 401406
18147 Rostock
GERMANY

Direct Cruises
Direct Holidays Plc
182 Upper Richmond Road
Putney
London SW15 2SH
ENGLAND

Discoverer Reederei GmbH
Marcusallee 9
28359 Bremen
GERMANY

Festival Cruises
99 Akti Miouli
GR 185 38
Piraeus
GREECE

Fred Olsen Cruise Lines
Fred Olsen House
White House Road
Ipswich
Suffolk IP1 5LL
ENGLAND

Golden Sea Cruises
Filonos 64
Piraeus 185 35
GREECE

Golden Sun Cruises
16 Voukourestiou Street
10671 Athens
GREECE

Hapag-Lloyd Seetouristik
Ballindamm 25
D-20095 Hamburg
GERMANY

Hebridean Island Cruises Ltd
Acorn Park
Skipton
North Yorkshire BD23 2UE
ENGLAND

Jadrolinija Cruises
Riva 16
P.O. Box 123
51000 Rijeka
CROATIA

Jahn Reisen GmbH
Eisenheimerstrasse 61
8000 Munich 21
GERMANY

Kristina Cruises
Korkeavuorenkatu 2
Kotka
FINLAND

Leisure Cruises
Meienbergstrasse 80
P.O. Box 1312
CH-8645 Rapperswil-Jona
SWITZERLAND

Louis Cruise Lines
54-58 Evangoros Avenue
(P.O. Box 1306)
Nicosia
CYPRUS

Marine Expeditions
13 Hazelton Avenue
Toronto, Ontario
CANADA M5R 2E1

Mediterranean Shipping Cruises
Piazza Garibaldi, 91
80142 Naples
ITALY

Mitsui OSK (Passenger Line) Ltd
Syosen Mitsui Building
1-1 Taramonon 2-Chome
Minato-ku
Tokyo 105
JAPAN

NYK Line (Nippon Yusen Kaisha)
Yusen Building
2-3-2 Marunouchi
Chiyoda-ku
Tokyo
JAPAN

Nihon Cruise Kyakusen
5-25, Umeda 2-chome
Kita-ku
Osaka
JAPAN

P&O Cruises
77 New Oxford Street
London WC1A 1PP
ENGLAND

P&O Holidays
P.O. Box 5287
Sydney 2001
New South Wales
AUSTRALIA

Croisieres Paquet
5 rue Gabriel Faure
06046 Nice - Cedex 1
FRANCE

Phoenix Seereisen
Kolnstrasse 80
53111 Bonn
GERMANY

Royal Olympic Cruises
Akti Miaouli 87
Piraeus 18538
GREECE

SAGA Cruises (Saga Shipping)
Folkestone
Kent
ENGLAND

Sea Cloud Kreutzfahrten GmbH
Ballindamm 17
D-200095 Hamburg
GERMANY

Seetours International GmbH
Seilerstrasse 23
60313 Frankfurt
GERMANY

Spice Island Cruises
Jalan Padang Galak No.25
Sanur
Denpasar 80228 (PO Box 3581)
Bali
INDONESIA

Star Cruises SDN BHD
Jalan Sultan Ismail
50250 Kuala Lumpur
MALAYSIA

Star Line Cruises
P.O. Box 81443
Mombasa
KENYA

Sun Cruises
304 Orchard Road,
#05-0-2 Lucky Plaza
SINGAPORE 238863

Swan Hellenic Cruises
77 New Oxford Street
London WC1A 1PP
ENGLAND

Thomson Cruises
Greater London House
Hampstead Road
London NW1 7SD
ENGLAND

Transocean Tours
Postfach 10 09 07
28009 Bremen
GERMANY

Transtours
49 avenue de l'Opera
75002 Paris
FRANCE

Dear Passenger,

You are welcome to send the author your observations concerning any recent cruises taken. Please complete the following basic information when sending comments (both positive and negative) concerning your recent cruise experience. The best Pet Peeves may be incorporated into the next edition of this book.

Although I cannot acknowledge receipt of this comment form due to my nonstop travel schedule, I thank you for your input, and for purchasing this book.

Cruise Date ________________

Ship Name ________________

Cruise Line ________________

Suite/Cabin Number ________

Dining Room Seating:

______(Open) ______(First) ______(Second)

Your Comments ____

____

Your Pet Peeves

(1) ____

____

(2) ____

____

(3) ____

____

Please send to the address below:
Mr. Douglas Ward
Canada House
1 Carrick Way
New Milton
Hampshire BH25 6UD
ENGLAND